IMPORTANT

HERE IS YOUR REGISTRATION CODE TO ACCESS MCGRAW-HILL PREMIUM CONTENT AND MCGRAW-HILL ONLINE RESOURCES

For key premium online resources you need THIS CODE to gain access. Once the code is entered, you will be able to use the web resources for the length of your course.

Access is provided only if you have purchased a new book.

If the registration code is missing from this book, the registration screen on our website, and within your WebCT or Blackboard course will tell you how to obtain your new code. Your registration code can be used only once to establish access. It is not transferable.

To gain access to these online resources

1. **USE** your web browser to go to: **www.mhhe.com/feldmanup7**

2. **CLICK** on "First Time User"

3. **ENTER** the Registration Code printed on the tear-off bookmark on the right

4. After you have entered your registration code, click on "Register"

5. **FOLLOW** the instructions to setup your personal UserID and Password

6. **WRITE** your UserID and Password down for future reference. Keep it in a safe place.

If your course is using WebCT or Blackboard, you'll be able to use this code to access the McGraw-Hill content within your instructor's online course.

To gain access to the McGraw-Hill content in your instructor's WebCT or Blackboard course simply log into the course with the user ID and Password provided by your instructor. Enter the registration code exactly as it appears to the right when prompted by the system. You will only need to use this code the first time you click on McGraw-Hill content.

These instructions are specifically for student access. Instructors are not required to register via the above instructions.

The McGraw-Hill Companies

McGraw Hill Higher Education

Thank you, and welcome to your McGraw-Hill Online Resources.

0-07-295462-0 t/a
Feldman
Understanding Psychology:
Concepts and Contexts, 7/e

REGISTRATION CODE

WRFW-JC9R-RWDL-PVTM-PK8G

SEVENTH EDITION

Understanding Psychology

Robert S. Feldman
University of Massachusetts at Amherst

Boston   Burr Ridge, IL   Dubuque, IA   Madison, WI   New York   San Francisco   St. Louis
Bangkok   Bogotá   Caracas   Kuala Lumpur   Lisbon   London   Madrid   Mexico City
Milan   Montreal   New Delhi   Santiago   Seoul   Singapore   Sydney   Taipei   Toronto

The McGraw-Hill Companies

Mc Graw Hill | **Higher Education**

UNDERSTANDING PSYCHOLOGY
Published by McGraw-Hill, an imprint of The McGraw-Hill Companies, Inc. 1221 Avenue of the
Americas, New York, NY, 10020. Copyright © 2005, 2002, 1999, 1996, 1993, 1990, 1987, by The
McGraw-Hill Companies, Inc. All rights reserved. No part of this publication may be reproduced
or distributed in any form or by any means, or stored in a data base or retrieval system, without
the prior written consent of The McGraw-Hill Companies, Inc., including, but not limited to, in
any network or other electronic storage or transmission, or broadcast for distance learning.
Some ancillaries, including electronic and print components, may not be available to customers
outside the United States.

This book is printed on acid-free paper.

4 5 6 7 8 9 0 VNH/VNH 0 9 8 7 6 5

ISBN 0-07-288665-X

Publisher: *Stephen Rutter*
Senior sponsoring editor: *John T. Wannemacher*
Director of development: *Judith Kromm*
Marketing manager: *Melissa S. Caughlin*
Lead media producer: *Erin Marean*
Lead project manager: *Susan Trentacosti*
Senior production supervisor: *Carol A. Bielski*
Freelance design coordinator: *Gino Cieslik*
Supplement producer: *Kathleen Boylan*
Supplement developmental editor: *Kirsten Stoller*
Photo research coordinator: *Alexandra Ambrose*
Art manager: *Robin K. Mouat*
Illustrators: *John Waller, Judy Waller, Kara Fellows*
Photo researcher: *Toni Michaels*
Cover and interior design: *Ellen Pettengell*
Typeface: *9.5/12 Palatino*
Compositor: *GTS–Los Angeles*
Printer: *Von Hoffmann Corporation*
Psychology Advisory Board:
   Sherree D'Amico, Senior Sales Representative   *Don Mason, Senior Account Manager*
   Steve Day, Field Publisher   *Jeff Neel, Senior Account Manager*
   Myron Flemming, Senior Sales Representative   *Robert E. Oakley, Senior Sales Representative*
   Tim Haak, Field Publisher   *Daniel Pellow, Senior Account Manager*
   John Kindler, Sales Representative   *Kathy Shackelford, Senior Account Manager*
   James Koch, Senior Sales Representative   *Emily Sparano, Sales Representative*

Library of Congress Control Number: 2004100110

www.mhhe.com

About the Author

ROBERT S. FELDMAN is a Professor in the Department of Psychology at the University of Massachusetts at Amherst, where he is Director of Undergraduate Studies. Professor Feldman, who is winner of the College Distinguished Teacher award, has also taught courses at Mount Holyoke College, Wesleyan University, and Virginia Commonwealth University.

As Director of Undergraduate Studies, he initiated the Minority Mentoring Program, and also teaches introductory psychology in the Talent Advancement Program to classes ranging in size from 20 to nearly 500 students. He also has served as a Hewlett Teaching Fellow and Senior Online Teaching Fellow, and he frequently gives talks on the use of technology in teaching. He initiated distance learning courses in psychology at the University of Massachusetts.

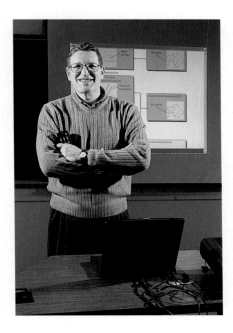

A Fellow of the American Psychological Association and the American Psychological Society, Professor Feldman received a B.A. from Wesleyan University and an M.S. and Ph.D. from the University of Wisconsin–Madison. He is a winner of a Fulbright Senior Research Scholar and Lecturer award, and has written more than 100 books, book chapters, and scientific articles. His books, which have been translated into languages ranging from Spanish and French to Chinese and Albanian, include *Fundamentals of Nonverbal Behavior, Development of Nonverbal Behavior in Children, Social Psychology, Development Across the Life Span,* and *P.O.W.E.R. Learning: Strategies for Success in College and Life.* His research interests include honesty and deception and the use of nonverbal behavior in impression management. His research has been supported by grants from the National Institute of Mental Health and the National Institute on Disabilities and Rehabilitation Research.

Professor Feldman's spare time is most often devoted to serious cooking and enthusiastic piano playing. He has three children and lives with his wife, also a psychologist, overlooking the Holyoke mountain range in Amherst, Massachusetts.

To
Jonathan, Joshua, Sarah,
and Kathy

Brief Contents

Contents

MODULE 6

3 ⊙ Neuroscience and Behavior 58

MODULE 7

MODULE 8

MODULE 9

4 ⊙ Sensation and Perception 98

MODULE 10

5 ▸ States of
    Consciousness 146

12 ⊚ Development 406

13 ⊚ Personality 464

14 ⊙ Health Psychology: Stress, Coping, and Well-Being 496

15 ⊙ Psychological Disorders 528

16 ● Treatment of Psychological Disorders 568

Preface

Psychology speaks with many voices to the students of the discipline, offering a personal message to each one. To some, the science of psychology provides a better understanding of others' behavior. Others view psychology as a pathway to self-understanding. Others see the potential for a future career, and some are drawn to psychology by the opportunity for intellectual discovery that its study provides. No matter what brings students into the introductory course and regardless of their initial motivation, *Understanding Psychology* is designed to engage and excite students about the field.

What's particularly exciting about this seventh edition is that I've had the opportunity to reinvent *Understanding Psychology,* using publishing and learning technologies that didn't exist when I originally wrote the book. This major revision integrates a variety of media elements that not only foster student understanding of psychology and how psychology impacts on students' everyday lives, but also allow students and instructors to assess students' mastery of psychology's key principles and concepts.

A Framework for Learning and Assessment

The multimedia package that is integral to this text includes print and electronic media that, together with the book, comprise a complete framework for learning and assessment. Conforming to recommendations of a 2002 APA task force report on undergraduate student competencies (Board of Educational Affairs, 2002), *every* component of the package is tied to specific psychological concepts and their application in everyday life. Though the book forms the core of this framework, its power to enrich and empirically demonstrate learning comes from a unique library of electronic interactivities with conceptually based quizzes and an easy-to-use electronic gradebook, all specifically created for this seventh edition. Instructors can create a seamless, custom set of assignments from the available resources, or they can opt for a traditional, text-based approach, depending on the needs of the specific course.

A very significant component of this framework responds to the need, described by many instructors, for a simple way to assess students' understanding of core concepts, in large and small introductory psychology classes, to assure that at the end of the course students have mastered a set of basic learning objectives. By identifying certain key concepts and using technology to deliver feedback to instructors as well as to students, the seventh edition of *Understanding Psychology* goes well beyond other texts in providing an innovative and effective means of accomplishing the general education goals of the course.

Psychological Science and Everyday Life

Understanding Psychology, seventh edition, provides broad coverage of the field of psychology, including the theories, research, and applications that constitute the discipline. Along with the traditional areas of psychology (the biological foundations of behavior, sensation and perception, states of consciousness, learning, memory, cognition, human development, personality, abnormal behavior and treatment, and social psychology), the applied topics of gender and sexuality and health psychology receive extensive attention.

Teaching students about the science of psychology and helping them make the connection between psychology and everyday life has been a goal of this text from the beginning. The prologues that open each set of modules, Becoming an Informed Consumer of Psychology sections, Applying Psychology in the 21st Century boxes, and examples presented throughout the text, help students see the real benefits of psychological research. With this edition, we have extended this theme to the interactivities and assessments on the *PsychInteractive* CD-ROM and the Online Learning Center to hone students' ability to apply psychological concepts to everyday situations.

A New Text Format

The book itself has undergone a change in format, as well as significant updating, to better serve the needs of instructors and students. Building on the strong pedagogy that has characterized previous editions, *Understanding Psychology,* seventh edition, is divided into 60 short, self-contained modules on the 17 major topics that formerly made up the chapters of the book. Now, rather than facing a long and potentially daunting chapter, students will be able to study material in smaller chunks, which psychological research long ago found to be the optimal way to learn. Moreover, instructors can customize assignments for their students by asking them to read only those modules that fit their course outline and in the sequence that matches their syllabus without being concerned about confusing references to other parts of the text.

At the beginning of each module, one or more questions introduce the key concepts covered in the module. At key points in the text, references and marginal icons direct students to multimedia activities that can be found on the PsychInteractive CD-ROM that comes with the text and on the Online Learning Center for the text (www.mhhe.com/feldmanup7), interactivities that reinforce the key concepts in a variety of ways and allow students to test their understanding of the concepts.

For example, consider the key concept of communication between neurons. The text presentation of this concept includes a verbal explanation and figures plus references and marginal icons that prompt students to complete a media interactivity on the nature of neural communication across synapses that includes a follow-up quiz, provides links to websites that offer additional information, and carry out an online review relevant to the key concepts and content for that section.

Very significantly, each interactivity includes assessment tools tied to key concepts, and instructors can elect to have the results of these concept quizzes automatically communicated to and recorded in an online, password-protected gradebook. Embedding assessment tools in every exercise allow both students and instructors to track progress in mastering the key concepts in a way that has not been possible until now. Additionally, suggestions for using the interactivities can be found in the Instructor's Manual and questions based on the interactivities are included in the Test Banks. *These resources, combined with other features of the book and the supplements package, comprise a complete framework for learning and assessment of key concepts.*

Finally, a number of unique *visual essays* summarizing key concepts have been added to the text. These essays present major, often difficult points through drawings and photographs, enhancing student understanding and aiding in their recall and application.

Additional Features of the Seventh Edition to Help Students Learn

In addition to the resources just described, *Understanding Psychology*, seventh edition, contains abundant features designed to help students learn, study, and master introductory psychology. Each set of modules includes the following:

- ▶ *Prologue.* Each set of modules starts with an account of a real-life situation that demonstrates the relevance of basic principles and concepts of psychology to pertinent issues and problems. These prologues depict well-known people and events, such as the tragic loss of the *Columbia* space shuttle crew, actor Christopher Reeve's struggle to walk again, and Aron Ralston's dramatic self-amputation of his arm in order to survive a mountain climbing accident.
- ▶ *Looking Ahead.* This section, following each prologue, expresses the key themes and issues discussed in the subsequent modules.
- ▶ *Key Concepts.* Each major section of a module begins with questions about the key concepts addressed in that section. These questions provide a framework for understanding and organizing the material that follows, as well as providing assessment benchmarks.
- ▶ *Interactivity Prompts.* Every set of modules includes several text references and marginal icons that guide readers to interactivities related to key concepts in psychology. In addition, marginal icons refer students to related readings found in the PowerWeb section of the book's website.
- ▶ *Applying Psychology in the 21st Century.* These boxes highlight the relevance of psychology by presenting current and potential applications of current psychological theory and research findings to real-world problems. For example, these discussions explore violence in television and video games, how a love for music may be genetically pre-programmed, and how positive thinking might increase life span.
- ▶ *Exploring Diversity.* In addition to substantial coverage of material relevant to diversity throughout the text, every set of modules also includes at least one special section devoted to an aspect of racial, ethnic, gender, or cultural diversity. These sections highlight the way in which psychology informs (and is informed by) issues relating to the increasing multiculturalism of our global society. Among the topics discussed in Exploring Diversity sections are culture and perception, cross-cultural differences in memory, cultural perspectives on female circumcision, and bilingual education.
- ▶ *Becoming an Informed Consumer of Psychology.* Every set of modules includes material designed to make readers more informed consumers of psychological information by giving them the ability to evaluate critically what the field of psychology offers. These discussions also provide sound, useful guidance concerning common problems. For example, these unique sections discuss ways to become better thinkers, to sleep better, to lose weight successfully, to lower the risks of date rape, and to choose the right therapist.
- ▶ *Recap/Evaluate/Rethink.* Each module concludes with a Recap/Evaluate/Rethink section. The *Recap* sections review the concept questions found at the beginning of each module. The *Evaluate* sections test recall of the material, assessing the degree of initial learning. The *Rethink* sections provide thought-provoking questions designed to provoke critical thinking about the material.

▶ **Running Glossary.** Key terms are highlighted in boldface type within the text where they are introduced, and definitions are given in the margin of the page, along with pronunciation guides for difficult words. To facilitate study, at the end of each module there is a list of the key terms and concepts introduced in that module. There is also a glossary of all key terms and concepts at the end of the book.

▶ **Looking Back** and **Epilogue.** Found at the end of every set of modules, a section called *Looking Back* contains critical thinking questions involving the use of Web resources and the interactivities that go with those modules. Critical thinking questions in the *Epilogue* that follows *Looking Back* relate to the *Prologue* at the opening of the set of modules. The thought-provoking questions in these sections provide a way of tying together a set of modules on one topic and illustrating how the concepts addressed in each module apply to the real-world situation described in the *Prologue*.

▶ **Visual Essays.** Following a number of modules, visual essays review key concepts in a format that is more pictorial than verbal. These features graphically summarize difficult concepts such as experimental design, emotional expression, and social influence.

Print and Media Complements

Several resources developed to enhance student mastery of the key concepts in *Understanding Psychology* are integral to the text. All are designed to meet the needs of new and veteran instructors, whether they favor traditional text-based instruction or a blend of traditional and electronic media.

FOR STUDENTS AND INSTRUCTORS

PsychInteractive This exciting new CD-ROM for students contains a unique library of electronic interactivities designed specifically to help students master the key concepts laid out in the book. Packaged free with each new copy of *Understanding Psychology, PsychInteractive* features more than 40 interactivities and more than 70 conceptual self-tests, as well as links to graded concept quizzes on the text's dedicated website. Using these assessment tools, both students and instructors can track students' progress in attaining course objectives. After completing each interactivity, students can also create and print a personalized study page, an excellent tool for reviewing the core concepts in *Understanding Psychology*.

Online Learning Center The Online Learning Center (www.mhhe.com/feldmanup7) includes the interactivities from the *PsychInteractive* student CD-ROM, along with the self-tests and the graded concept quizzes and much more. In addition, the Online Learning Center gives access to our PowerWeb Online Reader and *The New York Times* news feeds, which are updated daily.

The password-protected Instructor's Online Learning Center houses a gradebook where students' scores on the concept quizzes can be recorded automatically so that instructors can assess their understanding of the main concepts in the course. In addition, the site contains downloadable versions of the Instructor's Manual and Power-Point slides, a variety of other text-specific resources, including a gallery of 146 images and access to our acclaimed customized website creation tool, PageOut! Instructors in need of assistance can contact their McGraw-Hill sales representative via e-mail from the Online Learning Center. Visit us at www.mhhe.com/feldmanup7.

Besides the interactivities and assessment tools, the Student Online Learning Center provides an array of module-by-module study aids, including detailed module outlines, concepts and learning objectives, flashcards, self-quizzes (created by Kathleen McCormick of Ocean County College), answers to the text's Rethink questions, activities and projects, frequently asked questions, interesting Web links, interactive reviews, an Internet primer, a career appendix, and a statistics primer. Visit us at www.mhhe.com/feldmanup7.

FOR STUDENTS

Study Guide (by Barbara Radigan, Community College of Allegheny County, Pennsylvania). The printed Study Guide contains a comprehensive review of the text material. Features include an overview section and fill-in-the-blank, matching, and Rethink questions for each module. Multiple-choice and matching practice tests allow students to gauge their understanding of the material, and an answer key provides answers to all of the chapter's exercises, including feedback for all multiple-choice items. Also contained in the Study Guide is material created by Dr. Sheryl Hartman of Miami–Dade Community College to aid non-native speakers of English in understanding and retaining key course content.

PowerWeb This unique online reader provides current articles, curriculum-based materials, weekly updates with assessment, informative and timely world news, refereed Web links, research tools, study tools, and interactive exercises. Visit www.dushkin.com/powerweb for more information.

FOR INSTRUCTORS

Optional Modules For instructors who like to incorporate lectures on diversity or work issues in their introductory psychology course, optional full-color modules on these topics can be packaged, on request, with their students' copies of *Understanding Psychology*, seventh edition. The Diversity module discusses the roots of diversity and addresses related issues, such as conflict and cooperation. The module on Industrial–Organizational Psychology broadly introduces the psychology of work in the 21st century.

Instructor's Resource CD-ROM This CD-ROM contains the key instructor's resources for *Understanding Psychology*, seventh edition, in a flexible format. An easy-to-use interface for the design and delivery of multimedia classroom presentations makes the Instructor's Manual, two Test Banks, PowerPoint presentation slides, and Image Bank very customizable.

Instructor's Manual (by Susan Krauss Whitbourne, University of Massachusetts at Amherst). This thoroughly revised manual provides instructors of introductory psychology with all the tools and resources they need to present and enhance their course. The Instructor's Manual includes detailed lecture launchers, learning objectives, interesting lecture and media presentation ideas, student assignments and ready-to-use handouts, and descriptions of the new and exciting interactivities that have been developed to accompany *Understanding Psychology*, seventh edition. This manual contains many tips and activities that can be used with any class, regardless of size or teaching approach.

Test Banks (Test Bank I by Susan Krauss Whitbourne, University of Massachusetts at Amherst; Test Bank II by Jamie McMinn, Westminster College). Two test banks incorporate the new content in *Understanding Psychology*, seventh edition. Each test bank contains more than 1,800 multiple-choice items, classified by cognitive type and level of difficulty, and keyed to the appropriate learning objective and page in the textbook. Fill-in-the-blank, matching, and short-answer questions are provided for all modules.

Computerized Test Banks (Macintosh/Windows compatible) Available in a cross-platform format, the computerized test banks (on the Instructor's Resource CD-ROM) make all the items from Test Banks I and II easily available to instructors who like to create their own tests. The test-generating program facilitates the selection of questions from each Test Bank and the printing of tests and answer keys, and also allows instructors to import questions from other sources.

PowerPoint Slides For instructors using a computer monitor for demonstrations in the classroom, PowerPoint slides (which can be accessed from the Instructor's Resource CD-ROM or downloaded from the Online Learning Center) were specially created by Barbara Radigan from Community College of Allegheny County, Pennsylvania, to support the use of *Understanding Psychology,* seventh edition. Module-by-module PowerPoint presentations including illustrations from the Image Bank allow instructors to deliver their lectures in an effective manner.

Image Bank More than 145 illustrations are accessible on the Instructor's Resource CD-ROM for use on your course website or in PowerPoint presentations. These images also can be downloaded from the Image Bank on the Online Learning Center.

Overhead Transparencies A set of acetate transparencies containing key illustrations, graphs, and tables from *Understanding Psychology,* seventh edition, is available for instructors using projectors to deliver their lectures.

Classroom Performance System Booklet and CD-ROM The Classroom Performance System (CPS) from **eInstruction** allows instructors to gauge immediately what students are learning during lectures. With CPS, instructors can ask questions, take polls, or host classroom demonstrations, and get instant feedback. In addition, CPS makes it easy to take attendance, give and grade pop quizzes, or give formal paper-based class tests with multiple versions of the test using CPS for immediate grading.

For instructors who want to use CPS in their classroom, we are pleased to offer a new booklet containing strategies for implementing the system, specific multiple-choice questions designed for in-class use (tied to key concepts in the book), and classroom demonstrations that make use of the system. The accompanying CD-ROM includes footage of author Robert Feldman using this innovative teaching tool in his introductory course, as well as an electronic version of the multiple-choice questions and classroom demonstrations that can be easily ported into teaching notes. For a quick, easy demonstration of CPS, go to www.mhhe.com/wmg/cps/psychology.

Content Changes in the Seventh Edition

This edition incorporates a significant amount of new and updated information, reflecting the advances in the field and the suggestions of reviewers. *Well over 1,000 new citations have been added, and most of them refer to articles and books published in the 21st century.* For instance, studies in aggression and modeling from media and computer games, brain and behavior, human genome mapping, cognition, emotions, and cultural approaches to psychological phenomena receive expanded coverage. Additionally, this edition incorporates a wide range of new topics. The following sample of new and revised topics provides a good indication of the book's currency.

(1) Introduction to Psychology
- Prologue on *Columbia* space shuttle astronauts
- New section on careers in psychology (Module 1)
- Information on salaries for psychology major graduates (Module 1)
- Updated statistics on where psychologists work (Module 1)

(2) Psychological Research
- Prologue on bystander non-intervention

- Coverage of loaded survey questions (Module 5)
- *Applying Psychology in the 21st Century* box on using a video game to study racial bias (Module 5)

(3) Neuroscience and Behavior
- Prologue on Christopher Reeve's struggle to overcome paralysis
- Earlier coverage of endocrine system (Module 8)
- Material on hormone replacement therapy (Module 8)

- Discussion of steroid use (Module 8)
- *Applying Psychology in the 21st Century* box on robot rats and wired brains (Module 9)

(4) Sensation and Perception
- Use of baseball example to differentiate sensation and perception
- Questionnaire on sense sensitivity (Module 10)
- *Applying Psychology in the 21st Century* box on new technology for hearing and seeing (Module 12)
- Material on taste (including new taste: *umami*) (Module 12)

(5) States of Consciousness
- Emphasis on importance of sleep (Module 14)
- *Applying Psychology in the 21st Century* box on adolescent sleep deprivation (Module 14)
- Coverage of night terrors (Module 14)
- Role of *suprachiasmatic nucleus (SCN)* in circadian rhythm (Module 14)
- Data on dream content (Module 15)

(6) Learning
- Updated Prologue on dog trained to be helpmate
- Added examples of discrimination (Module 17)
- Increased coverage on "Little Albert" (Module 18)
- Revised explanation of Thorndike's law of effect (Module 18)
- Clarified presentation of punishment (Module 18)
- Added evolutionary explanation to Garcia data and constraints on learning (Module 18)
- Revised *Applying Psychology in the 21st Century* box on media aggression and modeling (Module 19)
- Added example of latent learning (Module 19)

(7) Memory
- Prologue on woman's loss of memory after accident
- Memory quiz (Module 20)
- Expanded discussion of brain structures related to memory consolidation (Module 20)
- Coverage of episodic buffer in working memory (Module 20)

- Coverage of serial position effect, primacy effect, recency effect (Module 20)
- New figures on working memory, spreading activation, and associative models of semantic memory (Module 20)
- *Applying Psychology in the 21st Century* box on the inaccuracies of memories (Module 21)
- Expanded discussion of amnesia (Module 22)

(8) Cognition and Language
- Prologue on retired dentist inventing new natural pesticide
- *Applying Psychology in the 21st Century* box on being genetically preprogrammed to like music
- Updated linguistic relativity hypothesis
- Material on "language gene"
- Recent data on number of phonemes
- Coverage of critical periods in language development
- New coverage of brain functioning in bilingual speakers, including figure showing brain activity in native language speakers vs. non-native language speakers

(9) Intelligence
- Updated Prologue on retarded and gifted students
- Discussion of different cultural conceptions of intelligence—e.g., Asian, African (Module 26)
- Added material on existential intelligence and classroom use of multiple intelligences (Module 26)
- Updated explanation for Flynn effect (Module 28)

(10) Motivation and Emotion
- *Applying Psychology in the 21st Century* box on using nonverbal behavior to expose terrorists (Module 31)
- Updated obesity statistics (Module 30)
- Coverage of BMI, including BMI calculator (Module 30)
- Material on role of leptin in obesity (Module 30)
- Recent findings on the role of the amygdala in emotion (Module 31)

(11) Sexuality and Gender
- ▶ Eagly's biosocial theory of gender differences (Module 33)
- ▶ Discussion of strength of women's sex drive compared to men's (Module 34)
- ▶ Recent research on homosexuality and mental health (Module 35)
- ▶ Added coverage of transgendersim (Module 36)

(12) Development
- ▶ Prologue on surviving preterm infant
- ▶ Examples of parenting styles (Module 39)
- ▶ Coverage of spermarche (Module 40)
- ▶ Current data on single-parent households with children living below the poverty line (Module 41)
- ▶ Discussion of resilience (Module 39)
- ▶ Added coverage of Alzheimer's (Module 41)

(13) Personality
- ▶ Revised Big Five dimensions of sample traits (Module 43)
- ▶ Questionnaire on optimism (Module 44)
- ▶ Clarified MMPI discussion and figure (Module 44)

(14) Health Psychology: Stress, Coping, and Well-Being
- ▶ Added material on avoidant coping styles (Module 45)
- ▶ Up-to-date discussion on psychoneuroimmunology and stress (Module 45)

- ▶ Material on resilience, terrorism, and PTSD (Module 45)
- ▶ Challenges to Selye's stress model (Module 45)
- ▶ Discussion of Type D personality (Module 46)
- ▶ *Applying Psychology in the 21st Century* box on how positive thinking might extend lifespan (Module 47)

(15) Psychological Disorders
- ▶ Prologue on person suffering with schizophrenia
- ▶ *Applying Psychology in the 21st Century* box on suicide bombers (Module 48)
- ▶ Coverage of childhood disorders (Module 49)

(16) Treatment of Psychological Disorders
- ▶ *Applying Psychology in the 21st Century* box on validity of online therapy (Module 52)
- ▶ Changes in brain function due to psychotherapy vs. drug therapy (Module 53)
- ▶ Interpersonal therapy (Module 52)

(17) Social Psychology
- ▶ Prologue on Good Samaritans saving lives
- ▶ Concept of self-serving bias (Module 54)
- ▶ *Applying Psychology in the 21st Century* box on name discrimination (Module 56)

Finally, several visual essays on key topics have been added to this edition of the text. These essays present major, often difficult points through drawings and photographs that will enhance student understanding and aid in recall and application.

▲ ▲ ▲

Based on extensive student feedback, systematic research involving a wide range of instructors, and endorsements received from reviewers at a variety of schools, I am confident that this edition reflects what instructors want and need: a book that motivates students to understand and apply psychology to their own lives. *Understanding Psychology*, seventh edition, is designed to expose readers to the content—and promise—of psychology, and to do so in a way that will nurture students' excitement about psychology and keep their enthusiasm alive for a lifetime.

Additional Resources for Introductory Psychology

Please see your McGraw-Hill sales representative for information on policy, price, and availability of the following supplements.

In-Class Activities Manual for Instructors of Introductory Psychology (By the Illinois State University team of Pat Jarvis, Cynthia Nordstrom, and Karen Williams). This activities manual covers every major topic in the course. Nineteen chapters include 58 separate activities, all of which have been used successfully in the authors' classes. Each activity includes a short description of the demonstration, the approximate time needed to complete the activity, the materials needed, step-by-step procedures, practical tips, and suggested readings related to the activity.

Annual Editions: Psychology 04/05 (Edited by Karen Duffy of SUNY–Geneseo). This annually updated reader is a compilation of carefully selected articles from magazines, newspapers, and journals. This title is supported by Dushkin Online, a student website that provides study support and tools and links to related sites. An *Instructor's Manual* and *Using Annual Editions in the Classroom* are available as support materials for instructors.

Sources: Notables Selections in Psychology, Third Edition (Edited by Terry Pettijohn of Ohio State University). This book includes more than 40 book excerpts, classic articles, and research studies that have shaped the study of psychology and our contemporary understanding of it.

Taking Sides: Clashing Views on Controversial Psychological Issues, Thirteenth Edition (Edited by Brent Slife of Brigham Young University). This debate-style reader is designed to introduce students to controversial viewpoints on the field's most crucial issues. Each issue is carefully framed for the student, and the pro and con essays represent the arguments of leading scholars and commentators in their fields.

Course Management Systems

WebCT and Blackboard Populated **WebCT** and **Blackboard** course cartridges are available free upon adoption of a McGraw-Hill textbook. Contact your McGraw-Hill sales representative for details.

PageOut! Build your own course website in less than an hour. You don't have to be a computer whiz to create a website with this exclusive McGraw-Hill product. It requires no prior knowledge of HTML, no long hours of coding, and no design skills on your part. With PageOut, even the most inexperienced computer user can quickly and easily create a professional-looking course website. Simply fill in templates with your information and with content provided by McGraw-Hill, choose a design, and you've got a website specifically designed for your course. Best of all, it's free! Visit us at **www.pageout.net** to find out more.

Video Resources

Media Resources for Teaching Psychology (Available as a DVD + CD-ROM set or as 2 VHS Tapes + CD-ROM) This exciting set of video segments and interactivities was designed to provide instructors of introductory psychology with a set of lecture tools that will enhance student interest and involvement. Fifty video segments and 22 interactivities have been carefully edited and arranged for undergraduate instruction. Thirty-six of the video segments—more than 2½ hours of footage—are available either on DVD or on 2 VHS videocassettes, through an exclusive partnership McGraw-Hill has established with **The Discovery Channel Education™**. The other video segments (animations) and interactivities are available on an accompanying CD-ROM. The video segments range in length from under 5 minutes to 12 minutes. Detailed teaching notes provide a summary of the activity, suggestions on how to use it in class, and discussion questions.

McGraw-Hill Introduction to Psychology Videos Taken from Films for Humanities & Sciences videos, each of these clips is 5–10 minutes in length and is designed to serve as a lecture launcher. Topics include Gestalt theories, classic and operant conditioning, eyewitness testimony, language development, Piaget's preoperational stage, and schizophrenia.

Acknowledgments

One of the central features of *Understanding Psychology* is the involvement of both professional and students in the review process. The seventh edition of *Understanding Psychology* has relied heavily—and benefited substantially—from the advice of instructors and students from a wide range of backgrounds.

I am extraordinarily grateful to the following reviewers, who provided their time and expertise to help insure that *Understanding Psychology,* seventh edition, reflects the best that psychology has to offer.

Carol Austad, *Central Connecticut State University*

Gary Biel, *Schreiner University*

Kathleen Brown, *Claremont McKenna College*

Nicole Judice Campbell, *University of Oklahoma*

Donna Dahlgren, *Indiana University Southeast*

Brenda Du Buc, *Wytheville Community College*

Lynda Federoff, *Indiana University of Pennsylvania*

Michael Firmin, *Cedarville University*

Leticia Flores, *Southwest Texas State University*

Stan Friedman, *Southwest Texas State University*

Christopher Frost, *Southwest Texas State University*

Bobbi Gabrenya, *Southern Vermont College*

Jay Garrett, *Kaskaskia College*

Harvey Ginsberg, *Southwest Texas State University*

Larry Goff, *Massachusetts Bay Community College*

Leslie Grout, *Hudson Valley Community College*

Christopher Hakala, *Western New England College*

Saera Khan, *University of San Francisco*

Richard Kimball, *Worcester State College*

A. Julie Kiotas, *Pasadena City College*

Art Kohn, *Portland State University*

Sara Levine, *Fitchburg State College*

Paul Lloyd, *Southeast Missouri State University*

Jamie McMinn, *University of Pittsburgh*

Dorothy Mercer, *Eastern Kentucky University*

Robert Moore, *Marshalltown Community College*

Melinda Myers, *Humboldt State University*

Ronald Mulson, *Hudson Valley Community College*

Geri Olson, *Sonoma State University*

Paul Richer, *Duquesne University*

Mark Seely, *St. Joseph's College*

Inger Thompson, *Glendale Community College*

Larry Welkowitz, *Keene State College*

Diane Wille, *Indiana University Southeast*

Many teachers along my educational path have shaped my thinking. I was introduced to psychology at Wesleyan University, where several committed and inspiring teachers—and in particular Karl Scheibe—conveyed their sense of excitement about the field and made its relevance clear to me. Karl epitomizes the teacher-scholar combination to which I aspire, and I continue to marvel at my good fortune in having such a role model.

By the time I left Wesleyan I could envision no other career but that of psychologist. Although the nature of the University of Wisconsin, where I did my graduate work, could not have been more different from the much smaller Wesleyan, the excitement and inspiration were similar. Once again, a cadre of excellent teachers—led, especially, by the late Vernon Allen—molded my thinking and taught me to appreciate the beauty and science of the discipline of psychology.

My colleagues and students at the University of Massachusetts at Amherst provide ongoing intellectual stimulation, and I thank them for making the university a fine place to work. Several people also provided extraordinary research and editorial help. In particular, I am grateful to my superb students, past and present, including Jim Tyler, Brent Weiss, and Chris Poirier. Chris, in particular, provided a good deal of help and advice on this edition of the book. Finally, I am extremely grateful to John Graiff, whose hard work and dedication helped immeasurably on just about everything involving this book.

I also offer great thanks to the McGraw-Hill editorial team that participated in this edition of the book. Steve Debow's and Thalia Dorwick's hands-on interest, as well as friendship, helped the project at every critical juncture. Publisher Steve Rutter and Senior Sponsoring Editor John Wannemacher created a creative, supportive environment, and I am grateful for their enthusiasm, commitment, and extremely good ideas. I also thank the very able Judith Kromm, Director of Development in Psychology, and Richard Mickey and Linda Bieze, all of who participated in development of the manuscript. And every reader of this book owes a debt to Rhona Robbin, developmental editor on prior editions of *Understanding Psychology*. Her relentless pursuit of excellence helped form this book, and she taught me a great deal about the craft and art of writing.

I am also grateful to the team that spent untold hours with me developing the teaching and learning tools that complement the book, including Art Kohn, Portland State University; Erin Marean, McGraw-Hill Lead Media Producer; Nick Barrett, McGraw-Hill Executive New Media Producer; Kirsten Stoller, McGraw-Hill Developmental Editor; and my master-of-all-pedagogies colleague Susan Whitbourne, University of Massachusetts at Amherst. I am convinced their efforts have created an instructional framework that is boundary-breaking.

Other people at McGraw-Hill were central to the design, production, and marketing process, including Lead Project Manager Susan Trentacosti, Senior Production Supervisor Carol Bielski, and Design Coordinators Mary Kazak and Gino Cieslik. Photo editor Toni Michaels did her usual superb job in choosing photos and was a pleasure to work with. I would also like to thank marketing manager Melissa Caughlin for her enthusiasm and commitment to this project. I am proud to be a part of this world-class team.

Finally, I remain completely indebted to my family. My parents, Leah Brochstein and the late Saul D. Feldman, provided a lifetime foundation of love and support, and I continue to see their influence in every corner of my life. My extended family also plays a central role in my life. They include, more or less in order of age, my nieces and nephews, my brother, assorted brothers- and sisters-in-law, Ethel Radler, and Harry Brochstein. Finally, my mother-in-law, the late Mary Evans Vorwerk, had an important influence on this book, and I remain ever grateful to her.

Ultimately, my children, Jonathan, Joshua, and Sarah; my daughter-in-law Leigh; and my wife, Katherine, remain the focal point of my life. I thank them, with immense love.

Robert S. Feldman
Amherst, Massachusetts

Using *Understanding Psychology*

If you're reading this page, you're probably taking an introductory psychology course. Maybe you're studying psychology because you've always been interested in what makes people tick. Or perhaps you've had a friend or family member who has sought assistance for a psychological disorder. Or maybe you have no idea of what psychology is all about, but you know that taking an introductory psychology course would fulfill a degree requirement.

Whatever your motivation for taking the course and reading this book, here's my commitment to you: by the time you finish this text, you will have a better understanding of why people—including you—behave the way they do. You will know how, and why, psychologists conduct research, and will have an understanding of the theories that guide their research. You will become acquainted with the breadth of the field and will obtain practical, useful information, as well as a wealth of knowledge that hopefully will excite your curiosity and increase your understanding of people's behavior.

To meet this commitment, *Understanding Psychology,* seventh edition, has been written with you, the reader, in mind. At every step in the development of the book, students and instructors have been consulted in an effort to identify the combination of learning tools that would maximize readers' ability to learn and retain the subject matter of psychology. The result is a book that contains features that will not only help you to understand psychology, but also make it a discipline that is part of your life.

Now it's your turn; you will need to take several steps to maximize the effectiveness of the learning tools in the book. These steps include familiarizing yourself with the scope and structure of the book, using the built-in learning aids, and employing a systematic study strategy.

Familiarize Yourself with the Scope and Organization of *Understanding Psychology*

Begin by reading the list of modules and skimming the detailed Contents. From this exercise, you will get a sense of the topics covered and the logic of the sequence of modules. Then take some time to flip through the book. Choose a section that looks particularly interesting to you, skim it, and see for yourself how the modules are laid out.

Each module provides logical starting and stopping points for reading and studying. You can plan your studying around the set of modules that encompasses a particular topic. For instance, if your instructor assigns a set of modules to read over the course of a week, you might plan to read and study one module each day, using later days in the week to review the material.

Use the Learning Aids Built Into the Book

Once you have acquired a broad overview of *Understanding Psychology*, you are ready to begin reading and learning about psychology. Each set of modules contains learning aids that will help you master the material.

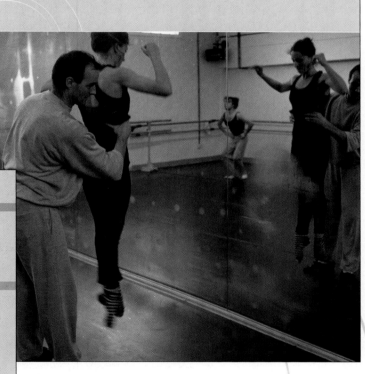

Learning

Prologue. Each set of modules begins with a Prologue and ends with an Epilogue. The Prologue sets the stage for the set of modules, providing a brief account of a real-life event that is relevant to the content of the modules, and demonstrating why the material in the set of modules is important.

Prologue
A Friend Named Bo

Any of us would be lucky to have a friend like Bo. Bo is a wonderful companion, loyal and giving unselfishly of time and affection. He is ever-ready to help, and in return, he asks for little.

But Bo was trained to be this way.

Bo is a 5-year-old golden retriever and Labrador mix, a dog trained to be a helpmate to his owner, Brad Gabrielson. Gabrielson has cerebral palsy, and he has little control over his muscles. Yet with the help of Bo, Gabrielson can lead a life of independence.

Bo's abilities are many. If the doorbell rings, he answers the door. If Gabrielson drops something, Bo will pick it up. If Gabrielson is thirsty, Bo brings him a drink. One time, when Gabrielson fell, Bo left the apartment, went across the hall to a neighbor's door, where he scratched and barked. When the neighbor proved not to be home, Bo went upstairs to another neighbor's apartment.

When that neighbor—who had never encountered Bo before—came to the door, Bo led him downstairs, carefully tugging his hand. As the neighbor helped Gabrielson, Bo stood careful watch at his side. Said Gabrielson later, "On my own, I would have had to lie there . . . until my fiancée got home six hours later." But, he continued, "Bo came over and licked my face, to make sure I was all right, that I responded. Then he went to look for help" (Ryan, 1991, p. 14). And Gabrielson stopped worrying.

Looking Ahead. The Looking Ahead sections, which follow the prologues, identify the key themes and issues addressed in the set of modules.

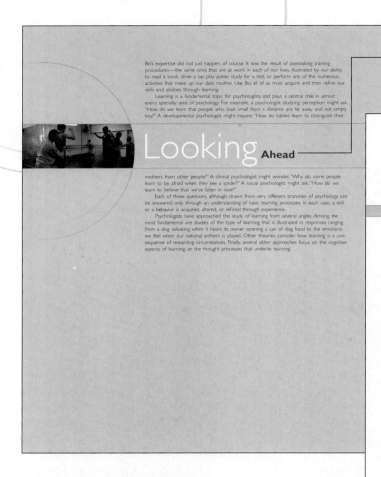

Bo's expertise did not just happen, of course. It was the result of painstaking training procedures—the same ones that are at work in each of our lives, illustrated by our ability to read a book, drive a car, play poker, study for a test, or perform any of the numerous activities that make up our daily routine. Like Bo, all of us must acquire and then refine our skills and abilities through learning.

Learning is a fundamental topic for psychologists and plays a central role in almost every specialty area of psychology. For example, a psychologist studying perception might ask, "How do we learn that people who look small from a distance are far away and not simply tiny?" A developmental psychologist might inquire, "How do babies learn to distinguish their

Looking Ahead

mothers from other people?" A clinical psychologist might wonder, "Why do some people learn to be afraid when they see a spider?" A social psychologist might ask, "How do we learn to believe that we've fallen in love?"

Each of these questions, although drawn from very different branches of psychology, can be answered only through an understanding of basic learning processes. In each case, a skill or a behavior is acquired, altered, or refined through experience.

Psychologists have approached the study of learning from several angles. Among the most fundamental are studies of the type of learning that is illustrated in responses ranging from a dog salivating when it hears its owner opening a can of dog food to the emotions we feel when our national anthem is played. Other theories consider how learning is a consequence of rewarding circumstances. Finally, several other approaches focus on the cognitive aspects of learning, or the thought processes that underlie learning.

Key Concepts. Each module begins with the key concepts discussed in that section. The key concepts, phrased as questions, provide a framework for understanding and organizing the material that follows. They will also help you to understand what the important content is.

Interactivity Prompts. Throughout the book, you find text references and marginal icons that will guide you to virtual interactivities that are part of a framework for learning surrounding the text. The multimedia and print components of this framework will help you fully understand the key concepts of psychology and will help illustrate how psychology affects your everyday life. The PsychInteractive CD-ROM packaged with the book and the text-specific website (www.mhhe.com/feldmanup7) contain visual interactivities and simulations, video and audio demonstrations, and mastery exercises that will enable you to achieve a richer and deeper understanding of the basic principles of the discipline.

Classical Conditioning

MODULE 17

What is learning?

How do we learn to form associations between stimuli and responses?

Does the mere sight of the golden arches in front of McDonald's make you feel pangs of hunger and think about hamburgers? If it does, you are displaying an elementary form of learning called classical conditioning. *Classical conditioning* helps explain such diverse phenomena as crying at the sight of a bride walking down the aisle, fearing the dark, and falling in love.

Classical conditioning is one of a number of different types of learning that psychologists have identified, but a general definition encompasses them all: **Learning** is a relatively permanent change in behavior that is brought about by experience.

Learning: A relatively permanent change in behavior brought about by experience.

How do we know when a behavior has been influenced by learning—or even is a result of learning? Part of the answer relates to the nature–nurture question, one of the fundamental issues underlying the field of psychology. In the acquisition of behaviors, experience—essential to the definition of learning—is the "nurture" part. However, some changes in behavior or performance come about through maturation: inherited, genetic factors representing the "nature" part of the nature–nurture question. For instance, children become better tennis players as they grow older partly because their strength increases with their size—a maturational phenomenon. Maturational changes have to be differentiated from improvements resulting from practice, which indicate that learning has taken place.

Similarly, we must distinguish short-term changes in behavior that are due to factors other than learning—such as declines in performance resulting from fatigue or lack of effort—from performance changes that are due to actual learning. If Venus Williams performs poorly in a tennis match because of tension or fatigue, this does not mean that she has not learned to play correctly or has "unlearned" how to play well. Because there is not always a one-to-one correspondence between learning and performance, understanding when true learning has occurred is difficult.

Although philosophers since the time of Aristotle have speculated on the foundations of learning, the first systematic research on learning was done at the beginning of the twentieth century, when Ivan Pavlov (does the name ring a bell?) developed the framework for learning called classical conditioning.

▲ ▲ ▲

PowerWeb: Memory and Learning
www.mhhe.com/feldmanup7

The Basics of Classical Conditioning

Ivan Pavlov, a Russian physiologist, never intended to do psychological research. In 1904 he won the Nobel Prize for his work on digestion, testimony to his contribution to that field. Yet Pavlov is remembered not for his physiological research, but for his experiments on basic learning processes—work that he began quite accidentally (Windholz, 1997).

Pavlov had been studying the secretion of stomach acids and salivation in dogs in response to the ingestion of varying amounts and kinds of food. While doing that, he observed a curious phenomenon: Sometimes stomach secretions and salivation would begin in the dogs when they had not yet eaten any food. The mere sight of the experimenter who normally brought the food, or even the sound of the experimenter's

187

---

tested. Hypotheses stem from theories; they help test the underlying validity of theories.

In the same way that we develop our own broad theories about the world, we also construct hypotheses about events and behavior. Those hypotheses can range from trivialities (such as why our English instructor wears those weird shirts) to more meaningful matters (such as what is the best way to study for a test). Although we rarely test these hypotheses systematically, we do try to determine whether they are right. Perhaps we try comparing two strategies: cramming the night before an exam versus spreading out our study over several nights. By assessing which approach yields better test performance, we have created a way to compare the two strategies.

Latané and Darley's hypothesis was a straightforward prediction from their more general theory of diffusion of responsibility: The more people who witness an emergency situation, the less likely it is that help will be given to a victim. They could, of course, have chosen another hypothesis (for instance, that people with more first-aid skills will be less affected by the presence of others and more likely to help than will those with fewer first-aid skills), but their initial formulation seemed to offer the most direct test of the theory.

Psychologists rely on formal theories and hypotheses for many reasons. For one thing, theories and hypotheses allow them to make sense of unorganized, separate observations and bits of information by permitting them to place the pieces within a structured and coherent framework. In addition, theories and hypotheses offer psychologists the opportunity to move beyond already known facts and principles and make deductions about unexplained phenomena. In this way, theories and hypotheses provide a reasoned guide to the direction that future investigation ought to take (Howitt & Cramer, 2000; Cohen, 2003).

In short, the scientific method, with its emphasis on theories and hypotheses, helps psychologists pose appropriate questions. With properly stated questions in hand, psychologists then can choose from a variety of research methods to find answers. (To get a better understanding of the scientific method used by psychologists, try **Interactivity 4–1**.)

INTERACTIVITY 4–1
The scientific method

APPLYING PSYCHOLOGY IN THE 21st CENTURY

Therapy Online: Is the Internet a Good Place to Get Treatment?

Amy, a first-year student at the University of Wisconsin at Eau Claire, was having some real personal difficulties. She told a friend about her problems, and her friend told Amy about a website that had been discussed during a campus orientation. The website was the university counseling center's homepage, where Amy located the email address of one of the counselors. She immediately composed and sent the following message: "I feel somewhat stupid even writing this but I need some help . . . Recently I made a very big mistake and I think I need someone to talk to" (Carlson, 2002, p. A35).

Amy claims she never knew the university's counseling center existed until she saw the website. And even if she had known about the center, she suspects that she wouldn't have gone there in person. It was only because of the offer of online help that she sought treatment for her psychological difficulties.

As people of all ages have grown increasingly comfortable turning to the Internet to find everything from mp3's and DVDs to new friends, why not online therapy too?

Although few people receive online therapy today, this form of treatment has become a growing trend. As various technologies become more advanced and affordable—including the development of inexpensive, high-quality two-way video links over the Web—experts predict that the popularity of online therapy will grow (Jerome et al., 2000).

Today, most online therapy occurs primarily through e-mail. Therapists and clients exchange messages, which are sometimes supplemented with phone calls or face-to-face visits. For people like Amy, online therapy may provide the treatment they need while safeguarding their privacy.

Proponents of virtual therapy say it will open new avenues of treatment for people with psychological disorders. For example, those who live in remote areas can receive online treatment, as can those who are disabled, concerned with privacy, or too embarrassed to seek out local therapists (Advances in Telepsychology/Telehealth, 2000; Jerome et al., 2000; Taylor et al., 2002).

Despite these advantages, Internet therapy has many critics. Because current technology limits online therapists' ability to see and hear their clients clearly, those therapists have no access to the valuable information provided by clients' nonverbal behavior. Moreover, virtual clients can misrepresent themselves more easily than can patients in face-to-face therapy sessions. Although the advent of more effective video links will reduce these limitations, they will remain problems as long as clients are physically distant from their therapists. Finally, online therapy guarantees privacy no more than face-to-face therapy does; we cannot ensure that highly personal information shared online will be completely protected from accidental disclosure or from hackers (Almer, 2000).

An even greater concern for people seeking virtual therapy is that no procedure exists for licensing individuals who provide treatment online. *Anyone* can call himself or herself a therapist and start providing therapy for—and collecting money from—clients. In addition, although a few studies suggest that Internet-based therapy is effective, psychologists need more research before they can be certain that online therapy is as effective as its face-to-face counterpart (Rabasca, 2000; Grohol & Zuckerman, 2002; Taylor & Luce, 2003).

Despite these drawbacks, online therapy in one form or another is likely to become an option for people seeking treatment for psychological disorders. Whether it will become routine—and be as effective as traditional face-to-face therapy—remains to be seen.

RETHINK

Do you think people are likely to be more honest when discussing their problems with an online therapist or with a face-to-face therapist? What kinds of clients do you think are more likely to find online therapy appealing? What kinds of clients might do better with traditional face-to-face therapy?

Exploring DIVERSITY
The Relative Influence of Genetics and Environment: Nature, Nurture, and IQ

Culture-fair IQ test: A test that does not discriminate against the members of any minority group.

In an attempt to produce a **culture-fair IQ test,** one that does not discriminate against the members of any minority group, psychologists have tried to devise test items that assess experiences common to all cultures or emphasize questions that do not require language usage. However, test makers have found this difficult to do, because past experiences, attitudes, and values almost always have an impact on respondents' answers. For example, children raised in Western cultures group things on the basis of what they *are* (such as putting *dog* and *fish* into the category of *animal*). In contrast, members of the Kpelle tribe in Africa see intelligence demonstrated by grouping things according to what they *do* (grouping *fish* with *swim*). Similarly, children in the United States asked to memorize the position of objects on a chess board perform better than do African children living in remote villages if household objects familiar to the U.S. children are used. But if rocks are used instead of household objects, the African children do better. In short, it is difficult to produce a test that is truly culture-fair (Samuda, 1998; Sandoval et al., 1998; Serpell, 2000; Valencia & Suzuki, 2003).

The efforts of psychologists to produce culture-fair measures of intelligence relate to a lingering controversy over differences in intelligence between members of minority and majority groups. In attempting to identify whether there are differences between such groups, psychologists have had to confront the broader issue of determining the relative contribution to intelligence of genetic factors (heredity) and experience (environment)—the nature-nurture issue that is one of the basic issues of psychology.

Richard Herrnstein, a psychologist, and Charles Murray, a sociologist, fanned the flames of the debate with the publication of their book *The Bell Curve* in the mid-1990s (Herrnstein & Murray, 1994). They argued that an analysis of IQ differences between whites and blacks demonstrated that although environmental factors played a role, there were also basic genetic differences between the two races. They based their argument on a number of findings. For instance, on average, whites score 15 points higher than do blacks on traditional IQ tests even when socioeconomic status (SES) is taken into account. According to Herrnstein and Murray, middle- and upper-SES blacks score lower than do middle- and upper-SES whites, just as lower-SES blacks score lower on average than do lower-SES whites. Intelligence differences between blacks and whites, they concluded, could not be attributed to environmental differences alone.

Heritability: A measure of the degree to which a characteristic is related to genetic, inherited factors.

Moreover, intelligence in general shows a high degree of **heritability,** a measure of the degree to which a characteristic is related to genetic, inherited factors (e.g., Plomin & Petrill, 1997; Grigorenko, 2000; Plomin, 2003). As can be seen in

Becoming an Informed Consumer of Psychology. One of the major goals of *Understanding Psychology* is to make readers more informed, critical consumers of information relating to psychological issues. These discussions give you the tools to evaluate information concerning human behavior that you may hear or read about in the media or on the Web.

Apart from the advantages of forgetting, say, a bad date, most of us still would like to find ways to improve our memories. Is it possible to find practical ways to increase our recall of information? Most definitely. Research has revealed a number of strategies that can help us develop a better memory (VanLehn, 1996; Hermann, Raybeck, & Gruneberg, 2002: West et al., 2003). Let's look at some of the best.

▶ *The keyword technique.* Suppose you are taking a foreign language class and need to learn vocabulary words. You can try the *keyword technique* of pairing a foreign word with a common English word that has a similar *sound*. This English word is known as the keyword. For example, to learn the Spanish word for duck (*pato*, pronounced *pot-o*), you might choose the keyword *pot*; for the Spanish word for horse (*caballo*, pronounced *cob-eye-yo*), the keyword might be *eye*.

Once you have thought of a keyword, imagine the Spanish word "interacting" with the English keyword. You might envision a duck taking a bath in a pot to remember the word *pato*, or a horse with a large, bulging eye in the center of its head to recall *caballo*. This technique has produced considerably superior results in learning foreign language vocabulary compared with more traditional techniques involving memorization of the words themselves (Pressley, 1987; Gruneberg & Pascoe, 1996; Carney & Levin, 1998).

▶ *Encoding specificity.* Some research suggests that we remember information best in an environment that is the same as or similar to the one where we initially learned it—a phenomenon known as *encoding specificity.* You may do better on a test, then, if you study in the classroom where the test will be given. However, if you must take a test in a room different from the one in which you studied, don't despair: The features of the test itself, such as the wording of the test questions, are sometimes so powerful that they overwhelm the subtler cues relating to the original encoding of the material (Bjork & Richardson-Klarehn, 1989).

▶ *Organization cues.* Many of life's important recall tasks involve texts that you have read. One proven technique for improving recall of written material is to organize the material in memory as you read it for the first time. Organize your reading on the basis of any advance information you have about the content and about its organization . You will then be able to make connections and see relationships among the various facts and process the material at a deeper level, which in turn will later aid recall.

▶ *Effective note taking.* "Less is more" is perhaps the best advice for taking lecture notes that facilitate recall. Rather than trying to jot down every detail of a lecture, it is better to listen and think about the material, and take down the main points. In effective note taking, thinking about the material initially is more important than writing it down. This is one reason that borrowing someone

---

Recap/Evaluate/Rethink segments. Every module ends with a *Recap/Evaluate/Rethink* segment. *Recap* sections review the key concepts found at the beginning of each module. *Evaluate* sections provide a series of questions on the module content that ask for concrete information, in a multiple choice, fill-in, or true-false format. The questions in the *Rethink* sections are designed to encourage you to think critically about a topic or issue, and they often have more than one correct answer.

Answer *Evaluate* and *Rethink* questions! Your responses will indicate both your degree of mastery of the material and the depth of your knowledge. If you have no trouble with the questions, you can be confident that you are studying effectively. Use questions with which you have difficulty as a basis for further study.

RECAP/EVALUATE/RETHINK

RECAP

What is sensation, and how do psychologists study it?

▶ Sensation is the activation of the sense organs by any source of physical energy. In contrast, perception is the process by which we sort out, interpret, analyze, and integrate stimuli to which our senses are exposed. (p. 100)

What is the relationship between a physical stimulus and the kinds of sensory responses that result from it?

▶ Psychophysics studies the relationship between the physical nature of stimuli and the sensory responses they evoke. (p. 101)

▶ The absolute threshold is the smallest amount of physical intensity at which a stimulus can be detected. Although under ideal conditions absolute thresholds are extraordinarily sensitive, the presence of noise (background stimuli that interfere with other stimuli) reduces detection capabilities. (p. 102)

▶ The difference threshold, or just noticeable difference, is the smallest change in the level of stimulation required to sense that a change has occurred. According to Weber's law, a just noticeable difference is a constant proportion of the intensity of an initial stimulus. (p. 103)

▶ Sensory adaptation occurs when we become accustomed to a constant stimulus and change our evaluation of it. Repeated exposure to a stimulus results in an apparent decline in sensitivity to it. (p. 103)

EVALUATE

1. _____ is the stimulation of the sense organs; _____ is the sorting out, interpretation, analysis, and integration of stimuli by the sense organs.
2. The term *absolute threshold* refers to the _____ intensity of a stimulus that must be present for the stimulus to be detected.
3. Weber discovered that for a difference between two stimuli to be perceptible, the stimuli must differ by at least a _____ proportion.
4. After completing a very difficult rock climb in the morning, Carmella found the afternoon climb unexpectedly easy. This case illustrates the phenomenon of _____

RETHINK

1. Do you think it is possible to have sensation without perception? Is it possible to have perception without sensation?
2. Do you think sensory adaptation is essential for everyday psychological functioning?

Answers to Evaluate Questions

1. sensation; perception; 2. smallest; 3. constant; 4. adaptation

KEY TERMS

sensation p. 101
perception p. 101
stimulus p. 101
psychophysics p. 101
absolute threshold p. 102
difference threshold (just noticeable difference) p. 103
Weber's law p. 103
adaptation p. 103

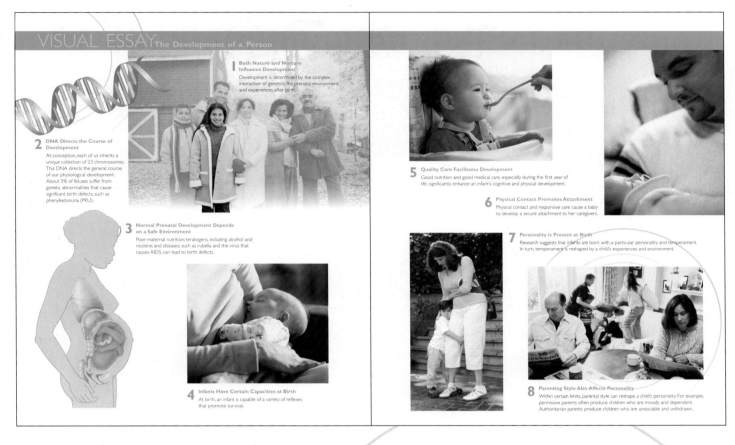

VISUAL ESSAY The Development of a Person

Both Nature and Nurture Influence Development
Development is determined by the complex interaction of genetics, the prenatal environment, and experiences after birth.

2 DNA Directs the Course of Development
At conception, each of us inherits a unique collection of 23 chromosomes. This DNA directs the general course of our physiological development. About 5% of fetuses suffer from genetic abnormalities that cause significant birth defects, such as phenylketonuria (PKU).

3 Normal Prenatal Development Depends on a Safe Environment
Poor maternal nutrition; teratogens, including alcohol and nicotine; and diseases, such as rubella and the virus that causes AIDS, can lead to birth defects.

4 Infants Have Certain Capacities at Birth
At birth, an infant is capable of a variety of reflexes that promote survival.

5 Quality Care Facilitates Development
Good nutrition and good medical care, especially during the first year of life, significantly enhance an infant's cognitive and physical development.

6 Physical Contact Promotes Attachment
Physical contact and responsive care cause a baby to develop a secure attachment to her caregivers.

7 Personality is Present at Birth
Research suggests that infants are born with a particular personality and temperament. In turn, temperament is reshaped by a child's experiences and environment.

8 Parenting Style Also Affects Personality
Within certain limits, parental style can reshape a child's personality. For example, permissive parents often produce children who are moody and dependent. Authoritarian parents produce children who are unsociable and withdrawn.

Looking Back, Epilogue, and Visual Essays. Each set of modules ends with a Looking Back section that involves an extension of the material to the Web. The Epilogue refers back to the Prologue at the start of the set of modules, placing it in the context of the modules' subject matter and asking questions designed to encourage you to think critically about what you've read.

In addition, a number of the Looking Back and Epilogue sections end with a Visual Essay. The Visual Essay summarizes key points covered in the set of modules in a verbal and pictorial way. Studying these Visual Essays will make recall and application of the material easier.

You'll find the same features in every set of modules, providing familiar landmarks to help you chart your way through new material. This structure will help you in organizing each set of modules' content, as well as learning and remembering the material.

One final note: This text uses a reference citation style endorsed by the American Psychological Association (APA). According to APA style, citations include a name and date, typically set off in parentheses at the end of a sentence specifying the author of the work being cited and the year of publication (e.g., Anderson & Dill, 2000). Each of these names and dates refers to a book or article included in the References section at the end of this book.

Understanding Psychology

Introduction to Psychology

Prologue

Seven Became One

Many months later, they would slip the surly bonds of earth, but on this summer day the seven *Columbia* crew members tried their best not to slip those bonds *just yet*. Assembled for an 11-day training mission in a remote Wyoming mountain range in August 2001, the astronauts were charged with scaling the craggy granite face of Wind River Peak, a challenging test of their endurance, leadership skills and cohesiveness as a group . . .

On the way up they passed a cow elk grazing peacefully; they paused to watch the sun rise gold over the mountain. "It was," says [climbing guide] John Kanengieter, "a magical morning." They finally reached the summit just after 11:00 A.M. Exhausted and triumphant, they placed a NASA patch on the peak, posed for a group photo and gaped as Kanengieter pulled out a secret cell phone and dialed NASA headquarters in Houston. Huddling around the phone, the astronauts delivered a message that now seems heartbreakingly poignant. "They all chimed in," says Kanengieter, "and said, '*Columbia* has landed'" (Hewitt et al., 2003, p. 92).

The actual *Columbia* space shuttle mission ended in tragedy as the shuttle attempted to land after a two-week journey in space. All seven astronauts died when the spacecraft disintegrated. While producing questions about its causes, the disaster also raises numerous issues of a psychological nature. Consider, for example, the ways in which different kinds of psychologists would look at the accident:

▶ Psychologists who study the biology that underlies behavior would consider changes in internal bodily activity as the crew members attempted to deal with the suddenly occurring problems on board.

Looking Ahead

▶ Psychologists who study learning and memory would examine what people remember afterward of the incident.

▶ Psychologists who focus on motivation would seek to explain why the crew members engaged in the demanding training necessary to become an astronaut.

▶ Developmental psychologists, who study growth and change throughout life, would ask how learning about the incident would later affect young people's lives.

▶ Clinical and counseling psychologists would try to identify the most effective ways to help family members cope with the loss of life of their loved ones.

▶ Social psychologists would examine the reasons for the outpouring of support for the astronauts' families after their deaths.

Clearly, the approaches that psychologists take are diverse, and so are the questions they address. Consider these examples: How long can we live without sleep? What is the best way to study? What is intelligence? What is normal sexual behavior? Can people change their dysfunctional behavior? Can aging be delayed? How does stress affect our lives? Are suicide bombers insane?

We'll begin to tackle the answers to these questions—and many, many more—as we begin our examination of psychology, the different types of psychologists, and the various roles that psychologists play.

Psychologists at Work

A month after losing his arm in an industrial accident, Henry Washington sits with his eyes closed as Hector Valdez, a research psychologist who studies the perception of touch, dribbles warm water on his cheek. Washington is startled as he reports feeling the water not only on his cheek but running down his missing arm. The sensation is so strong that he checks to be sure that the arm is still missing.

* * *

Evelyn Poirier welcomes to her lab the Chow brothers, a pair of identical twins who were adopted by different families just after they were born. They have come to participate in her study examining similarities in the behavioral and personality traits of twins. By comparing twins who have lived together virtually all their lives with those who have been separated from birth, Poirier is seeking to determine the relative influence of heredity and experience on human behavior.

* * *

Methodically—and painfully—recounting events that occurred in his youth, the college student discloses a childhood secret that he has revealed previously to no one. The listener, psychologist Jonnetta Pennybaker, responds with support, suggesting to him that in fact many people share his concern.

Although the last scene might be the only one that fits your image of the practice of psychology, each of these episodes describes work carried out by contemporary psychologists. Psychologists address extraordinarily different types of behavior, ranging from the most basic biological processes to the ways people are affected by their culture. This breadth is reflected in the definition of the field: **Psychology** is the scientific study of behavior and mental processes.

The simplicity of the definition is in some ways deceiving, concealing ongoing debates about what the scope of the field should be. Should psychologists limit themselves to the study of outward, observable behavior? Is it possible to study thinking scientifically? Should the field encompass the study of such diverse topics as physical and mental health, perception, dreaming, and motivation? Is it appropriate to focus solely on human behavior, or should the behavior of nonhumans be included?

Most psychologists have answered these questions with the argument that the field should be receptive to a variety of viewpoints and approaches. Consequently, the phrase *behavior and mental processes* in the definition of psychology must be understood to mean many things: It encompasses not just what people do but also their thoughts, feelings, perceptions, reasoning processes, memories, and even the biological activities that maintain bodily functioning.

When we speak of the *study* of behavior and mental processes, psychology's scope is equally broad. Psychologists try to describe, predict, and explain human behavior and mental processes, as well as help change and improve the lives of people and the world in which they live. The use of scientific methods allows psychologists to find answers that are far more valid and legitimate than those resulting from mere intuition and speculation, which are often inaccurate (see Figure 1).

The questions in Figure 1 provide just a hint of the various topics that we will encounter as we explore the field of psychology. Our discussions will take us through

Psychology: The scientific study of behavior and mental processes.

FIGURE 1 The scientific method is the basis of all psychological research and is used to find valid answers. Test your knowledge of psychology by answering these questions. (Source: Lamal, 1979.)

Psychological Truths?

To test your knowledge of psychology, try answering the following questions:

1. Infants love their mothers primarily because their mothers fulfill their basic biological needs, such as providing food. True or false? _____
2. Geniuses generally have poor social adjustment. True or false? _____
3. The best way to ensure that a desired behavior will continue after training is completed is to reward that behavior every single time it occurs during training rather than rewarding it only periodically. True or false? _____
4. People with schizophrenia have at least two distinct personalities. True or false? _____
5. If you are having trouble sleeping, the best way to get to sleep is to take a sleeping pill. True or false? _____
6. Children's IQ scores have little to do with how well they do in school. True or false? _____
7. Frequent masturbation can lead to mental illness. True or false? _____
8. Once people reach old age, their leisure activities change radically. True or false? _____
9. Most people would refuse to give painful electric shocks to other people. True or false? _____
10. One of the least important factors affecting how much we like another person is that person's physical attractiveness. True or false? _____

Scoring: The truth about each of these items: They are all false. Based on psychological research, each of these "facts" has been proved untrue. You will learn the reasons why as we explore what psychologists have discovered about human behavior.

the range of what is known about behavior and mental processes. At times we will explore animal behavior because it provides important clues about human behavior. Many psychologists study nonhuman species to determine general laws of behavior that pertain to *all* organisms. But we will always return to the everyday problems that confront human beings.

⓿⓿⓿

INTERACTIVITY 1–1

Multiple causes of behavior

The Subfields of Psychology: Psychology's Family Tree

The diversity of topical areas within psychology has resulted in the development of a number of subfields (described in Figure 2 and illustrated in **Interactivity 1–1**). The subfields of psychology can be likened to an extended family, with assorted nieces and nephews, aunts and uncles, and cousins who, although they may not interact on a day-to-day basis, are related to one another because they share a common goal: understanding behavior. One way to identify the key subfields is to look at some of the basic questions about behavior that they address.

WHAT ARE THE BIOLOGICAL FOUNDATIONS OF BEHAVIOR?

In the most fundamental sense, people are biological organisms. *Behavioral neuroscience* is the subfield of psychology that mainly examines how the brain and the nervous system—but other biological processes as well—determine behavior. Thus, neuroscientists consider how our bodies influence our behavior. For example, they

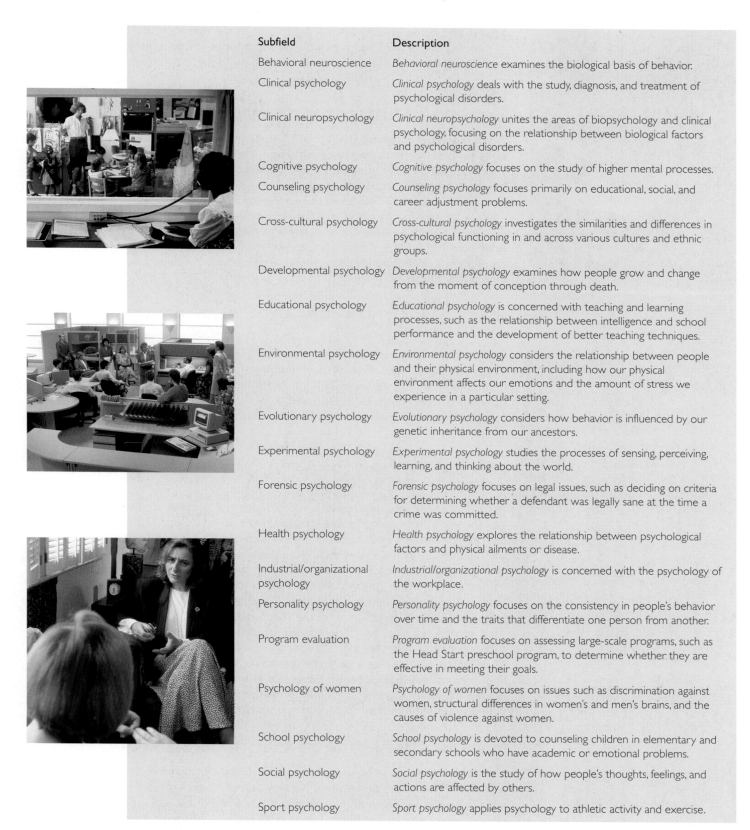

Subfield	Description
Behavioral neuroscience	*Behavioral neuroscience* examines the biological basis of behavior.
Clinical psychology	*Clinical psychology* deals with the study, diagnosis, and treatment of psychological disorders.
Clinical neuropsychology	*Clinical neuropsychology* unites the areas of biopsychology and clinical psychology, focusing on the relationship between biological factors and psychological disorders.
Cognitive psychology	*Cognitive psychology* focuses on the study of higher mental processes.
Counseling psychology	*Counseling psychology* focuses primarily on educational, social, and career adjustment problems.
Cross-cultural psychology	*Cross-cultural psychology* investigates the similarities and differences in psychological functioning in and across various cultures and ethnic groups.
Developmental psychology	*Developmental psychology* examines how people grow and change from the moment of conception through death.
Educational psychology	*Educational psychology* is concerned with teaching and learning processes, such as the relationship between intelligence and school performance and the development of better teaching techniques.
Environmental psychology	*Environmental psychology* considers the relationship between people and their physical environment, including how our physical environment affects our emotions and the amount of stress we experience in a particular setting.
Evolutionary psychology	*Evolutionary psychology* considers how behavior is influenced by our genetic inheritance from our ancestors.
Experimental psychology	*Experimental psychology* studies the processes of sensing, perceiving, learning, and thinking about the world.
Forensic psychology	*Forensic psychology* focuses on legal issues, such as deciding on criteria for determining whether a defendant was legally sane at the time a crime was committed.
Health psychology	*Health psychology* explores the relationship between psychological factors and physical ailments or disease.
Industrial/organizational psychology	*Industrial/organizational psychology* is concerned with the psychology of the workplace.
Personality psychology	*Personality psychology* focuses on the consistency in people's behavior over time and the traits that differentiate one person from another.
Program evaluation	*Program evaluation* focuses on assessing large-scale programs, such as the Head Start preschool program, to determine whether they are effective in meeting their goals.
Psychology of women	*Psychology of women* focuses on issues such as discrimination against women, structural differences in women's and men's brains, and the causes of violence against women.
School psychology	*School psychology* is devoted to counseling children in elementary and secondary schools who have academic or emotional problems.
Social psychology	*Social psychology* is the study of how people's thoughts, feelings, and actions are affected by others.
Sport psychology	*Sport psychology* applies psychology to athletic activity and exercise.

FIGURE 2 The major subfields of psychology.

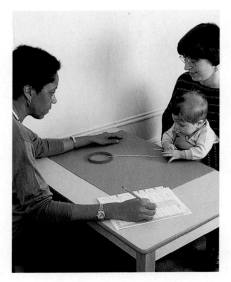

Experimental psychologists study how people sense the world. How do you think researchers adapt their experimental techniques when working with children?

may examine the link between specific sites in the brain and the muscular tremors of people affected by Parkinson's disease or attempt to determine how our emotions are related to physical sensations.

HOW DO PEOPLE SENSE, PERCEIVE, LEARN, AND THINK ABOUT THE WORLD?

If you have ever wondered why you are susceptible to optical illusions, how your body registers pain, or how you can study with the greatest effectiveness, an experimental psychologist can answer your questions. *Experimental psychology* is the branch of psychology that studies the processes of sensing, perceiving, learning, and thinking about the world. (The term *experimental psychologist* is somewhat misleading: Psychologists in every specialty area use experimental techniques.)

Several subspecialties of experimental psychology have become specialties in their own right. One example is *cognitive psychology,* which focuses on higher mental processes, including thinking, memory, reasoning, problem solving, judging, decision making, and language.

WHAT ARE THE SOURCES OF CHANGE AND STABILITY IN BEHAVIOR ACROSS THE LIFE SPAN?

A baby producing her first smile . . . taking her first step . . . saying her first word. These universal milestones in development are also singularly special and unique for each person. *Developmental psychology* studies how people grow and change from the moment of conception through death. *Personality psychology* focuses on the consistency in people's behavior over time and the traits that differentiate one person from another.

HOW DO PSYCHOLOGICAL FACTORS AFFECT PHYSICAL AND MENTAL HEALTH?

If you are frequently depressed, feel constant stress, or seek to overcome a fear that prevents you from carrying out your normal activities, your problems would interest either a health psychologist or a clinical psychologist. *Health psychology* explores the relationship between psychological factors and physical ailments or disease. For example, health psychologists are interested in how long-term stress (a psychological factor) can affect physical health and in identifying ways to promote behavior that brings about good health (Nelson & Simmons, 2003).

Clinical psychology deals with the study, diagnosis, and treatment of psychological disorders. Clinical psychologists are trained to diagnose and treat problems that range from the everyday crises of life, such as unhappiness over the breakup of a relationship, to more extreme conditions, such as profound, lingering depression. Some clinical psychologists also research and investigate issues that range from identifying the early signs of psychological disturbance to studying the relationship between family communication patterns and psychological disorders.

HOW DO OUR SOCIAL NETWORKS AFFECT BEHAVIOR?

Our complex networks of social interrelationships are the focus of study for a number of subfields of psychology. For example, *social psychology* is the study of how people's thoughts, feelings, and actions are affected by others. Social psychologists focus on such diverse topics as human aggression, liking and loving, persuasion, and conformity.

Cross-cultural psychology investigates the similarities and differences in psychological functioning in and across various cultures and ethnic groups. For example, cross-cultural psychologists examine how cultures differ in their use of punishment during child rearing or why certain cultures view academic success as being determined mostly by hard work while others see it as being determined mostly by innate ability (Matsumoto, 2001; Schoenpflug, 2003; Shweder, 2003).

EXPANDING PSYCHOLOGY'S FRONTIERS

As a science, psychology has boundaries that are constantly growing. Two newer members of the field's family tree—clinical neuropsychology and evolutionary psychology—have sparked particular excitement, and debate, within psychology (Adair & Vohra, 2003).

Clinical neuropsychology unites the areas of neuroscience and clinical psychology: It focuses on the origin of psychological disorders in biological factors. Building on advances in our understanding of the structure and chemistry of the brain, the specialty is leading to promising new treatments for psychological disorders as well as debates over the use of medication to control behavior.

Evolutionary psychology considers how behavior is influenced by our genetic inheritance from our ancestors. The evolutionary approach suggests that the chemical coding of information in our cells not only determines traits such as hair color and race but also holds the key to understanding a broad variety of behaviors that helped our ancestors survive and reproduce (Geary & Bjorklund, 2000; de Waal, 2002; Durrant & Ellis, 2003).

Evolutionary concepts have been used to explain similarities in behavior across cultures, such as the qualities desired in potential mates. However, such explanations have stirred controversy by suggesting that many significant behaviors are wired into the human species as a result of evolution and occur automatically.

Working at Psychology

Help Wanted: Assistant professor at a small liberal arts college. Teach undergraduate courses in introductory psychology and courses in specialty areas of cognitive psychology, perception, and learning. Strong commitment to quality teaching and student advising necessary. The candidate must also provide evidence of scholarship and research productivity.

* * *

Help Wanted: Industrial-organizational consulting psychologist. International firm is seeking psychologists for full-time career positions as consultants to management. Candidates must have the ability to establish a rapport with senior business executives and help them find innovative, practical, and psychologically sound solutions to problems concerning people and organizations.

* * *

Help Wanted: Clinical psychologist. Ph.D., internship experience, and license required. Comprehensive clinic seeks psychologist to work with children and adults providing individual and group therapy, psychological evaluations, crisis intervention, and development of behavior treatment plans on multidisciplinary team. Broad experience with substance-abuse problems is desirable.

As these advertisements suggest, psychologists are employed in a variety of settings. Many doctoral-level psychologists are employed by institutions of higher learning (universities and colleges) or are self-employed, usually working as private practitioners treating clients (see Figure 3). Other work sites include hospitals, clinics, mental health centers, counseling centers, government human-services organizations, and schools (APA, 2000).

Why do so many psychologists work in academic settings? Because these are effective settings for three major roles played by psychologists in society: teacher,

FIGURE 3 The breakdown of where U.S. psychologists (who have a Ph.D. or Psy.D. degree) work (APA, 2000). Why do you think so many psychologists work in college settings?

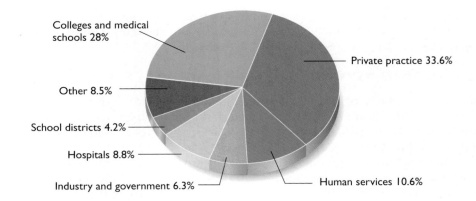

scientist, and clinical practitioner. Many psychology professors are also actively involved in research or in serving clients. Whatever the particular job site, however, psychologists share a commitment to improving individual lives as well as society in general.

PSYCHOLOGISTS: A STATISTICAL PORTRAIT

Is there an "average" psychologist in terms of personal characteristics? Probably not. About half of U.S. psychologists are men, and about half are women. It is predicted that by 2010 women will outnumber men in the field (Kite et al., 2001; Fowler, 2002; Harton & Lyons, 2003).

Although most psychologists today work in the United States, about one-third of the world's 500,000 psychologists are found elsewhere (see Figure 4). Psychologists outside the United States are increasingly influential in adding to the knowledge base and practices of psychology (Mays, Rubin, Sabourin, & Walker, 1996; Pawlik & d'Ydewalle, 1996; Peiro & Lunt, 2003).

An issue of great concern is the relative lack of racial and ethnic diversity among psychologists in the United States. According to figures compiled by the American Psychological Association (APA), the vast majority of psychologists are white. Only 6 percent of all psychologists are members of racial minority groups. Although the number of minority-group members entering the field is increasing, it has not kept up with the growth of the minority population at large (Kohout, 2001; Fowler, 2002).

The underrepresentation of racial and ethnic minorities among psychologists is significant for several reasons. First, the field of psychology is diminished by a lack of the diverse perspectives and talents that minority-group members can provide. Furthermore, minority-group psychologists serve as role models for members of minority communities, and their lack of representation in the profession might deter other minority-group members from entering the field. Finally, because members of minority groups often prefer to receive psychological therapy from treatment providers of their own race or ethnic group, the rarity of minority psychologists can discourage some members of minority groups from seeking treatment (Chamberlin, 1998; Bernal et al., 2002; Jenkins et al., 2003).

THE EDUCATION OF A PSYCHOLOGIST

How do people become psychologists? The most common route is a long one. Most psychologists have a doctorate, either a *Ph.D.* (doctor of philosophy) or, less frequently, a *Psy.D.* (doctor of psychology). The Ph.D. is a research degree that requires a dissertation based on an original investigation. The Psy.D. is obtained by psychologists who wish to focus on the treatment of psychological disorders. (Psychologists are distinct from psychiatrists, who are physicians who specialize in the treatment of psychological disorders.)

FIGURE 4 Origin of published research (APA, 2000). How do you think the heavy concentration of psychologists in North America affects the field of psychology?

Both the Ph.D. and the Psy.D. typically take four or five years of work past the bachelor's level. Some fields of psychology involve education beyond the doctorate. For instance, doctoral-level clinical psychologists, who deal with people with psychological disorders, typically spend an additional year doing an internship.

About a third of people working in the field of psychology have a master's degree as their highest degree, which is earned after two or three years of graduate work. These psychologists teach, provide therapy, conduct research, or work in specialized programs dealing with drug abuse or crisis intervention. Some work in universities, government, and business, collecting and analyzing data.

Although it takes a considerable amount of time to be trained as a psychologist, the number of psychologists continues to grow. Currently, there are close to 60,000 students enrolled in psychology graduate programs, a 10 percent increase from six years earlier. Some of these students are motivated by the desire to provide direct care to people facing psychological difficulties; others are driven by curiosity about the determinants of behavior. Some see themselves primarily as scientists, researching questions about human behavior, whereas others are more interested in providing help to specific individuals. Regardless of their specific interest, these students, along with current members of the field, share a desire to improve the human condition and believe that psychology provides a route to that goal (Chamberlin, 2000).

CAREERS FOR PSYCHOLOGY MAJORS

Although some psychology majors head for graduate school in psychology or an unrelated field, the majority join the workforce immediately after graduation. Most report that the jobs they take after graduation are related to their psychology background.

An undergraduate major in psychology provides excellent preparation for a variety of occupations. Because undergraduates who specialize in psychology develop good analytical skills, are trained to think critically, and are able to synthesize and evaluate information well, employers in business, industry, and the government value their preparation (Kuther, 2003).

The most common areas of employment for psychology majors are in the social services, including working in administration, serving as a counselor, and providing direct care. Some 20 percent of recipients of bachelor's degrees in psychology work in the social services or in some other form of public affairs. In addition, psychology majors often enter the fields of education or business or work for federal, state, and local governments (see Figure 5; APA, 2000; Murray, 2002).

What's the pay for psychology-related fields? In the early 2000s starting salaries for people with psychology majors who have just graduated with a B.A. degree have ranged from $20,000 to $45,000, depending on the type of job and location, with an average starting salary of around $30,000. Business-related fields pay the best, and social service jobs in nonprofit agencies are at the low end of the scale. But even in lower-paying jobs, salaries rise as employees move into administrative positions (Murray, 2002).

FIGURE 5 Although many psychology majors pursue employment in social services, a background in psychology can prepare one for many professions outside the social services field. What is it about the science of psychology that makes it such a versatile field? (Source: Kuther, 2003.)

Positions Obtained by Psychology Majors

Business Field	Education/Academic	Social Fields
Administrative assistant	Administration	Activities coordinator
Affirmative action officer	Child-care provider	Behavioral specialist
Advertising trainee	Child-care worker/	Career counselor
Benefits manager	supervisor	Case worker
Claims specialist	Data management	Child protection worker
Community relations officer	Laboratory assistant	Clinical coordinator
Customer relations	Parent/family education	Community outreach
Data management	Preschool teacher	worker
Employee recruitment	Public opinion surveyor	Corrections officer
Employee counselor	Research assistant	Counselor assistant
Human resources	Teaching assistant	Crisis intervention
coordinator/manager/specialist		counselor
Labor relations manager/specialist		Employment counselor
Loan officer		Group home attendant
Management trainee		Occupational therapist
Marketing		Probation officer
Personnel manager/officer		Program manager
Product and services research		Rehabilitation counselor
Programs/events coordination		Residence counselor
Public relations		Mental health assistant
Retail sales management		Social service assistant
Sales representative		Social worker assistant
Special features writing/reporting		Social worker
Staff training and development		Substance abuse counselor
Trainer/training officer		Youth counselor

RECAP/EVALUATE/RETHINK

RECAP

What is the science of psychology?

▶ Psychology is the scientific study of behavior and mental processes, encompassing not just what people do but their biological activities, feelings, perceptions, memory, reasoning, and thoughts. (p. 5)

What are the major specialties in the field of psychology?

▶ Behavioral neuroscientists focus on the biological basis of behavior, and experimental psychologists study the processes of sensing, perceiving, learning, and thinking about the world. (p. 6)

▶ Cognitive psychology, an outgrowth of experimental psychology, studies higher mental processes, including memory, knowing, thinking, reasoning, problem solving, judging, decision making, and language. (p. 8)

▶ Developmental psychologists study how people grow and change throughout the life span. (p. 8)

▶ Personality psychologists consider the consistency and change in an individual's behavior, as well as the individual differences that distinguish one person's behavior from another's. (p. 8)

▶ Health psychologists study psychological factors that affect physical disease, and clinical psychologists consider the study, diagnosis, and treatment of psychological disorders. (p. 8)

▶ Social psychology is the study of how people's thoughts, feelings, and actions are affected by others. (p. 8)

▶ Cross-cultural psychology examines the similarities and differences in psychological functioning among various cultures. (p. 8)

▶ Other increasingly important fields are clinical neuropsychology and evolutionary psychology. (p. 9)

Where do psychologists work?

▶ Psychologists are employed in a variety of settings. Although the primary sites of employment are private practice and colleges, many psychologists are found in hospitals, clinics, community mental health centers, and counseling centers. (p. 9)

EVALUATE

1. Match each subfield of psychology with the issues or questions posed below.

   a. Behavioral neuroscience
   b. Experimental psychology
   c. Cognitive psychology
   d. Developmental psychology
   e. Personality psychology
   f. Health psychology
   g. Clinical psychology
   h. Counseling psychology
   i. Educational psychology
   j. School psychology
   k. Social psychology
   l. Industrial psychology
   m. Consumer psychology

   1. Joan, a college freshman, is panicking. She needs to learn better organizational skills and study habits to cope with the demands of college.
   2. At what age do children generally begin to acquire an emotional attachment to their fathers?
   3. It is thought that pornographic films that depict violence against women may prompt aggressive behavior in some men.
   4. What chemicals are released in the human body as a result of a stressful event? What are their effects on behavior?
   5. Luis is unique in his manner of responding to crisis situations, with an even temperament and a positive outlook.
   6. The general public is more apt to buy products that are promoted by attractive and successful actors.
   7. The teachers of 8-year-old Jack are concerned that he has recently begun to withdraw socially and to show little interest in schoolwork.
   8. Janetta's job is demanding and stressful. She wonders if her lifestyle is making her more prone to certain illnesses, such as cancer and heart disease.
   9. A psychologist is intrigued by the fact that some people are much more sensitive to painful stimuli than others are.
   10. A strong fear of crowds leads a young woman to seek treatment for her problem.
   11. What mental strategies are involved in solving complex word problems?
   12. What teaching methods most effectively motivate elementary school students to successfully accomplish academic tasks?
   13. Jessica is asked to develop a management strategy that will encourage safer work practices in an assembly plant.

RETHINK

1. Why might the study of twins who were raised together and twins who were not be helpful in distinguishing the effects of heredity and environment?

2. Suppose you know a seven-year-old child who is having problems learning to read and you want to help. Imagine that you can consult as many psychologists as you want. How might each type of psychologist approach the problem?

3. Do you think intuition and common sense are sufficient for understanding why people act the way they do? In what ways is a scientific approach appropriate for studying human behavior?

Answers to Evaluate Question

1. a-4, b-9, c-11, d-2, e-5, f-8, g-10, h-1, i-12, j-7, k-3, l-13, m-6

KEY TERMS

psychology p. 5

A Science Evolves: The Past, the Present, and the Future

Some half million years ago people assumed that psychological problems were caused by evil spirits. To allow those spirits to escape from a person's body, ancient healers performed an operation called trephining. Trephining consisted of chipping away at a patient's skull with crude stone instruments until a hole was cut through the bone. Because archaeologists have found skulls with signs of healing around the opening, it's a fair guess that some patients survived the cure.

* * *

According to the seventeenth-century philosopher Descartes, nerves were hollow tubes through which "animal spirits" conducted impulses in the same way that water is transmitted through a pipe. When a person put a finger too close to a fire, heat was transmitted into the brain through the tubes.

* * *

Franz Josef Gall, an eighteenth-century physician, argued that a trained observer could discern intelligence, moral character, and other basic personality characteristics from the shape and number of bumps on a person's skull. His theory gave rise to the "science" of phrenology, employed by hundreds of devoted practitioners in the nineteenth century.

Although these explanations might sound far-fetched, in their own times they represented the most advanced thinking about what might be called the psychology of the era. Our understanding of behavior has advanced tremendously since those earlier views were formulated, yet most of the advances have been recent—for, as sciences go, psychology is one of the "new kids on the block." (For highlights in the development of the field, see Figure 1, and explore psychology's timeline further in **Interactivity 2–1**)

Psychology's roots can be traced back to the ancient Greeks and Romans, and philosophers argued for hundreds of years about some of the questions psychologists grapple with today. However, the formal beginning of psychology as a science is generally set at 1879, when Wilhelm Wundt established in Leipzig, Germany, the first experimental laboratory devoted to psychological phenomena. At about the same time, William James was setting up his laboratory in Cambridge, Massachusetts.

Ⓐ Ⓐ Ⓐ

INTERACTIVITY 2–1

Milestones in psychology

The Roots of Psychology

When Wilhelm Wundt set up the first psychology laboratory in 1879, his aim was to study the building blocks of the mind. He considered psychology to be the study of conscious experience, and he developed a perspective that came to be known as structuralism. **Structuralism** focused on the basic elements that constitute the foundation of perception, consciousness, thinking, emotions, and other kinds of mental states and activities.

To come to an understanding of how basic sensations combine to produce our perception of the world, Wundt and other structuralists used a procedure called **introspection** to study the mind. In this procedure, people were presented with a

Structuralism: Wundt's approach, which focuses on the fundamental elements that form the foundation of thinking, consciousness, emotions, and other kinds of mental states and activities.

Introspection: A procedure used to study the structure of the mind in which subjects are asked to describe in detail what they are experiencing when they are exposed to a stimulus.

FIGURE I This timeline illustrates the major milestones in the development of psychology.

◀ **500,000 BC** Trephining used to allow the escape of evil spirits

◀ **430 BC** Hippocrates argues for four temperaments of personality

1690 John Locke introduces idea of *tabula rasa*

1879 Wilhelm Wundt inaugurates first psychology laboratory in Leipzig, Germany

Forerunners of Psychology   1800

1637 Descartes describes animal spirits

1807 Franz Josef Gall proposes phrenology

1890 *Principles of Psychology* published by William James

Wilhelm Wundt

Functionalism: An early approach to psychology that concentrated on what the mind does—the functions of mental activity—and the role of behavior in allowing people to adapt to their environments.

stimulus—such as a bright green object or a sentence printed on a card—and were asked to describe, in their own words and in as much detail as they could, what they were experiencing. Wundt argued that by analyzing the reports people offered of their reactions, psychologists could come to a better understanding of the structure of the mind.

Over time, psychologists challenged Wundt's structuralism. They became increasingly dissatisfied with the assumption that introspection could unlock the fundamental elements of the mind. Introspection was not a truly scientific technique. There were few ways an outside observer could confirm the accuracy of others' introspections. Moreover, people had difficulty describing some kinds of inner experiences, such as emotional responses. Those drawbacks led to the evolution of new approaches, which largely supplanted structuralism.

However, the heritage of structuralism still exists, with some psychologists showing a renewed interest in people's descriptions of their inner experience. For example, cognitive psychologists, who focus on higher mental processes such as thinking, memory, and problem solving, have developed innovative techniques that help us understand people's conscious experience and overcome many of the difficulties inherent in introspection.

The main perspective that came to replace structuralism as psychology evolved is known as functionalism. Rather than focusing on the mind's components, **functionalism** concentrated on what the mind *does* and how behavior *functions*.

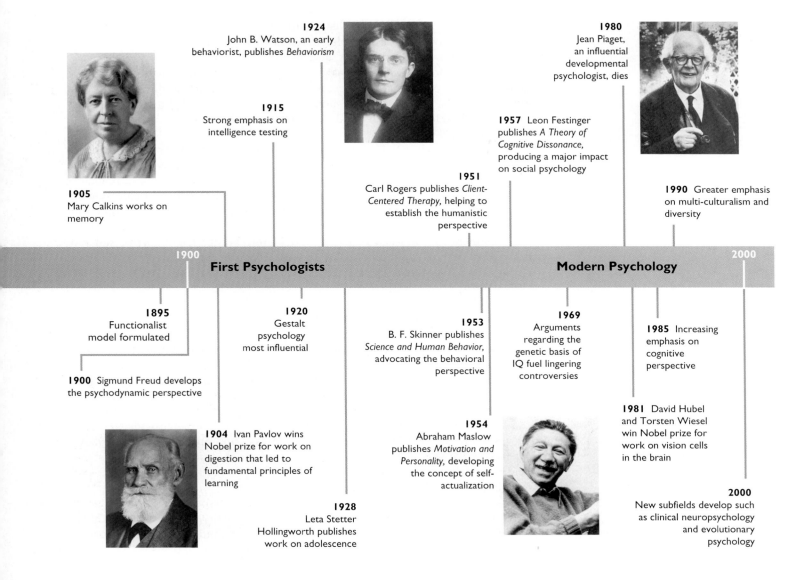

1924
John B. Watson, an early behaviorist, publishes *Behaviorism*

1915
Strong emphasis on intelligence testing

1980
Jean Piaget, an influential developmental psychologist, dies

1957 Leon Festinger publishes *A Theory of Cognitive Dissonance,* producing a major impact on social psychology

1951
Carl Rogers publishes *Client-Centered Therapy,* helping to establish the humanistic perspective

1905
Mary Calkins works on memory

1990 Greater emphasis on multi-culturalism and diversity

1900

First Psychologists

Modern Psychology

2000

1895
Functionalist model formulated

1920
Gestalt psychology most influential

1953
B. F. Skinner publishes *Science and Human Behavior,* advocating the behavioral perspective

1969
Arguments regarding the genetic basis of IQ fuel lingering controversies

1985 Increasing emphasis on cognitive perspective

1900 Sigmund Freud develops the psychodynamic perspective

1904 Ivan Pavlov wins Nobel prize for work on digestion that led to fundamental principles of learning

1954
Abraham Maslow publishes *Motivation and Personality,* developing the concept of self-actualization

1981 David Hubel and Torsten Wiesel win Nobel prize for work on vision cells in the brain

2000
New subfields develop such as clinical neuropsychology and evolutionary psychology

1928
Leta Stetter Hollingworth publishes work on adolescence

Functionalists, whose perspective became prominent in the early 1900s, asked what roles behavior plays in allowing people to better adapt to their environments. Led by the American psychologist William James, the functionalists examined how behavior allows people to satisfy their needs. The American educator John Dewey drew on functionalism to develop the field of school psychology, proposing ways to best meet students' educational needs.

Another important reaction to structuralism was the development of gestalt psychology in the early 1900s. **Gestalt psychology** is a perspective focusing on how perception is organized. Instead of considering the individual parts that make up thinking, gestalt psychologists took the opposite tack, concentrating on how people consider individual elements together as units or wholes. Their credo was "The whole is different from the sum of its parts," meaning that when considered together, the basic elements that compose our perception of objects produce something greater and more meaningful than those individual elements alone. Gestalt psychologists have made substantial contributions to our understanding of perception.

PowerWeb: The Principles of Psychology

www.mhhe.com/feldmanup7

Gestalt (geh SHTALLT) psychology: An approach to psychology that focuses on the organization of perception and thinking in a "whole" sense rather than on the individual elements of perception.

WOMEN IN PSYCHOLOGY: FOUNDING MOTHERS

As in many scientific fields, societal constraints hindered women's participation in the early development of psychology. Despite the hurdles they faced, several women made major contributions to psychology, although until recently their contributions were largely overlooked. For example, Margaret Floy Washburn was the first woman to receive a doctorate in psychology, and she did important work on animal behavior. Leta Stetter Hollingworth was one of the first psychologists to focus on child development and on women's issues. She collected data to refute the view, popular in the early 1900s, that women's abilities periodically declined during parts of the menstrual cycle (Hollingworth, 1943/1990; Denmark & Fernandez, 1993; Furumoto & Scarborough, 2002).

Mary Calkins, who studied memory in the early part of the twentieth century, became the first female president of the American Psychological Association. Karen Horney (pronounced "HORN-eye") focused on the social and cultural factors behind personality, and June Etta Downey spearheaded the study of personality traits and became the first woman to head a psychology department at a state university. Anna Freud (daughter of Sigmund Freud) also made notable contributions to the treatment of abnormal behavior, and Mamie Phipps Clark carried out pioneering work on how children of color grew to recognize racial differences (Horney, 1937; Stevens & Gardner, 1982; Lal, 2002).

Today's Perspectives

The women and the men who laid the foundations of psychology shared a common goal: to explain and understand behavior, using scientific methods. Seeking to achieve the same goal, the tens of thousands of psychologists who followed those early pioneers embraced—and often rejected—a variety of broad perspectives.

The various perspectives offer distinct outlooks and emphasize different factors. Just as we can use more than one map to find our way around a particular region—for instance, a map that shows roads and highways and another map that shows major landmarks—psychologists developed a variety of approaches to understanding behavior. When considered jointly, the different perspectives provide the means to explain behavior in its amazing variety.

Today, the field of psychology involves five major perspectives (summarized in Figure 2 and reviewed in **Interactivity 2–2**). Each of these broad perspectives emphasizes different aspects of behavior and mental processes, and each takes our understanding of behavior in a somewhat different direction.

INTERACTIVITY 2–2

Five perspectives of psychology

Key Characteristics of the Major Perspectives of Psychology

Neuroscience

Views behavior from the perspective of biological functioning

Psychodynamic

Believes behavior is motivated by inner, unconscious forces over which person has little control

Behavioral

Focuses on observable behavior

Cognitive

Examines how people understand and think about the world

Humanistic

Contends that people can control their behavior and that they naturally try to reach their full potential

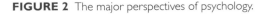

FIGURE 2 The major perspectives of psychology.

THE NEUROSCIENCE PERSPECTIVE: BLOOD, SWEAT, AND FEARS

When we get down to the basics, human beings are animals made of skin and bones. The **neuroscience perspective** considers how people and nonhumans function biologically: how individual nerve cells are joined together, how the inheritance of certain characteristics from parents and other ancestors influences behavior, how the functioning of the body affects hopes and fears, which behaviors are instinctual, and so forth. Even more complex kinds of behaviors, such as a baby's response to strangers, are viewed as having critical biological components by psychologists who work from the neuroscience perspective. This perspective includes the study of heredity and evolution, considering how heredity may influence behavior, and behavioral neuroscience, which examines how the brain and the nervous system affect behavior.

Because every behavior can be broken down to some extent into its biological components, the neuroscience perspective has broad appeal. Psychologists who subscribe to this perspective have made major contributions to the understanding and betterment of human life, ranging from developing cures for certain types of deafness to identifying medications to treat people with severe mental disorders.

Neuroscience perspective: The approach that views behavior from the perspective of the brain, the nervous system, and other biological functions.

THE PSYCHODYNAMIC PERSPECTIVE: UNDERSTANDING THE INNER PERSON

To many people who have never taken a psychology course, psychology begins and ends with the psychodynamic perspective. Proponents of the **psychodynamic perspective** believe that behavior is motivated by inner forces and conflicts about which we have little awareness or control. Dreams and slips of the tongue are viewed as indications of what a person is truly feeling within a seething cauldron of unconscious psychic activity.

The origins of the psychodynamic view are intimately linked with one individual: Sigmund Freud. Freud was a Viennese physician in the early 1900s whose ideas about unconscious determinants of behavior had a revolutionary effect on twentieth-century thinking, not just in psychology but in related fields as well. Although some of the original Freudian principles have been roundly criticized, the contemporary psychodynamic perspective has provided a means not only to understand and treat some kinds of psychological disorders but also to understand everyday phenomena such as prejudice and aggression.

Psychodynamic perspective: The approach based on the belief that behavior is motivated by unconscious inner forces over which the individual has little control.

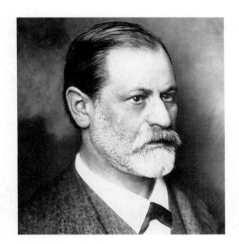

Sigmund Freud

THE BEHAVIORAL PERSPECTIVE: OBSERVING THE OUTER PERSON

Whereas the neuroscience and psychodynamic approaches look inside the organism to determine the causes of its behavior, the behavioral perspective takes a very different approach. The **behavioral perspective** grew out of a rejection of psychology's early emphasis on the inner workings of the mind, suggesting instead that the field should focus on observable behavior that can be measured objectively.

John B. Watson was the first major American psychologist to advocate a behavioral approach. Working in the 1920s, Watson was adamant in his view that one could gain a complete understanding of behavior by studying and modifying the environment in which people operate.

In fact, Watson believed rather optimistically that it was possible to elicit any desired type of behavior by controlling a person's environment. This philosophy is clear in his own words: "Give me a dozen healthy infants, well-formed, and my own specified world to bring them up in and I'll guarantee to take any one at random and train him to become any type of specialist I might select—doctor, lawyer, artist, merchant-chief, and yes, even beggar-man and thief, regardless of his talents, penchants,

Behavioral perspective: The approach that suggests that observable behavior should be the focus of study.

PowerWeb: Psychology as the Behaviorist Views It

www.mhhe.com/feldmanup7

tendencies, abilities, vocations and race of his ancestors" (Watson, 1924). The behavioral perspective was championed later by B. F. Skinner, who until his death in 1990 was probably the best-known psychologist. Much of our understanding of how people learn new behaviors is based on the behavioral perspective.

As we will see, the behavioral perspective crops up along every byway of psychology. Along with its influence in the area of learning processes, this perspective has made contributions in such diverse areas as treating mental disorders, curbing aggression, resolving sexual problems, and ending drug addiction.

THE COGNITIVE PERSPECTIVE: IDENTIFYING THE ROOTS OF UNDERSTANDING

Cognitive perspective: The approach that focuses on how people think, understand, and know about the world.

The route to understanding behavior leads some psychologists straight into the mind. Evolving in part from structuralism and in part as a reaction to behaviorism (which focused so heavily on observable behavior and the environment), the **cognitive perspective** focuses on how people think, understand, and know about the world. The emphasis is on learning how people comprehend and represent the outside world within themselves and how our ways of thinking about the world influence our behavior.

Many psychologists working from the cognitive perspective compare human thinking to the workings of a computer, considering how information is inputted, transformed, stored, and retrieved. In their view, thinking is *information processing.*

Psychologists who rely on the cognitive perspective ask questions ranging from how people make decisions to whether a person can watch television and study at the same time. The common elements that link cognitive approaches are an emphasis on how people understand and think about the world and an interest in describing the patterns and irregularities in the operation of our minds.

THE HUMANISTIC PERSPECTIVE: THE UNIQUE QUALITIES OF *HOMO SAPIENS*

Humanistic perspective: The approach that suggests that all individuals naturally strive to grow, develop, and be in control of their lives and behavior.

Rejecting the views that behavior is determined largely by automatically unfolding biological forces, unconscious processes, or the environment, the **humanistic perspective** instead suggests that all individuals naturally strive to grow, develop, and be in control of their lives and behavior. Humanistic psychologists maintain that each of us has the capacity to seek and reach fulfillment.

According to Carl Rogers and Abraham Maslow, who were central figures in the development of the humanistic perspective, people will strive to reach their full potential if they are given the opportunity. The emphasis of the humanistic perspective is on *free will,* the ability to freely make decisions about one's own behavior and life. The notion of free will stands in contrast to *determinism,* which sees behavior as caused, or determined, by things beyond a person's control.

The humanistic perspective assumes that people have the ability to make their own choices about their behavior rather than relying on societal standards. More than any other approach, it stresses the role of psychology in enriching people's lives and helping them achieve self-fulfillment. The humanistic perspective has had an important influence on psychologists, reminding them of their commitment to the individual person in society.

It is important not to let the abstract qualities of the broad approaches we have discussed lull you into thinking that they are purely theoretical: These perspectives underlie ongoing work of a practical nature, as we will discuss throughout this book. To start seeing how psychology can improve everyday life, read the *Applying Psychology in the 21st Century* box.

Psychology and the Reduction of Violence

"Hundreds of soldiers killed in fierce fighting."

"Investigators search for clues at site of terrorist attack."

"Police respond to domestic violence incident."

A quick survey of any day's news headlines reminds us that violence remains a significant problem in our world. From playground bullies to video games to genocide, violence is part of many people's daily experience.

Addressing this steady stream of violence and violent images, a considerable number of psychologists are devoting their energies and expertise to studying violence and aggression. Their work—coming from a variety of perspectives—is helping us better understand the causes and consequences of violence, as well as devise innovative ways of preventing it (Pettit & Dodge, 2003).

For example, Brad Bushman and Craig Anderson have been looking at the ways in which violent video games may result in heightened violence on the part of those who play those games. They have found that people who play such games have an altered view of the world, seeing it as a more violent place. In addition, they are more apt to respond to aggression even when provoked only minimally (Bushman & Anderson, 2001, 2002).

Other psychologists are working to limit the prevalence of violent behavior, and some have designed programs to teach people how to cope with exposure to violence. Because patterns of aggressive behavior can start early in life, many violence-reduction programs target school-age children, especially children

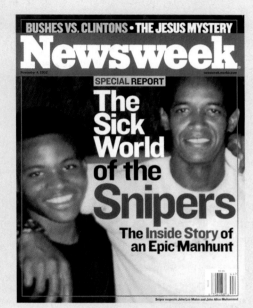

The role of guns in American culture is a widely discussed and controversial topic. What can psychologists add to the discussion?

from schools and neighborhoods where violence has occurred particularly frequently. For example, one promising psychology-based violence-reduction program is the *Fast Track Prevention Program* (Crawford, 2002). *Fast Track* begins working with students when they are first-graders and offers ten years' worth of workshops to them and their families. Focusing on improving many aspects of the children's lives, including academic skills, social skills, their parents' parenting skills, and much more, *Fast Track* has been

effective in reducing children's aggressive behavior at school and at home while contributing to gains in academic performance.

Of course, ten-year programs such as *Fast Track* are both expensive and time-consuming, making it difficult for many school districts to implement similar interventions. Psychologists are sensitive to these concerns and therefore are also working on less expensive, short-term programs. For instance, one group of researchers developed and tested a four-week conflict resolution training program for kindergarten students (Stevahn, Johnson, Johnson, Oberle, & Wahl, 2000). In a series of thirty-minute lessons, that program taught children about friendship and ways to resolve differences without resorting to aggression. Follow-up assessments showed that children who completed the conflict resolution program were willing and able to use the nonviolent conflict resolution techniques they learned and had a better understanding of the concept of friendship than did similar children who had not participated in the program.

Although violence-reduction programs like these may not in themselves be able to eliminate violent behavior completely, they make a positive difference in the lives of their participants. Furthermore, they represent only one of the many ways in which psychologists are striving to understand and curb violence in today's world (Flannery et al., 2003).

RETHINK

In addition to programs for schoolchildren, psychologists are designing violence-reduction programs for other social and demographic groups as well. For what other groups do you think such programs would be particularly helpful? How would the different perspectives of psychology be useful in designing such programs?

RECAP/EVALUATE/RETHINK

RECAP

What are the historical roots of the field of psychology?

- ▶ The foundations of psychology were established by Wilhelm Wundt in Germany in 1879. (p. 15)
- ▶ Early perspectives that guided the work of psychologists were structuralism, functionalism, and gestalt theory. (p. 16)

What are the major approaches used by contemporary psychologists?

- ▶ The neuroscience approach focuses on the biological functioning of people and animals, considering the most basic components of behavior. (p. 19)
- ▶ The psychodynamic perspective suggests that there are powerful, unconscious inner forces and conflicts about which people have little or no awareness and which are primary determinants of behavior. (p. 19)
- ▶ The behavioral perspective deemphasizes internal processes and concentrates instead on observable behavior, suggesting that understanding and control of a person's environment are sufficient to fully explain and modify behavior. (p. 19)
- ▶ Cognitive approaches to behavior consider how people know, understand, and think about the world. (p. 20)
- ▶ The humanistic perspective emphasizes that people are uniquely inclined toward psychological growth and higher levels of functioning and that they will strive to reach their full potential. (p. 26)

EVALUATE

1. Wundt described psychology as the study of conscious experience, a perspective he called _____.
2. Early psychologists studied the mind by asking people to describe what they were experiencing when exposed to various stimuli. This procedure was known as _____.

3. The statement "In order to study human behavior, we must consider the whole of perception rather than its component parts" might be made by a person subscribing to which perspective of psychology?
4. Jeanne's therapist asks her to recount a violent dream she recently experienced in order to gain insight into the unconscious forces affecting her behavior. Jeanne's therapist is working from a _____ perspective.
5. "It is behavior that can be observed that should be studied, not the suspected inner workings of the mind." This statement was most likely made by someone with which perspective?
   a. cognitive perspective
   b. neuroscience perspective
   c. humanistic perspective
   d. behavioral perspective

6. "My therapist is wonderful! She always points out my positive traits. She dwells on my uniqueness and strength as an individual. I feel much more confident about myself—as if I'm really growing and reaching my potential." The therapist being described most likely practices from a _____ perspective.

RETHINK

1. How might today's major perspectives of psychology be related to the earliest perspectives, such as structuralism, functionalism, and gestalt psychology?
2. Focusing on one of the five major perspectives in use today (i.e., neuroscience, psychodynamic, behavioral, cognitive, and humanistic), can you describe the sorts of research questions and studies that researchers using that perspective might pursue?

Answers to Evaluate Questions

1. structuralism; 2. introspection; 3. gestalt; 4. psychodynamic; 5. d;
6. humanistic

KEY TERMS

structuralism p. 15
introspection p. 15
functionalism p. 16
gestalt psychology p. 17

neuroscience perspective p. 19
psychodynamic perspective p. 19

behavioral perspective p. 19
cognitive perspective p. 20

humanistic perspective p. 20

Psychology's Key Issues and Controversies

What are psychology's key issues and controversies?

What is the future of psychology likely to hold?

INTERACTIVITY 3–1

Key issues in psychology

As you consider the many topics and perspectives that make up psychology, ranging from a narrow focus on minute biochemical influences on behavior to a broad focus on social behaviors, you might find yourself thinking that the discipline lacks cohesion. However, the field is more unified than a first glimpse might suggest. For one thing, no matter what topical area a psychologist specializes in, he or she will rely on one of the five major perspectives. For example, a developmental psychologist who specializes in the study of children could make use of the cognitive perspective *or* the psychodynamic perspective *or* any of the other major perspectives.

Psychologists also agree on what the key issues of the field are (Figure 1 and **Interactivity 3–1** summarize those issues). Although there are major arguments regarding how best to address and resolve those issues, psychology is a unified science because psychologists of all perspectives agree that the issues must be addressed for the field to advance. As you contemplate these key issues, try not to think of them in "either/or" terms. Instead, consider the opposing viewpoints on each issue as the opposite ends of a continuum, with the positions of individual psychologists typically falling somewhere between the two ends.

Nature (heredity) versus nurture (environment) is one of the major issues that psychologists address. How much of our behavior is due to heredity (or "nature") and how much is due to environment ("nurture"), and what is the interplay between the

Issue	Neuroscience	Psychodynamic	Behavioral	Cognitive	Humanistic
Nature (heredity) vs. nurture (environment)	Nature (heredity)	Nature (heredity)	Nurture (environment)	Both	Nurture (environment)
Conscious vs. unconscious determinants of behavior	Unconscious	Unconscious	Conscious	Both	Conscious
Observable behavior vs. internal mental processes	Internal emphasis	Internal emphasis	Observable emphasis	Internal emphasis	Internal emphasis
Free will vs. determinism	Determinism	Determinism	Determinism	Free will	Free will
Individual differences vs. universal principles	Universal emphasis	Universal emphasis	Both	Individual emphasis	Individual emphasis

FIGURE I Key issues in psychology and the positions taken by psychologists subscribing to the five major perspectives of psychology.

two forces? This question has deep philosophical and historical roots, and it is a factor in many topics in psychology.

A psychologist's take on this issue depends partly on which major perspective she or he subscribes to. For example, developmental psychologists, whose focus is on how people grow and change throughout the course of their lives, may be most interested in learning more about hereditary influences if they are employing a neuroscience perspective. In contrast, developmental psychologists who are proponents of the behavioral perspective would be more likely to focus on environment (Rutter, 2002).

However, every psychologist would agree that neither nature nor nurture alone is the sole determinant of behavior; rather, it is a combination of the two. In a sense, then, the real controversy involves how much of our behavior is caused by heredity and how much is caused by environmental influences.

A second major question addressed by psychologists is *conscious versus unconscious causes of behavior.* How much of our behavior is produced by forces of which we are fully aware, and how much is due to unconscious activity—mental processes that are not accessible to the conscious mind? This question represents one of the great controversies in the field of psychology. For example, clinical psychologists adopting a psychodynamic perspective argue that much of abnormal behavior is motivated by unconscious factors, whereas psychologists employing the cognitive perspective suggest that abnormal behavior is largely the result of faulty thinking processes. The specific approach taken has a clear impact on how abnormal behavior is diagnosed and treated.

The next issue is *observable behavior versus internal mental processes.* Should psychology concentrate solely on behavior that can be seen by outside observers, or should it focus on unseen thinking processes? Some psychologists, particularly those relying on the behavioral perspective, contend that the only legitimate source of information for psychologists is behavior that can be observed directly. Other psychologists, building on the cognitive perspective, argue that what goes on inside a person's mind is critical and that we cannot understand behavior without concerning ourselves with mental processes.

Free will: The idea that behavior is caused primarily by choices that are made freely by the individual.

Determinism: The idea that people's behavior is produced primarily by factors outside of their willful control.

Free will versus determinism is another key issue. How much of our behavior is a matter of **free will** (choices made freely by an individual), and how much is subject to **determinism,** the notion that behavior is largely produced by factors beyond people's willful control? An issue long debated by philosophers, the free-will/determinism argument is also central to the field of psychology (Dennett, 2003). For example, some psychologists who specialize in psychological disorders argue that people make intentional choices and that those who display so-called abnormal behavior should be considered responsible for their actions. Other psychologists disagree and contend that such individuals are the victims of forces beyond their control. The position psychologists take on this issue has important implications for the way they will treat abnormal behavior, especially in deciding whether treatment should be forced on individuals who reject it.

The last of the key issues is the question of *individual differences versus universal principles.* How much of our behavior is a consequence of our unique and special qualities, and how much reflects the culture and society in which we live? How much of our behavior is universally human? Psychologists who rely on the neuroscience perspective tend to look for universal principles of behavior, such as how the nervous system operates or the way certain hormones automatically prime us for sexual activity. Such psychologists concentrate on the similarities in our behavioral destinies despite vast differences in our upbringing. In contrast, psychologists who employ the humanistic perspective focus more on the uniqueness of every individual. They consider how every person's behavior is a reflection of distinct and special qualities.

The question of the degree to which psychologists can identify universal principles that apply to all people has taken on new significance in light of the tremendous demographic changes now occurring in the United States. For instance, the proportion of people of Hispanic descent in the United States in 2050 is projected to be more than twice what it is today. Soon after that, non-Hispanic whites will be a numerical minority in the United States. Similar demographic changes are under way around the world. As we discuss next, these and other changes raise new and critical issues for the discipline of psychology in the twenty-first century.

▲▲▲

Exploring DIVERSITY

Understanding How Culture, Ethnicity, and Race Influence Behavior

A mother in Burr Ridge, Illinois, helps her son with his math assignment. After he complains that he is "terrible at math," she tries to cheer him up by saying, "Don't feel bad; some people are born to do well in math, and others have a lot of trouble with it. It's just the way things are." At the same time, on the other side of the world in Taipei, Taiwan, a mother is helping her daughter with her math homework. When the daughter complains that she's no good at math, the mother tells her to keep at it because everyone has pretty much the same ability in math, and it is hard work that guarantees success.

These two apparently simple parent-child exchanges reveal a deep difference in perspectives on the world. People in Europe and North America are far more likely to attribute success to unchanging causes, such as intelligence, than are people in Asia, who are more likely to attribute school performance to temporary, situational factors such as the amount of effort expended.

These different perspectives may help explain the fact that Asian students often outperform U.S. students in international comparisons of student achievement. Asian students are taught that hard work and increased effort lead to academic success, and so they may be more willing to put in effort to achieve success. In contrast, North American students tend to believe that their ability is fixed at birth and largely determines their success, and so they may be less willing to work hard (Chen & Stevenson, 1995; Chao, 2000; Leung, 2002).

Our knowledge that people in different cultures can have very different views of the world underlines the importance of moving beyond North America and examining other cultural groups in order to identify universal principles of behavior. Furthermore, broad cultural differences are not the only ones taken into account by psychologists in their attempts to identify general principles of behavior. Subcultural,

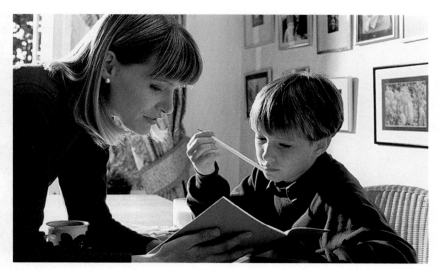

Members of different cultures attribute academic success to different factors. How might different cultural perspectives affect the performance of Asian versus North American students?

ethnic, racial, and socioeconomic differences are increasingly important targets of study by psychologists (Tucker & Herman, 2002).

Although the discipline is growing more aware of the importance of taking cultural and subcultural factors into account, progress has not been rapid in actual practice. For example, the amount of research conducted in the United States on groups other than white middle-class college students is woefully small. Furthermore, progress has been slowed by disagreement about what constitutes a culture or subculture. There isn't even universal agreement on the use of terms such as *race* and *ethnic group,* which sometimes have been used inappropriately. *Race,* for instance, is a biological concept that, technically, should be used only to refer to classifications based on the physical characteristics of an organism or species. In contrast, *ethnic group* and *ethnicity* are broader terms that refer to cultural background, nationality, religion, and language.

The notion of race has been particularly difficult to address. Despite the formal, biological meaning, *race* has been used to denote anything from skin color to culture. As a concept, it has remained quite imprecise. For example, depending on one's definition, anywhere from 3 to 300 races exist. In addition, no race is "pure" in a biological sense (Betancourt & Lopez, 1993; Winkler, 1997; Pääbo, 2001).

To compound the difficulty, there are no universally acceptable names for races and ethnic groups. Psychologists—like other members of society—are divided on whether they should use the label *African American* (which focuses on geographical origins) or *black* (which focuses on skin color), just as they disagree about whether to use *Caucasian* or *white, Hispanic* or *Latino,* and *Native American* or *American Indian* (Phinney, 1996; CNPAAEMI, 2000).

Psychologists also know that the consequences of race as a biological factor cannot be understood without taking into account environmental and cultural factors. Whatever aspects of people's behavior are based on race are a joint product of their race and of the treatment they receive from others because of it. In sum, only by examining behavior across ethnic, cultural, and racial lines can psychologists differentiate principles that are universal from those which are culture-bound.

Ⓐ Ⓐ Ⓐ

Psychology's Future

We have examined psychology's foundations, but what does the future hold for the discipline? Although the course of scientific development is difficult to predict, several trends seem likely. As its knowledge base grows, psychology will become increasingly specialized and new perspectives will evolve (Robins, Gosling, & Craik, 1999; Benjamin, 2001). As our understanding of the brain and the nervous system grows and scientific advances such as gene therapy become common, more psychologists will focus on the *prevention* of psychological disorders rather than on their treatment. Furthermore, it is likely that psychological treatment will become more available and socially acceptable as the number of psychologists increases (Evans, 1999).

Psychology's influence on issues of public interest also will grow. The major problems of our time—such as violence, racial and ethnic prejudice, poverty, and environmental and technological disasters—have important psychological aspects, and it is likely that psychologists will make important practical contributions toward their resolution (Lerner, Fisher, & Weinberg, 2000).

Finally, as the population of the United States becomes more diverse, issues of diversity—embodied in the study of racial, ethnic, linguistic, and cultural factors—will become more critical to psychologists providing services and doing research. The result will be a field that can provide an understanding of *human* behavior in its broadest sense (Sue et al., 1999; Leung & Blustein, 2000).

▶ An advertisement in a national magazine proclaims a cure for a major psychological problem: "The 8-week Phobia Treatment: A Complete Home-Treatment Guide to Phobia and Stress Relief." For only $29.95 (plus $3.05 for postage), a reader is furnished with an "amazing" book covering topics such as "why pills and medication won't help," "your own tests," and "much, much more."

▶ An advertisement selling computer software proclaims in bold type, "Announcing the new hi-tech program that gives you a short-cut to success."

▶ A World Wide Web site invites visitors to submit by e-mail confidential questions regarding their relationships, which will be answered by "cybershrinks."

▶ "Expand Your Mind Beyond Virtual Reality . . . & Learn at the Speed of Light!" declares the sales pitch that arrives in the mail with the day's bills and catalogs. "I have an astounding technology I'm going to share with you. Something so profound it will launch your brain beyond Virtual Reality . . . and transform your mind and soul forever."

BECOMING AN INFORMED CONSUMER

of Psychology

Thinking Critically About Psychology: Distinguishing Legitimate Psychology from Pseudo-Psychology

From advertisements, to television and radio talk shows, to the World Wide Web, we are subjected to a barrage of information about psychology. We are told that we can become better adjusted, smarter, more insightful, and happier individuals by learning the secrets that psychologists have revealed.

However, such promises are usually empty. If self-improvement were this easy, we would live in a country of happy-go-lucky, fully satisfied, fulfilled individuals. Obviously life is not quite so simple, and the quality of advice provided by self-styled experts—and even, on occasion, by some less-than-reputable psychologists—varies widely.

How can we separate accurate information from pseudo-psychology? The best approach is to employ critical thinking techniques. Developed by psychologists who specialize in learning, memory, cognition, intelligence, and education, critical thinking procedures provide the tools to scrutinize assumptions, evaluate assertions, and think with greater precision (Coats, Feldman, & Schwartzberg, 1994; Halpern & Riggio, 2002; Lilienfeld, Lynn, & Lohr, 2003).

We'll be considering ways to boost critical thinking skills in *Becoming an Informed Consumer of Psychology* sections throughout the book. To get started, let's consider what you need to evaluate information of a psychological nature whether the source is an advertisement, a television show, a magazine article, or even a book as seemingly reliable as a college textbook.

PowerWeb: Science and Pseudoscience

www.mhhe.com/feldmanup7

▶ For starters, know who is offering the information and advice. Are the providers of the information trained psychologists? What kinds of degrees do they have? Are they licensed? Are they affiliated with a particular institution? Before seriously relying on experts' advice, check out their credentials.

▶ Keep in mind that there is no free ride. If it is possible to solve major psychological ills by buying a $29.95 book, why do many people who suffer from such problems typically expend a considerable amount of time and money before they can be helped? If you could buy a computer program that would really "unlock the hidden truths" about others, wouldn't it be in widespread use? Be wary of simple, glib responses to major difficulties.

▶ Be aware that few universal cures exist for humankind's ills. No method or technique works for everyone. The range of difficulties attached to the human condition is so broad that any procedure that purports to resolve all problems is certain to disappoint.

▶ Finally, remember that no source of information or advice is definitive. The notion of infallibility is best left to the realm of religion, and you should approach psychological information and advice from a critical and thoughtful perspective.

Despite these cautions, you should remember that the field of psychology has contributed a wealth of information that people can draw upon for suggestions about every phase of life. One of the major goals of this book is to make you an informed consumer of psychological knowledge by enhancing your ability to evaluate what psychologists have to offer. Ultimately, this book will provide you with the tools you need to analyze critically the theories, research, and applications that psychologists have developed. As a result, you will be able to appreciate the real contributions that the field of psychology has made to improving human life.

RECAP/EVALUATE/RETHINK

RECAP

What are psychology's key issues and controversies?

▶ Psychology's key issues are the questions of nature versus nurture, conscious versus unconscious determinants of behavior, observable behavior versus internal mental processes, free will versus determinism, and individual differences versus universal principles. (p. 23)

What is the future of psychology likely to hold?

▶ Psychology will become increasingly specialized, will pay increasing attention to prevention instead of just treatment, will become increasingly concerned with the public interest, and will take the growing diversity of the country's population into account more fully. (p. 26)

EVALUATE

1. What perspective suggests that abnormal behavior may result largely from unconscious forces?

2. "Psychologists should worry only about behavior that is directly observable." This statement would most likely be made by a person using which psychological perspective?
3. Psychology is currently moving toward increased specialization. True or false?

RETHINK

1. "The fact that some businesses now promote their ability to help people 'expand their minds beyond virtual reality' shows the great progress psychology has made lately." Criticize this statement in light of what you know about professional psychology and pseudo-psychology.
2. How do some of psychology's key issues relate to law enforcement and criminal justice?

Answers to Evaluate Questions

1. psychodynamic; 2. behavioral; 3. true

KEY TERMS

free will p. 24
determinism p. 24

Looking Back

Psychology on the Web

1. Practice using several search strategies to find information on the Web about one of the key issues in psychology (e.g., free will versus determinism, nature versus nurture, or conscious versus unconscious determinants of behavior), using (a) a general-purpose search engine (such as Google at www.google.com) and (b) a more specialized search engine (such as Yahoo's Psychology section, under the "Social Science" heading, at www.yahoo.com). Summarize and then compare the kinds of information you have found through each strategy.

2. Search the Web for discussions of youth violence and try to find (a) an article in the general news media, (b) information from a psychological point of view (e.g., experimental information or recommendations for parents from a professional organization), and (c) political opinion or debate about how to address the issue of youth violence.

3. After completing Interactivity 1-1, identify a current news item (either from an online source or a daily newspaper) relating to human behavior. How would the different subfields of psychology be useful in explaining the behavior described in the news item? Which subfields are the most relevant, and which have the least relevance to the topic of the news item?

Epilogue

The field of psychology, as we have seen, is broad and diverse. It encompasses many different subfields and specialties practiced in a variety of settings, with new subfields continually arising. We have also seen that even within the various subfields of the field, it is possible to adopt several different approaches, including the neuroscience, psychodynamic, behavioral, cognitive, and humanistic perspectives.

For all its diversity, though, psychology focuses on certain key issues that serve to unify the field along common lines and shared findings. These issues will reappear as themes throughout this book as we discuss the work and accomplishments of psychologists in the many subfields of the discipline.

In light of what you've already learned about the field of psychology, reconsider the astronauts who were involved in the space shuttle *Columbia* disaster and answer the following questions:

1. How might a psychodynamic perspective explain why astronauts choose to take the risks of space travel? How would the explanation differ from the approach taken by a psychologist using the humanistic perspective?

2. Assume that two developmental psychologists are considering the effects of a child's observation of the shuttle disaster on television on that child's later development. How would the questions of interest to the psychologists differ if one employed the neuroscience perspective and the other employed the behavioral perspective?

3. What aspects of the *Columbia* disaster would a clinical psychologist probably focus on?

4. How might social psychologists explore the effects of watching news reports of the *Columbia* disaster on viewers' later helpfulness or aggression toward others?

Psychological Research

Prologue
The Bystanders' Dilemma

Like everyone else, Bob Munson always thought he'd do the right thing in a crisis. He never imagined he'd be standing there, watching helplessly as an 88-year-old man was being kicked to death, knowing he should be doing something but not sure what it was.

Munson still isn't sure what he should have done, what he could have done, as he stood outside a Shaw's supermarket in Portland, Maine . . . With a bag of groceries in one hand and a bouquet of flowers for his wife in the other, he watched a young man repeatedly kick John McCann in the face.

"Everybody wants to be a hero, but of course they were not in a situation when a murder was in progress. No one knows what they would do . . . You sit there for a moment frozen, and you try to analyze it . . . you don't dare approach" (Robertson, 2000, p. A1).

If Bob Munson's experience were an isolated incident, we might be able to attribute his—and the other bystanders'—inaction to something specific about the situation. However, events such as this one are all too common.

In one infamous case, a woman named Kitty Genovese was attacked by a man near an apartment building in Queens, New York. At one point during the assault, which lasted thirty minutes, she managed to free herself and screamed, "Oh, my God, he stabbed me. Please help me!" In the stillness of the night, no fewer than thirty-eight neighbors heard her screams. Windows opened, and lights went on. One couple pulled chairs up to the window and turned off the lights so that they could see better. Someone called out, "Let that girl alone." But

Looking **Ahead**

shouts were not enough to scare off the killer. He chased Genovese, stabbing her eight more times, and sexually molested her before leaving her to die. And how many of those thirty-eight witnesses came to her aid? As with the case of the 88-year-old who was beaten, not one person helped (Rogers & Eftimiades, 1995).

Such incidents remain dismaying—and puzzling. Why don't bystanders intervene in such situations, particularly when there are many of them who could potentially offer help? At the time of the Kitty Genovese murder, editorial writers suggested that the incidents could be attributed to the basic shortcomings of "human nature," but such an assumption is woefully inadequate. Many people have risked their own lives to help others in dangerous situations, and so "human nature" encompasses a wide range of both negative and positive responses.

Psychologists puzzled over the problem for many years. After much research they reached an unexpected conclusion: Kitty Genovese probably would have been better off if only a few people, rather than many, had heard her cries for help. In fact, if had only one bystander been present, the chances of that person's intervening might have been fairly high. It turns out that the *fewer* the witnesses to an assault, the *better* the victim's chances of getting help.

How did psychologists come to such a curious conclusion? After all, logic and common sense clearly suggest that *more* bystanders would produce a greater likelihood that someone would help a person in need. This seeming contradiction—and the way psychologists resolved it—illustrates a central challenge for the field of psychology: asking useful questions about the unknown, and getting valid answers.

Like professionals in any science, psychologists are vitally concerned with refining and expanding knowledge within their field. In the following modules we'll see how psychologists pose questions of interest and answer them through scientific research. We'll find that the answers psychologists obtain from their research not only advance our understanding of behavior, but also offer the potential to improve the human condition.

The Scientific Method

What is the scientific method?

How do psychologists use theory and research to answer questions of interest?

"Birds of a feather flock together" . . . or "opposites attract"? "Two heads are better than one" . . . or "if you want a thing done well, do it yourself"? "The more the merrier" . . . or "two's company, three's a crowd"?

If we were to rely on "common sense" to understand behavior, we'd have considerable difficulty—especially because commonsense views are often contradictory. In fact, one of the major undertakings for the field of psychology is to determine which suppositions about behavior are accurate and to develop those suppositions in the first place.

Psychologists—as well as scientists in other disciplines—meet the challenge of posing appropriate questions and properly answering them by relying on the scientific method. The **scientific method** is the approach used by psychologists to systematically acquire knowledge and understanding about behavior and other phenomena of interest. As illustrated in Figure 1, it consists of three main steps: (1) identifying questions of interest, (2) formulating an explanation, and (3) carrying out research designed to lend support to or refute the explanation.

Scientific method: The approach through which psychologists systematically acquire knowledge and understanding about behavior and other phenomena of interest.

▲▲▲

Theories: Specifying Broad Explanations

In using the scientific method, psychologists start by identifying questions of interest. We have all been curious at some time about our observations of everyday behavior. If you have ever asked yourself why a particular teacher is so easily annoyed, why a friend is always late for appointments, or how your dog understands your commands, you have been formulating questions about behavior.

Psychologists, too, ask questions about the nature and causes of behavior. They may wish to explore explanations for everyday behaviors or for various phenomena. They may also pose questions that build on findings from their previous research or from research carried out by other psychologists. Or they may produce new questions that are based on curiosity, creativity, or insight.

Once a question has been identified, the next step in the scientific method is to develop a theory to explain the phenomenon that has been observed. **Theories** are broad explanations and predictions concerning phenomena of interest. They provide a framework for understanding the relationships among a set of otherwise unorganized facts or principles.

Theories: Broad explanations and predictions concerning phenomena of interest.

All of us have developed our own informal theories of human behavior, such as "People are basically good" or "People's behavior is usually motivated by self-interest." However, psychologists' theories are more formal and focused. They are established on the basis of a careful study of the psychological literature to identify relevant research conducted and theories formulated previously, as

Identify questions of interest, stemming from

- Behavior and phenomenon requiring explanation
- Prior research findings
- Curiosity, creativity, insight

↓

Formulate an explanation

Specify a theory

↓

Develop a hypothesis

↓

Carry out research

Operationalize hypothesis

↓

Select a research method

↓

Collect the data

↓

Analyze the data

FIGURE 1 The scientific method, which encompasses the process of identifying, asking, and answering questions, is used by psychologists, and by researchers from every other scientific discipline, to come to an understanding about the world. What do you think are the advantages of this method?

well as psychologists' general knowledge of the field (Sternberg & Beall, 1991; McGuire, 1997).

Growing out of the diverse approaches employed by psychologists, theories vary both in their breadth and in their level of detail. For example, one theory might seek to explain and predict a phenomenon as broad as emotional experience in general. A narrower theory might attempt to explain why people display the emotion of fear nonverbally after receiving a threat.

Psychologists Bibb Latané and John Darley, responding to the failure of bystanders to intervene when Kitty Genovese was murdered in New York, developed what they called a theory of *diffusion of responsibility* (Latané & Darley, 1970). According to their theory, the greater the number of bystanders or witnesses to an event that calls for helping behavior is, the more the responsibility for helping is perceived to be shared by all the bystanders. Thus, the greater the number of bystanders in an emergency situation, the smaller the share of the responsibility each person feels—and the less likely it is that any single person will come forward to help.

Hypotheses: Crafting Testable Predictions

Hypothesis: A prediction, stemming from a theory, stated in a way that allows it to be tested.

Although the diffusion of responsibility theory seems to make sense, it represented only the beginning phase of Latané and Darley's investigative process. Their next step was to devise a way to test their theory. To do this, they needed to create a hypothesis. A **hypothesis** is a prediction stated in a way that allows it to be tested. Hypotheses stem from theories; they help test the underlying validity of theories.

In the same way that we develop our own broad theories about the world, we also construct hypotheses about events and behavior. Those hypotheses can range from trivialities (such as why our English instructor wears those weird shirts) to more meaningful matters (such as what is the best way to study for a test). Although we rarely test these hypotheses systematically, we do try to determine whether they are right. Perhaps we try comparing two strategies: cramming the night before an exam versus spreading out our study over several nights. By assessing which approach yields better test performance, we have created a way to compare the two strategies.

Latané and Darley's hypothesis was a straightforward prediction from their more general theory of diffusion of responsibility: The more people who witness an emergency situation, the less likely it is that help will be given to a victim. They could, of course, have chosen another hypothesis (for instance, that people with more first-aid skills will be less affected by the presence of others and more likely to help than will those with fewer first-aid skills), but their initial formulation seemed to offer the most direct test of the theory.

Psychologists rely on formal theories and hypotheses for many reasons. For one thing, theories and hypotheses allow them to make sense of unorganized, separate observations and bits of information by permitting them to place the pieces within a structured and coherent framework. In addition, theories and hypotheses offer psychologists the opportunity to move beyond already known facts and principles and make deductions about unexplained phenomena. In this way, theories and hypotheses provide a reasoned guide to the direction that future investigation ought to take (Howitt & Cramer, 2000; Cohen, 2003).

In short, the scientific method, with its emphasis on theories and hypotheses, helps psychologists pose appropriate questions. With properly stated questions in hand, psychologists then can choose from a variety of research methods to find answers. (To get a better understanding of the scientific method used by psychologists, try **Interactivity 4–1.**)

INTERACTIVITY 4–1

The scientific method

RECAP/EVALUATE/RETHINK

RECAP

What is the scientific method?

▶ The scientific method is the approach psychologists use to understand behavior. It consists of three steps: identifying questions of interest, formulating an explanation, and carrying out research that is designed to support or refute the explanation. (p. 33)

How do psychologists use theory and research to answer questions of interest?

▶ Research in psychology is guided by theories (broad explanations and predictions regarding phenomena of interest) and hypotheses (derivations of theories that are predictions stated in a way that allows them to be tested). (p. 34)

EVALUATE

1. An explanation for a phenomenon of interest is known as a _____.
2. To test this explanation, it must be stated in terms of a testable question known as a _____.

RETHINK

1. Starting with the theory that diffusion of responsibility causes responsibility for helping to be shared among bystanders, Latané and Darley derived the hypothesis that the more people who witness an emergency situation, the less likely it is that help will be given to a victim. How many other hypotheses can you think of that are based on the same theory of diffusion of responsibility?

2. Is it possible to formulate testable hypotheses from the theories behind the headlines in popular tabloid newspapers (e.g., about UFOs, Elvis's survival, or other popular notions)? Why or why not?

Answers to Evaluate Questions

1. theory; 2. hypothesis

KEY TERMS

scientific method p. 33   theories p. 33   hypothesis p. 34

Conducting Psychological Research

What are the different research methods employed by psychologists?

How do psychologists establish cause-and-effect relationships in research studies?

Research—systematic inquiry aimed at the discovery of new knowledge—is a central ingredient of the scientific method in psychology. It provides the key to understanding the degree to which hypotheses (and the theories behind them) are accurate.

Just as we can apply different theories and hypotheses to explain the same phenomena, we can use a number of alternative methods to conduct research (Ray, 2000). First, though, the hypothesis must be restated in a way that will allow it to be tested, a procedure known as operationalization. **Operationalization** is the process of translating a hypothesis into specific, testable procedures that can be measured and observed.

There is no single way to go about operationalizing a hypothesis; it depends on logic, the equipment and facilities available, the psychological perspective being employed, and ultimately the creativity of the researcher. For example, one researcher might develop a hypothesis in which she operationalizes "fear" as an increase in heart rate. In contrast, another psychologist might operationalize "fear" as a written response to the question "How much fear are you experiencing at this moment?"

Operationalization: The process of translating a hypothesis into specific, testable procedures that can be measured and observed.

We will consider several of the major tools in the psychologist's research kit. Keep in mind that their relevance extends beyond testing and evaluating hypotheses in psychology. Even people who do not have degrees in psychology, for instance, often carry out elementary forms of research on their own. A supervisor might need to evaluate an employee's performance; a physician might systematically test the effects of different doses of a drug on a patient; a salesperson might compare different persuasive strategies. Each of these situations draws on the research practices we are about to discuss.

Furthermore, knowledge of the research methods used by psychologists permits us to better evaluate the research that others conduct. The media constantly bombard us with claims about research studies and findings. Knowledge of research methods allows us to sort out what is credible from what should be ignored. Finally, there is evidence that by studying some kinds of research methods in depth, people learn to reason more critically and effectively. Understanding the methods by which psychologists conduct research can enhance our ability to analyze and evaluate the situations we encounter in our everyday lives (Shaughnessy, Zechmeister, & Zechmeister, 2000; Shadish, Cook, & Campbell, 2002; Tryon & Bernstein, 2003).

▲▲▲

Archival Research

Suppose that, like the psychologists Latané and Darley (1970), who were interested in bystander behavior in emergency situations, you were interested in finding out more about emergency situations in which bystanders did not provide help. One of the first places you might turn to would be historical accounts. By searching newspaper records, for example, you might find support for the notion that a decrease in helping behavior historically has accompanied an increase in the number of bystanders.

Archival research: Research in which existing data, such as census documents, college records, and newspaper clippings, are examined to test a hypothesis.

INTERACTIVITY 5–1

Naturalistic observation

Naturalistic observation: Research in which an investigator simply observes some naturally occurring behavior and does not make a change in the situation.

Dian Fossey, a pioneer in the study of endangered mountain gorillas in their native habitat, relied on naturalistic observation for her research. What are the advantages of this approach?

Survey research: Research in which people chosen to represent a larger population are asked a series of questions about their behavior, thoughts, or attitudes.

Using newspaper articles is an example of archival research. In **archival research,** existing data, such as census documents, college records, and newspaper clippings, are examined to test a hypothesis. For example, college records may be used to determine if there are gender differences in academic performance.

Archival research is a relatively inexpensive means of testing a hypothesis because someone else has already collected the basic data. Of course, the use of existing data has several drawbacks. For one thing, the data may not be in a form that allows the researcher to test a hypothesis fully. The information could be incomplete, or it could have been collected haphazardly (Stewart & Kamins, 1993; Riniolo, Koledin, Drakulic, & Payne, 2003).

Most attempts at archival research are hampered by the simple fact that records with the necessary information often do not exist. In these instances, researchers often turn to another research method: naturalistic observation.

Naturalistic Observation

In **naturalistic observation,** the investigator simply observes some naturally occurring behavior and does not make a change in the situation. For example, a researcher investigating helping behavior might observe the kind of help given to victims in a high-crime area of a city. The important point to remember about naturalistic observation is that the researcher simply records what occurs, making no modification in the situation that is being observed (Schmidt, 1999; Schutt, 2001).

Although the advantage of naturalistic observation is obvious—we get a sample of what people do in their "natural habitat"—there is also an important drawback: the inability to control any of the factors of interest. For example, we might find so few naturally occurring instances of helping behavior that we would be unable to draw any conclusions. Because naturalistic observation prevents researchers from making changes in a situation, they must wait until the appropriate conditions occur. Furthermore, if people know they are being watched, they may alter their reactions, producing behavior that is not truly representative of the group in question. (To get more information on research using naturalistic observation, try **Interactivity 5–1.**)

Survey Research

There is no more straightforward way of finding out what people think, feel, and do than asking them directly. For this reason, surveys are an important research method. In **survey research,** a *sample* of people chosen to represent a larger group of interest (a *population*) are asked a series of questions about their behavior, thoughts, or attitudes. Survey methods have become so sophisticated that even with a very small sample researchers are able to infer with great accuracy how a larger group would respond. For instance, a sample of just a few thousand voters is sufficient to predict within one or two percentage points who will win a presidential election—if the representative sample is chosen with care (Fink & Kosecoff, 1998; Sommer & Sommer, 2001).

Researchers investigating helping behavior might conduct a survey by asking people to complete a questionnaire in which they indicate their reasons for not wanting to come forward to help another individual. Similarly, researchers interested in learning about sexual practices have carried out surveys to learn which practices are common and which are not and to chart changing notions of sexual morality over the last several decades.

However, survey research has several potential pitfalls. For one thing, if the sample of people who are surveyed is not representative of the broader population of interest, the results of the survey will have little meaning (Daley, 2003).

People may also respond inaccurately if the survey includes *loaded questions,* questions that represent only one side of an issue or lead to biased responses. For

A portion of an online survey.

example, someone who answers the question "Do you support reducing welfare benefits in order to reduce the budget deficit?" positively may actually be against a reduction in welfare benefits but agree with the question because it is placed in the context of deficit reduction.

Finally, survey respondents may not want to admit to holding socially undesirable attitudes. To overcome participants' reluctance to be truthful, researchers are developing alternative, and often ingenious, research techniques, as we consider in the *Applying Psychology in the 21st Century* box. (See also **Interactivity 5–2** for information on self-report bias in surveys.)

INTERACTIVITY 5–2

Self-report bias in surveys

Case study: An in-depth, intensive investigation of an individual or small group of people.

The Case Study

When the snipers who terrorized the Washington, D.C., area for several weeks in the fall of 2002 were finally arrested, many people wondered what it was about the snipers' personalities or backgrounds that might have led to their behavior. To answer this question, psychologists might conduct a case study. In contrast to a survey, in which many people are studied, a **case study** is an in-depth, intensive investigation of an individual or a small group of people. Case studies often include *psychological testing,* a procedure in which a carefully designed set of questions is used to gain some insight into the personality of the individual or group (Breakwell, Hammond, & Fife-Schaw, 2000; Gass et al., 2000).

When case studies are used as a research technique, the goal is often not only to learn about the few individuals being examined but to use the insights gained from the study to improve our understanding of people in general. Sigmund Freud built his theories through case studies of individual patients. Similarly, case studies of the Washington, D.C.–area snipers might help identify others who are prone to violence.

"This is the New York 'Times' Business Poll again, Mr. Landau. Do you feel better or worse about the economy than you did twenty minutes ago?"

Serious Playtime: Using a Video Game to Study Racial Bias

You're a police officer, and you suddenly encounter someone holding what might be a dangerous weapon. Do you shoot first and ask questions later?

Your behavior is likely to depend on the race of the person you've encountered. At least that's the result of a research study by the psychologist Bernadette Park and colleagues, who used an innovative research technique to answer the question (Correll, Park, Judd, & Wittenbrink, 2002).

Using technology that is found more often in college dorms than in psychology labs, Park and colleagues had participants play a video game the psychologists developed to study the relationship between ethnic stereotypes and violent behavior. The participants were asked to play the role of a police officer who must instantly decide whether a man who appears on the screen is a criminal carrying a gun or an unarmed bystander who may be carrying an innocent object such as a cell phone, wallet, or aluminum can. If the participants concluded that the man was carrying a gun, they were to quickly press a button to "shoot" him. If they judged that he was unarmed, they were told to press a different button to avoid "shooting" the man. In the video game, half the men who

appeared on the screen were African American and half were white.

The results of the study were disturbing: The participants routinely viewed the African American men to be more threatening than the white men. They fired more quickly at images of armed African American men than at images of armed white men, and they decided more quickly not to shoot unarmed white men than was the case with unarmed African American men.

It was notable that the participants' tendency toward shooting the African American men in the video games was unrelated to their answers on a questionnaire assessment of racial prejudice, suggesting that the video game measured subtle biases that the questionnaire missed. This finding illustrates an important weakness in survey research: Because survey respondents are often unwilling to admit to socially undesirable behavior or attitudes—in this case ethnic prejudice—the results are not always a valid measure of the participants' actual views. The video game was an ingenious and engaging tool for measuring

underlying prejudice that people might not otherwise divulge.

Video games are only one example of the technologies psychologists have begun to use in their research into everyday human behavior. For example, researchers studying relationships have given palmtop computers to participants in studies to keep careful records of their feelings and social interactions (e.g., Feldman, Barrett, & Barrett, 2001). Other researchers have begun using sophisticated brain imaging equipment to learn how people form memories of visual information in television commercials (Rossiter, Silberstein, Harris, & Nield, 2001). In addition, many psychologists are using the Internet to gather data, running online studies to examine everything from procrastination to recreational drug use (Lavoie & Pychyl, 2001; Parrott et al., 2002; Sills & Song, 2002).

Whether using video games to assess stereotypes or the Internet to measure people's attitudes and experiences, psychologists are developing better and more innovative tools to learn about the biases and behaviors that we encounter every day.

RETHINK

Can you think of any other attitudes or behaviors psychologists could investigate by using video games? If you were a researcher, what other technologies from daily life could you use to study people's behavior?

These photos were used in an experiment in which participants viewed a photo of an African-American or white man holding a gun that was rapidly displayed as part of a video game. Participants were more likely to "shoot" the African-American man than the white man.

Correlational Research

In using the research methods we have described, researchers often wish to determine the relationship between two variables. **Variables** are behaviors, events, or other characteristics that can change, or vary, in some way. For example, we might want to find out if there is a relationship between the variable of attendance at religious services and the variable of helpfulness in emergency situations. If we did find such a relationship, we could say that there was an association—or correlation—between attendance at religious services and helpfulness in emergencies.

In **correlational research,** the relationship between two sets of variables is examined to determine whether they are associated, or "correlated." The strength and direction of the relationship between the two variables are represented by a mathematical score, known as a *correlation* (or, more formally, a *correlation coefficient*), that can range from +1.0 to −1.0.

A *positive correlation* indicates that as the value of one variable increases, we can predict that the value of the other variable will also increase. For example, if we predict that the more that students study for a test, the higher their subsequent grades on the test will be, and that the less they study, the lower their test scores will be, we are expecting to find a positive correlation. (Higher values of the variable "amount of study time" would be associated with higher values of the variable "test score," and lower values of "amount of study time" would be associated with lower values of "test score.") The correlation, then, would be indicated by a positive number, and the stronger the association was between studying and test scores, the closer the number would be to +1.0. For example, we might find a correlation of +.85 between test scores and amount of study time, indicating a strong positive association.

In contrast, a *negative correlation* tells us that as the value of one variable increases, the value of the other decreases. For instance, we might predict that as the number of hours spent studying increases, the number of hours spent in partying decreases. Here we are expecting a negative correlation, ranging between 0 and −1.0. More studying is associated with less partying, and less studying is associated with more partying. The stronger the association between studying and partying is, the closer the correlation will be to −1.0. For instance, a correlation of −.85 would indicate a strong negative association between partying and studying.

Of course, it's quite possible that little or no relationship exists between two variables. For instance, we would probably not expect to find a relationship between number of study hours and height. Lack of a relationship would be indicated by a correlation close to 0. For example, if we found a correlation of −.02 or +.03, it would indicate that there is virtually no association between the two variables; knowing how much someone studies does not tell us anything about how tall he or she is.

When we find that two variables are strongly correlated with each other, it is tempting to assume that one variable causes the other. For example, if we find that more study time is associated with higher grades, we might guess that more studying *causes* higher grades. Although this is not a bad guess, it remains just a guess—because finding that two variables are correlated does not mean that there is a causal relationship between them. Although the strong correlation suggests that knowing how much a person studies can help us predict how that person will do on a test, it does not mean that the studying causes the test performance. It might be, for instance, that people who are interested in the subject matter tend to study more than do those who are less interested, and that the amount of interest, not the number of hours spent studying, predicts test performance. The mere fact that two variables occur together does not mean that one causes the other. (To better understand this principle, try **Interactivity 5–3.**)

Another example illustrates the critical point that correlations tell us nothing about cause and effect but only provide a measure of the strength of a relationship between two variables. We might find that children who watch a lot of television

Variable: Behaviors, events, or other characteristics that can change, or vary, in some way.

Correlational research: Research in which the relationship between two sets of variables is examined to determine whether they are associated, or "correlated."

INTERACTIVITY 5–3

Correlation

FIGURE 1 If we find that frequent viewing of television programs having aggressive content is associated with high levels of aggressive behavior, we might cite several plausible causes, as suggested in this figure. For example, choosing to watch shows with aggressive content could produce aggression (a); or being a highly aggressive person might cause one to choose to watch televised aggression (b); or having a high energy level might cause a person to *both* choose to watch aggressive shows and act aggressively (c). Correlational findings, then, do not permit us to determine causality. Can you think of a way to study the effects of televised aggression on aggressive behavior that is not correlational?

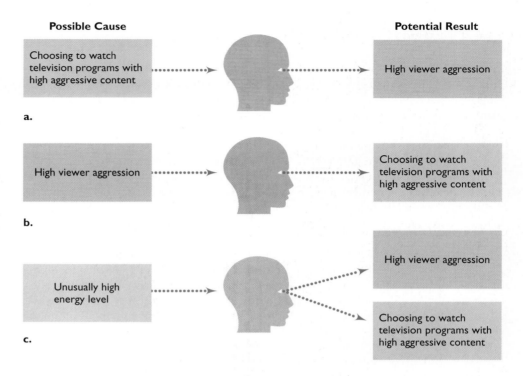

Possible Cause   **Potential Result**

Experiment: The investigation of the relationship between two (or more) variables by deliberately producing a change in one variable in a situation and observing the effects of that change on other aspects of the situation.

Experimental manipulation: The change that an experimenter deliberately produces in a situation.

Many studies show that the observation of violence in the media is associated with aggression in viewers. Can we conclude that the observation of violence causes aggression?

programs featuring high levels of aggression are likely to demonstrate a relatively high degree of aggressive behavior, and that those who watch few television shows that portray aggression are apt to exhibit a relatively low degree of such behavior (see Figure 1). But we cannot say that the aggression is *caused* by the TV viewing, because several other explanations are possible.

For instance, it could be that children who have an unusually high level of energy seek out programs with aggressive content *and* are more aggressive. The children's energy level, then, could be the true cause of the children's higher incidence of aggression. Finally, it is also possible that people who are already highly aggressive choose to watch shows with a high aggressive content *because* they are aggressive. Clearly, then, any number of causal sequences are possible—none of which can be ruled out by correlational research.

The inability of correlational research to demonstrate cause-and-effect relationships is a crucial drawback to its use. There is, however, an alternative technique that does establish causality: the experiment.

Experimental Research

The *only* way psychologists can establish cause-and-effect relationships through research is by carrying out an experiment. In a formal **experiment,** the relationship between two (or more) variables is investigated by deliberately producing a change in one variable in a situation and observing the effects of that change on other aspects of the situation. In an experiment, then, the conditions required to study a question of interest are created by an experimenter, who deliberately makes a change in those conditions in order to observe the effects of that change.

The change that an experimenter deliberately produces in a situation is called the **experimental manipulation.** Experimental manipulations are used to detect relationships between different variables.

Several steps are involved in carrying out an experiment, but the process typically begins with the development of one or more hypotheses for the experiment to test. For example, Latané and Darley, in testing their theory of the diffusion of responsibility in bystander behavior, developed this hypothesis: The higher the number of people who witness an emergency situation is, the less likely it is that any of them will help the victim. We can trace the way these researchers designed an experiment to test this hypothesis.

Their first step was to operationalize the hypothesis by conceptualizing it in a way that could be tested. Latané and Darley had to take into account the fundamental principle of experimental research mentioned earlier: Experimenters must manipulate at least one variable in order to observe the effects of the manipulation on another variable. However, the manipulation cannot be viewed by itself, in isolation; if a cause-and-effect relationship is to be established, the effects of the manipulation must be compared with the effects of no manipulation or a different kind of manipulation.

In this experiment, preschoolers' reactions to the puppet are monitored. Can you think of a hypothesis that might be tested in this way?

Experimental research requires, then, that the responses of at least two groups be compared. One group will receive some special **treatment**—the manipulation implemented by the experimenter—and another group will receive either no treatment or a different treatment. Any group that receives a treatment is called an **experimental group;** a group that receives no treatment is called a **control group.** (In some experiments there are multiple experimental and control groups, each of which is compared with another group.)

By employing both experimental and control groups in an experiment, researchers are able to rule out the possibility that something other than the experimental manipulation produced the results observed in the experiment. With no control group, we couldn't be sure that some other variable, such as the temperature at the time we were running the experiment, the color of the experimenter's hair, or even the mere passage of time, wasn't causing the changes observed.

For example, consider a medical researcher who thinks she has invented a medicine that cures the common cold. To test her claim, she gives the medicine one day to a group of twenty people who have colds, and finds that ten days later all of them are cured. Eureka? Not so fast. An observer viewing this flawed study might reasonably argue that the people would have gotten better even without the medicine. What the researcher obviously needed was a control group consisting of people with colds who *don't* get the medicine and whose health is also checked ten days later. Only if there is a difference between experimental and control groups can the effectiveness of the medicine be assessed. Through the use of control groups, then, researchers can isolate specific causes for their findings—and draw cause-and-effect inferences.

Returning to Latané and Darley's experiment, we note that the researchers needed a means of operationalizing their hypothesis in order to proceed. They decided to create a false emergency situation that would appear to require the aid of a bystander. As their experimental manipulation, they decided to vary the number of bystanders present. They could have had just one experimental group with, say, two people present, and a control group for comparison purposes with just one person present. Instead, they settled on a more complex procedure involving the creation of groups of three sizes—consisting of two, three, and six people—that could be compared with one another.

Latané and Darley had now identified what is called the independent variable. The **independent variable** is the variable that is manipulated by an experimenter. (You can think of the independent variable as being independent of the actions of those taking part in an experiment; it is controlled by the experimenter.) In the case of the Latané and Darley experiment, the independent variable was the number of people present, which was manipulated by the experimenters.

The next step was to decide how they were going to determine the effect that varying the number of bystanders had on behavior of those in the experiment.

Treatment: The manipulation implemented by the experimenter.

Experimental group: Any group participating in an experiment that receives a treatment.

Control group: A group participating in an experiment that receives no treatment.

Independent variable: The variable that is manipulated by an experimenter.

Dependent variable: The variable
that is measured and is expected to
change as a result of changes caused
by the experimenter's manipulation
of the independent variable.

Crucial to every experiment is the **dependent variable,** the variable that is measured and is expected to change as a result of changes caused by the experimenter's manipulation of the independent variable. The dependent variable is dependent on the actions of the *participants* or *subjects:* the people taking part in the experiment.

Latané and Darley had several possible choices for their dependent measure. One might have been a simple yes/no measure of the participants' helping behavior. But the investigators also wanted a more precise analysis of helping behavior. Consequently, they also measured the amount of time it took for a participant to provide help.

Latané and Darley now had all the necessary components of an experiment. The independent variable, manipulated by them, was the number of bystanders present in an emergency situation. The dependent variable was the measure of whether bystanders in each of the groups provided help and the amount of time it took them to do so. Consequently, like all experiments, this one had both an independent variable and a dependent variable. (To remember the difference, recall that a hypothesis predicts how a dependent variable *depends* on the manipulation of the independent variable.) *All* true experiments in psychology fit this straightforward model. (For more on experimental design, try **Interactivity 5–4.**)

INTERACTIVITY 5–4

Experimental design

THE FINAL STEP: RANDOM ASSIGNMENT OF PARTICIPANTS

To make the experiment a valid test of the hypothesis, the researchers needed to add a final step to the design: properly assigning participants to receive a particular treatment.

The significance of this step becomes clear when we examine various alternative procedures. For example, the experimenters might have assigned just males to the group with two bystanders, just females to the group with three bystanders, and both males and females to the group with six bystanders. If they had done this, however, any differences they found in helping behavior could not be attributed with any certainty solely to group size, because the differences might just as well have been due to the composition of the group. A more reasonable procedure would be to ensure that each group had the same composition in terms of gender; then the researchers would be able to make comparisons across groups with considerably more accuracy.

Participants in each of the experimental groups ought to be comparable, and it is easy enough to create groups that are similar in terms of gender. The problem becomes a bit more tricky, though, when we consider other participant characteristics. How can we ensure that participants in each experimental group will be equally intelligent, extroverted, cooperative, and so forth, when the list of characteristics— any one of which could be important—is potentially endless?

Random assignment to condition: A
procedure in which participants are
assigned to different experimental
groups or "conditions" on the basis
of chance and chance alone.

The solution is a simple but elegant procedure called **random assignment to condition:** Participants are assigned to different experimental groups or "conditions" on the basis of chance and chance alone. The experimenter might, for instance, flip a coin for each participant and assign a participant to one group when "heads" came up, and to the other group when "tails" came up. The advantage of this technique is that participant characteristics have an equal chance of being distributed across the various groups. When a researcher uses random assignment—which in practice is usually carried out using computer-generated random numbers—chances are that each of the groups will have approximately the same proportion of intelligent people, cooperative people, extroverted people, males and females, and so on.

Figure 2 provides another example of an experiment. Like all experiments, it includes the following set of key elements, which are important to keep in mind as you consider whether a research study is truly an experiment:

▶   An independent variable, the variable that is manipulated by the experimenter

| a. Identify participants | b. Randomly assign participants to a condition | c. Manipulate the independent variable | d. Measure the dependent variable | e. Compare the results of the two groups |

Group 1: Treatment group

Receive-drug condition

Group 2: Control group

No-drug condition

FIGURE 2 In this depiction of a study investigating the effects of the drug propranolol on stress, we can see the basic elements of all true experiments. The participants in the experiment were monkeys, who were randomly assigned to one of two groups. Monkeys assigned to the treatment group were given a drug, propranolol, hypothesized to prevent heart disease, whereas those in the control group were not given the drug. Administration of the drugs, then, was the independent variable.

All the monkeys were given a high-fat diet that was the human equivalent of two eggs with bacon every morning, and they occasionally were reassigned to different cages to provide a source of stress. To determine the effects of the drug, the monkeys' heart rates and other measures of heart disease were assessed after twenty-six months. These measures constituted the dependent variable. (The results? As hypothesized, monkeys that received the drug showed lower heart rates and fewer symptoms of heart disease than those who did not.) (Based on a study by Kaplan & Manuck, 1989.)

- ▶ A dependent variable, the variable that is measured by the experimenter and that is expected to change as a result of the manipulation of the independent variable
- ▶ A procedure that randomly assigns participants to different experimental groups or "conditions" of the independent variable
- ▶ A hypothesis that predicts the effect the independent variable will have on the dependent variable

Only if each of these elements is present can a research study be considered a true experiment in which cause-and-effect relationships can be determined.

WERE LATANÉ AND DARLEY RIGHT?

By now you must be wondering whether Latané and Darley were right when they hypothesized that increasing the number of bystanders in an emergency situation would lower the degree of helping behavior.

According to the results of the experiment they carried out, their hypothesis was right on target. To test the hypothesis, they placed the participants in a room and told them that the purpose of the experiment was to hold a discussion about personal

	Correlational Research	Experimental Research
General Process	Researcher observes a previously existing situation but does not make a change in the situation	Researcher manipulates a situation in order to observe the outcome of the manipulation
Intended Result	Identifies association between factors	Learns how changes in one variable cause changes in another variable
Type	Archival research (examines records to confirm hypothesis)	Experiment (investigator produces a change in one variable to observe the effects of that change on other variables)
	Naturalistic observation (observation of naturally occurring behavior, without making a change in the situation)	
	Survey research (a sample is chosen to represent a larger population and asked a series of questions)	
	Case study (intensive investigation of an individual or small group)	

FIGURE 3 Research strategies.

problems associated with college. The discussion was to be held over an intercom, supposedly to avoid the potential embarrassment of face-to-face contact. Chatting about personal problems was not, of course, the true purpose of the experiment, but the participants were told that it was a way of keeping their expectations about the experiment from biasing their behavior. (Consider how they would have been affected if they had been told that their helping behavior in emergencies was being tested. The experimenters could never have gotten an accurate assessment of what the participants would actually do in an emergency. By definition, emergencies are rarely announced in advance.)

The sizes of the discussion groups were two, three, and six people, which constituted the manipulation of the independent variable of group size. Participants were randomly assigned to these groups upon their arrival at the laboratory.

As the participants in each group were holding their discussion, they suddenly heard through the intercom one of the other participants (in reality a trained *confederate*, or employee, of the experimenters; in each group, one of the participants was a confederate, so that in each two-person group there was only one real "bystander") having what sounded like an epileptic seizure and calling for help.

The participants' behavior was now what counted. The dependent variable was the time that elapsed from the start of the "seizure" to the time a participant began trying to help the "victim." If six minutes went by without a participant's offering help, the experiment was ended.

As predicted by the hypothesis, the size of the group had a significant effect on whether a participant provided help. The more people who were present, the less likely it was that someone would supply help, as you can see in Figure 4 (Latané & Darley, 1970).

Because these results are so straightforward, it seems clear that the original hypothesis was confirmed. However, Latané and Darley could not be sure that the results were truly meaningful until they determined whether the results represented a **significant outcome.** Through various statistical analyses researchers can determine whether a numeric difference is meaningful or trivial. Only when differences between groups are large enough that statistical tests show them to be significant is it possible for researchers to confirm a hypothesis (Cwikel, Behar, & Rabson-Hare, 2000; Cohen, 2002).

Significant outcome: Meaningful results that make it possible for researchers to feel confident that they have confirmed their hypotheses.

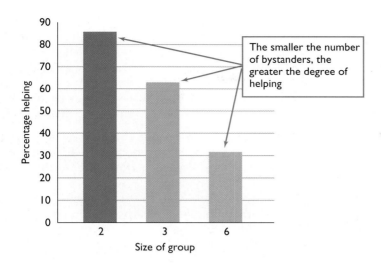

The smaller the number of bystanders, the greater the degree of helping

FIGURE 4 The Latané and Darley experiment showed that as the size of the group witnessing an emergency increased, helping behavior decreased.

MOVING BEYOND THE STUDY

The Latané and Darley study contains all the elements of an experiment: an independent variable, a dependent variable, random assignment to conditions, and multiple experimental groups. Consequently, we can say with some confidence that group size *caused* changes in the degree of helping behavior.

Of course, one experiment alone does not forever resolve the question of bystander intervention in emergencies. Psychologists require that findings be **replicated,** or repeated, sometimes using other procedures, in other settings, with other groups of participants, before full confidence can be placed in the validity of any single experiment. A procedure called *meta-analysis* permits psychologists to combine the results of many separate studies into one overall conclusion (Murphy, 2003).

In addition to replicating experimental results, psychologists need to test the limitations of their theories and hypotheses to determine under which specific circumstances they do and do not apply. It seems unlikely, for instance, that increasing the number of bystanders *always* results in less helping. Therefore, it is critical to continue carrying out experiments to understand the conditions in which exceptions to this general rule occur and other circumstances in which the rule holds (Aronson, 1988; Garcia et al., 2002).

Replication: The repetition of research, sometimes using other procedures, settings, and groups of participants, to increase confidence in prior findings.

RECAP/EVALUATE/RETHINK

RECAP

What are the different research methods employed by psychologists?

▶ Archival research uses existing records, such as old newspapers or other documents, to test a hypothesis. In naturalistic observation, the investigator acts mainly as an observer, making no change in a naturally occurring situation. In survey research, people are asked a series of questions about their behavior, thoughts, or attitudes. The case study is an in-depth interview and examination of one person or group. (p. 37)

▶ These methods rely on correlational techniques, which describe associations between variables but cannot determine cause-and-effect relationships. (p. 41)

How do psychologists establish cause-and-effect relationships in research studies?

▶ In a formal experiment, the relationship between variables is investigated by deliberately producing a change—called the experimental manipulation—in one of them and observing changes in the other. (p. 42)

▶ For a hypothesis to be tested, it must be operationalized: A researcher must translate the abstract concepts of the hypothesis into the actual procedures used in the study. (p. 42)

▶ In an experiment, at least two groups must be compared to assess cause-and-effect relationships. The group receiving the treatment (the special procedure devised by the experimenter) is the experimental group; the second group (which receives no treatment) is the control group. There also may be multiple experimental groups, each of which is subjected to a different procedure and then compared with the others. (p. 43)

▶ The variable that experimenters manipulate is the independent variable. The variable that they measure and expect to change as a result of manipulation of the independent variable is called the dependent variable. (p. 43)

▶ In a formal experiment, participants must be assigned to treatment conditions randomly so that participant characteristics are distributed evenly across the different conditions. (p. 44)

▶ Psychologists use statistical tests to determine whether research is significant in a formal sense. (p. 46)

EVALUATE

1. An experimenter is interested in studying the relationship between hunger and aggression. He defines aggression as the number of times a participant will hit a punching bag. What is the process of defining this variable called?

2. Match the following forms of research to their definition:

   1. Archival research   a. Directly asking a sample of people questions about their behavior

   2. Naturalistic observation   b. Examining existing records to test a hypothesis

   3. Survey research   c. Looking at behavior in its true setting without intervening in the setting

   4. Case study   d. Doing an in-depth investigation of a person or small group

3. Match each of the following research methods with a problem basic to it:

   1. Archival research   a. May not be able to generalize to the population at large.

   2. Naturalistic observation   b. People's behavior can change if they know they are being watched.

   3. Survey research   c. The data may not exist or may be unusable.

   4. Case study   d. People may lie in order to present a good image.

4. A friend tells you, "Anxiety about speaking in public and performance are negatively correlated. Therefore, high anxiety must cause low performance." Is this statement true or false, and why?

5. A psychologist wants to study the effect of attractiveness on willingness to help a person with a math problem. Attractiveness would be the _____ variable, and the amount of helping would be the _____ variable.

6. The group in an experiment that receives no treatment is called the _____ group.

RETHINK

1. Can you describe how a researcher might use naturalistic observation, case study methods, and survey research to investigate gender differences in aggressive behavior at the workplace? First state a hypothesis and then describe your research approaches. What positive and negative features does each method have?

2. Tobacco companies have frequently asserted that no experiment has ever proved that tobacco use causes cancer. Can you explain this claim in terms of the research procedures and designs discussed in this module? What sort of research would establish a cause-and-effect relationship between tobacco use and cancer? Is such a research study possible?

Answers to Evaluate Questions

1. Operationalization; 2. 1-b, 2-c, 3-a, 4-d; 3. 1-c, 2-b, 3-d, 4-a; 4. False. Correlation does not imply causation. Just because two variables are related does not mean that one causes the other. Poor performance may cause people to become more anxious, or a third variable may cause both of these effects; 5. independent, dependent; 6. control

Critical Research Issues

You probably realize by now that there are few simple formulas psychologists can follow as they carry out research. They must make choices about the type of study to conduct, the measures to take, and the most effective way to analyze the results. Even after they make these essential decisions, they must still consider several critical issues. We turn first to the most fundamental of these issues: ethics.

Ⓐ Ⓐ Ⓐ

The Ethics of Research

Put yourself in the place of one of the participants in the experiment conducted by Latané and Darley to examine the helping behavior of bystanders, in which another "bystander" simulating a seizure turned out to be a confederate of the experimenters (Latané & Darley, 1970). How would you feel when you learned that the supposed victim was in reality a paid accomplice?

Although you might at first experience relief that there had been no real emergency, you might also feel some resentment that you had been deceived by the experimenter. You might also experience concern that you had been placed in an embarrassing or compromising situation—one that might have dealt a blow to your self-esteem, depending on how you had behaved.

Most psychologists argue that deception is sometimes necessary to prevent participants from being influenced by what they think a study's true purpose is. (If you knew that Latané and Darley were actually studying your helping behavior, wouldn't you automatically have been tempted to intervene in the emergency?) To avoid such outcomes, a small proportion of research involves deception.

Nonetheless, because research has the potential to violate the rights of participants, psychologists are expected to adhere to a strict set of ethical guidelines aimed at protecting participants (American Psychological Association [APA], 2002). Those guidelines advocate the following:

- ⊙ Protection of participants from physical and mental harm
- ⊙ The right of participants to privacy regarding their behavior
- ⊙ The assurance that participation in research is completely voluntary
- ⊙ The necessity of informing participants about the nature of procedures before their participation in the experiment

All experiments that use humans as participants must be reviewed by an independent panel before being conducted, including the minority of studies that involve deception (Sales & Folkman, 2000; Fisher et al., 2002, 2003).

One of psychologists' key ethical principles is **informed consent.** Before participating in an experiment, the participants must sign a document affirming that they have been told the basic outlines of the study and are aware of what their participation will involve, what risks the experiment may hold, and the fact that their

**PowerWeb:
Psychology's Tangled
Web**

www.mhhe.com/feldmanup7

Informed consent: A document signed by participants affirming that they have been told the basic outlines of the study and are aware of what their participation will involve.

INTERACTIVITY 6–1

Ethical Dilemmas

participation is purely voluntary and they may terminate it at any time. Furthermore, after participation in a study, they must be given a *debriefing* in which they receive an explanation of the study and the procedures involved. The only time informed consent and a debriefing can be eliminated is in experiments in which the risks are minimal, as in a purely observational study in a public place (Koocher & Keith-Spiegel, 1998; Chastain & Landrum, 1999; DuBois, 2002). (To get a better understanding of ethics, try **Interactivity 6–1.**)

Exploring **DIVERSITY**

Choosing Participants Who Represent the Scope of Human Behavior

When Latané and Darley, both college professors, decided who should be chosen to participate in their experiment, they turned to the most available people: college students. In fact, college students are used so frequently in experiments that psychology has been called—somewhat contemptuously—the "science of the behavior of the college sophomore" (Rubenstein, 1982).

Using college students as participants has both advantages and drawbacks. The big benefit is that because most research occurs in university settings, college students are readily available. Typically, they cost the researcher very little: They participate for either extra course credit or a relatively small payment.

The problem is that college students may not represent the general population adequately. They tend to be younger and better educated than a significant percentage of the rest of the population of the United States. Compared with older adults, their attitudes are likely to be less well formed, and they are more apt to be influenced by authority figures and peers (Sears, 1986).

College students are also disproportionately white and middle class. However, even research that does not employ college students tends to use white, middle-class participants; the use of African Americans, Latinos, Asians, and other minorities as participants is low (Graham, 1992; Guthrie, 1998). Because psychology is a science that purports to explain human behavior in general, something is therefore amiss. Consequently, psychological researchers have become increasingly sensitive to the

Although readily available and widely used as research subjects, college students may not represent the population at large. What are some advantages and drawbacks of using college students as subjects?

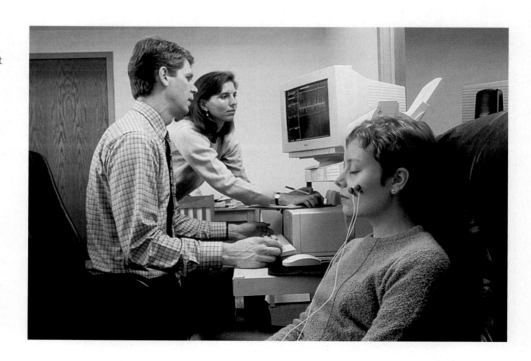

importance of using participants who are fully representative of the general population. Furthermore, the National Institute of Mental Health and the National Science Foundation—the primary U.S. funding sources for psychological research—now require that experiments address issues of diverse populations (Rogler, 1999; Carpenter, 2002).

▲▲▲

Should Animals Be Used in Research?

Like those who work with humans, researchers who use nonhuman animals in experiments have their own set of exacting guidelines to ensure that the animals do not suffer. Specifically, researchers must make every effort to minimize discomfort, illness, and pain, and procedures that subject animals to distress are permitted only when an alternative procedure is unavailable and when the research is justified by its prospective value. Moreover, there are federal regulations specifying how animals are to be housed, fed, and maintained. Not only must researchers strive to avoid causing physical discomfort, they are also required to promote the *psychological* well-being of some species of research animals, such as primates (Novak & Petto, 1991; APA, 1993).

Why should animals be used for research in the first place? Is it really possible to learn about human behavior from the results of research employing rats, gerbils, and pigeons? The answer is that psychological research that does employ animals has a different focus and is designed to answer different questions than is research that uses humans. For example, the shorter life span of animals (rats live an average of two years) allows researchers to learn about the effects of aging in a much smaller time frame than they could by using human participants. Moreover, some principles of behavior are similar across species, and so some basic behavioral phenomena can be studied more simply in nonhumans. Finally, some studies require large numbers

PowerWeb: Should Animals Be Used in Research?

www.mhhe.com/feldmanup7

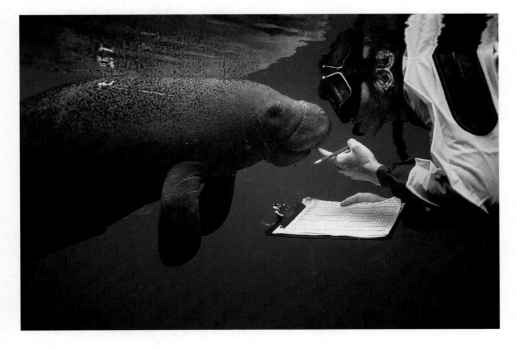

Research involving animals is controversial but, when conducted within ethical guidelines, yields significant benefits for humans.

of participants that share similar backgrounds or have been exposed to particular environments—conditions that could not practically be met with human beings (Gallagher & Rapp, 1997; Mukerjee, 1997).

Research using animals has provided psychologists with information that has profoundly benefited humans. For instance, it furnished the keys to detecting eye disorders in children early enough to prevent permanent damage, to communicating more effectively with severely retarded children, and to reducing chronic pain in people, to name just a few results (APA, 1988; Botting & Morrison, 1997).

Despite the value of research with animal participants, the use of animals in psychological research is highly controversial. For example, some critics believe that animals have rights no less significant than those of humans, and that because animals are unable to consent to participation in studies, their use is unethical. Others object to the use of animals on methodological grounds, saying it is impossible to generalize from findings on nonhuman species to humans (Plous & Herzog, 2000).

Because the issues involve complex moral and philosophical concerns, they are not easily resolved. As a consequence, review panels, which must approve all research before it is carried out, are particularly careful to ensure that research involving animals is conducted ethically (Plous, 1996a, 1996b; Barnard & Kaufman, 1997).

Threats to Experiment Validity: Experimenter and Participant Expectations

Experimental bias: Factors that distort how the independent variable affects the dependent variable in an experiment.

PowerWeb: The Minnesota Adoption Studies: Genetic Differences and Malleability

www.mhhe.com/feldmanup7

Even the best-laid experimental plans are susceptible to **experimental bias**—factors that distort the way the independent variable affects the dependent variable in an experiment. One of the most common forms of experimental bias is *experimenter expectations:* An experimenter unintentionally transmits cues to participants about the way they are expected to behave in a given experimental condition. The danger is that those expectations will bring about an "appropriate" behavior—one that otherwise might not have occurred (Rosnow & Rosenthal, 1997; Rosenthal, 2002).

A related problem is *participant expectations* about appropriate behavior. If you have ever been a participant in an experiment, you know that you quickly develop guesses about what is expected of you. In fact, it is typical for people to develop their own hypotheses about what the experimenter hopes to learn from the study. If participants form their own hypotheses, it may no longer be the experimental manipulation, but rather the participant's expectations, that produces an effect.

To guard against participant expectations biasing the results of an experiment, the experimenter may try to disguise the true purpose of the experiment. Participants who do not know that helping behavior is being studied, for example, are more apt to act in a "natural" way than they would if they knew.

Sometimes it is impossible to hide the actual purpose of research; when that is the case, other techniques are available to prevent bias. Suppose you were interested in testing the ability of a new drug to alleviate the symptoms of severe depression. If you simply gave the drug to half your participants and not to the other half, the participants who were given the drug might report feeling less depressed merely because they knew they were getting a drug. Similarly, the participants who got nothing might report feeling no better because they knew that they were in a no-treatment control group.

To solve this problem, psychologists typically use a procedure in which all the participants receive a treatment, but those in the control group receive only a

placebo, a false treatment, such as a pill, "drug," or other substance, that has no significant chemical properties or active ingredient. Because members of both groups are kept in the dark about whether they are getting a real or a false treatment, any differences that are found can be attributed to the quality of the drug and not to the possible psychological effects of being administered a pill or other substance (Kirsch, 1999; Enserink, 1999, 2000a; Kim & Holloway, 2003).

However, there is one more safeguard that a careful researcher must apply in an experiment such as this. To overcome the possibility that *experimenter* expectations will affect the participant, the person who administers the drug shouldn't know whether it is actually the true drug or the placebo. By keeping both the participant and the experimenter who interacts with the participant "blind" to the nature of the drug that is being administered, researchers can more accurately assess the effects of the drug. This method is known as the *double-blind procedure.*

> **Placebo:** A false treatment, such as a pill, "drug," or other substance, without any significant chemical properties or active ingredient.

If you were about to purchase an automobile, it is unlikely that you would stop at the nearest car dealership and drive off with the first car a salesperson recommended. Instead, you would probably mull over the purchase, read about automobiles, consider the alternatives, talk to others about their experiences, and ultimately put in a fair amount of thought before you made such a major purchase.

BECOMING AN INFORMED CONSUMER
of Psychology
Thinking Critically About Research

In contrast, many of us are considerably less conscientious when we expend our intellectual, rather than financial, assets. People often jump to conclusions on the basis of incomplete and inaccurate information, and only rarely do they take the time to critically evaluate the research and data to which they are exposed.

Because the field of psychology is based on an accumulated body of research, it is crucial for psychologists to scrutinize thoroughly the methods, results, and claims of researchers. Yet it is not just psychologists who need to know how to evaluate research critically; all of us are constantly exposed to the claims of others. Knowing how to approach research and data can be helpful in areas far beyond the realm of psychology.

Several basic questions can help us sort through what is valid and what is not. Among the most important questions to ask are the following:

PowerWeb: Taking Sides: The *Consumer Reports* Study

www.mhhe.com/feldmanup7

▶ *What was the purpose of the research?* Research studies should evolve from a clearly specified theory. Furthermore, we must take into account the specific hypothesis that is being tested. Unless we know what hypothesis is being examined, it is not possible to judge how successful a study has been.

▶ *How well was the study conducted?* Consider who the participants were, how many were involved, what methods were employed, and what problems in collecting the data the researcher encountered. There are important differences, for example, between a case study that reports the anecdotes of a handful of respondents and a survey that collects data from several thousand people.

▶ *Are the results presented fairly?* It is necessary to assess statements on the basis of the actual data they reflect and their logic. For instance, when the manufacturer of car X boasts that "no other car a has a better safety record than car X," this does not mean that car X is safer than every other car. It just means that no other car has been proved safer, though many other cars could be just as safe as car X. Expressed in the latter fashion, the finding doesn't seem worth bragging about.

These three basic questions can help you assess the validity of research findings you come across—both within and outside the field of psychology. The more you know how to evaluate research in general, the better you will be able to assess what the field of psychology has to offer.

RECAP/EVALUATE/RETHINK

RECAP

What major issues confront psychologists conducting research?

▶ One of the key ethical principles followed by psychologists is that of informed consent. Participants must be informed, before participation, about the basic outline of the experiment and the risks and potential benefits of their participation. (p. 49)

▶ Although the use of college students as participants has the advantage of easy availability, there are drawbacks too. For instance, students do not necessarily represent the population as a whole. The use of animals as participants may also have costs in terms of generalizability, although the benefits of using animals in research have been profound. (p. 50)

▶ Experiments are subject to a number of threats, or biases. Experimenter expectations can produce bias when an experimenter unintentionally transmits cues to participants about her or his expectations regarding their behavior in a given experimental condition. Participant expectations can also bias an experiment. Among the tools experimenters use to help eliminate bias are placebos and double-blind procedures. (p. 52)

EVALUATE

1. Ethical research begins with the concept of informed consent. Before signing up to participate in an experiment, participants should be informed of

   a. The procedure of the study, stated generally
   b. The risks that may be involved
   c. Their right to withdraw at any time
   d. All of the above

2. List three benefits of using animals in psychological research.
3. Deception is one means experimenters can use to try to eliminate participants' expectations. True or false?
4. A procedure in which neither the participants nor the experimenter knows whether the participants are or are not receiving an actual treatment is known as the _____ procedure.
5. According to a report, a study has shown that men differ from women in their preference for ice cream flavors. This study was based on a sample of two men and three women. What might be wrong with this study?

RETHINK

1. A pollster studies people's attitudes toward welfare programs by circulating a questionnaire via the Internet. Is this study likely to accurately reflect the views of the general population? Why or why not?
2. A researcher strongly believes that college professors tend to show female students less attention and respect in the classroom than they show male students. She sets up an experimental study involving observation of classrooms in different conditions. In explaining the study to the professors and students who will participate, what steps should the researcher take to eliminate experimental bias based on both experimenter expectations and participant expectations?

Answers to Evaluate Questions

1. d; 2. (1) We can study some phenomena in animals more easily than we can in people, because with animal subjects we have greater control over environmental and genetic factors. (2) Large numbers of similar participants can be easily obtained. (3) We can look at generational effects much more easily in animals, because of their shorter life span, than we can with people; 3. true; 4. double-blind; 5. There are far too few participants. Without a larger sample, no valid conclusions can be drawn about ice cream preferences based on gender.

KEY TERMS

Psychology on the Web

1. Identify a product or service that is advertised on the Internet using broad, unspecific claims, such as a weight-loss formula or body-building method. Find at least two advertisements on the Internet for that product or service and evaluate the claims they make according to the principles discussed in Modules 4 through 6. Summarize the evidence that is presented for those claims, and describe a method by which you might confirm the claims by using actual research.

2. Find a website that focuses on an important social issue (e.g., urban violence, gender differences in hiring or promotion, poverty) and locate descriptions of a research study about the issue. Evaluate the study by identifying the hypotheses that were tested, the methods used to test them, and the validity of the results reported.

3. After completing online Interactivity 6–1 on ethical issues in psychology, consult the most recent revision of the American Psychological Association ethical guidelines (found online at www.apa.org/ethics/code2002.html). If ethical standards for psychologists are based on enduring ethical principles, why do you think it is necessary to periodically revise the ethical standards?

 Epilogue We have been discussing the ways in which psychologists seek to understand phenomena and answer questions of interest. We've examined the scientific method and its reliance on posing good questions, creating productive theories, and crafting testable hypotheses. We have also looked at the basic methods psychologists use to conduct research studies and compared correlational methods and experimental methods. Finally, we've explored some of the major challenges that psychologists have to deal with when conducting research, including ethical considerations, the use of animals in research, and potential bias.

Before leaving this topic, reconsider the lack of bystander intervention in the case of the 88-year-old who was being beaten in plain view outside a supermarket. Reflect on the following questions in light of what you now know about conducting psychological research.

1. Suppose you were interested in studying aggressive behavior among criminals such as the one who was beating the 88-year-old. Can you formulate a theory that would provide an explanation for why criminals behave violently?

2. What hypotheses (testable predictions) can you construct to test your theory?

3. Can you design a correlational study to test one of your hypotheses? Which correlational method(s) (archival research, naturalistic observation, survey research, case study) would you use in your study?

4. Can you design an experimental study to test the same or another hypothesis? Describe the experiment, including the participants, the experimental manipulation, the treatment, and the independent and dependent variables.

Hypothesis Formation

Researchers develop theories to make predictions about the world. For example, they might theorize that viewing violent TV programs causes children to model aggression and to behave more aggressively. Based on the theory, they develop a hypothesis that can be tested using different research methods.

2 Archival and Survey Research

In archival research, researchers review existing data such as statistical reports and newspaper clippings about children's behavior. In survey research, experimenters ask children a series of questions about their behaviors and feelings.

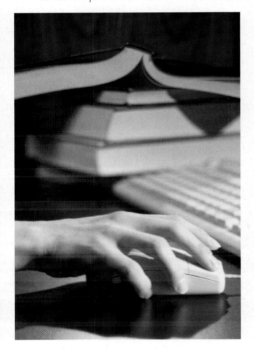

3 Naturalistic Observation and Case Study Methods

Using naturalistic observation, researchers can monitor children's behavior in a real-world setting. In the case study method, they focus on the actions of a single child. Researchers can use these observations to understand whether viewing violence on TV is related to aggression.

4 Correlational Research

Using correlational methods, researchers might measure children's viewing of violence on TV and the amount of their aggressive behavior. After assessing many children, they would compare the results to determine if children who watch more violent programming also tend to behave more aggressively.

Amount of violent TV

Amount of aggressive behavior

Experimental group

Control group

5 Experimental and Control Groups

An experiment (shown in the remaining frames) is the most powerful method for understanding behavior. Only through experiments can researchers determine the cause of the outcome. Researchers assign participants either to the experimental group or to the control group.

6 Independent Variable

During the experiment, the experimental group watches a violent video and the control group watches a nonviolent video. The different conditions (violent or nonviolent viewing) for the two groups is the independent variable.

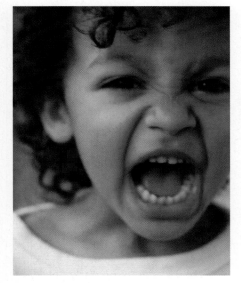

7 Dependent Variable

Next, all of the children are placed in a play environment, and the researchers measure the amount of aggressive behavior that they show. The specific aggressive behavior that is measured is referred to as the dependent variable.

8 Statistical Analysis

The researchers now use statistical methods to determine if there is a significant difference between the two groups. The researchers will then publish their results, and other researchers may try to replicate the experiment to ensure that the results are accurate.

Neuroscience and Behavior

Prologue

A Tiny Movement, But a Big Step

It was the tiniest of movements, barely even noticeable: a slight shift upward in the index finger of the left hand.

But for actor Christopher Reeve, who suffered a severe spinal cord injury that resulted in paralysis from the neck down, it was a major step forward in his recovery. For it signaled that the physicians who had initially told him that he would never be able to move any part of his body below the shoulders were wrong.

For the first five years after his 1995 accident, the pessimistic prediction had been correct, for he was totally paralyzed. However, he stuck to an ambitious regimen of exercise in which medical personnel repetitively moved parts of his body for hours at a time. In addition, he began a program in which his muscles were electrically stimulated.

The therapy has paid off. Although he still is confined to a wheelchair, he has retrieved the ability to move all his fingers on both hands. In addition, while floating in water, he is able to move some joints and can push against a therapist with both legs.

And due to an experimental procedure in which surgeons implanted electrodes into his diaphragm, he has been able to breathe by himself for short periods, without the help of a ventilator that has controlled his respiration nearly constantly since his accident (Blakeslee, 2002; Raymond, 2003).

Christopher Reeve's extraordinary progress is nothing short of miraculous. But the greater miracle is the organ that has provided him with his untiring energy, motivation, and spirit: the brain. The brain, an organ roughly half the size of a loaf of bread, controls our behavior through every waking and sleeping moment. Our movements, thoughts, hopes, aspirations, dreams—our very awareness that we are human—are all intimately related to the brain and the nerves that extend throughout the body, constituting the nervous system.

Because of the importance of the nervous system in controlling behavior, and because humans at their most basic level are biological beings, many researchers in psychology and other fields as diverse as computer science, zoology, and medicine have made the biological

Looking Ahead

Behavioral neuroscientists (or biopsychologists): Psychologists who specialize in considering the ways in which the biological structures and functions of the body affect behavior.

underpinnings of behavior their specialty. These experts collectively are called *neuroscientists* (Beatty, 2000; Posner & DiGiorlamo, 2000; Gazzaniga, Ivry, & Mangun, 2002).

Psychologists who specialize in considering the ways in which the biological structures and functions of the body affect behavior are known as **behavioral neuroscientists** (or **biopsychologists**). They seek to answer several key questions: What are the bases for voluntary and involuntary functioning of the body? How are messages communicated between the brain and other parts of the body? What is the physical structure of the brain, and how does this structure affect behavior? Can the causes of psychological disorders be traced to biological factors, and how can such disorders be treated?

As you consider the biological processes that we'll be discussing, it is important to keep in mind why behavioral neuroscience is an essential part of psychology: Our understanding of human behavior cannot be complete without knowledge of the fundamentals of the brain and other parts of the nervous system. Biological factors are central to our sensory experiences, states of consciousness, motivation and emotion, development throughout the life span, and physical and psychological health. Furthermore, advances in behavioral neuroscience have paved the way for the creation of drugs and other treatments for psychological and physical disorders. In short, we cannot understand behavior—the moods, motivations, goals, and desires that are central to the human condition—without an understanding of our biological makeup (Kosslyn et al., 2002).

Neurons: The Basic Elements of Behavior

Why do psychologists study the brain and nervous system?

What are the basic elements of the nervous system?

How does the nervous system communicate electrical and chemical messages from one part to another?

Watching Serena Williams hit a stinging backhand, Dario Vaccaro carry out a complex ballet routine, or Derek Jeter swing at a baseball, you may have marveled at the complexity—and wondrous abilities—of the human body. But even the most everyday tasks, such as picking up a pencil, writing, and speaking, depend on a sophisticated sequence of events in the body that is itself truly impressive. For instance, the difference between saying the words *dime* and *time* rests primarily on whether the vocal cords are relaxed or tense during a period lasting no more than one one-hundredth of a second, yet it is a distinction that almost everyone can make with ease.

The nervous system is the pathway for the instructions that permit our bodies to carry out such precise activities. To understand how it is able to exert such exacting control, we begin by examining neurons, the most basic parts of the nervous system, and considering how nerve impulses are transmitted throughout the brain and body.

▲▲▲

The Structure of the Neuron

Playing the piano, driving a car, or hitting a tennis ball depends, at one level, on exact muscle coordination. But if we consider *how* the muscles can be activated so precisely, we see that there are more fundamental processes involved. For the muscles to produce the complex movements that make up any meaningful physical activity, the brain has to provide the right messages to them and coordinate those messages.

Such messages—as well as those which enable us to think, remember, and experience emotion—are passed through specialized cells called neurons. **Neurons,** or nerve cells, are the basic elements of the nervous system. Their quantity is staggering—perhaps as many as 1 *trillion* neurons throughout the body are involved in the control of behavior. Although there are several types of neurons, they all have a similar basic structure, as illustrated in Figure 1. Like practically all cells in the body, neurons have a cell body that contains a nucleus. The nucleus incorporates the inherited material that ultimately determines how a cell will function. Neurons are physically held in place by *glial cells,* which provide nourishment and insulate them (Bear, Connors, & Paradiso, 2000; Vylings, 2002).

In contrast to most other cells, however, neurons have a distinctive feature: the ability to communicate with other cells and transmit information, sometimes across relatively long distances. Although many of the body's neurons receive signals from the environment or relay the nervous system's messages to muscles and other target cells, the vast majority of neurons communicate only with other neurons, making up the elaborate information system that regulates behavior.

Neurons: Nerve cells, the basic elements of the nervous system.

FIGURE I The primary components of the specialized cell called the neuron, the basic element of the nervous system (Van de Graaff, 2000). A neuron, like most types of cells in the body, has a cell body and a nucleus, but it also contains structures that carry messages: the dendrites, which receive messages from other neurons, and the axon, which carries messages to other neurons or body cells. In this neuron, as in most neurons, the axon is protected by the sausagelike myelin sheath. What advantages does the treelike structure of the neuron provide?

Dendrite: A cluster of fibers at one end of a neuron that receive messages form other neurons.

Axon: The part of the neuron that carries messages destined for other neurons.

Terminal buttons: Small bulges at the end of axons that send messages to other neurons.

Myelin sheath: A protective coat of fat and protein that wraps around the axon.

INTERACTIVITY 7–1

Structure of neurons

As you can see in Figure 1, neurons have clusters of fibers called **dendrites** at one end. Those fibers, which look like the twisted branches of a tree, receive messages from other neurons. At the opposite end, neurons have a long, slim, tubelike extension called an **axon,** the part of the neuron that carries messages destined for other neurons. The axon is considerably longer than the rest of the neuron. Although most axons are several millimeters in length, some can be as long as three feet. Axons end in small bulges called **terminal buttons** that send messages to other neurons.

The messages that travel through a neuron are purely electrical in nature. Although there are exceptions, those electrical messages generally move across neurons as if they were traveling on a one-way street. They follow a route that begins with the dendrites, continues into the cell body, and leads ultimately along the tubelike extension, the axon. Dendrites, then, *d*etect messages from other neurons; *a*xons carry signals *a*way from the cell body.

To prevent messages from short-circuiting one another, axons must be insulated in some fashion (just as electrical wires must be insulated). In most axons, this is done with a **myelin sheath,** a protective coating of fat and protein that wraps, like a sausage, around the axon.

The myelin sheath also serves to increase the velocity with which electrical impulses travel through axons. Those axons which carry the most important and most urgently required information have the greatest concentrations of myelin. If your hand touches a painfully hot stove, for example, the information regarding the pain is passed through axons in the hand and arm that have a relatively thick coating of myelin, speeding the message of pain so that you can react instantly. In certain diseases, such as multiple sclerosis, the myelin sheath surrounding the axon deteriorates, exposing parts of the axon that are normally covered. This short-circuits messages between the brain and muscles and results in symptoms such as the inability to walk, difficulties with vision, and general muscle impairment. (To review the structure of the neuron, try **Interactivity 7–1.**)

How Neurons Fire

Like a gun, neurons either fire—that is, transmit an electrical impulse along the axon—or don't fire. There is no in-between stage, just as pulling harder on a gun trigger doesn't make the bullet travel faster or move more surely. Similarly, neurons follow an **all-or-none law:** They are either on or off, with nothing in between the on state and the off state. Once there's enough force to pull the trigger, a neuron fires.

Before a neuron is triggered—that is, when it is in a **resting state**—it has a negative electrical charge of about −70 millivolts (a millivolt is one one-thousandth of a volt). This charge is caused by the presence of more negatively charged *ions* within the neuron than outside it. (An ion is an atom that is electrically charged.) You might compare the neuron to a miniature battery, with the inside of the neuron representing the negative pole and the outside representing the positive pole.

However, when a message arrives, the neuron's cell membrane opens briefly to allow positively charged ions to rush in at rates as high as 100 million ions per second. The sudden arrival of these positive ions causes the charge within the nearby part of the cell to change momentarily from negative to positive. When the positive charge reaches a critical level, the "trigger" is pulled, and an electrical nerve impulse, known as an **action potential,** travels along the axon of the neuron (see Figure 2).

The action potential moves from one end of the axon to the other like a flame moving along a fuse. As the impulse travels along the axon, the movement of ions causes a change in charge from negative to positive in successive sections of the axon

All-or-none law: The rule that neurons are either on or off.

Resting state: The state in which there is a negative electrical charge of about −70 millivolts within a neuron.

Action potential: An electric nerve impulse that travels through a neuron when it is set off by a "trigger," changing the neuron's charge from negative to positive.

Positive charge

Negative charge

Direction of impulse

FIGURE 2 Movement of an action potential across an axon. Just before Time 1, positively charged ions enter the cell membrane, changing the charge in the nearby part of the cell from negative to positive. The action potential is thus triggered, traveling along the axon, as illustrated in the changes occurring from Time 1 to Time 3 (from top to bottom in this drawing). Immediately after the action potential passes through a section of the axon, positive ions are pumped out, restoring the charge in that section to negative. The change in voltage illustrated at the top of the axon can be seen in greater detail in Figure 3 on page 64 (Stevens, 1979).

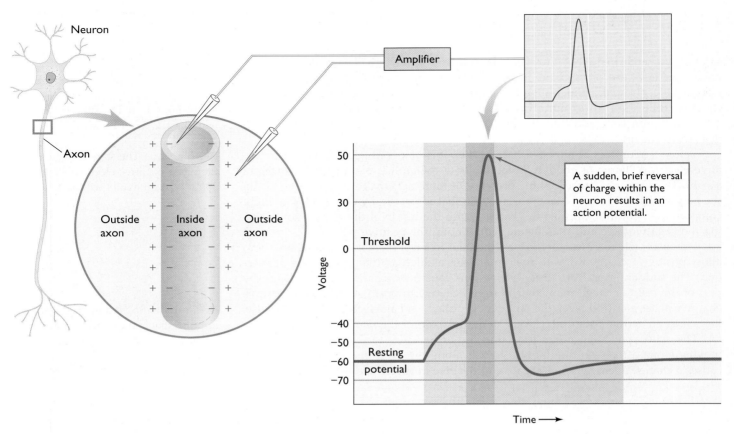

FIGURE 3 Changes in the electrical charge in a neuron during the passage of an action potential. In its normal resting state, a neuron has a negative charge of around −70 millivolts. When an action potential is triggered, however, the charge becomes positive, increasing to about +40 millivolts. Following the passage of the action potential, the charge becomes even more negative than it is in its typical state. It is not until the charge returns to its resting state that the neuron will be fully ready to be triggered once again.

(see Figure 3). After the impulse passes through a particular section of the axon, positive ions are pumped out of that section, and its charge returns to negative while the action potential continues along the neuron.

Just after an action potential has passed through a section of the axon, the cell membrane in that region cannot admit positive ions again for a few milliseconds, and so a neuron cannot fire again immediately no matter how much stimulation it receives. It is as if the gun has to be painstakingly reloaded after each shot. There then follows a period in which, though it is possible for the neuron to fire, a stronger stimulus is needed than would be needed if the neuron had reached its normal resting state. Eventually, though, the neuron is ready to fire once again.

These complex events can occur at dizzying speeds, although there is great variation among different neurons. The particular speed at which an action potential travels along an axon is determined by the axon's size and the thickness of its myelin sheath. Axons with small diameters carry impulses at about 2 miles per hour; longer and thicker ones can average speeds of more than 225 miles per hour.

Neurons differ not only in terms of how quickly an impulse moves along the axon but also in their potential rate of firing. Some neurons are capable of firing as many as a thousand times per second; others fire at much slower rates. The intensity of a stimulus that provokes a neuron determines how much of this potential rate is reached. A strong stimulus, such as a bright light or a loud sound, leads to a higher rate of firing than a less intense stimulus does. Thus, even though all impulses move at the same strength or speed through a particular axon—because of the all-or-none law—there is variation in the frequency of impulses, providing a mechanism by which we can distinguish the tickle of a feather from the weight of someone standing on our toes.

The structure, operation, and functions of the neuron are fundamental biological aspects of the body that underlie several primary psychological processes. Our understanding of the way we sense, perceive, and learn about the world would be greatly restricted without the information about the neuron that behavioral neuroscientists and other researchers have acquired.

Where Neurons Meet: Bridging the Gap

If you've ever looked inside a computer, you've seen that each part is physically connected to another part. In contrast, evolution has produced a neural transmission system that at some points has no need for a structural connection between its components. Instead, a chemical connection bridges the gap, known as a synapse, between two neurons (see Figure 4). The **synapse** is the space between two neurons where the axon of a sending neuron communicates with the dendrites of a receiving neuron by using chemical messages.

When a nerve impulse comes to the end of the axon and reaches a terminal button, the terminal button releases a chemical courier called a neurotransmitter. **Neurotransmitters** are chemicals that carry messages across the synapse to a dendrite (and sometimes the cell body) of a receiver neuron. Like a boat that ferries passengers across a river, these chemical messengers move toward the shorelines of other neurons. The chemical mode of message transmission that occurs between neurons is strikingly different from the means by which communication occurs inside neurons: Although messages travel in electrical form *within* a neuron, they move *between* neurons through a chemical transmission system.

There are several types of neurotransmitters, and not all receiver neurons are capable of making use of the chemical message carried by a particular neurotransmitter. In the same way that a jigsaw puzzle piece can fit in only one specific location in a puzzle, each kind of neurotransmitter has a distinctive configuration that allows it to fit into a specific type of receptor site on the receiving neuron (see Figure 4b). It is only when a neurotransmitter fits precisely into a receptor site that successful chemical communication is possible.

If a neurotransmitter does fit into a site on the receiving neuron, the chemical message it delivers is basically one of two types: excitatory or inhibitory. **Excitatory messages** make it more likely that a receiving neuron will fire and an action potential will travel down its axon. **Inhibitory messages,** in contrast, do just the opposite; they provide chemical information that prevents or decreases the likelihood that the receiving neuron will fire.

Because the dendrites of a neuron receive both excitatory and inhibitory messages simultaneously, the neuron must integrate the messages by using a kind of

Synapse: The space between two neurons where the axon of a sending neuron communicates with the dendrites of a receiving neuron by using chemical messages.

Neurotransmitters: Chemicals that carry messages across the synapse to the dendrite (and sometimes the cell body) of a receiver neuron.

Excitatory message: A chemical message that makes it more likely that a receiving neuron will fire and an action potential will travel down its axon.

Inhibitory message: A chemical message that prevents or decreases the likelihood that a receiving neuron will fire.

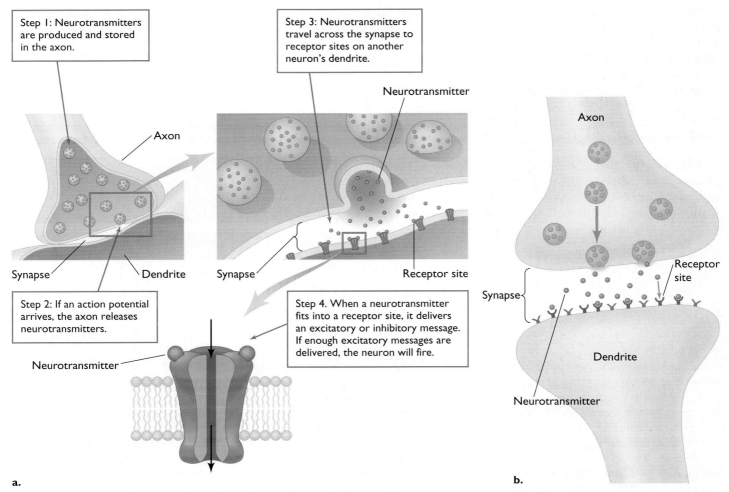

Step 1: Neurotransmitters are produced and stored in the axon.

Step 2: If an action potential arrives, the axon releases neurotransmitters.

Step 3: Neurotransmitters travel across the synapse to receptor sites on another neuron's dendrite.

Step 4. When a neurotransmitter fits into a receptor site, it delivers an excitatory or inhibitory message. If enough excitatory messages are delivered, the neuron will fire.

Axon

Synapse

Dendrite

Neurotransmitter

Neurotransmitter

Synapse

Receptor site

Axon

Receptor site

Synapse

Dendrite

Neurotransmitter

a.

b.

FIGURE 4 (a) A synapse is the junction between an axon and a dendrite. The gap between the axon and the dendrite is bridged by chemicals called neurotransmitters (Mader, 2000). (b) Just as the pieces of a jigsaw puzzle can fit in only one specific location in a puzzle, each kind of neurotransmitter has a distinctive configuration that allows it to fit into a specific type of receptor cell (Johnson, 2000). Why is it advantageous for axons and dendrites to be linked by temporary chemical bridges rather than by the hard wiring typical of a radio connection or telephone hookup?

Reuptake: The reabsorption of neurotransmitters by a terminal button.

chemical calculator. Put simply, if the concentration of excitatory messages is greater than the concentration of inhibitory ones, the neuron fires. In contrast, if the inhibitory messages outweigh the excitatory ones, nothing happens, and the neuron remains in its resting state (Miles, 2000; Mel, 2002).

If neurotransmitters remained at the site of the synapse, receptor neurons would be awash in a continual chemical bath, producing constant stimulation of the receptor neurons—and effective communication across the synapse would no longer be possible. To solve this problem, neurotransmitters are either deactivated by enzymes or—more frequently—reabsorbed by the terminal button in an example of chemical recycling called **reuptake.** Like a vacuum cleaner sucking up dust, neurons reabsorb the neurotransmitters that are now clogging the synapse. All this activity occurs at lightning speed, with the process taking just several milliseconds (Helmuth, 2000).

Neurotransmitters: Multitalented Chemical Couriers

Neurotransmitters are a particularly important link between the nervous system and behavior. Not only are they important for maintaining vital brain and body functions, a deficiency or an excess of a neurotransmitter can produce severe behavior disorders. More than a hundred chemicals have been found to act as neurotransmitters, and neuroscientists believe that more may ultimately be identified (Purves et al., 1997; Penney, 2000).

Neurotransmitters vary significantly in terms of how strong their concentration must be to trigger a neuron to fire. Furthermore, the effects of a particular neurotransmitter vary, depending on the area of the nervous system in which it is produced. The same neurotransmitter, then, can act as an excitatory message to a neuron located in one part of the brain and can inhibit firing in neurons located in another part. (The major neurotransmitters and their effects are described in Figure 5.)

One of the most common neurotransmitters is *acetylcholine* (or *ACh*, its chemical symbol), which is found throughout the nervous system. ACh is involved in our every move, because—among other things—it transmits messages relating to our skeletal muscles. ACh is also involved in memory capabilities, and diminished production of ACh may be related to Alzheimer's disease (Selkoe, 1997).

Another common excitatory neurotransmitter, *glutamate*, plays a role in memory. Memories appear to be produced by specific biochemical changes at particular

FIGURE 5 Some major neurotransmitters.

Dopamine pathways

Serotonin pathways

Name	Location	Effect	Function
Acetylcholine (ACh)	Brain, spinal cord, peripheral nervous system, especially some organs of the parasympathetic nervous system	Excitatory in brain and autonomic nervous system; inhibitory elsewhere	Muscle movement, cognitive functioning
Glutamate	Brain, spinal cord	Excitatory	Memory
Gamma-amino butyric acid (GABA)	Brain, spinal cord	Main inhibitory neuro-transmitter	Eating, aggression, sleeping
Dopamine (DA)	Brain	Inhibitory or excitatory	Muscle disorders, mental disorders, Parkinson's disease
Serotonin	Brain, spinal cord	Inhibitory	Sleeping, eating, mood, pain, depression
Endorphins	Brain, spinal cord	Primarily inhibitory, except in hippocampus	Pain suppression, pleasurable feelings, appetites, placebos

Michael J. Fox is free for the moment of the worst symptoms of Parkinson's after an operation called a thalamotomy.

synapses, and glutamate, along with other neurotransmitters, plays an important role in this process (Bennett, 2000; Riedel, Platt, & Micheau, 2003).

Gamma-amino butyric acid (GABA), which is found in both the brain and the spinal cord, appears to be the nervous system's primary inhibitory neurotransmitter. It moderates a variety of behaviors, ranging from eating to aggression. Several common substances, such as the tranquilizer Valium and alcohol, are effective because they permit GABA to operate more efficiently (Tabakoff & Hoffman, 1996).

Another major neurotransmitter is *dopamine (DA),* which is involved in movement, attention, and learning. The discovery that certain drugs can have a significant effect on dopamine release has led to the development of effective treatments for a wide variety of physical and mental ailments. For instance, Parkinson's disease, from which actor Michael J. Fox suffers, is caused by a deficiency of dopamine in the brain. Techniques for increasing the production of dopamine in Parkinson's patients are proving effective (Schapira, 1999; Heikkinen, Nutt, & LeWitt, 2001; Kaasinen & Rinne, 2002).

In other instances, *over*production of dopamine produces negative consequences. For example, researchers have hypothesized that schizophrenia and some other severe mental disturbances are affected or perhaps even caused by the presence of unusually high levels of dopamine. Drugs that block the reception of dopamine reduce the symptoms displayed by some people diagnosed with schizophrenia (Kahn, Davidson, & Davis, 1996; Baumeister & Francis, 2002).

Another neurotransmitter, *serotonin,* is associated with the regulation of sleep, eating, mood, and pain. A growing body of research points toward a broader role for serotonin, suggesting its involvement in such diverse behaviors as alcoholism, depression, suicide, impulsivity, aggression, and coping with stress (Smith, Williams, & Cowen, 2000; Maris, 2002; Zalsman & Apter, 2002).

Endorphins, another class of neurotransmitters, are a family of chemicals produced by the brain that are similar in structure to painkilling drugs such as morphine. The production of endorphins seems to reflect the brain's effort to deal with pain as well as to elevate mood. People who are afflicted with diseases that produce long-term, severe pain often develop large concentrations of endorphins in their brains.

PowerWeb: Serotonin, Motor Activity, and Depression-Related Disorders

www.mhhe.com/feldmanup7

Endorphins also may produce the euphoric feelings that runners sometimes experience after long runs. Although the research evidence is not firm, the exertion and perhaps the pain involved in a long run stimulate the production of endorphins, ultimately resulting in what has been called "runner's high" (Kremer & Scully, 1994; Kolata, 2002; Pert, 2002).

Endorphin release might also explain other phenomena that have long puzzled psychologists. For example, the act of taking placebos (pills or other substances that contain no actual drugs but that patients *believe* will make them better) may induce the release of endorphins, leading to the reduction of pain. In support of such reasoning, increasing evidence shows that people who are given placebos actually exhibit changes in brain functioning (Leuchter et al., 2002).

RECAP/EVALUATE/RETHINK

RECAP

Why do psychologists study the brain and nervous system?

▸ A full understanding of human behavior requires knowledge of the biological influences underlying that behavior, especially those originating in the nervous system. Psychologists who specialize in studying the effects of biological structures and functions on behavior are known as behavioral neuroscientists. (p. 60)

What are the basic elements of the nervous system?

▸ Neurons, the most basic elements of the nervous system, carry nerve impulses from one part of the body to another. Information in a neuron generally follows a route that begins with the dendrites, continues into the cell body, and leads ultimately down the tubelike extension, the axon. (p. 61)

How does the nervous system communicate electrical and chemical messages from one part to another?

▸ Most axons are insulated by a coating called the myelin sheath. When a neuron receives a message to fire, it releases an action potential, an electric charge that travels through the axon. Neurons operate according to an all-or-none law: Either they are at rest, or an action potential is moving through them. There is no in-between state. (p. 63)

▸ Once a neuron fires, nerve impulses are carried to other neurons through the production of chemical substances, neurotransmitters, that actually bridge the gaps—known as synapses—between neurons. Neurotransmitters may be either excitatory, telling other neurons to fire, or inhibitory, preventing or decreasing the likelihood of other neurons firing. Among the major neurotransmitters are acetylcholine (ACh), which produces contractions of skeletal muscles, and dopamine, which is involved in movement, attention, and learning and has been linked to Parkinson's disease and certain mental disorders, such as schizophrenia. (p. 65)

▸ Endorphins, another type of neurotransmitter, are related to the reduction of pain. Endorphins aid in the production of a natural painkiller and are probably responsible for creating the kind of euphoria that joggers sometimes experience after running. (p. 68)

EVALUATE

1. The _____ is the fundamental element of the nervous system.
2. Neurons receive information through their _____ and send messages through their _____.
3. Just as electrical wires have an outer coating, axons are insulated by a coating called the _____ _____.
4. The gap between two neurons is bridged by a chemical connection called a _____.
5. Endorphins are one kind of _____, the chemical "messengers" between neurons.

RETHINK

1. Can you use your knowledge of psychological research methods to suggest how researchers can study the effects of neurotransmitters on human behavior?
2. In what ways might endorphins help produce the placebo effect? Is there a difference between *believing* that one's pain is reduced and actually *experiencing* reduced pain? Why or why not?

Answers to Evaluate Questions

1. neuron; 2. dendrites, axons; 3. myelin sheath; 4. synapse; 5. neurotransmitter

KEY TERMS

behavioral neuroscientists
(or biopsychologists) p. 60
neurons p. 61
dendrites p. 62

axon p. 62
terminal buttons p. 62
myelin sheath p. 62
all-or-none law p. 63

resting state p. 63
action potential p. 63
synapse p. 65
neurotransmitters p. 65

excitatory message p. 65
inhibitory message p. 65
reuptake p. 66

The Nervous System and the Endocrine System: Communicating Within the Body

In light of the complexity of individual neurons and the neurotransmission process, it should come as no surprise that the connections and structures formed by the neurons are complicated. Because a neuron can be connected to 80,000 other neurons, the total number of possible connections is astonishing. For instance, estimates of the number of neural connections within the brain fall in the neighborhood of 1 quadrillion—a 1 followed by 15 zeros—and some experts put the number even higher. However, connections among neurons are not the only means of communication within the body; as we'll see, the endocrine system, which secretes chemical messages that circulate through the blood, also communicates messages that influence behavior and many aspects of biological functioning (Kandel, Schwartz, & Jessell, 2000).

⚠⚠⚠

The Nervous System

Whatever the actual number of neural connections, the human nervous system has both logic and elegance. We turn now to its basic structures.

CENTRAL AND PERIPHERAL NERVOUS SYSTEMS

As you can see from the schematic representation in Figure 1, the nervous system is divided into two main parts: the central nervous system and the peripheral nervous system. The **central nervous system (CNS)** is composed of the brain and spinal cord. The **spinal cord,** which is about the thickness of a pencil, contains a bundle of nerves that leaves the brain and runs down the length of the back (see Figure 2). It is the primary means for transmitting messages between the brain and the body. (Learn more about the organization of the nervous system in **Interactivity 8–1.**)

However, the spinal cord is not just a communications conduit. It also controls some simple kinds of behaviors on its own, without any involvement of the brain. An example is the way the knee jerks forward when it is tapped with a rubber hammer. Such behaviors, called **reflexes,** are automatic, involuntary responses to incoming stimuli. Similarly, when you touch a hot stove and immediately withdraw your hand, a reflex is at work. Although the brain eventually analyzes and reacts to the situation ("Ouch—hot stove—pull away!"), the initial withdrawal is directed only by neurons in the spinal cord.

Three sorts of neurons are involved in reflexes. **Sensory (afferent) neurons** transmit information from the perimeter of the body to the central nervous system. **Motor (efferent) neurons** communicate information from the nervous system to muscles and glands of the body. **Interneurons** connect sensory and motor neurons, carrying messages between the two.

The importance of the spinal cord and reflexes is illustrated by the outcome of accidents in which the cord is injured or severed. Actor Christopher Reeve, whose

---

In what way are the structures of the nervous system tied together?

How does the endocrine system distribute its messages?

INTERACTIVITY 8–1

Organization of the nervous system

Central nervous system (CNS): The part of the nervous system that includes the brain and spinal cord.

Spinal cord: A bundle of nerves that leaves the brain and runs down the length of the back and is the main means for transmitting messages between the brain and the body.

Reflexes: Automatic, involuntary responses to incoming stimuli.

Sensory (afferent) neurons: Neurons that transmit information from the perimeter of the body to the central nervous system.

Motor (efferent) neurons: Neurons that communicate information from the nervous system to muscles and glands of the body.

Interneurons: Neurons that connect sensory and motor neurons, carrying messages between the two.

FIGURE I A schematic diagram of the relationship of the parts of the nervous system.

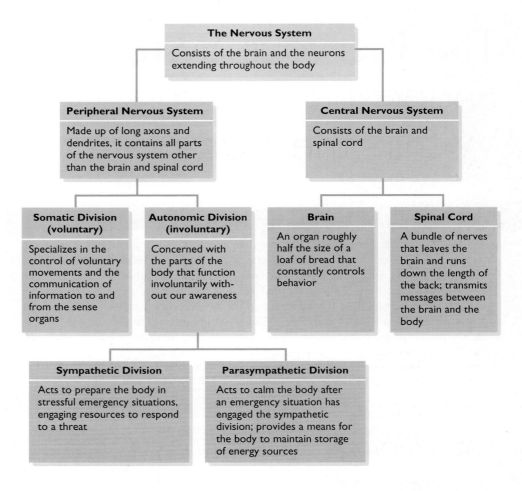

The Nervous System

Consists of the brain and the neurons extending throughout the body

Peripheral Nervous System

Made up of long axons and dendrites, it contains all parts of the nervous system other than the brain and spinal cord

Central Nervous System

Consists of the brain and spinal cord

Somatic Division (voluntary)

Specializes in the control of voluntary movements and the communication of information to and from the sense organs

Autonomic Division (involuntary)

Concerned with the parts of the body that function involuntarily without our awareness

Brain

An organ roughly half the size of a loaf of bread that constantly controls behavior

Spinal Cord

A bundle of nerves that leaves the brain and runs down the length of the back; transmits messages between the brain and the body

Sympathetic Division

Acts to prepare the body in stressful emergency situations, engaging resources to respond to a threat

Parasympathetic Division

Acts to calm the body after an emergency situation has engaged the sympathetic division; provides a means for the body to maintain storage of energy sources

injury was discussed in the Prologue, suffers from *quadriplegia,* a condition in which voluntary muscle movement below the neck is lost. In a less severe but still debilitating condition, *paraplegia,* people are unable to voluntarily move any muscles in the lower half of the body.

As suggested by its name, the **peripheral nervous system** branches out from the spinal cord and brain and reaches the extremities of the body. Made up of long axons and dendrites, the peripheral nervous system encompasses all the parts of the nervous system other than the brain and spinal cord. There are two major divisions—the somatic division and the autonomic division—both of which connect the central nervous system with the sense organs, muscles, glands, and other organs. The **somatic division** specializes in the control of voluntary movements—such as the motion of the eyes to read this sentence or those of the hand to turn this page—and the communication of information to and from the sense organs. On the other hand, the **autonomic division** is concerned with the parts of the body that keep us alive—the heart, blood vessels, glands, lungs, and other organs that function involuntarily without our awareness. As you are reading at this moment, the autonomic division of the peripheral nervous system is pumping blood through your body, pushing your lungs in and out, overseeing the digestion of the meal you had a few hours ago, and so on—all without a thought or care on your part.

Activating the Divisions of the Autonomic Nervous System. The autonomic division plays a particularly crucial role during emergency situations. Suppose as you are reading you suddenly sense that a stranger is watching you through the window. As you look up, you see the glint of something that might be a knife. As confusion races through your mind and fear overcomes your attempts to think rationally, what happens to your body? If you are like most people, you react immediately on a

Peripheral nervous system: The part of the nervous system that includes the autonomic and somatic subdivisions; made up of long axons and dendrites, it branches out from the spinal cord and brain and reaches the extremities of the body.

Somatic division: The part of the peripheral nervous system that specializes in the control of voluntary movements and the communication of information to and from the sense organs.

Autonomic division: The part of the peripheral nervous system that controls involuntary movement (the actions of the heart, glands, lungs, and other organs).

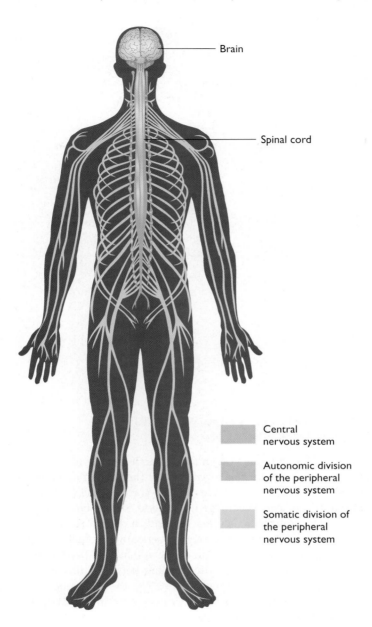

Brain

Spinal cord

Central
nervous system

Autonomic division
of the peripheral
nervous system

Somatic division of
the peripheral
nervous system

FIGURE 2 The central nervous system, consisting of the brain and spinal cord, and the peripheral nervous system.

physiological level. Your heart rate increases, you begin to sweat, and you develop goose bumps all over your body.

The physiological changes that occur result from the activation of one of the two parts that make up the autonomic division: the **sympathetic division.** The sympathetic division acts to prepare the body in stressful emergency situations, engaging all of the organism's resources to respond to a threat. This response often takes the form of "fight or flight." In contrast, the **parasympathetic division** acts to calm the body after the emergency situation has been resolved. When you find, for instance, that the stranger at the window is actually your roommate, who has lost his keys and is climbing in the window to avoid waking you, your parasympathetic division begins to predominate, lowering your heart rate, stopping your sweating, and returning your body to the state it was in before your fright. The parasympathetic division also provides a means for the body to maintain storage of energy sources such as nutrients and oxygen. The sympathetic and parasympathetic divisions work together to regulate many functions of the body (see Figure 3). For instance, sexual arousal is controlled by the parasympathetic division but sexual orgasm is a function of the sympathetic division.

Sympathetic division: The part of the autonomic division of the nervous system that acts to prepare the body in stressful emergency situations, engaging all the organism's resources to respond to a threat.

Parasympathetic division: The part of the autonomic division of the nervous system that acts to calm the body after an emergency situation has been resolved.

FIGURE 3 The major functions of the autonomic nervous system. The sympathetic division acts to prepare certain organs of the body for stressful emergency situations, and the parasympathetic division acts to calm the body after the emergency situation has been resolved. Can you explain why each response of the sympathetic division might be useful in an emergency?

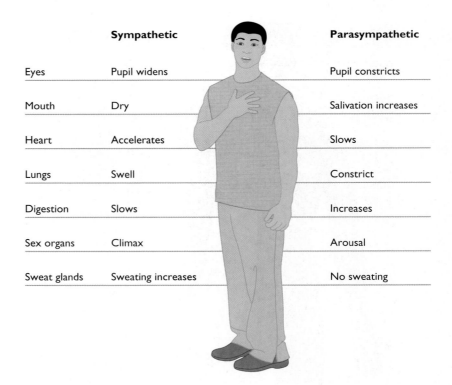

	Sympathetic		Parasympathetic
Eyes	Pupil widens		Pupil constricts
Mouth	Dry		Salivation increases
Heart	Accelerates		Slows
Lungs	Swell		Constrict
Digestion	Slows		Increases
Sex organs	Climax		Arousal
Sweat glands	Sweating increases		No sweating

THE EVOLUTIONARY FOUNDATIONS OF THE NERVOUS SYSTEM

The complexities of the nervous system can be understood only if we take the course of evolution into consideration. The forerunner of the human nervous system is found in the earliest simple organisms to have a spinal cord. Basically, those organisms were simple input-output devices: When the upper side of the spinal cord was stimulated by, for instance, being touched, they reacted with a simple response, such as jerking away. Such responses were completely a consequence of the organism's genetic makeup.

Over millions of years, the front end of the spinal cord became more specialized, and organisms became capable of distinguishing between different kinds of stimuli and responding appropriately to them. Ultimately, the front end of the spinal cord evolved into what we would consider a primitive brain. At first, it had just three parts, devoted to close stimuli (such as smell), more distant stimuli (such as sights and sounds), and the ability to maintain balance and bodily coordination. In fact, many animals, such as fish, still have a nervous system that is structured in roughly similar fashion today. In contrast, the human brain evolved from this three-part configuration into an organ that is far more complex and differentiated (Merlin, 1993).

Furthermore, the nervous system is *hierarchically organized*, meaning that relatively newer (from an evolutionary point of view) and more sophisticated regions of the brain regulate the older, and more primitive, parts of the nervous system. As we move up along the spinal cord and continue upward into the brain, then, the functions controlled by the various regions become progressively more advanced.

Why should we care about the evolutionary background of the human nervous system? The answer comes from researchers working in the area of **evolutionary psychology,** the branch of psychology that seeks to identify how behavior is influenced and produced by our genetic inheritance from our ancestors. Evolutionary psychologists argue that the course of evolution is reflected in the structure and functioning of the nervous system and that evolutionary factors consequently have a significant influence on our everyday behavior. Their work, along with that of other scientists, has led to the development of a new field: behavioral genetics.

Evolutionary psychology: The branch of psychology that seeks to identify behavior patterns that are a result of our genetic inheritance from our ancestors.

BEHAVIORAL GENETICS

Our evolutionary heritage manifests itself not only through the structure and functioning of the nervous system but through our behavior as well. In the view of a blossoming new area of study, people's personality and behavioral habits are affected in part by their genetic heritage. **Behavioral genetics** studies the effects of heredity on behavior. Behavioral genetics researchers are finding increasing evidence that cognitive abilities, personality traits, sexual orientation, and psychological disorders are determined to some extent by genetic factors (Craig et al., 2000; Reif & Lesch, 2003).

Behavioral genetics gets to the heart of the nature-nurture question, one of the key issues in the study of psychology. Although no one would argue that our behavior is *solely* determined by inherited factors, evidence collected by behavioral geneticists does suggest that our genetic inheritance predisposes us to respond in particular ways to our environment, and even to seek out particular kinds of environments. For instance, research indicates that genetic factors may be related to such diverse behaviors as level of family conflict, schizophrenia, learning disabilities, and general sociability (Berrettini, 2000; Cleveland, 2003; McGuire, 2003).

Furthermore, important human characteristics and behaviors are related to the presence (or absence) of particular *genes,* the inherited material that controls the transmission of traits. For example, researchers have found evidence that novelty-seeking behavior is determined, at least in part, by a certain gene.

Researchers have identified some 25,000 individual genes, each of which appears in a specific sequence on a particular *chromosome*, a rod-shaped structure that transmits genetic information across generations. Scientists only recently succeeded in mapping these genes as part of a massive multibillion-dollar project known as the Human Genome Project, which, after a decade of effort, identified the sequence of the 3 billion chemical pairs that make up human *DNA*, the basic genetic ingredient

Behavioral genetics: The study of the effects of heredity on behavior.

PowerWeb: The Tangled Skeins of Nature and Nurture in Human Evolution

www.mhhe.com/feldmanup7

PowerWeb: Decoding the Human Body

www.mhhe.com/feldmanup7

Chromosome 5: pTEL-D5S678

RH Map GB4 G3 | Genetic Map | Gene Density | Cytogenetic Ideogram

Part of the human DNA sequence, identified by the Human Genome Project, which has mapped the specific location and sequence of every gene.

of genes. By understanding the basic structure of the human *genome,* the "map" of humans' total genetic makeup, scientists are a giant step closer to understanding the biochemical recipes that direct human functioning (Corvin & Gill, 2003; Plomin, DeFries, Craig, & McGuffin, 2003; Plomin & McGuffin, 2003).

Despite its relative infancy, the field of behavioral genetics has already made substantial contributions. By understanding the relationship between our genetic heritage and the structures of the nervous system, we are gaining new knowledge about the development of various behavioral difficulties. Perhaps more important, behavioral genetics holds the promise of developing new diagnostic and treatment techniques to remedy genetic deficiencies that can lead to physical and psychological difficulties. Scientists have already developed genetic tests to determine whether someone is susceptible to certain types of cancer or heart disease, and it may not be long before analysis of a drop of blood can indicate whether a child is susceptible to certain psychological disorders.

The Endocrine System: Of Chemicals and Glands

Endocrine system: A chemical communication network that sends messages throughout the body via the bloodstream.

Hormones: Chemicals that circulate through the blood and affect the functioning or growth of other parts of the body.

Pituitary gland: The "master gland," the major component of the endocrine system, which secretes hormones that control growth.

The endocrine system represents another of the body's communication systems. The **endocrine system** is a chemical communication network that sends messages throughout the body via the bloodstream. Its job is to secrete **hormones,** chemicals that circulate through the blood and affect the functioning or growth of other parts of the body. It also influences—and is influenced by—the functioning of the nervous system. Although not a structure of the brain, the endocrine system is intimately tied to the hypothalamus.

As chemical messengers, hormones are like neurotransmitters, although their speed and mode of transmission are quite different. Whereas neural messages are measured in thousandths of a second, hormonal communications may take minutes to reach their destination. Furthermore, neural messages move through neurons in specific lines (like a signal carried by wires strung along telephone poles), whereas hormones travel throughout the body, similar to the way radio waves are transmitted across the entire landscape. Just as radio waves evoke a response only when a radio is tuned to the correct station, hormones flowing through the bloodstream activate only those cells which are receptive and "tuned" to the appropriate hormonal message.

A major component of the endocrine system is the **pituitary gland,** which is found near—and regulated by—the hypothalamus. The pituitary gland has sometimes been called the "master gland" because it controls the functioning of the rest of the endocrine system. But the pituitary gland is more than just the taskmaster of other glands; it has important functions in its own right. For instance, hormones secreted by the pituitary gland control growth. Extremely short people and unusually tall ones usually have pituitary gland abnormalities. Other endocrine glands, shown in Figure 4, affect emotional reactions, sexual urges, and energy levels.

Despite its designation as the "master gland," the pituitary is actually a servant of the brain, because the brain is ultimately responsible for the endocrine system's functioning. The brain regulates the internal balance of the body, ensuring that homeostasis is maintained through the hypothalamus.

Individual hormones can wear many hats, depending on circumstances. For example, the hormone oxytocin is at the root of many of life's satisfactions and pleasures. In new mothers, oxytocin produces an urge to nurse newborn offspring. The same hormone also seems to stimulate cuddling between species members. And—at least in rats—it encourages sexually active males to seek out females more passionately, and females to be more receptive to males' sexual advances (Angier, 1991; Quadros et al., 2002).

Structure   **Function**

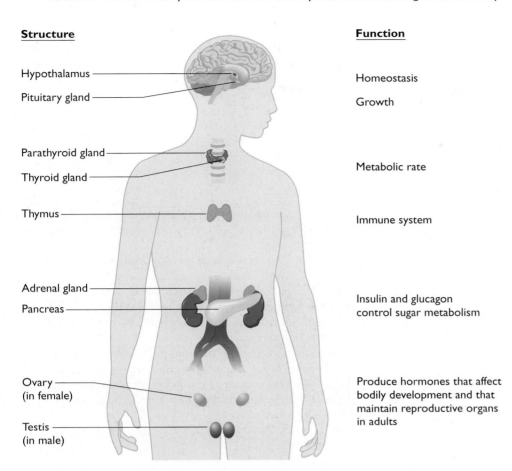

Hypothalamus

Pituitary gland

Homeostasis

Growth

Parathyroid gland

Thyroid gland

Metabolic rate

Thymus

Immune system

Adrenal gland

Pancreas

Insulin and glucagon
control sugar metabolism

Ovary
(in female)

Produce hormones that affect
bodily development and that
maintain reproductive organs
in adults

Testis
(in male)

FIGURE 4 Location and function of the major endocrine glands (Mader, 2000). The pituitary gland controls the functioning of the other endocrine glands and in turn is regulated by the hypothalamus.

Although hormones are produced naturally by the endocrine system, the ingestion of artificial hormones has proved to be both beneficial and potentially dangerous. For example, before the early 2000s, physicians frequently prescribed hormone replacement therapy (HRT) to treat severe symptoms of menopause in older women. However, because new research suggests that the treatment has potentially dangerous side effects, health experts now suggest that the dangers outweigh the benefits (Herrington & Howard, 2003).

The use of testosterone, a male hormone, and drugs known as *steroids*, which act like testosterone, is an increasingly common phenomenon. For athletes and others

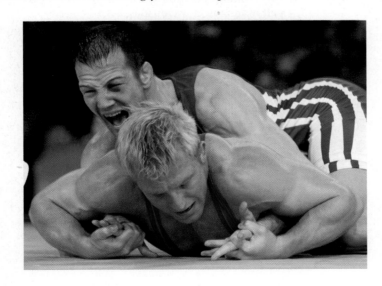

Steroids can provide added muscle and strength, but they have dangerous side effects.

who want to bulk up their appearance, steroids provide a way to add muscle weight and increase strength. However, researchers have raised strong suspicions that such drugs can lead to heart attacks, strokes, cancer, and even violent behavior, making them potentially extremely dangerous (Kolata, 2002).

RECAP/EVALUATE/RETHINK

RECAP

In what way are the structures of the nervous system tied to-gether?

▶ The nervous system is made up of the central nervous system (the brain and spinal cord) and the peripheral nervous system. The peripheral nervous system is made up of the somatic division, which controls voluntary movements and the communication of information to and from the sense organs, and the autonomic division, which controls involuntary functions such as those of the heart, blood vessels, and lungs. (p. 71)

▶ The autonomic division of the peripheral nervous sys-tem is further subdivided into the sympathetic and parasympathetic divisions. The sympathetic division prepares the body in emergency situations, and the parasympathetic division helps the body return to its typical resting state. (p. 72)

▶ Evolutionary psychology, the branch of psychology that seeks to identify behavior patterns that are a result of our genetic inheritance, has led to increased under-standing of the evolutionary basis of the structure and organization of the human nervous system. Behavioral genetics extends this study to include the evolutionary and hereditary basis of human personality traits and behavior. (p. 74)

How does the endocrine system distribute its messages?

▶ The endocrine system secretes hormones, chemicals that regulate the functioning of the body, via the blood-stream. A major component is the pituitary gland, which affects growth. (p. 76)

EVALUATE

1. If you put your hand on a red-hot piece of metal, the im-mediate response of pulling it away would be an example of a(n) _____.
2. The central nervous system is composed of the _____ and _____ _____.
3. In the peripheral nervous system, the _____ division controls voluntary movements, whereas the _____ division controls organs that keep us alive and function without our awareness.
4. Maria saw a young boy run into the street and get hit by a car. When she got to the fallen child, she was in a state of panic. She was sweating, and her heart was racing. Her bi-ological state resulted from the activation of what division of the nervous system?
   a. Parasympathetic
   b. Central
   c. Sympathetic
5. The increasing complexity and hierarchy of the nervous system over millions of years is the subject of study for re-searchers working in the field of _____.
6. The emerging field of _____ studies ways in which our genetic inheritance predisposes us to behave in certain ways.

RETHINK

1. How might communication within the nervous system re-sult in human consciousness?
2. In what ways is the "fight-or-flight" response helpful to organisms in emergency situations?

Answers to Evaluate Questions

5. evolutionary psychology; 6. behavioral genetics

1. reflex; 2. brain, spinal cord; 3. somatic, autonomic; 4. sympathetic;

KEY TERMS

central nervous system (CNS) p. 71
spinal cord p. 71
reflexes p. 71
sensory (afferent) neurons p. 71

motor (efferent) neurons p. 71
interneurons p. 71
peripheral nervous system p. 72
somatic division p. 72

autonomic division p. 72
sympathetic division p. 73
parasympathetic division p. 73
evolutionary psychology p. 74

behavioral genetics p. 75
endocrine system p. 76
hormones p. 76
pituitary gland p. 76

The Brain

It is not much to look at. Soft, spongy, mottled, and pinkish-gray in color, it hardly can be said to possess much in the way of physical beauty. Despite its physical appearance, however, it ranks as the greatest natural marvel that we know and has a beauty and sophistication all its own.

The object to which this description applies: the brain. The brain is responsible for our loftiest thoughts—and our most primitive urges. It is the overseer of the intricate workings of the human body. If one were to attempt to design a computer to mimic the range of capabilities of the brain, the task would be nearly impossible; in fact, it has proved difficult even to come close. The sheer quantity of nerve cells in the brain is enough to daunt even the most ambitious computer engineer. Many billions of nerve cells make up a structure weighing just three pounds in the average adult. However, it is not the number of cells that is the most astounding thing about the brain but its ability to allow the human intellect to flourish as it guides our behavior and thoughts.

We turn now to a consideration of the particular structures of the brain and the primary functions to which they are related. However, a caution is in order. Although we'll be discussing how specific brain areas are tied to specific behaviors, this approach is an oversimplification. No simple one-to-one correspondence between a distinct part of the brain and a particular behavior exists. Instead, behavior is produced by complex interconnections among sets of neurons in many areas of the brain: Our behavior, emotions, thoughts, hopes, and dreams are produced by a variety of neurons throughout the nervous system, working in concert.

▲▲▲

How do researchers identify the major parts and functions of the brain?

What are the major parts of the brain, and for what behaviors is each part responsible?

How do the two halves of the brain operate interdependently?

How can an understanding of the nervous system help us find ways to alleviate disease and pain?

The brain (shown here in cross section) may not be much to look at, but it represents one of the great marvels of human development. Why do most scientists believe that it will be difficult, if not impossible, to duplicate the brain's abilities?

Studying the Brain's Structure and Functions: Spying on the Brain

The brain has posed a continual challenge to those who wish to study it. For most of history, its examination was possible only after an individual was dead. Only then could the skull be opened and the brain cut into without serious injury. Although informative, such a limited procedure could hardly tell us much about the functioning of the healthy brain.

Today, however, important advances have been made in the study of the brain through the use of brain-scanning techniques. Investigators can take a "snapshot" of the internal workings of the brain without having to cut surgically into a person's skull. The major scanning techniques, illustrated in Figure 1, are the electroencephalogram (EEG), computerized tomography (CT), magnetic resonance imaging (MRI), the superconducting quantum interference device (SQUID), and positron emission tomography (PET).

The *electroencephalogram (EEG)* records electrical activity in the brain through electrodes placed on the outside of the skull. Although traditionally the EEG could produce only a graph of electrical wave patterns, new techniques are now used to transform the brain's electrical activity into a pictorial representation of the brain that, as a result of their greater detail, allows more precise diagnosis of problems such as epilepsy and learning disabilities.

The *computerized tomography (CT) scan* uses a computer to construct an image of the structures of the brain by combining thousands of separate X rays taken at slightly different angles. It is very useful for showing abnormalities in the structure of the brain, such as swelling and enlargement of certain parts, but does not provide information about brain activity.

a. EEG

b. CT scan

c. MRI scan

d. SQUID scan

e. PET scan

FIGURE 1 Brain scans produced by different techniques. (a) A computer-produced EEG image. (b) This CT scan shows the structures of the brain. (c) The MRI scan uses a magnetic field to detail the parts of the brain. (d) The SQUID scan shows the neural activity of the brain. (e) The PET scan displays the functioning of the brain at a given moment and is sensitive to the person's activities.

To get a better view of the brain, researchers are experimenting with various scanning techniques. This photo combines PET and MRI scans.

The *magnetic resonance imaging (MRI) scan* provides a detailed, three-dimensional computer-generated image of brain structures and activity by aiming a powerful magnetic field at the body. For example, it is capable of producing vivid images of individual bundles of nerves, opening the way for improved diagnosis of ailments such as chronic back pain.

The *superconducting quantum interference device (SQUID)* is sensitive to the tiny changes in magnetic fields that occur when neurons fire. Using SQUID, researchers can pinpoint the location of neural activity.

The *positron emission tomography (PET) scan* shows biochemical activity within the brain at a given moment. PET scans begin with the injection of a radioactive (but safe) liquid into the bloodstream, which makes its way to the brain. By locating radiation within the brain, a computer can determine which are the more active regions, providing a striking picture of the brain at work.

Each of these techniques offers exciting possibilities not only for the diagnosis and treatment of brain disease and injuries, but also for an increased understanding of the normal functioning of the brain. In addition, researchers are developing ways to combine separate scanning techniques (such as integrated, simultaneous PET and MRI scans) to produce even more effective portraits of the brain, such as three-dimensional reconstructions of the brain that can be used during surgery (Cacioppo, Tassinary, & Bernstson, 2000; Casey, 2002).

Advances in our understanding of the brain are also paving the way for the development of new methods for harnessing the brain's neural signals. We consider some of these intriguing findings in the *Applying Psychology in the 21st Century* box.

The Central Core: Our "Old Brain"

Although the capabilities of the human brain far exceed those of the brain of any other species, humans share some basic functions with more primitive animals, such as breathing, eating, and sleeping, and, not surprisingly, those activities are directed

Robot Rats and Wired Brains: Harnessing Brainpower to Improve Lives

Think of them as robots—rat robots, that is. Five rats, carrying miniature backpacks full of electronic equipment hooked to tiny wires leading to their brains, are following the commands of human scientists, relayed through a laptop computer. The rats can be guided through a maze or around obstacles in the same way that a child can guide a radio-controlled remote control car (Begley, 2002).

Robot rats like these are being tested for several different applications. By electrically stimulating specific areas in the rats' brains, researchers have learned to steer the rats through open areas, through a pile of debris, and even up trees. On the basis of these early results, robot rats may be used for search-and-rescue missions, helping people trapped in places that are too dangerous or too small for humans to reach easily (Talwar et al., 2002).

The arrival of robot rats represents one outcome of a growing area of research that promises to bring significant help for people with disabilities that restrict their mobility. In a reversal of the robot rat technique, researchers hope to develop ways in which people with injuries can command wheelchairs to roll or artificial limbs to move, simply through their thoughts.

To achieve these goals, researchers are carrying out experiments with monkeys that have been taught to use brainpower to move a robot arm. Using tiny wires implanted in their brains, monkeys have

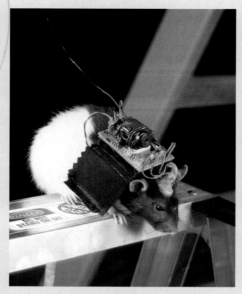

A rat's movements can be controlled by experimenters using implants into the rat's brain.

been taught to communicate with a computer that powers a mechanical arm. Using the patterns of brain activity transmitted through the wires, the mechanical arm mimics the monkeys' actual arms, moving at the same times and in the same directions. Eventually, the monkeys learned to move the robot arm simply by thinking about moving their own arms (Wessberg et al., 2000; Nicolelis & Chapin, 2002).

This research clearly has the potential to help people who have lost the use of their own arms or hands, allowing artificial limbs to be moved merely through thought. Scientists have already moved in this direction: Currently, it is possible for people to control computers by using only their thoughts. For example, using EEG scanning techniques that react to the pattern of brain waves originating in the brain, one patient learned to boost and curtail certain types of brain waves. After hundreds of hours of practice, he was able to select letters that appeared on a video screen. By stringing letters together, he could spell out messages. The process, which makes use of brain waves called slow cortical potentials, permitted the patient to communicate effectively for the first time in years. Although the method is slow and tedious—the patient can produce only about two characters per minute—it holds great promise (Birbaumer et al., 1999; Mitchener, 2001).

Clearly, much work remains before robot rats, thought-controlled machines, and brain-powered computers will be widely available. However, these technologies indicate the amazing possibilities that can result from harnessing the brain's power to control—whether the brains belong to rats, monkeys, or humans.

RETHINK

What additional uses might robot rats, thought-controlled robot arms, and thought-controlled computers have? How could such thought-controlled technology be utilized to improve people's daily lives?

Central core: The "old brain," which controls basic functions such as eating and sleeping and is common to all vertebrates.

by a relatively primitive part of the brain. A portion of the brain known as the **central core** (see Figure 2) is quite similar to that found in all vertebrates (species with backbones). The central core is sometimes referred to as the "old brain" because its evolutionary underpinnings can be traced back some 500 million years to primitive structures found in nonhuman species.

If we were to move up the spinal cord from the base of the skull to locate the structures of the central core of the brain, the first part we would come to would be the *hindbrain*, which contains the medulla, pons, and cerebellum (see Figure 3). The *medulla* controls a number of critical body functions, the most important of which are breathing and heartbeat. The *pons* comes next, joining the two halves of the cerebellum, which lies adjacent to it. Containing large bundles of nerves, the pons acts as a transmitter of motor information, coordinating muscles and integrating

Although the cerebellum is involved in several intellectual functions, its main duty is to control balance, constantly monitoring feedback from the muscles to coordinate their placement, movement, and tension. Do you think the cerebellum is under conscious or automatic control as people negotiate difficult balancing tasks?

FIGURE 2 The major divisions of the brain: the cerebral cortex and the central core. (Source: Seeley, Stephens, & Tate, 2000.)

movement between the right and left halves of the body. It is also involved in the control of sleep.

The **cerebellum** is found just above the medulla and behind the pons. Without the help of the cerebellum we would be unable to walk a straight line without staggering and lurching forward, for it is the job of the cerebellum to control bodily balance. It constantly monitors feedback from the muscles to coordinate their placement, movement, and tension. In fact, drinking too much alcohol seems to depress the activity of the cerebellum, leading to the unsteady gait and movement characteristic of drunkenness. The cerebellum is also involved in several intellectual functions, ranging from the analysis of sensory information to problem solving (Saab & Willis, 2003).

Cerebellum (ser uh BELL um): The part of the brain that controls bodily balance.

Hypothalamus
Responsible for regulating basic biological needs: hunger, thirst, temperature control

Pituitary gland
"Master" gland that regulates other endocrine glands

Pons
Involved in sleep and arousal

Reticular formation
A network of neurons related to sleep, arousal, and attention

Spinal cord
Responsible for communication between brain and rest of body; involved with simple reflexes

Cerebral cortex

Corpus callosum
Bridge of fibers passing information between the two cerebral hemispheres

Thalamus
Relay center for cortex; handles incoming and outgoing signals

Cerebellum

Medulla
Responsible for regulating largely unconscious functions such as breathing and circulation

FIGURE 3 The major structures in the brain. (Source: Johnson, 2000.)

Reticular formation: The part of the brain from the medulla through the pons made up of groups of nerve cells that can immediately activate other parts of the brain to produce general bodily arousal.

The **reticular formation** extends from the medulla through the pons, passing through the middle section of the brain—or *midbrain*—and into the front-most part of the brain, called the *forebrain*. Like an ever-vigilant guard, the reticular formation is made up of groups of nerve cells that can activate other parts of the brain immediately to produce general bodily arousal. If, for example, we are startled by a loud noise, the reticular formation can prompt a heightened state of awareness to determine whether a response is necessary. In addition, the reticular formation serves a different function when we are sleeping, seeming to filter out background stimuli to allow us to sleep undisturbed.

Thalamus: The part of the brain located in the middle of the central core that acts primarily as a busy relay station, mostly for information concerning the senses.

Hidden within the forebrain, the **thalamus** acts primarily as a busy relay station, mostly for information concerning the senses. Messages from the eyes, ears, and skin travel to the thalamus to be communicated upward to higher parts of the brain. The thalamus also integrates information from higher parts of the brain, sorting it out so that it can be sent to the cerebellum and medulla.

Hypothalamus: A tiny part of the brain, located below the thalamus, that maintains homostasis and produces and regulates vital, basic behavior such as eating, drinking, and sexual behavior.

The **hypothalamus** is located just below the thalamus. Although tiny—about the size of a fingertip—the hypothalamus plays an inordinantly important role. One of its major functions is to maintain *homeostasis*, a steady internal environment for the body. The hypothalamus helps provide a constant body temperature and monitors the amount of nutrients stored in the cells. A second major function is equally important: It produces and regulates behavior that is critical to the basic survival of the species, such as eating, self-protection, and sex.

The Limbic System: Beyond the Central Core

In an eerie view of the future, some science fiction writers have suggested that people someday will routinely have electrodes implanted in their brains. Those electrodes will permit them to receive tiny shocks that will produce the sensation of pleasure by stimulating certain centers of the brain. When they feel upset, people will simply activate their electrodes to achieve an immediate high.

Although far-fetched—and ultimately improbable—such a futuristic fantasy is based on fact. The brain does have pleasure centers in several areas, including some in the **limbic system**. Consisting of a series of doughnut-shaped structures that include the *amygdala, hippocampus,* and *fornix,* the limbic system borders the top of the central core and has connections with the cerebral cortex (see Figure 4).

Limbic system: The part of the brain located outside the "new brain" that controls eating, aggression, and reproduction.

The structures of the limbic system jointly control a variety of basic functions relating to emotions and self-preservation, such as eating, aggression, and reproduction. Injury to the limbic system can produce striking changes in behavior. It can turn animals that are usually docile and tame into belligerent savages. Conversely, those which are usually wild and uncontrollable may become meek and obedient (Bedard & Persinger, 1995).

Research examining the effects of mild electric shocks to parts of the limbic system and other parts of the brain has produced some thought-provoking findings (Olds & Milner, 1954; Olds & Fobes, 1981). In one experiment, rats that pressed a bar received mild electric stimulation through an electrode implanted in their brains, which produced pleasurable feelings. Even starving rats on their way to food would stop to press the bar as many times as they could. Some rats would actually stimulate themselves literally thousands of times an hour—until they collapsed with fatigue (Routtenberg & Lindy, 1965).

The extraordinarily pleasurable quality of certain kinds of stimulation has also been experienced by humans, who, as part of the treatment for certain kinds of brain disorders, have received electrical stimulation to certain areas of the limbic system. Although at a loss to describe just what it feels like, these people report the experience to be intensely pleasurable, similar in some respects to sexual orgasm.

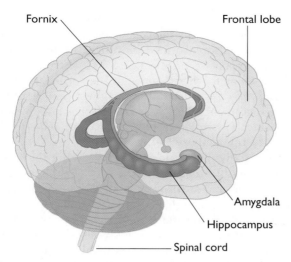

Fornix

Frontal lobe

Amygdala

Hippocampus

Spinal cord

FIGURE 4 The limbic system consists of a series of doughnut-shaped structures that are involved in self-preservation, learning, memory, and the experience of pleasure.

The limbic system also plays an important role in learning and memory, a finding demonstrated in patients with epilepsy. In an attempt to stop their seizures, such patients have had portions of the limbic system removed. One unintended consequence of the surgery is that individuals sometimes have difficulty learning and remembering new information. In one case, a patient who had undergone surgery was unable to remember where he lived, although he had resided at the same address for eight years. Further, even though the patient was able to carry on animated conversations, he was unable, a few minutes later, to recall what had been discussed (Milner, 1966).

The limbic system, then, is involved in several important functions, including self-preservation, learning, memory, and the experience of pleasure. These functions are hardly unique to humans; in fact, the limbic system is sometimes referred to as the "animal brain" because its structures and functions are so similar to those of other mammals. To identify the part of the brain that provides the complex and subtle capabilities that are uniquely human, we need to turn to another structure—the cerebral cortex.

The Cerebral Cortex: Our "New Brain"

As we have proceeded up the spinal cord and into the brain, our discussion has centered on areas of the brain that control functions similar to those found in less sophisticated organisms. But where, you may be asking, are the portions of the brain that enable humans to do what they do best and that distinguish humans from all other animals? Those unique features of the human brain—indeed, the very capabilities that allow you to come up with such a question in the first place—are embodied in the ability to think, evaluate, and make complex judgments. The principal location of these abilities, along with many others, is the **cerebral cortex.**

The cerebral cortex is referred to as the "new brain" because of its relatively recent evolution. It consists of a mass of deeply folded, rippled, convoluted tissue. Although only about one-twelfth of an inch thick, it would, if flattened out, cover an area more than two feet square. This configuration allows the surface area of the

Cerebral cortex: The "new brain," responsible for the most sophisticated information processing in the brain; contains the lobes.

cortex to be considerably greater than it would be if it were smoother and more uniformly packed into the skull. The uneven shape also permits a high level of integration of neurons, allowing sophisticated processing of information.

The cortex has four major sections called **lobes.** If we take a side view of the brain, the *frontal lobes* lie at the front center of the cortex and the *parietal lobes* lie behind them. The *temporal lobes* are found in the lower center of the cortex, with the *occipital lobes* lying behind them. These four sets of lobes are physically separated by deep grooves called sulci. Figure 5 shows the four areas, and—to further review the parts of the cortex—try **Interactivity 9–1.**

Another way to describe the brain is by considering the functions associated with a particular area. Figure 5 also shows the specialized regions within the lobes related to specific functions and areas of the body. Three major areas have been discovered: the motor areas, the sensory areas, and the association areas. Although we will discuss these areas as though they were separate and independent, keep in mind that this is an oversimplification. In most instances, behavior is influenced simultaneously by several structures and areas within the brain, operating interdependently. Furthermore, even within a given area, additional subdivisions exist. Finally, when people suffer certain kinds of brain injury, uninjured portions of the brain can sometimes take over the functions that were previously handled by the damaged area. In short, the brain is extraordinarily adaptable (Sharma, Angelucci, & Sur, 2000; Sacks, 2003).

Lobes: The four major sections of the cerebral cortex, frontal, parietal, temporal, and occipital.

INTERACTIVITY 9–1

Areas and functions of the brain

THE MOTOR AREA OF THE CORTEX

If you look at the frontal lobe in Figure 5, you will see a shaded portion labeled the **motor area.** This part of the cortex is largely responsible for the body's voluntary movement. Every portion of the motor area corresponds to a specific locale within the body. If we were to insert an electrode into a particular part of the motor area of the cortex and apply mild electrical stimulation, there would be involuntary movement in the corresponding part of the body. If we moved to another part of the motor area and stimulated it, a different part of the body would move.

Motor area: The part of the cortex that is largely responsible for the body's voluntary movement.

The motor area is so well mapped that researchers have identified the amount and relative location of cortical tissue used to produce movement in specific parts of the human body. For example, the control of movements that are relatively large scale and require little precision, such as the movement of a knee or a hip, is centered in a very small space in the motor area. In contrast, movements that must be precise and delicate, such as facial expressions and finger movements, are controlled by a considerably larger portion of the motor area.

In short, the motor area of the cortex provides a guide to the degree of complexity and the importance of the motor capabilities of specific parts of the body. It may do even more, in fact: Increasing evidence shows that not only does the motor cortex control different parts of the body, it may direct body parts into complex postures, such as the stance of a football center just before the ball is snapped to the quarterback (Graziano, Tyler, & Moore, 2002).

Ultimately, movement, like other behavior, is produced through the coordinated firing of a complex variety of neurons in the nervous system. The neurons that produce movement are linked in elaborate ways and work closely together.

THE SENSORY AREA OF THE CORTEX

Given the one-to-one correspondence between motor area and body location, it is not surprising to find a similar relationship between specific portions of the cortex and the senses. The **sensory area** of the cortex includes three regions: one that corresponds primarily to body sensations (including touch and pressure), one relating to sight, and a third relating to sound. For instance, the *somatosensory area* encompasses specific locations associated with the ability to perceive touch and pressure in a particular area of

Sensory area: The site in the brain of the tissue that corresponds to each of the senses, with the degree of sensitivity relating to the amount of tissue.

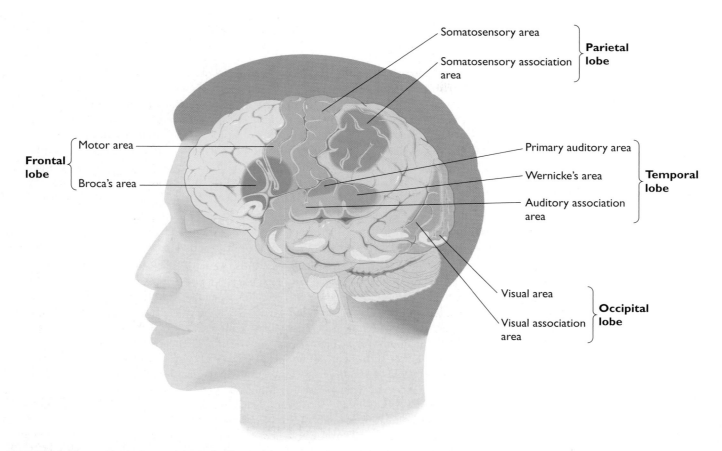

FIGURE 5 The cerebral cortex of the brain. The major physical *structures* of the cerebral cortex are called lobes. This figure also illustrates the *functions* associated with particular areas of the cerebral cortex. Are any areas of the cerebral cortex present in nonhuman animals?

the body. As with the motor area, the amount of brain tissue related to a particular location on the body determines the degree of sensitivity of that location. The greater the space within the cortex, the more sensitive that area of the body. As you can see from the weird-looking individual in Figure 6, parts such as the fingers are related to proportionally more space in the somatosensory area and are the most sensitive.

The senses of sound and sight are also represented in specific areas of the cerebral cortex. An *auditory area* located in the temporal lobe is responsible for the sense of hearing. If the auditory area is stimulated electrically, a person will hear sounds

FIGURE 6 The greater the amount of tissue in the somatosensory area of the brain that is related to a specific body part, the more sensitive is that body part. If the size of our body parts reflected the corresponding amount of brain tissue, we would look like this strange creature.

such as clicks or hums. It also appears that particular locations within the auditory area respond to specific pitches (deCharms, Blake, & Merzenich, 1998; Klinke et al., 1999; Hudspeth, 2000).

The *visual area* in the cortex, located in the occipital lobe, operates analogously to the other sensory areas. Stimulation by electrodes produces the experience of flashes of light or colors, suggesting that the raw sensory input of images from the eyes is received in this area of the brain and transformed into meaningful stimuli. The visual area also provides another example of how areas of the brain are intimately related to specific areas of the body: Particular areas of the eye's retina are related to a particular part of the cortex—with, as you might guess, more space in the brain given to the most sensitive portions of the retina (Wurtz & Kandel, 2000).

THE ASSOCIATION AREAS OF THE CORTEX

Consider the following case:

> Twenty-five-year-old Phineas Gage, a railroad employee, was blasting rock one day in 1848 when an accidental explosion punched a 3-foot-long spike, about an inch in diameter, completely through his skull. The spike entered just under his left cheek, came out the top of his head, and flew into the air. Gage immediately suffered a series of convulsions, yet a few minutes later was talking with rescuers. In fact, he was able to walk up a long flight of stairs before receiving any medical attention. Amazingly, after a few weeks his wound healed, and he was physically close to his old self again. Mentally, however, there was a difference: Once a careful and hard-working person, Phineas now became enamored with wild schemes and was flighty and often irresponsible. As one of his physicians put it, "Previous to his injury, though untrained in the schools, he possessed a well-balanced mind, and was looked upon by those who knew him as a shrewd, smart businessman, very energetic and persistent in executing all his plans of operation. In this regard his mind was radically changed, so decidedly that his friends and acquaintances said he was 'no longer Gage'" (Harlow, 1869, p. 14).

What had happened to the old Gage? Although there is no way of knowing for sure—science being what it was in the 1800s—we can speculate that the accident may have injured the association areas of Gage's cerebral cortex. The **association areas** generally are considered to be the site of higher mental processes such as thinking, language, memory, and speech (Rowe et al., 2000).

The association areas take up a large proportion of the cerebral cortex. Most of our understanding of the association areas comes from patients who have suffered some type of brain injury. In some cases, the injury stemmed from natural causes such as a tumor or a stroke, either of which would block certain blood vessels in the cerebral cortex. In other cases, accidental causes were the culprits, as was true with Phineas Gage. In any event, damage to these areas can result in unusual behavioral changes, indicating the importance of the association areas to normal functioning (Gannon et al., 1998; Macmillan, 2000).

Gage's case provides evidence that there are specialized areas for making rational decisions. When those areas are damaged, people undergo personality changes that affect their ability to make moral judgments and process emotions. At the same time, people with damage in those areas can still be capable of reasoning logically, performing calculations, and recalling information (Damasio et al., 1994).

Injuries to other parts of the association areas can produce a condition known as apraxia. *Apraxia* occurs when an individual is unable to integrate activities in a rational or logical manner. The disorder is most evident when people are asked to carry out a sequence of behaviors requiring a degree of planning and foresight, suggesting that the association areas act as "master planners," that is, organizers of actions.

Injuries to the association areas of the brain can also produce *aphasia*, problems with language. In *Broca's aphasia* (caused by damage to the part of the brain first identified by a French physician, Paul Broca, in 1861), speech becomes halting, laborious, and often ungrammatical. The speaker is unable to find the right words in a kind of

Association areas: One of the major areas of the cerebral cortex; the site of the higher mental processes, such as thought, language, memory, and speech.

A model of the injury sustained by Phineas Gage.

tip-of-the-tongue phenomenon that we all experience from time to time. People with aphasia, though, grope for words almost constantly, eventually blurting out a kind of "verbal telegram." A phrase like "I put the book on the table" comes out as "I . . . put . . . book . . . table" (Faroqui-Shah & Thompson, 2003).

Wernicke's aphasia is a disorder named for Carl Wernicke, who identified it in the 1870s. Wernicke's aphasia produces difficulties both in understanding others' speech and in the production of language. The disorder is characterized by speech that sounds fluent but makes no sense. For instance, one patient, asked what brought him to a hospital, gave this rambling reply: "Boy, I'm sweating, I'm awful nervous, you know, once in a while I get caught up, I can't mention the tarripoi, a month ago, quite a little, I've done a lot well, I impose a lot, while, on the other hand, you know what I mean, I have to run around, look it over, trebbin and all that sort of stuff" (Gardner, 1975, p. 68).

Brain injuries, such as those which result in aphasia, and brain disorders caused by disease and illness have given new impetus to scientists who are seeking to "map" the neural circuitry of the brain. Using sophisticated computer technology, researchers are seeking to create a database encompassing every facet of the brain (see Figure 7). Such efforts are producing significant innovations in the study of the brain.

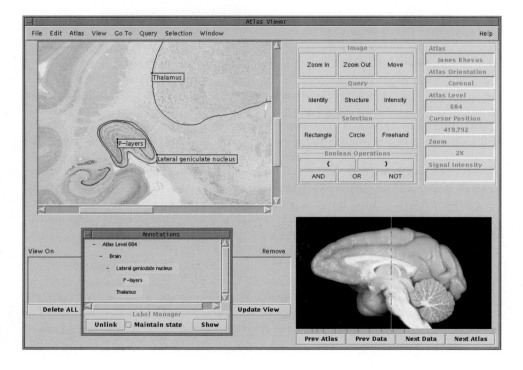

FIGURE 7 A sample computer screen from Atlas Viewer, a computerized database designed to make every aspect of the brain accessible.

Mending the Brain

Shortly after he was born, Jacob Stark's arms and legs started jerking every 20 minutes. Weeks later he could not focus his eyes on his mother's face. The diagnosis: uncontrollable epileptic seizures involving his entire brain.

His mother, Sally Stark, recalled: "When Jacob was two and a half months old, they said he would never learn to sit up, would never be able to feed himself. Nothing could be done to prevent profound retardation. They told us to take him home, love him and find an institution" (Blakeslee, 1992, p. C3).

Instead, the Starks brought Jacob to the University of California at Los Angeles for brain surgery when he was 5 months old. Surgeons removed 20 percent of his brain. The operation was a complete success. Three years later Jacob seemed normal in every way, with no sign of seizures.

Jacob's surgery is representative of increasingly daring approaches in the treatment of brain disorders. It also illustrates how our growing understanding of the processes that underlie brain functioning can be translated into solutions to difficult problems.

The surgery that helped Jacob was based on the premise that the diseased part of his brain was producing seizures throughout the brain. Surgeons reasoned that if they removed the misfiring portion, the remaining parts of the brain, which appeared intact in PET scans, would take over. They bet that Jacob could still lead a normal life after surgery, particularly because the surgery was being done at so young an age. Clearly, the gamble paid off.

The success of Jacob's surgery illustrates something that has been known for some time: The brain has the ability to shift functions to different locations after injury to a specific area or in cases of surgery. But equally encouraging are some new findings about the *regenerative* powers of the brain and nervous system. Scientists had assumed for decades that the neurons of the spinal cord and brain could never be replaced. However, new evidence is beginning to suggest otherwise. For instance, researchers have found that the cells from the brains of adult mice can produce new neurons, at least in a test tube environment.

Similarly, researchers have reported partial restoration of movement in rats who had a one-fifth-inch-long gap in their spinal cords and, as a result, were unable to move their hind limbs. The researchers transplanted neurons from the peripheral nervous system into the gap, and subsequently the rats were able to flex their legs. One year after the operation, they were able to support themselves and move their legs, and examination of the neurons in the spinal cord showed significant regeneration around the area of the transplantation (Cheng, Cao, & Olson, 1996; McDonald, 1999; Blakeslee, 2000).

The future also holds promise for people who suffer from the tremors and loss of motor control produced by Parkinson's disease. Because Parkinson's disease is caused by a gradual loss of cells that stimulate the production of dopamine in the brain, investigators reasoned that a procedure that would increase the supply of dopamine might be effective. They seem to be on the right track. When certain cells from human fetuses are injected directly into the brains of Parkinson's sufferers, they seem to take root, stimulating dopamine production. For most of those who have undergone this procedure, the preliminary results have been promising, with some patients showing great improvement. However, the technique remains experimental, and it also raises some thorny ethical issues, given that the source of the implanted fetal tissue is aborted fetuses (Pollack, 2000; Siderowf, 2003).

Neuroplasticity: Changes in the brain that occur throughout the life span relating to the addition of new neurons, more interconnections between neurons, and reorganization of information-processing areas.

The new research highlights the fact that the brain continually reorganizes itself in a process termed **neuroplasticity.** Not only does the number of neurons continue to grow throughout life, their interconnections become more complex. Furthermore, specific experiences can modify the way in which information is processed. For example, if you learn to read Braille, the amount of material in your cortex involved in relating to the fingertips will expand. Similarly, if you take up the violin, the area of the brain that receives messages from your fingers will grow—but only relating to the fingers that actually move across the violin's strings (Schwartz & Begley, 2002; Kolb, Gibb, & Robinson, 2003).

The Specialization of the Hemispheres: Two Brains or One?

The most recent development, at least in evolutionary terms, in the organization and operation of the human brain probably occurred in the last million years: a specialization of the functions controlled by the left and right sides of the brain.

The brain can be divided into two roughly mirror-image halves—just as we have two arms, two legs, and two lungs. Because of the way nerves are connected from the brain to the rest of the body, these two symmetrical left and right halves, called **hemispheres,** control motion in—and receive sensation from—the side of the body opposite to their location. The left hemisphere of the brain, then, generally controls the right side of the body, and the right hemisphere controls the left side of the body. Thus, damage to the right side of the brain is typically indicated by functional difficulties in the left side of the body.

Hemispheres: Two symmetrical left and right halves of the brain that control the side of the body opposite to their location.

Despite the appearance of similarity between the two hemispheres of the brain, they are somewhat different in the functions they control and the ways they control them. It appears that certain behaviors are more likely to reflect activity in one hemisphere than in the other. Early evidence for the functional differences between the halves of the brain came from studies of people with aphasia. Researchers found that people with the speech difficulties characteristic of aphasia tended to have physical damage to the left hemisphere of the brain. In contrast, physical abnormalities in the right hemisphere tended to produce far fewer problems with language. This finding led researchers to conclude that for most people, language is **lateralized,** or located more in one hemisphere than in the other—in this case, in the left side of the brain (Grossi, Samenza, Corazza, & Volterra, 1996; Ansaldo, Arguin, & Roch-Locours, 2002).

Lateralization: The dominance of one hemisphere of the brain in specific functions.

It now seems clear that the two hemispheres of the brain are somewhat specialized in the functions they carry out. The left hemisphere concentrates more on tasks that require verbal competence, such as speaking, reading, thinking, and reasoning. The right hemisphere has its own strengths, particularly in nonverbal areas such as the understanding of spatial relationships, recognition of patterns and drawings, music, and emotional expression. Cerebral specialization starts at a very early age. For example, even before infants under the age of 1 year have developed real language skills, their babbling involves left hemisphere specialization (Holowka & Petitto, 2002).

In addition, information is processed somewhat differently in each hemisphere. The left hemisphere tends to consider information sequentially, one bit at a time, while the right hemisphere tends to process information globally, considering it as a whole (Turkewitz, 1993; Banich & Heller, 1998).

However, it is important to keep in mind that the differences in specialization between the hemispheres are not great and that the degree and nature of lateralization vary from one person to another. If, like most people, you are right-handed, the control of language is probably concentrated more in your left hemisphere. By contrast, if you are among the 10 percent of people who are left-handed or are ambidextrous (you use both hands interchangeably), it is much more likely that the language centers of your brain are located more in the right hemisphere or are divided equally between the left and right hemispheres.

Researchers have also unearthed evidence that there may be subtle differences in brain lateralization patterns between males and females. In fact, some scientists have suggested that there are slight differences in the structure of the brain according to gender and culture. As we see next, such findings have led to a lively debate in the scientific community.

Exploring DIVERSITY
Human Diversity and the Brain

The interplay of biology and environment in behavior is particularly clear when we consider evidence suggesting that even in brain structure and function there are both sex and cultural differences. Let's consider sex first. Accumulating evidence seems to show intriguing differences in males' and females' brain lateralization and weight, although the nature of those differences—and even their existence—is the source of considerable controversy (Kimura, 1992; Dorion et al., 2000; Hugdaht & Davidson, 2002).

Some statements can be made with reasonable confidence. For instance, most males tend to show greater lateralization of language in the left hemisphere. For them, language is clearly relegated largely to the left side of the brain. In contrast, women display less lateralization, with language abilities apt to be more evenly divided between the two hemispheres (Gur et al., 1982; Shaywitz, Shaywitz, Pugh, Constable, et al., 1995; Kulynych, Vladar, Jones, & Weinberger, 1994). Such differences in brain lateralization may account, in part, for the superiority often displayed by females on certain measures of verbal skills, such as the onset and fluency of speech, and the fact that far more boys than girls have reading problems in elementary school (Kitterle, 1991).

Other research suggests that men's brains are somewhat bigger than women's brains even after taking differences in body size into account. In contrast, part of the *corpus callosum*, a bundle of fibers that connects the hemispheres of the brain, is proportionally larger in women than in men. Furthermore, some research suggests that women's brains have a higher proportion of the neurons that are actually involved in thinking compared with men's brains (Witelson, 1995; Falk et al., 1999; Gur et al., 1999).

Men and women also may process information differently. For example, MRI brain scans of men sounding out words show activation of a small area of the left side of the brain, whereas women use areas on both sides of the brain (Shaywitz et al., 1995; see Figure 8). Similarly, PET brain scans of men and women while they are not engaged in mental activity show differences in the use of glucose (Gur et al., 1995; Gur, 1996).

The meaning of such sex differences is far from clear. Consider one possibility related to the differences that have been found in the proportional size of the corpus callosum. Its increased proportion in women may permit stronger connections to

FIGURE 8 These composite MRI brain scans show the distribution of active areas in the brains of males (*left*) and females (*right*) during a verbal task involving rhyming. In males, activation is more lateralized, or confined, to the left hemisphere, whereas in females, activation is bilateralized, that is, occurring in both hemispheres of the brain. (Source: Shaywitz et al., 1995.)

develop between the parts of the brain that control speech. In turn, this would explain why speech tends to emerge slightly earlier in girls than in boys.

Before we rush to such a conclusion, though, it is important to consider an alternative hypothesis: The reason verbal abilities emerge earlier in girls may be that infant girls receive greater encouragement to talk than do infant boys. In turn, this greater early experience may foster the growth of certain parts of the brain. Hence, physical brain differences may be a *reflection* of social and environmental influences rather than a *cause* of the differences in men's and women's behavior. At this point, it is impossible to confirm which of these two alternative hypotheses is correct.

The culture in which people are raised also may give rise to differences in brain lateralization. Native speakers of Japanese seem to process information regarding vowel sounds primarily in the brain's left hemisphere. In contrast, North and South Americans, Europeans, and individuals of Japanese ancestry who learn Japanese later in life handle vowel sounds principally in the right hemisphere.

The reason for this cultural difference in lateralization? One explanation may be that certain characteristics of the Japanese language, such as the ability to express complex ideas by using only vowel sounds, result in the development of a specific type of brain lateralization in native speakers. Differences in lateralization may account for other dissimilarities between the ways in which native Japanese speakers and Westerners think about the world (Tsunoda, 1985; Kess & Miyamoto, 1994).

Scientists are just beginning to understand the extent, nature, and meaning of sex and cultural differences in lateralization and brain structure. In evaluating research on brain lateralization, keep in mind also that the two hemispheres of the brain function in tandem. It is a mistake to think of particular kinds of information as being processed solely in the right or the left hemisphere. The hemispheres work interdependently in deciphering, interpreting, and reacting to the world.

In addition, people who suffer injury to the left side of the brain and lose linguistic capabilities often recover the ability to speak: The right side of the brain often pitches in and takes over some of the functioning of the left side. This shift is especially true in young children; the extent of recovery increases the earlier the injury occurs (Gould et al., 1999; Kempermann & Gage, 1999). (For a first-hand experience with brain lateralization, complete **Interactivity 9–2.**)

INTERACTIVITY 9–2

Brain lateralization

The Split Brain: Exploring the Two Hemispheres

The patient, V.J., had suffered severe seizures. By cutting her corpus callosum, the fibrous portion of the brain that carries messages between the hemispheres, surgeons hoped to create a firebreak to prevent the seizures from spreading. The operation did decrease the frequency and severity of V.J.'s attacks. But V.J. developed an unexpected side effect: She lost the ability to write at will, although she could read and spell words aloud (Strauss, 1998, p. 287).

People like V.J., whose corpus callosum has been surgically cut to stop seizures and who are therefore called **split-brain patients,** offer a rare opportunity for researchers investigating the independent functioning of the two hemispheres of the brain. For example, psychologist Roger Sperry—who won the Nobel Prize for his work—developed a number of ingenious techniques for studying how each hemisphere operates (Sperry, 1982; Baynes et al., 1998; Gazzaniga, 1998).

In one experimental procedure, blindfolded subjects were allowed to touch an object with the right hand and were asked to name it. Because the right side of the body is connected to the left side of the brain—the hemisphere that is most responsible for language—the split-brain patient was able to name it. However, if the

Split-brain patient: A patient in whom the corpus callosum has been surgically cut and in whom the two halves of the brain function independently so that the two sides of the body work in disharmony.

PowerWeb: Hemisphere Disconnection and Unity in Conscious Awareness

www.mhhe.com/feldmanup7

blindfolded subject touched the object with his or her left hand, naming it aloud was not possible. However, the information had registered: When the blindfold was taken off, the subject could choose the object he or she had touched. Information can be learned and remembered, then, using only the right side of the brain. (By the way, unless you've had a split-brain operation, this experiment won't work with you, because the bundle of fibers connecting the two hemispheres of a normal brain immediately transfers the information from one hemisphere to the other.)

It is clear from experiments like this one that the right and left hemispheres of the brain specialize in handling different sorts of information. At the same time, it is important to realize that they are both capable of understanding, knowing, and being aware of the world, albeit in somewhat different ways. The two hemispheres, then, should be regarded as different in terms of the efficiency with which they process certain kinds of information, rather than as two entirely separate brains. Moreover, in people with normal, nonsplit brains, the hemispheres work interdependently to allow the full range and richness of thought of which humans are capable.

Biofeedback: A procedure in which a person learns to control through conscious thought internal physiological processes such as blood pressure, heart and respiration rate, skin temperature, sweating, and the constriction of particular muscles.

BECOMING AN
INFORMED CONSUMER
of Psychology

Learning to Control Your Heart—and
Mind—through Biofeedback

FIGURE 9 The traditional treatment for curvature of the spine employs an unsightly, cumbersome brace. In contrast, biofeedback treatment employs an unobtrusive set of straps attached to a small electronic device that produces tonal feedback when the patient is not standing straight. The person learns to maintain a position that gradually decreases the curvature of the spine until the device is no longer needed (Miller, 1985a). What other disorders might biofeedback devices like this one help treat?

Tammy DeMichael was cruising along the New York State Thruway with her fiancé when he fell asleep at the wheel. The car slammed into the guardrail and flipped, leaving DeMichael with what the doctors called a "splattered C-6, 7"—a broken neck and crushed spinal cord.

After a year of exhaustive medical treatment, she still had no function or feeling in her arms and legs. "The experts said I'd be a quadriplegic for the rest of my life, able to move only from the neck up," she recalls . . . But DeMichael proved the experts wrong. Today, feeling has returned to her limbs, her arm strength is normal or better, and she no longer uses a wheelchair. "I can walk about 60 feet with just a cane, and I can go almost anywhere with crutches," she says (Morrow & Wolf, 1991, p. 64).

The key to DeMichael's astounding recovery: biofeedback. **Biofeedback** is a procedure in which a person learns to control through conscious thought internal physiological processes such as blood pressure, heart and respiration rate, skin temperature, sweating, and the constriction of particular muscles. Although it traditionally had been thought that the heart rate, respiration rate, blood pressure, and other bodily functions are under the control of parts of the brain over which we have no influence, psychologists have discovered that these responses are actually susceptible to voluntary control (Bazell, 1998; Martin, 2002; Violani & Lombardo, 2003).

In biofeedback, a person is hooked up to electronic devices that provide continuous feedback relating to the physiological response in question. For instance, a person interested in controlling headaches through biofeedback might have electronic sensors placed on certain muscles on her head and learn to control the constriction and relaxation of those muscles. Later, when she felt a headache starting, she could relax the relevant muscles and abort the pain.

In DeMichael's case, biofeedback was effective because not all of the nervous system's connections between the brain and her legs were severed. Through biofeedback, she learned how to send messages to specific muscles, "ordering" them to move. Although it took more than a year, DeMichael was successful in restoring a large degree of her mobility.

Although the control of physiological processes through the use of biofeedback is not easy to learn, it has been employed with success in a variety of ailments, including emotional problems (such as anxiety, depression, phobias, tension headaches, insomnia, and hyperactivity), physical illnesses with a psychological component (such as asthma, high blood pressure, ulcers, muscle spasms, and migraine headaches), and physical problems (such as DeMichael's injuries, strokes, cerebral palsy, and—as we see in Figure 9—curvature of the spine).

RECAP

How do researchers identify the major parts and functions of the brain?

▶ Brain scans take a "snapshot" of the internal workings of the brain without having to cut surgically into a person's skull. Major brain-scanning techniques include the electroencephalogram (EEG), computerized tomography (CT), magnetic resonance imaging (MRI), the superconducting quantum interference device (SQUID), and positron emission tomography (PET). (p. 80)

What are the major parts of the brain, and for what behaviors is each part responsible?

▶ The central core of the brain is made up of the medulla (which controls functions such as breathing and the heartbeat), the pons (which coordinates the muscles and the two sides of the body), the cerebellum (which controls balance), the reticular formation (which acts to heighten awareness in emergencies), the thalamus (which communicates sensory messages to and from the brain), and the hypothalamus (which maintains homeostasis, or body equilibrium, and regulates behavior related to basic survival). The functions of the central core structures are similar to those found in other vertebrates. This central core is sometimes referred to as the "old brain." Increasing evidence also suggests that male and female brains may differ in structure in minor ways. (p. 81)

▶ The cerebral cortex—the "new brain"—has areas that control voluntary movement (the motor area); the senses (the sensory area); and thinking, reasoning, speech, and memory (the association area). The limbic system, found on the border of the "old" and "new" brains, is associated with eating, reproduction, and the experiences of pleasure and pain. (p. 85)

How do the two halves of the brain operate interdependently?

▶ The brain is divided into left and right halves, or hemispheres, each of which generally controls the opposite side of the body. Each hemisphere can be thought of as being specialized in the functions it carries out: The left is best at verbal tasks, such as logical reasoning, speaking, and reading; the right is best at nonverbal tasks, such as spatial perception, pattern recognition, and emotional expression. (p. 91)

How can an understanding of the nervous system help us find ways to alleviate disease and pain?

▶ Biofeedback is a procedure by which a person learns to control internal physiological processes. By controlling what were previously considered involuntary responses, people are able to relieve anxiety, tension, migraine headaches, and a wide range of other psychological and physical problems. (p. 94)

EVALUATE

1. Match the name of each brain scan with the appropriate description:
   a. EEG
   b. CT
   c. PET
   1. By locating radiation within the brain, a computer can provide a striking picture of brain activity.
   2. Electrodes placed around the skull record the electrical signals transmitted through the brain.
   3. A computer image combines thousands of X-ray pictures into one.

2. Match the portion of the brain with its function:
   a. medulla
   b. pons
   c. cerebellum
   d. reticular formation
   1. Maintains breathing and heartbeat
   2. Controls bodily balance
   3. Coordinates and integrates muscle movements
   4. Activates other parts of the brain to produce general bodily arousal

3. A surgeon places an electrode on a portion of your brain and stimulates it. Immediately, your right wrist involuntarily twitches. The doctor has most likely stimulated a portion of the _____ area of your brain.

4. Each hemisphere controls the _____ side of the body.

5. Nonverbal realms, such as emotions and music, are controlled primarily by the _____ hemisphere of the brain, whereas the _____ hemisphere is more responsible for speaking and reading.

6. The left hemisphere tends to consider information _____, whereas the right hemisphere tends to process information _____.

RETHINK

1. How would you answer the argument that "psychologists should leave the study of neurons and synapses and the nervous system to biologists?"

2. Before sophisticated brain-scanning techniques were developed, behavioral neuroscientists' understanding of the brain was based largely on the brains of people who had died. What limitations would this pose, and in what areas would you expect the most significant advances once brain-scanning techniques became possible?

3. Suppose that abnormalities in an association area of the brain were linked through research to serious criminal behavior. Would you be in favor of mandatory testing of individuals and surgery to repair or remove those abnormalities? Why or why not?

4. Could personal differences in people's specialization of right and left hemispheres be related to occupational success? For example, might an architect who relies on spatial skills have a different pattern of hemispheric specialization than a writer?

Answers to Evaluate Questions

1. a-2, b-3, c-1; 2. a-1, b-3, c-2, d-4; 3. motor; 4. opposite; 5. right, left; 6. sequentially, globally

KEY TERMS

central core p. 82
cerebellum p. 83
reticular formation p. 84
thalamus p. 84

hypothalamus p. 84
limbic system p. 84
cerebral cortex p. 85
lobes p. 86

motor area p. 86
sensory area p. 86
association areas p. 88
neuroplasticity p. 90

hemispheres p. 91
lateralization p. 91
split-brain patient p. 93
biofeedback p. 94

Looking Back

Psychology on the Web

1. Biofeedback research is continuously changing and being applied to new areas of human functioning. Find at least two websites that discuss recent research on biofeedback and summarize the research and any findings it has produced. Include in your summary your best estimate of future applications of this technique.
2. Find one or more websites on Parkinson's disease and learn more about this topic. Specifically, find reports of new treatments for Parkinson's disease that do not involve the use of fetal tissue. Write a summary of your findings.
3. After completing Interactivity 9–1, choose one of the structures of the brain that is discussed and enter it in one of the major search engines. After consulting at least three reputable websites, write a brief summary of recent findings about the particular structure in which you are interested.

Epilogue

In our examination of neuroscience, we've traced the ways in which biological structures and functions of the body affect behavior. Starting with neurons, we considered each of the components of the nervous system, culminating in an examination of how the brain permits us to think, reason, speak, recall, and experience emotions—the hallmarks of being human.

Before proceeding, consider the case of Christopher Reeve and his slow, painstaking recovery from his horse-riding accident, and reflect on the following questions:

1. Using what you know about the functioning of the nervous system, explain what happened to Christopher Reeve to produce his paralysis.
2. Accidents sometime produce paralysis on one side of the body while leaving the other side unaffected. What may have occurred in such cases?
3. To what do you attribute the success of Reeve's therapy? Do you think that there is a cognitive aspect involved in his recovery, as well as purely physical aspects?

Sensation and Perception

Prologue
Now Hear This!

With this much enthusiasm, Amy Ecklund might be a contestant on a television game show. "That's a glass!" she calls out as she hears a clinking noise in the restaurant where she's eating. As a fork clangs, she exclaims, "Silverware!" At the sound of a noisy hammer, Ecklund excitedly says, "Wow! That is loud!" (Ecklund, 1999, p. 68).

Ecklund, who played a deaf hospital administrator on the soap opera *Guiding Light*, lost her ability to hear at the age of six. But following a life-altering operation a few years ago, she no longer has to read lips in order to know what others are saying.

The operation inserted a Nucleus 24 cochlear implant in her right ear. It allows Ecklund to hear almost normally. According to Michael O'Leary, who played her husband on *Guiding Light*, "It's like watching a child being born" (Ecklund, 1999, p. 68).

Amy Ecklund is a beneficiary of a new generation of technological devices that offer the promise of restored hearing to the tens of thousands of people with hearing impairments. Still, no technological substitute has reached the ultimate level of sophistication of the human ear, or, for that matter, any of our other sense organs. In fact, our ability to sense the stimuli in our environment is remarkable, enabling us to feel the gentlest of breezes, see flickering lights miles away, and hear the soft murmuring of distant songbirds.

In the next four modules, we focus on the field of psychology that is concerned with the ways our bodies take in information through the senses and the ways we interpret that information. We will explore both sensation and perception. *Sensation* encompasses the

Looking Ahead

processes by which our sense organs receive information from the environment. *Perception* is the brain's and the sense organs' sorting out, interpretation, analysis, and integration of stimuli.

Although perception clearly represents a step beyond sensation, in practice it is sometimes difficult to find the precise boundary between the two. Indeed, psychologists—and philosophers as well—have argued for years over the distinction. The primary difference is that sensation can be thought of as an organism's first encounter with a raw sensory stimulus, whereas perception is the process by which that stimulus is interpreted, analyzed, and integrated with other sensory information.

For example, if we were considering sensation, we might ask about the loudness of a ringing fire alarm. If we were considering perception, we might ask whether someone recognizes the ringing sound as an alarm and identifies its meaning. Similarly, when baseball batters are judging whether they should swing the bat after a ball is pitched, they first make use of sensation in noting the moment when the ball is released from the pitcher's hand. But because a baseball is pitched at speeds faster than the eye can follow (it turns out that the old advice to keep your eye on the ball is impossible to follow), batters must depend on perception to anticipate when, and where, the ball is likely to arrive. Clearly, both sensation and perception are necessary for transforming the physical world into our psychological reality (Bayhill & Karnavas, 1993; Gray, 2002).

To a psychologist interested in understanding the causes of behavior, sensation and perception are fundamental topics because so much of our behavior is a reflection of how we react to and interpret stimuli from the world around us. The areas of sensation and perception deal with a wide range of questions—among them, how we respond to the characteristics of physical stimuli; what processes enable us to see, hear, and experience pain; why visual illusions fool us; and how we distinguish one person from another. As we explore these issues, we'll see how the senses work together to provide us with an integrated view and understanding of the world.

Sensing the World Around Us

What is sensation, and how do psychologists study it?

What is the relationship between a physical stimulus and the kinds of sensory responses that result from it?

As Isabel sat down to Thanksgiving dinner, her father carried the turkey in on a tray and placed it squarely in the center of the table. The noise level, already high from the talking and laughter of family members, grew louder still. As Isabel picked up her fork, the smell of the turkey reached her and she felt her stomach growl hungrily. The sight and sound of her family around the table, along with the smells and tastes of the holiday meal, made Isabel feel more relaxed than she had since starting school in the fall.

Put yourself in this setting and consider how different it might be if any one of your senses was not functioning. What if you were blind and unable to see the faces of your family members or the welcome shape of the golden-brown turkey? What if you had no sense of hearing and could not listen to the conversations of family members or were unable to feel your stomach growl, smell the dinner, or taste the food? Clearly, you would experience the dinner very differently than would someone whose sensory apparatus was intact.

Moreover, the sensations mentioned above barely scratch the surface of sensory experience. Although perhaps you were taught, as I was, that there are just five senses—sight, sound, taste, smell, and touch—that enumeration is too modest. Human sensory capabilities go well beyond the basic five senses. It is well established, for example, that we are sensitive not merely to touch but to a considerably wider set of stimuli—pain, pressure, temperature, and vibration, to name a few. In addition, vision has two subsystems—relating to day and night vision—and the ear is responsive to information that allows us not only to hear but also to keep our balance. Psychologists now believe there are at least a dozen distinct senses, all of which are interrelated.

To consider how psychologists understand the senses and, more broadly, sensation and perception, we first need a basic working vocabulary. In formal terms, **sensation** is the activation of the sense organs by a source of physical energy. **Perception** is the sorting out, interpretation, analysis, and integration of stumuli carried out by the sense organs and brain. A **stimulus** is any passing source of physical energy that produces a response in a sense organ.

Stimuli vary in both type and intensity. Different types of stimuli activate different sense organs. For instance, we can differentiate light stimuli (which activate the sense of sight and allow us to see the colors of a tree in autumn) from sound stimuli (which, through the sense of hearing, permit us to hear the sounds of an orchestra).

Each sort of stimulus that is capable of activating a sense organ can also be considered in terms of its strength, or *intensity*. How intense a light stimulus needs to be before it can be detected and how much perfume a person must wear before it is noticed by others are questions related to stimulus intensity.

The issue of how the intensity of a stimulus influences our sensory responses is considered in a branch of psychology known as psychophysics. **Psychophysics** is the study of the relationship between the physical aspects of stimuli and our psychological experience of them. Psychophysics played a central role in the development

Sensation: The activation of the sense organs by a source of physical energy.

Perception: The sorting out, interpretation, analysis, and integration of stimuli involving the sense organs and brain.

Stimulus: Energy that produces a response in a sense organ.

Psychophysics: The study of the relationship between the physical aspects of stimuli and our psychological experience of them.

of the field of psychology, and many of the first psychologists studied issues related to psychophysics (Chechile, 2003).

▲ ▲ ▲

Absolute Thresholds: Detecting What's Out There

Just when does a stimulus become strong enough to be detected by our sense organs? The answer to this question requires an understanding of the concept of absolute threshold. An **absolute threshold** is the smallest intensity of a stimulus that must be present for it to be detected.

Absolute threshold: The smallest intensity of a stimulus that must be present for a stimulus to be detected.

Our senses are extremely responsive to stimuli. For example, the sense of touch is so sensitive that we can feel a bee's wing falling on our cheeks when it is dropped from a distance of one centimeter. Test your knowledge of the absolute thresholds of other senses by completing the questionnaire in Figure 1.

In fact, our senses are so fine-tuned that we might have problems if they were any more sensitive. For instance, if our ears were slightly more acute, we would be able to hear the sound of air molecules in our ears knocking into the eardrum—a phenomenon that would surely prove distracting and might even prevent us from hearing sounds outside our bodies.

Of course, the absolute thresholds we have been discussing are measured under ideal conditions. Normally our senses cannot detect stimulation quite as well because of the presence of noise. *Noise,* as defined by psychophysicists, is background stimulation that interferes with the perception of other stimuli. Hence, noise refers not just to auditory stimuli, as the word suggests, but also to unwanted stimuli that interfere with other senses. Picture a talkative group of people crammed into a small, crowded, smoke-filled room at a party. The din of the crowd makes it hard to hear individual voices, and the smoke makes it difficult to see, or even taste, the food. In this case, the smoke and the crowded conditions would both be considered "noise" because they are preventing sensation at more discriminating levels.

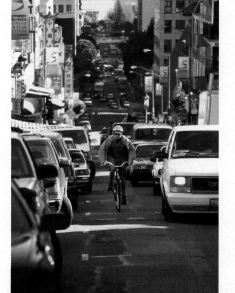

Crowded conditions, sounds, and sights can all be considered as noise that interferes with sensation. Can you think of other examples of noise that is not auditory in nature?

FIGURE 1 This test can shed some light on how sensitive the human senses are. (Source: Galanter, 1962.)

How Sensitive Are You?

To test your awareness of the capabilities of your senses, answer the following questions:

1. How far can a candle flame be seen on a clear, dark night:
   a. From a distance of 10 miles _____
   b. From a distance of 30 miles _____
2. How far can the ticking of a watch be heard under quiet conditions?
   a. From 5 feet away _____
   b. From 20 feet away _____
3. How much sugar is needed to allow it to be detected when dissolved in 2 gallons of water?
   a. 2 tablespoons_____
   b. 1 teaspoon_____
4. Over what area can a drop of perfume be detected?
   a. A 5-foot by 5-foot area _____
   b. A 3-room apartment _____

Scoring: In each case, the answer is b, illustrating the tremendous sensitivity of our senses.

Difference Thresholds: Noticing Distinctions Between Stimuli

Suppose you wanted to choose the six best apples from a supermarket display—the biggest, reddest, and sweetest apples. One approach would be to compare one apple with another systematically until you were left with a few so similar that you could not tell the difference between them. At that point, it wouldn't matter which ones you chose.

Psychologists have discussed this comparison problem in terms of the **difference threshold,** the smallest level of added (or reduced) stimulation required to sense that a *change* in stimulation has occurred. Thus, the difference threshold is the minimum change in stimulation required to detect the difference between two stimuli, and so it also is called a **just noticeable difference.**

The stimulus value that constitutes a just noticeable difference depends on the initial intensity of the stimulus. The relationship between changes in the original value of a stimulus and the degree to which a change will be noticed forms one of the basic laws of psychophysics: Weber's law. **Weber's law** (with *Weber* pronounced "vay-ber") states that a just noticeable difference is a *constant proportion* of the intensity of an initial stimulus.

For example, Weber found that the just noticeable difference for weight is 1:50. Consequently, it takes a 1-ounce increase in a 50-ounce weight to produce a noticeable difference, and it would take a 10-ounce increase to produce a noticeable difference if the initial weight were 500 ounces. In both cases, the same proportional increase is necessary to produce a just noticeable difference—1:50 = 10:500. Similarly, the just noticeable difference distinguishing changes in loudness between sounds is larger for sounds that are initially loud than it is for sounds that are initially soft, but the *proportional* increase remains the same.

Weber's law helps explain why a person in a quiet room is more apt to be startled by the ringing of a telephone than is a person in an already noisy room. To produce the same amount of reaction in a noisy room, a telephone ring might have to approximate the loudness of cathedral bells. Similarly, when the moon is visible during the late afternoon, it appears relatively dim—yet against a dark night sky, it seems quite bright.

Interactivity 10–1 asks you to test Weber's law for yourself and further explore the relationship between physical stimuli and sensation.

Difference threshold (just noticeable difference): The smallest level of added or reduced stimulation required to sense that a *change* in stimulation has occurred.

Weber's law: One of the basic laws of psychophysics, stating that a just noticeable difference is in constant proportion to the intensity of an initial stimulus.

INTERACTIVITY 10–1
Weber's law

Sensory Adaptation: Turning Down Our Responses

You enter a bar, and the odor of cigarettes assaults you. A few minutes later, though, you barely notice the smell.

The reason you acclimate to the odor is sensory adaptation. **Adaptation** is an adjustment in sensory capacity after prolonged exposure to unchanging stimuli. Adaptation occurs as people become accustomed to a stimulus and change their frame of reference. In a sense, our brains mentally turn down the volume of the stimulation they're experiencing.

One example of adaptation is the decrease in sensitivity that occurs after repeated exposure to a strong stimulus. If you were to hear a loud tone over and over again, eventually it would begin to sound softer. Similarly, although jumping into a cold lake may be temporarily unpleasant, eventually we probably will get used to the temperature.

This apparent decline in sensitivity to sensory stimuli is due to the inability of the sensory nerve receptors to fire off messages to the brain indefinitely. Because

Adaptation: An adjustment in sensory capacity after prolonged exposure to unchanging stimuli.

these receptor cells are most responsive to *changes* in stimulation, constant stimulation is not effective in producing a sustained reaction.

Judgments of sensory stimuli are also affected by the context in which the judgments are made. This is the case because judgments are made not in isolation from other stimuli but in terms of preceding sensory experience. You can demonstrate this for yourself by trying a simple experiment. Take two envelopes, one large and one small, and put fifteen nickels in each one. Now lift the large envelope, put it down, and lift the small one. Which seems to weigh more? Most people report that the small one is heavier, although, as you know, the weights are nearly identical. The reason for this misconception is that the visual context of the envelope interferes with the sensory experience of weight. Adaptation to the context of one stimulus (the size of the envelope) alters responses to another stimulus (the weight of the envelope) (Coren & Ward, 1989).

RECAP/EVALUATE/RETHINK

RECAP

What is sensation, and how do psychologists study it?

▶ Sensation is the activation of the sense organs by any source of physical energy. In contrast, perception is the process by which we sort out, interpret, analyze, and integrate stimuli to which our senses are exposed. (p. 100)

What is the relationship between a physical stimulus and the kinds of sensory responses that result from it?

▶ Psychophysics studies the relationship between the physical nature of stimuli and the sensory responses they evoke. (p. 101)

▶ The absolute threshold is the smallest amount of physical intensity at which a stimulus can be detected. Although under ideal conditions absolute thresholds are extraordinarily sensitive, the presence of noise (background stimuli that interfere with other stimuli) reduces detection capabilities. (p. 102)

▶ The difference threshold, or just noticeable difference, is the smallest change in the level of stimulation required to sense that a change has occurred. According to Weber's law, a just noticeable difference is a constant proportion of the intensity of an initial stimulus. (p. 103)

▶ Sensory adaptation occurs when we become accustomed to a constant stimulus and change our evaluation of it. Repeated exposure to a stimulus results in an apparent decline in sensitivity to it. (p. 103)

EVALUATE

1. _____ is the stimulation of the sense organs; _____ is the sorting out, interpretation, analysis, and integration of stimuli by the sense organs.
2. The term *absolute threshold* refers to the _____ intensity of a stimulus that must be present for the stimulus to be detected.
3. Weber discovered that for a difference between two stimuli to be perceptible, the stimuli must differ by at least a _____ proportion.
4. After completing a very difficult rock climb in the morning, Carmella found the afternoon climb unexpectedly easy. This case illustrates the phenomenon of _____.

RETHINK

1. Do you think it is possible to have sensation without perception? Is it possible to have perception without sensation?
2. Do you think sensory adaptation is essential for everyday psychological functioning?

Answers to Evaluate Questions

1. sensation; perception; 2. smallest; 3. constant; 4. adaptation

KEY TERMS

sensation p. 101
perception p. 101
stimulus p. 101

psychophysics p. 101
absolute threshold
p. 102

difference threshold (just
noticeable difference)
p. 103

Weber's law p. 103
adaptation p. 103

Vision: Shedding Light on the Eye

If, as poets say, the eyes provide a window to the soul, they also provide us with a window to the world. Our visual capabilities permit us to admire and react to scenes ranging from the beauty of a sunset, to the configuration of a lover's face, to the words written on the pages of a book.

Vision starts with light, the physical energy that stimulates the eye. Light is a form of electromagnetic radiation waves, which, as shown in Figure 1, are measured in wavelengths. The sizes of wavelengths correspond to different types of energy. The range of wavelengths that humans are sensitive to—called the *visual spectrum*—is relatively small. Many nonhuman species have different capabilities. For instance, some reptiles and fish sense energies of longer wavelengths than humans do, and certain insects sense energies of shorter wavelengths than humans do.

Light waves coming from some object outside the body (imagine the light reflected off the tree in Figure 2) are sensed by the only organ that is capable of responding to the visual spectrum: the eye. Our eyes shape light into a form that can be used by the neurons that serve as messengers to the brain. The neurons themselves take up a relatively small percentage of the total eye. In other words, most of the eye is a mechanical device that is similar in many respects to a camera without film, as you can see in Figure 2.

Despite the similarities between the eye and a camera, vision involves processes that are far more complex and sophisticated than those of any camera. Furthermore, once an image reaches the neuronal receptors of the eye, the eye/camera analogy ends, for the processing of the visual image in the brain is more reflective of a computer than it is of a camera. The animation of the eye in **Interactivity 11–1** will help you better understand how we are able to see.

Ⓐ Ⓐ Ⓐ

INTERACTIVITY 11–1

How do we see?

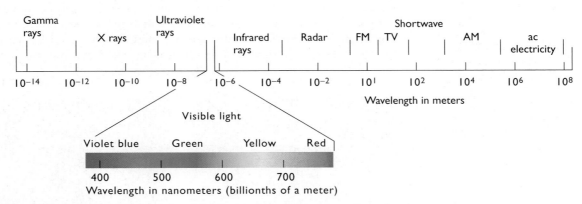

FIGURE 1 The visible spectrum—the range of wavelengths to which people are sensitive—is only a small part of the kinds of wavelengths present in our environment. Is it a benefit or disadvantage to our everyday lives that we aren't more sensitive to a broader range of visual stimuli? Why?

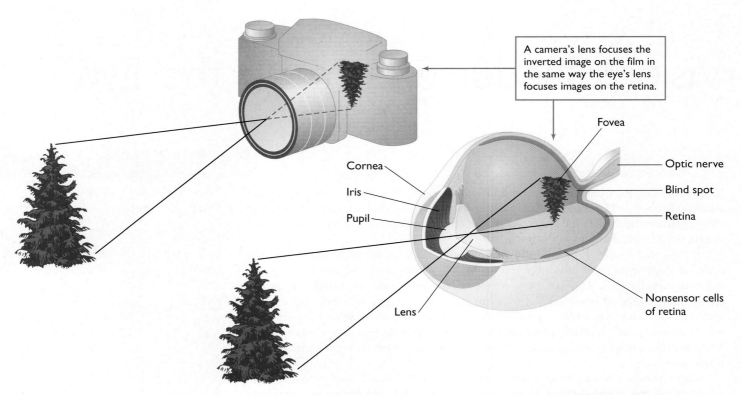

A camera's lens focuses the inverted image on the film in the same way the eye's lens focuses images on the retina.

FIGURE 2 Although human vision is far more complicated than the most sophisticated camera, in some ways basic visual processes are analogous to those used in photography.

Illuminating the Structure of the Eye

The ray of light we are tracing as it is reflected off the tree in Figure 2 first travels through the *cornea*, a transparent, protective window. The cornea, because of its curvature, bends (or *refracts*) light as it passes through to focus it more sharply. After moving through the cornea, the light traverses the pupil. The *pupil* is a dark hole in the center of the *iris,* the colored part of the eye, which in humans ranges from a light blue to a dark brown. The size of the pupil opening depends on the amount of light in the environment. The dimmer the surroundings are, the more the pupil opens to allow more light to enter.

Why shouldn't the pupil be open completely all the time, allowing the greatest amount of light into the eye? The answer relates to the basic physics of light. A small pupil greatly increases the range of distances at which objects are in focus. With a wide-open pupil, the range is relatively small, and details are harder to discern. The eye takes advantage of bright light by decreasing the size of the pupil and thereby

Like the automatic lighting system on a camera, the human eye dilates to let in more light (left) and contracts to block out light (right). Can humans adjust their ears to let in more or less sound in similar manner?

becoming more discerning. In dim light the pupil expands to enable us to view the situation better—but at the expense of visual detail. (Perhaps one reason candlelight dinners are thought of as romantic is that the dim light prevents one from seeing a partner's physical flaws.)

Once light passes through the pupil, it enters the *lens,* which is directly behind the pupil. The lens acts to bend the rays of light so that they are properly focused on the rear of the eye. The lens focuses light by changing its own thickness, a process called *accommodation:* It becomes flatter when viewing distant objects and rounder when looking at closer objects.

REACHING THE RETINA

Having traveled through the pupil and lens, our image of the tree finally reaches its ultimate destination in the eye—the **retina.** Here the electromagnetic energy of light is converted into the neural codes used by the brain. It is important to note that because of the physical properties of light, the image has reversed itself in traveling through the lens, and it reaches the retina upside down (relative to its original position). Although it might seem that this reversal would cause difficulties in understanding and moving about the world, this is not the case. The brain interprets the image in terms of its original position.

The retina consists of a thin layer of nerve cells at the back of the eyeball (see Figure 3). There are two kinds of light-sensitive receptor cells in the retina. The names they have been given describe their shapes: rods and cones. **Rods** are thin, cylindrical receptor cells that are highly sensitive to light. **Cones** are cone-shaped, light-sensitive receptor cells that are responsible for sharp focus and color perception, particularly in bright light. The rods and cones are distributed unevenly throughout the retina. The greatest concentration of cones is on the part of the retina called the *fovea.* The fovea is a particularly sensitive region of the retina. If you want to focus in on something of particular interest, you will automatically try to center the image from the lens onto the area of the fovea to see it more sharply.

The density of cones declines just outside the fovea, although cones are found throughout the retina in lower concentrations. In contrast, there are no rods in the very center of the fovea, but the density is greatest outside the fovea and then gradually declines toward the edges of the retina. Because the fovea covers only a small portion of the eye, we have fewer cones (between 5 million and 7 million) than rods (between 100 million and 125 million).

The rods and cones are not only structurally dissimilar but play distinctly different roles in vision. Cones are primarily responsible for the sharply focused perception of color, particularly in brightly lit situations; rods are related to vision in dimly lit situations and are largely insensitive to color and to details as sharp as those the cones are capable of recognizing. The rods play a key role in *peripheral vision*—seeing objects that are outside the main center of focus—and in night vision.

Rods and cones also are involved in *dark adaptation,* the phenomenon of adjusting to dim light after being in brighter light. (Think of the experience of walking into a dark movie theater and groping your way to a seat but a few minutes later seeing the seats quite clearly.) The speed at which dark adaptation occurs is a result of the rate of change in the chemical composition of the rods and cones. Although the cones reach their greatest level of adaptation in just a few minutes, the rods take 20 to 30 minutes to reach the maximum level. The opposite phenomenon—*light adaptation,* or the process of adjusting to bright light after exposure to dim light—occurs much faster, taking only a minute or so.

The distinctive abilities of rods and cones make the eye analogous to a camera that is loaded with two kinds of film. One type is a highly sensitive black-and-white film (the rods). The other type is a somewhat less sensitive color film (the cones).

Retina: The part of the eye that converts the electromagnetic energy of light into useful information for the brain.

Rods: Thin, cylindrical receptor cells in the retina that are highly sensitive to light.

Cones: Cone-shaped, light-sensitive receptor cells in the retina that are responsible for sharp focus and color perception, particularly in bright light.

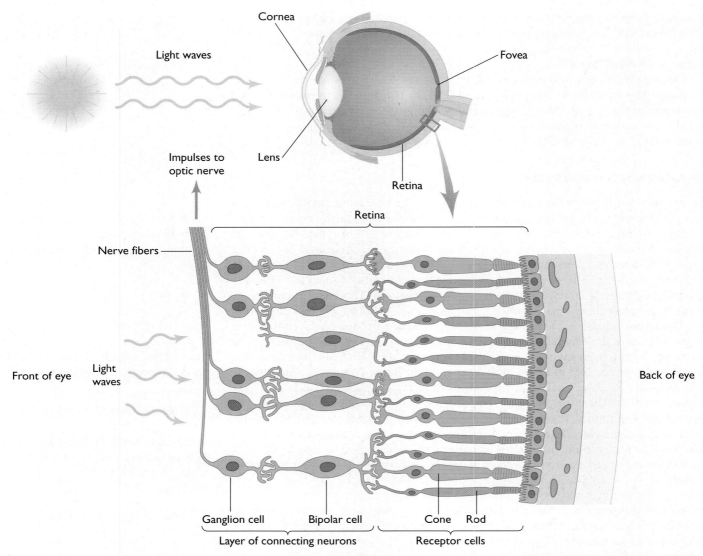

FIGURE 3 The basic cells of the eye. Light entering the eye travels through the ganglion and bipolar cells and strikes the light-sensitive rods and cones located at the back of the eye. The rods and cones then transmit nerve impulses to the brain via the bipolar and ganglion cells. (Source: Shier, Butler, & Lewis, 2000.)

SENDING THE MESSAGE FROM THE EYE TO THE BRAIN

When light energy strikes the rods and cones, it starts a chain of events that transforms light into neural impulses that can be communicated to the brain. Even before the neural message reaches the brain, however, some initial coding of the visual information takes place.

What happens when light energy strikes the retina depends in part on whether it encounters a rod or a cone. Rods contain *rhodopsin,* a complex reddish-purple substance whose composition changes chemically when energized by light. The substance in cone receptors is different, but the principles are similar. Stimulation of the nerve cells in the eye triggers a neural response that is transmitted to other nerve cells in the retina called *bipolar cells* and *ganglion cells.*

Bipolar cells receive information directly from the rods and cones and communicate that information to the ganglion cells. The ganglion cells collect and summarize visual information, which is then moved out of the back of the eyeball and sent to the brain through a bundle of ganglion axons called the **optic nerve**.

Optic nerve: A bundle of ganglion axons that carry visual information.

FIGURE 4 To find your blind spot, close your right eye and look at the haunted house with your left eye. You will see the ghost on the periphery of your vision. Now, while staring at the house, move the page toward you. When the book is about a foot from your eye, the ghost will disappear. At this moment, the image of the ghost is falling on your blind spot.

But also notice how, when the page is at that distance, not only does the ghost seem to disappear, but the line seems to run continuously through the area where the ghost used to be. This shows how we automatically compensate for missing information by using nearby material to complete what is unseen. That's the reason you never notice the blind spot. What is missing is replaced by what is seen next to the blind spot. Can you think of any advantages that this tendency to provide missing information gives humans as a species?

Because the opening for the optic nerve passes through the retina, there are no rods or cones in the area, and that creates a blind spot. Normally, however, this absence of nerve cells does not interfere with vision because you automatically compensate for the missing part of your field of vision (Ramachandran, 1995). To find your blind spot, see Figure 4.)

Once beyond the eye itself, the neural signals relating to the image move through the optic nerve. As the optic nerve leaves the eyeball, its path does not take the most direct route to the part of the brain right behind the eye. Instead, the optic nerves from each eye meet at a point roughly between the two eyes—called the *optic chiasm*—where each optic nerve then splits.

When the optic nerves split, the nerve impulses coming from the right half of each retina are sent to the right side of the brain, and the impulses arriving from the left half of each retina are sent to the left side of the brain. Because the image on the retinas is reversed and upside down, however, those images coming from the right half of each retina actually originated in the field of vision to the person's left, and the images coming from the left half of each retina originated in the field of vision to the person's right (see Figure 5).

PROCESSING THE VISUAL MESSAGE

By the time a visual message reaches the brain, it has passed through several stages of processing. One of the initial sites is the ganglion cells. Each ganglion cell gathers information from a group of rods and cones in a particular area of the eye and compares the amount of light entering the center of that area with the amount of light in the area around it. Some ganglion cells are activated by light in the center (and darkness in the surrounding area). Other ganglion cells are activated when there is darkness in the center and light in the surrounding areas. The ultimate effect of this process is to maximize the detection of variations in light and darkness. The neural image that is passed on to the brain, then, is an enhanced version of the actual visual stimulus outside the body (Kubovy, Epstein, & Gepshtein, 2003).

PowerWeb: Exploration of the Visual Cortex
www.mhhe.com/feldmanup7

The ultimate processing of visual images takes place in the visual cortex of the brain, and it is here that the most complex kinds of processing occur. Psychologists David Hubel and Torsten Wiesel won the Nobel Prize for their discovery that many neurons in the cortex are extraordinarily specialized, being activated only by visual stimuli of a particular shape or pattern—a process known as **feature detection.** They found that some cells are activated only by lines of a particular width, shape, or orientation. Other cells are activated only by moving, as opposed to stationary, stimuli (Hubel & Wiesel, 1979; Patzwahl, Zanker, & Altenmuller, 1994).

Feature detection: The activation of neurons in the cortex by visual stimuli of specific shapes or patterns.

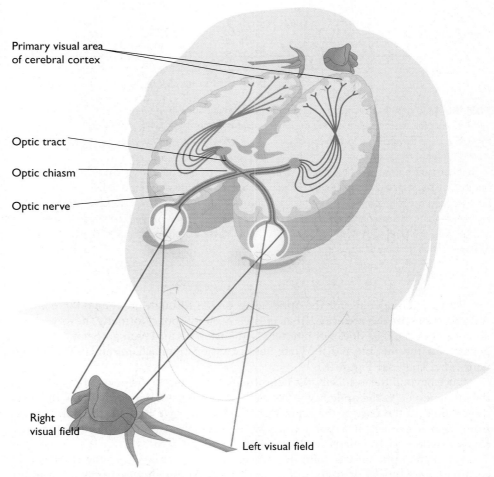

FIGURE 5 Because the optic nerve coming from each eye splits at the optic chiasm, the image to a person's right is sent to the left side of the brain and the image to the person's left is transmitted to the right side of the brain.

More recent work has added to our knowledge of the complex ways in which visual information coming from individual neurons is combined and processed. Different parts of the brain seem to process nerve impulses in several individual systems simultaneously. For instance, one system relates to shapes, one to colors, and others to movement, location, and depth. Furthermore, different parts of the brain appear to be involved in the perception of specific *kinds* of stimuli, showing distinctions between the perception of faces, cats, and inanimate stimuli (Moutoussis & Zeki, 1997; Haxby et al., 2001).

If separate neural systems exist for processing information about specific aspects of the visual world, how are all these data integrated by the brain? Although the exact process is not well understood, it seems likely that the brain makes use of information regarding the frequency, rhythm, and timing of the firing of particular sets of neural cells. Furthermore, it appears that the brain's integration of visual information does not occur in any single step or location in the brain but instead is a process that occurs on several levels simultaneously. The ultimate outcome, though, is indisputable: a vision of the world around us (deGelder, 2000; Macaluso, Frith, & Driver, 2000).

a.

b.

c.

FIGURE 6 (a) To someone with normal vision, the hot-air balloon in the foreground appears with regions of very pure red, orange, yellow, green, blue, and violet, as well as off-white; and the balloon in the rear is a bright shade of red-orange. (b) A person with red-green color blindness would see the scene in part (a) like this, in hues of blue and yellow. (c) A person who is blue-yellow blind, conversely, would see it in hues of red and green.

Color Vision and Color Blindness:
The Seven-Million-Color Spectrum

Although the range of wavelengths to which humans are sensitive is relatively narrow, at least in comparison with the entire electromagnetic spectrum, the portion to which we are capable of responding allows us great flexibility in sensing the world. Nowhere is this clearer than in terms of the number of colors we can discern. A person with normal color vision is capable of distinguishing no less than 7 million different colors (Bruce, Green, & Georgeson, 1997).

Although the variety of colors that people are generally able to distinguish is vast, there are certain individuals whose ability to perceive color is quite limited—the color-blind. Interestingly, the condition of these individuals has provided some of the most important clues to understanding how color vision operates (Neitz, Neitz, & Kainz, 1996).

Before continuing, though, look at the photos shown in Figure 6. If you have difficulty seeing the differences among the series of photos, you may well be one of the 1 in 50 men or 1 in 5,000 women who are color-blind.

For most people with color-blindness, the world looks quite dull. Red fire engines appear yellow, green grass seems yellow, and the three colors of a traffic light all look yellow. In fact, in the most common form of color blindness, all red and green objects are seen as yellow. There are other forms of color blindness as well, but they are quite rare. In yellow-blue blindness, people are unable to tell the difference between yellow and blue, and in the most extreme case an individual perceives no color at all. To such a person the world looks something like the picture on a black-and-white television set.

To understand why some people are color-blind, it is necessary to consider the basics of color vision. There appear to be two processes involved. The first process is explained by the **trichromatic theory of color vision.** This theory suggests that

Trichromatic theory of color vision: The theory that there are three kinds of cones in the retina, each of which responds primarily to a specific range of wavelengths.

there are three kinds of cones in the retina, each of which responds primarily to a specific range of wavelengths. One is most responsive to blue-violet colors, one to green, and the third to yellow-red (Brown & Wald, 1964). According to trichromatic theory, perception of color is influenced by the relative strength with which each of the three kinds of cones is activated. If we see a blue sky, the blue-violet cones are primarily triggered, and the others show less activity. The trichromatic theory provides a straightforward explanation of color-blindness. It suggests that one of the three cone systems malfunctions, and thus colors covered by that range are perceived improperly (Nathans et al., 1989).

However, there are phenomena that the trichromatic theory is less successful at explaining. For example, the theory does not explain what happens after you stare at something like the flag shown in Figure 7 for about a minute. Try this yourself and then look at a blank white page: You'll see an image of the traditional red, white, and blue U.S. flag. Where there was yellow, you'll see blue, and where there were green and black, you'll see red and white.

The phenomenon you have just experienced is called an *afterimage*. It occurs because activity in the retina continues even when you are no longer staring at the original picture. However, it also demonstrates that the trichromatic theory does not explain color vision completely. Why should the colors in the afterimage be different from those in the original?

Opponent-process theory of color vision: The theory that receptor cells for color are linked in pairs, working in opposition to each other.

Because trichromatic processes do not provide a full explanation of color vision, alternative explanations have been proposed. According to the **opponent-process theory of color vision,** receptor cells are linked in pairs, working in opposition to each other. Specifically, there is a blue-yellow pairing, a red-green pairing, and a black-white pairing. If an object reflects light that contains more blue than yellow, it will stimulate the firing of the cells sensitive to blue, simultaneously discouraging or inhibiting the firing of receptor cells sensitive to yellow—and the object will appear blue. If, in contrast, a light contains more yellow than blue, the cells that respond to yellow will be stimulated to fire while the blue ones are inhibited, and the object will appear yellow.

The opponent-process theory provides a good explanation for afterimages. When we stare at the yellow in the figure, for instance, our receptor cells for the

FIGURE 7 Stare at the dot in this flag for about a minute and then look at a piece of plain white paper. What do you see? Most people see an afterimage that converts the colors in the figure into the traditional red, white, and blue U.S. flag. If you have trouble seeing it the first time, blink once and try again.

yellow component of the yellow-blue pairing become fatigued and are less able to respond to yellow stimuli. In contrast, the receptor cells for the blue part of the pair are not tired, because they are not being stimulated. When we look at a white surface, the light reflected off it would normally stimulate both the yellow and the blue receptors equally. But the fatigue of the yellow receptors prevents this from happening. They temporarily do not respond to the yellow, which makes the white light appear to be blue. Because the other colors in the figure do the same thing relative to their specific opponents, the afterimage produces the opponent colors—for a while. The afterimage lasts only a short time, because the fatigue of the yellow receptors is soon overcome, and the white light begins to be perceived more accurately.

Both opponent processes and trichromatic mechanisms are at work in allowing us to see color. However, they operate in different parts of the visual sensing system. Trichromatic processes work within the retina itself, whereas opponent mechanisms operate both in the retina and at later stages of neuronal processing (de Valois & de Valois, 1993; Lee, Wachtler, & Sejnowski, 2002).

RECAP/EVALUATE/RETHINK

RECAP

What basic processes underlie the sense of vision?

▶ Vision depends on sensitivity to light, electromagnetic waves in the visible part of the spectrum (wavelengths of roughly 390 to 770 nm) that are either reflected off objects or produced by an energy source. The eye shapes the light into an image that is transformed into nerve impulses and interpreted by the brain. (p. 105)

▶ As light enters the eye, it passes through the cornea, pupil, and lens and ultimately reaches the retina, where the electromagnetic energy of light is converted into nerve impulses usable by the brain. These impulses leave the eye via the optic nerve. (p. 106)

▶ The visual information gathered by the rods and cones is transferred via bipolar and ganglion cells through the optic nerve, which leads to the optic chiasm—the point where the optic nerve splits. (p. 108)

How do we see colors?

▶ Color vision seems to be based on two processes described by the trichromatic theory and the opponent-process theory. (p. 111)

▶ The trichromatic theory suggests that there are three kinds of cones in the retina, each of which is responsive to a certain range of colors. The opponent-process theory presumes pairs of different types of cells in the eye. These cells work in opposition to each other. (p. 111)

EVALUATE

1. Light entering the eye first passes through the _____, a protective window.

2. The structure that converts light into usable neural messages is called the _____.

3. A woman with blue eyes could be described as having blue pigment in her _____.

4. What is the process by which the thickness of the lens is changed in order to focus light properly?

5. The proper sequence of structures that light passes through in the eye is the _____, _____, _____, and _____.

6. Match each type of visual receptor with its function.
   a. Rods   1. Used for dim light, largely insensitive to color.
   b. Cones   2. Detect color, good in bright light.

7. Paco was to meet his girlfriend in the movie theater. As was typical, he was late and the movie had begun. He stumbled down the aisle, barely able to see. Unfortunately, the woman he sat down beside and attempted to put his arm around was not his girlfriend. He sorely wished he had given his eyes a chance and waited for _____ adaptation to occur.

8. _____ theory states that there are three types of cones in the retina, each of which responds primarily to a different color.

RETHINK

1. If the eye were constructed with a second lens that "unre-versed" the image hitting the retina, do you think there would be changes in the way people perceive the world?
2. From an evolutionary standpoint, why might the eye have evolved so that the rods, which we rely on in low light, do not provide sharp images? Are there any advantages to this system?

Answers to Evaluate Questions

1. cornea; 2. retina; 3. iris; 4. accommodation; 5. cornea, pupil, lens, retina; 6. a-1, b-2; 7. dark; 8. trichromatic

KEY TERMS

retina p. 107
rods p. 107
cones p. 107

optic nerve p. 108
feature detection p. 109

trichromatic theory of color vision p. 111

opponent-process theory of color vision p. 112

Hearing and the Other Senses

The blast-off was easy compared with what the astronaut was experiencing now: space sickness. The constant nausea and vomiting were enough to make him wonder why he had worked so hard to become an astronaut. Even though he had been warned that there was a two-thirds chance that his first experience in space would cause these symptoms, he wasn't prepared for how terribly sick he really felt.

Whether or not the astronaut wishes he could head right back to earth, his experience, a major problem for space travelers, is related to a basic sensory process: the sense of motion and balance. This sense allows people to navigate their bodies through the world and keep themselves upright without falling. Along with hearing—the process by which sound waves are translated into understandable and meaningful forms—the senses of motion and balance are major functions of an intricate system of sensory organs: the ear.

⒜⒜⒜

What role does the ear play in the senses of sound, motion, and balance?

How do smell and taste function?

What are the skin senses, and how do they relate to the experience of pain?

Sensing Sound

Although many of us think primarily of the *outer ear* when we speak of the ear, that structure is only one simple part of the whole: a reverse megaphone, designed to collect and bring sounds into the internal portions of the ear (see Figure 1). The location of the outer ears on different sides of the head helps with *sound localization,* the process by which we identify the direction from which a sound is coming. Wave patterns in the air enter each ear at a slightly different time, and the brain uses the discrepancy as a clue to the sound's point of origin. In addition, the two outer ears delay or amplify sounds of particular frequencies to different degrees (Yost, 2000).

Sound is the movement of air molecules brought about by a source of vibration. Sounds travel through the air in wave patterns similar in shape to those made in water when a stone is thrown into a still pond. Sounds, arriving at the outer ear in the form of wave vibrations, are funneled into the *auditory canal,* a tubelike passage that leads to the eardrum. The **eardrum** is aptly named because it operates like a miniature drum, vibrating when sound waves hit it. The more intense the sound, the more the eardrum vibrates. These vibrations are then transferred into the *middle ear,* a tiny chamber containing three bones (the *hammer,* the *anvil,* and the *stirrup*) that transmit vibrations to the *oval window,* a thin membrane leading to the inner ear. Because the hammer, anvil, and stirrup act as a set of levers, they not only transmit vibrations but increase their strength. Moreover, because the opening into the middle ear (the eardrum) is considerably larger than the opening out of it (the oval window), the force of sound waves on the oval window becomes amplified. The middle ear, then, acts as a tiny mechanical amplifier.

The *inner ear* is the portion of the ear that changes the sound vibrations into a form in which they can be transmitted to the brain. (As you will see, it also contains the organs that allow us to locate our position and determine how we are moving

Sound: The movement of air molecules brought about by a source of vibration.

Eardrum: The part of the ear that vibrates when sound waves hit it.

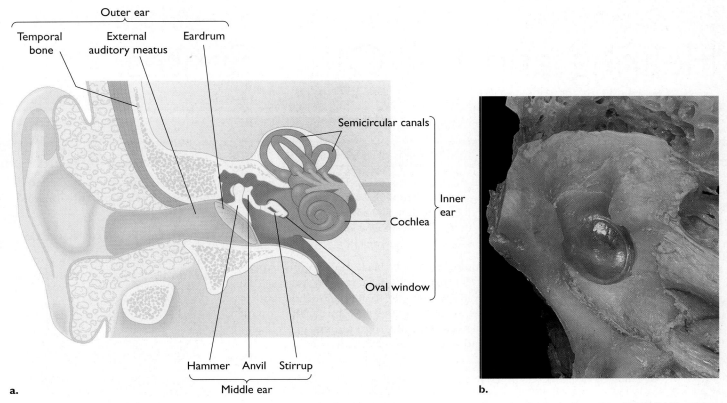

FIGURE I (a) The major regions and parts of the ear (Seeley, Stephens, & Tate, 2000). (b) The eardrum. This structure is aptly named because it operates like a miniature drum, vibrating when sound waves hit it.

Cochlea (KOKE lee uh): A coiled tube in the ear filled with fluid that vibrates in response to sound.

Basilar membrane: A vibrating structure that runs through the center of the cochlea, dividing it into an upper chamber and a lower chamber and containing sense receptors for sound.

Hair cells: Tiny cells covering the basilar membrane that, when bent by vibrations entering the cochlea, transmit neural messages to the brain.

through space.) When sound enters the inner ear through the oval window, it moves into the **cochlea,** a coiled tube that looks something like a snail and is filled with fluid that can vibrate in response to sound. Inside the cochlea is the **basilar membrane,** a structure that runs through the center of the cochlea, dividing it into an upper chamber and a lower chamber. The basilar membrane is covered with **hair cells.** When the hair cells are bent by the vibrations entering the cochlea, the cells send a neural message to the brain (Cho, 2000).

Although sound typically enters the cochlea via the oval window, there is an additional method of entry: bone conduction. Because the ear rests on a maze of bones in the skull, the cochlea is able to pick up subtle vibrations that travel across the bones from other parts of the head. For instance, one of the ways you hear your own voice is through bone conduction. This explains why you sound different to yourself than to other people who hear your voice. (Listen to a recording of your voice to hear what you *really* sound like!) The sound of your voice reaches you both through the air and via bone conduction and therefore sounds richer to you than to everyone else.

THE PHYSICAL ASPECTS OF SOUND

As we mentioned earlier, what we refer to as sound is actually the physical movement of air molecules in regular, wavelike patterns caused by a vibrating source. Sometimes it is even possible to view these vibrations: If you have ever seen an audio speaker that has no enclosure, you know that, at least when the lowest notes are playing, you can see the speaker moving in and out. What is less obvious is what

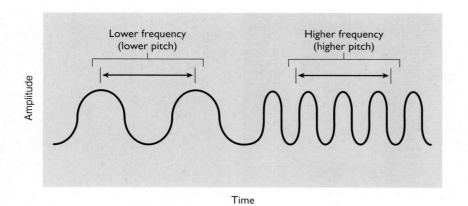

Lower frequency
(lower pitch)

Higher frequency
(higher pitch)

Amplitude

Time

FIGURE 2 The waves produced by different stimuli are transmitted—usually through the air—in different patterns, with lower frequencies indicated by fewer peaks and valleys per second.

happens next: The speaker pushes air molecules into waves with the same pattern as its movement. Those wave patterns soon reach your ear, although their strength has been weakened considerably during their travels. All other sources that produce sound work in essentially the same fashion, setting off wave patterns that move through the air to the ear. Air—or some other medium, such as water—is necessary to make the vibrations of objects reach us. This explains why there can be no sound in a vacuum.

We are able to see the audio speaker moving when low notes are played because of a primary characteristic of sound called frequency. *Frequency* is the number of wave cycles that occur in a second. With very low frequencies there are relatively few wave cycles per second (see Figure 2). These cycles are visible to the naked eye as vibrations in the speaker. Low frequencies are translated into a sound that is very low in pitch. (*Pitch* is the characteristic that makes sound seem "high" or "low.") For example, the lowest frequency that humans are capable of hearing is 20 cycles per second. Higher frequencies are heard as sounds of higher pitch. At the upper end of the sound spectrum, people can detect sounds with frequencies as high as 20,000 cycles per second.

Amplitude is a feature of wave patterns that allows us to distinguish between loud and soft sounds. Amplitude is the spread between the up-and-down peaks and valleys of air pressure in a sound wave as it travels through the air. Waves with small peaks and valleys produce soft sounds; those which are relatively large produce loud sounds (see Figure 2).

We are sensitive to broad variations in sound amplitudes. The strongest sounds we are capable of hearing are over a trillion times as intense as the very weakest sound we can hear. This range is measured in *decibels*. When sounds get higher than 120 decibels, they become painful to the human ear. (For more on hearing, try **Interactivity 12–1.**)

HEARING LOSS AND DEAF CULTURE

The delicacy of the organs involved in hearing makes the ear vulnerable to damage. For instance, exposure to intense levels of sound—coming from events ranging from rock concerts to overly loud headphones—eventually can result in hearing loss, as the hair cells of the basilar membrane lose their elasticity and bend and flatten (see Figure 3). Such hearing loss is often permanent.

Even without actual injury, many people eventually lose hearing acuity over the course of their lives. Some 28 million people in the United States have some degree of hearing impairment.

Although minor hearing impairment can be treated with hearing aids that increase the volume of sounds reaching the ear, more drastic measures are necessary in more severe cases. Certain forms of deafness, produced by damage to the hair

INTERACTIVITY 12–1

Hearing

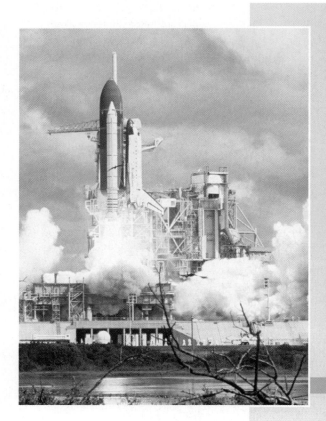

Sound	Decibel Level	Exposure Time Leading to Damage	
Whispering	25 dB		
Library	30 dB		
Average home	50 dB		
Normal conversation	60 dB		
Washing machine	65 dB		
Car	70 dB		
Vacuum cleaner	70 dB		
Busy traffic	75 dB		
Alarm clock	80 dB		
Noisy restaurant	80 dB		
Average factory	85 dB	16	hours
Live rock music (moderately loud)	90 dB	8	hours
Screaming child	90 dB	8	hours
Subway train	100 dB	2	hours
Jackhammer	100 dB	2	hours
Loud CD played through earphones	100 dB	30	minutes
Helicopter	105 dB	1	hour
Sandblasting	110 dB	30	minutes
Auto horn	120 dB	7.5	minutes
Live rock music (loud)	130 dB	3.75	minutes
Air raid siren	130 dB	3.75	minutes
THRESHOLD OF PAIN	140 dB	Immediate damage	
Jet engine	140 dB	Immediate damage	
Rocket launching	180 dB	Immediate damage	

FIGURE 3 Various sounds, their decibel levels, and the amount of exposure that results in hearing damage. Source: © 1998 Better Hearing Institute, Washington, DC. All rights reserved.

cells, can be treated through a *cochlear implant* like the one received by actress Amy Ecklund (the actor in the soap opera *Guiding Light*). Implants consist of a tiny receiver inside the ear and an electrode that stimulates hair cells, controlled by a small external sound processor worn behind the ear.

Although the restoration of hearing to a deaf person may seem like an unquestionably positive achievement, some advocates for the deaf suggest otherwise, especially when it comes to deaf children who are not old enough to provide informed consent. These critics suggest that deafness represents a legitimate culture—no better or worse than the hearing culture—and that providing even limited hearing to deaf children robs them of their natural cultural heritage. It is, without doubt, a controversial position, as we consider further in the *Applying Psychology in the 21st Century* box.

SORTING OUT THEORIES OF SOUND

How are our brains able to sort out wavelengths of different frequencies and intensities? One clue comes from studies of the basilar membrane, the area in the cochlea that translates physical vibrations into neural impulses. It turns out that sounds affect different areas of the basilar membrane, depending on the frequency of the sound wave. The part of the basilar membrane nearest to the oval window is most sensitive to high-frequency sounds, and the part nearest to the cochlea's inner end is most sensitive to low-frequency sounds. This finding has led to the **place theory of hearing,** which states that different areas of the basilar membrane respond to different frequencies.

Place theory of hearing: The theory that different areas of the basilar membrane respond to different frequencies.

Making Senses: New Technology for Hearing and Seeing

Thirty-one-year-old Chris Artinian and his older brother, Peter, have a disagreement that will impact their deaf children's lives forever. Chris, who has normal hearing, opted for his young son to receive a cochlear implant, a surgically implanted device that offers some deaf people the ability to hear. Peter, deaf since birth, does not want his young daughter to get an implant. He and his wife, who is also deaf, believe that the implants are unnatural and that the hours of speech therapy associated with using an implant would interfere with their daughter's education. Because of the disagreement, Peter says, his formerly close relationship with Chris has deteriorated (Hewitt, Gose, & Birkbeck, 2000).

With recent technological advances, more and more families may soon be facing choices like the one that has divided the Artinians. Researchers are developing ever more sophisticated electronic devices to enhance or restore sensory perception in people whose capability of hearing, seeing, speaking, or maintaining balance is impaired or damaged. For example, one new hearing-replacement technology makes use of tiny wires pressed into the brain stem, offering the ability to hear to people whose auditory nerves are too damaged to be helped even by cochlear implants. By working directly at the brain stem, the new device bypasses the auditory nerves and nerve endings that often degenerate soon after people lose their hearing (LeVay, 2000; McCreery, Yuen, & Bullara, 2000).

A range of new technologies also may help restore vision to blind people. For instance, scientists Alan and Vincent Chow have invented a tiny silicon chip that can help people suffering from retinitis pigmentosa, a disease that slowly damages light-sensitive cells in the eye. The chip, which can be implanted surgically underneath people's retinas,

Jerry, a 62-year-old man with blindness, is able to see as the result of electrodes implanted in his brain and connected to a camera mounted on a pair of glasses. A small computer on his hip permits him to read large letters and move around large objects in a room. Do you think modern technology will ever duplicate the functions of the human eye?

converts light into electrical energy that stimulates the damaged cells. The chip has restored some blind people's perception of light and shapes, allowing them to again see sights ranging from holiday lights to loved ones' faces (Charters, 2000; Chow et al., 2001).

Taking a more direct route, another experimental technique for restoring vision involves wiring a small digital camera directly into people's brains. Mounted on a pair of sunglasses, the camera connects to the brain's surface through a small opening in the skull behind the person's ear. The camera, equipped with an ultrasonic range finder, transmits information to a small computer, which in turn stimulates

an area on the person's brain associated with vision. The person perceives this stimulation as specks of light, but those specks provide enough vision for him or her to read two-inch-high letters or visually locate large objects. Although much research remains before techniques like this will re-create the vision provided by normal eyesight, the initial results have been promising (Dobelle, 2000; Gupta & Petersen, 2002).

Once they are perfected, these technologies will drastically change the way users perceive the world. By enhancing people's perceptual abilities, they present the opportunity to experience everyday life in an exciting new way.

RETHINK

Do you think Peter Artinian and his wife made the wrong decision by denying his daughter a cochlear implant? What are some possible negative effects of providing hearing and sight to people who have never experienced those senses? How might psychologists help people adjust to these new experiences?

Frequency theory of hearing: The theory that the entire basilar membrane acts like a microphone, vibrating as a whole in response to a sound.

However, place theory does not tell the full story of hearing, because very low frequency sounds trigger neurons across such a wide area of the basilar membrane that no single site is involved. Consequently, an additional explanation for hearing has been proposed: frequency theory. The **frequency theory of hearing** suggests that the entire basilar membrane acts like a microphone, vibrating as a whole in response to a sound. According to this explanation, the nerve receptors send out signals that are tied directly to the frequency (the number of wave crests per second) of the sounds to which we are exposed, with the number of nerve impulses being a direct function of a sound's frequency. Thus, the higher the pitch of a sound (and therefore the greater the frequency of its wave crests), the greater the number of nerve impulses that are transmitted up the auditory nerve to the brain.

Neither place theory nor frequency theory provides the full explanation for hearing (Hirsh & Watson, 1996; Hudspeth, 2000). Place theory provides a better explanation for the sensing of high-frequency sounds, whereas frequency theory explains what happens when low-frequency sounds are encountered. Medium-frequency sounds incorporate both processes.

After an auditory message leaves the ear, it is transmitted to the auditory cortex of the brain through a complex series of neural interconnections. As the message is transmitted, it is communicated through neurons that respond to specific types of sounds. Within the auditory cortex itself, there are neurons that respond selectively to very specific sorts of sound features, such as clicks and whistles. Some neurons respond only to a specific pattern of sounds, such as a steady tone but not an intermittent one. Furthermore, specific neurons transfer information about a sound's location through their particular pattern of firing (Hackett & Kass, 2003; Polyakov & Pratt, 2003).

If we were to analyze the configuration of the cells in the auditory cortex, we would find that neighboring cells are responsive to similar frequencies. The auditory cortex, then, provides us with a "map" of sound frequencies, just as the visual cortex furnishes a representation of the visual field.

BALANCE: THE UPS AND DOWNS OF LIFE

Semicircular canals: Three tubelike structures of the inner ear containing fluid that sloshes through them when the head moves, signaling rotational or angular movement to the brain.

Several structures of the ear are related more to our sense of balance than to our hearing. The **semicircular canals** of the inner ear (refer to Figure 1) consist of three

The weightlessness of the ear's otoliths produces space sickness in most astronauts.

tubes containing fluid that sloshes through them when the head moves, signaling rotational or angular movement to the brain. The pull on our bodies caused by the acceleration of forward, backward, or up-and-down motion, as well as the constant pull of gravity, is sensed by the **otoliths,** tiny, motion-sensitive crystals. When we move, these crystals shift like sands on a windy beach. The brain's inexperience in interpreting messages from the weightless otoliths is the cause of the space sickness commonly experienced by two-thirds of all space travelers (Flam, 1991; Stern & Koch, 1996).

Otoliths: Tiny, motion-sensitive crystals within the semicircular canals that sense body acceleration.

Smell and Taste

Until he bit into a piece of raw cabbage on that February evening . . . , Raymond Fowler had not thought much about the sense of taste.

The cabbage, part of a pasta dish he was preparing for his family's dinner, had an odd, burning taste, but he did not pay it much attention. Then a few minutes later, his daughter handed him a glass of cola, and he took a swallow. "It was like sulfuric acid," he said. "It was like the hottest thing you could imagine boring into your mouth" (Goode, 1999b, pp. D1–D2).

It was evident that something was very wrong with Fowler's sense of taste. After extensive testing, it became clear that he had damaged the nerves involved in his sense of taste, probably because of a viral infection or a medicine he was taking. (Luckily for him, a few months later his sense of taste returned to normal.)

Even without disruptions in our ability to perceive the world such as those experienced by Fowler, we all know the important roles that taste and smell play. We'll consider these two senses next.

SMELL

Although many animals have keener abilities to detect odors than we do, the human sense of smell *(olfaction)* permits us to detect more than 10,000 separate smells. We also have a good memory for smells, and long-forgotten events and memories can be brought back with the mere whiff of an odor associated with a memory (Gillyatt, 1997; Schiffman et al., 2002; DiLorenzo & Youngentob, 2003).

Results of "sniff tests" have shown that women generally have a better sense of smell than men do (Engen, 1987). People also seem to have the ability to distinguish males from females on the basis of smell alone. In one experiment, blindfolded students who were asked to sniff the breath of a female or male volunteer who was hidden from view were able to distinguish the sex of the donor at better than chance levels. People can also distinguish happy from sad emotions by sniffing underarm smells, and women are able to identify their babies solely on the basis of smell just a few hours after birth (Doty et al., 1982; Haviland-Jones & Chen, 1999).

Our understanding of the mechanisms that underlie the sense of smell is just beginning to emerge. We do know that the sense of smell is sparked when the molecules of a substance enter the nasal passages and meet *olfactory cells,* the receptor neurons of the nose, which are spread across the nasal cavity. More than 1,000 separate types of receptors have been identified on those cells so far. Each of these receptors is so specialized that it responds only to a small band of different odors. The responses of the separate olfactory cells are then transmitted to the brain, where they are combined into recognition of a particular smell (Rubin & Katz, 1999).

There is increasing evidence that smell can also act as a hidden means of communication for humans. It has long been known that nonhumans release *pheromones,*

More than 1000 receptor cells, known as olfactory cells, are spread across the nasal cavity. The cells are specialized to react to particular odors. Do you think it is possible to "train" the nose to pick up a greater number of odors?

chemicals secreted into the environment by individuals that produce a reaction in other members of the same species, permitting the transmission of messages such as sexual availability. For instance, the vaginal secretions of female monkeys contain pheromones that stimulate sexual interest in male monkeys (Holy, Dulac, & Meister, 2000).

Although it seems reasonable that humans might also communicate through the release of pheromones, the evidence is still scanty. Women's vaginal secretions contain chemicals similar to those found in monkeys, but in humans the smells do not seem to be related to sexual activity. However, the presence of these substances may explain why women who live together for long periods of time tend to start their menstrual cycles on the same day (McCoy & Pitino, 2002; McClintock et al., 2002).

TASTE

The sense of taste *(gustation)* involves receptor cells that respond to just four basic stimulus qualities: sweet, sour, salty, and bitter. (There also may be a fifth stimulus category, which is a flavor called *umami*—involving food stimuli with amino acids—but the evidence is not firm; Smith & Margolskee, 2001).

Although the specialization of the receptor cells leads them to respond most strongly to a particular type of taste, they also seem capable of responding to other tastes as well. Ultimately, every taste is simply a combination of the basic flavor qualities, in the same way that the primary colors blend into a vast variety of shades and hues (Gilberson, Damak, & Margolskee, 2000; Dilorenzo & Youngentob, 2003).

The receptor cells for taste are located in roughly 10,000 *taste buds,* which are distributed across the tongue and other parts of the mouth and throat. The taste buds wear out and are replaced every ten days or so. That's a good thing, because if our taste buds weren't constantly reproducing, we'd lose the ability to taste after we'd accidentally burned our tongues.

The sense of taste differs significantly from one person to another, largely as a result of genetic factors. Some people, dubbed "supertasters," are highly sensitive to taste; they have twice as many taste receptors as "nontasters," who are relatively insensitive to taste. Supertasters (who, for unknown reasons, are more likely to be female than male) find sweets sweeter, cream creamier, and spicy dishes spicier, and weaker concentrations of flavor are enough to satisfy any cravings they may have. In contrast, because they aren't so sensitive to taste, nontasters may seek out relatively

There are 10,000 taste buds on the tongue and other parts of the mouth. Taste buds wear out and are replaced every ten days. What would happen if taste buds were not regenerated?

Take a Taste Test

1. Taste Bud Count
   Punch a hole with a standard hole punch in a square of wax paper. Paint the front of your tongue with a cotton swab dipped in blue food coloring. Put wax paper on the tip of your tongue, just to the right of center. With a flashlight and magnifying glass, count the number of pink, unstained circles. They contain taste buds.
2. Sweet Taste
   Rinse your mouth with water before tasting each sample. Put 1/2 cup sugar in a measuring cup, and then add enough water to make 1 cup. Mix. Coat front half of your tongue, including the tip, with a cotton swab dipped in the solution. Wait a few moments. Rate the sweetness according to the scale shown below.
3. Salt Taste
   Put 2 teaspoons of salt in a measuring cup and add enough water to make 1 cup. Repeat the steps listed above, rating how salty the solution is.
4. Spicy Taste
   Add 1 teaspoon of Tabasco sauce to 1 cup of water. Apply with a cotton swab to first half inch of the tongue, Including the tip. Keep your tongue out of your mouth until the burn reaches a peak, then rate the burn according to the scale.

TASTE SCALE

Barely Detectable	**Weak**	**Moderate**	**Strong**	**Very Strong**	**Strongest Imaginable Sensation**

0	10	20	30	40	50	60	70	80	90	100

	SUPERTASTERS	NONTASTERS
No. of taste buds	25 on Average	10
Sweet rating	56 on Average	32
Tabasco	64 on Average	31

Average tasters lie in between supertasters and nontasters. Bartoshuk and Lucchina lack the data at this time to rate salt reliably, but you can compare your results with others taking the test.

FIGURE 4 All tongues are not created equal, according to taste researchers Linda Bartoshuk and Laurie Lucchina. Instead, they suggest that the intensity of a flavor experienced by a given person is determined by that person's genetic background. This taste test can help determine if you are a nontaster, average taster, or supertaster. (Source: Bartoshuk & Lucchina, 1997.)

sweeter and fattier foods in order to maximize the taste. As a consequence, they may be prone to obesity (Bartoshuk & Drewnowski, 1997; Bartoshuk, 2000). To determine your own taste sensitivity, try the test in Figure 4.

The Skin Senses: Touch, Pressure, Temperature, and Pain

It started innocently when Jennifer Darling hurt her right wrist during gym class. At first it seemed like a simple sprain. But even though the initial injury healed, the excruciating, burning pain accompanying it did not go away. Instead, it spread to her other arm and then to her legs. The pain, which Jennifer described as similar to "a hot iron on your arm," was unbearable—and never stopped.

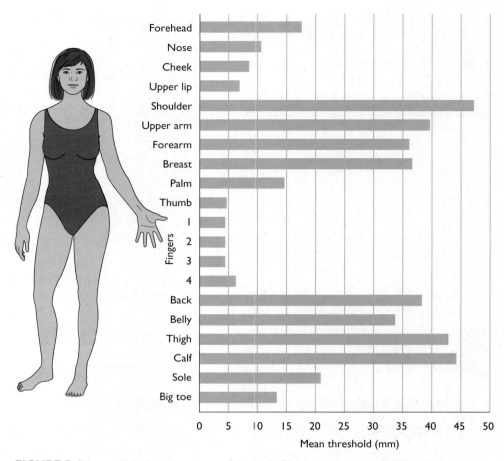

FIGURE 5 Skin sensitivity in various areas of the body. The lower the mean threshold is, the more sensitive a body part is. The fingers and thumb, lips, nose, cheeks, and big toe are the most sensitive. Why do you think certain areas are more sensitive than others? (Source: From Kenshalo, *The Skin Senses*, 1968. Courtesy of Charles C Thomas, Publisher, Ltd., Springfield, Illinois.)

The source of Darling's pain turned out to be a rare condition known as "reflex sympathetic dystrophy syndrome," or RSDS for short. For a victim of RSDS, a stimulus as mild as a gentle breeze or the touch of a feather can produce agony. Even bright sunlight or a loud noise can trigger intense pain.

Pain like Darling's can be devastating, yet a lack of pain can be equally bad. If you never experienced pain, for instance, you might not notice that your arm had brushed against a hot pan, and you would suffer a severe burn. Similarly, without the warning sign of abdominal pain that typically accompanies an inflamed appendix, your appendix might eventually rupture, spreading a fatal infection throughout your body.

In fact, all our **skin senses**—touch, pressure, temperature, and pain—play a critical role in survival, making us aware of potential danger to our bodies. Most of these senses operate through nerve receptor cells located at various depths throughout the skin, distributed unevenly throughout the body. For example, some areas, such as the fingertips, have many more receptor cells sensitive to touch and as a consequence are notably more sensitive than other areas of the body (Gardner & Kandel, 2000; see Figure 5).

Probably the most extensively researched skin sense is pain, and with good reason: People consult physicians and take medication for pain more than for any other symptom or condition. Some $1.8 billion is spent annually on painkillers (Price, 2000; Kalb, 2001a).

Skin senses: The senses of touch, pressure, temperature, and pain.

PowerWeb: Pain and Its Mysteries

www.mhhe.com/feldmanup7

Pain is a response to a great variety of different kinds of stimuli. A light that is too bright can produce pain, and sound that is too loud can be painful. One explanation is that pain is an outcome of cell injury; when a cell is damaged, regardless of the source of damage, it releases a chemical called *substance P* that transmits pain messages to the brain.

But the experience of pain is not just a physical reaction to particular stimuli. For example, women report that the pain experienced in childbirth is moderated to some degree by the joyful nature of the situation. In contrast, even a minor stimulus can produce the perception of strong pain if it is accompanied by anxiety (like a visit to the dentist). Clearly, then, pain is a perceptual response that depends heavily on our emotions and thoughts (Turk, 1994; Gatchel & Weisberg, 2000; Montgomery & Bovbjerg, 2003).

According to the **gate-control theory of pain,** particular nerve receptors in the spinal cord lead to specific areas of the brain related to pain. When these receptors are activated because of an injury or problem with a part of the body, a "gate" to the brain is opened, allowing us to experience the sensation of pain.

However, another set of neural receptors is able, when stimulated, to close the "gate" to the brain, thereby reducing the experience of pain. The gate can be shut in two different ways. First, other impulses can overwhelm the nerve pathways relating to pain, which are spread throughout the brain. In this case, nonpainful stimuli compete with and sometimes displace the neuronal message of pain, thereby shutting off the painful stimulus. This explains why rubbing the skin around an injury helps reduce pain. The competing stimuli from the rubbing can overpower the painful ones (Wall & Melzack, 1989; Kakigi, Matsuda, & Kuroda, 1993).

Psychological factors account for the second way a gate can be shut. Depending on an individual's current emotions, interpretation of events, and previous experience, the brain can close a gate by sending a message down the spinal cord to an injured area, producing a reduction in or relief from pain. Thus, soldiers who are injured in battle may experience no pain—the surprising situation in more than half of all combat injuries. The lack of pain probably occurs because a soldier experiences such relief at still being alive that the brain sends a signal to the injury site to shut down the pain gate (Turk, 1994; Gatchel & Weisberg, 2000; Pincus & Morley, 2001).

Gate-control theory also may explain cultural differences in the experience of pain. Some of these variations are astounding. For example, in India people who participate in the "hook-swinging" ritual to celebrate the power of the gods have steel hooks embedded under the skin and muscles of their backs. During the ritual, they swing from a pole, suspended by the hooks. What would seem likely to induce excruciating pain instead produces a state of celebration and near euphoria. In fact, when the hooks are later removed, the wounds heal quickly, and after two weeks almost no visible marks remain (Kosambi, 1967; Melzack & Wall, 2001).

Gate-control theory suggests that the lack of pain is due to a message from the participant's brain, which shuts down the pain pathways. Gate-control theory also may explain the effectiveness of *acupuncture*, an ancient Chinese technique in which sharp needles are inserted into various parts of the body. The sensation from the needles may close the gateway to the brain, reducing the experience of pain. It is also possible that the body's own painkillers, the endorphins, as well as positive and negative emotions, can play a role in opening and closing the gate (Daitz, 2002; Fee et al., 2002).

Gate-control theory of pain: The theory that particular nerve receptors lead to specific areas of the brain related to pain.

Pain—whether a pounding, aching, stinging soreness or a burning feeling—is one sensation you cannot easily overlook. For many people, pain is unceasing: According to the American Pain Foundation, some 50 million people in the United States suffer from chronic pain (Clay, 2002).

To fight pain, psychologists and medical specialists have devised several strategies. Among the most important

BECOMING AN INFORMED CONSUMER

of Psychology

Managing Pain

The ancient practice of acupuncture is still used in the twenty-first century. How does the gate-control theory of pain explain how acupuncture works?

approaches (Gatchel & Turk, 1996; Keefe & France, 1999; Kalb, 2001b) are the following:

- *Medication.* Painkilling drugs are the most popular treatment in fighting pain. Drugs range from those which directly treat the source of the pain—such as reducing swelling in painful joints—to those which work on the symptoms. Medication can be in the form of pills, injections, or liquids. In a recent innovation, drugs are pumped directly into the spinal cord (Wallace, 2002).

- *Nerve and brain stimulation.* Pain can sometimes be relieved when a low-voltage electric current is passed through the specific part of the body that is in pain. In even more severe cases, electrodes can be implanted surgically directly into the brain, or a handheld battery pack can stimulate nerve cells to provide direct relief. This process is known as *transcutaneous electrical nerve stimulation,* or *TENS* (Ross, 2000; Campbell & Ditto, 2002).

- *Light therapy.* One of the newest forms of pain reduction involves exposure to specific wavelengths of red or infrared light. Certain kinds of light increase the production of enzymes that may promote healing (Whelan et al., 2001; Under-wood, 2003).

- *Hypnosis.* For people who can be hypnotized, hypnosis can greatly relieve pain (Nash, 2001; Ketterhagen, VandeVusse, & Berner, 2002).

- *Biofeedback and relaxation techniques.* Using *biofeedback,* people learn to control "involuntary" functions such as heartbeat and respiration. If the pain involves muscles, as in tension headaches or back pain, sufferers can be trained to relax their bodies systematically (National Institutes of Health, 1996; Middaugh & Pawlick, 2002).

- *Surgery.* In one of the most extreme methods, nerve fibers that carry pain messages to the brain can be cut surgically. Still, because of the danger that other bodily functions will be affected, surgery is a treatment of last resort, used most frequently with dying patients (Cullinane, Chu, & Mamelak, 2002).

- *Cognitive restructuring.* Cognitive treatments are effective for people who continually say to themselves, "This pain will never stop," "The pain is ruining my life," or "I can't take it anymore" and are thereby likely to make their pain even worse. By substituting more positive ways of thinking, people can increase their sense of control—and actually reduce the pain they experience. Teaching people to rewrite their pain "script" through therapy can result in significant reductions in their perception of pain (Mufson, 1999; Pincus & Morley, 2001).

To learn more about chronic pain, you can consult the American Pain Society (847-375-4715; www.ampainsoc.org) or the American Chronic Pain Association (916-632-0922; www.theacpa.org). Many hospitals have clinics that specialize in the treatment of pain. Any pain clinic, though, should be approved by the Commission for the Accreditation of Rehabilitative Facilities or the Joint Commission on the Accreditation of Health-Care Organizations.

RECAP/EVALUATE/RETHINK

RECAP

What role does the ear play in the senses of sound, motion, and balance?

- ▶ Sound, motion, and balance are centered in the ear. Sounds, in the form of vibrating air waves, enter through the outer ear and travel through the auditory canal until they reach the eardrum. (p. 115)
- ▶ The vibrations of the eardrum are transmitted into the middle ear, which consists of three bones: the hammer, the anvil, and the stirrup. These bones transmit vibrations to the oval window. (p. 115)
- ▶ In the inner ear, vibrations move into the cochlea, which encloses the basilar membrane. Hair cells on the basilar membrane change the mechanical energy of sound waves into nerve impulses that are transmitted to the brain. The ear is also involved in the sense of balance and motion. (p. 116)
- ▶ Sound has a number of physical characteristics, including frequency and amplitude. The place theory of hearing and the frequency theory of hearing explain the processes by which we distinguish sounds of varying frequency and intensity. (p. 118)

How do smell and taste function?

- ▶ Smell employs olfactory cells (the receptor cells of the nose), and taste is centered in the tongue's taste buds. (p. 121)

What are the skin senses, and how do they relate to the experience of pain?

- ▶ The skin senses are responsible for the experiences of touch, pressure, temperature, and pain. Gate-control theory suggests that particular nerve receptors, when activated, open a "gate" to specific areas of the brain related

to pain, and that another set of receptors closes the gate when stimulated. (p. 123)
- ▶ Among the techniques used most frequently to alleviate pain are medication, hypnosis, biofeedback, relaxation techniques, surgery, nerve and brain stimulation, and cognitive therapy. (p. 126)

EVALUATE

1. The tubelike passage leading from the outer ear is known as the _____ _____.
2. The purpose of the eardrum is to protect the sensitive nerves underneath it. It serves no purpose in actual hearing. True or false?
3. The three middle ear bones transmit their sound to the _____.
4. The _____ theory of hearing states that the entire basilar membrane responds to a sound, vibrating more or less, depending on the nature of the sound.
5. The three fluid-filled tubes in the inner ear that are responsible for our sense of balance are known as the _____ _____.
6. The _____ - _____ theory states that when certain skin receptors are activated as a result of an injury, a "pathway" to the brain is opened, allowing pain to be experienced.

RETHINK

1. Much research is being conducted on repairing faulty sensory organs through devices such as personal guidance systems and eyeglasses, among others. Do you think that researchers should attempt to improve normal sensory capabilities beyond their "natural" range (e.g., make human visual or audio capabilities more sensitive than

normal)? What benefits might this bring? What problems might it cause?

2. Why might sensitivity to pheromones have evolved differently in humans than in other species? What cultural factors might have played a role?

Answers to Evaluate Questions

1. auditory canal; 2. false; it vibrates when sound waves hit it, and transmits the sound; 3. oval window; 4. frequency; 5. semicircular canals; 6. gate-control

KEY TERMS

sound p. 115
eardrum p. 115
cochlea (KOKE lee uh) p. 116

basilar membrane p. 116
hair cells p. 116
place theory of hearing p. 118

frequency theory of hearing p. 120
semicircular canals p. 120
otoliths p. 121

skin senses p. 124
gate-control theory of pain p. 125

Perceptual Organization: Constructing Our View of the World

Consider the vase shown in Figure 1a for a moment. Or is it a vase? Take another look, and instead you may see the profiles of two people.

Now that an alternative interpretation has been pointed out, you will probably shift back and forth between the two interpretations. Similarly, if you examine the shapes in Figure 1b and 1c long enough, you will probably experience a shift in what you're seeing. The reason for these reversals is this: Because each figure is two-dimensional, the usual means we employ for distinguishing the *figure* (the object being perceived) from the *ground* (the background or spaces within the object) do not work.

The fact that we can look at the same figure in more than one way illustrates an important point. We do not just passively respond to visual stimuli that happen to fall on our retinas. Instead, we actively try to organize and make sense of what we see.

We turn now from a focus on the initial response to a stimulus (sensation) to what our minds make of that stimulus—perception. Perception is a constructive process by which we go beyond the stimuli that are presented to us and attempt to construct a meaningful situation.

▲ ▲ ▲

What principles underlie our organization of the visual world, allowing us to make sense of our environment?

How are we able to perceive the world in three dimensions when our retinas are capable of sensing only two-dimensional images?

What clues do visual illusions give us about our understanding of general perceptual mechanisms?

a. b. c.

FIGURE 1 When the usual cues we use to distinguish figure from ground are absent, we may shift back and forth between different views of the same figure. If you look at each of these objects long enough, you'll probably experience a shift in what you're seeing. In (a), you can see either a vase or the profiles of two people. In (b), the shaded portion of the figure, called a Necker cube, can appear to be either the front or the back of the cube. Finally, in (c), you'll be able to see a face of a woman if you look at the drawing long enough.

The Gestalt Laws of Organization

Some of the most basic perceptual processes can be described by a series of principles that focus on the ways we organize bits and pieces of information into meaningful wholes. These are known as **gestalt laws of organization,** set forth in the early 1900s by a group of German psychologists who studied patterns, or *gestalts* (Wertheimer, 1923). Those psychologists discovered a number of important principles that are valid for visual (as well as auditory) stimuli, illustrated in Figure 2: closure, proximity, similarity, and simplicity.

Figure 2a illustrates *closure*. We usually group elements to form enclosed or complete figures rather than open ones. We tend to ignore the breaks in Figure 2a and concentrate on the overall form. Figure 2b demonstrates the principle of *proximity*: We perceive elements that are closer together as grouped together. As a result, we tend to see pairs of dots rather than a row of single dots in Figure 2b.

Elements that are *similar* in appearance we perceive as grouped together. We see, then, horizontal rows of circles and squares in Figure 2c instead of vertical mixed columns. Finally, in a general sense, the overriding gestalt principle is *simplicity*: When we observe a pattern, we perceive it in the most basic, straightforward manner that we can. For example, most of us see Figure 2d as a square with lines on two sides, rather than as the block letter *W* on top of the letter *M.* If we have a choice of interpretations, we generally opt for the simpler one.

Although gestalt psychology no longer plays a prominent role in contemporary psychology, its legacy endures. One fundamental gestalt principle that remains influential is that two objects considered together form a whole that is different from the simple combination of the objects. Gestalt psychologists argued, quite convincingly, that the perception of stimuli in our environment goes well beyond the individual elements that we sense. Instead, it represents an active, constructive process carried out within the brain. There, bits and pieces of sensations are put together to make something more meaningful than the separate elements (Humphreys & Muller, 2000; Lehar, 2003; see Figure 3).

Gestalt laws of organization: A series of principles that describe how we organize bits and pieces of information into meaningful wholes.

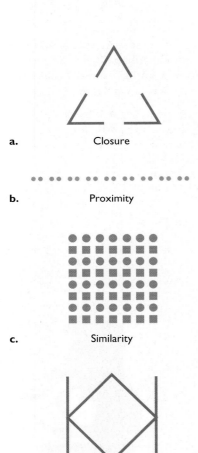

a.   Closure

b.   Proximity

c.   Similarity

d.   Simplicity

FIGURE 2 Organizing these various bits and pieces of information into meaningful wholes constitutes some of the most basic processes of perception, which are summed up in the gestalt laws of organization. Do you think any other species share this organizational tendency? How might we find out?

FIGURE 3 Although at first it is difficult to distinguish anything in this drawing, keep looking, and eventually you'll probably be able to see the figure of a dog (James, 1966). The dog represents a *gestalt*, or perceptual whole, which is something greater than the sum of the individual elements.

Feature Analysis: Focusing on the Parts of the Whole

A more recent approach to perception—**feature analysis**—considers how we perceive a shape, pattern, object, or scene by reacting first to the individual elements that make it up. We then use those individual components to understand the overall nature of what we are perceiving. Feature analysis begins with the evidence that individual neurons in the brain are sensitive to specific spatial configurations, such as angles, curves, shapes, and edges. The presence of these neurons suggests that any stimulus can be broken down into a series of component features. For example, the letter *R* is a combination of a vertical line, a diagonal line, and a half circle (see Figure 4).

According to feature analysis, when we encounter a stimulus—such as a letter—the brain's perceptual processing system initially responds to its component parts. Each of those parts is compared with information about components that is stored in memory. When the specific components we perceive match up with a particular set of components we have encountered previously, we are able to identify the stimulus (Spillmann & Werner, 1990; Ullman, 1996).

According to some research, the way we perceive complex objects is similar to the way we perceive simple letters—viewing them in terms of their component elements. For instance, just 36 fundamental components seem to be capable of producing over 150 million objects—more than enough to describe the 30,000 separate objects that the average person can recognize (see Figure 5). Ultimately, these component features are combined into a representation of the whole object in the brain. This representation is compared to existing memories, thereby permitting us to identify the object (Biederman, 1987, 1990).

Psychologist Anne Treisman has a different perspective. She suggests that the perception of objects is best understood in terms of a two-stage process. In the *preattentive*

Feature analysis: A theory of perception according to which we perceive a shape, pattern, object, or scene by reacting first to the individual elements that make it up.

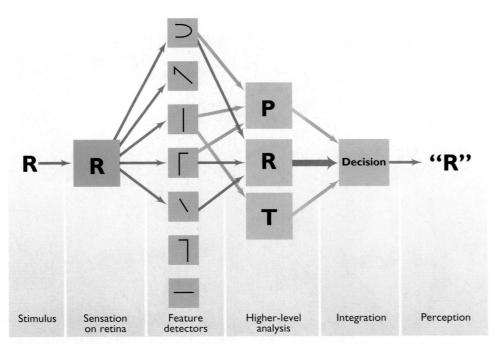

FIGURE 4 According to feature analysis approaches to perception, we break down stimuli into their component parts and then compare those parts to information that is stored in memory. When we find a match, we are able to identify the stimulus. In this example, the process by which we recognize the letter *R* is illustrated (Goldstein, 1984).

FIGURE 5 Components and simple objects created from them. (Source: Adapted from Biederman, 1990.)

stage, we focus on the physical features of a stimulus, such as its size, shape, color, orientation, and direction of movement. This initial stage takes little or no conscious effort. In the *focused-attention stage,* we pay attention to particular features of an object, choosing and emphasizing features that were initially considered separately (Treisman, 1988, 1993).

For example, take a look at the two upside-down photos in Figure 6. Probably, your first impression is that you're viewing two similar photos of the Mona Lisa. But now look at them right side up, and you'll be surprised to note that one of the photos has distorted features. In Treisman's terms, your initial scanning of the photos took place at the preattentive stage. When you turned them over, however, you

FIGURE 6 Double Mona Lisas? These pictures appear similar at first glance because only our preattentive process is active. When the pictures are seen upright, the true detail in the two faces is revealed. (Source: Julesz, 1986.)

immediately progressed to the focused-attention stage, where you were able to consider the actual nature of the stimuli more carefully.

Treisman's perspective (and other approaches to feature analysis), compared with that of proponents of the gestaltist perspective, raises a fundamental question about the nature of perceptual processes: Is perception based mainly on consideration of the component parts of a stimulus, or is it grounded primarily in perception of the stimulus as a whole? This is the issue to which we turn next.

Top-Down and Bottom-Up Processing

Ca- yo- re-d t-is -en-en-e, w-ic- ha- ev-ry -hi-d l-tt-r m-ss-ng? It probably won't take you too long to figure out that it says, "Can you read this sentence, which has every third letter missing?"

If perception were based primarily on breaking down a stimulus into its most basic elements, understanding the sentence, as well as other ambiguous stimuli, would not be possible. The fact that you were probably able to recognize such an imprecise stimulus illustrates that perception proceeds along two different avenues, called top-down processing and bottom-up processing.

In **top-down processing,** perception is guided by higher-level knowledge, experience, expectations, and motivations. You were able to figure out the meaning of the sentence with the missing letters because of your prior reading experience, and because written English contains redundancies. Not every letter of each word is necessary to decode its meaning. Moreover, your expectations played a role in your being able to read the sentence. You were probably expecting a statement that had *something* to do with psychology, not the lyrics to an Eminem song.

Top-down processing is illustrated by the importance of context in determining how we perceive objects. Look, for example, at Figure 7. Most of us perceive that the first row consists of the letters *A* through *F,* while the second contains the numbers 10 through 14. But take a more careful look and you'll see that the "B" and the "13" are identical. Clearly, our perception is affected by our expectations about the two sequences—even though the two stimuli are exactly the same.

However, top-down processing cannot occur on its own. Even though top-down processing allows us to fill in the gaps in ambiguous and out-of-context stimuli, we would be unable to perceive the meaning of such stimuli without bottom-up processing. **Bottom-up processing** consists of recognizing and processing information about the individual components of the stimuli. We would make no headway in our recognition of the sentence without being able to perceive the individual shapes that make up the letters. Some perception, then, occurs at the level of the patterns and features of each of the separate letters.

It should be apparent that top-down and bottom-up processing occur simultaneously, and interact with each other, in our perception of the world around us. Bottom-up processing permits us to process the fundamental characteristics of stimuli,

Top-down processing: Perception that is guided by higher-level knowledge, experience, expectations, and motivations.

Bottom-up processing: Perception that consists of recognizing and processing information about the individual components of stimuli.

A B C D E F
10 11 12 13 14

FIGURE 7 The power of context is shown in this figure. Note how the B and the 13 are identical. (Source: Coren & Ward, 1989.)

whereas top-down processing allows us to bring our experience to bear on perception. As we learn more about the complex processes involved in perception, we are developing a better understanding of how the brain continually interprets information from the senses and permits us to make responses appropriate to the environment.

Perceptual Constancy

Consider what happens as you finish a conversation with a friend and she begins to walk away from you. As you watch her walk down the street, the image on your retina becomes smaller and smaller. Do you wonder why she is shrinking?

Of course not. Despite the very real change in the size of the retinal image, you factor into your thinking the knowledge that your friend is moving farther away from you because of perceptual constancy. *Perceptual constancy* is a phenomenon in which physical objects are perceived as unvarying and consistent despite changes in their appearance or in the physical environment.

One of the most dramatic examples of perceptual constancy involves the rising moon. When the moon first appears at night, close to the horizon, it seems to be huge—much larger than when it is high in the sky later in the evening. You may have thought that the apparent size of the moon was caused by the moon's being physically closer to the earth when it first appears. In fact, though, this is not the case at all.

Instead, the moon appears to be larger when it is close to the horizon primarily because of the phenomenon of perceptual constancy. When the moon is near the horizon, the perceptual cues of intervening terrain and objects such as trees on the horizon produce a misleading sense of distance. Because perceptual constancy leads us to take that distance into account when we view the moon, we perceive the moon as relatively large. In contrast, when the moon is high in the sky, we see it by itself, and perceptual constancy leads us to perceive it as relatively small. To prove this, try looking at the moon when it is relatively low on the horizon through a paper-towel tube; the moon suddenly will appear to "shrink" back to normal size (Coren & Aks, 1990; Coren, 1992b).

In addition to size constancy, other factors have been hypothesized to produce the moon illusion. For example, some scientists suggest observers consider the moon seen on the horizon to be further away than when they see the moon overhead. Their brains then use this information to conclude that because the moon on the horizon

When the moon is near the horizon, we do not see it by itself and perceptual constancy leads us to take into account a misleading sense of distance.

is so far away, it must be very large, and consequently their brains exaggerate its size (Kaufman & Kaufman, 2000).

Although we don't know which explanation for the moon illusion is most accurate, it is clear that perceptual constancy is a primary ingredient in our susceptibility to the illusion. Furthermore, perceptual constancy occurs not just in terms of size (as with the moon illusion) but with shape and color as well. Despite the varying images on the retina as a plane approaches, flies overhead, and disappears, we do not perceive the plane as changing shape (Redding, 2002).

Depth Perception: Translating 2-D to 3-D

As sophisticated as the retina is, the images projected onto it are flat and two-dimensional. Yet the world around us is three-dimensional, and we perceive it that way. How do we make the transformation from 2-D to 3-D?

The ability to view the world in three dimensions and to perceive distance—a skill known as *depth perception*—is due largely to the fact that we have two eyes. Because there is a certain distance between the eyes, a slightly different image reaches each retina. The brain then integrates the two images into one composite view. However, it does not ignore the difference in images, which is known as *binocular disparity*. The disparity allows the brain to estimate the distance of an object from us.

You can get a sense of binocular disparity for yourself. Hold a pencil at arm's length and look at it first with one eye and then with the other. There is little difference between the two views relative to the background. Now bring the pencil just six inches away from your face, and try the same thing. This time you will perceive a greater difference between the two views. You can also learn more about depth perception by trying **Interactivity 13–1.**

INTERACTIVITY 13–1

Depth perception

The fact that the discrepancy between the images in the two eyes varies according to the distance of objects that we view provides us with a means of determining distance. If we view two objects and one is considerably closer to us than the other is, the retinal disparity will be relatively large and we will have a greater sense of depth between the two. However, if the two objects are a similar distance from us, the retinal disparity will be minor, and we will perceive them as being a similar distance from us.

In some cases, certain cues permit us to obtain a sense of depth and distance with just one eye. These cues are known as *monocular cues.* One monocular cue—*motion parallax*—is the change in position of an object on the retina caused by movement of your body relative to the object. For example, suppose you are a passenger in a moving car, and you focus your eye on a stable object such as a tree. Objects that are closer than the tree will appear to move backward, and the nearer the object is, the more quickly it will appear to move. In contrast, objects beyond the tree will seem to move at a slower speed, but in the same direction as you are. Your brain is able to use these cues to calculate the relative distances of the tree and other objects.

Similarly, experience has taught us that if two objects are the same size, the one that makes a smaller image on the retina is farther away than is the one that provides a larger image—an example of the monocular cue of *relative size.* But it's not just size of an object that provides information about distance; the quality of the image on the retina helps us judge distance. The monocular cue of *texture gradient* provides information about distance because the details of things that are far away are less distinct.

Railroad tracks that seem to join together in the distance are an example of linear perspective.

Finally, anyone who has ever seen railroad tracks that seem to join together in the distance knows that distant objects appear to be closer together than are nearer ones, a phenomenon called linear perspective. People use *linear perspective* as a monocular cue in estimating distance, allowing the two-dimensional image on the retina to record the three-dimensional world (Bruce, Green, & Georgeson, 1997; Dobbins et al., 1998; Shimono & Wade, 2002).

Motion Perception: As the World Turns

When a batter tries to hit a pitched ball, the most important factor is the motion of the ball. How is a batter able to judge the speed and location of a target that is moving at some 90 miles per hour?

The answer rests in part on several cues that provide us with relevant information about the perception of motion. For one thing, the movement of an object across the retina is typically perceived relative to some stable, unmoving background. Moreover, if the stimulus is heading toward us, the image on the retina will expand in size, filling more and more of the visual field. In such cases, we assume that the stimulus is approaching—not that it is an expanding stimulus viewed at a constant distance.

It is not, however, just the movement of images across the retina that brings about the perception of motion. If it were, we would perceive the world as moving every time we moved our heads. Instead, one of the critical things we learn about perception is to factor information about our own head and eye movements along with information about changes in the retinal image.

Perceptual Illusions: The Deceptions of Perceptions

If you look carefully at the Parthenon, one of the most famous buildings of ancient Greece, still standing at the top of an Athens hill, you'll see that it was built with a bulge on one side. If it didn't have that bulge—and quite a few other "tricks" like it, such as columns that incline inward—it would look as if it were crooked and about to fall down. Instead, it appears to stand completely straight, at right angles to the ground.

The fact that the Parthenon appears to be completely upright is the result of a series of visual illusions. **Visual illusions** are physical stimuli that consistently produce errors in perception. In the case of the Parthenon, the building appears to be completely square, as illustrated in Figure 8a. However, if it had been built that way, it would look to us as it does in Figure 8b. The reason for this is an illusion that makes right angles placed above a line appear as if they were bent. To offset the illusion, the Parthenon was constructed as in Figure 8c, with a slight upward curvature.

Visual illusions: Physical stimuli that consistently produce errors in perception.

Such perceptual insights did not stop with the Greeks. Modern-day architects and designers also take visual distortions into account in their planning. For example, the New Orleans Superdome makes use of several visual tricks. Its seats vary in color throughout the stadium to give the appearance, from a distance, that there is always a full house. The carpeting in some of the sloping halls has stripes that make people slow their pace by producing the perception that they are moving faster than they actually are. The same illusion is used at toll booths on superhighways. Stripes painted on the pavement in front of the toll booths make drivers feel that they are moving more rapidly than they actually are and cause them to decelerate quickly.

The implications of visual illusions go beyond the attractiveness of buildings. For instance, suppose you were an air traffic controller watching a radar screen like the one shown in Figure 9a. You might be tempted to sit back and relax as the two planes, whose flight paths are indicated in the figure, drew closer and closer together. If you did, however, the result might be an air disaster. Although it looks as if the two planes will miss each other, they are headed for a collision. Investigation has suggested that some 70 to 80 percent of all airplane accidents are caused by pilot errors of one sort or another (Krause, 2003; Shappell & Wiegmann, 2003).

The flight-path illustration provides an example of a well-known visual illusion called the *Poggendorf illusion*. As you can see in Figure 9b, the Poggendorf illusion, when stripped down to its basics, gives the impression that line X would pass *below* line Y if it were extended through the pipelike figure, instead of heading directly toward line Y as it actually does.

The Poggendorf illusion is just one of many that consistently fool the eye (Perkins, 1983; Greist-Bousquet & Schiffman, 1986). Another, illustrated in Figure 10,

a.

b.

c.

FIGURE 8 In building the Parthenon, the Greeks constructed an architectural wonder that looks perfectly straight, with right angles at every corner, as in (a). However, if it had been built with completely true right angles, it would have looked as it does in (b). To compensate for this illusion, the Parthenon was designed to have a slight upward curvature, as shown in (c). (Source: Coren & Ward, 1989, p. 5.)

FIGURE 9 (*a*) Put yourself in the shoes of a flight controller and look at the flight paths of the two planes on this radar screen. A first glance suggests that they are headed on different courses and will not hit each other. But now take a ruler and lay it along the two paths. Your career as a flight controller might well be over if you were guiding the two planes and allowed them to continue without a change in course (Coren, Porac, & Ward, 1984, p. 7). (*b*) The Poggendorf illusion, in which the two diagonal lines appear (incorrectly) as if they would not meet if extended toward each other.

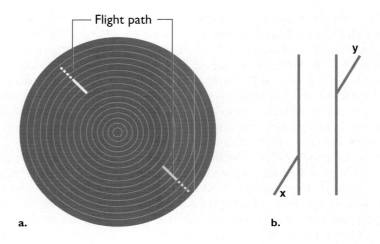

is called the *Müller-Lyer illusion*. Although the two lines are the same length, the one with the arrow tips pointing inward (Figure 10a, top) appears to be longer than the one with the arrow tips pointing outward (Figure 10a, bottom).

Although all kinds of explanations for visual illusions have been suggested, most concentrate either on the physical operation of the eye or on our misinterpretation of the visual stimulus. For example, one explanation for the Müller-Lyer illusion is that eye movements are greater when the arrow tips point inward, making us perceive the line as longer than it is when the arrow tips face outward. In contrast, a

FIGURE 10 In the Müller-Lyer illusion (*a*), the upper horizontal line appears longer than the lower one. One explanation for the Müller-Lyer illusion suggests that the line with arrow points directed inward is to be interpreted as the inside corner of a rectangular room extending away from us (*b*), and the line with arrow points directed outward is viewed as the relatively close corner of a rectangular object, such as the building corner in (*c*). Our previous experience with distance cues leads us to assume that the outside corner is closer than the inside corner and that the inside corner must therefore be longer.

different explanation for the illusion suggests that we unconsciously attribute particular significance to each of the lines (Gregory, 1978; Redding & Hawley, 1993). When we see the top line in Figure 10a, we tend to perceive it as if it were the inside corner of a room extending away from us, as illustrated in Figure 10b. In contrast, when we view the bottom line in Figure 10a, we perceive it as the relatively close outside corner of a rectangular object such as the building corner in Figure 10c. Because previous experience leads us to assume that the outside corner is closer than the inside corner, we make the further assumption that the inside corner must therefore be larger.

Despite the complexity of the latter explanation, a good deal of evidence supports it. For instance, cross-cultural studies show that people raised in areas where there are few right angles—such as the Zulu in Africa—are much less susceptible to the illusion than are people who grow up where most structures are built using right angles and rectangles (Segall, Campbell, & Herskovits, 1966).

To learn more about illusions and the reasons why we're susceptible to them, try **Interactivity 13–2.**

INTERACTIVITY 13–2
Visual illusions

As the example of the Zulu indicates, the particular culture in which we are raised has clear consequences for how we perceive the world. Consider the drawing in Figure 11. Sometimes called the "devil's tuning fork," it is likely to produce a mind-boggling effect, as the center tine of the fork alternates between appearing and disappearing.

Exploring DIVERSITY
Culture and Perception

Now try to reproduce the drawing on a piece of paper. Chances are that the task is nearly impossible for you—unless you are a member of an African tribe with little exposure to Western cultures. For such individuals, the task is simple; they have no trouble reproducing the figure. The reason seems to be that Western people automatically interpret the drawing as something that cannot exist in three dimensions, and they therefore are inhibited from reproducing it. The African tribal members, in contrast, do not make the assumption that the figure is "impossible" and instead view it in two dimensions; that enables them to copy the figure with ease (Deregowski, 1973).

Cultural differences are also reflected in depth perception. A Western viewer of Figure 12 would interpret the hunter in the drawing as aiming for the antelope in the foreground, while an elephant stands under the tree in the background. A member of an isolated African tribe, however, interprets the scene very differently by

FIGURE 11 The "devil's tuning fork" has three prongs . . . or does it have two?

FIGURE 12 Is the man aiming for the elephant or the antelope? Westerners assume that the differences in size between the two animals indicate that the elephant is farther away, and therefore the man is aiming for the antelope. In contrast, members of some African tribes, not used to depth cues in two-dimensional drawings, assume that the man is aiming for the elephant. (The drawing is based on Deregowski, 1973.) Do you think Westerners, who view the picture in three dimensions, could explain what they see to someone who views the scene in two dimensions and eventually get that person to view it in three dimensions?

assuming that the hunter is aiming at the elephant. Westerners use the difference in sizes between the two animals as a cue that the elephant is farther away than the antelope (Hudson, 1960).

The misinterpretations created by visual illusions are ultimately due, then, to errors in both fundamental visual processing and the way the brain interprets the information it receives. But visual illusions, by illustrating something fundamental about perception, become more than mere psychological curiosities. There is a basic connection between our prior knowledge, needs, motivations, and expectations about how the world is put together and the way we perceive it. Our view of the world is very much a function, then, of fundamental psychological factors. Furthermore, each person perceives the environment in a way that is unique and special—a fact that allows each of us to make our own special contribution to the world.

Ⓐ Ⓐ Ⓐ

Subliminal Perception

Can stimuli that we're not even aware we've been exposed to change our behavior in a significant way? Probably not.

Subliminal perception refers to the perception of messages about which we have no awareness. The stimulus could be a word, a sound, or even a smell that activates the sensory system but that is not intense enough for a person to report having experienced it. For example, in some studies people are exposed to a descriptive label—called a *prime*—about a person (such as the word *smart* or *happy*) so briefly that they cannot report seeing the label. Later, however, they form impressions that are influenced by the content of the prime. Somehow, they have been influenced by the prime that they say they couldn't see, providing some evidence for subliminal perception (Greenwald, Draine, & Abrams, 1996; Key, 2003).

Does this mean that subliminal messages can actually lead to significant changes in attitudes or behavior? Most research suggests that they cannot. Although we are able to perceive at least some kinds of information of which we are unaware, no evidence demonstrates that subliminal messages can change our attitudes or behavior in any substantial way (Greenwald et al., 1991; Greenwald, 2002).

EXTRASENSORY PERCEPTION (ESP)

Given the lack of evidence that subliminal perception can meaningfully affect our behavior, psychologists are even more skeptical of reports of *extrasensory perception*, or *ESP*—perception that does not involve our known senses. Although half of the general population of the United States believes it exists, most psychologists reject the existence of ESP, asserting that there is no sound documentation of the phenomenon (Swets & Bjork, 1990; Hyman, 1994; Gallup Poll, 2001).

A short-lived scandal of the 2000 U.S. presidential campaign involved a George Bush political advertisement in which the word "RATS" appeared for one-thirtieth of a second while a voice-over criticized his opponent Al Gore's prescription drug plan. Critics argued that the ad sought to take advantage of subliminal perception. Based on the research evidence, do you think this use of "RATS" could have been effective in influencing voters?

However, an ongoing debate in one of the most prestigious psychology journals, *Psychological Bulletin,* has heightened interest in the area. According to proponents of ESP, reliable evidence exists for an "anomalous process of information transfer," or *psi.* These researchers, who painstakingly reviewed considerable evidence, argue that a cumulative body of research shows reliable support for the existence of psi (Bem & Honorton, 1994; Storm & Ertel, 2001).

However, their conclusion has been challenged on several counts. For example, critics suggest that the research methodology was inadequate, and that the experiments supporting psi are flawed (Hyman, 1994; Milton & Wiseman, 1999).

Because of questions about the quality of the research, as well as a lack of any credible theoretical explanation for how extrasensory perception might take place, most psychologists continue to believe that there is no reliable scientific support for ESP (Rose & Blackmore, 2002; Wiseman & Greening, 2002). Still, the exchanges in *Psychological Bulletin* are likely to heighten the debate. More important, the renewed interest in ESP among psychologists is likely to inspire more research, which is the only way the issue can be resolved.

PowerWeb: Is There a Sixth Sense?

www.mhhe.com/feldmanup7

RECAP/EVALUATE/RETHINK

RECAP

What principles underlie our organization of the visual world, allowing us to make sense of our environment?

▶ Perception is a constructive process in which people go beyond the stimuli that are physically present and try to construct a meaningful situation. (p. 129)

▶ The gestalt laws of organization are used to describe the way in which we organize bits and pieces of information into meaningful wholes, known as gestalts, through closure, proximity, similarity, and simplicity. (p. 130)

▶ Feature analysis pertains to how we consider a shape, pattern, object, or scene in terms of the individual elements that make it up. (p. 131)

▶ In top-down processing, perception is guided by higher-level knowledge, experience, expectations, and motivations. In bottom-up processing, perception involves recognizing and processing information about the individual components of stimuli. (p. 133)

▶ Perceptual constancy permits us to perceive stimuli as unvarying in size, shape, and color despite changes in the environment or the appearance of the objects being perceived. (p. 134)

How are we able to perceive the world in three dimensions when our retinas are capable of sensing only two-dimensional images?

▶ Depth perception is the ability to perceive distance and view the world in three dimensions even though the images projected on our retinas are two-dimensional. We are able to judge depth and distance as a result of binocular disparity and monocular cues, such as motion parallax, the relative size of images on the retina, and linear perspective. (p. 135)

▶ Motion perception depends on cues such as the perceived movement of an object across the retina and information about how the head and eyes are moving. (p. 136)

What clues do visual illusions give us about our understanding of general perceptual mechanisms?

▶ Visual illusions are physical stimuli that consistently produce errors in perception, causing judgments that do not reflect the physical reality of a stimulus accurately. Two of the best-known illusions are the Poggendorf illusion and the Müller-Lyer illusion. (p. 137)

▶ Visual illusions are usually the result of errors in the brain's interpretation of visual stimuli. Furthermore, culture clearly affects how we perceive the world. (p. 139)

▶ Subliminal perception refers to the perception of messages about which we have no awareness. The reality of the phenomenon, as well as of ESP, is open to question and debate. (p. 140)

EVALUATE

1. Match each of the following organizational laws with its meaning:

a. Closure   1. Elements close together are grouped together.

b. Proximity   2. Patterns are perceived in the most basic, direct manner possible.

c. Similarity   3. Groupings are made in terms of complete figures.

d. Simplicity   4. Elements similar in appearance are grouped together.

2. _____ analysis deals with the way in which we break an object down into its component pieces in order to understand it.

3. Processing that involves higher functions such as expectations and motivations is known as _____, whereas processing that recognizes the individual components of a stimulus is known as _____ .

4. When a car passes you on the road and appears to shrink as it gets farther away, the phenomenon of _____ _____ permits you to realize that the car is not in fact getting smaller.

5. _____ _____ is the ability to view the world in three dimensions instead of two.

6. The brain makes use of a phenomenon known as _____ _____ , or the difference in the images the two eyes see, to give three dimensions to sight.

7. Match the monocular cues with their definitions.

a. Relative size

1. Straight lines seem to join together as they become more distant.

b. Linear perspective

2. An object changes position on the retina as the head moves.

c. Motion parallax

3. If two objects are the same size, the one producing the smaller retinal image is farther away.

RETHINK

1. Can you think of examples of the combined use of top-down and bottom-up processing in everyday life? Is one type of processing superior to the other?

2. In what ways do painters represent three-dimensional scenes in two dimensions on a canvas? Do you think artists in non-Western cultures use the same or different principles to represent three-dimensionality? Why?

Answers to Evaluate Questions

1. a-3, b-1, c-4, d-2; 2. feature; 3. top-down, bottom-up; 4. perceptual constancy; 5. depth perception; 6. binocular disparity; 7. a-3, b-1, c-2

KEY TERMS

gestalt law of
organization p. 130

feature analysis p. 131
top-down processing p. 133

bottom-up
processing p. 133

visual illusions p. 137

Looking Back

Psychology on the Web

1. Select one topic of personal interest to you that was mentioned in this set of modules (e.g., psi, cochlear implants, visual/optical illusions). Find one "serious" or scientific website and one "popular" or commercial website with information about the chosen topic. Compare the type, level, and reliability of the information that you find on each site. Write a summary of your findings.

2. Are there more gestalt laws of organization than the four we've considered (i.e., closure, proximity, similarity, and simplicity)? Find the answer to this question on the Web and write a summary of any additional gestalt laws you find.

3. After completing Interactivity 11–1 on the eye, search the Web for a recent research finding about the eye. Summarize the findings in several paragraphs, describing why you think it is important.

Epilogue

We have noted the important distinction between sensation and perception, and we have examined the processes that underlie both of them. We've seen how external stimuli evoke sensory responses and how our different senses process the information contained in those responses. We also have focused on the physical structure and internal workings of the individual senses, including vision, hearing, balance, smell, taste, and the skin senses, and we've explored how our brains organize and process sensory information to construct a consistent, integrated picture of the world around us.

To complete our investigation of sensation and perception, let's reconsider the story of Amy Ecklund, whose cochlear implant had a profound effect on her life. Using your knowledge of sensation and perception, answer the following questions:

1. What do you think happens when a formerly deaf person such as Amy Ecklund first hears a sound that is new to her, such as the "chirping" of a cell phone? What differences would there be in her *sensation* of the sound and her *perception* of it?

2. Do you think that Ecklund's cochlear implant is capable of sensory adaptation—a decrease in sensitivity after repeated exposure to a strong stimulus? If it is not, how would this affect her experience of the world?

3. Do you think Ecklund will gradually lose her ability to read lips? Will she necessarily lose her sense of belonging in the culture of the deaf? What disadvantages would this have for her?

1 When light enters the eye, it initiates a complex series of neural impulses. The brain analyzes these impulses and combines them with memories and experiences to construct an individual's perceptual reality.

2 Visual receptors in the retina, which is on the back of the eye, transform light energy into neural impulses. These raw impulses are the visual sensation that travels to the brain for analysis by successive visual processing areas. These processing areas convert the sensation into a complete perception.

Impulses transmitted to the brain

neural transduction

3 In bottom-up processing, neural information travels first to the thalamus and then to the visual cortex for preliminary analysis. The first level of analysis identifies only basic angles, features, and shapes.

bottom-up processing

4 Next, the signals are sent to another area of the brain for additional processing. At this point, basic features and shapes are combined and assembled into complete objects, such as a building.

5 The brain also interprets distance cues in the visual field and uses these cues to convert the 2-dimensional sensations into 3-dimensional perception. After analyzing distance cues, the brain assigns each object both a relative distance and a corresponding size.

top-down processing

6 The brain then organizes all of the objects into a coherent whole using gestalt laws of organization. For example, similar objects are perceived as a unit. Here, the vertical columns and the roughly triangular roof above them are perceived as a building.

7 In top-down processing, the brain modifies perception based on previous personal experiences and memories. For example, the brain might contain a memory of a friend's face which the brain uses to enhance facial features and fill in missing information.

8 Finally, top-down processing incorporates personal expectations, needs, and drives to enhance what we see. For example, if we expect a place or person to be beautiful, our perception might be altered to match our expectation.

States of Consciousness

Prologue
A Deadly Binge

The Massachusetts Institute of Technology is known as a demanding school, and Scott Krueger was ready for it. He had graduated near the top of his high school class and no one doubted that he could balance his freshman engineering classes with early-morning crew practice. But in Boston, there is another side to MIT: its 30 fraternities are a magnet for whiz kids who like to party.

Scott Krueger wasn't ready for that. During a Greek Week celebration, the Phi Gamma Delta pledge passed out after downing the equivalent of 16 shots in an hour. His frat brothers carried him back to his basement room in their stately Boston mansion, then noticed he wasn't breathing well. Rescue workers found Krueger comatose. His blood-alcohol level was a staggering .41; the state's legal driving limit is .08. Either Krueger's blood got so thick from alcohol that the oxygen wasn't able to reach his brain or he choked on his own vomit. Days later, his anguished parents took their son off life support (Rosenberg & Bai, 1997, p. 69).

Binge drinking—defined as five drinks in a row for men, and four for women—is commonplace on college campuses. Although most binge drinkers are luckier than Krueger, all put themselves at serious risk. In fact, each year thousands of people die from complications of alcohol and drug overdoses, and many more are addicted to various kinds of drugs.

What leads people to use alcohol and other types of consciousness-altering drugs? In the following modules we will seek to answer this question by considering the nature of both normal and altered states of consciousness.

Consciousness is the awareness of the sensations, thoughts, and feelings being experienced at a given moment. Consciousness is our subjective understanding of both

Looking Ahead

the environment around us and our private internal world, unobservable to outsiders.

In *waking consciousness,* we are awake and aware of our thoughts, emotions, and perceptions. All other states of consciousness are considered *altered states of consciousness.* Among these, sleeping and dreaming occur naturally; drug use and hypnosis, in contrast, are methods of deliberately altering one's state of consciousness.

Because consciousness is so personal a phenomenon, psychologists sometimes have been reluctant to study it. After all, who can say that your consciousness is similar to or, for that matter, different from anyone else's? Although the earliest psychologists, such as William James (1890), saw the study of consciousness as central to the field, later psychologists suggested that it was out of bounds for the discipline. They argued that consciousness could be understood only by relying "unscientifically" on what experimental participants said they were experiencing. Philosophers and not psychologists, they suggested, were the ones who should speculate on such knotty issues as whether consciousness is separate from the physical body, how people know they exist, how the body and mind are related to each other, and how we identify what state of consciousness we are in at any given moment (Rychlak, 1997).

Contemporary psychologists reject the view that the study of consciousness is unsuitable for the field of psychology. Instead, they argue that several approaches permit the scientific study of consciousness. For example, behavioral neuroscientists can measure brain-wave patterns under conditions of consciousness ranging from sleep to waking to hypnotic trances. And new understanding of the chemistry of drugs such as marijuana and alcohol has provided insights into the way they produce their pleasurable—as well as adverse—effects (Shear, 1997; Damasio, 1999; Sommerhof, 2000).

Whatever state of consciousness we are in—be it waking, sleeping, hypnotic, or drug-induced—the complexities of consciousness are profound.

Sleep and Dreams

MODULE 14

What are the different states of consciousness?

What happens when we sleep, and what are the meaning and function of dreams?

What are the major sleep disorders, and how can they be treated?

How much do we daydream?

The crowd roared as running back Donald Dorff, age 67, took the pitch from his quarterback and accelerated smoothly across the artificial turf. As Dorff braked and pivoted to cut back over a tackle, a huge defensive lineman loomed in his path. One hundred twenty pounds of pluck, Dorff did not hesitate. But let the retired grocery merchandiser from Golden Valley, Minnesota, tell it:

"There was a 280-pound tackle waiting for me, so I decided to give him my shoulder. When I came to, I was on the floor in my bedroom. I had smashed into the dresser and knocked everything off it and broke the mirror and just made one heck of a mess. It was 1:30 a.m." (Long, 1987, p. 787).

Dorff, it turned out, was suffering from a rare condition (called *REM sleep behavior disorder*) in which the mechanism that usually shuts down bodily movement during dreams does not function properly. People with the malady have been known to hit others, smash windows, punch holes in walls—all while fast asleep.

Luckily, Dorff's problem had a happy ending. With the help of clonazepam, a drug that suppresses movement during dreams, his malady vanished, permitting him to sleep through the night undisturbed.

Despite the success of Dorff's treatment, many unanswered questions about sleep remain, along with a considerable number of myths. Test your knowledge of sleep and dreams by answering the questionnaire in Figure 1.

▲ ▲ ▲

The Stages of Sleep

Most of us consider sleep a time of tranquillity, as we set aside the tensions of the day and spend the night in uneventful slumber. However, a closer look at sleep shows that a good deal of activity occurs throughout the night, and that what at first appears to be a unitary state is, in fact, quite diverse.

Much of our knowledge of what happens during sleep comes from the *electroencephalogram,* or *EEG,* a measurement of electrical activity in the brain. When probes from an EEG machine are attached to the surface of a sleeping person's scalp and face, it becomes clear that the brain is active throughout the night. It produces electrical discharges with systematic, wavelike patterns that change in height (or amplitude) and speed (or frequency) in regular sequences. Instruments that measure muscle and eye movements also reveal a good deal of physical activity.

People progress through five distinct stages of sleep during a night's rest— known as *stage 1* through *stage 4* and *REM sleep*—moving through the stages in cycles lasting about ninety minutes. Each of these sleep stages is associated with a unique pattern of brain waves, which you can see in Figure 2.

When people first go to sleep, they move from a waking state in which they are relaxed with their eyes closed into **stage 1 sleep,** which is characterized by relatively rapid, low-amplitude brain waves. This is actually a stage of transition between

Stage 1 sleep: The state of transition between wakefulness and sleep, characterized by relatively rapid, low-amplitude brain waves.

149

FIGURE I There are many unanswered questions about sleep. Taking this quiz can help you clear up some of the myths.

Sleep Quiz

Although sleeping is something we all do for a significant part of our lives, myths and misconceptions about the topic abound. To test your own knowledge of sleep and dreams, try answering the following questions before reading further.

_____	1. Some people never dream. *True or false?*	_____	6. If we lose some sleep, we will eventually make up all the lost sleep the next night or another night. *True or false?*
_____	2. Most dreams are caused by bodily sensations such as an upset stomach. *True or false?*	_____	7. No one has been able to go for more than 48 hours without sleep. *True or false?*
_____	3. It has been proved that people need eight hours of sleep to maintain mental health. *True or false?*	_____	8. Everyone is able to sleep and breathe at the same time. *True or false?*
_____	4. When people do not recall their dreams, it is probably because they are secretly trying to forget them. *True or false?*	_____	9. Sleep enables the brain to rest, because little brain activity takes place during sleep. *True or false?*
_____	5. Depriving someone of sleep will invariably cause the individual to become mentally imbalanced. *True or false?*	_____	10. Drugs have been proved to provide a long-term cure for sleeplessness. *True or false?*

Scoring: This is an easy set of questions to score, for every item is false. But don't lose any sleep if you missed them; they were chosen to represent the most common myths regarding sleep.

Stage 2 sleep: A sleep deeper than that of stage 1, characterized by a slower, more regular wave pattern, along with momentary interruptions of "sleep spindles."

Stage 3 sleep: A sleep characterized by slow brain waves, with greater peaks and valleys in the wave pattern than in stage 2 sleep.

Stage 4 sleep: The deepest stage of sleep, during which we are least responsive to outside stimulation.

INTERACTIVITY 14–1

Sleep stages

wakefulness and sleep and lasts only a few minutes. During stage 1, images sometimes appear, as if we were viewing still photos, although this is not true dreaming, which occurs later in the night.

As sleep becomes deeper, people enter **stage 2 sleep,** which makes up about half of the total sleep of those in their early twenties and is characterized by a slower, more regular wave pattern. However, there are also momentary interruptions of sharply pointed, spiky waves that are called, because of their configuration, *sleep spindles*. It becomes increasingly difficult to awaken a person from sleep as stage 2 progresses.

As people drift into **stage 3 sleep,** the brain waves become slower, with higher peaks and lower valleys in the wave pattern. By the time sleepers arrive at **stage 4 sleep,** the pattern is even slower and more regular, and people are least responsive to outside stimulation.

As you can see in Figure 3, and learn more about in **Interactivity 14–1,** stage 4 sleep is most likely to occur during the early part of the night. In the first half of the night, sleep is dominated by stages 3 and 4. The second half is characterized by stages 1 and 2 of sleep—as well as a fifth stage during which dreams occur.

REM Sleep: The Paradox of Sleep

Several times a night, when sleepers have cycled back to a shallower state of sleep, something curious happens. Their heart rate increases and becomes irregular, their

FIGURE 2 Brain-wave patterns (measured by an EEG apparatus) vary significantly during the different stages of sleep (Hobson, 1989). As sleep moves from stage 1 through stage 4, brain waves become slower.

blood pressure rises, their breathing rate increases, and males—even male infants—have erections. Most characteristic of this period is the back-and-forth movement of their eyes, as if they were watching an action-filled movie. This period of sleep is called **rapid eye movement,** or **REM, sleep,** and contrasts with stages 1 through 4, which are grouped together under the label of *non-REM* (or *NREM*) sleep. REM sleep occupies a little over 20 percent of adults' total sleeping time.

Paradoxically, while all this activity is occurring, the major muscles of the body appear to be paralyzed—except in rare cases such as Donald Dorff's. In addition, and most important, REM sleep is usually accompanied by dreams, which—whether or not people remember them—are experienced by *everyone* during some part of the night. Although some dreaming occurs in non-REM stages of sleep, dreams are most likely to occur in the REM period, where they are the most vivid and easily remembered (Dement, 1999; Schwartz & Maquet, 2002; Titone, 2002).

There is good reason to believe that REM sleep plays a critical role in everyday human functioning. In fact, REM sleep is so important that the other four stages of

Rapid eye movement (REM) sleep: Sleep occupying 20 percent of an adult's sleeping time, characterized by increased heart rate, blood pressure, and breathing rate; erections; eye movements; and the experience of dreaming.

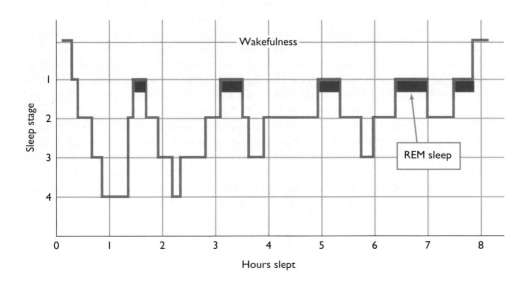

FIGURE 3 During the night, the typical sleeper passes through all four stages of sleep and several REM periods. (Source: Hartmann, 1967.)

People progress through four distinct stages of sleep during a night's rest spread over cycles lasting about ninety minutes. REM sleep, which occupies only 20 percent of adults' sleeping time, occurs in stage 1 sleep. These photos, taken at different times of night, show the synchronized patterns of a couple accustomed to sleeping in the same bed.

sleep are often collectively labeled "non-REM" sleep. People deprived of REM sleep—by being awakened every time they begin to display the physiological signs of that stage—show a *rebound effect* when allowed to rest undisturbed. With this rebound effect, REM-deprived sleepers spend significantly more time in REM sleep than they normally would.

Why Do We Sleep, and How Much Sleep Is Necessary?

Sleep is a requirement for normal human functioning, although, surprisingly, we don't know exactly why. It is reasonable to expect that our bodies would require a tranquil "rest and relaxation" period to revitalize themselves, and experiments with rats show that total sleep deprivation results in death. Some researchers, using an evolutionary perspective, suggest that sleep permitted our ancestors to conserve energy at night, a time when food was relatively hard to come by. Still, this explanation is speculative, and although we know that *some* sleep is necessary, we don't fully know why we must sleep (Webb, 1992; Porkka-Heiskanen et al., 1997).

Scientists have been unable to establish just how much sleep is absolutely required. For instance, today most people sleep seven to eight hours each night, but they sleep three hours a night *less* than people did a hundred years ago. In addition, there is wide variability among individuals, with some people needing as little as three hours. Sleep requirements also vary over the course of a lifetime: As they age, people generally need less and less sleep (see Figures 4 and 5).

People who participate in sleep deprivation experiments, in which they are kept awake for stretches as long as 200 hours, show no lasting effects. It's no fun—they feel weary and irritable, can't concentrate, and show a loss of creativity, even after only minor deprivation. They also show a decline in logical reasoning ability. However, after being allowed to sleep normally, they bounce back quickly and are able to perform at predeprivation levels after just a few days (Dinges et al., 1997; Veasey et al., 2002).

In short, as far as we know, most people suffer no permanent consequences of such temporary sleep deprivation. But—and this is an important but—a lack of sleep

FIGURE 4 Although most people report sleeping between eight and nine hours per night, the amount varies a great deal (Borbely, 1996). Where would you place yourself on this graph, and why do you think you need more or less sleep than others?

can make us feel edgy, slow our reaction time, and lower our performance on academic and physical tasks. In addition, we put ourselves, and others, at risk when we carry out routine activities, such as driving, when we're very sleepy (Macchi et al., 2002; Walker et al., 2002; Thiffault & Bergeron, 2003). (For more on the importance of sleep, see the *Applying Psychology in the 21st Century* box.)

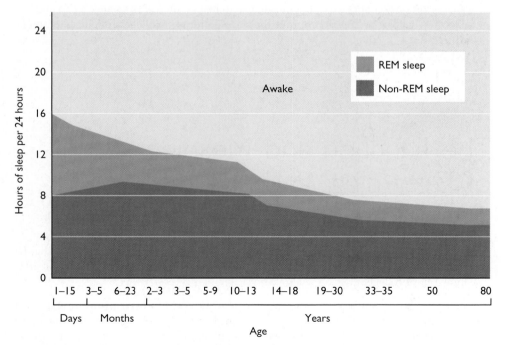

FIGURE 5 As people get older, they spend less time sleeping (Roffwarg, Muzio, & Dement, 1966). In addition, the proportion of REM sleep decreases with age.

Tired Teens: Adolescents Struggle to Balance Sleep and School

Like many other high school juniors in her Michigan school district, Molly Melamed kept her alarm clock set at 5:45 A.M. to wake her in time for her first class—at 7:20 A.M. At the end of her last class, she regularly threw herself into a busy afternoon schedule of student council meetings, pompom practice, guitar lessons, teaching horseback riding, and waitressing. After a further few hours of homework and conversations with friends, she tried to be asleep by 11 P.M. She definitely noticed that she needed more sleep. Nevertheless, until one of her friends fell asleep while driving and was killed in a car crash, she says, "no one understood how dangerous it was not to get your sleep" (Hellmich, 2000, p. 1A).

As Molly's schedule indicates, many adolescents live in a sleep-deprived stupor that carries a range of potential negative consequences. In addition to their increased risk for auto accidents, sleepy teens earn lower grades, experience more negative moods, have difficulty controlling their emotions, and use more stimulants and alcohol (National Sleep Foundation, 2000).

Of course, adolescents do not hold a monopoly on sleep deprivation: More than two-thirds of adults sleep fewer than eight hours each weeknight (National Sleep Foundation, 2002). However, psychologists have discovered that teens may be particularly vulnerable to sleep deprivation. In a number of studies, sleep researchers Mary Carskadon and colleagues have shown that adolescents require over nine hours of sleep per night and that they undergo a biological shift in their bodies' timing systems, making older teens go to bed later and wake up later than do preadolescents (Carpenter, 2001). Therefore, adolescents do not feel sleepy until late at night, and their prime sleeping time is disrupted by early morning classes, which can set the stage for a pattern of chronic sleep deprivation.

On the basis of research findings like these, psychologists and educators are developing strategies to help adolescents get the sleep they need. These proposals include limiting the times of day when teens can work, teaching teens about their sleep needs and patterns, and educating teens about the dangers of drowsy driving (National Sleep Foundation, 2000). Perhaps the most talked-about proposal— and probably the favorite of sleepy teens—involves simply moving high school classes so that they start later in the morning. When a Minneapolis, Minnesota, school district changed its opening time from 7:15 A.M. to 8:40 A.M., students began getting more sleep on school nights, missing fewer classes, and earning slightly better grades (Wahlstrom, Davison, Choi, & Ross, 2001). These students go to bed at the same time as before—about 11 P.M.— but they now sleep for an additional hour each morning. This strongly suggests that they were not getting enough sleep before the schedule change.

As a result of successes like the Minneapolis experiment and because 80 percent of adults believe that high schools should start no earlier than 8:00 A.M., politicians have begun introducing legislation to help school districts make the transition to a later starting time (Carpenter, 2001; National Sleep Foundation, 2002). As more and more school districts make this shift, teenagers' schedules and moods are changing for the better, and the days (and nights) of adolescent sleepiness may be numbered.

RETHINK

What additional changes would you suggest to help adolescents balance sleep and school? What can be done to improve the sleep patterns of college students and other adults?

The Function and Meaning of Dreaming

I was sitting at my desk when I remembered that this was the day of my chemistry final! I was terrified, because I hadn't studied a bit for it. In fact, I had missed every lecture all semester. In a panic, I began running across campus desperately searching for the classroom, to which I'd never been. It was hopeless; I knew I was going to fail and flunk out of college.

If you have had a similar dream—a surprisingly common dream among people involved in academic pursuits—you know how utterly convincing are the panic and fear that the events in the dream can bring about. *Nightmares,* unusually frightening dreams, occur fairly often. In one survey, almost half of a group of college students who kept records of their dreams over a two-week period reported having at least one nightmare. This works out to some twenty-four nightmares per person each year, on average (Wood & Bootzin, 1990; Berquier & Ashton, 1992; Tan & Hicks, 1995).

However, most of the 150,000 dreams the average person experiences by the age of 70 are much less dramatic (Webb, 1992). They typically encompass everyday events such as going to the supermarket, working at the office, and preparing a meal. Students dream about going to class; professors dream about lecturing. Dental patients dream of getting their teeth drilled; dentists dream of drilling the wrong tooth. The English take tea with the queen in their dreams; in the United States, people go to a bar with the president (Webb, 1992; Potheraju & Soper, 1995; Domhoff, 1996). See Figure 6 for the most common themes found in people's dreams.

But what, if anything, do all these dreams mean? Whether dreams have a specific significance and function is a question that scientists have considered for many years, and they have developed several alternative theories.

DO DREAMS REPRESENT UNCONSCIOUS WISH FULFILLMENT?

Sigmund Freud viewed dreams as a guide to the unconscious (Freud, 1900). In his **unconscious wish fulfillment theory,** he proposed that dreams represent unconscious wishes that dreamers desire to see fulfilled. However, because these wishes are threatening to the dreamer's conscious awareness, the actual wishes—called the **latent content of dreams**—are disguised. The true subject and meaning of a dream, then, may have little to do with its overt story line, which Freud called the **manifest content of dreams.**

To Freud, it was important to pierce the armor of a dream's manifest content to understand its true meaning. To do this, Freud tried to get people to discuss their dreams, associating symbols in the dreams with events in the past. He also suggested that certain common symbols with universal meanings appear in dreams. For example,

THE FAR SIDE® BY GARY LARSON

"I've got it again, Larry ... an eerie feeling like there's something on top of the bed."

Unconscious wish fulfillment theory: Sigmund Freud's theory that dreams represent unconscious wishes that dreamers desire to see fulfilled.

Latent content of dreams: According to Freud, the "disguised" meanings of dreams, hidden by more obvious subjects.

Manifest content of dreams: According to Freud, the overt story line of dreams.

FIGURE 6 Although dreams tend to be subjective to the person having them, there are common elements that frequently occur in everyone's dreams. Why do you think so many common dreams are unpleasant and so few are pleasant? Do you think this tells us anything about the function of dreams?

Thematic Element	Percentage of Respondents Reporting at Least One	
	Males	**Females**
Aggression	47%	44%
Friendliness	38	42
Sexuality	12	4
Misfortune	36	33
Success	15	8
Failure	15	10

Source: Schneider, A., & Domhoff, G. W. (2002).

Freud suggested that certain common symbols with universal meanings appear in dreams. According to his symbolism, a plane flying across the sky might represent the dreamer's wish for sexual intercourse. Can this claim be proved?

PowerWeb: The Dream as a Wish-Fulfillment

www.mhhe.com/feldmanup7

to Freud, dreams in which a person is flying symbolize a wish for sexual intercourse. (See Figure 7 for other common symbols.)

Many psychologists reject Freud's view that dreams typically represent unconscious wishes and that particular objects and events in a dream are symbolic. Instead, they believe that the direct, overt action of a dream is the focal point of its meaning. For example, a dream in which we are walking down a long hallway to take an exam for which we haven't studied does not relate to unconscious, unacceptable wishes. Instead, it simply may mean that we are concerned about an impending test. Even more complex dreams can often be interpreted in terms of everyday concerns and stress (Domhoff, 1996; Nikles et al., 1998; Picchioni et al., 2002).

Moreover, some dreams reflect events occurring in the dreamer's environment as he or she is sleeping. For example, sleeping participants in one experiment were sprayed with water while they were dreaming. Those unlucky volunteers reported more dreams involving water than did a comparison group of participants who were left to sleep undisturbed (Dement & Wolpert, 1958). Similarly, it is not unusual to wake up to find that the doorbell that was being rung in a dream is actually an alarm clock telling us it is time to get up.

However, recent research lends some support for the wish fulfillment view. For instance, according to work by Allen Braun and colleagues, the parts of the brain associated with emotions and visual imagery are strongly activated during REM sleep. Using position emission tomography (PET) scans that show brain activity, Braun's research team found that the limbic and paralimbic regions of the brain,

FIGURE 7 According to Freud, dreams contain common symbols with universal meanings.

Symbol (Manifest Content of Dream)	Interpretation (Latent Content)
Climbing up a stairway, crossing a bridge, riding an elevator, flying in an airplane, walking down a long hallway, entering a room, train traveling through a tunnel	Sexual intercourse
Apples, peaches, grapefruits	Breasts
Bullets, fire, snakes, sticks, umbrellas, guns, hoses, knives	Male sex organs
Ovens, boxes, tunnels, closets, caves, bottles, ships	Female sex organs

which are associated with emotion and motivation, are particularly active during REM sleep. At the same time, the association areas of the prefrontal cortex, which control logical analysis and attention, are inactive during REM sleep (Braun et al., 1998; see Figure 8).

These results can be viewed as consistent with several aspects of Freudian theory. For example, the high activation of emotional and motivational centers of the brain during dreaming makes it more plausible that dreams may reflect unconscious wishes and instinctual needs, just as Freud suggested. Similarly, the fact that the areas of the brain responsible for emotions are highly active, whereas the brain regions responsible for rational thought are offline during REM sleep, suggests that conscious parts of personality (what Freud calls the ego and the superego) are inactive. This inactivity permits unconscious thoughts to dominate.

Areas active during REM sleep

FIGURE 8 The parts of the brain that are associated with emotions and visual imagery are strongly activated during REM sleep. Why might this be the case?

DREAMS-FOR-SURVIVAL THEORY

According to the **dreams-for-survival theory,** dreams permit information that is critical for our daily survival to be reconsidered and reprocessed during sleep. Dreaming is seen as an inheritance from our animal ancestors, whose small brains were unable to sift sufficient information during waking hours. Consequently, dreaming provided a mechanism that permitted the processing of information twenty-four hours a day.

According to this theory, dreams represent concerns about our daily lives, illustrating our uncertainties, indecisions, ideas, and desires. Dreams are seen, then, as consistent with everyday living. Rather than being disguised wishes, as Freud suggested, they represent key concerns growing out of our daily experiences (Pavlides & Winson, 1989; Winson, 1990).

Research supports the dreams-for-survival theory, suggesting that certain dreams permit people to focus on and consolidate memories, particularly dreams that pertain to "how-to-do-it" memories related to motor skills. For example, rats seem to dream about mazes that they learned to run through during the day, at least according to the patterns of brain activity that appear while they are sleeping (Kenway & Wilson, 2001; Stickgold, Hobson, Fosse, & Fosse, 2001)

A similar phenomenon appears to operate in humans. For instance, in one experiment, participants learned a visual memory task late in the day. They were then sent to bed but were awakened at certain times during the night. When they were awakened at times that did not interrupt dreaming, their performance on the memory task typically improved the next day. But when they were awakened during rapid eye movement sleep—the stage of sleep when people dream—their performance declined. The implication: Dreaming can play a role in helping us remember material to which we have been previously exposed (Karni et al., 1992, 1994).

Dreams-for-survival theory: The theory suggesting that dreams permit information that is critical for our daily survival to be reconsidered and reprocessed during sleep.

PowerWeb: Brains in Dreamland

www.mhhe.com/feldmanup7

ACTIVATION-SYNTHESIS THEORY

According to psychiatrist J. Allan Hobson, who proposed **activation-synthesis theory,** the brain produces random electrical energy during REM sleep, possibly as a result of changes in the production of particular neurotransmitters. This electrical energy randomly stimulates memories lodged in various portions of the brain. Because we have a need to make sense of our world even while asleep, the brain takes these chaotic memories and weaves them into a logical story line, filling in the gaps to produce a rational scenario (Hobson, 1996; Porte & Hobson, 1996).

However, Hobson does not entirely reject the view that dreams reflect unconscious wishes. He suggests that the particular scenario a dreamer produces is not random but instead is a clue to the dreamer's fears, emotions, and concerns. Hence, what starts out as a random process culminates in something meaningful.

Activation-synthesis theory: Hobson's theory that the brain produces random electrical energy during REM sleep that stimulates memories lodged in various portions of the brain.

FIGURE 9 Three theories of dreams. Researchers have yet to agree on the fundamental meaning of dreams, and so several theories about dreaming have emerged.

Theory	Basic Explanation	Meaning of Dreams	Is Meaning of Dream Disguised?
Unconscious wish fulfillment theory (Freud)	Dreams represent unconscious wishes the dreamer wants to fulfill	Latent content reveals unconscious wishes	Yes, by manifest content of dreams
Dreams-for-survival theory	Information relevant to daily survival is reconsidered and reprocessed	Clues to everyday concerns about survival	Not necessarily
Activation-synthesis theory	Dreams are the result of random activation of various memories, which are tied together in a logical story line	Dream scenario that is constructed is related to dreamer's concerns	Not necessarily

DREAM THEORIES IN PERSPECTIVE

The range of theories about dreaming clearly illustrates that researchers have yet to agree on the fundamental meaning of dreams. Figure 9 summarizes the three major theories. In fact, there are quite a few additional theories of dreaming, probably reflecting the fact that dream research ultimately must rely on self-reports of hidden phenomena that are not directly observable. For now, the true meaning of dreams remains a mystery (Domhoff, 2001, 2003; Stern, 2001).

Sleep Disturbances: Slumbering Problems

At one time or another, almost all of us have difficulty sleeping—a condition known as *insomnia*. It could be due to a particular situation, such as the breakup of a relationship, concern about a test score, or the loss of a job. Some cases of insomnia, however, have no obvious cause. Some people are simply unable to fall asleep easily, or they go to sleep readily but wake up frequently during the night. Insomnia is a problem that afflicts about a quarter of the population of the United States (Hauri, 1991; Pressman & Orr, 1997).

Interestingly, some people who *think* they have sleeping problems are mistaken. For example, researchers in sleep laboratories have found that some people who report being up all night actually fall asleep in thirty minutes and stay asleep all night. Furthermore, some people with insomnia accurately recall sounds that they heard while they were asleep, which gives them the impression that they were awake during the night. In fact, some researchers suggest that future drugs for insomnia could function by changing people's *perceptions* of how much they have slept, rather than by making them sleep more (Engle-Friedman, Baker, & Bootzin, 1985; Klinkenborg, 1997).

Other sleep problems are less common than insomnia, although they are still widespread. For instance, some 20 million people suffer from *sleep apnea,* a condition in which a person has difficulty breathing while sleeping. The result is disturbed, fitful sleep, as the person is constantly reawakened when the lack of oxygen becomes great enough to trigger a waking response. Some people with apnea wake as many as 500 times during the course of a night, although they may not even be aware that they have wakened. Not surprisingly, such disturbed sleep results in complaints of fatigue the next day. Sleep apnea also may play a role in *sudden infant death syndrome (SIDS),* a mysterious killer of seemingly normal infants who die while sleeping (Ball et al., 1997).

Night terrors are sudden awakenings from non-REM sleep that are accompanied by extreme fear, panic, and strong physiological arousal. Usually occurring in stage 4 sleep, night terrors may be so frightening that a sleeper awakens with a shriek. Although night terrors initially produce great agitation, victims usually can get back to sleep fairly quickly. They occur most frequently in children between the ages of 3 and 8, although adults may suffer from them as well. Their cause is not known, but they are unrelated to emotional disturbance.

Narcolepsy is uncontrollable sleeping that occurs for short periods while a person is awake. No matter what the activity—holding a heated conversation, exercising, or driving—a narcoleptic will suddenly fall asleep. People with narcolepsy go directly from wakefulness to REM sleep, skipping the other stages. The causes of narcolepsy are not known, although there could be a genetic component because narcolepsy runs in families (Siegel, 2000; Silber, 2001; Witmans & Kirk, 2002).

We know relatively little about sleeptalking and sleepwalking, two sleep disturbances that are usually harmless. Both occur during stage 4 sleep and are more common in children than in adults. Sleeptalkers and sleepwalkers usually have a vague consciousness of the world around them, and a sleepwalker may be able to walk with agility around obstructions in a crowded room. Unless a sleepwalker wanders into a dangerous environment, sleepwalking typically poses little risk (Hobson & Silverstri, 1999; Oksenberg et al., 2002; Baruss, 2003).

Circadian Rhythms: Life Cycles

The fact that we cycle back and forth between wakefulness and sleep is one example of the body's circadian rhythms. **Circadian rhythms** (from the Latin *circa diem*, or "around the day") are biological processes that occur repeatedly on approximately a twenty-four-hour cycle. Sleep and waking, for instance, occur naturally to the beat of an internal pacemaker that works on a cycle of about twenty-four hours. Several other bodily functions, such as body temperature and the female menstrual cycle, also work on circadian rhythms (Oren & Terman, 1998; Czeisler et al., 1999; Young, 2000).

Circadian rhythms: Biological processes that occur repeatedly on approximately a twenty-four-hour cycle.

Circadian cycles are complex, and they involve a variety of behaviors (see Figure 10). For instance, sleepiness occurs not just in the evening but throughout the day in regular patterns, with most of us getting drowsy in midafternoon—regardless of whether we have eaten a heavy lunch. By making an afternoon siesta part of their everyday habit, people in several cultures take advantage of the body's natural inclination to sleep at this time (Ezzel, 2002; Macchi et al., 2002; Wright, 2002).

The brain's *suprachiasmatic nucleus (SCN)* controls the beat of circadian rhythms. However, the relative amount of light and darkness, which differs with the seasons of the year, also plays a role in determining circadian rhythms. In fact, some people experience *seasonal affective disorder,* a form of severe depression in which feelings of despair and hopelessness increase during the winter and lift during the rest of the year. The disorder appears to be a result of the brevity and gloom of winter days. Daily exposure to bright lights is sometimes sufficient to improve the mood of those with the disorder (Roush, 1995; Oren & Terman, 1998; Young, 2000; Eagles, 2001).

Circadian rhythms explain the difficulty people have in flying through multiple time zones—the phenomenon of *jet lag*. Pilots, as well as others who must work on constantly changing time shifts (police officers and physicians), must fight their internal clocks. The result can be fatigue, irritability, and, even worse, outright error. In fact, an analysis of major disasters caused by human error finds that many, such as the *Exxon Valdez* oil spill in Alaska and the Chernobyl nuclear reactor accident, occurred late at night (Mapes, 1990; Moore-Ede, 1993).

7:00 A.M.
• Hay fever symptoms are worst

8:00 A.M.
• Risk for heart attack and stroke is highest
• Symptoms of rheumatoid arthritis are worst
• Helper T lymphocytes are at their lowest daytime level

Noon
• Level of hemoglobin in the blood is at its peak

6:00 A.M.
• Onset of menstruation is most likely
• Insulin levels in the bloodstream are lowest
• Blood pressure and heart rate begin to rise
• Levels of the stress hormone cortisol increase
• Melatonin levels begin to fall

3:00 P.M.
• Grip strength, respiratory rate, and reflex sensitivity are highest

4:00 A.M.
• Asthma attacks are most likely to occur

4:00 P.M.
• Body temperature, pulse rate, and blood pressure peak

2:00 A.M.
• Levels of growth hormone are highest

6:00 P.M.
• Urinary flow is highest

1:00 A.M.
• Pregnant women are most likely to go into labor
• Immune cells called helper T lymphocytes are at their peak

9:00 P.M.
• Pain threshold is lowest

11:00 P.M.
• Allergic responses are most likely

FIGURE 10 Day times, night times: regular body changes over every 24-hour period. Over the course of the day, our circadian rhythms produce a wide variety of effects. (Source: Young, 2000.)

Daydreams: Dreams Without Sleep

Daydreams: Fantasies that people construct while awake.

Daydreams are fantasies that people construct while they are awake. What are the similarities and differences between daydreams and night dreams?

It is the stuff of magic: Our past mistakes can be wiped out and the future filled with noteworthy accomplishments. Fame, happiness, and wealth can be ours. In the next moment, though, the most horrible tragedies can occur, leaving us devastated, alone, and penniless.

The source of these scenarios is **daydreams,** fantasies that people construct while awake. Unlike dreaming that occurs during sleep, daydreams are more under people's control. Therefore, their content is often more closely related to immediate events in the environment than is the content of the dreams that occur during sleep. Although they may include sexual content, daydreams also pertain to other activities or events that are relevant to a person's life.

Daydreams are a typical part of waking consciousness, even though our awareness of the environment around us declines while we are daydreaming. People vary considerably in the amount of daydreaming they do. For example, around 2 to 4 percent of the population spend at least half their free time fantasizing. Although most people daydream much less frequently, almost everyone fantasizes to some degree. Studies that ask people to identify what they are doing at random times during the day have shown that they are daydreaming about 10 percent of the time. As for the content of fantasies, most concern such mundane, ordinary events as paying the telephone bill, picking up the groceries, and solving a romantic problem (Singer, 1975; Lynn & Rhue, 1988; Lynn et al., 1996).

Frequent daydreaming may seem to suggest psychological difficulties, but there appears to be little relationship between psychological disturbance and daydreaming. Except in those rare cases in which a daydreamer is unable to distinguish a fantasy from reality (a mark of serious psychological problems), daydreaming seems to be a normal part of waking consciousness. Indeed, fantasy can contribute to the psychological well-being of some people by enhancing their creativity and permitting them to use their imagination to understand what other people are experiencing (Lynn & Rhue, 1988; Pihlgren, Gidycz, & Lynn, 1993; Lynn et al., 1996).

Do you have trouble sleeping? You're not alone—70 million people in the United States have sleep problems. For those of us who spend hours tossing and turning in bed, psychologists studying sleep disturbances have a number of suggestions for overcoming insomnia (National Institutes of Health, 1996; Scharf, 1999; Edinger et al., 2001). Here are some ideas.

BECOMING AN INFORMED CONSUMER
of Psychology
Sleeping Better

- ▶ *Exercise during the day (at least six hours before bedtime) and avoid naps*. Not surprisingly, it helps to be tired before going to sleep! Moreover, learning systematic relaxation techniques and biofeedback can help you unwind from the day's stresses and tensions.
- ▶ *Choose a regular bedtime and stick to it*. Adhering to a habitual schedule helps your internal timing mechanisms regulate your body more effectively.
- ▶ *Don't use your bed as an all-purpose area*. Leave studying, reading, eating, watching TV, and other recreational activities to some other part of your living quarters. If you follow this advice, your bed will become a cue for sleeping.
- ▶ *Avoid drinks with caffeine after lunch*. The effects of beverages such as coffee, tea, and some soft drinks can linger for as long as eight to twelve hours after they are consumed.
- ▶ *Drink a glass of warm milk at bedtime*. Your grandparents were right when they dispensed this advice: Milk contains the chemical tryptophan, which helps people fall asleep.
- ▶ *Avoid sleeping pills*. Even though 25 percent of U.S. adults report having taken medication for sleep in the previous year, in the long run sleep medications can do more harm than good because they disrupt the normal sleep cycle.
- ▶ *Try* not *to sleep*. This approach works because people often have difficulty falling asleep because they are trying so hard. A better strategy is to go to bed only when you feel tired. If you don't get to sleep within ten minutes, leave the bedroom and do something else, returning to bed only when you feel sleepy. Continue this process all night if necessary. But get up at your usual hour in the morning, and don't take any naps during the day. After three or four weeks, most people become conditioned to associate their beds with sleep—and fall asleep rapidly at night (Sloan et al., 1993; Ubell, 1993; Smith, 2001).

For long-term problems with sleep, you might consider visiting a sleep disorders center. For information on accredited clinics, consult the American Academy of Sleep Medicine at www.aasmnet.org.

RECAP/EVALUATE/RETHINK

RECAP

What are the different states of consciousness?

- ▶ Consciousness is a person's awareness of the sensations, thoughts, and feelings at a given moment. Waking consciousness can vary from more active to more passive states. (p. 148)

- ▶ Altered states of consciousness include naturally occurring sleep and dreaming, as well as hypnotic and drug-induced states. (p. 148)

What happens when we sleep, and what are the meaning and function of dreams?

- ▶ Using the electroencephalogram, or EEG, to study sleep, scientists have found that the brain is active throughout the night, and that sleep proceeds through a series of stages identified by unique patterns of brain waves. (p. 149)

- ◉ REM (rapid eye movement) sleep is characterized by an increase in heart rate, a rise in blood pressure, an increase in the rate of breathing, and, in males, erections. Dreams occur during this stage. (p. 151)

- ◉ According to Freud, dreams have both a manifest content (their apparent story line) and a latent content (their true meaning). He suggested that the latent content provides a guide to a dreamer's unconscious, revealing unfulfilled wishes or desires. (p. 154)

- ◉ The dreams-for-survival theory suggests that information relevant to daily survival is reconsidered and reprocessed in dreams. The activation-synthesis theory proposes that dreams are a result of random electrical energy that stimulates different memories, which then are woven into a coherent story line. (p. 157)

What are the major sleep disorders, and how can they be treated?

- ◉ Insomnia is a sleep disorder characterized by difficulty sleeping. Sleep apnea is a condition in which people have difficulty sleeping and breathing at the same time. People with narcolepsy have an uncontrollable urge to sleep. Sleepwalking and sleeptalking are relatively harmless. (p. 158)

- ◉ Psychologists and sleep researchers advise people with insomnia to increase exercise during the day, avoid caffeine and sleeping pills, drink a glass of warm milk before bedtime, and try to avoid going to sleep. (p. 158)

How much do we daydream?

- ◉ Wide individual differences exist in the amount of time devoted to daydreaming. Almost everyone daydreams or fantasizes to some degree. (p. 160)

EVALUATE

1. _____ is the term used to describe our understanding of the world external to us, as well as our own internal world.

2. A great deal of neural activity goes on during sleep. True or false?

3. Dreams occur in _____ sleep.

4. _____ _____ are internal bodily processes that occur on a daily cycle.

5. Freud's theory of unconscious _____ _____ states that the actual wishes an individual expresses in dreams are disguised because they are threatening to the person's conscious awareness.

6. Match the theory of dreaming with its definition.
   1. Activation-synthesis theory
   2. Dreams-for-survival theory
   3. Dreams as wish fulfillment
   a. Dreams permit important information to be reprocessed during sleep.
   b. The manifest content of dreams disguises the latent content of the dreams.
   c. Electrical energy stimulates random memories, which are woven together to produce dreams.

7. Match the sleep problem with its definition.

1. Insomnia	a. Condition that makes breathing while sleeping difficult
2. Narcolepsy	b. Difficulty sleeping
3. Sleep apnea	c. Uncontrollable need to sleep during the day

RETHINK

1. How would studying the sleep patterns of nonhuman species potentially help us figure out which of the theories of dreaming provide the best account of the functions of dreaming?

2. Suppose that a new "miracle pill" is developed that will allow a person to function with only one hour of sleep per night. However, because a night's sleep is so short, a person who takes the pill will never dream again. Knowing what you do about the functions of sleep and dreaming, what would be some advantages and drawbacks of such a pill from a personal standpoint? Would you take such a pill?

Answers to Evaluate Questions

1. consciousness; 2. true; 3. REM; 4. circadian rhythms; 5. wish fulfillment; 6. 1-c, 2-a, 3-b; 7. 1-b, 2-c, 3-a

KEY TERMS

consciousness p. 148
stage 1 sleep p. 149
stage 2 sleep p. 150
stage 3 sleep p. 150
stage 4 sleep p. 150
rapid eye movement (REM)
sleep p. 151

unconscious wish fulfillment theory p. 155
latent content
of dreams p. 155

manifest content
of dreams p. 155
dreams-for-survival
theory p. 157

activation-synthesis
theory p. 157
circadian rhythms p. 159
daydreams p. 160

Hypnosis and Meditation

What is hypnosis, and are hypnotized people in a different state of consciousness?

What are the effects of meditation?

You are feeling relaxed and drowsy. You are getting sleepier and sleepier. Your body is becoming limp. Now you are starting to become warm, at ease, more comfortable. Your eyelids are feeling heavier and heavier. Your eyes are closing; you can't keep them open anymore. You are totally relaxed.

Now, as you listen to my voice, do exactly as I say. Place your hands above your head. You will find they are getting heavier and heavier—so heavy you can barely keep them up. In fact, although you are straining as hard as you can, you will be unable to hold them up any longer.

An observer watching the above scene would notice a curious phenomenon occurring. Many of the people listening to the voice would, one by one, drop their arms to their sides, as if they were holding heavy lead weights. The reason for this strange behavior? Those people have been hypnotized.

It is only recently that hypnotism has become an area considered worthy of scientific investigation. In part, the initial rejection of hypnosis relates to its bizarre eighteenth-century origins, in which Franz Mesmer argued that a form of "animal magnetism" could be used to influence people and cure their illnesses. After a commission headed by Benjamin Franklin discredited the phenomenon, it fell into disrepute, only to rise again to respectability in the nineteenth century. But even today, as we will see, the nature of hypnosis is controversial.

⚫ ⚫ ⚫

Hypnosis: A Trance-Forming Experience?

People under **hypnosis** are in a trancelike state of heightened susceptibility to the suggestions of others. In some respects, it appears that they are asleep. Yet other aspects of their behavior contradict this notion, for people are attentive to the hypnotist's suggestions and may carry out bizarre or silly suggestions.

Despite their compliance when hypnotized, people do not lose all will of their own. They will not perform antisocial behaviors, and they will not carry out self-destructive acts. People will not reveal hidden truths about themselves, and they *are* capable of lying. Moreover, people cannot be hypnotized against their will—despite popular misconceptions (Gwynn & Spanos, 1996).

There are wide variations in people's susceptibility to hypnosis. About 5 to 20 percent of the population cannot be hypnotized at all, and some 15 percent are very easily hypnotized. Most people fall somewhere in between. Moreover, the ease with which a person is hypnotized is related to a number of other characteristics. People who are hypnotized readily are also easily absorbed while reading books or listening to music, becoming unaware of what is happening around them, and they often spend an unusual amount of time daydreaming. In sum, then, they show a high ability to concentrate and to become completely absorbed

Hypnosis: A trancelike state of heightened susceptibility to the suggestions of others.

Despite common misconceptions, people such as these cannot be hypnotized against their will, nor do they lose all will of their own. In what ways is hypnosis beneficial?

INTERACTIVITY 15–1

Hypnosis

in what they are doing (Rhue, Lynn, & Kirsch, 1993; Weitzenhoffer, 1999; Kirsch & Braffman, 2001). (To investigate hypnosis more, try **Interactivity 15–1**.)

A DIFFERENT STATE OF CONSCIOUSNESS?

The question of whether hypnosis is a state of consciousness that is qualitatively different from normal waking consciousness is controversial. Psychologist Ernest Hilgard presented one side of the argument when he argued convincingly that hypnosis represents a state of consciousness that differs significantly from other states. He contended that particular behaviors clearly differentiate hypnosis from other states, including higher suggestibility, increased ability to recall and construct images, and acceptance of suggestions that clearly contradict reality. Moreover, changes in electrical activity in the brain are associated with hypnosis, supporting the position that hypnosis is a state of consciousness different from normal waking (Hilgard, 1975, 1992; Graffin, Ray, & Lundy, 1995).

On the other side of the controversy were theorists who rejected the notion that hypnosis is a state significantly different from normal waking consciousness. They argued that altered brain wave patterns are not sufficient to demonstrate a qualitative difference in light of the fact that no other specific physiological changes occur when a person is in a trance. Furthermore, little support exists for the contention that adults can recall memories of childhood events accurately while hypnotized. That lack of evidence suggests that there is nothing qualitatively special about the hypnotic trance (Spanos et al., 1993; Kirsch & Lynn, 1998).

There is increasing agreement that the controversy over the nature of hypnosis has led to extreme positions on both sides of the issue (Kirsch & Lynn, 1995). More recent approaches suggest that the hypnotic state may best be viewed as lying along a continuum in which hypnosis is neither a totally different state of consciousness nor totally similar to normal waking consciousness.

As arguments about the true nature of hypnosis continue, though, one thing is clear: Hypnosis has been used successfully to solve practical human problems. In fact, psychologists working in many different areas have found hypnosis to be a reliable, effective tool (Rhue, Lynn, & Kirsch, 1993). It has been applied to a number of areas, including the following:

- ▶ *Controlling pain.* Patients suffering from chronic pain may be given the suggestion, while hypnotized, that their pain is gone or reduced. They also may be taught to hypnotize themselves to relieve pain or gain a sense of control over their symptoms. Hypnosis has proved to be particularly useful during childbirth and dental procedures (Nash, 2001; Cosser, 2002; Ketterhagen, Vande-Vusse, & Berner, 2002).
- ▶ *Reducing smoking.* Although it hasn't been successful in stopping drug and alcohol abuse, hypnosis sometimes helps people stop smoking through hypnotic suggestions that the taste and smell of cigarettes are unpleasant (Speigel et al., 1993; Barber, 2001; Zarren & Eimer, 2002).
- ▶ *Treating psychological disorders.* Hypnosis sometimes is used during treatment for psychological disorders. For example, it may be employed to heighten relaxation, reduce anxiety, increase expectations of success, or modify self-defeating thoughts (Fromm & Nash, 1992; Zarren & Eimer, 2002).
- ▶ *Assisting in law enforcement.* Witnesses and victims are sometimes better able to recall the details of a crime when hypnotized. In one case, a witness to the kidnapping of a group of California schoolchildren was placed under hypnosis and was able to recall all but one digit of the license number on the kidnapper's vehicle (Geiselman et al., 1985). However, sometimes hypnotic recollections are inaccurate, and the legal status of hypnosis is unresolved (Lynn, Lock, Myers, & Payne, 1997; Baker, 1998; Newman & Thompson, 2001).
- ▶ *Improving athletic performance.* Athletes sometimes turn to hypnosis to improve their performance. For example, some baseball players have used hypnotism to increase their concentration when batting, with considerable success (Stanton, 1994; Edgette & Edgette, 1995).

Meditation: Regulating Our Own State of Consciousness

When traditional practitioners of the ancient Eastern religion of Zen Buddhism want to achieve greater spiritual insight, they turn to a technique that has been used for centuries to alter their state of consciousness. This technique is called meditation.

Meditation is a learned technique for refocusing attention that brings about an altered state of consciousness. Meditation typically consists of the repetition of a *mantra*—a sound, word, or syllable—over and over. In other forms of meditation, the focus is on a picture, flame, or specific part of the body. Regardless of the nature of the particular initial stimulus, the key to the procedure is concentrating on it so thoroughly that the meditator becomes unaware of any outside stimulation and reaches a different state of consciousness.

After meditation, people report feeling thoroughly relaxed. They sometimes relate that they have gained new insights into themselves and the problems they are facing. The long-term practice of meditation may even improve health because of the biological changes it produces. For example, during meditation, oxygen usage decreases, heart rate and blood pressure decline, and brain-wave patterns may change (Zamarra et al., 1996; Arambula, Peper, Kawakami, & Gibney, 2001; see Figure 1).

Meditation: A learned technique for refocusing attention that brings about an altered state of consciousness.

FIGURE 1 The body's use of oxygen declines significantly during meditation. (Source: Benson, 1993.)

Anyone can meditate by following a few simple procedures. The fundamentals include sitting in a quiet room with the eyes closed, breathing deeply and rhythmically, and repeating a word or sound—such as the word *one*—over and over. Practiced twice a day for twenty minutes, the technique is effective in bringing about relaxation (Benson & Friedman, 1985; Benson, 1993; Benson et al., 1994). For more information on meditation, contact the Mind/Body Medical Institute at www.mbmi.org or call (866) 509-0732.

As you may have gathered from this discussion, meditation is a means of altering consciousness that is practiced in many different cultures, though it can take different forms and serve different purposes across cultures. In fact, one impetus for the study of consciousness is the realization that people in many different cultures routinely seek ways to alter their states of consciousness.

Exploring DIVERSITY

Cross-Cultural Routes to Altered States of Consciousness

A group of Native American Sioux men sit naked in a steaming sweat lodge as a medicine man throws water on sizzling rocks to send billows of scalding steam into the air.

Aztec priests smear themselves with a mixture of crushed poisonous herbs, hairy black worms, scorpions, and lizards. Sometimes they drink the potion.

During the sixteenth century, a devout Hasidic Jew lies across the tombstone of a celebrated scholar. As he murmurs the name of God repeatedly, he seeks to be possessed by the soul of the dead wise man's spirit. If successful, he will attain a mystical state, and the deceased's words will flow out of his mouth.

Each of these rituals has a common goal: suspension from the bonds of everyday awareness and access to an altered state of consciousness (Furst, 1977; Fine, 1994). Although they may seem exotic from the vantage point of many Western cultures, these rituals represent an apparently universal effort to alter consciousness.

Some scholars suggest that the quest to alter consciousness represents a basic human desire (Siegel, 1989). Whether or not one accepts such an extreme view, it is clear that variations in states of consciousness share some basic characteristics across a variety of cultures (Ludwig, 1969; Martindale, 1981). One is an alteration in thinking, which may become shallow, illogical, or otherwise different from normal. In addition, people's sense of time can become disturbed, and their perceptions of the world and of themselves may be changed. They may experience a loss of self-control, doing things that they would never otherwise do. Finally, they may feel a sense of *ineffability*—the inability to understand an experience rationally or describe it in words.

Of course, realizing that efforts to produce altered states of consciousness are widespread throughout the world's societies does not answer a fundamental question: Is the experience of *un*altered states of consciousness similar across different cultures?

There are two possible responses to this question. Because humans share basic biological commonalties in the ways their brains and bodies are wired, we might assume that the fundamental experience of consciousness is similar across cultures. As a result, we could suppose that consciousness shows some basic similarities across cultures.

However, the ways in which certain aspects of consciousness are interpreted and viewed show substantial differences among different cultures. For example, people in various cultures view the experience of the passage of time in varying ways. One study found, for instance, that Mexicans view time as passing more slowly than other North Americans do (Diaz-Guerrero, 1979).

Whatever the true nature of consciousness and the reasons why people try to alter it, it is clear that people often seek the means to alter their everyday experience of the world. In some cases that need becomes overwhelming, as when people use consciousness-altering drugs, sometimes to a destructive extent.

RECAP/EVALUATE/RETHINK

RECAP

What is hypnosis, and are hypnotized people in a different state of consciousness?

▶ Hypnosis produces a state of heightened susceptibility to the suggestions of the hypnotist. Under hypnosis, significant behavioral changes occur, including increased concentration and suggestibility, heightened ability to recall and construct images, lack of initiative, and acceptance of suggestions that clearly contradict reality. (p. 163)

What are the effects of meditation?

▶ Meditation is a learned technique for refocusing attention that brings about an altered state of consciousness. (p. 165)

▶ Different cultures have developed their own unique ways to alter states of consciousness. (p. 166)

EVALUATE

1. _____ is a state of heightened susceptibility to the suggestions of others.
2. A friend tells you, "I once heard of a person who was murdered by being hypnotized and then told to jump from the Golden Gate Bridge!" Could such a thing have happened? Why or why not?
3. _____ is a learned technique for refocusing attention to bring about an altered state of consciousness.
4. Leslie repeats a unique sound, known as a _____, when she engages in meditation.

RETHINK

1. Meditation produces several physical and psychological benefits. Does this suggest that we are physically and mentally burdened in our normal state of waking consciousness? Why?

2. Why do you think people in almost every culture use psychoactive drugs and search for altered states of consciousness?

Answers to Evaluate Questions

1. hypnosis; 2. no; people who are hypnotized cannot be made to perform self-destructive acts; 3. meditation; 4. mantra

Drug Use: The Highs and Lows of Consciousness

John Brodhead's bio reads like a script for an episode of VH1's *Behind the Music*. A young rebel from the New Jersey suburbs falls in with a fast crowd, gets hooked on parties and booze and, with intensive counseling and a bit of tough love, manages to get his life back together.

What makes his story different? Just one thing: his age. John is 13 (Rogers, 2002).

John Brodhead was lucky. Now in recovery, John had begun to drink when he was in the sixth grade. He is not alone: The number of kids who start drinking by the eighth grade has increased by almost a third since the 1970s, even though alcohol consumption overall has stayed fairly steady among the general population.

Drugs of one sort or another are a part of almost everyone's life. From infancy on, most people take vitamins, aspirin, cold-relief medicine, and the like, and surveys find that 80 percent of adults in the United States have taken an over-the-counter pain reliever in the last six months. However, these drugs rarely produce an altered state of consciousness (Dortch, 1996).

In contrast, some substances, known as psychoactive drugs, lead to an altered state of consciousness. **Psychoactive drugs** influence a person's emotions, perceptions, and behavior. Yet even this category of drugs is common in most of our lives. If you have ever had a cup of coffee or sipped a beer, you have taken a psychoactive drug.

A large number of individuals have used more potent—and dangerous—psychoactive drugs than coffee and beer (see Figure 1); for instance, surveys find that 41 percent of high school seniors have used an illegal drug in the last year. In addition, 30 percent report having been drunk on alcohol. The figures for the adult population are even higher (Johnston, O'Malley, & Bachman, 2002).

Of course, drugs vary widely in the effects they have on users, in part because they affect the nervous system in very different ways. Some drugs alter the limbic system, and others affect the operation of specific neurotransmitters across the synapses of neurons. For example, some drugs block or enhance the release of neurotransmitters, others block the receipt or the removal of a neurotransmitter, and still others mimic the effects of a particular neurotransmitter (see Figure 2, and learn more by trying **Interactivity 16–1**).

The most dangerous drugs are addictive. **Addictive drugs** produce a biological or psychological dependence in the user, and withdrawal from them leads to a craving for the drug that, in some cases, may be nearly irresistible. Addictions may be *biologically based:* The body becomes so accustomed to functioning in the presence of a drug that it cannot function in its absence. Or they may be *psychologically based*, in which case people believe that they need the drug to respond to the stresses of daily living. Although we generally associate addiction with drugs such as heroin, everyday sorts of drugs such as caffeine (found in coffee) and nicotine (found in cigarettes) have addictive aspects as well.

We know surprisingly little about the underlying causes of addiction. One of the problems in identifying those causes is that different drugs (such as alcohol and cocaine) affect the brain in very different ways—yet may be equally addicting. Furthermore, it takes longer to become addicted to some drugs than to others, even though the ultimate consequences of addiction may be equally grave (Wickelgren, 1998; Thombs, 1999).

What are the major classifications of drugs, and what are their effects?

Psychoactive drugs: Drugs that influence a person's emotions, perceptions, and behavior.

Addictive drugs: Drugs that produce a biological or psychological dependence in the user so that withdrawal from them leads to a craving for the drug that, in some cases, may be nearly irresistible.

INTERACTIVITY 16–1

Drug effects

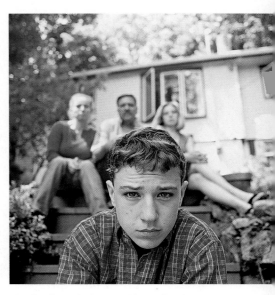

John Brodhead began to drink heavily when he was in the sixth grade.

FIGURE 1 How many teenagers use drugs? The results of the most recent comprehensive survey of 14,000 high school seniors across the United States show the percentage of respondents who have used various substances for nonmedical purposes at least once (Johnston, O'Malley, & Bachman, 2002). Can you think of any reasons why teenagers—as opposed to older people—might be particularly likely to use drugs?

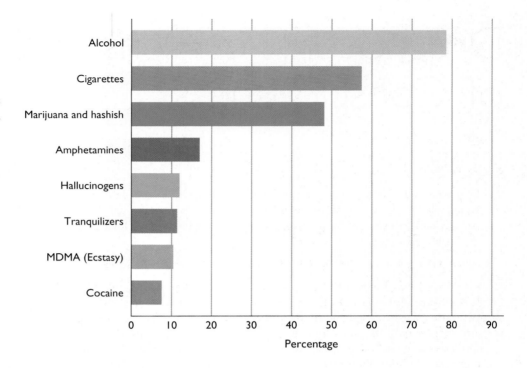

Why do people take drugs in the first place? There are many reasons, ranging from the perceived pleasure of the experience itself, to the escape a drug-induced high affords from the everyday pressures of life, to an attempt to achieve a religious or spiritual state. However, other factors, ones that have little to do with the nature of the experience itself, also lead people to try drugs (McDowell & Spitz, 1999).

For instance, the alleged drug use of well-known role models (such as baseball player Darryl Strawberry and film star Robert Downey, Jr.), the easy availability of some illegal drugs, and peer pressure all play a role in the decision to use drugs. In some cases, the motive is simply the thrill of trying something new. Finally, the sense of helplessness experienced by unemployed individuals trapped in lives of poverty may lead them to try drugs as a way of escaping from the bleakness of their lives.

FIGURE 2 Different drugs affect different parts of the nervous system and brain and each drug functions in one of these specific ways.

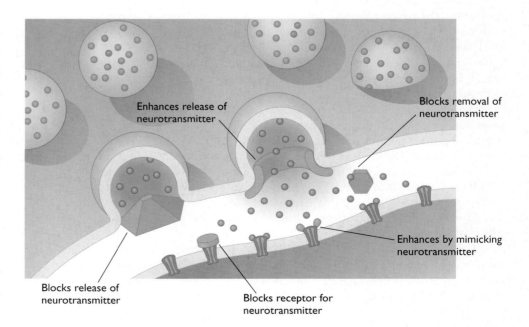

Regardless of the forces that lead a person to begin using drugs, drug addiction is among the most difficult of all behaviors to modify, even with extensive treatment (Tucker, Donovan, & Marlatt, 1999; Lemonick, 2000).

Because of the difficulty in treating drug problems, there is little disagreement that the best hope for dealing with the overall societal problem of substance abuse is to prevent people from becoming involved with drugs in the first place. However, there is little accord on how to accomplish this goal. Even programs widely publicized for their effectiveness—such as D.A.R.E. (Drug Abuse Resistance Education)—are of questionable helpfulness. Used in more than 80 percent of school districts in the United States, D.A.R.E consists of a series of seventeen lessons on the dangers of drugs, alcohol, and gangs taught to fifth- and sixth-graders by a police officer. The program is highly popular with school officials, parents, and politicians.

The problem: Several well-controlled evaluations have been unable to demonstrate that the D.A.R.E. program is effective in reducing drug use over the long term. In fact, one study even showed that D.A.R.E. graduates were *more* likely to use marijuana than was a comparison group of nongraduates (Clayton et al., 1996; Lynam et al., 1999; Kalb, 2001b).

⒜⒜⒜

Stimulants: Drug Highs

It's one o'clock in the morning, and you still haven't finished reading the last chapter of the text on which you will be tested in the morning. Feeling exhausted, you turn to the one thing that may help you stay awake for the next two hours: a cup of strong black coffee.

If you have ever found yourself in such a position, you have been relying on a major *stimulant*, caffeine, to stay awake. *Caffeine* is one of a number of **stimulants,** drugs whose effect on the central nervous system causes a rise in heart rate, blood pressure, and muscular tension. Caffeine is present not only in coffee; it is an important ingredient in tea, soft drinks, and chocolate as well (see Figure 3).

Caffeine produces several reactions. The major behavioral effects are an increase in attentiveness and a decrease in reaction time. Caffeine can also bring about an

Stimulants: Drugs whose effect on the central nervous system causes a rise in heart rate, blood pressure, and muscular tension.

FIGURE 3 How much caffeine do you consume? This chart shows the range of caffeine found in common foods and drinks (*The New York Times*, 1991). The average person in the United States consumes about 200 milligrams of caffeine each day.

improvement in mood, most likely by mimicking the effects of a natural brain chemical, adenosine. Too much caffeine, however, can result in nervousness and insomnia. People can build up a biological dependence on the drug. Regular users who suddenly stop drinking coffee may experience headaches or depression. Many people who drink large amounts of coffee on weekdays have headaches on weekends because of the sudden drop in the amount of caffeine they are consuming (Silverman et al., 1992, 1994; James, 1997).

Nicotine, found in cigarettes, is another common stimulant. The soothing effects of nicotine help explain why cigarette smoking is addictive. Smokers develop a dependence on nicotine, and those who suddenly stop smoking develop strong cravings for the drug. This is not surprising: Nicotine activates neuronal mechanisms similar to those activated by cocaine, which, as we see next, is also highly addictive (Murray, 1990; Pich et al., 1997).

COCAINE

Although its use has declined over the last decade, the stimulant *cocaine* and its derivative crack still represent a serious concern. Cocaine is inhaled or "snorted" through the nose, smoked, or injected directly into the bloodstream. It is rapidly absorbed into the body and takes effect almost immediately.

When used in relatively small quantities, cocaine produces feelings of profound psychological well-being, increased confidence, and alertness. Cocaine produces this "high" through the neurotransmitter dopamine. Dopamine is one of the chemicals that transmit between neurons messages that are related to ordinary feelings of pleasure. Normally when dopamine is released, excess amounts of the neurotransmitter are reabsorbed by the releasing neuron. However, when cocaine enters the brain, it blocks reabsorption of leftover dopamine. As a result, the brain is flooded with dopamine-produced pleasurable sensations (Landry, 1997; Bolla, Cadet, & London, 1998). Figure 4 provides a summary of the effects of cocaine and other illegal drugs.

However, there is a steep price to be paid for the pleasurable effects of cocaine. The brain may become permanently rewired, triggering a psychological and physical addiction in which users grow obsessed with obtaining the drug. Cocaine addicts indulge in binge use, administering the drug every ten to thirty minutes if it is available. During these binges, they think of nothing but cocaine; eating, sleeping, family, friends, money, and even survival have no importance. Their lives become tied

During the late nineteenth century, and even into the early twentieth century, cocaine was used in numerous home remedies and medicines.

FIGURE 4 Drugs and their effects. A comprehensive breakdown of effects of the most commonly used drugs.

Drug	Street Name	Effects	Withdrawal Symptoms	Adverse/Overdose Reactions
Stimulants				
Cocaine	Coke, blow, snow, lady, crack	Increased confidence, mood elevation, sense of energy and alertness, decreased appetite, anxiety, irritability, insomnia, transiet drowsiness, delayed orgasm	Apathy, general fatigue, prolonged sleep, depression, disorientation, suicidal thoughts, agitated motor activity, irritability, bizarre dreams	Elevated blood pressure, increase in body temperature, face picking, suspiciousness, bizarre and repetitious behavior, vivid hallucinations, convulsions, possible death
Amphetamines				
Benzedrine	Speed			
Dexedrine	Speed			
Depressants				
Alcohol	Booze	Anxiety reduction, impulsive-ness, dramatic mood swings, bizarre thoughts, suicidal behavior, slurred speech, disorientation, slowed mental and physical functioning, limited attention span	Weakness, restlessness, nausea and vomiting, headaches, nightmares, irritability, depression, acute anxiety, hallucinations, seizures, possible death	Confusion, decreased response to pain, shallow respiration, dilated pupils, weak and rapid pulse, coma, possible death
Barbiturates				
Nembutal	Yellowjackets, yellows			
Seconal	Reds			
Phenobarbital				
Rohypnol	Roofies, rope, "date-rape drug"	Muscle relaxation, amnesia, sleep	Seizures	Seizures, coma, incapacitation, inability to resist sexual assault
Narcotics				
Heroin	H, hombre, junk, smack, dope, crap, horse	Anxiety and pain reduction, apathy, difficulty in concentration, slowed speech, decreased physical activity, drooling, itching, euphoria, nausea	Anxiety, vomiting, sneezing, diarrhea, lower back pain, watery eyes, runny nose, yawning, irritability, tremors, panic, chills and sweating, cramps	Depressed levels of consciousness, low blood pressure, rapid heart rate, shallow breathing, convulsions, coma, possible death
Morphine	Drugstore dope, cube, first line, mud			
Hallucinogens				
Cannabis	Bhang, kif, ganja, dope, grass, pot, hemp, joint, weed, bone, Mary Jane reefer	Euphoria, relaxed inhibitions, increased appetite, disoriented behavior	Hyperactivity, insomnia, decreased, appetite, anxiety	Severe reactions rare but include panic, paranoia, fatigue, bizarre and dangerous behavior, decreased testosterone over long term; immune-system effects
Marijuana				
Hashish				
Hash oil				
MDMA	Ecstasy	Heightened sense of oneself and insight, feelings of peace, empathy, energy	Depression, anxiety, sleeplessness	Increase in body temperature, memory difficulties
LSD	Acid, quasey, microdot, white lightning	Heightened aesthetic responses; vision and depth distortion; heightened sensitivity to faces and gestures; magnified feelings; paranoia; panic; euphoria	Not reported	Nausea and chills; increased pulse, temperature, and blood pressure; slow, deep breathing; loss of appetite; insomnia; bizarre, dangerous behavior

to the drug. Over time, users deteriorate mentally and physically. In extreme cases, cocaine can cause hallucinations—a common one is of insects crawling over one's body. Ultimately, an overdose of cocaine can lead to death (Carpenter, 2001; Nestler, 2001).

Almost 2.5 million people in the United States are occasional cocaine users, and as many as 1.8 million people use the drug regularly. Given the strength of cocaine, withdrawal from the drug is difficult, and people pass through several distinct

Phase 1 Crash 9 hours to 4 days	Phase 2 Withdrawal 1 to 10 weeks	Phase 3 Extinction Indefinite

FIGURE 5 Phases of cocaine deprivation. In the first stage, users crave cocaine, feel depressed and agitated, and experience increasing anxiety. In the second stage, which begins from nine hours to four days later, heavy users begin the process of "withdrawal." If addicts are able to pass through the withdrawal stage, they move into the third stage, in which craving for cocaine is further reduced. However, they remain highly sensitive to cues related to cocaine use, and relapses are common. (Source: Based on Gawin, 1991.)

phases (see Figure 5). Although the use of cocaine among high school students has declined in recent years, the drug still represents a major problem (Johnston, O'Malley, & Bachman, 2002).

AMPHETAMINES

Amphetamines are strong stimulants, such as Dexedrine and Benzedrine, popularly known as speed. When their use soared in the 1970s, the phrase "speed kills" became prevalent as the drugs caused an increasing number of deaths. Although amphetamine use has declined from its 1970s peak, many drug experts believe that speed would quickly resurface in large quantities if cocaine supplies were interrupted.

In small quantities, amphetamines—which stimulate the central nervous system— bring about a sense of energy and alertness, talkativeness, heightened confidence, and a mood "high." They increase concentration and reduce fatigue. Amphetamines also cause a loss of appetite, increased anxiety, and irritability. When taken over long periods of time, amphetamines can cause feelings of being persecuted by others, as well as a general sense of suspiciousness. People taking amphetamines may lose interest in sex. If taken in too large a quantity, amphetamines overstimulate the central nervous system to such an extent that convulsions and death can occur.

Amphetamines (shown here greatly magnified) are strong stimulants that increase alertness and energy and provide a sense of heightened confidence.

Depressants: Drug Lows

Depressants: Drugs that slow down the nervous system.

In contrast to the initial effect of stimulants, which is an increase in arousal of the central nervous system, the effect of **depressants** is to impede the nervous system by causing neurons to fire more slowly. Small doses result in at least temporary feelings of *intoxication*—drunkenness—along with a sense of euphoria and joy. When large amounts are taken, however, speech becomes slurred and muscle control becomes disjointed, making motion difficult. Ultimately, heavy users may lose consciousness entirely.

ALCOHOL

The most common depressant is *alcohol*, which is used by more people than is any other drug. Based on liquor sales, the average person over the age of 14 drinks 2½ gallons of pure alcohol over the course of a year. This works out to more than 200 drinks per person. Although alcohol consumption has declined steadily over the last decade, surveys show that more than three-fourths of college students indicate that they have had a drink within the last thirty days (Center on Addiction and Substance Abuse, 1994; Jung, 2002).

One of the more disturbing trends is the high frequency of binge drinking among college students. For men, *binge drinking* is defined as having five or more drinks in one sitting; for women, who generally weigh less than men and whose bodies absorb alcohol less efficiently, binge drinking is defined as having four or more drinks at one sitting.

As shown in Figure 6, some 50 percent of male college students and 40 percent of female college students responding to a nationwide survey said they had engaged in binge drinking within the prior two weeks. Some 17 percent of female students and 31 percent of male students admitted drinking on ten or more occasions during the last 30 days. Furthermore, even light drinkers were affected by the high rate of alcohol use: Two-thirds of lighter drinkers said that they had had their studying or sleep disturbed by drunk students, and around one-third had been insulted or humiliated by a drunk student. A quarter of the women said they had been the target of an unwanted sexual advance by a drunk classmate (Wechsler et al., 1994, 2000, 2002).

Although alcohol consumption is widespread, there are significant gender and cultural variations in its use. For example, women are typically somewhat lighter drinkers than men—although the gap between the sexes is narrowing for older women and has closed completely for teenagers. In addition, not only are women usually more susceptible to the effects of alcohol, because of differences in blood volume and body fat that permit more alcohol to go directly into the bloodstream, alcohol abuse may harm the brains of women more than those of men (National Center on Addiction and Substance Abuse, 1996; Blume, 1998; Wuethrich, 2001).

There are also ethnic differences in alcohol consumption. For example, people of East Asian backgrounds who live in the United States tend to drink significantly less than do Caucasians and African Americans, and their incidence of alcohol-related problems is lower. It may be that physical reactions to drinking, which may include

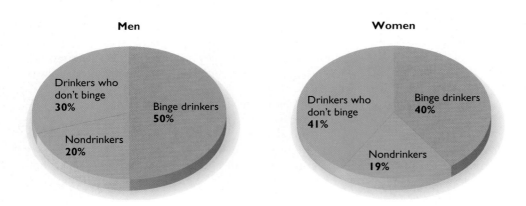

Men

Drinkers who don't binge 30%

Binge drinkers 50%

Nondrinkers 20%

Women

Drinkers who don't binge 41%

Binge drinkers 40%

Nondrinkers 19%

FIGURE 6 Drinking habits of college students (Wechsler et al., 2002). For men, binge drinking was defined as consuming five or more drinks in one sitting; for women, the total was four or more.

FIGURE 7 The effects of alcohol. The quantities represent only rough benchmarks; the effects vary significantly depending on an individual's weight, height, recent food intake, genetic factors, and even psychological state.

Number of drinks consumed in two hours	Alcohol in blood (percentage)	Typical effects
2	0.05	Judgment, thought, and restraint weakened; tension released, giving carefree sensation
3	0.08	Tensions and inhibitions of everyday life lessened; cheerfulness
4	0.10	Voluntary motor action affected, making hand and arm movements, walk, and speech clumsy
7	0.20	Severe impairment—staggering, loud, incoherent, emotionally unstable, 100 times greater traffic risk; exuberance and aggressive inclinations magnified
9	0.30	Deeper areas of brain affected, with stimulus-response and understanding confused; stuporous; blurred vision
12	0.40	Incapable of voluntary action; sleepy, difficult to arouse; equivalent of surgical anesthesia
15	0.50	Comatose; centers controlling breathing and heartbeat anesthetized; death increasingly probable

Note: A drink refers to a typical 12-ounce bottle of beer, a 1.5-ounce shot of hard liquor, or a 5-ounce glass of wine.

sweating, a quickened heartbeat, and flushing, are more unpleasant for East Asians than for other groups (Akutsu et al., 1989; Smith & Lin, 1996; Garcia-Andrade, Wall, & Ehlers, 1997).

Although alcohol is a depressant, most people claim that it increases their sense of sociability and well-being. The discrepancy between the actual and the perceived effects of alcohol lies in the initial effects it produces in the majority of individuals who use it: release of tension and stress, feelings of happiness, and loss of inhibitions (Steele & Josephs, 1990; Sayette, 1993).

As the dose of alcohol increases, however, the depressive effects become more pronounced (see Figure 7). People may feel emotionally and physically unstable. They also show poor judgment and may act aggressively. Moreover, memory is impaired, brain processing of spatial information is diminished, and speech becomes slurred and incoherent. Eventually they may fall into a stupor and pass out. If they drink enough alcohol in a short time, they may die of alcohol poisoning (Bushman, 1993; Chin & Pisoni, 1997; Murphy et al., 1998).

Although most alcohol consumers are casual users, there are more than 14 million alcoholics in the United States. The effects of alcohol vary significantly, depending on who is drinking it and the setting in which people drink. If alcohol were a newly discovered drug, do you think its sale would be legal?

Although most people fall into the category of casual users, there are some 14 million alcoholics in the United States. *Alcoholics*, people with alcohol-abuse problems, come to rely on alcohol and continue to drink even though it causes serious difficulties. In addition, they become increasingly immune to the effects of alcohol. Consequently, alcoholics must drink progressively more to experience the initial positive feelings that alcohol produces (Galanter & Kleber, 1999; Jung, 2002).

In some cases of alcoholism, people must drink constantly in order to feel well enough to function in their daily lives. In other cases, though, people drink inconsistently, but occasionally go on sporadic binges in which they consume large quantities of alcohol.

It is not clear why certain people become alcoholics and develop a tolerance for alcohol, whereas others do not. Some evidence suggests a genetic cause, although the question whether there is a specific inherited gene that produces alcoholism is controversial. What is clear is that the chances of becoming an alcoholic are considerably higher if alcoholics are present in earlier generations of a person's family. However, not all alcoholics have close relatives who are alcoholics. In these cases, environmental stressors are suspected of playing a larger role (Pennisi, 1997b; McGue, 1999).

BARBITURATES

Barbiturates, which include drugs such as Nembutal, Seconal, and phenobarbital, are another form of depressant. Frequently prescribed by physicians to induce sleep or reduce stress, barbiturates produce a sense of relaxation. Yet they too are psychologically and physically addictive and, when combined with alcohol, can be deadly, since such a combination relaxes the muscles of the diaphragm to such an extent that the user stops breathing.

ROHYPNOL

Rohypnol is sometimes called the "date rape drug," because when it is mixed with alcohol, it can prevent victims from resisting sexual assault. Sometimes people who are unknowingly given the drug are so incapacitated that they have no memory of the assault.

Even legal drugs, when used improperly, can lead to addiction.

Narcotics: Relieving Pain and Anxiety

Narcotics are drugs that increase relaxation and relieve pain and anxiety. Two of the most powerful narcotics, *morphine* and *heroin*, are derived from the poppy seed pod. Although morphine is used medically to control severe pain, heroin is illegal in the United States. This has not prevented its widespread use.

Heroin users usually inject the drug directly into their veins with a hypodermic needle. The immediate effect has been described as a "rush" of positive feeling, similar in some respects to a sexual orgasm—and just as difficult to describe. After the rush, a heroin user experiences a sense of well-being and peacefulness that lasts three to five hours. When the effects of the drug wear off, however, the user feels extreme anxiety and a desperate desire to repeat the experience. Moreover, larger amounts of heroin are needed each time to produce the same pleasurable effect. These last two properties are all the ingredients necessary for biological and psychological addiction: The user is constantly either shooting up or attempting to obtain ever-increasing amounts of the drug. Eventually, the life of the addict revolves around heroin.

Because of the powerful positive feelings the drug produces, heroin addiction is particularly difficult to cure. One treatment that has shown some success is the use of methadone. *Methadone* is a synthetic chemical that satisfies a heroin user's physiological cravings for the drug without providing the "high" that accompanies heroin. When heroin users are placed on regular doses of methadone, they may be able to function relatively normally. The use of methadone has one substantial drawback, however: Although it removes the psychological dependence on heroin, it replaces the biological addiction to heroin with a biological addiction to methadone. Researchers are attempting to identify nonaddictive chemical substitutes for heroin as well as substitutes for other addictive drugs that do not replace one addiction with another (Waldrop, 1989; Sinclair, 1990; Pulvirenti & Koob, 1994).

Hallucinogens: Psychedelic Drugs

What do mushrooms, jimsonweed, and morning glories have in common? Besides being fairly common plants, each can be a source of a powerful **hallucinogen**, a drug that is capable of producing hallucinations, or changes in the perceptual process.

The most common hallucinogen in widespread use today is *marijuana*, whose active ingredient—tetrahydrocannabinol (THC)—is found in a common weed, cannabis. Marijuana is typically smoked in cigarettes or pipes, although it can be cooked and eaten. Just over 36 percent of high school seniors and 14 percent of eighth-graders report having used marijuana in the last year (Johnston, O'Malley, & Bachman, 2002; see Figure 8).

The effects of marijuana vary from person to person, but they typically consist of feelings of euphoria and general well-being. Sensory experiences seem more vivid and intense, and a person's sense of self-importance seems to grow. Memory may be impaired, causing the user to feel pleasantly "spaced out." However, the effects are not universally positive. Individuals who use marijuana when they feel depressed can end up even more depressed, because the drug tends to magnify both good and bad feelings.

There are clear risks associated with long-term, heavy marijuana use. Although marijuana does not seem to produce addiction by itself, some evidence suggests that there are similarities in the way marijuana and drugs such as cocaine and heroin affect the brain. Furthermore, there is some evidence that heavy use at least temporarily decreases the production of the male sex hormone testosterone, potentially affecting sexual activity and sperm count (DiChiara, Reinhart, 1997; Block, 2000; Iverson, 2000).

The use of heroin creates a cycle of biological and physical dependence. Combined with the strong positive feelings produced by the drug, this makes heroin addiction especially difficult to cure.

Narcotics: Drugs that increase relaxation and relieve pain and anxiety.

Hallucinogen: A drug that is capable of producing hallucinations, or changes in the perceptual process.

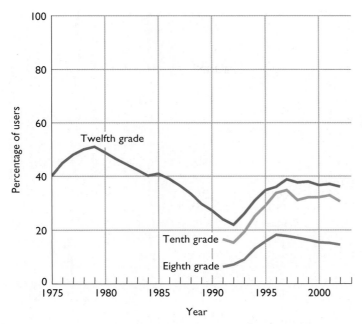

FIGURE 8 Although the level of marijuana use has declined slightly in recent years, overall the absolute number of teenagers who have used the drug in the last year remains relatively high. (Source: Johnston, O'Malley, & Bachman, 2002.)

In addition, marijuana smoked during pregnancy may have lasting effects on children who are exposed prenatally, although the results are inconsistent. Heavy use also affects the ability of the immune system to fight off germs and increases stress on the heart, although it is unclear how strong these effects are. There is one unquestionably negative consequence of smoking marijuana: The smoke damages the lungs much the way cigarette smoke does, producing an increased likelihood of developing cancer and other lung diseases (Cornelius et al., 1995; Julien, 2001).

Despite the possible dangers of marijuana use, there is little scientific evidence for the popular belief that users "graduate" from marijuana to more dangerous drugs. Furthermore, the use of marijuana is routine in certain cultures. For instance, some people in Jamaica habitually drink a marijuana-based tea related to religious practices. In addition, marijuana has several medical uses; it can be used to prevent nausea from chemotherapy, treat some AIDS symptoms, and relieve muscle spasms for people with spinal cord injuries. In a controversial move, several states have made the use of the drug legal if it is prescribed by a physician—although it remains illegal under U.S. federal law (Brookhiser, 1997; National Academy of Sciences, 1999; Iverson, 2000).

MDMA (ECSTASY) AND LSD

MDMA ("Ecstasy") and *lysergic acid diethylamide* (LSD, or "acid") fall into the category of hallucinogens. Both drugs affect the operation of the neurotransmitter serotonin in the brain, causing an alteration in brain-cell activity and perception (Aghajanian, 1994; Cloud, 2000).

Ecstasy users report a sense of peacefulness and calm. People on the drug report experiencing increased empathy and connection with others, as well as feeling more relaxed, yet energetic. Although the data are not conclusive, some researchers have found declines in memory and performance on intellectual tasks, and such findings suggest that there may be long-term changes in serotonin receptors in the brain (Murray, 2001; Gowing, Henry-Edwards, Irvine, & Ali, 2002; Kish, 2002; Parrott, 2002).

What are the effects of a hallucinogen on thinking? Artists have tried to depict the hallucinogenic experience, as in this yarn painting.

LSD, which is structurally similar to serotonin, produces vivid hallucinations. Perceptions of colors, sounds, and shapes are altered so much that even the most mundane experience—such as looking at the knots in a wooden table—can seem moving and exciting. Time perception is distorted, and objects and people may be viewed in a new way, with some users reporting that LSD increases their understanding of the world. For others, however, the experience brought on by LSD can be terrifying, particularly if users have had emotional difficulties in the past. Furthermore, people occasionally experience flashbacks, in which they hallucinate long after they initially used the drug (Baruss, 2003).

BECOMING AN INFORMED CONSUMER of Psychology
Identifying Drug and Alcohol Problems

In a society bombarded with commercials for drugs that are guaranteed to do everything from curing the common cold to giving new life to "tired blood," it is no wonder that drug-related problems are a major social issue. Yet many people with drug and alcohol problems deny they have them, and even close friends and family members may fail to realize when occasional social use of drugs or alcohol has turned into abuse.

Certain signs, however, indicate when use becomes abuse (Archambault, 1992; National Institute on Drug Abuse, 2000). Among them are the following:

- ▶ Always getting high to have a good time
- ▶ Being high more often than not
- ▶ Getting high to get oneself going
- ▶ Going to work or class while high
- ▶ Missing or being unprepared for class or work because you were high
- ▶ Feeling bad later about something you said or did while high
- ▶ Driving a car while high
- ▶ Coming in conflict with the law because of drugs
- ▶ Doing something while high that you wouldn't do otherwise
- ▶ Being high in nonsocial, solitary situations

- ⊚ Being unable to stop getting high
- ⊚ Feeling a need for a drink or a drug to get through the day
- ⊚ Becoming physically unhealthy
- ⊚ Failing at school or on the job
- ⊚ Thinking about liquor or drugs all the time
- ⊚ Avoiding family or friends while using liquor or drugs

Any combination of these symptoms should be sufficient to alert you to the potential of a serious drug problem. Because drug and alcohol dependence are almost impossible to cure on one's own, people who suspect that they have a problem should seek immediate attention from a psychologist, physician, or counselor.

You can also get help from national hotlines. For alcohol difficulties, call the National Council on Alcoholism at (800) 622-2255. For drug problems, call the National Institute on Drug Abuse at (800) 662-4357. You can also check your telephone book for a local listing of Alcoholics Anonymous or Narcotics Anonymous. Finally, check out the websites of the National Institute on Alcohol Abuse and Alcoholism (www.niaaa.nih.gov) and the National Institute on Drug Abuse (www.nida.nih.gov).

RECAP/EVALUATE/RETHINK

RECAP

What are the major classifications of drugs, and what are their effects?

- ⊚ Drugs can produce an altered state of consciousness. However, they vary in how dangerous they are and in whether they are addictive. (p. 169)
- ⊚ Stimulants cause arousal in the central nervous system. Two common stimulants are caffeine and nicotine. More dangerous are cocaine and amphetamines, which in large quantities can lead to convulsions and death. (p. 171)
- ⊚ Depressants decrease arousal in the central nervous system. They can cause intoxication along with feelings of euphoria. The most common depressants are alcohol and barbiturates. (p. 174)
- ⊚ Alcohol is the most frequently used depressant. Its initial effects of released tension and positive feelings yield to depressive effects as the dose of alcohol increases. Both genetic causes and environmental stressors can lead to alcoholism. (p. 175)
- ⊚ Morphine and heroin are narcotics, drugs that produce relaxation and relieve pain and anxiety. Because of their addictive qualities, morphine and heroin are particularly dangerous. (p. 178)
- ⊚ Hallucinogens are drugs that produce hallucinations or other changes in perception. The most frequently used hallucinogen is marijuana, which has several long-term risks. Two other hallucinogens are LSD and Ecstasy. (p. 178)

- ⊚ A number of signals indicate when drug use becomes drug abuse. A person who suspects that he or she has a drug problem should get professional help. People are almost never capable of solving drug problems on their own. (p. 180)

EVALUATE

1. Drugs that affect a person's consciousness are referred to as _____.
2. Match the type of drug to an example of that type.

   1. Narcotic—a pain reliever
   2. Amphetamine—a strong stimulant
   3. Hallucinogen—capable of producing hallucinations
   a. LSD
   b. Heroin
   c. Dexedrine or speed

3. Classify each drug listed as a stimulant (S), depressant (D), hallucinogen (H), or narcotic (N).

   1. Nicotine
   2. Cocaine
   3. Alcohol
   4. Morphine
   5. Marijuana

4. The effects of LSD can recur long after the drug has been taken. True or false?
5. _____ is a drug that has been used to cure people of heroin addiction.

RETHINK

1. Why have drug education campaigns largely been ineffective in stemming the use of illegal drugs? Should the use of certain now-illegal drugs be made legal? Would it be more effective to stress reduction of drug use rather than a complete prohibition of drug use?

2. People often use the word *addiction* loosely, speaking of an addiction to candy or a television show. Can you explain the difference between this type of "addiction" and a true physiological addiction? Is there a difference between this type of addiction and a psychological addiction?

Answers to Evaluate Questions

1. psychoactive; 2. 1-b, 2-c, 3-a; 3. 1-S, 2-S, 3-D, 4-N, 5-H; 4. true; 5. methadone

KEY TERMS

psychoactive drugs p. 169   stimulants p. 171   narcotics p. 178   hallucinogen p. 178
addictive drugs p. 169   depressants p. 174

Looking Back

Psychology on the Web

1. Find a resource on the Web that interprets dreams and another that reports the results of scientific dream research. Compare the nature and content of the two sites in terms of the topics covered, the reliability of information provided, and the promises made about the use of the site and its information. Write a summary of what you found.
2. There is considerable debate about the effectiveness of D.A.R.E., the Drug Abuse Resistance Education program. Find a discussion of both sides of the issue on the Web and summarize the arguments on each side. State your own preliminary conclusions about the D.A.R.E. program.
3. After completing Interactivity 16–1, use the Web to investigate one of the illegal drugs that are described in the chapter. Consult several websites and summarize the way that the drug operates on the nervous system and brain.

Epilogue

An examination of states of consciousness ranges widely, as we have seen. It focuses both on natural factors such as sleep, dreaming, and daydreaming and on more intentional modes of altering consciousness, including hypnosis, meditation, and drugs. As we consider why people seek to alter their consciousness, we need to reflect on the uses and abuses of the various consciousness-altering strategies in which people engage.

Return briefly to the case of Scott Kreuger, the college student who died from binge drinking. Consider the following questions in light of your understanding of alcohol use and abuse:

1. How does alcohol affect the state of consciousness of users such as Kreuger?
2. What do you think might have caused Kreuger's excessive drinking the evening he overdosed on alcohol? Given his excessive alcohol consumption, do you believe he should have been considered an alcoholic?
3. How do college norms about drinking affect alcohol use among students?
4. Do you think that more effective alcohol and drug education might have prevented his behavior?

Learning

Prologue

A Friend Named Bo

Any of us would be lucky to have a friend like Bo. Bo is a wonderful companion, loyal and giving unselfishly of time and affection. He is ever-ready to help, and in return, he asks for little.

But Bo was trained to be this way.

Bo is a 5-year-old golden retriever and Labrador mix, a dog trained to be a helpmate to his owner, Brad Gabrielson. Gabrielson has cerebral palsy, and he has little control over his muscles. Yet with the help of Bo, Gabrielson can lead a life of independence.

Bo's abilities are many. If the doorbell rings, he answers the door. If Gabrielson drops something, Bo will pick it up. If Gabrielson is thirsty, Bo brings him a drink. One time, when Gabrielson fell, Bo left the apartment, went across the hall to a neighbor's door, where he scratched and barked. When the neighbor proved not to be home, Bo went upstairs to another neighbor's apartment.

When that neighbor—who had never encountered Bo before—came to the door, Bo led him downstairs, carefully tugging his hand. As the neighbor helped Gabrielson, Bo stood careful watch at his side. Said Gabrielson later, "On my own, I would have had to lie there ... until my fiancée got home six hours later." But, he continued, "Bo came over and licked my face, to make sure I was all right, that I responded. Then he went to look for help" (Ryan, 1991, p. 14). And Gabrielson stopped worrying.

Bo's expertise did not just happen, of course. It was the result of painstaking training procedures—the same ones that are at work in each of our lives, illustrated by our ability to read a book, drive a car, play poker, study for a test, or perform any of the numerous activities that make up our daily routine. Like Bo, all of us must acquire and then refine our skills and abilities through learning.

Learning is a fundamental topic for psychologists and plays a central role in almost every specialty area of psychology. For example, a psychologist studying perception might ask, "How do we learn that people who look small from a distance are far away and not simply tiny?" A developmental psychologist might inquire, "How do babies learn to distinguish their

Looking Ahead

mothers from other people?" A clinical psychologist might wonder, "Why do some people learn to be afraid when they see a spider?" A social psychologist might ask, "How do we learn to believe that we've fallen in love?"

Each of these questions, although drawn from very different branches of psychology, can be answered only through an understanding of basic learning processes. In each case, a skill or a behavior is acquired, altered, or refined through experience.

Psychologists have approached the study of learning from several angles. Among the most fundamental are studies of the type of learning that is illustrated in responses ranging from a dog salivating when it hears its owner opening a can of dog food to the emotions we feel when our national anthem is played. Other theories consider how learning is a consequence of rewarding circumstances. Finally, several other approaches focus on the cognitive aspects of learning, or the thought processes that underlie learning.

Classical Conditioning

Does the mere sight of the golden arches in front of McDonald's make you feel pangs of hunger and think about hamburgers? If it does, you are displaying an elementary form of learning called classical conditioning. *Classical conditioning* helps explain such diverse phenomena as crying at the sight of a bride walking down the aisle, fearing the dark, and falling in love.

Classical conditioning is one of a number of different types of learning that psychologists have identified, but a general definition encompasses them all: **Learning** is a relatively permanent change in behavior that is brought about by experience.

How do we know when a behavior has been influenced by learning—or even is a result of learning? Part of the answer relates to the nature-nurture question, one of the fundamental issues underlying the field of psychology. In the acquisition of behaviors, experience—essential to the definition of learning—is the "nurture" part. However, some changes in behavior or performance come about through maturation: inherited, genetic factors representing the "nature" part of the nature-nurture question. For instance, children become better tennis players as they grow older partly because their strength increases with their size—a maturational phenomenon. Maturational changes have to be differentiated from improvements resulting from practice, which indicate that learning has taken place.

Similarly, we must distinguish short-term changes in behavior that are due to factors other than learning—such as declines in performance resulting from fatigue or lack of effort—from performance changes that are due to actual learning. If Venus Williams performs poorly in a tennis match because of tension or fatigue, this does not mean that she has not learned to play correctly or has "unlearned" how to play well. Because there is not always a one-to-one correspondence between learning and performance, understanding when true learning has occurred is difficult.

Although philosophers since the time of Aristotle have speculated on the foundations of learning, the first systematic research on learning was done at the beginning of the twentieth century, when Ivan Pavlov (does the name ring a bell?) developed the framework for learning called classical conditioning.

Ⓐ Ⓐ Ⓐ

What is learning?

How do we learn to form associations between stimuli and responses?

Learning: A relatively permanent change in behavior brought about by experience.

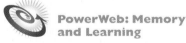

PowerWeb: Memory and Learning
www.mhhe.com/feldmanup7

The Basics of Classical Conditioning

Ivan Pavlov, a Russian physiologist, never intended to do psychological research. In 1904 he won the Nobel Prize for his work on digestion, testimony to his contribution to that field. Yet Pavlov is remembered not for his physiological research, but for his experiments on basic learning processes—work that he began quite accidentally (Windholz, 1997).

Pavlov had been studying the secretion of stomach acids and salivation in dogs in response to the ingestion of varying amounts and kinds of food. While doing that, he observed a curious phenomenon: Sometimes stomach secretions and salivation would begin in the dogs when they had not yet eaten any food. The mere sight of the experimenter who normally brought the food, or even the sound of the experimenter's

Ivan Pavlov (center) developed the principles of classical conditioning.

Classical conditioning: A type of learning in which a neutral stimulus comes to bring about a response after it is paired with a stimulus that naturally brings about that response.

Neutral stimulus: A stimulus that, before conditioning, does not naturally bring about the response of interest.

Unconditioned stimulus (UCS): A stimulus that naturally brings about a particular response without having been learned.

Unconditioned response (UCR): A response that is natural and needs no training (e.g., salivation at the smell of food).

Conditioned stimulus (CS): A once-neutral stimulus that has been paired with an unconditioned stimulus to bring about a response formerly caused only by the unconditioned stimulus.

Conditioned response (CR): A response that, after conditioning, follows a previously neutral stimulus (e.g., salivation at the ringing of a bell).

footsteps, was enough to produce salivation in the dogs. Pavlov's genius lay in his ability to recognize the implications of this discovery. He saw that the dogs were responding not only on the basis of a biological need (hunger), but also as a result of learning—or, as it came to be called, classical conditioning. **Classical conditioning** is a type of learning in which a neutral stimulus (such as the experimenter's footsteps) comes to bring about a response after it is paired with a stimulus (such as food) that naturally brings about that response.

To demonstrate and analyze classical conditioning, Pavlov conducted a series of experiments (Pavlov, 1927). In one, he attached a tube to the salivary gland of a dog; that would allow him to measure precisely the dog's salivation. He then rang a bell and, just a few seconds later, presented the dog with meat. This pairing occurred repeatedly and was carefully planned so that each time exactly the same amount of time elapsed between the presentation of the bell and the meat. At first the dog would salivate only when the meat was presented, but soon it began to salivate at the sound of the bell. In fact, even when Pavlov stopped presenting the meat, the dog still salivated after hearing the sound. The dog had been classically conditioned to salivate to the bell.

As you can see in Figure 1, the basic processes of classical conditioning that underlie Pavlov's discovery are straightforward, although the terminology he chose is not simple. Consider first the diagram in Figure 1a. Before conditioning, there are two unrelated stimuli: the ringing of a bell and meat. We know that normally the ringing of a bell does not lead to salivation but to some irrelevant response, such as perking up the ears or perhaps a startle reaction. The bell is therefore called the **neutral stimulus** because it is a stimulus that, before conditioning, does not naturally bring about the response in which we are interested. We also have meat, which, because of the biological makeup of the dog, naturally leads to salivation—the response we are interested in conditioning. The meat is considered an **unconditioned stimulus**, or **UCS**, because food placed in a dog's mouth automatically causes salivation to occur. The response that the meat elicits (salivation) is called an **unconditioned response**, or **UCR**—a natural, innate, reflexive response that is not associated with previous learning. Unconditioned responses are always brought about by the presence of unconditioned stimuli.

Figure 1b illustrates what happens during conditioning. The bell is rung just before each presentation of the meat. The goal of conditioning is for the bell to become associated with the unconditioned stimulus (meat) and therefore to bring about the same sort of response as the unconditioned stimulus. After a number of pairings of the bell and meat, the bell alone causes the dog to salivate.

When conditioning is complete, the bell has evolved from a neutral stimulus to what is now called a **conditioned stimulus**, or **CS**. At this time, salivation that occurs as a response to the conditioned stimulus (bell) is considered a **conditioned response**, or **CR**. This situation is depicted in Figure 1c. After conditioning, then, the conditioned stimulus evokes the conditioned response.

The sequence and timing of the presentation of the unconditioned stimulus and the conditioned stimulus are particularly important (Rescorla, 1988; Wasserman & Miller, 1997). Like a malfunctioning warning light at a railroad crossing that goes on after the train has passed by, a neutral stimulus that *follows* an unconditioned stimulus has little chance of becoming a conditioned stimulus. However, just as a warning light works best if it goes on right before a train passes, a neutral stimulus that is presented *just before* the unconditioned stimulus is most apt to result in successful

a. Before conditioning

b. During conditioning

c. After conditioning

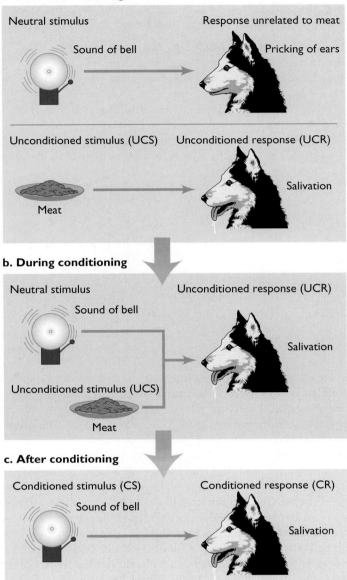

FIGURE 1 The basic process of classical conditioning. (a) Before conditioning, the ringing of a bell does not bring about salivation—making the bell a neutral stimulus. In contrast, meat naturally brings about salivation, making the meat an unconditioned stimulus and salivation an unconditioned response. (b) During conditioning, the bell is rung just before the presentation of the meat. (c) Eventually, the ringing of the bell alone brings about salivation. We now can say that conditioning has been accomplished: The previously neutral stimulus of the bell is now considered a conditioned stimulus that brings about the conditioned response of salivation.

conditioning. Research has shown that conditioning is most effective if the neutral stimulus (which will become a conditioned stimulus) precedes the unconditioned stimulus by between a half second and several seconds, depending on what kind of response is being conditioned.

PowerWeb:
Conditioned Reflexes:
An Investigation of the
Physiological Activity
of the Cerebral Cortex

www.mhhe.com/feldmanup7

INTERACTIVITY 17–1

Classical conditioning

PowerWeb:
Conditioned
Emotional Reactions

www.mhhe.com/feldmanup7

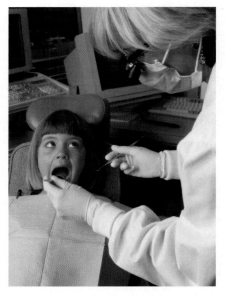

Because of a previous unpleasant experience, a person may expect a similar occurrence when faced with a comparable situation in the future, a process known as stimulus generalization. Can you think of ways this process is used in everyday life?

Although the terminology Pavlov used to describe classical conditioning at first may seem confusing, the following summary rules can help make the relationships between stimuli and responses easier to understand and remember:

- Conditioned = learned, and unconditioned = not learned.
- An *un*conditioned stimulus leads to an *un*conditioned response.
- *Un*conditioned stimulus–*un*conditioned response pairings are *un*learned and *un*trained.
- During conditioning, a previously neutral stimulus is transformed into the conditioned stimulus.
- A conditioned stimulus leads to a conditioned response, and a conditioned stimulus–conditioned response pairing is a consequence of learning and training.
- An unconditioned response and a conditioned response are similar (such as salivation in the example described earlier), but the unconditioned response occurs naturally, whereas the conditioned response is learned.

Interactivity 17–1 will help you understand these principles and classical conditioning in general.

Applying Conditioning Principles to Human Behavior

Although the initial conditioning experiments were carried out with animals, classical conditioning principles were soon found to explain many aspects of everyday human behavior. Recall, for instance, the earlier illustration of how people may experience hunger pangs at the sight of McDonald's golden arches. The cause of this reaction is classical conditioning: The previously neutral arches have become associated with the food inside the restaurant (the unconditioned stimulus), causing the arches to become a conditioned stimulus that brings about the conditioned response of hunger.

Emotional responses are particularly likely to be learned through classical conditioning processes. For instance, how do some of us develop fears of mice, spiders, and other creatures that are typically harmless? In a now-infamous case study, psychologist John B. Watson and colleague Rosalie Rayner (1920) showed that classical conditioning was at the root of such fears by conditioning an 11-month-old infant named Albert to be afraid of rats. "Little Albert," like most infants, initially was frightened by loud noises but had no fear of rats.

In the study, the experimenters sounded a loud noise just as they showed Little Albert a rat. The noise (the unconditioned stimulus) evoked fear (the unconditioned response). However, after just a few pairings of noise and rat, Albert began to show fear of the rat by itself, bursting into tears when he saw it. The rat, then, had become a CS that brought about the CR, fear. Furthermore, the effects of the conditioning lingered: five days later, Albert reacted with fear not only when shown a rat, but when shown objects that looked similar to the white, furry rat, including a white rabbit, a white sealskin coat, and even a white Santa Claus mask. (By the way, we don't know what happened to the unfortunate Little Albert. We do know that Watson, the experimenter, has been condemned for using ethically questionable procedures and that such studies would never be conducted today.)

Learning via classical conditioning also occurs during adulthood. For example, you may not go to a dentist as often as you should because of prior associations of dentists with pain. Or you may have a particular fondness for the smell of a certain perfume or aftershave lotion because the feelings and thoughts of an early lover come rushing back whenever you encounter it. Classical conditioning, then, explains many of the reactions we have to stimuli in the world around us (Woodruff-Pak, 1999; Herman et al., 2002).

Extinction

What do you think would happen if a dog that had become classically conditioned to salivate at the ringing of a bell never again received food when the bell was rung? The answer lies in one of the basic phenomena of learning: extinction. **Extinction** occurs when a previously conditioned response decreases in frequency and eventually disappears.

Extinction: A basic phenomenon of learning that occurs when a previously conditioned response decreases in frequency and eventually disappears.

To produce extinction, one needs to end the association between conditioned stimuli and unconditioned stimuli. For instance, if we had trained a dog to salivate (the conditioned response) at the ringing of a bell (the conditioned stimulus), we could produce extinction by repeatedly ringing the bell but *not* providing meat. At first the dog would continue to salivate when it heard the bell, but after a few such instances, the amount of salivation would probably decline, and the dog would eventually stop responding to the bell altogether. At that point, we could say that the response had been extinguished. In sum, extinction occurs when the conditioned stimulus is presented repeatedly without the unconditioned stimulus.

We should keep in mind that extinction can be a helpful phenomenon. Consider, for instance, what it would be like if the fear you experienced while watching the shower murder scene in the classic movie *Psycho* never was extinguished. You might well tremble with fright every time you took a shower.

Once a conditioned response has been extinguished, has it vanished forever? Not necessarily. Pavlov discovered this when he returned to his dog a few days after the conditioned behavior had seemingly been extinguished. If he rang a bell, the dog once again salivated—an effect known as **spontaneous recovery**, or the reemergence of an extinguished conditioned response after a period of rest and with no further conditioning.

Spontaneous recovery: The reemergence of an extinguished conditioned response after a period of rest and with no further conditioning.

Spontaneous recovery helps explain why it is so hard to overcome drug addictions. For example, cocaine addicts who are thought to be "cured" can experience an irresistible impulse to use the drug again if they are subsequently confronted by a stimulus with strong connections to the drug, such as a white powder (O'Brien et al., 1992; Drummond et al., 1995; DiCano & Everitt, 2002).

Generalization and Discrimination

Despite differences in color and shape, to most of us a rose is a rose is a rose. The pleasure we experience at the beauty, smell, and grace of the flower is similar for different types of roses. Pavlov noticed a similar phenomenon. His dogs often salivated not only at the ringing of the bell that was used during their original conditioning but at the sound of a buzzer as well.

Such behavior is the result of stimulus generalization. **Stimulus generalization** is what takes place when a conditioned response follows a stimulus that is similar to the original conditioned stimulus. The greater the similarity between the two stimuli, the greater the likelihood of stimulus generalization. Little Albert, who, as we mentioned earlier, was conditioned to be fearful of rats, grew afraid of other furry white things as well. However, according to the principle of stimulus generalization, it is unlikely that he would have been afraid of a black dog, because its color would have differentiated it sufficiently from the original fear-evoking stimulus (Prokasy & Hall, 1963).

Stimulus generalization: Tendency to respond to a stimulus that is similar to but different from a conditioned stimulus; the more similar the two stimuli are, the more likely generalization is to occur.

The conditioned response elicited by the new stimulus is usually not as intense as the original conditioned response, although the more similar the new stimulus is to the old one, the more similar the new response will be. It is unlikely, then, that Little Albert's fear of the Santa Claus mask was as great as his learned fear of a rat. Still, stimulus generalization permits us to know, for example, that we ought to brake at all red lights, even if there are minor variations in size, shape, and shade.

If two stimuli are sufficiently distinct from one another that one evokes a conditioned response but the other does not, we can say that stimulus discrimination has occurred. **Stimulus discrimination** is the ability to differentiate between stimuli. For example, my dog Cleo comes running into the kitchen when she hears the sound of the electric can opener, which she has learned is used to open her dog food when her dinner is about to be served. She does not bound into the kitchen at the sound of the food processor, although it sounds similar. In other words, she discriminates between the stimuli of can opener and food processor. Similarly, our ability to discriminate between the behavior of a growling dog and that of one whose tail is wagging can lead to adaptive behavioral reactions.

Stimulus discrimination: The ability to differentiate between stimuli.

Beyond Traditional Classical Conditioning: Challenging Basic Assumptions

Although Pavlov hypothesized that all learning is nothing more than long strings of conditioned responses, this notion has not been supported by subsequent research. It turns out that classical conditioning provides us with only a partial explanation of how people and animals learn and that Pavlov was wrong in some of his basic assumptions (Rizley & Rescorla, 1972; Hollis, 1997).

For example, according to Pavlov, the process of linking stimuli and responses occurs in a mechanistic, unthinking way. In contrast to this perspective, learning theorists influenced by cognitive psychology have argued that learners actively develop an understanding and expectancy about which particular unconditioned stimuli are matched with specific conditioned stimuli. A ringing bell, for instance, gives a dog something to think about: the impending arrival of food (Rescorla, 1988; Clark & Squire, 1998; Woodruff-Pak, 1999).

Traditional explanations of how classical conditioning operates have also been challenged by learning psychologist John Garcia, whose research was initially concerned with the effects of exposure to nuclear radiation on laboratory animals. In the course of his experiments, he realized that rats placed in a radiation chamber drank almost no water, even though in their home cage they drank eagerly. The most obvious explanation—that it had something to do with the radiation—was soon ruled out. Garcia found that even when the radiation was not turned on, the rats still drank little or no water in the radiation chamber (Garcia, Hankins, & Rusiniak, 1974; Garcia, 1990).

Initially puzzled by the rats' behavior, Garcia eventually figured out that the drinking cups in the radiation chamber were made of plastic, giving the water an unusual, plastic-like taste. In contrast, the drinking cups in the home cage were made of glass and left no abnormal taste.

As a result, the plastic-tasting water had become repeatedly paired with illness brought on by exposure to radiation, and that had led the rats to form a classically conditioned association. The process began with the radiation acting as an unconditioned stimulus evoking the unconditioned response of sickness. With repeated pairings, the plastic-tasting water had become a conditioned stimulus that evoked the conditioned response of sickness.

This finding violated one of the basic rules of classical conditioning—that an unconditioned stimulus should *immediately* follow a conditioned stimulus for optimal conditioning to occur. Instead, Garcia's findings showed that conditioning could

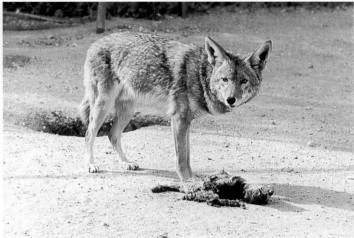

Because of prior experience with meat that had been laced with a mild poison, this coyote does not obey its natural instincts and ignores what otherwise would be a tasty meal. What principles of classical conditioning does this phenomenon contradict?

occur even when there was an interval of as long as eight hours between exposure to the conditioned stimulus and the response of sickness. Furthermore, the conditioning persisted over very long periods and sometimes occurred after just one exposure to water that was followed later on by illness.

These findings have had important practical implications. For example, to prevent coyotes from killing their sheep, some ranchers now routinely lace a sheep carcass with a drug and leave the carcass in a place where coyotes will find it. The drug temporarily makes the coyotes quite ill, but it does not harm them permanently. After just one exposure to a drug-laden sheep carcass, coyotes avoid sheep, which are normally one of their primary natural victims (Green, Henderson, & Collinge, 2003).

The ease with which animals can be conditioned to avoid certain kinds of dangerous stimuli, such as tainted food, supports evolutionary theory. As Darwin suggested, organisms that have traits and characteristics that aid survival are more likely to thrive and have descendents. Consequently, organisms that ingest unpalatable foods (whether coyotes that eat a carcass laced with a drug or humans who suffer food poisoning after eating spoiled sushi in a restaurant) are likely to avoid similar foods in the future, making their survival more likely (Steinmetz, Kim, & Thompson, 2003).

RECAP/EVALUATE/RETHINK

RECAP

What is learning?

▶ Learning, a relatively permanent change in behavior resulting from experience, is a basic topic of psychology. (p. 187)

How do we learn to form associations between stimuli and responses?

▶ One major form of learning is classical conditioning, which occurs when a neutral stimulus—one that normally brings about no relevant response—is repeatedly paired with a stimulus (called an unconditioned stimulus) that brings about a natural, untrained response. (p. 187)

▶ Conditioning occurs when the neutral stimulus is repeatedly presented just before the unconditioned stimulus. After repeated pairings, the neutral stimulus brings about the same response that the unconditioned stimulus brings about. When this occurs, the neutral stimulus has become a conditioned stimulus, and the response a conditioned response. (p. 188)

▶ Learning is not always permanent. Extinction occurs when a previously learned response decreases in frequency and eventually disappears. (p. 191)

▶ Stimulus generalization is the tendency for a conditioned response to follow a stimulus that is similar to, but not the same as, the original conditioned stimulus. The converse phenomenon, stimulus discrimination, occurs when an organism learns to distinguish between stimuli. (p. 191)

EVALUATE

1. _____ involves changes brought about by experience, whereas maturation describes changes resulting from biological development.

2. _____ is the name of the scientist responsible for discovering the learning phenomenon known as _____ conditioning, in which an organism learns a response to a stimulus to which it normally would not respond.

Refer to the passage below to answer questions 3 through 5:

The last three times little Theresa visited Dr. Lopez for checkups, he administered a painful preventive immunization shot that left her in tears. Today, when her mother takes her for another checkup, Theresa begins to sob as soon as she comes face to face with Dr. Lopez, even before he has had a chance to say hello.

3. The painful shot that Theresa received during each visit was a(n) _____ _____ that elicited the _____ _____, her tears.

4. Dr. Lopez is upset because his presence has become a _____ _____ for Theresa's crying.

5. Fortunately, Dr. Lopez gave Theresa no more shots for quite some time. Over that period she gradually stopped crying and even came to like him. _____ had occurred.

6. _____ _____ occurs when a stimulus that is fairly similar to the conditioned stimulus produces the same response.

7. In contrast, _____ _____ occurs when there is no response to a stimulus that is slightly distinct from the conditioned stimulus.

RETHINK

1. Can you think of ways in which classical conditioning is used by politicians? advertisers? moviemakers? Do ethical issues arise from any of these uses?

2. How likely is it that Little Albert, Watson's experimental subject, went through life afraid of Santa Claus? Describe what could have happened to prevent his continual dread of Santa.

Answers to Evaluate Questions

1. learning; 2. Pavlov, classical; 3. unconditioned stimulus, unconditioned response; 4. conditioned stimulus; 5. extinction; 6. stimulus generalization; 7. stimulus discrimination

KEY TERMS

learning p. 187
classical conditioning p. 188
neutral stimulus p. 188
unconditioned stimulus (UCS) p. 188

unconditioned response (UCR) p. 188
conditioned stimulus (CS) p. 188

conditioned response (CR) p. 188
extinction p. 191
spontaneous recovery p. 191

stimulus generalization p. 191
stimulus discrimination p. 192

Operant Conditioning

What is the role of reward and punishment in learning?

What are some practical methods for bringing about behavior change, both in ourselves and in others?

Very good ... What a clever idea ... Fantastic ... I agree ... Thank you ... Excellent ... Super ... Right on ... This is the best paper you've ever written; you get an A ... You are really getting the hang of it ... I'm impressed ... You're getting a raise ... Have a cookie ... You look great ... I love you ...

Few of us mind being the recipient of any of the above comments. But what is especially noteworthy about them is that each of these simple statements can be used, through a process known as operant conditioning, to bring about powerful changes in behavior and to teach the most complex tasks. Operant conditioning is the basis for many of the most important kinds of human, and animal, learning.

Operant conditioning is learning in which a voluntary response is strengthened or weakened, depending on its favorable or unfavorable consequences. When we say that a response has been strengthened or weakened, we mean that it has been made more or less likely to recur regularly.

Unlike classical conditioning, in which the original behaviors are the natural, biological responses to the presence of a stimulus such as food, water, or pain, operant conditioning applies to voluntary responses, which an organism performs deliberately to produce a desirable outcome. The term *operant* emphasizes this point: The organism *operates* on its environment to produce a desirable result. Operant conditioning is at work when we learn that toiling industriously can bring about a raise or that studying hard results in good grades.

As with classical conditioning, the basis for understanding operant conditioning was laid by work with animals. We turn now to some of that early research, which began with a simple inquiry into the behavior of cats.

Operant conditioning: Learning in which a voluntary response is strengthened or weakened, depending on its favorable or unfavorable consequences.

▲▲▲

Thorndike's Law of Effect

If you placed a hungry cat in a cage and then put a small piece of food outside the cage, just beyond the cat's reach, chances are that the cat would eagerly search for a way out of the cage. The cat might first claw at the sides or push against an opening. Suppose, though, you had rigged things so that the cat could escape by stepping on a small paddle that released the latch to the door of the cage (see Figure 1). Eventually, as it moved around the cage, the cat would happen to step on the paddle, the door would open, and the cat would eat the food.

What would happen if you then returned the cat to the box? The next time, it would probably take a little less time for the cat to step on the paddle and escape. After a few trials, the cat would deliberately step on the paddle as soon as it was placed in the cage. What would have occurred, according to Edward L. Thorndike (1932), who studied this situation extensively, was that the cat would have learned that pressing the paddle was associated with the desirable consequence of getting food. Thorndike summarized that relationship by formulating the *law of effect*: Responses that lead to satisfying consequences are more likely to be repeated.

FIGURE 1 Edward L. Thorndike devised this puzzle box to study the process by which a cat learns to press a paddle to escape from the box and receive food. Do you think Thorndike's work has relevance to the question of why humans voluntarily solve puzzles, such as crossword puzzles and jigsaw puzzles? Do they receive any rewards?

Thorndike believed that the law of effect operates as automatically as leaves fall off a tree in autumn. It was not necessary for an organism to understand that there was a link between a response and a reward. Instead, Thorndike believed, over time and through experience the organism would make a direct connection between the stimulus and the response without any awareness that the connection existed.

The Basics of Operant Conditioning

Thorndike's early research served as the foundation for the work of one of the twentieth century's most influential psychologists, B. F. Skinner, who died in 1990. You may have heard of the Skinner box (shown in Figure 2), a chamber with a highly controlled environment that was used to study operant conditioning processes with laboratory animals. Whereas Thorndike's goal was to get his cats to learn to obtain

FIGURE 2 A Skinner box, used to study operant conditioning. Laboratory rats learn to press the lever in order to obtain food, which is delivered in the tray.

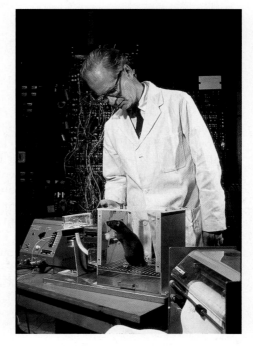

food by leaving the box, animals in a Skinner box learn to obtain food by operating on their environment within the box. Skinner became interested in specifying how behavior varies as a result of alterations in the environment.

Skinner, whose work went far beyond perfecting Thorndike's earlier apparatus, is considered the inspiration for a whole generation of psychologists studying operant conditioning (Bjork, 1993; Keehn, 1996). To illustrate Skinner's contribution, let's consider what happens to a rat in the typical Skinner box.

Suppose you want to teach a hungry rat to press a lever that is in its box. At first the rat will wander around the box, exploring the environment in a relatively random fashion. At some point, however, it will probably press the lever by chance, and when it does, it will receive a food pellet. The first time this happens, the rat will not learn the connection between pressing a lever and receiving food and will continue to explore the box. Sooner or later the rat will press the lever again and receive a pellet, and in time the frequency of the pressing response will increase. Eventually, the rat will press the lever continually until it satisfies its hunger, thereby demonstrating that it has learned that the receipt of food is contingent on pressing the lever.

REINFORCING DESIRED BEHAVIOR

Skinner called the process that leads the rat to continue pressing the key "reinforcement." **Reinforcement** is the process by which a stimulus increases the probability that a preceding behavior will be repeated. In other words, pressing the lever is more likely to occur again because of the stimulus of food.

In a situation such as this one, the food is called a reinforcer. A **reinforcer** is any stimulus that increases the probability that a preceding behavior will occur again. Hence, food is a reinforcer because it increases the probability that the behavior of pressing (formally referred to as the *response* of pressing) will take place.

What kind of stimuli can act as reinforcers? Bonuses, toys, and good grades can serve as reinforcers—if they strengthen the probability of the response that occurred before their introduction. What makes something a reinforcer depends on individual preferences. Although a Hershey bar can act as a reinforcer for one person, an individual who dislikes chocolate may find 75 cents more desirable. The only way we can know if a stimulus is a reinforcer for a particular organism is to observe whether the frequency of a previously occurring behavior increases after the presentation of the stimulus.

Of course, we are not born knowing that 75 cents can buy us a candy bar. Rather, through experience we learn that money is a valuable commodity because of its association with stimuli, such as food and drink, that are naturally reinforcing. This fact suggests a distinction between primary reinforcers and secondary reinforcers. A *primary reinforcer* satisfies some biological need and works naturally, regardless of a person's prior experience. Food for a hungry person, warmth for a cold person, and relief for a person in pain all would be classified as primary reinforcers. A *secondary reinforcer*, in contrast, is a stimulus that becomes reinforcing because of its association with a primary reinforcer. For instance, we know that money is valuable because we have learned that it allows us to obtain other desirable objects, including primary reinforcers such as food and shelter. Money thus becomes a secondary reinforcer. (To learn more about operant conditioning, try **Interactivity 18–1.**)

Positive Reinforcers, Negative Reinforcers, and Punishment

In many respects, reinforcers can be thought of in terms of rewards; both a reinforcer and a reward increase the probability that a preceding response will occur again. But the term *reward* is limited to *positive* occurrences, and this is where it differs from a reinforcer—for it turns out that reinforcers can be positive or negative.

PowerWeb: Shaping and Maintaining Operant Behavior
www.mhhe.com/feldmanup7

Reinforcement: The process by which a stimulus increases the probability that a preceding behavior will be repeated.

Reinforcer: Any stimulus that increases the probability that a preceding behavior will occur again.

INTERACTIVITY 18–1
Operant conditioning

Positive reinforcer: A stimulus added to the environment that brings about an increase in a preceding response.

Negative reinforcer: An unpleasant stimulus whose removal leads to an increase in the probability that a preceding response will occur again in the future.

PowerWeb: Do Rewards Facilitate Learning?

www.mhhe.com/feldmanup7

Punishment: A stimulus that decreases the probability that a previous behavior will occur again.

A **positive reinforcer** is a stimulus *added* to the environment that brings about an increase in a preceding response. If food, water, money, or praise is provided after a response, it is more likely that that response will occur again in the future. The paychecks that workers get at the end of the week, for example, increases the likelihood that they will return to their jobs the following week.

In contrast, a **negative reinforcer** refers to an unpleasant stimulus whose *removal* from the environment leads to an increase in the probability that a preceding response will occur again in the future. For example, if you have cold symptoms (an unpleasant stimulus) that are relieved when you take medicine, you are more likely to take the medicine when you experience such symptoms again. Taking medicine, then, is negatively reinforcing, because it removes the unpleasant cold symptoms. Similarly, if the radio volume is so loud that it hurts your ears, you are likely to find that turning it down relieves the problem. Lowering the volume is negatively reinforcing, and you are more apt to repeat the action in the future. Negative reinforcement, then, teaches the individual that taking an action removes a negative condition that exists in the environment. Like positive reinforcers, negative reinforcers increase the likelihood that preceding behaviors will be repeated.

It is important to note that negative reinforcement is not the same as punishment. **Punishment** refers to a stimulus that *decreases* the probability that a prior behavior will occur again. Unlike negative reinforcement, which produces an *increase* in behavior, punishment reduces the likelihood of a prior response. If we receive a shock that is meant to decrease a certain behavior, then, we are receiving punishment, but if we are already receiving a shock and do something to stop that shock, the behavior that stops the shock is considered to be negatively reinforced. In the first case, the specific behavior is apt to decrease because of the punishment; in the second, it is likely to increase because of the negative reinforcement.

Punishment can weaken a response either through the application of an unpleasant stimulus or by the removal of something pleasant. For instance, spanking a child for misbehaving is punishment in the form of the application of an unpleasant stimulus. In contrast, when a teenager is told she is "grounded" and will no longer be able to use the family car because of her poor grades, punishment is in the form of the removal of something pleasant. In both cases, punishment is meant to result in a decrease in the likelihood that a prior behavior will be repeated.

The distinctions between positive reinforcement, negative reinforcement, and punishment may seem confusing initially, but the following rules (and the summary

FIGURE 3 Types of reinforcement and punishment.

	Positive reinforcement	Negative reinforcement	Punishment
Stimulus is	Added	Removed	Added or removed
Desired effect on behavior	Increase in response strength	Increase in response strength	Decrease in response strength
Example	Giving a raise for good performance leads to increase in good performance	Taking an aspirin to relieve a headache leads to a higher future likelihood of taking aspirin	Penalizing for misbehavior leads to a decrease in frequency of that behavior

in Figure 3) can help you distinguish these concepts from one another:

- ⊙ Reinforcement *increases* the frequency of the behavior preceding it; punishment *decreases* the frequency of the behavior preceding it.
- ⊙ The *application* of a *positive* stimulus brings about an increase in the frequency of behavior and is referred to as positive reinforcement; the *application* of a *negative* stimulus decreases or reduces the frequency of behavior and is called punishment.
- ⊙ The *removal* of a *negative* stimulus that results in an increase in the frequency of behavior is termed negative reinforcement; the *removal* of a *positive* stimulus that decreases the frequency of behavior is punishment.

The Pros and Cons of Punishment: Why Reinforcement Beats Punishment

Is punishment an effective way to modify behavior? Punishment often presents the quickest route to changing behavior that, if allowed to continue, might be dangerous to an individual. For instance, a parent may not have a second chance to warn a child not to run into a busy street, and so punishing the first incidence of this behavior may prove to be wise. Moreover, the use of punishment to suppress behavior, even temporarily, provides an opportunity to reinforce a person for subsequently behaving in a more desirable way.

There are some rare instances in which punishment can be the most humane approach to treating certain severe disorders. For example, some children suffer from *autism*, a psychological disorder that can lead them to abuse themselves by tearing at their skin or banging their heads against the wall, injuring themselves severely in the process. In such cases—and when all other treatments have failed—punishment in the form of a quick but intense electric shock has been used to prevent self-injurious behavior. Such punishment, however, is used only to keep the child safe and to buy time until positive reinforcement procedures can be initiated (Lovaas & Koegel, 1973; Linscheid et al., 1990; Siegel, 1996b).

Several disadvantages make the routine use of punishment questionable. For one thing, punishment is frequently ineffective, particularly if it is not delivered shortly after the undesired behavior or if the individual is able to leave the setting in which the punishment is being given. An employee who is reprimanded by the boss may quit; a teenager who loses the use of the family car may borrow a friend's car instead. In such instances, the initial behavior that is being punished may be replaced by one that is even less desirable.

Even worse, physical punishment can convey to the recipient the idea that physical aggression is permissible and perhaps even desirable. A father who yells at and hits his son for misbehaving teaches the son that aggression is an appropriate, adult response. The son soon may copy his father's behavior by acting aggressively toward others. In addition, physical punishment is often administered by people who are themselves angry or enraged. It is unlikely that individuals in such an emotional state will be able to think through what they are doing or control carefully the degree of punishment they are inflicting. Ultimately, those who resort to physical punishment run the risk that they will grow to be feared. Punishment can also reduce the self-esteem of recipients unless they can understand the reasons for it (Baumrind, Larzelere, & Cowan, 2002; Gershoff, 2002; Holden, 2002; Parke, 2002).

Finally, punishment does not convey any information about what an alternative, more appropriate behavior might be. To be useful in bringing about more desirable behavior in the future, punishment must be accompanied by specific information about the behavior that is being punished, along with specific suggestions concerning a more desirable behavior. Punishing a child for staring out the window in school could merely lead her to stare at the floor instead. Unless we teach her appropriate ways to respond, we have merely managed to substitute one undesirable behavior for another. If punishment is not followed up with reinforcement for subsequent behavior that is more appropriate, little will be accomplished.

In short, reinforcing desired behavior is a more appropriate technique for modifying behavior than using punishment. Both in and out of the scientific arena, then, reinforcement usually beats punishment (Sulzer-Azaroff & Mayer, 1991; Seppa, 1996; Cicero & Pfadt, 2002; Pogarsky & Piquero, 2003).

Schedules of Reinforcement: Timing Life's Rewards

The world would be a different place if poker players never played cards again after the first losing hand, fishermen returned to shore as soon as they missed a catch, or door-to-door salespeople turned in their samples after their first experience of being turned away. The fact that such unreinforced behaviors continue, often with great frequency and persistence, illustrates that reinforcement need not be received continually for behavior to be learned and maintained. In fact, behavior that is reinforced only occasionally can ultimately be learned better than can behavior that is always reinforced.

When we refer to the frequency and timing of reinforcement that follows desired behavior, we are talking about **schedules of reinforcement**. Behavior that is reinforced every time it occurs is said to be on a **continuous reinforcement schedule**; if it is reinforced some but not all of the time, it is on a **partial (or intermittent) reinforcement schedule**. Although learning occurs more rapidly under a continuous reinforcement schedule, behavior lasts longer after reinforcement stops when it is learned under a partial reinforcement schedule (Staddon & Cerutti, 2003).

Why should intermittent reinforcement result in stronger, longer-lasting learning than continuous reinforcement? We can answer the question by examining how we might behave when using a candy vending machine compared with a Las Vegas slot

Schedules of reinforcement: Different patterns of frequency and timing of reinforcement following desired behavior.

Continuous reinforcement schedule: Reinforcing of a behavior every time it occurs.

Partial (or intermittent) reinforcement schedule: Reinforcing of a behavior some but not all of the time.

machine. When we use a vending machine, prior experience has taught us that every time we put in the appropriate amount of money, the reinforcement, a candy bar, ought to be delivered. In other words, the schedule of reinforcement is continuous. In comparison, a slot machine offers intermittent reinforcement. We have learned that after putting in our cash, most of the time we will not receive anything in return. At the same time, though, we know that we will occasionally win something.

Now suppose that, unknown to us, both the candy vending machine and the slot machine are broken, and so neither one is able to dispense anything. It would not be very long before we stopped depositing coins into the broken candy machine. Probably at most we would try only two or three times before leaving the machine in disgust. But the story would be quite different with the broken slot machine. Here, we would drop in money for a considerably longer time, even though there would be no payoff.

In formal terms, we can see the difference between the two reinforcement schedules: Partial reinforcement schedules (such as those provided by slot machines) maintain performance longer than do continuous reinforcement schedules (such as those established in candy vending machines) before extinction—the disappearance of the conditioned response—occurs.

Certain kinds of partial reinforcement schedules produce stronger and lengthier responding before extinction than do others. Although many different partial reinforcement schedules have been examined, they can most readily be put into two categories: schedules that consider the *number of responses* made before reinforcement is given, called fixed-ratio and variable-ratio schedules, and those which consider the *amount of time* that elapses before reinforcement is provided, called fixed-interval and variable-interval schedules (Svartdal, 2003).

FIXED- AND VARIABLE-RATIO SCHEDULES

In a **fixed-ratio schedule**, reinforcement is given only after a specific number of responses. For instance, a rat might receive a food pellet every tenth time it pressed a lever; here, the ratio would be 1:10. Similarly, garment workers are generally paid on fixed-ratio schedules: They receive a specific number of dollars for every blouse they sew. Because a greater rate of production means more reinforcement, people on fixed-ratio schedules are apt to work as quickly as possible (see Figure 4).

In a **variable-ratio schedule**, reinforcement occurs after a varying number of responses rather than after a fixed number. Although the specific number of responses necessary to receive reinforcement varies, the number of responses usually hovers around a specific average. A good example of a variable-ratio schedule is a telephone salesperson's job. She might make a sale during the third, eighth, ninth, and twentieth calls without being successful during any call in between. Although the number of responses that must be made before making a sale varies, it averages out to a 20 percent success rate. Under these circumstances, you might expect that the salesperson would try to make as many calls as possible in as short a time as possible. This is the case with all variable-ratio schedules, which lead to a high rate of response and resistance to extinction.

Fixed-ratio schedule: A schedule by which reinforcement is given only after a specific number of responses are made.

Variable-ratio schedule: A schedule by which reinforcement occurs after a varying number of responses rather than after a fixed number.

FIXED- AND VARIABLE-INTERVAL SCHEDULES: THE PASSAGE OF TIME

In contrast to fixed- and variable-ratio schedules, in which the crucial factor is the number of responses, fixed-*interval* and variable-*interval* schedules focus on the amount of time that has elapsed since a person or animal was rewarded. One example of a fixed-interval schedule is a weekly paycheck. For people who receive regular, weekly paychecks, it typically makes relatively little difference exactly how much they produce in a given week.

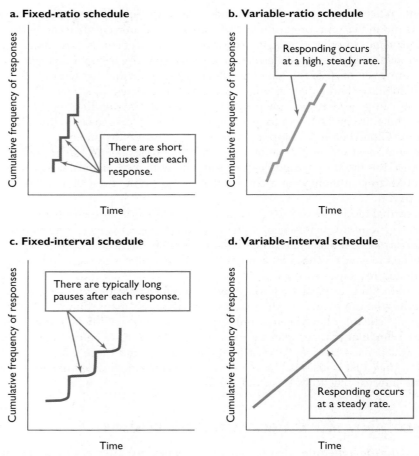

FIGURE 4 Typical outcomes of different reinforcement schedules. (a) In a fixed-ratio schedule, short pauses occur after each response. Because the more responses, the more reinforcement, fixed-ratio schedules produce a high rate of responding. (b) In a variable-ratio schedule, responding also occurs at a high rate. (c) A fixed-interval schedule produces lower rates of responding, especially just after reinforcement has been presented, because the organism learns that a specified time period must elapse between reinforcements. (d) A variable-interval schedule produces a fairly steady stream of responses.

Fixed-interval schedule: A schedule that provides reinforcement for a response only if a fixed time period has elapsed, making overall rates of response relatively low.

Variable-interval schedule: A schedule by which the time between reinforcements varies around some average rather than being fixed.

Because a **fixed-interval schedule** provides reinforcement for a response only if a fixed time period has elapsed, overall rates of response are relatively low. This is especially true in the period just after reinforcement, when the time before another reinforcement is relatively great. Students' study habits often exemplify this reality. If the periods between exams are relatively long (meaning that the opportunity for reinforcement for good performance is given fairly infrequently), students often study minimally or not at all until the day of the exam draws near. Just before the exam, however, students begin to cram for it, signaling a rapid increase in the rate of their studying response. As you might expect, immediately after the exam there is a rapid decline in the rate of responding, with few people opening a book the day after a test.

One way to decrease the delay in responding that occurs just after reinforcement, and to maintain the desired behavior more consistently throughout an interval, is to use a variable-interval schedule. In a **variable-interval schedule**, the time between reinforcements varies around some average rather than being fixed. For example, a professor who gives surprise quizzes that vary from one every three days to one every three weeks, averaging one every two weeks, is using a variable-interval schedule. Compared to the study habits we observed with a fixed-interval schedule, students' study habits under such a variable-interval schedule would most likely be

INTERACTIVITY 18–2
Schedules of reinforcement

very different. Students would be apt to study more regularly because they would never know when the next surprise quiz was coming. Variable-interval schedules, in general, are more likely to produce relatively steady rates of responding than are fixed-interval schedules, with responses that take longer to extinguish after reinforcement ends. (To better understand schedules of reinforcement, try **Inter-activity 18–2**.)

Discrimination and Generalization in Operant Conditioning

It does not take a child long to learn that a red light at an intersection means stop and a green light indicates that it is permissible to continue, in the same way that a pigeon can learn to peck a key when a green light goes on, but not when a red light appears. Just as in classical conditioning, then, operant learning involves the phenomena of discrimination and generalization.

The process by which people learn to discriminate stimuli is known as stimulus control training. In *stimulus control training*, a behavior is reinforced in the presence of a specific stimulus, but not in its absence. For example, one of the most difficult discriminations many people face is determining when someone's friendliness is not mere friendliness, but a signal of romantic interest. People learn to make the discrimination by observing the presence of certain nonverbal cues—such as increased eye contact and touching—that indicate romantic interest. When such cues are absent, people learn that no romantic interest is indicated. In this case, the nonverbal cue acts as a discriminative stimulus, one to which an organism learns to respond during stimulus control training. A *discriminative stimulus* signals the likelihood that reinforcement will follow a response. For example, if you wait until your roommate is in a good mood before you ask to borrow her favorite compact disc, your behavior can be said to be under stimulus control because you can discriminate between her moods.

Just as in classical conditioning, the phenomenon of *stimulus generalization,* in which an organism learns a response to one stimulus and then exhibits the same response to slightly different stimuli, is found in operant conditioning. If you have learned that being polite produces the reinforcement of getting your way in a certain situation, you are likely to generalize your response to other situations. Sometimes, though, generalization can have unfortunate consequences, as occurs when people behave negatively toward all members of a racial group because they have had an unpleasant experience with one member of that group.

Shaping: Reinforcing What Doesn't Come Naturally

Consider the difficulty of using operant conditioning to teach people to repair an automobile transmission. If you had to wait until they chanced to fix a transmission perfectly before you provided them with reinforcement, the Model T might be back in style long before they mastered the repair process.

There are many complex behaviors, ranging from auto repair to zoo management, that we would not expect to occur naturally as part of anyone's spontaneous behavior. For such behaviors, for which there might otherwise be no opportunity to provide reinforcement (because the behavior would never occur in the first place), a procedure known as shaping is used. **Shaping** is the process of teaching a complex behavior by rewarding closer and closer approximations of the desired behavior. In

Shaping: The process of teaching a complex behavior by rewarding closer and closer approximations of the desired behavior.

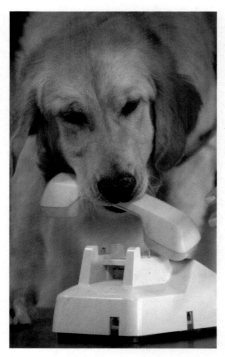

Shaping is often used to train animals to be companions for people with disabilities.

shaping, you start by reinforcing any behavior that is at all similar to the behavior you want the person to learn. Later, you reinforce only responses that are closer to the behavior you ultimately want to teach. Finally, you reinforce only the desired response. Each step in shaping, then, moves only slightly beyond the previously learned behavior, permitting the person to link the new step to the behavior learned earlier.

Shaping allows even lower animals to learn complex responses that would never occur naturally, ranging from lions jumping through hoops to dolphins rescuing divers lost at sea. Shaping also underlies the learning of many complex human skills. For instance, the organization of most textbooks is based on the principles of shaping. Typically, information is presented so that new material builds on previously learned concepts or skills. Thus, the concept of shaping could not be presented until we had discussed the more basic principles of operant learning.

Biological Constraints on Learning: You Can't Teach an Old Dog Just Any Trick

Psychologists Keller and Marian Breland were pleased with their idea: As professional animal trainers, they came up with the notion of having a pig pick up a wooden disk and place it into a piggy bank. With their experience in training animals through operant conditioning, they thought the task would be easy to teach, because it was certainly well within the range of the pig's physical capabilities. Yet almost every time they tried the procedure, it failed. Rather than picking up the disk, the pigs generally pushed it along the ground, something that they appeared to be biologically programmed to do.

To remedy the problem, the Brelands substituted a raccoon. Although the procedure worked fine with one disk, when two disks were used, the raccoon refused to deposit either of them and instead rubbed the two together, as if it were washing them. Once again, it appeared that the disks evoked biologically innate behaviors that were impossible to replace through even the most exhaustive training (Breland & Breland, 1961).

The Brelands' difficulties illustrate an important point: Not all behaviors can be trained in all species equally well. Instead, there are *biological constraints*, built-in limitations in the ability of animals to learn particular behaviors. In some cases, an organism will have a special predisposition that will aid in its learning a behavior (such as pecking behaviors in pigeons); in other cases, biological constraints will act to prevent or inhibit an organism from learning a behavior.

The existence of biological constraints is consistent with evolutionary explanations of behavior. Clearly, there are adaptive benefits that promote survival for organisms that quickly learn—or avoid—certain behaviors. For example, our ability to rapidly learn to avoid touching hot surfaces increases our chances of survival (Barkow, Cosmides, & Tooby, 1992; Terry, 2003).

Furthermore, some psychologists, taking a neuroscience perspective, believe that we may be genetically predisposed to be fearful of certain stimuli—such as snakes. Taking an evolutionary approach, they argue that stimuli such as snakes posed a potential danger to early humans, and that there may be an evolved fear module in the brain that is sensitized to be afraid of such threats—although the notion remains quite speculative (Oehman & Mineka, 2003).

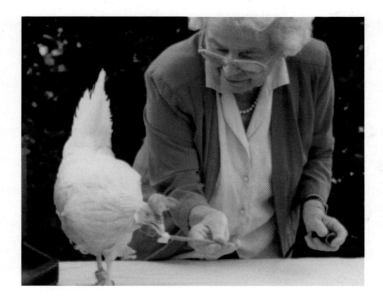

Biological constraints make it nearly impossible for animals to learn certain behaviors. Here, psychologist Marian Breland attempts to overcome the natural limitations that inhibit the success of conditioning in this rooster.

What is clear is that the study of operant conditioning has provided us with a variety of tools for understanding and modifying behavior, many of which directly improve the human condition.

BECOMING AN
INFORMED CONSUMER

of Psychology

Using Behavior Analysis and Behavior Modification

A couple who had been living together for three years began to fight more and more frequently. The issues of disagreement ranged from the seemingly petty, such as who was going to do the dishes, to the more profound, such as the quality of their love life and whether they found each other interesting. Disturbed about this increasingly unpleasant pattern of interaction, the couple went to a behavior analyst, a psychologist who specialized in behavior-modification techniques. After interviewing each of them alone and then speaking to them together, he asked them to keep a detailed written record of their interactions over the next two weeks—focusing in particular on the events that preceded their arguments.

When they returned two weeks later, he carefully went over the records with them. In doing so, he noticed a pattern that the couple themselves had observed after they had started keeping their records: Each of their arguments had occurred just after one or the other had left a household chore undone. For instance, the woman would go into a fury when she came home from work and found that the man, a student, had left his dirty lunch dishes on the table and had not even started dinner preparations. The man would get angry when he found the woman's clothes draped on the only chair in the bedroom. He insisted it was her responsibility to pick up after herself.

Using the data the couple had collected, the behavior analyst devised a system for the couple to try out. He asked them to list all the chores that could possibly arise and assign each one a point value depending on how long it took to complete. Then he had them divide the chores equally and agree in a written contract to fulfill the ones assigned to them. If either failed to carry out one of the assigned chores, he or she would have to place $1 per point in a fund for the other to spend. They also agreed to a program of verbal praise, promising to reward each other verbally for completing a chore.

Although skeptical about the value of such a program, the couple agreed to try it for a month and to keep careful records of the number of arguments they had during that period. To their surprise, the number declined rapidly, and even the more basic issues in their relationship seemed on the way to being resolved.

This case provides an illustration of **behavior modification**, a formalized technique for promoting the frequency of desirable behaviors and decreasing the incidence of unwanted ones. Using the basic principles of learning theory, behavior-modification techniques have proved to be helpful in a variety of situations. People with severe mental retardation have learned the rudiments of language and, for the first time in their lives, have started dressing and feeding themselves. Behavior modification has also helped people lose weight, give up smoking, and behave more safely (Bellack, Hersen, & Kazdin, 1990; Sulzer-Azaroff & Mayer, 1991; Malott, Whaley, & Malott, 1993; Walter, Vaughan, & Wynder, 1994).

The techniques used by behavior analysts are as varied as the list of processes that modify behavior. They include reinforcement scheduling, shaping, generalization training, discrimination training, and extinction. Participants in a behavior-change program do, however, typically follow a series of similar basic steps that include the following:

- ⊙ *Identifying goals and target behaviors.* The first step is to define *desired behavior.* Is it an increase in time spent studying? A decrease in weight? An increase in the use of language? A reduction in the amount of aggression displayed by a child? The goals must be stated in observable terms and lead to specific targets. For instance, a goal might be "to increase study time," whereas the target behavior would be "to study at least two hours per day on weekdays and an hour on Saturdays."

- ⊙ *Designing a data-recording system and recording preliminary data.* To determine whether behavior has changed, it is necessary to collect data before any changes are made in the situation. This information provides a baseline against which future changes can be measured.

- ⊙ *Selecting a behavior-change strategy.* The most crucial step is to select an appropriate strategy. Because all the principles of learning can be employed to bring about behavior change, a "package" of treatments is normally used. This might include the systematic use of positive reinforcement for desired behavior (verbal praise or something more tangible, such as food), as well as a program of extinction for undesirable behavior (ignoring a child who throws a tantrum). Selecting the right reinforcers is critical; it may be necessary to experiment a bit to find out what is important to a particular individual. It is best for participants to avoid threats, because they are merely punishing and ultimately not very effective in bringing about long-term changes in behavior.

- ⊙ *Implementing the program.* The next step is to institute the program. Probably the most important aspect of program implementation is consistency. It is also important to make sure that one is reinforcing the behavior he or she wants to reinforce. For example, suppose a mother wants her daughter to spend more time on her homework, but as soon as the child sits down to study, she asks for a snack. If the mother gets a snack for her, she is likely to be reinforcing her daughter's delaying tactic, not her studying. Instead, the mother might tell her child that she will provide her with a snack after a certain time interval has gone by during which she has studied—thereby using the snack as a reinforcement for studying.

- ⊙ *Keeping careful records after the program is implemented.* Another crucial task is record keeping. If the target behaviors are not monitored, there is no way of knowing whether the program has actually been successful. Participants are advised not to rely on memory, because memory lapses are all too common.

- ⊙ *Evaluating and altering the ongoing program.* Finally, the results of the program should be compared with baseline, preimplementation data to determine its

Behavior modification: A formalized technique for promoting the frequency of desirable behaviors and decreasing the incidence of unwanted ones.

effectiveness. If the program has been successful, the procedures employed can be phased out gradually. For instance, if the program called for reinforcing every instance of picking up one's clothes from the bedroom floor, the reinforcement schedule could be modified to a fixed-ratio schedule in which every third instance was reinforced. However, if the program has not been successful in bringing about the desired behavior change, consideration of other approaches might be advisable.

Behavior-change techniques based on these general principles have enjoyed wide success and have proved to be one of the most powerful means of modifying behavior (Greenwood et al., 1992). Clearly, it is possible to employ the basic notions of learning theory to improve our lives.

RECAP/EVALUATE/RETHINK

RECAP

What is the role of reward and punishment in learning?

- Operant conditioning is a form of learning in which a voluntary behavior is strengthened or weakened. According to B. F. Skinner, the major mechanism underlying learning is reinforcement, the process by which a stimulus increases the probability that a preceding behavior will be repeated. (p. 195)
- Primary reinforcers involve rewards that are naturally effective without prior experience because they satisfy a biological need. Secondary reinforcers begin to act as if they were primary reinforcers through association with a primary reinforcer. (p. 197)
- Positive reinforcers are stimuli that are added to the environment and lead to an increase in a preceding response. Negative reinforcers are stimuli that remove something unpleasant from the environment, also leading to an increase in the preceding response. (p. 198)
- Punishment decreases the probability that a preceding prior behavior will occur. In contrast to reinforcement, in which the goal is to increase the incidence of behavior, punishment is meant to decrease or suppress behavior. (p. 199)
- Schedules and patterns of reinforcement affect the strength and duration of learning. Generally, partial reinforcement schedules—in which reinforcers are not delivered on every trial—produce stronger and longer-lasting learning than do continuous reinforcement schedules. (p. 200)
- Among the major categories of reinforcement schedules are fixed- and variable-ratio schedules, which are based on the number of responses made, and fixed- and variable-interval schedules, which are based on the time interval that elapses before reinforcement is provided. (p. 201)

- Stimulus control training (similar to stimulus discrimination in classical conditioning) is reinforcement of a behavior in the presence of a specific stimulus but not in its absence. In stimulus generalization, an organism learns a response to one stimulus and then exhibits the same response to slightly different stimuli. (p. 202)
- Shaping is a process for teaching complex behaviors by rewarding closer and closer approximations of the desired final behavior. (p. 203)
- There are biological constraints, or built-in limitations, on the ability of an organism to learn: Certain behaviors will be relatively easy for individuals of a species to learn, whereas other behaviors will be either difficult or impossible for them to learn. (p. 204)

What are some practical methods for bringing about behavior change, both in ourselves and in others?

- Behavior modification is a method for formally using the principles of learning theory to promote the frequency of desired behaviors and to decrease or eliminate unwanted ones. (p. 206)

EVALUATE

1. _____ conditioning describes learning that occurs as a result of reinforcement.
2. Match the type of operant learning with its definition:
   1. An unpleasant stimulus is presented to decrease behavior.
   2. An unpleasant stimulus is removed to increase behavior.
   3. A pleasant stimulus is presented to increase behavior.
      a. Positive reinforcement
      b. Negative reinforcement
      c. Punishment

3. Sandy had had a rough day, and his son's noisemaking was not helping him relax. Not wanting to resort to scolding, Sandy told his son in a serious manner that he was very tired and would like the boy to play quietly for an hour. This approach worked. For Sandy, the change in his son's behavior was
   a. Positively reinforcing
   b. Negatively reinforcing
4. In a _____ reinforcement schedule, behavior is reinforced some of the time, whereas in a _____ reinforcement schedule, behavior is reinforced all the time.
5. Match the type of reinforcement schedule with its definition.
   1. Reinforcement occurs after a set time period.
   2. Reinforcement occurs after a set number of responses.
   3. Reinforcement occurs after a varying time period.
   4. Reinforcement occurs after a varying number of responses.
      a. Fixed-ratio
      b. Variable-interval
      c. Fixed-interval
      d. Variable-ratio

6. Fixed reinforcement schedules produce greater resistance to extinction than do variable reinforcement schedules. True or false?

RETHINK

1. How might operant conditioning be used to address serious personal concerns, such as smoking and unhealthy eating?
2. Using the scientific literature as a guide, what would you tell parents who wish to know if the routine use of physical punishment is a necessary and acceptable form of child rearing?

Answers to Evaluate Questions

1. operant; 2. 1-c, 2-b, 3-a; 3. b; 4. partial (or intermittent), continuous; 5. 1-c, 2-a, 3-b, 4-d; 6. false; variable ratios are more resistant to extinction

KEY TERMS

operant
conditioning p. 195
reinforcement p. 197
reinforcer p. 197
positive reinforcer p. 198
negative reinforcer p. 198
punishment p. 198

schedules of
reinforcement p. 200
continuous reinforcement
schedule p. 200
partial (or intermittent)
reinforcement
schedule p. 200

fixed-ratio schedule p. 201
variable-ratio
schedule p. 201
fixed-interval
schedule p. 202

variable-interval
schedule p. 202
shaping p. 203
behavior
modification p. 206

Cognitive-Social Approaches to Learning

Consider what happens when people learn to drive a car. They don't just get behind the wheel and stumble around until they randomly put the key into the ignition, and later, after many false starts, accidentally manage to get the car to move forward, thereby receiving positive reinforcement. Instead, they already know the basic elements of driving from prior experience as passengers, when they more than likely noticed how the key was inserted into the ignition, the car was put in drive, and the gas pedal was pressed to make the car go forward.

Clearly, not all learning is due to operant and classical conditioning. In fact, instances such as learning to drive a car imply that some kinds of learning must involve higher-order processes in which people's thoughts and memories and the way they process information account for their responses. Such situations argue against regarding learning as the unthinking, mechanical, and automatic acquisition of associations between stimuli and responses, as in classical conditioning, or the presentation of reinforcement, as in operant conditioning.

Instead, some psychologists view learning in terms of the thought processes, or cognitions, that underlie it—an approach known as **cognitive-social learning theory**. Although psychologists working from the cognitive-social learning perspective do not deny the importance of classical and operant conditioning, they have developed approaches that focus on the unseen mental processes that occur during learning, rather than concentrating solely on external stimuli, responses, and reinforcements.

Cognitive-social learning theory: An approach to the study of learning that focuses on the thought processes that underlie learning.

In its most basic formulation, cognitive-social learning theory suggests that it is not enough to say that people make responses because there is an assumed link between a stimulus and a response as a result of a past history of reinforcement for a response. Instead, according to this point of view, people—and even animals—develop an *expectation* that they will receive a reinforcer after making a response. Support for this point of view comes from several quarters.

Ⓐ Ⓐ Ⓐ

Latent Learning

Evidence for the importance of cognitive processes comes from a series of animal experiments that revealed a type of cognitive-social learning called latent learning. In **latent learning**, a new behavior is learned but not demonstrated until some incentive is provided for displaying it (Tolman & Honzik, 1930). In short, latent learning occurs without reinforcement.

Latent learning: Learning in which a new behavior is acquired but is not demonstrated until some incentive is provided for displaying it.

In the studies demonstrating latent learning, psychologists examined the behavior of rats in a maze such as the one shown in Figure 1a. In one experiment, a group of rats was allowed to wander around the maze once a day for seventeen days without ever receiving a reward. Understandably, those rats made many errors and spent a relatively long time reaching the end of the maze. A second group, however, was always given food at the end of the maze. Not surprisingly, those rats learned to run quickly and directly to the food box, making few errors.

a.

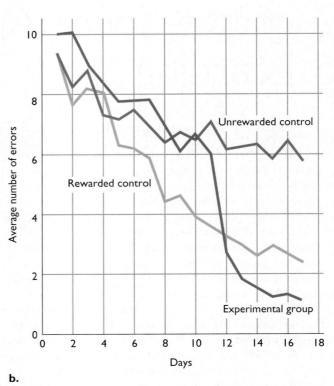

b.

FIGURE I (a) In an attempt to demonstrate latent learning, rats were allowed to roam through a maze of this sort once a day for seventeen days. (b) The rats that were never rewarded (the non-rewarded control condition) consistently made the most errors, whereas those which received food at the finish every day (the rewarded control condition) consistently made far fewer errors. But the results also showed latent learning: Rats that were initially unrewarded but began to be rewarded only after the tenth day (the experimental group) showed an immediate reduction in errors and soon became similar in error rate to the rats that had been rewarded consistently. According to cognitive-social learning theorists, the reduction in errors indicates that the rats had developed a cognitive map—a mental representation—of the maze. Can you think of other examples of latent learning?

A third group of rats started out in the same situation as the unrewarded rats, but only for the first ten days. On the eleventh day, a critical experimental manipulation was introduced: From that point on, the rats in this group were given food for completing the maze. The results of this manipulation were dramatic, as you can see from the graph in Figure 1b. The previously unrewarded rats, which had earlier seemed to wander about aimlessly, showed such reductions in running time and declines in error rates that their performance almost immediately matched that of the group that had received rewards from the start.

To cognitive-social theorists, it seemed clear that the unrewarded rats had learned the layout of the maze early in their explorations; they just never displayed their latent learning until the reinforcement was offered. Instead, those rats seemed to develop a *cognitive map* of the maze—a mental representation of spatial locations and directions.

People, too, develop cognitive maps of their surroundings. For example, latent learning may permit you to know the location of a kitchenware store at a local mall you've frequently visited, even though you've never entered the store and don't even like to cook.

The possibility that we develop our cognitive maps through latent learning presents something of a problem for strict operant conditioning theorists. If we consider the results of Tolman's maze experiment, for instance, it is unclear what the specific reinforcement was that permitted the rats that initially received no reward to learn about the layout of the maze, because there was no obvious reinforcer present. Instead, the results support a cognitive-social view of learning, in which learning may have resulted in changes in unobservable mental processes (Beatty, 2002; Voicu & Schmajuk, 2002).

Observational Learning: Learning Through Imitation

Let's return for a moment to the case of a person learning to drive. How can we account for instances in which an individual with no direct experience in carrying out a particular behavior learns the behavior and then performs it? To answer this question, psychologists have proposed another form of cognitive-social learning: observational learning.

According to psychologist Albert Bandura and colleagues, a major part of human learning consists of **observational learning**, which they define as learning through observing the behavior of another person called a *model* (Bandura, 1977). Bandura and his colleagues demonstrated rather dramatically the ability of models to stimulate learning. In what is now considered a classic experiment, young children saw a film of an adult wildly hitting a five-foot-tall inflatable punching toy called a Bobo doll (Bandura, Ross, & Ross, 1963a, 1963b). Later the children were given the opportunity to play with the Bobo doll themselves, and, sure enough, most displayed the same kind of behavior, in some cases mimicking the aggressive behavior almost identically. (See more about how people learn aggressive behavior through observation in **Interactivity 19–1.**)

Not only negative behaviors are acquired through observational learning. In one experiment, for example, children who were afraid of dogs were exposed to a model—dubbed the Fearless Peer—playing with a dog (Bandura, Grusec, & Menlove, 1967). After exposure, observers were considerably more likely to approach a strange dog than were children who had not viewed the Fearless Peer.

According to Bandura, observational learning takes place in four steps: (1) paying attention and perceiving the most critical features of another person's behavior, (2) remembering the behavior, (3) reproducing the action, and (4) being motivated to learn and carry out the behavior in the future. Instead of learning occurring through trial and error, then, with successes being reinforced and failures being punished, many important skills are learned through observational processes (Bandura, 1986).

Observational learning is particularly important in acquiring skills in which the operant conditioning technique of shaping is inappropriate. Piloting an airplane and performing brain surgery, for example, are behaviors that could hardly be learned by using trial-and-error methods without grave cost—literally—to those involved in the learning.

Not all behavior that we witness is learned or carried out, of course. One crucial factor that determines whether we later imitate a model is whether the model is

Albert Bandura examined the principles of observational learning.

Observational learning: Learning through observing the behavior of another person called a *model*.

INTERACTIVITY 19–1

Observational learning

As this boy watches his father, he is engaged in observational learning. How does observational learning contribute to defining gender roles?

Illustrating observational learning, this infant observes an adult on the television and then is able to imitate his behavior. Learning has obviously occurred through the mere observation of the television model.

rewarded for his or her behavior. If we observe a friend being rewarded for putting more time into her studies by receiving higher grades, we are more likely to imitate her behavior than we would be if her behavior resulted only in her being stressed and tired. Models who are rewarded for behaving in a particular way are more apt to be mimicked than are models who receive punishment. Interestingly, though, observing the punishment of a model does not necessarily stop observers from learning the behavior. Observers can still describe the model's behavior—they are just less apt to perform it (Bandura, 1977, 1986, 1994).

Observational learning is central to a number of important issues relating to the extent to which people learn simply by watching the behavior of others. For instance, the degree to which observation of media aggression produces subsequent aggression on the part of viewers is a crucial—and controversial—question, as we discuss in the *Applying Psychology in the 21st Century* box.

Exploring DIVERSITY
Does Culture Influence How We Learn?

When a member of the Chilcotin Indian tribe teaches her daughter to prepare salmon, at first she only allows the daughter to observe the entire process. A little later, she permits her child to try out some basic parts of the task. Her response to questions is noteworthy. For example, when the daughter asks about how to do "the backbone part," the mother's response is to repeat the entire process with

Violence in Television and Video Games: Does the Media's Message Matter?

In an episode of HBO's "The Sopranos," fictional mobster Tony Soprano murdered one of his associates. To make identification of the victim's body difficult, Soprano, along with one of his henchmen, dismembered the body and dumped the body parts.

A few months later, two real-life half brothers in Riverside, California, strangled their mother and then cut her head and hands from her body. Victor Bautista, 20, and Matthew Montejo, 15, who were caught by police after a security guard noticed that the bundle they were attempting to throw in a dumpster had a foot sticking out of it, told police that the plan to dismember their mother was inspired by "The Sopranos" episode (Martelle, Hanley, & Yoshino, 2003).

Like other "media copycat" killings, the brothers' cold-blooded brutality raises a critical issue: Does observing violent and antisocial acts in the media lead viewers to behave in similar ways? Because research on modeling shows that people frequently learn and imitate the aggression that they observe, this question is among the most important being addressed by psychologists.

Certainly, the amount of violence in the mass media is enormous. By the time of elementary school graduation, the average child in the United States will have viewed more than 8,000 murders and more than 800,000 violent acts on network television. Adult television shows also contain significant violence, with cable television leading the way with such shows as "When Animals Attack" and "World's Scariest Police Shootouts" (Huston et al., 1992; Mifflin, 1998).

Most experts agree that watching high levels of media violence makes viewers more susceptible to acting aggressively, and recent research supports this claim. For example, a recent survey of serious and violent young male offenders incarcerated in Florida showed that one-fourth of them had attempted to commit a media-inspired copycat crime (Surette, 2002). A significant proportion of those teenage offenders noted that they paid close attention to the media.

Does violence in television shows like "The Sopranos" lead to real-life violence? Most research suggests that watching high levels of violence makes viewers more susceptible to acting aggressively.

Research using video games has also linked violent media with actual aggression. According to a recent series of studies by psychologist Craig Anderson and colleagues, playing violent video games is associated with later aggressive behavior. In one study, for example, they found that college students who frequently played violent video games, such as *Postal* or *Doom*, were more likely to have been involved in delinquent behavior and aggression. Furthermore, college students—particularly men—also were more apt to act aggressively toward another student if they'd played a violent video game. Frequent players also had lower academic achievement (Anderson & Dill, 2000; Bartholow & Anderson, 2002).

However, such results do not show that playing violent games *causes* delinquency, aggression, and lower academic performance; the research only found that the various variables were *associated with* one another. To explore the question of whether violent game play actually caused aggression, Anderson and Dill subsequently conducted a laboratory study. In it, they had participants play either a violent

video game (*Wolfenstein 3D*) or one that was nonviolent (*Myst*). The results were clear: Exposure to the graphically violent video game increased aggressive thoughts and actual aggression.

Several aspects of media violence may contribute to real-life aggressive behavior (Bushman & Anderson, 2001; Johnson et al., 2002). For one thing, experiencing violent media content seems to lower inhibitions against carrying out aggression—watching television portrayals of violence or using violence to win a video game makes aggression seem a legitimate response to particular situations. Exposure to media violence also may distort our understanding of the meaning of others' behavior, predisposing us to view even nonaggressive acts by others as aggressive. Finally, a continuous diet of aggression may leave us desensitized to violence, and what previously would have repelled us now produces little emotional response. Our sense of the pain and suffering brought about by aggression may be diminished (Anderson & Bushman, 2002; Anderson, Carnagey, & Eubanks, 2003; Huesmann et al., 2003).

RETHINK

If a conclusive causal link between watching violent television or playing violent video games and subsequent aggressive acts were established, would you support a ban on such media? Why or why not? What could be done to decrease the likelihood that media-related aggression would spill over into everyday life?

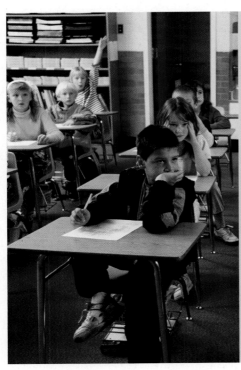

Relational Style

1. Perceive information as part of total picture

2. Exhibit improvisational and intuitive thinking

3. More easily learn materials that have a human, social content and are characterized by experimental/cultural relevance

4. Have a good memory for verbally presented ideas and information, especially if relevant

5. Are more task-oriented concerning nonacademic areas

6. Are influenced by authority figures' expression of confidence or doubt in students' ability

7. Prefer to withdraw from unstimulating task performance

8. Style conflicts with the traditional school environment

Analytical Style

1. Able to dis-embed information from total picture (focus on detail)

2. Exhibit sequential and structured thinking

3. More easily learn materials that are inanimate and impersonal

4. Have a good memory for abstract ideas and irrelevant information

5. Are more task-oriented concerning academics

6. Are not greatly affected by the opinions of others

7. Show ability to persist at unstimulating tasks

8. Style matches most school environments

FIGURE 2 A comparison of analytical versus relational approaches to learning offers one example of how learning styles differ along several dimensions.

another fish. The reason? The mother feels that one cannot learn the individual parts of the task apart from the context of preparing the whole fish (Tharp, 1989).

It should not be surprising that children raised in the Chilcotin tradition, which stresses instruction that starts by communicating the entire task, may have difficulty with traditional Western schooling. In the approach to teaching most characteristic of Western culture, tasks are broken down into their component parts. Only after each small step is learned is it thought possible to master the complete task.

Do the differences in teaching approaches between cultures affect how people learn? Some psychologists, taking a cognitive-social perspective on learning, suggest that people develop particular *learning styles*, characteristic ways of approaching material, based on their cultural background and unique pattern of abilities (Anderson & Adams, 1992; Chi-Ching & Noi, 1994; Furnham, 1995; Sternberg & Grigorenko, 1997).

Learning styles differ along several dimensions. For example, one central dimension is analytical versus relational approaches to learning (Anderson, 1988; Tharp, 1989). As illustrated in Figure 2, people with a relational learning style master material best through exposure to a full unit or phenomenon. Parts of the unit are comprehended only when their relationship to the whole is understood.

In contrast, people with an analytical learning style do best when they can carry out an initial analysis of the principles and components underlying a phenomenon or situation. By developing an understanding of the fundamental principles and components, they are best able to understand the full picture.

Although research findings are mixed, some evidence suggests that particular minority groups in Western societies display characteristic learning styles. For instance, James Anderson and Maurianne Adams (1992) argue that Caucasian females and African American, Native American, and Hispanic American males and females are more apt to use a relational style of learning than Caucasian and Asian American males, who are more likely to employ an analytical style.

The conclusion that members of particular ethnic and gender groups have similar learning styles is controversial. Because there is so much diversity within each particular racial and ethnic group, critics argue that generalizations about learning styles cannot be used to predict the style of any single individual, regardless of group membership. Many psychologists contend that a discussion of group learning styles is a misguided undertaking. (This argument echoes an ongoing controversy about the usefulness of intelligence tests.) Instead, they suggest that it is more fruitful to concentrate on determining each individual's particular learning style and pattern of academic and social strengths.

Still, it is clear that values about learning, which are communicated through a person's family and cultural background, have an impact on how successful students are in school. One theory suggests that members of minority groups who were voluntary immigrants are more apt to be successful in school than those who are were brought into a majority culture against their will. For example, Korean children in the United States—the sons and daughters of voluntary immigrants—perform quite well, as a group, in school. In contrast, Korean children in Japan—often the sons and daughters of people who were forced to immigrate during World War II, essentially as forced laborers—tend to do poorly in school. Presumably, children in the forced immigration group are less motivated to succeed than those in the voluntary immigration group (Ogbu, 1992; Gallagher, 1994).

⏶ ⏶ ⏶

RECAP/EVALUATE/RETHINK

RECAP

What is the role of cognition and thought in learning?

▶ Cognitive-social approaches consider learning in terms of thought processes or cognition. Phenomena such as latent learning—in which a new behavior is learned but not performed until some incentive is provided for its performance—and the apparent development of cognitive maps support cognitive-social approaches. Learning also occurs through observation of the behavior of models. (p. 209)

▶ The major factor that determines whether an observed behavior will actually be performed is the nature of reinforcement or punishment a model receives. (p. 211)

▶ Learning styles are characteristic ways of approaching material, based on a person's cultural background and unique pattern of abilities. One major dimension relates to analytical versus relational approaches to learning. (p. 214)

EVALUATE

1. Cognitive-social learning theorists are concerned only with overt behavior, not with its internal causes. True or false?

2. In cognitive-social learning theory, it is assumed that people develop a(n) _____ about receiving a reinforcer when they behave a certain way.

3. In _____ learning, a new behavior is learned but is not shown until appropriate reinforcement is presented.

4. Bandura's theory of _____ learning states that people learn through watching a(n) _____— another person displaying the behavior of interest.

RETHINK

1. What is the relationship between a model (in Bandura's sense) and a role model (as the term is used popularly)? Celebrities often complain that their actions should not be scrutinized closely because they do not want to be role models. How would you respond?
2. The relational style of learning sometimes conflicts with the traditional school environment. Could a school be created that takes advantage of the characteristics of the relational style? How? Are there types of learning for which the analytical style is clearly superior?

Answers to Evaluate Questions

1. false; cognitive-social learning theorists are primarily concerned with mental processes; 2. expectation; 3. latent; 4. observational, model

KEY TERMS

cognitive-social learning theory p. 209

latent learning p. 209

observational learning p. 211

Looking Back

Psychology on the Web

1. B. F. Skinner had an impact on society and on thought that is only hinted at in our discussion of learning. Find additional information on the Web about Skinner's life and influence. See what you can find out about his ideas for an ideal, utopian society based on the principles of conditioning and behaviorism. Write a summary of your findings.

2. Select a topic discussed in this set of modules that is of interest to you (reinforcement versus punishment, teaching complex behaviors by shaping, violence in video games, relational versus analytical learning styles, behavior modification, etc.). Find at least two sources of information on the Web about your topic and summarize the results of your quest. It may be most helpful to find two different approaches to your topic and compare them.

3. After completing Interactivity 18–1, search the Web for three examples of animal training procedures that employ operant conditioning. Summarize the training techniques, identifying each use of operant conditioning.

Epilogue

Here we have discussed several kinds of learning, ranging from classical conditioning, which depends on the existence of natural stimulus-response pairings, to operant conditioning, in which reinforcement is used to increase desired behavior. These approaches to learning focus on outward, behavioral learning processes. We have also been introduced to more cognitive-social approaches to learning, which focus on mental processes that enable learning.

We have also noted that learning is affected by culture and individual differences, with individual learning styles potentially affecting the ways in which people learn most effectively. And we saw some ways in which our learning about learning can be put to practical use, through such means as behavior-modification programs designed to decrease negative behaviors and increase positive ones.

Return to the prologue of this set of modules and consider the following questions in relation to Bo, the helpful dog who served Brad Gabrielson.

1. Is Bo's learning primarily an example of classical conditioning, operant conditioning, or cognitive-social learning? Why?

2. Do you think punishment would be an effective teaching strategy for Bo? Why?

3. How might different schedules of reinforcement be used to train Bo? Which schedule probably would have been most effective?

4. In what way would shaping have been used to teach Bo some of his more complex behaviors, such as signaling neighbors by scratching at their doors?

1 Operant Conditioning

Our behavior elicits rewards and punishments from our environment. In turn, these rewards and punishments increase or decrease the frequency of our behavior. This process, known as operant conditioning, occurs repeatedly in our daily lives.

2 Negative and Positive Reinforcement

When a mother hears her baby cry, she picks him up and strokes him. In turn, he stops crying. The removal of the undesirable stimulus (crying) reinforces the mother's behavior. As a result, this negative reinforcement makes it more likely that the mother will repeat her nurturing behavior in the future. From the baby's point of view, whenever he cries, he gets picked up and stroked. Therefore, stroking acts as a positive reinforcement for him. In turn, this positive reinforcement makes it more likely that he will cry in the future.

3 Punishment by Applying Aversive Stimuli

One way to punish a behavior is by delivering a painful or aversive stimulus, such as making a child write "I will not talk in class" 25 times on the blackboard.

4 **Punishment by Removing Positive Stimuli**

A second way to punish behavior is by removing a positive stimulus. An example is keeping a child in class while her classmates are playing outdoors.

5 **Punishment vs. Reinforcement**

A father used to yell at his son when he did not put away his toys. The father learned, however, that punishment usually fails to produce the desired behavior. Now he positively reinforces cooperative behavior and his son is more helpful.

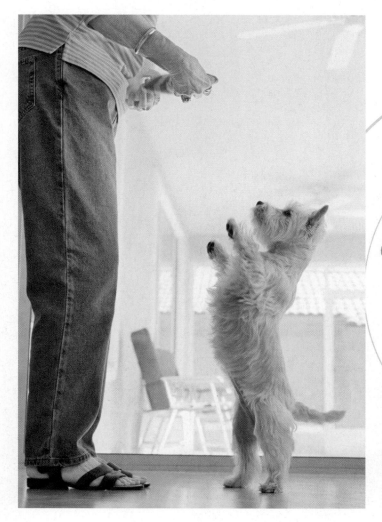

6 **Shaping**

Shaping can be used to teach a dog to perform tricks. Shaping is a gradual process in which you reinforce closer and closer approximations of the desired behavior. At first, a trainer reinforces anything that resembles sitting up. Later, only the complete behavior is reinforced.

7 **Continuous vs. Partial Reinforcement**

If the trainer rewards the dog after every trick, we call it continuous reinforcement. If she rewards him after every third or fourth trick, we call it partial reinforcement.

Memory

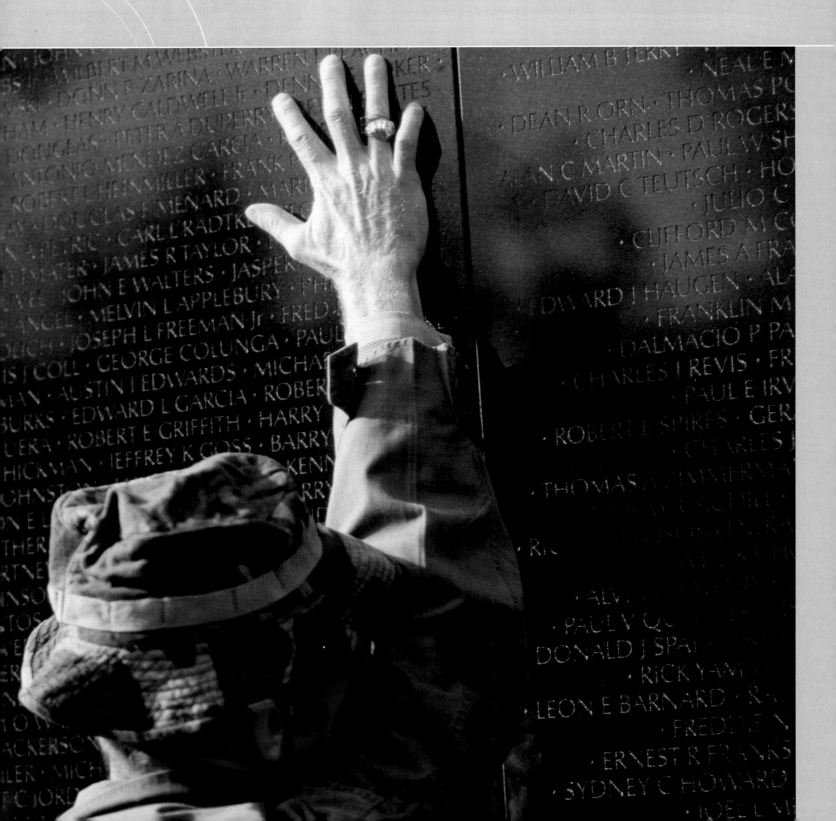

Prologue
The Wife Who Forgot She Had a Husband

In wedding portraits on the walls of their Las Vegas, New Mexico, living room, Kim and Krickitt Carpenter look like any young newly-weds—deeply in love and filled with hope for their new life together. But Krickitt admits it causes her some pain now to look at the pictures or to see herself in the wedding video, walking down the aisle in her lacy white gown. "I would almost rather not watch it," she says. "It makes me miss the girl in the picture more and more."

In a sense, that Krickitt is gone, lost forever. Less than 10 weeks after the September, 1993, ceremony, the Carpenters were in a nightmarish auto accident that badly injured them both and left Krickitt comatose. Though doctors initially doubted she would survive, she rallied, regaining consciousness and, eventually, most of her physical abilities. But the trauma to her brain caused retrograde amnesia, erasing virtually her entire memory of the previous 18 months—including any recollection of the man she had fallen in love with and married. "The last 2½ years have been based on a story I'm told," says Krickitt, 26, "because I don't remember any of it" (Fields-Meyer & Haederle, 1996, p. 48).

For Krickitt Carpenter, the road to recovery has been a slow one. Although she retained most of her long-term memories after the accident, she had no recent recollections of her marriage or her husband. Initially, when she returned to living with Kim, it was like being with a stranger toward whom she felt no emotion, and the marriage faltered. However, by retracing the origins of their relationship—the Carpenters began by having "dates"—they were able to reforge the bonds that had been shattered. On Valentine's Day three years after the accident, Kim proposed to Krickitt again, and she accepted. A short time later, the couple exchanged rings and recited new vows.

The Carpenters' story raises several issues regarding the nature of memory loss: What

Looking **Ahead**

specifically was the nature of the physical trauma that devastated Krickitt's memories? Will the lost memories ever return? Why were only recent memories lost and older ones retained?

Stories like this illustrate not only the important role memory plays in our lives but also its fragility. Memory allows us to retrieve a vast amount of information. We are able to remember the name of a friend we haven't talked with for years and recall the details of a picture that hung in our bedroom as a child. At the same time, though, memory failures are common. We forget where we left the keys to the car and fail to answer an exam question about material we studied only a few hours earlier.

We turn now to the nature of memory, considering the ways in which information is stored and retrieved. We examine the problems of retrieving information from memory, the accuracy of memories, and the reasons information is sometimes forgotten. We also consider the biological foundations of memory and discuss some practical means of increasing memory capacity.

Encoding, Storage, and Retrieval of Memory

What is memory?

Are there different kinds of memory?

You are playing a game of Trivial Pursuit, and winning the game comes down to one question: On what body of water is Bombay located?

As you rack your brain for the answer, several fundamental processes relating to memory come into play. You may never, for instance, have been exposed to information regarding Bombay's location, or if you have been exposed to it, it may simply not have registered in a meaningful way. In other words, your difficulty in answering the question may be traced to the initial encoding stage of memory. *Encoding* refers to the process by which information initially is recorded in a form usable to memory.

However, even if you had been exposed to the information and originally knew the name of the body of water, you may still be unable to recall it during the game because of a failure in the retention process. Memory specialists speak of *storage*, the maintenance of material saved in the memory system. If the material is not stored adequately, it cannot be recalled later.

Memory also depends on one last process—retrieval: Material in memory storage has to be located and brought into awareness to be useful. Your failure to recall Bombay's location, then, may rest on your inability to retrieve information that you learned earlier.

In sum, psychologists consider **memory** to be the process by which we encode, store, and retrieve information (see Figure 1). Each of the three parts of this definition—encoding, storage, and retrieval—represents a different process. You can think of these processes as being analogous to a computer's keyboard (encoding), hard drive (storage), and software that accesses the information for display on the screen (retrieval). Only if all three processes have operated will you experience success and be able to recall the body of water on which Bombay is located: the Arabian Sea.

However, before continuing, we should keep in mind the value of memory *failures*. Forgetting is essential to the proper functioning of memory. The ability to forget inconsequential details about experiences, people, and objects helps us avoid being burdened and distracted by trivial stores of meaningless data.

Furthermore, forgetting permits us to form general impressions and recollections. For example, the reason our friends consistently look familiar to us is our ability to

Memory: The process by which we encode, store, and retrieve information.

Encoding
(Initial recording of information)

Storage
(Information saved for future use)

Retrieval
(Recovery of stored information)

loading from/ drive a

FIGURE 1 Memory is built on three basic processes—encoding, storage, and retrieval—that are analogous to a computer's keyboard, hard drive, and software that accesses the information for display on the screen. The analogy is not perfect, however, because human memory is less precise than a computer. How might you modify the analogy to make it more accurate?

forget their clothing, facial blemishes, and other transient features that change from one occasion to the next. Instead, our memories are based on a summary of various critical features—a far more economical use of our memory capabilities. Forgetting unnecessary information, then, is as essential to the proper functioning of memory as is remembering more important material. If you're uneasy about your own forgetfulness, try the quiz in Figure 2.

▲ ▲ ▲

FIGURE 2 If you're concerned about your memory not being what it should be, try this quiz. It is similar to tests used to determine if someone has a serious loss of memory—from which you, as a college student, are unlikely to suffer. (Source: Adapted from Devi, 2002.)

Take a Measure of Your Memory

If you're concerned your memory is not what is should be (or used to be), try this quiz.

PART I

1. a. What year is it? _____
   b. What season is it? _____
   c. What month is it? _____
   d. What day of the week is it? _____
   e. What is today's date? _____ Example: 12
2. Remember these words: apple, table, penny
3. Without looking at your watch, write down what time it is: _____ hh:mm
   Now look at your watch and write down the actual time: _____ hh:mm
4. Give the names of the current and previous four U.S. presidents:
   _____
   _____
   _____
   _____
   _____

5. Give the names of the following items:

   a. _____

   b. _____

   c. _____

   d. _____

   e. _____

   f. _____

   g. _____

   h. _____

FIGURE 2 concluded

PART II

6. Do you remember the address of the last place you lived?
   ☐ Yes ☐ No
7. Do you find that you repeat yourself more often?
   ☐ Yes ☐ No
8. Do people get annoyed with you due to your memory?
   ☐ Yes ☐ No
9. Do you have more trouble remembering lists, such as shopping lists?
   ☐ Yes ☐ No
10. Do you have trouble remembering events that happened this morning or last week?
    ☐ Yes ☐ No
11. Do you now have more trouble following directions?
    ☐ Yes ☐ No
12. Have you been getting lost more often than usual?
    ☐ Yes ☐ No
13. Do you have trouble finding words?
    ☐ Yes ☐ No
14. Do you find that you lose or misplace things more often?
    ☐ Yes ☐ No
15. Do your memory difficulties impair work/social life?
    ☐ Yes ☐ No
16. Without going back to the previous page, write down the three words you were told to remember at the beginning of the quiz: _____ _____ _____

SCORING FOR MEMORY QUIZ

PART I OF QUIZ (SUBSECTION SCORE 18):

1. Give yourself 1 point for remembering the **exact** date (date, day of week, month, season, and year). (1 point)
2. Did you remember the three words (apple, table, penny) asked in question 16?
   Give yourself 1 point for each correct answer. (3 points)
3. If the difference between your guessed time and the correct time is less than 30 minutes, give yourself 1 point.
4. Give yourself 1 point for each president named correctly. (5 points): Bush, Clinton, Bush, Reagan, Carter. The order in which you remembered them is not important.
5. Give yourself a point for each correct answer. (total 8 points)
   5a Abacus (1 point); **5b** Acorn (1 point); **5c** Escalator (1 point); **5d** Igloo (1 point); **5e** Pencil (1 point); **5f** Protractor (1 point); **5g** Pyramid (1 point); **5h** Watch (1 point)

PART II OF QUIZ (SUBSECTION SCORE 10):

6. 1 point for remembering your last address.
7–15. Give yourself 1 point each for every question answered "No."

INTERPRETATION:

Note that poor scores may be due to factors such as anxiety and inattention and not just from memory difficulties. Doing well on this simple quiz also does not ensure that you have no memory or cognitive difficulties.

The best indicator of your memory is your own assessment of your abilities. A perceived consistent change in your mental capacity is a far more sensitive indicator of cognitive difficulties than most tests, including this one. You should seek further help if this is the case.

If you scored a 27 or 28, congratulations!

If you scored between 22 and 26, you may have some memory difficulties that, if persistent and interfering with function, may need to be evaluated.

If you scored 21 or below, and you have noticed that you have difficulty with your memory or thinking abilities of sufficient severity to interfere with functioning, you probably would benefit from a good evaluation.

The Three Systems of Memory: Memory Storehouses

Although the processes of encoding, storing, and retrieving information are necessary for memory to operate successfully, they do not describe *how* information enters into memory. According to the three-system theory of memory that dominated memory research for several decades, there are different memory storage systems or stages through which information must travel if it is to be remembered. Although the theory is no longer fully accepted, its terminology is often employed, and it has been enormously influential (Atkinson & Shiffrin, 1968, 1971).

The three-system memory theory proposes the existence of the three separate memory stores shown in Figure 3. **Sensory memory** refers to the initial, momentary storage of information, lasting only an instant. Information is recorded by the person's sensory system as an exact replica of the stimulus. In a second stage, **short-term memory** holds information for fifteen to twenty-five seconds and stores it according to its meaning rather than as mere sensory stimulation. The third type of storage system is **long-term memory**. Information is stored in long-term memory on a relatively permanent basis, although it may be difficult to retrieve.

Although we'll be discussing the three types of memory as separate memory stores, keep in mind that these are not mini-warehouses located in particular portions of the brain. Instead, they represent three different types of memory systems with different characteristics. Furthermore, although the three-part model of memory dominated the field of memory research for several decades, recent studies have suggested several newer models, as we'll discuss later. Still, considering memory in terms of three major kinds of stores provides us with a useful framework for understanding how information is both recalled and forgotten.

SENSORY MEMORY

A momentary flash of lightning, the sound of a twig snapping, and the sting of a pinprick all represent stimulation of exceedingly brief duration, but they may nonetheless provide important information that can require a response. Such stimuli

Sensory memory: The initial, momentary storage of information, lasting only an instant.

Short-term memory: Memory that holds information for fifteen to twenty-five seconds.

Long-term memory: Memory that stores information on a relatively permanent basis, although it may be difficult to retrieve.

FIGURE 3 In this three-stage model of memory, information initially recorded by the person's sensory system enters sensory memory, which momentarily holds the information. The information then moves to short-term memory, which stores it for fifteen to twenty-five seconds. Finally, the information can move into long-term memory, which is relatively permanent. Whether the information moves from short-term to long-term memory depends on the kind and amount of rehearsal of the material that is carried out. (Source: Atkinson & Shifrin, 1968.)

are initially—and briefly—stored in sensory memory, the first repository of the information the world presents to us. Actually, the term *sensory memory* encompasses several types of sensory memories, each related to a different source of sensory information. There is **iconic memory**, which reflects information from the visual system; **echoic memory**, which stores auditory information coming from the ears; and corresponding memories for each of the other senses.

Regardless of the individual subtypes, sensory memory in general is able to store information for only a very short time. If information does not pass to short-term memory, it is lost for good. For instance, iconic memory seems to last less than a second, and echoic memory typically fades within two or three seconds. However, despite the brief duration of sensory memory, its precision is high: Sensory memory can store an almost exact replica of each stimulus to which it is exposed (Darwin, Turvey, & Crowder, 1972; Long & Beaton, 1982; Sams et al., 1993).

A momentary flash of lightning leaves a sensory visual memory, a fleeting but exact replica of the stimulus that fades rapidly.

If the storage capabilities of sensory memory are so limited and information stored within sensory memory so fleeting, it would seem almost impossible to find evidence for its existence; new information would constantly be replacing older information, even before a person could report its presence. Not until psychologist George Sperling (1960) conducted a series of clever and now-classic studies was sensory memory well understood. Sperling briefly exposed people to a series of twelve letters arranged in the following pattern:

Iconic memory: Sensory memory that reflects information from the visual system.

Echoic memory: Sensory memory that stores auditory information coming from the ears.

F T Y C
K D N L
Y W B M

When exposed to this pattern of letters for just one-twentieth of a second, most people could recall only four or five of the letters accurately. Although they knew that they had seen more, the memory of those letters had faded by the time they reported the first few letters. It was possible, then, that the information had initially been accurately stored in sensory memory, but during the time it took to verbalize the first four or five letters the memory of the other letters faded.

To test that possibility, Sperling conducted an experiment in which a high, medium, or low tone sounded just after a person had been exposed to the full pattern of letters. People were told to report the letters in the highest line if a high tone was sounded, the middle line if the medium tone occurred, or the lowest line at the sound of the low tone. Because the tone occurred after the exposure, people had to rely on their memories to report the correct row.

The results of the study clearly showed that people had been storing the complete pattern in memory. They were accurate in their recollection of the letters in the line that had been indicated by the tone regardless of whether it was the top, middle, or bottom line. Obviously, *all* the lines they had seen had been stored in sensory memory. Despite its rapid loss, then, the information in sensory memory was an accurate representation of what people had seen.

By gradually lengthening the time between the presentation of the visual pattern and the tone, Sperling was able to determine with some accuracy the length of time that information was stored in sensory memory. The ability to recall a particular row of the pattern when a tone was sounded declined progressively as the period between the visual exposure and the tone increased. This decline continued until the period reached about one second in duration, at which point the row could not be recalled accurately at all. Sperling concluded that the entire visual image was stored in sensory memory for less than a second. Go to **Interactivity 20–1** to convince yourself of Sperling's results.

INTERACTIVITY 20–1

Sensory memory

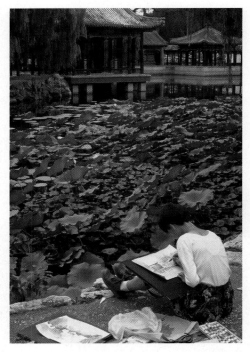

An artist must repeatedly view the subject of a painting in order to capture the image as viewed, using both short-term and long-term memory. Why do you think people tend to close their eyes when recalling a scene or picture?

Chunk: A meaningful grouping of stimuli that can be stored as a unit in short-term memory.

In sum, sensory memory operates as a kind of snapshot that stores information—which may be of a visual, auditory, or other sensory nature—for a brief moment in time. But it is as if each snapshot, immediately after being taken, is destroyed and replaced with a new one. Unless the information in the snapshot is transferred to some other type of memory, it is lost.

SHORT-TERM MEMORY: GIVING MEMORY MEANING

Because the information that is stored briefly in sensory memory consists of representations of raw sensory stimuli, it is not meaningful to us. For us to make sense of it and to allow for the possibility of long-term retention, the information must be transferred to the next stage of memory: short-term memory. Short-term memory is the memory store in which information first has meaning, although the maximum length of retention is relatively short.

The specific process by which sensory memories are transformed into short-term memories is not clear. Some theorists suggest that the information is first translated into graphical representations or images, and others hypothesize that the transfer occurs when the sensory stimuli are changed to words (Baddeley & Wilson, 1985). What is clear, however, is that unlike sensory memory, which holds a relatively full and detailed—if short-lived—representation of the world, short-term memory has incomplete representational capabilities.

In fact, the specific amount of information that can be held in short-term memory has been identified as seven items, or "chunks," of information, with variations up to plus or minus two chunks. A **chunk** is a meaningful grouping of stimuli that can be stored as a unit in short-term memory. According to George Miller (1956), it can be individual letters or numbers, permitting us to hold a seven-digit phone number (like 226-4610) in short-term memory.

But a chunk also may consist of larger categories, such as words or other meaningful units. For example, consider the following list of twenty-one letters:

P B S F O X C N N A B C C B S M T V N B C

Because the list exceeds seven chunks, it is difficult to recall the letters after one exposure. But suppose they were presented as follows:

PBS FOX CNN ABC CBS MTV NBC

In this case, even though there are still twenty-one letters, you'd be able to store them in short-term memory, since they represent only seven chunks.

Chunks can vary in size from single letters or numbers to categories that are far more complicated. The specific nature of what constitutes a chunk varies according to one's past experience. You can see this for yourself by trying an experiment that was first carried out as a comparison between expert and inexperienced chess players and is illustrated in Figure 4 (deGroot, 1966; Huffman, Matthews, & Gagne, 2001; Saariluoma & Laine, 2001).

Although it is possible to remember seven or so relatively complicated sets of information entering short-term memory, the information cannot be held there very long. Just how brief is short-term memory? Anyone who has looked up a telephone number at a pay phone, struggled to find coins, and forgotten the number at the sound of the dial tone knows that information in short-term memory does not remain there very long. Most psychologists believe that information in short-term memory is lost after fifteen to twenty-five seconds—unless it is transferred to long-term memory.

REHEARSAL

Rehearsal: The repetition of information that has entered short-term memory.

The transfer of material from short- to long-term memory proceeds largely on the basis of **rehearsal**, the repetition of information that has entered short-term memory. Rehearsal accomplishes two things. First, as long as the information is repeated, it is maintained in short-term memory. More important, however, rehearsal allows us to

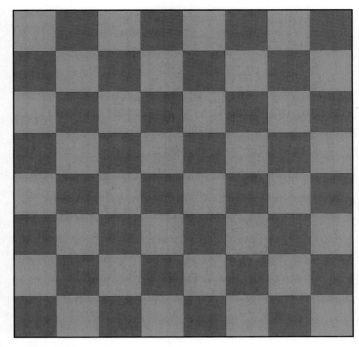

FIGURE 4 Examine the chessboard containing the chess pieces for about five seconds, and then, after covering up the board, try to draw the position of the pieces on the blank chessboard. (You could also use a chessboard of your own and place the pieces in the same positions.) Unless you are an experienced chess player, you are likely to have great difficulty carrying out such a task. Yet chess masters—the kind who win tournaments—do this quite well (deGroot, 1966). They are able to reproduce correctly 90 percent of the pieces on the board. In comparison, inexperienced chess player are typically able to reproduce only 40 percent of the board properly. The chess masters do not have superior memories in other respects; they generally test normally on other measures of memory. What they can do better than others is see the board in terms of chunks or meaningful units and reproduce the position of the chess pieces by using those units.

transfer the information into long-term memory, as you can see for yourself in **Interactivity 20–2.**

Whether the transfer is made from short- to long-term memory seems to depend largely on the kind of rehearsal that is carried out. If the information is simply repeated over and over again—as we might do with a telephone number while we rush from the phone book to the phone—it is kept current in short-term memory, but it will not necessarily be placed in long-term memory. Instead, as soon as we stop punching in the phone numbers, the number is likely to be replaced by other information and will be completely forgotten.

In contrast, if the information in short-term memory is rehearsed using a process called elaborative rehearsal, it is much more likely to be transferred into long-term memory (Craik & Lockhart, 1972). *Elaborative rehearsal* occurs when the information is considered and organized in some fashion. The organization might include expanding the information to make it fit into a logical framework, linking it to another memory, turning it into an image, or transforming it in some other way. For example, a list of vegetables to be purchased at a store could be woven together in memory as items being used to prepare an elaborate salad, could be linked to the items bought on an earlier shopping trip, or could be thought of in terms of the image of a farm with rows of each item.

By using organizational strategies such as these—called *mnemonics*—we can vastly improve our retention of information. Mnemonics (pronounced "neh MON ix") are formal techniques for organizing information in a way that makes it more likely to be

INTERACTIVITY 20–2

Short-term memory

remembered. For instance, when a beginning musician learns that the spaces on the music staff spell the word *FACE*, or when we learn the rhyme "Thirty days hath September, April, June, and November...," we are using mnemonics (Mastropieri & Scruggs, 1991; Bellezza, Six, & Phillips, 1992; Goldstein et al., 1996; Schoen, 1996; Carney, Levin, Levin, & Schoen, 2000).

LONG-TERM MEMORY: THE FINAL STOREHOUSE

Material that makes its way from short-term memory to long-term memory enters a storehouse of almost unlimited capacity. Like a new file we save on a hard drive, the information in long-term memory is filed and coded so that we can retrieve it when we need it.

Evidence of the existence of long-term memory, as distinct from short-term memory, comes from a number of sources. For example, people with certain kinds of brain damage have no lasting recall of new information after the damage, although people and events stored in memory before the injury remain intact (Milner, 1966). Because information that was encoded and stored before the injury can be recalled and because short-term memory after the injury appears to be operational—new material can be recalled for a very brief period—we can infer that there are two distinct types of memory: one for short-term and one for long-term storage.

Results from laboratory experiments are also consistent with the notion of separate short-term and long-term memory. For example, in one set of studies people were asked to recall a relatively small amount of information (such as a set of three letters). Then, to prevent practice of the initial information, participants were required to recite some extraneous material aloud, such as counting backward by threes (Brown, 1958; Peterson & Peterson, 1959). By varying the amount of time between the presentation of the initial material and the need for its recall, investigators found that recall was quite good when the interval was very short but declined rapidly thereafter. After fifteen seconds had gone by, recall hovered at around 10 percent of the material initially presented.

Apparently, the distraction of counting backward prevented almost all the initial material from reaching long-term memory. Initial recall was good because it was coming from short-term memory, but those memories were lost at a rapid rate. Eventually, all that could be recalled was the small amount of material that had made its way into long-term storage despite the distraction of counting backward.

The distinction between short- and long-term memory is also supported by the *serial position effect*, in which the ability to recall information in a list depends on where in the list an item appears. For instance, often a *primacy effect* occurs, in which items presented early in a list are remembered better. There is also a *recency effect*, in which items presented late in a list are remembered best.

PowerWeb: Storage and Retrieval Processes in Long-Term Memory

www.mhhe.com/feldmanup7

Contemporary Approaches to Memory: Working Memory, Memory Modules, and Associative Models of Memory

So far, we have relied on the traditional model of memory that suggests that the processing of information in memory proceeds in three sequential stages, starting with sensory memory, advancing to short-term memory, and potentially ending in long-term memory. However, many contemporary approaches suggest that this traditional model provides an incomplete account of memory. For instance, rather than information being processed sequentially from sensory to short-term to long-term memory stores (a *serial* process), increasing evidence suggests that the brain may process information simultaneously in different memory components (a *parallel* process). These views are exemplified by approaches to short- and long-term memory that we consider next.

WORKING MEMORY

Rather than seeing short-term memory as an independent way station through which memories travel, some theorists conceive of short-term memory as an information-processing system known as working memory. **Working memory** is a set of temporary memory stores that actively manipulate and rehearse information (Baddeley, 2001; Engle, 2002).

> Working memory: A set of active, temporary memory stores that rehearse information.

Working memory is thought to contain a *central executive* processor that is involved in reasoning and decision making. The central executive coordinates three distinct storage-and-rehearsal systems: the visual store, the verbal store, and the episodic buffer. The *visual store* specializes in visual and spatial information, whereas the *verbal store* is responsible for holding and manipulating material relating to speech, words, and numbers. The *episodic buffer* contains information that represents episodes or occurrences (Baddeley, 2001; see Figure 5).

Working memory permits us to maintain information in an active state briefly so that we can do something with the information. For instance, we use working memory when we're doing a multistep arithmetic problem in our heads, storing the result of one calculation while getting ready to move to the next stage. (I make use of my working memory when I figure a 20 percent tip in a restaurant by first calculating 10 percent of the total bill and then doubling it.)

Although working memory aids in the recall of information, it uses a significant amount of cognitive resources during its operation. In turn, this can make us less

FIGURE 5 Working memory is an active "workspace" in which information is retrieved and manipulated, and in which information is held through rehearsal (Gathercole & Baddeley, 1993). It consists of a "central executive" that coordinates the visual store (which concentrates on visual and spatial information), the verbal store (concentrating on speech, words, and numbers), and the episodic buffer (which represents episodes or occurrences that are encountered). (Source: Adapted from Baddeley, 2001.)

The ability to remember specific skills and the order in which they are used is known as procedural memory. If driving involves procedural memory, is it safe to use a cell phone while driving?

INTERACTIVITY 20–3

Working memory

Declarative memory: Memory for factual information: names, faces, dates, and the like.

Procedural memory: Memory for skills and habits, such as riding a bike or hitting a baseball, sometimes referred to as "nondeclarative memory."

Semantic memory: Memory for general knowledge and facts about the world, as well as memory for the rules of logic that are used to deduce other facts.

aware of our surroundings—something that has implications for the debate about the use of cellular telephones in automobiles. If a phone conversation requires thinking, it will burden working memory, leaving people less aware of their surroundings, an obviously dangerous state of affairs for a driver (deFockert et al., 2001; Wickelgren, 2001). (To learn more about working memory, try **Interactivity 20–3.**)

LONG-TERM MEMORY MODULES

Just as short-term memory is often viewed in terms of working memory, many contemporary researchers now see long-term memory as made up of several different components, or memory modules. Each of these modules is related to a separate memory system in the brain.

For instance, one major distinction within long-term memory is between declarative memory and procedural memory. **Declarative memory** is memory for factual information: names, faces, dates, and facts such as "a bike has two wheels." In contrast, **procedural memory** (sometimes referred to as "nondeclarative memory") refers to memory for skills and habits, such as how to ride a bike or hit a baseball. Information *about* things is stored in declarative memory; information regarding *how to do* things is stored in procedural memory (Eichenbaum, 1997; Schacter, Wagner, & Buckner, 2000).

In addition to procedural memory, driving a car involves what is known as declarative or explicit memory, which permits us to remember how to get to our destination.

The facts in declarative memory can be further subdivided into semantic memory and episodic memory (Tulving, 1993; Nyberg & Tulving, 1996). **Semantic memory** is memory for general knowledge and facts about the world, as well as memory for the rules of logic that are used to deduce other facts. Because of semantic memory, we remember that $2 \times 2 = 4$, that the ZIP code for Beverly Hills is 90210, and that *memoree* is misspelled. Thus, semantic memory is somewhat like a mental almanac of facts.

Long-term memory

Declarative memory
(factual information)
Example: George Washington was
the first U.S. president

Procedural memory
(skills and habits)
Example: Riding a bicycle

Semantic memory
(general memory)
Example: Math facts

Episodic memory
(personal knowledge)
Example: Your car accident

FIGURE 6 Long-term memory can be subdivided into several different types. What type of long-term memory is involved in your recollection of the moment you first arrived on your campus at the start of college? What type of long-term memory is involved in remembering the lyrics to a song, compared with the tune of a song?

In contrast, **episodic memory** is memory for the biographical details of our individual lives. Memories of what we have done and the kinds of experiences we have had constitute episodic memory. Consequently, our recall of the first time we rode a bike or our first date is based on episodic memories. (To help your long-term memory keep the distinctions between the different types of long-term memory straight, look at Figure 6.)

Episodic memories can be surprisingly detailed. Consider, for instance, how you'd respond if you were asked to identify what you were doing on a specific day two years ago. Impossible? You may think otherwise as you read the following exchange between a researcher and a participant in a study who was asked, in a memory experiment, what he was doing "on Monday afternoon in the third week of September two years ago."

PARTICIPANT: Come on. How should I know?

EXPERIMENTER: Just try it anyhow.

PARTICIPANT: OK. Let's see: Two years ago . . . I would be in high school in Pittsburgh . . . That would be my senior year. Third week in September—that's just after summer—that would be the fall term . . . Let me see. I think I had chemistry lab on Mondays. I don't know. I was probably in chemistry lab. Wait a minute—that would be the second week of school. I remember he started off with the atomic table—a big fancy chart. I thought he was crazy trying to make us memorize that thing. You know, I think I can remember sitting . . . (Lindsay & Norman, 1977).

Episodic memory, then, can provide information from events that happened long in the past (Reynolds & Takooshian, 1988). But semantic memory is no less impressive, permitting us to dredge up tens of thousands of facts ranging from the date of our birthday to the knowledge that $1 is less than $5.

ASSOCIATIVE MODELS OF MEMORY

Our ability to recall detailed information has led some memory researchers to view memory primarily in terms of associations between different pieces of information. **Associative models of memory** suggest that memory consists of mental representations of clusters of interconnected information (e.g., Collins & Quillian, 1969; Collins & Loftus, 1975).

Consider, for example, Figure 7, which shows some of the relationships in memory relating to fire engines, the color red, and a variety of other concepts. Associative

Episodic memory: Memory for the biographical details of our individual lives.

PowerWeb: What Is Episodic Memory?

www.mhhe.com/feldmanup7

Associative models of memory: Theory that memory consists of mental representations of interconnected information.

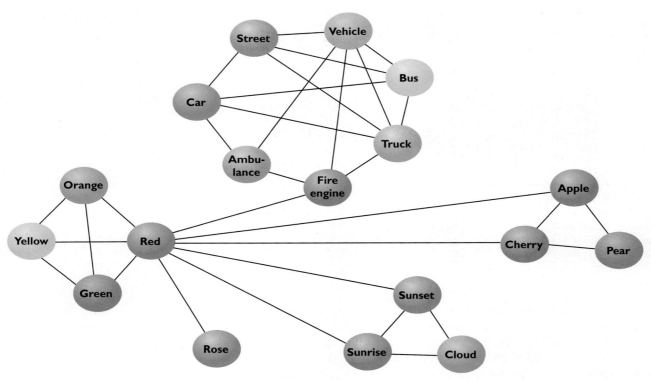

FIGURE 7 Associative models suggest that semantic memory consists of relationships between pieces of information, such as those relating to the concept of a fire engine. The lines suggest the connections that indicate how the information is organized within memory. (Source: Collins & Loftus, 1975.)

Priming: A phenomenon in which exposure to a word or concept (called a *prime*) later makes it easier to recall related information, even when there is no conscious memory of the word or concept.

memory models suggest that thinking about a particular concept leads to recall of related concepts. For example, seeing a fire engine may activate our recollections of other kinds of emergency vehicles, such as an ambulance, which in turn may activate recall of the related concept of a vehicle. And thinking of a vehicle may lead us to think about a bus that we've seen in the past. Activating one memory triggers the activation of related memories in a process known as *spreading activation*.

Associative memory models help account for **priming,** a phenomenon in which exposure to a word or concept (called a *prime*) later makes it easier to recall related information. Priming effects occur even when people have no conscious memory of the original word or concept (Tulving & Schacter, 1990; Toth & Reingold, 1996; Schacter, 1998).

The typical experiment designed to illustrate priming helps clarify the phenomenon. In priming experiments, participants are rapidly exposed to a stimulus such as a word, an object, or perhaps a drawing of a face. The second phase of the experiment is done after an interval ranging from several seconds to several months. At that point, participants are exposed to incomplete perceptual information that is related to the first stimulus, and they are asked whether they recognize it. For example, the new material may consist of the first letter of a word that had been presented earlier, or a part of a face that had been shown earlier. If participants are able to identify the stimulus more readily than they identify stimuli that have not been presented earlier, priming has taken place.

Priming occurs even when participants report no conscious awareness of having been exposed to a stimulus earlier. For instance, studies have found that people who are anesthetized during surgery can sometimes recall snippets of conversations they heard during surgery—even though they have no conscious recollection of the information (Kihlstrom et al., 1990; Sebel, Bonke, & Winogard, 1993).

Explicit memory: Intentional or conscious recollection of information.

The discovery that people have memories about which they are unaware has been an important one. It has led to speculation that two forms of memory, explicit and implicit, may exist side by side. **Explicit memory** refers to intentional or

"The matters about which I'm being questioned, Your Honor, are all things I should have included in my long-term memory but which I mistakenly inserted in my short-term memory."

conscious recollection of information. When we try to remember a name or date we have encountered or learned about previously, we are searching our explicit memory. In contrast, **implicit memory** refers to memories of which people are not consciously aware, but which can affect subsequent performance and behavior. Skills that operate automatically and without thinking, such as jumping out of the path of an automobile coming toward us as we walk down the side of a road, are stored in implicit memory. Similarly, a feeling of vague dislike for an acquaintance, without knowing why we have that feeling, may be a reflection of implicit memories. In short, when an event that we are unable to consciously recall affects our behavior, implicit memory is at work (Graf & Masson, 1993; Schacter, Chiu, & Ochsner, 1993; Schacter, 1994b, 1995; Underwood, 1996; Tulving, 2000).

Implicit memory: Memories of which people are not consciously aware, but which can affect subsequent performance and behavior.

THE MULTIPLE MODELS OF MEMORY

We've seen that the way memory is viewed has been expanded from the three-stage model of memory. Although this traditional view of memory has not been rejected, contemporary views take a broader approach, considering memory in terms of multiple interdependent systems, operating simultaneously, that are responsible for different types of recall. Moreover, greater emphasis has been placed on working memory, in an effort to determine how different types of information can be stored and processed simultaneously.

You might be asking which of these views of memory is most accurate. It's a fair question, but one that is not easily answered at this point. More than most areas of psychology, memory has attracted a great deal of theorizing, and it is probably too early to tell—let alone remember—which of the multiple models proposed by different memory psychologists provides the most accurate characterization of memory (Wolters, 1995; Bjork & Bjork, 1996; Conway, 1997).

RECAP/EVALUATE/RETHINK

RECAP

What is memory?

▶ Memory is the process by which we encode, store, and retrieve information. (p. 223)

Are there different kinds of memory?

▶ Sensory memory, corresponding to each of the sensory systems, is the first place where information is saved. Sensory memories are very brief, but they are precise, storing a nearly exact replica of a stimulus. (p. 226)

▶ Roughly seven (plus or minus two) chunks of information can be transferred and held in short-term memory. Information in short-term memory is held from fifteen to twenty-five seconds and, if not transferred to long-term memory, is lost. (p. 226)

▶ Memories are transferred into long-term storage through rehearsal. If memories are transferred into long-term memory, they become relatively permanent. (p. 226)

▶ Some theorists view short-term memory as a working memory, in which information is retrieved and manipulated, and held through rehearsal. In this view, it is a central executive processor involved in reasoning and decision making; it coordinates a visual store, a verbal store, and an episodic buffer. (p. 231)

▶ Newer memory models view long-term memory in terms of memory modules, each of which is related to separate memory systems in the brain. For instance, we can distinguish between declarative memory and procedural memory. Declarative memory is further divided into episodic memory and semantic memory. (p. 232)

▶ Associative models of memory suggest that memory consists of mental representations of clusters of interconnected information. (p. 233)

▶ Explicit memory refers to intentional or conscious recollection of information. In contrast, implicit memory refers to memories of which people are not consciously aware, but which can affect subsequent performance and behavior. (p. 234)

EVALUATE

1. Match the type of memory with its definition:
   1. Long-term memory
   2. Short-term memory
   3. Sensory memory
   a. Holds information fifteen to twenty-five seconds.
   b. Can be difficult to retrieve.
   c. Direct representation of a stimulus.
2. A(n) _____ is a meaningful group of stimuli that can be stored together in short-term memory.
3. _____ are strategies used to organize information for retrieval.
4. There appear to be two types of declarative memory: _____ memory, for knowledge and facts, and _____ memory, for personal experiences.
5. _____ models of memory state that long-term memory is stored as associations between pieces of information.

RETHINK

1. It is a truism that "you never forget how to ride a bicycle." Why might this be so? Where is information about bicycle riding stored? What happens when a person has to retrieve that information after not using it for a long time?
2. Priming often occurs without conscious awareness. How might this effect be used by advertisers and others to promote their products? What ethical principles are involved? Can you think of a way to protect yourself from unethical advertisers?

Answers to Evaluate Questions

1. 1-b, 2-a, 3-c 2. chunk; 3. mnemonics; 4. semantic, episodic; 5. associative

KEY TERMS

memory p. 223
sensory memory p. 226
short-term memory p. 226
long-term memory p. 226
iconic memory p. 227

echoic memory p. 227
chunk p. 228
rehearsal p. 228
working memory p. 231
declarative memory p. 232

procedural memory p. 232
semantic memory p. 232
episodic memory p. 233
associative models of
memory p. 233

priming p. 234
explicit memory p. 234
implicit memory p. 235

Recalling Long-Term Memories

An hour after his job interview, Ricardo was sitting in a coffee shop, telling his friend Laura how well it had gone, when the woman who had interviewed him walked in.

"Well, hello, Ricardo. How are you doing?" Trying to make a good impression, Ricardo began to make introductions, but suddenly realized he could not remember the name of the interviewer. Stammering, he desperately searched his memory, but to no avail. "I *know* her name," he thought to himself, "but here I am, looking like a fool. I can kiss this job good-bye."

Have you ever tried to remember someone's name, convinced that you knew it, but were unable to recall it no matter how hard you tried? This common occurrence—known as the **tip-of-the-tongue phenomenon**—exemplifies the difficulties that can occur in retrieving information stored in long-term memory (Schwartz, Travis, Castro, & Smith, 2000; Schwartz, 2001, 2002).

The tip-of-the-tongue phenomenon is especially frustrating in situations in which a person cannot recall the name of someone he or she has just met. Can you think of ways to avoid this common occurrence?

Retrieval Cues

One reason recall is not perfect is the sheer quantity of recollections that are stored in long-term memory. Although the issue is far from settled, many psychologists have suggested that the material that makes its way to long-term memory is relatively permanent (Tulving & Psotka, 1971). If they are correct, this suggests that the capacity of long-term memory is vast, given the broad range of people's experiences

Tip-of-the-tongue phenomenon: The inability to recall information that one realizes one knows—a result of the difficulty of retrieving information from long-term memory.

FIGURE 1 Try to recall the names of these characters. Because this is a recall task, it is relatively difficult.

FIGURE 2 Naming the characters in Figure 1 (a recall task) is more difficult than solving the recognition problem posed in this list.

| **Answer this recognition question:** |
| **Which of the following are the names of the seven dwarfs in the Disney** |
| **movie *Snow White and the Seven Dwarfs*?** |

Goofy	Bashful
Sleepy	Meanie
Smarty	Doc
Scaredy	Happy
Dopey	Angry
Grumpy	Sneezy
Wheezy	Crazy

and educational backgrounds. For instance, if you are like the average college student, your vocabulary includes some 50,000 words, you know hundreds of mathematical "facts," and you are able to conjure up images—such as the way your childhood home looked—with no trouble at all. In fact, simply cataloging all your memories would probably take years of work.

How do we sort through this vast array of material and retrieve specific information at the appropriate time? One of the major ways is through retrieval cues. A *retrieval cue* is a stimulus that allows us to recall more easily information that is in long-term memory (Tulving & Thompson, 1973; Ratcliff & McKoon, 1989). It may be a word, an emotion, or a sound; whatever the specific cue, a memory will suddenly come to mind when the retrieval cue is present. For example, the smell of roasting turkey may evoke memories of Thanksgiving or family gatherings (Schab & Crowder, 1995).

Retrieval cues guide people through the information stored in long-term memory in much the same way that the cards in an old-fashioned card catalog guided people through a library, or a search engine such as "Yahoo" guides people through the World Wide Web. They are particularly important when we are making an effort to *recall* information, as opposed to being asked to *recognize* material stored in memory. In *recall*, a specific piece of information must be retrieved—such as that needed to answer a fill-in-the-blank question or write an essay on a test. In contrast, *recognition* occurs when people are presented with a stimulus and asked whether they have been exposed to it previously, or are asked to identify it from a list of alternatives.

As you might guess, recognition is generally a much easier task than recall (see Figures 1 and 2). Recall is more difficult because it consists of a series of processes: a search through memory, retrieval of potentially relevant information, and then a decision regarding whether the information you have found is accurate. If the information appears to be correct, the search is over, but if it does not, the search must continue. In contrast, recognition is simpler because it involves fewer steps (Anderson & Bower, 1972; Miserando, 1991).

Levels of Processing

Levels-of-processing theory: The theory of memory that emphasizes the degree to which new material is mentally analyzed.

One determinant of how well memories are recalled is the way in which material is first perceived, processed, and understood. The **levels-of-processing theory** emphasizes the degree to which new material is mentally analyzed (Craik & Lockhart, 1972; Craik, 1990). Levels-of-processing theory suggests that the amount of information processing that occurs when material is initially encountered is central in determining how much of the information is ultimately remembered. According to this approach, the depth of information processing during exposure to material—

meaning the degree to which it is analyzed and considered—is critical; the greater the intensity of its initial processing is, the more likely we are to remember it.

Because we do not pay close attention to much of the information to which we are exposed, typically only scant mental processing takes place, and we forget new material almost immediately. However, information to which we pay greater attention is processed more thoroughly. Therefore, it enters memory at a deeper level—and is less apt to be forgotten than is information processed at shallower levels.

The theory goes on to suggest that there are considerable differences in the ways information is processed at various levels of memory. At shallow levels, information is processed merely in terms of its physical and sensory aspects. For example, we may pay attention only to the shapes that make up the letters in the word *dog*. At an intermediate level of processing, the shapes are translated into meaningful units—in this case, letters of the alphabet. Those letters are considered in the context of words, and specific phonetic sounds may be attached to the letters.

At the deepest level of processing, information is analyzed in terms of its meaning. We may see it in a wider context and draw associations between the meaning of the information and broader networks of knowledge. For instance, we may think of dogs not merely as animals with four legs and a tail, but also in terms of their relationship to cats and other mammals. We may form an image of our own dog, thereby relating the concept to our own lives. According to the levels-of-processing approach, the deeper the initial level of processing of specific information is, the longer the information will be retained.

Although the concept of depth of processing has proved difficult to test experimentally and the levels-of-processing theory has its critics (e.g., Baddeley, 1990), it is clear that there are considerable practical implications to the notion that the degree to which information is initially processed affects recall. For example, the depth at which information is processed is critical when one is learning and studying course material. Rote memorization of a list of key terms for a test is unlikely to produce long-term recollection of information, because processing is being carried out at a shallow level. In contrast, thinking about the meaning of the terms and reflecting on how they relate to information that one currently knows is a far more effective route to long-term retention. The experiment in **Interactivity 21–1** will help you understand levels-of-processing theory.

INTERACTIVITY 21–1

Levels of processing

Flashbulb Memories

Where were you on February 1, 2003? You will most likely draw a blank until this piece of information is added: February 1, 2003, was the date the Space Shuttle *Columbia* broke up in space and fell to Earth.

You probably have little trouble recalling your exact location and a variety of other trivial details that occurred when you heard the news, even though the incident happened months ago. The reason is a phenomenon known as flashbulb memory. **Flashbulb memories** are memories around a specific, important, or surprising event that are so vivid they represent a virtual snapshot of the event.

Several types of flashbulb memories are common among college students. For example, involvement in a car accident, meeting one's roommate for the first time, and the night of high school graduation are all typical focuses of flashbulb memories (Rubin, 1985; Tekcan, 2001; Davidson & Glisky, 2002; see Figure 3).

Of course, flashbulb memories do not contain every detail of an original scene. I remember vividly that some four decades ago I was sitting in Mr. Sharp's tenth-grade geometry class when I heard that President John Kennedy had been shot. However, although I recall where I was sitting and how my classmates reacted to the news, I do not recollect what I was wearing or what I had for lunch that day.

Furthermore, the details recalled in flashbulb memories are often inaccurate. For example, three days after the O. J. Simpson murder case verdict was announced, a

Flashbulb memories: Memories centered on a specific, important, or surprising event that are so vivid it is as if they represented a snapshot of the event.

FIGURE 3 These are the most common flashbulb memory events, based on a survey of college students (Rubin, 1985). What are some of your flashbulb memories?

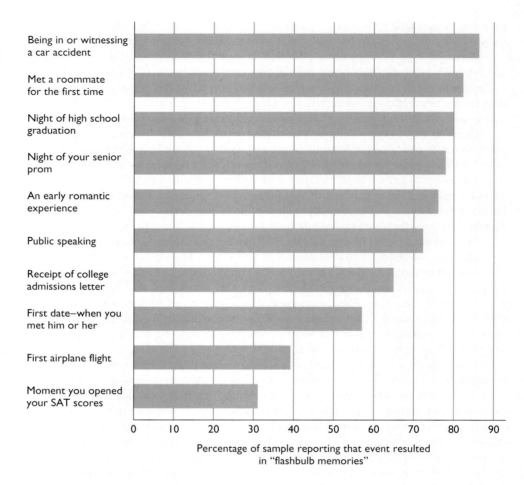

Being in or witnessing a car accident

Met a roommate for the first time

Night of high school graduation

Night of your senior prom

An early romantic experience

Public speaking

Receipt of college admissions letter

First date—when you met him or her

First airplane flight

Moment you opened your SAT scores

0 10 20 30 40 50 60 70 80 90

Percentage of sample reporting that event resulted in "flashbulb memories"

group of college students were asked how they had heard the news. When the same people were asked the identical question fifteen months later, half the recollections were highly accurate, with only 11 percent containing major errors. But after thirty-two months, fewer than a third of the recollections were highly accurate, and over 40 percent had major distortions (Schmolck, Buffalo, & Squire, 2000; Winningham, Hyman, & Dinnel, 2000).

Flashbulb memories illustrate a more general phenomenon about memory: Memories that are exceptional are more easily retrieved (although not necessarily accurately) than are those relating to events that are commonplace. The more distinctive a stimulus is, then, the more likely we are to recall it later (von Restorff, 1933; Winningham, Hyman, & Dinnel, 2000).

Even with a distinctive stimulus, however, we may not remember where the information came from. *Source amnesia* occurs when an individual has a memory for some material but cannot recall where he or she encountered it before. For example, you may have experienced source amnesia when meeting a very familiar person, but you just can't remember where you'd met that person initially.

Constructive Processes in Memory: Rebuilding the Past

Constructive processes: Processes in which memories are influenced by the meaning we give to events.

As we have seen, although it is clear that we can have detailed recollections of significant and distinctive events, it is difficult to gauge the accuracy of such memories. In fact, it is apparent that our memories reflect, at least in part, **constructive processes,**

processes in which memories are influenced by the meaning we give to events. When we retrieve information, then, the memory that is produced is affected not just by the direct prior experience we have had with the stimulus, but also by our guesses and inferences about its meaning.

The notion that memory is based on constructive processes was first put forward by Sir Frederic Bartlett, a British psychologist. He suggested that people tend to remember information in terms of **schemas**, organized bodies of information stored in memory that bias the way new information is interpreted, stored, and recalled (Bartlett, 1932). Our reliance on schemas means that memories often consist of a general reconstruction of previous experience. Bartlett argued that schemas are based not only on the specific material to which people are exposed, but also on their understanding of the situation, their expectations about the situation, and their awareness of the motivations underlying the behavior of others.

One of the earliest demonstrations of schemas came from a classic study that involved a procedure similar to the children's game of "telephone," in which information from memory is passed sequentially from one person to another. In the study, a participant viewed a drawing in which there were a variety of people of differing racial and ethnic backgrounds on a subway car, one of whom—a white person—was shown with a razor in his hand (Allport & Postman, 1958). The first participant was asked to describe the drawing to someone else without looking back at it. Then that person was asked to describe it to another person (without looking at the drawing), and then the process was repeated with still one more participant.

The report of the last person differed in significant, yet systematic, ways from the initial drawing. Specifically, many people described the drawing as depicting an African American with a knife—an incorrect recollection, given that the drawing showed a razor in the hand of a Caucasian person. The transformation of the Caucasian's razor into an African American's knife clearly indicates that the participants held a schema that included the unwarranted prejudice that African Americans are more violent than Caucasians and thus more apt to be holding a knife.

In short, our expectations and knowledge affect the reliability of our memories (Katz, 1989; Ross & Newby, 1996; McDonald & Hirt, 1997). (For more on the imperfections of people's recollections, see the *Applying Psychology in the 21st Century* box.)

Schemas: Organized bodies of information stored in memory that bias the way new information is interpreted, stored, and recalled.

Memory in the Courtroom: The Eyewitness on Trial

For William Jackson, the inadequate memories of two people cost him five years of his life. Jackson was the victim of mistaken identity when two witnesses picked him out of a lineup as the perpetrator of a crime. On that basis, he was convicted and sentenced to serve fourteen to fifty years in jail.

Five years later the actual criminal was identified, and Jackson was released. For Jackson, though, it was too late. In his words, "They took away part of my life, part of my youth. I spend five years down there, and all they said was 'we're sorry'" (*Time*, 1982).

Unfortunately, Jackson is not the only victim to whom apologies have had to be made; there have been many cases of mistaken identity that have led to unjustified legal actions. Research on eyewitness identification of suspects, as well as on memory for other details of crimes, has shown that eyewitnesses are apt to make substantial errors when they try to recall details of criminal activity—even if they are highly confident about their recollections. To find out just how unreliable memory can be, try **Interactivity 21–2** (Miller, 2000; Thompson, 2000; Wells, Olson, & Charman, 2002).

One reason is the impact of the weapons used in crimes. When a criminal perpetrator displays a gun or knife, it acts like a perceptual magnet, attracting the eyes

PowerWeb: Leading Questions and the Eyewitness Report

www.mhhe.com/feldmanup7

INTERACTIVITY 21–2

Eyewitness fallibility

(Mis)Remembering Tragic Events

Think back to the tragic day the World Trade Center in New York was attacked by suicidal terrorists. Do you remember watching television that morning and seeing images of the first plane, and then the second plane, striking the towers?

If you do, you are among the 73 percent of Americans who recall viewing the initial television images of both planes on September 11. However, that recollection is wrong: In fact, television broadcasts showed images only of the second plane on September 11. No video of the first plane was available until the following day, September 12, when it was shown on television early that morning (Begley, 2002).

The terrorist attack on the World Trade Center is not the only tragedy to be misremembered. On November 12, 2001, American Airlines Flight 587 crashed soon after taking off from Kennedy International Airport, killing over 250 people. As investigators sought to determine the cause of the crash, they collected 349 reports from eyewitnesses. Over half the eyewitnesses indicated seeing a fire while the plane was in the air, and 8 percent noted seeing a wing fall off the plane. However, based on their analysis of the crash, investigators showed that the plane was not on fire while it was in the air—and neither of the plane's wings fell off (Wald, 2002).

Although you may be surprised that such powerful memories of high-profile events contain inaccuracies, psychologists who specialize in memory are not. Research has shown that even traumatic

On September 11, 2001, did you see videos of both planes hitting the World Trade Center towers?

memories function much like memories of everyday, mundane events. Although they are mostly accurate, traumatic memories—like all memories—are reconstructions of experiences, and they can be biased or distorted. Memories of trauma and tragedy may be somewhat more detailed than memories of less-distressing incidents, but our recollections of powerful negative events are no more vivid than are our more mundane memories (Porter & Birt, 2001; Pezdek & Taylor, 2002).

Even if they are misremembered, memories of trauma and tragedy forcefully affect people's lives. For example, long after September 11, 2001, many people continued to suffer from posttraumatic stress and other difficulties related to their memories of that day's terrorist attacks. Moreover, eyewitness memories can play critical roles in investigations related to traumatic or tragic events. However, it is always important to balance the necessity of relying on such memories with their potential for inaccuracy (Schlenger et al., 2002).

RETHINK

Why do you think so many Americans incorrectly remember seeing video on September 11 of the first plane striking the World Trade Center? What is the impact of such inaccurate, yet powerful, memories on the individuals who hold them?

of the witnesses. As a consequence, witnesses pay less attention to other details of the crime and are less able to recall what actually occurred (Loftus, Loftus, & Messo, 1987; Steblay, 1992).

Even when weapons are not involved, eyewitnesses are prone to errors relating to memory. For instance, viewers of a twelve-second film of a mugging that was shown on a New York City television news program were later given the opportunity to pick out the assailant from a six-person lineup (Buckhout, 1974). Of some 2,000 viewers who called the station after the program, only 15 percent were able to pick out the right person—a percentage similar to random guessing.

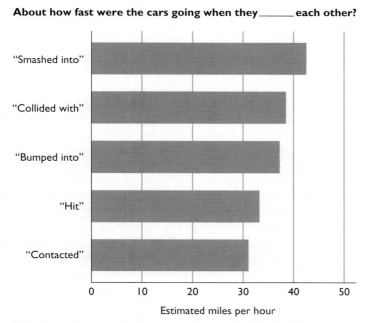

About how fast were the cars going when they _____ each other?

FIGURE 4 After viewing an accident involving two cars, the participants in a study were asked to estimate the speed of the two cars involved in the collision. Estimates varied substantially, depending on the way the question was worded. (Source: Loftus & Palmer, 1974.)

One reason eyewitnesses are prone to memory-related errors is that the specific wording of questions posed to them by police officers or attorneys can affect the way they recall information, as a number of experiments illustrate. For example, in one experiment the participants were shown a film of two cars crashing into each other. Some were then asked the question, "About how fast were the cars going when they *smashed* into each other?" On average, they estimated the speed to be 40.8 miles per hour. In contrast, when another group of participants was asked, "About how fast were the cars going when they *contacted* each other?" the average estimated speed was only 31.8 miles per hour (Loftus & Palmer, 1974; see Figure 4).

The problem of memory reliability becomes even more acute when children are witnesses, because increasing evidence suggests that children's memories are highly vulnerable to the influence of others (Loftus, 1993; Cassel, Roebers, & Bjorklund, 1996). For instance, in one experiment, 5- to 7-year-old girls who had just had a routine physical examination were shown an anatomically explicit doll. The girls were shown the doll's genital area and asked, "Did the doctor touch you here?" Three of the girls who did not have a vaginal or anal exam said that the doctor had in fact touched them in the genital area, and one of those three made up the detail "The doctor did it with a stick" (Saywitz & Goodman, 1990).

Children's memories are especially susceptible to influence when the situation is highly emotional or stressful. For example, in trials in which there is significant pretrial publicity or in which alleged victims are questioned repeatedly, often by untrained interviewers, the memories of the alleged victims may be influenced by the types of questions they are asked (Scullin, Kanaya, & Ceci, 2002; Lamb & Garretson, 2003).

In short, the memories of witnesses are far from infallible, and this is especially true when children are involved (Howe, 1999; Goodman et al., 2002; Schaaf et al., 2002). The question of the accuracy of memories becomes even more complex, however, when we consider the possibility of triggering memories of events that people at first don't even recall happening.

As the result of testimony from Eileen Franklin, based on repressed memory, her father was found guilty of murder. The validity of repressed memory, especially in investigating crimes, remains controversial. Can you think of a test to tell whether a recovered memory is accurate?

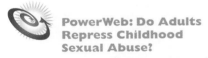

PowerWeb: Do Adults Repress Childhood Sexual Abuse?

www.mhhe.com/feldmanup7

Autobiographical memories: Our recollections of circumstances and episodes from our own lives.

Repressed Memories: Truth or Fiction?

Guilty of murder in the first degree.

That was the jury's verdict in the case of George Franklin, Sr., who was charged with murdering his daughter's playmate. But this case was different from most other murder cases: It was based on memories that had been repressed for twenty years. Franklin's daughter claimed that she had forgotten everything she had once known about her father's crime until two years earlier, when she began to have flashbacks of the event. Gradually, though, the memories became clearer in her mind, until she recalled her father lifting a rock over his head and then seeing her friend lying on the ground, covered with blood. On the basis of her memories, her father was convicted—and later cleared of the crime after an appeal of the conviction.

Although the prosecutor and jury clearly believed Franklin's daughter, there is good reason to question the validity of *repressed memories*, recollections of events that are initially so shocking that the mind responds by pushing them into the unconscious. Supporters of the notion of repressed memory (who draw on Freud's psychoanalytic approach) suggest that such memories may remain hidden, possibly throughout a person's lifetime, unless they are triggered by some current circumstance, such as the probing that occurs during psychological therapy.

However, memory researcher Elizabeth Loftus (1998, 2003) maintains that so-called repressed memories may well be inaccurate or even wholly false—representing *false memory*. For example, false memories develop when people are unable to recall the source of a memory of a particular event about which they have only vague recollections. When the source of the memory becomes unclear or ambiguous, people may begin to confuse whether they actually experienced the event or whether it was imagined. Ultimately, people come to believe that the event actually occurred (Clancy, Schacter, McNally, & Pitman, 2000).

In fact, some therapists have been accused of accidentally encouraging people who come to them with psychological difficulties to re-create false chronicles of childhood sexual experiences. Furthermore, the publicity surrounding well-publicized declarations of supposed repressed memories, such as those of people who claim to be the victims of satanic rituals, makes the possibility of repressed memories seem more legitimate and ultimately may prime people to recall memories of events that never happened (Loftus, 1997).

The controversy regarding the legitimacy of repressed memories is unlikely to be resolved soon. Many psychologists, particularly those who provide therapy, give great weight to the reality of repressed memories. On the other side of the issue are memory researchers who maintain that there is no scientific support for the existence of such memories. There is also a middle ground: memory researchers who suggest that false memories are a result of normal information processing. The challenge for those on all sides of the issue is to distinguish truth from fiction (Brown & Pope, 1996; Roediger & McDermott, 2000; Walcott, 2000; Leavitt, 2002; McNally, 2003).

Autobiographical Memory: Where Past Meets Present

Your memory of experiences in your own past may well be a fiction—or at least a distortion of what actually occurred. The same constructive processes that act to make us inaccurately recall the behavior of others also reduce the accuracy of autobiographical memories. **Autobiographical memories** are our recollections of circumstances and episodes from our own lives. Autobiographical memories encompass the episodic memories we hold about ourselves (Stein et al., 1997; Rubin, 1999).

For example, we tend to forget information about our past that is incompatible with the way in which we currently see ourselves. One study found that adults who were well adjusted but who had been treated for emotional problems during the early years of their lives tended to forget important but troubling childhood events, such as being in foster care. College students misremember their bad grades—but remember their good ones (see Figure 5; Bahrick et al., 1996; Stein et al., 1996; D'Argembeau, Comblain, & Van der Linden, 2003).

Similarly, when a group of 48-year-olds were asked to recall how they had responded on a questionnaire they had completed when they were high school freshman, their accuracy was no better than chance. For example, although 61 percent of the questionnaire respondents said that playing sports and other physical activities was their favorite pastime, only 23 percent of the adults recalled it accurately (Offer et al., 2000).

It is not just certain kinds of events that are distorted; particular periods of life are remembered more easily than others are. For example, when people reach late adulthood, they remember periods of life in which they experienced major transitions, such as attending college and working at their first job, better than they remember their middle-age years. Similarly, although most adults' earliest memories of their own lives are of events that occurred when they were toddlers, toddlers show evidence of recall of events that occurred when they were as young as 6 months old (Rubin, 1985; Newcombe et al., 2000; Simcock & Hayne, 2002; Wang, 2003).

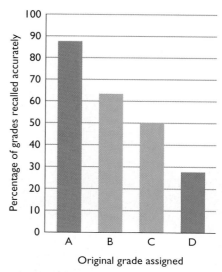

FIGURE 5 We distort memories of unpleasant events. For example, college students are much more likely to accurately recall their good grades, while inaccurately recalling their poor ones (Bahrick et al, 1996). Now that you know this, how well do you think you can recall your high school grades?

Exploring DIVERSITY

Are There Cross-Cultural Differences in Memory?

Travelers who have visited areas of the world in which there is no written language often have returned with tales of people with phenomenal memories. For instance, storytellers in some preliterate cultures can recount long chronicles that recall the names and activities of people over many generations. Those feats led experts to argue initially that people in preliterate societies develop a different, and perhaps better, type of memory than do those in cultures that employ a written language. They suggested that in a society that lacks writing, people are motivated to recall information with accuracy, particularly information relating to tribal histories and traditions that would be lost if they were not passed down orally from one generation to another (Bartlett, 1932; Rubin, 1995; Daftary & Meri, 2002).

However, more recent approaches to cultural differences suggest a different conclusion. For one thing, preliterate peoples don't have an exclusive claim to amazing memory feats. Some Hebrew scholars memorize thousands of pages of text and can recall the locations of particular words on the page. Similarly, poetry singers in the Balkans can recall thousands of lines of poetry. Even in cultures in which written language exists, then, astounding feats of memory are possible (Neisser, 1982; Strathern & Stewart, 2003).

Storytellers in many cultures can recount hundreds of years of history in vivid detail. Research has found that this amazing ability is due less to basic memory processes than to the ways in which they acquire and retain information.

Memory researchers now suggest that there are both similarities and differences in memory across cultures. Basic memory processes such as short-term memory capacity and the structure of long-term memory—the "hardware" of memory—are universal and operate similarly in people in all cultures. In contrast, cultural differences can be seen in the way information is acquired and rehearsed—the "software" of memory. Culture determines how people frame information initially, how much they practice learning and recalling it, and the strategies they use to try to recall it (Wagner, 1982; Mack, 2003).

▲ ▲ ▲

RECAP/EVALUATE/RETHINK

RECAP

What causes difficulties and failures in remembering?

▶ The tip-of-the-tongue phenomenon is the temporary inability to remember information that one is certain one knows. Retrieval cues are a major strategy for recalling information successfully. (p. 237)

▶ The levels-of-processing approach to memory suggests that the way in which information is initially perceived and analyzed determines the success with which it is recalled. The deeper the initial processing, the greater the recall. (p. 238)

▶ Flashbulb memories are memories centered on a specific, important event. The more distinctive a memory is, the more easily it can be retrieved. (p. 239)

▶ Memory is a constructive process: We relate memories to the meaning, guesses, and expectations we give to events. Specific information is recalled in terms of schemas, organized bodies of information stored in memory that bias the way new information is interpreted, stored, and recalled. (p. 240)

▶ Eyewitnesses are apt to make substantial errors when they try to recall the details of crimes. The problem of memory reliability becomes even more acute when the witnesses are children. (p. 241)

▶ Autobiographical memory is influenced by constructive processes. (p. 244)

EVALUATE

1. While with a group of friends at a dance, Eva bumps into a man she dated last month, but when she tries to introduce him to her friends, she cannot remember his name. What is the term for this occurrence?

2. _____ is the process of retrieving a specific item from memory.

3. A friend of your mother's tells you, "I know exactly where I was and what I was doing when I heard that John Lennon died." What phenomenon explains this type of recollection?

4. The same person could probably also accurately describe in detail what she was wearing when she heard about John Lennon's death, right down to the color of her shoes. True or false?

5. _____ are organized bodies of information stored in memory that bias the way new information is interpreted, stored, and recalled.

6. _____ theory states that the more a person analyzes a statement, the more likely he or she is to remember it later.

RETHINK

1. How do schemas help people process information during encoding, storage, and retrieval? In what ways are they helpful? Can they contribute to inaccurate autobiographical memories?

2. How might courtroom procedure be improved, based on what you've learned about memory errors and biases?

Answers to Evaluate Questions

1. tip-of-the-tongue phenomenon; 2. recall; 3. flashbulb memory; 4. false; small details probably won't be remembered through flashbulb memory; 5. schemas; 6. levels-of-processing

KEY TERMS

tip-of-the-tongue
phenomenon p. 237
levels-of-processing
theory p. 238

flashbulb memories p. 239
constructive
processes p. 240

schemas p. 241
autobiographical
memories p. 244

Forgetting: When Memory Fails

He could remember, quite literally, nothing—nothing, that is, that had happened since the loss of his brain's temporal lobes and hippocampus during experimental surgery to reduce epileptic seizures. Until that time, his memory had been quite normal. But after the operation he was unable to recall anything for more than a few minutes, and then the memory was seemingly lost forever. He did not remember his address, or the name of the person to whom he was talking. He would read the same magazine over and over again. According to his own description, his life was like waking from a dream and being unable to know where he was or how he got there (Milner, 1966).

Why do we forget information?

What are the biological bases of memory?

What are the major memory impairments?

As this case illustrates, a person without a normal memory faces severe difficulties. All of us who have experienced even routine instances of forgetting—such as not remembering an acquaintance's name or a fact on a test—understand the very real consequences of memory failure.

The first attempts to study forgetting were made by German psychologist Hermann Ebbinghaus about a hundred years ago. Using himself as the only participant in his study, Ebbinghaus memorized lists of three-letter nonsense syllables— meaningless sets of two consonants with a vowel in between, such as FIW and BOZ. By measuring how easy it was to relearn a given list of words after varying periods of time had passed since the initial learning, he found that forgetting occurred systematically, as shown in Figure 1. As the figure indicates, the most rapid forgetting occurs in the first nine hours, particularly in the first hour. After nine hours, the rate of forgetting slows and declines little, even after the passage of many days.

Despite his primitive methods, Ebbinghaus's study had an important influence on subsequent research, and his basic conclusions have been upheld (Wixted & Ebbesen,

FIGURE 1 In his classic work, Ebbinghaus found that the most rapid forgetting occurs in the first nine hours after exposure to new material. However, the rate of forgetting then slows down and declines very little even after many days have passed (Ebbinghaus, 1885, 1913). Check your own memory: What were you doing exactly two hours ago? What were you doing last Tuesday at 5 P.M.? Which information is easier to retrieve?

FIGURE 2 One of these pennies is the real thing. Can you find it? Why is this task harder than it seems at first? (Source: Nickerson & Adams, 1979.)

If you don't have a penny handy, the correct answer is "A."

1991). There is almost always a strong initial decline in memory, followed by a more gradual drop over time. Furthermore, relearning of previously mastered material is almost always faster than starting from scratch, whether the material is academic information or a motor skill such as serving a tennis ball.

Why do we forget? One reason is that we may not have paid attention to the material in the first place—a failure of *encoding*. For example, if you live in the United States, you probably have been exposed to thousands of pennies during your life. Despite this experience, you probably don't have a clear sense of the details of the coin. (See this for yourself by looking at Figure 2.) Consequently, the reason for your memory failure is that you probably never encoded the information into long-term memory initially. Obviously, if information hasn't been placed in memory initially, there is no way the information can be recalled.

But what about material that has been encoded into memory and that can't later be remembered? Several processes account for memory failures, including decay, interference, and cue-dependent forgetting.

PowerWeb: Memory's Mind Games

www.mhhe.com/feldmanup7

Decay: The loss of information in memory through its nonuse.

Memory trace: An actual physical change in the brain that occurs when new material is learned.

Interference: The phenomenon by which information in memory disrupts the recall of other information.

Decay is the loss of information through nonuse. This explanation for forgetting assumes that when new material is learned, a **memory trace**—an actual physical change in the brain—appears. In decay, the trace simply fades away with nothing left behind, because of the mere passage of time.

Although there is evidence that decay does occur, this does not seem to be the complete explanation for forgetting. Often there is no relationship between how long ago a person was exposed to information and how well that information is recalled. If decay explained all forgetting, we would expect that the longer the time was between the initial learning of information and our attempt to recall it, the harder it would be to remember it, because there would be more time for the memory trace to decay. Yet people who take several consecutive tests on the same material often recall more of the initial information when taking later tests than they did on earlier tests. If decay were operating, we would expect the opposite to occur (Payne, 1986).

Because decay does not fully account for forgetting, memory specialists have proposed an additional mechanism: **interference.** In interference, information in memory disrupts the recall of other information.

To distinguish between decay and interference, think of the two processes in terms of a row of books on a library shelf. In decay, the old books are constantly crumbling and rotting away, leaving room for new arrivals. Interference processes suggest that new books knock the old ones off the shelf, where they become inaccessible.

Finally, forgetting may occur because of **cue-dependent forgetting**, forgetting that occurs when there are insufficient retrieval cues to rekindle information that is in memory (Tulving & Thompson, 1983). For example, you may not be able to remember where you lost a set of keys until you mentally walk through your day, thinking of each place you visited. When you think of the place where you lost the keys—say, the library—the retrieval cue of the library may be sufficient to help you recall that you left them on the desk in the library. Without that retrieval cue, you may be unable to recall the location of the keys.

Most research suggests that interference and cue-dependent forgetting are key processes in forgetting (Mel'nikov, 1993; Bower, Thompson, & Tulving, 1994). We forget things mainly because new memories interfere with the retrieval of old ones or because appropriate retrieval cues are unavailable, not because the memory trace has decayed.

Cue-dependent forgetting: Forgetting that occurs when there are insufficient retrieval cues to rekindle information that is in memory.

Proactive and Retroactive Interference: The Before and After of Forgetting

There are actually two sorts of interference that influence forgetting: proactive and retroactive. In *proactive interference*, information learned earlier disrupts the recall of newer material. Suppose, as a student of foreign languages, you first learned French in the tenth grade, and then in the eleventh grade you took Spanish. When in the twelfth grade you take a college achievement test in Spanish, you may find you have difficulty recalling the Spanish translation of a word because all you can think of is its French equivalent.

In contrast, *retroactive interference* refers to difficulty in the recall of information because of later exposure to different material. If, for example, you have difficulty on a French achievement test because of your more recent exposure to Spanish, retroactive interference is the culprit (see Figure 3). One way to remember the difference between

Proactive interference:
Spanish test performance
impaired by study of French

Retroactive interference:
French test performance
impaired by study of Spanish

FIGURE 3 Proactive interference occurs when material learned earlier interferes with the recall of newer material. In this example, studying French before studying Spanish interferes with performance on a Spanish test. In contrast, retroactive interference exists when material learned after initial exposure to other material interferes with the recall of the first material. In this case, retroactive interference occurs when recall of French is impaired because of later exposure to Spanish.

proactive and retroactive interference is to keep in mind that *pro*active interference progresses in time—the past interferes with the present—whereas *retro*active interference retrogresses in time, working backward as the present interferes with the past.

Although the concepts of proactive and retroactive interference help illustrate how material may be forgotten, they still do not explain whether forgetting is caused by the actual loss or modification of information or by problems in the retrieval of information. Most research suggests that material that has apparently been lost because of interference can eventually be recalled if appropriate stimuli are presented (Tulving & Psotka, 1971; Anderson, 1981), but the question has not been fully answered. In an effort to resolve the issue, some psychologists have begun to study the biological bases of memory to better understand what is remembered and what is forgotten—an increasingly important avenue of investigation that we turn to now.

The Biological Bases of Memory

What are the biological foundations of memory? One answer comes from work on *long-term potentiation*, which shows that certain neural pathways become easily excited while a new response is being learned. At the same time, changes occur in the number of synapses between neurons as the dendrites branch out to receive messages. These changes reflect a process called *consolidation*, in which memories become fixed and stable in long-term memory. Long-term memories take some time to stabilize; this explains why events and other stimuli are not suddenly fixed in memory. Instead, consolidation may continue for days and even years (McGaugh, 2000; Rioult-Pedotti, Friedman, & Donoghue, 2000).

The location of *memory traces*, the physical record of memory in the brain, depends on the kind of material being learned and the specific neural systems that process the information when it is first learned. Because a stimulus may contain different sensory aspects, visual, auditory, and other areas of the brain may be involved simultaneously in processing information about that stimulus. Information storage appears to be linked to the sites in which this processing occurs, and is therefore located in the particular areas that initially processed the information in terms of its visual, auditory, and other sensory stimuli.

In short, because several brain processing systems are involved in any learning situation, memory traces are distributed throughout the brain (Desimone, 1992; Squire, 1993; Brewer et al., 1998). Investigators using position emission tomography (PET) scans, which measure biochemical activity in the brain, also have found that neuronal memory traces are highly specialized. For instance, the participants in one

FIGURE 4 PET scans of a participant in an experiment who was first asked to read a list of nouns and produce a related verb (left scan). When the participant was asked to carry out the task repeatedly with the same list of nouns, different areas of the brain became active (center). However, when the participant was given a new list of nouns, the regions of the brain that were initially involved became reactivated (right). (Source: Peterson, 1993.)

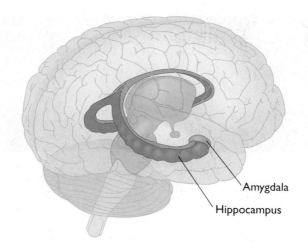

FIGURE 5 The hippocampus and amygdala, parts of the brain's limbic system, play a central role in the consolidation of memories. (Source: Van De Graff, 2000.)

Amygdala

Hippocampus

experiment were given a list of nouns to read aloud. After reading each noun, they were asked to suggest a related verb. After reading the noun *dog*, for example, they might have proposed the verb *bark*.

Several distinct areas of the brain showed increased neural activity as the participants first did the task (see Figure 4). However, if they repeated the task with the same nouns several times, the activity in the brain shifted to another area. Most interestingly, if they were given a new list of nouns, the activity in the brain returned to the areas that were initially activated.

These results suggest that a particular part of the brain is involved in the production of words, but another part takes over when the process becomes routine—in other words, when memory comes into play. It also suggests that memory is distributed in the brain not just in terms of its content, but also in terms of its function (Corbetta et al., 1993; Horgan, 1993; Petersen & Fiez, 1993).

Certain areas and structures of the brain also specialize in different types of memory-related activities. The *hippocampus*, a part of the brain's limbic system (see Figure 5), plays a central role in the consolidation of memories. Located within the brain's *medial temporal lobes*, just behind the eyes, the hippocampus aids in the initial encoding of information, acting like a kind of neurological e-mail system. That information is subsequently passed along to the cerebral cortex of the brain, where it is actually stored (Smith, 2000; Wheeler, Petersen, & Buckner, 2000; Wilson, 2002).

The *amygdala*, another part of the limbic system, also plays a role in memory. The amygdala is especially involved with memories involving emotion (Adolphs, Denburg, & Tranel, 2001; Hamann, 2001). For example, if you are frightened by a large Doberman, you're likely to remember the event vividly—an outcome related to the functioning of the amygdala. Encountering the Doberman, or any large dog, in the future is likely to reactivate the amygdala and bring back the unpleasant memory.

Memory Dysfunctions: Afflictions of Forgetting

First you notice that you're always misplacing things, or that common nouns are evading you as stubbornly as the names of new acquaintances. Pretty soon you're forgetting appointments and getting flustered when you drive in traffic. On bad days you find you can't hold numbers in your mind long enough to dial the phone. You try valiantly to conceal your lapses, but they become ever more glaring. You crash your car. You spend whole mornings struggling to dress yourself properly. And even as you lose the ability to read or play the piano, you're painfully aware of what's happening to you (Cowley, 2000b, p. 46).

Initially	6 months later	12 months later	18 months later

FIGURE 6 This series of brain images clearly show the deterioration caused by the spreading of Alzheimer's disease over a period of eighteen months.

INTERACTIVITY 22–1

Alzheimer's disease

The problem is *Alzheimer's disease,* an illness that includes among its symptoms severe memory problems. Alzheimer's is the fourth leading cause of death among adults in the United States. One in five people between the ages of 75 and 84, and almost half of those 85 and older, have the disease.

In its initial stages, Alzheimer's symptoms appear as simple forgetfulness of things such as appointments and birthdays. As the disease progresses, memory loss becomes more profound, and even the simplest tasks—such as how to dial a telephone—are forgotten. Ultimately, victims may lose their ability to speak or comprehend language, and physical deterioration sets in, leading to death.

Some researchers argue that a breakdown in working memory's central executive may result in the memory losses that are characteristic of Alzheimer's disease, the progressively degenerative disorder that produces loss of memory and confusion (Cherry, Buckwalter, & Henderson, 1996).

The causes of Alzheimer's disease are not fully understood. However, increasing evidence suggests that it results from an inherited susceptibility to a defect in the production of the protein beta amyloid, which is necessary for the maintenance of nerve cell connections. When the manufacture of beta amyloid goes awry, large clumps of cells grow that trigger inflammation and the deterioration of nerve cells in the brain (Cooper, Kalaria, McGeer, & Rogers, 2000; Hardy & Selkoe, 2002; Selkoe, 2002; see Figure 6).

Alzheimer's disease (about which you can learn more in **Interactivity 22–1**) is just one of several memory dysfunctions that plague their victims. Another is *amnesia,* memory loss that occurs without other mental difficulties. The type of amnesia immortalized in countless Hollywood films involves a victim who receives a blow to the head and is unable to remember anything from his or her past. In reality, amnesia of this type, known as retrograde amnesia, is quite rare. In *retrograde amnesia,* memory is lost for occurrences prior to a certain event. Usually, lost memories gradually reappear, although full restoration may take as long as several years. In certain cases, some memories are lost forever. But even in cases of severe memory loss, the loss is generally selective. For example, although people suffering from retrograde amnesia may be unable to recall friends and family members, they still may be able to play complicated card games or knit a sweater quite well (Markowitsch, 2000; Verfaellie & Keane, 2002).

A second type of amnesia is exemplified by people who remember nothing of their current activities. In *anterograde amnesia,* loss of memory occurs for events that follow an injury. Information cannot be transferred from short-term to long-term memory, resulting in the inability to remember anything other than what was in long-term storage before the accident.

Amnesia is also displayed by people who suffer from *Korsakoff's syndrome,* a disease that afflicts long-term alcoholics. Although many of their intellectual abilities may be intact, Korsakoff's sufferers display a strange array of symptoms, including hallucinations and repetition of the same story over and over.

Fortunately, most of us have intact memory, and the occasional failures we suffer may actually be preferable to having a perfect memory. Consider, for instance, the case of a man who had total recall. After reading passages of the *Divine Comedy* in Italian—a language he did not speak—he was able to repeat them from memory some fifteen years later. He could memorize lists of fifty unrelated words and recall them at will more than a decade later. He could even repeat the same list of words backward, if asked (Luria, 1968).

Such a skill at first may seem to be enviable, but it actually presented quite a problem. The man's memory became a jumble of lists of words, numbers, and names, and when he tried to relax, his mind was filled with images. Even reading was difficult, since every word evoked a flood of thoughts from the past that interfered with his ability to understand the meaning of what he was reading. Partially as a consequence of the man's unusual memory, psychologist A. R. Luria, who studied his case, found him to be a "disorganized and rather dull-witted person" (Luria, 1968, p. 65).

We may be grateful, then, that forgetfulness plays a role in our lives.

Apart from the advantages of forgetting, say, a bad date, most of us still would like to find ways to improve our memories. Is it possible to find practical ways to increase our recall of information? Most definitely. Research has revealed a number of strategies that can help us develop a better memory (VanLehn, 1996; Hermann, Raybeck, & Gruneberg, 2002: West et al., 2003). Let's look at some of the best.

BECOMING AN INFORMED CONSUMER
of Psychology
Improving Your Memory

- *The keyword technique.* Suppose you are taking a foreign language class and need to learn vocabulary words. You can try the *keyword technique* of pairing a foreign word with a common English word that has a similar *sound*. This English word is known as the keyword. For example, to learn the Spanish word for duck (*pato*, pronounced *pot-o*), you might choose the keyword *pot*; for the Spanish word for horse (*caballo*, pronounced *cob-eye-yo*), the keyword might be *eye*.

  Once you have thought of a keyword, imagine the Spanish word "interacting" with the English keyword. You might envision a duck taking a bath in a pot to remember the word *pato*, or a horse with a large, bulging eye in the center of its head to recall *caballo*. This technique has produced considerably superior results in learning foreign language vocabulary compared with more traditional techniques involving memorization of the words themselves (Pressley, 1987; Gruneberg & Pascoe, 1996; Carney & Levin, 1998).

- *Encoding specificity.* Some research suggests that we remember information best in an environment that is the same as or similar to the one where we initially learned it—a phenomenon known as *encoding specificity*. You may do better on a test, then, if you study in the classroom where the test will be given. However, if you must take a test in a room different from the one in which you studied, don't despair: The features of the test itself, such as the wording of the test questions, are sometimes so powerful that they overwhelm the subtler cues relating to the original encoding of the material (Bjork & Richardson-Klarehn, 1989).

- *Organization cues.* Many of life's important recall tasks involve texts that you have read. One proven technique for improving recall of written material is to organize the material in memory as you read it for the first time. Organize your reading on the basis of any advance information you have about the content and about its organization . You will then be able to make connections and see relationships among the various facts and process the material at a deeper level, which in turn will later aid recall.

- *Effective note taking.* "Less is more" is perhaps the best advice for taking lecture notes that facilitate recall. Rather than trying to jot down every detail of a lecture, it is better to listen and think about the material, and take down the main points. In effective note taking, thinking about the material initially is more important than writing it down. This is one reason that borrowing someone else's notes is a bad proposition; you will have no framework in memory that you can use to understand them (Feldman, 2003).

- ► *Practice and rehearse.* Although practice does not necessarily make perfect, it helps. By studying and rehearsing material past initial mastery—a process called *overlearning*—people are able to show better long-term recall than they show if they stop practicing after their initial learning of the material. Keep in mind that as research clearly demonstrates, fatigue and other factors prevent long practice sessions from being as effective as distributed practice.
- ► *Don't believe claims about drugs that improve memory.* Advertisements for One-A-Day vitamins with ginkgo biloba or Quanterra Mental Sharpness Product would have you believe that taking a drug can improve your memory. Not so, according to the results of studies. No research has shown that commercial memory enhancers are effective (Meier, 1999; Gold, Cahill, & Wenk, 2002; McDaniel, Maier, & Einstein, 2002). Save your money!

RECAP/EVALUATE/RETHINK

RECAP

Why do we forget information?

- ► Several processes account for memory failure, including decay, interference (both proactive and retroactive), and cue-dependent forgetting. (p. 248)

What are the biological bases of memory?

- ► Memory processes are distributed across the brain, relating to different information-processing systems involved during the initial exposure to a stimulus. The hippocampus is particularly important in the establishment of memory. (p. 250)

What are the major memory impairments?

- ► Among the memory dysfunctions are Alzheimer's disease, which leads to a progressive loss of memory, and amnesia, a memory loss that occurs without other mental difficulties and that can take two forms: retrograde amnesia and anterograde amnesia. Korsakoff's syndrome is a disease that afflicts long-term alcoholics, resulting in memory impairment. (p. 251)
- ► Among the techniques for improving memory are the keyword technique to memorize foreign language vocabulary; using the encoding specificity phenomenon; organizing text material and lecture notes; and practice and rehearsal, leading to overlearning. (p. 253)

EVALUATE

1. If, after learning the history of the Middle East for a class two years ago, you now find yourself unable to recall what you learned, you are experiencing memory _____, caused by nonuse.
2. Difficulty in accessing a memory because of the presence of other information is known as _____.
3. _____ interference occurs when material is difficult to retrieve because of exposure to later material; _____ interference refers to difficulty in retrieving material as a result of the interference of previous material.
4. Match the following memory disorders with the correct information:
    1. Affects alcoholics; may result in hallucinations.
    2. Memory loss occurring without other mental problems.
    3. Beta amyloid defect; progressive forgetting and physical deterioration.
    a. Alzheimer's disease
    b. Korsakoff's syndrome
    c. Amnesia

RETHINK

1. Does the phenomenon of interference help explain the unreliability of autobiographical memory? Why?
2. How might findings on the biological mechanisms of memory aid in the treatment of memory disorders such as amnesia?

Answers to Evaluate Questions

1. decay; 2. interference; 3. retroactive, proactive; 4. 1-b, 2-c, 3-a

KEY TERMS

decay p. 248
memory trace p. 248

interference p. 248

cue-dependent
forgetting p. 249

Looking Back

Psychology on the Web

1. The study of repressed memories can lead down unusual pathways—even more unusual than the criminal investigation pathway. Two other areas in which repressed memories play a large part are alien abduction and reincarnation. Find two sources on the Web that deal with one of these issues—one supportive and one skeptical. Read what they say and relate it to your knowledge of memory. Summarize your findings and indicate which side of the controversy your study of memory leads you to favor.

2. Memory is a topic of serious interest to psychologists, but it is also a source of amusement. Find a website that focuses on the amusing side of memory (such as memory games, tests of recall, or lists of mnemonics; hint: there's even a mnemonics generator out there!). Write down the address of any interesting sites that you encounter and summarize what you found.

3. After completing Interactivity 21–2, find two actual cases of failures of eyewitness memory in a courtroom situation. Summarize each case briefly.

 Our examination of memory has highlighted how memory includes the processes of encoding, storage, and retrieval. We also encountered several phenomena relating to memory, including the tip-of-the-tongue phenomenon and flashbulb memories. Above all we observed that memory is a constructive process by which interpretations, expectations, and guesses contribute to the nature of our memories.

Before moving on to the next module, return to the prologue that discusses Krickitt Carpenter and her lost memories of courtship and marriage. Consider the following questions in light of what you know about memory.

1. Krickitt Carpenter's memory loss is called retrograde amnesia. What does this mean?
2. What would have been the effects on Carpenter's life if her accident had caused anterograde amnesia?
3. What are the chances that Carpenter will recover her lost memories of the eighteen-month period preceding the accident? How might this happen? Do you think the process can be accelerated by associative techniques?
4. If Krickitt Carpenter suddenly announces that she has recovered her memory, how will doctors know that she is really recalling the past rather than simply accepting as her own memories the stories others have told her?
5. How might investigators examine Carpenter during her recovery to answer questions about the biological bases of memory? Assuming Carpenter gave her consent to PET scans and other means of looking inside her cerebral cortex, what sorts of questions might be explored?

Cognition and Language

Prologue
Eureka!

Clifford Matson's "Eureka!" moment arrived the day the silverfish invaded his bathroom.

Dr. Matson, tall, white-haired and retired after 50 years of practicing dentistry in his hometown of Junction City, Oregon, was fretting about the insects skittering around the bathroom. Then several seemingly unrelated thoughts collided in his mind.

One was about the pesky silverfish. One concerned a book he was reading about neem trees, tropical trees grown in India and Burma that have seeds with their own natural pesticides. The third thought arrived when Dr. Matson noticed the small cork squares separating the double-pane windows in the bathroom.

A couple of drops of neem oil on one of those little cork squares ought to be just the ticket to get rid of silverfish, Dr. Matson thought.

He tried it, and the silverfish died. Then he tried the cork squares on cockroaches, and they bit the dust as well . . .

Two years ago the U.S. Patent and Trademark Office granted Dr. Matson Patent No. 6,093,413 for Cork-EZ, an adhesive-backed piece of cork the size of a Scrabble square that delivers a natural pesticide derived from cedar bark (Richardson, 2002, p. R7).

Cognitive psychology: The branch of psychology that focuses on the study of higher mental processes, including thinking, language, memory, problem solving, knowing, reasoning, judging, and decision making.

Clifford Matson has big plans for his invention. But whether or not Cork-EZ revolutionizes the extermination field, it is clear that Matson has the elusive quality that marks successful inventors: creativity.

Where does Matson's creativity come from? More generally, how do people use information to devise innovative solutions to problems? And how do people think about, understand, and, through language, describe the world?

Answers to these questions come from **cognitive psychology,** the branch of psychology that focuses on the study of higher mental processes, including thinking, language, memory, problem solving, knowing, reasoning, judging, and decision making. Clearly, the realm of

Looking Ahead

cognitive psychology is broad.

Cognitive psychology centers on three major topics: thinking and reasoning, problem solving and creativity, and language. First we consider concepts, which are the building blocks of thinking, and various kinds of reasoning. Then we examine different strategies for approaching problems, means of generating solutions, and ways of making judgments about the usefulness and accuracy of solutions. Finally, we consider how language is developed and acquired, its basic characteristics, and the relationship between language and thought.

Thinking and Reasoning

What is thinking?

What processes underlie reasoning and decision making?

What are you thinking about at this moment?

The mere ability to pose such a question underscores the distinctive nature of the human ability to think. No other species contemplates, analyzes, recollects, or plans as humans do. Understanding what thinking is, however, goes beyond knowing that we think. Philosophers, for example, have argued for generations about the meaning of thinking, with some placing it at the core of human beings' understanding of their own existence.

Psychologists define **thinking** as the manipulation of mental representations of information. A representation may be in the form of a word, a visual image, a sound, or data in any other modality. Thinking transforms a particular representation of information into new and different forms in order to answer questions, solve problems, or reach goals.

Although a clear sense of what specifically occurs when we think remains elusive, our understanding of the nature of the fundamental elements involved in thinking is growing. We begin by considering our use of mental images and concepts, the building blocks of thought.

▲▲▲

"What do you think I think about what you think I think you've been thinking about?"

Mental Images: Examining the Mind's Eye

Think of your best friend.

Chances are that you "see" some kind of visual image when asked to think of her or him, or any other person or object, for that matter. To some cognitive psychologists, such mental images constitute a major part of thinking.

Mental images are representations in the mind in the form of the object or event being represented. They are not just visual representations; our ability to "hear" a tune in our heads also relies on a mental image. In fact, every sensory modality may produce corresponding mental images (Paivio, 1971, 1975; Kosslyn & Shin, 1994).

Research has found that our mental images have many of the properties of the actual perception of the objects being represented. For example, it takes the mind longer to scan mental images of large objects than of small ones, just as the eye takes longer to scan an actual large object than an actual small one. Similarly, we are able to manipulate and rotate mental images of objects, just as we are able to manipulate and rotate them in the real world (Shepard et al., 2000; Mast & Kosslyn, 2002; see Figure 1).

Some have heralded the production of mental images as a way to improve various skills. For instance, many athletes use mental imagery in training. Basketball players may try to produce vivid and detailed images of the court, the basket, the ball, and the noisy crowd. They may visualize themselves taking a foul shot, watching the

Thinking: The manipulation of mental representations of information.

Mental images: Representations in the mind that resemble the object or event being represented.

FIGURE 1 Try to mentally rotate one of each pair of patterns to see if it is the same as the other member of that pair. It's likely that the farther you have to mentally rotate a pattern, the longer it will take to decide if the patterns match one another. (Source: Based on Shepard & Metzler, 1971.) Does this mean that it will take you longer to visualize a map of the world than a map of the United States? Why or why not?

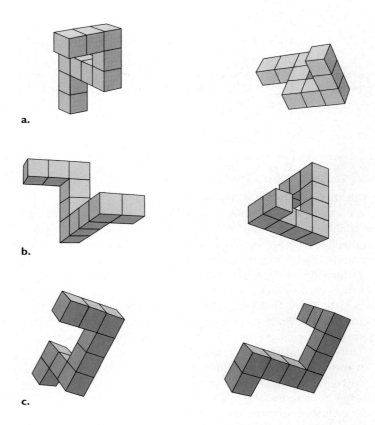

a.

b.

c.

ball, and hearing the swish as it goes through the net. And it works: The use of mental imagery can lead to improvements in sports performance (Druckman & Bjork, 1991; Cummings & Hall, 2002; MacIntyre, Moran, & Jennings, 2002).

Using mental imagery may improve other types of skills as well. In music, for example, researcher Alvaro Pascual-Leone taught groups of people to play a five-finger exercise on the piano. One group practiced the exercise every day for five days, while a control group played daily without any training, just hitting the keys at random. Finally, the members of a third group were taught the exercise but were not allowed to try it out on the piano. Instead, they rehearsed it mentally, sitting at the piano every day and looking at the keys, but not actually touching them.

Comparing brain scans of people in the groups, researchers found a distinct difference between those who manually practiced the exercise and those who just randomly hit keys. However, the most surprising finding came from the group that mentally rehearsed: Their brain scans were virtually identical to those of the people who had actually practiced the exercise manually (see Figure 2). Apparently, carrying out

FIGURE 2 Compared with the brain scans of people who actually practiced a piano finger exercise, the brain scans of those who only used mental rehearsal but did not touch the piano were nearly identical. The results of the experiment clearly show the value of mental imagery. (Source: Pascual-Leone et al., 1995.)

the task involved the same network of brain cells as the network used in mentally rehearsing it (Chase, 1993; Pascual-Leone et al., 1995).

Such research suggests that children whose parents nag them about practicing an instrument, a dance routine, or some other skill can now employ a new excuse: They *are* practicing—mentally.

Concepts: Categorizing the World

If someone asked you what was in your kitchen cabinet, you might answer with a detailed list of items ("a jar of peanut butter, three boxes of macaroni and cheese, six unmatched dinner plates," and so forth). More likely, though, you would respond by naming some broader categories, such as "food" and "dishes."

Using such categories reflects the operation of concepts. **Concepts** are categorizations of objects, events, or people that share common properties. By employing concepts, we are able to organize complex phenomena into simpler, and therefore more easily usable, cognitive categories (Margolis & Laurence, 1999; Goldstone & Kersten, 2003).

Concepts help us classify newly encountered objects on the basis of our past experience. For example, we can surmise that someone tapping a handheld screen is probably using some kind of computer or PDA, even if we have never encountered that specific brand before. Ultimately, concepts influence behavior; we would assume, for instance, that it might be appropriate to pet an animal after determining that it is a dog, whereas we would behave differently after classifying the animal as a wolf.

When cognitive psychologists first studied concepts, they focused on those which were clearly defined by a unique set of properties or features. For example, an equilateral triangle is a closed shape that has three sides of equal length. If an object has these characteristics, it is an equilateral triangle; if it does not, it is not an equilateral triangle.

Other concepts—often those with the most relevance to our everyday lives—are more ambiguous and difficult to define. For instance, concepts such as "table" and "bird" share a set of general, relatively loose characteristic features, rather than unique, clearly defined properties that distinguish an example of the concept from a nonexample. When we consider these more ambiguous concepts, we usually think in terms of examples called prototypes. **Prototypes** are typical, highly representative examples of a concept that represent our mental image or best example of the concept. For instance, although a robin and an ostrich are both examples of birds, the robin is an example that comes to most people's mind far more readily. Consequently, robin is a prototype of the concept "bird." Similarly, when we think of the concept of a table, we're likely to think of a coffee table before we think of a drafting table, making a coffee table closer to our prototype of a table.

Relatively high agreement exists among people in a particular culture about which examples of a concept are prototypes, as well as which examples are not. For instance, most people in Western cultures consider cars and trucks good examples of vehicles, whereas elevators and wheelbarrows are not considered very good examples. Consequently, cars and trucks are prototypes of the concept of a vehicle (see Figure 3).

Concepts enable us to think about and understand more readily the complex world in which we live. For example, the suppositions we make about the reasons

Many athletes, such as Reggie Miller (shown here), use mental imagery to focus on a task, a process they call "getting in the zone." What are some other occupations that require the use of strong mental imagery?

Concepts: Categorizations of objects, events, or people that share common properties.

Prototypes: Typical, highly representative examples of a concept.

How do you view these structures? Whether you categorize them as two houses of workship (left & middle), as two similar examples of architecture (middle & right), or simply as three buildings, you are using concepts.

Ranking of Prototype from Most to Least Typical	Concept Category			
	Furniture	Vehicle	Weapon	Vegetable
1—Most Typical	Chair	Car	Gun	Peas
2	Sofa	Truck	Knife	Carrots
3	Table	Bus	Sword	String beans
4	Dresser	Motorcycle	Bomb	Spinach
5	Desk	Train	Hand grenade	Broccoli
6	Bed	Trolley car	Spear	Asparagus
7	Bookcase	Bicycle	Cannon	Corn
8	Footstool	Airplane	Bow and arrow	Cauliflower
9	Lamp	Boat	Club	Brussels sprouts
10	Piano	Tractor	Tank	Lettuce
11	Cushion	Cart	Tear gas	Beets
12	Mirror	Wheelchair	Whip	Tomato
13	Rug	Tank	Ice pick	Lima beans
14	Radio	Raft	Fists	Eggplant
15—Least Typical	Stove	Sled	Rocket	Onion

FIGURE 3 Prototypes are typical, highly representative examples of a concept. For instance, a highly typical prototype of the concept "furniture" is a chair, whereas a stove is not a good prototype. High agreement exists within a culture about which examples of a concept are prototypes. (Source: Adapted from Rosch & Mervis, 1975.)

for other people's behavior are based on the ways in which we classify behavior. Hence, our conclusion that a person who washes her hands twenty times a day could vary, depending on whether we place her behavior within the conceptual framework of a health-care worker or a mental patient. Similarly, physicians make diagnoses by drawing on concepts and prototypes of symptoms that they learned about in medical school. Finally, concepts and prototypes facilitate our efforts to draw suitable conclusions through the cognitive process we turn to next: reasoning.

Reasoning: Making Up Your Mind

Professors deciding when students' assignments are due.
An employer determining who to hire out of a pool of job applicants.
The president concluding that it is necessary to send troops to a foreign nation.

What do these three situations have in common? Each requires *reasoning*, the process by which information is used to draw conclusions and make decisions.

Although philosophers and logicians have considered the foundations of reasoning for centuries, it is only relatively recently that cognitive psychologists have begun to investigate how people reason and make decisions. Their efforts have contributed to our understanding of formal reasoning processes as well as the cognitive shortcuts we routinely use—shortcuts that sometimes may lead our reasoning capabilities astray.

SYLLOGISTIC REASONING: THE FORMAL RULES OF LOGIC

If you've ever played a card game like poker and tried to figure out what cards your opponent was holding, you probably used **syllogistic reasoning,** a kind of formal reasoning in which a person draws a conclusion from a set of assumptions. In using syllogistic reasoning, we begin with a general assumption that we believe is true and then derive specific implications from that assumption. If the assumption is true, the conclusions must also be true (Fisk & Sharp, 2002).

A major technique for studying syllogistic reasoning involves asking people to evaluate a series of statements that present two assumptions, or *premises*, that are used to derive a conclusion. For example, consider the following syllogism:

> All men are mortal.   *[premise]*
> Socrates is a man.   *[premise]*
> Therefore, Socrates is mortal.   *[conclusion]*

Because both premises are true, by applying logic appropriately we come to an accurate conclusion. More abstractly, we can state the syllogism as the following:

> All A's are B.   *[premise]*
> C is an A.   *[premise]*
> Therefore, C is a B.   *[conclusion]*

However, even if the premises are correct, people may apply logic incorrectly. For example, consider the following syllogism:

> All A's are B.   *[premise]*
> C is an A.   *[premise]*
> Therefore, all A's are C.   *[conclusion]*

Although it may not be immediately apparent, the conclusion is illogical—something seen more readily if we make the syllogism more concrete:

> All men are mortal.   *[premise]*
> Socrates is a man.   *[premise]*
> Therefore, all men are Socrates.   *[conclusion]*

In short, syllogistic reasoning is only as accurate as the accuracy of the premises and the validity of the logic applied to the premises.

ALGORITHMS AND HEURISTICS

When faced with making a decision, we often turn to various kinds of cognitive shortcuts, known as algorithms and heuristics, to help us. An **algorithm** is a rule that, if applied appropriately, guarantees a solution to a problem. We can use an algorithm even if we cannot understand why it works. For example, you may know that the length of the third side of a right triangle can be found by using the formula $a^2 + b^2 = c^2$, although you may not have the foggiest notion of the mathematical principles behind the formula.

For many problems and decisions, however, no algorithm is available. In those instances, we may be able to use heuristics to help us. A **heuristic** is a cognitive shortcut that may lead to a solution. Heuristics enhance the likelihood of success in coming to a solution, but, unlike algorithms, they cannot ensure it. For example, when I play tic-tac-toe, I follow the heuristic of placing an X in the center square when I start the game. This tactic doesn't guarantee that I will win, but experience has taught me that it will increase my chances of success. Similarly, some students follow the heuristic of preparing for a test by ignoring the assigned textbook reading and only studying their lecture notes—a strategy that may or may not pay off. Practice using heuristics in **Interactivity 23–1.**

Although heuristics often help people solve problems and make decisions, certain kinds of heuristics may lead to inaccurate conclusions. For example, we sometimes use

Syllogistic reasoning: Formal reasoning in which people draw a conclusion from a set of assumptions.

Algorithm: A rule that, if applied appropriately, guarantees a solution to a problem.

Heuristic: A cognitive shortcut that may lead to a solution.

INTERACTIVITY 23–1

Heuristics

the *availability heuristic*, which involves judging the probability of an event on the basis of how easily the event can be recalled from memory. According to this heuristic, we assume that events we remember easily are likely to have occurred more frequently in the past—and are more likely to occur in the future—than events that are harder to remember. For instance, people are usually more afraid of dying in a plane crash than in an auto accident, despite statistics clearly showing that airplane travel is much safer than auto travel. The reason is that plane crashes receive far more publicity than car crashes do, and they are therefore more easily remembered. The availability heuristic leads people to conclude that they are in greater jeopardy in an airplane than in a car (Schwarz et al., 1991; Vaughn & Weary, 2002).

RECAP/EVALUATE/RETHINK

RECAP

What is thinking?

▸ Cognitive psychology encompasses the higher mental processes, including the way people know and understand the world, process information, make decisions and judgments, and describe their knowledge and understanding to others. (p. 258)

▸ Thinking is the manipulation of mental representations of information. Thinking transforms such representations into novel and different forms, permitting people to answer questions, solve problems, and reach goals. (p. 259)

▸ Mental images are representations in the mind that resemble the object or event being represented. (p. 259)

▸ Concepts are categorizations of objects, events, or people that share common properties. Prototypes are representative examples of concepts. (p. 261)

What processes underlie reasoning and decision making?

▸ In syllogistic reasoning, people derive implications from a set of assumptions that they know to be true. (p. 263)

▸ Decisions sometimes (but not always) may be improved through the use of algorithms and heuristics. An algorithm is a rule that, if applied appropriately, guarantees a solution; a heuristic is a cognitive shortcut that may lead to a solution but is not guaranteed to do so. (p. 263)

EVALUATE

1. _____ _____ are representations in the mind that resemble the object or event being represented.
2. _____ are categorizations of objects that share common properties.
3. When you think of the concept "chair," you immediately think of a comfortable easy chair. A chair of this type could be thought of as a _____ of the category "chair."
4. When you ask your friend how best to study for your psychology final, he tells you, "I've always found it best to skim over the notes once, then read the book, then go over the notes again." What decision-making tool might this be an example of? _____

RETHINK

1. How might the availability heuristic contribute to prejudices based on race, age, and gender? Can awareness of this heuristic prevent this from happening?
2. In what ways might prototypes for the category "vehicle" differ between tribe members living in a rural African village and people living in an urban, Western city?

Answers to Evaluate Questions

1. mental images; 2. concepts; 3. prototype; 4. heuristic

KEY TERMS

cognitive
psychology p. 258
thinking p. 259

mental images p. 259
concepts p. 261

prototypes p. 261
syllogistic reasoning p. 263

algorithm p. 263
heuristic p. 263

Problem Solving

According to an old legend, a group of Vietnamese monks guard three towers on which sit sixty-four golden rings. The monks believe that if they succeed in moving the rings from the first tower to the third according to a series of rigid rules, the world as we know it will come to an end. (Should you prefer that the world remain in its present state, there's no need for immediate concern: The puzzle is so complex that it will take the monks about a trillion years to solve it.)

In the Tower of Hanoi puzzle, a simpler version of the task facing the monks, three disks are placed on three posts in the order shown in Figure 1. The goal of the puzzle is to move all three disks to the third post, arranged in the same order, by using as few moves as possible. There are two restrictions: Only one disk can be moved at a time, and no disk can ever cover a smaller one during a move.

Why are cognitive psychologists interested in the Tower of Hanoi problem? Because the way people go about solving such puzzles helps illuminate how people solve complex, real-life problems. Psychologists have found that problem solving typically involves three major steps: preparing to create solutions, producing solutions, and evaluating the solutions that have been generated (Sternberg & Frensch, 1991).

▲ ▲ ▲

How do people approach and solve problems?

What are the major obstacles to problem solving?

"I don't know about hair care, Rapunzel, but I'm thinking a good cream rinse plus protein conditioner might just solve both our problems."

Start Finish

FIGURE I The goal of the Tower of Hanoi puzzle is to move all three disks from the first post to the third and still preserve the original order of the disks, using the fewest number of moves possible while following the rules that only one disk at a time can be moved and no disk can cover a smaller one during a move. Try it yourself before you look at the solution, which is listed according to the sequence of moves. (Solution: Move C to 3, B to 2, C to 2, A to 3, C to 1, B to 3, and C to 3.)

Preparation: Understanding and Diagnosing Problems

When approaching a problem like the Tower of Hanoi, most people begin by trying to understand the problem thoroughly. If the problem is a novel one, they probably will pay particular attention to any restrictions placed on coming up with a solution—such as the rule for moving only one disk at a time in the Tower of Hanoi problem. If, by contrast, the problem is a familiar one, they are apt to spend considerably less time in this preparation stage.

Problems vary from well defined to ill defined (Reitman, 1965; Arlin, 1989). In a *well-defined problem*—such as a mathematical equation or the solution to a jigsaw puzzle—both the nature of the problem itself and the information needed to solve it are available and clear. Thus, we can make straightforward judgments about whether a potential solution is appropriate. With an *ill-defined problem*, such as how to increase morale on an assembly line or bring peace to the Middle East, not only may the specific nature of the problem be unclear, the information required to solve the problem may be even less obvious.

KINDS OF PROBLEMS

Typically, a problem falls into one of the three categories shown in Figure 2: arrangement, inducing structure, and transformation (Greeno, 1978; Spitz, 1987). Solving each type requires somewhat different kinds of psychological skills and knowledge.

Arrangement problems require the problem solver to rearrange or recombine elements in a way that will satisfy a certain criterion. Usually, several different arrangements can be made, but only one or a few of the arrangements will produce a solution. Anagram problems and jigsaw puzzles are examples of arrangement problems (Coventry, Venn, Smith, & Morley, 2003).

In *problems of inducing structure*, a person must identify the existing relationships among the elements presented and then construct a new relationship among them. In such a problem, the problem solver must determine not only the relationships among the elements but also the structure and size of the elements involved. In the example shown in Figure 2, a person must first determine that the solution requires the numbers to be considered in pairs (14-24-34-44-54-64). Only after identifying that part of the problem can a person determine the solution rule (the first number of each pair increases by one, while the second number remains the same).

The Tower of Hanoi puzzle represents the third kind of problem—*transformation problems*—which consist of an initial state, a goal state, and a method for changing the initial state into the goal state. In the Tower of Hanoi problem, the initial state is the original configuration, the goal state is to have the three disks on the third peg, and the method is the rules for moving the disks (Mataix-Cols & Bartres-Faz, 2002).

Whether the problem is one of arrangement, inducing structure, or transformation, the preparation stage of understanding and diagnosing is critical in problem solving because it allows us to develop our own cognitive representation of the problem and to place it within a personal framework. We may divide the problem into subparts or ignore some information as we try to simplify the task. Winnowing out nonessential information is often a critical step in the preparation stage of problem solving.

FIGURE 2 The three major categories of problems: (a) arrangement, (b) inducing structure, and (c) transformation. (Sources: Bourne et al., 1986; hobbit problem: Solso, 1991, p. 448.) Solutions appear in Figure 3 on p. 268.

a. Arrangement problems

1. Anagrams: Rearrange the letters in each set to make an English word:

2. Two strings hang from a ceiling but are too far apart to allow a person to hold one and walk to the other. On the floor are a book of matches, a screwdriver, and a few pieces of cotton. How could the strings be tied together?

b. Problems of inducing structure

1. What number comes next in the series?

   1 4 2 4 3 4 4 4 5 4 6 4

2. Complete these analogies:

   baseball is to bat as tennis is to _____

   merchant is to sell as customer is to _____

c. Transformation problems

1. Hobbits and orcs: Three hobbits and three orcs want to cross a river. However, they have only one boat, which will hold only two individuals. There is no other way to cross the river. If more orcs than hobbits are left on either bank, the orcs will eat the hobbits. What is the most efficient way that the six hobbits and orcs can get to the other side of the river without harm?

Hobbit

Orc

2. Water jars: A person has three jars with the following capacities:

 Jar A: 28 ounces   Jar B: 7 ounces   Jar C: 5 ounces

   How can the person measure exactly 11 ounces of water?

a. Arrangement problems

1. FACET, DOUBT, THICK, NAIVE, ANVIL

2. The screwdriver is tied to one of the strings. This makes a pendulum that can be swung to reach the other string.

b. Problems of inducing structure

1. 7

2. racket; buy

c. Transformation problems

1.

Hobbit

Orc

Boat

2. Fill jar A; empty into jar B once and into jar C twice. What remains in jar A is 11 ounces.

FIGURE 3 Solutions to the problems in Figure 2.

REPRESENTING AND ORGANIZING THE PROBLEM

A crucial aspect of the initial encounter with a problem is the way in which we represent it to ourselves and organize the information presented to us (Brown & Walter, 1993; Davidson, Deuser, & Sternberg, 1994). Consider the following problem:

> A man climbs a mountain on Saturday, leaving at daybreak and arriving at the top near sundown. He spends the night at the top. The next day, Sunday, he leaves at daybreak and heads down the mountain, following the same path that he climbed the day before. The question is this: Will there be any time during the second day when he will be at exactly the same point on the mountain as he was at exactly that time on the first day?

If you try to solve this problem by using algebraic or verbal representations, you will have a good deal of trouble. However, if you represent the problem with the kind of simple diagram shown in Figure 4, the solution will become apparent.

Our ability to represent a problem—and the kind of solution we eventually come to—depends on the way a problem is phrased, or *framed*. Consider, for example, if you were a cancer patient having to choose between surgery and radiation and were given the two sets of treatment options shown in Figure 5 (Tversky & Kahneman, 1987). When the options are framed in terms of the likelihood of survival, only 18 percent of participants in a study chose radiation over surgery. However, when the choice was framed in terms of the likelihood of dying, 44 percent chose radiation over surgery—even though the outcomes are identical in both sets of framing conditions.

Production: Generating Solutions

After preparation, the next stage in problem solving is the production of possible solutions. If a problem is relatively simple, we may already have a direct solution stored in long-term memory, and all we need to do is retrieve the appropriate information. If we cannot retrieve or do not know the solution, we must generate possible solutions and compare them with information in long- and short-term memory.

At the most basic level, we can solve problems through trial and error. Thomas Edison invented the light bulb only because he tried thousands of different kinds

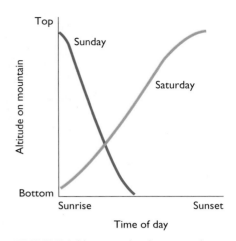

FIGURE 4 You can solve the mountain-climbing problem by using a graph. Keep in mind that the goal is not to determine the time, but just to indicate whether an exact time exists. Consequently, the speed at which the traveler is moving is unimportant (Anderson, 1980). Can you think of other approaches that might lead to a solution?

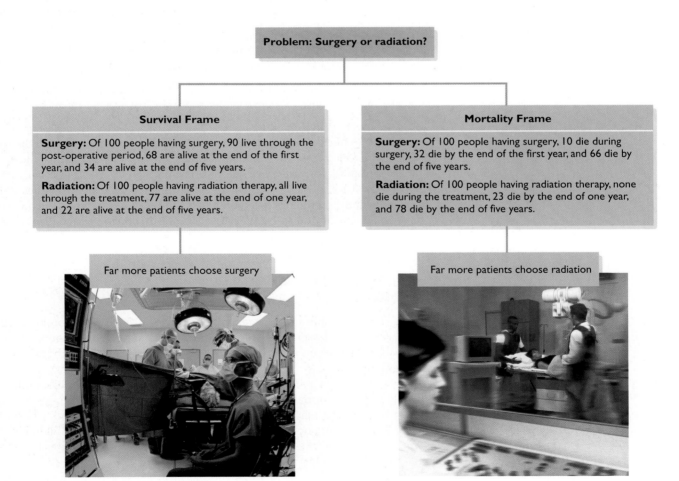

Problem: Surgery or radiation?

Survival Frame

Surgery: Of 100 people having surgery, 90 live through the post-operative period, 68 are alive at the end of the first year, and 34 are alive at the end of five years.

Radiation: Of 100 people having radiation therapy, all live through the treatment, 77 are alive at the end of one year, and 22 are alive at the end of five years.

Far more patients choose surgery

Mortality Frame

Surgery: Of 100 people having surgery, 10 die during surgery, 32 die by the end of the first year, and 66 die by the end of five years.

Radiation: Of 100 people having radiation therapy, none die during the treatment, 23 die by the end of one year, and 78 die by the end of five years.

Far more patients choose radiation

FIGURE 5 A decision often is affected by the way a problem is framed. In this case, most would choose radiation over surgery.

of materials for a filament before he found one that worked (carbon). The difficulty with trial and error, of course, is that some problems are so complicated that it would take a lifetime to try out every possibility. For example, according to some estimates, there are some 10^{120} possible sequences of chess moves (Fine & Fine, 2003).

In place of trial and error, complex problem solving often involves the use of heuristics, cognitive shortcuts that can generate solutions. Probably the most frequently applied heuristic in problem solving is a **means-ends analysis,** which involves repeated tests for differences between the desired outcome and what currently exists. Consider this simple example (Newell & Simon, 1972):

> I want to take my son to nursery school. What's the difference between what I have and what I want? One of distance. What changes distance? My automobile. My automobile won't work. What is needed to make it work? A new battery. What has new batteries? An auto repair shop . . .

In a means-end analysis, each step brings the problem solver closer to a resolution. Although this approach is often effective, if the problem requires indirect steps that temporarily *increase* the discrepancy between a current state and the solution, means-ends analysis can be counterproductive. For example, sometimes the fastest route to a summit requires a mountain climber to backtrack temporarily; a means-end approach—which implies that the mountain climber should always forge ahead and upward—will be ineffective in such instances.

For other problems, the best approach is to work backward by focusing on the goal, rather than the starting point, of the problem. Consider, for example, the water lily problem:

> Water lilies are growing on Blue Lake. The water lilies grow rapidly, so that the amount of water surface covered by lilies *doubles* every 24 hours.
>
> On the first day of summer, there was just one water lily. On the 90th day of the summer, the lake was entirely covered. On what day was the lake *half covered*? (Reisberg, 1997).

If you start searching for a solution to the problem by thinking about the initial state on day 1 (one water lily) and move forward from there, you're facing a daunting task of trial-and-error estimation. But try taking a different approach: Start with day 90, when the entire lake was covered with lilies. Given that the lilies double their coverage daily, on the prior day only half the lake was covered. The answer, then, is day 89, a solution found by working backward (Bourne et al., 1986; Hunt, 1994).

FORMING SUBGOALS: DIVIDING PROBLEMS INTO THEIR PARTS

Another heuristic commonly used to generate solutions is to divide a problem into intermediate steps, or *subgoals*, and solve each of those steps. For instance, in our modified Tower of Hanoi problem, we could choose several obvious subgoals, such as moving the largest disk to the third post.

If solving a subgoal is a step toward the ultimate solution to a problem, identifying subgoals is an appropriate strategy. In some cases, however, forming subgoals is not all that helpful and may actually increase the time needed to find a solution (Hayes, 1966; Reed, 1996). For example, some problems cannot be subdivided. Others are so complex that it takes longer to identify the appropriate subdivisions than to solve the problem by other means.

Means-ends analysis: Repeated testing for differences between the desired outcome and what currently exists.

(a)　　　　　　　　　　　　　　　(b)　　　　　　　　　　　　　　　(c)

In an impressive display of insight, Sultan, one of the chimpanzees in Köhler's experiments in problem solving, sees a bunch of bananas that is out of his reach (a). He then carries over several crates (b), stacks them, and stands on them to reach the bananas (c).

INSIGHT: SUDDEN AWARENESS

Some approaches to generating possible solutions focus less on step-by-step heuristics than on the sudden bursts of comprehension that one may experience during efforts to solve a problem. Just after World War I, German psychologist Wolfgang Köhler examined learning and problem-solving processes in chimpanzees (Köhler, 1927). In his studies, Köhler exposed chimps to challenging situations in which the elements of the solution were all present; all the chimps needed to do was put them together.

In one of Köhler's studies, chimps were kept in a cage in which boxes and sticks were strewn about, with a bunch of tantalizing bananas hanging from the ceiling out of reach. Initially, the chimps made trial-and-error attempts to get to the bananas: They would throw the sticks at the bananas, jump from one of the boxes, or leap wildly from the ground. Frequently, they would seem to give up in frustration, leaving the bananas dangling temptingly overhead. But then, in what seemed like a sudden revelation, they would stop whatever they were doing and stand on a box to reach the bananas with a stick. Köhler called the cognitive process

Insight: A sudden awareness of the relationships among various elements that had previously appeared to be independent of one another.

INTERACTIVITY 24–1

Insight

underlying the chimps' new behavior **insight,** a sudden awareness of the relationships among various elements that had previously appeared to be unrelated.

Although Köhler emphasized the apparent suddenness of insightful solutions, subsequent research has shown that prior experience and initial trial-and-error practice in problem solving must precede "insight" (Metcalfe, 1986; Windholz & Lamal, 2002). One study demonstrated that only chimps that had experience playing with sticks could successfully solve the problem; inexperienced chimps never made the connection between standing on the box and reaching the bananas with a stick (Birch, 1945). Some researchers have suggested that the chimps' behavior was simply chaining together previously learned responses, no different from the way a pigeon learns, by trial and error, to peck a key (Epstein, 1987, 1996). Such studies clearly show that insight depends on previous experience with the elements involved in a problem. (For more on insight, try **Interactivity 24–1.**)

Judgment: Evaluating the Solutions

The final stage in problem solving is judging the adequacy of a solution. Often this is a simple matter: If the solution is clear—as in the Tower of Hanoi problem—we will know immediately whether we have been successful.

If the solution is less concrete or if there is no single correct solution, evaluating solutions becomes more difficult. In such instances, we must decide which alternative solution is best. Unfortunately, we often quite inaccurately estimate the quality of our own ideas (Johnson, Parrott, & Stratton, 1968). For instance, a team of drug researchers working for a particular company may feel that their remedy for an illness is superior to all others, overestimating the likelihood of their success and downplaying the approaches of competing drug companies.

Theoretically, if we rely on appropriate heuristics and valid information to make decisions, we can make accurate choices among alternative solutions. However, as we see next, several kinds of obstacles to and biases in problem solving affect the quality of the decisions and judgments we make.

Impediments to Solutions: Why Is Problem Solving Such a Problem?

Consider the following problem-solving test (Duncker, 1945):

> You are given a set of tacks, candles, and matches each in a small box, and told your goal is to place three candles at eye level on a nearby door, so that wax will not drip on the floor as the candles burn [see Figure 6]. How would you approach this challenge?

FIGURE 6 The problem here is to place three candles at eye level on a nearby door so that the wax will not drip on the floor as the candles burn—using only material in the figure. For a solution turn to Figure 8 on p. 274.

If you have difficulty solving the problem, you are not alone. Most people cannot solve it when it is presented in the manner illustrated in the figure, in which the objects are *inside* the boxes. However, if the objects were presented *beside* the boxes, just resting on the table, chances are that you would solve the problem much more readily—which, in case you are wondering, requires tacking the boxes to the door and then placing the candles inside them (see Figure 8 on page 274).

The difficulty you probably encountered in solving this problem stems from its presentation, which misled you at the initial preparation stage. Actually, significant obstacles to problem solving can exist at each of the three major stages. Although cognitive approaches to problem solving suggest that thinking proceeds along fairly rational, logical lines as a person confronts a problem and considers various solutions, several factors can hinder the development of creative, appropriate, and accurate solutions.

FUNCTIONAL FIXEDNESS AND MENTAL SET

The difficulty most people experience with the candle problem is caused by **functional fixedness,** the tendency to think of an object only in terms of its typical use. For instance, functional fixedness probably leads you to think of this book as something to read, instead of its potential use as a doorstop or as kindling for a fire. In the candle problem, because the objects are first presented inside the boxes, functional fixedness leads most people to see the boxes simply as containers for the objects they hold rather than as a potential part of the solution. They cannot envision another function for the boxes.

Functional fixedness is an example of a broader phenomenon known as **mental set,** the tendency for old patterns of problem solving to persist. A classic experiment (Luchins, 1946) demonstrated this phenomenon. As you can see in Figure 7, the object of the task is to use the jars in each row to measure out the designated amount of liquid. (Try it yourself to get a sense of the power of mental set before moving on.)

If you have tried to solve the problem, you know that the first five rows are all solved in the same way: First fill the largest jar (B) and then from it fill the middle-size jar (A) once and the smallest jar (C) two times. What is left in B is the designated amount. (Stated as a formula, the designated amount is B − A − 2C.) The demonstration of mental set comes in the sixth row of the problem, a point at which

Functional fixedness: The tendency to think of an object only in terms of its typical use.

Mental set: The tendency for old patterns of problem solving to persist.

Given jars with these capacities (in ounces):

	A	B	C	Obtain:
1.	21	127	3	100
2.	14	163	25	99
3.	18	43	10	5
4.	9	42	6	21
5.	20	59	4	31
6.	28	76	3	25

FIGURE 7 Try this classic demonstration, which illustrates the importance of mental set in problem solving. The object is to use the jars in each row to measure out the designated amount of liquid. After you figure out the solution for the first five rows, you'll probably have trouble with the sixth row—even though the solution is actually easier. In fact, if you had tried to solve the problem in the sixth row first, you probably would have had no difficulty at all.

FIGURE 8 A solution to the problem in Figure 6 involves tacking the boxes to the door and placing the candles in the boxes.

you probably encountered some difficulty. If you are like most people, you tried the formula and were perplexed when it failed. Chances are, in fact, that you missed the simple (but different) solution to the problem, which involves merely subtracting C from A. Interestingly, people who were given the problem in row 6 *first* had no difficulty with it at all.

Mental set can affect perceptions, as well as patterns of problem solving. It can prevent you from seeing beyond the apparent constraints of a problem. For example, try to draw four straight lines so that they pass through all nine dots in the grid below—without lifting your pencil from the page.

•   •   •

•   •   •

•   •   •

If you had difficulty with the problem, it was probably because you felt compelled to keep your lines within the grid. If you had gone outside the boundaries, however, you would have succeeded by using the solution shown in Figure 9 on page 276. (The phrase "thinking outside the box"—a term commonly used in business today to encourage creativity—stems from research on overcoming the constraining effects of mental set.)

INACCURATE EVALUATION OF SOLUTIONS

When the nuclear power plant at Three Mile Island in Pennsylvania suffered its initial malfunction in 1979, a disaster that almost led to a nuclear meltdown, the plant operators immediately had to solve a problem of the most serious kind. Several monitors indicated contradictory information about the source of the problem: One suggested that the pressure was too high, leading to the danger of an explosion; others indicated that the pressure was too low, which could lead to a meltdown. Although the pressure was, in fact, too low, the supervisors on duty relied on the one monitor—which turned out to be faulty—that suggested that the pressure was too high. Once they had made their decision and acted on it, they ignored the contradictory evidence from the other monitors (Wickens, 1984).

The operators' mistake exemplifies *confirmation bias*, in which problem solvers favor initial hypotheses and ignore contradictory information that supports alternative hypotheses or solutions. Even when we find evidence that contradicts a solution we have chosen, we are apt to stick with our original hypothesis.

Confirmation bias occurs for several reasons. For one, rethinking a problem that appears to be solved already takes extra cognitive effort, and so we are apt to stick with our first solution. For another, we give greater weight to subsequent information that supports our initial position than to information that is not supportive of it (Gilovitch, Griffin, & Kahneman, 2002).

Creativity and Problem Solving

Despite obstacles to problem solving, many people adeptly discover creative solutions to problems. One enduring question that cognitive psychologists have sought to answer is what factors underlie **creativity,** the ability to combine responses or ideas in novel ways.

Although identifying the stages of problem solving helps us understand how people approach and solve problems, it does little to explain why some people come up with better solutions than others do. For instance, even the possible solutions to a simple problem often show wide discrepancies. Consider, for example, how you might respond to the question "How many uses can you think of for a newspaper?"

Now compare your solution with this one proposed by a 10-year-old boy:

> You can read it, write on it, lay it down and paint a picture on it . . . You could put it in your door for decoration, put it in the garbage can, put it on a chair if the chair is messy. If you have a puppy, you put newspaper in its box or put it in your backyard for the dog to play with. When you build something and you don't want anyone to see it, put newspaper around it. Put newspaper on the floor if you have no mattress, use it to pick up something hot, use it to stop bleeding, or to catch the drips from drying clothes. You can use a newspaper for curtains, put it in your shoe to cover what is hurting your foot, make a kite out of it, shade a light that is too bright. You can wrap fish in it, wipe windows, or wrap money in it . . . You put washed shoes in newspaper, wipe eyeglasses with it, put it under a dripping sink, put a plant on it, make a paper bowl out of it, use it for a hat if it is raining, tie it on your feet for slippers. You can put it on the sand if you had no towel, use it for bases in baseball, make paper airplanes with it, use it as a dustpan when you sweep, ball it up for the cat to play with, wrap your hands in it if it is cold (Ward, Kogan, & Pankove, 1972).

This list shows extraordinary creativity. Unfortunately, it is much easier to identify *examples* of creativity than to determine its causes. Several factors, however, seem to be associated with creativity (Csikszentmihalyi, 1997; Simonton, 2000; Niu & Sternberg, 2003).

One of these factors is **divergent thinking,** the ability to generate unusual, yet nonetheless appropriate, responses to problems or questions. This type of thinking contrasts with **convergent thinking,** which produces responses that are based primarily on knowledge and logic. For instance, someone relying on convergent thinking would answer "You read it" to the query "What can you do with a newspaper?" In contrast,

Creativity: The combining of responses or ideas in novel ways.

PowerWeb: Creativity: Its Nature and Assessment

www.mhhe.com/feldmanup7

Divergent thinking: The ability to generate unusual, yet nonetheless appropriate, responses to problems or questions.

Convergent thinking: The ability to produce responses that are based primarily on knowledge and logic.

Pablo Picasso is considered one of the greatest creative artists of the twentieth century. Do you think he relied more on convergent or divergent thinking in his art?

FIGURE 9 A solution to the nine-dot problem requires the use of lines drawn beyond the boundaries of the figure—something that our mental set may prevent us from seeing easily.

"You use it as a dustpan" is a more divergent—and creative—response (Baer, 1993; Runco & Sakamoto, 1993; Finke, 1995; Sternberg, 2001).

Another aspect of creativity is its *cognitive complexity*, or preference for elaborate, intricate, and complex stimuli and thinking patterns. For instance, creative people often have a wider range of interests and are more independent and more interested in philosophical or abstract problems than are less creative individuals (Barron, 1990).

One factor that is *not* closely related to creativity is intelligence. Traditional intelligence tests, which ask focused questions that have only one acceptable answer, tap convergent thinking skills. Highly creative people may therefore find that such tests penalize their divergent thinking. This may explain why researchers consistently find that creativity is only slightly related to school grades and intelligence, when intelligence is measured using traditional intelligence tests (Hong, Milgram, & Gorsky, 1995; Sternberg & O'Hara, 2000).

BECOMING AN INFORMED CONSUMER
of Psychology
Thinking Critically and Creatively

Can we learn to be better thinkers?

Cognitive researchers have found that people can learn the abstract rules of logic and reasoning and that such knowledge can improve our reasoning about the underlying causes of everyday events in our lives.

In short, research suggests that critical and creative thinkers are made, not born. Consider, for instance, some of these suggestions for increasing critical thinking and creativity (Feldman, Coats, & Schwartzberg, 1994; Levy, 1997; Halpern, 1998):

- ▶ *Redefine problems.* We can modify boundaries and assumptions by rephrasing a problem at either a more abstract or a more concrete level.
- ▶ *Use fractionation.* Fractionation breaks down an idea or concept into its component parts. Through fractionation, we can examine each part for new possibilities and approaches, leading to a novel solution for the problem as a whole.
- ▶ *Adopt a critical perspective.* Rather than passively accepting assumptions or arguments, we can evaluate material critically, consider its implications, and think about possible exceptions and contradictions.
- ▶ *Consider the opposite.* By considering the opposite of a concept we're seeking to understand, we can sometimes make progress. For example, to define "good mental health," it may be useful to consider what "bad mental health" means.

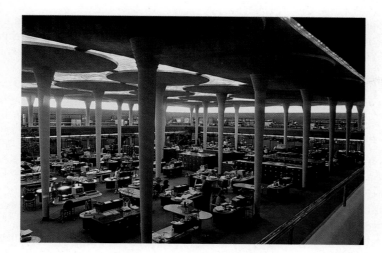

The use of analogies is a characteristic of creativity. Frank Lloyd Wright incorporated into his architecture many analogies to nature, as you can see in this building he designed. How are analogies used by other creative artists?

- ▶ *Use analogies.* Analogies provide alternative frameworks for the interpretation of facts and help us uncover new understanding. One particularly effective means of coming up with analogies is to look for examples in the animal world. For instance, architects discovered how to construct the earliest skyscrapers by noting how lily pads on a pond could support the weight of a person (Shouler, 1992; Getner & Holyoak, 1997; Reisberg, 1997).

- ▶ *Think divergently.* Instead of the most logical or common use for an object, consider how you might use the object if you were forbidden to use it in the usual way.

- ▶ *Take the perspective of another person.* By temporarily adopting another person's point of view, you may gain a fresh view of the situation.

- ▶ *Use heuristics.* Heuristics are cognitive shortcuts that can help bring about a solution to a problem. If the problem has a single correct answer and you can use or construct a heuristic, you can often find the solution more rapidly and effectively.

- ▶ *Experiment with various solutions.* Don't be afraid to use different routes to find solutions for problems (verbal, mathematical, graphic, even dramatic). For instance, try to come up with every conceivable idea you can, no matter how wild or bizarre it may seem at first. After you've come up with a list of solutions, review each one and try to think of ways to make what at first appeared impractical seem more feasible.

RECAP/EVALUATE/RETHINK

RECAP

How do people approach and solve problems?

- ▶ Problem solving typically involves three major stages: preparation, production of solutions, and evaluation of solutions that have been generated. (p. 265)

- ▶ Preparation involves placing the problem in one of three categories. In arrangement problems, a group of elements must be rearranged or recombined in a way that will satisfy a certain criterion. In problems of inducing structure, a person first must identify the existing relationships among the elements presented and then con-

struct a new relationship among them. Finally, transformation problems consist of an initial state, a goal state, and a method for changing the initial state into the goal state. (p. 266)

- ▶ A crucial aspect of the preparation stage is the representation and organization of the problem. (p. 268)

- ▶ In the production stage, people try to generate solutions. They may find solutions to some problems in long-term memory. Alternatively, they may solve some problems through simple trial and error and use algorithms and heuristics to solve more complex problems. (p. 269)

▶ Using the heuristic of a means-ends analysis, a person will repeatedly test for differences between the desired outcome and what currently exists, trying each time to come closer to the goal. (p. 270)

▶ Köhler's research with chimpanzees illustrates insight, a sudden awareness of the relationships among elements that had previously seemed unrelated. (p. 271)

What are the major obstacles to problem solving?

▶ Several factors hinder effective problem solving. Mental set, of which functional fixedness is an example, is the tendency for old patterns of problem solving to persist. Inappropriate use of algorithms and heuristics can also act as an obstacle to the production of solutions. Confirmation bias, in which initial hypotheses are favored, can hinder the accurate evaluation of solutions to problems. (p. 272)

▶ Creativity is the ability to combine responses or ideas in novel ways. Creativity is related to divergent thinking (the ability to generate unusual, but still appropriate, responses to problems or questions) and cognitive complexity. (p. 275)

EVALUATE

1. Solving a problem by trying to reduce the difference between the current state and the goal state is known as a _____.

2. _____ is the term used to describe the sudden "flash" of revelation that often accompanies the solution to a problem.

3. Thinking of an object only in terms of its typical use is known as _____ _____. A broader, related tendency for old problem-solving patterns to persist is known as a _____ _____.

4. _____ describes the phenomenon of favoring an initial hypothesis and ignoring subsequent competing hypotheses.

5. Generating unusual but appropriate approaches to a question is known as _____ _____.

RETHINK

1. Is the reasoning in the following syllogism correct or incorrect? Why?
   Creative people often have trouble with traditional intelligence tests.
   I have trouble with traditional intelligence tests.
   Therefore, I am a creative person.

2. Are divergent thinking and convergent thinking mutually exclusive or complementary? Why? Are there situations in which one way of thinking is clearly superior? How can the two ways of thinking be combined?

Answers to Evaluate Questions

1. transformation; 2. insight; 3. functional fixedness, mental set; 4. confirmation bias; 5. divergent thinking.

KEY TERMS

means-ends analysis p. 270
insight p. 272

functional fixedness p. 273
mental set p. 273

creativity p. 275
divergent thinking p. 275

convergent thinking p. 275

Language

'Twas brillig, and the slithy toves

Did gyre and gimble in the wabe:

All mimsy were the borogoves,

And the mome raths outgrabe.

MODULE 25

How do people use language?

How does language develop?

Although few of us have ever come face to face with a tove, we have little difficulty in discerning that in Lewis Carroll's (1872) poem "Jabberwocky," the expression *slithy toves* contains an adjective, *slithy*, and the noun it modifies, *toves.*

Our ability to make sense out of nonsense, if the nonsense follows typical rules of language, illustrates the complexity of both human language and the cognitive processes that underlie its development and use. The use of **language**—the communication of information through symbols arranged according to systematic rules—is an important cognitive ability, one that is indispensable for communicating with others. Not only is language central to communication, it is also closely tied to the very way in which we think about and understand the world. No wonder psychologists have devoted considerable attention to studying language (Barrett, 1999; Owens, 2001; Hoff, 2003; Saffran & Schwartz, 2003).

Language: The communication of information through symbols arranged according to systematic rules.

⊛⊛⊛

Grammar: Language's Language

To understand how language develops and relates to thought, we first need to review some of the formal elements of language. The basic structure of language rests on **grammar,** the system of rules that determine how our thoughts can be expressed.

Grammar deals with three major components of language: phonology, syntax, and semantics. **Phonology** is the study of the smallest basic units of speech, called **phonemes,** that affect meaning, and of the way we use those sounds to form words and produce meaning. For instance, the *a* sound in *fat* and the *a* sound in *fate* represent two different phonemes in English (Vihman, 1996; Baddeley, Gathercole, & Pagano, 1998).

Linguists have identified more than 800 different phonemes among all the world's languages. Although English speakers use just 52 phonemes to produce words, other languages use from as few as 15 to as many as 141. Differences in phonemes are one reason people have difficulty learning other languages. For example, to a Japanese speaker, whose native language does not have an *r* phoneme, English words such as *roar* present some difficulty (Gibbs, 2002; Iverson et al., 2003).

Syntax refers to the rules that indicate how words and phrases can be combined to form sentences. Every language has intricate rules that guide the order in which words may be strung together to communicate meaning. English speakers have no difficulty recognizing that "Radio down the turn" is not a meaningful sequence, whereas "Turn down the radio" is. To understand the effect of syntax in English,

Grammar: The system of rules that determine how our thoughts can be expressed.

Phonology: The study of the smallest units of speech, called phonemes.

Phonemes: The smallest units of speech.

PowerWeb: Listening to Speech in the First Year of Life

www.mhhe.com/feldmanup7

Syntax: Ways in which words and phrases can be combined to form sentences.

consider the changes in meaning caused by the different word orders in the following three utterances: "John kidnapped the boy," "John, the kidnapped boy," and "The boy kidnapped John" (Lasnik, 1990).

The third major component of language is **semantics,** the meanings of words and sentences (Larson, 1990; Hipkiss, 1995; O'Grady & Dobrovolsky, 1996). Semantic rules allow us to use words to convey the subtlest nuances. For instance, we are able to make the distinction between "The truck hit Laura" (which we would be likely to say if we had just seen the vehicle hitting Laura) and "Laura was hit by a truck" (which we would probably say if someone asked why Laura was missing class while she recuperated).

Despite the complexities of language, most of us acquire the basics of grammar without even being aware that we have learned its rules (Pinker, 1994). Moreover, even though we may have difficulty explicitly stating the rules of grammar, our linguistic abilities are so sophisticated that we can utter an infinite number of different statements. How do we acquire such abilities?

Language Development: Developing a Way with Words

To parents, the sounds of their infant babbling and cooing are music to their ears (except, perhaps, at three o'clock in the morning). These sounds also serve an important function. They mark the first step on the road to the development of language.

BABBLING

Children **babble**—make speechlike but meaningless sounds—from around the age of 3 months through 1 year. While babbling, they may produce, at one time or another, any of the sounds found in all languages, not just the one to which they are exposed. Even deaf children display their own form of babbling, for infants who are unable to hear yet who are exposed to sign language from birth "babble" with their hands (Petitto & Marentette, 1991; Pettito, 1993; Meier & Willerman, 1995).

An infant's babbling increasingly reflects the specific language being spoken in the infant's environment, initially in terms of pitch and tone and eventually in terms of specific sounds. Young infants can distinguish among all 869 phonemes that have been identified across the world's languages. However, after the age of 6 to 8 months, that ability begins to decline. Infants begin to "specialize" in the language to which they are exposed as neurons in their brains reorganize to respond to the particular phonemes infants routinely hear.

Some theorists argue that a *critical period* exists for language development early in life, in which a child is particularly sensitive to language cues and most easily acquires language. In fact, if children are not exposed to language during this critical period, later they will have great difficulty overcoming this deficit (Bortfeld & Whitehurst, 2001; Bruer, 2001; Newport, Bavelier, & Neville, 2001).

Cases in which abused children have been isolated from contact with others support the theory of such critical periods. In one case, for example, a girl named Genie was exposed to virtually no language from the age of 20 months until she was rescued at age 13 years. She was unable to speak at all. Despite intensive instruction, she learned only some words and was never able to master the complexities of language (Rymer, 1994; Veltman & Browne, 2001).

Semantics: The rules governing the meaning of words and sentences.

Babble: Speechlike but meaningless sounds made by children from around the age of 3 months through 1 year.

A syllable in signed language, similar to the ones seen in the manual babbling of deaf infants and in the spoken babbling of hearing infants. The similarities in language structure suggest that language has biological roots.

PRODUCTION OF LANGUAGE

By the time children are approximately 1 year old, they stop producing sounds that are not in the language to which they have been exposed. It is then a short step to the production of actual words. In English, these are typically short words that start with a consonant sound such as *b, d, m, p,* and *t*—this helps explain why *mama* and *dada* are so often among babies' first words. Of course, even before they produce their first words, children can understand a fair amount of the language they hear. Language comprehension precedes language production.

After the age of 1 year, children begin to learn more complicated forms of language. They produce two-word combinations, the building blocks of sentences, and sharply increase the number of different words they are able to use. By age 2, the average child has a vocabulary of more than fifty words. Just six months later, that vocabulary has grown to several hundred words. At that time, children can produce short sentences, although they use **telegraphic speech**—sentences that sound as if they were part of a telegram, in which words not critical to the message are left out. Rather than saying, "I showed you the book," a child using telegraphic speech may say, "I show book," and "I am drawing a dog" may become "Drawing dog." As children get older, of course, they use less telegraphic speech and produce increasingly complex sentences (Volterra et al., 2003).

By age 3, children learn to make plurals by adding *s* to nouns and to form the past tense by adding *-ed* to verbs. This also leads to errors, since children tend to apply rules inflexibly. In such **overgeneralization,** children employ rules even when doing so results in an error. Thus, although it is correct to say "he walked" for the past tense of *walk,* the *-ed* rule doesn't work quite so well when children say "he runned" for the past tense of *run* (Marcus, 1996; Howe, 2002).

By age 5, children have acquired the basic rules of language. However, they do not attain a full vocabulary and the ability to comprehend and use subtle grammatical rules until later. For example, a 5-year-old boy who sees a blindfolded doll and is asked, "Is the doll easy or hard to see?" would have great trouble answering the question. In fact, if he were asked to make the doll easier to see, he would probably try to remove the doll's blindfold. By the time they are 8 years old, however, children have little difficulty understanding this question, because they realize that the doll's blindfold has nothing to do with an observer's ability to see the doll (Chomsky, 1969; Hoff, 2003).

Telegraphic speech: Sentences in which words not critical to the message are left out.

Overgeneralization: The phenomenon by which children apply language rules even when the application results in an error.

Understanding Language Acquisition: Identifying the Roots of Language

Anyone who spends even a little time with children will notice the enormous strides that they make in language development throughout childhood. However, the reasons for this rapid growth are far from obvious. Psychologists have offered two major explanations, one based on learning theory and the other based on innate processes.

The **learning-theory approach** suggests that language acquisition follows the principles of reinforcement and conditioning discovered by psychologists who study learning. For example, a child who says "mama" receives hugs and praise from her mother, which reinforces the behavior of saying "mama" and makes its repetition more likely. This view suggests that children first learn to speak by being rewarded for making sounds that approximate speech. Ultimately, through a process of shaping, language becomes more and more like adult speech (Skinner, 1957).

Learning-theory approach: The theory suggesting that language acquisition follows the principles of reinforcement and conditioning.

FIGURE 1 The more words that parents say to their children before the age of 3, the larger the children's vocabulary. (Source: Courtesy of Drs. Betty Hart and Todd Risley, 1997.)

Noam Chomsky argues that all languages share a universal grammar.

Universal grammar: Noam Chomsky's theory that all the world's languages share a common underlying structure.

Language-acquisition device: A neural system of the brain hypothesized to permit understanding of language.

To support the learning-theory approach, research shows that the more parents speak to their young children, the more proficient the children become in language use (see Figure 1). In addition, by the time they are 3 years old, children who hear higher levels of linguistic sophistication in their parents' speech show a greater rate of vocabulary growth, vocabulary use, and even general intellectual achievement than do children whose parents' speech is more simple (Hart & Risley, 1997).

The learning-theory approach is less successful in explaining how children acquire language rules. Children are reinforced not only when they use language correctly, but also when they use it incorrectly. For example, parents answer a child's "Why the dog won't eat?" as readily as they do the correctly phrased question, "Why won't the dog eat?" Listeners understand both sentences equally well. Learning theory, then, has difficulty fully explaining language acquisition.

Pointing to such problems with learning-theory approaches to language acquisition, linguist Noam Chomsky (1968, 1978, 1991) provided a groundbreaking alternative. Chomsky argued that humans are born with an innate linguistic capability that emerges primarily as a function of maturation. According to his analysis, all the world's languages share a common underlying structure called a **universal grammar.** Chomsky suggested that the human brain has a neural system, the **language-acquisition device,** that not only lets us understand the structure language provides but also gives us strategies and techniques for learning the unique characteristics of our native language (McGilvray, 2004).

Chomsky used the concept of the language-acquisition device as a metaphor, and he did not identify a specific area of the brain in which it resides. However, some

Music on the Mind

We spend a great amount of time listening to music. Most college students listen to music at least three or four times a week, and more than 50 percent of them go to at least one concert per year, collectively spending over $675 million on concert tickets (Harris Interactive, 2002). What's the attraction?

According to new research, we may be born liking music, because human beings appear to be genetically preprogrammed to find certain combinations of sounds attractive. For example, infants can recognize a familiar melody even when its key is changed or its tempo is altered. Likewise, infants respond with more emotion to their mothers' singing than to their mothers' speech. Careful analysis of mothers' infant-directed songs indicates that each mother's songs remain remarkably stable from one "performance" to the next, and this may encourage infants' engagement with the songs (Trehub, 2001; Trehub & Nakata, 2001–02; Bergeson & Trehub, 2002).

Research with adults suggests that music grabs our attention by activating brain pathways that are more suited to processing music than to processing other kinds of sound. Specifically, music appreciation relies on the auditory cortex on the right side of the brain, which is specialized to process the variations in pitch that characterize music—in contrast to the left auditory cortex, which processes the stop-and-start bursts of sound that characterize speech (Peretz, 2001; Janata, Tillman, & Bharucha, 2002; Zatorre, Belin, & Penhune, 2002).

Are we genetically prewired to enjoy music? Recent research suggests humans are.

Music also may have powerful effects on our thinking. Although some psychologists remain skeptical, a number of studies have shown that listening to music can enhance people's spatial reasoning abilities. Furthermore, it is clear that music can profoundly influence our emotions. Personally significant music activates areas of the brain associated with pleasure and reward, the same areas that are stimulated by sex and good food (Blood & Zatorre, 2001; Abbot, 2002; McKelvie & Low, 2002; Rauscher, 2002).

Researchers do not agree about whether humans' abilities to process and enjoy music are products of evolutionary design or by-products of our highly evolved auditory systems. Either way, the next time you enjoy listening to a piece of music, remember that the most complex pieces of audio equipment are the ones between your headphones.

RETHINK

Why do you think humans have developed the abilities to experience and create music? How would you be affected if you could no longer appreciate music?

---

evidence suggests that the ability to use language, which was a significant evolutionary advance in human beings, is tied to specific neurological developments. For example, scientists have discovered a gene related to the development of language abilities that may have emerged as recently—in evolutionary terms—as 100,000 years ago (Enard et al., 2002; Hauser, Chomsky, & Fitch, 2002).

Chomsky thus argues that language is a uniquely human phenomenon made possible by the presence of the language-acquisition device. Furthermore, as we consider in the accompanying *Applying Psychology in the 21st Century* box, it's not just language that may be prewired; music may also be a critical part of our human makeup.

INTERACTIVITY 25–1

Language development

Chomsky's view, as you might suspect, has its critics. For instance, learning theorists contend that the apparent ability of certain animals, such as chimpanzees, to learn the fundamentals of human language (as we discuss later in this module) contradicts the innate linguistic capability view. To reconcile such data, some theorists suggest that the brain's hardwired language-acquisition device that Chomsky and geneticists posit provides the hardware for our acquisition of language, whereas the exposure to language in our environment that learning theorists observe allows us to develop the appropriate software. But the issue of how language is acquired remains hotly contested (Pinker, 1994, 2002; Fromkin, 2000; Lana, 2002). Go to **Interactivity 25–1** to further investigate language development.

The Influence of Language on Thinking: Do Eskimos Have More Words for Snow Than Texans Do?

Do Eskimos living in the frigid Arctic have a more expansive vocabulary for discussing snow than people living in warmer climates?

It makes sense, and arguments that the Eskimo language has many more words than English for snow have been made since the early 1900s. At that time, linguist Benjamin Lee Whorf contended that because snow is so relevant to Eskimos' lives, their language provides a particularly rich vocabulary to describe it—considerably larger than what we find in other languages, such as English (Martin & Pullum, 1991; Pinker, 1994).

The contention that the Eskimo language is particularly abundant in snow-related terms led to the *linguistic-relativity hypothesis*, the notion that language shapes and, in fact, may determine the way people in a particular culture perceive and understand the world. According to this view, language provides us with categories that we use to construct our view of people and events in the world around us. Consequently, language shapes and produces thought (Whorf, 1956; Smith, 1996; Oezgen & Davies, 2002).

Let's consider another possibility, however. Suppose that instead of language being the *cause* of certain ways of thinking, thought *produces* language. The only reason to expect that Eskimo language might have more words for snow than English does is that snow is considerably more relevant to Eskimos than it is to people in other cultures.

Which view is correct? Most recent research refutes the linguistic-relativity hypothesis and suggests, instead, that thinking produces language. In fact, new analyses of the Eskimo language suggest that Eskimos have no more words for snow than English speakers, for if one examines the English language closely, one sees that it is hardly impoverished when it comes to describing snow (consider, for example, *sleet, slush, blizzard, dusting,* and *avalanche*).

Still, the linguistic relativity hypothesis has not been entirely discarded. A newer version of the hypothesis suggests that speech patterns may influence certain aspects of thinking. For example, in some languages, such as English, speakers distinguish between nouns that can be counted (such as "five chairs") and nouns that require a measurement unit to be quantified (such as "a liter of water"). In some other languages, however, such as the Mayan language called Yucatec, all nouns require a measurement unit. In such cultures, people appear to think more closely about what things are made of than do people in cultures in which languages such as English are spoken. In contrast, English speakers focus more on the shape of objects (Gentner, Goldin, & Goldin-Meadow, 2003).

In short, although research does not support the linguistic-relativity hypothesis that language *causes* thought, it is clear that language influences how we think. And, of course, it certainly is the case that thought influences language, suggesting that language and thinking interact in complex ways (Heyman & Diesendruck, 2002; Kim, 2002).

Do Animals Use Language?

One question that has long puzzled psychologists is whether language is uniquely human or if other animals are able to acquire it as well. Many animals communicate with one another in rudimentary forms. For instance, fiddler crabs wave their claws to signal, bees dance to indicate the direction in which food will be found, and certain birds call "zick, zick" during courtship and "kia" when they are about to fly away. However, researchers have yet to demonstrate con-clusively that these animals use true language, which is characterized in part by the ability to produce and com-municate new and unique meanings by following a formal grammar.

Psychologists have, however, been able to teach chimps to communicate at surprisingly high levels. For instance, after four years of training, a chimp named Washoe learned to make signs for 132 words and combine those signs into simple sentences. Even more impressively, Kanzi, a pygmy chimpanzee, has linguistic skills that some psychologists claim are close to those of a 2-year-old human being. Kanzi's trainers suggest that he can create grammatically sophisti-cated sentences and can even invent new rules of syntax (Gardner & Gardner, 1969; Savage-Rumbaugh et al., 1993).

Despite the skills displayed by primates such as Kanzi, critics contend that the language such animals use still lacks the grammar and the complex and novel constructions of human language. Instead, they maintain that the chimps are displaying a skill no different from that of a dog that learns to lie down on command to get a reward. Furthermore, we lack firm evidence that animals can recognize and respond

"He's pretty good at rote categorization and single-object relational tasks, but he's not so hot at differentiating between representational and associa-tional signs, and he's very weak on syntax."

Sue Savage-Rumbaugh with a primate friend, Panbanisha. Does the use of sign language by primates indicate true mastery of language?

to the mental states of others of their species, an important aspect of human communication (Seidenberg & Petitto, 1987; Seyfarth & Cheney, 1992, 1996; Tattersall, 2002).

Most evidence supports the contention that humans are better equipped than other animals to produce and organize language in the form of meaningful sentences. But the issue of whether other animals can be taught to communicate in a way that resembles human language remains controversial (Gilbert, 1996; Savage-Rumbaugh & Brakke, 1996).

Exploring DIVERSITY

Teaching with Linguistic Variety: Bilingual Education

For Picture Day at New York's P.S. 217, a neighborhood elementary school in Brooklyn, the notice to parents was translated into five languages. That was a nice gesture, but insufficient: More than 40 percent of the children are immigrants whose families speak any one of twenty-six languages, ranging from Armenian to Urdu (Leslie, 1991, p. 56).

From the biggest cities to the most rural areas, the face—and voice—of education in the United States is changing. More schoolchildren today have last names like Kim, Valdez, and Karachnicoff as the wave of immigration during the 1980s, larger than that of the early 1900s, hits the country's schools. In seven states, including Texas, New York, and Colorado, more than one-quarter of the students are not native English speakers. For some 32 million Americans, English is their second language (see Figure 2).

How to appropriately and effectively teach the increasing number of children who do not speak English is not always clear. Many educators maintain that *bilingual education* is best. With a bilingual approach, students learn some subjects in their native language while simultaneously learning English. Proponents of bilingualism believe that students must develop a sound footing in basic subject areas and that, initially at least, teaching those subjects in their native language is the only way to provide them with that foundation. During the same period, they learn English, with the eventual goal of shifting all instruction into English.

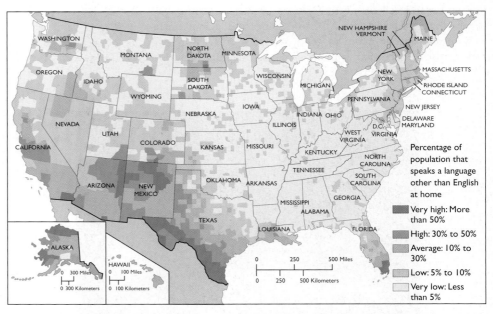

FIGURE 2 The language of diversity. Some 14 percent of the people in the United States speak a language other than English at home. Most of them speak Spanish, with the rest speaking an astounding variety of different languages. Where are the largest clusters of non-English speakers in the United States, and what do you think explains these concentrations? (Source: *Time*, January 30, 1995).

FIGURE 3 Brain functioning in bilingual speakers. When bilingual speakers carried out language tasks in their native and second languages, brain activity differed depending on when in life each speaker learned the second language. For example, the brain scan in (a), which shows two separate areas of the brain activated, is from a native English speaker who learned French in adulthood. In contrast, the brain scan in (b) is from a speaker who learned both English and Turkish in infancy. For that person, substantial overlap exists between the areas of the brain that are activated. (Source: Kim, Relkin, Lee, & Hirsch, 1997).

In contrast, other educators insist that all instruction ought to be in English from the moment students, including those who speak no English at all, enroll in school. In *immersion programs*, students are immediately plunged into English instruction in all subjects. The reasoning—endorsed by voters in California in a referendum designed to end bilingual education—is that teaching students in a language other than English simply hinders nonnative English speakers' integration into society and ultimately does them a disservice. Proponents of English immersion programs point as evidence to improvements in standardized test scores that followed the end of bilingual education programs (Wildavsky, 2000).

Although the controversial issue has strong political undercurrents, evidence shows that the ability to speak two languages provides significant cognitive benefits over speaking only one language. For example, bilingual speakers show more cognitive flexibility and may understand concepts more easily than those who speak only one language. They have more linguistic tools for thinking because of their multiple-language abilities. In turn, this makes them more creative and flexible in solving problems (Hong, 2000; Sanz, 2000; Heyman & Diesendruck, 2002).

Research also suggests that speaking several languages changes the organization of the brain, as does the timing of the acquisition of a second language. For example, one study compared bilingual speakers on linguistic tasks in their native and second languages. The study found that those who had learned their second language as adults showed different areas of brain activation compared with those who had learned their second language in childhood (Kim et al., 1997; see Figure 3).

A related question is this: What is the psychological impact of *biculturalism*, that is, being a member of two cultures? Some psychologists argue that society should promote an *alternation model* of bicultural competence. Such a model supports members of a culture in their efforts to maintain their original cultural identity, as well as in their integration into the adopted culture. In this view, a person can belong to two cultures and have two cultural identities without having to choose between them. Whether society will adopt the alternation model remains to be seen (LaFromboise, Coleman, & Gerton, 1995; Calderon & Minaya-Rowe, 2003; Carter, 2003).

⚠⚠⚠

RECAP/EVALUATE/RETHINK

RECAP

How do people use language?

▶ Language is the communication of information through symbols arranged according to systematic rules. All languages have a grammar—a system of rules that determines how thoughts can be expressed—that encompasses the three major components of language: phonology, syntax, and semantics. (p. 279)

How does language develop?

▶ Language production, which follows language comprehension, develops out of babbling, which then leads to the production of actual words. After 1 year of age, children use two-word combinations, increase their vocabulary, and use telegraphic speech, which drops words not critical to the message. By age 5, acquisition of language rules is relatively complete. (p. 280)

▶ Learning theorists suggest that language is acquired through reinforcement and conditioning. In contrast, Chomsky and other linguists suggest that an innate language-acquisition device guides the development of language. (p. 281)

▶ The linguistic-relativity hypothesis suggests that language shapes and may determine the way people think about the world. Most evidence suggests that although language does not determine thought, it does affect the way people store information in memory and how well they can retrieve it. (p. 284)

▶ The degree to which language is a uniquely human skill remains controversial. Some psychologists contend that even though certain primates communicate at a high level, those animals do not use language; other psychologists suggest that those primates truly understand and produce language in much the same way humans. (p. 285)

▶ People who speak more than one language may have a cognitive advantage over those who speak only one. (p. 286)

EVALUATE

1. Match the component of grammar with its definition:
   1. Syntax
   2. Phonology
   3. Semantics
   a. Rules showing how words can be combined into sentences
   b. Rules governing the meaning of words and sentences
   c. The study of the sound units that affect speech
2. Language production and language comprehension develop in infants at about the same time. True or false?
3. _____ _____ refers to the phenomenon in which young children omit nonessential portions of sentences.
4. A child knows that adding -ed to certain words puts them in the past tense. As a result, instead of saying "He came," the child says "He comed." This is an example of
   _____.
5. _____ theory assumes that language acquisition is based on principles of operant conditioning and shaping.
6. In his theory of language acquisition, Chomsky argues that language acquisition is an innate ability tied to the structure of the brain. True or false?

RETHINK

1. Why is overgeneralization seen as an argument against a strict learning-theory approach to explaining language acquisition?
2. Do people who use two languages, one at home and one at school, automatically have two cultures? Why might people who speak two languages have cognitive advantages over those who speak only one?

Answers to Evaluate Questions

1. 1-a, 2-c, 3-b; 2. false; language comprehension precedes language production; 3. telegraphic speech; 4. overgeneralization; 5. learning; 6. true

KEY TERMS

language p. 279
grammar p. 279
phonology p. 279
phonemes p. 279

syntax p. 279
semantics p. 280
babble p. 280
telegraphic speech p. 281

overgeneralization p. 281
learning-theory approach p. 281

universal grammar p. 282
language-acquisition device p. 282

Psychology on the Web

1. In addition to mental images of sights and sounds, are there mental representations that correspond to the other senses? See whether you can answer this question by searching the Web. Summarize your findings in writing.

2. Do animals think? What evidence is there on either side of this question? Search the Web for at least one example of research and/or argument on each side of this question. Summarize your findings and use your knowledge of cognitive psychology to state your own position on this question.

3. After completing Interactivity 23–1, which illustrates how the use of heuristics can sometimes lead to the wrong conclusion, consider how employing heuristics can also be helpful. Describe at least two ways in which the use of heuristics helps us in everyday life.

Epilogue

The study of cognition occupies a central place in the field of psychology, encompassing a variety of areas— including thinking, problem solving, decision making, creativity, language, memory, and intelligence. Specialists in cognitive psychology have made significant advances in the last decade that have influenced the entire field of psychology.

Before proceeding, turn back to the prologue about Clifford Matson's "Eureka!" moment. Answer the following questions in light of what you have learned about reasoning, problem solving, and creativity:

1. What factors led up to Matson's invention of Cork-EZ?

2. How do the concepts of functional fixedness and mental set relate to Matson's inventiveness? Are they related to the notion of prototypes?

3. How do you think insight is involved in Matson's inventiveness?

4. In what ways do you think divergent and convergent thinking are involved in the processes of invention? Do they play different roles in the various stages of the act of invention, including identifying the need for an invention, devising possible solutions, and creating a practical invention?

Intelligence

Prologue
Chris Burke and Vino Vasudevan

When Chris Burke was born, physicians suggested to his parents that he immediately be institutionalized. He had Down Syndrome, a common birth defect that produces mental retardation, and the physicians predicted that the chances of his leading anything like a normal life were slim. Chris's parents ignored the advice, and raised Chris like their other children.

It was a decision that led to an extraordinary life, in which Chris has made significant contributions to society. He speaks regularly on behalf of people with developmental disabilities, has co-authored book chapters, and has appeared regularly in a variety of television shows, including starring roles on *Life Goes On* and *Touched by an Angel* (Hassold & Patterson, 1999; McDaniel & Burke, 2001).

▲▲▲

Most aspiring college students wait until they are in high school to take the SAT test, but when Vino Vasudevan took it, she was only 13. Vino, a middle-school student, took the test as part of a program to identify gifted children (Fields-Meyer, 1999).

Vino achieved perfect 800 math and 800 verbal scores. Her performance was not totally surprising, though. Vino had read 100 books by the time she was 5. At the age of 7 she had mastered seventh-grade math. When she was 8, she took a college algebra class.

Chris Burke

Vino Vasudevan

Two very different people, with widely different intellectual capabilities and strengths—and yet, at their core, Chris Burke and Vino Vasudevan share basic aspects of humanity and even, one could argue, intelligence that ultimately make them more similar than different.

In the following modules, we consider intelligence in all its many varieties. Intelligence represents a focal point for psychologists intent on understanding how people are able to adapt their behavior to the environment in which they live. It also represents a key aspect of how individuals differ from one another in the way in which they learn about and understand the world.

We begin by considering the challenges involved in defining and measuring intelligence.

Looking Ahead

If you are like most people, you have probably wondered how smart you are compared with others. Psychologists, too, have pondered the nature of intelligence. We examine some of their conceptions of intelligence as well as efforts to develop and use standardized tests as a means of measuring intelligence. We also consider the two extremes of individual differences in intelligence: people with mental retardation and the gifted. Finally, we explore what are probably the two most controversial issues surrounding intelligence: the degree to which intelligence is influenced by heredity and by the environment, and whether traditional tests of intelligence are biased toward the dominant cultural groups in society—difficult issues that have both psychological and social significance.

What Is Intelligence?

What are the different definitions and conceptions of intelligence?

What are the major approaches to measuring intelligence, and what do intelligence tests measure?

It is typical for the Trukese, people of a small tribe in the South Pacific, to sail a hundred miles in open ocean waters. Although their destination may be just a small dot of land less than a mile wide, the Trukese are able to sail unerringly toward it without the aid of a compass, chronometer, sextant, or any of the other sailing tools that are indispensable to modern Western navigation. They are able to sail accurately, even when prevailing winds do not allow a direct approach to the island and they must take a zigzag course (Gladwin, 1964; Mytinger, 2001).

How are the Trukese able to navigate so effectively? If you asked them, they could not explain it. They might tell you that they use a process that takes into account the rising and setting of the stars and the appearance, sound, and feel of the waves against the side of the boat. But at any given moment as they are sailing along, they could not identify their position or say why they are doing what they are doing. Nor could they explain the navigational theory underlying their sailing technique.

Some might say that the inability of the Trukese to explain in Western terms how their sailing technique works is a sign of primitive or even unintelligent behavior. In fact, if we gave Trukese sailors a Western standardized test of navigational knowledge and theory or, for that matter, a traditional test of intelligence, they might do poorly on it. Yet, as a practical matter, it is not possible to accuse the Trukese of being unintelligent: Despite their inability to explain how they do it, they are able to navigate successfully through the open ocean waters.

Trukese navigation points out the difficulty in coming to grips with what is meant by intelligence. To a Westerner, traveling in a straight line along the most direct and quickest route by using a sextant and other navigational tools is likely to represent the most "intelligent" kind of behavior; in contrast, a zigzag course, based on the "feel" of the waves, would not seem very reasonable. To the Trukese, who are used to their own system of navigation, however, the use of complicated navigational tools might seem so overly complex and unnecessary that they might think of Western navigators as lacking in intelligence.

What does the Trukese people's method of navigation—which is done without maps or instruments—tell us about the nature of intelligence?

It is clear that the term *intelligence* can take on many different meanings. If, for instance, you lived in a remote part of the Australian outback, the way you would differentiate between more intelligent and less intelligent people might have to do with successfully mastering hunting skills, whereas to someone living in the heart of urban Miami, intelligence might be exemplified by being "street-wise" or by business success.

Each of these conceptions of intelligence is reasonable. Each represents an instance in which more intelligent people are better able to use the resources of their environment than are less intelligent people, a distinction that is presumably basic to any definition of intelligence. Yet it is also clear that these conceptions represent very different views of intelligence.

That two such different sets of behavior can exemplify the same psychological concept has long posed a challenge to psychologists. For years they have grappled with the issue of devising a general definition of intelligence. Interestingly, laypersons have fairly clear ideas of what intelligence is, although the nature of their ideas is related to their culture. Westerners view intelligence as people's ability to form categories and debate rationally. In contrast, people in Eastern cultures view intelligence more in terms of understanding and relating to one another. And members of some African communities are more likely to view intelligence and social competence as similar (Yang & Sternberg, 1997; Serpell, 2000; Nisbett, 2003).

Intelligence: The capacity to understand the world, think rationally, and use resources effectively when faced with challenges.

The definition of intelligence that psychologists employ contains some of the same elements found in the layperson's conception. To psychologists, **intelligence** is the capacity to understand the world, think rationally, and use resources effectively when faced with challenges.

This definition does not lay to rest a key question asked by psychologists: Is intelligence a unitary attribute, or are there different kinds of intelligence? We turn now to various theories of intelligence that address the issue.

▲▲▲

Theories of Intelligence: Are There Different Kinds of Intelligence?

G or g-factor: The single, general factor for mental ability assumed to underlie intelligence in some early theories of intelligence.

Fluid intelligence: Intelligence that reflects information-processing capabilities, reasoning, and memory.

Crystallized intelligence: The accumulation of information, skills, and strategies that are learned through experience and can be applied in problem-solving situations.

Perhaps you see yourself as a good writer but as someone who lacks ability in math. Or maybe you view yourself as a "science" person who easily masters physics but has few strengths in literature. Perhaps you view yourself as generally fairly smart, with intelligence that permits you to excel across domains.

The different ways in which people view their own talents mirrors a question that psychologists have grappled with: Is intelligence a single, general ability, or is it multifaceted and related to specific abilities? Early psychologists interested in intelligence assumed that there was a single, general factor for mental ability, which they called **g,** or the **g-factor** (Spearman, 1927). This general intelligence factor was thought to underlie performance in every aspect of intelligence, and it was the g-factor that was presumably being measured on tests of intelligence. However, more recent theories see intelligence in multidimensional terms (Sternberg & Hedlund, 2002; Tenopyr, 2002; Stankov, 2003).

FLUID AND CRYSTALLIZED INTELLIGENCE

Some psychologists suggest that there are two different kinds of intelligence: fluid intelligence and crystallized intelligence. **Fluid intelligence** reflects information-processing capabilities, reasoning, and memory. If we were asked to solve an analogy, group a series of letters according to some criterion, or remember a set of numbers, we would be using fluid intelligence (Catell, 1987; Kane & Engle, 2002).

In contrast, **crystallized intelligence** is the accumulation of information, skills, and strategies that people have learned through experience and that they can apply in problem-solving situations. We would be likely to rely on crystallized intelligence, for instance, if we were asked to participate in a discussion about the solution to the causes of poverty, a task that allows us to draw on our own past experiences and knowledge of the world. In contrast to fluid intelligence, which reflects a more general kind of intelligence, crystallized

Piloting a helicopter requires the use of both fluid intelligence and crystallized intelligence. Which of the two kinds of intelligence do you believe is more important for such a task?

intelligence is more a reflection of the culture in which a person is raised. The differences between fluid intelligence and crystallized intelligence become particularly evident in the elderly, who show declines in fluid, but not crystallized, intelligence (Schaie, 1993, 1994; Schretlen et al., 2000; Zimprich & Martin, 2002).

Other theoreticians conceive of intelligence as encompassing even more components. For example, Louis Thurstone (1938) suggested there are seven factors, which he called primary mental abilities, and J. P. Guilford (1985) said there are 150!

"To be perfectly frank, I'm not nearly as smart as you seem to think I am."

GARDNER'S MULTIPLE INTELLIGENCES: THE MANY WAYS OF SHOWING INTELLIGENCE

In his consideration of intelligence, psychologist Howard Gardner has taken an approach very different from traditional thinking about the topic. Gardner argues that rather than asking "How smart are you?" we should be asking a different question: "How are you smart?" In answering the latter question, Gardner has developed a theory of *multiple intelligences* that has become quite influential (Gardner, 2000).

Gardner argues that we have at a minimum eight different forms of intelligence, each relatively independent of the others: musical, bodily kinesthetic, logical-mathematical, linguistic, spatial, interpersonal, intrapersonal, and naturalist. (Figure 1 describes the eight types of intelligence, with some of Gardner's examples of people who excel in each type.) In Gardner's view, each of the multiple intelligences is linked to an independent system in the brain. Furthermore, he suggests that there may be even more types of intelligence, such as *existential intelligence,* which involves identifying and thinking about the fundamental questions of human existence. For example, the Dalai Lama might exemplify this type of intelligence (Gardner, 1999, 2000).

Although Gardner illustrates his conception of the specific types of intelligence with descriptions of well-known people, each person has the same eight kinds of intelligence, although in different degrees. Moreover, although the eight basic types of intelligence are presented individually, Gardner suggests that these separate intelligences do not operate in isolation. Normally, any activity encompasses several kinds of intelligence working together.

The concept of multiple intelligences has led to the development of intelligence tests that include questions in which more than one answer can be correct, providing an opportunity for test takers to demonstrate creative thinking. In addition, many educators have embraced the concept of multiple intelligences, designing classroom curricula that are meant to draw on different aspects of intelligence (Armstrong, 2000, 2003).

PowerWeb: Should Psychology Adopt a Theory of Multiple Intelligences?

www.mhhe.com/feldmanup7

PowerWeb: Who Owns Intelligence?

www.mhhe.com/feldmanup7

IS INFORMATION PROCESSING INTELLIGENCE?

One of the newer contributions to understanding intelligence comes from the work of cognitive psychologists who take an *information-processing approach.* They assert that the way people store material in memory and use that material to solve intellectual tasks provides the most accurate measure of intelligence. Consequently, rather than focusing on the structure of intelligence or its underlying content or dimensions, information-processing approaches examine the *processes* involved in producing intelligent behavior (Sternberg, 1990; Deary & Stough, 1996; Embretson, 1996).

For example, research shows that people with high scores on tests of intelligence spend more time on the initial encoding stages of problems, identifying the parts of a problem and retrieving relevant information from long-term memory, than do

1. Musical intelligence (skills in tasks involving music). Case example:

When he was 3, Yehudi Menuhin was smuggled into San Francisco Orchestra concerts by his parents. By the time he was 10 years old, Menuhin was an international performer.

2. Bodily kinesthetic intelligence (skills in using the whole body or various portions of it in the solution of problems or in the construction of products or displays, exemplified by dancers, athletes, actors, and surgeons). Case example:

Fifteen-year-old Babe Ruth played third base. During one game, his team's pitcher was doing very poorly and Babe loudly criticized him from third base. Brother Matthias, the coach, called out, "Ruth, if you know so much about it, *you* pitch!" Ruth said later that at the very moment he took the pitcher's mound, he *knew* he was supposed to be a pitcher.

3. Logical-mathematical intelligence (skills in problem-solving and scientific thinking). Case example:

Barbara McClintock, who won the Nobel Prize in medicine, describes one of her breakthroughs, which came after thinking about a problem for half an hour . . .: "Suddenly I jumped and ran back to the (corn) field. At the top of the field (the others were still at the bottom) I shouted, 'Eureka, I have it!'"

4. Linguistic intelligence (skills involved in the production and use of language). Case example:

At the age of 10, T. S. Eliot created a magazine called *Fireside*, to which he was the sole contributor.

5. Spatial intelligence (skills involving spatial configurations, such as those used by artists and architects). Case example:

Natives of the Truk Islands navigate at sea without instruments. During the actual trip, the navigator must envision mentally a reference island as it passes under a particular star and from that he computes the number of segments completed, the proportion of the trip remaining, and any corrections in heading.

6. Interpersonal intelligence (skills in interacting with others, such as sensitivity to the moods, tempera-ments, motivations, and intentions of others). Case example:

When Anne Sullivan began instructing the deaf and blind Helen Keller, her task was one that had eluded others for years. Yet, just two weeks after begin-ning her work with Keller, Sullivan achieved great success.

7. Intrapersonal intelligence (knowledge of the internal aspects of oneself; access to one's own feelings and emotions). Case example:

In her essay "A Sketch of the Past," Virginia Woolf displays deep insight into her own inner life through these lines, describing her reaction to several specific memories from her childhood that still, in adulthood, shock her: "Though I still have the peculiarity that I receive these sudden shocks, they are now always welcome; after the first surprise, I always feel instantly that they are particularly valuable. And so I go on to suppose that the shock-receiving capacity is what makes me a writer."

8. Naturalist intelligence (ability to identify and classify patterns in nature). Case example:

During prehistoric times, hunter/gatherers would rely on naturalist intelligence to identify what flora and fauna were edible. People who are adept at distinguishing nuances between large numbers of similar objects may be expressing naturalist intelligence abilities.

FIGURE 1 Howard Gardner believes that there are eight major kinds of intelligences, correspon-ding to abilities in different domains. In what area does your greatest intelligence reside, and why do you think you have particular strengths in that area? (Source: Adapted from Gardner, 2000.)

people with lower scores. This initial emphasis on recalling relevant information pays off in the end; those who use this approach are more successful in finding solutions than are those who spend relatively less time on the initial stages (Sternberg, 1982, 1990; Deary & Stough, 1996).

Other information-processing approaches examine the sheer speed of processing. For example, research shows that the speed with which people are able to retrieve information from memory is related to verbal intelligence. In general, people with high scores on measures of intelligence react more quickly on a variety of information-processing tasks, ranging from reactions to flashing lights to distinguishing between letters. The speed of information processing, then, may underlie differences in intelligence (Hunt, 1983; Deary & Stough, 1996; Siegler, 1998).

The Biological Basis of Intelligence

Using brain-scanning methods, researchers have identified several areas of the brain that relate to the intelligence. For example, according to the findings of cognitive scientist John Duncan and colleagues, the brains of people completing intelligence test questions in both verbal and spatial domains show activation in a similar location: the lateral prefrontal cortex (see Figure 2). That area is above the outer edge of the eyebrow, about where people rest their heads in the palms of their hands if they are thinking hard about a problem. This area of the brain is critical to juggling many pieces of information simultaneously and solving new problems (Duncan et al., 2000; Duncan & Miller, 2002).

These findings suggest that there is a global "workspace" in the brain that organizes and coordinates information, helping to transfer material to other parts of the brain. In this view, the functioning of the workspace represents general intelligence, with the workspace integrating and coordinating specialized processing that is being carried out in other areas of the brain (Gray, Chabris, & Braver, 2003).

Spatial domains

Verbal domains

FIGURE 2 The lateral prefrontal cortex is activated when the brain is confronted with problems that involve both verbal and spatial domains. These results suggest that there is a specific area of the brain that serves as the brain's center for organizing and coordinating information. (Source: Duncan et al., 2000.)

Research using nonhumans has also begun to help us better understand the biological underpinnings of intelligence. For example, rats raised in enriched environments (meaning an environment containing more toys, tunnels, and so on) develop more complex connections between neurons, along with more rapid learning and better memory. Other studies show differences in metabolism (the rate at which food is converted to energy and expended by the body) that seem to be related to intelligence (Haier, 1993; Rampon et al., 2000).

Ultimately, the search for the biological underpinnings of intelligence will not lead in a single direction. Instead, the most plausible scenario is that there are multiple areas of the brain, as well as multiple kinds of functioning, that are related to intelligent behavior.

Practical Intelligence and Emotional Intelligence: Toward a More Intelligent View of Intelligence

Consider the following situation:

> An employee who reports to one of your subordinates has asked to talk with you about waste, poor management practices and possible violations of both company policy and the law on the part of your subordinate. You have been in your present position only a year, but in that time you have had no indications of trouble about the subordinate in question. Neither you nor your company has an "open door" policy, so it is expected that employees should take their concerns to their immediate supervisors before bringing a matter to the attention of anyone else. The employee who wishes to meet with you has not discussed this matter with her supervisors because of its delicate nature (Sternberg, 1998, p. 17).

Your response to this situation has a lot to do with your future success in a business career, according to its author, psychologist Robert Sternberg. The question is one of a series designed to help give an indication of your intelligence. However, it is not traditional intelligence that the question is designed to tap, but rather intelligence of a particular kind: practical intelligence. **Practical intelligence** is intelligence related to overall success in living (Wagner, 1997, 2000; Sternberg, 2000, 2002; Sternberg & Hedlund, 2002).

Practical intelligence: Intelligence related to overall success in living.

Noting that traditional tests were designed to relate to academic success, Sternberg points to evidence showing that most traditional measures of intelligence do not relate particularly well to *career* success (McClelland, 1993). Specifically, although successful business executives usually score at least moderately well on intelligence tests, the rate at which they advance and their ultimate business achievements are only minimally associated with traditional measures of their intelligence.

Sternberg argues that career success requires a very different type of intelligence from that required for academic success. Whereas academic success is based on knowledge of a particular information base obtained from reading and listening, practical intelligence is learned mainly through observation of others' behavior. People who are high in practical intelligence are able to learn general norms and principles and apply them appropriately. Consequently, practical intelligence tests, like the one shown in Figure 3, measure the ability to employ broad principles in solving everyday problems (Sternberg et al., 1995; Polk, 1997).

Some psychologists broaden the concept of practical intelligence even further beyond the intellectual realm and consider intelligence involving emotions.

You are given a map of an entertainment park. You walk from the lemonade stand to the computer games arcade. Your friend walks from the shooting gallery to the roller coaster. Which of these are you BOTH most likely to pass? (a) the merry-go-round, (b) the music hall, (c) the pizza stand, or (d) the dog show.

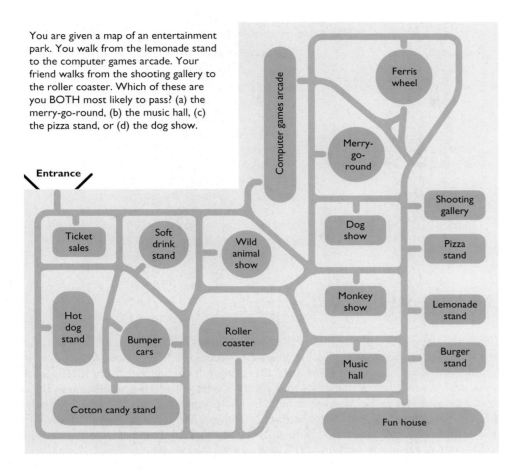

FIGURE 3 Most standard tests of intelligence primarily measure analytical skills; more comprehensive tests measure creative and practical abilities as well. (Source: Sternberg, 2000, p. 389.)

Emotional intelligence is the set of skills that underlie the accurate assessment, evaluation, expression, and regulation of emotions (Matthews, Zeidner, & Roberts, 2003; Mayer et al., 2003).

According to psychologist Daniel Goleman (1995), emotional intelligence underlies the ability to get along well with others. It provides us with an understanding of what other people are feeling and experiencing and permits us to respond appropriately to others' needs. Emotional intelligence is the basis of empathy for others, self-awareness, and social skills.

Abilities in emotional intelligence may help explain why people with only modest scores on traditional intelligence tests can be quite successful, despite their lack of traditional intelligence. High emotional intelligence may enable an individual to tune into others' feelings, permitting a high degree of responsiveness to others.

Although the notion of emotional intelligence makes sense, it has yet to be quantified in a rigorous manner. Furthermore, the view that emotional intelligence is so important that skills related to it should be taught in school has raised concerns among some educators. They suggest that the nurturance of emotional intelligence is best left to students' families, especially because there is no well-specified set of criteria for what constitutes emotional intelligence (Sleek, 1997; Becker, 2003).

Still, the notion of emotional intelligence reminds us that there are many ways to demonstrate intelligent behavior—just as there are multiple views of the nature of intelligence (Fox & Spector, 2000). Figure 4 presents a summary of the different approaches used by psychologists.

Emotional intelligence: The set of skills that underlie the accurate assessment, evaluation, expression, and regulation of emotions.

PowerWeb: What's Your Emotional IQ?

www.mhhe.com/feldmanup7

FIGURE 4 Just as there are many views of the nature of intelligence, there are also numerous ways to demonstrate intelligent behavior. This summary provides an overview of the various approaches used by psychologists.

Major Approaches to Intelligence	
Approach	**Characteristics**
IQ tests	General measures of intelligence.
Fluid and crystallized intelligence	Fluid intelligence relates to reasoning, memory, and information-processing capabilities; crystallized intelligence relates to information, skills, and strategies learned through experience.
Gardner's multiple intelligences	Eight independent forms of intelligence.
Information-processing approaches	Intelligence is reflected in the ways people store and use material to solve intellectual tasks.
Practical intelligence	Intelligence in terms of nonacademic, career, and personal success.
Emotional intelligence	Intelligence that provides an understanding of what other people are feeling and experiencing, and permits us to respond appropriately to others' needs.

Assessing Intelligence

Given the variety of approaches to the components of intelligence, it is not surprising that measuring intelligence has proved challenging. Psychologists who study intelligence have focused much of their attention on the development of **intelligence tests,** and have relied on such tests to quantify a person's level of intelligence. These tests have proved to be of great benefit in identifying students in need of special attention in school, diagnosing cognitive difficulties, and helping people make optimal educational and vocational choices. At the same time, their use has proved quite controversial, raising important social and educational issues.

Historically, the first effort at intelligence testing was based on an uncomplicated, but completely wrong, assumption: that the size and shape of a person's head could be used as an objective measure of intelligence. The idea was put forward by Sir Francis Galton (1822–1911), an eminent English scientist whose ideas in other domains proved to be considerably better than his notions about intelligence.

Galton's motivation to identify people of high intelligence stemmed from his prejudices. He sought to demonstrate the natural superiority of people of high social class (of which he was one) by showing that intelligence is inherited. He hypothesized that head configuration, being genetically determined, is related to brain size, and therefore related to intelligence.

Galton's theories proved wrong on virtually every count. Head size and shape are not related to intellectual performance, and subsequent research has found little relationship between brain size and intelligence. However, Galton's work did have at least one desirable result: He was the first person to suggest that intelligence could be quantified and measured in an objective manner (Jensen, 2002).

BINET AND THE DEVELOPMENT OF IQ TESTS

After Galton's efforts, the first real intelligence tests were developed by the French psychologist Alfred Binet (1857–1911). His tests followed from a simple premise: If performance on certain tasks or test items improved with *chronological*, or physical, age, performance could be used to distinguish more intelligent people from less intelligent ones within a particular age group. On the basis of this principle, Binet devised the first formal intelligence test, which was designed to identify the "dullest" students in the Paris school system in order to provide them with remedial aid.

Binet began by presenting tasks to same-age students who had been labeled "bright" or "dull" by their teachers. If a task could be completed by the bright students but not by the dull ones, he retained that task as a proper test item; otherwise it was discarded. In the end he came up with a test that distinguished between the

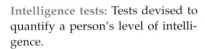

Intelligence tests: Tests devised to quantify a person's level of intelligence.

Alfred Binet

bright and dull groups, and—with further work—one that distinguished among children in different age groups (Binet & Simon, 1916; Sternberg & Jarvin, 2003).

On the basis of the Binet test, children were assigned a score relating to their **mental age,** the average age of individuals who achieve a particular level of performance on a test. For example, if the average 8-year-old answered, say, 45 items correctly on a test, anyone who answered 45 items correctly would be assigned a mental age of 8 years. Consequently, whether the person taking the test was 20 years old or 5 years old, he or she would have the same mental age of 8 years.

Assigning a mental age to students provided an indication of their general level of performance. However, it did not allow for adequate comparisons among people of different chronological ages. By using mental age alone, for instance, we might assume that a 20-year-old responding at a 18-year-old's level would be as bright as a 5-year-old answering at a 3-year-old's level, when actually the 5-year-old would be displaying a much greater *relative* degree of slowness.

A solution to the problem came in the form of the **intelligence quotient,** or **IQ,** a score that takes into account an individual's mental *and* chronological ages. To calculate an IQ score, the following formula is used, in which *MA* stands for mental age and *CA* for chronological age:

$$\text{IQ score} = \frac{\text{MA}}{\text{CA}} \times 100$$

Using this formula, we can return to the earlier example of an 20-year-old performing at a mental age of 18 and calculate an IQ score of $(18/20) \times 100 = 90$. In contrast, the 5-year-old performing at a mental age of 3 comes out with a considerably lower IQ score: $(3/5) \times 100 = 60$.

As a bit of trial and error with the formula will show you, anyone who has a mental age equal to his or her chronological age will have an IQ equal to 100. Moreover, people with a mental age that is greater than their chronological age will have IQs that exceed 100.

Although the basic principles behind the calculation of an IQ score still hold, today IQ scores are figured in a different manner and are known as *deviation IQ scores.* First, the average test score for everyone of the same age who takes the test is determined, and that average score is assigned an IQ of 100. Then, with the aid of statistical techniques that calculate the differences (or "deviations") between each score and the average, IQ scores are assigned.

As you can see in Figure 5, approximately two-thirds of all individuals fall within 15 IQ points above and below the average score of 100. As scores increase or fall beyond that range, the percentage of people in a category falls considerably.

Mental age: The average age of individuals who achieve a particular level of performance on a test.

Intelligence quotient (IQ): A score that takes into account an individual's mental *and* chronological ages.

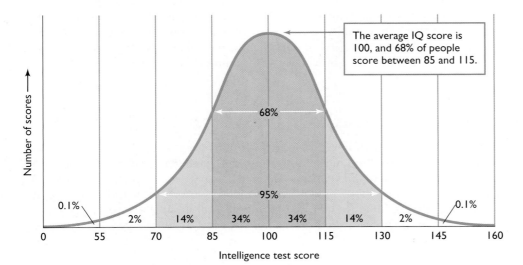

FIGURE 5 The average and most common IQ score is 100, and 68 percent of all people are within a 30-point range centered on 100. Some 95 percent of the population have scores that are within 30 points above or below 100, and 99.8 percent have scores that are between 55 and 145.

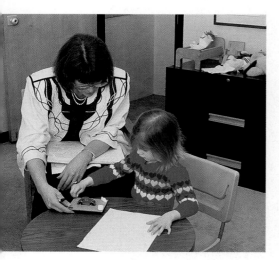

Now in its fifth edition, the Stanford-Binet test consists of a series of items that vary in nature according to the age of the person being tested. What can we learn about a person from a test of this type?

CONTEMPORARY IQ TESTS: GAUGING INTELLIGENCE

Remnants of Binet's original intelligence test are still with us, although the test has been revised in significant ways. Now in its fifth edition and called the *Stanford-Binet Intelligence Scale, Fifth Edition,* the test consists of a series of items that vary in nature according to the age of the person being tested (Roid, 2003). For example, young children are asked to copy figures or answer questions about everyday activities. Older people are asked to solve analogies, explain proverbs, and describe similarities that underlie sets of words.

The test is administered orally. An examiner begins by finding a mental age level at which a person is able to answer all the questions correctly, and then moves on to successively more difficult problems. When a mental age level is reached at which no items can be answered, the test is over. By examining the pattern of correct and incorrect responses, the examiner is able to compute an IQ score for the person being tested. In addition, the Stanford-Binet test provides separate subscores, providing clues to a test-taker's particular strengths and weaknesses.

The IQ test most frequently used in the United States was devised by psychologist David Wechsler and is known as the *Wechsler Adult Intelligence Scale–III,* or, more commonly, the *WAIS-III.* There is also a children's version, the *Wechsler Intelligence Scale for Children–IV,* or *WISC-IV.* Both the WAIS-III and the WISC-IV have two major parts: a verbal scale and a performance (or nonverbal) scale.

As you can see from the sample questions in Figure 6, the verbal and performance scales include questions of very different types. Verbal tasks consist of more traditional kinds of problems, including vocabulary definition and comprehension of various concepts. In contrast, the performance (nonverbal) part involves the timed assembly of small objects and the arrangement of pictures in a logical order. Although an individual's scores on the verbal and performance sections of the test are generally within close range of each other, the scores of a person with a language deficiency or a background of severe environmental deprivation may show a relatively large discrepancy between the two sections. By providing separate scores, the WAIS-III and WISC-IV give a more precise picture of a person's specific abilities compared with other IQ tests (Kaufman & Lichtenberger, 1999).

Because the Stanford-Binet, WAIS-III, and WISC-IV all require individualized, one-on-one administration, it is relatively difficult and time-consuming to administer and score them on a large-scale basis. Consequently, there are now a number of IQ tests that allow group administration. Rather than having one examiner ask one person at a time to respond to individual items, group IQ tests are strictly paper-and-pencil tests. The primary advantage of group tests is their ease of administration (Anastasi & Urbina, 1997).

However, sacrifices are made in group testing that in some cases may outweigh the benefits. For instance, group tests generally offer fewer kinds of questions than do tests administered individually. Furthermore, people may be more motivated to perform at their highest ability level when working on a one-to-one basis with a test administrator than they are in a group. Finally, in some cases, it is simply impossible to employ group tests, particularly with young children or people with unusually low IQs (Aiken, 1996).

ACHIEVEMENT AND APTITUDE TESTS

IQ tests are not the only kind of tests that you may have taken during the course of your schooling. Two other kinds of tests, related to intelligence but designed to measure somewhat different phenomena, are achievement tests and aptitude tests. An **achievement test** is a test designed to determine a person's level of knowledge in a specific subject area. Rather than measuring general ability, as an intelligence test does, an achievement test concentrates on the specific material a person has learned.

Achievement test: A test designed to determine a person's level of knowledge in a given subject area.

WAIS-III		
NAME	**GOAL OF ITEM**	**EXAMPLE**
VERBAL SCALE		
Information	Assess general information	Who wrote Tom Sawyer?
Comprehension	Assess understanding and evaluation of social norms and past experience	Why is copper often used for electrical wires?
Arithmetic	Assess math reasoning through verbal problems	Three women divided eighteen golf balls equally among themselves. How many golf balls did each person receive?
Similarities	Test understanding of how objects or concepts are alike, tapping abstract reasoning	In what way are a circle and a triangle alike?
PERFORMANCE SCALE		
Digit symbol	Assess speed of learning	Test-taker must learn what symbols correspond to what digits, and then must replace a multidigit number with the appropriate symbols.
Matrix reasoning	Tests spatial reasoning	Test-taker must decide which of the five possibilities replaces the question mark and completes the sequence.
Block design item	Tests understanding of relationship of parts to whole	Problems require test-takers to reproduce a design in fixed amount of time.

(continues)

FIGURE 6 Typical kinds of items found on the verbal and performance (nonverbal) scales of the Wechsler Adult Intelligence Scales (WAIS-III) and the Wechsler Intelligence Scale for Children (WISC-IV).

WISC-IV		
NAME	**GOAL OF ITEM**	**EXAMPLE**
VERBAL SCALE		
Information	Assess general information	How many nickels make a dime?
Comprehension	Assess understanding and evaluation of social norms and past experience	What is the advantage of keeping money in the bank?
Arithmetic	Assess math reasoning through verbal problems	If two buttons cost 15 cents, what will be the cost of a dozen buttons?
Similarities	Test understanding of how objects or concepts are alike, tapping abstract reasoning	In what way are an hour and a week alike?
PERFORMANCE SCALE		
Digit symbol	Assess speed of learning	Match symbols to numbers using key.
Picture completion	Visual memory and attention	Identify what is missing.
Object assembly	Test understanding of relationship of parts to wholes	Put pieces together to form a whole.

FIGURE 6 concluded

Source: Simulated items similar to those in the *Wechsler Intelligence Scale for Children.* Copyright © 1949, 1955, 1974, 1981, 1991, 1997 by The Psychological Corporation, a Harcourt Assessment Company. Reproduced by permission. All rights reserved. *"Wechsler Intelligence Scale for Children,"* "WISC," "WISC-III," *"Wechsler Adult Intelligence Scale,"* and "WAIS" are trademarks of The Psychological Corporation registered in the United States of America and/or other jurisdictions.

High school students sometimes take specialized achievement tests in particular areas such as world history and chemistry as a college entrance requirement; lawyers must pass an achievement test (in the form of the bar exam) in order to practice law.

An **aptitude test** is designed to predict a person's ability in a particular area or line of work. Most of us take one or the other of the best-known aptitude tests in the process of pursuing admission to college: the SAT and the ACT. The SAT and ACT are meant to predict how well people will do in college, and the scores have proved over the years to be moderately correlated with college grades (Hoffman, 2001).

Although in theory the distinction between aptitude tests and achievement tests is precise, it is difficult to develop an aptitude test that does not rely at least in part on past achievement. For example, the SAT has been strongly criticized for being less an aptitude test (predicting college success) than an achievement test (assessing prior performance). (For more on how tests are used, see the *Applying Psychology in the 21st Century* box.)

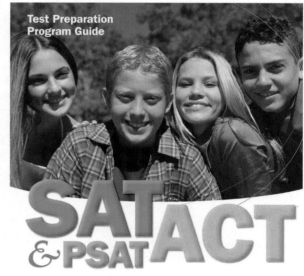

Real expertise. Real strategies. Real results.

Thousands of students enroll in courses in an effort to boost their SAT and GRE scores.

RELIABILITY AND VALIDITY: TAKING THE MEASURE OF TESTS

When we use a ruler, we expect to find that it measures an inch in the same way it did the last time we used it. When we weigh ourselves on the bathroom scale, we hope that the variations we see on the scale are due to changes in our weight and not to errors on the part of the scale (unless the change in weight is in an unwanted direction!).

In the same way, we hope that psychological tests have **reliability**—that they measure consistently what they are trying to measure. We need to be sure that each time we administer the test, a test-taker will achieve the same results—assuming that nothing about the person has changed relevant to what is being measured.

Aptitude test: A test designed to predict a person's ability in a particular area or line of work.

Reliability: The property by which tests measure consistently what they are trying to measure.

When High IQ Keeps You from Getting a Job: Are You Too Smart for the Job You Want?

Wanted: One not-so-smart police officer.

Although that is not what the advertisement for police officers in New London, Connecticut, said, the sentiment would not have been inaccurate. The official hiring policy prevents people who score too low or too *high* on an employment test administered by the town to be considered for a position as a police officer (Allen, 1999).

The hiring standards came to light during a three-year court battle concerning an applicant for a position as a police officer who was refused even an interview. The reason? He scored 33 out of 50 on an exam used by the police department to screen applicants, and anyone who scored over 27 was considered too skilled to do a good job as a police officer.

The screening test used by the police department, the Wonderlic Personnel Test (WPT), has been utilized by thousands of employers throughout the United States and has been given to many millions of people since it was devised. The WPT, which consists of fifty items that must be answered in twelve minutes, is designed to provide a range of scores for people who are likely to thrive in a specific profession, with the particular range dependent on the nature of the particular job (see Figure 7). Although it is not a traditional IQ measure, the test gauges cognitive abilities, such as learning ability, skill in understanding instructions, and problem-solving potential. To do well on the test, applicants must rely upon both fluid intelligence and crystallized intelligence (Bell et al., 2002; Wonderlic, 2003).

The WPT is typically used to provide minimum scores for particular professions, allowing employers to screen out potential employees who lack the skills to succeed on the job. The use of a test to

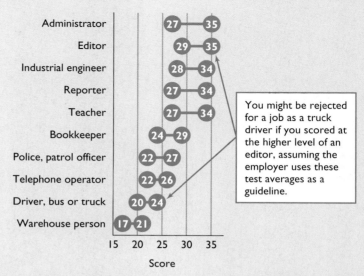

FIGURE 7 Based on a scale from 1 to 50, these are suggested minimum and maximum scores for selected professions as determined by a pre-employment test developed by a private human resources firm. (Source: Wonderlic, 1999.)

screen out people who score too high is less common. The rationale for excluding applicants who score too high, according to the New London police department, is that much police work is routine: Highly intelligent police officers become bored and leave the job soon after they have received their expensive initial training.

Critics of the police department's position point out that it takes considerable intelligence to deal with the complex situations that often face police officers, such as the complicated social predicaments involved in domestic disputes. Moreover, some decisions must be made instantly and under enormous pressure—situations in which intelligence would clearly be beneficial. Furthermore, research suggests that intelligent workers

are useful as "insurance" in crisis situations, as they may be better equipped than their less intelligent colleagues to assume extra responsibilities and improvise creative solutions. In addition, one could argue that it is better to have relatively frequent turnover of intelligent workers than to be burdened with not-so-intelligent employees for long periods (Bulmahn & Krakel, 2002).

Despite these criticisms, courts have ruled that employers have the right to exclude potential workers on the basis of their being too skilled, as long as the guidelines are applied uniformly to all job seekers. As a consequence, job applicants have a new worry to add to their many anxieties—that they may score too high on a job test.

RETHINK

How do you think employers established that some scores on the tests described above were too high for certain jobs? Do you think it is reasonable to exclude people from certain jobs on the basis of high test scores? How might a workforce segregated on the basis of intelligence affect the quality of the goods you buy?

Suppose, for instance, that when you first took the SAT exams, you scored a 400 on the verbal section of the test. Then, after taking the test again a few months later, you scored a 700. Upon receiving your new score, you might well stop celebrating for a moment to question whether the test is reliable, for it is unlikely that your abilities could have changed enough to raise your score by 300 points.

But suppose your score changed hardly at all, and both times you received a score of about 400. You couldn't complain about a lack of reliability. However, if you knew your verbal skills were above average, you might be concerned that the test did not adequately measure what it was supposed to measure. In sum, the question has now become one of validity rather than reliability. A test has **validity** when it actually measures what it is supposed to measure.

Validity: The property by which tests actually measure what they are supposed to measure.

Knowing that a test is reliable is no guarantee that it is also valid. For instance, Sir Francis Galton assumed that skull size is related to intelligence, and he was able to measure skull size with great reliability. However, the measure of skull size was not valid—it had nothing to do with intelligence. In this case, then, we have reliability without validity.

However, if a test is unreliable, it cannot be valid. Assuming that all other factors—motivation to score well, knowledge of the material, health, and so forth—are similar, if a person scores high the first time he or she takes a specific test and low the second time, the test cannot be measuring what it is supposed to measure. Therefore, the test is both unreliable and not valid.

Test validity and reliability are prerequisites for accurate assessment of intelligence—as well as for any other measurement task carried out by psychologists. Consequently, the measures of personality carried out by personality psychologists, clinical psychologists' assessments of psychological disorders, and social psychologists' measures of attitudes must meet the tests of validity and reliability for the results to be meaningful (Thompson, 2002; Feldt, 2003).

Assuming that a test is both valid and reliable, one further step is necessary in order to interpret the meaning of a particular test-taker's score: the establishment of norms. **Norms** are standards of test performance that permit the comparison of one person's score on a test to the scores of others who have taken the same test. For example, a norm permits test-takers to know that they have scored, say, in the top 15 percent of those who have taken the test previously. Tests for which norms have been developed are known as *standardized tests.*

Norms: Standards of test performance that permit the comparison of one person's score on a test with the scores of others who have taken the same test.

The basic scheme for developing norms is for test designers to calculate the average score achieved by a particular group of people for whom the test has been designed. The test designers then can determine the extent to which each person's score differs from the scores of the others who have taken the test in the past. Test-takers are then able to consider the meaning of their raw scores relative to the scores of others who have taken the test, giving them a qualitative sense of their performance.

Obviously, the samples of test-takers who are employed in the establishment of norms are critical to the norming process. The people used to determine norms must be representative of the individuals to whom the test is directed. (To learn more about testing issues, try **Interactivity 26–1.**)

INTERACTIVITY 26–1

Testing issues

ADAPTIVE TESTING: USING COMPUTERS TO ASSESS PERFORMANCE

Ensuring that tests are reliable and valid, and are based on appropriate norms, has become even more critical with the introduction of computers to administer standardized tests. The Educational Testing Service (ETS)—the company that devises the SAT and the Graduate Record Examination (GRE), used for college and graduate school admission—is moving to computer administration of all its standardized tests.

In computerized versions, not only are test questions viewed and answered on a computer, the test itself is individualized. Under *adaptive testing,* students do not necessarily receive identical sets of test questions. Instead, the computer first presents a randomly selected question of moderate difficulty. If the test-taker answers it correctly, the computer will then present a randomly chosen item of slightly greater difficulty. If the answer is wrong, the computer will present a slightly easier item. Each question becomes slightly harder or easier than the question preceding it, depending on whether the previous response is correct. Ultimately, the greater the number of difficult questions answered correctly, the higher the score (Wainer et al., 2000; Chang & Ansley, 2003; see Figure 8).

Because the test is able to pinpoint a test-taker's level of proficiency fairly quickly, the total time spent taking the exam is shorter than it is with a traditional exam. Test-takers are not forced to spend a great deal of time answering questions that are either much easier or much harder than they can handle.

Critics of computerized adaptive testing suggest that it may discriminate against test takers who have limited access to computers and thus may have less practice

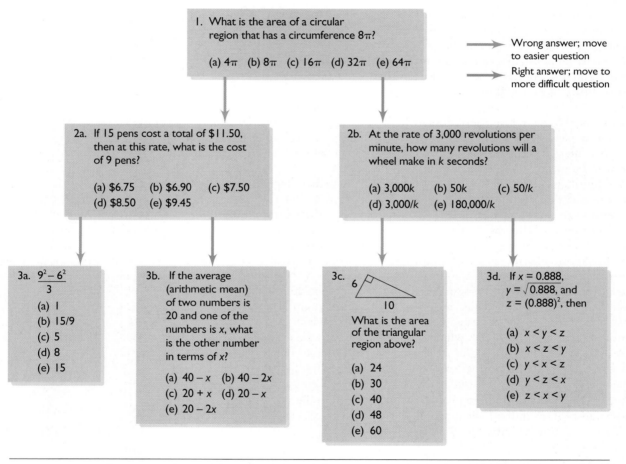

Answers: 1. 16π, 2a. $6.90, 2b. 50k, 3a. 15, 3b. $40 - x$, 3c. 24, 3d. $z < x < y$

FIGURE 8 Adaptive testing. In the Graduate Record Examination, the computer randomly selects a first question of medium difficulty. If the test-taker answers the question correctly, the computer poses a more difficult question. Once the test-taker gives an incorrect answer, he or she is given a question at the next easiest level, as illustrated in this example (*The New York Times,* 1993, p. B9). Test-takers are graded based on the level of difficulty of the questions they answer correctly, meaning that two test-takers who answer the same number of questions correctly can end up with very different scores. What do you think are the drawbacks of adaptive testing of this sort? Do you think such tests may discriminate against test-takers who are less familiar with computers compared with those who have easy access to them?

with them or may be more intimidated by the testing medium. ETS disputes this claim, although some of its own research shows that women and older test-takers display greater anxiety at the beginning of the test. Despite this anxiety, however, their performance ultimately is not affected, and most research suggests that computerized adaptive testing provides scores equivalent to those of traditional paper-and-pencil measures for most types of testing (Tonidandel, Quinones, & Adams, 2002).

Even though psychologists disagree about the nature of intelligence, intelligence tests—as well as many other kinds of tests—are still widely used in a variety of situations. For example, if you are thinking about becoming a physician, a lawyer, or almost any other kind of professional in a field that requires advanced training, you will have to take a formal exam in order to be accepted for postundergraduate training.

BECOMING AN INFORMED CONSUMER
of Psychology
Scoring Better on Standardized Tests

If you do have to take such an exam, you can do several things to maximize your score, including the following (Holmes & Keffer, 1995; Bronner, 1998; Lurie, 2002):

▶ *Learn as much as you can about the test before you take it.* Know what sections will be on the test and how much each section is worth.

▶ *Practice.* Try as many practice tests as you can find. The more practice you have, the easier it will be when you actually take the test.

▶ *If the test is administered on a computer, as it probably will be, take practice tests on a computer.* The more familiar you are with computers, the more at ease you will feel when you sit down to take the test.

▶ *Time yourself carefully.* Don't spend too much time on early items at the expense of later ones. Your goal should be not perfection, but maximizing the number of correct responses you get.

▶ *Be aware of the scoring policy.* If you are not penalized for wrong answers, guess. If there are penalties, be more conservative about guessing.

▶ *If it is a paper-and-pencil test, complete answer sheets accurately.* Check and check again. If the test is on a computer, check your answer thoroughly before going on to the next question, because you won't be able to go back and change your answer once you've submitted it.

RECAP/EVALUATE/RETHINK

RECAP

What are the different definitions and conceptions of intelligence?

▶ Because intelligence can take many forms, defining it is challenging. One commonly accepted view is that intelligence is the capacity to understand the world, think rationally, and use resources effectively when faced with challenges. (p. 294)

▶ The earliest psychologists assumed that there is a general factor for mental ability called *g*. However, later psychologists disputed the view that intelligence is unidimensional. (p. 294)

▶ Some researchers suggest that intelligence can be broken down into fluid intelligence and crystallized intelligence. Gardner's theory of multiple intelligences proposes that there are eight spheres of intelligence. (p. 294)

▶ Information-processing approaches examine the processes underlying intelligent behavior rather than focusing on the structure of intelligence. (p. 295)

▶ Practical intelligence is intelligence related to overall success in living; emotional intelligence is the set of skills that underlie the accurate assessment, evaluation, expression, and regulation of emotions. (p. 298)

What are the major approaches to measuring intelligence, and what do intelligence tests measure?

▶ Intelligence tests have traditionally compared a person's mental age and chronological age to yield an IQ, or intelligence quotient, score. (p. 300)

▶ Specific tests of intelligence include the Stanford-Binet test, the Wechsler Adult Intelligence Scale–III (WAIS-III), and the Wechsler Intelligence Scale for Children–III (WISC-IV). Achievement tests and aptitude tests are other types of standardized tests. (p. 302)

▶ Tests are expected to be both reliable and valid. Reliability refers to the consistency with which a test measures what it is trying to measure. A test has validity when it actually measures what it is supposed to measure. (p. 305)

EVALUATE

1. _____ is a measure of intelligence that takes into account a person's chronological and mental ages.

2. _____ tests predict a person's ability in a specific area; _____ tests determine the specific level of knowledge in an area.

3. Some psychologists make the distinction between _____ intelligence, which reflects reasoning, memory, and information-processing capabilities, and _____ intelligence, which is the information, skills, and strategies that people have learned through experience.

4. Cognitive psychologists use a(n) _____-_____ approach to measure intelligence.

RETHINK

1. Job interviews are really a kind of test. In what ways does a job interview resemble an aptitude test? An achievement test? Do you think job interviews can be shown to have validity? Reliability?

2. If such concepts as fluid and crystallized intelligence do exist, how might they be tested? What applications would each of these types of intelligence have?

Answers to Evaluate Questions

1. IQ; 2. aptitude, achievement; 3. fluid, crystallized; 4. information-processing

KEY TERMS

intelligence p. 294
g or g-factor p. 294
fluid intelligence p. 294
crystallized
intelligence p. 294

practical intelligence p. 298
emotional
intelligence p. 299
intelligence tests p. 300

mental age p. 301
intelligence
quotient (IQ) p. 301
achievement test p. 302

aptitude test p. 305
reliability p. 305
validity p. 307
norms p. 307

Variations in Intellectual Ability

"Hey, hey, hey, Fact Track!" The 11-year-old speaker chose one of his favorite programs . . .

"What is your name?" appeared on the monitor.

"Daniel Skandera," he typed. A menu scrolled up listing the program's possibilities. Daniel chose multiplication facts, Level 1 . . .

Randomly generated multiplication facts flashed on the screen: "4 × 6," "2 × 9," "3 × 3," "7 × 6." Daniel responded, deftly punching in his answers on the computer's numeric key-pad . . .

The computer tallied the results. "You completed 20 problems in 66 seconds. You beat your goal. Problems correct = 20. Congratulations Daniel!" And with that the 11-year-old retreated hastily to the TV room. The Lakers and 76ers were about to tip off for an NBA championship game, and Daniel wanted to see the first half before bedtime (Heward & Orlansky, 1988, p. 100).

If you view people with mental retardation as inept and dull, it is time to revise your perceptions. As in the case of Daniel Skandera, described above, individuals with deficits of intellectual abilities can lead full, rounded lives and in some cases perform well in certain kinds of academic endeavors.

More than 7 million people in the United States have been identified as far enough below average in intelligence that they can be regarded as having a serious deficit. Both those individuals with such low IQs—people with mental retardation—and those with unusually high IQs, or the intellectually gifted, require special attention if they are to reach their full potential.

⒜ ⒜ ⒜

Mental Retardation

Although sometimes thought of as a rare phenomenon, mental retardation occurs in 1 to 3 percent of the population. There is wide variation among those labeled as mentally retarded, in large part because of the inclusiveness of the definition developed by the American Association on Mental Retardation (AAMR). The association suggests that **mental retardation** is a disability characterized by significant limitations both in intellectual functioning and in adaptive behavior involving conceptual, social, and practical adaptive skills (AAMR, 2002).

Although below-average intellectual functioning can be measured in a relatively straightforward manner—using standard IQ tests—it is more difficult to determine how to gauge limitations in particular adaptive skill areas. Ultimately, this imprecision leads to a lack of uniformity in how experts apply the label *mental retardation*. Furthermore, it has resulted in significant variation in the abilities of people who are categorized as mentally retarded, ranging from those who can be taught to work and function with little special attention to those who virtually cannot be trained and

Mental retardation: A condition characterized by significant limitations both in intellectual functioning and in adaptive behavior involving conceptual, social, and practical adaptive skills.

must receive institutional treatment throughout their lives (Negrin & Capute, 1996; Detterman, Gabriel, & Ruthsatz, 2000).

Most people with mental retardation have relatively minor deficits and are classified as having *mild retardation.* These individuals, who have IQ scores ranging from 55 to 69, constitute some 90 percent of all people with mental retardation. Although their development is typically slower than that of their peers, they can function quite independently by adulthood and are able to hold jobs and have families of their own (Bates, Cuvo, Miner, & Korabeck, 2001).

At greater levels of retardation—*moderate retardation* (IQs of 40 to 54), *severe retardation* (IQs of 25 to 39), and *profound retardation* (IQs below 25)—the difficulties are more pronounced. For people with moderate retardation, deficits are obvious early, with language and motor skills lagging behind those of peers. Although these individuals can hold simple jobs, they need to have a moderate degree of supervision throughout their lives. Individuals with severe and profound mental retardation are generally unable to function independently and typically require care for their entire lives.

IDENTIFYING THE ROOTS OF MENTAL RETARDATION

What are the causes of mental retardation? In nearly one-third of the cases there is an identifiable biological reason. The most common biological cause of retardation is Down syndrome. *Down syndrome* results from the presence of an extra chromosome. Fetal alcohol syndrome (caused by a mother's use of alcohol while pregnant) also can produce retardation.

In other cases of mental retardation, an abnormality occurs in the structure of a chromosome. Birth complications, such as a temporary lack of oxygen, may also cause retardation. In some cases, mental retardation occurs after birth, following a head injury, a stroke, or infections such as meningitis (Selikowitz, 1997; Gualtiere, 2003; Plomin, 2003).

However, the majority of cases of mental retardation are classified as *familial retardation,* in which no apparent biological defect exists but there is a history of retardation in the family. Whether the family background of retardation is caused by environmental factors, such as extreme continuous poverty leading to malnutrition, or by some underlying genetic factor is usually impossible to determine (Zigler et al., 2002). Learn more about the causes of mental retardation in **Interactivity 27–1.**

INTERACTIVITY 27–1

Mental retardation

INTEGRATING INDIVIDUALS WITH MENTAL RETARDATION

Regardless of the cause of mental retardation, important advances in the care and treatment of those with retardation have been made in the last several decades. Much of this change was instigated by the Education for All Handicapped Children Act of 1975 (Public Law 94-142). In this federal law, Congress ruled that people with retardation are entitled to a full education and that they must be educated and trained in the *least restrictive environment.* The law increased the educational opportunities for individuals with mental retardation, facilitating their integration into regular classrooms as much as possible—a process known as *mainstreaming* (Lloyd, Kameenui, & Chard, 1997; Katsiyannis, Zhang, & Archwamety, 2002).

The philosophy behind mainstreaming suggests that the interaction of students with and without mental retardation in regular classrooms will improve educational opportunities for those with retardation, increase their social acceptance, and facilitate their integration into society as a whole. Of course, special education classes still exist; some individuals with retardation function at too low a level to benefit from placement in regular classrooms. Moreover, children with mental retardation who are mainstreamed into regular classes typically attend special classes for at least part of the day (Guralnick et al., 1996; Hastings & Oakford, 2003).

Some educators argue that an alternative to mainstreaming, called full inclusion, might be more effective. *Full inclusion* is the integration of all students, even those with the most severe educational disabilities, into regular classes and an avoidance of special, segregated special education classes. Teacher aides are assigned to help the children with special needs progress. Schools with full inclusion have no separate special education classes. However, full inclusion is a controversial practice, and it is not widely applied (Kavale, 2002; Hastings & Oakford, 2003; Praisner, 2003).

The Intellectually Gifted

Another group of people—the intellectually gifted—differ from those with average intelligence as much as do individuals with mental retardation, although in a different manner. Accounting for 2 to 4 percent of the population, the **intellectually gifted** have IQ scores greater than 130.

Although the stereotype associated with the gifted suggests that they are awkward, shy social misfits who are unable to get along well with peers, most research indicates that just the opposite is true. The intellectually gifted are most often outgoing, well-adjusted, popular people who are able to do most things better than the average person can (Winner, 1997, 2000; Harden, 2000; Rizza & Morrison, 2003).

For example, in a long-term study by psychologist Lewis Terman that started in the early 1920s and is still going on, 1,500 children who had IQ scores above 140 were followed and examined periodically over the next sixty years (Terman & Oden, 1947; Sears, 1977). From the start, the members of this group were more physically, academically, and socially capable than their nongifted peers. They were generally healthier, taller, heavier, and stronger than average. Not surprisingly, they did better in school as well. They also showed better social adjustment than average. All these advantages paid off in terms of career success: As a group, the gifted received more awards and distinctions, earned higher incomes, and made more contributions in art and literature than typical individuals. For example, by the time the members of the group were 40 years old, they had collectively written more than 90 books, 375 plays and short stories, and 2,000 articles, and had registered more than 200 patents. Perhaps most important, they reported greater satisfaction in life than the nongifted.

Of course, not every member of the group Terman studied was successful. Furthermore, high intelligence is not a homogeneous quality; a person with a high overall IQ is not necessarily gifted in every academic subject, but may excel in just one or two. A high IQ, then, is not a universal guarantee of success (Shurkin, 1992; Winner, 2000).

Although special programs attempting to overcome the deficits of people with mental retardation abound, programs targeted at the intellectually gifted are more rare. One reason for this lack of attention is that although there are as many gifted individuals as there are those with mental retardation, the definition of *gifted* is vague, especially compared with definitions of mental retardation. Furthermore, there is a persistent view that the gifted ought to be able to "make it on their own"; if they can't, they really weren't gifted in the first place (Robinson, Zigler, & Gallagher, 2000; Parke, 2003).

More enlightened approaches, however, have acknowledged that without some form of special attention, the gifted become bored and frustrated with the pace of their schooling and may never reach their potential. Consequently, programs for the gifted are designed to provide enrichment that allows participants' talents to flourish (Winner, 2000; Moon, Swift, & Shallenberger, 2002; Neber & Heller, 2002).

Intellectually gifted: The 2 to 4 percent of the population who have IQ scores greater than 130.

RECAP/EVALUATE/RETHINK

RECAP

How can the extremes of intelligence be characterized?

▶ The levels of mental retardation include mild, moderate, severe, and profound retardation. (p. 312)

▶ About one-third of the cases of retardation have a known biological cause; Down syndrome is the most common. Most cases, however, are classified as familial retardation, for which there is no known biological cause. (p. 312)

▶ The intellectually gifted are people with IQ scores greater than 130. Intellectually gifted people tend to be healthier and more successful than are the nongifted. (p. 313)

How can we help people reach their full potential?

▶ Advances in the treatment of people with mental retardation include mainstreaming, or the integration of individuals with mental retardation into regular education classrooms as much as possible (along with some participation in segregated special education classes), and full inclusion, in which all students, even those with the most severe educational disabilities, are fully integrated into regular classes (and separate classes are avoided). (p. 313)

EVALUATE

1. The term *mental retardation* is applied specifically to people with an IQ below 60. True or false?
2. _____ is a disorder caused by an extra chromosome that is responsible for some cases of mental retardation.
3. _____ is the process by which students with mental retardation are placed in normal classrooms to facilitate learning and reduce isolation.
4. Most forms of retardation have no identifiable biological cause. True or false?
5. People with high intelligence are generally shy and socially withdrawn. True or false?

RETHINK

1. What advantages and disadvantages do you think full inclusion programs would present for students with mental retardation? For students without mental retardation?
2. Why do you think negative stereotypes persist of gifted individuals and people with mental retardation, even in the face of contrary evidence? How can these stereotypes be changed?

Answers to Evaluate Questions

1. false; the term is used to describe a wide range of people with various degrees of mental impairment; 2. Down syndrome; 3. mainstreaming; 4. true; 5. false; the gifted are generally more socially adept than those with a lower IQ

KEY TERMS

mental retardation p. 311   intellectually gifted p. 313

Group Differences in Intelligence: Genetic and Environmental Determinants

Are traditional IQ tests culturally biased?

Are there racial differences in intelligence?

To what degree is intelligence influenced by the environment, and to what degree by heredity?

Kwang is often washed with a pleck tied to a:

(a) rundel

(b) flink

(c) pove

(d) quirj

If you found this kind of item on an intelligence test, you would probably complain that the test was totally absurd and had nothing to do with your intelligence or anyone else's—and rightly so. How could anyone be expected to respond to items presented in a language that was so unfamiliar?

Yet to some people, even more reasonable questions may appear just as nonsensical. Consider the example of a child raised in a city who is asked about procedures for milking cows, or someone raised in a rural area who is asked about subway ticketing procedures. Obviously, the previous experience of the test-takers would affect their ability to answer correctly. And if such types of questions were included on an IQ test, a critic could rightly contend that the test had more to do with prior experience than with intelligence.

Although IQ tests do not include questions that are so clearly dependent on prior knowledge as questions about cows and subways, the background and experiences of test-takers do have the potential to affect results. In fact, the issue of devising fair intelligence tests that measure knowledge unrelated to culture and family background and experience is central to explaining an important and persistent finding: Members of certain racial and cultural groups consistently score lower on traditional intelligence tests than do members of other groups. For example, as a group, blacks tend to average 10 to 15 IQ points lower than whites. Does this reflect a true difference in intelligence, or are the questions biased in regard to the kinds of knowledge they test? Clearly, if whites perform better because of their greater familiarity with the kind of information that is being tested, their higher IQ scores are not necessarily an indication that they are more intelligent than members of other groups (Kamieniecki & Lynd-Stevenson, 2002; Miele, 2002; Jensen, 2003)

There is good reason to believe that some standardized IQ tests contain elements that discriminate against minority-group members whose experiences differ from those of the white majority. Consider the question "What should you do if another child grabbed your hat and ran off with it?" Most white middle-class children answer that they would tell an adult, and this response is scored as correct. However, a reasonable response might be to chase the person and fight to get the hat back, the answer that is chosen by many urban black children—but one that is scored as incorrect (Miller-Jones, 1989; Aiken, 1996; Reynolds & Ramsay, 2003).

Furthermore, tests may include even subtler forms of bias against minority groups. For example, psychologist Janet Helms (1992) argues that assessments of cognitive ability developed in the United States are sometimes constructed to favor responses that implicitly reflect North American or European values, customs, or traditions. At the same time, such tests are biased against African and other cultural value systems (Byrne & Watkins, 2003).

More specifically, Helms suggests that the traditional Western value of "rugged individualism" means that correct answers to test items may require a test-taker to reason independently of a particular social context. In contrast, the African cultural value of communalism, in which one's group is valued more than individuals are, may leave test-takers from that tradition unable to answer a question that provides no information about the social context (Greenfield, 1997).

▲▲▲

Exploring DIVERSITY

The Relative Influence of Genetics and Environment: Nature, Nurture, and IQ

Culture-fair IQ test: A test that does not discriminate against the members of any minority group.

In an attempt to produce a **culture-fair IQ test,** one that does not discriminate against the members of any minority group, psychologists have tried to devise test items that assess experiences common to all cultures or emphasize questions that do not require language usage. However, test makers have found this difficult to do, because past experiences, attitudes, and values almost always have an impact on respondents' answers. For example, children raised in Western cultures group things on the basis of what they *are* (such as putting *dog* and *fish* into the category of *animal*). In contrast, members of the Kpelle tribe in Africa see intelligence demonstrated by grouping things according to what they *do* (grouping *fish* with *swim*). Similarly, children in the United States asked to memorize the position of objects on a chess board perform better than do African children living in remote villages if household objects familiar to the U.S. children are used. But if rocks are used instead of household objects, the African children do better. In short, it is difficult to produce a test that is truly culture-fair (Samuda, 1998; Sandoval et al., 1998; Serpell, 2000; Valencia & Suzuki, 2003).

The efforts of psychologists to produce culture-fair measures of intelligence relate to a lingering controversy over differences in intelligence between members of minority and majority groups. In attempting to identify whether there are differences between such groups, psychologists have had to confront the broader issue of determining the relative contribution to intelligence of genetic factors (heredity) and experience (environment)—the nature-nurture issue that is one of the basic issues of psychology.

Richard Herrnstein, a psychologist, and Charles Murray, a sociologist, fanned the flames of the debate with the publication of their book *The Bell Curve* in the mid-1990s (Herrnstein & Murray, 1994). They argued that an analysis of IQ differences between whites and blacks demonstrated that although environmental factors played a role, there were also basic genetic differences between the two races. They based their argument on a number of findings. For instance, on average, whites score 15 points higher than do blacks on traditional IQ tests even when socioeconomic status (SES) is taken into account. According to Herrnstein and Murray, middle- and upper-SES blacks score lower than do middle- and upper-SES whites, just as lower-SES blacks score lower on average than do lower-SES whites. Intelligence differences between blacks and whites, they concluded, could not be attributed to environmental differences alone.

Heritability: A measure of the degree to which a characteristic is related to genetic, inherited factors.

Moreover, intelligence in general shows a high degree of **heritability,** a measure of the degree to which a characteristic is related to genetic, inherited factors (e.g., Plomin & Petrill, 1997; Grigorenko, 2000; Plomin, 2003). As can be seen in

Relationship	Genetic overlap	Rearing	Correlation
Monozygotic (identical) twins	100%	Together	.86
Dizygotic (fraternal) twins	50%	Together	.62
Siblings	50%	Together	.41
Siblings	50%	Apart	.24
Parent-child	50%	Together	.35
Parent-child	50%	Apart	.31
Adoptive parent-child	0%	Together	.16
Unrelated children	0%	Together	.25
Spouses	0%	Apart	.29

The difference between these two correlations shows the impact of the environment

The relatively low correlation for unrelated children raised together shows the importance of genetic factors

FIGURE 1 The relationship between IQ and closeness of genetic relationship. In general, the more similar the genetic and environmental background of two people, the greater the correlation. Note, for example, that the correlation for spouses, who are genetically unrelated and have been reared apart, is relatively low, whereas the correlation for identical twins reared together is substantial. (Source: Adapted from Henderson, 1982.)

Figure 1, the closer the genetic link between two related people, the greater the correspondence of IQ scores. Using data such as these, Herrnstein and Murray argued that differences between races in IQ scores were largely caused by genetically based differences in intelligence.

However, many psychologists reacted strongly to the arguments laid out in *The Bell Curve*, refuting several of the book's basic arguments (e.g., Nisbett, 1994; American Psychological Association Task Force on Intelligence, 1996; Fish, 2002; Hall, 2002; Horn, 2002). For one thing, even when attempts are made to hold socioeconomic conditions constant, wide variations remain among individual households. Furthermore, no one can convincingly assert that the living conditions of blacks and whites are identical even when their socioeconomic status is similar. In addition, as we discussed earlier, there is reason to believe that traditional IQ tests may discriminate against lower-SES urban blacks by asking for information pertaining to experiences they are unlikely to have had.

Moreover, blacks who are raised in economically enriched environments have similar IQ scores to whites in comparable environments. For example, a study by Sandra Scarr and Richard Weinberg (1976) examined black children who had been adopted at an early age by white middle-class families of above-average intelligence. The IQ scores of those children averaged 106—about 15 points above the average IQ scores of unadopted black children in the study. Other research shows that the racial gap in IQ narrows considerably after a college education, and cross-cultural data demonstrate that when racial gaps exist in other cultures, it is the economically disadvantaged groups that typically have lower scores. In short, the evidence that genetic factors play the major role in determining racial differences in IQ is not compelling, although the question still evokes considerable controversy (Neisser et al., 1996; Myerson et al., 1998; Fish, 2002).

It is also crucial to remember that IQ scores and intelligence have the greatest relevance in terms of individuals, not groups. In fact, considering group *racial* differences presents some conceptually troublesome distinctions. *Race* was originally meant to be a biological concept, referring to classifications based on the physical and structural characteristics of a species. Despite its biological origins, however, the term *race* has taken on additional meanings and is used in a variety of ways, ranging from skin color to culture. In short, race is an extraordinarily inexact concept (Betancourt & Lopez, 1993; Yee et al., 1993; Beutler et al., 1996).

Consequently, drawing comparisons between different races on any dimension, including IQ scores, is an imprecise, potentially misleading, and often fruitless venture. By far, the greatest discrepancies in IQ scores occur when comparing *individuals*, not when comparing mean IQ scores of different *groups*. There are blacks who score high on IQ tests and whites who score low, just as there are whites who score high and blacks who score low. For the concept of intelligence to aid in the betterment of society, we must examine how *individuals* perform, not the groups to which they belong. We need to focus on the degree to which intelligence can be enhanced in an individual person, not in members of a particular group (Angoff, 1988; Fagan & Holland, 2002). (For more study on the issues surrounding group IQ differences, complete **Interactivity 28–1.**)

Other issues make the heredity-versus-environment debate somewhat irrelevant to practical concerns. For example, there are multiple kinds of intelligence, and traditional IQ scores do not tap many of them. Furthermore, IQ scores are often inadequate predictors of ultimate occupational success.

It also appears that intelligence is more flexible and modifiable than originally envisioned. For instance, researchers have been puzzled by data showing a long-term increase in IQ scores that has occurred since the early 1900s. Because the average person today gets more items correct than did the average person several generations ago on IQ tests, scores have risen significantly—a phenomenon known as the *Flynn effect* after its discoverer, psychologist James Flynn. The Flynn effect is not trivial, with the performance of the average 20-year-old today measuring some 15 points higher than the performance of the average 20-year-old in 1940 (Flynn, 1999, 2000; see Figure 2).

The explanation for the Flynn effect is not clear. Flynn and a colleague, economist William Dickens, argue that the higher scores have resulted as people have matched their genetic gifts with their environment. Because society is increasingly complex and driven by technology, it is increasingly making demands that people with high intelligence are particularly good at meeting. Consequently, society provides greater opportunities for people with high IQs to excel, and that environment

INTERACTIVITY 28–1

IQ issues

Improvements in technology and the general social environment are factors that may contribute to the Flynn effect

FIGURE 2 Although average IQ scores increased steadily during the 1900s—a phenomenon known as the Flynn effect—the reason for the rise is not at all clear. Do you think this trend is likely to continue in the twenty-first century? (Source: Horgan, 1995, p. 12.)

pushes them intellectually, creating an increase overall in IQ scores (Dickens & Flynn, 2001).

Other explanations for the Flynn effect suggest that it may due to better nutrition, better parenting, or improvements in the general social environment, including education. Whatever the cause, the change in IQ scores over the century is *not* due to evolutionary changes in human genetics: The period over which the Flynn effect has occurred is far too short for people to have evolved into a more intelligent species (Neisser, 1996; Loehlin, 2002).

ⓐ ⓐ ⓐ

Placing the Heredity–Environment Question in Perspective

Ultimately, there is no absolute answer to the question of the degree to which intelligence is influenced by heredity and by the environment. We are dealing with an issue for which experiments to unambiguously determine cause and effect cannot be devised. (A moment's thought about how we might experimentally assign infants to enriched or deprived environments will reveal the impossibility of devising ethically reasonable experiments!)

The more critical question to ask, then, is not whether hereditary or environmental factors primarily underlie intelligence, but whether there is anything we can do to maximize the intellectual development of each individual. If we can find ways to do this, we will be able to make changes in the environment—which may take the form of enriched home and school environments—that can lead each person to reach his or her potential.

RECAP/EVALUATE/RETHINK

RECAP

Are traditional IQ tests culturally biased?

▶ Traditional intelligence tests have frequently been criticized for being biased in favor of the white middle-class population. This controversy has led to attempts to devise culture-fair tests, IQ measures that avoid questions that depend on a particular cultural background. (p. 316)

Are there racial differences in intelligence?

▶ Issues of racial differences in intelligence represent a major controversy, in part because of the difficulty of defining the concept of race scientifically and disagreement over what constitutes an unbiased measure of race. (p. 317)

To what degree is intelligence influenced by the environment, and to what degree by heredity?

▶ Attempting to distinguish environmental from hereditary factors in intelligence is probably futile and certainly misguided. Because individual IQ scores vary far more than do group IQ scores, it is more critical to ask what can be done to maximize the intellectual development of each individual. (p. 318)

EVALUATE

1. Intelligence tests may be biased toward the prevailing culture in such a way that minorities are put at a disadvantage when taking these tests. True or false?
2. A(n) _____-_____ test tries to use only questions appropriate to all the people taking the test.
3. IQ tests can accurately determine the intelligence of entire groups of people. True or false?
4. Intelligence can be seen as a combination of _____ and _____ factors.

RETHINK

1. Why might a test that identifies a disproportionate number of minority-group members for special educational services and remedial assistance be considered potentially biased? Isn't the purpose of the test to help persons at risk

of falling behind academically? How can a test created for a good purpose be biased?

2. What ideas do you have for explaining the Flynn effect, the steady rise in IQ scores over several decades? How would you test your ideas?

KEY TERMS

culture-fair IQ test p. 316   heritability p. 316

Looking Back

Psychology on the Web

1. Many sites on the Web permit you to assess your IQ. Take at least two such tests and compare (a) your results, (b) what mental qualities seemed to be tested on the test, and (c) your impression of the reliability and validity of the tests. Write up your conclusions.
2. Find a way to assess at least one other of your multiple intelligences (i.e., one not tested by the IQ tests you took) on the Web. What sort of intelligence was the test supposed to be testing? What sorts of items were included? How valid and reliable do you think it was, both in and of itself and compared with the IQ tests you took?
3. After completing Interactivity 27–1 on mental retardation, search the Web for further information on the causes of mental retardation. Summarize the most recent evidence you find.

Epilogue

We've just examined one of the most controversial areas of psychology—intelligence. Some of the most heated discussions in all of psychology are focused on this topic, engaging educators, policymakers, politicians, and psychologists. The issues include the very meaning of intelligence, its measurement, individual extremes of intelligence, and, finally, the heredity–environment question. We saw that the quest to partition intelligence into hereditary factors versus environmental factors is generally pointless. In the area of intelligence, the focus of our efforts should be on making sure that every individual has the opportunity to achieve his or her potential.

Before we leave the topic of intelligence, return to the stories of the two persons of widely different intellectual capabilities discussed in the Prologue, Chris Burke and Vino Vasudevan. Consider the following questions on the basis of what you have learned about intelligence.

1. Chris Burke's physicians concluded in his infancy that he would never be able to function effectively in society and should be institutionalized immediately. How do you think the physicians came to their conclusions, and why do you think they were proved wrong?
2. In what ways would placing Burke in a separate educational program have helped or hurt his chances of reaching his full potential?
3. How might the educational acceleration of Vino Vasudevan help and hinder her later development? Do you think slowing down her educational progress might be beneficial? How?
4. Based on research relating to individuals who have unusually high IQ scores, what do you think Vino's emotional intelligence is like?

The Normal Distribution of IQ Scores

Intelligence is measured with IQ tests. Most people have an IQ near the average of 100. A smaller number of people have scores that are significantly above or below the average. What factors contribute to differences in IQ scores?

IQ=100

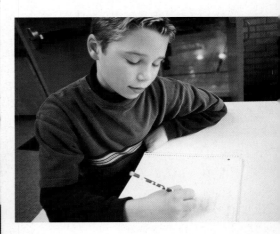

2 Test Biases

Questions on some IQ tests focus on topics that might be more familiar to a particular group, and the "correct" answers might reflect the dominant culture in society. These biases might lead to higher test scores for one group of test-takers.

Genetic Contributions to IQ 3

Genetics contributes to every human characteristic, including intelligence. In general, an individual's IQ score is associated with the IQ scores of his or her ancestors.

4 Prenatal Biochemical Contributions

Prenatal factors can affect not only fetal development but also adult characteristics. A healthy prenatal environment can promote the development of intelligence, whereas an unhealthy environment (for example, smoking or alchohol consumption by the mother) can have a negative effect on intelligence.

5 Nutritional Influences

During infancy, nutrition affects all aspects of a child's development. An inadequate diet that results from a family's financial limitations might reduce a person's IQ score.

6 School and Social Opportunities

Social and economic inequality are also associated with differences in IQ. People who have greater educational opportunities and who suffer fewer economic constraints are able to maximize their intelligence.

7 Potential for Everyone

Test bias and differences in nature and nurture contribute to differences in people's IQ scores. It is crucial, therefore, for society to focus on ways of promoting opportunities for all children to maximize their potential.

Motivation and Emotion

Prologue

Armed with Bravery

In just a moment, 27-year-old Aron Ralston's life changed. An 800-pound boulder dislodged in a narrow canyon where Ralston was hiking in an isolated Utah canyon, pinning his lower arm to the ground.

For the next five days, Ralston lay in the dense, lonely forest, unable to escape. An experienced climber who had search-and-rescue training, he had ample time to consider his options. He tried unsuccessfully to chip away at the rock, and he rigged up ropes and pulleys around the boulder in a vain effort to move it.

Finally, out of water and nearly dehydrated, Ralston reasoned there was only one option left short of dying. In acts of incredible bravery, Ralston broke two bones in his wrist, applied a tourniquet, and used a dull pen knife to amputate his arm beneath the elbow.

Freed from his entrapment, Ralston climbed down from where he had been pinned, and then hiked five miles to safety (Cox, 2003; Lofholm, 2003).

Aron Ralston

Ralston, who now has a prosthetic arm, recovered from his ordeal. He remains an active outdoorsman and hiker.

The topics of motivation and emotion are central in attempting to explain Ralston's extraordinary courage and will to live. Psychologists who study motivation seek to discover the particular desired goals—the *motives*—that underlie behavior. Behaviors as basic as drinking to satisfy thirst and as inconsequential as taking a stroll to get exercise exemplify motives. Psychologists specializing in the study of motivation assume that such underlying motives steer our choices of activities.

While motivation concerns the forces that direct future behavior, emotion pertains to

Looking Ahead

the feelings we experience throughout our lives. The study of emotions focuses on our internal experiences at any given moment. All of us feel a variety of emotions: happiness at succeeding at a difficult task, sadness over the death of a loved one, anger at being treated unfairly. Because emotions not only play a role in motivating our behavior but also act as a reflection of our underlying motivation, they play an important role in our lives.

We begin this set of modules by focusing on the major conceptions of motivation, discussing how different motives and needs jointly affect behavior. We consider motives that are biologically based and universal in the animal kingdom, such as hunger, as well as motives that are unique to humans, such as the need for achievement.

We then turn to emotions. We consider the roles and functions that emotions play in people's lives and discuss several approaches that explain how people understand their emotions. Finally, we look at how nonverbal behavior communicates emotions.

Explaining Motivation

When Lance Armstrong completed the final leg of the Tour de France before a cheering crowd of a half million people, it meant more than winning the world's most prestigious cycling race. The moment represented a triumph of human motivation and spirit—with a dash of miracle.

How does motivation direct and energize behavior?

Only 33 months earlier, no one would have thought that Armstrong would be the winner of the Tour de France. In fact, the odds were against him ever cycling again. At that time, he learned he had testicular cancer that had spread to his lungs and brain, which contained 12 tumors and two lesions. Doctors gave him a 50–50 chance of surviving.

His treatment was grueling. He suffered through surgery and four rounds of intense chemotherapy, separated by a month each. But he never gave up. Pushing himself, he would ride 20 to 50 miles a day following each of the one-week chemotherapy sessions.

Motivation: The factors that direct and energize the behavior of humans and other organisms.

Instincts: Inborn patterns of behavior that are biologically determined rather than learned.

Then the unexpected happened: The cancer disappeared, surprising everyone. And Armstrong picked up where he had left off, training hours each day and entering cycling competitions (Abt, 1999, p. D4).

Several years later, Armstrong was not only healthy but crossing the finish line at the Tour de France—a testament to his enormous will to succeed.

What motivation lay behind Armstrong's resolve? Was it anticipating the emotional thrill of winning the Tour de France? The potential rewards that would follow if he succeeded? The excitement of participating? The satisfaction of achieving a long-sought goal?

To answer such questions, psychologists employ the concept of **motivation,** the factors that direct and energize the behavior of humans and other organisms. Motivation has biological, cognitive, and social aspects, and the complexity of the concept has led psychologists to develop a variety of approaches. All seek to explain the energy that guides people's behavior in particular directions.

▲▲▲

Instinct Approaches: Born to Be Motivated

When psychologists first tried to explain motivation, they turned to **instincts,** inborn patterns of behavior that are biologically determined rather than learned. According to instinct approaches to motivation, people and animals are born preprogrammed with sets of behaviors essential to their survival. Those instincts provide the energy that channels behavior in appropriate directions. Hence, sexual behavior may be a response to an instinct to reproduce, and exploratory behavior may be motivated by an instinct to examine one's territory.

This conception presents several difficulties, however. For one thing, psychologists do not agree on what, or even how many, primary instincts exist. One early

Did the same motivation that drove Lance Armstrong to battle cancer help him win the Tour de France?

psychologist, William McDougall (1908), suggested that there are eighteen instincts. Other theorists came up with even more—with one sociologist (Bernard, 1924) claiming that there are exactly 5,759 distinct instincts!

Furthermore, explanations based on the concept of instincts do not go very far toward explaining *why* one specific pattern of behavior, and not others, has appeared in a given species. In addition, although it is clear that much animal behavior is based on instincts, because much of the variety and complexity of human behavior is learned, that behavior cannot be seen as instinctual.

As a result of these shortcomings, newer explanations have replaced conceptions of motivation based on instincts. However, instinct approaches still play a role in certain theories, particularly those based on evolutionary approaches that focus on our genetic inheritance. Furthermore, Freud's work suggests that instinctual drives of sex and aggression motivate behavior (Katz, 2001).

Drive-Reduction Approaches: Satisfying Our Needs

Drive-reduction approaches to motivation: Theories suggesting that a lack of a basic biological requirement such as water produces a drive to obtain that requirement (in this case, the thirst drive).

Drive: Motivational tension, or arousal, that energizes behavior to fulfill a need.

After rejecting instinct theory, psychologists first proposed simple drive-reduction theories of motivation to take its place (Hull, 1943). **Drive-reduction approaches** suggest that a lack of some basic biological requirement such as water produces a drive to obtain that requirement (in this case, the thirst drive).

To understand this approach, we begin with the concept of drive. A **drive** is motivational tension, or arousal, that energizes behavior to fulfill a need. Many basic drives, such as hunger, thirst, sleep, and sex, are related to biological needs of the body or of the species as a whole. These are called *primary drives*. Primary drives contrast with *secondary drives*, in which behavior fulfills no obvious biological need. In secondary drives, prior experience and learning bring about needs. For instance, some people have strong needs to achieve academically and professionally. We can say that their achievement need is reflected in a secondary drive that motivates their behavior (McMillan & Katz, 2002).

We usually try to satisfy a primary drive by reducing the need underlying it. For example, we become hungry after not eating for a few hours and may raid the refrigerator, especially if the next scheduled meal is not imminent. If the weather turns cold, we put on extra clothing or raise the setting on the thermostat to keep warm. If our bodies need liquids to function properly, we experience thirst and seek out water.

HOMEOSTASIS

Homeostasis: The body's tendency to maintain a steady internal state.

Homeostasis, the body's tendency to maintain a steady internal state, underlies primary drives. Using feedback loops, homeostasis brings deviations in body functioning back to an optimal state, similar to the way a thermostat and a furnace work in a home heating system to maintain a steady temperature (see Figure 1). Receptor cells throughout the body constantly monitor factors such as temperature and nutrient levels, and when deviations from the ideal state occur, the body adjusts in an effort to return to an optimal state. Many fundamental needs, including the needs for food, water, stable body temperature, and sleep, operate via homeostasis (Canteras, 2002).

Although drive-reduction theories provide a good explanation of how primary drives motivate behavior, they cannot fully explain a behavior in which the goal is not to reduce a drive, but rather to maintain or even increase the level of excitement or arousal. For instance, some behaviors seem to be motivated by nothing more than curiosity, such as rushing to check e-mail messages. Similarly, many people pursue thrilling activities such as riding a roller coaster and steering a raft down the rapids

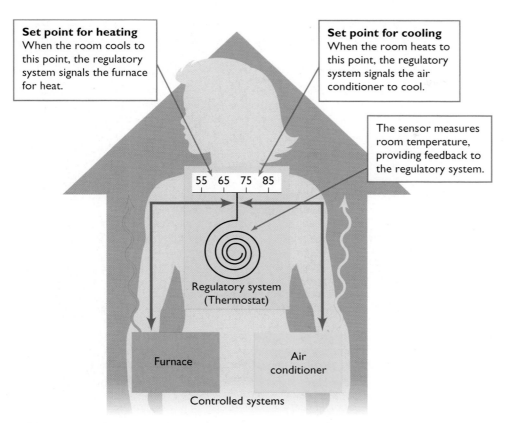

Set point for heating
When the room cools to this point, the regulatory system signals the furnace for heat.

Set point for cooling
When the room heats to this point, the regulatory system signals the air conditioner to cool.

The sensor measures room temperature, providing feedback to the regulatory system.

55 65 75 85

Regulatory system (Thermostat)

Furnace

Air conditioner

Controlled systems

FIGURE I With homeostasis, a series of feedback loops is used to regulate body functions, similar to the way a thermostat turns on the furnace when a room's air temperature becomes too cool and turns it off when the air temperature becomes too warm. Similarly, when body temperature becomes too low, the blood vessels constrict, causing shivering and making us seek warmth. When body temperature becomes too high, the blood vessels expand, and we sweat as our bodies try to lower the temperature. Can you think of other internal systems that operate via homeostasis?

of a river. Such behaviors certainly don't suggest that people seek to reduce all drives, as drive-reduction approaches would indicate (Loewenstein, 1994; Begg & Langley, 2001; Rosenbloom & Wolf, 2002).

Both curiosity and thrill-seeking behavior, then, shed doubt on drive-reduction approaches as a complete explanation for motivation. In both cases, rather than seeking to reduce an underlying drive, people and animals appear to be motivated to *increase* their overall level of stimulation and activity. To explain this phenomenon, psychologists have devised an alternative: arousal approaches to motivation.

Arousal Approaches: Beyond Drive Reduction

Arousal approaches seek to explain behavior in which the goal is to maintain or increase excitement (Berlyne, 1967; Brehm & Self, 1989). According to **arousal approaches to motivation,** each person tries to maintain a certain level of stimulation and activity. As with the drive-reduction model, this model suggests that if our stimulation and activity levels become too high, we try to reduce them. But in contrast to the drive-reduction model, the arousal model also suggests that if levels of stimulation and activity are too low, we will try to *increase* them by seeking stimulation.

Arousal approaches to motivation: The belief that we try to maintain certain levels of stimulation and activity, increasing or reducing them as necessary.

FIGURE 2 Some people seek high levels of arousal, while others are more easygoing. You can get a sense of your own preferred level of stimulation by completing this questionnaire. (Source: Zuckerman, 1978, 1994.)

Do You Seek Out Sensation?

How much stimulation do you crave in your everyday life? You will have an idea after you complete the following questionnaire, which lists some items from a scale designed to assess your sensation-seeking tendencies. Circle either A or B in each pair or statements.

1. A I would like a job that requires a lot of travelling.
   B I would prefer a job in one location.
2. A I am invigorated by a brisk, cold day.
   B I can't wait to get indoors on a cold day.
3. A I get bored seeing the same old faces.
   B I like the comfortable familiarity of everyday friends.
4. A I would prefer living in an ideal society in which everyone was safe, secure, and happy.
   B I would have preferred living in the unsettled days of our history.
5. A I sometimes like to do things that are a little frightening.
   B A sensible person avoids activities that are dangerous.
6. A I would not like to be hypnotized.
   B I would like to have the experience of being hypnotized.
7. A The most important goal of life is to live it to the fullest and to experience as much as possible.
   B The most important goal of life is to find peace and happiness.
8. A I would like to try parachute jumping.
   B I would never want to try jumping out of a plane, with or without a parachute.
9. A I enter cold water gradually, giving myself time to get used to it.
   B I like to dive or jump right into the ocean or a cold pool.
10. A When I go on a vacation, I prefer the comfort of a good room and bed.
    B When I go on a vacation, I prefer the change of camping out.
11. A I prefer people who are emotionally expressive, even if they are a bit unstable.
    B I prefer people who are calm and even-tempered.
12. A A good painting should shock or jolt the senses.
    B A good painting should give one a feeling of peace and security.
13. A People who ride motorcycles must have some kind of unconscious need to hurt themselves.
    B I would like to drive or ride a motorcycle.

Scoring Give yourself one point for each of the following responses: 1A, 2A, 3A, 4B, 5A, 6B, 7A, 8A, 9B, 10B, 11A, 12A, 13B. Find your total score by adding up the number of points and then use the following scoring key:

0–3 very low sensation seeking
4–5 low
6–9 average
10–11 high
12–13 very high

Keep in mind, of course, that this short questionnaire, for which the scoring is based on the results of college students who have taken it, provides only a rough estimate of your sensation-seeking tendencies. Moreover, as people get older, their sensation-seeking scores tend to decrease. Still, the questionnaire will at least give you an indication of how your sensation-seeking tendencies compare with those of others.

INTERACTIVITY 29–1

Sensation-seeking behavior

People vary widely in the optimal level of arousal they seek out, with some people looking for especially high levels of arousal. For example, people who participate in daredevil sports, high-stakes gamblers, and criminals who pull off high-risk robberies may be exhibiting a particularly high need for arousal (see Figure 2 and try **Interactivity 29–1;** Farley, 1986; Zuckerman & Kuhlman, 2000; Zuckerman, 2002).

Incentive Approaches: Motivation's Pull

When a luscious dessert appears on the table after a filling meal, its appeal has little or nothing to do with internal drives or the maintenance of arousal. Rather, if we choose to eat the dessert, such behavior is motivated by the external stimulus of the dessert itself, which acts as an anticipated reward. This reward, in motivational terms, is an *incentive*.

Incentive approaches to motivation suggest that motivation stems from the desire to obtain valued external goals, or incentives. In this view, the desirable properties of external stimuli—whether grades, money, affection, food, or sex—account for a person's motivation.

Although the theory explains why we may succumb to an incentive (such as a mouthwatering dessert) even though we lack internal cues (such as hunger), it does not provide a complete explanation of motivation, because organisms sometimes seek to fulfill needs even when incentives are not apparent. Consequently, many psychologists believe that the internal drives proposed by drive-reduction theory work in tandem with the external incentives of incentive theory to "push" and "pull" behavior, respectively. Thus, at the same time that we seek to satisfy our underlying hunger needs (the push of drive-reduction theory), we are drawn to food that appears particularly appetizing (the pull of incentive theory). Rather than contradicting each other, then, drives and incentives may work together in motivating behavior (Petri, 1996; Pinel, Assanand, & Lehman, 2000; Lowery, Fillingim, & Wright, 2003).

> **Incentive approaches to motivation:** Theories suggesting that motivation stems from the desire to obtain valued external goals, or incentives.

Cognitive Approaches: The Thoughts Behind Motivation

Cognitive approaches to motivation suggest that motivation is a product of people's thoughts, expectations, and goals—their cognitions. For instance, the degree to which people are motivated to study for a test is based on their expectation of how well studying will pay off in terms of a good grade (Wigfield & Eccles, 2000).

Cognitive theories of motivation draw a key distinction between intrinsic and extrinsic motivation. *Intrinsic motivation* causes us to participate in an activity for our own enjoyment rather than for any concrete, tangible reward that it will bring us. In contrast, *extrinsic motivation* causes us to do something for money, a grade, or some other concrete, tangible reward. For example, when a physician works long hours because she loves medicine, intrinsic motivation is prompting her; if she works hard to make a lot of money, extrinsic motivation underlies her efforts (Rawsthorne & Elliot, 1999; Ryan & Deci, 2000; Pedersen, 2002).

We are more apt to persevere, work harder, and produce work of higher quality when motivation for a task is intrinsic rather than extrinsic. In fact, in some cases providing rewards for desirable behavior (thereby increasing extrinsic motivation) actually may decrease intrinsic motivation (Sansone & Harackiewicz, 2000; Deci, Koestner, & Ryan, 2001; Henderlong & Lepper, 2002).

> **Cognitive approaches to motivation:** Theories suggesting that motivation is a product of people's thoughts and expectations—their cognitions.

Maslow's Hierarchy: Ordering Motivational Needs

What do Eleanor Roosevelt, Abraham Lincoln, and Albert Einstein have in common? The common thread, according to a model of motivation devised by psychologist Abraham Maslow, is that each of them fulfilled the highest levels of motivational needs underlying human behavior.

FIGURE 3 Maslow's hierarchy shows how our motivation progresses up the pyramid from the broadest, most fundamental biological needs to higher-order ones. (After Maslow, 1970.) Do you agree that lower-order needs must be satisfied before higher-order needs? Do hermits and monks who attempt to fulfill spiritual needs while denying basic physical needs contradict Maslow's hierarchy?

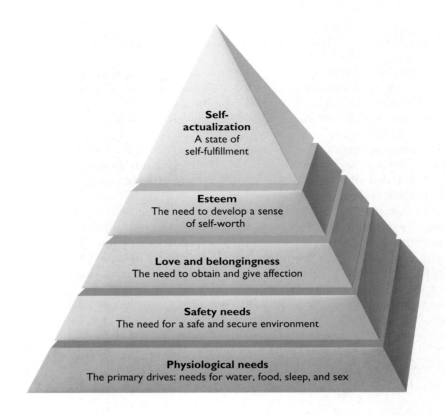

Self-actualization
A state of self-fulfillment

Esteem
The need to develop a sense of self-worth

Love and belongingness
The need to obtain and give affection

Safety needs
The need for a safe and secure environment

Physiological needs
The primary drives: needs for water, food, sleep, and sex

PowerWeb: A Theory of Human Motivation

www.mhhe.com/feldmanup7

Self-actualization: A state of self-fulfillment in which people realize their highest potential, each in his or her own unique way.

Maslow's model places motivational needs in a hierarchy and suggests that before more sophisticated, higher-order needs can be met, certain primary needs must be satisfied (Maslow, 1970, 1987). A pyramid can represent the model, with the more basic needs at the bottom and the higher-level needs at the top (see Figure 3). To activate a particular higher-order need, thereby guiding behavior, a person must first fulfill the more basic needs in the hierarchy.

The basic needs are primary drives: needs for water, food, sleep, sex, and the like. To move up the hierarchy, a person must first meet these basic physiological needs. Safety needs come next in the hierarchy; Maslow suggests that people need a safe, secure environment in order to function effectively. Physiological and safety needs compose the lower-order needs.

Only after meeting the basic lower-order needs can a person consider fulfilling higher-order needs, such as the needs for love and a sense of belonging, esteem, and self-actualization. Love and belongingness needs include the need to obtain and give affection and to be a contributing member of some group or society. After fulfilling these needs, a person strives for esteem. In Maslow's thinking, esteem relates to the need to develop a sense of self-worth by knowing that others know and value one's competence.

Once these four sets of needs are fulfilled—no easy task—a person is able to strive for the highest-level need, self-actualization. **Self-actualization** is a state of self-fulfillment in which people realize their highest potentials, each in his or her own unique way. Although Maslow first suggested that self-actualization occurred in only a few, famous individuals, he later expanded the concept to encompass everyday people. For example, a parent with excellent nurturing skills who raises a family, a teacher who year after year creates an environment that maximizes students' opportunities for success, and an artist who realizes his creative potential all may be self-actualized. The important thing is that people feel at ease with themselves and satisfied that they are using their talents to the fullest. In a sense, achieving self-actualization reduces the striving and yearning for greater fulfillment that mark most people's lives and instead provides a sense of satisfaction with the current state of affairs (Jones & Crandall, 1991; Hamel, Leclerc, & Lefrancois, 2003; Piechowski, 2003).

Although research has been unable to validate the specific ordering of Maslow's stages, and although it is difficult to measure self-actualization objectively, Maslow's model is important for two reasons: It highlights the complexity of human needs, and it emphasizes the idea that until more basic biological needs are met, people will be relatively unconcerned with higher-order needs. For example, if people are hungry, their first interest will be in obtaining food; they will not be concerned with needs such as love and self-esteem (Hanley & Abell, 2002; Samantaray, Srivastava, & Misbra, 2002).

Applying the Different Approaches to Motivation

The various theories of motivation (summarized in Figure 4) give several different perspectives on motivation. Which provides the fullest account of motivation? Actually, many of the approaches are complementary, rather than contradictory. In fact, employing more than one approach can help us understand motivation in a particular instance.

Consider, for example, Aron Ralston's accident while hiking (described at the beginning of the module). His interest in climbing in an isolated and potentially dangerous area may be explained by arousal approaches to motivation. From the

Instinct

People and animals are born with preprogrammed sets of behaviors essential to their survival.

Drive reduction

When some basic biological requirement is lacking, a drive is produced.

Arousal

People seek an optimal level of stimulation. If the level of stimulation is too high, they act to reduce it; if it is too low, they act to increase it.

Incentive

External stimuli direct and energize behavior.

Cognitive

Thoughts, expectations, and understanding of the world direct motivation.

Hierarchy of needs

Needs form a hierarchy; before higher-order needs are met, lower-order needs must be fulfilled.

FIGURE 4 The major approaches to motivation.

perspective of instinct approaches, we see that Aron had an overwhelming instinct to preserve his life at all costs. From a cognitive perspective, we see his careful consideration of various strategies to extricate himself from the boulder.

In short, applying multiple approaches to motivation in a given situation provides a broader understanding than we might obtain by employing only a single approach. We'll see this again when we consider specific motives—such as the needs for food, achievement, affiliation, and power—and draw on several of the theories for the fullest account of what motivates our behavior.

RECAP/EVALUATE/RETHINK

RECAP

How does motivation direct and energize behavior?

- ▶ Motivation relates to the factors that direct and energize behavior. (p. 327)
- ▶ Drive is the motivational tension that energizes behavior to fulfill a need. (p. 328)
- ▶ Homeostasis, the maintenance of a steady internal state, often underlies motivational drives. (p. 328)
- ▶ Arousal approaches suggest that we try to maintain a particular level of stimulation and activity. (p. 329)
- ▶ Incentive approaches focus on the positive aspects of the environment that direct and energize behavior. (p. 331)
- ▶ Cognitive approaches focus on the role of thoughts, expectations, and understanding of the world in producing motivation. (p. 331)
- ▶ Maslow's hierarchy suggests that there are five basic needs: physiological, safety, love and belongingness, esteem, and self-actualization. Only after the more basic needs are fulfilled can a person move toward meeting higher-order needs. (p. 332)

EVALUATE

1. _____ are forces that guide a person's behavior in a certain direction.
2. Biologically determined, inborn patterns of behavior are known as _____.
3. Your psychology professor tells you, "Explaining behavior is easy! When we lack something, we are motivated to get it." Which approach to motivation does your professor subscribe to?

4. By drinking water after running a marathon, a runner tries to keep his or her body at an optimal level of functioning. This process is called _____.
5. I help an elderly person cross the street because doing a good deed makes me feel good. What type of motivation is at work here? What type of motivation would be at work if I were to help an elderly man across the street because he paid me $20?
6. According to Maslow, a person with no job, no home, and no friends can become self-actualized. True or false?

RETHINK

1. Which approaches to motivation are more commonly used in the workplace? How might each approach be used to design employment policies that can sustain or increase motivation?
2. A writer who works all day composing copy for an advertising firm has a hard time keeping her mind on her work and continually watches the clock. After work she turns to a collection of stories she is creating and writes long into the night, completely forgetful of the clock. What ideas from your reading on motivation help explain this phenomenon?

Answers to Evaluate Questions

1. motives; 2. instincts; 3. drive reduction; 4. homeostasis; 5. intrinsic, extrinsic; 6. false; lower-order needs must be fulfilled before self-actualization can occur.

KEY TERMS

motivation p. 327
instincts p. 327
drive-reduction approaches
to motivation p. 328

drive p. 328
homeostasis p. 328
arousal approaches to
motivation p. 329

incentive approaches to
motivation p. 331
cognitive approaches to
motivation p. 331

self-actualization p. 332

Human Needs and Motivation: Eat, Drink, and Be Daring

As a sophomore at the University of California, Santa Cruz, Lisa Arndt followed a menu of her own making: For breakfast she ate cereal or fruit, with 10 diet pills and 50 chocolate-flavored laxatives. Lunch was a salad or sandwich; dinner: chicken and rice. But it was the feast that followed that Arndt relished most. Almost every night at about 9 P.M., she would retreat to her room and eat an entire small pizza and a whole batch of cookies. Then she'd wait for the day's laxatives to take effect. "It was extremely painful," says Arndt of those days . . . "But I was that desperate to make up for my bingeing. I was terrified of fat the way other people are afraid of lions or guns" (Hubbard, O'Neill, & Cheakalos, 1999, p. 59).

Lisa was one of the 5 to 10 million females (and 1 million males) who suffer from an eating disorder. These disorders, which usually appear during adolescence, can bring about extraordinary weight loss and other forms of physical deterioration. Extremely dangerous, they sometimes result in death.

Why are Lisa and others like her subject to such disordered eating, which revolves around the motivation to avoid weight gain at all costs? And why do so many other people engage in overeating, which leads to obesity?

To answer these questions, we must consider some of the specific needs that underlie behavior. In this module, we examine several of the most important human needs. We begin with hunger, the primary drive that has received the most attention from researchers, and then turn to secondary drives—those uniquely human endeavors, based on learned needs and past experience, that help explain why people strive to achieve, to affiliate with others, and to seek power over others.

⏶⏶⏶

The Motivation Behind Hunger and Eating

Two-thirds of the people in the United States are overweight. Among those people, nearly half are so heavy that they have **obesity,** body weight that is more than 20 percent above the average weight for a person of a particular height. And the rest of the world is not far behind: A billion people around the globe are overweight or obese. The World Health Organization has said that worldwide obesity has reached epidemic proportions (Taubes, 1998; Flegal, 2002; Grady, 2002).

The most widely used measure of obesity is *body mass index (BMI)*, which is based on a ratio of weight to height. People with a BMI greater than 30 are considered obese, whereas those with a BMI between 25 and 30 are overweight. (Use the calculations in Figure 1 to determine your own BMI.)

Although the definition of obesity is clear from a scientific point of view, people's perceptions of what an ideal body looks like vary significantly across different cultures and, within Western cultures, from one time period to another. For instance,

Obesity: Body weight that is more than 20 percent above the average weight for a person of a particular height.

335

FIGURE I Use this procedure to find your body mass index.

To calculate your body mass index, follow these steps:

1. Indicate your weight in pounds: _____ pounds
2. Indicate your height in inches: _____ inches
3. Divide your weight (item 1) by your height (item 2), and write the outcome here:
   _____
4. Divide the result above (item 3) by your height (item 2), and write the outcome here:
   _____
5. Multiply the number above by 703, and write the product here: _____ . This is your body mass index.

Example:

For a person who weights 210 pounds and who is 6 feet tall, divide 210 pounds by 72 inches, which equals 2.917. Then divide 2.917 by 72 inches (item 3), which yields .041. Multiplying .041 (from item 4) by 703 yields a BMI of 28.5.

Interpretation:
- Underweight = less than 18.5
- Normal weight = 18.5–24.9
- Overweight = 25–29.9
- Obesity = BMI of 30 or greater

Keep in mind that a BMI greater than 25 may or may not be due to excess body fat. For example, professional athletes may have little fat but weigh more than the average person because they have greater muscle mass.

"Gee, I had no idea you were married to a supermodel."

many contemporary Western cultures stress the importance of slimness in women—a relatively recent view. In nineteenth-century Hawaii, the most attractive women were those who were the heaviest. Furthermore, for most of the twentieth century—except for periods in the 1920s and the most recent decades—the ideal female figure was relatively full. Even today, weight standards differ among different cultural groups. For instance, African Americans generally judge heavier women more positively than whites do (Hebl & Hetherton, 1998; Crandall et al., 2001; Gluck & Geliebter, 2002; Mills et al., 2002).

Regardless of cultural standards for appearance and weight, no one doubts that being overweight represents a major health risk. However, controlling weight is complicated, because eating behavior involves a variety of mechanisms. In our discussion of what motivates people to eat, we'll start with the biological aspects of eating.

BIOLOGICAL FACTORS IN THE REGULATION OF HUNGER

In contrast to human beings, other species are unlikely to become obese. Internal mechanisms regulate not only the quantity of food they take in but also the kind of food they desire. For example, rats that have been deprived of particular foods seek out alternatives that contain the specific nutrients their diet is lacking, and many species, given the choice of a wide variety of foods, select a well-balanced diet (Bouchard & Bray, 1996; Woods et al., 2000; Jones & Corp, 2003).

Complex mechanisms tell organisms whether they require food or should stop eating. It's not just a matter of an empty stomach causing hunger pangs and a full one alleviating those pangs. (Even individuals who have had their stomachs removed

FIGURE 2 The hypothalamus acts as the brain's "feeding center," being primarily responsible for the monitoring of food intake.

still experience the sensation of hunger.) One important factor is changes in the chemical composition of the blood. In particular, changes in levels of glucose, a kind of sugar, regulate feelings of hunger (Inglefinger, 1944; Campfield et al., 1996; Mulligan et al., 2002).

The brain's *hypothalamus* (see Figure 2) monitors glucose levels. Increasing evidence suggests that the hypothalamus carries the primary responsibility for monitoring food intake. Injury to the hypothalamus has radical consequences for eating behavior, depending on the site of the injury. For example, rats whose *lateral hypothalamus* is damaged may literally starve to death. They refuse food when it is offered, and unless they are force-fed, they eventually die. Rats with an injury to the *ventromedial hypothalamus* display the opposite problem: extreme overeating. Rats with this injury can increase in weight by as much as 400 percent. Similar phenomena occur in humans who have tumors of the hypothalamus (Woods, Seeley, Porte, & Schwartz, 1998; Woods & Seeley, 2002).

Although the important role the hypothalamus plays in regulating food intake is clear, the exact way this organ operates is still unclear. One hypothesis suggests that injury to the hypothalamus affects the **weight set point,** or the particular level of weight that the body strives to maintain, which in turn regulates food intake. Acting as a kind of internal weight thermostat, the hypothalamus calls for either greater or less food intake (Capaldi, 1996; Woods et al., 2000; Berthoud, 2002).

In most cases, the hypothalamus does a good job. Even people who are not deliberately monitoring their weight show only minor weight fluctuations in spite of substantial day-to-day variations in how much they eat and exercise. However, injury to the hypothalamus can alter the weight set point, and a person then struggles to meet the internal goal by increasing or decreasing food consumption. Even temporary exposure to certain drugs can alter the weight set point (Cabanac & Frankham, 2002).

Genetic factors determine the weight set point, at least in part. People seem destined, through heredity, to have a particular **metabolism,** the rate at which food is converted to energy and expended by the body. People with a high metabolic rate can eat virtually as much as they want without gaining weight, whereas others, with low metabolism, may eat literally half as much yet gain weight readily (Woods, Seeley, Porte, & Schwartz, 1998; Jequier, 2002).

Weight set point: The particular level of weight that the body strives to maintain.

Metabolism: The rate at which food is converted to energy and expended by the body.

SOCIAL FACTORS IN EATING

You've just finished a full meal and feel completely stuffed. Suddenly your host announces with great fanfare that he will be serving his "house specialty" dessert, bananas flambé, and that he has spent the better part of the afternoon preparing it.

Cultural influences on eating habits vary tremendously. Grasshoppers, red agave worms, and excamola may be considered a delicacy in Mexico, but most people in the United States would feel differently. Have you ever overcome your culture-based dislike of a food after exposure to another culture's eating habits?

Even though you are full and don't even like bananas, you accept a serving of his dessert and eat it all.

Clearly, internal biological factors do not fully explain our eating behavior. External social factors, based on societal rules and on what we have learned about appropriate eating behavior, also play an important role. Take, for example, the simple fact that people customarily eat breakfast, lunch, and dinner at approximately the same times every day. Because we tend to eat on schedule every day, we feel hungry as the usual hour approaches, sometimes quite independently of what our internal cues are telling us.

Similarly, we put roughly the same amount of food on our plates every day, even though the amount of exercise we may have had, and consequently our need for energy replenishment, varies from day to day. We also tend to prefer particular foods over others. Rats and dogs may be a delicacy in certain Asian cultures, but few people in Western cultures find them appealing despite their potentially high nutritional value. In sum, cultural influences and our individual habits play important roles in determining when, what, and how much we eat (Rozin, 1990; Capaldi, 1996; Miller & Pumariega, 2001).

Other social factors relate to our eating behavior as well. Some of us head toward the refrigerator after a difficult day, seeking solace in a pint of Heath Bar Crunch ice cream. Why? Perhaps when we were children, our parents gave us food when we were upset. Eventually, we may have learned, through the basic mechanisms of classical and operant conditioning, to associate food with comfort and consolation. Similarly, we may learn that eating, which focuses our attention on immediate pleasures, provides an escape from unpleasant thoughts. Consequently, we may eat when we feel distressed (McManus & Waller, 1995; Hill & Peters, 1998; Bulik et al., 2003).

THE ROOTS OF OBESITY

Given that both biological and social factors influence eating behavior, determining the causes of obesity has proved to be a challenging task. Researchers have followed several paths.

Some psychologists suggest that oversensitivity to external eating cues based on social factors, coupled with insensitivity to internal hunger cues, produces obesity. Others argue that overweight people have higher weight set points than other people do. Because their set points are unusually high, their attempts to lose weight by eating less may make them especially sensitive to external, food-related cues and therefore more apt to overeat, perpetuating their obesity (Nisbett, 1968; Schachter, 1971; Hill & Peters, 1998).

But why may some people's weight set points be higher than those of others? One biological explanation is that obese individuals have a higher level of the hormone *leptin*, which appears to be designed, from an evolutionary standpoint, to "protect" the body against weight loss. The body's weight-regulation system thus appears to be designed more to protect against losing weight than to protect against gaining it, meaning that it's easier to gain weight than to lose it (Friedman, 2003).

Another biologically based explanation for obesity relates to the size and number of fat cells in the body, which increase as a function of weight increase. Because the set-point level appears to reflect the number of fat cells a person has, any increase in weight—which raises the number of fat cells—may also raise the set point. Furthermore, any loss of weight after the age of 2 years does not decrease the number of fat cells in the body, although it may cause them to shrink in size. In short, according to the weight-set-point hypothesis, the presence of too many fat cells may result in the set point becoming "stuck" at a higher level than is desirable. In such circumstances, losing weight becomes a difficult proposition, because one is constantly at odds with one's own internal set point when dieting (Freedman, 1995; Leibel, Rosenbaum & Hirsch, 1995).

Not everyone agrees with the set-point explanation for obesity. Pointing to the rapid rise in obesity over the last several decades in the United States, some researchers suggest that the body does not try to maintain a fixed weight set point. Instead, they suggest, the body has a *settling point*, determined by a combination of our genetic heritage and the nature of the environment in which we live. If high-fat foods are prevalent in our environment and we are genetically predisposed to obesity, we settle into an equilibrium that maintains relatively high weight. In contrast, if our environment is nutritionally healthier, a genetic predisposition to obesity will not be triggered, and we will settle into an equilibrium in which our weight is lower (Comuzzie & Allison, 1998; Pi-Sunyer, 2003).

Eating Disorders

One devastating weight-related disorder is **anorexia nervosa.** In this severe eating disorder, people may refuse to eat while denying that their behavior and appearance—which can become skeleton-like—are unusual. Some 10 percent of people with anorexia literally starve themselves to death.

Anorexia nervosa mainly afflicts females between the ages of 12 and 40, although both men and women of any age may develop it. People with the disorder typically come from stable homes, and they are often successful, attractive, and relatively affluent. The disorder often occurs after serious dieting, which somehow gets out of control. Life begins to revolve around food: Although people with the disorder eat little, they may cook for others, go shopping for food frequently, or collect cookbooks (Lask & Bryant-Waugh, 1999; Rosen, 1999; Reijonen et al., 2003).

A related problem, **bulimia,** from which Lisa Arndt (described earlier) suffered, is a disorder in which people binge on large quantities of food. For instance, they may consume an entire gallon of ice cream and a whole pie in a single sitting. After such a binge, sufferers feel guilt and depression and often induce vomiting or take laxatives to rid themselves of the food—behavior known as purging. Constant bingeing-and-purging cycles and the use of drugs to induce vomiting or diarrhea can lead to heart failure. Often, though, the weight of a person with bulimia remains normal (Phillips et al., 2003).

Eating disorders represent a growing problem: Estimates show that between 1 and 4 percent of high school-age and college-age women have either anorexia nervosa or bulimia. As many as 10 percent of women suffer from bulimia at some point in their lives. Furthermore, an increasing number of men are diagnosed with eating disorders; an estimated 10 to 13 percent of all cases occur in males (NIMH, 2000; DeAngelis, 2002; Morgan, 2002).

What are the causes of anorexia nervosa and bulimia? Some researchers suspect a biological cause such as a chemical imbalance in the hypothalamus or pituitary gland, perhaps brought on by genetic factors. Others believe that the cause has roots in society's valuation of slenderness and the parallel notion that obesity is undesirable. These researchers maintain that people with anorexia nervosa and bulimia become preoccupied with their weight and take to heart the cliché that one can never be too thin. This may explain why, as countries become more developed and Westernized, and dieting becomes more popular, eating disorders increase. Finally, some psychologists suggest that the disorders result from overly demanding parents or other family problems (Goldner, Cockell, & Srikameswaran, 2002; Polivy & Herman, 2002; Grilo et al., 2003).

The complete explanations for anorexia nervosa and bulimia remain elusive. These disorders probably stem from both biological and social causes, and successful treatment probably encompasses several strategies, including therapy and dietary changes (Striegel-Moore & Smolak, 2001; Wilson & Fairburn, 2002; Patel, Pratt, & Greydanus, 2003). If you or a family member needs advice or help with an eating problem, contact the American Anorexia Bulimia Association at www.aabainc.org or

Despite looking skeleton-like to others, people with the weight disorder anorexia nervosa see themselves as overweight.

Anorexia nervosa: A severe eating disorder in which people may refuse to eat while denying that their behavior and appearance—which can become skeleton-like—are unusual.

Bulimia: A disorder in which a person binges on incredibly large quantities of food.

call 212-575-6200. You can get more information at www.nlm.nih.gov/medlineplus/ eatingdisorders.html.

BECOMING AN INFORMED CONSUMER of Psychology

Dieting and Losing Weight Successfully

PowerWeb: Psychology

www.mhhe.com/feldmanup7

Although 60 percent of the people in the United States say they want to lose weight, it's a losing battle for most of them. Most people who diet eventually regain the weight they have lost, and so they try again and get caught in a seemingly endless cycle of weight loss and gain. Given what we know about the causes of obesity, this is not entirely surprising, because so many factors affect eating behavior and weight (Lowe, 1993; Newport & Carroll, 2002; Parker-Pope, 2003).

According to diet experts, you should keep several things in mind when trying to lose weight (CR, 1993; Gatchel & Oordt, 2003; Heshka et al., 2003):

- ⊙ *There is no easy route to weight control.* You will have to make permanent changes in your life to lose weight without gaining it back. The most obvious strategy—cutting down on the amount of food you eat—is just the first step toward a lifetime commitment to changing your eating habits. You must consider the nutrient content, as well as the overall quantity, of the food you consume.
- ⊙ *Keep track of what you eat and what you weigh.* Unless you keep careful records, you won't really know how much you are eating and whether any diet is working.
- ⊙ *Eat "big" foods.* Eat foods that are bulky and heavy but low in calories, such as grapes and soup. Such foods trick your body into thinking you've eaten more, decreasing hunger.
- ⊙ *Exercise.* When you exercise, you use up fat stored in your body as fuel for muscles, which is measured in calories. As you use up this fat, you will probably lose weight. Almost any activity helps burn calories (see Figure 3). The weight-set-point hypothesis suggests another advantage to moderate exercise: It may lower your set point. Although just how much exercise is sufficient to lower weight is disputed, most experts recommend at least thirty consecutive minutes of moderate exercise at least three times a week. (If nothing else, the release of endorphins, neurotransmitters involved in pain reduction, after exercise will make you feel better even if you don't lose weight.)
- ⊙ *Decrease the influence of external, social stimuli on your eating behavior.* For instance, serve yourself smaller portions of food, and leave the table before you see what is being served for dessert. Don't even buy snack foods such as nachos and potato chips; if they're not readily available in the kitchen cupboard, you're not apt to eat them. Wrap refrigerated foods in aluminum foil so that you cannot see the contents and be tempted every time you open the refrigerator.
- ⊙ *Avoid fad diets.* No matter how popular they are at a particular time, extreme diets, including liquid diets, usually don't work in the long run and can be dangerous to your health.
- ⊙ *Maintain good eating habits.* When you have reached your desired weight, maintain the new habits you learned while dieting to avoid gaining back the weight you have lost.
- ⊙ *Set reasonable goals.* Know how much weight you want to lose before you start to diet. Don't try to lose too much weight too quickly or you may doom yourself to failure. Even small changes in behavior—such as walking fifteen minutes a day or eating a few less bites at each meal—can prevent weight gain (Hill et al., 2003).
- ⊙ *Don't feel guilty!* Above all, don't blame yourself if you don't succeed in losing weight. Given the evidence that obesity may be genetically determined, the

More vigorous/ less time

Stair walking for 15 minutes

Shoveling snow for 15 minutes

Running 1½ miles in 15 minutes (10 min./mile)

Jumping Rope for 15 minutes

Bicycling 4 miles in 15 minutes

Basketball (playing a game) for 15–20 minutes

Wheelchair basketball for 20 minutes

Swimming laps for 20 minutes

Water aerobics for 30 minutes

Walking 2 miles in 30 minutes (15 min./mile)

Raking leaves for 30 minutes

Pushing a stroller 1½ miles in 30 minutes

Dancing fast (social) for 30 minutes

Bicycling 5 miles in 30 minutes

Basketball (shooting baskets) for 30 minutes

Walking 1¾ miles in 35 minutes (20 min./mile)

Wheeling self in wheelchair for 30-45 minutes

Gardening for 35–45 minutes

Playing touch football for 30–45 minutes

Playing volleyball for 45 minutes

Washing windows or floors for 45–60 minutes

Washing and waxing a car for 45–60 minutes

Less vigorous/ more time

FIGURE 3 Ways to burn 150 calories: People can expend 150 calories by spending more time at a less vigorous activity or spending less time at a more vigorous activity. (Source: Adapted from Lertola, 1997.)

inability to lose weight should not be seen as a moral failing. Indeed, you are in good company, for some 90 to 95 percent of dieters regain the weight they have lost (Fritsch, 1999; Friedman, 2003).

In light of the difficulty of losing weight, psychologists Janet Polivy and C. Peter Herman suggest—paradoxically—that the best approach may be to avoid dieting in the first place. They recommend that people eat what they really want to eat, even if this means indulging in candy or ice cream every so often. This freedom to eat anything may reduce binge eating, which is more likely to occur when dieters feel that bingeing represents their only opportunity to eat what they really wish to eat. Although such an approach may not produce major weight loss, even a relatively small weight loss is better than none: Just a ten- to fifteen-pound drop in body weight may lower the major health risks that are associated with obesity (Polivy & Herman, 1991, 2002; Bruce & Wilfley, 1996).

The Need for Achievement: Striving for Success

Although hunger may be one of the more potent primary drives in our day-to-day lives, powerful secondary drives that have no clear biological basis also motivate us. Among the more prominent of these is the need for achievement.

The **need for achievement** is a stable, learned characteristic in which a person obtains satisfaction by striving for and attaining a level of excellence (McClelland

Need for achievement: A stable, learned characteristic in which a person obtains satisfaction by striving for and attaining a level of excellence.

et al., 1953). People with a high need for achievement seek out situations in which they can compete against some standard—be it grades, money, or winning at a game—and prove themselves successful. But they are not indiscriminate when it comes to picking their challenges: They tend to avoid situations in which success will come too easily (which would be unchallenging) and situations in which success is unlikely. Instead, people high in achievement motivation generally choose tasks that are of intermediate difficulty.

In contrast, people with low achievement motivation tend to be motivated primarily by a desire to avoid failure. As a result, they seek out easy tasks, being sure to avoid failure, or seek out very difficult tasks for which failure has no negative implications, because almost anyone would fail at them. People with a high fear of failure will stay away from tasks of intermediate difficulty, because they may fail where others have been successful (Atkinson & Feather, 1966; Martin & Marsh, 2002).

A high need for achievement generally produces positive outcomes, at least in a success-oriented society such as ours. For instance, people motivated by a high need for achievement are more likely to attend college than are their low-achievement counterparts, and once they are in college, they tend to receive higher grades in classes that are related to their future careers. Furthermore, high achievement motivation indicates future economic and occupational success (McClelland, 1985; Thrash & Elliot, 2002). (To learn more about need for achievement, try **Interactivity 30–1.**)

MEASURING ACHIEVEMENT MOTIVATION

How can we measure a person's need for achievement? The measuring instrument used most frequently is the *Thematic Apperception Test (TAT)* (Spangler, 1992). In the TAT, an examiner shows a series of ambiguous pictures, such as the one in Figure 4. The examiner tells participants to write a story that describes what is happening, who the people are, what led to the situation, what the people are thinking or wanting, and what will happen next. Researchers then use a standard scoring system to determine the amount of achievement imagery in people's stories. For example, someone who writes a story in which the main character strives to beat an opponent, studies in order to do well at some task, or works hard in order to get a promotion shows clear signs of an achievement orientation. The inclusion of such achievement-related imagery in the participants' stories is assumed to indicate an unusually high degree of concern with—and therefore a relatively strong need for—achievement (Tuerlinckx, DeBoeck, & Lens, 2002).

The Need for Affiliation: Striving for Friendship

Few of us choose to lead our lives as hermits. Why?

One main reason is that most people have a **need for affiliation,** an interest in establishing and maintaining relationships with other people. Individuals with a high need for affiliation write TAT stories that emphasize the desire to maintain or reinstate friendships and show concern over being rejected by friends.

People who have higher affiliation needs are particularly sensitive to relationships with others. They desire to be with their friends more of the time, and alone less often, compared with people who are lower in the need for affiliation. However, gender is a greater determinant of how much time is actually spent with friends: Regardless of their affiliative orientation, female students spend significantly more time with their friends and less time alone than male students do (Wong & Csikszentmihalyi, 1991; O'Connor & Rosenblood, 1996; Cantwell & Andrews, 2002).

FIGURE 4 This ambiguous picture is similar to those used in the Thematic Apperception Test to determine people's underlying motivation (© 1943 by the President and Fellows of Harvard College; 1971 by Henry A. Murray.) What do you see? Do you think your response is related to your motivation?

INTERACTIVITY 30–1

Need for achievement

Need for affiliation: An interest in establishing and maintaining relationships with other people.

The Need for Power: Striving for Impact on Others

If your fantasies include becoming president of the United States or running Microsoft, your dreams may reflect a high need for power. The **need for power,** a tendency to seek impact, control, or influence over others and to be seen as a powerful individual, is an additional type of motivation (Winter, 1973, 1987; Lee-Chai & Bargh, 2001).

As you might expect, people with strong needs for power are more apt to belong to organizations and seek office than are those low in the need for power. They also tend to work in professions in which their power needs may be fulfilled, such as business management and—you may or may not be surprised—teaching (Jenkins, 1994). In addition, they seek to display the trappings of power. Even in college, they are more likely to collect prestigious possessions, such as electronic equipment and sports cars.

Some significant gender differences exist in the display of need for power. Men with high power needs tend to show unusually high levels of aggression, drink heavily, act in a sexually exploitative manner, and participate more frequently in competitive sports—behaviors that collectively represent somewhat extravagant, flamboyant behavior. In contrast, women display their power needs with more restraint; this is congruent with traditional societal constraints on women's behavior. Women with high power needs are more apt than men are to channel those needs in a socially responsible manner, such as by showing concern for others or displaying highly nurturing behavior (Winter, 1988, 1995).

> **Need for power:** A tendency to seek impact, control, or influence over others, and to be seen as a powerful individual.

RECAP/EVALUATE/RETHINK

RECAP

What biological and social factors underlie hunger?

- ▶ Eating behavior is subject to homeostasis, as most people's weight stays within a relatively stable range. The hypothalamus in the brain is central to the regulation of food intake. (p. 337)
- ▶ Social factors, such as mealtimes, cultural food preferences, and other learned habits, also play a role in the regulation of eating, determining when, what, and how much one eats. An oversensitivity to social cues and an insensitivity to internal cues may also be related to obesity. In addition, obesity may be caused by an unusually high weight set point—the weight the body attempts to maintain—and genetic factors. (p. 338)

How are needs relating to achievement, affiliation, and power motivation exhibited?

- ▶ Need for achievement refers to the stable, learned characteristic in which a person strives to attain a level of excellence. Need for achievement is usually measured through the Thematic Apperception Test (TAT), a series of pictures about which a person writes a story. (p. 341)

- ▶ The need for affiliation is a concern with establishing and maintaining relationships with others, whereas the need for power is a tendency to seek to exert an impact on others. (p. 342)

EVALUATE

1. Match the following terms with their definitions:
   1. Hypothalamus   a. Leads to refusal of food and starvation
   2. Lateral hypothalamic damage   b. Responsible for monitoring food intake
   3. Ventromedial hypothalamic damage   c. Causes extreme overeating
2. The _____ _____ _____ is the particular level of weight the body strives to maintain.
3. _____ is the rate at which energy is produced and expended by the body.
4. Julio is the type of person who constantly strives for excellence. He feels intense satisfaction when he is able to master a new task. Julio most likely has a high need for _____.

5. Debbie's Thematic Apperception Test (TAT) story depicts a young girl who is rejected by one of her peers and seeks to regain her friendship. What major type of motivation is Debbie displaying in her story?
   a. Need for achievement
   b. Need for motivation
   c. Need for affiliation
   d. Need for power

RETHINK

1. In what ways do societal expectations, expressed by television shows and commercials, contribute to both obesity and excessive concern about weight loss? How could television contribute to better eating habits and attitudes toward weight? Should it be required to do so?

2. Can hiring managers use traits such as need for achievement, need for power, and need for affiliation to select workers for jobs? What other criteria, both motivational and personal, would managers have to consider when making such a selection?

Answers to Evaluate Questions

1. 1-b, 2-a, 3-c; 2. weight set point; 3. metabolism; 4. achievement; 5. c.

Understanding Emotional Experiences

Karl Andrews held in his hands the envelope he had been waiting for. It could be the ticket to his future: an offer of admission to his first-choice college. But what was it going to say? He knew it could go either way; his grades were pretty good and he had been involved in some extracurricular activities, but his SAT scores had been not so terrific. He felt so nervous that his hands shook as he opened the thin envelope (not a good sign, he thought). Here it comes. "Dear Mr. Andrews," it read. "The Trustees of the University are pleased to admit you . . ." That was all he needed to see. With a whoop of excitement, Karl found himself jumping up and down gleefully. A rush of emotion overcame him as it sank in that he had, in fact, been accepted. He was on his way.

At one time or another, all of us have experienced the strong feelings that accompany both very pleasant and very negative experiences. Perhaps we have felt the thrill of getting a sought-after job, the joy of being in love, sorrow over someone's death, or the anguish of inadvertently hurting someone. Moreover, we experience such reactions on a less intense level throughout our daily lives: the pleasure of a friendship, the enjoyment of a movie, and the embarrassment of breaking a borrowed item.

Despite the varied nature of these feelings, they all represent emotions. Although everyone has an idea of what an emotion is, formally defining the concept has proved to be an elusive task. We'll use a general definition: **Emotions** are feelings that generally have both physiological and cognitive elements and that influence behavior.

Think, for example, about how it feels to be happy. First, we obviously experience a feeling that we can differentiate from other emotions. It is likely that we also experience some identifiable physical changes in our bodies: Perhaps the heart rate increases, or—as in the example of Karl Andrews—we find ourselves "jumping for joy." Finally, the emotion probably encompasses cognitive elements: Our understanding and evaluation of the meaning of what is happening prompts our feelings of happiness.

It is also possible, however, to experience an emotion without the presence of cognitive elements. For instance, we may react with fear to an unusual or novel situation (such as coming into contact with an erratic, unpredictable individual), or we may experience pleasure over sexual excitation without having cognitive awareness or understanding of just what it is about the situation that is exciting.

Some psychologists argue that entirely separate systems govern cognitive responses and emotional responses. A current controversy focuses on whether the emotional response predominates over the cognitive response or vice versa. Some theorists suggest that we first respond to a situation with an emotional reaction and later try to understand it (Zajonc, 1985; Zajonc & McIntosh, 1992; Murphy & Zajonc, 1993). For example, we may enjoy a complex modern symphony without at first understanding it or knowing why we like it.

In contrast, other theorists propose that people first develop cognitions about a situation and then react emotionally. This school of thought suggests that we must think about and understand a stimulus or situation, relating it to what we already know, before we can react on an emotional level (Lazarus, 1991a, 1991b, 1994, 1995).

Emotions: Feelings that generally have both physiological and cognitive elements and that influence behavior.

Proponents of both sides of this debate can cite research to support their viewpoints, and so the question is far from resolved. Perhaps the sequence varies from situation to situation, with emotions predominating in some instances and cognitive processes occurring first in others. Both sides agree that we can experience emotions that involve little or no conscious thought. We may not know why we're afraid of mice, understanding objectively that they represent no danger, but we may still be frightened out of our wits when we see them (Lewis & Haviland-Jones, 2000).

⊕⊕⊕

The Functions of Emotions

Imagine what it would be like if we didn't experience emotion—no depths of despair, no depression, no remorse, but at the same time no happiness, joy, or love. Obviously, life would be considerably less satisfying, and even dull, if we lacked the capacity to sense and express emotion.

But do emotions serve any purpose beyond making life interesting? Indeed they do. Psychologists have identified several important functions that emotions play in our daily lives (Averill, 1994; Scherer, 1994; Oatley & Jenkins, 1996). Among the most important of those functions are the following:

▶ *Preparing us for action.* Emotions act as a link between events in our environment and our responses. For example, if we saw an angry dog charging toward us, the emotional reaction (fear) would be associated with physiological arousal of the sympathetic division of the autonomic nervous system, the activation of the "fight-or-flight" response. The role of the sympathetic division is to prepare us for emergency action, which presumably would get us moving out of the dog's way—quickly.

▶ *Shaping our future behavior.* Emotions promote learning that will help us make appropriate responses in the future. For example, the emotional response that occurs when we experience something unpleasant—such as a threatening dog—teaches us to avoid similar circumstances in the future. In the same way, pleasant emotions act as positive reinforcement for prior behavior and therefore may lead an individual to seek out similar situations in the future.

▶ *Helping us interact more effectively with others.* We often communicate the emotions we experience through our verbal and nonverbal behaviors, making our emotions obvious to observers. These behaviors can act as a signal to observers, allowing them to understand better what we are experiencing and to predict our future behavior. In turn, this promotes more effective and appropriate social interaction.

Determining the Range of Emotions: Labeling Our Feelings

If we were to list the words in the English language that have been used to describe emotions, we would end up with at least 500 examples (Averill, 1975). The list would range from such obvious emotions as *happiness* and *fear* to less common ones, such as *adventurousness* and *pensiveness*.

One challenge for psychologists has been to sort through this list to identify the most important, fundamental emotions. Theorists have hotly contested the issue of cataloging emotions and have come up with different lists, depending on how they define the concept of emotion. In fact, some reject the question entirely, saying that *no* set of emotions should be singled out as most basic, and that emotions are best

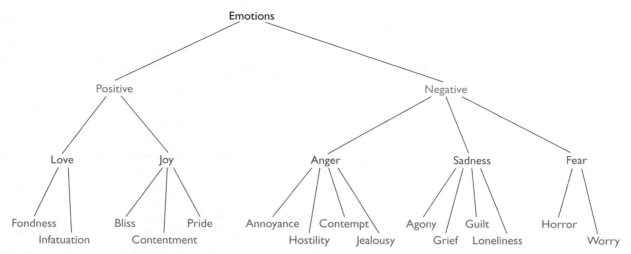

FIGURE 1 One approach to organizing emotions is to use a hierarchy, which divides emotions into increasingly narrow subcategories. (Source: Adapted from Fischer, Shaver, & Carnochan, 1990.)

understood by breaking them down into their component parts. Other researchers argue for looking at emotions in terms of a hierarchy, dividing them into positive and negative categories, and then organizing them into increasingly narrower subcategories (see Figure 1; Carroll & Russell, 1997; Manstead, Frijda, & Fischer, 2003).

Still, most researchers suggest that a list of basic emotions would include, at a minimum, happiness, anger, fear, sadness, and disgust. Other lists are broader, including emotions such as surprise, contempt, guilt, and joy (Plutchik, 1980; Ortony & Turner, 1990; Russell, 1991; Ekman, 1994a; Shweder, 1994).

One difficulty in defining a basic set of emotions is that substantial differences exist in descriptions of emotions among various cultures. For instance, Germans report experiencing *schadenfreude*, a feeling of pleasure over another person's difficulties, and the Japanese experience *hagaii*, a mood of vulnerable heartache colored by frustration. In Tahiti, people experience *musu*, a feeling of reluctance to yield to unreasonable demands made by one's parents.

Finding *schadenfreude*, *hagaii*, or *musu* in a particular culture doesn't mean that the members of other cultures are incapable of experiencing such emotions, of course. It does suggest, though, that fitting a particular emotion into a linguistic category to describe that emotion may make it easier to discuss, contemplate, and perhaps experience (Russell, 1991; Mesquita & Frijda, 1992; Russell & Sato, 1995).

The Roots of Emotions

I've never been so angry before; I feel my heart pounding, and I'm trembling all over . . . I don't know how I'll get through the performance. I feel like my stomach is filled with butterflies . . . That was quite a mistake I made! My face must be incredibly red . . . When I heard the footsteps in the night, I was so frightened that I couldn't catch my breath.

If you examine our language, you will find that there are literally dozens of ways to describe how we feel when we experience an emotion, and that the language we use to describe emotions is, for the most part, based on the physical symptoms that are associated with a particular emotional experience (Koveces, 1987; Manstead & Wagner, 2004).

Consider, for instance, the experience of fear. Pretend that it is late on New Year's Eve. You are walking down a dark road, and you hear a stranger approaching behind you. It is clear that he is not trying to hurry by but is coming directly toward you.

You think about what you will do if the stranger attempts to rob you or, worse, hurt you in some way.

While these thoughts are running through your head, something rather dramatic will be happening to your body. The most likely reactions, which are associated with activation of the autonomic nervous system, include an increase in your rate of breathing, an acceleration of your heart rate, a widening of your pupils (to increase visual sensitivity), and a dryness in your mouth as the functioning of your salivary glands, and in fact of your entire digestive system, ceases. At the same time, though, your sweat glands probably will increase their activity, because increased sweating will help you rid yourself of the excess heat developed by any emergency activity in which you engage.

Of course, all these physiological changes are likely to occur without your awareness. At the same time, though, the emotional experience accompanying them will be obvious to you: You most surely would report being fearful.

Although it is easy to describe the general physical reactions that accompany emotions, defining the specific role that those physiological responses play in the experience of emotions has proved to be a major puzzle for psychologists. As we shall see, some theorists suggest that specific bodily reactions *cause* us to experience a particular emotion—we experience fear, for instance, *because* the heart is pounding and we are breathing deeply. In contrast, other theorists suggest that the physiological reaction *results* from the experience of an emotion. In this view, we experience fear, and as a result the heart pounds and our breathing deepens.

THE JAMES-LANGE THEORY: DO GUT REACTIONS EQUAL EMOTIONS?

To William James and Carl Lange, who were among the first researchers to explore the nature of emotions, emotional experience is, very simply, a reaction to instinctive bodily events that occur as a response to some situation or event in the environment. This view is summarized in James's statement, "we feel sorry because we cry, angry because we strike, afraid because we tremble" (James, 1890).

James and Lange took the view that the instinctive response of crying at a loss leads us to feel sorrow, that striking out at someone who frustrates us results in our feeling anger, that trembling at a menacing threat causes us to feel fear. They suggested that for every major emotion there is an accompanying physiological or "gut" reaction of internal organs—called a *visceral experience*. It is this specific pattern of visceral response that leads us to label the emotional experience.

James-Lange theory of emotion: The belief that emotional experience is a reaction to bodily events occurring as a result of an external situation ("I feel sad because I am crying").

In sum, James and Lange proposed that we experience emotions as a result of physiological changes that produce specific sensations. The brain interprets these sensations as particular kinds of emotional experiences (see Figure 2). This view has come to be called the **James-Lange theory of emotion** (Laird & Bresler, 1990; Cobo et al., 2002).

The James-Lange theory has some serious drawbacks, however. For the theory to be valid, visceral changes would have to occur relatively quickly, because we experience some emotions—such as fear upon hearing a stranger rapidly approaching on a dark night—almost instantaneously. Yet emotional experiences frequently occur even before there is time for certain physiological changes to be set into motion. Because of the slowness with which some visceral changes take place, it is hard to see how they could be the source of immediate emotional experience.

The James-Lange theory poses another difficulty: Physiological arousal does not invariably produce emotional experience. For example, a person who is jogging has an increased heartbeat and respiration rate, as well as many of the other physiological changes associated with certain emotions. Yet joggers typically do not think of such changes in terms of emotions. There cannot be a one-to-one correspondence,

FIGURE 2 A comparison of three models of emotion.

then, between visceral changes and emotional experience. Visceral changes by themselves may not be sufficient to produce emotion.

Finally, our internal organs produce a relatively limited range of sensations. Although some types of physiological changes are associated with specific emotional experiences, it is difficult to imagine how each of the myriad emotions that people are capable of experiencing could be the result of a unique visceral change. Many emotions actually are associated with relatively similar sorts of visceral changes, a fact that contradicts the James-Lange theory (Davidson et al., 1994; Cameron, 2002).

THE CANNON-BARD THEORY: PHYSIOLOGICAL REACTIONS AS THE RESULT OF EMOTIONS

In response to the difficulties inherent in the James-Lange theory, Walter Cannon, and later Philip Bard, suggested an alternative view. In what has come to be known as the **Cannon-Bard theory of emotion,** they proposed the model illustrated in the second part of Figure 2 (Cannon, 1929). This theory rejects the view that physiological arousal alone leads to the perception of emotion. Instead, the theory assumes that both physiological arousal *and* the emotional experience are produced simultaneously by the same nerve stimulus, which Cannon and Bard suggested emanates from the thalamus in the brain.

The theory states that after we perceive an emotion-producing stimulus, the thalamus is the initial site of the emotional response. Next, the thalamus sends a signal to the autonomic nervous system, thereby producing a visceral response. At the same time, the thalamus also communicates a message to the cerebral cortex regarding the nature of the emotion being experienced. Hence, it is not necessary for different emotions to have unique physiological patterns associated with them—as long as the message sent to the cerebral cortex differs according to the specific emotion.

Cannon-Bard theory of emotion: The belief that both physiological arousal and emotional experience are produced simultaneously by the same nerve stimulus.

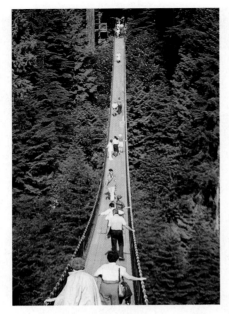

This is the high, swaying suspension bridge that was used to increase the physiological arousal of male subjects. What other types of behavior can be explained by the Schachter-Singer theory of emotion?

Schachter-Singer theory of emotion: The belief that emotions are determined jointly by a nonspecific kind of physiological arousal and its interpretation, based on environmental cues.

The Cannon-Bard theory seems to have been accurate in rejecting the view that physiological arousal alone accounts for emotions. However, more recent research has led to some important modifications of the theory. For one thing, we now understand that the hypothalamus and the limbic system, not the thalamus, play a major role in emotional experience. In addition, the simultaneous occurrence of the physiological and emotional responses, which is a fundamental assumption of the Cannon-Bard theory, has yet to be demonstrated conclusively. This ambiguity has allowed room for yet another theory of emotions: the Schachter-Singer theory.

THE SCHACHTER-SINGER THEORY: EMOTIONS AS LABELS

Suppose that, as you are being followed down a dark street on New Year's Eve, you notice a man being followed by another shady figure on the other side of the street. Now assume that instead of reacting with fear, the man begins to laugh and act gleeful. Would the reactions of this other individual be sufficient to lay your fears to rest? Might you, in fact, decide there is nothing to fear, and get into the spirit of the evening by beginning to feel happiness and glee yourself?

According to an explanation that focuses on the role of cognition, the **Schachter-Singer theory of emotion,** this might very well happen. This approach to explaining emotions emphasizes that we identify the emotion we are experiencing by observing our environment and comparing ourselves with others (Schachter & Singer, 1962).

Schachter and Singer's classic experiment found evidence for this hypothesis. In the study, participants were told that they would receive an injection of a vitamin. In reality, they were given epinephrine, a drug that causes an increase in physiological arousal, including higher heart and respiration rates and a reddening of the face, responses that typically occur during strong emotional reactions. The members of both groups were then placed individually in a situation where a confederate of the experimenter acted in one of two ways. In one condition he acted angry and hostile, and in the other condition he behaved as if he were exuberantly happy.

The purpose of the experiment was to determine how the participants would react emotionally to the confederate's behavior. When they were asked to describe their own emotional state at the end of the experiment, the participants exposed to the angry confederate reported that they felt angry, while those exposed to the happy confederate reported feeling happy. In sum, the results suggest that participants turned to the environment and the behavior of others for an explanation of the physiological arousal they were experiencing.

The results of the Schachter-Singer experiment, then, supported a cognitive view of emotions, in which emotions are determined jointly by a relatively nonspecific kind of physiological arousal *and* the labeling of that arousal on the basis of cues from the environment (refer to the third part of Figure 2).

Although later research has found that arousal is not as nonspecific as Schachter and Singer assumed, it is clear that arousal can magnify, and be mistaken for, many emotions. For example, in one experiment, men who crossed a swaying 450-foot suspension bridge spanning a deep canyon were more attracted to a woman they encountered at the other end than were those who crossed a stable bridge spanning a shallow stream. Apparently, the men who crossed the frightening bridge attributed their subsequent high arousal to the woman, rather than to the swaying bridge (Dutton & Aron, 1974; Schorr, 2001).

In short, the Schachter-Singer theory of emotions is important because it suggests that, at least under some circumstances, emotional experiences are a joint function of physiological arousal and the labeling of that arousal. When the source of physiological arousal is unclear, we may look to our surroundings to determine just what we are experiencing.

CONTEMPORARY PERSPECTIVES ON THE NEUROLOGICAL UNDERPINNINGS OF EMOTIONS

When Schachter and Singer carried out their groundbreaking experiment in the early 1960s, the ways in which they could evaluate the physiology that accompanies emotion were relatively limited. However, advances in the measurement of the nervous system and other parts of the body have allowed researchers to examine more closely the biological responses involved in emotion. As a result, contemporary research on emotion points to a revision of earlier views that physiological responses associated with emotions are undifferentiated. Instead, evidence is growing that specific patterns of biological arousal are associated with individual emotions (Levenson, 1994; Franks & Smith, 2000).

For instance, researchers have found that specific emotions produce activation of very different portions of the brain. In one study, participants undergoing positron emission tomography (PET) brain scans were asked to recall events, such as deaths and funerals, that made them feel sad, or events that made them feel happy, such as weddings and births. They also looked at photos of faces that appeared to be happy or sad. The results of the PET scans were clear: Happiness was related to a decrease in activity in certain areas of the cerebral cortex, whereas sadness was associated with increases in activity in particular portions of the cortex (see Figure 3). Ultimately, it may be possible to map each particular emotion to specific a site in the brain (George et al., 1995; Hamann, Ely, Hoffman, & Kilts, 2002).

The *amygdala*, in the brain's temporal lobe, also is important in the experience of emotions, for it provides a link between the perception of an emotion-producing stimulus and the recall of that stimulus later (Adolphs, 2002). For example, if we've once been attacked by a vicious pit bull, the amygdala processes that information and leads us to react with fear when we see a pit bull later—an example of a classically conditioned fear response. Because neural pathways connect the amygdala, the visual cortex, and the *hippocampus* (which plays an important role in the consolidation of memories), some scientists speculate that emotion-related stimuli can be processed and responded to almost instantaneously (see Figure 4). This immediate response occurs so rapidly that higher-order, more rational thinking, which

FIGURE 3 Experiencing different emotions activates particular areas of the brain, as these scans illustrate. (Source: Mark George, NIMH.)

FIGURE 4 Connections from the amygdala, seen here in red, allow it to mediate many of the autonomic expressions of emotional states through the hippocampus (blue) and visual cortex (orange). (Source: Dolan, 2002.)

The Appearance of Deception: Can Nonverbal Behavior Be Used to Reveal Terrorists?

FBI agents were looking for a six-month-old boy whose mother reported that he had been kidnapped from a Wal-Mart in Tampa, Florida. Joe Navarro, a body language expert for the FBI, watched as the tearful mother told agents about her son's disappearance. But Navarro immediately suspected the woman was lying: Despite her tears, her body language seemed too calm and calculated for a mother whose infant son had just been kidnapped. When agents called her back for further questioning, she confessed that she had suffocated her child with a plastic garbage bag (Davis, Pereira, & Bulkeley, 2002).

When people are being deceitful, do their faces or body language give them away? According to some psychologists, such nonverbal cues can indicate deceptive or malicious intent. Looking at a range of lies—from workers faking pain to get a few days off from their jobs to criminals attempting to deceive police detectives—researchers have shown that careful analysis of facial expressions and body language sometimes can differentiate truth from fiction. For example, compared with expressions of true pain, faked pain is characterized by more

facial activity and longer-lasting expressions (Vrij, 2001; Hill & Craig, 2002).

However, nonverbal behaviors do not invariably provide indications of deception. Skilled liars can control their nonverbal behavior, thereby making detection difficult or impossible. In addition, the cues that may indicate that someone is lying, such as acting tense or fidgeting, may signal that an honest person is simply anxious. In fact, a careful analysis of the nonverbal behavior of lying people shows two things: Few cues consistently reveal deception, and untrained people can seldom detect deception. Even *polygraphs*, electronic lie detectors that measure physiological arousal, can be inaccurate, because there is no foolproof technique for assessing the extent of the physiological changes that may indicate a lie (Committee to Review the Scientific Evidence on the Polygraph, 2003; DePaulo et al., 2003).

Furthermore, training people to be more aware of the nonverbal cues indicative of deception is difficult and time-consuming. Although psychologist Paul Ekman, who studies deceptive facial expressions, has developed a program that can teach trainees to recognize subtle

facial expressions that untrained eyes miss, even trained security agents and law enforcement officials who are fatigued or inattentive may miss subtle cues given off by hostile individuals (Davis, Pereira, & Bulkeley, 2002).

Consequently, researchers are developing automated equipment that can instantly analyze the nonverbal behaviors of large numbers of people with the goal of identifying suspects who then can be further investigated. For instance, one research group has developed a high-definition thermal-imaging technique that can detect deceit by examining the thermal patterns on people's faces. Soon, airports and other high-traffic public areas will be able to use imaging techniques like this in conjunction with other technologies, such as voice analysis equipment, surveillance video analysis software, and instantaneous background checks, to quickly screen large crowds for criminals or terrorists. At security checkpoints, people may eventually pass through nonverbal behavior detectors just as they pass through metal detectors today (Pavlidis, Eberhardt, & Levine, 2002).

RETHINK

In addition to their security and law enforcement uses, how might nonverbal behavior analysis technologies be used in other contexts? How might such technologies be misused?

takes more time, seems not to be involved initially. In a slower, but more thoughtful, response to emotion-evoking stimuli, emotion-related sensory information is first evaluated and then sent on to the amygdala. It appears that the quicker system offers an immediate response to emotion-evoking stimuli, whereas the slower system helps confirm a threat and prepare a more thoughtful response (Dolan, 2002).

MAKING SENSE OF THE MULTIPLE PERSPECTIVES ON EMOTION

As new approaches to emotion continue to develop, it is reasonable to ask why so many theories of emotion exist and, perhaps more important, which one provides the most complete explanation. Actually, we have only scratched the surface. There are almost as many explanatory theories of emotion as there are individual emotions (e.g., Lewis & Haviland-Jones, 2000; Mayne & Bonanno, 2001; DeCoster, 2003; Manstead, Frijda, & Fischer, 2003).

Why are theories of emotion so plentiful? For one thing, emotions are not a simple phenomenon but are intertwined closely with motivation, cognition, neuroscience, and a host of related branches of psychology. For example, evidence from brain imaging studies shows that even when people come to supposedly rational, nonemotional decisions—such as making moral, philosophical judgments—emotions come into play (Greene et al., 2001).

In short, emotions are such complex phenomena, encompassing both biological and cognitive aspects, that no single theory has been able to explain fully all the facets of emotional experience. Furthermore, contradictory evidence of one sort or another challenges each approach, and therefore no theory has proved invariably accurate in its predictions.

This abundance of perspectives on emotion is not a cause for despair—or unhappiness, fear, or any other negative emotion. It simply reflects the fact that psychology is an evolving, developing science. As we gather more evidence, the specific answers to questions about the nature of emotions will become clearer. Furthermore, even as our understanding of emotions continues to grow, ongoing efforts are applying our knowledge of emotions to practical problems, as we consider in the *Applying Psychology in the 21st Century* box and in **Interactivity 31–1.**

INTERACTIVITY 31–1

Detection of deception

RECAP/EVALUATE/RETHINK

RECAP

What are emotions, and how do we experience them?

- ▶ Emotions are broadly defined as feelings that may affect behavior and generally have both a physiological component and a cognitive component. Debate continues over whether separate systems govern cognitive and emotional responses and whether one has primacy over the other. (p. 345)

What are the functions of emotions?

- ▶ Emotions prepare us for action, shape future behavior through learning, and help us interact more effectively with others. (p. 346)

What are the explanations for emotions?

- ▶ Several theories explain emotions. The James-Lange theory suggests that emotional experience is a reaction to bodily, or visceral, changes that occur as a response to an environmental event and are interpreted as an emotional response. (p. 348)
- ▶ In contrast, the Cannon-Bard theory contends that both physiological arousal *and* an emotional experience are produced simultaneously by the same nerve stimulus and that the visceral experience does not necessarily differ among differing emotions. (p. 349)
- ▶ The Schachter-Singer theory suggests that emotions are determined jointly by a relatively nonspecific physiological arousal and the subsequent labeling of that arousal,

using cues from the environment to determine how others are behaving in the same situation. (p. 350)
- ▶ The most recent approaches to emotions focus on their biological aspects. For instance, it now seems that specific patterns of biological arousal are associated with individual emotions. Furthermore, new scanning techniques have identified the specific parts of the brain that are activated during the experience of particular emotions. (p. 351)

EVALUATE

1. Emotions are always accompanied by a cognitive response. True or false?
2. The _____-_____ theory of emotions states that emotions are a response to instinctive bodily events.
3. According to the _____-_____ theory of emotion, both an emotional response and physiological arousal are produced simultaneously by the same nerve stimulus.
4. Your friend—a psychology major—tells you, "I was at a party last night. During the course of the evening, my general level of arousal increased. Since I was at a party where people were enjoying themselves, I assume I must have felt happy." What theory of emotion does your friend subscribe to?
5. The _____, or "lie detector," is an instrument used to measure physiological responses associated with answers to questions.

RETHINK

1. Many people enjoy watching movies, sporting events, and music performances in crowded theaters and arenas more than they like watching them at home alone. Which theory of emotions may help explain this? How?
2. If researchers learned how to control emotional responses so that targeted emotions could be caused or prevented, what ethical concerns might arise? Under what circumstances, if any, should such techniques be used?

Answers to Evaluate Questions

1. false; emotions may occur without a cognitive response; 2. James-Lange; 3. Cannon-Bard; 4. Schachter-Singer; 5. polygraph

KEY TERMS

emotions p. 345
James-Lange theory of emotion p. 348

Cannon-Bard theory of emotion p. 349

Schachter-Singer theory of emotion p. 350

Nonverbal Behavior and the Expression of Emotions

How does nonverbal behavior relate to the expression of emotions?

Some years ago, John Yarbrough was working patrol for the Los Angeles Country Sheriff's Department. It was about two in the morning. He and his partner were in the Willowbrook section of South Central Los Angeles, and they pulled over a sports car . . . [Yarbrough] opened the door and stepped out onto the street, walking toward the vehicle with his weapon drawn. Suddenly, a man jumped out of the passenger side and pointed a gun directly at him. The two of them froze, separated by no more than a few yards. "There was a tree behind him, to his right," Yarbrough recalls. "He was about seventeen. He had the gun in his right hand. He was on the curb side. I was on the other side, facing him. It was just a matter of who was going to shoot first. I remember it clear as day. But for some reason I didn't shoot him . . . [Was] he a danger? Sure. He's standing there with a gun, and what person in his right mind does that facing a uniformed armed policeman? If you looked at it logically, I should have shot him. But logic had nothing to do with it. Something just didn't feel right. It was a gut reaction not to shoot—a hunch that at that exact moment he was not an imminent threat to me" (Gladwell, 2002, p. 38).

Yarbrough's hunch was right: The man with the gun backed down. But that hunch was based on the officer's reading of the man's nonverbal behavior—the gunman's facial expressions, his body movements, and his gestures. And that reading was, fortunately, an accurate one.

Reliance on nonverbal behavior to "read" others is nothing new. Ancient Sanskrit writings speak of someone who, on giving an evasive answer, "rubs the great toe along the ground, and shivers." Shakespeare describes Macbeth's face as "a place where men may read strange matters." An old love song claims that "your eyes are the eyes of a woman in love." Such examples demonstrate how nonverbal behavior has long had the reputation of revealing people's emotions. Only recently, though, have psychologists demonstrated the validity of such claims, finding that nonverbal behavior is an important way in which we communicate our emotions.

Nonverbal behavior communicates messages simultaneously across several *channels*, or paths. For example, facial expressions, eye contact, body movements, tone of voice, and even less obvious behaviors such as the positioning of the eyebrows are separate nonverbal channels of communication. Furthermore, each channel can carry a particular message—which may or may not be related to the messages being carried by the other channels. Because facial expressions represent the primary means of communicating emotional states, we will examine their role in the experience of emotions.

▲ ▲ ▲

Consider, for a moment, the six photos displayed in Figure 1. Can you identify the emotions being expressed by the person in each of the photos?

If you are a good judge of facial expressions, you will conclude that these expressions display six of the basic emotions: happiness, anger, sadness, surprise, disgust, and

Exploring DIVERSITY

Do People in All Cultures Express Emotion Similarly?

FIGURE I These photos demonstrate six of the primary emotions: happiness, anger, sadness, surprise, disgust, and fear.

fear. Hundreds of studies of nonverbal behavior show that these emotions are consistently distinct and identifiable, even by untrained observers (Ekman & O'Sullivan, 1991).

It is particularly interesting that these six emotions are not unique to members of Western cultures; rather, they constitute the basic emotions expressed universally by members of the human race, regardless of where individuals have been raised and what learning experiences they have had. Psychologist Paul Ekman convincingly demonstrated this point when he studied the members of an isolated New Guinea jungle tribe who had had almost no contact with Westerners (Ekman, 1972). The people of the tribe did not speak or understand English, had never seen a movie, and had had very limited experience with Caucasians before Ekman's arrival. Yet their nonverbal responses to emotion-evoking stories, as well as their ability to identify basic emotions, were quite similar to those of Westerners.

Being so isolated, the New Guineans could not have learned from Westerners to recognize or produce similar facial expressions. Instead, their similar abilities

"And just exactly what is that expression intended to convey?"

and manner of responding emotionally appear to have been present innately. Although one could argue that similar experiences in both cultures led the members of each one to learn similar types of nonverbal behavior, this appears unlikely, because the two cultures are so very different. The expression of basic emotions, then, seems to be universal (Ekman, 1994b; Izard, 1994; Matsumoto, 2002). To learn more about the expression of emotions and nonverbal behavior, try **Interactivity 32–1.**

▲ ▲ ▲

THE FACIAL-AFFECT PROGRAM

Why do people across cultures express emotions similarly? A hypothesis known as the **facial-affect program** gives one explanation (Ekman, 1972, 2003).

The facial-affect program—which is assumed to be universally present at birth—is analogous to a computer program that is turned on when a particular emotion is experienced. When set in motion, the "program" activates a set of nerve impulses that make the face display an appropriate expression. Each primary emotion produces a unique set of muscular movements, forming the kinds of expressions shown in Figure 1. For example, the emotion of happiness is universally displayed by movement of the zygomatic major, a muscle that raises the corners of the mouth—forming what we would call a smile (Ekman, Davidson, & Friesen, 1990; Ekman, 2003).

DISPLAY RULES

If you've ever traveled in another culture, you've probably encountered people whose nonverbal behavior is quite different from what you are accustomed to. For instance, perhaps you've been to Japan or other Asian countries, where effusive

INTERACTIVITY 32–1

Emotions and nonverbal behavior

Facial-affect program: Activation of a set of nerve impulses that make the face display the appropriate expression.

PowerWeb: What's in a Face?

www.mhhe.com/feldmanup7

a.   b.

c.   d.

FIGURE 2 Which is the real smile? In comparison to a true happy smile—the smile in (a)—the smiles in the other photos are false. In (b) and (c) the person is actually experiencing disgust; in (d), the person is actually feeling sad. (Source: Ekman, Friesen, & O'Sullivan, 1988.)

emotional displays tend to be rarer than they are in Western countries. How do such differences correspond with the evidence showing that the expression of basic emotions is similar across cultures?

Some cultural differences in emotional expression are analogous to the way in which spoken languages show regional differences. For example, even though English is spoken in both the United States and Australia, speakers in the two countries show clear differences in accent. Similarly, people in different cultures may display basic emotions in slightly different ways; for this reason, we recognize emotions more accurately when the emotion is displayed by a member of our own national, ethnic, or regional group (Elfenbein & Ambady, 2002).

The use of different display rules provides another reason for these cultural differences. **Display rules** are the guidelines that govern the appropriateness of showing emotion nonverbally. Display rules, which are learned during childhood, act to exaggerate, minimize, or mask emotional expressions (Feldman, 1991; Eid & Diener, 2001; Diefendorff & Richard, 2003).

Display rules: Guidelines that govern the appropriateness of showing emotion nonverbally.

People use display rules fairly well, because we all have plenty of practice. For instance, people who receive an unwanted gift learn to paste a smile on their faces, at least in the presence of the gift giver. Similarly, card players learn to avoid gloating when they have a good hand (instead displaying a "poker face").

However, we do not always successfully mask our true feeling, and subtle indications may give away our actual emotions. For instance, you may observe slight differences in true and sham smiles when you compare the photos in Figure 2.

The nature of display rules varies considerably from one culture to another. For instance, Asians, by and large, consider it less desirable to express emotions than do people in Mediterranean and Latin cultures. Although the evidence is sketchy, some research also suggests that differences in display rules exist between whites and African Americans within the United States. For instance, one study suggests that whites display more restrained emotional than African Americans do. Still, research has not fully established the scope and reliability of such within-culture findings (Hanna, 1984; Manstead, 1991; Matsumoto, 2001).

The Facial-Feedback Hypothesis: Smile, Though You're Feeling Blue

If you want to feel happy, try smiling. That is the implication of an intriguing notion known as the **facial-feedback hypothesis.** According to this hypothesis, facial expressions not only *reflect* emotional experience, they also help *determine* how people experience and label emotions (Izard, 1990). Basically put, "wearing" an emotional expression provides muscular feedback to the brain that helps produce an emotion congruent with that expression. For instance, the muscles activated when we smile may send a message to the brain indicating the experience of happiness—even if there is nothing in the environment that would produce that particular emotion. Some theoreticians have gone further, suggesting that facial expressions are *necessary* for an emotion to be experienced (Rinn, 1984, 1991). According to this view, if no facial expression is present, the emotion cannot be felt.

Support for the facial-feedback hypothesis comes from a classic experiment carried out by psychologist Paul Ekman and colleagues (Ekman, Levenson, & Friesen, 1983). In the study, professional actors were asked to follow very explicit instructions regarding the movements of muscles in their faces. You might try this example yourself:

- ▶ Raise your brows and pull them together.
- ▶ Raise your upper eyelids.
- ▶ Now stretch your lips horizontally back toward your ears.

After carrying out these directions—which, as you may have guessed, are meant to produce an expression of fear—the actors' heart rates rose and their body temperatures declined, physiological reactions that characterize fear. Overall, facial expressions representing the primary emotions produced physiological effects similar to those accompanying the genuine emotions in other circumstances (Keillor et al., 2002; Soussignan, 2002).

> **Facial-feedback hypothesis:** The hypothesis that facial expressions not only *reflect* emotional experience but also help *determine* how people experience and label emotions.

PowerWeb: Facial Expressions of Emotion
www.mhhe.com/feldmanup7

RECAP/EVALUATE/RETHINK

RECAP

How does nonverbal behavior relate to the expression of emotions?

- ▶ A person's facial expressions can reveal emotions. In fact, members of different cultures understand the emotional expressions of others in similar ways. One explanation for this similarity is that an innate facial-affect program activates a set of muscle movements representing the emotion being experienced. (p. 356)

- ▶ The facial-feedback hypothesis suggests that facial expressions not only reflect, but also produce, emotional experiences. (p. 359)

EVALUATE

1. What are the six primary emotions that can be identified from facial expressions?
2. Viewed as similar to a computer program, the
   _____ - _____ program

provides a possible explanation for the universality in the expression of emotions.

3. According to the _____ - _____ hypothesis, an emotion cannot be felt without an accompanying facial response.

RETHINK

1. What might be the biological reasons for the fact that the six basic emotions are associated with universal facial expressions? The facial-affect program is said to be

"universally present at birth"; how can this be confirmed through experimentation?

2. How might differences in nonverbal display rules between people of different cultures or between racial groups be responsible for misunderstandings during social interaction?

Answers to Evaluate Questions

1. surprise, sadness, happiness, anger, disgust, and fear; 2. facial-affect; 3. facial-feedback

KEY TERMS

facial-affect program p. 357
display rules p. 358

facial-feedback
hypothesis p. 359

Looking Back

Psychology on the Web

1. Find two different websites that deal with nonverbal behavior. One site should present a fairly "academic" discussion of the topic, and the other should be more informal. (Hint: The terms *nonverbal behavior* and *nonverbal communication* may lead you to more formal discussions of the topic, whereas *body language* may lead you to less formal discussions.) Compare and contrast your findings from the two sites.

2. Find one or more websites that offer information on polygraphs (lie detectors). The sites should be intended either to advertise (i.e., sell) lie detectors or lie detection services or to debunk lie detector tests (e.g., by showing how to cheat on them). Evaluate the information on the website(s), using your understanding of the lie detection techniques discussed earlier. Summarize your findings and conclusions.

3. After completing Interactivity 31–1, use the Web to find two examples of attempts to identify potential terrorists via their nonverbal behavior. Summarize what you find and consider the feasibility of these efforts based on what you have learned about nonverbal behavior and deception detection.

Epilogue

Motivation and emotions are two interrelated aspects of psychology. In these modules, we first considered the topic of motivation, which has spawned a great deal of theory and research examining primary and secondary drives. We then turned to a discussion of emotions, beginning with their functions and proceeding to a review of three major theories that seek to explain what emotions are and how they, and their associated physiological symptoms, emerge in the individual. Finally, we looked at cultural differences in the expression and display of emotions and discussed the facial-affect program, which seems to be innate and to regulate the nonverbal expression of the basic emotions.

Return to the opening scenario of this group of modules, which describes how hiker Aron Ralston amputated his arm to free himself from being trapped by a boulder. Using your knowledge of motivation and emotion, consider the following questions:

1. Which approach or approaches to motivation—instinctual, drive-reduction, arousal, incentive, or cognitive—most effectively explains Ralston's decision to amputate his arm to free himself?

2. Many observers commented on Ralston's "will to live" as they attempted to explain his decision to amputate his arm. How could you translate the concept of "will to live" into motivational terms?

3. What function might Ralston's emotions have served in helping or impeding his decision-making processes when he found that his arm was trapped under the boulder?

4. After he was rescued, Ralston said that once he had made the decision to sever his arm, "all the desires and joys and euphorias of a future life came rushing into me, and maybe this is how I handled the pain." How would you interpret this comment in terms of your understanding of motivation and emotion?

Sexuality and Gender

Prologue
From Boy to Girl and Back

It was a gruesome accident. A physician botched the routine circumcision of Bruce Reimer, an 8-month-old infant boy, slicing off his penis.

The distraught parents consulted with leading experts, whose predictions were unremittingly grim. Not only could he never have sex, they said, he could never marry or live a normal life in any way. The radical solution the experts suggested: The Reimers should turn their son into a daughter.

Following the experts' advice, the Reimers began calling Bruce "Brenda." What was left of his genitals was removed, and he had a series of operations meant to build an artificial vagina. Bruce/Brenda was clothed in dresses and given dolls to play with. He was taught how to be "clean" and "tidy"—in order, it was thought, to be more girl-like. He was given female hormones when he was a teenager to make him develop breasts.

But it never worked. Bruce/Brenda was beset by anxiety and depression growing up, and he didn't feel or even look like a girl. And when he learned the truth about his past when he was 14, he renounced his female identity. He became a boy again (Diamond & Simundson, 1997; Colapinto, 2000).

Although Bruce Reimer's story is a painful one, his life ultimately turned out well. After plastic surgeons crafted partially functional male genitals for him, he married a woman he deeply loved. He has adopted his wife's three children and leads, by his account, a normal life.

Reimer's experience raises a host of issues. How does heredity account for our sexual identity? How flexible is that identity? What is the relationship between gender (the sense of being male or female) and physical sexual characteristics? How do sex and gender affect our everyday behavior?

Issues like these are central to people's lives. Exemplifying major personal, as well as societal, concerns, sex and gender are also key topics for psychologists in a variety of specialties.

Looking Ahead

For instance, psychologists interested in motivation view sexuality in terms of sexual needs, drives, and gratification. Neuroscientists consider sexuality from the perspective of the relationship of the brain and nervous system to the functioning of the sexual organs. Social psychologists and psychologists who specialize in the study of women focus on society's rules of sexual conduct and the role sexual behavior plays in interpersonal behavior.

In this set of modules, we consider human sexuality from several of these vantage points. We begin by examining gender, discussing differences in societal expectations about how men and women should behave and the impact of those expectations on behavior and attitudes. Next we turn to sexual behavior. We describe the biological aspects of sexual excitement and arousal and then examine the variety of sexual activities in which people engage. We conclude with a discussion of nonconsenting sex, sexually transmitted diseases, and the psychological aspects of sexual difficulties.

Gender and Sex

What are the major differences between male and female gender roles?

"It's a girl!" "It's a boy!"

One of these exclamations, or some variant, is typically the first sentence uttered upon the birth of a child. However, the consequences of whether we are born with male or female sex organs extend well beyond the moment of birth. Throughout our lives, the ways that others think of us, and even the ways in which we view ourselves, are based to a large extent on whether we are labeled as a woman or a man by society—our gender.

Gender is the perception of being male or female. Although there is a good deal of overlap between the concepts of sex and gender, they are not the same: *Sex* typically refers to sexual anatomy and sexual behavior, whereas *gender* refers to the sense of maleness or femaleness related to our membership in a given society.

Gender: The perception of being male or female.

⧫⧫⧫

Gender Roles: Society's Expectations for Women and Men

Our conclusions about what is or is not "appropriate" behavior for others and ourselves are based on gender roles. **Gender roles** are the set of expectations, defined by a particular society, that indicate what is appropriate behavior for men and women.

If men's and women's gender roles were equivalent, they would have only a minor impact on our lives. However, expectations about men and women differ significantly, and this may result in favoritism toward members of one of the sexes. Gender roles also may produce *stereotyping*, judgments about individual members of a group on the basis of their membership in that group. Stereotypes about gender roles are reflected in **sexism**, negative attitudes and behavior toward a person that are based on that person's gender.

People in Western societies like ours generally hold well-defined stereotypes about men and women, which prevail regardless of age, economic status, and social and educational background. Men are more apt to be viewed as having traits involving competence, such as independence, objectivity, and competitiveness. In contrast, women tend to be seen as having traits involving warmth and expressiveness, such as gentleness and awareness of others' feelings. Because Western society traditionally values competence more than warmth and expressiveness, the perceived differences between men and women are biased in favor of men (Eagly & Wood, 1999).

From the moment of birth, gender differences are defined by outside influences. Is it possible for a family to block these influences completely? Would it be desirable to do so?

Gender roles: The set of expectations, defined by a particular society, that indicate what is appropriate behavior for men and women.

Sexism: Negative attitudes and behavior toward a person based on that person's gender.

Items Associated with Males		Items Associated with Females
Active	Initiative	Affected
Adventurous	Inventive	Affectionate
Aggressive	Lazy	Attractive
Ambitious	Logical	Charming
Arrogant	Loud	Curious
Assertive	Masculine	Dependent
Autocratic	Opportunistic	Dreamy
Clear-thinking	Progressive	Emotional
Coarse	Rational	Fearful
Courageous	Realistic	Feminine
Cruel	Reckless	Gentle
Daring	Robust	Mild
Determined	Rude	Sensitive
Disorderly	Self-confident	Sentimental
Dominant	Serious	Sexy
Egotistical	Severe	Softhearted
Energetic	Stern	Submissive
Enterprising	Stolid	Superstitious
Forceful	Strong	Talkative
Hardheaded	Unemotional	Weak
Hardhearted	Wise	
Independent		

FIGURE I In spite of numerous differences among cultures, research has found strong similarities in the content of gender stereotypes. (Source: Williams & Best, 1990.)

What's more, cross-cultural research finds remarkable similarity in the content of gender stereotypes in different societies. For example, a twenty-five-nation study identified a core set of descriptors that were consistently used to describe men and women (Williams & Best, 1990). Women were seen as sentimental, submissive, and superstitious, whereas men were seen as adventurous, forceful, and independent (see Figure 1). These stereotypical similarities across cultures may be due to similarities in status between men and women across the cultures; in most, men receive somewhat higher status than women (Lips, 2003).

Stereotypes about women and men have proved to be remarkably enduring. Even though the number of women in the workforce has expanded dramatically in the last few decades and the feminist movement's influence has been far-reaching, gender stereotypes regarding women's and men's personal characteristics have shown little change (Allen, 1995; Fan & Marini, 2000).

Such stereotypes matter. By shaping beliefs about how men and women should behave, they potentially keep inequalities between the genders alive. Stereotypes put pressure on people to fulfill the stereotypes, and they may lead people to perform in accordance with the stereotypes rather than in accordance with their own abilities (Lips, 2003). To learn more about gender stereotypes, try **Interactivity 33–1**.

INTERACTIVITY 33–1

Gender stereotypes

SEXISM ON THE JOB

Substantial differences still exist regarding which occupations are deemed appropriate for men and for women. Women continue to be viewed as best suited for traditionally female jobs: "pink-collar" jobs such as secretary, nurse, cashier, and other female-dominated professions that often feature low pay and low status. Men and women alike still report that they expect greater success when they enter a profession viewed as appropriate for their gender (Crawford & Unger, 1999; MacPherson, 2002).

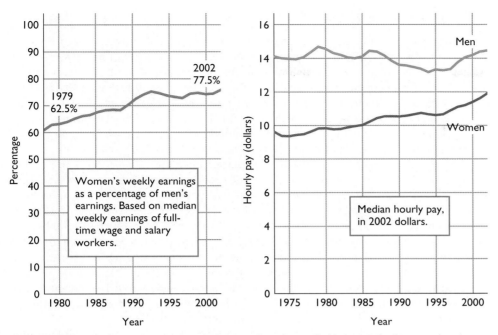

FIGURE 2 In spite of the fact that women's wages have been climbing over the last two decades, a recent survey found that women's earnings as a percentage of men's are still just above 75 percent and had not improved over the previous three years. What factors account for the continuing gap between men and women's wages? (Source: U.S. Bureau of Labor Statistics, 2003.)

The extent of gender stereotyping is illustrated by surveys designed to gauge the attitudes of men and women. For example, when women in the first year of college are asked to name a probable career choice, they are much less likely than men to choose careers traditionally dominated by men, such as engineering and computer programming. Women also hold significantly lower expectations than do men about their entering and peak salaries. Those expectations reflect the reality that, over the last five decades, women, on average, earn less than men. Although the gap has been decreasing, women overall earn an average of 78 cents for every dollar that men earn. (Women who are members of minority groups are even worse off: Black women earn 62 cents for every dollar men make, and Hispanic women earn just 54 cents for every dollar men earn.) Furthermore, even when they are in the same professions as men, women generally make less than men in comparable positions earn (Holden, 2000; Leonhardt, 2003; U.S. Bureau of Labor Statistics, 1999; see Figure 2).

Even when women move into upper-level, high-status positions, they may face significant hurdles in their efforts to move up the corporate ladder, eventually hitting what has come to be called the glass ceiling. The *glass ceiling* is an invisible barrier within an organization that, because of gender discrimination, may prevent women from being promoted beyond a certain level (Austin, 2000; Rudman & Glick, 2001; Whisenant, Pedersen, & Obenour, 2002).

As phenomena such as the glass ceiling make clear, male gender stereotypes are typically more positive than female stereotypes. Although such stereotypes reflect people's perceptions and not necessarily the reality of the world, people often act as if they were real and modify their behavior to conform to the stereotypes. As a result, gender stereotypes limit both women's and men's behavior and ultimately lead to the unfortunate consequence of preferential treatment of men.

SEXUAL HARASSMENT

In addition to pay inequity and limited job advancement, women—even those in high-status professions—may face workplace sexism in the form of *sexual harassment*, defined as unwanted sexual attention, the creation of a hostile or abusive environment, or explicit coercion to engage in unwanted sexual activity. Sexual harassment is not a minor problem. One-fifth of women surveyed in polls say that they have been sexually harassed at work. And it is not just women who encounter harassment: Some 10 percent of men report experiencing sexual harassment on the job (Burgess & Borgida, 1997; Matchen & De Souza, 2000; Fineran, 2002).

Sexual harassment is not just a workplace issue. Thirty percent of the female graduates of one large California university reported being the recipients of some form of harassment. Such harassment begins earlier in life: In one survey, more than three-quarters of girls in junior and senior high school reported receiving unwelcome sexual comments or looks, and two-thirds said they had been touched, grabbed, or pinched in a sexual way (see Figure 3). Overall, estimates suggest that one of every two women will be harassed at some point during her academic or working life. Although boys also reported being the recipients of similar behavior, it occurs less frequently, and boys perceive the behavior as being considerably less harmful than girls do. For instance, one-third of all the girls surveyed reacted by not wanting to go to school or speak in class (AAUW, 1993; Fitzgerald, 1993).

Sexual harassment often has less to do with sex than with power (similar to the motivation behind many cases of rape). In this view, higher-status persons who

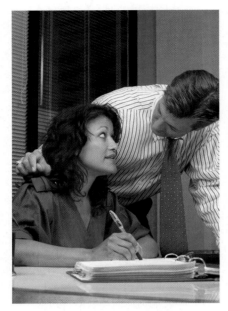

Sexual harassment consists of unwanted sexual attention. How is it possible for men and women to perceive this issue so differently?

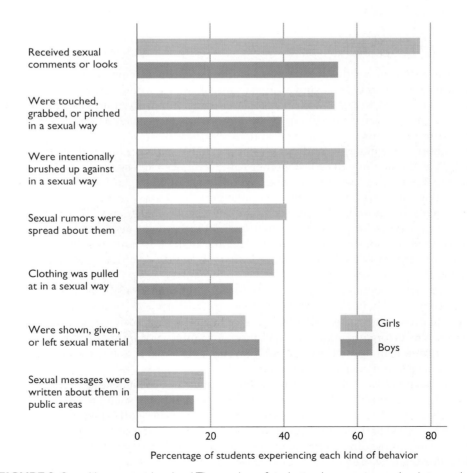

FIGURE 3 Sexual harassment in school. The number of students who report experiencing unwelcomed sexual attention at school is significant. (Source: American Association of University Women, 1994.)

engage in harassment may be less interested in receiving sexual favors than in demonstrating their power over the victim (Paludi, 1996; O'Donohue, 1997).

In some cases, harassment stems from *benevolent sexism*, stereotyped and restrictive attitudes that appear, on the surface, to be beneficial to women. For example, a male employer may compliment a woman on her attractiveness or offer her an easy job so that she won't have to "work so hard." The reality, however, is that such comments or "favors" may undermine the employee's sense of competence, and she may feel that she is not being taken seriously (Glick & Fiske, 1996; Munson, Hulin, & Drasgow, 2000).

Regardless of the motivation that lies behind sexual harassment, the consequences for the victim are clear. Feelings of shame and embarrassment are standard. Because targets of harassment are typically in lower-status positions, such feelings may be compounded by a sense of helplessness and powerlessness. People in these situations often suffer emotional and physical consequences, and the quality of their work may decline (Gutek, Cohen, & Tsui, 1996; Jorgenson & Wauhl, 2000; Magley, 2002).

Gender Differences: More Similar Than Dissimilar

Not surprisingly, gender stereotyping, combined with other factors, results in actual behavior differences between men and women. Before we consider the nature of gender differences, however, it is important to keep in mind that in most respects men and women are more similar to one another than they are different. Furthermore, the differences that have been found reflect *average* male and female *group* differences, and this tells us little or nothing about any *individual* male or female (Tavris, 1992; Deaux, 1995).

For example, even if we find that males, on the whole, generally tend to be more talkative than females—as they do, according to research findings (Matlin, 2000)—an individual man can be less talkative than most women. Similarly, an individual woman may be more talkative than most men. When we consider any single person, our focus should be on the individual rather than on his or her gender group. It is important to take this into account as we examine the findings on gender differences.

PERSONALITY FACTORS

One of the most pronounced differences between men and women lies in their degree of aggressive behavior. By the time they are 2 years old, boys tend to display more aggression than girls do, and this higher level of aggression persists throughout the life span. Furthermore, compared with men, women experience greater anxiety and guilt about their aggressiveness and are more concerned about its effects on their victims (Feingold, 1994; Hyde, 1994; Munroe et al., 2000).

Men generally seem to have higher self-esteem than women do, although the size of the difference is not great and is based on different factors. Women's self-esteem is influenced to a large extent by their perception of their sense of interdependence and connection with others. In contrast, men's self-esteem stems from their assessment of their unique characteristics and abilities, traits that help them distinguish themselves from other people (Feingold, 1994; Kling et al., 1999; Stetsenko et al., 2000).

Research has shown that boys from age 2 tend to be more aggressive than girls, a pattern that continues throughout the life span.

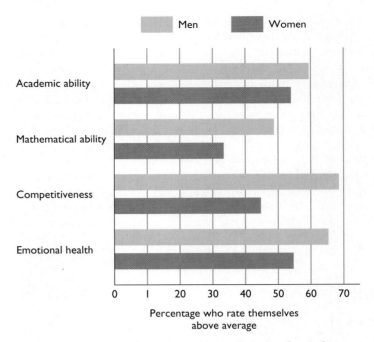

FIGURE 4 Male first-year college students are much more likely than female first-year college students to rate themselves as above average in academic ability, mathematical ability, competitiveness, and emotional health. (Source: *The American Freshman: National Norms for Fall 1990.* Astin, Korn, & Berz. Higher Education Research Council, UCLA.)

Men and women differ in how positively they view their own abilities and how they estimate the probability of their future success. In general, women evaluate themselves more harshly than do men. For example, a survey of first-year college students compared men's and women's views of whether they were above or below average. As you can see in Figure 4, more men than women considered themselves above average in overall academic and mathematical ability, competitiveness, and emotional health. Such self-perceptions matter, because they influence motivation, as well as academic and career choices. They even influence performance. For example, when women experience *stereotype threat*—the perception that a performance measure is sensitive to gender differences—their performance declines (Orenstein, 2001; Nosek, Banaji, & Greenwald, 2002; Steele, Spencer, & Aronson, 2002).

The content of men's and women's speech also differs, with women's speech being more precise. However, women's speech patterns lead others to view them as more tentative and less assertive. Women more often raise their pitch at the end of a sentence, and add "tags" at the end of an opinion, rather than stating the opinion outright. For example, instead of saying "It's awfully warm today," a female speaker might say instead "It's awfully warm today, *isn't it?"* thereby appearing less certain of her opinion. When females use such tentative language, they are judged to be less competent and knowledgeable than they are when they speak assertively (Matlin, 1987; Carli, 1990; Crawford, 1995).

Women's and men's nonverbal behavior differs as well in several significant respects. In conversations with people of the other sex, women look at their partner significantly more while listening than while speaking, whereas men's levels of looking while speaking and listening are about the same. The effect of the male's pattern is to communicate power and dominance, whereas the woman's pattern is associated more with cooperation. Women, however, are generally better than men at decoding the facial expressions of others (Ellyson, Dovidio, & Brown, 1992; Burgoon & Dillman, 1995; Coats & Feldman, 1996).

COGNITIVE ABILITIES

No general differences exist between men and women in overall IQ scores, learning, memory, problem solving, and concept-formation tasks. A few differences in more specific cognitive areas have been identified, although the true nature of those differences—and even their existence—has been called into question by more recent research (Halpern, 2000).

When Eleanor Maccoby and Carol Jacklin carried out a pioneering study of sex differences in 1974, they concluded that girls outperformed boys in verbal abilities and that boys had superior quantitative and spatial abilities. That conclusion was accepted widely as one of the truisms of the psychological literature.

However, recent and more sophisticated analyses have questioned the specific nature and magnitude of those differences. Psychologist Janet Shibley Hyde and colleagues, for instance, examined the mathematical performance of males and females in 100 studies encompassing some 4 million subjects (Hyde, Fennema, & Lamon, 1990). Contrary to traditional wisdom, females slightly outperformed males in math in elementary and middle school. The finding was reversed in high school, where males scored higher in mathematical problem solving. At all ages, however, the differences were quite small, and they became even smaller when studies of the general adult population were considered. In sum, the differences in mathematical performance between men and women are relatively insignificant and, if anything, appear to be declining (Benbow, Lubinski, & Hyde, 1997; Nosek, Banaji, & Greenwald, 2002).

Psychologists have drawn a similar conclusion about the extent of gender differences in verbal skills. Despite the earlier view that women show greater verbal abilities than men, a more recent analysis of 165 studies of gender differences in verbal ability, representing the testing of close to 1.5 million subjects, has led to the conclusion that verbal gender differences are insignificant (Hyde & Linn, 1988; Hedges & Nowell, 1995).

Current evidence suggests, then, that gender differences in cognitive skills are minimal. Meanwhile, particular tests of mathematical and verbal skills do elicit differences in performance, as in the example of the mathematics part of the SAT, where very high scorers are predominantly male. Differences such as these illustrate the fact that we still do not have the full story on gender differences in cognitive abilities (Halpern, 2000).

PowerWeb:Gender and Relationships: A Developmental Account.

www.mhhe.com/feldmanup7

Sources of Gender Differences: Where Biology and Society Meet

If the identification of gender differences has presented a difficult challenge for researchers, the search for their causes has proved even more daunting. Given the indisputable fact that sex is a biological variable, it would seem reasonable to look at factors involving biological differences between men and women. It is also true that, from the time they are born, people are treated differently on the basis of their sex. Consequently, we must take into account both biological and social factors when we try to understand the source of gender differences.

Although we'll consider biological and environmental variables separately, neither alone can provide a full explanation for gender differences. Some combination of the two, interacting with each other, will ultimately provide us with an understanding of why men and women may behave differently.

BIOLOGICAL AND EVOLUTIONARY FACTORS

Do differences between male and female brains underlie sex and gender differences? This intriguing hypothesis has been put forward by some psychologists studying brain structure and functioning. For instance, girls who were exposed before birth to unusually high levels of *androgen*, a male hormone, because their mothers accidentally took a drug containing that hormone while pregnant, preferred different toys from those preferred by girls not exposed to androgens. Specifically, they were more likely to play with toys that are stereotypically preferred by boys (such as cars) and less likely to play with toys stereotypically associated with girls (such as dolls). Although you can probably think of several alternative explanations for these results, one possibility is that exposure to the male hormone may have affected the development of the girls' brains, making them favor toys that involve certain kinds of skills, such as those related to spatial abilities (Levine et al., 1999; Mealey, 2000; Hines et al., 2002).

Similarly, some evidence suggests that women perform better on tasks involving verbal skill and muscular coordination during periods when their production of the female sex hormone *estrogen* is relatively high, compared with periods when it is low. In contrast, they perform better on tasks involving spatial relationships when the estrogen level is relatively low (Kimura, 1999; Rosenberg & Park, 2002).

Some psychologists argue that evolutionary forces lead to certain differences between men's and women's behavior. For example, David Buss and colleagues point to differences in the nature of jealousy between men and women. Men are more jealous in cases of sexual infidelity than in cases of emotional infidelity; women are more jealous in cases of emotional infidelity than in cases of sexual infidelity (Buss et al., 1992; Buss, 2003).

According to Buss's controversial explanation, the root cause for the differences in jealousy lies in the evolutionary implications of sexual, versus emotional, infidelity for men and women. He argues that for males, sexual infidelity represents a threat to their ability to ensure that their children are actually their own (and are the ones who have inherited their genes). In contrast, females have no doubt that a child that they carry through pregnancy is their own. However, their major concern is ensuring the male's protection and support during child rearing. Thus, to females, maintaining males' emotional attachment is crucial.

Psychologists relying on the evolutionary approach also argue that similarities in the division of labor between men and women across different cultures suggest that sex differences are due to evolutionary factors. Their argument is that even in very different types of cultures, men tend to be more aggressive, competitive, and prone to taking risks than women are—traits that had an evolutionary advantage (Buss & Kenrick, 1998; Mealey, 2000).

However, many critics question the assumptions of the evolutionary approach. Rather than assuming that the differences are due to evolutionary forces, some psychologists suggest that differences in males' and females' beliefs about the meaning of infidelity are the actual cause of their jealousy differences. For instance, men may believe that women have sex only when they are in love. Consequently, sexual infidelity may be seen as a sign that a woman is in love with another man, and may produce more jealousy than emotional infidelity alone would. In contrast, women may believe that men are capable of having sex without being in love, and consequently they may find a man's sexual infidelity less bothersome because it does not necessarily mean that he is in love with someone else (DeSteno & Salovey, 1996; Harris & Christenfeld, 1996).

Psychologists Alice Eagly and Wendy Wood criticize evolutionary explanations for gender differences on different grounds. They argue, in their *biosocial approach*, that one important source of gender differences is the difference in the physical capabilities of men and women. Consistently across cultures, the division of labor between men and women is based largely on men's size, strength, and speed and women's capacity for pregnancy and caring for children. However, the specific nature

Boy's World	Girl's World
• Action figures	• Barbie
• Sports collectibles	• Baby dolls
• Radio remote-control cars	• Doll houses
• Tonka trucks	• Collectible horses
• Boy's role play	• Play kitchens
• Walkie-talkies	• Housekeeping toys
	• Girl's dress-up
	• Jewelry
	• Cosmetics
	• Bath and body

FIGURE 5 The placement of toys according to gender was commonplace until protests forced a nationwide chain to discontinue the practice.

of activities in which men and women specialize varies from one culture to another, depending on the specifics of a culture (Wood & Eagly, 2002).

The extent to which biological and evolutionary factors may underlie gender differences is an unanswered, and highly controversial, question. One thing is clear, however: Biological factors and evolutionary factors alone do not explain the complete range of differences between male and female behavior. To fully understand the source of gender differences, we also must consider the social environment, as we do next.

THE SOCIAL ENVIRONMENT

Starting from the moment of birth, with blue blankets for boys and pink ones for girls, most parents and other adults provide environments that differ in important respects according to gender. For example, boys and girls are given different kinds of toys, and—until protests recently brought the practice to an end—items in the largest toy store chain in the United States were laid out according to the gender appropriateness of particular toys (see Figure 5; Bannon, 2000; Wood, Desmarais, & Gugula, 2002).

Parents interact with their children differently, depending on their sex. Fathers play more roughly with their infant sons than with their infant daughters. Middle-class mothers tend to talk more to their daughters than to their sons. It is clear that adults frequently treat children differently on the basis of gender (McHale, Crouter, & Tucker, 1999; Tenenbaum & Leaper, 2002).

Such differences in behavior, and there are many more, produce different socialization experiences for men and women. *Socialization* is the process by which an individual learns the rules and norms of appropriate behavior. In this case, it refers to learning what society considers appropriate behavior for men and women. According to the processes of social learning theory, boys and girls are taught, and rewarded for performing, the socially perceived appropriate behaviors for men and for women, respectively (Philpot, 2000; Archer & Lloyd, 2002; Liben & Bigler, 2002).

It is not just parents, of course, who provide socialization experiences for children. Society as a whole communicates clear messages to children as they are growing up. Children's reading books traditionally have portrayed girls in stereotypically

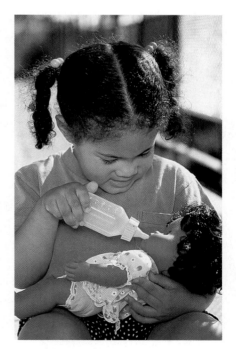

Children's reading books have traditionally portrayed girls in stereotypically nurturing roles using photos such as this, whereas boys have been given more physical and action-oriented roles. Do you think there are cultures in which this is not the case?

Androgynous individuals tend to defy stereotypes by combining the psychological and behavioral characteristics thought typical of both sexes.

nurturing roles, whereas boys have been given more physical and action-oriented roles. Television, too, acts as a particularly influential source of socialization. Men outnumber women on television, and women are often cast in such stereotypical roles as housewife, secretary, and mother. The potency of television as an agent of socialization is underscored by data indicating that the more television children watch, the more sexist they become (Coltraine & Messineo, 2000; Furnham, Pallangyo, & Gunter, 2001; Turkel, 2002).

Our educational system also treats boys and girls differently. For example, in elementary school, boys are five times more likely to receive attention from classroom teachers than girls. Boys receive significantly more praise, criticism, and remedial help than girls do. They are also more likely to be praised for the intelligence shown in their work, whereas girls are more apt to be commended for their neatness. Even in college classes, male students receive more eye contact from their professors than female students, men are called upon more frequently in class, and men are more apt to receive extra help from their professors (AAUW, 1992; Sadker & Sadker, 1994; Einarsson & Granstroem, 2002; Koch, 2003).

Gender schema: A mental framework that organizes and guides a child's understanding of information relevant to gender.

According to Sandra Bem (1998), socialization produces a **gender schema,** a mental framework that organizes and guides a child's understanding of information relevant to gender. On the basis of their schemas for appropriate and inappropriate behavior for males and females, children begin to behave in ways that reflect society's gender roles. Hence, a child who goes to summer camp and is offered the opportunity to sew a costume may evaluate the activity not in terms of the intrinsic components of the process (such as the mechanics of using a needle and thread), but in terms of whether the activity is compatible with his or her gender schema (Bem, 1993, 1998; Martin, Ruble, & Szkrybalo, 2002).

Androgynous: Characterized by gender roles that encompass psychological and behavioral traits thought typical of both sexes.

Bem suggests that one way to decrease the likelihood that children will develop gender schemas is to encourage them to be androgynous. **Androgynous** individuals combine the psychological and behavioral characteristics thought typical of both sexes. Specifically, an androgynous individual may be forceful, assertive, and self-reliant (characteristics typically viewed by society as masculine) in certain circumstances and

"Sometimes it would be helpful if you were a bit more androgynous."

compassionate, gentle, and soft-spoken (characteristics typically thought of as feminine) when the situation calls for such behavior.

The concept of androgyny does not suggest that there should be no differences between men and women. Far from it: Androgyny proposes that differences should be based on choices, freely made, of the best *human* characteristics, not on an artificially restricted inventory of characteristics deemed by society to be appropriate only for men or only for women.

RECAP/EVALUATE/RETHINK

RECAP

What are the major differences between male and female gender roles?

- ▶ Gender is the perception of being male or female. Gender roles are the expectations, defined by society, of what is appropriate behavior for men and women. When gender roles reflect favoritism toward one sex, they lead to stereotyping and produce sexism. (p. 365)
- ▶ The gender-role stereotype for men suggests that they are endowed with competence-related traits, whereas women are seen in terms of their capacity for warmth and expressiveness. Actual sex differences are much less clear, and of smaller magnitude, than the stereotypes would suggest. The differences that do exist are produced by a combination of biological and environmental factors. (p. 365)
- ▶ Biological causes of sex difference are reflected by evidence suggesting a possible difference in brain structure and functioning between men and women and may be associated with differential exposure to hormones before birth. (p. 371)
- ▶ An evolutionary approach explains gender differences in terms of different male-female concerns regarding the inheritance of genes and the need for child rearing, but this approach is highly controversial. (p. 372)
- ▶ Socialization experiences produce gender schemas, mental frameworks that organize and guide a child's understanding of information relevant to gender. (p. 374)

EVALUATE

1. _____ _____ are sets of societal expectations about what is appropriate behavior for men and women.

2. Gender stereotypes seem to be much less prevalent today than they were several decades ago. True or false?

3. Which of the following statements about male-female differences in aggression is true?
   a. Males are physically more aggressive than females only during childhood.
   b. Male-female differences in aggression first become evident during adolescence.
   c. Males are more aggressive than females throughout the life span.
   d. Females and males feel equally anxious about their aggressive acts.
4. _____ _____ are frameworks that organize understanding of gender-specific information.

RETHINK

1. The U.S. Congress has enacted laws prohibiting women in the armed forces from participating directly in combat, in the interest of keeping them safe. Do you think such laws are protective or sexist? Is this an example of "benevolent sexism"?
2. If you wished to raise a child in as androgynous a manner as possible, how would you do it? What problems might the child encounter in the everyday world? Do you think this is the best way to raise a child in today's society?

Answers to Evaluate Questions

1. gender roles; 2. false; they are still prevalent; 3. c; 4. gender schemas

KEY TERMS

gender p. 365
gender roles p. 365

sexism p. 365
gender schema p. 374

androgynous p. 374

Understanding Human Sexual Response: The Facts of Life

MODULE 34

Why, and under what circumstances, do we become sexually aroused?

When I started "tuning out," teachers thought I was sick—physically sick that is. They kept sending me to the school nurse to have my temperature taken. If I'd told them I was carrying on with Cindy Crawford in their classes, while supposedly learning my Caesar and my Latin vocabulary, they'd have thought I was—well, delirious. I *was!* (based on Coles & Stokes, 1985, pp. 18–19).

Not everyone's sexual fantasies are as consuming as those reported by this teenage boy. Yet sex is an important consideration in most people's lives, for although the physical aspects of human sex are not all that different from those of other species, the meaning, values, and feelings that humans place on sexual behavior elevate it to a special plane. To fully appreciate this difference, however, it is necessary to understand the basic biology underlying sexual responses.

▲ ▲ ▲

The Basic Biology of Sexual Behavior

Anyone who has seen two dogs mating knows that sexual behavior has a biological basis. Their sexual behavior appears to occur naturally, without much prompting on the part of others. A number of genetically controlled factors influence the sexual behavior of nonhuman animals. For instance, animal behavior is affected by the presence of certain hormones in the blood. Moreover, female animals are receptive to sexual advances only during certain relatively limited periods of the year.

Human sexual behavior, by comparison, is more complicated, although the underlying biology is not all that different from that of related species. In males, for example, the *testes* begin to secrete **androgens**, male sex hormones, at puberty. (See Figure 1 for the basic anatomy of the male and female **genitals,** or sex organs.) Not only do androgens produce secondary sex characteristics, such as the growth of body hair and a deepening of the voice, they also increase the sex drive. Because the level of androgen production by the testes is fairly constant, men are capable of (and interested in) sexual activities without any regard to biological cycles. Given the proper stimuli leading to arousal, male sexual behavior can occur (Goldstein, 2000).

Women show a different pattern. When they reach maturity at puberty, the two *ovaries* begin to produce **estrogens** and **progesterone**, female sex hormones. However, those hormones are not produced consistently; instead, their production follows a cyclical pattern. The greatest output occurs during **ovulation**, when an egg is released from the ovaries, making the chances of fertilization by a sperm cell highest. While in nonhumans the period around ovulation is the only time the female is receptive to sex, people are different. Although there are variations in reported sex drive, women are receptive to sex throughout their cycles. In addition, although some evidence suggests that males have a stronger sex drive than females, the difference may be the result of society's discouragement of female sexuality rather than of innate differences between men and women (Baumeister, 2000; Baumeister, Catanese, & Vohs, 2001; Baumeister & Twenge, 2002).

Androgens: Male sex hormones secreted by the testes.

Genitals: The male and female sex organs.

Estrogens: Class of female sex hormones.

Progesterone: A female sex hormone secreted by the ovaries.

Ovulation: The point at which an egg is released from the ovaries.

FIGURE 1 Cutaway side views of the female and male sex organs.

Ovary
Uterus
Bladder
Pubic bone
Urethra
Clitoris
Cervix
Vagina
Anus

Female

Bladder
Pubic bone
Vas deferens
Urethra
Penis
Glans
Large intestine
Seminal vesicle
Ejaculatory duct
Prostate
Anus
Testis
Scrotum

Male

Though biological factors "prime" people for sex, it takes more than hormones to motivate and produce sexual behavior (McClintock & Herdt, 1996). In animals the presence of a partner who provides arousing stimuli leads to sexual activity. Humans are considerably more versatile; not only other people but nearly any object, sight, smell, sound, or other stimulus can lead to sexual excitement. Because of prior associations, then, people may be turned on sexually by the smell of Chanel No. 5 or Brut or the sound of a favorite song hummed softly in their ears. The reaction to a specific, potentially arousing stimulus, as we shall see, is highly individual—what turns one person on may do just the opposite for another (Benson, 2003).

Psychological Aspects of Sexual Excitement: What Turns People On?

If you were to argue that the major human sex organ is the brain, in a sense you would be right. Much of what is considered sexually arousing in our society has little or nothing to do with our genitals, but instead is related to external stimuli that, through a process of learning, have come to be labeled as *erotic*, or sexually stimulating.

For example, there are no areas of the body that *automatically* produce sexual arousal when touched. Areas of the body, called **erogenous zones,** that have an unusually rich array of nerve receptors are particularly sensitive not just to sexual touch but to any kind of touch. When a physician touches a breast or a penis, the information sent to the brain by the nerve cells is essentially the same as that sent when a sexual partner touches that spot. What differs is the interpretation given to the touch. Sexual arousal is likely only when a certain part of the body is touched in what people define as a sexual manner and when a person is receptive to sexual activity (Gagnon, 1977; Goldstein, 2000).

Although people can learn to respond sexually to almost any stimulus, there is a good deal of agreement within a society or culture about what usually represents an erotic stimulus. In many Western societies breast size is often the standard by which female appeal is measured, but in many other cultures breast size is irrelevant (Rothblum, 1990).

Sexual fantasies also play an important role in producing sexual arousal. Not only do people have fantasies of a sexual nature during their everyday activities, about 60 percent of all people have fantasies during sexual intercourse. Interestingly, such fantasies often include having sex with someone other than one's partner of the moment (Hicks & Leitenberg, 2001; Trudel, 2002).

Men's and women's fantasies differ little from each other in terms of content or quantity, although men seem to fantasize about sex more than women do (Jones & Barlow, 1990; Hsu et al., 1994). As you can see in Figure 2 , thoughts of being sexually irresistible and of engaging in oral-genital sex are most common for both sexes. It is important to note that fantasies do not represent an actual desire for their fulfillment in the real world. Thus, we should not assume from data about female fantasies that women want to be sexually overpowered or assume from data about male fantasies that every male is desirous of forcing sexual overtures on a submissive victim. (To get a deeper understanding of sexual arousal, try **Interactivity 34–1.**)

Erogenous zones: Areas of the body that are particularly sensitive because of the presence of an unusually rich array of nerve receptors.

INTERACTIVITY 34–1

Sexual response

The Phases of Sexual Response: The Ups and Downs of Sex

Although the kinds of stimuli that produce sexual arousal are to some degree unique to each individual, there are some basic aspects of sexual responsiveness that we all share. According to pioneering work done by William Masters and Virginia Johnson (1966), who studied sexual behavior in carefully controlled laboratory settings, sexual responses follow a regular pattern consisting of four phases: excitement, plateau, orgasm, and resolution. Although other researchers argue that sexual responses proceed somewhat differently (e.g., Kaplan, 1974; Zilbergeld & Ellison, 1980), Masters and Johnson's research is the most widely accepted account of what happens when people become sexually excited (Masters & Johnson, 1994).

In the **excitement phase,** which can last from just a few minutes to over an hour, an arousing stimulus begins a sequence that prepares the genitals for sexual intercourse. In the male, the *penis* becomes erect when blood flows into it; in the female, the *clitoris* swells because of an increase in the blood supply to that area, and the *vagina* becomes lubricated. Women may also experience a "sex flush," a red rash that typically spreads over the chest and throat.

Next comes the **plateau phase,** the body's preparation for orgasm. During this stage, the maximum level of sexual arousal is attained as the penis and clitoris swell with blood. Women's breasts and vaginas expand, heartbeat and blood pressure rise, and breathing rate increases. Muscle tension becomes greater as the body prepares

Excitement phase: The interval at which an arousing stimulus begins a sequence that prepares the genitals for sexual intercourse.

Plateau phase: The period in which the maximum level of arousal is attained, the penis and clitoris swell with blood, and the body prepares for orgasm.

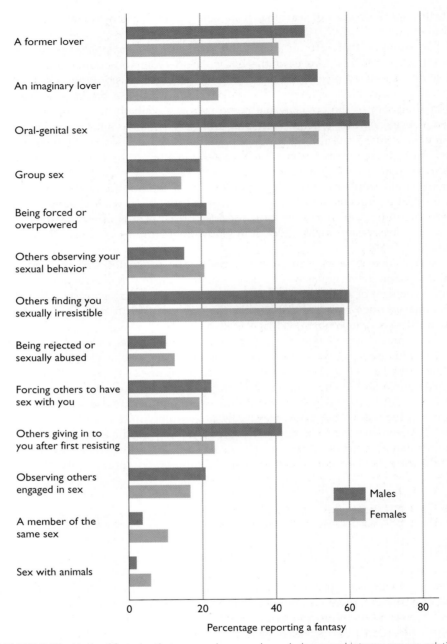

FIGURE 2 The kinds of fantasies that men and women have during sexual intercourse are relatively similar (Sue, 1979). Why do you think this is true, and do you think the fantasies are similar in non-Western cultures?

Orgasm: The peak of sexual excitement, during which rhythmic muscular contractions occur in the genitals.

itself for the next stage, orgasm. Although it is difficult to explain the sensation of **orgasm** beyond saying that it is an intense, highly pleasurable experience, the biological events that accompany the feeling are fairly straightforward. When the orgasm stage is reached, rhythmic muscular contractions occur in the genitals every eight-tenths of a second. In the male, the contractions expel *semen,* a fluid containing sperm, from the penis—a process known as *ejaculation.* For women and men, breathing and heart rates reach their maximum.

What does it feel like to have an orgasm? The following ten descriptions were written by men and women in an introductory psychology class. As you read through them, see if you can tell which were written by men and which by women.

1. Your heart pounds more than 100 miles per hour, your body tenses up, you feel an overwhelming sensation of pleasure and joy.

2. An orgasm feels like blood pulsating through my body, rushing essentially to the genital area, a surge of contraction-like waves paired with a rapidly beating heart and strong pulse; my heart feels like someone is squeezing it, painful, and I have trouble breathing deeply.

3. Feels like being plugged into an electrical socket, but pleasurable rather than painful. Nearly indescribable!

4. It's as if every muscle in your body is being charged with intense electricity; your mind is incapable of thinking about anything, and you become totally incoherent. All the nerves in your body tremble, and you have trouble breathing, and get the urge to scream, or yell, or do something wild.

5. An orgasm to me is like the sensations of hot and cold coming together in one throbbing, thrusting, prolonged moment. It is the ultimate excitement of my passion.

6. Like exquisite torture. The sudden release of all the primal urges in the body. The gladness and yet the sadness that the fun is over.

7. An orgasm is that point when you don't care if anyone hears you screaming out your pleasures of ecstasy.

8. It's like all the cells in my brain popping at once and whirling around, while all the muscles in my body heave upward till I reach ultimate sensory bliss.

9. Tingling, throbbing, pleasurable feeling. Breathing is very fast and not rhythmic. Tend to hold my breath at peak. Possible shaking afterward and tightening/contraction of muscles.

10. An orgasm is a heavenly experience. It can be compared to nothing.

If you thought that men and women experience orgasm differently, you may be surprised at how hard it is to tell the difference from these descriptions. The correct answers: 1. Male 2. Female 3. Male 4. Female 5. Female 6. Male 7. Female 8. Male 9. Female 10. Male

FIGURE 3 There appears to be little difference between men and women when it comes to their subjective experience of orgasm. The photo, from the movie *When Harry Met Sally*, illustrates the actress Meg Ryan's portrayal of an orgasm.

Although we can't be sure, the subjective experience of orgasm seems identical for males and females despite the differences in the organs that are involved. In one experiment, a group of men and women wrote down their descriptions of how an orgasm felt to them. Those descriptions were given to a group of experts, who were asked to identify the sex of each writer. The results showed that the experts were correct at no better than chance levels, suggesting that there was little means to distinguish the descriptions of orgasms on the basis of gender (Vance & Wagner, 1976). To get a sense of how people describe orgasms, see Figure 3.

After orgasm, people move into the last stage of sexual arousal, the **resolution stage.** The body returns to its resting state, reversing the changes brought about by arousal. The genitals resume their unaroused size and shape, and blood pressure, breathing, and heart rate return to normal.

Male and female responses differ significantly during the resolution stage; these differences are depicted in Figure 4. Women are able to cycle back to the orgasm phase and experience repeated orgasms. Ultimately, of course, females enter the final resolution stage, and then they return to their prestimulation state. In contrast, it generally is thought that men enter a refractory period during the resolution stage.

Resolution stage: The interval after orgasm in which the body returns to its unaroused state, reversing the changes brought about by arousal.

a. Male pattern

Time

b. Female patterns

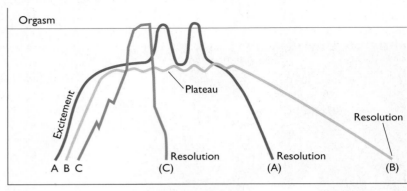

Time

FIGURE 4 A four-stage model of the sexual response cycle for males and females based on the findings of Masters and Johnson (1966). Note how the male pattern (a) includes a refractory period. Part (b) shows three possible female patterns. In A, the pattern is closest to the male cycle, except that the woman has two orgasms in a row. In B, there is no orgasm, whereas in C orgasm is reached quickly and the woman rapidly returns to an unaroused state. (Source: After Masters & Johnson, 1966.)

Refractory period: A temporary period that follows the resolution stage and during which the male cannot develop an erection again.

During the **refractory period,** men are unable to develop an erection and therefore are unable to have another orgasm and ejaculate. The refractory period may last from a few minutes to several hours, although in the elderly it may continue for several days (Goldstein, 2000).

Exploring DIVERSITY

Female Circumcision: A Celebration of Culture—or Genital Mutilation?

Waris Dirie was just an innocent, unknowing child of 5 when she begged her mother to let her be circumcised like virtually all females in Somalia. "When you've been told over and over that, until this happens, you're filthy and no man would ever marry you, you believe what everybody says," Dirie explains. "I just wanted to be like the other girls."

Months later her awful wish came true. As her mother held down the crying, blindfolded Diri, a gypsy performed the circumcision using a dirty, dull razor and no anesthetic. She sewed the ragged wound with thorns and thread. "It's not a pain you forget," says Dirie, in a whisper. She was left with only a tiny opening, and urinating became torture. Later, menstruation was so unbearable that Dirie routinely fainted (Cheakalos & Heyn, 1998, p. 149).

The operation in question—female circumcision—represents one of the most controversial procedures relating to sex throughout the world. In such an operation, the clitoris is removed, resulting in permanent inability to experience sexual pleasure.

Some 80 million women, living mostly in Africa and Asia, have undergone female circumcision. More than 90 percent of Nigerian women have been circumcised during childhood, and more than 90 percent intend to circumcise their daughters. Furthermore, in some cases, more extensive surgery is carried out, in which additional parts of the female genitals are removed or are sewn together with catgut or thorns (French, 1997; Obermeyer, 2001; Lacey, 2002).

Those who practice female circumcision say it upholds an ancient societal tradition and is no different from other cultural customs. Its purpose, they say, is to preserve virginity before marriage, keep women faithful to their husbands after marriage, and enhance a woman's beauty. Furthermore, proponents believe that it differs little from the common Western practice of male circumcision, in which the foreskin of the penis is surgically removed soon after birth.

Critics, in contrast, argue that female circumcision is nothing less than female mutilation. Not only does the practice permanently eliminate sexual pleasure, it can also lead to constant pain and infection, depending on the nature of the surgery. In fact, because the procedure is traditionally conducted in a ritualistic fashion without an anesthetic, using a razor blade, sawtooth knife, or glass, the circumcision itself can be physically traumatic (Dugger, 1996).

The procedure raises some difficult issues, which have been brought to light in various court cases. For instance, a Nigerian immigrant, living temporarily in the United States, went to court to argue that she should be allowed to remain permanently. Her plea: If she and her young daughters were sent back to Nigeria, her daughters would face circumcision upon their return. The court agreed and permitted her to stay indefinitely (Gregory, 1994; Dugger, 1996).

In reaction to the controversy about female circumcision, Congress recently passed laws that make the practice illegal in the United States. Still, some argue that female circumcision is a valued cultural custom, and that no one, particularly someone judging from the perspective of another culture, should prevent people from carrying out the customs they think are important. In addition, critics point to the practice of *male* circumcision, in which the foreskin of the penis is surgically removed. They suggest that male circumcision provides few significant health benefits, and that the decision to have male infants circumcised—an accepted practice in U.S. society—rests on religious, social, and cultural traditions (American Academy of Pediatrics, 1999b; Boyle, Goldman, Svoboda, & Fernandez, 2002).

⚛ ⚛ ⚛

RECAP/EVALUATE/RETHINK

RECAP

Why, and under what circumstances, do we become sexually aroused?

▶ Although biological factors, such as the presence of androgens (male sex hormones) and estrogens and progesterone (female sex hormones), prime people for sex, almost any kind of stimulus can produce sexual arousal, depending on a person's prior experience. (p. 377)

▶ People's sexual responses follow a regular pattern consisting of four phases: excitement, plateau, orgasm, and resolution. (p. 379)

EVALUATE

1. Match the phase of sexual arousal with its characteristics
   1. Excitement phase
   2. Plateau phase
   3. Orgasm phase
   4. Resolution phase
   a. Maximum level of sexual arousal
   b. Erection and lubrication
   c. Rhythmic muscular contractions and ejaculation
   d. Return of body to resting state
2. Men are generally thought to enter a _____ period after sex, in which orgasm is impossible for a period of time.
3. Whereas men are interested in sexual activity regardless of their biological cycles, women are truly receptive to sex only during ovulation, when the production of their sex hormones is greatest. True or false?
4. Men's and women's sexual fantasies are essentially similar to each other. True or false?

RETHINK

1. Why do you think humans differ from other species in their year-round receptivity to sex and in the number and variety of stimuli they perceive as sexual? What evolutionary purpose might this difference serve in humans?

2. How do people learn to be aroused by the stimuli that their society considers erotic? When do they learn this, and where does the message come from?

Answers to Evaluate Questions

1. 1-b, 2-a, 3-c, 4-d; 2. refractory; 3. false; women are receptive through-out their cycle; 4. true

KEY TERMS

androgens p. 377
genitals p. 377
estrogens p. 377

progesterone p. 377
ovulation p. 377
erogenous zones p. 379

excitement phase p. 379
plateau phase p. 379
orgasm p. 380

resolution stage p. 381
refractory period p. 382

The Varieties of Sexual Behavior

A boy who practices this habit can never be the best that Nature intended him to be. His wits are not so sharp. His memory is not so good. His power of fixing his attention on whatever he is doing is lessened . . . A boy like this is a poor thing to look at . . . [He is] untrustworthy, unreliable, untruthful, and probably even dishonest (Schofield & Vaughan-Jackson, 1913, pp. 30–42).

The cause of this condition: masturbation—at least according to the authors of the early 1900s sex manual *What Every Boy Should Know.* The consequences of masturbation for women were considered no less severe. In the words of one nineteenth-century physician, "There is hardly an end to the diseases caused by masturbation: dyspepsia, spinal disease, headache, epilepsy, various kinds of fits . . . impaired eyesight, palpitation of the heart, pain in the side and bleeding at the lungs, spasm of the heart, and sometimes sudden death" (Gregory, 1856).

Such views may seem bizarre and far-fetched to you, as they do to contemporary experts on human sexual behavior. However, at one time they were considered perfectly sound by quite reasonable people. Indeed, trivia buffs might be interested to learn that corn flakes owe their invention to a nineteenth-century physician, J. W. Kellogg, who believed that because the enjoyment of tasty food provoked sexual excitation, an alternative of "unstimulating" grains was needed.

Clearly, sex and sex-related behavior are influenced by expectations, attitudes, beliefs, and the state of medical and biological knowledge in a given period. Today we know that sexual behavior may take a variety of forms, and much of what was once seen as "unnatural" and "lewd" is often more likely to be accepted in contemporary

Times change: The veiled sexuality of Victorian-era paintings has given way to a more frank acknowledgment of sexual behavior.

society. Similarly, sexual behavior that is commonplace in one culture is seen as appalling in others. For instance, seven societies are known in which kissing never occurs (Ford & Beach, 1951; Mason, 1994). In sum, distinctions between normal and abnormal sexual behavior are not easy to draw. That certainly hasn't prevented people from trying to draw them, however.

△ △ △

Approaches to Sexual Normality

One approach is to define abnormal sexual behavior in terms of deviation from the average, or typical, behavior. To determine abnormality, we simply observe what behaviors are rare and uncommon in a society and label those deviations from the norm as abnormal.

The difficulty with such an approach, however, is that some behaviors that are statistically unusual hardly seem worthy of concern. Even though most people have sexual intercourse in the bedroom, does the fact that someone prefers sex in the dining room imply abnormality? If some people prefer portly sexual partners, are they abnormal in a society that holds slimness in high regard? Clearly, the answer to both of these questions is no, and so an approach that defines sexual abnormality in terms of deviation from the average is inappropriate. (The same difficulties are encountered in considering definitions of psychological abnormality.)

An alternative approach would be to compare sexual behavior against some standard or ideal. But here, again, there is a problem: What standard should we use? Some might suggest philosophy, some might turn to the Bible, and some might even consider psychology the ultimate determinant. The trouble is that none of these potential sources of standards is universally acceptable. Furthermore, since standards change radically with shifts in societal attitudes and new knowledge, such an approach is undesirable. For instance, forty years ago, the American Psychiatric Association labeled homosexuality a mental illness. However, as evidence to the contrary accumulated, in 1973 the organization determined that homosexuality should no longer be considered a mental disorder. Obviously the behavior had not changed. Only the label placed on it by the psychiatric profession had been modified.

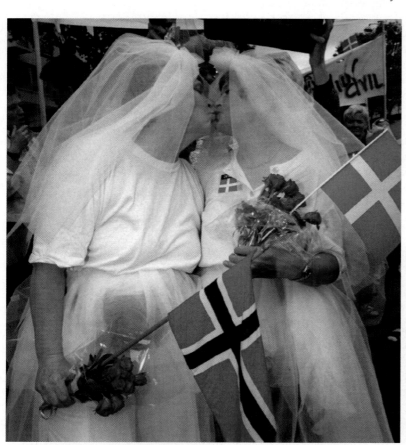

Same-sex marriages, already legal in some countries, represent a significant social issue dividing people in the United States.

In light of the difficulties with other approaches, probably the most reasonable definition of sexual normality is one that considers the psychological consequences of the behavior. In this approach, sexual behavior is considered abnormal if it produces a sense of distress, anxiety, or guilt—or if it is harmful to some other person. According to this view, then, sexual behaviors can be viewed as abnormal only when they have a negative impact on a person's sense of well-being or if they hurt someone else.

It is important to recognize that what is seen as normal and what is seen as abnormal sexual behavior are dictated primarily by societal values, and that there have been dramatic shifts from one generation to another in definitions of what constitutes appropriate sexual behavior. People can and should make their own personal value judgments about what is appropriate in their own sex lives, but there are few universally accepted absolute rights and wrongs.

Surveying Sexual Behavior: What's Happening Behind Closed Doors?

For most of recorded history, the vast variety of sexual practices remained shrouded in ignorance. However, in the late 1930s, biologist Albert Kinsey launched a series of surveys on the sexual behavior of people in the United States. The result was the first comprehensive attempt to see what people were actually doing sexually, highlighted by the publication of Kinsey's landmark volumes *Sexual Behavior in the Human Male* (Kinsey et al., 1948) and *Sexual Behavior in the Human Female* (Kinsey et al., 1953).

Kinsey's efforts represented the first major systematic approach to learning about human sexual behavior. Kinsey and his colleagues interviewed tens of thousands of individuals, and the interview techniques they devised are still regarded as exemplary because of their ability to elicit sensitive information without causing embarrassment.

On the other hand, Kinsey's samples reflected an overrepresentation of college students, young people, well-educated individuals, urban dwellers, and people living in Indiana and the northeast (Kirby, 1977). Furthermore, as with all surveys involving volunteer participants, it is unclear how representative his data are of people who refused to participate in the study. Similarly, because no survey observes behavior directly, it is difficult to assess how accurately people's descriptions of what they do in private match their actual sexual practices.

Kinsey's work set the stage for later surveys, although because of political reasons (the use of government funding for sex surveys is controversial), surprisingly few comprehensive large-scale, representative surveys—either in the United States or in other countries—have been carried out since Kinsey did his initial work (Pinkerton et al., 2003). However, by examining the common results gleaned from different samples of subjects, we now have a reasonably complete picture of contemporary sexual practices—to which we turn next.

Masturbation: Solitary Sex

If you listened to physicians seventy-five years ago, you would have been told that **masturbation,** sexual self-stimulation, often using the hand to rub the genitals, would lead to a wide variety of physical and mental disorders, ranging from hairy palms to insanity. If those physicians had been correct, however, most of us would be wearing gloves to hide the sight of our hair-covered palms—for masturbation is one of the most frequently practiced sexual activities. Some 94 percent of all males and 63 percent of all females have masturbated at least once, and among college students, the frequency ranges from "never" to "several times a day" (Hunt, 1974; Michael et al., 1994; Laqueur, 2003).

Masturbation: Sexual self-stimulation.

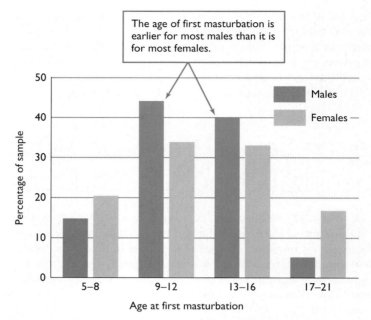

FIGURE I The age at which a sample of college students first masturbated. The percentages are based on only those people who had experience with masturbation. (Source: Arafat & Cotton, 1974.)

Men and women typically begin to masturbate for the first time at different ages, as you can see in Figure 1. Furthermore, men masturbate considerably more often than women, although there are differences in frequency according to age. Male masturbation is most common in the early teens and then declines, whereas females both begin and reach a maximum frequency later. There are also some racial differences: African American men and women masturbate less than whites do (Oliver & Hyde, 1993; Pinkerton, Bogart, Cecil, & Abramson, 2002).

Although masturbation is often considered an activity to engage in only if no other sexual outlets are available, this view bears little relationship to reality. Close to three-quarters of married men (age 20 to 40) report masturbating an average of twenty-four times a year, and 68 percent of the married women in the same age group masturbate an average of ten times a year (Hunt, 1974; Michael et al., 1994).

Despite the high incidence of masturbation, attitudes toward it still reflect some of the negative views of yesteryear. For instance, one survey found that around 10 percent of people who masturbated experienced feelings of guilt, and 5 percent of the males and 1 percent of the females considered their behavior perverted (Arafat & Cotton, 1974). Despite these negative attitudes, however, most experts on sex view masturbation as a healthy and legitimate—and harmless—sexual activity. In addition, masturbation is seen as providing a means of learning about one's own sexuality and a way of discovering changes in one's body such as the emergence of precancerous lumps (Coleman, 2002).

Heterosexuality

Heterosexuality: Sexual attraction and behavior directed to the other sex.

People often believe that the first time they have sexual intercourse they have achieved one of life's major milestones. However, **heterosexuality,** sexual attraction and behavior directed to the other sex, consists of far more than male-female intercourse. Kissing, petting, caressing, massaging, and other forms of sex play are all components of heterosexual behavior. Still, the focus of sex researchers has been on the act of intercourse, particularly in terms of its first occurrence and its frequency.

PREMARITAL SEX

Until fairly recently, premarital sexual intercourse, at least for women, was considered one of the major taboos in our society. Traditionally, women have been warned by society that "nice girls don't do it"; men have been told that although premarital sex is okay for them, they should make sure they marry virgins. This view that premarital sex is permissible for males but not for females is called the **double standard.**

Although as recently as the 1960s the majority of adult Americans believed that premarital sex was always wrong, since that time there has been a dramatic change in public opinion. For example, as you can see in Figure 2, the percentage of middle-age people who say sex before marriage is "not wrong at all" has increased considerably, and overall 60 percent of Americans say premarital sex is okay. More than half say that living together before marriage is morally acceptable (C&F Report, 2001; Thornton & Young-DeMarco, 2001).

Changes in attitudes toward premarital sex were matched by changes in actual rates of premarital sexual activity. For instance, the most recent figures show that just over one-half of women between the ages of 15 and 19 have had premarital sexual intercourse. These figures are close to double the number of women in the same age range who reported having intercourse in 1970. Clearly, the trend over the last several decades has been toward more women engaging in premarital sexual activity (Singh & Carroch 1999).

Double standard: The view that premarital sex is permissible for males but not for females.

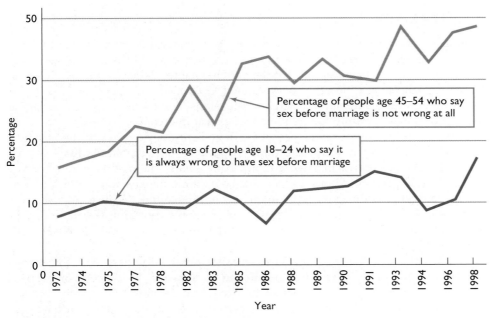

FIGURE 2 The percentage of adults who find premarital sex is not wrong at all has risen dramatically over the last 25 years, whereas the percentage adults who think premarital sex is always wrong has increased only slightly. (Source: Gallup Poll News Service, 1998.) What changes in society account for this shift in attitudes toward intercourse?

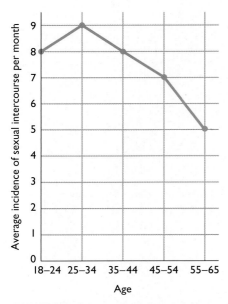

FIGURE 3 Once a couple is past their midthirties, the average number of times per month they have sexual intercourse declines (Clements, 1994). Why do older couples have intercourse less frequently than do younger ones?

Males, too, have shown an increase in the incidence of premarital sexual intercourse, although the increase has not been as dramatic as it has been for females—probably because the rates for males were higher to begin with. For instance, the first surveys of premarital intercourse carried out in the 1940s showed an incidence of 84 percent across males of all ages; recent figures put the figure at closer to 95 percent. Moreover, the average age of males' first sexual experience has been declining steadily. Almost half of males have had sexual intercourse by the age of 18, and by the time they reach age 20, 88 percent have had intercourse. There also are race and ethnicity differences: African Americans tend to have sex for the first time earlier than do Puerto Ricans, who have sex earlier than whites do. Racial and ethnic differences probably reflect differences in socioeconomic opportunities and family structure (Arena, 1984; CDC, 1992; Singh et al., 2000; Hyde, 2003).

What may be most interesting about the patterns of premarital sex is that they show a convergence of male and female attitudes and behavior. But is the change sufficient to signal an end to the double standard?

Probably. For many people, particularly younger individuals, the double standard has been succeeded by a new view: *permissiveness with affection.* According to those holding this view, premarital intercourse is permissible for both men and women if it occurs within a long-term, committed, or loving relationship (DeGaton, Week, & Jensen, 1996; Hyde, 2003).

Still, the double standard has not disappeared completely. Where differing standards remain, the attitudes are almost always more lenient toward the male than toward the female (Sprecher & Hatfield, 1996).

Furthermore, there are substantial cultural differences regarding the incidence and acceptability of premarital intercourse. For instance, the proportions of male teenagers who have intercourse before the seventeenth birthday in Jamaica, the United States, and Brazil are about 10 times the level reported in the Philippines. And in some cultures, such as those in sub-Saharan Africa, women become sexually active at an earlier age than do men—although this may be due to the fact that they marry at a younger age than men do (Singh et al., 2000).

MARITAL SEX

To judge by the number of articles about sex in marriage, one would think that sexual behavior was the number one standard by which marital bliss is measured. Married couples are often concerned that they are having too little sex, too much sex, or the wrong kind of sex (Sprecher & McKinney, 1993).

Although there are many different dimensions along which sex in marriage is measured, one is certainly the frequency of sexual intercourse. What is typical? As with most other types of sexual activities, there is no easy answer to the question, because there are such wide variations in patterns between individuals. We do know that 43 percent of married couples have sexual intercourse a few times a month and 36 percent of couples have it two or three times a week. With increasing age and length of marriage, the frequency of intercourse declines. Still, sex continues into late adulthood, with almost half of people reporting that they engage in sexual activity at least once a month and that its quality is high (Michael et al., 1994; see Figure 3).

Extramarital sex: Sexual activity between a married person and someone who is not his or her spouse.

Although early research found **extramarital sex** to be widespread, the current reality appears to be otherwise. According to surveys, 85 percent of married women and more than 75 percent of married men are faithful to their spouses. Furthermore, the median number of sex partners, inside and outside of marriage, since the age of 18 for men was six, and for women two. Accompanying these numbers is a high, consistent degree of disapproval of extramarital sex, with nine of ten people saying that it is "always" or "almost always" wrong (Michael et al., 1994; Calmes, 1998; Allan & Harrison, 2002).

Homosexuality and Bisexuality

Homosexuals are sexually attracted to members of their own sex, whereas **bisexuals** are sexually attracted to people of the same sex *and* the other sex. (Many male homosexuals prefer the term *gay* and female homosexuals the label *lesbian*, because they refer to a broader array of attitudes and lifestyles than the term *homosexual*, which focuses on the sexual act.)

The number of people who choose same-sex sexual partners at one time or another is considerable. Estimates suggest that around 20 to 25 percent of males and about 15 percent of females have had at least one homosexual experience during adulthood. The exact number of people who identify themselves as exclusively homosexual has proved difficult to gauge, with some estimates as low as 1.1 percent and some as high as 10 percent. Most experts suggest that between 5 and 10 percent of both men and women are exclusively homosexual during extended periods of their lives (Hunt, 1974; Sells, 1994; Firestein, 1996).

Although people often view homosexuality and heterosexuality as two completely distinct sexual orientations, the issue is not that simple. Pioneering sex researcher Alfred Kinsey acknowledged this when he considered sexual orientation along a scale or continuum, with "exclusively homosexual" at one end and "exclusively heterosexual" at the other. In the middle were people who showed both homosexual and heterosexual behavior (see Figure 4). Kinsey's approach suggests that sexual orientation is dependent on a person's sexual feelings and behaviors and romantic feelings (Weinberg, Williams, & Pryor, 1991).

What determines whether people become homosexual or heterosexual? Although there are a number of theories, none has proved completely satisfactory.

Some explanations for sexual orientation are biological in nature, suggesting that there are genetic causes. Evidence for a genetic origin of sexual orientation comes from studies of identical twins, which have found that when one twin identified himself or herself as homosexual, the occurrence of homosexuality in the other twin was higher than it was in the general population. Such results occur even for twins who have been separated early in life and who therefore are not necessarily raised in similar social environments (Hamer et al., 1993; Turner, 1995; Bailey, et al., 1997).

Hormones may also play a role in determining sexual orientation. For example, research shows that women exposed to DES, or diethylstilbestrol, before birth (their mothers took the drug to avoid miscarriage) were more likely to be homosexual or bisexual (Meyer-Bahlburg, 1997).

Furthermore, some evidence suggests that differences in brain structures may be related to sexual orientation. For instance, the structure of the anterior hypothalamus, an area of the brain that governs sexual behavior, differs in male homosexuals and heterosexuals. Similarly, other research shows that, compared with heterosexual men or women, homosexual men have a larger anterior commissure, which is a bundle of neurons connecting the right and left hemispheres of the brain (LeVay, 1993; Byne, 1996).

Homosexuals: Persons who are sexually attracted to members of their own sex.

Bisexuals: Persons who are sexually attracted to people of the same sex *and* the other sex.

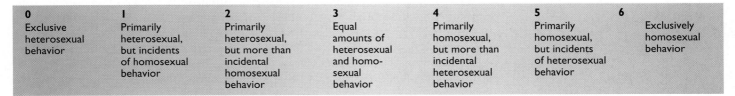

0	1	2	3	4	5	6
Exclusive heterosexual behavior	Primarily heterosexual, but incidents of homosexual behavior	Primarily heterosexual, but more than incidental homosexual behavior	Equal amounts of heterosexual and homosexual behavior	Primarily homosexual, but more than incidental heterosexual behavior	Primarily homosexual, but incidents of heterosexual behavior	Exclusively homosexual behavior

FIGURE 4 The Kinsey scale is designed to define the degree to which sexual orientation is heterosexual, homosexual, or bisexual. Although Kinsey saw people as falling along a continuum, most people believe that they belonged to a specific category. (Source: After Kinsey, Pomeroy, & Martin, 1948.)

"Frankly, I've repressed my sexuality so long I've actually forgotten what my orientation is."

However, research suggesting that biological causes are at the root of homosexuality is not conclusive because most findings are based on only small samples of individuals. Still, the possibility is real that some inherited or biological factor exists that predisposes people toward homosexuality, if certain environmental conditions are met (Rice et al., 1999; Veniegas, 2000; Teodorov et al., 2002).

There is little evidence suggesting that sexual orientation is brought about by child-rearing practices or family dynamics. Although classic psychoanalytic theories argued that the nature of the parent-child relationship can produce homosexuality (e.g., Freud, 1922/1959), research evidence does not support such explanations (Isay, 1990; Roughton, 2002).

Another explanation for homosexuality rests on learning theory (Masters & Johnson, 1979). According to this view, sexual orientation is learned through rewards and punishments in much the same way that we may learn to prefer swimming over tennis. For example, a young adolescent who had an unpleasant heterosexual experience might learn to link unpleasant associations with the other sex. If the same person had a rewarding, pleasant homosexual experience, homosexuality might be incorporated into his or her sexual fantasies. If such fantasies are used during later sexual activities—such as masturbation—they may be positively reinforced through orgasm, and the association of homosexual behavior and sexual pleasure eventually may cause homosexuality to become the preferred form of sexual behavior.

Although the learning-theory explanation is plausible, several difficulties rule it out as a definitive explanation. Because our society tends to hold homosexuality in low esteem, one ought to expect that the punishments involved in homosexual behavior would outweigh the rewards attached to it. Furthermore, children growing up with a homosexual parent are statistically unlikely to become homosexual, thus contradicting the notion that homosexual behavior may be learned from others (Golombok, 1995; Victor & Fish, 1995; Golombok & Tasker, 1996).

Because of the difficulty of finding a consistent explanation, most researchers reject the notion that any single factor orients a person toward homosexuality or heterosexuality. Most experts suspect that a combination of biological and environmental factors is at work (Greene & Herek, 1994; Bem, 1996).

Although we don't know at this point exactly why people develop a particular sexual orientation, one thing is clear: There is no relationship between sexual orientation and psychological adjustment. Bisexuals and homosexuals generally enjoy the same

Extensive research has found that bisexuals and homosexuals enjoy the same overall degree of mental and physical health as heterosexuals.

INTERACTIVITY 35–1

Attitudes toward sexuality

quality of mental and physical health that heterosexuals do, although the discrimination they experience may produce higher rates of some disorders, such as depression. Bisexuals and homosexuals also hold equivalent ranges and types of attitudes about themselves, independent of sexual orientation. For such reasons, the American Psychological Association and most other mental health organizations have endorsed efforts to reduce discrimination against gays and lesbians, such as revoking the ban against homosexuals in the military (Cochran, 2000; Perez, DeBord, & Bieschke, 2000; Morris, Waldo, & Rothblum, 2001). (For more on attitudes regarding sexuality, try **Interactivity 35–1.**)

PowerWeb: Is Treating Homosexuality Ethical and Effective?

www.mhhe.com/feldmanup7

RECAP/EVALUATE/RETHINK

RECAP

What is "normal" sexual behavior?

▶ There are a number of approaches to determining normality: deviation from the average, comparison of sexual behavior with some standard or ideal, and consideration of the psychological and physical consequences of the behavior to the person and to others. (p. 386)

How do most people behave sexually?

▶ The frequency of masturbation is high, particularly for males. Although increasingly liberal, attitudes toward masturbation have traditionally been negative even though no negative consequences have been detected. (p. 387)

▶ Heterosexuality, or sexual attraction to members of the other sex, is the most common sexual orientation. (p. 388)

▶ The double standard by which premarital sex is thought to be more permissible for men than for women has declined, particularly among young people. For many people, the double standard has been replaced by endorsement of "permissiveness with affection," the view that premarital intercourse is permissible if it occurs in the context of a loving and committed relationship. (p. 389)

▶ The frequency of marital sex varies widely. However, younger couples tend to have sexual intercourse more frequently than older ones. In addition, most men and women do not engage in extramarital sex. (p. 390)

▶ Homosexuals are sexually attracted to members of their own sex; bisexuals are sexually attracted to people of the same sex and the other sex. No explanation for why people become homosexual has been confirmed; among the possibilities are genetic or biological factors, childhood and family influences, and prior learning experiences and conditioning. However, no relationship exists between sexual orientation and psychological adjustment. (p. 391)

EVALUATE

1. The work carried out by _____ in the 1930s was the first systematic study of sexual behavior ever undertaken.
2. Although the incidence of masturbation among young adults is high, once men and women become involved in intimate relationships, they typically cease masturbating. True or false?
3. The increase in premarital sex in recent years has been greater for women than for men. True or false?
4. _____ _____ _____ refers to the view that premarital sex is acceptable within a loving, long-term re-lationship.
5. Research comparing homosexuals and heterosexuals clearly demonstrates that there is no difference in the level of adjustment or psychological functioning between the two groups. True or false?

RETHINK

1. In what ways might a sample of respondents to a survey about sexual practices be biased? How might bias in such a survey be reduced?
2. What societal factors have led to a reduction in the double standard by which sexuality in men and women is re-garded differently? Do you think the double standard has completely vanished?

Answers to Evaluate Questions

1. Kinsey; 2. false; even people in married relationships show a contin-ued incidence of masturbation; 3. true; 4. permissiveness with affection; 5. true

KEY TERMS

masturbation p. 387
heterosexuality p. 388

double standard p. 389
extramarital sex p. 390

homosexuals p. 391
bisexuals p. 391

Sexual Difficulties: When Sex Goes Wrong

It was a warm Friday evening in autumn, the kind of night that makes a college campus seem a magical place, full of excitement and promise. Exhilarated by her new independence, Casey Letvin, like hundreds of other recently arrived University of Colorado freshmen, was looking for a party. The students milling about the streets of Boulder seemed convivial, and Casey and her roommate thought nothing of stopping four upperclassmen to ask where the parties were . . . The four young men offered to take them to a nearby off-campus house where about twenty students were gathered. But approximately four hours later, the evening ended in a brutal breach of trust. At 12:30 a.m., Casey Letvin was taken back to her dormitory and raped on her own narrow bed by a man she might never have spoken to had he not been a fellow student (Freeman, 1990, p. 94).

What happened to Casey Letvin unfortunately is not rare. Rapes occur among women of all ages, from all economic levels, and from all ethnic groups. Female college students, who enjoy newfound freedoms while living in a community of strangers, have a particular vulnerability to rape.

When sex—an activity that should be pleasurable, joyful, and intimate—is forced on someone, it becomes one of the ultimate acts of aggression and brutality, and few crimes produce such profound and long-lasting consequences. But sexual crimes are not the only category of serious problems related to sex. Few personal difficulties produce as much anxiety, embarrassment, and even shame as do sexually transmitted diseases and sexual dysfunctions. We now turn to the major types of problems related to sex.

▲▲▲

> **How prevalent are rape and other forms of nonconsenting sex, and what are their causes?**
>
> **What are the major sexually transmitted diseases?**
>
> **What sexual difficulties do people most frequently encounter?**

Rape

Rape occurs when one person forces another person to submit to sexual activity such as intercourse or oral-genital sex. Although it usually applies to a male forcing a female, rape can be said to occur when members of either sex are forced into sexual activities without their consent.

Most people think of rape as a rare crime committed by strangers. Unfortunately, they are wrong on both counts. In fact, rape occurs far more frequently than is commonly thought, and rapists are typically acquaintances of their victims. Although it is hard to obtain reliable estimates, most research suggests that there is a 14 to 25 percent chance that a woman will be the victim of a rape during her lifetime. Furthermore, more than half a million sexual assaults are directed against women each year in the United States (Kilpatrick, Edmunds, & Seymour, 1992; Wiehe & Richards, 1995).

Furthermore, a national survey conducted at thirty-five universities revealed the startling finding that one out of eight female college students reported having been raped. Among the women who had been raped, about half said the rapists were first dates, casual dates, or romantic acquaintances—a phenomenon called **date rape.** Girls in high school also suffer both sexual and physical abuse: In one survey, 9 percent of 14- to 18-year-old girls said they had been forced into sexual activity by a date, and

Rape: The act by which one person forces another person to submit to sexual activity.

Date rape: Rape in which the rapist is either a date or a romantic acquaintance.

395

in more than half of those cases the incident had been accompanied by hitting, slapping, or shoving (Koss, 1993; Silverman, 2001; Ackard & Neumark-Sztainer, 2002).

Women in some segments of society are more at risk for rape than are others. Although the likelihood of sexual assault is considerably lower among Latino women in comparison to non-Latino white women, the rate for black women is slightly higher in comparison to white women. Such racial differences may stem from differing cultural views of women and male dominance (Sorenson & Siegel, 1992; Wyatt, 1992; Koss, 1993).

Although on the surface it might appear that rape is primarily a crime of sex, other types of motivation also underlie the behavior. In many cases, the rapist uses sex as a means of demonstrating power and control over the victim. In such cases, there is little that is sexually satisfying about rape to the rapist; instead, the pleasure comes from forcing someone else to be submissive (Hall & Barongan, 1997; Zurbriggen, 2000).

In other cases of rape, the primary motivation is anger. Sexual behavior is used to show the male rapist's rage at women in general, usually because of some perceived rejection or hurt that he has suffered in the past. Such rapes are likely to include physical violence and degrading acts against the victim.

Some rapes *are* based on a desire for sexual gratification. Some men hold the attitude that it is appropriate and desirable for them to actively seek out sex. To them, sexual encounters represent a form of "war" between the sexes—with winners and losers—and violence is sometimes considered an appropriate way to obtain what they want. According to their reasoning, using force to obtain sexual gratification is permissible (Malamuth et al., 1995; Hall, 1996).

Finally, there is a common, although unfounded, societal belief that many women offer token resistance to sex, saying no to sex when they mean yes. If a man holds such a view, he may ignore a woman's protestations that she doesn't want sex (Muehlenhard & Hollabaugh, 1988; Anderson, Cooper, & Okamura, 1997).

The repercussions of rape are devastating for the victims. During a rape, women experience fear, terror, and physical pain. Later, victims report shock, disbelief, panic, extreme anxiety, and suspiciousness—reactions that are sometimes intensified by implications that somehow the victim was to blame because of her style of dress or her presence in the wrong neighborhood

The psychological reactions to rape are no different whether it is date rape or rape by a stranger. These feelings may continue for years, even though the victim outwardly appears to have recovered. However, immediate psychological intervention, such as that provided by rape crisis centers, may be helpful in diminishing the long-term reactions to rape (Golding, 1999; Monnier, Resnick, Kilpatrick, & Seals, 2002).

Childhood Sexual Abuse

One form of sexual behavior that is surprisingly common, yet little understood, is the sexual abuse of children. Each year a half million children are sexually abused. In fact, between 5 and 10 percent of boys and 20 percent of girls will be abused (Villarosa, 2002; see Figure 1).

Who commits child sexual abuse? In most cases it is a relative or acquaintance; in only about one-quarter of the cases is the abuse carried out by a stranger. The most vulnerable age for being molested is between 7 and 13 years old, and the abusers tend to be about twenty years older than their victims. In most instances, the abuser is a male heterosexual (Finkelhor, 1984; Wolfe, 1999).

The short- and longer-term consequences of childhood sexual abuse can be extremely damaging. In terms of initial effects, victims report fear, anxiety, depression, anger, and hostility. Long-term effects may include depression, self-destructive behavior, feelings of isolation, poor self-esteem, and substance abuse. Although they may experience sexual difficulties later in life, the victims are not more likely to become sexual abusers themselves. Ultimately, the consequences of childhood sexual

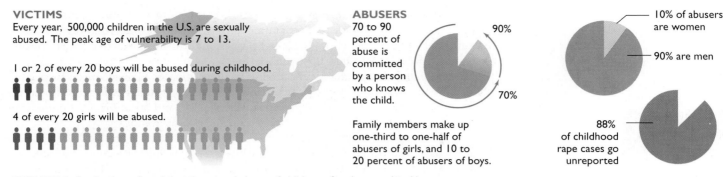

VICTIMS
Every year, 500,000 children in the U.S. are sexually abused. The peak age of vulnerability is 7 to 13.

1 or 2 of every 20 boys will be abused during childhood.

4 of every 20 girls will be abused.

ABUSERS
70 to 90 percent of abuse is committed by a person who knows the child.

90%
70%

Family members make up one-third to one-half of abusers of girls, and 10 to 20 percent of abusers of boys.

10% of abusers are women
90% are men

88% of childhood rape cases go unreported

FIGURE 1 Studies have found that the sexual abuse of children often is committed by a person who knows the child, with almost a third of the abusers being family members. (Source: Dr. David Finkelhor, University of New Hampshire.)

abuse are related to the specific nature of the abuse. Experiences involving fathers, genital contact, and the use of force are the most damaging (Berkowitz, 2000; Hawke, Jainchill, & De Leon, 2000; Berliner & Elliott, 2002).

Sexually Transmitted Diseases (STDs)

Millions of people suffer the discomfort—not to mention the psychological distress—of a **sexually transmitted disease (STD),** a medical condition acquired through sexual contact. Estimates suggest that one of five people in the United States is infected with some form of STD, and at least one of four will probably contract a STD during their lifetimes. The United States has the highest rate of sexually transmitted diseases of all the economically developed countries in the world, in part because people in the United States don't talk about sex as frankly or provide as much sex education as people in other developed nations do (see Figure 2; Centers for Disease Control and Prevention, 2000).

The most widespread STD is *chlamydia,* a disease that in women initially produces no symptoms and in men causes a burning sensation during urination and a discharge from the penis. If it is left untreated, chlamydia can lead to pelvic inflammation, urethral damage, arthritis, and even sterility. Chlamydia affects some 4 million women and men each year, but it can be cured with a new antibiotic, azithromycin (Ku et al., 2002).

Genital herpes is a virus related to the cold sores that sometimes appear around the mouth. Herpes first appears as small blisters or sores around the genitals that

Sexually transmitted disease (STD): A disease acquired through sexual contact.

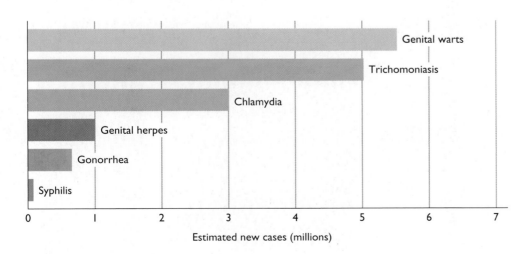

Genital warts

Trichomoniasis

Chlamydia

Genital herpes

Gonorrhea

Syphilis

0   1   2   3   4   5   6   7

Estimated new cases (millions)

FIGURE 2 Estimates of the numbers of new cases annually of sexually transmitted diseases in the United States. Although—as the figure shows—there are more new cases of genital warts and trichomoniasis diagnosed each year, overall there are more existing cases of chlamydia among people in the United States. (Source: Centers for Disease Control and Prevention, 2000.)

later break open, causing severe pain. These sores heal after a few weeks, but the disease can and often does reappear after an indeterminate interval, and the cycle repeats itself. There is no cure for genital herpes, and during the active phases of the disease it can be transmitted to sexual partners.

Trichomoniasis is an infection occurring in the vagina or penis. Caused by a parasite, it is often without symptoms, especially in men. Eventually, it can cause painful urination and intercourse, a discharge from the vagina, and an unpleasant odor. The 5 million cases reported each year can be treated with antibiotics.

Gonorrhea and *syphilis* are the two STDs that have been recognized the longest by scientists. Gonorrhea can lead to fertility problems and infection. Syphilis, if untreated, may affect the brain, the heart, and a developing fetus, and can even be fatal. Syphilis reveals itself first through a small sore at the point of sexual contact. In its secondary stage, it may include a rash. Both gonorrhea and syphilis can be treated successfully with antibiotics if they are diagnosed early enough.

Another common STD is *genital warts* (caused by *human papilloma virus)*. Genital warts are small, lumpy warts that form on or near the penis or vagina. The warts are easy to diagnose because of their distinctive appearance: They look like small cauliflower bulbs. They usually form about two months after exposure and can be treated with a drug called metronidazole (Cothran & White, 2002).

Acquired immune deficiency syndrome (AIDS): A fatal, sexually transmitted disease caused by a virus that destroys the body's immune system.

In the last two decades, no sexually transmitted disease has had a greater impact on sexual behavior—and society as a whole—than **acquired immune deficiency syndrome (AIDS).** Although in the United States AIDS at first was found primarily in homosexual men, it has spread to other populations, such as intravenous drug users. In some parts of the world, such as Africa, it mainly affects heterosexuals. In the United States, AIDS is the leading cause of death among men 25 to 44 years of age and the third leading cause of death among women in that age range. The worldwide figures are even more daunting: Already, 25 million people have died from AIDS, and people living with the disease number 42 million worldwide (see Figure 3; UNAIDS, 2002).

The extent of the AIDS epidemic has led to significant changes in sexual behavior. People are less likely to engage in "casual" sex with new acquaintances, and the use of condoms during sexual intercourse has increased. Nonetheless, the only foolproof method of avoiding AIDS is total abstinence—an alternative that many people

FIGURE 3 The number of people carrying the AIDS virus varies substantially by geographic region. By far the most cases are found in Africa and the Middle East, although the disease is a growing problem in Asia. (Source: United Nations AIDS Program, 2001.)

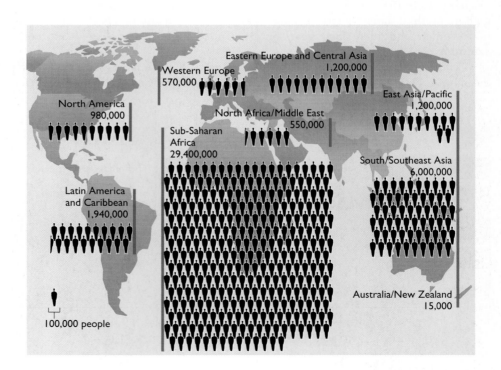

find unrealistic. However, there are several ways to reduce the risk of contracting AIDS (as well as other sexually transmitted diseases); these methods have come to be called "safer sex" practices (Carr, 2002):

- ▶ *Know your sexual partner—well.* Before having sex with someone, learn about his or her sexual history.
- ▶ *Use condoms.* For those in sexual relationships, condoms are the most reliable means of preventing transmission of the AIDS virus.
- ▶ *Avoid the exchange of bodily fluids, particularly semen.* In particular, avoid anal intercourse. The AIDS virus can spread through small tears in the rectum, making anal intercourse without condoms particularly dangerous. Oral sex, once thought relatively safe, is now viewed as potentially dangerous.
- ▶ *Stay sober.* Using alcohol and drugs impairs judgment and can lead to poor decisions—and it makes using a condom correctly more difficult.
- ▶ *Consider the benefits of monogamy.* People in long-term, monogamous relationships with partners who have been faithful are at a lower risk of contracting AIDS.

Sexual Problems

Few people would feel embarrassed by a case of appendicitis or a broken leg. In contrast, sexual difficulties are often a source of concern and self-consciousness because of the importance that society places on "desirable" sexual conduct. And such difficulties are surprisingly common, with 43 percent of women and 31 percent of men experiencing problems associated with sexual performance. Among the most widespread are the disorders we discuss below (Laumann et al., 1999; Goldstein, 2000; Rosner, 2001).

Erectile dysfunction is the inability of a male to achieve or maintain an erection. The rare case is a male who has never been able to have an erection, and the more common case is a male who, though now unable to have an erection, has had one at least once in the past. Erectile dysfunction is not an uncommon problem, and it is the rare man who has never experienced it at least once during his lifetime. This is hardly surprising, because the ability to achieve and hold an erection is sensitive to alcohol, drugs, performance fears, anxiety, and a host of other factors. Erectile dysfunction becomes a more serious problem when it occurs more than occasionally. As we consider in the *Applying Psychology in the 21st Century* box, drugs such as Viagra have brought about significant advances in the treatment of erectile dysfunction.

In **premature ejaculation,** a male is unable to delay orgasm as long as he wishes. Because "as long as he wishes" is dependent on a man's—and his partner's—attitudes and opinions about how long is appropriate, this is a difficult disorder to diagnose, and sometimes the problem can be resolved simply by having a male redefine how long he wants to delay ejaculation. Premature ejaculation is most often a psychological problem, as there are rarely physical reasons for it. One cause may be early sexual learning: Because sexual experiences during adolescence are often accompanied by a fear of being caught, some men learn early in their lives to reach orgasm as quickly as possible (Astbury-Ward, 2002).

Inhibited ejaculation is the opposite problem. In this case, the male is unable to ejaculate when he wants to, if at all. Sometimes learning general relaxation techniques is sufficient to allow men to overcome the difficulty.

Some women experience **anorgasmia,** or a lack of orgasm. In *primary orgasmic dysfunction,* a woman has never experienced orgasm. In *secondary orgasmic dysfunction,* a woman has had an orgasm at some point but no longer does, or does so only under certain conditions—such as during masturbation but not during sexual intercourse. Because the lack of orgasm during sexual intercourse is so common (some one-third of women report they do not receive sufficient stimulation to reach orgasm during sexual intercourse), this state of affairs is not dysfunctional at all but is merely a normal variation of female sexuality.

Erectile dysfunction: The inability of a male to achieve or maintain an erection.

Premature ejaculation: The inability of a male to delay orgasm as long as he wishes.

Inhibited ejaculation: The inability of a male to ejaculate when he wants to, if at all.

Anorgasmia (an or GAZ mee uh): A female's lack of orgasm.

Bringing Sexual Dysfunction into the Open: The Newest Sexual Revolution

Bob Dole [was] on "The Larry King Show" to discuss his prostate-cancer operation. During a commercial break, so the story goes, King leaned over to ask his old friend, confidentially, how he was dealing with the operation's grimmest side effect, impotence. Dole cheerfully informed the talk-show host that there was a new drug, Viagra, and miraculously, it had cured the problem. King asked Dole if he would discuss it on the air, and Dole said sure, why not?

The world was about to become a very different place (Hitt, 2000, p. 43).

It was not too long ago that talk of sexual dysfunction was rare even among close friends, let alone on network television. That time has passed as discussions of Viagra have become commonplace, and the drug can be ordered almost as easily as aspirin over the World Wide Web. Almost 200,000 prescriptions are filled each week, and 17 million men in the United States have used the drug.

Viagra treats erectile dysfunction by increasing the flow of blood through a man's penis, producing an erection relatively quickly. It is also being used experimentally to treat women's sexual dysfunction by increasing blood flow to parts of the genitals and thus improving the chances of reaching orgasm.

Critics of Viagra suggest that the drug may become the Prozac of sex: prescribed indiscriminately and without sufficient consideration for the underlying condition that produced the sexual problem in the first place. In this view, although Viagra may treat the symptoms of erectile dysfunction successfully, it does not address underlying psychological difficulties, which may have produced the dysfunction in the first place (Sigmund, 2002).

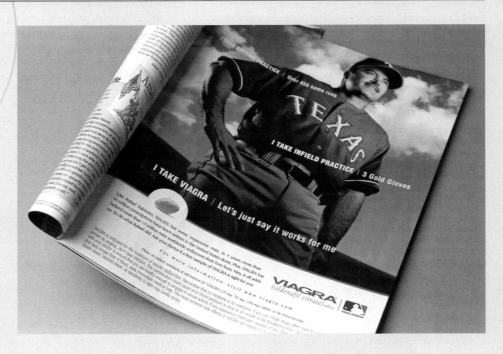

The controversy over the use of Viagra has not stopped pharmaceutical companies from working on the next generation of sexual-arousal aids. They include such possibilities as the following:

- *Testosterone patches.* These patches deliver the male hormone testosterone in slow doses, potentially helping people who have inhibited sexual desire.
- *Prostaglandin E-1 cream.* By stimulating blood flow to the genital area, this cream is meant to treat arousal and orgasm dysfunction in women.
- *Clitoral blood flow device.* This tiny device nestles, like a thimble, over a woman's clitoris and stimulates blood flow. This produces greater sensitivity and lubrication, making it easier to have an orgasm (Hitt, 2000).

These products offer the potential of providing improved treatment to those with sexual dysfunction. All of them, though, address only the biological aspects of sexual behavior. The ultimate effectiveness of treatments for sexual dysfunction that do not take into account psychological issues such as relationship and intimacy considerations remains an open question (Leland, 2000; Weeks & Gambescia, 2000; Sigmund, 2002).

RETHINK

Should sexually enhancing drugs such as Viagra be routinely prescribed—or even sold over the counter without a prescription? Why or why not? Is the restricted availability of such drugs an example of medical caution, or is it mainly "puritanical" disapproval of sexuality?

Finally, **inhibited sexual desire** occurs when the motivation for sexual activity is restrained or lacking entirely. When people with inhibited sexual desire find themselves in circumstances that typically would evoke sexual feelings, they begin to turn off sexually and may even experience a kind of "sexual anesthesia." Ultimately they may begin to avoid situations of a sexual nature, thereby forgoing intimacy with others (Meston, 2003).

It is important to note that many of the problems we have discussed turn up at one time or another in most people's sex lives. It is only when these problems persist, cause undue anxiety, and turn sex from play into work that they are cause for concern. Furthermore, treatments for common sexual problems have a good rate of success (Masters & Johnson, 1994; Rosner, 2001). (To explore sexual disorders in greater depth, complete **Interactivity 36–1.**)

Inhibited sexual desire: A sexual dysfunction in which the motivation for sexual activity is restrained or lacking entirely.

INTERACTIVITY 36–1

Sexual disorders

Transgenderism

Transgendered individuals (also known as transsexuals) are people who believe they are trapped in the body of the other gender. In important ways, transgenderism represents less a sexual difficulty than a gender issue involving one's sexual identity.

Transgendered people may seek sex-change operations in which their existing genitals are surgically removed and the genitals of the desired sex are fashioned. Several steps, including intensive counseling and hormone injections, along with living as a member of the desired sex for several years, precede surgery, which is, not surprisingly, highly complicated. The outcome, though, can be quite positive (Fields-Meyer & Wihlborg, 2003; O'Keefe & Fox, 2003; Stegerwald & Janson, 2003).

As we have seen, surveys of college women make clear that the greatest danger of rape comes not from some unknown assailant but from a fellow student. There are ways, however, to reduce the likelihood of date rape. The following suggestions provide some guidance for women and men (American College Health Association, 1989; Jackson, 1996; Shultz, Scherman, & Marshall, 2000):

BECOMING AN INFORMED CONSUMER

of Psychology

Lowering the Risks of Date Rape

- ▶ Women should believe in their rights to set limits and communicate those limits clearly, firmly, and early on. They should say no when they mean no.
- ▶ Women should be assertive when someone is pressuring them to engage in an activity in which they don't want to engage. They should keep in mind that men may interpret passivity as permission.
- ▶ Women should be aware of situations in which they are at risk.
- ▶ Women should keep in mind the fact that some men interpret certain kinds of dress as sexually provocative, and that not all men subscribe to the same standards of sex as they do.
- ▶ Women should keep close tabs on what they are given to drink in social situations; victims of date rape have sometimes been given mind-altering drugs.
- ▶ Men should be aware of their dates' views on sexual behavior.
- ▶ Men should not hold the view that the goal of dating is to "score."
- ▶ The word *no* should be understood to mean no and not be interpreted as an invitation to continue. Men should know that a woman who says no is not rejecting them, but is rejecting a specific act at a specific time.
- ▶ Men should not assume that certain kinds of dress or flirtatious behavior are an invitation to sex.
- ▶ Both men and women should understand that alcohol and drugs cloud judgment and hinder communication between them.

RECAP/EVALUATE/RETHINK

RECAP

How prevalent are rape and other forms of nonconsenting sex, and what are their causes?

▶ Rape occurs when one person forces another person to submit to sexual activity. Often the victim is acquainted with the rapist. The motivation for rape is only sometimes sexual gratification. More frequently it is power, aggression, or anger. (p. 395)

▶ Childhood sexual abuse is surprisingly widespread. Most often the perpetrator is an acquaintance or a family member. (p. 396)

What are the major sexually transmitted diseases?

▶ Acquired immune deficiency syndrome, or AIDS, is bringing about profound changes in people's sexual practices. Other sexually transmitted diseases include chlamydia, genital herpes, trichomoniasis, gonorrhea, syphilis, and genital warts. (p. 398)

What sexual difficulties do people most frequently encounter?

▶ Among the major sexual problems reported by males are erectile dysfunction, premature ejaculation, and inhibited ejaculation. For females, the major problem is anorgasmia, or a lack of orgasm. Both men and women may suffer from inhibited sexual desire. (p. 399)

EVALUATE

1. A college woman is more likely to be raped by an acquaintance than by a stranger. True or false?
2. Which of the following is unlikely to be a motivation for the act of rape?
   a. Need for power
   b. Desire for sexual intimacy
   c. Desire for sexual gratification
   d. Anger against women in general

3. Which of the following STDs is the most widespread?
   a. Genital herpes
   b. Gonorrhea
   c. Chlamydia
   d. Syphilis
4. Which of the following is *not* true about changes in sexual behavior as a result of the AIDS epidemic?
   a. The use of condoms has increased.
   b. People are less likely to engage in casual sex.
   c. HIV infection rates are dropping because most unmarried people have adopted abstinence.
   d. The risk of contracting AIDS may be reduced by engaging in safer sex practices.
5. Sexual dysfunctions, even if they occur only once, are cause for considerable concern and should be treated immediately. True or false?

RETHINK

1. Should women be free to dress any way they want without being concerned about "giving off the wrong signals"? Is it reasonable for men to assume that women sometimes give off signals that indicate that they really want sex even when they say they don't?
2. What responsibilities do people who learn they have a sexually transmitted disease have to their sexual partners?

Answers to Evaluate Questions

1. true; 2. b; 3. c; 4. c; 5. false; sexual dysfunction is experienced by almost everyone at one time or another

KEY TERMS

rape p. 395
date rape p. 395
sexually transmitted disease (STD) p. 397

acquired immune deficiency syndrome (AIDS) p. 398
erectile dysfunction p. 399

premature ejaculation p. 399
inhibited ejaculation p. 399

anorgasmia p. 399
inhibited sexual desire p. 401

Looking Back

Psychology on the Web

1. Find at least two recent news articles or discussions on the Web dealing with the issue of gender equality in school or the workplace, especially unequal treatment of individuals because of their gender. Summarize in writing what you found, and discuss your own attitudes toward this issue.

2. Find information on the Web about date rape, including guidelines or suggestions published by other colleges, for preventing rape among students. Summarize your findings, including recommendations for behavioral or policy changes that might be effective at your college. If your college's policies toward or publications about this topic could benefit from your findings, bring them to the attention of the appropriate office at your institution and suggest specific changes.

3. After completing Interactivity 36–1, search the Web for the latest statistics on the spread of AIDS around the world. Where is the incidence of AIDS growing most rapidly and why is it increasing in those areas?

Epilogue

We have seen how the subjects of gender and sex are dealt with by psychologists, first with regard to gender roles, gender stereotyping, gender schemas, and sexism. The expectations of society regarding male and female characteristics and behaviors lead to inequities in the treatment of men and women in school, the workplace, and the rest of society—inequities that largely favor men.

With regard to sexuality, we discussed the nature of the physical processes that surround sexuality and addressed the controversial issue of "normality" in sexual behavior. We saw the varieties of sexual behavior, and we discussed premarital sex and marital sex, as well as heterosexuality, homosexuality, and bisexuality. We also examined rape and other forms of nonconsenting sex, including childhood sexual abuse.

Finally, we looked at the sexual problems that people may have, including sexually transmitted diseases and sexual dysfunctions. We explored the nature of these problems and discussed ways to treat and deal with them.

Before we turn to the subject of human development in the next few modules, return to the Prologue of this chapter, concerning the case of Bruce Reimer, the boy who was temporarily transformed into a girl. Using your knowledge of gender and sex, consider the following questions.

1. What might Bruce's parents have done differently after the accident that cut off Bruce's penis?

2. Is it reasonable to generalize from a single case such as this one to broader issues of sex and gender? Why or why not?

3. "Brenda" was given dolls to play with and taught to be clean and tidy in order to be more like a girl. How were such efforts misguided, and what do they say about society's expectations about male and female behavior?

4. What conclusions can you draw from the lack of success in changing Bruce into Brenda in terms of the relative influence of heredity and environment on sexual identity?

1 Gender Differences in Nature

Throughout the animal kingdom, an animal's gender affects its behavior. For example, males tend to be more competitive and aggressive, whereas females tend to be more cooperative and nurturing. Many factors contribute to this gender difference.

2 Evolution

Some psychologists believe that evolution has predisposed males and females to behave differently. For example, males tend to be more concerned about physical infidelity, whereas females are more concerned with emotional infidelity, a difference that evolutionary psychologists believe reflects evolutionary factors.

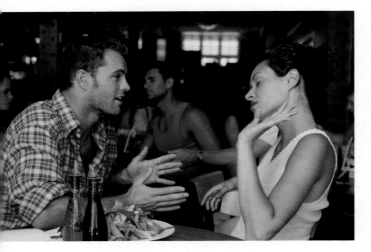

3 Development of Human Sex Organs

At four weeks, a human fetus has undifferentiated sexual organs. During the next 8 weeks, the organs develop into either male or female organs.

Male

7th–8th week

Female

12th week

4 Prenatal Hormones

During prenatal development, male and female fetuses secrete different hormones. In turn, these hormones may "masculinize" and "feminize" their respective brains.

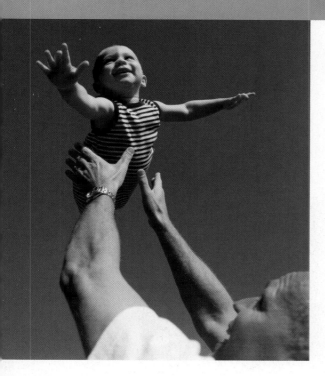

5 Socialization

Every culture treats girls and boys differently. For example, fathers play more roughly with their sons than mothers do, and mothers talk more to their infant daughters than to their sons. These differences socialize infants into gender roles.

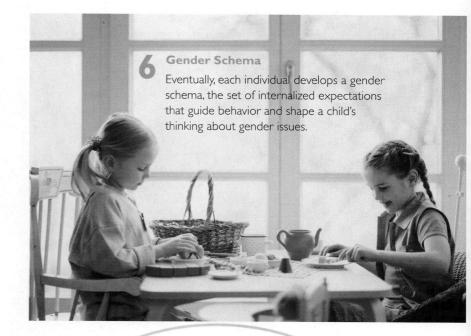

6 Gender Schema

Eventually, each individual develops a gender schema, the set of internalized expectations that guide behavior and shape a child's thinking about gender issues.

7 Puberty and Gender Roles

Physical changes during puberty include the rapid development of sexual organs, body changes, and first menstruation. In turn, these changes increase the magnitude of sex role differences between the genders.

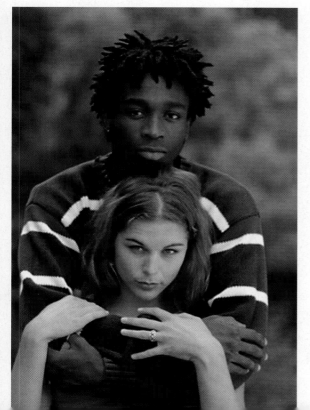

8 Androgyny

Some psychologists argue that androgynous children are more emotionally healthy than those who are socialized to traditional gender roles. Androgynous individuals exhibit some traits that are traditionally thought of as masculine and other traits that are typically thought of as feminine.

Development

Prologue
The One-Pound Wonder

Courtney Rose Jackson's parents placed her on the dining room table, smack in front of her first birthday cake. She fixed on the confection with an expression of utmost seriousness. Then, just as her mother, Jennifer, 26, remarked, "Uh-oh, she's going to grab the cake," the 1-year-old lunged.

After tasting her icing-coated fingers, Courtney opened her blue eyes wide and burst out laughing. A circle of relatives looked just as amazed. "A year ago it was hard to believe she was even going to make it," said her father, Chris, 27. "She was so small."

Courtney, soon after birth, weighing a fraction over a pound.

When Courtney came into the world, after only 23 weeks in her mother's womb, she weighed 460 grams—a fraction over 1 pound. Her heart was the size of a child's knuckle and a mere eight teaspoons of blood flowed through her 11-inch body (Cheakalos & Breu, 2002, p. 60).

Courtney at her first birthday.

Ten years ago, Courtney would have been unlikely to live for long. But thanks to advances in medical technology and our understanding of how children develop, Courtney not only survived, but has thrived.

Welcome to the brave new world of childhood—or, rather, one of the brave new worlds. From new ways of caring for newborns to learning how to raise children most sensibly, the issues involved in human development touch each of us.

Developmental psychology, the branch of psychology that studies the patterns of growth and change that occur throughout life, addresses these issues, along with many others. In large part, developmental psychologists study the interaction between the unfolding of

Looking Ahead

biologically predetermined patterns of behavior and a constantly changing, dynamic environment. They ask how our genetic background affects our behavior throughout our lives and whether our potential is limited by heredity. Similarly, they seek to understand the way in which the environment works with—or against—our genetic capabilities, how the world we live in affects our development, and how we can be encouraged to reach our full potential.

We begin by examining the approaches developmental psychologists use to study the environmental and genetic factors: the nature–nurture issue. Then we consider the very start of development, beginning with conception and the nine months of life before birth. We describe both genetic and environmental influences on the unborn individual and the way they can affect behavior throughout the remainder of the life cycle.

Next, we examine development that occurs after birth, witnessing the enormous and rapid growth that takes place during the early stages of life, focusing on physical, social, and cognitive change throughout infancy, toddlerhood, and middle childhood. We then move on to development from adolescence through adulthood. We end with a discussion of the ways in which people prepare themselves for death.

Nature and Nurture: The Enduring Developmental Issue

How many bald, six-foot-six, 250-pound volunteer firefighters in New Jersey wear droopy mustaches, aviator-style eyeglasses, and a key ring on the right side of the belt?

The answer is two: Gerald Levey and Mark Newman. They are twins who were separated at birth. Each twin did not even know the other existed until they were reunited—in a fire station—by a fellow firefighter who knew Newman and was startled to see his double, Levey, at a firefighters' convention.

The lives of the twins, although separate, took remarkably similar paths. Levey went to college, studying forestry; Newman planned to study forestry in college but instead took a job trimming trees. Both had jobs in supermarkets. One had a job installing sprinkler systems; the other installed fire alarms.

Both men are unmarried and find the same kind of woman attractive: "tall, slender, long hair." They share similar hobbies, enjoying hunting, fishing, going to the beach, and watching old John Wayne movies and professional wrestling. Both like Chinese food and drink the same brand of beer. Their mannerisms are also similar—for example, each one throws his head back when he laughs. And, of course, there is one more thing: They share a passion for fighting fires.

How do psychologists study the degree to which development is an interaction of hereditary and environmental factors?

The similarities we see in twins Gerald Levey and Mark Newman vividly raise one of the fundamental questions posed by **developmental psychology,** the study of the patterns of growth and change that occur throughout life. The question is this: How can we distinguish between the *environmental* causes of behavior (the influence of parents, siblings, family, friends, schooling, nutrition, and all the other experiences to which a child is exposed) and *hereditary* causes (those based on the genetic makeup of an individual that influence growth and development throughout life)? This question embodies the **nature–nurture issue.** In this context, nature refers to hereditary factors, and nurture to environmental influences.

Although the question was first posed as a nature-*versus*-nurture issue, developmental psychologists today agree that *both* nature and nurture interact to produce specific developmental patterns and outcomes. Consequently, the question has evolved into *How and to what degree* do environment and heredity both produce their effects? No one grows up free of environmental influences, nor does anyone develop without being affected by his or her inherited *genetic makeup.* However, the debate over the comparative influence of the two factors remains active, with different approaches and theories of development emphasizing the environment or heredity to a greater or lesser degree (de Waal, 1999; Pinker, 2002).

For example, some developmental theories rely on basic psychological principles of learning and stress the role learning plays in producing changes in behavior in a developing child. Such theories emphasize the role of the environment in development. In contrast, other developmental theories emphasize the influence of one's physiological makeup and functioning on development. Such theories stress the role of heredity and *maturation*—the unfolding of biologically predetermined patterns of behavior—in producing developmental change. Maturation can be seen, for instance, in the development of sex characteristics (such as breasts and body hair) that occurs at the start of adolescence. Furthermore, the work of behavioral geneticists, who study the effects of

Gerald Levey and Mark Newman

Developmental psychology: The branch of psychology that studies the patterns of growth and change that occur throughout life.

Nature–nurture issue: The issue of the degree to which environment and heredity influence behavior.

FIGURE 1 Characteristics influenced significantly by genetic factors. Although these characteristics have strong genetic components, they are also affected by environmental factors.

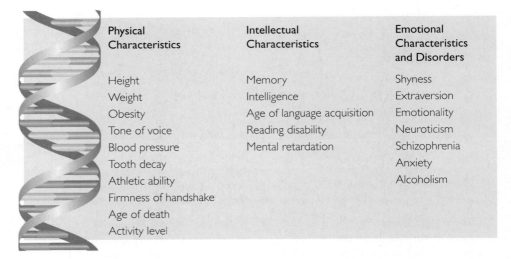

Physical Characteristics	Intellectual Characteristics	Emotional Characteristics and Disorders
Height	Memory	Shyness
Weight	Intelligence	Extraversion
Obesity	Age of language acquisition	Emotionality
Tone of voice	Reading disability	Neuroticism
Blood pressure	Mental retardation	Schizophrenia
Tooth decay		Anxiety
Athletic ability		Alcoholism
Firmness of handshake		
Age of death		
Activity level		

heredity on behavior, and the theories of evolutionary psychologists, who identify behavior patterns that result from our genetic inheritance, have influenced developmental psychologists. Both behavioral geneticists and evolutionary psychologists have highlighted the importance of heredity in influencing human behavior (Bjorklund, 1997).

Despite their differences over theory, developmental psychologists concur on some points. They agree that genetic factors not only provide the potential for particular behaviors or traits to emerge, but also place limitations on the emergence of such behavior or traits. For instance, heredity defines people's general level of intelligence, setting an upper limit that—regardless of the quality of the environment—people cannot exceed. Heredity also places limits on physical abilities; humans simply cannot run at a speed of sixty miles an hour, nor will they grow as tall as ten feet, no matter what the quality of their environment (Plomin & McClearn, 1993; Steen, 1996; Pinker, 2002).

Figure 1 lists some of the characteristics most affected by heredity. As you consider these items, it is important to keep in mind that these characteristics are not *entirely* determined by heredity, but that environmental factors also play a role.

Developmental psychologists also agree that in most instances environmental factors play a critical role in enabling people to reach the potential capabilities that their genetic background makes possible. If Albert Einstein had received no intellectual stimulation as a child and had not been sent to school, it is unlikely that he would have reached his genetic potential. Similarly, a great athlete such as basketball star Michael Jordan would have been unlikely to display much physical skill if he had not been raised in an environment that nurtured his innate talent and gave him the opportunity to train and perfect his natural abilities.

Clearly, the relationship between heredity and environment is far from simple. As a consequence, developmental psychologists typically take an *interactionist* position on the nature–nurture issue, suggesting that a combination of hereditary and environmental factors influences development. Developmental psychologists face the challenge of identifying the relative strength of each of these influences on the individual, as well as that of identifying the specific changes that occur over the course of development (Plomin & Neiderhiser, 1992; Wozniak & Fischer, 1993; Saudino & Plomin, 1996).

PowerWeb: Environment and Genes: Determinants of Behavior

www.mhhe.com/feldmanup7

Ⓐ Ⓐ Ⓐ

Determining the Relative Influence of Nature and Nurture

Developmental psychologists use several approaches to determine the relative influence of genetic and environmental factors on behavior. In one approach, researchers can experimentally control the genetic makeup of laboratory animals by carefully breeding them for specific traits. For instance, by observing animals with identical genetic backgrounds placed in varied environments, researchers can learn the effects of particular kinds of environmental stimulation. Although researchers must be careful when generalizing the findings of nonhuman research to a human population, findings from animal research provide important information that cannot be obtained, for ethical reasons, by using human participants.

Human twins serve as another important source of information about the relative effects of genetic and environmental factors. If **identical twins** (those who are genetically identical) display different patterns of development, those differences have to be attributed to variations in the environment in which the twins were raised. The most useful data come from identical twins (such as Gerald Levey and Mark Newman) who are adopted at birth by different sets of adoptive parents and raised apart in differing environments. Studies of nontwin siblings who are raised in totally different environments also shed some light on the issue. Because they have relatively similar genetic backgrounds, siblings who show similarities a as adults provide strong evidence for the importance of heredity (Gottesman, 1997; Sternberg, 2002a).

Researchers can also take the opposite tack. Instead of concentrating on people with similar genetic backgrounds who are raised in different environments, they may consider people raised in similar environments who have totally dissimilar genetic backgrounds. If they find, for example, similar courses of development in two adopted children who have different genetic backgrounds and have been raised in the same family, they have evidence for the importance of environmental influences on development. Moreover, psychologists can carry out research involving animals with dissimilar genetic backgrounds; by experimentally varying the environment in which they are raised, we can determine the influence of environmental factors (independent of heredity) on development (Segal, 1993; Vernon et al., 1997). (To better understand the nature-nurture issue, complete **Interactivity 37–1.**)

Identical twins: Twins who are genetically identical.

INTERACTIVITY 37–1

Nature and nurture

Specific Research Approaches

Because of the demands of measuring behavioral change across different ages, developmental researchers have designed several unique methodologies. The most frequently used, **cross-sectional research,** compares people of different ages at the same point in time. Cross-sectional studies provide information about differences in development between different age groups.

Suppose, for instance, we were interested in the development of intellectual ability in adulthood. To carry out a cross-sectional study, we might compare a sample of 25-, 45-, and 65-year-olds who all take the same IQ test. We then can determine whether average IQ test scores differ in each age group.

Cross-sectional research has limitations, however. For instance, we cannot be sure that the differences in IQ scores we might find in our example are due to age differences alone. Instead, the scores may reflect differences in the educational attainment of the cohorts represented. A *cohort* is a group of people who grow up at similar times, in similar places, and in similar conditions. In the case of IQ differences, any age differences we find in a cross-sectional study may reflect educational differences among the cohorts studied: People in the older age group may belong to a cohort that was less likely to attend college than were the people in the younger groups.

A longitudinal study, the second major research strategy used by developmental psychologists, provides one way around this problem. **Longitudinal research** traces the behavior of one or more participants as the participants age. Longitudinal studies assess *change* in intellectual ability over time, unlike cross-sectional studies, which assess *differences* among groups of people.

For instance, consider how we might investigate intellectual development during adulthood by using a longitudinal research strategy. First, we might give an IQ test to a group of 25-year-olds. We'd then come back to the same people twenty years

Cross-sectional research: A research method that compares people of different ages at the same point in time.

Longitudinal research: A research method that investigates behavior as participants age.

later and retest them at age 45. Finally, we'd return to them once more when they were 65 years old and test them again.

By examining changes at several points in time, we can clearly see how individuals develop. Unfortunately, longitudinal research requires an enormous expenditure of time (as the researcher waits for the participants to get older), and participants who begin a study at an early age may drop out, move away, or even die as the research continues. Moreover, participants who take the same test at several points in time may become "test-wise" and perform better each time they take it, having become more familiar with the test.

Sequential research: A research method that combines cross-sectional and longitudinal research by considering a number of different age groups and examining them at several points in time.

To make up for the limitations in both cross-sectional and longitudinal research, investigators have devised an alternative strategy. Known as **sequential research,** it combines cross-sectional and longitudinal approaches by taking a number of different age groups and examining them at several points in time. For example, investigators might use a group of 3-, 5-, and 7-year-olds, examining them every six months for a period of several years. This technique allows a developmental psychologist to tease out the specific effects of age changes from other possibly influential factors.

RECAP/EVALUATE/RETHINK

RECAP

How do psychologists study the degree to which development is an interaction of hereditary and environmental factors?

- ▶ Developmental psychology studies growth and change throughout life. One fundamental question is how much developmental change is due to heredity and how much is due to environment—the nature–nurture issue. Heredity seems to define the upper limits of our growth and change, whereas the environment affects the degree to which the upper limits are reached. (p. 409)
- ▶ Cross-sectional research compares people of different ages with one another at the same point in time. In contrast, longitudinal research traces the behavior of one or more participants as the participants become older. Finally, sequential research combines the two methods by taking several different age groups and examining them at several points in time. (p. 411)

EVALUATE

1. Developmental psychologists are interested in the effects of both _____ and _____ on development.

2. Environment and heredity both influence development, with genetic potentials generally establishing limits on environmental influences. True or false?
3. By observing genetically similar animals in differing environments, we can increase our understanding of the influences of hereditary and environmental factors in humans. True or false?
4. _____ research studies the same individuals over a period of time, whereas _____-_____ research studies people of different ages at the same time.

RETHINK

1. Consider what factors might determine when a child learns to walk. What kinds of environmental influences might be involved? What kinds of genetic influences might be involved?
2. When researchers find similarities in development between very different cultures, what implications might such findings have for the nature–nurture issue?

Answers to Evaluate Questions

4. longitudinal, cross-sectional
1. heredity (or nature), environment (or nurture); 2. true; 3. true;

KEY TERMS

developmental
psychology p. 409
nature–nurture
issue p. 409

identical twins p. 411
cross-sectional
research p. 411

longitudinal
research p. 411

sequential
research p. 412

Prenatal Development: Conception to Birth

A few years ago, when Elizabeth Carr's class was learning how an egg combines with sperm in the mother's body to create a child, she felt compelled to interrupt.

"I piped up to say that not all babies are conceived like that and explained about sperm and eggs and petri dishes," said Elizabeth . . . , the first child in the United States born through *in vitro* fertilization.

Because her mother's landmark pregnancy was documented in great detail by a film crew, Elizabeth has seen pictures of the egg and sperm that united to become her, the petri dish where she was conceived, the embryonic blob of cells that grew into the bubbly young woman who now plays field hockey and sings in the school chorus (Rosenthal, 1996, pp. A1, B8).

Now a young adult, Elizabeth is just "one of a crowd," as her mother predicted when she was born in 1981—a crowd of some 60,000 children in the United States who were born thanks to the technology of in vitro fertilization. Yet our increasing understanding of the biology of *conception*—when a male's sperm cell penetrates a female's egg cell—makes conception no less of a miracle. At that single moment, an individual's genetic endowment is established for the rest of his or her life.

⊕⊕⊕

The Basics of Genetics

The one-cell entity established at conception contains twenty-three pairs of **chromosomes**, rod-shaped structures that contain all basic hereditary information. One member of each pair is from the mother, and the other is from the father.

Each chromosome contains thousands of **genes**—smaller units through which genetic information is transmitted. Either individually or in combination, genes produce the particular characteristics of each person. Composed of sequences of *DNA (deoxyribonucleic acid)* molecules, genes are the biological equivalent of "software" that programs the future development of all parts of the body's hardware. Humans have some 25,000 different genes (see Figure 1).

Some genes control the development of systems common to all members of the human species—the heart, circulatory system, brain, lungs, and so forth; others shape the characteristics that make each human unique, such as facial configuration, height, and eye color. The child's sex is also determined by a particular combination of genes. Specifically, a child inherits an X chromosome from its mother and either an X or a Y chromosome from its father. When it receives an XX combination, it is a female; with an XY combination, it develops as a male. Male development is triggered by a single gene on the Y chromosome, and without the presence of that specific gene, the individual will develop as a female (see Figure 2).

As behavioral geneticists have discovered, genes are also at least partially responsible for a wide variety of personal characteristics, including cognitive abilities, personality traits, and psychological disorders. Of course, few of these characteristics are determined by a single gene. Instead, most traits result from a combination of

What is the nature of development before birth?

What factors affect a child during the mother's pregnancy?

Elizabeth Carr

PowerWeb: Fetal Psychology

www.mhhe.com/feldmanup7

Chromosomes: Rod-shaped structures that contain all basic hereditary information.

Genes: The parts of the chromosomes through which genetic information is transmitted.

a. Conception

b. 23 pairs of chromosomes

c. DNA sequence

d. Genes

FIGURE 1 Every individual's characteristics are determined by the individual's specific genetic information. At the moment of conception (a), humans receive twenty-three pairs of chromosomes (b), half from the mother and half from the father. These chromosomes are made up of coils of DNA (c). Each chromosome contains thousands of genes (d) that "program" the future development of the body.

multiple genes, which operate together with environmental influences (Gilger, 1996; Pillard, 1996; Rieder, Kaufmann, & Knowles, 1996; Funder, 1997).

To better understand how genes influence human characteristics and behavior, in the last few years scientists have mapped the specific location and sequence of every human gene. The *Applying Psychology in the 21st Century* box considers how our increasing understanding of genetics is likely to produce a revolution in health care, as scientists identify the particular genes responsible for genetically caused disorders.

FIGURE 2 When an egg and a sperm meet at the moment of fertilization, the egg provides an X chromosome, and the sperm provides either an X or a Y chromosome. If the sperm contributes an X chromosome, the child will have an XX pairing on the 23rd chromosome and will be a girl. If the sperm contributes a Y chromosome, the result will be an XY paring—a boy.

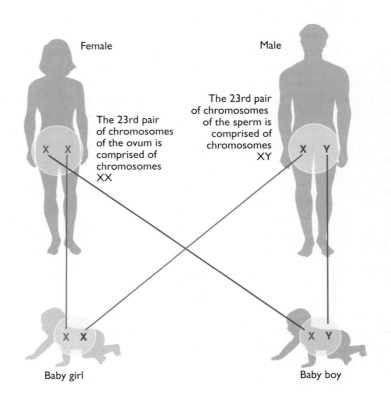

Female

Male

The 23rd pair of chromosomes of the ovum is comprised of chromosomes XX

The 23rd pair of chromosomes of the sperm is comprised of chromosomes XY

X X

X Y

X X

X Y

Baby girl

Baby boy

Cloning, Gene Therapy, and the Coming Medical Revolution

As he chats with the young mother, the doctor flicks a cotton swab into the mouth of her infant son, collecting a small sample of mucus from inside his cheek. In the back room of his office, he inserts the sample into a machine, which extracts DNA from the mucus cells and compares it with the genetic material on a dime-size chip. Minutes later, a computer printer begins to spit out a list of the infant's genes. Fortunately, all but a few of the genes are labeled "normal." It is those few that the doctor discusses as he explains the results to the mother. "Your son's genetic inheritance is generally good," he says, "but he is somewhat predisposed to skin lesions. So starting right away, he should be protected against excessive exposure to the sun." And the doctor warns, "he may well be susceptible to cardiovascular disease later in life. To lessen his risk, after about age two he should begin a lifelong low-fat, high-fiber diet" (Jaroff, 1996, p. 24).

This view of a visit to a pediatrician's office is not so futuristic, for it may become reality within the next decade. Our increasing understanding of genetics is leading not only to the identification of risk factors in children, but also to the development of new treatments for everything from serious physical illnesses such as cancer to psychological disorders such as schizophrenia and depression.

This potential medical revolution has been heralded, in part, by a series of achievements, such as the birth of Dolly (a sheep that was the first mammal to be cloned from the cells of an adult) and the birth of ANDi (named for "inserted DNA" in reverse), the first genetically modified primate. ANDi received a jellyfish gene inserted into monkey eggs and fertilized with monkey sperm in the lab. Ultimately, three baby monkeys were born, one of which—ANDi—included the new gene in his DNA (Chan et al., 2001).

ANDi, the first genetically modified primate, has a gene from a jellyfish.

ANDi, a result of genetic engineering, joins fruit flies, rabbits, sheep, and cows that carry genes from other species. Other genetically engineered animals have been produced as exact genetic replicas, or clones, of members of the same species (Kolata, 1998; Pennisi & Vogel, 2000; Lanza et al., 2001).

The ability of scientists to produce genetically engineered clones raises new possibilities of correcting genetic flaws, not only in animals but in humans, and is accelerating the pace of developments in the new field of gene therapy. In gene therapy, genes are introduced into existing cells to prevent or cure a disorder. For instance, genes developed to treat a particular disease can be injected into a patient's bloodstream. When the injected genes reach the site of the problem—such as a cancerous tumor—they give the existing cells a set of new instructions that modify their functioning, thereby potentially curing the disease. It also may be possible to "harvest" defective cells from a child be-

fore birth. Those cells could be treated by gene therapy and reintroduced into the unborn child, thereby repairing the defect (Kmiec, 1999; Levy, 2000; Yan, Kinzler, & Vogelstein, 2000).

Although the list of diseases currently being treated by gene therapy is not long, the number is likely to grow rapidly. For example, disorders such as AIDS, cystic fibrosis, and rheumatoid arthritis already are strong candidates for gene therapy. In addition, even more promising therapies are coming. For example, a process called *germ-line gene therapy* can be used to correct problems not only for unborn individuals, but for future generations as well. In germ-line gene therapy, scientists "harvest" defective cells soon after conception, removing them from the fertilized egg within the mother, placing them in a test-tube culture, repairing the defects in the cells, and returning them to the mother. In a more extreme possibility, cells from one parent might be altered genetically to remove any defects, and this clone could then be permitted to grow. The result would be offspring genetically identical to the parent except for a lack of the genetic defect (Begley, 1998b; Weiner, 2000).

Cloning advances raise significant ethical issues. In one radical possibility, cloning might be employed if both a husband and a wife were infertile. In such a case, they might consider cloning one or the other of themselves in order to have at least one child who was genetically similar (in this case, genetically identical) to one of them. The ethical and moral issues of such a procedure, of course, are profound. Although polls show most people in the United States oppose cloning, the rapid advances in cloning and gene therapy suggest that the ethical issues need to be dealt with (Gordon, 1999; Stolberg, 2001; Saad, 2002; Tennant, 2002).

RETHINK

Would you choose to be genetically tested so that you could know your susceptibility to future genetic diseases? Would you be tested if you might learn that you had a genetic disorder that was likely to shorten your life? Why or why not?

The Earliest Development

Zygote: The new cell formed by the union of an egg and sperm.

When the egg becomes fertilized by the sperm, the resulting one-celled entity, called a **zygote,** immediately begins to develop. The zygote starts out as a microscopic speck. Three days after fertilization, though, the zygote increases to around 32 cells, and within a week it has grown to 100–150 cells. These first two weeks are known as the *germinal period.*

Two weeks after conception, the developing individual enters the *embryonic period,* which lasts from week 2 through week 8, and he or she is now called an

Embryo: A developed zygote that has a heart, a brain, and other organs.

embryo. As an embryo develops through an intricate, preprogrammed process of cell division, it grows 10,000 times larger by 4 weeks of age, attaining a length of about one-fifth of an inch. At this point it has developed a rudimentary beating heart, a brain, an intestinal tract, and a number of other organs. Although all these organs are at a primitive stage of development, they are clearly recognizable. Moreover, by week 8, the embryo is about an inch long, and has discernible arms and legs and a face.

Fetus: A developing individual, from eight weeks after conception until birth.

From week 8 and continuing until birth, the developing individual enters the *fetal period* and is called a **fetus.** At the start of this period, it begins to be responsive to touch; it bends its fingers when touched on the hand. At 16 to 18 weeks, its movements become strong enough for the mother to sense them. At the same time, hair may begin to grow on the fetus's head, and the facial features become similar to those the child will display at birth. The major organs begin functioning, although the fetus could not be kept alive outside the mother. In addition, a lifetime's worth of brain neurons are produced—although it is unclear whether the brain is capable of thinking at this early stage.

By week 24, a fetus has many of the characteristics it will display as a newborn. In fact, when an infant is born prematurely at this age, it can open and close its eyes; suck; cry; look up, down, and around; and even grasp objects placed in its hands, although it is still unable to survive for long outside the mother.

Age of viability: The point at which a fetus can survive if born prematurely.

The fetus continues to develop before birth. It begins to grow fatty deposits under the skin, and it gains weight. The fetus reaches the **age of viability,** the point at which it can survive if born prematurely, at about prenatal age 22 weeks, although through advances in medical technology this crucial age is getting earlier. At prenatal

These remarkable photos of live fetuses display the degree of physical development at prenatal ages 4 and 15 weeks.

age 28 weeks, the fetus weighs less than three pounds and is about sixteen inches long. It may be capable of learning: One study found that the infants of mothers who had repeatedly read aloud the Dr. Seuss story *The Cat in the Hat* before the infants' birth preferred the sound of that particular story to other stories after they were born (Spence & DeCasper, 1982).

Before birth, a fetus passes through several *critical periods* (sometimes referred to as *sensitive periods*). A critical period is a time span when specific events have their greatest impact. For example, fetuses are particularly susceptible to environmental influences such as drugs during certain critical periods before birth. If they are exposed to a particular drug before or after the critical period, it may have relatively little impact, but if exposure comes during a critical period, the impact will be significant. Critical periods can also occur after birth; some language specialists suggest, for instance, that there is a period in which children are particularly receptive to developing language (deVilliers & deVilliers, 1999).

In the final weeks of pregnancy, the fetus continues to gain weight and grow. At the end of the normal thirty-eight weeks of pregnancy the fetus typically weighs around seven pounds and is about twenty inches in length. However, the story is different for *preterm infants,* who are born before week 38. Because they have not been able to develop fully, they are at higher risk for illness, future problems, and even death. For infants who have been in the womb for more than thirty weeks, the prospects are relatively good. However, for those born before week 30, the story is often less positive. Such newborns, who may weigh as little as two pounds at birth, are in grave danger because they have immature organs; they have less than a 50–50 chance of survival. If they do survive—and it takes extraordinarily heroic (and expensive) medical intervention to assure this—they may later experience significant developmental delays.

GENETIC INFLUENCES ON THE FETUS

The process of fetal growth that we have just described reflects normal development, which occurs in 95 to 98 percent of all pregnancies. Some individuals are less fortunate, for in the remaining 2 to 5 percent of cases, children are born with serious birth defects. A major cause of such defects is faulty genes or chromosomes. Here are some of the more common genetic and chromosomal difficulties.

- ▶ *Phenylketonuria (PKU).* A child born with the inherited disease phenylketonuria cannot produce an enzyme that is required for normal development. This results in an accumulation of poisons that eventually cause profound mental retardation. The disease is treatable, however, if it is caught early enough. Most infants today are routinely tested for PKU, and children with the disorder can be placed on a special diet that allows them to develop normally (Walter et al., 2002).
- ▶ *Sickle-cell anemia.* About 10 percent of the African American population has the possibility of passing on sickle-cell anemia, a disease that gets its name from the abnormally shaped red blood cells it causes. Children with the disease may have poor appetites, swollen stomachs, yellowish eyes, and cognitive difficulties; they frequently die during childhood (Schatz, Finke, Kellett, & Kramer, 2002; Helps, Fuggle, Udwin, & Dick, 2003).
- ▶ *Tay-Sachs disease.* Children born with Tay-Sachs disease, a disorder most often found in Jews of eastern European ancestry, usually die by age 3 or 4 because of the body's inability to break down fat. If both parents carry the genetic defect that produces the fatal illness, their child has a one in four chance of being born with the disease (Navon & Proia, 1989).
- ▶ *Down syndrome.* Down syndrome, one of the causes of mental retardation, occurs when the zygote receives an extra chromosome at the moment of

conception. Down syndrome is often related to the mother's age; mothers over 35 and younger than 18, in particular, stand a higher risk than other women of having a child with the syndrome (Roizen & Patterson, 2003).

PRENATAL ENVIRONMENTAL INFLUENCES

Genetic factors are not the only causes of difficulties in fetal development. Environmental influences—the *nurture* part of the nature–nurture equation—also affect the fetus. Some of the more profound consequences are brought about by **teratogens,** environmental agents such as a drug, chemical, virus, or other factor that produce a birth defect. Among the major prenatal environmental influences on the fetus are the following:

Teratogens: Environmental agents such as a drug, chemical, virus, or other factor that produce a birth defect.

- ▶ *Mother's nutrition and emotional state.* What a mother eats during her pregnancy can have important implications for the health of her baby. Seriously undernourished mothers cannot provide adequate nutrition to a growing fetus, and they are likely to give birth to underweight babies. Poorly nourished babies are also more susceptible to disease, and a lack of nourishment may have an adverse impact on their mental development (Adams & Parker, 1990; Ricciuti, 1993; Sigman, 1995; Zigler, Finn-Stevenson, & Hall, 2002). Moreover, the mother's emotional state affects the baby. Mothers who are anxious and tense during the last months of their pregnancies are more apt to have irritable infants who sleep and eat poorly. The reason? The autonomic nervous system of the fetus becomes especially sensitive as a result of chemical changes produced by the mother's emotional state (Relier, 2001).
- ▶ *Mother's illness.* Several diseases that have a relatively minor effect on the health of a mother can have devastating consequences for a developing fetus if they are contracted during the early part of a pregnancy. For example, rubella (German measles), syphilis, diabetes, and high blood pressure may each produce a permanent effect on the fetus. The virus that causes AIDS can also be

FIGURE 3 A variety of environmental factors can play a role in prenatal development.

Environmental Factor	Possible Effect on Prenatal Development
Rubella (German measles)	Blindness, deafness, heart abnormalities, stillbirth
Syphilis	Mental retardation, physical deformities, maternal miscarriage
Addictive drugs	Low birth weight, addiction of infant to drug, with possible death, after birth, from withdrawal
Smoking	Premature birth, low birth weight and length
Alcohol	Mental retardation, lower-than-average birth weight, small head, limb deformities
Radiation from X-rays	Physical deformities, mental retardation
Inadequate diet	Reduction in growth of brain, smaller-than-average weight and length at birth
Mother's age—younger than 18 at birth of child	Premature birth, increased incidence of Down syndrome
Mother's age—older than 35 at birth of child	Increased incidence of Down syndrome
DES (diethylstilbestrol)	Reproductive difficulties and increased incidence of genital cancer in children of mothers who were given DES during pregnancy to prevent miscarriage
AIDS	Possible spread of AIDS virus to infant; facial deformities; growth failure
Accutane	Mental retardation and physical deformities

passed from mother to child before birth. The virus also can be passed through breast-feeding after birth (Heyward & Curran, 1988).

▶ *Mother's use of drugs.* Mothers who take illegal, physically addictive drugs such as cocaine run the risk of giving birth to babies who are similarly addicted. Their newborns suffer painful withdrawal symptoms and sometimes show permanent physical and mental impairment as well. Even legal drugs taken by a pregnant women (who may not know that she has become pregnant) can have a tragic effect. For example, drugs such as the acne medicine Accutane can produce abnormalities (Streissguth et al., 1999; Ikonomidou et al, 2000).

▶ *Alcohol and nicotine use.* Alcohol and nicotine are dangerous to fetal development. For example, *fetal alcohol syndrome,* a condition resulting in mental and growth retardation, has been found in the children of mothers who consumed heavy or sometimes even moderate amounts of alcohol during pregnancy. Pregnant mothers who smoke also put their children at considerable risk (Mills, 1999; Secker-Walker & Vacek, 2003).

Several other environmental factors have an impact on the child before and during birth (see Figure 3). Keep in mind, however, that although we have been discussing the influences of genetics and environment separately, neither factor works alone. (Complete **Interactivity 38–1** to gain a fuller understanding of prenatal development.) Furthermore, despite the emphasis here on some of the ways in which development can go wrong, the vast majority of births occur without difficulty. And in most instances, subsequent development also proceeds normally, as we discuss next.

INTERACTIVITY 38–1

Prenatal development

RECAP/EVALUATE/RETHINK

RECAP

What is the nature of development before birth?

▶ At the moment of conception, a male's sperm cell and a female's egg cell unite, with each contributing to the new individual's genetic makeup. The union of sperm and egg produces a zygote, which contains 23 pairs of chromosomes—with one member of each pair coming from the father and the other coming from the mother. (p. 413)

▶ Each chromosome contains genes, through which genetic information is transmitted. Genes, which are composed of DNA sequences, are the "software" that programs the future development of the body's hardware. (p. 414)

▶ After two weeks the zygote becomes an embryo. By week 8, the embryo is called a fetus and is responsive to touch and other stimulation. At about week 22 it reaches the age of viability, which means it may survive if born prematurely. A fetus is normally born after thirty-eight weeks of pregnancy, weighing around seven pounds and measuring about twenty inches. (p. 416)

▶ Genes affect not only physical attributes but also a wide array of personal characteristics such as cognitive abilities, personality traits, and psychological disorders. (p. 417)

What factors affect a child during the mother's pregnancy?

▶ Genetic abnormalities produce birth defects such as phenylketonuria (PKU), sickle-cell anemia, Tay-Sachs disease, and Down syndrome. (p. 417)

▶ Among the environmental influences on fetal growth are the mother's nutrition, illnesses, drug intake, and birth complications. (p. 418)

EVALUATE

1. Match each of the following terms with its definition:
   1. Zygote
   2. Gene
   3. Chromosome
   a. Smallest unit through which genetic information is passed
   b. Fertilized egg
   c. Rod-shaped structure containing genetic information
2. Specific kinds of growth must take place during a _____ period if the embryo is to develop normally.
3. A _____ is an environmental agent such as a drug, chemical, virus, or other factor that produces a birth defect.

RETHINK

1. Describe the policy you might create to notify persons who have genetically based disorders that can be identified by genetic testing. Would your policy treat potentially fatal disorders differently from less serious ones? Would it make a distinction between treatable and untreatable disorders?
2. Given the possible effects of the environment on a developing fetus, do you think pregnant women should be prosecuted for the use of alcohol and other drugs that may do serious harm to their unborn children? Defend your position.

Answers to Evaluate Questions

1. 1-b, 2-a, 3-c; 2. critical; 3. teratogen

KEY TERMS

chromosomes p. 413

genes p. 413

zygote p. 416

embryo p. 416

fetus p. 416

age of viability p. 416

teratogens p. 418

Infancy and Childhood

His head was molded into a long melon shape and came to a point at the back . . . He was covered with a thick greasy white material known as "vernix," which made him slippery to hold, and also allowed him to slip easily through the birth canal. In addition to a shock of black hair on his head, his body was covered with dark, fine hair known as "lanugo." His ears, his back, his shoulders, and even his cheeks were furry . . . His skin was wrinkled and quite loose, ready to scale in creased places such as his feet and hands . . . His ears were pressed to his head in unusual positions—one ear was matted firmly forward on his cheek. His nose was flattened and pushed to one side by the squeeze as he came through the pelvis (Brazelton, 1969, p. 3).

What kind of creature is this? Although the description hardly fits that of the adorable babies seen in advertisements for baby food, we are in fact talking about a normal, completely developed child just after the moment of birth. Called a **neonate,** a newborn arrives in the world in a form that hardly meets the standards of beauty against which we typically measure babies. Yet ask any parents: Nothing is more beautiful or exciting than the first glimpse of their newborn.

⚈⚈⚈

What are the major competencies of newborns?

What are the milestones of physical and social development during childhood?

How does cognitive development proceed during childhood?

Neonate: A newborn child.

The Extraordinary Newborn

Several factors cause a neonate's strange appearance. The trip through the mother's birth canal may have squeezed the incompletely formed bones of the skull together and squashed the nose into the head. The skin secretes *vernix,* a white, greasy covering, for protection before birth, and the baby may have *lanugo,* a soft fuzz, over the entire body for a similar purpose. The infant's eyelids may be puffy with an accumulation of fluids because of the upside-down position during birth.

All this changes during the first two weeks of life as the neonate takes on a more familiar appearance. Even more impressive are the capabilities a neonate begins to display from the moment of birth—capabilities that grow at an astounding rate over the ensuing months.

Reflexes: Unlearned, involuntary responses that occur automatically in the presence of certain stimuli.

REFLEXES

A neonate is born with a number of **reflexes**—unlearned, involuntary responses that occur automatically in the presence of certain stimuli. Critical for survival, many of those reflexes unfold naturally as part of an infant's ongoing maturation. The *rooting reflex,* for instance, causes neonates to turn their heads toward things that touch their cheeks—such as the

Many of the reflexes that a neonate is born with are critical for survival and unfold naturally as a part of an infant's ongoing maturation. Do you think humans have more or fewer reflexes than other animals?

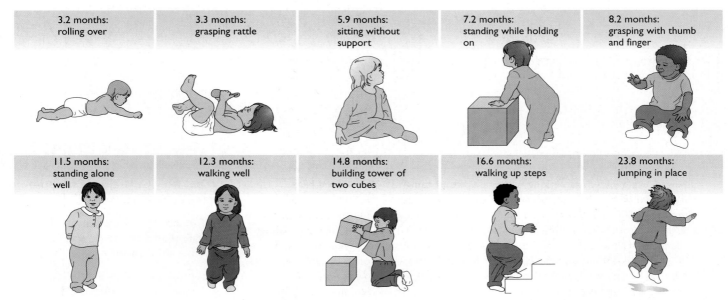

FIGURE 1 Although at birth a neonate can make only jerky, limited voluntary movements, during the first year of life the ability to move independently grows enormously. The ages indicate the time when 50 percent of children are able to perform each skill (Frankenburg et al., 1992). Remember, however, that the time when each skill appears can vary considerably. For example, 25 percent of children are able to walk well at age 11 months, and by 15 months 90 percent of children are walking well.

mother's nipple or a bottle. Similarly, a *sucking reflex* prompts infants to suck at things that touch their lips. Among other reflexes are a *gag reflex* (to clear the throat), the *startle reflex* (a series of movements in which an infant flings out the arms, fans the fingers, and arches the back in response to a sudden noise), and the *Babinski reflex* (a baby's toes fan out when the outer edge of the sole of the foot is stroked).

Infants lose these primitive reflexes after the first few months of life, replacing them with more complex and organized behaviors. Although at birth a neonate is capable of only jerky, limited voluntary movements, during the first year of life the ability to move independently grows enormously. The typical baby rolls over by the age of 3 months, sits without support at 6 months, stands alone at about 11 months, and walks at just over a year old. Not only does the ability to make large-scale movements improve during this time, fine-muscle movements become increasingly sophisticated (see Figure 1).

DEVELOPMENT OF THE SENSES: TAKING IN THE WORLD

When proud parents peer into the eyes of their neonate, is the child able to return their gaze? Although it was thought for some time that newborns can see only a hazy blur, most current findings indicate that the capabilities of neonates are far more impressive. Although their eyes have a limited capacity to focus on objects that are not within a seven- to eight-inch distance from the face, neonates can follow objects moving within their field of vision. They also show the rudiments of depth perception, as they react by raising their hands when an object appears to be moving rapidly toward the face (Gelman & Kit-Fong Au, 1996; Maurer et al., 1999).

You might think that it would be hard to figure out just how well neonates can see, because their lack of both language and reading ability clearly prevents them from saying what direction the *E* on a vision chart is facing. However, researchers have devised a number of ingenious methods, relying on the newborn's biological responses and innate reflexes, to test perceptual skills.

For instance, infants who see a novel stimulus typically pay close attention to it, and, as a consequence, their heart rates increase. But if they repeatedly see the same stimulus, their attention to it decreases, as indicated by a return to a slower heart rate. This phenomenon is known as **habituation,** the decrease in the response to a stimulus that occurs after repeated presentations of the same stimulus. By studying habituation, developmental psychologists can tell when a stimulus can be detected and discriminated by a child who is too young to speak (Gurnwald et al., 2003).

Researchers have developed many other methods for measuring neonate and infant perception. One technique, for instance, involves babies sucking on a nipple attached to a computer. A change in the rate and vigor with which the babies suck helps researchers infer that babies can perceive variations in stimuli. Other approaches include examining babies' eye movements and observing which way babies move their heads in response to a visual stimulus (George, 1999).

Through the use of such research techniques, we now know that infants' visual perception is remarkably sophisticated from the start of life. At birth, babies prefer patterns with contours and edges over less distinct patterns, indicating that they can respond to the configuration of stimuli. Furthermore, even newborns are aware of size constancy, because they are apparently sensitive to the phenomenon by which objects stay the same size even though the image on the retina may change size as the distance between the object and the retina varies (Slater, Mattock, & Brown, 1990; Slater, 1996).

In fact, neonates can discriminate facial expressions—and even imitate them. As you can see in Figure 2, newborns who see an adult with a happy, sad, or surprised facial expression can produce a good imitation of the adult's expression. Even very young infants, then, can respond to the emotions and moods that their caregivers' facial expressions reveal. This capability provides the foundation for social interaction skills in children (Meltzoff, 1996; Montague & Walker-Andrews, 2002).

Habituation: The decrease in the response to a stimulus that occurs after repeated presentations of the same stimulus.

FIGURE 2 This newborn infant is clearly imitating the expressions of the adult model in these amazing photos. How does this ability contribute to social development? (Courtesy of Dr. Tiffany Field.)

Other visual abilities grow rapidly after birth. By the end of their first month, babies can distinguish some colors from others, and after four months they can focus on near or far objects. By age 4 or 5 months they are able to recognize two-and three-dimensional objects, and they can perceive the gestalt organizing principles discovered by psychologists who study perception. Furthermore, their perceptual abilities rapidly improve: Sensitivity to visual stimuli, for instance, becomes three to four times greater at 1 year of age than it was at birth (Slater, 1996; Vital-Durand, Atkinson, & Braddick, 1996).

In addition to vision, infants display other impressive sensory capabilities. Newborns can distinguish different sounds to the point of being able to recognize their own mothers' voices at the age of 3 days. They can also make the subtle perceptual distinctions that underlie language abilities. For example, at 2 days of age, infants can distinguish between their native tongue and foreign languages, and they can discriminate between such closely related sounds as *ba* and *pa* when they are 4 days old. By 6 months of age, they can discriminate virtually any difference in sound that is relevant to the production of language. Moreover, they can recognize different tastes and smells at a very early age. There even seems to be something of a built-in sweet tooth: Neonates prefer liquids that have been sweetened with sugar over their unsweetened counterparts (Bornstein & Arterberry, 1999; Akman et al., 2002).

The Growing Child: Infancy Through Middle Childhood

It was during the windy days of March that the problem in the day care center first arose. Its source: 10-month-old Russell Ruud. Otherwise a model of decorum, Russell had somehow learned how to unzip the Velcro chin strap to his winter hat. He would remove the hat whenever he got the urge, seemingly oblivious to the potential health problems that might follow.

But that was just the start of the real difficulty. To the chagrin of the teachers in the day care center, not to speak of the children's parents, soon other children were following his lead, removing their own caps at will.

Russell's mother, made aware of the anarchy at the day care center—and the other parents' distress over Russell's behavior—pleaded innocent. "I never showed Russell how to unzip the Velcro," claimed his mother, Judith Ruud, an economist with the Congressional Budget Office in Washington, D.C. "He learned by trial and error, and the other kids saw him do it one day when they were getting dressed for an outing" (Goleman, 1993a, C10).

At the age of 10 months, Russell asserted his personality, illustrating the tremendous growth that occurs in a variety of domains during the first year of life. Throughout the remainder of childhood, moving from infancy into middle childhood and the start of adolescence around age 11 or 12, children develop physically, socially, and cognitively in extraordinary ways. In the remainder of this module, we'll consider this development.

PHYSICAL DEVELOPMENT

Children's physical growth provides the most obvious sign of development. During the first year of life, children typically triple their birthweight, and their height increases by about half. This rapid growth slows down as the child gets older—think how gigantic adults would be if that rate of growth were constant—and from age 3 to the beginning of adolescence at around age 13, growth averages a gain of about five pounds and three inches a year (see Figure 3).

FIGURE 3 The average heights and weights of males and females in the United States from birth through age 20. At what ages are girls typically heavier and taller than boys? (Source: National Center for Health Statistics, 2000.)

The physical changes that occur as children develop are not just a matter of increasing growth; the relationship of the size of the various body parts to one another changes dramatically as children age. As you can see in Figure 4, the head of a fetus (and a newborn) is disproportionately large. However, the head soon becomes more proportional in size to the rest of the body as growth occurs mainly in the trunk and legs.

DEVELOPMENT OF SOCIAL BEHAVIOR: TAKING ON THE WORLD

As anyone who has seen an infant smiling at the sight of his or her mother can guess, at the same time that infants grow physically and hone their perceptual abilities, they also develop socially. The nature of a child's early social development provides the foundation for social relationships that will last a lifetime.

Attachment, the positive emotional bond that develops between a child and a particular individual, is the most important form of social development that occurs during infancy. The earliest studies of attachment were carried out by animal ethologist Konrad Lorenz (1966). Lorenz focused on newborn goslings, which under

Attachment: The positive emotional bond that develops between a child and a particular individual.

FIGURE 4 As development progresses, the size of the head relative to the rest of the body decreases until the individual reaches adulthood. Why do you think the head starts out so large?

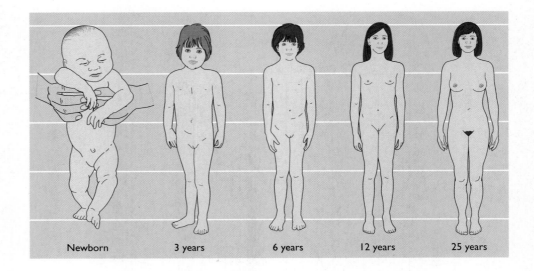

Newborn   3 years   6 years   12 years   25 years

FIGURE 4 As development progresses, the size of the head relative to the rest of the body decreases until the individual reaches adulthood. Why do you think the head starts out so large?

normal circumstances instinctively follow their mother, the first moving object they perceive after birth. Lorenz found that goslings whose eggs were raised in an incubator and which viewed him immediately after hatching would follow his every movement, as if he were their mother. He labeled this process *imprinting*, behavior that takes place during a critical period and involves attachment to the first moving object that is observed.

Our understanding of attachment progressed when psychologist Harry Harlow, in a classic study, gave infant monkeys the choice of cuddling a wire "monkey" that provided milk or a soft, terry-cloth "monkey" that was warm but did not provide milk. Their choice was clear: They spent most of their time clinging to the warm cloth "monkey," although they made occasional forays to the wire monkey to nurse. Obviously, the cloth monkey provided greater comfort to the infants; milk alone was insufficient to create attachment (Harlow & Zimmerman, 1959; Blum, 2002; see Figure 5).

FIGURE 5 Although the wire "mother" dispensed milk to the hungry infant monkey, the infant preferred the soft, terry-cloth "mother." Do you think human babies would react the same way? What does this tell us about attachment? (Source: Harry Harlow Primate Laboratory/University of Wisconsin.)

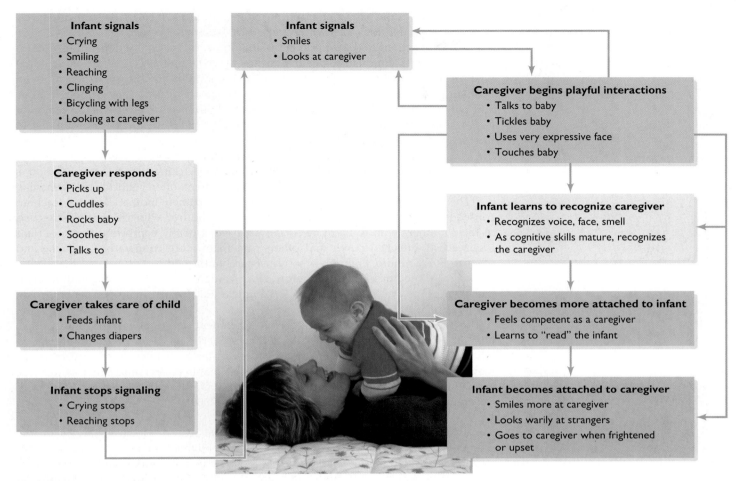

FIGURE 6 The Attachment Behavioral System shows the sequence of activities that infants employ to keep their primary caregivers physically close and bring about attachment. Early in life, crying is the most effective behavior. Later, though, infants keep the caregiver near through other, more socially appropriate behaviors such as smiling, looking, and reaching. After they are able to walk, children play a more active role in staying close to the caregiver. At the same time, the caregiver's behavior interacts with the baby's activities to promote attachment. (Source: Tomlinson-Keasey, 1985.)

Building on this pioneering work with nonhumans, developmental psychologists have suggested that human attachment grows through the responsiveness of infants' caregivers to the signals the babies provide, such as crying, smiling, reaching, and clinging. The greater the responsiveness of the caregiver to the child's signals, the more likely it is that the child will become securely attached. Full attachment eventually develops as a result of the complex series of interactions between caregiver and child illustrated in Figure 6. In the course of these interactions, the infant plays as critical and active a role as the caregiver in the formation of the bond. Infants who respond positively to a caregiver produce more positive behavior on the part of the caregiver, which in turn produces an even stronger degree of attachment in the child.

Measuring Attachment. Developmental psychologists have devised a quick and direct way to measure attachment. Developed by Mary Ainsworth, the *Ainsworth strange situation* consists of a sequence of events involving a child and (typically) his or her mother. Initially, the mother and baby enter an unfamiliar room, and the mother permits the baby to explore while she sits down. An adult stranger then enters the room, after which the mother leaves. The mother returns, and the stranger leaves. The mother

PowerWeb: Infant-Mother Attachment

www.mhhe.com/feldmanup7

once again leaves the baby alone, and the stranger returns. Finally, the stranger leaves, and the mother returns (Ainsworth et al., 1978; Waters & Beauchaine, 2003).

Babies' reactions to the experimental situation vary drastically, depending, according to Ainsworth, on their degree of attachment to the mother. One-year-old children who are *securely attached* employ the mother as a kind of home base, exploring independently but returning to her occasionally. When she leaves, they exhibit distress, and they go to her when she returns. *Avoidant* children do not cry when the mother leaves, and they seem to avoid her when she returns, as if they were indifferent to her. *Ambivalent* children display anxiety before they are separated and are upset when the mother leaves, but they may show ambivalent reactions to her return, such as seeking close contact but simultaneously hitting and kicking her. A fourth reaction is *disorganized-disoriented;* these children show inconsistent, often contradictory behavior.

The nature of attachment between children and their mothers has far-reaching consequences for later development. For example, children who are securely attached to their mothers tend to be more socially and emotionally competent than are their less securely attached peers, and others find them more cooperative, capable, and playful. Furthermore, children who are securely attached at age 1 show fewer psychological difficulties when they grow older compared with avoidant and ambivalent youngsters (Waters, Hamilton, & Weinfield, 2000; Bakermans-Kranenburg, van Ijzendoorn, & Juffer, 2003).

In contrast, children who lack secure attachment do not always have difficulties later in life, and being securely attached at an early age does not guarantee good adjustment later. Furthermore, some cultures foster higher levels of secure attachment than others do. In short, the social environment children encounter as they are growing up influences their attachment style (Hamilton, 2000; Lewis, Feiring, & Rosenthal, 2000; Waters, Hamilton, & Wienfield, 2000).

The Father's Role. Although early developmental research focused largely on the mother-child relation, more recent research has highlighted the father's role in parenting, and with good reason: The number of fathers who are primary caregivers for their children has grown significantly, and fathers play an increasingly important role in their children's lives. For example, in almost 20 percent of families with children, the father is the parent who stays at home to care for preschoolers (Fitzgerald et al., 2003).

When fathers interact with their children, their play often differs from that of mothers. Fathers engage in more physical, rough-and-tumble sorts of activities, whereas mothers play more verbal and traditional games, such as peekaboo. Despite such behavioral differences, the nature of attachment between fathers and children compared with that between mothers and children can be similar. In fact, children can form multiple attachments simultaneously (Larson, Richards, & Perry-Jenkins, 1994; Genuis & Violato, 2000; Sagi et al., 2002).

Social Relationships with Peers. By the time they are 2 years old, children become less dependent on their parents and more self-reliant, increasingly preferring to play with friends. Initially, play is relatively independent: Even though they may be sitting side by side, 2-year-olds pay more attention to toys than to one another when playing. Later, however, children actively interact, modifying one another's behavior and later exchanging roles during play (Bukowski, Newcomb, & Hartup, 1996).

As children reach school age, their social interactions begin to follow set patterns, as well as becoming more frequent. They may engage in elaborate games involving teams and rigid rules. This play serves purposes other than mere enjoyment. It allows children to become increasingly competent in their social interactions with others. Through play they learn to take the perspective of other people and to infer others' thoughts and feelings, even when those thoughts and feelings are not directly expressed (Asher & Parker, 1991; Royzman, Cassidy, & Baron, 2003).

In short, social interaction help children interpret the meaning of others' behavior and develop the capacity to respond appropriately. Furthermore, children learn physical and emotional self-control: They learn to avoid hitting a playmate who beats them at a game, be polite, and control their emotional displays and facial expressions (e.g., smiling even when receiving a disappointing gift). Situations that provide children with opportunities for social interaction, then, may enhance their social development (Feldman, 1982, 1993; Lengua & Long, 2002).

The Consequences of Day Care. Research on the importance of social interaction is corroborated by work that examines the benefits of day care, which is an important part of an increasing number of children's lives. For instance, almost 30 percent of preschool children whose mothers work outside the home spend their days in day-care centers. More than 80 percent of infants are cared for by people other than their mothers for part of the day during the first year of life. Most of these infants begin day care before the age of 4 months and are enrolled for almost thirty hours per week (NICHD Early Child Care Research Network, 1997; National Research Council, 2000; see Figure 7).

Do out-of-the-home child-care arrangements benefit children's development? If the programs are of high quality, they can. According to the results of a large study supported by the U.S. National Institute of Child Health and Development, children who attend high-quality child-care centers may not only do as well as children who stay at home with their parents, but in some respects may actually do better. Children in child care are generally more considerate and sociable than other children are, and they interact more positively with teachers. They may also be more compliant and regulate their own behavior more effectively, and their mothers show increased sensitivity to their children (Lamb, 1996; NICHD Early Child Care Research Network, 1997, 1998, 1999, 2001).

In addition, especially for children from poor or disadvantaged homes, child care in specially enriched environments—those with many toys, books, a variety of children, and high-quality care providers—often proves to be more intellectually stimulating than the home environment. Such child care can lead to increased intellectual achievement, demonstrated in higher IQ scores and better language development. In fact, children in care centers sometimes are found to score higher on tests of cognitive abilities than those who are cared for by their mothers or by sitters or home day-care providers—effects lasting into adulthood (Wilgoren, 1999; Burchinal et al., 2000).

However, child care does not have universally positive outcomes. Children may be less likely to feel secure when they are placed in low-quality child care or in multiple child-care arrangements. Furthermore, although the findings are not consistent, some research suggests that infants who are involved in outside care more than twenty hours a week in the first year show less secure attachment to their mothers than do those who have not been in day care. Finally, some studies find negative associations between young children's cognitive development and full-time employment of their mothers (Belsky & Rovine, 1988; NICHD Early Child Care Research Network, 1997, 1998, 2001; Belsky, 2002; Brooks-Gunn, Han, & Waldfogel, 2002).

The key to the success of day care is its quality. High-quality day care produces benefits; low-quality day care provides little or no gain, and may even hinder children's development. In short, significant benefits result from the social interaction and intellectual stimulation provided by high-quality day-care centers—particularly for children from impoverished environments (Harvey, 1999; Campbell, Lamb, & Hwang, 2000; NICHD Early Child Care Research Network, 2000, 2002; Ghazvini & Mullis, 2002).

Parenting Styles and Social Development. Parents' child-rearing practices are critical in shaping their children's social competence, and—according to classic research by developmental psychologist Diana Baumrind—four main categories describe different parenting styles (Figure 8). Rigid and punitive, **authoritarian parents** value unquestioning obedience from their children. They have strict standards and discourage expressions of disagreement. **Permissive parents** give their children relaxed or inconsistent direction and, although warm, require little of them. In contrast,

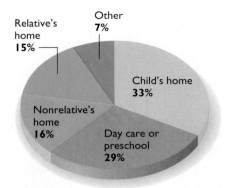

FIGURE 7 Almost 30 percent of children younger than 5 years of age whose mothers work outside the home spend their days in day care or preschool centers; the remainder receive care in their own or someone else's home. (Source: U.S. Bureau of the Census, 1997.)

Authoritarian parents: Parents who are rigid and punitive and value unquestioning obedience from their children.

Permissive parents: Parents who give their children relaxed or inconsistent direction and, although warm, require little of them.

Parenting Style	Parent Behavior	Type of Behavior Produced in Child
Authoritarian	Rigid, punitive, strict standards (example: "If you don't clean your room, I'm going to take away your Walkman for good and ground you.")	Unsociable, unfriendly, withdrawn
Permissive	Lax, inconsistent, undemanding (example: "It might be good to clean your room, but I guess it can wait.")	Immature, moody, dependent, low self-control
Authoritative	Firm, sets limits and goals, uses reasoning, encourages independence (example: "You'll need to clean your room before we can go out to the restaurant. As soon as you finish, we'll leave.")	Good social skills, likeable, self-reliant, independent
Uninvolved	Detached emotionally, sees role only as providing food, clothing, and shelter (example: "I could care less if your room is a pigsty.")	Indifferent, rejecting behavior

FIGURE 8 According to developmental psychologist Diana Baumrind (1971), four main parenting styles characterize child rearing.

Authoritative parents: Parents who are firm, set clear limits, reason with their children, and explain things to them.

Uninvolved parents: Parents who show little interest in their children and are emotionally detached.

Temperament: Basic, innate disposition.

authoritative parents are firm, setting limits for their children. As the children get older, these parents try to reason and explain things to them. They also set clear goals and encourage their children's independence. Finally, **uninvolved parents** show little interest in their children. Emotionally detached, they view parenting as nothing more than providing food, clothing, and shelter for children. At their most extreme, uninvolved parents are guilty of neglect, a form of child abuse (Baumrind, 1971, 1980; Maccoby & Martin, 1983.)

As you might expect, the four kinds of child-rearing styles seem to produce very different kinds of behavior in children (with many exceptions, of course). Children of authoritarian parents tend to be unsociable, unfriendly, and relatively withdrawn. In contrast, permissive parents' children show immaturity, moodiness, dependence, and low self-control. The children of authoritative parents fare best: With high social skills, they are likable, self-reliant, independent, and cooperative. Worst off are the children of uninvolved parents; they feel unloved and emotionally detached, and their physical and cognitive development is impeded (Howes, Galinsky, & Kontos, 1998; Saarni, 1999).

Before we rush to congratulate authoritative parents and condemn authoritarian, permissive, and uninvolved ones, it is important to note that in many cases nonauthoritative parents also produce perfectly well adjusted children. Moreover, children are born with a particular **temperament**—a basic, innate disposition. Some children are naturally easygoing and cheerful, whereas others are irritable and fussy. The kind of temperament a baby is born with may in part bring about particular kinds of parental child-rearing styles (Chess, 1997; Porter & Hsu, 2003).

In addition, children vary considerably in their degree of *resilience,* the ability to overcome circumstances that place them at high risk for psychological or even physical harm. Highly resilient children have temperaments that evoke positive responses from caregivers. Such children display unusual social skills: outgoingness, intelligence, and a feeling that they have control over their lives. In a sense, resilient children try to shape their own environment, rather than being victimized by it (Werner, 1995; Luthar, Cicchetti, & Becker, 2000).

We also need to keep in mind that these findings regarding child-rearing styles apply primarily to U.S. society, which highly values children's growing independence and diminishing reliance on their parents. In contrast, Japanese parents encourage dependence to promote the values of cooperation and community life. These differences in cultural values result in very different philosophies of child rearing. For example, Japanese mothers believe it is a punishment to make a young child sleep alone, and so many children sleep next to their mothers throughout infancy and toddlerhood (Miyake, Chen, & Campos, 1985; Kawasaki et al., 1994; Dennis et al., 2002).

In sum, a child's upbringing results from the child-rearing philosophy parents hold, the specific practices they use, and the nature of their own and their child's personalities. As is the case with other aspects of development, then, behavior is a function of a complex interaction of environmental and genetic factors.

"Please, Jason, Don't you want to grow up to be an autonomous person?"

Erikson's Theory of Psychosocial Development. In tracing the course of social development, some theorists have considered how the challenges of society and culture change as an individual matures. Following this path, psychoanalyst Erik Erikson developed one of the more comprehensive theories of social development. Erikson (1963) viewed the developmental changes occurring throughout life as a series of eight stages of psychosocial development, of which four occur during childhood. **Psychosocial development** involves changes in our interactions and understanding of one another as well as in our knowledge and understanding of ourselves as members of society.

Erikson suggests that passage through each of the stages necessitates the resolution of a crisis or conflict. Accordingly, Erikson represents each stage as a pairing of the most positive and most negative aspects of the crisis of that period. Although each crisis is never resolved entirely—life becomes increasingly complicated as we grow older—it has to be resolved sufficiently to equip us to deal with demands made during the following stage of development.

In the first stage of psychosocial development, the **trust-versus-mistrust stage** (ages birth to 1½ years), infants develop feelings of trust if their physical requirements and psychological needs for attachment are consistently met and their interactions with the world are generally positive. In contrast, inconsistent care and unpleasant interactions with others can lead to mistrust and leave an infant unable to meet the challenges required in the next stage of development.

In the second stage, the **autonomy-versus-shame-and-doubt stage** (ages 1½ to 3 years), toddlers develop independence and autonomy if exploration and freedom are encouraged, or they experience shame, self-doubt, and unhappiness if they are overly restricted and protected. According to Erikson, the key to the development of autonomy during this period is for the child's caregivers to provide the appropriate amount of control. If parents provide too much control, children cannot assert themselves and develop their own sense of control over their environment; if parents provide too little control, the children become overly demanding and controlling.

Next, children face the crises of the **initiative-versus-guilt stage** (ages 3 to 6). In this stage, children's desire to act independently conflicts with the guilt that comes from the unintended and unexpected consequences of such behavior. Children in this period come to understand that they are persons in their own right, and they begin to make decisions about their behavior. If parents react positively to children's attempts at independence, they will help their children resolve the initiative-versus-guilt crisis positively.

The fourth and last stage of childhood is the **industry-versus-inferiority stage** (ages 6 to 12). During this period, increasing competency in all areas, whether social interactions or academic skills, characterizes successful psychosocial development. In contrast, difficulties in this stage lead to feelings of failure and inadequacy.

Erikson's theory suggests that psychosocial development continues throughout life, and he proposes four more crises that are faced after childhood. Although his theory has been criticized on several grounds—such as the imprecision of the concepts he employs and his greater emphasis on male development than female development—it remains influential and is one of the few theories that encompass the entire life span.

Psychosocial development: Development of individuals' interactions and understanding of each other and of their knowledge and understanding of themselves as members of society.

Trust-versus-mistrust stage: According to Erikson, the first stage of psychosocial development, occurring from birth to age 1½ years, during which time infants develop feelings of trust or lack of trust.

Autonomy-versus-shame-and-doubt stage: The period during which, according to Erikson, toddlers (ages 1½ to 3 years) develop independence and autonomy if exploration and freedom are encouraged, or shame and self-doubt if they are restricted and overprotected.

Initiative-versus-guilt stage: According to Erikson, the period during which children ages 3 to 6 years experience conflict between independence of action and the sometimes negative results of that action.

Industry-versus-inferiority stage: According to Erikson, the last stage of childhood, during which children age 6 to 12 years may develop positive social interactions with others or may feel inadequate and become less sociable.

COGNITIVE DEVELOPMENT: CHILDREN'S THINKING ABOUT THE WORLD

Suppose you had two drinking glasses of different shapes—one short and broad and one tall and thin. Now imagine that you filled the short, broad one with soda about halfway and then poured the liquid from that glass into the tall one. The soda would appear to fill about three-quarters of the second glass. If someone asked you whether there was more soda in the second glass than there had been in the first, what would you say?

You might think that such a simple question hardly deserves an answer; of course there is no difference in the amount of soda in the two glasses. However, most 4-year-olds would be likely to say that there is more soda in the second glass. If you then poured the soda back into the short glass, they would say there is now less soda than there was in the taller glass.

Why are young children confused by this problem? The reason is not immediately obvious. Anyone who has observed preschoolers must be impressed by how far they have progressed from the early stages of development. They speak with ease, know the alphabet, count, play complex games, use tape players, tell stories, and communicate ably. Yet despite this seeming sophistication, there are deep gaps in children's understanding of the world. Some theorists have suggested that children cannot understand certain ideas and concepts until they reach a particular stage of **cognitive development**—the process by which a child's understanding of the world changes as a function of age and experience. In contrast to the theories of physical and social development discussed earlier (such as those of Erikson), theories of cognitive development seek to explain the quantitative and qualitative intellectual advances that occur during development.

Piaget's Theory of Cognitive Development. No theory of cognitive development has had more impact than that of Swiss psychologist Jean Piaget. Piaget (1970) suggested that children around the world proceed through a series of four stages in a fixed order. He maintained that these stages differ not only in the *quantity* of information acquired at each stage but in the *quality* of knowledge and understanding as well. Taking an interactionist point of view, he suggested that movement from one stage to the next occurs when a child reaches an appropriate level of maturation *and* is exposed to relevant types of experiences. Piaget assumed that, without having such experiences, children cannot reach their highest level of cognitive growth.

Piaget proposed four stages: the sensorimotor, preoperational, concrete operational, and formal operational (see Figure 9). Let's examine each of them and the approximate ages that they span.

Cognitive development: The process by which a child's understanding of the world changes as a function of age and experience.

PowerWeb: The Stages of the Intellectual Development of the Child

www.mhhe.com/feldmanup7

Cognitive Stage	Approximate Age Range	Major Characteristics
Sensorimotor	Birth–2 years	Development of object permanence, development of motor skills, little or no capacity for symbolic representation
Preoperational	2–7 years	Development of language and symbolic thinking, egocentric thinking
Concrete operational	7–12 years	Development of conservation, mastery of concept of reversibility
Formal operational	12 years–adulthood	Development of logical and abstract thinking

FIGURE 9 According to Piaget, all children pass through four stages of cognitive development.

Sensorimotor Stage: Birth to 2 Years. During the **sensorimotor stage,** children base their understanding of the world primarily on touching, sucking, chewing, shaking, and manipulating objects. In the initial part of the stage, children have relatively little competence in representing the environment by using images, language, or other kinds of symbols. Consequently, infants lack what Piaget calls **object permanence,** the awareness that objects—and people—continue to exist even if they are out of sight.

How can we know that children lack object permanence? Although we cannot ask infants, we can observe their reactions when a toy they are playing with is hidden under a blanket. Until the age of about 9 months, children will make no attempt to locate the hidden toy. However, soon after that age they will begin to search actively for the missing object, indicating that they have developed a mental representation of the toy. Object permanence, then, is a critical development during the sensorimotor stage.

Preoperational Stage: 2 to 7 Years. The most important development during the **preoperational stage** is the use of language. Children develop internal representational systems that allow them to describe people, events, and feelings. They even use symbols in play, pretending, for example, that a book pushed across the floor is a car.

Although children use more advanced thinking in this stage than they did in the earlier sensorimotor stage, their thinking is still qualitatively inferior to that of adults. We see this when we observe a preoperational child using **egocentric thought,** a way of thinking in which the child views the world entirely from his or her own perspective. Preoperational children think that everyone shares their perspective and knowledge. Thus, children's stories and explanations to adults can be maddeningly uninformative, as they are delivered without any context. For example, a preoperational child may start a story with "He wouldn't let me go," neglecting to mention who "he" is or where the storyteller wanted to go. We also see egocentric thinking when children at the preoperational stage play hiding games. For instance, 3-year-olds frequently hide with their faces against a wall, covering their eyes—although they are still in plain view. It seems to them that if *they* cannot see, then no one else will be able to see them, because they assume that others share their view.

In addition, preoperational children have not yet developed the ability to understand the **principle of conservation,** which is the knowledge that quantity is unrelated to the arrangement and physical appearance of objects. Children who have not mastered this concept do not know that the amount, volume, or length of an object does not change when its shape or configuration changes. The question about the two glasses—one short and broad and the other tall and thin—with which we began our discussion of cognitive development illustrates this point clearly. Children who do not understand the principle of conservation invariably state that the amount of liquid changes as it is poured back and forth. They cannot comprehend that a transformation in appearance does not imply a transformation in amount. Instead, it seems as reasonable to the child that there is a change in quantity as it does to the adult that there is no change.

In a number of other ways, some quite startling, the failure to understand the principle of conservation affects children's responses. Research demonstrates that principles that are obvious to and unquestioned by adults may be completely misunderstood by children during the preoperational period, and that it is not until the next stage of cognitive development that children grasp the concept of conservation. (To get a deeper understanding of the concept of conservation, examine Figure 10 and complete **Interactivity 39–1.**)

Concrete Operational Stage: 7 to 12 Years. Mastery of the principle of conservation marks the beginning of the **concrete operational stage.** However, children do not fully understand some aspects of conservation—such as conservation of weight and volume—for a number of years.

During the concrete operational stage, children develop the ability to think in a more logical manner, and begin to overcome some of the egocentrism characteristic of the preoperational period. One of the major principles children learn during this

Sensorimotor stage: According to Piaget, the stage from birth to 2 years, during which a child has little competence in representing the environment by using images, language, or other symbols.

Object permanence: The awareness that objects—and people—continue to exist even if they are out of sight.

Preoperational stage: According to Piaget, the period from 2 to 7 years of age that is characterized by language development.

Egocentric thought: A way of thinking in which a child views the world entirely from his or her own perspective.

Principle of conservation: The knowledge that quantity is unrelated to the arrangement and physical appearance of objects.

INTERACTIVITY 39–1

Conservation

Concrete operational stage: According to Piaget, the period from 7 to 12 years of age that is characterized by logical thought and a loss of egocentrism.

FIGURE 10 These tests are frequently used to assess whether children have learned the principle of conservation across a variety of dimensions. Do you think children in the preoperational stage can be *taught* to avoid conservation mistakes before the typical age of mastery?

Conservation of...	Modality	Change in physical appearance	Average age at full mastery
Number	Number of elements in a collection	Rearranging or dislocating elements	6–7 years
Substance (mass)	Amount of a malleable substance (e.g., clay or liquid)	Altering shape	7–8 years
Length	Length of a line or object	Altering shape or configuration	7–8 years
Area	Amount of surface covered by a set of plane figures	Rearranging the figures	8–9 years
Weight	Weight of an object	Altering shape	9–10 years
Volume	Volume of an object (in terms of water displacement)	Altering shape	14–15 years

Children who have not mastered the principle of conservation assume that the volume of a liquid increases when it is poured from a short, wide container to a tall, thin one. What other tasks might a child under age 7 have difficulty comprehending?

Formal operational stage: According to Piaget, the period from age 12 to adulthood that is characterized by abstract thought.

stage is reversibility, the idea that some changes can be undone by reversing an earlier action. For example, they can understand that when someone rolls a ball of clay into a long sausage shape, that person can re-create the original ball by reversing the action. Children can even conceptualize this principle in their heads, without having to see the action performed before them.

Although children make important advances in their logical capabilities during the concrete operational stage, their thinking still displays one major limitation: They are largely bound to the concrete, physical reality of the world. For the most part, they have difficulty understanding questions of an abstract or hypothetical nature.

Formal Operational Stage: 12 Years to Adulthood. The **formal operational stage** produces a new kind of thinking that is abstract, formal, and logical. Thinking is no longer tied to events that individuals observe in the environment but makes use of logical techniques to resolve problems.

The way in which children approach the "pendulum problem" devised by Piaget (Piaget & Inhelder, 1958) illustrates the emergence of formal operational thinking. The problem solver is asked to figure out what determines how fast a pendulum swings. Is it the length of the string, the weight of the pendulum, or the force with which the pendulum is pushed? (For the record, the answer is the length of the string.)

Children in the concrete operational stage approach the problem haphazardly, without a logical or rational plan of action. For example, they may simultaneously change the length of the string *and* the weight on the string *and* the force with which they push the pendulum. Because they are varying all the factors at once, they cannot tell which factor is the critical one. In contrast, people in the formal operational stage approach the problem systematically. Acting as if they were scientists conducting an experiment, they examine the effects of changes in one variable at a time. This ability to rule out competing possibilities characterizes formal operational thought.

Although formal operational thought emerges during the teenage years, some individuals use this type of thinking only infrequently. Moreover, it appears that many individuals never reach this stage at all; most studies show that only 40 to 60 percent of college students and adults fully reach it, with some estimates running as low as 25 percent of the general population. In addition, in certain cultures—particularly those which are less technologically sophisticated than most Western societies—almost no one reaches the formal operational stage (Chandler, 1976; Keating & Clark, 1980; Super, 1980).

Stages versus Continuous Development: Is Piaget Right? No other theorist has given us as comprehensive a theory of cognitive development as that of Piaget. Still, many contemporary theorists suggest that a better explanation of how children develop cognitively can be provided by theories that do not involve a stage approach. For instance, children are not always consistent in their performance of tasks that—if Piaget's theory is accurate—ought to be performed equally well at a particular stage (Feldman, 2003).

Furthermore, some developmental psychologists suggest that cognitive development proceeds in a more continuous fashion than Piaget's stage theory implies. They propose that cognitive development is primarily quantitative in nature, rather than qualitative. They argue that although there are differences in when, how, and to what extent a child can use specific cognitive abilities—reflecting quantitative changes—the underlying cognitive processes change relatively little with age (Gelman & Baillargeon, 1983; Case & Okamoto, 1996).

Piaget also underestimated the age at which infants and children can understand specific concepts and principles; in fact, they seem to be more sophisticated in their cognitive abilities than Piaget believed. For instance, some evidence suggests that infants as young as 5 months have rudimentary mathematical skills (Wynn, 1995, 2000; Wynn, Bloom, & Chiang, 2002).

Despite such criticisms, most developmental psychologists agree that although the processes that underlie changes in cognitive abilities may not unfold in the manner suggested by his theory, Piaget has generally provided us with an accurate account of age-related changes in cognitive development. Moreover, his theory has had an enormous influence in education. For example, Piaget suggests that individuals cannot increase their cognitive performance unless both cognitive readiness brought about by maturation and appropriate environmental stimulation are present. This view has inspired the nature and structure of educational curricula and teaching methods. Researchers have also used Piaget's theory and methods to investigate issues surrounding animal cognition, such as whether primates show object permanence (they seem to; Funk, 1996; Hauser, 2000).

Information-Processing Approaches: Charting Children's Mental Programs. If cognitive development does not proceed as a series of stages, as Piaget suggested, what does underlie the enormous growth in children's cognitive abilities that even the most untutored eye can observe? To many developmental psychologists, changes in **information processing,** the way in which people take in, use, and store information, account for cognitive development (Siegler, 1998).

According to this approach, quantitative changes occur in children's ability to organize and manipulate information. From this perspective, children become increasingly adept at information processing, much as a computer program may

Information processing: The way in which people take in, use, and store information.

become more sophisticated as a programmer modifies it on the basis of experience. Information-processing approaches consider the kinds of "mental programs" that children invoke when approaching problems (Reyna, 1997).

Several significant changes occur in children's information-processing capabilities. For one thing, speed of processing increases with age, as some abilities become more automatic. The speed at which children can scan, recognize, and compare stimuli increases with age. As they grow older, children can pay attention to stimuli longer and discriminate between different stimuli more readily, and they are less easily distracted (Miller & Vernon, 1997; Rose, Feldman, & Jankowski, 2002; Myerson et al., 2003).

Memory also improves dramatically with age. Preschoolers can hold only two or three chunks of information in short-term memory, 5-year-olds can hold four, and 7-year-olds can hold five. (Adults are able to keep seven, plus or minus two, chunks in short-term memory.) The size of chunks also grows with age, as does the sophistication and organization of knowledge stored in memory (see Figure 11). Still, memory capabilities are impressive at a very early age: Even before they can speak, infants can remember for months events in which they actively participated (Rovee-Collier, 1993; Bauer, 1996; Cowan et al., 2003).

Metacognition: An awareness and understanding of one's own cognitive processes.

Finally, improvement in information processing relates to advances in **metacognition,** an awareness and understanding of one's own cognitive processes. Metacognition involves the planning, monitoring, and revising of cognitive strategies. Younger children, who lack an awareness of their own cognitive processes, often do not realize their incapabilities. Thus, when they misunderstand others, they may fail to recognize their own errors. It is only later, when metacognitive abilities become more sophisticated, that children are able to know when they *don't* understand. Such increasing sophistication reflects a change in children's *theory of mind,* their knowledge and beliefs about the way the mind operates (Taylor, 1996; Flavell, 2002; McCormick, 2003).

Vygotsky's View of Cognitive Development: Considering Culture. According to Russian developmental psychologist Lev Vygotsky, the culture in which we are raised has an important influence on our cognitive development. In an increasingly influential view, Vygotsky suggests that the focus on individual performance of both Piagetian and information-processing approaches is misplaced. Instead, he holds that we cannot understand cognitive development without taking into account the social aspects of learning (Vygotsky, 1926/1997; Beilin, 1996; John-Steiner & Mahn, 2003).

FIGURE 11 Memory span increases with age for both numbers and letters. (Source: Adapted from Dempster, 1981.)

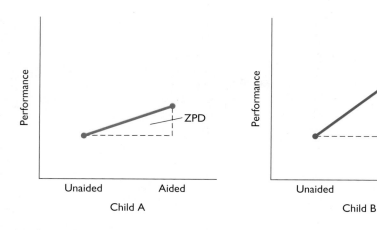

FIGURE 12 Although the performances of the two children working at a task without aid are similar, the second child benefits more from aid and thus has a larger zone of proximal development (ZPD).

Vygotsky argues that cognitive development occurs as a consequence of social interactions in which children work with others to jointly solve problems. Through such interactions, children's cognitive skills increase, and they gain the ability to function intellectually on their own. More specifically, he suggests that children's cognitive abilities increase when they encounter information that falls within their zone of proximal development. The **zone of proximal development,** or **ZPD,** is the level at which a child can almost, but not fully, comprehend or perform a task on his or her own. When children receive information that falls within the ZPD, they can increase their understanding or master a new task. In contrast, if the information lies outside children's ZPD, they will not be able to master it (see Figure 12).

In short, cognitive development occurs when parents, teachers, or skilled peers assist a child by presenting information that is both new and within the ZPD. This type of assistance, called *scaffolding,* provides support for learning and problem solving that encourages independence and growth. Vygotsky claims that scaffolding not only promotes the solution of specific problems, but also aids in the development of overall cognitive abilities (Steward, 1995).

More than other approaches to cognitive development, Vygotsky's theory considers how an individual's specific cultural and social context affects intellectual growth. The way in which children understand the world grows out of interactions with parents, peers, and other members of a specific culture (Tomasello, 2000; John-Steiner & Mahn, 2003).

Zone of proximal development (ZPD): According to Vygotsky, the level at which a child can almost, but not fully, comprehend or perform a task on his or her own.

RECAP/EVALUATE/RETHINK

RECAP

What are the major competencies of newborns?

- ▶ Newborns, or neonates, have reflexes that include a rooting reflex, the startle reflex, and the Babinski reflex. After birth, physical development is rapid; children typically triple their birthweight in a year. (p. 421)
- ▶ Sensory abilities also increase rapidly; infants can distinguish color, depth, sound, tastes, and smells relatively soon after birth. (p. 422)

What are the milestones of physical and social development during childhood?

- ▶ Attachment—the positive emotional bond between a child and a particular individual—marks social development in infancy. Measured in the laboratory by means of the Ainsworth strange situation, attachment relates to later social and emotional adjustment. (p. 425)
- ▶ As children become older, the nature of their social interactions with peers changes. Initially play occurs relatively independently, but it becomes increasingly cooperative. (p. 428)
- ▶ The different child-rearing styles include authoritarian, permissive, authoritative, and uninvolved. (p. 429)
- ▶ According to Erikson, eight stages of psychosocial development involve people's changing interactions and

understanding of themselves and others. During childhood, the four stages are trust-versus-mistrust (birth to
1½ years), autonomy-versus-shame-and-doubt (1½ to
3 years), initiative-versus-guilt (3 to 6 years), and
industry-versus-inferiority (6 to 12 years). (p. 431)

How does cognitive development proceed during childhood?

▶ Piaget's theory suggests that cognitive development proceeds through four stages in which qualitative changes
occur in thinking: the sensorimotor stage (birth to
2 years), the preoperational stage (2 to 7 years), the concrete operational stage (7 to 12 years), and the formal
operational stage (12 years to adulthood). (p. 432)

▶ Information-processing approaches suggest that quantitative changes occur in children's ability to organize and
manipulate information about the world, such as significant increases in speed of processing, attention span, and
memory. In addition, children advance in metacognition,
the awareness and understanding of one's own cognitive
processes. (p. 435)

▶ Vygotsky argued that children's cognitive development
occurs as a consequence of social interactions in which
children and others work together to solve problems.
(p. 436)

EVALUATE

1. Researchers studying newborns use _____, or the decrease in the response to a stimulus that occurs after repeated presentations of the same stimulus, as an indicator
of a baby's interest.
2. The emotional bond that develops between a child and its
caregiver is known as _____.
3. Match the parenting style with its definition:
   1. Permissive
   2. Authoritative
   3. Authoritarian
   4. Uninvolved
   a. Rigid; highly punitive; demand obedience
   b. Give little direction; lax on obedience

c. Firm but fair; try to explain parental decisions
d. Emotionally detached and unloving
4. Erikson's theory of _____ development involves a
series of eight stages, each of which must be resolved for a
person to develop optimally.
5. Match the stage of development with the thinking style
characteristic of that stage:
   1. Egocentric thought
   2. Object permanence
   3. Abstract reasoning
   4. Conservation; reversibility
   a. Sensorimotor
   b. Formal operational
   c. Preoperational
   d. Concrete operational
6. _____-_____ theories of development suggest
that the way in which a child handles information is critical to his or her development.
7. According to Vygotsky, information that is within a child's
_____ _____ _____ _____ is most likely to
result in cognitive development.

RETHINK

1. In what ways might an infant's major reflexes—the rooting, sucking, gagging, and Babinski reflexes—have had
survival value from an evolutionary perspective? What
value might the infant's ability to mimic the facial expressions of adults have?
2. Do you think the widespread use of IQ testing in the
United States contributes to parents' views that their children's academic success is due largely to the children's innate intelligence? Why? Would it be possible (or desirable)
to change this view?

Answers to Evaulate Questions

1. habituation; 2. attachment; 3. 1-b, 2-c, 3-a, 4-d; 4. psychosocial; 5. 1-c, 2-a, 3-b, 4-d; 6. information-processing; 7. zone of proximal development

KEY TERMS

neonate p. 421
reflexes p. 421
habituation p. 423
attachment p. 425
authoritarian parents p. 429
permissive parents p. 429
authoritative parents p. 430
uninvolved parents p. 430
temperament p. 430

psychosocial development p. 431
trust-versus-mistrust stage p. 431
autonomy-versus-shame-and-doubt stage p. 431
initiative-versus-guilt stage p. 431
industry-versus-inferiority stage p. 431

cognitive development p. 432
sensorimotor stage p. 433
object permanence p. 433
preoperational stage p. 433
egocentric thought p. 433
principle of conservation p. 433
concrete operational stage p. 433

formal operational stage p. 434
information processing p. 435
metacognition p. 436
zone of proximal development (ZPD) p. 437

Adolescence: Becoming an Adult

What major physical, social, and cognitive transitions characterize adolescence?

Diana Leary, Age 17: "The school is divided into different groups of kids: the break-dancers, the people who listen to heavy metal, the pretty girls, the ravers and the hip-hop people. But there's no pressure to be in one group or another. If a person is a break-dancer, they can still chill with the ravers. I'm a hip-hopper. We wear baggy jeans and sweatshirts. But if I'm really good friends with a person in the heavy-metal group, I can go chill with them and it's just like, whatever" (Gordon et al., 1999, p. 48).

* * *

Trevor Kelson, Age 15: "Keep the Hell Out of my Room!" says a sign on Trevor's bedroom wall, just above an unmade bed, a desk littered with dirty T-shirts and candy wrappers, and a floor covered with clothes. Is there a carpet? "Somewhere," he says with a grin. "I think it's gold" (Fields-Meyer, 1995, p 53).

* * *

Lauren Barry, Age 18: "I went to a National Honor Society induction. The parents were just staring at me. I think they couldn't believe someone with pink hair could be smart. I want to be a high-school teacher, but I'm afraid that, based on my appearance, they won't hire me" (Gordon et al., 1999, p. 47).

Although Diana, Trevor, and Lauren have never met, they share anxieties that are common to adolescence—concerns about friends, parents, appearance, independence, and their futures. **Adolescence,** the developmental stage between childhood and adulthood, is a crucial period. It is a time of profound changes and, occasionally, turmoil. Considerable biological change occurs as adolescents attain sexual and physical maturity. At the same time, and rivaling these physiological changes, important social, emotional, and cognitive changes occur as adolescents strive for independence and move toward adulthood.

Because many years of schooling precede most people's entry into the workforce in Western societies, the stage of adolescence is fairly long, beginning just before the teenage years and ending just after them. No longer children but considered by society to be not quite adults, adolescents face a period of rapid physical, cognitive, and social change that affects them for the rest of their lives.

Dramatic changes in society also affect adolescents' development. More than half of all children in the United States will spend all or some of their childhood and adolescence in single-parent families. Furthermore, adolescents spend considerably less time with their parents, and more with their peers, than they did several decades ago. Finally, the ethnic and cultural diversity of adolescents as a group is increasing dramatically. A third of all adolescents today are of non-European descent, and by the year 2050 the number of adolescents of Hispanic, African American, Native American, and Asian origin will have grown significantly (Carnegie Council on Adolescent Development, 1995; Dreman, 1997).

▲▲▲

Adolescence: The developmental stage between childhood and adulthood.

Physical Development: The Changing Adolescent

Although puberty begins around age 11 or 12 for girls and 13 or 14 for boys, there are wide variations. What are some advantages and disadvantages of early puberty?

Puberty: The period at which maturation of the sexual organs occurs, beginning at about age 11 or 12 for girls and 13 or 14 for boys.

If you think back to the start of your own adolescence, the most dramatic changes you probably remember are physical ones. A spurt in height, the growth of breasts in girls, deepening voices in boys, the development of body hair, and intense sexual feelings cause curiosity, interest, and sometimes embarrassment for individuals entering adolescence.

The physical changes that occur at the start of adolescence result largely from the secretion of various hormones, and they affect virtually every aspect of an adolescent's life. Not since infancy has development been so dramatic. Weight and height increase rapidly because of a growth spurt that typically begins around age 10 for girls and age 12 for boys. Adolescents may grow as much as five inches in one year.

Puberty, the period at which maturation of the sexual organs occurs, begins at about age 11 or 12 for girls, when menstruation starts. However, there are wide variations (see Figure 1). For example, some girls begin to menstruate as early as age 8 or 9 or as late as age 16. Furthermore, in Western cultures, the average age at which adolescents reach sexual

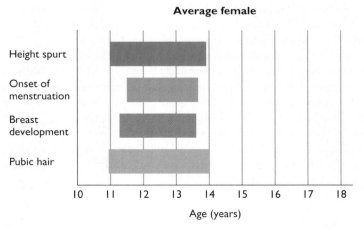

FIGURE 1 The range of ages during which major sexual changes occur during adolescence is shown by the colored bars. (Source: Based on Tanner, 1978.)

maturity has been steadily decreasing over the last century, most likely as a result of improved nutrition and medical care. Sexual *attraction* to others begins even before the maturation of the sexual organs, at around age 10 (see Figure 1; Tanner, 1990; Finlay, Jones, & Coleman, 2002).

For boys, the onset of puberty is marked by their first ejaculation, known as *spermarche*. Spermarche usually occurs around the age of 13 (see Figure 1). At first, relatively few sperm are produced during an ejaculation, but the amount increases significantly within a few years.

The age at which puberty begins has implications for the way adolescents feel about themselves—as well as the way others treat them. Early-maturing boys have a distinct advantage over later-maturing boys. They do better in athletics, are generally more popular with peers, and have more positive self-concepts (Duncan et al., 1985; Peterson, 1985; Anderson & Magnusson, 1990).

The picture differs for girls. Although early-maturing girls are more sought after as dates and have better self-esteem than do later-maturing girls, some consequences of early physical maturation may be less positive. For example, early breast development may set them apart from their peers and be a source of ridicule (Simmons & Blyth, 1987; Ge, Conger, & Elder, 1996).

Late physical maturation may produce certain psychological difficulties for both boys and girls. Boys who are smaller and less coordinated than their more mature peers tend to feel ridiculed and less attractive. Similarly, late-maturing girls are at a disadvantage in middle school and early high school. They hold relatively low social status and may be overlooked in dating (Clarke-Stewart & Friedman, 1987; Lanza & Collins, 2002).

Clearly, the rate at which physical changes occur during adolescence can affect the way in which people are viewed by others and the way they view themselves. Just as important as physical changes, however, are the psychological and social changes that unfold during adolescence.

Moral and Cognitive Development: Distinguishing Right from Wrong

In a European country, a woman is near death from a special kind of cancer. The one drug that the doctors think might save her is a medicine that a medical researcher has recently discovered. The drug is expensive to make, and the researcher is charging ten times the cost, or $5,000, for a small dose. The sick woman's husband, Henry, approaches everyone he knows in hopes of borrowing money, but he can get together only about $2,500. He tells the researcher that his wife is dying and asks him to lower the price of the drug or let him pay later. The researcher says, "No, I discovered the drug, and I'm going to make money from it." Henry is desperate and considers stealing the drug for his wife.

What would you tell Henry to do?

KOHLBERG'S THEORY OF MORAL DEVELOPMENT

In the view of psychologist Lawrence Kohlberg, the advice you give Henry reflects your level of moral development. According to Kohlberg, people pass through a series of stages in the evolution of their sense of justice and in the kind of reasoning they use to make moral judgments (Kohlberg, 1984). Largely because of the various cognitive limitations that Piaget described, preadolescent children tend to think either in terms of concrete, unvarying rules ("It is always wrong to steal" or "I'll be punished if I steal") or in terms of the rules of society ("Good people don't steal" or "What if everyone stole?").

Adolescents, however, can reason on a higher plane, having typically reached Piaget's formal operational stage of cognitive development. Because they are able to

Sample Moral Reasoning of Subjects

Level	In Favor of Stealing the Drug	Against Stealing the Drug
Level 1 Preconventional morality: At this level, the concrete interests of the individual are considered in terms of rewards and punishments.	"If you let your wife die, you will get in trouble. You'll be blamed for not spending the money to save her, and there'll be an investigation of you and the druggist for your wife's death."	"You shouldn't steal the drug because you'll be caught and sent to jail if you do. If you do get away, your conscience will bother you thinking how the police will catch up with you at any minute."
Level 2 Conventional morality: At this level, people approach moral problems as members of society. They are interested in pleasing others by acting as good members of society.	"If you let your wife die, you'll never be able to look anybody in the face again."	"After you steal the drug, you'll feel bad thinking how you've brought dishonor on your family and yourself; you won't be able to face anyone again."
Level 3 Postconventional morality: At this level, people use moral principles which are seen as broader than those of any particular society.	"If you don't steal the drug, and if you let your wife die, you'll always condemn yourself for it afterward. You won't be blamed and you'll have lived up to the outside rule of the law, but you won't have lived up to your own conscience and standards of honesty."	"If you steal the drug, you won't be blamed by other people, but you'll condemn yourself because you won't have lived up to your own conscience and standards of honesty."

FIGURE 2 Developmental psychologist Lawrence Kohlberg theorized that people move through a three-level sequence of moral reasoning in a fixed order. However, he contended that few people ever reach the highest level of moral reasoning.

comprehend broad moral principles, they can understand that morality is not always black and white and that conflict can exist between two sets of socially accepted standards.

Kohlberg (1984) suggests that the changes in moral reasoning can be understood best as a three-level sequence (see Figure 2). His theory assumes that people move through the levels in a fixed order, and that they cannot reach the highest level until about age 13—primarily because of limitations in cognitive development before that age. However, many people never reach the highest level of moral reasoning. In fact, Kohlberg found that only a relatively small percentage of adults rise above the second level of his model (Kohlberg & Ryncarz, 1990).

Although Kohlberg's theory has had a substantial influence on our understanding of moral development, the research support is mixed. One difficulty with the theory is that it pertains to moral *judgments,* not moral *behavior.* Knowing right from wrong does not mean that we will always act in accordance with our judgments. In addition, the theory applies primarily to Western society and its moral code; cross-cultural research conducted in cultures with different moral systems suggests that Kohlberg's theory is not necessarily relevant (Coles, 1997; Damon, 1999; Nucci, 2002).

MORAL DEVELOPMENT IN WOMEN

One glaring shortcoming of Kohlberg's research is that he primarily used male participants. Furthermore, psychologist Carol Gilligan (1996) argues that because of men's and women's distinctive socialization experiences, a fundamental difference exists in the way each gender views moral behavior. According to Gilligan, men view morality primarily in terms of broad principles, such as justice and fairness. In contrast, women see it in terms of responsibility toward individuals and willingness to make sacrifices to help a specific individual within the context of a particular relationship. Compassion for individuals is a more salient factor in moral behavior for women than it is for men.

Because Kohlberg's model defines moral behavior largely in terms of abstract principles such as justice, Gilligan finds it inadequately describes the moral development of females. She suggests that women's morality centers on individual well-being and social relationships—a morality of *caring*. In her view, compassionate concern for the welfare of others represents the highest level of morality.

The fact that Gilligan's conception of morality differs greatly from Kohlberg's suggests that gender plays an important role in determining what a person sees as moral. Although the research evidence is not definitive, it seems plausible that their differing conceptions of what constitutes moral behavior may lead men and women to regard the morality of a particular behavior in different ways (Wark & Krebs, 1996; Jaffee & Hyde, 2000).

To check your understanding of moral development, complete **Interactivity 40–1.**

INTERACTIVITY 40–1

Stages of moral development

Social Development: Finding Oneself in a Social World

"Who am I?" "How do I fit into the world?" "What is life all about?"

Questions such as these assume particular significance during the teenage years, as adolescents seek to find their place in the broader social world. As we will see, this quest takes adolescents along several routes.

ERIKSON'S THEORY OF PSYCHOSOCIAL DEVELOPMENT: THE SEARCH FOR IDENTITY

Erikson's theory of psychosocial development emphasizes the search for identity during the adolescent years. As was noted earlier, psychosocial development encompasses the way people's understanding of themselves, one another, and the world around them changes during the course of development (Erikson, 1963).

The fifth stage of Erikson's theory (summarized, with the other stages, in Figure 3), the **identity-versus-role-confusion stage,** encompasses adolescence. During this

Identity-versus-role-confusion stage: According to Erikson, a time in adolescence of major testing to determine one's unique qualities.

FIGURE 3 Erikson's stages of psychosocial development. According to Erikson, people proceed through eight stages of psychosocial development across their lives. He suggested that each stage requires the resolution of a crisis or conflict and may produce both positive and negative outcomes.

Stage	Approximate Age	Positive Outcomes	Negative Outcomes
1. Trust-vs.-mistrust	Birth–1 1/2 years	Feelings of trust from environmental support	Fear and concern regarding others
2. Autonomy-vs.-shame-and-doubt	1 1/2–3 years	Self-sufficiency if exploration is encouraged	Doubts about self, lack of independence
3. Initiative-vs.-guilt	3–6 years	Discovery of ways to initiate actions	Guilt from actions and thoughts
4. Industry-vs.-inferiority	6–12 years	Development of sense of competence	Feelings of inferiority, no sense of mastery
5. Identity-vs.-role-confusion	Adolescence	Awareness of uniqueness of self, knowledge of role to be followed	Inability to identify appropriate roles in life
6. Intimacy-vs.-isolation	Early adulthood	Development of loving, sexual relationships and close friendships	Fear of relationships with others
7. Generativity-vs.-stagnation	Middle adulthood	Sense of contribution to continuity of life	Trivialization of one's activities
8. Ego-integrity-vs.-despair	Late adulthood	Sense of unity in life's accomplishments	Regret over lost opportunities of life

Identity: The distinguishing character of the individual: who each of us is, what our roles are, and what we are capable of.

Intimacy-versus-isolation stage: According to Erikson, a period during early adulthood that focuses on developing close relationships.

Generativity-versus-stagnation stage: According to Erikson, a period in middle adulthood during which we take stock of our contributions to family and society.

Ego-integrity-versus-despair stage: According to Erikson, a period from late adulthood until death during which we review life's accomplishments and failures.

stage, a time of major testing, people try to determine what is unique about themselves. They attempt to discover who they are, what their strengths are, and what kinds of roles they are best suited to play for the rest of their lives—in short, their **identity.** A person confused about the most appropriate role to play in life may lack a stable identity, adopt an unacceptable role such as that of a social deviant, or have difficulty maintaining close personal relationships later in life (Brendgen, Vitaro, & Bukowski, 2000).

During the identity-versus-role-confusion period, an adolescent feels pressure to identify what to do with his or her life. Because these pressures come at a time of major physical changes as well as important changes in what society expects of them, adolescents can find the period a particularly difficult one. The identity-versus-role-confusion stage has another important characteristic: declining reliance on adults for information, with a shift toward using the peer group as a source of social judgments. The peer group becomes increasingly important, enabling adolescents to form close, adultlike relationships and helping them clarify their personal identities. According to Erikson, the identity-versus-role-confusion stage marks a pivotal point in psychosocial development, paving the way for continued growth and the future development of personal relationships.

During early adulthood, people enter the **intimacy-versus-isolation stage.** Spanning the period of early adulthood (from postadolescence to the early thirties), this stage focuses on developing close relationships with others. Difficulties during this stage result in feelings of loneliness and a fear of such relationships, whereas successful resolution of the crises of the stage results in the possibility of forming relationships that are intimate on a physical, intellectual, and emotional level.

Development continues during middle adulthood as people enter the **generativity-versus-stagnation stage.** Generativity is the ability to contribute to one's family, community, work, and society, and assist the development of the younger generation. Success in this stage results in a person feeling positive about the continuity of life, whereas difficulties lead a person to feel that his or her activities are trivial or stagnant and have done nothing for upcoming generations. In fact, if a person has not successfully resolved the identity crisis of adolescence, he or she may still be foundering as far as identifying an appropriate career is concerned.

Finally, the last stage of psychosocial development, the **ego-integrity-versus-despair stage,** spans later adulthood and continues until death. Now a sense of accomplishment signifies success in resolving the difficulties presented by this stage of life; failure to resolve the difficulties results in regret over what might have been achieved but was not.

Notably, Erikson's theory suggests that development does not stop at adolescence but continues throughout adulthood, a view that a substantial amount of research now confirms. For instance, a 22-year study by psychologist Susan Whitbourne found considerable support for the fundamentals of Erikson's theory, determining that psychosocial development continues through adolescence and adulthood. In sum, adolescence is not an end point but rather a way station on the path of psychosocial development (Whitbourne et al., 1992; McAdams et al., 1997).

STORMY ADOLESCENCE: MYTH OR REALITY?

Does puberty invariably foreshadow a stormy, rebellious period of adolescence?

At one time, psychologists thought most children entering adolescence were beginning a period fraught with stress and unhappiness. However, research now shows that this characterization is largely a myth, that most young people pass through adolescence without appreciable turmoil in their lives, and that parents speak easily—and fairly often—with their children about a variety of topics (Klein, 1998; van Wel, Linssen, & Abma, 2000).

This does not mean that adolescence is completely calm. In most families with adolescents, the amount of arguing and bickering clearly rises. Most young teenagers, as part of their search for identity, experience tension between their attempts to become independent from their parents and their actual dependence on them. They may experiment with a range of behaviors, flirting with a variety of activities that their parents, and even society as a whole, find objectionable. Happily, though, for most families such tensions stabilize during middle adolescence—around age 15 or 16—and eventually decline around age 18 (Eccles, Lord, & Roeser, 1996; Gullotta, Adams, & Markstrom, 1999).

One reason for the increase in discord during adolescence appears to be the protracted period in which children stay at home with their parents. In prior historical periods—and in some non-Western cultures today—children leave home immediately after puberty and are considered adults. Today, however, sexually mature adolescents may spend as many as seven or eight years with their parents. Current social trends even hint at an extension of the conflicts of adolescence beyond the teenage years, because a significant number of young adults—known as *boomerang children*—return to live with their parents after leaving home for some period. Although some parents welcome the return of their children, others are less sympathetic, and this opens the way to conflict (Bianchi & Casper, 2000).

Another source of strife with parents lies in the way adolescents think. Adolescence fosters *adolescent egocentrism*, a state of self-absorption in which a teenager views the world from his or her own point of view. Egocentrism leads adolescents to be highly critical of authority figures, unwilling to accept criticism, and quick to fault others. It also makes them believe that they are the center of everyone else's attention, leading to self-consciousness. Furthermore, they develop *personal fables*, the belief that their experience is unique, exceptional, and shared by no one else. Such personal fables may make adolescents feel invulnerable to the risks that threaten others (Elkind, 1985; Goossens, et al., 2002).

Adolescence also introduces a variety of stresses outside the home. Typically, adolescents change schools at least twice (from elementary to middle school or junior high, then to senior high school), and relationships with friends and peers are particularly volatile. Many adolescents hold part-time jobs, increasing the demands of school, work, and social activities on their time. Such stressors can lead to tensions at home (Steinberg & Dornbusch, 1991; Dworkin, Larson, & Hansen, 2003).

ADOLESCENT SUICIDE

Although the vast majority of teenagers pass through adolescence without major psychological difficulties, some experience unusually severe psychological problems. Sometimes those problems become so extreme that adolescents take their own lives. Suicide is the third leading cause of death for adolescents (after accidents and homicide) in the United States. More teenagers and young adults die from suicide than from cancer, heart disease, AIDS, birth defects, stroke, pneumonia and influenza, and chronic lung disease *combined* (CDC, 2000).

A teenager commits suicide every ninety minutes—a rate that has tripled over the last two decades. Furthermore, the reported rate of suicide may actually be understated, because medical personnel hesitate to report suicide as a cause of death. Instead, they frequently label a death as an accident in an effort to protect the survivors.

These students are mourning the deaths of two classmates who committed suicide. The rate of suicide among teenagers has risen significantly over the last few decades. Can you think of any reasons for this phenomenon?

Male adolescents are five times more likely to commit suicide than are females, although females *attempt* suicide more often than males do. Overall, as many as 200 adolescents may attempt suicide for every one who actually takes his or her own life (Berman & Jobes, 1991; Gelman, 1994; CDC, 2000).

The rate of adolescent suicide is significantly greater among whites than among nonwhites. However, the suicide rate of African American males has increased much more rapidly than has that of white males over the last two decades. Native Americans have the highest suicide rate of any ethnic group in the United States, and Asian Americans have the lowest rate (MMWR, 1998; NIMH, 1999).

It is not clear why suicide has increased so dramatically over the last few decades. Some psychologists suggest that the sharp rise in stress that teenagers experience—in terms of academic and social pressure, alcoholism, drug abuse, and family difficulties—provokes the most troubled adolescents to take their own lives. However, that is not the whole story, for the suicide rate for other age groups has remained fairly stable in the last few decades. It is unlikely that stress has increased only for adolescents and not for the rest of the population (HMHL, 1996).

Although the question of why adolescent suicide has risen remains unanswered, several factors put adolescents at risk. One factor is depression, characterized by unhappiness, extreme fatigue, and—a variable that seems particularly important—a profound sense of hopelessness. In other cases, adolescents who commit suicide are perfectionists, inhibited socially and prone to extreme anxiety when they face any social or academic challenge (Rierdan, 1996; Ayyash-Abdo, 2002; see Figure 4).

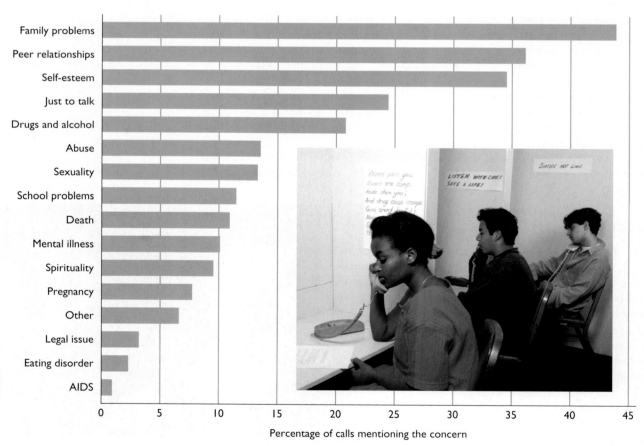

FIGURE 4 According to a review of phone calls to one telephone help line, adolescents who were considering suicide most often mentioned family, peer relationships, and self-esteem problems. (Source: Boehm & Campbell, 1995.)

Family background and adjustment difficulties are also related to suicide. A long-standing history of conflicts between parents and children may lead to adolescent behavior problems, such as delinquency, dropping out of school, and aggressive tendencies. In addition, teenage alcoholics and abusers of other drugs have a relatively high rate of suicide (Wagner, 1997; Stronski et al., 2000).

Several warning signs indicate when a teenager's problems may be severe enough to warrant concern about the possibility of a suicide attempt. They include the following:

- ▶ School problems, such as missing classes, truancy, and a sudden change in grades
- ▶ Frequent incidents of self-destructive behavior, such as careless accidents
- ▶ Loss of appetite or excessive eating
- ▶ Withdrawal from friends and peers
- ▶ Sleeping problems
- ▶ Signs of depression, tearfulness, or overt indications of psychological difficulties, such as hallucinations
- ▶ A preoccupation with death, an afterlife, or what would happen "if I died"
- ▶ Putting affairs in order, such as giving away prized possessions or making arrangements for the care of a pet
- ▶ An explicit announcement of thoughts of suicide

If you know some who shows signs that he or she is suicidal, urge that person to seek professional help. You may need to take assertive action, such as enlisting the assistance of family members or friends. Talk of suicide is a serious signal for help, not a confidence to be kept. (For immediate help with a suicide problem, call 800-448-3000, a national help line. To get practice in understanding the causes of suicide, complete **Interactivity 40–2**.)

INTERACTIVITY 40–2

Suicide risk factors

Exploring DIVERSITY

Rites of Passage: Coming of Age Around the World

It is not easy for male members of the Awa tribe in New Guinea to make the transition from childhood to adulthood. First come whippings with sticks and prickly branches, both for the boys' own past misdeeds and in honor of those tribesmen who were killed in warfare. In the next phase of the ritual, adults jab sharpened sticks into the boys' nostrils. Then they force a five-foot length of vine into the boys' throats, until they gag and vomit. Finally, tribesmen cut the boys' genitals, causing severe bleeding.

Although the rites that mark the coming of age of boys in the Awa tribe sound horrifying to Westerners, they are comparable to those in other cultures. In some, youths must kneel on hot coals without displaying pain. In others, girls must toss wads of burning cotton from hand to hand and allow themselves to be bitten by hundreds of ants (Selsky, 1997).

Other cultures have less fearsome, although no less important, ceremonies that mark the passage from childhood to adulthood. For instance, when a girl first menstruates in traditional Apache tribes, the event is marked by dawn-to-dusk chanting. Western religions, too, have several types of celebrations, including bar and bat mitzvahs at age 13 for Jewish boys and girls and confirmation ceremonies for children in many Christian denominations (Myerhoff, 1982; Dunham, et al., 1986; Rakoff, 1995).

In most societies, males, but not females, are the focus of coming-of-age ceremonies. The renowned anthropologist Margaret Mead remarked, only partly in jest, that the preponderance of male ceremonies might reflect the fact that "the worry that boys will not grow up to be men is much more widespread than that girls will not grow up to be women" (1949, p. 195). Said another way, it may be that in most cultures men traditionally have higher status than women, and therefore those cultures regard boys' transition into adulthood as more important.

However, another fact may explain why most cultures place greater emphasis on male rites than on female ones. For females, the transition from childhood is marked by a definite, biological event: menstruation. For males, in contrast, no single event can be used to pinpoint entry into adulthood. Thus, men are forced to rely on culturally determined rituals to acknowledge their arrival into adulthood.

Ⓐ Ⓐ Ⓐ

RECAP/EVALUATE/RETHINK

RECAP

What major physical, social, and cognitive transitions characterize adolescence?

▶ Adolescence, the developmental stage between childhood and adulthood, is marked by the onset of puberty, the point at which sexual maturity occurs. The age at which puberty begins has implications for the way people view themselves and the way others see them. (p. 439)

▶ Moral judgments during adolescence increase in sophistication, according to Kohlberg's three-level model. Although Kohlberg's levels provide an adequate description of males' moral judgments, Gilligan suggests that women view morality in terms of caring for individuals rather than in terms of broad, general principles of justice. (p. 441)

▶ According to Erikson's model of psychosocial development, adolescence may be accompanied by an identity crisis. Adolescence is followed by three more stages of psychosocial development that cover the remainder of the life span. (p. 443)

▶ Suicide is the third leading cause of death in adolescents. (p. 445)

EVALUATE

1. _____ is the period during which the sexual organs begin to mature.

2. Delayed maturation typically provides both males and females with a social advantage. True or false?

3. _____ proposed a set of three levels of moral development ranging from reasoning based on rewards and punishments to abstract thinking involving concepts of justice.

4. Erikson believed that during adolescence, people must search for _____, whereas during the early adulthood, the major task is _____.

RETHINK

1. In what ways do school cultures help or hurt teenage students who are going through adolescence? What school policies might benefit early-maturing girls and late-maturing boys? Explain how same-sex schools could help, as some have argued.

2. Many cultures have "rites of passage" that officially recognize young people as adults. Do you think such rites can be beneficial? Does the United States have any such rites? Would setting up an official designation that one has achieved "adult" status have benefits?

Answers to Evaluate Questions

1. puberty; 2. false; both male and female adolescents suffer if they mature late; 3. Kohlberg; 4. identity, intimacy

KEY TERMS

adolescence p. 439
puberty p. 440
identity-versus-role-
confusion stage p. 443

identity p. 444
intimacy-versus-isolation
stage p. 444

generativity-versus-
stagnation stage p. 444

ego-integrity-versus-despair
stage p. 444

Adulthood

MODULE 41

What are the principal kinds of physical, social, and intellectual changes that occur in early and middle adulthood, and what are their causes?

How does the reality of late adulthood differ from the stereotypes about that period?

How can we adjust to death?

I thought I got better as I got older. I found out that wasn't the case in a real hurry last year. After going twelve years in professional football and twelve years before that in amateur football without ever having surgery performed on me, the last two seasons of my career I went under the knife three times. It happened very quickly and without warning, and I began to ask myself, "Is this age? Is this what's happening?" Because up until that moment, I'd never realized that I was getting older (Kotre & Hall, 1990, p. 257, 259–260).

As a former professional football player, Brian Sipes intensely felt the changes in his body brought about by aging. But the challenges he experienced are part of a normal process that affects all people as they move through adulthood.

Psychologists generally agree that early adulthood begins around age 20 and lasts until about age 40 to 45, with middle adulthood beginning then and continuing until around age 65. Despite the enormous importance of these periods of life in terms of both the accomplishments that occur in them and their overall length (together they span some forty-five years), they have been studied less than has any other stage. For one reason, the physical changes that occur during these periods are less apparent and more gradual than are those at other times during the life span. In addition, the diverse social changes that arise during this period defy simple categorization. However, developmental psychologists have recently begun to focus on the period, particularly on the social changes in the family and women's careers.

⚠⚠⚠

Physical Development: The Peak of Health

For most people, early adulthood marks the peak of physical health. From about 18 to 25 years of age, people's strength is greatest, their reflexes are quickest, and their chances of dying from disease are quite slim. Moreover, reproductive capabilities are at their highest level.

Around age 25, the body becomes slightly less efficient and more susceptible to disease. Overall, however, ill health remains the exception; most people stay remarkably healthy during early adulthood. (Can you think of any machine other than the body that can operate without pause for so long a period?)

During middle adulthood people gradually become aware of changes in their bodies. People often begin to put on weight (although this can be avoided through diet and exercise). Furthermore, the sense organs gradually become less sensitive, and reactions to stimuli are slower. But generally, the physical declines that occur during middle adulthood are minor and often unnoticeable (DiGiovanna, 1994; Forzanna et al., 1994).

The major biological change that does occur pertains to reproductive capabilities during middle adulthood. On average, during their late forties or early fifties, women

Menopause: The period during which women stop menstruating and are no longer fertile.

begin **menopause,** during which they stop menstruating and are no longer fertile. Because menopause is accompanied by a significant reduction in the production of estrogen, a female hormone, women sometimes experience symptoms such as hot flashes, sudden sensations of heat. However, many symptoms can be treated through *hormone replacement therapy (HRT),* in which menopausal women take the hormones estrogen and progesterone. However, hormone replacement therapy poses several dangers, such as an increase in the risk of breast cancer, blood clots, and heart disease. These uncertainties make the routine use of HRT controversial (Kittell & Mansfield, 2000; National Heart, Lung, & Blood Institute, 2002; Rymer, Wilson, & Ballard, 2003).

Menopause was once blamed for a variety of psychological symptoms, including depression and memory loss. However, such difficulties, if they do occur, may be caused by women's expectations about reaching an "old" age in a society that highly values youth.

Furthermore, women's reactions to menopause vary significantly across cultures. According to anthropologist Yewoubdar Beyene (1989), the more a society values old age, the less difficulty its women have during menopause. In a study of women in Mayan villages, she found that women looked forward to menopause, because they then stopped having children. In addition, they didn't experience some of the classic symptoms of menopause; hot flashes, for example, were unheard of (Beck, 1992; Mingo, Herman, & Jasperse, 2000; Elliot, Berman, & Kim, 2002).

For men, the aging process during middle adulthood is somewhat subtler. There are no physiological signals of increasing age equivalent to the end of menstruation in women, and so no male menopause exists. In fact, men remain fertile and are capable of fathering children until well into late adulthood. However, some gradual physical decline occurs: Sperm production decreases, and the frequency of orgasm tends to decline. Once again, though, any psychological difficulties associated with these changes are usually brought about not so much by physical deterioration as by the inability of an aging individual to meet the exaggerated standards of youthfulness.

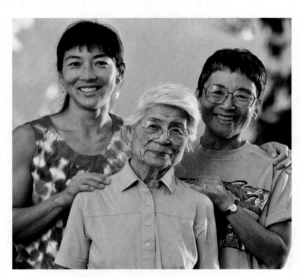

Women's reactions to menopause vary significantly across cultures, and according to one study, the more a society values old age, the less difficulty its women have during menopause. Why do you think this would be the case?

Social Development: Working at Life

Whereas physical changes during adulthood reflect development of a quantitative nature, social developmental transitions are qualitative and more profound. During this period, people typically launch themselves into careers, marriage, and families.

The entry into early adulthood is usually marked by leaving one's childhood home and entering the world of work. People envision life goals and make career choices. Their lives often center on their careers, which form an important part of their identity (Vaillant & Vaillant, 1990; Levinson, 1990, 1992).

In their early forties, however, people may begin to question their lives as they enter a period called the *midlife transition.* The idea that life will end at some point becomes increasingly influential in their thinking, and they may question their past accomplishments (Gould, 1978). Facing signs of physical aging and feeling dissatisfaction with their lives, some individuals experience what has been popularly labeled a *midlife crisis.*

In most cases, though, the passage into middle age is relatively calm. Most 40 year-olds view their lives and accomplishments positively enough to proceed relatively smoothly through midlife, and the forties and fifties are often a particularly rewarding period. Rather than looking to the future, people concentrate on the present, and their involvement with their families, friends, and other social groups takes on new importance. A major developmental thrust of this period is coming to terms with one's circumstances (Whitbourne, 2000).

Finally, during the last stages of adulthood people become more accepting of others and of their own lives and are less concerned about issues or problems that once bothered them. People come to accept the fact that death is inevitable, and they try to understand their accomplishments in terms of the broader meaning of life. Although people may begin, for the first time, to label themselves as "old," many also develop a sense of wisdom and feel freer to enjoy life (Baltes & Kunzmann, 2003).

Marriage, Children, and Divorce: Family Ties

In the typical fairy tale, a dashing young man and a beautiful young woman marry, have children, and live happily ever after. However, that scenario does not match the realities of love and marriage in the twenty-first century. Today, it is just as likely that the man and woman would first live together, then get married and have children, but ultimately end up getting divorced.

The percentage of U.S. households made up of unmarried couples has increased dramatically over the last two decades. At the same time, the average age at which marriage takes place is higher than at any time since the turn of the last century. These changes have been dramatic, and they suggest that the institution of marriage has changed considerably from earlier historical periods (see Figure 1).

When people do marry, the probability of divorce is high, particularly for younger couples. Even though divorce rates have been declining since they peaked in 1981, about half of all first marriages end in divorce. Before they are 18 years old, two-fifths of children will experience the breakup of their parents' marriages. Moreover, the rise in divorce is not just a U.S. phenomenon: The divorce rate has accelerated over the last several decades in most industrialized countries except Japan and Italy (Cherlin, 1993; Ahrons, 1995; Schaefer, 2000).

Changes in marriage and divorce trends have doubled the number of single-parent households in the United States over the last two decades. More than one-quarter of all family households are now headed by one parent, compared with 13 percent in 1970, and half of all black children and almost one-third of Hispanic

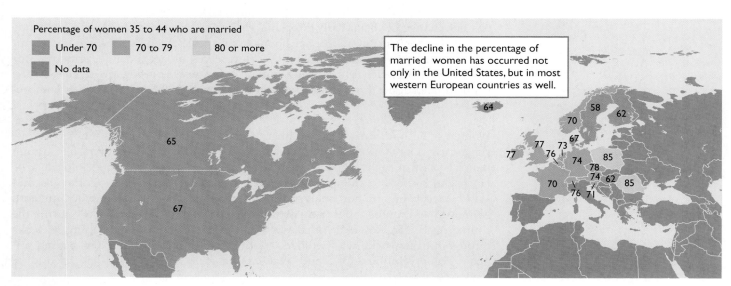

FIGURE I The percentage of women who are married has declined in most Western countries over previous decades. What do you think are some of the reasons for the declines, and do you think they will be permanent? (Source: Statistical Office of the European Communities, 1998.)

children live in homes with only one parent. Furthermore, in most single-parent families, it is the mother, rather than the father, with whom the children reside—a phenomenon that is consistent across racial and ethnic groups throughout the industrialized world (Burns & Scott, 1994; U.S. Bureau of the Census, 1997).

What are the economic and emotional consequences for children living in homes with only one parent? Single-parent families are often economically less well off, and this has an impact on children's opportunities. Over a third of single-mother families with children have incomes below the poverty line (U.S. Bureau of the Census, 2000). In addition, good child care is often hard to find. Time is always at a premium in single-parent families. Furthermore, for children of divorce, the parents' separation is often a painful experience that may result in obstacles to establishing close relationships later in life. Children may blame themselves for the breakup or feel pressure to take sides (Hetherington, 1999; Wallerstein, Lewis, Blakeslee & Lewis, 2000).

Most evidence, however, suggests that children from single-parent families are no less well adjusted than are those from two-parent families. In fact, children may be more successful growing up in a harmonious single-parent family than in a two-parent family that engages in continuous conflict (Harold et al., 1997; Clarke-Stewart et al., 2000; Kelly, 2000).

CHANGING ROLES OF MEN AND WOMEN: THE TIME OF THEIR LIVES

One of the major changes in family life in the last two decades has been the evolution of men's and women's roles. More women than ever before act simultaneously as wives, mothers, and wage earners—in contrast to women in traditional marriages, in which the husband is the sole wage earner and the wife assumes primary responsibility for care of the home and children.

Close to 75 percent of all married women with school-age children are now employed outside the home, and 55 percent of mothers with children under age 6 are working. In the mid-1960s, only 17 percent of mothers of 1-year-olds worked full-time; now, more than half are in the labor force (Carnegie Task Force, 1994; U.S, Bureau of the Census, 2001).

Most married working women are not free of household responsibilities. Even in marriages in which the spouses hold jobs that have similar status and require similar hours, the distribution of household tasks between husbands and wives has not changed substantially. Working wives are still more likely than husbands to feel responsible for traditional homemaking tasks such as cooking and cleaning. In contrast, husbands still view themselves as responsible primarily for household tasks such as repairing broken appliances, putting up screens in the summer, and doing yard work (Ganong & Coleman, 1999; Juster, Ono, & Stafford, 2002).

Women's "Second Shift." The number of hours put in by working mothers can be staggering. One survey, for instance, found that employed mothers of children under 3 years of age worked an average of ninety hours per week! Sociologist Arlie Hochschild refers to the additional work performed by women as the "second shift." According to her analysis of national statistics, women who are both employed and mothers put in an extra month of twenty-four-hour days during the course of a year. Researchers see similar patterns in many developing societies throughout the world, with women working at full-time jobs and also having primary responsibilities for child care (Hochschild, 1990, 2001; Hochschild & Machung, 2001).

Consequently, rather than careers being a substitute for what women do at home, they often exist in addition to the role of homemaker. It is not surprising that some wives feel resentment toward husbands who spend less time on child care and housework than the wives had expected before the birth of their children (Stier & Lewin-Epstein, 2000; Kiecolt, 2003).

The Later Years of Life: Growing Old

I've always enjoyed doing things in the mountains—hiking or, more recently, active cliff-climbing. When climbing a route of any difficulty at all, it's absolutely necessary to become entirely absorbed in what you're doing. You look for a crack that you can put your hand in. You have to think about whether the foothold over there will leave you in balance or not. Otherwise you can get trapped in a difficult situation. And if you don't remember where you put your hands or feet a few minutes before, then it's very difficult to climb down.

The more difficult the climb, the more absorbing it is. The climbs I really remember are the ones I had to work on. Maybe a particular section where it took two or three tries before I found the right combination of moves that got me up easily—and, preferably, elegantly. It's a wonderful exhilaration to get to the top and sit down and perhaps have lunch and look out over the landscape and be so grateful that it's still possible for me to do that sort of thing (Lyman Spitzer, age 74, quoted in Kotre & Hall, 1990, pp. 358–359).

If you can't quite picture a 74-year-old climbing rocks, some rethinking of your view of old age may be in order. In spite of the societal stereotype of "old age" as a time of inactivity and physical and mental decline, *gerontologists,* specialists who study aging, are beginning to paint a very different portrait of late adulthood.

By focusing on the period of life that starts at around age 65, gerontologists are making important contributions to clarifying the capabilities of older adults. Their work is demonstrating that significant developmental processes continue even during old age. And as life expectancy increases, the number of people who reach older adulthood will continue to grow substantially (see Figure 2). Consequently, developing

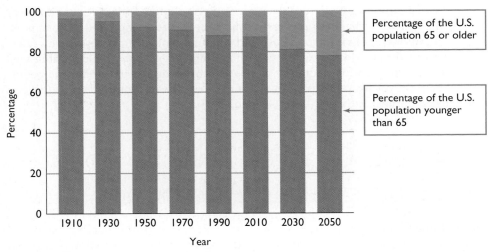

FIGURE 2 Projections suggest that by the year 2050, 20 percent of the U.S. population will be over age 65. What implications does this statistic have for U.S. society?

an understanding of late adulthood has become a critical priority for psychologists (Birren, 1996; Moody, 2000).

Physical Changes in Late Adulthood: The Aging Body

INTERACTIVITY 41–1

Attitudes toward aging

Napping, eating, walking, conversing. It probably doesn't surprise you that these relatively nonstrenuous activities represent the typical pastimes of late adulthood. But it is striking that these activities are identical to the most common leisure activities reported in a survey of college students (Harper, 1978). Although the students cited more active pursuits—such as sailing and playing basketball—as their favorite activities, in actuality they engaged in such sports relatively infrequently, spending most of their free time napping, eating, walking, and conversing. (To learn more about age stereotypes, complete **Interactivity 41–1**.)

Although the leisure activities in which older adults engage may not differ all that much from those which younger people pursue, many physical changes are, of course, brought about by the aging process. The most obvious are those of appearance—hair thinning and turning gray, skin wrinkling and folding, and sometimes a slight loss of height as the thickness of the disks between vertebrae in the spine decreases—but subtler changes also occur in the body's biological functioning. For example, sensory capabilities decrease as a result of aging: Vision, hearing, smell, and taste become less sensitive. Reaction time slows, and physical stamina changes (DiGiovanna, 1994; Whalley, 2003).

What are the reasons for these physical declines? **Genetic preprogramming theories of aging** suggest that human cells have a built-in time limit to their reproduction. These theories suggest that after a certain time cells stop dividing or become harmful to the body—as if a kind of automatic self-destruct button had been pushed. In contrast, **wear-and-tear theories of aging** suggest that the mechanical functions of the body simply stop working efficiently as people age. Waste by-products of energy production eventually accumulate, and mistakes are made when cells divide. Eventually the body, in effect, wears out, just as an old automobile does (Hayflick, 1994; Ly et al., 2000).

Evidence supports both the genetic preprogramming and the wear-and-tear views, and it may be that both processes contribute to natural aging. It is clear, however, that physical aging is not a disease, but a natural biological process. Many physical functions do not decline with age. For example, sex remains pleasurable well into old age (although the frequency of sexual activity decreases), and some people report that the pleasure they derive from sex increases during late adulthood (Olshansky, Carnes, & Cassel, 1990; Gelfand, 2000).

Genetic preprogramming theories of aging: Theories that suggest that human cells have a built-in time limit to their reproduction, and that after a certain time they are no longer able to divide.

Wear-and-tear theories of aging: Theories that suggest that the mechanical functions of the body simply stop working efficiently.

Cognitive Changes: Thinking About—and During—Late Adulthood

At one time, many gerontologists would have agreed with the popular view that older adults are forgetful and confused. Today, however, most research indicates that this is far from an accurate assessment of older people's capabilities.

One reason for the change in view is that more sophisticated research techniques exist for studying the cognitive changes that occur in late adulthood. For example, if we were to give a group of older adults an IQ test, we might find that the average score was lower than the score achieved by a group of younger people. We might

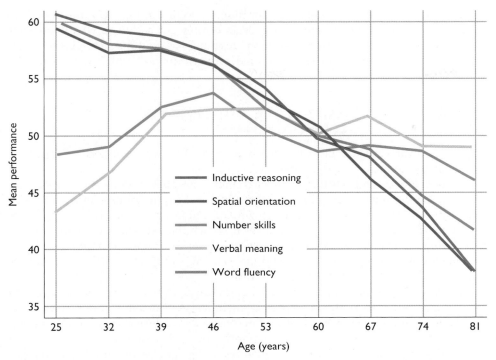

Inductive reasoning

Spatial orientation

Number skills

Verbal meaning

Word fluency

FIGURE 3 Age-related changes in intellectual skills vary according to the specific cognitive ability in question. (Source: Schaie, 1994.)

conclude that this signifies a decline in intelligence. Yet if we looked a little more closely at the specific test, we might find that that conclusion was unwarranted. For instance, many IQ tests include portions based on physical performance (such as arranging a group of blocks) or on speed. In such cases, poorer performance on the IQ test may be due to gradual decreases in reaction time—a physical decline that accompanies late adulthood and has little or nothing to do with the intellectual capabilities of older adults (Schaie, 1991).

Other difficulties hamper research into cognitive functioning during late adulthood. For example, older people are often less healthy than younger ones; when only *healthy* older adults are compared to healthy younger adults, intellectual differences are far less evident. Furthermore, the average number of years in school is often lower in older adults (for historical reasons) than in younger ones, and older adults may be less motivated to perform well on intelligence tests than younger people. Finally, traditional IQ tests may be inappropriate measures of intelligence in late adulthood. Older adults sometimes perform better on tests of practical intelligence than do younger individuals (Cornelius & Caspi, 1987; Kausler, 1994; Willis & Schaie, 1994; Dixon & Cohen, 2003).

Still, some declines in intellectual functioning during late adulthood do occur, although the pattern of age differences is not uniform for different types of cognitive abilities (see Figure 3). In general, skills relating to *fluid intelligence* (which involves reasoning, memory, and information processing) show declines in late adulthood. In contrast, skills relating to *crystallized intelligence* (intelligence based on information, skills, and problem-solving strategies) remain steady and in some cases actually improve (Schaie, 1994; Salthouse, 1996; Stankov, 2003).

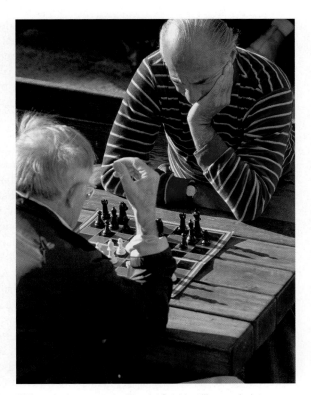

Although there are declines in fluid intelligence in late adulthood, skills relating to crystallized intelligence remain steady and may actually improve.

Even when changes in intellectual functioning occur during late adulthood, people often are able to compensate for any decline. They can still learn what they want to; it may just take more time. Furthermore, teaching older adults strategies for dealing with new problems can prevent declines in performance (Willis & Nesselroade, 1990; Coffey et al., 1999).

MEMORY CHANGES IN LATE ADULTHOOD: ARE OLDER ADULTS FORGETFUL?

One of the characteristics most frequently attributed to late adulthood is forgetfulness. How accurate is this assumption?

Most evidence suggests that memory change is *not* an inevitable part of the aging process. For instance, research shows that older people in cultures in which older adults are held in high esteem, such as mainland China, are less likely to show memory losses than are those living in cultures in which the expectation is that memory will decline. Similarly, when older people in Western societies are reminded of the advantages of age (for example, "age brings wisdom"), they tend to do better on tests of memory (Levy & Langer, 1994; Levy, 1996).

Even when people show memory declines during late adulthood, their deficits tend to be limited to particular types of memory. For instance, losses tend to be limited to episodic memories, which relate to specific experiences in people's lives. Other types of memories, such as semantic memories (which refer to general knowledge and facts) and implicit memories (memories of which we are not consciously aware), are largely unaffected by age (Graf, 1990; Russo & Parkin, 1993).

Declines in episodic memories can often be traced to changes in the lives of older adults. For instance, it is not surprising that a retired person, who may no longer face the same kind of consistent intellectual challenges encountered on the job, may be less practiced in using memory or even be less motivated to remember things, leading to an apparent decline in memory. Even in cases in which long-term memory declines, older adults can usually profit from compensatory efforts. Training older adults to use the mnemonic strategies developed by psychologists studying memory not only may prevent their long-term memory from deteriorating, but may actually improve it (Verhaeghen, Marcoen, & Goossens, 1992; West, 1995).

In the past, older adults with severe cases of memory decline, accompanied by other cognitive difficulties, were said to suffer from senility. *Senility* is a broad, imprecise term typically applied to older adults who experience progressive deterioration of mental abilities, including memory loss, disorientation to time and place, and general confusion. Once thought to be an inevitable state that accompanies aging, senility is now viewed by most gerontologists as a label that has outlived its usefulness. Rather than senility being the cause of certain symptoms, the symptoms are deemed to be caused by some other factor.

Alzheimer's disease: A progressive brain disorder that leads to a gradual and irreversible decline in cognitive abilities.

Some cases of memory loss, however, are produced by actual disease. For instance, **Alzheimer's disease** is a progressive brain disorder that leads to a gradual and irreversible decline in cognitive abilities. Nineteen percent of people age 75 to 84 have Alzheimer's, and almost 50 percent of people over age 85 are affected by the disease. Unless a cure is found, some 14 million people will experience Alzheimer's by 2050—more than three times the current number (Cowley, 2000b; Feinberg, 2002).

In other cases, cognitive declines may be caused by temporary anxiety and depression, which can be treated successfully, or may even be due to overmedication. The danger is that people with such symptoms may be labeled senile and left

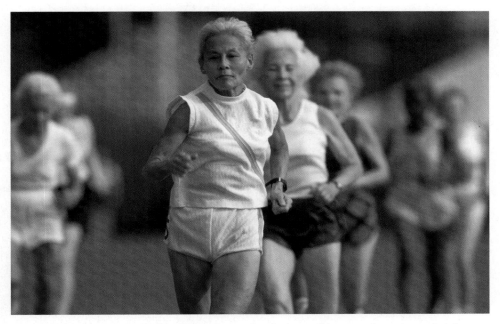

People in late adulthood usually see themselves as functioning, well-integrated members of society, and many maintain activities in which they participated earlier in life.

untreated, thereby continuing their decline—even though treatment would have been beneficial (Selkoe, 1997).

In sum, declines in cognitive functioning in late adulthood are, for the most part, not inevitable. The key to maintaining cognitive skills may lie in intellectual stimulation. Like the rest of us, older adults need a stimulating environment in order to hone and maintain their skills (Bosma et al., 2002; Bosma, van Boxtel, Ponds, Houx, & Jolles, 2003).

The Social World of Late Adulthood: Old but Not Alone

Just as the view that old age predictably means mental decline has proved to be wrong, so has the view that late adulthood inevitably brings loneliness. People in late adulthood most often see themselves as functioning members of society, with only a small number of them reporting that loneliness is a serious problem (Binstock & George, 1996).

There is no single way to age successfully. According to the **disengagement theory of aging,** aging produces a gradual withdrawal from the world on physical, psychological, and social levels (Cummings & Henry, 1961). However, such disengagement serves an important purpose, providing an opportunity for increased reflectiveness and decreased emotional investment in others at a time of life when social relationships will inevitably be ended by death.

The **activity theory of aging** presents an alternative view of aging, holding that the people who age most successfully are those who maintain the interests, activities, and level of social interaction they experienced during middle adulthood (Blau, 1973). According to activity theory, late adulthood should reflect a continuation, as

Disengagement theory of aging: A theory that suggests that aging produces a gradual withdrawal from the world on physical, psychological, and social levels.

Activity theory of aging: A theory that suggests that the elderly who are most successful while aging are those who maintain the interests and activities they had during middle age.

much as possible, of the activities in which people participated during the earlier part of their lives.

Both disengagement and activity can lead to successful aging. Not all people in late adulthood need a life filled with activities and social interaction to be happy; as in every stage of life, some older adults are just as satisfied leading a relatively inactive, solitary existence. What may be more important is how people view the aging process: Evidence shows that positive self-perceptions of aging are associated with increased longevity (Charles, Reynolds, & Gatz, 2001; Levy et al., 2002).

Life review: The process by which people examine and evaluate their lives.

Regardless of whether people become disengaged or maintain their activities from earlier stages of life, most engage in a process of **life review,** in which they examine and evaluate their lives. Remembering and reconsidering what has occurred in the past, people in late adulthood often come to a better understanding of themselves, sometimes resolving lingering problems and conflicts, and facing their lives with greater wisdom and serenity.

Clearly, people in late adulthood are not just marking time until death. Rather, old age is a time of continued growth and development, as important as any other period of life.

BECOMING AN INFORMED CONSUMER of Psychology

Adjusting to Death

At some time in our lives, we all face death—certainly our own, as well as the deaths of friends, loved ones, and even strangers. Although there is nothing more inevitable in life, death remains a frightening, emotion-laden topic. Certainly, little is more stressful than the death of a loved one or the contemplation of our own imminent death, and preparing for death is one of our most crucial developmental tasks (Aiken, 2000).

A generation ago, talk of death was taboo. The topic was never mentioned to dying people, and gerontologists had little to say about it. That changed, however, with the pioneering work of Elisabeth Kübler-Ross (1969), who brought the subject of death into the open with her observation that those facing impending death tend to move through five broad stages:

- ▶ *Denial.* In this stage, people resist the idea that they are dying. Even if told that their chances for survival are small, they refuse to admit that they are facing death.
- ▶ *Anger.* After moving beyond the denial stage, dying people become angry—angry at people around them who are in good health, angry at medical professionals for being ineffective, angry at God.
- ▶ *Bargaining.* Anger leads to bargaining, in which the dying try to think of ways to postpone death. They may decide to dedicate their lives to religion if God saves them; they may say, "If only I can live to see my son married, I will accept death then."
- ▶ *Depression.* When dying people come to feel that bargaining is of no use, they move to the next stage: depression. They realize that their lives really are coming to an end, leading to what Kübler-Ross calls "preparatory grief" for their own deaths.
- ▶ *Acceptance.* In this stage, people accept impending death. Usually they are unemotional and uncommunicative; it is as if they have made peace with themselves and are expecting death with no bitterness.

It is important to keep in mind that not everyone experiences each of these stages in the same way. In fact, Kübler-Ross's stages pertain only to people who are fully aware that they are dying and have the time to evaluate their impending death. Furthermore, vast differences occur in the way individuals react to impending death. The specific cause and duration of dying, as well as the person's sex, age, and personality and the type of support received from family and friends, all have an impact on how people respond to death (Zautra, Reich, & Guarnaccia, 1990; Stroebe, Stroebe, & Hansson, 1993).

Few of us enjoy the contemplation of death. Yet awareness of its psychological aspects and consequences can make its inevitable arrival less anxiety-producing and perhaps more understandable.

RECAP/EVALUATE/RETHINK

RECAP

What are the principal kinds of physical, social, and intellectual changes that occur in early and middle adulthood, and what are their causes?

- ▶ Early adulthood marks the peak of physical health. Physical changes occur relatively gradually in men and women during adulthood (p. 449)
- ▶ One major physical change occurs at the end of middle adulthood for women: They begin menopause, after which they are no longer fertile. (p. 450)
- ▶ During middle adulthood, people typically experience a midlife transition in which the notion that life is not unending becomes more important. In some cases this may lead to a midlife crisis, although the passage into middle age is typically relatively calm. (p. 450)
- ▶ As aging continues during middle adulthood, people realize in their fifties that their lives and accomplishments are fairly well set, and they try to come to terms with them. (p. 450)
- ▶ Among the important developmental milestones during adulthood are marriage, family changes, and divorce. Another important determinant of adult development is work. (p. 451)

How does the reality of late adulthood differ from the stereotypes about that period?

- ▶ Old age may bring marked physical declines caused by genetic preprogramming or physical wear and tear. Although the activities of people in late adulthood are not all that different from those of younger people, older adults experience declines in reaction time, sensory abilities, and physical stamina. (p. 453)
- ▶ Intellectual declines are not an inevitable part of aging. Fluid intelligence does decline with age, and long-term memory abilities are sometimes impaired. In contrast, crystallized intelligence shows slight increases with age, and short-term memory remains at about the same level. (p. 455)
- ▶ Disengagement theory sees successful aging as a process of gradual withdrawal from the physical, psychological, and social worlds. In contrast, activity theory suggests that the maintenance of interests and activities from earlier years leads to successful aging. (p. 457)

How can we adjust to death?

- ▶ According to Kübler-Ross, dying people move through five stages as they face death: denial, anger, bargaining, depression, and acceptance. (p. 458)

EVALUATE

1. Rob recently turned 40 and surveyed his goals and accomplishments to date. Although he has accomplished a lot, he realized that many of his goals will not be met in his lifetime. This stage is called a _____ _____.

2. In households where both partners have similar jobs, the division of labor that generally occurs is the same as in "traditional" households where the husband works and the wife stays at home. True or false?

3. _____ _____ theories suggest that there is a maximum time span in which cells are able to reproduce. This time limit explains the eventual breakdown of the body during old age.

4. Lower IQ test scores during late adulthood do not necessarily mean a decrease in intelligence. True or false?

5. During old age, a person's _____ intelligence continues to increase, whereas _____ intelligence may decline.

6. In Kübler-Ross's _____ stage, people resist the idea of death. In the _____ stage, they attempt to make deals to avoid death, and in the _____ stage, they passively await death.

RETHINK

1. Is the possibility that life may be extended for several decades a mixed blessing? What societal consequences might an extended life span bring about?
2. Does the finding that people in late adulthood require intellectual stimulation have implications for the societies in which older people live? In what way might stereotypes about older individuals contribute to their isolation and lack of intellectual stimulation?

Answers to Evaulate Questions

1. midlife transition; 2.true; 3. genetic preprogramming; 4. true; 5. crystallized, fluid; 6. denial, bargaining, acceptance

KEY TERMS

menopause p. 450
genetic preprogramming theories of aging p. 454

wear-and-tear theories of aging p. 454
Alzheimer's disease p. 456

disengagement theory of aging p. 457

activity theory of aging p. 457
life review p. 458

Looking Back

Psychology on the Web

1. Find information on the Web about cloning. What recent advances in cloning have been made by researchers? What developments appear to be on the horizon? What ethical issues have been raised regarding the cloning of humans?

2. Find different answers to the question "Why do people die?" Search the Web for scientific, philosophical, and spiritual/religious answers. Write a summary in which you compare the different approaches to this question. Does the thinking in any one realm influence the thinking in the others? How?

3. After completing Interactivity 40–2, search the Web for the most recent statistics on adolescent suicide. How have the trends changed over the last 10 years, and what factors explain those changes?

Epilogue

We have traced major events in the development of physical, social, and cognitive growth throughout the life span. Clearly, people change throughout their lives.

As we explored each area of development, we encountered anew the nature–nurture issue, concluding in every significant instance that both nature and nurture contribute to a person's development of skills, personality, and interactions. Specifically, our genetic inheritance—nature—lays down general boundaries within which we can advance and grow, and our environment—nurture—helps determine the extent to which we take advantage of our potential.

Turn once again to the Prologue to this set of modules on Courtney Rose Jackson, who was born prematurely. Using your knowledge of development, consider the following questions.

1. Courtney Rose Jackson was born at twenty-three weeks from the time of conception. Why was the fact that she has survived (and thrived) surprising? Discuss her birth in terms of the age of viability.

2. What dangers was Courtney subject to immediately after birth because of her high degree of prematurity? What dangers would be likely to continue into her childhood?

3. How might you design a longitudinal study to examine the risks that Courtney, and other preterm infants, may face? How would you design a cross-sectional study to study the same issue?

4. What ethical considerations affect the assessment of whether the substantial costs of medical interventions for highly premature babies are justifiable? Who should pay those costs?

1 Both Nature and Nurture Influence Development

Development is determined by the complex interaction of genetics, the prenatal environment, and experiences after birth.

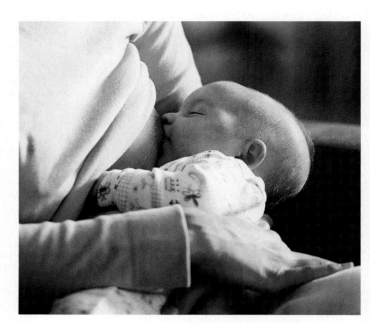

2 DNA Directs the Course of Development

At conception, each of us inherits a unique collection of 23 chromosomes. This DNA directs the general course of our physiological development. About 5% of fetuses suffer from genetic abnormalities that cause significant birth defects, such as phenylketonuria (PKU).

3 Normal Prenatal Development Depends on a Safe Environment

Poor maternal nutrition; teratogens, including alcohol and nicotine; and diseases, such as rubella and the virus that causes AIDS, can lead to birth defects.

4 Infants Have Certain Capacities at Birth

At birth, an infant is capable of a variety of reflexes that promote survival.

5 **Quality Care Facilitates Development**
Good nutrition and good medical care, especially during the first year of life, significantly enhance an infant's cognitive and physical development.

6 **Physical Contact Promotes Attachment**
Physical contact and responsive care cause a baby to develop a secure attachment to her caregivers.

7 **Personality is Present at Birth**
Research suggests that infants are born with a particular personality and temperament. In turn, temperament is reshaped by a child's experiences and environment.

8 **Parenting Style Also Affects Personality**
Within certain limits, parental style can reshape a child's personality. For example, permissive parents often produce children who are moody and dependent. Authoritarian parents produce children who are unsociable and withdrawn.

Personality

Prologue
The Dapper Don

In many ways, John Gotti appeared to be an ordinary fellow. He described himself as a salesman who sold plumbing and heating supplies to builders, and zippers to dressmakers. He lived in a modest home with a satellite dish on the roof. His friends and admirers—of whom there were many—said he was just an ordinary guy, and it wouldn't have been unusual to find him at a local bar, drinking a few beers. He hung out at the neighborhood Bergin Hunt and Fish Social Club.

There was another side to Gotti, though. He frequented expensive restaurants, wearing custom-made $1,800 suits and designer socks. His hair was always freshly barbered, and his nails were meticulously manicured. If you met him at such a nightspot, you'd probably guess he was a rich, highly successful businessman. You might approach him for a contribution to your favorite charity, and you might receive a generous donation.

But there was still another side to John Gotti. To U.S. prosecutors, he was the head of a crime family similar to that portrayed in the film *The Godfather*. They considered him a vicious, cold-hearted killer who was responsible for the deaths of scores of people. And they convinced a jury: Based on testimony from an informant, Sammy "the Bull" Gravano, Gotti was convicted for the murder of five people and was given a life sentence. He died in prison in June 2002 (Poniewozik, 2002).

Just who was John Gotti?

A warm, friendly neighbor? A wealthy businessman? A ruthless, greedy mobster, willing to do anything to keep control of his crime family?

Many people, like Gotti, have different sides to their personalities, appearing one way to some people and quite differently to others. Yet to any one group of people who were acquainted with Gotti, his behavior was probably so consistent that (they thought) they could predict how he would behave, no matter what the situation.

Psychologists who specialize in personality seek to understand the characteristic ways in which people behave. **Personality** is the pattern of enduring characteristics that differentiate

Personality: The pattern of enduring characteristics that differentiate people—the behaviors that make each individual unique.

Looking Ahead

people—the behaviors that make all of us the unique individuals we are. It is also personality that leads us to act consistently in different situations and over extended periods.

We will consider a number of approaches to personality. We begin with psychodynamic theories of personality that emphasize the importance of the unconscious. Next, we consider approaches that concentrate on identifying the most fundamental personality traits, theories that view personality as a set of learned behaviors, biological and evolutionary perspectives on personality, and approaches, known as humanistic theories, that highlight the uniquely human aspects of personality. We end our discussion by focusing on how personality is measured and how personality tests can be used.

Psychodynamic Approaches to Personality

MODULE 42

How do psychologists define and use the concept of personality?

What do the theories of Freud and his successors tell us about the structure and development of personality?

The college student was intent on making a good first impression on an attractive woman he had spotted across a crowded room at a party. As he walked toward her, he mulled over a line he had heard in an old movie the night before: "I don't believe we've been properly introduced yet." To his horror, what came out was a bit different. After threading his way through the crowded room, he finally reached the woman and blurted out, "I don't believe we've been properly seduced yet."

Although this student's error may seem to be merely an embarrassing slip of the tongue, according to some personality theorists, such a mistake is not an error at all (Motley, 1987). Instead, *psychodynamic personality theorists* might argue that the error illustrates one way in which behavior is triggered by forces within the personality of which we are not aware. These hidden drives, shaped by childhood experiences, play an important role in energizing and directing everyday behavior.

Psychodynamic approaches to personality are founded on the idea that personality is motivated by inner forces and conflicts about which people have little awareness or control. The most important pioneer of the psychodynamic approach was Sigmund Freud.

▲ ▲ ▲

Freud's Psychoanalytic Theory

Sigmund Freud, an Austrian physician, originated **psychoanalytic theory** in the early 1900s. Freud believed that conscious experience is just the tip of our psychological makeup and experience. In fact, he thought that much of our behavior is motivated by the **unconscious,** a part of the personality of which a person is not aware.

Like the unseen mass of a floating iceberg, the memories, knowledge, beliefs, and feelings in the unconscious far surpass in quantity the information about which we are aware. Freud argued that to understand personality, it is necessary to expose what is in the unconscious. But because the unconscious disguises the meaning of the material it holds, the content of the unconscious cannot be observed directly. It is therefore necessary to interpret clues to the unconscious— slips of the tongue, fantasies, and dreams—to understand the unconscious processes that direct behavior. A slip of the tongue such as the one quoted earlier (sometimes termed a *Freudian slip*) may be interpreted as revealing the speaker's unconscious sexual desires.

To Freud, much of our personality is determined by our unconscious. Some of the unconscious is made up of the *preconscious,* which contains material that is not threatening and is easily brought to mind, such as the knowledge that 2 + 2 = 4. But deeper in the unconscious are instinctual drives, the wishes, desires, demands, and needs that are hidden from conscious awareness because of the conflicts and pain they would cause if they were part of our everyday lives. The unconscious provides a "safe haven" for our recollections of threatening events.

Psychoanalytic theory: Freud's theory that unconscious forces act as determinants of personality.

Unconscious: A part of the personality of which a person is not aware and which is a potential determinant of behavior.

**PowerWeb:
Psychoanalyst:
Sigmund Freud**

www.mhhe.com/feldmanup7

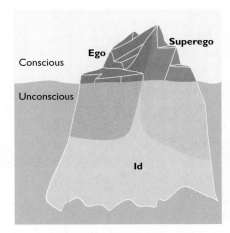

FIGURE 1 In Freud's model of personality, there are three major components: the id, the ego, and the superego. As the iceberg analogy shows, only a small portion of personality is conscious. Why do you think that only the ego and superego have conscious components?

STRUCTURING PERSONALITY: ID, EGO, AND SUPEREGO

To describe the structure of personality, Freud developed a comprehensive theory that held that personality consists of three separate but interacting components: the id, the ego, and the superego. Freud suggested that the three structures can be diagrammed to show how they are related to the conscious and the unconscious (see Figure 1).

Although it may appear that Freud is describing the three components of personality as actual physical structures in the nervous system, they are not. Instead, they represent abstract conceptions of a general *model* of personality that describes the interaction of forces that motivate behavior.

If personality consisted only of primitive, instinctual cravings and longings, it would have just one component: the id. The **id** is the raw, unorganized, inborn part of personality. From the time of birth, the id attempts to reduce tension created by primitive drives related to hunger, sex, aggression, and irrational impulses. Those drives are fueled by "psychic energy," which can be thought of as a limitless energy source constantly putting pressure on the various parts of the personality.

The id operates according to the *pleasure principle*, in which the goal is the immediate reduction of tension and the maximization of satisfaction. However, reality prevents the fulfillment of the demands of the pleasure principle in most cases: We cannot always eat when we are hungry, and we can discharge our sexual drives only when the time and place are appropriate. To account for this fact of life, Freud suggested a second component of personality, which he called the ego.

The **ego** strives to balance the desires of the id and the realities of the objective, outside world. In contrast to the pleasure-seeking nature of the id, the ego operates according to the *reality principle*, in which instinctual energy is restrained to maintain the safety of the individual and help integrate the person into society. In a sense, then, the ego is the "executive" of personality: It makes decisions, controls actions, and allows thinking and problem solving of a higher order than the id's capabilities permit.

The **superego,** the final personality structure to develop, represents the rights and wrongs of society as taught and modeled by a person's parents, teachers, and other significant individuals. The superego actually has two components, the *conscience* and the *ego-ideal*. The conscience prevents us from behaving in a morally improper way by making us feel guilty if we do wrong, whereas the ego-ideal, which represents the "perfect person" we wish we were, motivates us to do what is morally right. The superego helps us control impulses coming from the id, making our behavior less selfish and more virtuous.

The superego and id share an important feature: Both are unrealistic in that they do not consider the practical realities imposed by society. The superego, if left to operate without restraint, would create perfectionists unable to make the compromises that life requires. Similarly, an unrestrained id would create a primitive, pleasure-seeking, thoughtless individual seeking to fulfill every desire without delay. As a result, the ego must compromise between the demands of the superego and the demands of the id.

Freud suggests that the superego, the part of personality that represents the rights and wrongs of society, develops from direct teaching and from the models of parents, teachers, and other significant individuals.

Id: The raw, unorganized, inborn part of personality whose sole purpose is to reduce tension created by primitive drives related to hunger, sex, aggression, and irrational impulses.

Ego: The part of the personality that provides a buffer between the id and the outside world.

DEVELOPING PERSONALITY: A STAGE APPROACH

Freud also provided us with a view of how personality develops in childhood through a series of stages. The sequence he proposed is noteworthy because it explains how experiences and difficulties during a particular childhood stage may predict specific characteristics in the adult personality. The theory is also unique in

Stage	Age	Major Characteristics
Oral	Birth to 12–18 months	Interest in oral gratification from sucking, eating, mouthing, biting
Anal	12–18 months to 3 years	Gratification from expelling and withholding feces; coming to terms with society's controls relating to toilet training
Phallic	3 to 5–6 years	Interest in the genitals; coming to terms with Oedipal conflict, leading to identification with same-sex parent
Latency	5–6 years to adolescence	Sexual concerns largely unimportant
Genital	Adolescence to adulthood	Reemergence of sexual interests and establishment of mature sexual relationships

FIGURE 2 Freud's theory of personality development suggests that there are several distinct stages.

focusing each stage on a major biological function, which Freud assumed to be the focus of pleasure in a given period.

In the first stage of development, called the **oral stage,** the baby's mouth is the focal point of pleasure (see Figure 2 for a summary of the stages). During the first 12 to 18 months of life, children suck, mouth, and bite anything that will fit into their mouths. To Freud, this behavior suggested that the mouth is the primary site of a kind of sexual pleasure, and that weaning (withdrawing the breast or bottle) represents the main conflict during the oral stage. If infants are either overly indulged (perhaps by being fed every time they cry) or frustrated in their search for oral gratification, they may become fixated at this stage. **Fixation** refers to conflicts or concerns that persist beyond the developmental period in which they first occur. Such conflicts may be due to having needs ignored or (conversely) being overly indulged during the earlier period. For example, fixation might occur if an infant's oral needs were constantly gratified immediately at the first sign of hunger, rather than the infant learning that feeding takes place on a schedule because eating whenever an infant wants to eat is not always realistic. Fixation at the oral stage might produce an adult who was unusually interested in oral activities—eating, talking, smoking—or who showed symbolic sorts of oral interests: being either "bitingly" sarcastic or very gullible ("swallowing" anything).

From around age 12 to 18 months until 3 years of age—a period when the emphasis in Western cultures is on toilet training—a child enters the **anal stage.** At this point, the major source of pleasure changes from the mouth to the anal region, and children obtain considerable pleasure from both retention and expulsion of feces. If toilet training is particularly demanding, the result may be fixation. If fixation occurs during the anal stage, Freud suggested that adults may show unusual rigidity, orderliness, punctuality—or extreme disorderliness or sloppiness.

At about age 3, the **phallic stage** begins, at which point there is another major shift in the primary source of pleasure for the child. This time, interest focuses on the genitals and the pleasures derived from fondling them. This is also the stage of one of the most important points of personality development, according to Freudian theory: the **Oedipal conflict.** As children focus their attention on their genitals, the differences between male and female anatomy become more salient. Furthermore, at this time, according to Freud, the male unconsciously begins to develop a sexual interest in his mother, starts to see his father as a rival, and harbors a wish to kill his father—as Oedipus did in the ancient Greek tragedy. But because he views his father as too powerful, he develops a fear that his father may retaliate drastically by removing the source of the threat: the son's penis. The fear of losing one's penis leads to *castration anxiety,* which ultimately becomes so powerful that the child represses his

Superego: According to Freud, the final personality structure to develop; it represents the rights and wrongs of society as handed down by a person's parents, teachers, and other important figures.

Oral stage: According to Freud, a stage from birth to age 12 to 18 months, in which an infant's center of pleasure is the mouth.

Fixations: Conflicts or concerns that persist beyond the developmental period in which they first occur.

Anal stage: According to Freud, a stage from age 12 to 18 months to 3 years of age, in which a child's pleasure is centered on the anus.

Phallic stage: According to Freud, a period beginning around age 3 during which a child's pleasure focuses on the genitals.

Oedipal conflict: A child's sexual interest in his or her opposite-sex parent, typically resolved through identification with the same-sex parent.

Imitating a person's behavior and adopting similar beliefs and values is part of Freud's concept of identification. How can this concept be applied to the definition of gender roles? Is identification similar in all cultures?

According to Freud, a child goes through the anal stage from age 12 to 18 months until 3 years of age. Toilet training is a crucial event at this stage, one that psychoanalytic theory claims directly influences the formation for an individual's personality.

Identification: The process of wanting to be like another person as much as possible, imitating that person's behavior and adopting similar beliefs and values.

Latency period: According to Freud, the period between the phallic stage and puberty during which children's sexual concerns are temporarily put aside.

Genital stage: According to Freud, the period from puberty until death, marked by mature sexual behavior (i.e., sexual intercourse).

Defense mechanisms: Unconscious strategies that people use to reduce anxiety by concealing the source of the anxiety from themselves and others.

desires for his mother and identifies with his father. **Identification** is the process of wanting to be like another person as much as possible, imitating that person's behavior and adopting similar beliefs and values. By identifying with his father, a son seeks to obtain a woman like his unattainable mother.

For girls, the process is different. Freud reasoned that girls begin to experience sexual arousal toward their fathers and—in a suggestion that was later to bring serious accusations that he viewed women as inferior to men—begin to experience *penis envy.* They wish they had the anatomical part that, at least to Freud, seemed most clearly "missing" in girls. Blaming their mothers for their lack of a penis, girls come to believe that their mothers are responsible for their "castration." As with males, though, they find that to resolve such unacceptable feelings, they must identify with the same-sex parent by behaving like her and adopting her attitudes and values. In this way, a girl's identification with her mother is completed.

At this point, the Oedipal conflict is said to be resolved, and Freudian theory assumes that both males and females move on to the next stage of development. If difficulties arise during this period, however, all sorts of problems are thought to occur, which include improper sex-role behavior and the failure to develop a conscience.

After the resolution of the Oedipal conflict, typically at around age 5 or 6, children move into the **latency period,** which lasts until puberty. During this period, sexual interests become dormant, even in the unconscious. Then, during adolescence, sexual feelings re-emerge, marking the start of the final period, the **genital stage,** which extends until death. The focus during the genital stage is on mature, adult sexuality, which Freud defined as sexual intercourse.

DEFENSE MECHANISMS

Freud's efforts to describe and theorize about the underlying dynamics of personality and its development were motivated by very practical problems that his patients faced in dealing with *anxiety,* an intense, negative emotional experience. According to Freud, anxiety is a danger signal to the ego. Although anxiety may arise from realistic fears—such as seeing a poisonous snake about to strike—it may also occur in the form of *neurotic anxiety,* in which irrational impulses emanating from the id threaten to burst through and become uncontrollable.

Because anxiety, obviously, is unpleasant, Freud believed that people develop a range of defense mechanisms to deal with it. **Defense mechanisms** are unconscious strategies that people use to reduce anxiety by concealing the source from themselves and others.

FIGURE 3 According to Freud, people are able to use a wide range of defense mechanisms to cope with anxieties.

Freud's Defense Mechanisms		
Defense Mechanism	**Explanation**	**Example**
Repression	Unacceptable or unpleasant impulses are pushed back into the unconscious	A woman is unable to recall that she was raped.
Regression	People behave as if they were at an earlier stage of development	A boss has a temper tantrum when an employee makes a mistake.
Displacement	The expression of an unwanted feeling or thought is redirected from a more threatening, powerful person to a weaker one.	A brother yells at his younger sister after a teacher gives him a bad grade.
Rationalization	People provide self-justifying explanations in place of the actual, but threatening, reason for their behavior.	A student who goes out drinking the night before a big test rationalizes his behavior by saying the test isn't all that important.
Denial	People refuse to accept or acknowledge an anxiety-producing piece of information.	A student refuses to believe that he has flunked a course.
Projection	People attribute unwanted impulses and feelings to someone else.	A man who is angry at his father acts lovingly to his father but complains that his father is angry with him.
Sublimation	People divert unwanted impulses into socially approved thoughts, feelings, or behaviors.	A person with strong feelings of aggression becomes a soldier.
Reaction formation	Unconscious impulses are expressed as their opposite in consciousness.	A mother who unconsciously resents her child acts in an overly loving way toward the child.

The primary defense mechanism is *repression,* in which unacceptable or unpleasant id impulses are pushed back into the unconscious. Repression is the most direct method of dealing with anxiety; instead of handling an anxiety-producing impulse on a conscious level, one simply ignores it. For example, a college student who feels hatred for her mother may repress those personally and socially unacceptable feelings. The feelings remain lodged within the unconscious, because acknowledging them would provoke anxiety. Similarly, memories of childhood abuse may be repressed. Although such memories may not be consciously recalled, they can affect later behavior, and they may be revealed through dreams or slips of the tongue or symbolically in some other fashion.

If repression is ineffective in keeping anxiety at bay, other defense mechanisms may be used. Freud, and later his daughter Anna Freud (who became a well-known psychoanalyst), formulated an extensive list of potential defense mechanisms. The major defense mechanisms are summarized in Figure 3 (Conte & Plutchik, 1995; Basch, 1996; Cramer, 2000). To clearly understand these defense mechanisms, complete **Interactivity 42–1.**

All of us employ defense mechanisms to some degree, according to Freudian theory, and they can serve a useful purpose by protecting us from unpleasant information. Yet some people fall prey to them to such an extent that a large amount of psychic energy must constantly be directed toward hiding and rechanneling unacceptable impulses. When this occurs, everyday living becomes difficult. In such cases, the result is a mental disorder produced by anxiety—what Freud called "neurosis" (a term rarely used by psychologists today, although it endures in everyday conversation).

INTERACTIVITY 42–1

Defense mechanisms

EVALUATING FREUD'S LEGACY

Freud's theory has had a significant impact on the field of psychology—and even more broadly on Western philosophy and literature. The ideas of the unconscious, defense mechanisms, and childhood roots of adult psychological difficulties have become accepted by many. Furthermore, Freud's emphasis on the unconscious has been partially supported by current research on dreams and implicit memory, and neuroscientists have found evidence suggesting that the brain's limbic system may be the source of unconscious motivations. Finally, Freud generated an important method—psychoanalysis—to treat psychological disturbances (Westen & Gabbard, 1999; Guterl, 2002; Messer & McWilliams, 2003).

However, personality psychologists have leveled significant criticisms against the theory. Among the most important is the lack of compelling scientific data to support the theory. Although individual case studies *seem* supportive, we lack conclusive evidence showing that the personality is structured and operates along the lines Freud laid out. This is due, in part, to the fact that Freud's conception of personality is built on unobservable abstract concepts. Moreover, it is not clear that the stages of personality that Freud laid out provide an accurate description of personality development. We also know now that important changes in personality can occur in adolescence and adulthood—something that Freud did not believe happened, thinking that personality largely is set by adolescence.

The vague nature of Freud's theory also makes it difficult to predict how certain developmental difficulties will be displayed in an adult. For instance, if a person is fixated at the anal stage, he or she may, according to Freud, be unusually messy— or may be unusually neat. Freud's theory offers no way to predict in what way the difficulty will be exhibited (Macmillan, 1991; Crews, 1996). Furthermore, Freud can be faulted for seeming to view women as inferior to men, because he argues that women have weaker superegos than men do and in some ways unconsciously yearn to be men (the concept of penis envy).

Finally, Freud made his observations—admittedly insightful ones—and derived his theory from a limited population. His theory was based almost entirely on upper-class Austrian women living in the strict, puritanical era of the early 1900s who had come to him seeking treatment for psychological and physical problems. How far one can generalize beyond this population is a matter of considerable debate. For instance, in some Pacific Island societies, the role of disciplinarian is played by the mother's oldest brother, not the father. In such a culture, it is unreasonable to argue that the Oedipal conflict will progress in the same way that it did in Austrian society, where the father typically was the major disciplinarian. In short, a cross-cultural perspective raises questions about the universality of Freud's view of personality development (Doi, 1990; Brislin, 1993; Altman, 1996).

The Neo-Freudian Psychoanalysts

One important outgrowth of Freud's theorizing was the work done by a series of successors who were trained in traditional Freudian theory but later rejected some of its major points. These theorists are known as **neo-Freudian psychoanalysts.**

The neo-Freudians placed greater emphasis than Freud had on the functions of the ego, suggesting that it has more control than does the id over day-to-day activities, and less emphasis on sex as a driving force in people's lives. They also paid greater attention to social factors and the effects of society and culture on personality development.

JUNG'S COLLECTIVE UNCONSCIOUS

One of the most influential neo-Freudians, Carl Jung (pronounced "yoong"), rejected the notion of the primary importance of unconscious sexual urges. Instead he looked at the primitive urges of the unconscious more positively, suggesting that people have a **collective unconscious,** a common set of ideas, feelings, images, and symbols that we inherit from our relatives, the whole human race, and even nonhuman animal ancestors from the distant past. This collective unconscious is shared by everyone and is displayed by behavior that is common across diverse cultures—such as love of mother, belief in a supreme being, and even behavior as specific as fear of snakes (Oehman & Mineka, 2003).

Neo-Freudian psychoanalysts: Psychoanalysts who were trained in traditional Freudian theory but later rejected some of its major points.

Collective unconscious: A common set of ideas, feelings, images, and symbols that we inherit from our ancestors, the whole human race, and even animal ancestors from the distant past.

Jung went on to propose that the collective unconscious contains *archetypes*, universal symbolic representations of a particular person, object, or experience (Jung, 1961). For instance, a mother archetype, which contains reflections of our ancestors' relationships with mother figures, is suggested by the prevalence of mothers in art, religion, literature, and mythology. (Think of the Virgin Mary, Earth Mother, wicked stepmothers in fairy tales, Mother's Day, and so forth!) Jung also suggested that men possess an unconscious feminine archetype affecting how they behave, whereas women have a male archetype that colors their behavior.

To Jung, archetypes play an important role in determining our day-to-day reactions, attitudes, and values. For example, Jung might explain the popularity of the *Star Wars* movies as being due to their use of broad archetypes of good (Luke Skywalker) and evil (Darth Vader).

ADLER AND THE OTHER NEO-FREUDIANS

Alfred Adler, another important neo-Freudian psychoanalyst, also considered Freudian theory's emphasis on sexual needs misplaced. Instead, Adler proposed that the primary human motivation is a striving for superiority, not in terms of superiority over others but as a quest to achieve self-improvement and perfection.

Adler used the term **inferiority complex** to describe situations in which adults have not been able to overcome the feelings of inferiority they developed as children, when they were small and limited in their knowledge about the world. Early social relationships with parents have an important effect on how well children are able to outgrow feelings of personal inferiority and instead orient themselves toward attaining more socially useful goals, such as improving society.

Inferiority complex: According to Adler, a situation in which adults have not been able to overcome the feelings of inferiority that they developed as children, when they were small and limited in their knowledge about the world.

Other neo-Freudians, such as Erik Erikson, Freud's daughter Anna Freud, and Karen Horney (1937), also focused less than Freud did on inborn sexual and aggressive drives and more on the social and cultural factors behind personality. Horney (pronounced "HORN-eye") was one of the first psychologists who championed women's issues. She suggested that personality develops in terms of social relationships and depends particularly on the relationship between parents and child and how well the child's needs are met. She rejected Freud's suggestion that women have penis envy, asserting that what women envy most in men is not their anatomy but the independence, success, and freedom that women often are denied (Miletic, 2002).

Horney was also one of the first to stress the importance of cultural factors in the determination of personality. For example, she suggested that society's rigid gender roles for women lead them to experience ambivalence about success, fearing that they will lose their friends. Her conceptualizations, developed in the 1930s and 1940s, laid the groundwork for many of the central ideas of feminism that were to emerge decades later.

In Jungian terms, Luke Skywalker and Darth Vader are archetypes, or universally recognizable symbols of good and evil.

RECAP/EVALUATE/RETHINK

RECAP

How do psychologists define and use the concept of personality?

▶ Personality is the pattern of enduring characteristics that differentiate people—the behaviors that make each person unique. (p. 466)

What do the theories of Freud and his successors tell us about the structure and development of personality?

▶ According to psychodynamic explanations for personality, much of behavior is caused by parts of personality that are found in the unconscious and of which we are unaware. (p. 467)

▶ Freud's theory suggests that personality is composed of the id, the ego, and the superego. The id is the unorganized, inborn part of personality whose purpose is to immediately reduce tensions relating to hunger, sex, aggression, and other primitive impulses. The ego restrains instinctual energy to maintain the safety of the individual and help the person be a member of society. The superego represents the rights and wrongs of society and consists of the conscience and the ego-ideal. (p. 468)

▶ Freud's psychoanalytic theory suggests that personality develops through a series of stages, each of which is associated with a primary biological function. (p. 469)

▶ Defense mechanisms, according to Freudian theory, are unconscious strategies with which people reduce anxieties relating to impulses from the id. (p. 470)

▶ Freud's psychoanalytic theory has provoked a number of criticisms, including a lack of supportive scientific data, the theory's inadequacy in making predictions, and its reliance on a highly restricted population. (p. 471)

▶ Neo-Freudian psychoanalytic theorists built on Freud's work, although they placed greater emphasis on the role of the ego and paid more attention to the role of social factors in determining behavior. (p. 472)

EVALUATE

1. _____ approaches state that behavior is motivated primarily by unconscious forces.
2. Match each section of the personality (according to Freud) with its description:
   1. Ego
   2. Id
   3. Superego
   a. Determines right from wrong on the basis of cultural standards.
   b. Operates according to the "reality principle"; energy is redirected to integrate the person into society.
   c. Seeks to reduce tension brought on by primitive drives.
3. Within the superego, the _____-_____ motivates us to do what is right, and the _____ restrains us from doing what is unacceptable.
4. Which of the following represents the proper order of personality development, according to Freud?
   a. Oral, phallic, latency, anal, genital
   b. Anal, oral, phallic, genital, latency
   c. Oral, anal, phallic, latency, genital
   d. Latency, phallic, anal, genital, oral
5. In the resolution of the _____ complex, Freud believed that boys learn to repress their desire for their mothers and identify with their fathers.
6. _____ _____ is the term Freud used to describe unconscious strategies used to reduce anxiety.

RETHINK

1. Can you think of ways in which Freud's theories of unconscious motivations are commonly used in popular culture? How accurately do you think such popular uses of Freudian theories reflect Freud's ideas?
2. What are some examples of archetypes in addition to those mentioned in this module? Can you think of an evolutionary purpose that archetypes serve?

Answers to Evaluate Questions

1. psychodynamic; 2. 1-b, 2-c, 3-a; 3. ego-ideal, conscience; 4. c; 5. Oedipal; 6. defense mechanisms

KEY TERMS

personality p. 466
psychoanalytic
theory p. 467
unconscious p. 467
id p. 468
ego p. 468

superego p. 469
oral stage p. 469
fixations p. 469
anal stage p. 469
phallic stage p. 469
Oedipal conflict p. 469

identification p. 470
latency period p. 470
genital stage p. 470
defense
mechanisms p. 470

neo-Freudian
psychoanalysts p. 472
collective
unconscious p. 472
inferiority complex p. 473

Other Major Approaches to Personality: In Search of Human Uniqueness

"Tell me about Nelson," said Johnetta.

"Oh, he's just terrific. He's the friendliest guy I know—goes out of his way to be nice to everyone. He hardly ever gets mad. He's just so even-tempered, no matter what's happening. And he's really smart, too. About the only thing I don't like is that he's always in such a hurry to get things done. He seems to have boundless energy, much more than I have."

"He sounds great to me, especially in comparison to Rico," replied Johnetta. "He is so self-centered and arrogant that it drives me crazy. I sometimes wonder why I ever started going out with him."

Friendly. Even-tempered. Smart. Energetic. Self-centered. Arrogant.

The interchange above is made up of a series of trait characterizations of the boyfriends being discussed. In fact, much of our own, personal understanding of the reasons behind others' behavior is based on the premise that people possess certain traits that are consistent across different situations. For example, we generally assume that if someone is outgoing and sociable in one situation, he or she is outgoing and sociable in other situations (Gilbert et al., 1992; Gilbert, Miller, & Ross, 1998).

A number of formal theories of personality employ variations of this approach. We turn now to a discussion of these and other personality approaches, each of which provides an alternative to the psychoanalytic emphasis on unconscious processes in determining behavior.

⟨▲⟩⟨▲⟩⟨▲⟩

Trait Approaches: Placing Labels on Personality

If someone asked you to characterize another person, it is probable that—like the two people in the conversation just presented—you would come up with a list of that individual's personal qualities, as you see them. But how would you know which of those qualities are most important to an understanding of that person's behavior?

Personality psychologists have asked similar questions. To answer them, they have developed a model of personality known as **trait theory. Traits** are enduring dimensions of personality characteristics along which people differ.

Trait theorists do not assume that some people have a trait and others do not; rather, they propose that all people possess certain traits, but that the degree to which a particular trait applies to a specific person varies and can be quantified. For instance, you may be relatively friendly, whereas I may be relatively unfriendly. But we both have a "friendliness" trait, although your degree of "friendliness" is higher

Trait theory: A model of personality that seeks to identify the basic traits necessary to describe personality.

Traits: Enduring dimensions of personality characteristics along which people differ.

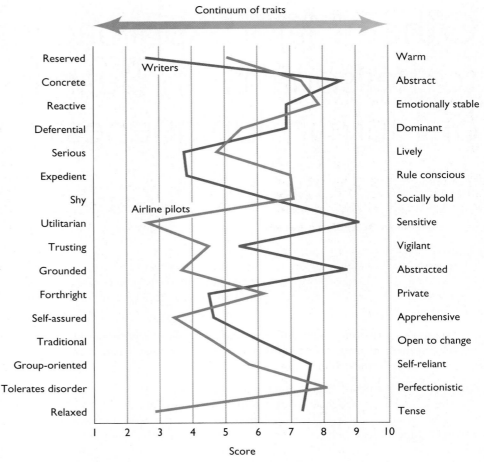

FIGURE 1 Personality profiles for source traits developed by Cattell for two groups of subjects: writers, and airline pilots. The average score for the general population is between 4.5 and 6.5 on each scale. On what traits do airline pilots and writers differ most? How do these differences contribute to their chosen work? (Source: Data derived from Cattell, Eber, and Tatsuoka: *Handbook for the 16PF*, Copyright © 1970, 1988, 1992 by the Institute for Personality and Ability Testing Inc., Champaign, Illinois, USA. All rights reserved.)

than mine. The major challenge for trait theorists taking this approach has been to identify the specific primary traits necessary to describe personality. As we shall see, different theorists have come up with surprisingly different sets of traits.

ALLPORT'S TRAIT THEORY: IDENTIFYING THE BASICS

When personality psychologist Gordon Allport systematically pored over an unabridged dictionary, he came up with some 18,000 separate terms that could be used to describe personality. Although he was able to pare down the list to a mere 4,500 descriptors after eliminating words with the same meaning, he was obviously left with a problem crucial to all trait approaches: Which of those traits were the most basic?

Allport answered this question by suggesting that there are three basic categories of traits: cardinal, central, and secondary (Allport, 1961, 1966). A *cardinal trait* is a single characteristic that directs most of a person's activities. For example, a totally selfless woman may direct all her energy toward humanitarian activities; an intensely power-hungry person may be driven by an all-consuming need for control.

Most people, however, do not develop a single, comprehensive cardinal trait. Instead, they possess a handful of central traits that make up the core of personality. *Central traits,* such as honesty and sociability, are the major characteristics of an individual; they usually number from five to ten in any one person. Finally, *secondary traits* are characteristics that affect behavior in fewer situations and are less influential than central or cardinal traits. For instance, a reluctance to eat meat and a love of modern art would be considered secondary traits (Nicholson, 2003).

CATTELL, EYSENCK, AND THE BIG FIVE: FACTORING OUT PERSONALITY

More recent attempts to identify primary traits have centered on a statistical technique known as factor analysis. *Factor analysis* is a method of summarizing the relationships among a large number of variables into fewer, more general patterns. For example, a personality researcher might administer a questionnaire to many participants, asking them to describe themselves by referring to an extensive list of traits. By statistically combining responses and computing which traits are associated with one another in the same person, a researcher can identify the most fundamental patterns or combinations of traits—called factors—that underlie participants' responses.

Using factor analysis, personality psychologist Raymond Cattell (1965) suggested that sixteen pairs of *source traits* represent the basic dimensions of personality. Using those source traits, he developed the Sixteen Personality Factor Questionnaire, or 16 PF, a measure that provides scores for each of the source traits. Figure 1 shows the pattern of average scores on each of the source traits for two different groups of participants—airplane pilots, and writers (Cattell, Cattell, & Cattell, 1993; 2000).

Another trait theorist, psychologist Hans Eysenck (1995, 1994b; Eysenck et al., 1992), also used factor analysis to identify patterns of traits, but he came to a very different conclusion about the nature of personality. He found that personality could best be described in terms of just three major dimensions: *extraversion, neuroticism,* and *psychoticism.* The extraversion dimension relates to the degree of sociability, whereas the neurotic dimension encompasses emotional stability. Finally, psychoticism refers to the degree to which reality is distorted. By evaluating people along these three dimensions, Eysenck was able to predict behavior accurately in a variety of types of situations. Figure 2 illustrates specific traits associated with each of the dimensions.

The most influential trait approach today contends that five broad trait factors—called the "Big Five"—lie at the core of personality. The five factors, described in Figure 3, are *openness to experience, conscientiousness, extraversion, agreeableness,* and *neuroticism* (emotional stability).

The Big Five emerge quite consistently in different populations of individuals, including children, college students, older adults, and speakers of different languages. Furthermore, cross-cultural research conducted in countries as diverse as Canada, Finland, Poland, and the Philippines also has been supportive. In short, although the evidence is not conclusive, a growing consensus exists that the "Big Five" represent the best description of personality. Still, the debate over the specific number and kinds of traits that are fundamental to personality remains a lively one (Katigbak et al., 2002; Roccas et al., 2002; Paunonen, 2003).

EVALUATING TRAIT APPROACHES TO PERSONALITY

Trait approaches have several virtues. They provide a clear, straightforward explanation of people's behavioral consistencies. Furthermore, traits allow us to readily compare one person with another. Because of these advantages, trait approaches to personality have had an important influence on the development of several useful

Extraversion
- Sociable
- Lively
- Active
- Assertive
- Sensation-seeking

Neuroticism
- Anxious
- Depressed
- Guilt feelings
- Low self-esteem
- Tense

Psychoticism
- Aggressive
- Cold
- Egocentric
- Impersonal
- Impulsive

FIGURE 2 According to Eysenck, personality could best be described in terms of just three major dimensions: extraversion, neuroticism, and psychoticism. Eysenck was able to predict behavior accurately in a variety of types of situations by evaluating people along these three dimensions (Eysenck, 1990). How do you think an airline pilot would score on Eysenck's scale?

Agreeableness is one of the "Big Five" broad trait factors that are the core of personality.

FIGURE 3 Five broad trait factors, referred to as the "Big Five," are considered to be the core of personality. You can memorize these traits by using the mnemonic *OCEAN*, representing the first letter of each trait. (Source: Adapted from Pervin, 1990, Chapter 3, and McCrae & Costa, 1986, p. 1002.)

The Big Five Personality Factors and Dimensions of Sample Traits
Openness to experience
Independent—Conforming
Imaginative—Practical
Preference for variety—Preference for routine
Conscientiousness
Careful—Careless
Disciplined—Impulsive
Organized—Disorganized
Extraversion
Talkative—Quiet
Fun-loving—Sober
Sociable—Retiring
Agreeableness
Sympathetic—Fault-finding
Kind—Cold
Appreciative—Unfriendly
Neuroticism (Emotional Stability)
Stable—Tense
Calm—Anxious
Secure—Insecure

personality measures (Funder, 1991; Wiggins, 1997). Furthermore, they have been helpful in identifying people who have particular traits for specialized jobs, as we discuss in the *Applying Psychology in the 21st Century box.*

However, trait approaches also have some drawbacks. For example, we have seen that various trait theories describing personality come to very different conclusions about which traits are the most fundamental and descriptive. The difficulty in determining which of the theories is the most accurate has led some personality psychologists to question the validity of trait conceptions of personality in general.

Actually, there is an even more fundamental difficulty with trait approaches. Even if we are able to identify a set of primary traits, we are left with little more than a label or description of personality—rather than an explanation of behavior. If we say that someone donates money to charity because he or she has the trait of generosity, we still do not know *why* that person became generous in the first place, or the reasons for displaying generosity in a specific situation. In the view of some critics, then, traits do not provide explanations for behavior; they merely describe it.

Learning Approaches: We Are What We've Learned

The psychodynamic and trait approaches we've discussed concentrate on the "inner" person—the stormy fury of an unobservable but powerful id or a hypothetical but critical set of traits. In contrast, learning approaches to personality focus on the "outer" person. To a strict learning theorist, personality is simply the sum of learned responses to the external environment. Internal events such as thoughts, feelings, and motivations

The A-Team: What Personality Does it Take to Travel into Space?

There are two kinds of people, the ones who say, "Sign me up tomorrow" and the ones who say, "Never in a million years."—Dr. Rhea Seddon, one of the first women in NASA's astronaut program (Goode, 2003a, p. F1).

Although countless children dream of becoming astronauts when they grow up, only a handful of people actually realize this aspiration. Most of those who initially aim to become astronauts end up reluctant to accept the necessary risks of the profession, and many of those who apply to the astronaut program do not make it through the intensive screening process.

A central focus of the astronaut screening process involves a search for people with a particular personality type. In general, astronauts must be willing to take calculated risks, be able to keep their anxieties under control, and maintain a positive, optimistic outlook.

In addition, to successfully pass through the screening process, a potential astronaut must be free from psychological problems. However, the ideal astronaut demonstrates a number of positive personality traits too. For example, astronauts need to work well with team members, including the other astronauts as well as the crew members on the ground. Also, astronauts must have put in the work required to have been an excellent student, as research indicates that a high grade point average in college and graduate school is one of the best predictors of success as an astronaut (Fogg & Rose, 1999; Kanas et al., 2002).

As astronauts are spending more and more time with space travelers from a variety of nations, they also must be able to work side by side with people from cultures different from their own. Astronauts must be good communicators and be open to using whatever language is being spoken on a particular mission. Moreover, they must be accepting of other crew members' cultural differences with respect to everything from culturally influenced management styles to religious beliefs (Kring, 2001).

Regardless of how many positive personality traits they have, astronauts still experience considerable stress from the dangerous conditions in which they work. Consequently, NASA researchers are energetically engaged in developing support services to maintain astronauts' social and psychological well-being (Kanas et al., 2002).

RETHINK

Are there additional traits that you think would be important in the ideal astronaut? Who among your acquaintances has the ideal astronaut's personality?

---

are ignored. Although the existence of personality is not denied, learning theorists say that it is best understood by looking at features of a person's environment.

According to the most influential of the learning theorists, B. F. Skinner (who carried out pioneering work on operant conditioning), personality is a collection of learned behavior patterns (Skinner, 1975). Similarities in responses across different situations are caused by similar patterns of reinforcement that have been received in such situations in the past. If I am sociable both at parties and at meetings, it is because I have been reinforced for displaying social behaviors—not because I am fulfilling an unconscious wish based on experiences during my childhood or because I have an internal trait of sociability.

Strict learning theorists such as Skinner are less interested in the consistencies in behavior across situations, however, than in ways of modifying behavior. Their view is that humans are infinitely changeable through the process of learning new behavior patterns. If one is able to control and modify the patterns of reinforcers in a situation, behavior that other theorists would view as stable and unyielding can be changed and ultimately improved. Learning theorists are optimistic in their attitudes about the potential for resolving personal and societal problems through treatment strategies based on learning theory.

SOCIAL COGNITIVE APPROACHES TO PERSONALITY

Not all learning theories of personality take such a strict view in rejecting the importance of what is "inside" a person by focusing solely on the "outside." Unlike other learning approaches to personality, **social cognitive approaches** emphasize the influence of a person's cognitions—thoughts, feelings, expectations, and values—in determining personality. According to Albert Bandura, one of the main proponents of this point of view, people are able to foresee the possible outcomes of certain behaviors

Social cognitive approaches to personality: Theories that emphasize the influence of a person's cognitions—thoughts—feelings, expectations, and values-in determining personality.

479

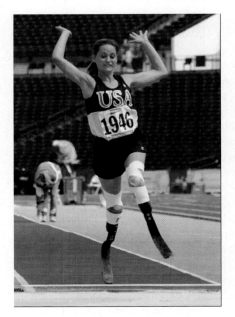

Self-efficacy, the belief in one's own capabilities, leads to higher aspirations and greater persistence.

PowerWeb: Self-Efficacy: Toward a Unifying Theory of Behavioral Change

www.mhhe.com/feldmanup7

in a particular setting without actually having to carry them out. This takes place mainly through the mechanism of *observational learning*—viewing the actions of others and observing the consequences (Bandura, 1986, 1999).

For instance, children who view a model behaving in, say, an aggressive manner tend to copy the behavior if the consequences of the model's behavior are seen to be positive. If, in contrast, the model's aggressive behavior has resulted in no consequences or negative consequences, children are considerably less likely to act aggressively. According to social cognitive approaches, personality thus develops through repeated observation of the behavior of others.

Bandura places particular emphasis on the role played by *self-efficacy,* belief in one's personal capabilities. Self-efficacy underlies people's faith in their ability to carry out a particular behavior or produce a desired outcome. People with high self-efficacy have higher aspirations and greater persistence in working to attain goals and ultimately achieve greater success than do those with lower self-efficacy (Bandura, 1997, 1999; Pajares, 2003).

How do we develop self-efficacy? One way is by paying close attention to our prior successes and failures. If we try snowboarding and experience little success, we'll be less likely to try it again. However, if our initial efforts appear promising, we'll be more likely to attempt it again. Direct reinforcement and encouragement from others also play a role in developing self-efficacy (Bandura, 1988; Jenkins & Gortner, 1998).

Compared with other learning theories of personality, social cognitive approaches are distinctive in their emphasis on the reciprocity between individuals and their environment. Not only is the environment assumed to affect personality, people's behavior and personalities are assumed to "feed back" and modify the environment (Bandura, 1999, 2000).

Our behavior also reflects the view we have of ourselves and the way we value the various parts of our personalities. *Self-esteem* is the component of personality that encompasses our positive and negative self-evaluations. Although people have a general level of self-esteem, it is not unidimensional. Specifically, we may see ourselves positively in one domain but negatively in others. For example, a good student may have high self-esteem in academic domains but more negative self-esteem in athletic areas (Moretti & Higgins, 1990; Baumeister, 1998).

Self-esteem has strong cultural components. For example, having high *relationship harmony*—a sense of success in forming close bonds with other people—is more important to self-esteem in Asian cultures than it is in more individualistic Western societies (Kwan, Bond, & Singelis, 1997; Twenge & Crocker, 2002).

Although almost everyone goes through periods of low self-esteem (after, for instance, an undeniable failure), some people are chronically low in self-esteem. For them, failure seems to be an inevitable part of life. In fact, low self-esteem may lead to a cycle of failure in which past failure breeds future failure. Consider students with low self-esteem who are studying for a test. Because of their low self-esteem, they expect to do poorly on the test. In turn, this raises their anxiety level, making it increasingly difficult to study and perhaps even leading them to work less hard. Because of these attitudes, the ultimate outcome is that they do, in fact, do badly on the test. Ultimately, the failure reinforces their low self-esteem, and the cycle is perpetuated, as illustrated in Figure 4. In short, low self-esteem can lead to a cycle of failure that is self-destructive.

FIGURE 4 The cycle of low self-esteem begins with an individual's already having low self-esteem. As a consequence, the person will have low performance expectations and expect to fail a test, thereby producing anxiety and reduced effort. As a result, the person will actually fail, and failure in turn reinforces low self-esteem.

EVALUATING LEARNING APPROACHES TO PERSONALITY

Because they ignore the internal processes that are uniquely human, traditional learning theorists such as Skinner have been accused of oversimplifying personality to such an extent that the concept becomes meaningless. In the eyes of their critics, reducing behavior to a series of stimuli and responses, and excluding thoughts and feelings from the realm of personality, leaves behaviorists practicing an unrealistic and inadequate form of science.

Of course, some of these criticisms are blunted by social cognitive approaches, which explicitly consider the role of cognitive processes in personality. Still, learning approaches tend to share a highly *deterministic* view of human behavior, maintaining that behavior is shaped primarily by forces beyond the control of the individual. As in psychoanalytic theory (which suggests that personality is determined by the unconscious forces) and trait approaches (which view personality in part as an mixture of genetically determined traits), learning theory's reliance on deterministic principles deemphasizes the ability of people to pilot their own course through life.

Nonetheless, learning approaches have had a major impact in a variety of ways. For one thing, they have helped make the study of personality an objective, scientific venture by focusing on observable behavior and environment. In addition, they have produced important, successful means of treating a variety of psychological disorders. The degree of success of these treatments is a testimony to the merits of learning theory approaches to personality.

Biological and Evolutionary Approaches: Are We Born with Personality?

Do we inherit our personalities?

That's the question raised by **biological and evolutionary approaches** to personality, which suggest that important components of personality are influenced by our genetic inheritance from our ancestors. Building on the work of behavioral geneticists, researchers using biological and evolutionary approaches argue that

Biological and evolutionary approaches to personality: Theories that suggest that important components of personality are inherited.

Biological and evolutionary approaches to personality seek to explain the consistencies in personality that are found in some families.

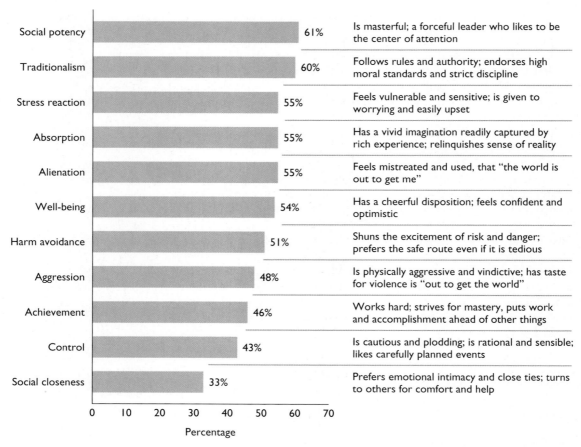

Social potency	61%	Is masterful; a forceful leader who likes to be the center of attention
Traditionalism	60%	Follows rules and authority; endorses high moral standards and strict discipline
Stress reaction	55%	Feels vulnerable and sensitive; is given to worrying and easily upset
Absorption	55%	Has a vivid imagination readily captured by rich experience; relinquishes sense of reality
Alienation	55%	Feels mistreated and used, that "the world is out to get me"
Well-being	54%	Has a cheerful disposition; feels confident and optimistic
Harm avoidance	51%	Shuns the excitement of risk and danger; prefers the safe route even if it is tedious
Aggression	48%	Is physically aggressive and vindictive; has taste for violence is "out to get the world"
Achievement	46%	Works hard; strives for mastery, puts work and accomplishment ahead of other things
Control	43%	Is cautious and plodding; is rational and sensible; likes carefully planned events
Social closeness	33%	Prefers emotional intimacy and close ties; turns to others for comfort and help

Percentage

FIGURE 5 The roots of personality. The percentages indicate the degree to which eleven personality characteristics reflect the influence of heredity. (Source: Tellegen et al., 1988.)

personality is determined at least in part by particular combinations of genes, in much the same way that our height is largely a result of genetic contributions from our ancestors. The evolutionary perspective assumes that personality traits that led to survival and reproductive success of our ancestors are more likely to be preserved and passed on to subsequent generations (Buss, 2001).

The importance of genetic factors in personality has been illustrated by studies of twins. For instance, personality psychologists Auke Tellegen and colleagues at the University of Minnesota examined the personality traits of pairs of twins who were genetically identical but were raised apart from each other (Tellegen et al., 1988). In the study, each of the twins was given a battery of personality tests, including one that measured eleven key personality traits.

The results of the personality tests indicated that in major respects the twins were quite similar in personality, despite having been raised separately from an early age. Moreover, certain traits were more influenced by heredity than were others. For example, social potency (the degree to which a person assumes mastery and leadership roles in social situations) and traditionalism (the tendency to follow authority) had particularly strong genetic components, whereas achievement and social closeness had relatively weak genetic components (see Figure 5).

Furthermore, it is increasingly clear that the roots of adult personality emerge in the earliest periods of life. Infants are born with a particular **temperament,** a basic,

Temperament: A basic, innate disposition that emerges early in life.

innate disposition. Temperament encompasses several dimensions, including general activity level and mood. For instance, some individuals are quite active, while others are relatively calm. Similarly, some are relatively easygoing, while others are irritable, easily upset, and difficult to soothe. Temperament is quite consistent, with significant stability from infancy well into adolescence (Caspi et al., 1995; Clark & Watson, 1999; Molfese & Molfese, 2000).

Some researchers believe that specific genes are related to personality. For example, people with a longer variety of a dopamine-4 receptor gene are more likely to be thrill seekers than are those without such a gene. These thrill seekers tend to be extroverted, impulsive, quick-tempered, and always on the prowl for excitement and novel situations (Hamer et al., 1993; Zuckerman & Kuhlman, 2000).

Does the identification of specific genes linked to personality, coupled with the existence of temperaments from the time of birth, mean that we are destined to have certain types of personalities? Hardly. First, it is unlikely that any single gene is linked to a specific trait. For instance, the dopamine-4 receptor accounts for only around 10 percent of the variation in novelty seeking between different individuals. The rest of the variation is accounted for by other genes and environmental factors (Angier, 1996).

More importantly, genes and the environment never work in isolation. As we see in discussions of the heritability of intelligence and the nature–nurture issue, it is impossible to completely divorce genetic factors from environmental factors. Although studies of identical twins raised in different environments are helpful, they are not definitive, because it is impossible to assess and control environmental factors fully. Furthermore, estimates of the influence of genetics are just that—estimates— and apply to groups, not individuals. Consequently, findings such as those shown in Figure 5 must be regarded as approximations.

Finally, even if more genes are found to be linked to specific personality characteristics, genes still cannot be viewed as the sole cause of personality. For one thing, genetically determined characteristics may not be expressed if they are not "turned on" by particular environmental experiences. Furthermore, the appearance of behaviors produced by genes in some ways may create a particular environment. For instance, a cheerful, smiley baby may lead her parents to smile more and be more responsive, thereby creating an environment that is supportive and pleasant. In contrast, the parents of a cranky, fussy baby may be less inclined to smile at the child; in turn, the environment in which that child is raised will be a less supportive and pleasant one. In a sense, then, genes not only influence a person's behavior—they also help produce the environment in which a person is raised (Scarr, 1992, 1993; Plomin & Caspi, 1999).

Although an increasing number of personality theorists are taking biological and evolutionary factors into account, no comprehensive, unified theory that considers biological and evolutionary factors is widely accepted. Still, it is clear that certain personality traits have substantial genetic components, and that heredity and environment interact to determine personality (Plomin & Caspi, 1999; Buss, 2000; Ebstein, Benjamin, & Belmaker, 2003).

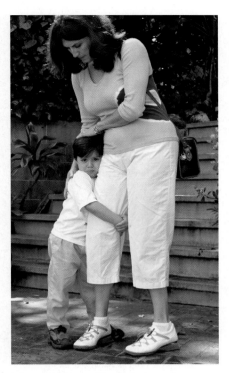

Infants are born with particular temperaments, dispositions that are consistent throughout childhood.

Humanistic Approaches: The Uniqueness of You

Where, in all these approaches to personality, is there an explanation for the saintliness of a Mother Teresa, the creativity of a Michelangelo, and the brilliance and perseverance of an Einstein? An understanding of such unique individuals—as well as more ordinary sorts of people who have some of the same attributes—comes from humanistic theory.

According to humanistic theorists, all the approaches to personality we have discussed share a fundamental misperception in their views of human nature. Instead of seeing people as controlled by unconscious, unseen forces (as do psychodynamic approaches), a set of stable traits (trait approaches), situational reinforcements and punishments (learning theory), or inherited factors (biological and evolutionary approaches), **humanistic approaches** emphasize people's basic goodness and their tendency to grow to higher levels of functioning. It is this conscious, self-motivated ability to change and improve, along with people's unique creative impulses, that make up the core of personality.

The major proponent of the humanistic point of view is Carl Rogers (1971). Rogers, along with other humanistic theorists, such as Abraham Maslow, believes that all people have a fundamental need for **self-actualization,** a state of self-fulfillment in which people realize their highest potential, each in his or her own unique way. He further suggests that people develop a need for positive regard that reflects the desire to be loved and respected. Because others provide this positive regard, we grow dependent on them. We begin to see and judge ourselves through the eyes of other people, relying on their values and preoccupied with what they think of us.

Humanistic approaches to personality: Theories that emphasize people's basic goodness and tendency to grow to higher levels of functioning.

Self-actualization: A state of self-fulfillment in which people realize their highest potential, each in his or her own unique way.

According to Rogers, one outgrowth of placing importance on the opinions of others is that a conflict may grow between people's actual experiences and their *self-concepts,* or self-impressions. If the discrepancies are minor, so are the consequences. But if the discrepancies are great, they will lead to psychological disturbances in daily functioning, such as the experience of frequent anxiety. (To better understand this, complete **Interactivity 43–1.**)

Rogers suggests that one way of overcoming the discrepancy between experience and self-concept is through the receipt of unconditional positive regard from another person—a friend, a spouse, or a therapist. **Unconditional positive regard** refers to an attitude of acceptance and respect on the part of an observer, no matter what a person says or does. This acceptance, says Rogers, gives people the opportunity to evolve and grow both cognitively and emotionally and to develop more realistic self-concepts. You may have experienced the power of unconditional positive regard when you opened up to someone, revealing embarrassing secrets because you knew the listener would still love and respect you, even after hearing the worst about you (Snyder, 2002).

"So, while extortion, racketeering, and murder may be bad acts, they don't make you a bad person."

Unconditional positive regard: An attitude of acceptance and respect on the part of an observer, no matter what a person says or does.

In contrast, when you are getting *conditional positive regard,* others' view of you is dependent on your behavior. In such cases, others withdraw their love and acceptance if you do something of which they don't approve. The result is a discrepancy between your true self and what others wish you would be, leading to anxiety and frustration (see Figure 6).

INTERACTIVITY 43–1

Your ideal self

	Others' behavior toward you	Your response
Need for positive regard	Unconditional positive regard	Self-actualization
	Conditional positive regard	Anxiety and frustration

FIGURE 6 According to the humanistic view of Carl Rogers, people have a basic need to be loved and respected. If you have unconditional positive regard from others, you will develop a more realistic self-concept, but if the response is conditional it may lead to anxiety and frustration.

EVALUATING HUMANISTIC APPROACHES

Although humanistic theories suggest the value of providing unconditional positive regard toward people, unconditional positive regard toward humanistic theories has been less forthcoming. The criticisms have centered on the difficulty of verifying the basic assumptions of the approach, as well as on the question of whether unconditional positive regard does, in fact, lead to greater personality adjustment.

Humanistic approaches have also been criticized for making the assumption that people are basically "good"—a notion that is unverifiable—and, equally important, for using nonscientific values to build supposedly scientific theories. Still, humanistic theories have been important in highlighting the uniqueness of human beings and guiding the development of a significant form of therapy designed to alleviate psychological difficulties (Cain, 2002).

Comparing Approaches to Personality

In light of the multiple approaches we have discussed, you may be wondering which of the theories provides the most accurate description of personality. That is a question that cannot be answered precisely. Each theory is built on different assumptions and focuses on somewhat different aspects of personality (see Figure 7). Given the complexity of every individual, it seems reasonable that personality can be viewed from a number of perspectives simultaneously (Pervin & John, 1999).

Theoretical Approach and Major Theorists	Conscious Versus Unconscious Determinants of Personality	Nature (Hereditary Factors) Versus Nurture (Environmental Factors)	Free Will Versus Determinism	Stability Versus Modifiability
Psychodynamic (Freud)	Emphasizes the unconscious	Stresses innate, inherited structure of personality while emphasizing importance of adulthood experience	Stresses determinism, the view that behavior is directed and caused by factors outside one's control	Emphasizes the stability of characteristics throughout a person's life
Trait (Allport, Cattell, Eysenck)	Disregards both conscious and unconscious	Approaches vary	Stresses determinism, the view that behavior is directed and caused by factors outside one's control	Emphasizes the stability of characteristics throughout a person's life
Learning (Skinner, Bandura)	Disregards both conscious and unconscious	Focuses on the environment	Stresses determinism, the view that behavior is directed and caused by factors outside one's control	Stresses that personality remains flexible and resilient throughout one's life
Biological and Evolutionary (Tellegen)	Disregards both conscious and unconscious	Stresses the innate, inherited determinants of personality	Stresses determinism, the view that behavior is directed and caused by factors outside one's control	Emphasizes the stability of characteristics throughout a person's life
Humanistic (Rogers, Maslow)	Stresses the conscious more than unconscious	Stresses the interaction between both nature and nurture	Stresses the freedom of individuals to make their own choices	Stresses that personality remains flexible and resilient throughout one's life

FIGURE 7 Personality as understood from multiple perspectives.

RECAP/EVALUATE/RETHINK

RECAP

What are the major aspects of trait, learning, biological and evolutionary, and humanistic approaches to personality?

- ▶ Trait approaches have been used to identify the most basic and relatively enduring dimensions along which people differ from one another—dimensions known as traits. (p. 475)
- ▶ Learning approaches to personality concentrate on observable behavior. To a strict learning theorist, personality is the sum of learned responses to the external environment. (p. 478)
- ▶ Social cognitive approaches concentrate on the role of cognitions in determining personality. Those approaches pay particular attention to self-efficacy in determining behavior. (p. 479)
- ▶ Biological and evolutionary approaches to personality focus on the way personality characteristics are inherited. (p. 481)
- ▶ Humanistic approaches emphasize the basic goodness of people. They consider the core of personality in terms of a person's ability to change and improve. (p. 483)
- ▶ The major personality approaches differ substantially from one another; that may reflect both their focus on different aspects of personality and the overall complexity of personality (p. 485)

EVALUATE

1. Carl's determination to succeed is the dominant force in all his activities and relationships. According to Gordon Allport's theory, this is an example of a _____ trait. In contrast, Cindy's fondness for old western movies is an example of a _____ trait.

2. A person who enjoys activities such as parties and hang gliding might be described by Eysenck as high on what trait?

3. Proponents of which approach to personality would be most likely to agree with the statement "Personality can be thought of as learned responses to a person's upbringing and environment"?
   a. Humanistic
   b. Biological and evolutionary
   c. Learning
   d. Trait

4. A person who would make the statement "I know I can't do it" would be rated by Bandura as low on _____-_____.

5. Which approach to personality emphasizes the innate goodness of people and their desire to grow?
   a. Humanistic
   b. Psychodynamic
   c. Learning
   d. Biological and evolutionary

RETHINK

1. If personality traits are merely descriptive and not explanatory, of what use are they? Can assigning a trait to a person be harmful—or helpful? Why or why not?

2. In what ways are Cattell's sixteen source traits, Eysenck's three dimensions, and the "Big Five" factors similar, and in what ways are they different? Which traits seem to appear in all three schemes (under one name or another), and which are unique to one scheme? Is this significant?

Answers to Evaluate Questions

1. cardinal, secondary; 2. extraversion; 3. c; 4. self-efficacy; 5. a

KEY TERMS

trait theory p. 475
traits p. 475
social cognitive approaches to personality p. 479

biological and evolutionary approaches to personality p. 481

temperament p. 482
humanistic approaches to personality p. 484

self-actualization p. 484
unconditional positive regard p. 484

Assessing Personality: Determining What Makes Us Special

You have a need for other people to like and admire you.

You have a tendency to be critical of yourself.

You have a great deal of unused potential that you have not turned to your advantage.

Although you have some personality weaknesses, you generally are able to compensate for them.

Relating to members of the opposite sex has presented problems to you.

Although you appear to be disciplined and self-controlled to others, you tend to be anxious and insecure inside.

At times you have serious doubts about whether you have made the right decision or done the right thing.

You prefer a certain amount of change and variety and become dissatisfied when hemmed in by restrictions and limitations.

You do not accept others' statements without satisfactory proof.

You have found it unwise to be too frank in revealing yourself to others.

If you think these statements provide a surprisingly accurate account of your personality, you are not alone: Most college students think that the descriptions are tailored just to them. In fact, the statements were designed intentionally to be so vague that they apply to just about anyone (Forer, 1949; Russo, 1981).

The ease with which we can agree with such imprecise statements underscores the difficulty in coming up with accurate and meaningful assessments of people's personalities (also see **Interactivity 44–1**). Just as trait theorists were faced with the problem of determining the most critical and important traits, psychologists interested in assessing personality must be able to define the most meaningful ways of discriminating between one person's personality and another's. To do this, they use **psychological tests,** standard measures devised to assess behavior objectively. With the results of such tests, psychologists can help people make decisions about their lives and understand more about themselves. Psychological tests are also employed by researchers interested in the causes and consequences of personality (Groth-Marnat, 1996; Aiken, 1997; Kaplan & Saccuzzo, 1997).

Like the intelligence assessments that seek to measure intelligence, all psychological tests must have reliability and validity. *Reliability* refers to the measurement consistency of a test. If a test is reliable, it yields the same result each time it is administered to a particular person or group. In contrast, unreliable tests give different results each time they are administered.

For meaningful conclusions to be drawn, tests also must be valid. Tests have *validity* when they actually measure what they are designed to measure. If a test is constructed to measure sociability, for instance, we need to know that it actually measures sociability, not some other trait.

Finally, psychological tests are based on *norms,* standards of test performance that permit the comparison of one person's score on a test with the scores of others

INTERACTIVITY 44–1

Personality assessment

Psychological tests: Standard measures devised to assess behavior objectively; used by psychologists to help people make decisions about their lives and understand more about themselves.

who have taken the same test. For example, a norm permits test takers who have received a particular score on a test to know that they have scored in the top 10 percent of all those who have taken the test.

Norms are established by administering a particular test to a large number of people and determining the typical scores. It is then possible to compare a single person's score with the scores of the group, providing a comparative measure of test performance against the performance of others who have taken the test.

The establishment of appropriate norms is not a simple endeavor. For instance, the specific group that is employed to determine norms for a test has a profound effect on the way an individual's performance is evaluated. In fact, as we discuss next, the process of establishing norms can take on political overtones.

Exploring DIVERSITY

Should Race and Ethnicity Be Used to Establish Norms?

The passions of politics may confront the objectivity of science when test norms are established, at least in the realm of standardized tests that are meant to predict future job performance. In fact, a national controversy has developed around the question of whether different norms should be established for members of various racial and ethnic groups (Kilborn, 1991; Brown, 1994; Babrina & Bondi, 2003).

At issue is the U.S. government's fifty-year-old General Aptitude Test Battery, a test that measures a broad range of abilities from eye-hand coordination to reading proficiency. The problem that sparked the controversy is that African Americans and Hispanics tend to score lower on the test, on average, than do members of other groups. The lower scores often are due to a lack of prior relevant experience and job opportunities, which in turn has been due to prejudice and discrimination.

To promote the employment of minority racial groups, the government developed a separate set of norms for African Americans and Hispanics. Rather than using the pool of all people who took the test, the scores of African American and Hispanic applicants were compared only with the scores of other African Americans and Hispanics. Consequently, a Hispanic who scored in the top 20 percent of the Hispanics taking the test was considered to have performed equivalently to a white job applicant who scored in the top 20 percent of the whites who took the test, even though the absolute score of the Hispanic might be lower than that of the white.

Critics of the adjusted norming system suggest that such a procedure discriminates in favor of certain racial and ethnic groups at the expense of others, thereby fanning the flames of racial bigotry. The practice was challenged legally, and with the passage of the Civil Rights Act in 1991, race norming on the General Aptitude Test Battery was discontinued (Galef, 2001).

However, proponents of race norming continue to argue that norming procedures that take race into account are an affirmative action tool that simply permits minority job seekers to be placed on an equal footing with white job seekers. Furthermore, a panel of the National Academy of Sciences concurred with the practice of adjusting test norms. It suggested that the unadjusted test norms are not terribly useful in predicting job performance, and that they would tend to screen out otherwise qualified minority-group members. And a U.S. federal court opinion ruled in 2001 that using "bands" of score ranges was not necessarily discriminatory, unless the bands were designed on the basis of race (Fleming, 2000; Seventh U.S. Circuit Court of Appeals, 2001).

Job testing is not the only area in which issues arise regarding norms and the meaning of test scores. Like the meaning of racial differences in IQ scores, the issue of how to treat racial differences in test scores is both controversial and divisive. Clearly, race norming raises profound and intense feelings that may come into conflict with scientific objectivity, and the controversy is far from over (American Psychological Association, 1993; Greenlaw & Jensen, 1996; Leiter & Leiter, 2003).

The issue of establishing norms for tests is further complicated by the existence of a wide array of personality measures and approaches to assessment. We consider some of these measures, which have a variety of characteristics and purposes, next.

⒜⒜⒜

Self-Report Measures of Personality

If someone wanted to assess your personality, one possible approach would be to carry out an extensive interview with you to determine the most important events in your childhood, your social relationships, and your successes and failures. Obviously, though, such a technique would be extraordinarily costly in time and effort.

It is also unnecessary. Just as physicians draw only a small sample of your blood to test it, psychologists can utilize **self-report measures** that ask people about a relatively small sample of their behavior. This sampling of self-report data is then used to infer the presence of particular personality characteristics. For example, a researcher who was interested in assessing a person's orientation to life might administer the questionnaire shown in Figure 1. Although the questionnaire consists of only a few questions, the answers can be used to generalize about personality characteristics. (Try it yourself!)

One of the best examples of a self-report measure, and one of the most frequently used personality tests, is the **Minnesota Multiphasic Personality Inventory-2 (MMPI-2).** Although the original purpose of the measure was to differentiate people with specific sorts of psychological difficulties from those without disturbances, it has been found to predict a variety of other behaviors. For instance, MMPI scores

Self-report measures: A method of gathering data about people by asking them questions about a sample of their behavior.

Minnesota Multiphasic Personality Inventory-2 (MMPI-2): A widely used self-report test that identifies people with psychological difficulties and is employed to predict some everyday behaviors.

FIGURE 1 The Life Orientation Test. Try this scale by indicating the degree to which you agree with each of the ten statements, using the scale from 0 to 4 for each item. Try to be as accurate as possible. There are no right or wrong answers. (Source: Adapted from Scheier, Carver, & Bridges, 1994.)

The Life Orientation Test

Use the following scale to answer the items below:

0	1	2	3	4
Strongly disagree	Disagree	Neutral	Agree	Strongly agree

1. In uncertain times, I usually expect the best.
2. It's easy for me to relax.
3. If something can go wrong for me, it will.
4. I'm always optimistic about my future.
5. I enjoy my friends a lot.
6. It's important for me to keep busy.
7. I hardly ever expect things to go my way.
8. I don't get upset too easily.
9. I rarely count on good things happening to me.
10. Overall, I expect more good things to happen to me than bad.

Scoring. First, reverse your answers to questions 3, 7, and 9. Do this by changing a 0 to a 4, a 1 to a 3, a 3 to a 1, and a 4 to a 0 (answers of 2 stay as 2). Then sum the reversed scores, and add them to the scores you gave to questions 1, 4, and 10. (Ignore questions 2, 5, 6, and 8, which are filler items.)

The total score you get is a measure of a particular orientation to life: your degree of optimism. The higher your scores, the more positive and hopeful you generally are about life. For comparison purposes the average score for college students is 14.3, according to the results of a study by Scheier, Carver, and Bridges (1994). People with a higher degree of optimism generally deal with stress better than do those with lower scores.

FIGURE 2 A profile on the MMPI-2 of a person who suffers from obsessional anxiety, social withdrawal, and delusional thinking. (Source: Based on data from Halgin & Whitbourne, 1994, p. 72, and Minnesota Multiphasic Personality Inventory-2. Copyright © by the Regents of the University of Minnesota, 1942, 1943 (renewed 1970, 1989).)

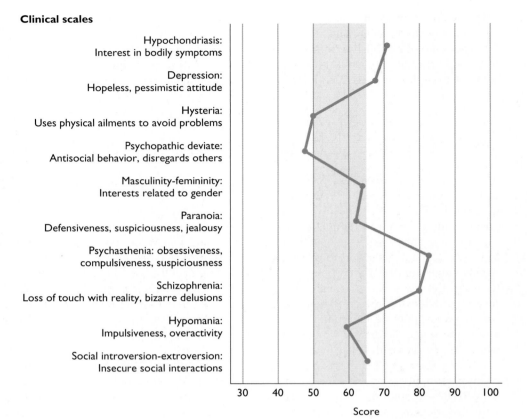

Clinical scales

Hypochondriasis: Interest in bodily symptoms

Depression: Hopeless, pessimistic attitude

Hysteria: Uses physical ailments to avoid problems

Psychopathic deviate: Antisocial behavior, disregards others

Masculinity-femininity: Interests related to gender

Paranoia: Defensiveness, suspiciousness, jealousy

Psychasthenia: obsessiveness, compulsiveness, suspiciousness

Schizophrenia: Loss of touch with reality, bizarre delusions

Hypomania: Impulsiveness, overactivity

Social introversion-extroversion: Insecure social interactions

30 40 50 60 70 80 90 100

Score

Test standardization: A technique used to validate questions in personality tests by studying the responses of people with known diagnoses.

have been shown to be good predictors of whether college students will marry within ten years and will get an advanced degree. Police departments use the test to measure whether police officers are prone to use their weapons. Psychologists in Russia administer a modified form of the MMPI to their astronauts and Olympic athletes (Butcher, 1995, 1999; Craig, 1999; Friedman et al., 2000).

The test consists of a series of 567 items to which a person responds "true," "false," or "cannot say." The questions cover a variety of issues, ranging from mood ("I feel useless at times") to opinions ("People should try to understand their dreams") to physical and psychological health ("I am bothered by an upset stomach several times a week" and "I have strange and peculiar thoughts").

There are no right or wrong answers. Instead, interpretation of the results rests on the pattern of responses. The test yields scores on ten separate scales, plus three scales meant to measure the validity of the respondent's answers. For example, there is a "lie scale" that indicates when people are falsifying their responses in order to present themselves more favorably (through items such as "I can't remember ever having a bad night's sleep") (Butcher et al., 1990; Butcher, 1999; Graham, 1999).

How did the authors of the MMPI determine what specific patterns of responses indicate? The procedure they used is typical of personality test construction—a process known as **test standardization.** To create the test, groups of psychiatric patients with a specific diagnosis, such as depression or schizophrenia, were asked to complete a large number of items. The test authors then determined which items best differentiated members of those groups from a comparison group of normal participants, and those specific items were included in the final version of the test. By systematically carrying out this procedure on groups with different diagnoses, the test authors were able to devise a number of subscales that identified different forms of abnormal behavior (see Figure 2).

When the MMPI is used for the purpose for which it was devised—identification of personality disorders—it does a reasonably good job. However, like other personality tests, it presents an opportunity for abuse. For instance, employers who use it as a screening tool for job applicants may interpret the results improperly, relying too heavily on the results of individual scales instead of taking into account the overall patterns of results, which require skilled interpretation. Furthermore, critics point out that the individual scales overlap, making their interpretation difficult. In sum, although the MMPI remains the most widely used personality test and has been translated into more than 100 different languages, it must be used with caution (Greene & Clopton, 1994; Graham, 1999; Holden, 2000).

Projective Methods

If you were shown the shape presented in Figure 3 and asked what it represented to you, you might not think that your impressions would mean very much. But to a psychodynamic theoretician, your responses to such an ambiguous figure would provide valuable clues to the state of your unconscious, and ultimately to your general personality characteristics.

The shape in the figure is representative of inkblots used in **projective personality tests,** in which a person is shown an ambiguous stimulus and asked to describe it or tell a story about it. The responses are considered to be "projections" of what the person is like.

The best-known projective test is the **Rorschach test.** Devised by Swiss psychiatrist Hermann Rorschach (1924), the test involves showing a series of symmetrical stimuli, similar to the one in Figure 3, to people who are then asked what the figures

"Rorschach! What's to become of you?"

Projective personality test: A test in which a person is shown an ambiguous stimulus and asked to describe it or tell a story about it.

Rorschach test: A test developed by Swiss psychiatrist Hermann Rorschach that involves showing a series of symmetrical visual stimuli to people who then are asked what the figures represent to them.

FIGURE 3 This inkblot is similar to the type used in the Rorschach personality test. (Source: Alloy, Jacobson, & Acocella, 1999.) What do you see in it?

Although projective tests such as the Rorschach test and the Thematic Apperception Test (TAT) are frequently employed in testing situations, their reliability and validity have been questioned.

Thematic Apperception Test (TAT): A test consisting of a series of pictures about which a person is asked to write a story.

Behavioral assessment: Direct measures of an individual's behavior used to describe characteristics indicative of personality.

INTERACTIVITY 44–2

Projective tests

represent to them. Their responses are recorded, and through a complex set of clinical judgments on the part of the examiner, people are classified into different personality types. For instance, respondents who see a bear in one inkblot are thought to have a strong degree of emotional control, according to the rules developed by Rorschach (Aronow, Reznikoff, & Moreland, 1994; Weiner, 1998).

The **Thematic Apperception Test (TAT)** is another well-known projective test. The TAT consists of a series of pictures about which a person is asked to write a story. The stories are then used to draw inferences about the writer's personality characteristics (Cramer, 1996; F. D. Kelly, 1997).

Tests with stimuli as ambiguous as those used in the Rorschach and TAT require particular skill and care in their interpretation—too much, in many critics' estimation. (To see for yourself, and to learn about projective tests in general, complete **Interactivity 44–2.**) The Rorschach in particular has been criticized for requiring too much inference on the part of the examiner, and attempts to standardize scoring have frequently failed. Furthermore, many critics complain that the Rorschach does not provide much valid information about underlying personality traits. Despite such problems, both the Rorschach and the TAT are widely used, particularly in clinical settings, and their proponents suggest that their reliability and validity are great enough to provide useful inferences about personality (Meyer, 2000; Garb, 2002, 2003; Wood et al., 2003).

Behavioral Assessment

If you were a psychologist subscribing to a learning approach to personality, you would be likely to object to the indirect nature of projective tests. Instead, you would be more apt to use **behavioral assessment**—direct measures of an individual's behavior designed to describe characteristics indicative of personality. As with observational research, behavioral assessment may be carried out naturalistically by observing people in their own settings: in the workplace, at home, or in school. In other cases, behavioral assessment occurs in the laboratory, under controlled conditions in which a psychologist sets up a situation and observes an individual's behavior (Ramsay, Reynolds, & Kamphaus, 2002).

Regardless of the setting in which behavior is observed, an effort is made to ensure that behavioral assessment is carried out objectively, quantifying behavior as much as possible. For example, an observer may record the number of social contacts a person initiates, the number of questions asked, or the number of aggressive acts. Another method is to measure the duration of events: the duration of a temper tantrum in a child, the length of a conversation, the amount of time spent working, or the time spent in cooperative behavior.

Behavioral assessment is particularly appropriate for observing—and eventually remedying—specific behavioral difficulties, such as increasing socialization in shy children. It provides a means of assessing the specific nature and incidence of a problem and subsequently allows psychologists to determine whether intervention techniques have been successful.

Behavioral assessment techniques based on learning theories of personality have also made important contributions to the treatment of certain kinds of psychological difficulties. Indeed, the knowledge of normal personality provided by the various personality theories has led to significant advances in our understanding and treatment of both physical and psychological disorders.

Wanted: People with "kinetic energy," "emotional maturity," and the ability to "deal with large numbers of people in a fairly chaotic situation."

Although this job description may seem most appropriate for the job of cohost of *Wheel of Fortune,* in actuality it is part of an advertisement for managers for American MultiCinema's (AMC) theaters (Dentzer, 1986). To find people with such qualities, AMC has developed a battery of personality measures for job applicants to complete. In developing its own tests, AMC joined scores of companies, ranging from General Motors to J. C. Penney, that employ personality tests to help determine who gets hired (Hogan, Hogan, & Roberts, 1996).

Individuals, too, have come to depend on personality testing. Many organizations will—for a hefty fee—administer a battery of personality tests that claim to steer people toward a career for which their personalities are particularly suited. Before relying too heavily on the results of such personality testing in the role of potential employee, employer, or consumer of testing services, you should keep several points in mind:

▶ *Understand what the test claims to measure.* Standard personality measures are accompanied by information that discusses how the test was developed, to whom it is most applicable, and how the results should be interpreted. Read any explanations of the test; they will help you understand the meaning of any results.

▶ *Base no decision only on the results of any one test.* Test results should be interpreted in the context of other information—academic records, social interests, and home and community activities.

▶ *Remember that test results are not always accurate.* The results may be in error; the test may be unreliable or invalid. You may, for example, have had a "bad day" when you took the test, or the person scoring and interpreting the test may have made a mistake. You should not place undue stock in the results of a single administration of any test.

In sum, it is important to keep in mind the complexity of human behavior—particularly your own. No single test can provide an understanding of the intricacies of someone's personality without considering a good deal more information than can be provided in a single testing session.

RECAP/EVALUATE/RETHINK

RECAP

How can we most accurately assess personality?

▶ Psychological tests such as the MMPI are standard assessment tools that measure behavior objectively. They must be reliable, measuring what they are trying to measure consistently, and valid, measuring what they are supposed to measure. (p. 489)

What are the major types of personality measures?

▶ Self-report measures ask people about a sample range of their behaviors. These reports are used to infer the presence of particular personality characteristics. (p. 489)

▶ Projective personality tests (such as the Rorschach and the Thematic Apperception Test) present an ambiguous stimulus; the observer's responses are used to infer information about the observer. (p. 491)

▶ Behavioral assessment is based on the principles of learning theory. It employs direct measurement of an individual's behavior to determine characteristics related to personality. (p. 492)

EVALUATE

1. _____ is the consistency of a personality test; _____ is the ability of a test to actually measure what it is designed to measure.
2. _____ are standards used to compare scores of different people taking the same test.
3. Tests such as the MMPI-2, in which a small sample of behavior is assessed to determine larger trends, are examples of
   a. Cross-sectional tests
   b. Projective tests
   c. Achievement tests
   d. Self-report tests

4. A person shown a picture and asked to make up a story about it would be taking a _____ personality test.

RETHINK

1. What do you think are some of the problems that developers and interpreters of self-report personality tests must deal with in their effort to provide useful information about test-takers? Why is a "lie scale" included on such measures?
2. Should personality tests be used for personnel decisions? Should they be used for other social purposes, such as identifying individuals at risk for certain types of personality disorders? What sorts of policies would you devise to ensure that such tests were used ethically?

Answers to Evaluate Questions

1. reliability, validity; 2. norms; 3. d; 4. projective

KEY TERMS

psychological tests p. 487
self-report measures p. 489
Minnesota Multiphasic
Personality Inventory-2
(MMPI-2) p. 489

test standardization p. 490
projective personality
test p. 491

Rorschach test p. 491
Thematic Apperception Test
(TAT) p. 492

behavioral
assessment p. 492

Looking Back

Psychology on the Web

1. Sigmund Freud is one of the towering figures in psychology, with an influence far beyond his psychoanalytic work. Find further information on the Web about Freud. Pick one aspect of his work or influence (e.g., on therapy, medicine, literature, film, or culture and society) and summarize in writing what you have found, including your attitude toward your findings.

2. Find a website that links to personality tests and take one or two tests—remembering to take them with skepticism. For each test, summarize in writing the aspects of personality that were tested, the theoretical approach the test appeared to be based on, and your assessment of the trustworthiness of the information you received.

3. After completing Interactivity 44–2 on the Rorschach and projective tests, go to the Web to search both pro and con arguments on the use of the Rorschach. Summarize the arguments.

Epilogue

We have discussed the different ways in which psychologists have interpreted the development and structure of personality. The perspectives we examined ranged from Freud's analysis of personality based primarily on internal, unconscious factors to the externally based view of personality as a learned set of traits and actions that is championed by learning theorists. We also noted that there are many ways to interpret personality, and by no means does a consensus exist on what the key traits are that are central to personality.

Return to the Prologue and consider the case of John Gotti, who was—depending on your experience with him—either awfully nice or just awful. Use your understanding of personality to consider the following questions.

1. How might a psychoanalytic approach to personality, using the concepts of id, ego, and superego, help explain Gotti's criminal behavior?

2. Using Cattell's sixteen source traits, what sort of profile do you think Gotti would have displayed if he had been tested? Where would he fall on Eysenck's major personality dimensions?

3. Would a personality profile of Gotti administered during the time he was involved in mob activities have been different from one administered when he was visiting friends? Why?

4. How would an advocate of a social cognitive approach to personality interpret and explain Gotti's seemingly contradictory behavior? How might the concepts of observational learning apply to a case like Gotti's?

Health Psychology: Stress, Coping, and Well-Being

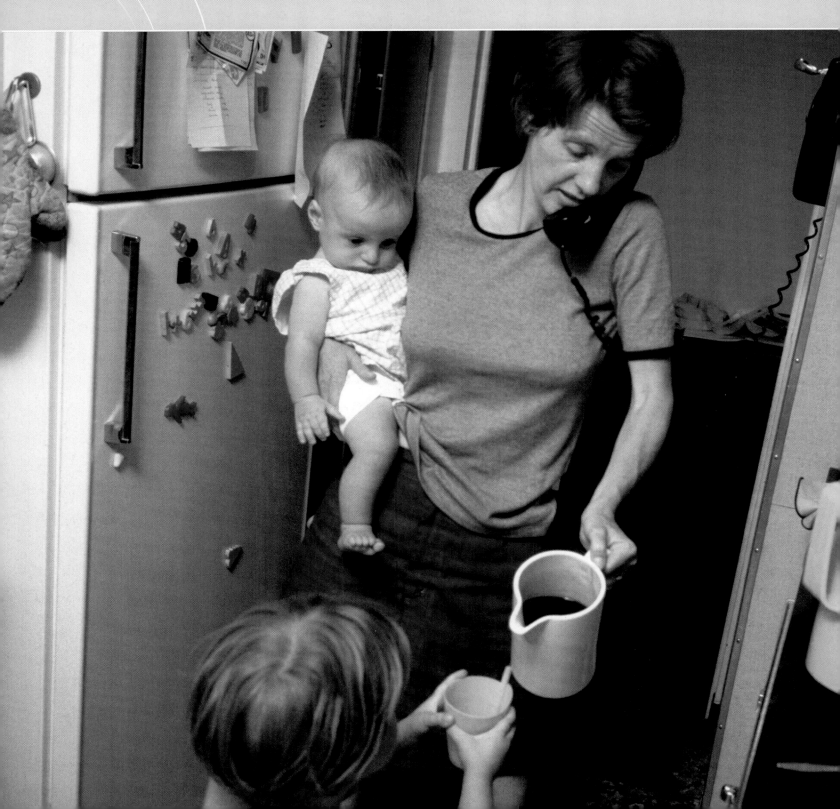

Prologue
So Much To Do, So Little Time To Do It

Here's a typical day in the life of Elizabeth Oettinger, minister and single mother, with two daughters, Jessie, 16, and Sarah, 14, living in Corvallis, Oregon:

5:30 a.m. Elizabeth wakes to the sound of Jessie's alarm clock, but stays in bed for 15 minutes to "work things out."

5:48 a.m. Feeds the dog and four cats. Puts in a load of laundry.

6:55 a.m. Drives Sarah (and her cello) to orchestra practice.

7:40 a.m. Arrives back home, showers, then checks her e-mail to see if her friend from Idaho will visit today. No word.

8:10 a.m. Does another load of laundry, cleans the kitchen.

8:25 a.m. Drives to church, stopping at the Starbucks downtown for a tall latte: 2% and sweetener. . . .

10:40 a.m. Drives to Sarah's school to drop off her lunch, which she forgot. Leaves her car with her "whatever he is, soon-to-be-ex-husband," whose own ride is in the shop.

11:00 a.m. Back at the monthly clergy meeting, she finds her friend from Idaho in attendance. Under discussion: the role of female pastors.

2:30 p.m. Speaks with a new parishioner about the congregation. Assures her that the church has an "open and affirming" attitude toward lesbians and gay men.

3:45 p.m. Catches a lift home. Talks with Jessie about her lesson and her physics class, where she was disappointed to receive her first B. Leaves, in Jessie's car, to visit a sick parishioner.

4:47 p.m. Drives home, praying on the way.

5:21 p.m. Leaves for her first session with her therapist, to whom the church referred her after her separation. "They just wanted to make sure I had a place to take my stuff."

6:31 p.m. Returns home and heats up a quick dinner of beef-and-vegetable soup.

7:31 p.m. Leaves for a meeting of the Corvallis Youth Symphony, for which she's arranging a fund-raiser.

9:15 p.m. Back home, helps Jessie with a speech she's writing for school, then watches the last half of "E.R."

11:04 p.m. Tucks the girls in.

11:16 p.m. Gets into bed. Prays. "There are people I promise to pray for during the day. This is when I get to do it." Sleeps (D'Antoni, 1999, p. 26).

Health psychology: The branch of psychology that investigates the psychological factors related to wellness and illness, including the prevention, diagnosis, and treatment of medical problems.

It's not hard to guess what Elizabeth Oettinger was experiencing during the course of her long day: stress. For people like her—and that probably includes most of us—the intensity of juggling multiple roles leads to feelings of never having sufficient time and, in some cases, takes a toll on both physical and psychological well-being.

Stress and ways of coping with it have long been central topics of interest for psychologists. However, in recent years the focus has broadened as psychology has come to view stress in the broader context of one of psychology's newer subfields: health psychology. **Health psychology** investigates the psychological factors related to wellness and illness, including the prevention, diagnosis, and treatment of medical problems. Health psychologists

Looking Ahead

investigate how illness is influenced by psychological factors such as stress. They examine the psychological principles underlying treatments for disease and illness. They are also concerned with issues of prevention: how health problems such as heart disease and stress can be avoided by means of more healthful behavior.

Health psychologists take a decisive stand on the enduring mind-body issue that philosophers, and later psychologists, have debated since the time of the ancient Greeks. In their view, the mind and the body are clearly linked, rather than representing two distinct systems (Sternberg, 2000).

Health psychologists recognize that good health and the ability to cope with illness are affected by psychological factors such as thoughts, emotions, and the ability to manage stress. They have paid particular attention to the *immune system,* the complex of organs, glands, and cells that constitute our bodies' natural line of defense in fighting disease.

In fact, health psychologists are among the primary investigators in a growing field called (somewhat awkwardly) *psychoneuroimmunology,* or *PNI,* the study of the relationship among psychological factors, the immune system, and the brain. PNI has led to discoveries such as the existence of an association between a person's emotional state and the success of the immune system in fighting disease (Baum, Revenson, & Singer, 2000; Ader, 2001; Ader, Felton, & Cohen, 2001).

In sum, health psychologists view the mind and the body as two parts of a whole human being that cannot be considered independently. This more recent view marks a sharp departure from earlier thinking. Previously, disease was seen as a purely biological phenomenon, and psychological factors were of little interest to most health-care workers. In the early twentieth century, the primary causes of death were short-term infections from which one either rapidly recovered—or died. Now, however, the major causes of death, such as heart disease, cancer, and diabetes, are chronic illnesses that often cannot be cured and may linger for years, posing significant psychological issues (Delahanty & Baum, 2000).

In these modules we discuss the ways in which psychological factors affect health. We first focus on the causes and consequences of stress, as well as on the means of coping with it. Next, we explore the psychological aspects of several major health problems, including heart disease, cancer, and ailments resulting from smoking. Finally, we examine the ways in which patient-physician interactions influence our health and offer suggestions for increasing people's compliance with recommendations about behavior that will improve their well-being.

Stress and Coping

Louisa Denby's day began badly: She slept through her alarm and had to skip breakfast in order to catch the bus to campus. Then, when she went to the library to catch up on the reading she had to do before taking a test the next day, the one article she needed was missing. The librarian told her that replacing it would take 24 hours. Feeling frustrated, she walked to the computer lab to print out the paper she had completed at home the night before.

The computer wouldn't read her disk. She searched for someone to help her, but she was unable to find anyone who knew any more about computers than she did.

It was only 9:42 a.m., and Louisa had a wracking headache. Apart from that pain, she was conscious of only one feeling: stress (Feldman, 2003, p. 364).

ⒶⒶⒶ

How is health psychology a union between medicine and psychology?

What is stress, how does it affect us, and how can we best cope with it?

Stress: Reacting to Threat and Challenge

Most of us need little introduction to the phenomenon of **stress,** people's response to events that threaten or challenge them. Whether it be a paper or an exam deadline, a family problem, or even a cumulative series of events such as those faced by Elizabeth Oettinger, life is full of circumstances and events, known as *stressors*, that produce threats to our well-being. Even pleasant events—such as planning a party or beginning a sought-after job—can produce stress, although negative events result in greater detrimental consequences than do positive ones.

All of us face stress in our lives. Some health psychologists believe that daily life actually involves a series of repeated sequences of perceiving a threat, considering ways to cope with it, and ultimately adapting to the threat, with greater or lesser success. Although adaptation is often minor and occurs without our awareness, adaptation requires a major effort when stress is more severe or longer lasting. Ultimately, our attempts to overcome stress may produce biological and psychological responses that result in health problems (Gatchel & Baum, 1983; Fink, 2000).

Stress: A person's response to events that are threatening or challenging.

THE HIGH COST OF STRESS

Stress can take its toll in many ways, producing both biological and psychological consequences. Often the most immediate reaction to stress is a biological one. Exposure to stressors generates a rise in certain hormones secreted by the adrenal glands, an increase in heart rate and blood pressure, and changes in how well the skin conducts electrical impulses. On a short-term basis, these responses may be adaptive because they produce an "emergency reaction" in which the body prepares to defend itself through activation of the sympathetic nervous system. Those responses may allow more effective coping with the stressful situation (Akil & Morano, 1996; McEwen, 1998).

However, continued exposure to stress results in a decline in the body's overall level of biological functioning because of the constant secretion of stress-related hormones. Over time, stressful reactions can promote deterioration of body tissues such as blood vessels and the heart. Ultimately, we become more susceptible to disease as our ability to fight off infection is lowered (Sapolsky, 1996; Shapiro, 1996; McCabe et al., 2000).

Furthermore, an entire class of physical problems known as **psychophysiological disorders** often result from or are worsened by stress. Once referred to as *psychosomatic disorders* (a term dropped because people assumed that the disorders were somehow unreal), psychophysiological disorders are actual medical problems that are influenced by an interaction of psychological, emotional, and physical difficulties. The more common psychophysiological disorders range from major problems such as high blood pressure to usually less serious difficulties such as headaches, backaches, skin rashes, indigestion, fatigue, and constipation. Stress has even been linked to the common cold (Cohen, 1996; Rice, 2000).

On a psychological level, high levels of stress prevent people from adequately coping with life. Their view of the environment can become clouded (e.g., a minor

Psychophysiological disorders: Medical problems influenced by an interaction of psychological, emotional, and physical difficulties.

FIGURE 1 To get a sense of the level of stress in your life, complete this questionnaire. (Source: Cohen, 1999.)

How Stressful Is Your Life?

Test your level of stress by answering these questions, and adding the score from each box. Questions apply to the last month only. A key below will help you determine the extent of your stress.

1. How often have you been upset because of something that happened unexpectedly?
   0 = never, 1 = almost never, 2 = sometimes, 3 = fairly often, 4 = very often

2. How often have you felt that you were unable to control the important things in your life?
   0 = never, 1 = almost never, 2 = sometimes, 3 = fairly often, 4 = very often

3. How often have you felt nervous and "stressed"?
   0 = never, 1 = almost never, 2 = sometimes, 3 = fairly often, 4 = very often

4. How often have you felt confident about your ability to handle your personal problems?
   4 = never, 3 = almost never, 2 = sometimes, 1 = fairly often, 0 = very often

5. How often have you felt that things were going your way?
   4 = never, 3 = almost never, 2 = sometimes, 1 = fairly often, 0 = very often

6. How often have you been able to control irritations in your life?
   4 = never, 3 = almost never, 2 = sometimes, 1 = fairly often, 0 = very often

7. How often have you found that you could not cope with all the things that you had to do?
   0 = never, 1 = almost never, 2 = sometimes, 3 = fairly often, 4 = very often

8. How often have you felt that you were on top of things?
   4 = never, 3 = almost never, 2 = sometimes, 1 = fairly often, 0 = very often

9. How often have you been angered because of things that were outside your control?
   0 = never, 1 = almost never, 2 = sometimes, 3 = fairly often, 4 = very often

10. How often have you felt difficulties were piling up so high that you could not overcome them?
    0 = never, 1 = almost never, 2 = sometimes, 3 = fairly often, 4 = very often

How You Measure Up:
Stress levels vary among individuals—compare your total score to the averages below:

AGE		GENDER	
18-29	14.2	Men	12.1
30-44	13.0	Women	13.7
45-54	12.6		
55-64	11.9		
65 & over	12.0		

MARITAL STATUS

Widowed	12.6
Married or living with	12.4
Single or never wed	14.1
Divorced	14.7
Separated	16.6

criticism made by a friend is blown out of proportion). Moreover, at the highest levels of stress, emotional responses may be so extreme that people are unable to act at all. People under a lot of stress also become less able to deal with new stressors.

In short, stress affects us in multiple ways. It may increase the risk that we will become ill, it may directly produce illness, it may make us less able to recover from a disease, and it may reduce our ability to cope with future stress. (See Figure 1 and try **Interactivity 45–1** to get a measure of your own level of stress.)

INTERACTIVITY 45–1

College stress test

THE GENERAL ADAPTATION SYNDROME MODEL: THE COURSE OF STRESS

The effects of stress are illustrated in a model devised by Hans Selye (pronounced "sell-yay"), a pioneering stress theorist (Selye, 1976, 1993). This model, the **general adaptation syndrome (GAS),** suggests that the same set of physiological stress reactions to stress occurs regardless of the particular cause of stress.

As shown in Figure 2, the model has three phases. The first stage—the *alarm and mobilization stage*—occurs when people become aware of the presence of a stressor. On a biological level, the sympathetic nervous system becomes energized, helping a person cope initially with the stressor.

However, if the stressor persists, people move into the next stage of the model. In the *resistance stage,* people prepare themselves to fight the stressor. During resistance, people use a variety of means to cope with the stressor—sometimes successfully but at a cost of some degree of physical or psychological well-being.

If resistance is inadequate, people enter the last stage of the model, the *exhaustion stage.* During the exhaustion stage, a person's ability to adapt to the stressor declines to the point where negative consequences of stress appear: physical illness, psychological symptoms in the form of an inability to concentrate, heightened irritability, or, in severe instances, disorientation and a loss of touch with reality. In a sense, people wear out, and their physical reserves are taxed to the limit.

How do people move out of the third stage after they have entered it? In some cases, exhaustion allows people to avoid a stressor. For example, people who become ill from overwork may be excused from their duties for a time, giving them a temporary respite from their responsibilities. At least for a time, then, the immediate stress is reduced.

The GAS model has had a substantial impact on our understanding of stress. By suggesting that the exhaustion of resources in the third stage of the model produces biological damage, it has provided a specific explanation of how stress can lead to illness. Furthermore, the model can be applied to both people and nonhuman species.

General adaptation syndrome (GAS): A theory developed by Selye that suggests that a person's response to a stressor consists of three stages: alarm and mobilization, resistance, and exhaustion.

Power Web: The Evolution of the Stress Concept

www.mhhe.com/feldmanup7

Stressor ▶ 1. Alarm and mobilization
Meeting and resisting stressor. ▶ 2. Resistance
Coping with stress and resistance to stressor. ▶ 3. Exhaustion
Negative consequences of stress (such as illness) occur when coping is inadequate.

FIGURE 2 The general adaptation syndrome (GAS) suggests that there are three major stages to stress responses. (Source: Selye, 1976.)

Selye's theory has not gone unchallenged. For example, whereas the theory suggests that regardless of the stressor, the biological reaction is similar, some health psychologists disagree. They believe that people's biological response is specific to the way they appraise a stressful event. For example, if a stressor is seen as unpleasant but not unusual, the biological response may be different than it will be if the stressor is seen as unpleasant, out of the ordinary, and unanticipated. This approach has led to an increased focus on psychoneuroimmunology (Lazarus, 2000; Taylor et al., 2000).

PSYCHONEUROIMMUNOLOGY AND STRESS

Psychoneuroimmunology (PNI): The study of the relationship among psychological factors, the immune system, and the brain.

Contemporary health psychologists specializing in **psychoneuroimmunology (PNI)**— the study of the relationship among psychological factors, the immune system, and the brain—have taken a broader approach. Focusing on the outcomes of stress, they have identified three main consequences (see Figure 3).

First, stress has direct physiological results, including an increase in blood pressure, an increase in hormonal activity, and an overall decline in the functioning of the immune system. Second, stress leads people to engage in behavior that is harmful to their health, including increased nicotine, drug, and alcohol use; poor eating habits; and decreased sleep. Finally, stress produces indirect consequences that result in declines in health: a reduction in the likelihood of obtaining health care and decreased compliance with medical advice when it is sought (McCabe et al., 2000; Gevirtz, 2000; Marsland et al., 2002).

Why is stress so damaging to the immune system? One reason is that stress may overstimulate the immune system. Rather than fighting invading bacteria, viruses, and other foreign invaders, it may begin to attack the body itself, damaging healthy tissue. When that happens, it can lead to disorders such as arthritis and an allergic reaction.

Stress can also make the immune system react inadequately, permitting germs that produce colds to reproduce more easily or allowing cancer cells to spread more rapidly. In normal circumstances, our bodies produce *lymphocytes,* specialized white

FIGURE 3 Three major types of consequences result from stress: direct physiological effects, harmful behaviors, and indirect health-related behaviors (Source: Adapted from Baum, 1994.)

blood cells that fight disease, at an extraordinary rate—some 10 million every few seconds—and it is possible that stress can alter this level of production (Ader, Felten, & Cohen, 2001; Miller & Cohen, 2001; Cohen et al., 2002).

THE NATURE OF STRESSORS: MY STRESS IS YOUR PLEASURE

Although our increasing knowledge about the immune system helps us understand how people respond to stress, it is less helpful when it comes to specifying what constitutes a stressor for a particular person. Although certain kinds of events, such as the death of a loved one or participation in combat during a war, are universally stressful, other situations may or may not be stressful to a particular person (Affleck et al., 1994; Krohne, 1996; Robert-McComb, 2001).

Consider, for instance, bungee jumping. Some people would find jumping off a bridge while attached to a slender rubber tether extremely stressful. However, there are those who see such an activity as challenging and fun-filled. Whether bungee jumping is stressful depends in part, then, on individual perceptions of the activity.

The ability to fight off disease is related to psychological factors. Here a cell from the body's immune system engulfs and destroys disease-producing bacteria.

For people to consider an event stressful, they must perceive it as threatening and must lack the resources to deal with it effectively. Consequently, the same event may at some times be stressful and at other times provoke no stressful reaction at all. A young man may experience stress when he is turned down for a date—if he attributes the refusal to his unattractiveness or unworthiness. But if he attributes it to some factor unrelated to his self-esteem, such as a previous commitment by the woman he asked, the experience of being refused may create no stress at all. Hence, a person's interpretation of events plays an important role in the determination of what is stressful (Folkman & Moskowitz, 2000).

The severity of stress is greatest when important goals are threatened, the threat is immediate, or the anticipation of a threatening event extends over a long period. For example, members of minority groups who feel they are potentially the targets of racist behavior experience significant stress (Clark et al., 1999; Taylor & Turner, 2002; Troxel et al., 2003).

CATEGORIZING STRESSORS

What kinds of events tend to be seen as stressful? There are three general classes of events: cataclysmic events, personal stressors, and background stressors.

Cataclysmic events are strong stressors that occur suddenly and typically affect many people simultaneously. Disasters such as tornadoes and plane crashes, as well as terrorist attacks like that at the World Trade Center, are examples of cataclysmic events that can affect hundreds or thousands of people simultaneously.

Although it might seem that cataclysmic events would produce potent, lingering stress, in many cases this is not true. In fact, cataclysmic events involving natural disasters may produce less stress in the long run than do events that are initially not as devastating. One reason is that natural disasters have a clear resolution. Once they are over and done with, people can look to the future knowing that the worst is behind them. Moreover, the stress induced by cataclysmic events is shared by others who have also experienced the disaster. This permits people to offer one another social support and a firsthand understanding of the difficulties others are going through (Kaniasty & Norris, 1995; Hobfoll et al., 1996).

In contrast, terrorist attacks like the one on the World Trade Center are cataclysmic events that produce considerable stress. Terrorist attacks are deliberate, and

Cataclysmic events: Strong stressors that occur suddenly, affecting many people at once (e.g., natural disasters).

Even positive events can produce significant stress.

Personal stressors: Major life events, such as the death of a family member, that have immediate negative consequences that generally fade with time.

Everyone confronts daily hassles, or background stressors, at some point. At what point do daily hassles become more than mere irritants?

victims (and observers) know that future attacks are likely. Government warnings in the form of heightened terror alerts may further increase the stress (Graham, 2001; Pomponio, 2002; Murphy, Wismar, & Freeman, 2003).

The second major category of stressor is the personal stressor. **Personal stressors** include major life events such as the death of a parent or spouse, the loss of one's job, a major personal failure, or even something positive such as getting married. Typically, personal stressors produce an immediate major reaction that soon tapers off. For example, stress arising from the death of a loved one tends to be greatest just after the time of death, but people begin to feel less stress and are better able to cope with the loss after the passage of time.

Some victims of major catastrophes and severe personal stressors experience **posttraumatic stress disorder,** or **PTSD,** in which a person has experienced a significantly stressful event that has long-lasting effects that may include re-experiencing the event in vivid flashbacks or dreams. An episode of PTSD may be triggered by an otherwise innocent stimulus, such as the sound of a honking horn, that leads someone to re-experience a past event that produced considerable stress.

Depending on what statistics one accepts, between 5 and 60 percent of the veterans of the Vietnam War have PTSD. Furthermore, those who have experienced child abuse or rape, rescue workers facing overwhelming situations, and victims of any sudden natural disaster or accidents that produce feelings of helplessness and shock may suffer from the same disorder (Woods, 2000; Southwick & Friedman, 2001; Schlenger et al., 2002).

Terrorist attacks produce high levels of PTSD. For example, overall 11 percent of the people in New York City had some form of PTSD in the months after the September 11 terrorist attacks. But the responses varied significantly with a resident's proximity to the attacks, as illustrated in Figure 4; the closer someone lived to ground zero, the greater the likelihood of PTSD (Susser, Herman, & Aaron, 2002).

Symptoms of posttraumatic stress disorder include reexperiencing the event, emotional numbing, sleep difficulties, problems relating to others, alcohol and drug abuse, and—in some cases—suicide. For instance, the suicide rate for Vietnam veterans is as much as 25 percent higher than it is for the general population (Wilson & Keane, 1996; Mazza, 2000; Orr, Metzger, & Pitman, 2002; Ozer et al., 2003).

Background stressors, or more informally, *daily hassles,* are the third major category of stressors. Exemplified by standing in a long line at a bank and getting stuck in a traffic jam, daily hassles are the minor irritations of life that we all face time and time again: delays, noisy cars and trucks, broken appliances, other people's irritating behavior, and so on. Another type of background stressor is a long-term, chronic problem, such as experiencing dissatisfaction with school or a job, being in an unhappy relationship, or living in crowded quarters without privacy (van Eck, Nicolson, & Berkhof, 1998; Lazarus, 2000).

By themselves, daily hassles do not require much coping or even a response on the part of the individual, although they certainly produce unpleasant emotions and moods. Yet daily hassles add up—and ultimately they may produce as great a toll as a single, more stressful incident does. In fact, the number of daily hassles people face is associated with psychological symptoms and health problems such as flu, sore throat, and backaches.

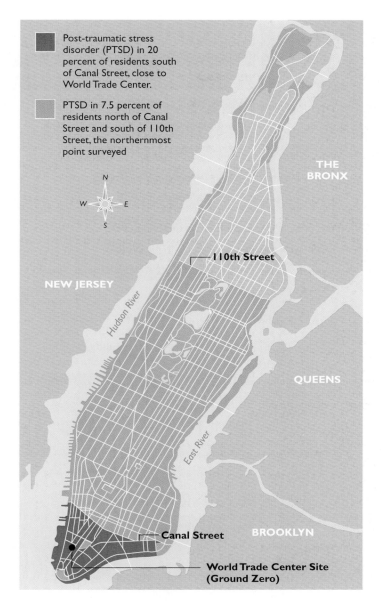

Post-traumatic stress disorder (PTSD) in 20 percent of residents south of Canal Street, close to World Trade Center.

PTSD in 7.5 percent of residents north of Canal Street and south of 110th Street, the northernmost point surveyed

THE BRONX

NEW JERSEY

Hudson River

110th Street

East River

QUEENS

BROOKLYN

Canal Street

World Trade Center Site (Ground Zero)

FIGURE 4 The closer people lived to the site of the World Trade Center terrorist attack, the greater the rate of posttraumatic stress disorder. (Source: Susser, Herman, & Aaron, 2002.)

PowerWeb: Little Hassles Can Be Hazardous to Your Health

www.mhhe.com/feldmanup7

The flip side of hassles is **uplifts,** the minor positive events that make one feel good—even if only temporarily. As indicated in Figure 5, uplifts range from relating well to a companion to finding one's surroundings pleasing. What is especially intriguing about uplifts is that they are associated with people's psychological health in just the opposite way that hassles are: The greater the number of uplifts experienced, the fewer the psychological symptoms people later report (Chamberlain & Zika, 1990; Roberts, 1995; Ravindran et al., 2002).

LEARNED HELPLESSNESS

Have you ever faced an intolerable situation that you just couldn't resolve, where you finally just gave up and accepted things the way they were? This example illustrates one of the possible consequences of being in an environment in which control over a situation is not possible—a state that produces learned helplessness.

Posttraumatic stress disorder (PTSD): A phenomenon in which victims of major catastrophes or strong personal stressors feel long-lasting effects that may include reexperiencing the event in vivid flashbacks or dreams.

Background stressors ("daily hassles"): Everyday annoyances, such as being stuck in traffic, that cause minor irritations and may have long-term ill effects if they continue or are compounded by other stressful events.

Uplifts: Minor positive events that make one feel good.

FIGURE 5 The most common everyday hassles and uplifts (hassles: Chamberlain & Zika, 1990; uplifts: Kanner et al., 1981.) How many of these are part of *your* life, and how do you cope with them?

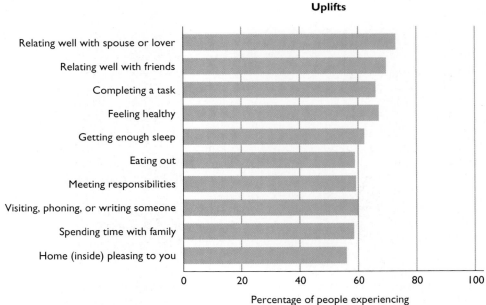

Learned helplessness: A state in which people conclude that unpleasant or aversive stimuli cannot be controlled—a view of the world that becomes so ingrained that they cease trying to remedy the aversive circumstances, even if they actually can exert some influence.

According to psychologist Martin Seligman, **learned helplessness** occurs when people conclude that unpleasant or aversive stimuli cannot be controlled—a view of the world that becomes so ingrained that they cease trying to remedy the aversive circumstances, even if they actually can exert some influence (Seligman, 1975; Peterson, Maier, & Seligman, 1993). Victims of the phenomenon of learned helplessness have concluded that there is no link between the responses they make and the outcomes that occur.

Take, for example, what often happens to elderly persons when they are placed in a nursing home or hospital. One of the most striking features of their new environment is that they are no longer independent: They do not have control over the most basic activities in their lives. They are told what and when to eat and told when they may watch TV or participate in recreational activities. In addition, their sleeping schedules are arranged by someone else. It is not hard to see how this loss of control can have negative effects on people suddenly placed, often reluctantly, in such a situation.

The results of this loss of control and the ensuing stress are frequently poorer health and even the likelihood of earlier death. These outcomes were confirmed in a classic experiment conducted in a nursing home in which elderly residents in one group were encouraged to make more choices and take greater control of their day-to-day activities (Langer & Janis, 1979). As a result, the members of that group were more active and happier than were those in a comparison group of residents who were encouraged to let the nursing home's staff take care of them. Moreover, an analysis of the residents' medical records revealed that six months after the experiment, the group encouraged to be self-sufficient showed significantly greater health improvement than did the comparison group. Even more startling was an examination of the death rate: Eighteen months after the experiment began, only 15 percent of the "independent" group had died—compared with 30 percent of the comparison group.

Other research confirms that learned helplessness has negative consequences, and not just for elderly people. People of all ages report more physical symptoms and depression when they perceive that they have little or no control than they do when they feel a sense of control over a situation (Joiner & Wagner, 1995; Shnek et al., 1995).

Coping with Stress

Stress is a normal part of life—and not necessarily a completely bad part. For example, without stress, we might not be sufficiently motivated to complete the activities we need to accomplish. However, it is also clear that too much stress can take a toll on both physical and psychological health. How do people deal with stress? Is there a way to reduce its negative effects?

Efforts to control, reduce, or learn to tolerate the threats that lead to stress are known as **coping.** We habitually use certain coping responses to help deal with stress. Most of the time, we're not aware of these responses—just as we may be unaware of the minor stressors of life until they build up to sufficiently aversive levels (Snyder, 1999; Folkman & Moscowitz, 2000).

One means of dealing with stress that occurs on an unconscious level is the use of defense mechanisms. As personality psychologists have discovered, **defense mechanisms** are unconscious reactions that maintain a person's sense of control and self-worth by distorting or denying the actual nature of the situation. For example, one study examined California students who lived in dormitories close to a geological fault. Those who lived in dorms that were rated as being unlikely to withstand an earthquake were significantly more likely to doubt experts' predictions of an impending earthquake than were those who lived in safer structures (Lehman & Taylor, 1988).

Another defense mechanism used to cope with stress is *emotional insulation,* in which a person stops experiencing any emotions at all, thereby remaining unaffected and unmoved by both positive and negative experiences. The problem with defense mechanisms, of course, is that they do not deal with reality but merely hide the problem.

People also have other, more direct, and potentially more positive means for coping with stress. Specifically, coping strategies generally fall into two categories: emotion-focused coping and problem-focused coping. In *emotion-focused coping,* people try to manage their emotions in the face of stress, seeking to change the way they feel about or perceive a problem. Examples of emotion-focused coping include strategies such as accepting sympathy from others and looking at the bright side of a situation. In contrast, *problem-focused coping* attempts to modify the stressful problem or source of stress. Problem-focused strategies lead to changes in

Coping: Efforts to control, reduce, or learn to tolerate the threats that lead to stress.

Defense mechanisms: Unconscious strategies people use to reduce anxiety by concealing its source from themselves and others.

behavior or to the development of a plan of action to deal with stress. Starting a study group to improve poor classroom performance is an example of problem-focused coping.

In most stressful incidents, people employ *both* emotion-focused and problem-focused strategies. However, they use emotion-focused strategies more frequently when they perceive circumstances as being unchangeable, and problem-focused approaches more often in situations they see as relatively modifiable (Folkman & Moskowitz, 2000; Stanton et al., 2000; Penley, Tomaka, & Wiebe, 2002).

One of the least effective forms of coping is avoidant coping. In *avoidant coping,* a person may use wishful thinking to reduce stress or use more direct escape routes, such as drug use, alcohol use, and overeating. For example, people may hope to "will" a problem away by means of wishful thinking (saying to themselves, "Maybe it will snow so hard tomorrow that the test will be canceled"). In other cases, they may get drunk to avoid a problem. Either way, avoidant coping usually results in a postponement of dealing with a stressful situation, and often makes it even worse (Appelhans & Schmeck, 2002).

COPING STYLES: THE HARDY PERSONALITY

Most of us cope with stress in a characteristic manner, employing a *coping style* that represents our general tendency to deal with stress in a specific way. For example, you may know people who habitually react to even the smallest amount of stress with hysteria, and others who calmly confront even the greatest stress in an unflappable manner. These kinds of people clearly have quite different coping styles (Gallaher, 1996; Taylor & Aspinwall, 1996; Taylor, 2003).

Hardiness: A personality characteristic associated with a lower rate of stress-related illness, consisting of three components: commitment, challenge, and control.

Among those who cope with stress most successfully are people who are equipped with **hardiness,** a personality characteristic associated with a lower rate of stress-related illness. Hardiness consists of three components (Kobasa et al., 1994; Baumgartner, 2002):

- ▶ *Commitment.* Commitment is a tendency to throw ourselves into whatever we are doing with a sense that our activities are important and meaningful.
- ▶ *Challenge.* Hardy people believe that change, rather than stability, is the standard condition of life. To them, the anticipation of change serves as an incentive rather than a threat to their security.
- ▶ *Control.* Hardiness is marked by a sense of control—the perception that people can influence the events in their lives.

Hardy individuals approach stress in an optimistic manner and take direct action to learn about and deal with stressors, thereby changing stressful events into less threatening ones. As a consequence, hardiness acts as a defense against stress-related illness.

For those who confront the most profound difficulties, such as the death of a loved one and a permanent injury such as paralysis after an accident, a key ingredient in their psychological recovery is their degree of resilience. *Resilience* is the ability to withstand, overcome, and actually thrive after profound adversity (Werner, 1995; Ryff & Singer, 2003).

Resilient people are generally easygoing and good-natured and have good social skills. They are usually independent, and they have a sense of control over their own destiny—even if fate has dealt them a devastating blow. In short, they work with what they have and make the best of whatever situation they find themselves in (Staudinger et al., 1999; Humphreys, 2003).

"Today, we examined our life style, we evaluated our diet and our exercise program, and we also assessed our behavioral patterns. Then we felt we needed a drink."

SOCIAL SUPPORT: TURNING TO OTHERS

Our relationships with others also help us cope with stress. Researchers have found that **social support,** the knowledge that we are part of a mutual network of caring, interested others, enables us to experience lower levels of stress and be better able to cope with the stress we do undergo (Uchino, Uno, & Holt-Lunstad, 1999; Bolger, Zuckerman, & Kessler, 2000; McCabe et al., 2000).

Social support: A mutual network of caring, interested others.

The social and emotional support people provide each other helps in dealing with stress in several ways. For instance, such support demonstrates that a person is an important and valued member of a social network. Similarly, other people can provide information and advice about appropriate ways of dealing with stress (Day & Livingstone, 2003).

Finally, people who are part of a social support network can provide actual goods and services to help others in stressful situations. For instance, they can supply a person whose house has burned down with temporary living quarters, or they can help a student who is experiencing stress because of poor academic performance study for a test (Hobfoll et al., 1996; Lepore, Ragan, & Jones, 2000; Natvig, Albrektsen, & Ovamstrom, 2003).

Surprisingly, the benefits of social support are not limited to the comfort provided by other humans. One study found that owners of pets were less likely to require medical care after exposure to stressors than were those without pets! Dogs, in particular, helped diminish the effects of stress (Siegel, 1990, 1993).

How does one cope most effectively with stress? Researchers have made a number of recommendations for dealing with the problem. There is no universal solution, of course, because effective coping depends on the nature of the stressor and the degree to which control is possible. Still, some general guidelines can be followed (Zeidner & Endler, 1996; Aspinwall & Taylor, 1997; Folkman & Moskowitz, 2000):

BECOMING AN INFORMED CONSUMER of Psychology

Effective Coping Strategies

- ▶ *Turn threat into challenge.* When a stressful situation may be controllable, the best coping strategy is to treat the situation as a challenge, focusing on ways to control it. For instance, if you experience stress because your car is always breaking down, you might take a course in auto mechanics and learn to deal directly with the car's problems.
- ▶ *Make a threatening situation less threatening.* When a stressful situation seems to be uncontrollable, a different approach must be taken. It is possible to change one's appraisal of the situation, view it in a different light, and modify one's attitude toward it. The old truism "Look for the silver lining in every cloud" is supported by research (Salovey et al., 2000; Smith & Lazarus, 2001).
- ▶ *Change your goals.* When one is faced with an uncontrollable situation, a reasonable strategy is to adopt new goals that are practical in view of the particular situation. For example, a dancer who has been in an automobile accident and has lost full use of her legs may no longer aspire to a career in dance but might modify her goals and try to become a dance instructor.
- ▶ *Take physical action.* Changing your physiological reaction to stress can help with coping. For example, biofeedback (in which a person learns to control internal physiological processes through conscious thought) can alter basic physiological processes, allowing people to reduce blood pressure, heart rate, and other consequences of heightened stress. In addition, exercise can be effective in reducing stress. Regular exercise improves overall health and may even reduce the risk of certain diseases, such as breast cancer. Finally, exercise gives people a sense of control over their bodies, as well as a feeling of accomplishment (Barinaga, 1997; Tkachuk & Martin, 1999; Hong, 2000; Langreth, 2000).

▶ *Prepare for stress before it happens.* A final strategy for coping with stress is *proactive coping*, anticipating and preparing for stress *before* it is encountered. For example, if you're expecting to go through a one-week period in which you must take a number of major tests, you can try to arrange your schedule so you have more time to study. Through proactive coping, people can ready themselves for upcoming stressful events and thereby reduce their consequences (Aspinwall & Taylor, 1997).

RECAP/EVALUATE/RETHINK

RECAP

How is health psychology a union between medicine and psychology?

▶ The field of health psychology considers how psychology can be applied to the prevention, diagnosis, and treatment of medical problems. (p. 498)

What is stress, how does it affect us, and how can we best cope with it?

▶ Stress is a response to threatening or challenging environmental conditions. People encounter stressors—the circumstances that produce stress—of both a positive and a negative nature. (p. 499)

▶ Stress produces immediate physiological reactions. In the short term those reactions may be adaptive, but in the long term they may have negative consequences, including the development of psychophysiological disorders. (p. 501)

▶ The consequences of stress can be explained in part by Selye's general adaptation syndrome (GAS), which suggests that there are three stages in stress responses: alarm and mobilization, resistance, and exhaustion. (p. 501)

▶ The way an environmental circumstance is interpreted affects whether it will be considered stressful. Still, there are general classes of events that provoke stress: cataclysmic events, personal stressors, and background stressors (daily hassles). (p. 503)

▶ Stress can be reduced by developing a sense of control over one's circumstances. In some cases, however, people develop a state of learned helplessness. (p. 505)

▶ Coping with stress can take a number of forms, including the unconscious use of defense mechanisms and the use of emotion-focused or problem-focused coping strategies. (p. 507)

EVALUATE

1. _____ is defined as a response to challenging or threatening events.
2. Match each portion of the GAS with its definition
   1. Alarm and mobilization
   2. Exhaustion
   3. Resistance
   a. Ability to adapt to stress diminishes; symptoms appear.
   b. Activation of sympathetic nervous system.
   c. Various strategies are used to cope with a stressor.
3. Stressors that affect a single person and produce an immediate major reaction are known as
   a. Personal stressors
   b. Psychic stressors
   c. Cataclysmic stressors
   d. Daily stressors
4. People with the personality characteristic of _____ seem to be better able to successfully combat stressors.

RETHINK

1. Why are cataclysmic stressors less stressful in the long run than are other types of stressors? Does the reason relate to the coping phenomenon known as social support? How?
2. Given what you know about coping strategies, how would you train people to avoid stress in their everyday lives? How would you use this information with a group of veterans from the war in Iraq suffering from posttraumatic stress disorder?

Answers to Evaluate Questions

1. stress; 2. 1-b; 2-a; 3-c; 3. a; 4. hardiness.

KEY TERMS

Psychological Aspects of Illness and Well-Being

M O D U L E 4 6

How do psychological factors affect health-related problems such as coronary heart disease, cancer, and smoking?

Once a week they meet to talk, to cry, sometimes to laugh together. "Is the pain still worse in the mornings?" Margaret asks Kate today.

A petite, graceful woman in her late forties, Kate shakes her head no. "It's getting bad all the time," she says in a voice raw with worry and fatigue. A few weeks ago she learned that the cancer that began in her breast had spread into her bones. Since then she's hardly slept. She knows, as do the other women in the group, that her prognosis isn't good. "Sometimes I'm afraid I'm not going to do that well because it all came on so fast," she tells them. "It's like being in the ocean and the waves are just coming too fast, and you can't get your breath."

They nod in tacit understanding, eight women sitting in a loose circle of chairs here in a small, sparely furnished room at Stanford University Medical Center. They know. All of them have been diagnosed with recurrent breast cancer . . .

They gather here each Wednesday afternoon to talk with each other and to listen. It's a chance to discuss their fears and find some small comfort, a time to feel they're not alone. And in some way that no one has been able to explain, it may be keeping them alive (Jaret, 1992, p. 87).

As recently as two decades ago, most psychologists and health-care providers would have scoffed at the notion that a discussion group could improve a cancer patient's chances of survival. Today, however, such methods have gained increasing acceptance.

Growing evidence suggests that psychological factors have a substantial impact both on major health problems that were once seen in purely physiological terms and on our everyday sense of health, well-being, and happiness. We'll consider the psychological components of three major health problems—heart disease, cancer, and smoking—and then consider the nature of people's well-being and happiness.

ⒶⒶⒶ

The A's and B's of Coronary Heart Disease

Tim knew it wasn't going to be his day when he got stuck in traffic behind a slow-moving farm truck. How could the driver dawdle like that? Didn't he have anything of any importance to do? Things didn't get any better when Tim arrived on campus and discovered the library didn't have the books he needed. He could almost feel the tension rising. "I need that material to finish my paper," he thought to himself. He knew that meant he wouldn't be able to get his paper done early, and that meant he wouldn't have the time he wanted to revise the paper. He wanted it to be a first-class paper. *This* time Tim wanted to get a better grade than his roommate, Luis; although Luis didn't know it, Tim felt they were in direct competition and was always trying to better him, whether it was academically or just playing cards. "In fact," Tim mused to himself, "I feel like I'm in competition with with everyone, no matter what I'm doing."

FIGURE I No one is totally a Type A or Type B personality; rather, everyone is a combination of the two types. Take this quick test to determine which type is strongest in you. (Source: Adapted from Jenkins, Zyzanski, & Rosenman, 1978.)

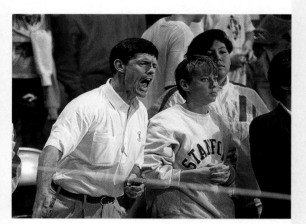

Type Yourself

To get an idea of whether you have the characteristics of a Type A or Type B personality, answer the following questions:

1. When you listen to someone talking and this person takes too long to come to the point, how often do you feel like hurrying the person along?
   _____ Frequently
   _____ Occasionally
   _____ Never

2. Do you ever set deadlines or quotas for yourself at work or at home?
   _____ No
   _____ Yes, but only occasionally
   _____ Yes, once a week or more

3. Would people you know well agree that you tend to get irritated easily?
   _____ Definitely yes
   _____ Probably yes
   _____ Probably no
   _____ Definitely no

4. Would people who know you well agree that you tend to do most things in a hurry?
   _____ Definitely yes
   _____ Probably yes
   _____ Probably no
   _____ Definitely no

Scoring: The more frequently your answers reflect affirmative responses, the more Type A characteristics you hold.

Type A behavior pattern: A pattern of behavior characterized by competitiveness, impatience, a tendency toward frustration, and hostility.

Type B behavior pattern: A pattern of behavior characterized by cooperation, patience, noncompetitiveness, and nonaggression.

INTERACTIVITY 46–1

Type A behavior

Have you, like Tim, ever seethed impatiently at being caught behind a slow-moving vehicle, felt anger and frustration at not finding material you needed at the library, or experienced a sense of competitiveness with your classmates?

Many of us experience these sorts of feelings at one time or another, but for some people they represent a pervasive, characteristic set of personality traits known as the **Type A behavior pattern.** Type A individuals are competitive, show a continuous sense of urgency about time, are aggressive, exhibit a driven quality regarding their work, and are hostile, both verbally and nonverbally—especially when interrupted while trying to complete a task. In contrast, people who show the **Type B behavior pattern** are more cooperative, far less competitive, not especially time-oriented, and not usually aggressive, driven, or hostile. Although people are typically not "pure" Type A's or Type B's, showing instead a combination of both behavior types, they generally fall into one or the other category (Rosenman, 1990; Strube, 1990). See Figure 1 and complete **Interactivity 46–1** to learn more about Type A and B tendencies.

Type A people lead fast-paced, driven lives. They put in longer hours at work than do Type B's and are impatient with other people's performance, which they typically perceive as too slow. They also engage in "multitasking," concentrating on several activities simultaneously, such as running on a treadmill, watching television, and reading a magazine all at the same time.

The importance of the Type A behavior pattern lies in its links to coronary heart disease. Studies have found that men who display the Type A pattern develop coronary heart disease twice as often and suffer significantly more fatal heart attacks than do those classified as having the Type B pattern. Moreover, the Type A pattern predicts who is going to develop heart disease at least as well as—and independently of—any other single factor, including age, blood pressure, smoking habits, and cholesterol levels in the body (Rosenman et al., 1976; 1994; Wielgosz & Nolan, 2000).

Not every component of the Type A behavior pattern is bad. Hostility and anger seem to be the key factors in the link between coronary heart disease and the Type A behavior pattern (Mittleman et al., 1995; McCabe et al., 2000; Williams et al., 2000).

Why are the hostility and anger behind the Type A behavior so toxic? The most convincing theory is that the Type A behavior pattern produces excessive physiological arousal in stressful situations. That arousal, in turn, results in increased production of the hormones epinephrine and norepinephrine, as well as increases in heart rate and blood pressure. Such exaggerated physiological responsivity ultimately produces an increased incidence of coronary heart disease (Sundin et al., 1995; Black & Barbutt, 2002).

It's important to keep in mind that not everyone who displays Type A behaviors is destined to have coronary heart disease. For one thing, a firm association between Type A behaviors and coronary heart disease has not been established for women; most findings pertain to males, not to females. In addition, other types of negative emotions, besides the hostility and anger found in Type A behavior, appear to be related to heart attacks. For example, psychologist Johan Denollet has found evidence that what he calls *Type D*—for "distressed"—behavior is linked to coronary heart disease. In his view, insecurity, anxiety, and the negative outlook displayed by Type D's puts them at risk for repeated heart attacks (Denollet & Brutsaert, 1998).

Furthermore, the evidence relating Type A behavior (and other personality types) to coronary heart disease is correlational. Consequently, we cannot say for sure whether Type A behavior *causes* heart disease or whether, instead, some other factor causes both heart disease and Type A behavior. In fact, rather than focusing on Type A behavior as the cause of heart disease, it may make more sense to ask whether Type B behavior *prevents* heart disease (Powell et al., 1993; Orth-Gomér, Chesney, & Wenger, 1996; Snieder et al., 2002).

Psychological Aspects of Cancer

Hardly any disease is feared more than cancer. Most people think of cancer in terms of lingering pain, and being diagnosed with the disease is typically viewed as receiving a death sentence.

Although a diagnosis of cancer is not as grim as one might at first suspect—several kinds of cancer have a high cure rate if detected early enough—cancer remains the second leading cause of death after coronary heart disease. The precise trigger for the disease is not well understood, but the process by which cancer spreads is straightforward. Certain cells in the body become altered and multiply rapidly and in an uncontrolled fashion. As those cells grow, they form tumors, which, if left unchecked, suck nutrients from healthy cells and body tissue, ultimately destroying the body's ability to function properly.

Although the processes involved in the spread of cancer are basically physiological, accumulating evidence suggests that the emotional responses of cancer patients to their disease may have a critical effect on its course. For example, one experiment found that people who adopt a fighting spirit are more likely to recover than are those who pessimistically suffer and resign themselves to death (Pettingale et al., 1985). The study analyzed the survival rates of women who had undergone the removal of a breast because of cancer.

The results suggested that the survival rates were related to the psychological response of the women three months after surgery (see Figure 2). Women who stoically accepted their fate, trying not to complain, and those who felt the situation was hopeless and that nothing could be done showed the lowest survival rates; most

FIGURE 2 The relationship between women's psychological response to breast cancer three months after surgery and their survival ten years after the operation (Pettingale et al., 1985). What implications do these findings have for the treatment of people with cancer?

According to this study, having a fighting spirit helped increase the survival rate of women who have been treated for breast cancer.

Women's psychological reactions three months after the operation

Increasing evidence suggests that the way a cancer patient emotionally deals with the disease may have an impact on its effects and treatment and may slow the growth of cancer cells such as these. Which is the better strategy: stoic acceptance or denial? Why?

of those women were dead after ten years. In comparison, the survival rates of women who showed a fighting spirit (predicting that they would overcome the disease and planning to take steps to prevent its recurrence) and the survival rates of women who (erroneously) denied that they had ever had cancer (saying that the breast removal was merely a preventive step) were significantly higher. In sum, according to this study, cancer patients with a positive attitude were more likely to survive than were those with a more negative one.

On the other hand, other research contradicts the notion that the course of cancer is affected by patients' attitudes and emotions. For example, some findings show that although a "fighting spirit" leads to better coping, the long-term survival rate is no better than it is for patients with a less positive attitude (Watson et al., 1999).

Despite the conflicting evidence, health psychologists believe that patients' emotions may at least partially determine the course of their disease. For example, psychologists specializing in psychoneuroimmunology (PNI) suggest that a patient's emotional state affects the immune system in the same way that stress affects it. For instance, in the case of cancer, it is possible that positive emotional responses may help generate specialized "killer" cells that help control the size and spread of cancerous tumors. Conversely, negative emotions may suppress the ability of those cells to fight tumors (Andersen, Kiecolt-Glaser, & Glaser, 1994; Seligman, 1995; Schedlowski & Tewes, 1999).

Other research suggests that "joy"—referring to mental resilience and vigor—is related to the likelihood of survival of patients with recurrent breast cancer. Similarly, cancer patients who are characteristically optimistic report less distress throughout the course of their treatment (Levy et al., 1988; Carver et al., 2000).

Is a particular personality type linked to cancer? Some findings suggest that cancer patients are less emotionally reactive, suppress anger, and lack outlets for emotional release. However, the data are too tentative and inconsistent to suggest firm conclusions about a link between personality characteristics and cancer. Certainly no conclusive evidence suggests that people who develop cancer would not have done so if their personality had been of a different sort or if their attitudes had been more positive (Smith, 1988; Zevon & Corn, 1990; Holland & Lewis, 2001).

What is increasingly clear, however, is that certain types of psychological therapy have the potential for extending the lives of cancer patients. For example, the results of one study showed that women with breast cancer who received psychological treatment lived at least a year and a half longer, and experienced less anxiety and pain, than did women who did not participate in therapy. Research on patients with other health problems, such as heart disease, also has found that therapy can be beneficial, both psychologically and medically (Spiegel, 1993, 1996b; Galavotti et al., 1997; Frasure-Smith, Lesperance, & Talajic, 2000).

Smoking

Would you stroll into a convenience store and buy an item with a label warning you that its use could kill you? Although most people would probably answer no, millions make such a purchase every day: a pack of cigarettes. Furthermore, they do this despite clear, well-publicized evidence that smoking is linked to cancer, heart attacks, strokes, bronchitis, emphysema, and a host of other serious illnesses. Smoking is the greatest preventable cause of death in the United States; one in five U.S. deaths is caused by smoking. Worldwide, 3 million people die prematurely each year from the effects of smoking (Mackay & Eriksen, 2002).

Why do people smoke despite all the evidence showing that it is bad for their health? It is not that they are somehow unaware of the link between smoking and disease; surveys show that most *smokers* agree with the statement "Cigarette smoking frequently causes disease and death." And almost three-quarters of the 48 million smokers in the United States say they would like to quit (CDC, 1994; Wetter et al., 1998).

Heredity seems to determine, in part, whether people will become smokers, how much they will smoke, and how easily they can quit. Genetics also influences how susceptible people are to the harmful effects of smoking. For instance, there is an almost 50 percent higher rate of lung cancer in African American smokers than in white smokers. This difference may be due to genetically produced variations in the efficiency with which enzymes are able to reduce the effects of the cancer-causing chemicals in tobacco smoke (Heath & Madden, 1995; Pomerlau, 1995; Li et al., 2003).

However, although genetics plays a role in smoking, most research suggests that environmental factors are the primary cause of the habit. Smoking at first may be seen as "cool" or sophisticated, as a rebellious act, or as facilitating calm performance in stressful situations. In addition, smoking a cigarette is sometimes viewed as a "rite of passage" for adolescents, undertaken at the urging of friends and viewed as a sign of growing up. But this may be changing: Since 1997, the percentage of U.S. teenagers who smoke has declined significantly (Koval et al., 2000; Wagner & Atkins, 2000; Johnston, O'Malley, & Bachman, 2003).

Ultimately, smoking becomes a habit. People begin to label themselves smokers, and smoking becomes part of their self-concept. Moreover, they become dependent physiologically as a result of smoking, because nicotine, a primary ingredient of tobacco, is highly addictive. Ultimately, a complex relationship develops among smoking, nicotine levels, and a smoker's emotional state, in which a certain nicotine level becomes associated with a positive emotional state. As a result, people smoke in an effort to regulate *both* emotional states and nicotine levels in the blood (Leventhal & Cleary, 1980; Gilbert, 1995; Kassel, Stroud, & Paronis, 2003).

QUITTING SMOKING

Because smoking has both psychological and biological components, few habits are as difficult to break. Long-term successful treatment typically occurs in just 15 percent of those who try to stop smoking, and once smoking becomes a habit, it is as hard to stop as an addiction to cocaine or heroin. In fact, some of the biochemical reactions to nicotine are similar to those to cocaine, amphetamines, and morphine. Many people try to quit and fail, as you can see in Figure 3 (Glassman & Koob, 1996; Piasecki et al., 1997; Harris Poll, 2000).

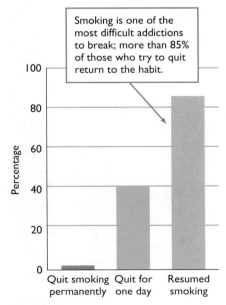

FIGURE 3 The difficulty of quitting smoking is evident in this graph. More than 85 percent of those who tried to quit returned to smoking. (Source: Centers for Disease Control, 1993.)

Changes in society's attitudes, and strong antismoking campaigns, can go a long way toward reducing tobacco use.

Among the most effective tools for ending the smoking habit are drugs that replace the nicotine found in cigarettes. Whether in the form of gum, patches, nasal sprays, or inhalers, these products provide a dose of nicotine that reduces dependence on cigarettes. Another approach is exemplified by the drug Zyban, which, rather than replacing nicotine, raises dopamine levels in the brain, thereby reducing the desire to smoke (Rock, 1999; Mitchell, 2000; Barringer & Weaver, 2002).

Behavioral strategies, which view smoking as a learned habit and concentrate on changing the smoking response, can also be effective. Initial "cure" rates of 60 percent have been reported, and one year after treatment more than half of those who quit have not resumed smoking. Counseling, either individually or in groups, also increases the rate of success in breaking the habit. The best treatment seems to be a combination of nicotine replacement *and* counseling. What doesn't work? Going it alone: Only 5 percent of smokers who quit cold-turkey on their own are successful (Wetter et al., 1998; Noble, 1999; Rock, 1999).

In the long term, the most effective means of reducing smoking may be changes in societal norms and attitudes toward the habit. For instance, many cities and towns have made smoking in public places illegal, and legislation banning smoking in places such as college classrooms and buildings—based on strong popular sentiment—is being passed with increasing frequency (Gibson, 1997; Jacobson, Wasserman, & Anderson, 1997).

The long-term effect of the barrage of information regarding the negative consequences of smoking on people's health has been substantial; overall, smoking has declined over the last two decades, particularly among males. Still, more than one-fourth of students enrolled in high school are active smokers by the time they graduate. Among these students, more than 10 percent become active smokers as early as the eighth grade (see Figure 4; Johnston, O'Malley, & Bachman, 2003).

Hucksters of Death: Promoting Smoking Throughout the World

In Dresden, Germany, three women in miniskirts offer passers-by a pack of Lucky Strikes and a leaflet that reads: "You just got hold of a nice piece of America." Says a local doctor, "Adolescents time and again receive cigarettes at such promotions."

A Jeep decorated with the Camel logo pulls up to a high school in Buenos Aires. A woman begins handing out free cigarettes to 15- and 16-year-olds during their lunch recess.

At a video arcade in Taipei, free American cigarettes are strewn atop each game. At a disco filled with high school students, free packs of Salems are on each table (Ecenbarger, 1993, p. 50).

As the number of smokers has declined in the United States, cigarette manufacturers have turned to new markets in an effort to increase the number of people who smoke. In the process, they have employed some dubious marketing techniques.

For instance, the tobacco company RJ Reynolds developed a new cigarette brand it named Uptown in the early 1990s. Because of the nature of the advertising that initiated the distribution of the cigarette, it soon became apparent that the product was targeted at African Americans (Jhally et al., 1995; Ringold, 1996). Because of the questionable ethics of targeting a potentially life-threatening product to a minority population, the product introduction caused considerable controversy. Ultimately, the secretary of the U.S. Department of Health and Human Services condemned the tactic, and the manufacturer stopped distributing the brand soon afterward.

Because of legal constraints on smoking in the United States, manufacturers have turned their sights to other parts of the world, where they see a fertile market of

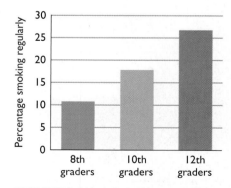

FIGURE 4 Although smoking among teenagers is lower than 20 years ago, a significant number still report smoking regularly. What factors might account for the continued high use of tobacco by teenagers, despite the increase in antismoking advertising? (Source: Monitoring the Future Study, 2003.)

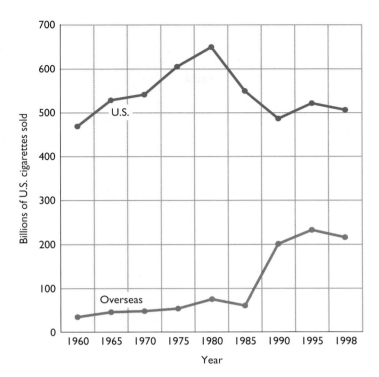

FIGURE 5 Despite the plummeting in sales of cigarettes in the United States, the number sold overseas has dramatically increased. (Source: U.S. Department of Agriculture, 1998).

In some countries, children as young as 6 smoke regularly.

nonsmokers. Although they must often sell cigarettes more cheaply than they do in the United States, the number of potential smokers still makes it financially worthwhile for the tobacco companies. For instance, China has opened its market of 320 million smokers—more than the entire U.S. population—to American brands. As can be seen in Figure 5, overseas sales have surged since the mid-1980s, as sales in the United States have declined (Bartecchi, MacKenzie, & Schrier, 1995; Brown, 2001).

Clearly, the push into worldwide markets has been successful. In some Latin American cities, as many as 50 percent of teenagers smoke. Children as young as age 7 smoke in Hong Kong, and 30 percent of children smoked their first whole cigarette before the age of 10 in India, Ghana, Jamaica, and Poland. The World Health Organization predicts that smoking will prematurely kill some 200 million of the world's children, and that ultimately 10 percent of the world's population will die as a result of smoking. Of everyone alive today, 500 million will eventually die from tobacco use. Clearly, smoking represents one of the world's greatest health problems (Mackay & Eriksen, 2002).

RECAP/EVALUATE/RETHINK

RECAP

How do psychological factors affect health-related problems such as coronary heart disease, cancer, and smoking?

▶ Hostility and anger, part of the Type A behavior pattern, are linked to coronary heart disease. Type A individuals tend to be competitive, show a sense of time urgency

and hurriedness, are hostile and aggressive, and seem to be driven. (p. 511)

▶ Increasing evidence suggests that people's attitudes and emotional responses affect the course of cancer through links to the immune system. (p. 513)

▶ Smoking, the leading preventable cause of health problems, has proved to be difficult to quit, even though most smokers are aware of the dangerous consequences of the behavior. (p. 515)

EVALUATE

1. Type _____ behavior is characterized by cooperativeness and by being easy going; Type _____ behavior is characterized by aggression and competitiveness.

2. Type A behavior is known to directly cause heart attacks. True or false?

3. A cancer patient's attitude and emotions may affect that person's _____ system, helping or hindering the patient's fight against the disease.

4. Smoking is used to regulate both nicotine levels and emotional states in smokers. True or false?

RETHINK

1. Do you think Type A or Type B behavior is more widely encouraged in the United States? Why?

2. Is there a danger of "blaming the victim" when we argue that the course of cancer can be improved if a person with the disease holds particular beneficial attitudes or beliefs? Why?

Answers to Evaluate Questions

1. B, A; 2. false; Type A behavior is related to a higher incidence of coronary heart disease but does not necessarily cause it directly; 3. immune; 4. true

KEY TERMS

Type A behavior
pattern p. 512

Type B behavior
pattern p. 512

Promoting Health and Wellness

When Stuart Grinspoon first noticed the small lump in his arm, he assumed it was just a bruise from the touch football game he had played the previous week. But as he thought about it more, he considered more serious possibilities and decided that he'd better get it checked out at the university health service. But the visit was less than satisfactory. A shy person, Stuart felt embarrassed talking about his medical condition. Even worse, after answering a string of questions, he couldn't even understand the physician's diagnosis and was too embarrassed to ask for clarification.

Stuart Grinspoon's attitudes toward health care are shared by many of us. We approach physicians the same way we approach auto mechanics. When something goes wrong with the car, we want the mechanic to figure out the problem and then fix it. In the same way, when something isn't working right with our bodies, we want a diagnosis of the problem and then a (hopefully quick) repair.

Yet such an approach ignores the fact that—unlike auto repair—good health care requires taking psychological factors into account. Health psychologists have sought to determine the factors involved in the promotion of good health and, more broadly, a sense of well-being and happiness. Let's take a closer look at two areas they have tackled: producing compliance with health-related advice and identifying the determinants of well-being and happiness.

▲ ▲ ▲

Following Medical Advice

We're not very good at taking medical advice. Consider these figures:

- ▶ As many as 85 percent of patients do not fully comply with a physician's recommendations.
- ▶ Between 14 and 21 percent of patients don't fill their drug prescriptions.
- ▶ Some 10 percent of adolescent pregnancies result from noncompliance with birth control medication.
- ▶ Sixty percent of all patients cannot identify their own medicines.
- ▶ From 30 percent to 50 percent of all patients ignore instructions or make errors in taking medication (Zuger, 1998; Christensen & Johnson, 2002; Health Pages, 2003).

Noncompliance with medical advice can take many forms. For example, patients may fail to show up for scheduled appointments, not follow diets or not give up smoking, or discontinue medication during treatment. In some cases, they fail to take prescribed medicine at all.

Patients also may practice *creative nonadherence,* in which they adjust a treatment prescribed by a physician, relying on their own medical judgment and experience. In many cases patients' lack of medical knowledge may be harmful (Weintraub, 1976; Taylor, 1995).

Noncompliance is sometimes a result of psychological reactance. **Reactance** is a negative emotional and cognitive reaction that results from the restriction of one's

How do our interactions with physicians affect our health and compliance with medical treatment?

What leads to a sense of well-being?

Reactance: A disagreeable emotional and cognitive reaction that results from the restriction of one's freedom and that can be associated with medical regimens.

519

INTERACTIVITY 47–1

Compliance with medical advice

freedom. People who experience reactance feel hostility and anger. Because of such emotions, they may seek to restore their sense of freedom, but in a self-destructive manner by refusing to accept medical advice and perhaps acting in a way that worsens their medical condition. For instance, a man who is placed on a strict diet may experience reactance and tend to eat even more than he did before his diet was restricted (Fogarty & Young, 2000). To get a better understanding of the reasons behind compliance with medical advice, complete **Interactivity 47–1.**

FAILURE TO COMMUNICATE

I was lying on a gurney, trying to prepare myself for a six-hour breast-reconstruction surgery. A few months earlier, I'd had a mastectomy for breast cancer. Because I'm small-boned, my doctor told me I needed to have a muscle sliced from my back and moved to my chest to create a proper foundation for an implant. I knew the operation would slow me down—bad news for someone who swims, runs and chases three young kids. But as the surgeon diagramed incision points on my chest with a felt-tip pen, my husband asked a question: "Is it really necessary to transfer this back muscle?" (Halpert, 2003, p. 63).

The surgeon's answer shocked the patient: No, it wasn't necessary. And if she didn't have the procedure, her recovery time would be cut in half. The surgeon had simply assumed, without asking the patient, that she would prefer the more complicated procedure, because cosmetically it would be preferable. But after a hurried consultation with her husband, the patient opted for the less invasive procedure.

Lack of communication between medical care providers and patients can be a major obstacle to good medical care. Such communication failures occur for several reasons. One is that physicians make assumptions about what patients prefer, or they push a particular treatment that they prefer without consulting patients. Furthermore, the relatively high prestige of physicians may intimidate patients. Patients may also be reluctant to volunteer information that might cast them in a bad light, and physicians may have difficulties encouraging their patients to provide information. In many cases, physicians dominate an interview with questions of a technical nature, whereas patients attempt to communicate a personal sense of their illness and the impact it is having on their lives, as illustrated in Figure 1 (Graugaard, Eide, & Finset, 2003; Ihler, 2003).

Furthermore, the view held by many patients that physicians are "all-knowing" can result in serious communication problems. Many patients do not understand their treatments yet fail to ask their physicians for clearer explanations of a prescribed course of action. About half of all patients are unable to report accurately how long they are to continue taking a medication prescribed for them, and about a quarter do not even know the purpose of the drug. In fact, some patients are not even sure, as they are about to be rolled into the operating room, why they are having surgery (Svarstad, 1976; Atkinson, 1997; Halpert, 2003)!

Sometimes patient-physician communication difficulties occur because the material that must be communicated is too technical for patients, who may lack fundamental knowledge about the body and basic medical practices. In response to

"Give it to me straight, Doc. How long do I have to ignore your advice?"

FIGURE 1 Effective communication between patient and physician is important, but often proves frustrating for both.

A Patient Talks to Her Physician

The following excerpt from a case study used at the Harvard Medical School is an example of poor interviewing technique on the part of the physician.

Patient: I can hardly drink water.
Doctor: Um hum.
Patient: Remember when it started? . . . It was pains in my head. It must have been then.
Doctor: Um hum.
Patient: I don't know what it is. The doctor looked at it . . . said something about glands.
Doctor: Ok. Um hum, aside from this, how have you been feeling?
patient: Terrible.
Doctor: Yeah.
Patient: Tired . . . there's pains . . . I don't know what it is.
Doctor: Ok. . . . Fever or chills?
Patient: No.
Doctor: Ok. . . . Have you been sick to your stomach or anything?
Patient: (Sniffles, crying) I don't know what's going on. I get up in the morning tired. The only time I feel good. . . . maybe like around suppertime . . . and everything (crying) and still the same thing.
Doctor: Um hum. You're getting the nausea before you eat or after? (Goleman, 1988, p. B16)

Although the frequent "um hums" suggest that the physician is listening to the patient, in fact he does not encourage the patient to disclose more pertinent details. Even more, late in the interview, the physician ignores the patient's emotional distress and coldly continues through the list of questions.

this problem, some health-care providers routinely use baby talk (calling patients "honey" or telling them to go "night-night") and assume that patients are unable to understand even simple information (Whitbourne & Wills, 1993; DiMatteo, 1997; Basset et al., 1998).

The amount of physician-patient communication also is related to the sex of a physician. Overall, female primary care physicians provide more patient-centered communications than do male primary care physicians (Roter, Hall, & Aoki, 2002).

Cultural values and expectations also contribute to communication barriers between patients and their physicians. Providing medical advice to a patient whose native language is not English may be problematic. Furthermore, medical practices differ between cultures, and medical practioners need to be familiar with a patient's culture to produce compliance with medical recommendations (Bush & Osterweis, 1978; Dressler & Oths, 1997; Whaley, 2000).

INCREASING COMPLIANCE WITH HEALTH-RELATED ADVICE

Although compliance with medical advice does not guarantee that a patient's medical problems will go away, it does optimize the possibility that the patient's condition will improve. What, then, can health-care providers do to produce greater compliance on the part of their patients? One strategy is to provide clear

Positively framed messages suggest that a change in behavior will lead to a health-related gain.

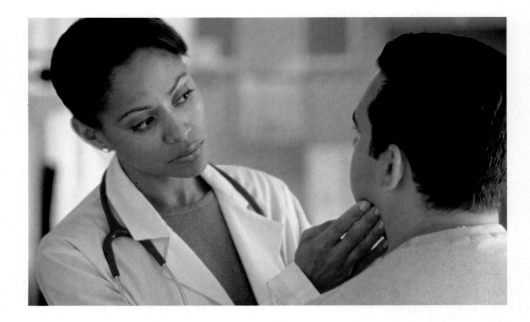

instructions to patients regarding drug regimens. Maintaining good, warm relations between physicians and patients also leads to increased compliance (Cramer, 1995; Cheney, 1996).

In addition, honesty helps. Patients generally prefer to be well informed—even if the news is bad—and their degree of satisfaction with their medical care is linked to how well and how accurately physicians are able to convey the nature of their medical problems and treatments (Hall, Roter, & Katz, 1988; Haley, Clair, & Saulsberry, 1992).

The way in which a message is framed also can result in more positive responses to health-related information. *Positively framed messages* suggest that a change in behavior will lead to a gain, emphasizing the benefits of carrying out a health-related behavior. For instance, suggesting that skin cancer is curable if it is detected early, and that you can reduce your chances of getting the disease by using a sunscreen, places information in a positive frame. In contrast, *negatively framed messages* highlight what you can lose by not performing a behavior. For instance, one might say that if you don't use sunscreen, you're more likely to get skin cancer, which can kill you if it's not detected early—an example of a negative frame.

What type of message is more effective? According to psychologists Alex Rothman and Peter Salovey, it depends on the type of health behavior one is trying to bring about. Negatively framed messages are best for motivating *preventive* behavior. However, positively framed messages are most effective in producing behavior that will lead to the detection of a disease (Rothman & Salovey, 1997; Apanovich, McCarthy, & Salovey, 2003; McCaul, Johnson, & Rothman, 2003).

Well-Being and Happiness

Subjective well-being: People's own evaluation of their lives in terms of both their thoughts and their emotions.

What makes for a good life?

It's a question that has been pondered by philosophers and theologians for centuries, and now health psychologists are turning their spotlight on the question. They are doing that by investigating **subjective well-being,** people's evaluations of their lives in terms of both their thoughts and their emotions. Considered another way, subjective well-being is the measure of how happy people are (Oishi & Diener, 2001; Diener, Lucas, & Oishi, 2002).

Research on the subject of well-being shows that happy people share several characteristics (Myers & Diener, 1996; Myers, 2000; Diener & Seligman, 2002):

- *Happy people have high self-esteem.* Particularly in Western cultures, which emphasize the importance of individuality, people who are happy like themselves. They see themselves as more intelligent and better able to get along with others than is the average person.
- *Happy people have a firm sense of control.* They feel more in control of events in their lives, unlike those who feel they are the pawns of others and who experience learned helplessness.
- *Happy individuals are optimistic.* Their optimism permits them to persevere at tasks and ultimately to achieve more. In addition, their health is better (Peterson, 2000).
- *Happy people like to be around other people.* They tend to be extroverted and have a supportive network of close relationships.

Perhaps most important, most people are at least moderately happy most of the time. In both national and international surveys, people living in a wide variety of circumstances report being happy. Furthermore, life-altering events that one might expect would produce long-term spikes in happiness, such as winning the lottery, probably won't make you much happier than you already are, as we discuss next.

DOES MONEY BUY HAPPINESS?

If you won the lottery, would you be happier?

Probably not. At least that's the implication of health psychologists' research on subjective well-being. That research shows that although winning the lottery brings an initial surge in happiness, a year later winners' level of happiness seems to return to what it was before. The converse phenomenon occurs for people who have had serious injuries in accidents: Despite an initial decline in happiness, in most cases victims return to their prior levels of happiness after the passage of time (Srivastava, Locke, & Bartol, 2001; Diener & Biswas Diener, 2002; Nissle & Bschor, 2002).

Why is the level of subjective well-being so stable? One explanation is that people have a general "set point" for happiness, a marker that establishes the tone for one's life. Although particular events may temporarily elevate or depress one's mood (a surprise promotion or a job loss, for example), ultimately people return to their general level of happiness.

Although it is not certain how people's happiness set points are initially established, some evidence suggests that the set point is determined at least in part by genetic factors. Specifically, identical twins who grow up in widely different circumstances turn out to have very similar levels of happiness (Lykken & Tellegen, 1996; Kahneman, Diener, & Schwarz, 1998).

Most people's well-being set point is relatively high. For example, some 30 percent of people in the United States rate themselves as "very happy," and only one in ten rates himself or herself as "not too happy." Most people declare themselves to be "pretty happy." Such feelings are graphically confirmed by people who are asked to place themselves on the measure of happiness illustrated in Figure 2. The scale clearly illustrates that most people view their lives quite positively.

Similar results are found when people are asked to compare themselves with others. For example, when asked, "Who of the following people do you think is

Happy Thoughts: Thinking Positively May Help You Live Longer

Imagine you wrote an autobiography of your life from birth up through today. If someone were to read your autobiography, would that person be struck by the number of positive emotions you described? Or would your reader come away depressed by the negative emotions you have experienced?

If your imaginary autobiography were full of positive emotions, you might experience yet another positive emotion when you learned that research suggests that you may be in for a long life. Specifically, a recent study of the handwritten autobiographies of young Catholic nuns showed that the nuns whose journals focused on positive emotions actually lived longer than did those who focused on more negative feelings. An emphasis on positive emotions probably is an indicator of a life long habit of responding positively to life events, a habit that appears to affect people's health positively and thereby extend their lives (Danner, Snowdon, & Friesen, 2001).

Positive emotions also can be helpful even in the face of severe adversity. For example, the more people were able to experience positive emotions in the days after the World Trade Center terrorist attack (such as gratitude that loved ones were safe), the better able they were to rebound from the attack (Fredrickson et al., 2003).

A generally optimistic outlook on life also seems to help people live longer,

Positive thinking is associated with health and long life.

healthier lives. In a longitudinal study that tracked people's health and personality for thirty years, the optimists in the study consistently outlived their pessimistic counterparts. Although no one can explain how optimism can extend

people's lives (or, conversely, how pessimism can shorten them), some researchers speculate that positive thinking itself may somehow keep optimists healthier or that pessimists may be reluctant to seek health care, fearing that they will hear bad news (Maruta, Colligan, Malinchoc, & Offord, 2000).

Further highlighting the power of positive thinking, helping other people—even as infrequently as once per year—appears to improve one's chances for living longer (Brown, 2003). Likewise, as people grow older, maintaining a positive attitude toward aging is associated with an increased likelihood for long life. Similarly, among older people, simply feeling in control of the aspects of their lives that are most important to them has a positive influence on their longevity (Krause & Shaw, 2001; Levy, Slade, Kunkel, & Kasl, 2002).

The research trend is clear: Increasing evidence is revealing relationships among positive thinking, health, and a long life. It's important to keep in mind that a person's life span is determined by many factors, including genetics, diet, and lifestyle, not just positive thinking. Still, evidence continues to mount that positive thinking is a healthy contributor to a long, happy life.

RETHINK

How do you think that positive thinking can influence the length of people's lives? Do you believe that people can be taught to think positively? Why or why not? Do you believe that people *should* be taught to think positively? Why or why not?

the happiest?" survey respondents answered "Oprah Winfrey" (23 percent), "Bill Gates" (7 percent), "the Pope" (12 percent), "Chelsea Clinton" (3 percent), and "yourself" (49 percent), with 6 percent saying they didn't know (Black & McCafferty, 1998).

Few differences exist between members of different demographic groups. Men and women report being equally happy, and African Americans are only slightly less likely than European Americans to rate themselves as "very happy." Furthermore, happiness is hardly unique to U.S. culture. Even countries that are far from

Faces Scale: "Which face comes closest to expressing how you feel about your life as a whole?"

20%	46%	27%	4%	2%	1%	0%

FIGURE 2 Most people in the United States rate themselves as happy, while only a small minority indicate they are "not too happy." (*Source:* Myers, 2000, p. 57, drawn from *Social Indicators of Well-Being: Americans' Perceptions of Life Quality* (pp. 207 and 306), by F. M. Andrews and S. B. Withey, 1976. New York, Plenum. Copyright 1976 by Plenum.)

economically prosperous have, on the whole, happy residents (Myers & Diener, 1996; Diener & Clifton, 2002; Suh, 2002).

The bottom line: Money does *not* seem to buy happiness. Despite the ups and downs of life, most people tend to be reasonably happy, and they adapt to the trials and tribulations—and joys and delights—of life by returning to a steady-state level of happiness. That habitual level of happiness can have profound—perhaps life-prolonging—implications, as we discuss in the *Applying Psychology in the 21st Century* box.

RECAP/EVALUATE/RETHINK

RECAP

How do our interactions with physicians affect our health and compliance with medical treatment?

- ▶ Although patients would often like physicians to base a diagnosis only on a physical examination, communicating one's problem to the physician is equally important. (p. 519)
- ▶ Patients may find it difficult to communicate openly with their physicians because of the high social prestige of physicians and the technical nature of medical information. (p. 520)

What leads to a sense of well-being?

- ▶ Subjective well-being, the measure of how happy people are, is highest in people with high self-esteem, a sense of control, optimism, and a supportive network of close relationships. (p. 523)

EVALUATE

1. Health psychologists are most likely to focus on which of the following problems with health care?

   a. Incompetent health-care providers
   b. Rising health-care costs
   c. Ineffective communication between physician and patient
   d. Scarcity of medical research funding

2. If you wish for people to floss more to prevent gum disease, the best approach is to
   a. Use a negatively framed message
   b. Use a positively framed message
   c. Have a dentist deliver an encouraging message on the pleasures of flossing
   d. Provide people with free dental floss

3. Winning the lottery is likely to
   a. Produce an immediate and long-term increase in the level of well-being
   b. Produce an immediate, but not lingering, increase in the level of well-being
   c. Produce a decline in well-being over the long run
   d. Lead to an increase in greed over the long run

RETHINK

1. Do you think stress plays a role in making communication between physicians and patients difficult? Why?

2. You are given the job of instructing a group of medical school students in a lecture called "Physician-Patient Interactions." How would you set up your class, and what kind of information would you provide?

3. If money doesn't buy happiness, what *can* you do to make yourself happier? As you answer, consider the research findings on stress and coping, as well as on emotions.

Answers to Evaluate Questions

1. c; 2. a; 3. b

KEY TERMS

reactance p. 519

subjective well-being p. 522

Psychology on the Web

1. Find three or more websites that deal with stress reduction. Gather at least five techniques for reducing stress and summarize them. Write a critique and evaluation of those techniques, using the information you learned about stress. Which ones seem to have a sound basis in psychological theory and/or research?
2. Are you closer to a Type A personality or a Type B? Find two websites offering tests that claim to provide the answer. Summarize the quality of the tests from a scientific point of view and compare the results you received from each one.
3. After completing Interactivity 45–1 on stress, investigate reports on the Web of posttraumatic stress disorder in soldiers returning from the war in Iraq. Summarize your findings.

Epilogue

In this set of modules, we have explored the intersection of psychology and biology. We saw how the emotional and psychological experience of stress can lead to physical symptoms of illness, how personality factors may be related to major health problems, and how psychological factors can interfere with effective communication between physician and patient. We also looked at the other side of the coin, noting that some relatively simple strategies can help us control stress, affect illness, and improve our interactions with physicians.

Turn back to the Prologue to this set of modules, about Elizabeth Oettinger and her hectic schedule, and use your understanding of health psychology and stress to consider these questions.

1. Based on the description of Elizabeth Oettinger's day, which stressors are personal and which are background stressors? What might happen to "elevate" the stress level of a background stressor to a more serious level? Are there likely to be any uplifts in Oettinger's day?
2. How does the general adaptation syndrome (GAS) apply to Oettinger's situation? How might events in her life move her along the three stages of the model?
3. What steps would you advise Oettinger to take to keep her level of stress under control? How might others in her life be involved in such an effort?
4. Does Oettinger appear more likely to have a Type A or Type B personality? Why?

Psychological Disorders

Prologue
Chris Coles

Chris Coles heard the voice in his head for the first time late one evening. The voice told him to meet a friend at that moment, and to apologize to the friend for planning to date the friend's girlfriend.

Although Chris had never thought about dating the girlfriend, he nonetheless did as he was told, arriving at the beach at two o'clock in the morning. No one was there.

Chris put the incident out of his mind, attributing it to a trick of imagination, like something in a dream. However, the voice kept intruding in Chris's thoughts. And then he started to see visions. He would see whales and dolphins swimming up to the beach, and there would be a golden Buddha shining from the bushes. He also began to think he could control nature.

As Chris later said, "I felt that I had power over things in nature, influence over the whales and dolphins and waves. I thought I could make things happen magically in the water" (Begley, 2002, p. 44).

Chris Coles

Chris Coles was losing his grip on reality. It turned out that he was suffering from schizophrenia, one of the more severe psychological disorders. Although drug treatments eventually stilled the voices in his head, his experience raises several questions. What caused his disorder? Were genetic factors involved, or were stressors in his life primarily responsible? Were there signs that others should have noticed earlier? Could his schizophrenia have been prevented? And, more generally, how do we distinguish normal from abnormal behavior, and how can Chris's behavior be categorized and classified in a way that can pinpoint the specific nature of his problem?

We address the issues raised by Chris Coles's case in this set of modules. We begin by

Looking Ahead

discussing the difference between normal and abnormal behavior, which can be surprisingly indistinct. We then turn to a consideration of the most significant kinds of psychological disorders. Finally, we consider ways of evaluating behavior—one's own and that of others—to determine whether seeking help from a mental health professional is warranted.

Normal Versus Abnormal: Making the Distinction

Universally that person's acumen is esteemed very little perceptive concerning whatsoever matters are being held as most profitable by mortals with sapience endowed to be studied who is ignorant of that which the most in doctrine erudite and certainly by reason of that in them high mind's ornament deserving of veneration constantly maintain when by general consent they affirm that other circumstances being equal by no exterior splendour is the prosperity of a nation . . .

It would be easy to conclude that these words are the musings of a madman. To most people, the passage does not seem to make any sense at all. But literary scholars would disagree. Actually, this passage is from James Joyce's classic *Ulysses*, hailed as one of the major works of twentieth-century literature (Joyce, 1934, p. 377).

As this example illustrates, casually examining a person's writing is insufficient to determine the degree to which that person is "normal." But even when we consider more extensive samples of a person's behavior, we find that there may be only a fine line between behavior that is considered normal and that which is considered abnormal.

How can we distinguish normal from abnormal behavior?

What are the major perspectives on psychological disorders used by mental health professionals?

What classification system is used to categorize psychological disorders?

Ⓐ Ⓐ Ⓐ

Defining Abnormality

Because of the difficulty in distinguishing normal from abnormal behavior, psychologists have struggled to devise a precise, scientific definition of "abnormal behavior." For instance, consider the following definitions, each of which has advantages and disadvantages:

▶ *Abnormality as deviation from the average*. To employ this statistically based approach, we simply observe what behaviors are rare or occur infrequently in a particular society or culture and label those deviations from the norm "abnormal."

  The difficulty with such a definition is that some statistically rare behaviors clearly do not lend themselves to classification as abnormal. If most people prefer to have corn flakes for breakfast but you prefer raisin bran, this hardly makes your behavior abnormal. Similarly, such a concept of abnormality unreasonably labels a person who has an unusually high IQ as abnormal, simply because a high IQ is statistically rare. A definition of abnormality that rests on deviation from the average, then, is insufficient.

▶ *Abnormality as deviation from the ideal*. An alternative approach considers abnormality in relation to the standard toward which most people are striving—the ideal. This sort of definition considers behavior abnormal if it deviates enough from some kind of ideal or cultural standard. However, because society has so few standards on which people agree, and because the standards that do arise tend to change over time and vary across cultures, the deviation-from-the-ideal approach is inadequate.

▶ *Abnormality as a sense of personal discomfort*. A more useful definition concentrates on the psychological consequences of the behavior for the individual. In

Andrea Yates was sane when she drowned her five children in a bathtub, according to the jury that heard her case.

this approach, behavior is considered abnormal if it produces a sense of personal distress, anxiety, or guilt in an individual—or if it is harmful to others in some way.

Even a definition that relies on personal discomfort has drawbacks, though, because in some particularly severe forms of mental disturbance, people report feeling wonderful, even though their behavior seems bizarre to others. In such cases, a personal state of well-being exists, yet most people would consider the behavior abnormal.

▶ *Abnormality as the inability to function effectively.* Most people are able to feed themselves, hold a job, get along with others, and in general live as productive members of society. Yet there are those who are unable to adjust to the demands of society or function effectively.

According to this view of abnormality, people who are unable to function effectively and adapt to the demands of society are considered abnormal. For example, an unemployed, homeless woman living on the street may be considered unable to function effectively. Therefore, her behavior can be viewed as abnormal, even if she has chosen to live this way. Her inability to adapt to the requirements of society is what makes her "abnormal," according to this approach.

▶ *Abnormality as a legal concept.* According to the jury that heard her case, Andrea Yates was sane when she drowned her five children in a bathtub.

Although you might question this view, it reflects the way in which the law defines abnormal behavior. To the judicial system, the distinction between normal and abnormal behavior rests on the definition of *insanity,* which is a legal, but not a psychological, term. The definition of insanity varies from one jurisdiction to another. In some states, insanity simply means that defendants cannot understand the difference between right and wrong at the time they commit a criminal act. Other states consider whether defendants are substantially incapable of understanding the criminality of their behavior or unable to control themselves. And in some jurisdictions pleas of insanity are not allowed at all (Steadman et al., 1993; Weiner & Wettstein, 1993; Frost & Bonnie, 2001).

IDENTIFYING NORMAL AND ABNORMAL BEHAVIOR: DRAWING THE LINE ON PSYCHOLOGICAL DISORDERS

Clearly, none of the previous definitions is broad enough to cover all instances of abnormal behavior. Consequently, the distinction between normal and abnormal behavior often remains ambiguous even to trained professionals. Furthermore, to a large extent, cultural expectations for "normal" behavior in a particular society influence the understanding of "abnormal behavior" (Scheff, 1999; also see the *Applying Psychology in the 21st Century* box).

Probably the best way to deal with this imprecision is to view abnormal and normal behavior as marking two ends of a continuum rather than as absolute states. Behavior should be evaluated in terms of gradations, ranging from completely normal functioning to extremely abnormal behavior. Behavior typically falls somewhere between those extremes.

Perspectives on Abnormality: From Superstition to Science

Until recently, people linked abnormal behavior to superstition and witchcraft. Individuals who displayed abnormal behavior were accused of being possessed by the devil or some sort of demonic god. Authorities felt justified in "treating" abnormal

Suicide Bombers: Normal or Abnormal?

When American soldiers marched on Baghdad, Iraq, one of Syria's most prominent religious leaders issued a call to action for suicide bombers willing to carry out "martyrdom operations" against the American invaders (Begley, 2003, p. B1).

What kinds of people are willing to answer an invitation to strap explosives to their bodies and blow themselves up? Are only those with some sort of psychological disorder likely to do this with the aim of killing as many people as possible, taking their own lives in the process?

According to most psychologists studying the issue, the answers are clear: Suicide bombers are *not* psychologically disordered. Almost no real-life suicide attackers are the deranged, maniacal loners portrayed in movies and on television. According to psychologist Ariel Merai (1985), who has carefully profiled many Palestinian and Lebanese suicide bombers, such attackers are usually males in their early twenties who come from a wide range of backgrounds. Some bombers are wealthy whereas others are poor, and some are highly educated whereas others are uneducated. Although suicide bombers are generally unmarried, they are otherwise similar to the average members of their societies (Goode, 2001).

Generally, research suggests that most suicide bombers are sociable. They have close friends and family members, and they are sometimes described as extroverted. Moreover, their psychological functioning seems generally normal: Before their attacks, they show no suicidal symptoms, and they do not express feelings of hopelessness or of having "nothing to lose" (Atran, 2003, p. 1537). In short, psychological studies of suicide bombers provide little evidence that those individuals are suffering from any type of diagnosable psychological disorder.

Are suicide bombers psychologically disordered? Most research suggests that they are not.

If they're not psychologically disordered, why do they volunteer for suicide missions? In arguing against the idea that suicide bombers are necessarily dysfunctional or pathological, psychologist Charles Ruby (2002) contends that terrorist acts differ from conventional military operations only in terms of their methods. He suggests that because terrorists do not have access to enough weapons to attack their enemy conventionally, they use a different strategy. Terrorist leaders target innocent civilians, hoping to cultivate fear and persuade governments to change specific policies that the terrorists despise.

However, although terrorist leaders orchestrate strategy, suicide bombers are not focused only on political objectives; they are also motivated by commitment to a particular group or cause. Suicide bombers often belong to political or religious groups, and leaders of those groups work tirelessly to inspire potential bombers' loyalty to the group, to other group members, and to the leaders themselves. Although the group leaders may calmly select targets for the bombers to attack, the suicide bombers' decision is probably based on emotion as much as on politics (Atran, 2003).

For those charged with stopping suicide bombers' attacks and other types of terrorism, it becomes quite problematic that suicide attackers are driven not by psychological disorder, but by a complex web of emotions, loyalties, and politics. Terrorist attacks motivated by mental illness probably would be a much simpler problem to solve than are terrorist attacks inflamed by emotional, political, and religious group conflict. As psychologist Clark McCauley puts it, "If only it were true that only psychopaths can be terrorists, the terrorist problem would be nothing" (Goode, 2001, p. A13).

RETHINK

If it were your job to combat suicide bombings, how would you do it? What kinds of psychological, political, or social interventions might help discourage potential suicide attackers from volunteering?

FIGURE 1 In considering the case of Chris Coles, discussed in the Prologue, we can employ each of the different perspectives on abnormal behavior. Note, however, that because of the nature of his psychological disorder, some of the perspectives are more applicable than others.

Perspectives on Psychological Disorder		
Perspective	**Description**	**Possible Application of Perspective to Chris Coles' Case**
Medical perspective	Assumes that physiological causes are at the root of psychological disorders	Examine Coles for medical problems, such as brain tumor, chemical imbalance in the brain, or disease
Psychoanalytic perspective	Argues that psychological disorders stem from childhood conflicts	Seek out information about Coles' past, considering possible childhood conflicts
Behavioral perspective	Assumes that abnormal behaviors are learned responses	Concentrate on rewards and punishments for Coles' behavior, and identify environmental stimuli that reinforce his behavior
Cognitive perspective	Assumes that cognitions (people's thoughts and beliefs) are central to psychological disorders	Focus on Coles' perceptions of himself and his environment
Humanistic perspective	Emphasizes people's responsibility for their own behavior and the need to self-actualize	Consider Coles' behavior in terms of his choices and efforts to reach his potential
Sociocultural perspective	Assumes that behavior is shaped by family, society, and culture	Focus on how societal demands contributed to Coles' disorder

behavior by attempting to drive out the source of the problem. This typically involved whipping, immersion in hot water, starvation, or other forms of torture in which the cure was often worse than the affliction (Howells & Osborn, 1984; Berrios, 1996).

Contemporary approaches take a more enlightened view. Today, six major perspectives are used to understand psychological disorders. These perspectives suggest not only different causes of abnormal behavior but different treatment approaches as well. Furthermore, some perspectives are more applicable to particular disorders than are others. Figure 1 summarizes the perspectives and the way in which they can be applied to the case of Chris Coles described in the Prologue.

THE MEDICAL PERSPECTIVE

Medical perspective: The perspective that suggests that when an individual displays symptoms of abnormal behavior, the root cause will be found in a physical examination of the individual, which may reveal a hormonal imbalance, a chemical deficiency, or a brain injury.

When people display the symptoms of tuberculosis, we generally find tubercular bacteria in their body tissue. In the same way, the **medical perspective** suggests that when an individual displays symptoms of abnormal behavior, the fundamental cause will be found through a physical examination of the individual, which may reveal a hormonal imbalance, a chemical deficiency, or a brain injury. Indeed, when we speak of mental "illness," "symptoms" of abnormal behavior, and mental "hospitals," we are using terminology associated with the medical perspective.

Because many abnormal behaviors have been linked to biological causes, the medical perspective is a reasonable approach, yet serious criticisms have been leveled against it. For one thing, no biological cause has been identified for many forms of abnormal behavior. In addition, some critics have argued that the use of the term *illness* implies that people who display abnormal behavior have no responsibility for their actions (Szasz, 1982, 1994).

Still, recent advances in our understanding of the biological bases of behavior have supported the importance of considering physiological factors in abnormal behavior. For instance, some of the more severe forms of psychological disturbance, such as major depression and schizophrenia, are influenced by genetic factors and malfunctions in neurotransmitter signals (Pennington, 2002; Plomin & McGuffin, 2003).

THE PSYCHOANALYTIC PERSPECTIVE

Whereas the medical perspective suggests that biological causes are at the root of abnormal behavior, the **psychoanalytic perspective** holds that abnormal behavior stems from childhood conflicts over opposing wishes regarding sex and aggression. Freud believed that children pass through a series of stages in which sexual and aggressive impulses take different forms and produce conflicts that require resolution. If these childhood conflicts are not dealt with successfully, they remain unresolved in the unconscious and eventually bring about abnormal behavior during adulthood.

To understand the roots of people's disordered behavior, the psychoanalytic perspective scrutinizes their early life history. However, because there is no conclusive way to link people's childhood experiences with the abnormal behaviors they display as adults, we can never be sure that the causes suggested by psychoanalytic theory are accurate. Moreover, psychoanalytic theory paints a picture of people as having relatively little control over their behavior, because much of it is guided by unconscious impulses.

On the other hand, the contributions of psychoanalytic theory have been significant. More than any other approach to abnormal behavior, this perspective highlights the fact that people can have a rich, involved inner life and that prior experiences can have a profound effect on current psychological functioning (Horgan, 1996; Bornstein, 2001; Elliott, 2002).

> **Psychoanalytic perspective:** The perspective that suggests that abnormal behavior stems from childhood conflicts over opposing wishes regarding sex and aggression.

THE BEHAVIORAL PERSPECTIVE

Both the medical and psychoanalytic perspectives look at abnormal behaviors as *symptoms* of an underlying problem. In contrast, the **behavioral perspective** looks at the behavior itself as the problem. Using the basic principles of learning, behavioral theorists see both normal and abnormal behaviors as responses to various stimuli, responses that have been learned through past experience and that are guided in the present by stimuli in the individual's environment. To explain why abnormal behavior occurs, we must analyze how an individual has learned abnormal behavior and observe the circumstances in which it is displayed.

The emphasis on observable behavior represents both the greatest strength and the greatest weakness of the behavioral approach to abnormal behavior. This perspective provides the most precise and objective approach for examining behavioral displays of particular disorders, such as attention-deficit hyperactivity disorder (ADHD). At the same time, though, critics charge that the perspective ignores the rich inner world of thoughts, attitudes, and emotions that may contribute to abnormal behavior.

> **Behavioral perspective:** The perspective that looks at the behavior itself as the problem.

THE COGNITIVE PERSPECTIVE

The medical, psychoanalytic, and behavioral perspectives view people's behavior as being caused by factors largely beyond their control. To many critics of these views, however, people's thoughts cannot be ignored.

In response to such concerns, some psychologists employ a **cognitive perspective**. Rather than considering only external behavior, as in traditional behavioral approaches, the cognitive approach assumes that *cognitions* (people's thoughts and beliefs) are central to a person's abnormal behavior. A primary goal of treatment using the cognitive perspective is to explicitly teach new, more adaptive ways of thinking.

For instance, suppose a student forms the erroneous belief that "doing well on this exam is crucial to my entire future" whenever he or she takes an exam. Through therapy, that person might learn to hold the more realistic, and less anxiety-producing, thought "My entire future is not dependent on this one exam." By changing cognitions in this way, psychologists working within a cognitive

> **Cognitive perspective:** The perspective that suggests that people's thoughts and beliefs are a central component of abnormal behavior.

framework help people free themselves from thoughts and behaviors that are potentially maladaptive (Frost & Steketee, 2002).

The cognitive perspective is not without critics. For example, it is possible that maladaptive cognitions are the symptoms or consequences of disorders, rather than their cause. Furthermore, there are circumstances in which negative beliefs may not be irrational at all, but simply reflect the unpleasant environments in which people live—after all, there are times when a single exam may be extremely important. Still, cognitive theorists would argue that one can find a more adaptive way of framing beliefs even in the most negative circumstances.

THE HUMANISTIC PERSPECTIVE

Humanistic perspective: The perspective that emphasizes the responsibility people have for their own behavior, even when such behavior is abnormal.

Psychologists who subscribe to the **humanistic perspective** emphasize the responsibility people have for their own behavior, even when such behavior is seen as abnormal. The humanistic perspective—growing out of the work of Carl Rogers and Abraham Maslow—concentrates on what is uniquely human, viewing people as basically rational, oriented toward a social world, and motivated to seek self-actualization (Rogers, 1980).

Humanistic approaches focus on the relationship of the individual to society, considering the ways in which people view themselves in relation to others and see their place in the world. The humanistic perspective views people as having an awareness of life and of themselves that leads them to search for meaning and self-worth. Rather than assuming that individuals require a "cure," the humanistic perspective suggests that they can, by and large, set their own limits of what is acceptable behavior. As long as they are not hurting others and do not feel personal distress, people should be free to choose the behaviors in which they engage.

Sociocultural perspective: The perspective that assumes that people's behavior—both normal and abnormal—is shaped by the kind of family group, society, and culture in which they live.

Although the humanistic perspective has been criticized for its reliance on unscientific, unverifiable information and its vague, almost philosophical formulations, it offers a distinctive view of abnormal behavior. It stresses the unique aspects of being human and provides a number of important suggestions for helping those with psychological problems.

THE SOCIOCULTURAL PERSPECTIVE

The **sociocultural perspective** assumes that people's behavior—both normal and abnormal—is shaped by the kind of family group, society, and culture in which they live. According to this view, the nature of one's relationships with others may support abnormal behaviors and even cause them. Consequently, the kinds of stresses and conflicts people experience as part of their daily interactions with others in their environment can promote and maintain abnormal behavior.

This perspective finds statistical support for the position that sociocultural factors shape abnormal behavior in the fact that some kinds of abnormal behavior are far more prevalent among certain social classes than they are in others. For instance, diagnoses of schizophrenia tend to be higher among members of lower socioeconomic groups than among members of more affluent groups. Proportionally more African American individuals are hospitalized involuntarily for psychological disorders than are whites. Furthermore, poor economic times seem to be linked to general declines in psychological functioning, and social problems such as homelessness are associated with psychological disorders (Kiesler, 1999; López & Guarnaccia, 2000; Conger et al., 2002).

"First off, you're not a nut. You're a legume."

On the other hand, alternative explanations abound for the association between abnormal behavior and social factors. For example, people from lower socioeconomic levels may be less likely than those from higher levels to seek help, gradually reaching a point where their symptoms become severe and warrant a more serious diagnosis. Furthermore, sociocultural explanations provide relatively little specific guidance for the treatment of individuals showing mental disturbance, because the focus is on broader societal factors (Paniagua, 2000).

Classifying Abnormal Behavior: The ABCs of *DSM*

Crazy. Whacked. Mental. Loony. Insane. Neurotic. Psycho. Strange. Demented. Odd. Possessed.

Society has long placed labels on people who display abnormal behavior. Unfortunately, most of the time these labels have reflected intolerance and have been used with little thought to what each label signifies.

Providing appropriate and specific names and classifications for abnormal behavior has presented a major challenge to psychologists. It is not hard to understand why, given the difficulties discussed earlier in simply distinguishing normal from abnormal behavior. Yet we need classification systems to describe and ultimately diagnose abnormal behavior.

DSM-IV-TR: Determining Diagnostic Distinctions

Over the years, mental health workers have used many different classification systems that vary in terms of their utility and how universally they have been accepted. Today, however, one standard system, devised by the American Psychiatric Association, has emerged in the United States; most professionals use it to diagnose and classify abnormal behavior. The classification system is known as the ***Diagnostic and Statistical Manual of Mental Disorders, Fourth Edition (DSM-IV-TR).***

DSM-IV-TR presents comprehensive and relatively precise definitions for more than 200 disorders, organizing them into seventeen major categories. It also includes five types of information, known as *axes*, that have to be considered in assessing a patient. For example, Axis I relates to clinical disorders, and Axis III relates to general medical conditions that may be relevant to a psychological disorder.

By following the criteria presented in the *DSM-IV-TR* classification system, diagnosticians can clearly describe the specific problem an individual is experiencing. (Figure 2 provides a brief outline of the major diagnostic categories, and **Interactivity 48–1** provides practice in classifying different behaviors.)

DSM-IV-TR is designed to be primarily descriptive and avoids suggesting an underlying cause for an individual's behavior and problems. For instance, the term *neurotic*—a label that is commonly used by people in their everyday descriptions of abnormal behavior—is not listed as a *DSM-IV-TR* category. Because the term refers to problems associated with a specific cause based in Freud's theory of personality, neurosis is not included in *DSM-IV-TR*.

DSM-IV-TR has the advantage, then, of providing a descriptive system that does not specify the cause of or reason behind a problem. Instead, it paints a picture of the behavior that is being displayed. Why should this be important? For one thing, it allows communication between mental health professionals of diverse backgrounds and theoretical approaches. In addition, precise classification enables researchers to make progress on exploring the causes of a problem. If displays of an abnormal behavior cannot be reliably described, researchers will be hard-pressed to find ways to investigate the disorder. Finally, *DSM-IV-TR* provides a kind of conceptual

Diagnostic and Statistical Manual of Mental Disorders, Fourth Edition (DSM-IV-TR): A system, devised by the American Psychiatric Association, used by most professionals to diagnose and classify abnormal behavior.

INTERACTIVITY 48–1

DSM-IV-TR classification system

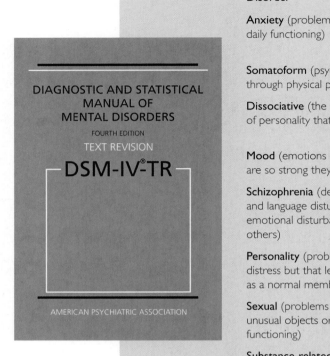

Disorder	Subcategories
Anxiety (problems in which anxiety impedes daily functioning)	Generalized anxiety disorder, panic disorder, phobic disorder, obsessive-compulsive disorder, posttraumatic stress disorder
Somatoform (psychological difficulties displayed through physical problems)	Hypochondriasis, conversion disorder
Dissociative (the splitting apart of crucial parts of personality that are usually integrated)	Dissociative identity disorder (multiple personality), dissociative amnesia, dissociative fugue
Mood (emotions of depression or euphoria that are so strong they intrude on everyday living)	Major depression, bipolar disorder
Schizophrenia (declines in functioning, thought and language disturbances, perception disorders, emotional disturbances, and withdrawal from others)	Disorganized, paranoid, catatonic, undifferentiated, residual
Personality (problems that create little personal distress but that lead to an inability to function as a normal member of society)	Antisocial (sociopathic) personality disorder, narcissistic personality disorder
Sexual (problems related to sexual arousal from unusual objects or problems related to functioning)	Paraphilia, sexual dysfunction
Substance-related (problems related to drug dependence and abuse)	Alcohol, cocaine, hallucinogens, marijuana
Delirium, dementia, amnesia, and other cognitive disorders	

FIGURE 2 This list of disorders represents the major categories from the *DSM-IV-TR*. It is only a partial list of the more than 200 disorders included there.

shorthand through which professionals can describe the behaviors that tend to occur together in an individual (Frances, First, & Pincus, 1995; Halling & Goldfarb, 1996; Widiger & Clark, 2000).

CONNING THE CLASSIFIERS: THE SHORTCOMINGS OF *DSM-IV-TR*

When clinical psychologist David Rosenhan and eight colleagues sought admission to separate mental hospitals across the United States in the 1970s, each stated that he or she was hearing voices—"unclear voices" that said "empty," "hollow," and "thud"—and each was immediately admitted to the hospital (Rosenhan, 1973).

However, the truth was that they actually were conducting a study, and none of them was really hearing any voices. Aside from these misrepresentations, *everything* else they did and said represented their true behavior, including the responses they gave during extensive admission interviews and their answers to the battery of tests they were asked to complete. In fact, as soon as they were admitted, they said they no longer heard any voices. In short, each of the pseudo-patients acted in a "normal" way.

We might assume that Rosenhan and his colleagues would have been quickly discovered as the impostors they were, but this was not the case. Instead, each of them was diagnosed as severely abnormal on the basis of observed behavior. Mental health workers labeled most as suffering from schizophrenia and kept them in the hospital

PowerWeb: On Being Sane in Insane Places

www.mhhe.com/feldmanup7

from three to fifty-two days, with the average stay being nineteen days. Even when they were discharged, most of the "patients" left with the label *schizophrenia—in remission*, implying that the abnormal behavior had only temporarily subsided and could recur at any time. Most disturbing, hospital staff members identified none of the pseudo-patients as impostors—although some of the actual patients figured out the ruse.

The results of Rosenhan's classic study illustrate that placing labels on individuals powerfully influences the way mental health workers perceive and interpret individuals' actions. It also points out that determining who is psychologically disordered is not always a clear-cut, or accurate, process.

Although the *DSM-IV-TR* was developed to provide more accurate and consistent determinations of psychological disorders, it has not been entirely successful. For instance, critics charge that it relies too much on the medical perspective on psychological disorders. Because it was drawn up by psychiatrists—who are physicians—some condemn it for viewing psychological disorders primarily in terms of the symptoms of an underlying physiological disorder. Moreover, critics suggest that *DSM-IV-TR* compartmentalizes people into inflexible, all-or-none categories, rather than considering the degree to which a person displays psychologically disordered behavior.

Other concerns with *DSM-IV-TR* are more subtle, but equally important. For instance, some critics argue that labeling an individual as abnormal provides a dehumanizing, lifelong stigma. Furthermore, after a person receives an initial diagnosis, mental health professionals, who may concentrate on the initial diagnostic category, could overlook other diagnostic possibilities (Kirk, 1992; Szasz, 1994; Duffy, Gillig, Tureen, & Ybarra, 2002).

Still, despite the drawbacks inherent in any labeling system, *DSM-IV* has had an important influence on the way in which mental health professionals consider psychological disorders. It has increased both the reliability and the validity of diagnostic categorization. In addition, it offers a logical way to organize our examination of the major types of mental disturbance.

PowerWeb: Classic Dialogue: Do Diagnostic Labels Hinder Treatment?

www.mhhe.com/feldmanup7

RECAP/EVALUATE/RETHINK

RECAP

How can we distinguish normal from abnormal behavior?

⊙ Definitions of abnormality include deviation from the average, deviation from the ideal, a sense of personal discomfort, the inability to function effectively, and legal conceptions. (p. 531)

⊙ No single definition is totally adequate, suggesting that abnormal and normal behavior be considered in terms of a continuum. (p. 532)

What are the major perspectives on psychological disorders used by mental health professionals?

⊙ The medical perspective views abnormality as a symptom of an underlying disease that requires a cure. (p. 534)

⊙ Psychoanalytic perspectives suggest that abnormal behavior stems from conflicts in the unconscious that are produced by past experience. (p. 535)

⊙ Behavioral approaches view abnormal behavior not as a symptom of an underlying problem, but as the problem itself. To resolve the problem, one must change the behavior. (p. 535)

⊙ The cognitive approach suggests that abnormal behavior is the result of faulty cognitions (thoughts and beliefs). In this view, abnormal behavior can be remedied through a change in cognitions. (p. 535)

⊙ Humanistic approaches emphasize the responsibility people have for their own behavior, even when such behavior is seen as abnormal. (p. 536)

⊙ Sociocultural approaches view abnormal behavior in terms of difficulties arising from family and other social relationships. (p. 538)

What classification system is used to categorize psychological disorders?

⊙ The most widely used system for classifying psychological disorders is *DSM-IV-TR—Diagnostic and Statistical Manual of Mental Disorders, Fourth Edition.* (p. 537)

EVALUATE

1. One problem in defining abnormal behavior is that
   a. Statistically rare behavior may not be abnormal.
   b. Not all abnormalities are accompanied by feelings of discomfort.
   c. Cultural standards are too general to use as a measuring tool.
   d. All of the above.
2. If abnormality is defined as experiencing personal discomfort or causing harm to others, which of the following people is most likely to need treatment?
   a. An executive is afraid to accept a promotion because it would require moving from his ground-floor office to the top floor of a tall office building.
   b. A woman decides to quit her job and chooses to live on the street in order to live a "simpler life."
   c. A man believes that friendly spacemen visit his house every Thursday.
   d. A photographer lives with nineteen cats in a small apartment, lovingly caring for them.
3. Virginia's mother thinks that her daughter's behavior is clearly abnormal because, despite being offered admission to medical school, Virginia decides to become a waitress. What approach is Virginia's mother using to define abnormal behavior?
4. Which of the following is a strong argument against the medical perspective on abnormality?
   a. Physiological abnormalities are almost always impossible to identify.
   b. There is no conclusive way to link past experience and behavior.

c. The medical perspective rests too heavily on the effects of nutrition.
d. Assigning behavior to a physical problem takes responsibility away from the individual for changing his or her behavior.

5. Cheryl is painfully shy. According to the behavioral perspective, the best way to deal with her "abnormal" behavior is to
   a. Treat the underlying physical problem
   b. Use the principles of learning theory to modify her shy behavior
   c. Express a great deal of caring
   d. Uncover her negative past experiences through hypnosis

RETHINK

1. Imagine that an acquaintance of yours was recently arrested for shoplifting a $15 necktie. What sort of explanation for this behavior would be provided by the proponents of *each* perspective on abnormality: the medical perspective, the psychoanalytic perspective, the behavioral perspective, the cognitive perspective, the humanistic perspective, and the sociocultural perspective?
2. Do you agree or disagree that *DSM* should be updated every several years? What makes abnormal behavior so variable? Why can't there be one definition of abnormal behavior that is unchanging?

Answers to Evaluate Questions

1. d; 2. a; 3. deviation from the ideal; 4. d; 5. b

KEY TERMS

medical
perspective p. 534
psychoanalytic
perspective p. 535

behavioral
perspective p. 535
cognitive
perspective p. 535

humanistic
perspective p. 536
sociocultural
perspective p. 536

Diagnostic and Statistical Manual of Mental Disorders, Fourth Edition (DSM-IV-TR) p. 537

The Major Psychological Disorders

Sally experienced her first panic attack out of the blue, 3 weeks after completing her senior year in college. She had just finished a job interview and was meeting some friends for dinner. In the restaurant, she began to feel dizzy. Within a few seconds, her heart was pounding, and she was feeling breathless, as though she might pass out. Her friends noticed that she did not look well and offered to drive her home. Sally suggested they stop at the hospital emergency room instead. Although she felt better by the time they arrived at the hospital, and tests indicated nothing wrong, Sally experienced a similar episode a week later while at a movie . . .

Her attacks became more and more frequent. Before long, she was having several attacks per week. In addition, she constantly worried about having attacks. She began to avoid exercise and other activities that produced physical sensations. She also noticed the attacks were worse when she was alone. She began to avoid driving, shopping in large stores, and eating in all restaurants. Some weeks she avoided leaving the house completely (Antony, Brown, & Barlow, 1992, p. 79).

Sally suffered from panic disorder, one of the specific psychological disorders we'll consider in this module. Keep in mind that although we'll be discussing these disorders in a dispassionate manner, each represents a very human set of difficulties that influence, and in some cases considerably disrupt, people's lives.

⊛⊛⊛

Anxiety Disorders

All of us, at one time or another, experience *anxiety*, a feeling of apprehension or tension, in reaction to stressful situations. There is nothing "wrong" with such anxiety. It is a normal reaction to stress that often helps, rather than hinders, our daily functioning. Without some anxiety, for instance, most of us probably would not have much motivation to study hard, undergo physical exams, or spend long hours at our jobs.

But some people experience anxiety in situations in which there is no external reason or cause for such distress. When anxiety occurs without external justification and begins to affect people's daily functioning, mental health professionals consider it a psychological problem known as an **anxiety disorder.** We'll discuss four types of anxiety disorders: phobic disorder, panic disorder, generalized anxiety disorder, and obsessive-compulsive disorder.

Anxiety disorder: The occurrence of anxiety without an obvious external cause, affecting daily functioning.

PHOBIC DISORDER

It's not easy moving through the world when you're terrified of electricity. "Donna," 45, a writer, knows that better than most. Get her in the vicinity of an appliance or a light switch or—all but unthinkable—a thunderstorm, and she is overcome by a terror so blinding she can think of nothing but fleeing. That, of course, is not always possible, so

Phobia	Trigger	Phobia	Trigger
Acrophobia	Heights	Herpetophobia	Reptiles
Aerophobia	Flying	Hydrophobia	Water
Agoraphobia	Entering public spaces	Mikrophobia	Germs
Ailurophobia	Cats	Murophobia	Mice
Amaxophobia	Vehicles, driving	Mysophobia	Dirt or germs
Anthophobia	Flowers	Numerophobia	Numbers
Aquaphobia	Water	Nyctophobia	Darkness
Arachnophobia	Spiders	Ochlophobia	Crowds
Astraphobia	Lightning	Ophidiophobia	Snakes
Brontophobia	Thunder	Ornithophobia	Birds
Claustrophobia	Closed spaces	Phonophobia	Speaking out loud
Cynophobia	Dogs	Pyrophobia	Fire
Dementophobia	Insanity	Thanatophobia	Death
Electrophobia	Electricity	Trichophobia	Hair
Gephyrophobia	Bridges	Xenophobia	Strangers

FIGURE 1 Phobic disorders differ from generalized anxiety and panic disorders because a specific stimulus can be identified. Listed here are a number of phobias and their triggers.

over time, Donna has come up with other answers. When she opens the refrigerator door, rubber-sole shoes are a must. If a light bulb blows, she will tolerate the dark until someone else changes it for her. Clothes shopping is done only when necessary, lest static on garments send her running from the store. And swimming at night is absolutely out of the question, lest underwater lights electrocute her (Kluger, 2001, p. 51).

Phobias: Intense, irrational fears of specific objects or situations.

Donna suffers from a **phobia,** an intense, irrational fear of specific objects or situations. For example, claustrophobia is a fear of enclosed places, acrophobia is a fear of high places, xenophobia is a fear of strangers, and—as in Donna's case—electrophobia is a fear of electricity. Although the objective danger posed by an anxiety-producing stimulus (which can be just about anything, as you can see from the list in Figure 1) is typically small or nonexistent, to the individual suffering from the phobia the danger is great, and a full-blown panic attack may follow exposure to the stimulus. Phobic disorders differ from generalized anxiety disorders and panic disorders in that there is a specific, identifiable stimulus that sets off the anxiety reaction.

Phobias may have only a minor impact on people's lives if those who suffer from them can avoid the stimuli that trigger fear. Unless one is a professional firefighter or tightrope walker, for example, a fear of heights will have little impact on one's daily life. On the other hand, a fear of strangers presents a more serious problem. In one extreme case, a Washington woman left her home just three times in thirty years—once to visit her family, once for a medical operation, and once to purchase ice cream for a dying companion (Adler, 1984). (To get a fuller understanding of phobias, complete **Interactivity 49–1.**)

INTERACTIVITY 49–1

Phobia

PANIC DISORDER

Panic disorder: Anxiety that reveals itself in the form of panic attacks that last from a few seconds to as long as several hours.

In another type of anxiety disorder, **panic disorder,** *panic attacks* occur that last from a few seconds to several hours. Unlike phobias, which are stimulated by specific objects or situations, panic disorders do not have any identifiable stimuli. Instead, during an attack, such as the ones experienced by Sally in the case described earlier, anxiety suddenly—and often without warning—rises to a peak, and an individual feels a sense of impending, unavoidable doom. Although the physical symptoms differ from person to person, they may include heart palpitations, shortness of breath, unusual amounts of sweating, faintness and dizziness, an urge to urinate, gastric sensations, and—in extreme cases—a sense of imminent death. After such an attack, it is no wonder that people tend to feel exhausted (Rachman & deSilva, 1996; Pollack & Marzol, 2000).

Panic attacks seemingly come out of nowhere and are unconnected to any specific stimulus. Because they don't know what triggers their feelings of panic, victims of panic attacks may become fearful of going places. In fact, some people with panic disorder develop a complication called *agoraphobia*, the fear of being in a situation in which escape is difficult, and in which help for a possible panic attack would not be available. In extreme cases, people with agoraphobia never leave their homes (Smith, Friedman, & Paradis, 2002; Marcaurelle, Belanger, & Marchand, 2003).

Acrophobia, the fear of heights, is not an uncommon phobia. What sort of behavior-modification approaches might be used to deal with acrophobia?

GENERALIZED ANXIETY DISORDER

People with **generalized anxiety disorder** experience long-term, persistent anxiety and worry. Sometimes their concerns are about identifiable issues involving family, money, work, or health. In other cases, though, people with the disorder feel that something dreadful is about to happen but can't identify the reason, experiencing "free-floating" anxiety.

Because of their persistent anxiety, they cannot concentrate, cannot set their worry and fears aside; their lives become centered on their worry. Their anxiety may eventually cause medical problems. Because of heightened muscle tension and arousal, individuals with generalized anxiety disorder may develop headaches, dizziness, heart palpitations, or insomnia. Figure 2 shows the most common symptoms of generalized anxiety disorder.

Generalized anxiety disorder: The experience of long-term, persistent anxiety and worry.

OBSESSIVE-COMPULSIVE DISORDER

In **obsessive-compulsive disorder,** people are plagued by unwanted thoughts, called obsessions, or feel that they must carry out actions, termed compulsions, against their will.

An **obsession** is a persistent, unwanted thought or idea that keeps recurring. For example, a student may be unable to stop thinking that she has neglected to put her name on a test and may think about it constantly for the two weeks it takes to get the paper back. A man may go on vacation and wonder the whole time whether he locked his house. A woman may hear the same tune running through her head over and over. In each case, the thought or idea is unwanted and difficult to put out of mind. Of course, many people suffer from mild obsessions from time to time, but usually such thoughts persist only for a short period. For people with serious obsessions, however, the thoughts persist for days or months and may consist of bizarre, troubling images (Lee & Kwon, 2003).

As part of an obsessive-compulsive disorder, people may also experience **compulsions,** irresistible urges to repeatedly carry out some act that seems strange and unreasonable, even to them. Whatever the compulsive behavior is, people

Obsessive-compulsive disorder: A disorder characterized by obsessions or compulsions.

Obsession: A persistent, unwanted thought or idea that keeps recurring.

Compulsion: An irresistible urge to repeatedly carry out some act that seems strange and unreasonable.

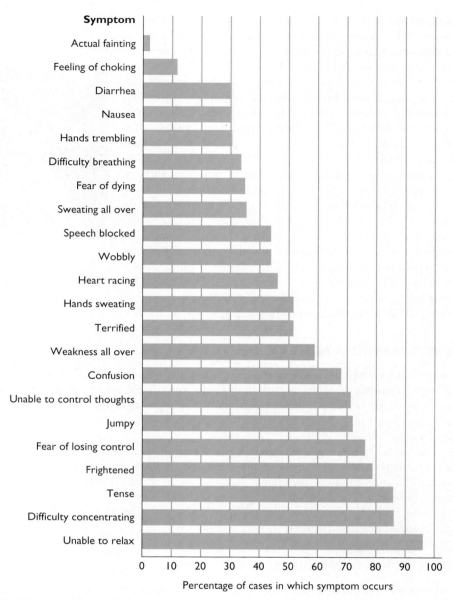

FIGURE 2 Frequency of symptoms in cases of generalized anxiety disorder. (Source: Adapted from Beck & Emery, 1985, pp. 87–88.)

experience extreme anxiety if they cannot carry it out, even if it is something they want to stop. The acts involved may be relatively trivial, such as repeatedly checking the stove to make sure all the burners are turned off, or more unusual, such as continuously washing oneself (Carter, Pauls, & Leckman, 1995; Frost & Steketee, 2002).

For example, consider this case report of a 27-year-old woman with a cleaning ritual:

> Bess would first remove all of her clothing in a preestablished sequence. She would lay out each article of clothing at specific spots on her bed, and examine each one for any indications of "contamination." She would then thoroughly scrub her body, starting at her feet and working meticulously up to the top of her head, using certain washcloths for certain areas of her body. Any articles of clothing that appeared to have been

"contaminated" were thrown into the laundry. Clean clothing was put in the spots that were vacant. She would then dress herself in the opposite order from which she took the clothes off (Meyer & Osborne, 1987, p. 156).

Although such compulsive rituals lead to some immediate reduction of anxiety, in the long term the anxiety returns. In fact, people with severe cases lead lives filled with unrelenting tension (Goodman, Rudorfer, & Maser, 1999; Penzel, 2000).

THE CAUSES OF ANXIETY DISORDERS

No single cause fully explains all cases of anxiety disorders. Genetic factors clearly are part of the picture. For example, if one member of a pair of identical twins has panic disorder, there is a 30 percent chance that the other twin will have it also. Furthermore, a person's characteristic level of anxiety is related to a specific gene involved in the production of the neurotransmitter serotonin. This is consistent with findings indicating that certain chemical deficiencies in the brain appear to produce some kinds of anxiety disorder (Lesch et al., 1996; Rieder, Kaufmann, & Knowles, 1996).

Other researchers believe that an overactive autonomic nervous system may be at the root of panic attacks. Specifically, they suggest that poor regulation of the brain's locus ceruleus may lead to panic attacks, which lead the limbic system to be overstimulated. In turn, the overstimulated limbic system produces chronic anxiety, which ultimately leads the locus ceruleus to generate still more panic attacks (Gorman, Papp, & Coplan, 1995; Balaban, 2002).

Psychologists who employ the behavioral perspective have taken a different approach, emphasizing environmental factors. They consider anxiety to be a learned response to stress. For instance, suppose a dog bites a young girl. When the girl next sees a dog, she is frightened and runs away—a behavior that relieves her anxiety and thereby reinforces her avoidance behavior. After repeated encounters with dogs in which she is reinforced for her avoidance behavior, she may develop a full-fledged phobia regarding dogs.

Finally, the cognitive perspective suggests that anxiety disorders grow out of inappropriate and inaccurate thoughts and beliefs about circumstances in a person's world. For example, people with anxiety disorders may view a friendly puppy as a ferocious and savage pit bull, or they may see an air disaster looming every moment they are in the vicinity of an airplane. According to the cognitive perspective, people's maladaptive thoughts about the world are at the root of an anxiety disorder (Frost & Steketee, 2002; Wang & Clark, 2002).

Somatoform Disorders

Somatoform disorders are psychological difficulties that take on a physical (somatic) form, but for which there is no medical cause. Even though an individual with a somatoform disorder reports physical symptoms, no biological cause exists, or if there is a medical problem, the person's reaction is greatly exaggerated.

One type of somatoform disorder is **hypochondriasis,** in which people have a constant fear of illness and a preoccupation with their health. These individuals believe everyday aches and pains are the symptoms of a dread disease. It is not that the "symptoms" are faked; instead, it is the misinterpretation of those sensations as evidence of some serious illness—often in the face of inarguable medical evidence to the contrary—that characterizes hypochondriasis (Noyes et al., 1993, 2002, 2003; Cantor & Fallon, 1996).

Another somatoform disorder is conversion disorder. Unlike hypochondriasis, in which there is no physical problem, **conversion disorders** involve an actual physical

Somatoform disorder: Psychological difficulties that take on a physical (somatic) form, but for which there is no medical cause.

Hypochondriasis: A disorder in which people have a constant fear of illness and a preoccupation with their health.

Conversion disorder: A major somatoform disorder that involves an actual physical disturbance, such as the inability to use a sensory organ or the complete or partial inability to move an arm or leg.

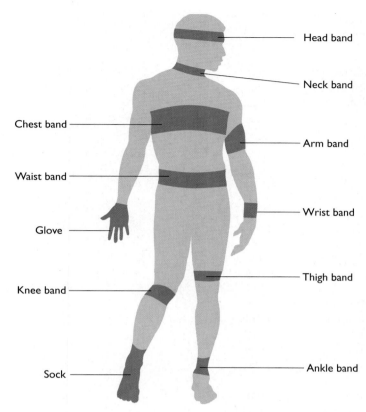

Head band

Neck band

Chest band

Arm band

Waist band

Wrist band

Glove

Thigh band

Knee band

Ankle band

Sock

FIGURE 3 Conversion disorders sometimes produce numbness in particular isolated areas of the body (indicated by the shaded areas in the figure). For instance, in glove anesthesia, the area of the body covered by a glove feels numb. However, the condition is biologically implausible because of the nerves involved, suggesting that the problem results from a psychological disorder rather than from actual nerve damage.

PowerWeb: Do Multiple Personalities Exist?

www.mhhe.com/feldmanup7

Dissociative disorders: Psychological dysfunctions characterized by the separation of critical personality facets that are normally integrated, allowing stress avoidance through escape.

Dissociative identity disorder (or multiple personality): A disorder in which a person displays characteristics of two or more distinct personalities.

Dissociative amnesia: A disorder in which a significant, selective memory loss occurs.

disturbance, such as the inability to see or hear or to move an arm or leg. The *cause* of such a physical disturbance is purely psychological; no biological reason produces the problem. Some of Freud's classic cases involved conversion disorders. For instance, one patient of Freud's suddenly became unable to use her arm, without any apparent physiological cause. Later, just as abruptly, she regained its use.

Conversion disorders often begin suddenly. People wake up one morning blind or deaf, or they experience numbness that is restricted to a certain part of the body. Someone's hand, for example, may become entirely numb, while an area above the wrist, controlled by the same nerves, remains sensitive to touch—something that is physiologically implausible. Mental health professionals refer to such a condition as "glove anesthesia," because the numb area is the part of the hand covered by a glove, not a region related to pathways of the nervous system (see Figure 3).

Surprisingly, people who experience conversion disorders frequently remain unconcerned about symptoms that most of us would expect to be highly anxiety-producing. For instance, a person in good health who wakes up blind may react in a bland, matter-of-fact way. Considering how most of us would feel if we woke up unable to see, this unemotional reaction (called *"la belle indifférence,"* a French phrase meaning "a beautiful indifference") hardly seems appropriate (Brasic, 2002).

Dissociative Disorders

The classic movie *The Three Faces of Eve* and the book *Sybil* (about a girl who allegedly had sixteen personalities) represent a highly dramatic class of disorders: dissociative disorders. **Dissociative disorders** are characterized by the separation (or dissociation) of critical parts of personality that are normally integrated and work together. By dissociating key parts of personality, people are able to keep disturbing memories or perceptions from reaching conscious awareness, thereby reducing their anxiety (Putnam, 1995a; Spiegel, 1996a; Ishikura & Tashiro, 2002).

Several dissociative disorders exist, all of which are rare. A person with a **dissociative identity disorder** (or multiple personality) displays characteristics of two or more distinct personalities, identities, or personality fragments. Individual personalities often have a unique set of likes and dislikes and their own reactions to situations. Some people with multiple personalities even carry several pairs of glasses because their vision changes with each personality. Moreover, each individual personality can be well adjusted when considered on its own (Kluft, 1996; Ross, 1996; Lilienfeld & Lynn, 2003).

The problem, of course, is that the various personalities reside in only one body, forcing the personalities to take turns. Because the personalities can vary greatly from each other, the person's behavior—considered as a whole—can appear very inconsistent. For instance, in the famous case portrayed in *The Three Faces of Eve*, the meek, bland Eve White provided a stunning contrast to the dominant and carefree Eve Black (Sizemore, 1989).

Dissociative amnesia is another dissociative disorder in which a significant, selective memory loss occurs. Dissociative amnesia is unlike simple amnesia, which involves an actual loss of information from memory, typically resulting from a physiological cause. In contrast, in cases of dissociative amnesia, the "forgotten" material is still present in memory—it simply cannot be recalled. The term *repressed* *memories* is sometimes used to describe the lost memories of people with dissociative amnesia.

In the most severe form, individuals cannot recall their names, are unable to recognize parents and other relatives, and do not know their addresses. In other respects, though, they may appear quite normal. Apart from an inability to remember certain facts about themselves, they may be able to recall skills and abilities that they developed earlier. For instance, even though a chef may not remember where he grew up and received training, he may still be able to prepare gourmet meals.

In some cases of dissociative amnesia, the memory loss is quite profound. For example, in one well-known case, a Florida park ranger found a woman who was dubbed Jane Doe by her rescuers (Carson, Butcher, & Coleman, 1992). Incoherent, thin, and only partially clothed, Doe was unable to recall her name, her past, and even how to read and write. On the basis of her accent, authorities thought the woman was from Illinois, and interviews conducted while she was given tranquilizing drugs revealed that she had had a Catholic education. However, the childhood memories she revealed were so universal that her background could not be pinpointed further. In a desperate attempt to rediscover her identity, she appeared on the television show "Good Morning America," and ultimately a couple from Roselle, Illinois, whose daughter had moved to Florida stepped forward, saying they were her parents. However, Jane Doe never regained her memory.

A more unusual form of amnesia is a condition known as **dissociative fugue.** In this state, people take sudden, impulsive trips, sometimes assuming a new identity. After a period of time—days, months, or sometimes even years—they suddenly realize that they are in a strange place and completely forget the time they have spent wandering. Their last memories are those from the time just before they entered the fugue state.

The common thread among dissociative disorders is that they allow people to escape from some anxiety-producing situation. Either the person produces a new personality to deal with stress, or the individual forgets or leaves behind the situation that caused the stress as he or she journeys to some new—and perhaps less anxiety-ridden—environment (Spiegel & Cardena, 1991; Putnam, 1995b).

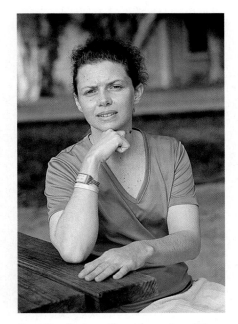

"Jane Doe," who suffered from dissociative amnesia, was found wandering in a Florida park, unable to recall who she was or anything about her past.

Dissociative fugue: A form of amnesia in which people take sudden, impulsive trips, sometimes assuming a new identity.

Mood Disorders

> From the time I woke up in the morning until the time I went to bed at night, I was unbearably miserable and seemingly incapable of any kind of joy or enthusiasm. Everything—every thought, word, movement—was an effort. Everything that once was sparkling now was flat. I seemed to myself to be dull, boring, inadequate, thick brained, unlit, unresponsive, chill skinned, bloodless, and sparrow drab. I doubted, completely, my ability to do anything well. It seemed as though my mind had slowed down and burned out to the point of being virtually useless (Jamison, 1995a, p. 110).

We all experience mood swings. Sometimes we are happy, perhaps even euphoric; at other times we feel upset, saddened, or depressed. Such changes in mood are a normal part of everyday life. In some people, however, moods are so pronounced and lingering—like the feelings described above by writer (and psychiatrist) Kay Jamison—that they interfere with the ability to function effectively. In extreme cases a mood may become life-threatening, and in others it may cause the person to lose touch with reality. Situations such as these represent **mood disorders,** disturbances in emotional feelings strong enough to intrude on everyday living.

Mood disorder: A disturbance in emotional feelings strong enough to intrude on everyday living.

Major depression: A severe form of depression that interferes with concentration, decision making, and sociability.

MAJOR DEPRESSION

President Abraham Lincoln. Queen Victoria. Newscaster Mike Wallace.

The common link among these people? Each suffered from periodic attacks of **major depression,** one of the more common forms of mood disorders. Some 15 million people in the United States suffer from major depression, and at any one time, 6 to 10 percent of the U.S. population is clinically depressed. Almost one in five people in the United States experiences major depression at some point in life. The cost of depression to society approaches $50 billion a year (Dryden, 2003; Ghaemi, 2003).

Women are twice as likely to experience major depression as men, with one-fourth of all females apt to encounter it at some point during their lives. Furthermore, although no one is sure why, the rate of depression is going up throughout the world. Results of in-depth interviews conducted in the United States, Puerto Rico, Taiwan, Lebanon, Canada, Italy, Germany, and France indicate that the incidence of depression has increased significantly over previous rates in every area. In fact, in some countries, the likelihood that individuals will have major depression at some point in their lives is three times higher than it was for earlier generations. In addition, people are developing major depression at increasingly young ages (Beckham & Leber, 1997; Hoffman, Baldwin, & Cerbone, 2003).

When psychologists speak of major depression, they do not mean the sadness that comes from experiencing one of life's disappointments, something that we all have experienced. Some depression is normal after the breakup of a long-term relationship, the death of a loved one, or the loss of a job. It is normal even after less serious problems: doing badly on a test or having a romantic partner forget one's birthday.

People who suffer from major depression experience similar sorts of feelings, but the severity tends to be considerably greater. They may feel useless, worthless, and lonely and may despair over the future. Moreover, they may experience such feelings for months or even years. They may cry uncontrollably, have sleep disturbances, and be at risk for suicide. The depth of such behavior and the length of time it lasts are the hallmarks of major depression. (Figure 4 provides a self-assessment of depression.)

MANIA AND BIPOLAR DISORDERS

Mania: An extended state of intense, wild elation.

While depression leads to the depths of despair, mania leads to emotional heights. **Mania** is an extended state of intense, wild elation. People experiencing mania feel intense happiness, power, invulnerability, and energy. They may become involved in wild schemes, believing they will succeed at anything they attempt. Consider, for example, the following description of an individual who experienced a manic episode:

FIGURE 4 This is a version of a test distributed by mental health organizations during the annual National Depression Screening Day, a nationwide event that seeks to identify people who are suffering from depression that is severe enough to warrant psychological intervention. (Source: National Depression Screening Day, 2003.)

A Test for Depression

To complete the questionnaire, count the number of statements with which you agree:

1. I feel downhearted, blue, and sad.
2. I don't enjoy the things that I used to.
3. I feel that others would be better off if I were dead.
4. I feel that I am not useful or needed.
5. I notice that I am losing weight.
6. I have trouble sleeping through the night.
7. I am restless and can't keep still.
8. My mind isn't as clear as it used to be.
9. I get tired for no reason.
10. I feel hopeless about the future.

Scoring: If you agree with at least five of the statements, including either item 1 or 2, and if you have had these symptoms for at least two weeks, help from a professional is strongly recommended. If you answer yes to number 3, you should get help immediately.

FIGURE 5 The number of pieces written by composer Robert Schumann in a given year is related to his periods of depression and mania (Slater & Meyer, 1959; reprinted in Jamison, 1993). Why do you think mania might be associated with creative productivity in some people?

Mr. O'Reilly took a leave of absence from his civil service job. He purchased a large number of cuckoo clocks and then an expensive car, which he planned to use as a mobile showroom for his wares, anticipating that he would make a great deal of money. He proceeded to "tear around town" buying and selling clocks and other merchandise, and when he was not out, he was continuously on the phone making "deals." He rarely slept and, uncharacteristically, spent every evening in neighborhood bars drinking heavily and, according to him, "wheeling and dealing."... He was $3,000 in debt and had driven his family to exhaustion with his excessive activity and talkativeness. He said, however, that he felt "on top of the world" (Spitzer et al., 1983, p. 115).

Frequently, a person sequentially experiences periods of mania and depression. This alternation of mania and depression is called **bipolar disorder** (or, as it used to be known, manic-depressive disorder). The swings between highs and lows may occur a few days apart or may alternate over a period of years. In addition, periods of depression are usually longer than periods of mania. (To learn more about bipolar symptoms, complete **Interactivity 49–2.**)

Ironically, some of society's most creative individuals may suffer from forms of bipolar disorder. The imagination, drive, excitement, and energy that they display during manic stages allow them to make unusually creative contributions. For instance, historical analysis of the composer Robert Schumann's music shows that he was most prolific during the periods of mania he had periodically. In contrast, his output dropped off drastically during periods of depression (see Figure 5). On the other hand, the high output associated with mania does not necessarily lead to higher quality: Some of Schumann's greatest works were created outside his periods of mania (Ludwig, 1996; Szegedy-Maszak, 2003).

Despite the creative fires that may be lit by mania, persons who experience this disorder often show a recklessness that produces self-injury—emotionally and sometimes physically. They may alienate others with their talkativeness, inflated self-esteem, and indifference to the needs of others.

Bipolar disorder: A disorder in which a person alternates between periods of euphoric feelings of mania and periods of depression.

INTERACTIVITY 49–2

Bipolar disorder

CAUSES OF MOOD DISORDERS

Because they represent a major mental health problem, mood disorders—and, in particular, depression—have received a good deal of study. Several approaches have been used to explain the disorder. Proponents of psychoanalytic approaches, for example, see depression as the result of feelings of loss (real or potential) or of anger directed at oneself. One psychoanalytic approach, for instance, suggests that depression is produced by the loss or threatened loss of a parent early in life. Another psychoanalytic view maintains that people feel responsible for the bad things that happen to them and direct their anger inward.

On the other hand, convincing evidence has been found that both bipolar disorder and major depression may have genetic and biochemical roots. For example, heredity plays a role in bipolar disorder: The affliction clearly runs in some families. Furthermore, several neurotransmitters appear to play a role in depression. For instance, alterations in the functioning of serotonin and norepinephrine in the brain are related to the disorder (Leonard, 2000; Vogel, 2000; Plomin & McGuffin, 2003).

Behavioral theories of depression argue that the stresses of life produce a reduction in positive reinforcers. As a result, people begin to withdraw, which only serves to reduce positive reinforcers further. In addition, people receive attention for their depressive behavior, which leads to further reinforcement of the depression (Lewinsohn & Essau, 2002; Lewinsohn et al., 2003).

Some explanations for mood disorders rely on cognitive factors. For example, psychologist Martin Seligman suggests that depression is largely a response to learned helplessness. *Learned helplessness* is a learned expectation that events in one's life are uncontrollable and that one cannot escape from the situation. As a consequence, people simply give up fighting aversive events and submit to them, thereby producing depression. Other theorists go a step further, suggesting that depression results from *hopelessness*, a combination of learned helplessness and an expectation that negative outcomes in one's life are inevitable (Peterson, Maier, & Seligman, 1993; Abramson et al., 2002; Kwon & Laurenceau, 2002).

Clinical psychologist Aaron Beck has proposed that faulty cognitions underlie people's depressed feelings. Specifically, his cognitive theory of depression suggests that depressed individuals typically view themselves as life's losers, blaming themselves whenever anything goes wrong. By focusing on the negative side of situations, they feel inept and unable to act constructively to change their environment. In sum, their negative cognitions lead to feelings of depression (Newman et al., 2002).

The most recent explanation of depression derives from evolutionary psychology, which considers how behavior is influenced by our genetic inheritance from our ancestors. In the evolutionary view, depression is an adaptive response to unattainable goals. When people fruitlessly pursue an ever-elusive goal, depression begins, ending pursuit of the goal. Ultimately, when the depression lifts, people can turn to other, more reasonable goals. In this view, depression serves a positive function, in the long run increasing the chances of survival for particular individuals, who can then pass the behavior to their offspring. Such reasoning, of course, is highly speculative (Nesse, 2000, Siegert & Ward, 2002).

The various theories of depression have not provided a complete answer to an elusive question that has dogged researchers: Why does depression occur in approximately twice as many women as men—a pattern (shown in Figure 6) that is similar across a variety of cultures? One explanation suggests that the stress experienced by women may be greater than that experienced by men at certain points in

**PowerWeb:
Helplessness: On
Depression,
Development, and
Death**

www.mhhe.com/feldmanup7

Several areas of the brain are involved in producing the symptoms of depression.

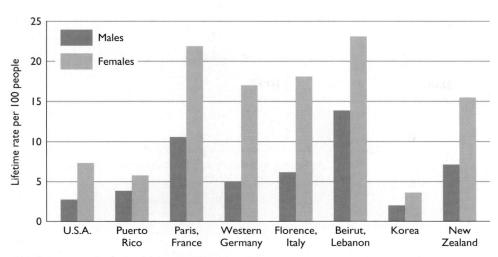

FIGURE 6 Across different places and cultures, women are diagnosed more frequently with depression than men. (Source: Weissman & Olfson, 1995.)

their lives—such as when a woman must simultaneously earn a living and be the primary caregiver for her children. In addition, women have a higher risk for physical and sexual abuse, typically earn lower wages than men, report greater unhappiness with their marriages, and generally experience chronic negative circumstances (Joiner & Coyne, 1999; Nolen-Hoeksema, Larson, & Grayson, 1999; Antonucci et al., 2002).

Biological factors may also explain some women's depression. For example, 25 to 50 percent of women who take oral contraceptives report symptoms of depression, and depression that occurs after the birth of a child is linked to hormonal changes (Strickland, 1992).

It is clear, ultimately, that researchers have discovered no definitive solutions to the puzzle of depression, and there are many alternative explanations. Most likely, a complex interaction of several factors causes these mood disorders.

Schizophrenia

> I'm a doctor, you know . . . I don't have a diploma, but I'm a doctor. I'm glad to be a mental patient, because it taught me how to be humble. I use Cover Girl creamy natural makeup. Oral Roberts has been here to visit me . . . This place is where *Mad* magazine is published. The Nixons make Noxon metal polish. When I was a little girl, I used to sit and tell stories to myself. When I was older, I turned off the sound on the TV set and made up dialogue to go with the shows I watched . . . I'm a week pregnant. I have schizophrenia—cancer of the nerves. My body is overcrowded with nerves. This is going to win me the Nobel Prize for medicine. I don't consider myself schizophrenic anymore. There's no such thing as schizophrenia, there's only mental telepathy. I once had a friend named Camilla Costello (Sheehan, 1982, pp. 72–73).

This excerpt illustrates the efforts of a woman with schizophrenia, one of the more severe forms of mental disturbance, to hold a conversation with a clinician. People with schizophrenia account for by far the largest percentage of those hospitalized for mental disorders. They are also in many respects the least likely to recover from their psychological difficulties.

FIGURE 7 The distinctions among the different types of schizophrenia are not always clear-cut, and symptoms may vary considerably over time.

Types of Schizophrenia	
Type	**Symptoms**
Disorganized (hebephrenic) schizophrenia	Innappropriate laughter and giggling, silliness, incoherent speech, infantile behavior, strange and sometimes obscene behavior
Paranoid schizophrenia	Delusions and hallucinations of persecution or of greatness, loss of judgment, erratic and unpredictable behavior
Catatonic schizophrenia	Major disturbances in movement; in some phases, loss of all motion, with patient frozen into a single position, remaining that way for hours and sometimes even days; in other phases, hyperactivity and wild, sometimes violent, movement
Undifferentiated schizophrenia	Variable mixture of major symptoms of schizophrenia; classification used for patients who cannot be typed into any of the more specific categories
Residual schizophrenia	Minor signs of schizophrenia after a more serious episode

Schizophrenia: A class of disorders in which severe distortion of reality occurs.

Schizophrenia refers to a class of disorders in which severe distortion of reality occurs. Thinking, perception, and emotion may deteriorate; the individual may withdraw from social interaction; and the person may display bizarre behavior. Although several types of schizophrenia (see Figure 7) have been observed, the distinctions between them are not always clear-cut (Bentall, 1992; Cannon, 1998). Moreover, the symptoms displayed by persons with schizophrenia may vary considerably over time, and people with schizophrenia show significant differences in the pattern of their symptoms even when they are labeled with the same diagnostic category. Nonetheless, a number of characteristics reliably distinguish schizophrenia from other disorders. They include the following:

- *Decline from a previous level of functioning.* An individual can no longer carry out activities he or she was once able to do.
- *Disturbances of thought and language.* People with schizophrenia use logic and language in a peculiar way. Their thinking often does not make sense, and their information processing is frequently faulty. They also do not follow conventional linguistic rules (Penn et al., 1997). Consider, for example, the following response to the question "Why do you think people believe in God?"

> Uh, let's, I don't know why, let's see, balloon travel. He holds it up for you, the balloon. He don't let you fall out, your little legs sticking down through the clouds. He's down to the smokestack, looking through the smoke trying to get the balloon gassed up you know. Way they're flying on top that way, legs sticking out. I don't know, looking down on the ground, heck, that'd make you so dizzy you just stay and sleep you know, hold down and sleep there. I used to be sleep outdoors, you know, sleep outdoors instead of going home (Chapman & Chapman, 1973, p. 3).

As this selection illustrates, although the basic grammatical structure may be intact, the substance of thinking characteristic of schizophrenia is often illogical, garbled, and lacking in meaningful content (see Figure 8).

- ▶ *Delusions.* People with schizophrenia often have *delusions*, firmly held, unshakable beliefs with no basis in reality. Among the common delusions experienced by people with schizophrenia are the beliefs that they are being controlled by someone else, they are being persecuted by others, and their thoughts are being broadcast so that others know what they are thinking (Siddle et al., 2002; Stompe et al., 2003).

- ▶ *Hallucinations and perceptual disorders.* People with schizophrenia do not perceive the world as most other people do. They also may have *hallucinations*, the experience of perceiving things that do not actually exist. Furthermore, they may see, hear, or smell things differently from others (see Figure 9) and do not even have a sense of their bodies in the way that others do, having difficulty determining where their bodies stop and the rest of the world begins (Reichman & Rabins, 1996; Roehricht & Priebe, 2002; Copolov et al., 2003).

- ▶ *Emotional disturbances.* People with schizophrenia sometimes show a bland lack of emotion in which even the most dramatic events produce little or no emotional response. Conversely, they may display emotion that is inappropriate to a situation. For example, a person with schizophrenia may laugh uproariously at a funeral or react with anger when being helped by someone.

- ▶ *Withdrawal.* People with schizophrenia tend to have little interest in others. They tend not to socialize or hold real conversations with others, although they may talk *at* another person. In the most extreme cases they do not even acknowledge the presence of other people, appearing to be in their own isolated world.

The symptoms of schizophrenia follow two primary courses. In *process schizophrenia*, the symptoms develop relatively early in life, slowly and subtly. There may be a gradual withdrawal from the world, excessive daydreaming, and a blunting of emotion, until eventually the disorder reaches the point where others cannot overlook it. In other cases, known as *reactive schizophrenia*, the onset of symptoms is sudden and conspicuous. The

FIGURE 8 This shows an excerpt from the diary of the killer of Senator Robert Kennedy who, like his brother President John Kennedy, was assassinated in the 1960s. The diary entry shows disturbances of thought and language characteristic of schizophrenia. Kennedy's killer is still in prison, but he is seeking parole on the grounds that his schizophrenia is no longer a problem. Would you permit him to go free? (Source: World Wide Photos.)

PowerWeb: The Schizophrenic Mind

www.mhhe.com/feldmanup7

FIGURE 9 This unusual art was created by an individual suffering from severe mental disturbance.

FIGURE 10 The closer the genetic links between two people, the greater the likelihood that if one experiences schizophrenia, so will the other some time during his or her lifetime. However, genetics is not the full story, because if it were, the risk of identical twins having schizophrenia would be 100 percent, not the 48 percent shown in this figure. (Source: Gottesman, 1991.)

Risk of Developing Schizophrenia, Based on Genetic Relatedness to a Person with Schizophrenia		
Relationship	**Genetic Relatedness, %**	**Risk of Developing Schizophrenia, %**
Identical twin	100	48
Child of two schizophrenic parents	100	46
Fraternal twin	50	17
Offspring of one schizophrenic parent	50	17
Sibling	50	9
Nephew or niece	25	4
Spouse	0	2
Unrelated person	0	1

INTERACTIVITY 49–3

Schizophrenia

treatment outlook for reactive schizophrenia is relatively favorable; process schizophrenia has proved to be much more difficult to treat.

The symptoms of schizophrenia can be classified into two types. Positive-symptom schizophrenia is indicated by the presence of disordered behavior such as hallucinations, delusions, and emotional extremes. In contrast, negative-symptom schizophrenia shows an absence or loss of normal functioning, such as social withdrawal or blunted emotions. The distinction is important because it suggests that two different underlying processes may explain the roots of schizophrenia—which remains one of the greatest mysteries facing psychologists who deal with disordered behavior. To increase your understanding of schizophrenia, work on **Interactivity 49–3.**

SOLVING THE PUZZLE OF SCHIZOPHRENIA: BIOLOGICAL CAUSES

Although schizophrenic behavior clearly departs radically from normal behavior, its causes are less apparent. It does appear, however, that schizophrenia has both biological and environmental origins (Sawa & Snyder, 2002).

Let's first consider the evidence pointing to a biological cause. Because schizophrenia is more common in some families than in others, genetic factors seem to be involved in producing at least a susceptibility to or readiness for developing schizophrenia. For example, research has shown that the closer the genetic link between a person with schizophrenia and another individual, the greater the likelihood that the other person will experience the disorder (see Figure 10; Gottesman & Moldin, 1998; Brzustowicz et al., 2000; Plomin & McGuffin, 2003).

On the other hand, if genetics alone was responsible, the chance of both of two identical twins having schizophrenia would be 100 percent instead of just under 50 percent, because identical twins have the same genetic makeup. Moreover, attempts to find a link between schizophrenia and a particular gene have been only partly successful. Apparently, more than genetic factors alone produces schizophrenia (Franzek & Beckmann, 1996; Lenzenweger & Dworkin, 1998).

One intriguing biological hypothesis to explain schizophrenia is that the brains of people with the disorder may harbor either a biochemical imbalance or a structural abnormality. For example, the *dopamine hypothesis* suggests that schizophrenia occurs when there is excess activity in the areas of the brain that use dopamine as a neurotransmitter. This hypothesis came to light after the discovery that drugs that block dopamine action in brain pathways can be highly effective in reducing the symptoms of schizophrenia. Other research suggests that dopamine may operate in

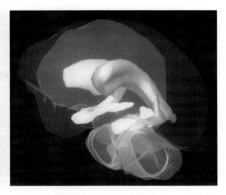

FIGURE 11 Structural changes in the brain have been found in people with schizophrenia. In the first MRI reconstruction of the brain of a patient with schizophrenia (left), the hippocampus (yellow) is shrunken, and the ventricles (gray) are enlarged and fluid-filled. In contrast, the brain of a person without the disorder (right) appears structurally different. (Source: N.C. Andreasen, University of Iowa.)

conjunction with other neurotransmitters, such as serotonin (Kapur & Remington, 1996; Baumeister & Francis, 2002).

Some biological explanations propose that structural abnormalities exist in the brains of people with schizophrenia, perhaps as a result of exposure to a virus during prenatal development. For example, some research shows abnormalities in the neural circuits of the cortex and limbic systems of individuals with schizophrenia. Consistent with such research, people with schizophrenia and those without the disorder show different brain functioning (see Figures 11 and 12; Brown et al., 1996; Lenzenweger & Dworkin, 1998; Bartzokis et al., 2003).

Further evidence for the importance of biological factors shows that when people with schizophrenia hear voices during hallucinations, the parts of the brain responsible for hearing and language processing become active. When they have visual hallucinations, the parts of the brain involved in movement and color are active. At the same time, people with schizophrenia often have unusually low activity in the brain's frontal lobes—the parts of the brain involved with emotional regulation, insight, and the evaluation of sensory stimuli (Stern & Silbersweig, 2001).

ENVIRONMENTAL PERSPECTIVES ON SCHIZOPHRENIA

Although biological factors provide some pieces of the puzzle of schizophrenia, we still need to consider past and current experiences in the environments of people who develop the disturbance. For instance, psychoanalytic approaches suggest that

FIGURE 12 Compare these PET scans, which show differences in functioning between two people, one of whom has been diagnosed with schizophrenia. Both are performing a vigilance task. In the non-schizophrenic, the task increases prefrontal cortex metabolism (the scan on the right labeled "control"). For the person with schizophrenia, however, this does not occur (the scan labeled "schizophrenic"). (Source: M.S. Buchsbaum, University of California–Irvine.)

schizophrenia is a form of regression to earlier experiences and stages of life. Freud believed, for instance, that people with schizophrenia lack strong enough egos to cope with their unacceptable impulses. They regress to the oral stage—a time when the id and ego are not yet separated. Therefore, individuals with schizophrenia essentially lack an ego and act out impulses without concern for reality.

Although this reasoning is theoretically plausible, little evidence supports psychoanalytic explanations. Somewhat more convincing theories look toward the emotional and communication patterns of the families of people with schizophrenia. For instance, some researchers suggest that schizophrenia results from high levels of expressed emotion. *Expressed emotion* is an interaction style characterized by criticism, hostility, and emotional intrusiveness by family members. Other researchers suggest that faulty communication patterns lie at the heart of schizophrenia (Bayer, 1996; Linszen et al., 1997; Miklowitz & Tompson, 2003).

Psychologists who take a cognitive perspective on schizophrenia suggest that the problems in thinking experienced by people with the disorder point to a cognitive cause. Some suggest that schizophrenia results from *overattention* to stimuli in the environment. Rather than being able to screen out unimportant or inconsequential stimuli and focus on the most important things in the environment, people with schizophrenia may be excessively receptive to virtually everything in their environment. As a consequence, their information-processing capabilities become overloaded and eventually break down. Other cognitive experts argue that schizophrenia results from *underattention* to certain stimuli. According to this explanation, people with schizophrenia fail to focus sufficiently on important stimuli, and pay attention to other, less important information in their surroundings (Braff, 1993).

Although it is plausible that overattention and underattention are related to different forms of schizophrenia, these phenomena do not explain the origins of such information-processing disorders. Consequently, cognitive approaches—like other environmental explanations—do not provide a full explanation of the disorder.

THE MULTIPLE CAUSES OF SCHIZOPHRENIA

We have seen that several different biological and environmental factors are related to schizophrenia. It is likely, then, that not just one but several causes jointly explain the onset of the disorder. The predominant approach used today, the *predisposition model of schizophrenia*, considers a number of factors simultaneously. This model suggests that individuals may inherit a predisposition or an inborn sensitivity to schizophrenia that makes them particularly vulnerable to stressful factors in the environment. The stressors may vary—social rejection or dysfunctional family communication patterns—but if they are strong enough and are coupled with a genetic predisposition, the result will be the onset of schizophrenia. Similarly, if the genetic predisposition is strong enough, schizophrenia may occur even when the environmental stressors are relatively weak.

In short, the models used today associate schizophrenia with several kinds of biological and environmental factors. It is increasingly clear, then, that no single factor, but a combination of interrelated variables, produces schizophrenia (Lenzenweger & Dworkin, 1998; McDonald & Murray, 2000; Meltzer, 2000).

Personality Disorders

I had always wanted lots of things; as a child I can remember wanting a bullet that a friend of mine had brought in to show the class. I took it and put it into my school bag and when my friend noticed it was missing, I was the one who stayed after school with him and searched the room, and I was the one who sat with him and bitched about the other kids and how one of them took his bullet. I even went home with him to help him break the news to his uncle, who had brought it home from the war for him.

But that was petty compared with the stuff I did later. I wanted a Ph.D. very badly, but I didn't want to work very hard—just enough to get by. I never did the experiments I reported; hell, I was smart enough to make up the results. I knew enough about statistics to make anything look plausible. I got my master's degree without even spending one hour in a laboratory. I mean, the professors believed anything. I'd stay out all night drinking and being with my friends, and the next day I'd get in just before them and tell 'em I'd been in the lab all night. They'd actually feel sorry for me (Duke & Nowicki, 1979, pp. 309–310).

This excerpt provides a graphic first-person account of a person with a personality disorder. A **personality disorder** is characterized by a set of inflexible, maladaptive personality traits that keep a person from functioning properly in society. Personality disorders differ from the other problems we have discussed because those affected by them often have little sense of personal distress associated with the psychological maladjustment. In fact, people with personality disorders frequently lead seemingly normal lives. However, just below the surface lies a set of inflexible, maladaptive personality traits that do not permit these individuals to function appropriately as members of society (Clarkin & Lenzenweger, 1996; Millon & Davis, 1996, 1999).

The best-known type of personality disorder, illustrated by the case above, is the **antisocial personality disorder** (sometimes referred to as a sociopathic personality). Individuals with this disturbance show no regard for the moral and ethical rules of society or the rights of others. Although they can appear quite intelligent and likable (at least at first), upon closer examination they turn out to be manipulative and deceptive. Moreover, they lack any guilt or anxiety over their wrongdoing. When those with an antisocial personality behave in a way that injures someone else, they understand intellectually that they have caused the harm but feel no remorse (Lykken, 1995; Goodwin & Hamilton, 2003).

People with antisocial personalities are often impulsive and lack the ability to withstand frustration. They can be extremely manipulative. They also may have excellent social skills; they can be charming, engaging, and highly persuasive. Some of the best con artists have antisocial personalities.

What causes such an unusual constellation of problems? A variety of factors have been suggested, ranging from a biologically induced inability to experience emotions appropriately to problems in family relationships. For example, in many cases of antisocial behavior, the individual has come from a home in which a parent has died or left, or one in which there is a lack of affection, a lack of consistency in discipline, or outright rejection. Other explanations concentrate on sociocultural factors, because an unusually high proportion of people with antisocial personalities come from lower socioeconomic groups. Still, no one has been able to pinpoint the specific causes of antisocial personalities, and it is likely that some combination of factors is responsible (Nigg & Goldsmith, 1994; Rosenstein & Horowitz, 1996; Costa & Widiger, 2002).

People with **borderline personality disorder** have difficulty developing a secure sense of who they are. As a consequence, they tend to rely on relationships with others to define their identity. The problem with this strategy is that rejections are devastating. Furthermore, people with this disorder distrust others and have difficulty controlling their anger. Their emotional volatility leads to impulsive and self-destructive behavior. Individuals with borderline personality disorder often feel empty and alone. They may form intense, sudden, one-sided relationships, demanding the attention of another person and then feeling angry when they don't receive it. One reason for this behavior is that they may have a background in which others discounted or criticized their emotional reactions, and they may have not learned to regulate their emotions effectively (Linehan, Cochran, & Kehrer, 2001; Trull, Stepp, & Durrett, 2003). You can learn more about borderline personality disorders by completing **Interactivity 49–4.**

Personality disorder: A disorder characterized by a set of inflexible, maladaptive personality traits that keep a person from functioning properly in society.

Antisocial personality disorder: A disorder in which individuals show no regard for the moral and ethical rules of society or the rights of others.

Borderline personality disorder: A disorder in which individuals have difficulty developing a secure sense of who they are.

INTERACTIVITY 49–4
Borderline personality disorder

Narcissistic personality disorder: A personality disturbance characterized by an exaggerated sense of self-importance.

Another example of a personality disturbance is the **narcissistic personality disorder,** which is characterized by an exaggerated sense of self-importance. Those with the disorder expect special treatment from others, while at the same time disregarding others' feelings. In some ways, in fact, the main attribute of the narcissistic personality is an inability to experience empathy for other people.

There are several other categories of personality disorder, ranging in severity from individuals who may simply be regarded by others as eccentric, obnoxious, or difficult to people who act in a manner that is criminal and dangerous to others. Although they are not out of touch with reality in the way that people with schizophrenia are, people with personality disorders lead lives that put them on the fringes of society (Millon et al., 2000; Trull & Widiger, 2003).

Childhood Disorders

We typically view childhood as a time of innocence and relative freedom from stress. In reality, though, almost 20 percent of children and 40 percent of adolescents experience significant emotional or behavioral disorders (Romano et al., 2001; Nolen-Hoeksema, 2004)

For example, although major depression is more prevalent in adults, around 2.5 percent of children and more than 8 percent of adolescents suffer from the disorder. In fact, by the time they reach age 20, between 15 and 20 percent of children and adolescents will experience an episode of major depression (Garber & Horowitz, 2002).

Children do not always display depression in the same way adults do. Rather than showing profound sadness or hopelessness, childhood depression may produce the expression of exaggerated fears, clinginess, or avoidance of everyday activities. In older children, the symptoms may be sulking, school problems, and even acts of delinquency (Prieto, Cole, & Tageson, 1992; Wenar, 1994; Koplewicz, 2002).

Attention-deficit hyperactivity disorder (ADHD): A disorder marked by inattention, impulsiveness, a low tolerance for frustration, and a great deal of inappropriate activity.

A considerably more common childhood disorder is **attention-deficit hyperactivity disorder,** or **ADHD,** a disorder marked by inattention, impulsiveness, a low tolerance for frustration, and generally a great deal of inappropriate activity. Although all children show such behavior some of the time, it is so common in children diagnosed with ADHD that it interferes with their everyday functioning (Barkley, 1998a; Brown, 2000; Swanson, Harris, & Graham, 2003).

ADHD is surprisingly widespread, with estimates ranging between 3 and 5 percent of the school-age population—or some 3.5 million children under the age of 18 in the United States. Children diagnosed with the disorder are often exhausting to parents and teachers, and even their peers find them difficult to deal with.

The cause of ADHD is not known, although most experts feel that it is produced by dysfunctions in the nervous system. For example, one theory suggests that unusually low levels of arousal in the central nervous system cause ADHD. To compensate, children with ADHD seek out stimulation to increase arousal. Still, such theories are speculative. Furthermore, because many children occasionally show behaviors characteristic of ADHD, it often is misdiagnosed. Only the frequency and persistence of the symptoms of ADHD allow for a correct diagnosis, which can be done only by a trained professional (Hinshaw et al., 1997; Barkley, 2000).

Other Disorders

It's important to keep in mind that the various forms of abnormal behavior described in *DSM-IV-TR* cover much more ground than we have been able to discuss in this module. Some relate to topics previously considered in other contexts, such as *psychoactive substance-use disorder*, in which problems arise from the abuse of drugs; *eating disorders;* and *sexual disorders*, in which one's sexual activity is unsatisfactory.

Another important class of disorders previously touched upon is *organic mental disorders*. These are problems that have a purely biological basis. There are other disorders we have not mentioned at all, and each of the classes we have discussed can be divided into several subcategories (Kopelman & Fleminger, 2002; Pratt et al., 2003; Reijonen et al., 2003).

RECAP/EVALUATE/RETHINK

RECAP

What are the major psychological disorders?

- Anxiety disorders are present when a person experiences so much anxiety that it affects daily functioning. Specific types of anxiety disorders include phobic disorder, panic disorder, generalized anxiety disorder, and obsessive-compulsive disorder. (p. 541)
- Somatoform disorders are psychological difficulties that take on a physical (somatic) form, but for which there is no medical cause. Examples are hypochondriasis and conversion disorders. (p. 545)
- Dissociative disorders are marked by the separation, or dissociation, of crucial parts of personality that are usually integrated. The major kinds of dissociative disorders are dissociative identity disorder (multiple personalities), dissociative amnesia, and dissociative fugue. (p. 546)
- Mood disorders are characterized by emotional states of depression or euphoria so strong that they intrude on everyday living. They include major depression and bipolar disorder. (p. 547)
- Schizophrenia is one of the more severe forms of mental illness. Symptoms of schizophrenia include declines in functioning, thought and language disturbances, perceptual disorders, emotional disturbance, and withdrawal from others. (p. 551)
- Strong evidence links schizophrenia to genetic, biochemical, and environmental factors. According to the predisposition model, an interaction among various factors produces the disorder. (p. 554)
- People with personality disorders experience little or no personal distress, but they do suffer from an inability to function as normal members of society. These disorders include antisocial personality disorder, borderline personality disorder, and narcissistic personality disorder. (p. 556)
- Childhood disorders include major depression and attention-deficit hyperactivity disorder (ADHD), which is marked by inattention, impulsiveness, a low tolerance for frustration, and inappropriate activity. (p. 557)

EVALUATE

1. Kathy is terrified of elevators. She is likely to be suffering from a(n)
   a. Obsessive-compulsive disorder
   b. Phobic disorder
   c. Panic disorder
   d. Generalized anxiety disorder
2. Carmen described an incident in which her anxiety suddenly rose to a peak and she felt a sense of impending doom. Carmen experienced a(n) _____ _____.
3. Troubling thoughts that persist for days or months are known as
   a. Obsessions
   b. Compulsions
   c. Rituals
   d. Panic attacks
4. An overpowering urge to carry out a strange ritual is called a(n) _____.
5. In what major way does conversion disorder differ from hypochondriasis?
6. The separation of the personality, providing escape from stressful situations, is the key factor in _____ disorders.
7. States of extreme euphoria and energy paired with severe depression characterize _____ disorder.
8. _____ schizophrenia is characterized by symptoms that are sudden and of easily identifiable onset; _____ schizophrenia develops gradually over a person's life span.
9. The _____ _____ states that schizophrenia may be caused by an excess of certain neurotransmitters in the brain.
10. Which of the following theories states that schizophrenia is caused by the combination of a genetic predisposition and environmental stressors?
    a. Learned-inattention theory
    b. Predisposition model
    c. Dopamine hypothesis
    d. Learned-helplessness theory

RETHINK

1. What cultural factors might contribute to the rate of anxiety disorders found in a culture? How might the *experience* of anxiety differ among people of different cultures?
2. Personality disorders are often not apparent to others, and many people with these problems seem to live basically

normal lives and are not a threat to others. Because these people can function well in society, why should they be considered psychologically disordered?

KEY TERMS

anxiety disorder p. 541
phobias p. 542
panic disorder p. 542
generalized anxiety
disorder p. 543
obsessive-compulsive
disorder p. 543
obsession p. 543
compulsion p. 543

somatoform
disorder p. 545
hypochondriasis p. 545
conversion disorder p. 545
dissociative disorder p. 546
dissociative identity
disorder (or multiple
personality) p. 546
dissociative amnesia p. 546

dissociative fugue p. 547
mood disorder p. 547
major depression p. 547
mania p. 548
bipolar disorder p. 549
schizophrenia p. 552
personality disorder p. 557
antisocial personality
disorder p. 557

borderline personality
disorder p. 557
narcissistic personality
disorder p. 558
attention-deficit
hyperactivity disorder
(ADHD) p. 558

Psychological Disorders in Perspective

MODULE 50

How prevalent are psychological disorders?

What indicators signal a need for the help of a mental health practitioner?

The Prevalence of Psychological Disorders: The Mental State of the Union

How common are the kinds of psychological disorders we've been discussing? Here's one answer: Every second person you meet in the United States is likely to suffer, at some point during his or her life, from a psychological disorder.

That's the conclusion drawn from a massive study on the prevalence of psychological disorders. In that study, researchers conducted face-to-face interviews with more than 8,000 men and women between the ages of 15 and 54 years. The sample was designed to be representative of the population of the United States. According to results of the study, 48 percent of those interviewed had experienced a disorder at some point in their lives. In addition, 30 percent experience a disorder in any particular year, and the number of people who experience simultaneous multiple disorders (known as *comorbidity*) is significant (Kessler et al., 1994; Welkowitz et al., 2000).

The most common disorder was depression, with 17 percent of those surveyed reporting at least one major episode. Ten percent of those surveyed had suffered from depression during the current year. The next most common disorder was alcohol dependence, which occurred at a lifetime incidence rate of 14 percent. In addition, 7 percent of those interviewed had experienced alcohol dependence during the last year. Other frequently occurring psychological disorders were drug dependence, disorders involving panic (such as an overwhelming fear of talking to strangers and terror of heights), and posttraumatic stress disorder.

Although some researchers think the estimates of severe disorders may be too high (Narrow et al., 2002), the national findings are consistent with studies of college students and their psychological difficulties. For example, in one study of the problems of students who visited a college counseling center, more than 40 percent of students reported being depressed (see Figure 1). Remember, though, that these figures include only students who sought help from the counseling center, not those who did not seek treatment. Consequently, the figures are not representative of the entire college population (Benton et al., 2003).

Also, keep in mind that these results differ significantly in other cultures. For instance, cross-cultural surveys show that the incidence of major depression varies significantly from one culture to another. The probability of having at least one episode of depression is only 1.5 percent in Taiwan and 2.9 percent in Korea, compared with 11.6 percent in New Zealand and 16.4 percent in France. Such notable differences underscore the importance of considering the cultural context of psychological disorders (Weissman et al., 1996).

The prevalence figures for the United States suggest that psychological disorders are far from rare, yet society directs significant prejudice and discrimination toward

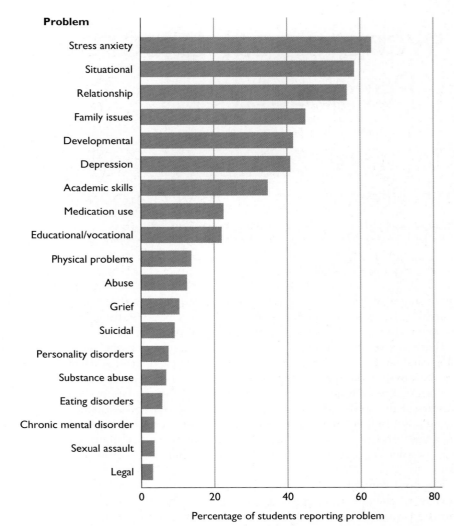

Problem

Stress anxiety
Situational
Relationship
Family issues
Developmental
Depression
Academic skills
Medication use
Educational/vocational
Physical problems
Abuse
Grief
Suicidal
Personality disorders
Substance abuse
Eating disorders
Chronic mental disorder
Sexual assault
Legal

0   20   40   60   80

Percentage of students reporting problem

FIGURE 1 The problems reported by students visiting a college counseling center. Would you have predicted this pattern of psychological difficulties? (Source: Benton et al., 2003.)

INTERACTIVITY 50–1

Prevalence of psychological disorders

people with psychological disorders. The stigma (a label that leads people to be seen as different and therefore defective) that marks people who experience a psychological disorder remains real. (You can learn more about the prevalence of psychological disorders by completing **Interactivity 50–1.**)

The Social and Cultural Context of Psychological Disorders

In considering the nature of the psychological disorders described in *DSM-IV-TR*, it's important to keep in mind that the specific disorders reflect turn-of-the-twenty-first-century Western cultures. The classification system provides a snapshot of how its authors viewed mental disorder when it was published in 1994. In fact, the development of the most recent version of *DSM* was a source of great debate, in part reflecting issues that divide society.

For example, two disorders caused particular controversy during the revision process. One, known as the "self-defeating personality disorder," was ultimately was removed from the appendix, where it had appeared in the previous revision. The term *self-defeating personality disorder* had been applied to cases in which people who were treated unpleasantly or demeaningly in relationships neither left nor took other action. It was typically used to describe people who remained in abusive relationships.

Although some clinicians argued that it was a valid category, one that they observed in clinical practice, the disorder seemed to lack enough research evidence to support its existence. Furthermore, some critics complained that use of the label had the effect of condemning targets of abuse for their plight—a blame-the-victim phenomenon—and as a result, the category was removed from the manual.

A second and even more controversial category was "premenstrual dysphoric disorder." That disorder is characterized by severe, incapacitating mood changes or depression related to a woman's menstrual cycle. Some critics argued that the classification simply labels normal female behavior as a disorder. Former U.S. Surgeon General Antonia Novello suggested that what "in women is called PMS [premenstrual syndrome, a similar classification] in men is called healthy aggression and initiative" (Cotton, 1993, p. 270). Advocates for including the disorder prevailed, however, and "premenstrual dysphoric disorder" appears in the appendix of *DSM-IV-TR* (Hartung & Widiger, 1998).

Such controversies underline the fact that our understanding of abnormal behavior reflects the society and culture in which we live. Future revisions of *DSM* may include a different catalog of disorders. Even now, other cultures might include a list of disorders that look very different from the list that appears in the current *DSM*, as we discuss next.

Exploring DIVERSITY

DSM and Culture—and the Culture of DSM

In most people's estimation, a person who hears voices of the recently deceased is probably a victim of a psychological disturbance. Yet some Plains Indians routinely hear the voices of the dead calling to them from the afterlife.

This is only one example of the role of culture in labeling behavior as "abnormal." In fact, among all the major adult disorders included in the *DSM* categorization, just four are found across all cultures of the world: schizophrenia, bipolar disorder, major depression, and anxiety disorders. *All* the rest are particular to North America and Western Europe (Kleinman, 1996; López & Guarnaccia, 2000; Cohen et al., 1999).

Take, for instance, anorexia nervosa, the disorder in which people develop inaccurate views of their body appearance, become obsessed with their weight, and refuse to eat, sometimes starving in the process. This disorder occurs only in cultures that hold the societal standard that slender female bodies are the most desirable. In most of the world, where such a standard does not exist, anorexia nervosa does not occur. Interestingly, there is no anorexia nervosa in all of Asia, with two exceptions: the upper and upper-middle classes of Japan and Hong Kong, where Western influence tends to be great. In fact, anorexia nervosa developed fairly recently even in Western cultures. In the 1600s and 1700s it did not occur because the ideal female body in Western cultures at that time was a full-figured one.

Similarly, dissociative identity (multiple personality) disorder makes sense as a problem only in societies in which a sense of self is fairly concrete. In India, the self is based more on external factors that are relatively independent of the person. There, when an individual displays symptoms of what people in a Western society would call dissociative identity disorder, Indians assume that that person is possessed either by demons (which they view as a malady) or by gods (which does not require treatment).

Furthermore, even though disorders such as schizophrenia are found throughout the world, cultural factors influence the particular symptoms of the disorder. Hence, catatonic schizophrenia, in which unmoving patients appear to be frozen in the same position, sometimes for days, is rare in North America and Western Europe. In contrast, in India, 80 percent of those with schizophrenia are catatonic.

Other cultures have disorders that do not appear in the West. For example, in Malaysia, a behavior called *amok* is characterized by a wild outburst in which a person, usually quiet and withdrawn, kills or severely injures another. *Koro* is a condition found in Southeast Asian males who develop an intense panic that the penis is about to withdraw into the abdomen. Some West African men develop a disorder when they first attend college that they call "brain fag"; it includes feelings of heaviness or heat in the head, as well as depression and anxiety. Finally, *ataque de nervios* is a disorder found most often among Latinos from the Caribbean, characterized by trembling, crying, uncontrollable screams, and incidents of verbal or physical aggression (Stix, 1996; Cohen et al., 1999; López & Guarnaccia, 2000).

In sum, we should not assume that the *DSM* provides the final word on psychological disorders. The disorders it includes are very much a creation and function of Western cultures at a particular moment in time, and its categories should not be seen as universally applicable.

▲▲▲

BECOMING AN INFORMED CONSUMER
of Psychology
Deciding When You Need Help

After you consider the range and variety of psychological disturbances that can afflict people, you may begin to feel that you suffer from one (or more) of the problems we have discussed. In fact, this perception has a name: *medical student's disease*. Although in this case it might more aptly be labeled "psychology student's disease," the basic symptoms are the same: feeling that you suffer from the same sorts of problems you are studying.

Most often, of course, your concerns will be unwarranted. As we have discussed, the differences between normal and abnormal behavior are often so fuzzy that it is easy to jump to the conclusion that one has the same symptoms that are involved in serious forms of mental disturbance.

Before coming to such a conclusion, though, keep in mind that from time to time we all experience a wide range of emotions, and it is not unusual to feel deeply unhappy, fantasize about bizarre situations, or feel anxiety about life's circumstances. It is the persistence, depth, and consistency of such behavior that set normal reactions apart from abnormal ones. If you have not previously had serious doubts about the normality of your behavior, it is unlikely that reading about others' psychological disorders will prompt you to reevaluate your earlier conclusion.

On the other hand, many people do have problems that merit concern, and in such cases it is important to consider the possibility that professional help is warranted. The following list of symptoms can serve as a guideline to help you determine whether outside intervention might be useful (Engler & Goleman, 1992):

▶ Long-term feelings of distress that interfere with your sense of well-being, competence, and ability to function effectively in daily activities

▶ Occasions in which you experience overwhelmingly high stress, accompanied by feelings of inability to cope with the situation

▶ Prolonged depression or feelings of hopelessness, particularly when they do not have any clear cause (such as the death of someone close)

▶ Withdrawal from other people

▶ A chronic physical problem for which no physical cause can be determined

▶ A fear or phobia that prevents you from engaging in everyday activities

▶ Feelings that other people are out to get you or are talking about and plotting against you

▶ Inability to interact effectively with others, preventing the development of friendships and loving relationships

This list offers a rough set of guidelines for determining when the normal problems of everyday living have escalated beyond your ability to deal with them by yourself. In such situations, the least reasonable approach would be to pore over the psychological disorders we have discussed in an attempt at self-diagnosis. A more reasonable strategy is to consider seeking professional help.

RECAP/EVALUATE/RETHINK

RECAP

How prevalent are psychological disorders?

▶ About half the people in the United States are likely to experience a psychological disorder at some point in their lives, and 30 percent experience a disorder in any specific year. (p. 561)

What indicators signal a need for the help of a mental health practitioner?

▶ The signals that indicate a need for professional help include long-term feelings of psychological distress, feelings of inability to cope with stress, withdrawal from other people, prolonged feelings of hopelessness, chronic physical problems with no apparent causes, phobias and compulsions, paranoia, and an inability to interact with others. (p. 564)

EVALUATE

1. The latest version of *DSM* is considered to be the conclusive guideline on defining mental disorders. True or false?

2. _____ _____ _____, characterized by severe, incapacitating mood changes or depression related to a woman's menstrual cycle, was eventually added to the appendix of *DSM-IV-TR* despite controversy surrounding its inclusion.

3. Match the disorder with the culture in which it is most common:
   1. amok
   2. anorexia nervosa
   3. brain frag
   4. catatonic schizophrenia
   a. India
   b. Malaysia
   c. United States
   d. West Africa

4. Recent research on the prevalence of psychological disorders has found that _____ is the most common disorder, with 17 percent of those surveyed reporting at least one major episode.

RETHINK

1. Why is inclusion in the *DSM-IV-TR* of "borderline" disorders such as self-defeating personality disorder and

premenstrual dysphoric disorder so controversial and political? What disadvantages does inclusion bring? Does inclusion bring any benefits?

2. What societal changes would have to occur for psychological disorders to be regarded as the equivalent of appendicitis or another treatable physical disorder? Would you have reservations about voting for someone who has been treated for a major psychological disorder for president of the United States? Why?

Answers to Evaluate Questions

1. false; the development of the latest version of *DSM* was a source of great controversy, in part reflecting issues that divide society; 2. premenstrual dysphoric disorder; 3. 1-b, 2-c, 3-d, 4-a; 4. depression

Looking Back

Psychology on the Web

1. On the Web, research the insanity defense as it is used in U.S. courts of law, consulting at least two sources. Summarize your findings, evaluating them against the perspectives on psychological disorders. Are there differences between legal and psychological interpretations of "sanity"? If so, what are they? Do you think such differences are appropriate?
2. Find information on the Web about the controversy surrounding dissociative (or multiple) personality disorder. Summarize both sides of the controversy. Using your knowledge of psychology, state your opinion on the matter.
3. After completing Interactivities 49–1 and 49–3 on bipolar disorders and schizophrenia, use the Web to investigate the current status of the case of Andrea Yates, who drowned all five of her children in a bathtub. From what disorder does she suffer? In your opinion, does the fact she has a diagnosed psychological disorder fit with the determination that she was legally sane at the time of the killings? Why?

Epilogue

We've discussed some of the many types of psychological disorders to which people are prone, noting the difficulty psychologists and physicians have in clearly differentiating normal from abnormal behavior and looking at some of the approaches mental health professionals have taken to explain and treat psychological disorders. We considered today's most commonly used classification scheme, categorized in *DSM-IV-TR*, and examined some of the more prevalent forms of psychological disorders. To gain a perspective on the topic of psychological disorders, we discussed the surprisingly broad incidence of psychological disorders in U.S. society and the cultural nature of such disorders.

Turn back to the Prologue, in which the case of Chris Coles was described. Using the knowledge you've gained about psychological disorders, consider the following questions.

1. Coles was diagnosed as having schizophrenia. What elements of his behavior seem to fit the description of schizophrenia provided by *DSM-IV-TR*?
2. From which type of schizophrenia (i.e., disorganized, paranoid, catatonic, undifferentiated, residual) do you think Coles was suffering? Why?
3. Which perspective (i.e., medical, psychoanalytic, behavioral, cognitive, humanistic, sociocultural) provides the most useful explanation for Coles's case, in your opinion? Why?
4. What advantages might there be in using multiple perspectives to address Coles's case?

Treatment of Psychological Disorders

Prologue

Conquering Schizophrenia

For weeks they had practiced dance steps, shopped for formals, fretted about hairstyles and what on earth to say to their partners. Now the Big City band was pumping up the volume, and the whole ballroom was beginning to shake. Brandon Fitch, wearing a pinstripe suit and an ear-to-ear grin, shimmied with a high-stepping blond. Daphne Moss, sporting a floral dress and white corsage, delighted her dad by letting him cut in. The usually quiet Kevin Buchberger leaped onto the dance floor and flat-out boogied for the first time in his life, while Kevin Namkoong grabbed an electric guitar and jammed with the band. The prom at Case Western Reserve University had hit full tilt.

But this was a prom that almost never was. Most of the 175 participants were in their 30s; they had missed the proms of their youth—along with other adolescent rites of passage. Don't ask where they were at 18 or 21. The memories are too bleak, too fragmented to convey. They had organized this better-late-than-never prom to celebrate their remarkable "awakening" to reality after many years of being lost in the darkness of schizophrenia.

Moss, Buchberger, Fitch, and their fellow promgoers were awakened from their long nightmare of insanity by a remarkable drug called clozapine (brand name: Clozaril). The dinner dance, organized with help from psychiatrists and counselors at Case Western Reserve's affiliated University Hospitals, in Cleveland, served as a bittersweet celebration of shared loss and regained hope. (Wallis & Willwerth, 1992, p. 53).

Prom night

PowerWeb: Are We Nuts?
www.mhhe.com/feldmanup7

The drug that has brought new life to people like Daphne Moss, Kevin Buchberger, and Brandon Fitch is just one of many that, along with other new treatment approaches, have revolutionized the treatment of psychological disorders in the last several decades. Although treatment can take literally hundreds of different approaches, ranging from one-meeting informal counseling sessions to long-term drug therapy, all the approaches have a common objective: the relief of psychological disorder, with the ultimate aim of enabling individuals to achieve richer, more meaningful, and more fulfilling lives.

Despite their diversity, approaches to treating psychological disorders fall into two main categories: psychologically based and biologically based therapies. Psychologically based

Looking Ahead

Psychotherapy: Treatment in which a trained professional—a therapist—uses psychological techniques to help a person overcome psychological difficulties and disorders, resolve problems in living, or bring about personal growth.

Biomedical therapy: Therapy that relies on drugs and other medical procedures to improve psychological functioning.

therapy, or **psychotherapy,** is treatment in which a trained professional—a therapist—uses psychological techniques to help someone overcome psychological difficulties and disorders, resolve problems in living, or bring about personal growth. In psychotherapy, the goal is to produce psychological change in a person (called a "client" or "patient") through discussions and interactions with the therapist. In contrast, **biomedical therapy** relies on drugs and other medical procedures to improve psychological functioning.

As we describe the various approaches to therapy, keep in mind that although the distinctions may seem clear-cut, the classifications and procedures overlap a good deal. In fact, many therapists today use a variety of methods with an individual patient, taking an *eclectic approach to therapy.* Assuming that both psychological and biological processes often produce psychological disorders, eclectic therapists may draw from several perspectives simultaneously to address both the psychological and the biological aspects of a person's problems (Nathan & Gorman, 1997; Wachtel & Messer, 1997).

Psychotherapy: Psychodynamic, Behavioral, and Cognitive Approaches to Treatment

Therapists use some 400 different varieties of psychotherapy, approaches to therapy that focus on psychological factors. Although diverse in many respects, all psychological approaches see treatment as a way of solving psychological problems by modifying people's behavior and helping them gain a better understanding of themselves and their past, present, and future.

In light of the variety of psychological approaches, it is not surprising that the people who provide therapy vary considerably in educational background and training (see Figure 1). Many have doctoral degrees in psychology (meaning that they have attended graduate school, learned clinical and research techniques, and held an internship). But therapy is also provided by people in fields allied with psychology, such as psychiatry and social work.

Regardless of their specific training, almost all psychotherapists employ one of four major approaches to therapy: psychodynamic, behavioral, cognitive, and humanistic treatments. These approaches are based on the models of personality and psychological disorders developed by psychologists. We'll consider each approach in turn.

▲▲▲

What are the goals of psychologically and biologically based treatment approaches?

What are the basic kinds of psychotherapies?

Psychodynamic Approaches to Therapy

Psychodynamic therapy is based on the premise, first suggested by Freud in his psychoanalytic approach to personality, that the primary sources of abnormal behavior are unresolved past conflicts and the possibility that unacceptable unconscious impulses will enter a person's consciousness. To guard against this anxiety-provoking possibility, individuals employ *defense mechanisms*, psychological strategies to protect themselves from those unconscious impulses.

The most common defense mechanism is repression, which pushes threatening conflicts and impulses back into the unconscious. However, since unacceptable conflicts and impulses can never be completely buried, some of the anxiety associated with them can produce abnormal behavior in the form of what Freud called *neurotic symptoms*.

How does one rid oneself of the anxiety produced by unconscious, unwanted impulses and drives? To Freud, the answer was to confront the conflicts and impulses by bringing them out of the unconscious part of the mind and into

Psychodynamic therapy: First suggested by Freud, therapy that is based on the premise that the primary sources of abnormal behavior are unresolved past conflicts and the possibility that unacceptable unconscious impulses will enter consciousness.

"Look, call it denial if you like, but I think what goes on in my personal life id none of my own domn business."

FIGURE 1 A variety of professionals provide therapy and counseling. Each could be expected to give helpful advice and direction. However, the nature of the problem a person is experiencing may make one or another therapy more appropriate. For example, a person who is suffering from a severe disturbance and who has lost touch with reality will typically require some sort of biologically based drug therapy. In that case, a psychiatrist—who is a physician—would be the professional of choice. In contrast, those suffering from milder disorders, such as difficulty adjusting to the death of a family member, have a broader choice that might include any of the professionals listed below. The decision can be made easier by initial consultations with professionals in mental health facilities in communities, colleges, and health organizations, who can provide guidance in selecting an appropriate therapist.

Getting Help from the Right Person

Clinical Psychologists

Psychologists with a Ph.D. or Psy.D. who have also completed a postgraduate internship. They specialize in assessment and treatment of psychological difficulties.

Counseling Psychologists

Psychologists with a Ph.D. or Ed.D. who typically treat day-to-day adjustment problems, often in a university mental health clinic

Psychiatrists

M.D.s with postgraduate training in abnormal behavior. Because they can prescribe medication, they often treat the most severe disorders

Psychoanalysts

Either M.D.s or psychologists who specialize in psychoanalysis, the treatment technique first developed by Freud

Licensed Professional Counselors or Clinical Mental Health Counselors

Professionals with a master's degree who provide therapy to individuals, couples, and families and who hold a national or state certification

Clinical or Psychiatric Social Workers

Professionals with a master's degree and specialized training who may provide therapy, usually regarding common family and personal problems

the conscious part. Freud assumed that this technique would reduce anxiety stemming from past conflicts and that the patient could then participate in his or her daily life more effectively.

A psychodynamic therapist, then, faces the challenge of finding a way to assist patients' attempts to explore and understand the unconscious. The technique that has evolved has a number of components, but basically it consists of guiding patients to consider and discuss their past experiences, in explicit detail, from the time of their first memories. This process assumes that patients will eventually stumble upon long-hidden crises, traumas, and conflicts that are producing anxiety in their adult lives. They will then be able to "work through"—understand and rectify—those difficulties.

PSYCHOANALYSIS: FREUD'S THERAPY

Psychoanalysis: Classic Freudian psychodynamic therapy that involves frequent sessions and often lasts for many years.

Classic Freudian psychodynamic therapy, called **psychoanalysis,** tends to be a lengthy and expensive affair. Patients typically meet with the therapist an hour a day, four to six days a week, for several years. In their sessions, they often use a technique developed by Freud called *free association.* Psychoanalysts tell patients to say aloud whatever comes to mind, regardless of its apparent irrelevance or senselessness, and the analysts attempt to recognize and label the connections between what a patient says and the patient's unconscious. Therapists also use *dream interpretation,* examining dreams to find clues to unconscious conflicts and problems. Moving beyond the surface description of a dream (called the *manifest content*), therapists seek its underlying meaning (the *latent content*), thereby revealing the true unconscious meaning of the dream (Galatzer-Levy & Cohler, 1997).

The processes of free association and dream interpretation do not always move forward easily. The same unconscious forces that initially produced repression may keep past difficulties out of the conscious mind, producing resistance. *Resistance* is an inability or unwillingness to discuss or reveal particular memories, thoughts, or motivations. Patients can express resistance in many ways. For instance, patients may be discussing a childhood memory and suddenly forget what they were saying, or they may change the subject completely. It is the therapist's job to pick up instances of resistance and interpret their meaning, as well as to ensure that patients return to the subject—which is likely to hold difficult or painful memories for the patients.

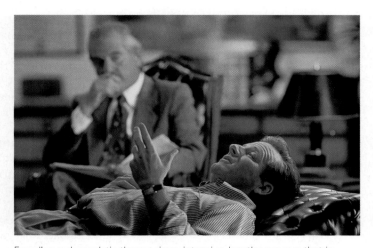

Freud's psychoanalytic therapy is an intensive, lengthy process that includes techniques such as free association and dream interpretation. What are some advantages and disadvantages of psychoanalysis compared with other approaches?

Because of the close, almost intimate interaction between patient and psychoanalyst, the relationship between the two often becomes emotionally charged and takes on a complexity unlike most other relationships. Patients may eventually think of the analyst as a symbol of a significant other in their past, perhaps a parent or a lover, and apply some of their feelings for that person to the analyst—a phenomenon known as *transference* (Mann, 1997; Gordon, 2000).

A therapist can use transference to help a patient re-create past relationships that were psychologically difficult. For instance, if a patient undergoing transference views her therapist as a symbol of her father—with whom she had a difficult relationship—the patient and therapist may "redo" an earlier interaction, this time including more positive aspects. Through this process, the patient may resolve conflicts regarding her real father—something that is beginning to happen in the following therapy session:

> Sandy: My father . . . never took any interest in any of us . . . It was my mother—rest her soul—who loved us, not our father. He worked her to death. Lord, I miss her . . . I must sound angry at my father. Don't you think I have a right to be angry?
>
> Therapist: Do you think you have a right to be angry?
>
> Sandy: Of course, I do! Why are you questioning me? You don't believe me, do you?
>
> Therapist: You want me to believe you.
>
> Sandy: I don't care whether you believe me or not . . . I know what you're thinking— you think I'm crazy—you must be laughing at me—I'll probably be a case in your next book! You're just sitting there—smirking—making me feel like a bad person— thinking I'm wrong for being mad, that I have no right to be mad.
>
> Therapist: Just like your father.
>
> Sandy: Yes, you're just like my father.—Oh my God! Just now—I—I—thought I was talking to him (Sue, Sue, & Sue, 1990, pp. 514–515).

CONTEMPORARY ALTERNATIVES TO PSYCHOANALYSIS

Few people have the time, money, or patience that participating in years of traditional psychoanalysis requires. Moreover, no conclusive evidence shows that psychoanalysis, as originally conceived by Freud in the nineteenth century, works better than other, more recent versions of psychodynamic therapy. Today, for instance, psychodynamic therapy tends to be shorter, usually lasting no longer than three months or twenty sessions. The therapist takes a more active role than Freud would have liked, controlling the course of therapy and prodding and advising the patient with considerable directness. Finally, the therapist puts less emphasis on a patient's past history and childhood, concentrating instead on an individual's current relationships and specific complaints (Bornstein, 2001; Goode, 2003b).

Even with its current modifications, psychodynamic therapy has its critics. In its longer versions, it can be time-consuming and expensive, especially in comparison with other forms of psychotherapy, such as behavioral and cognitive approaches. Furthermore, less articulate patients may not do as well as more verbal ones do.

Ultimately, the most important concern about psychodynamic treatment is whether it actually works, and here there is no simple answer. Psychodynamic treatment techniques have been controversial since Freud introduced them. Part of the problem is the difficulty in establishing whether patients have improved after psychodynamic therapy. Determining effectiveness depends on reports from the therapist or the patients themselves, reports that are obviously open to bias and subjective interpretation.

Critics have questioned the entire theoretical basis of psychodynamic theory, maintaining that constructs such as the unconscious have not been proved to exist. Despite the criticism, though, the psychodynamic treatment approach has remained viable. To proponents, it not only provides effective treatment in many cases of psychological disturbance but also permits the potential development of an unusual degree of insight into one's life (Barber & Lane, 1995; Clay, 2000).

Behavioral Approaches to Therapy

Behavioral treatment approaches:
Treatment approaches that build on the basic processes of learning, such as reinforcement and extinction.

Perhaps, when you were a child, your parents rewarded you with an ice cream cone when you were especially good . . . or sent you to your room if you misbehaved. Sound principles back up such a child-rearing strategy: Good behavior is maintained by reinforcement, and unwanted behavior can be eliminated by punishment.

These principles represent the basic underpinnings of **behavioral treatment approaches.** Building on the basic processes of learning, behavioral treatment approaches make this fundamental assumption: Both abnormal behavior and normal behavior are *learned*. People who act abnormally have either failed to learn the skills they need to cope with the problems of everyday living or have acquired faulty skills and patterns that are being maintained through some form of reinforcement. To modify abnormal behavior, then, behavioral approaches propose that people must learn new behavior to replace the faulty skills they have developed and unlearn their maladaptive behavior patterns (Bergin & Garfield, 1994; Agras & Berkowitz, 1996).

Behavioral psychologists do not need to delve into people's pasts or their psyches. Rather than viewing abnormal behavior as a symptom of an underlying problem, they consider the abnormal behavior as the problem in need of modification. Changing people's behavior to allow them to function more effectively solves the problem—with no need for concern about the underlying cause. In this view, then, if you can change abnormal behavior, you've cured the problem.

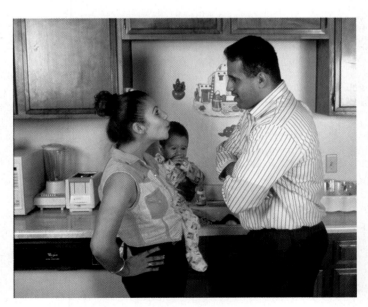

Behavioral approaches to treatment would seek to modify the behavior of this couple, rather than focusing on the underlying causes of the behavior.

AVERSIVE CONDITIONING

Suppose you bite into your favorite candy bar and find that it is not only infested with ants but that you've swallowed a bunch of them. You immediately become sick to your stomach and throw up. Your long-term reaction? You never eat that kind of candy bar again, and it may be months before you eat any type of candy.

This simple example demonstrates how therapists may employ classical conditioning to modify behavior. Using a procedure known as *aversive conditioning,* a person with a drinking problem may be given an alcoholic drink along with a drug that causes severe nausea and vomiting. After the two are paired a few times, the person associates the alcohol alone with the vomiting and finds alcohol less appealing.

Although aversion therapy works reasonably well in inhibiting substance-abuse problems such as alcoholism and certain kinds of sexual disorders, critics question its long-term effectiveness. Also, important ethical concerns surround aversion techniques that employ such potent stimuli as electric shock, which therapists use only in the most extreme cases, such as patient self-mutilation. Clearly, though, aversion therapy offers an important procedure for eliminating maladaptive responses for some period of time—a respite that provides, even if only temporarily, an opportunity to encourage more adaptive behavior patterns (Yuskauskas, 1992; Linscheid & Reichenbach, 2002).

SYSTEMATIC DESENSITIZATION

The most successful treatment based on classical conditioning is systematic desensitization. **Systematic desensitization** is a technique in which gradual exposure to an anxiety-producing stimulus is paired with relaxation to extinguish the response of anxiety (Wolpe, 1990; St. Onge, 1995b).

Suppose, for instance, you were extremely afraid of flying. The very thought of being in an airplane would make you begin to sweat and shake, and you'd never even be able to get yourself near enough to an airport to know how you'd react if you actually had to fly somewhere. Using systematic desensitization to treat your problem, you would first be trained in relaxation techniques by a behavior therapist (see Figure 2), learning to relax your body fully—a highly pleasant state, as you might imagine.

Systematic desensitization: A behavioral technique in which gradual exposure to an anxiety-producing stimulus is paired with relaxation to extinguish the response of anxiety.

Step 1. Pick a focus word or short phrase that's firmly rooted in your personal belief system. For example, a nonreligious individual might choose a neutral word like *one* or *peace* or *love.* A Christian person desiring to use a prayer could pick the opening words of Psalm 23. *The Lord is my shepherd;* a Jewish person could choose *Shalom.*

Step 2. Sit quietly in a comfortable position.

Step 3. Close your eyes.

Step 4. Relax your muscles.

Step 5. Breathe slowly and naturally, repeating your focus word or phrase silently as you exhale.

Step 6. Throughout, assume a passive attitude. Don't worry about how well you're doing. When other thoughts come to mind, simply say to yourself, "Oh, well," and gently return to the repetition.

Step 7. Continue for 10 to 20 minutes. You may open your eyes to check the time, but do not use an alarm. When you finish, sit quietly for a minute or so, at first with your eyes closed and later with your eyes open. Then do not stand for one or two minutes.

Step 8. Practice the technique once or twice a day.

FIGURE 2 Following these basic steps will help you achieve a sense of calmness by employing the relaxation response.

The next step would involve constructing a *hierarchy of fears*—a list, in order of increasing severity, of the things you associate with your fears. For instance, your hierarchy might resemble this one:

1. Watching a plane fly overhead.
2. Going to an airport.
3. Buying a ticket.
4. Stepping into the plane.
5. Seeing the plane door close.
6. Having the plane taxi down the runway.
7. Taking off.
8. Being in the air.

These participants in a systematic desensitization program have worked to overcome their fear of flying and are about to "graduate" by taking a brief flight. In what ways is this approach based on classical conditioning?

INTERACTIVITY 51–1

Systematic desensitization

Once you had developed this hierarchy and had learned relaxation techniques, you would learn to associate the two sets of responses. To do this, your therapist might ask you to put yourself into a relaxed state and then imagine yourself in the first situation identified in your hierarchy. After you were able to consider that first step while remaining relaxed, you would move on to the next situation, eventually moving up the hierarchy in gradual stages until you could imagine yourself being in the air without experiencing anxiety. Ultimately, you would be asked to make a visit to an airport and later to take a flight. (For more practice with systematic desensitization, complete **Interactivity 51–1.**)

Systematic desensitization has proved to be an effective treatment for a number of problems, including phobias, anxiety disorders, and even impotence and fear of sexual contact. In short, we *can* learn to enjoy the things we once feared (Kluger, 2001; Waldrep & Waits, 2002).

OPERANT CONDITIONING TECHNIQUES

Behavioral approaches that use operant conditioning techniques (which demonstrate the effects of rewards and punishments on future behavior) are based on the notion that we should reward people for carrying out desirable behavior and extinguish behavior that we wish to eliminate by either ignoring or punishing it (Kazdin, 1994).

One example of the systematic application of operant conditioning principles is the *token system,* which rewards a person for desired behavior with a token such as a poker chip or some kind of play money. Although it is most frequently employed in institutional settings for individuals with relatively serious problems, and sometimes with children as a classroom management technique, the system resembles what parents do when they give children money for being well behaved—money that the children can later exchange for something they want. The desired behavior may range from simple things such as keeping one's room neat to personal grooming and interacting with other people. In institutions, patients can exchange tokens for some object or activity, such as snacks, new clothes, or, in extreme cases, being able to sleep in one's own bed rather than on the floor.

Contingency contracting, a variant of the more extensive token system, has proved quite effective in producing behavior modification. In *contingency contracting,* the therapist and client (or teacher and student, or parent and child) draw up a written agreement. The contract states a series of behavioral goals the client hopes to achieve. It also specifies the positive consequences for the client if the client reaches goals—usually an explicit reward such as money or additional privileges. Contracts frequently state negative consequences if the client does not meet the goals. For example, clients who are trying to quit smoking might write out a check to a cause they have no interest in supporting (for instance, the National Rifle Association if they are strong supporters of gun control). If the client smokes on a given day, the therapist will mail the check.

Behavior therapists also use *observational learning,* the process in which the behavior of other people is modeled, to systematically teach people new skills and ways of handling their fears and anxieties. For example, modeling helps when therapists are teaching basic social skills such as maintaining eye contact during conversation and acting assertively. Similarly, children with dog phobias have been able to overcome their fears by watching another child— called the "Fearless Peer"—repeatedly walk up to a dog, touch it, pet it, and finally play with it. Modeling, then, can play an effective role in resolving some kinds of behavior difficulties, especially if the model receives a reward for his or her behavior (Bandura, Grusec, & Menlove, 1967; St. Onge, 1995a).

A "Fearless Peer" who models appropriate and effective behavior can help children overcome their fears.

HOW DOES BEHAVIOR THERAPY STACK UP?

Behavior therapy works particularly well for treating phobias and compulsions, establishing control over impulses, and learning complex social skills to replace maladaptive behavior. More than any of the other therapeutic techniques, it has produced methods that nonprofessionals can use to change their own behavior. Moreover, it is efficient, because it focuses on solving carefully defined problems (Wilson & Agras, 1992).

Behavior therapy has its disadvantages. For instance, it cannot treat deep depression or personality disorders successfully (Brody, 1990). In addition, because it emphasizes changing external behavior, people receiving behavior therapy do not necessarily gain insight into thoughts and expectations that may be fostering their maladaptive behavior. Because of such concerns, some psychologists have turned to cognitive approaches.

Cognitive Approaches to Therapy

If you assumed that illogical thoughts and beliefs lie at the heart of psychological disorders, wouldn't the most direct treatment route be to teach people new, more adaptive modes of thinking? The answer is yes, according to psychologists who take a cognitive approach to treatment.

Cognitive treatment approaches teach people to think in more adaptive ways by changing their dysfunctional cognitions about the world and themselves. Unlike behavior therapists, who focus on modifying external behavior, cognitive therapists attempt to change the way people think as well as their behavior. Because they often use basic principles of learning, the methods they employ are sometimes referred to as the **cognitive-behavioral approach** (Beck, 1991; McCullough, 1999; Frost & Steketee, 2002).

Although cognitive treatment approaches take many forms, they all share the assumption that anxiety, depression, and negative emotions develop from maladaptive thinking. Accordingly, cognitive treatments seek to change the thought patterns that lead to getting "stuck" in dysfunctional ways of thinking. Therapists systematically teach clients to challenge their assumptions and adopt new approaches to old problems.

Cognitive therapy is relatively short-term, usually lasting a maximum of twenty sessions. Therapy tends to be highly structured and focused on concrete problems.

Cognitive treatment approaches: Treatment approaches that teach people to think in more adaptive ways by changing their dysfunctional cognitions about the world and themselves.

Cognitive-behavioral approach: An approach used by cognitive therapists that attempts to change the way people think through the use of basic principles of learning.

FIGURE 3 In the A-B-C model of rational-emotive behavior therapy, negative activating conditions (A) lead to the activation of an irrational belief system (B), which leads to emotional consequences (C). Those emotional consequences then feed back and support the belief system. At what steps in the model could change occur as a result of rational-emotive behavior therapy?

Rational-emotive behavior therapy: A form of therapy that attempts to restructure a person's belief system into a more realistic, rational, and logical set of views.

Therapists often begin by teaching the theory behind the approach and then continue to take an active role throughout the course of therapy, acting as a combination of teacher, coach, and partner.

One good example of cognitive treatment, **rational-emotive behavior therapy,** attempts to restructure a person's belief system into a more realistic, rational, and logical set of views. According to psychologist Albert Ellis (2002), many people lead unhappy lives and suffer from psychological disorders because they harbor irrational, unrealistic ideas such as these:

- ⊙ We need the love or approval of virtually every significant other person for everything we do.
- ⊙ We should be thoroughly competent, adequate, and successful in all possible respects in order to consider ourselves worthwhile.
- ⊙ It is horrible when things don't turn out the way we want them to.

Such irrational beliefs trigger negative emotions, which in turn support the irrational beliefs, leading to a self-defeating cycle. Ellis calls it the A-B-C model, in which negative activating conditions (A) lead to the activation of an irrational belief system (B), which in turn leads to emotional consequences (C). For example, if a person experiences the breakup of a close relationship (A) and holds the irrational belief (B) that "I'll never be loved again," this triggers negative emotions (C) that in turn feed back into support of the irrational belief (see Figure 3).

Rational-emotive behavior therapy aims to help clients eliminate maladaptive thoughts and beliefs and adopt more effective thinking. To accomplish this goal, therapists take an active, directive role during therapy, openly challenging patterns of thought that appear to be dysfunctional. Consider this example:

Martha: The basic problem is that I'm worried about my family. I'm worried about money. And I never seem to be able to relax.

Therapist: Why are you worried about your family? . . . What's to be concerned about? They have certain demands which you don't want to adhere to.

Martha: I was brought up to think that I mustn't be selfish.

Therapist: Oh, we'll have to knock that out of your head!

Martha: My mother feels that I shouldn't have left home—that my place is with them. There are nagging doubts about what I should—

Therapist: Why are there doubts? Why *should* you?

Martha: I think it's a feeling I was brought up with that you always have to give of yourself. If you think of yourself, you're wrong.

PowerWeb: Cognitive Therapy and the Emotional Disorders

www.mhhe.com/feldmanup7

Therapist: That's a *belief*. Why do you have to keep believing that—at *your* age? You believed a lot of superstitions when you were younger. Why do you have to retain them? Your parents indoctrinated you with this nonsense, because that's *their* belief . . . Who needs that philosophy? All it's gotten you, so far, is guilt (Ellis, 1974, pp. 223–286).

By poking holes in Martha's reasoning, the therapist is attempting to help her adopt a more realistic view of herself and her circumstances (Dryden, 1999; Ellis, 2002).

Another form of therapy that builds on a cognitive perspective is that of Aaron Beck (Beck, 1991, 1995). Like rational-emotive behavior therapy, Beck's *cognitive therapy* aims to change people's illogical thoughts about themselves and the world. However, cognitive therapy is considerably less confrontational and challenging than rational-emotive behavior therapy. Instead of the therapist actively arguing with clients about their dysfunctional cognitions, cognitive therapists more often play the role of teacher. Therapists urge clients to obtain information on their own that will lead them to discard their inaccurate thinking. During the course of treatment, therapists help clients discover ways of thinking more appropriately about themselves and others (Alford & Beck, 1997; Greenberg, 2000; Rosen, 2000).

Cognitive approaches to therapy have proved successful in dealing with a broad range of disorders. The ability of cognitive therapy to incorporate additional treatment approaches (e.g., combining cognitive and behavioral techniques in cognitive behavioral therapy) has made it a particularly effective form of treatment (McMullin, 2000).

Check your understanding of the cognitive and other therapeutic approaches in **Interactivity 51–2.**

"*To this day, I can hear my mother's voice—harsh, accusing. 'Lost your mittens? You naughty kittens! Then you shall have no pie!'*"

INTERACTIVITY 51–2

Compare and contrast approaches to therapy

RECAP/EVALUATE/RETHINK

RECAP

What are the goals of psychologically and biologically based treatment approaches?

▶ Psychotherapy (psychologically based therapy) and biomedical therapy (biologically based therapy) share the goal of resolving psychological problems by modifying people's thoughts, feelings, expectations, evaluations, and ultimately behavior. (p. 570)

What are the basic kinds of psychotherapies?

▶ Psychoanalytic treatment seeks to bring unresolved past conflicts and unacceptable impulses from the unconscious into the conscious, where patients may deal with the problems more effectively. To do this, therapists use techniques such as free association and dream interpretation. (p. 571)

▶ Behavioral approaches to treatment view abnormal behavior as the problem, rather than viewing that behavior as a symptom of some underlying cause. To bring about a "cure," this view suggests that the outward behavior must be changed by using methods such as aversive conditioning, systematic desensitization, observational learning, token systems, and contingency contracting. (p. 574)

▶ Cognitive approaches to treatment suggest that the goal of therapy should be to help a person restructure his or her belief system into a more realistic, rational, and logical view of the world. Two examples of cognitive treatments are the rational-emotive behavior therapy and cognitive therapy. (p. 577)

EVALUATE

1. Match the following mental health practitioners with the appropriate description.
   1. Psychiatrist
   2. Clinical psychologist

3. Counseling psychologist
4. Psychoanalyst
a. Ph.D. specializing in the treatment of psychological disorders
b. Professional specializing in Freudian therapy techniques
c. M.D. trained in abnormal behavior
d. Ph.D. specializing in the adjustment of day-to-day problems

2. According to Freud, people use _____ _____ as a means to ensure that unwanted impulses will not intrude on conscious thought.

3. In dream interpretation, a psychoanalyst must learn to distinguish between the _____ content of a dream, which is what appears on the surface, and the _____ content, its underlying meaning.

4. Which of the following treatments deals with phobias by gradual exposure to the item producing the fear?
a. Systematic desensitization
b. Partial reinforcement
c. Behavioral self-management
d. Aversion therapy

RETHINK

1. In what ways are psychoanalysis and cognitive therapy similar, and how do they differ?
2. How might you examine the reliability of dream interpretation?

Answers to Evaluate Questions

1. 1-c, 2-a, 3-d, 4-b; 2. defense mechanisms; 3. manifest, latent; 4. a

KEY TERMS

psychotherapy p. 570
biomedical therapy p. 570
psychodynamic therapy p. 571
psychoanalysis p. 572

behavioral treatment approaches p. 574
systematic desensitization p. 575

cognitive treatment approaches p. 577
cognitive-behavioral approach p. 577

rational-emotive behavior therapy p. 578

Psychotherapy: Humanistic, Interpersonal, and Group Approaches to Treatment

Humanistic Therapy

What are the humanistic approaches to treatment?

What is interpersonal therapy?

How does group therapy differ from individual types of therapy?

How effective is therapy, and which kind of therapy works best in a given situation?

As you know from your own experience, a student cannot master the material covered in a course without some hard work, no matter how good the teacher and the textbook are. *You* must take the time to study, memorize the vocabulary, and learn the concepts. Nobody else can do it for you. If you choose to put in the effort, you'll succeed; if you don't, you'll fail. The responsibility is primarily yours.

Humanistic therapy draws on this philosophical perspective of self-responsibility in developing treatment techniques. The many different types of therapy that fit into this category have a similar rationale: We have control of our own behavior, we can make choices about the kinds of lives we want to live, and it is up to us to solve the difficulties we encounter in our daily lives.

Instead of being the directive figures seen in some psychodynamic and behavioral approaches, humanistic therapists view themselves as guides or facilitators. Therapists using humanistic techniques seek to help people understand themselves and find ways to come closer to the ideal they hold for themselves. In this view, psychological disorders are the result of people's inability to find meaning in life and of their feeling lonely and unconnected to others (Cain, 2002).

Humanistic approaches have produced many therapeutic techniques. Among the most important is person-centered therapy.

Humanistic therapy: Therapy in which the underlying rationale is that people have control of their behavior, can make choices about their lives, and are essentially responsible for solving their own problems.

PERSON-CENTERED THERAPY

Consider the following therapy session excerpt:

> Alice: I was thinking about this business of standards. I somehow developed a sort of a knack, I guess, of—well—habit—of trying to make people feel at ease around me, or to make things go along smoothly . . .
>
> Therapist: In other words, what you did was always in the direction of trying to keep things smooth and to make other people feel better and to smooth the situation.
>
> Alice: Yes. I think that's what it was. Now the reason why I did it probably was—I mean, not that I was a good little Samaritan going around making other people happy, but that was probably the role that felt easiest for me to play . . .
>
> Therapist: You feel that for a long time you've been playing the role of kind of smoothing out the frictions or differences or what not . . .
>
> Alice: M-hm.
>
> Therapist: Rather than having any opinion or reaction of your own in the situation. Is that it? (Rogers, 1951, pp. 152–153).

PowerWeb: On Becoming a Person: A Therapist's View of Psychotherapy

www.mhhe.com/feldmanup7

The therapist does not interpret or answer the questions the client has raised. Instead, the therapist clarifies or reflects back what the client has said (e.g., "In other words, what you did . . ."; "You feel that . . ."; "Is that it?"). This therapeutic technique, known as *nondirective counseling,* is at the heart of person-centered therapy, which was first practiced by Carl Rogers (Rogers, 1951, 1980; Raskin & Rogers, 1989).

Person-centered therapy (also called *client-centered therapy*) aims to enable people to reach their potential for self-actualization. By providing a warm and accepting environment, therapists hope to motivate clients to air their problems and feelings. In turn, this enables clients to make realistic and constructive choices and decisions about the things that bother them in their current lives (Bozarth, Zimring, & Tausch, 2002).

Person-centered therapy: Therapy in which the goal is to reach one's potential for self-actualization.

Instead of directing the choices clients make, therapists provide what Rogers calls *unconditional positive regard*—expressing acceptance and understanding, regardless of the feelings and attitudes the client expresses. By doing this, therapists hope to create an atmosphere that enables clients to come to decisions that can improve their lives (Farber, Brink, & Raskin, 1996).

Furnishing unconditional positive regard does not mean that therapists must approve of everything their clients say or do. Rather, therapists need to communicate that they are caring, nonjudgmental, and *empathetic*—understanding of a client's emotional experiences (Fearing & Clark, 2000).

Person-centered therapy is rarely used today in its purest form. Contemporary approaches tend to be somewhat more directive, with therapists nudging clients toward insights rather than merely reflecting back their statements. However, therapists still view clients' insights as central to the therapeutic process.

HUMANISTIC APPROACHES IN PERSPECTIVE

The notion that psychological disorders result from restricted growth potential appeals philosophically to many people. Furthermore, when humanistic therapists acknowledge that the freedom we possess can lead to psychological difficulties, clients find an unusually supportive environment for therapy. In turn, this atmosphere can help clients discover solutions to difficult psychological problems.

However, humanistic treatments lack specificity, a problem that has troubled their critics. Humanistic approaches are not very precise and are probably the least scientifically and theoretically developed type of treatment. Moreover, this form of treatment works best for the same type of highly verbal client who profits most from psychoanalytic treatment.

Interpersonal Therapy

Interpersonal therapy (IPT): Short-term therapy that focuses on the context of social relationships, focusing on the here and now.

Interpersonal therapy (IPT) considers therapy in the context of social relationships. Growing out of contemporary psychodynamic approaches, interpersonal therapy focuses more on the here and now, considering how to improve a client's current relationships.

Interpersonal therapy is more directive than traditional psychodynamic approaches. It also tends to be shorter, typically lasting a dozen weeks. Therapists make concrete suggestions on improving relations with others, and the process tends to be short-term. Research has shown that interpersonal therapy is particularly effective in dealing with depression, anxiety, and addictions (MacKenzie & Grabovac, 2001; Ablon & Jones, 2002; Markowitz, 2003).

Group Therapy

Group therapy: Therapy in which people meet with a therapist to discuss problems with a group.

Although most treatment takes place between a single individual and a therapist, some forms of therapy involve groups of people seeking treatment. In **group therapy,** several unrelated people meet with a therapist to discuss some aspect of their psychological functioning.

People typically discuss their problems with the group, which is often centered on a common difficulty, such as alcoholism or a lack of social skills. The other members of the group provide emotional support and dispense advice on ways in which they have coped effectively with similar problems (Yalom, 1997; Free, 2000; Alonso, Alonso, & Piper, 2003).

Groups vary greatly in terms of the particular model they employ; one finds psychoanalytic groups, humanistic groups, and groups corresponding to the other therapeutic approaches. Furthermore, groups also differ in regard to the degree of guidance the therapist provides. In some, the therapist is quite directive, while in others, the members of the group set their own agenda and determine how the group will proceed (Spira, 1997; Earley, 1999; Beck & Lewis, 2000).

Because in group therapy several people are treated simultaneously, it is a much more economical means of treatment than individual psychotherapy. On the other hand, critics argue that group settings lack the individual attention inherent in one-to-one therapy, and that especially shy and withdrawn individuals may not receive the attention they need in a group setting.

In group therapy, people with psychological difficulties meet with a therapist to discuss their problems.

FAMILY THERAPY

One specialized form of group therapy is family therapy. As the name implies, **family therapy** involves two or more family members, one (or more) of whose problems led to treatment. But rather than focusing simply on the members of the family who present the initial problem, family therapists consider the family as a unit, to which each member contributes. By meeting with the entire family simultaneously, family therapists try to understand how the family members interact with one another (Rolland & Walsh, 1996; Cooklin, 2000).

Family therapy: An approach that focuses on the family and its dynamics.

Family therapists view the family as a "system," and assume that individuals in the family cannot improve without understanding the conflicts found in interactions among family members. Thus, the therapist expects each member to contribute to the resolution of the problem being addressed.

Many family therapists believe that family members fall into rigid roles or set patterns of behavior, with one person acting as the scapegoat, another as a bully, and so forth. In their view, that system of roles perpetuates family disturbances. One goal of this type of therapy, then, is to get the family members to adopt new, more constructive roles and patterns of behavior (Minuchin & Nichols, 1992; Sprenkle & Moon, 1996).

In family therapy, the family system as a whole—not just one family member identified as the "problem"—is treated. Why is this advantageous?

Evaluating Psychotherapy: Does Therapy Work?

Your best friend, Ben, comes to you because he just hasn't been feeling right about things lately. He's upset because he and his girlfriend aren't getting along, but his difficulties go beyond that. He can't concentrate on his studies, has a lot of trouble getting to sleep, and—this is what really bothers him—has begun to think that people are ganging up on him, talking about him behind his back. It seems that no one really cares about or understands him or makes any effort to see why he's become so miserable.

Ben knows that he ought to get *some* kind of help, but he is not sure where to turn. He is fairly skeptical of psychologists, thinking that a lot of what they say is just mumbo jumbo, but he's willing to put his doubts aside and try anything to feel better. He also knows there are many different types of therapy, and he doesn't have a clue about which would be best for him. He turns to you for advice, because he knows you are taking a psychology course. He asks, "Which kind of therapy works best?"

IS THERAPY EFFECTIVE?

This question requires a complex response. In fact, identifying the single most appropriate form of treatment is a controversial, and still unresolved, task for psychologists specializing in psychological disorders. In fact, even before considering whether one form of therapy works better than another, we need to determine whether therapy in *any* form effectively alleviates psychological disturbances.

Until the 1950s, most people simply assumed that therapy was effective. But in 1952 psychologist Hans Eysenck published what has become a classic article that challenged that assumption. He claimed that people who received psychodynamic treatment and related therapies were no better off at the end of treatment than were people who were placed on a waiting list for treatment but never received it. According to his analysis, about two-thirds of the people who reported suffering from "neurotic" symptoms believed that those symptoms had disappeared after two years, regardless of whether they had been in therapy. Eysenck concluded that people would go into **spontaneous remission,** recovery without treatment, if they were simply left alone—certainly a cheaper and simpler process.

Although others quickly challenged Eysenck's conclusions, his review stimulated a continuing stream of better controlled, more carefully crafted studies on the effectiveness of psychotherapy, and today most psychologists agree: Therapy does work. Several comprehensive reviews indicate that therapy brings about greater improvement than does no treatment at all, with the rate of spontaneous remission being fairly low. In most cases, then, the symptoms of abnormal behavior do not go away by themselves if left untreated—although the issue continues to be hotly debated (Bergin & Garfield, 1994; Seligman, 1996; Sohn, 1996). (You can explore the question of the effectiveness of therapy further in **Interactivity 52–1.**)

WHICH KIND OF THERAPY WORKS BEST?

Although most psychologists feel confident that psychotherapeutic treatment *in general* is more effective than no treatment at all, the question of whether any specific form of treatment is superior to any other has not been answered definitively (Barber & Lane, 1995; Pratt & Moreland, 1996; Nathan, Stuart, & Dolan, 2000).

For instance, one classic study comparing the effectiveness of various approaches found that although success rates vary somewhat by treatment form, most treatments show fairly equal success rates. As Figure 1 indicates, the rates ranged from about 70 to 85 percent greater success for treated compared with untreated individuals. Behavioral and cognitive approaches tended to be slightly more successful, but that result may have been due to differences in the severity of the cases treated (Smith, Glass, & Miller, 1980; Orwin & Condray, 1984).

Other research, relying on *meta-analysis,* in which data from a large number of studies are statistically combined, yields similar general conclusions. Furthermore, a large-scale survey of 186,000 individuals found that although survey respondents felt they had benefited substantially from psychotherapy (see Figure 2), there was little difference in "consumer satisfaction" on the basis of the specific type of treatment they had received (CR, 1995; Seligman, 1995; Strupp, 1996).

PowerWeb: The Effectiveness of Psychotherapy: The *Consumer Reports* Study

www.mhhe.com/feldmanup7

Spontaneous remission: Recovery without treatment.

INTERACTIVITY 52–1

Effectiveness of therapy

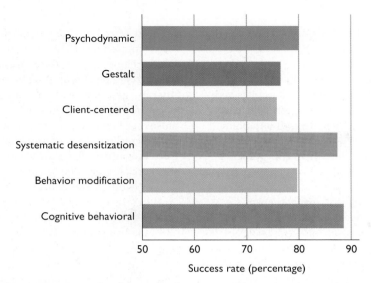

FIGURE 1 Estimates of the effectiveness of different types of treatment, in comparison to control groups of untreated people (Smith, Glass, & Miller, 1980). The percentile score shows how much more effective a particular type of treatment is for the average patient than is no treatment. For example, people given psychodynamic treatment score, on average, more positively on outcome measures than about three-quarters of untreated people.

FIGURE 2 A large survey of 186,000 individuals found that while the respondents had benefited substantially from psychotherapy, there was little difference in "consumer satisfaction" based on the specific type of treatment they had received. (Source: "Mental Health: Does Therapy Help?" *Consumer Reports*, 1995.)

In short, converging evidence allows us to draw several conclusions about the effectiveness of psychotherapy (Strupp & Binder, 1992; Seligman, 1996):

- ▶ *For most people, psychotherapy is effective.* This conclusion holds over different lengths of treatment, specific kinds of psychological disorders, and various types of treatment. Thus, the question "Does psychotherapy work?" appears to have been answered convincingly: It does (Lipsey & Wilson, 1993; Seligman, 1996; Spiegel, 1999).

- ▶ *On the other hand, psychotherapy doesn't work for everyone.* As many as 10 percent of people treated show no improvement or actually deteriorate (Lambert, Shapiro, & Bergin, 1986; Luborsky, 1988).

- ▶ *Certain specific types of treatments are somewhat, although not invariably, better for specific types of problems.* For example, cognitive therapy works particularly well for panic disorders, and systematic desensitization relieves specific phobias effectively. However, there are many exceptions, and often the differences in success rates for different types of treatment are not substantial (Hubble, Duncan, & Miller, 1999; Miller & Magruder, 1999).

- ▶ *No single form of therapy works best for every problem.* Consequently, we can give no definitive answer to the question "Which therapy works best?"—nor may we find one soon—because of the difficulties in sorting out the various factors that enter into the success of therapy. Furthermore, new types of therapy continue to emerge (see, for example, the *Applying Psychology in the 21st Century* box for a discussion of online therapy), making it difficult to draw sweeping conclusions about treatment effectiveness.

Because no single type of psychotherapy is invariably effective, eclectic approaches to therapy have become increasingly popular. In an **eclectic approach to therapy,** a therapist uses a variety of techniques, integrating several perspectives, to treat a person's problems. By using eclectic procedures, a therapist can choose the appropriate mix of treatments to match the specific needs of the individual. Furthermore, therapists with certain personal characteristics may work better with particular individuals and types of treatments, and even racial and

Eclectic approach to therapy: An approach to therapy that uses techniques taken from a variety of treatment methods, rather than just one.

Therapy Online: Is the Internet a Good Place to Get Treatment?

Amy, a first-year student at the University of Wisconsin at Eau Claire, was having some real personal difficulties. She told a friend about her problems, and her friend told Amy about a website that had been discussed during a campus orientation. The website was the university counseling center's homepage, where Amy located the email address of one the counselors. She immediately composed and sent the following message: "I feel somewhat stupid even writing this but I need some help . . . Recently I made a very big mistake and I think I need someone to talk to" (Carlson, 2002, p. A35).

Amy claims she never knew the university's counseling center existed until she saw the website. And even if she had known about the center, she suspects that she wouldn't have gone there in person. It was only because of the offer of online help that she sought treatment for her psychological difficulties.

As people of all ages have grown increasingly comfortable turning to the Internet to find everything from mp3's and DVDs to new friends, why not online therapy too?

Although few people receive online therapy today, this form of treatment has become a growing trend. As various technologies become more advanced and affordable—including the development of inexpensive, high-quality two-way video links over the Web—experts predict that the popularity of online therapy will grow (Jerome et al., 2000).

Today, most online therapy occurs primarily through e-mail. Therapists and clients exchange messages, which are sometimes supplemented with phone calls or face-to-face visits. For people like Amy, online therapy may provide the treatment they need while safeguarding their privacy.

Proponents of virtual therapy say it will open new avenues of treatment for people with psychological disorders. For example, those who live in remote areas can receive online treatment, as can those who are disabled, concerned with privacy, or too embarrassed to seek out local therapists (Advances in Telepsychology/ Telehealth, 2000; Jerome et al., 2000; Taylor et al., 2002).

Despite these advantages, Internet therapy has many critics. Because current technology limits online therapists' ability to see and hear their clients clearly, those therapists have no access to the valuable information provided by clients' nonverbal behavior. Moreover, virtual clients can misrepresent themselves more easily than can patients in face-to-face therapy sessions. Although the advent of more effective video links will reduce these limitations, they will remain problems as long as clients are physically distant from their therapists. Finally, online therapy guarantees privacy no more than face-to-face therapy does; we cannot ensure that highly personal information shared online will be completely protected from accidental disclosure or from hackers (Almer, 2000).

An even greater concern for people seeking virtual therapy is that no procedure exists for licensing individuals who provide treatment online. *Anyone* can call himself or herself a therapist and start providing therapy for—and collecting money from—clients. In addition, although a few studies suggest that Internet-based therapy is effective, psychologists need more research before they can be certain that online therapy is as effective as its face-to-face counterpart (Rabasca, 2000; Grohol & Zuckerman, 2002; Taylor & Luce, 2003).

Despite these drawbacks, online therapy in one form or another is likely to become an option for people seeking treatment for psychological disorders. Whether it will become routine—and be as effective as traditional face-to-face therapy—remains to be seen.

RETHINK

Do you think people are likely to be more honest when discussing their problems with an online therapist or with a face-to-face therapist? What kinds of clients do you think are more likely to find online therapy appealing? What kinds of clients might do better with traditional face-to-face therapy?

---

ethnic factors may be related to the success of treatment (Roth & Fonagy, 1996; Cheston, 2000).

Exploring DIVERSITY

Racial and Ethnic Factors in Treatment: Should Therapists Be Color-Blind?

Consider the following case report, written by a school counselor about Jimmy Jones, a 12-year-old student who was referred to a counselor because of his lack of interest in schoolwork:

Jimmy does not pay attention, daydreams often, and frequently falls asleep during class. There is a strong possibility that Jimmy is harboring repressed rage that needs to be ventilated and

Treatment for psychological disorders must take into account the individual's environmental, cultural, and socioeconomic background. What are the potential dangers in not considering these factors when providing treatment?

dealt with. His inability to directly express his anger had led him to adopt passive aggressive means of expressing hostility, i.e., inattentiveness, daydreaming, falling asleep. It is recommended that Jimmy be seen for intensive counseling to discover the basis of the anger (Sue & Sue, 1990, p. 44).

The counselor was wrong, however. Rather than suffering from "repressed rage," Jimmy lived in a poverty-stricken and disorganized home. Because of overcrowding at his house, he did not get enough sleep and consequently was tired the next day. Frequently, he was also hungry. In short, the stresses arising from his environment caused his problems, not any deep-seated psychological disturbances.

This incident underscores the importance of taking people's environmental and cultural backgrounds into account during treatment for psychological disorders. In particular, members of racial and ethnic minority groups, especially those who are also poor, may behave in ways that help them deal with a society that discriminates against them. As a consequence, behavior that may signal psychological disorder in middle- and upper-class whites may simply be adaptive in people from other racial and socioeconomic groups. For instance, characteristically suspicious and distrustful people may be displaying a survival strategy to protect themselves from psychological and physical injury, rather than suffering from a psychological disturbance (Sue & Sue, 1999; Aponte & Wohl, 2000; Paniagua, 2000).

In fact, therapists must question some basic assumptions of psychotherapy when dealing with racial, ethnic, and cultural minority-group members. For example, compared with the dominant culture, Asian and Latino cultures typically place much greater emphasis on the group, family, and society. When an Asian or Latino faces a critical decision, the family helps make it—suggesting that family members should also play a role in psychological treatment. Similarly, the traditional Chinese recommendation for dealing with depression or anxiety is to urge people who experience such problems to avoid thinking about whatever is upsetting them. Consider how this advice contrasts with treatment approaches that emphasize the value of insight (Okun, 1996; Kleinman & Cohen, 1997; Ponterotto et al., 2001).

Consequently, therapists *cannot* be "color-blind." Instead, they must take into account the racial, ethnic, cultural, and social class backgrounds of their clients in determining the nature of a psychological disorder and the course of treatment (Sue & Sue, 1999; Aponte & Wohl, 2000; Pedersen et al., 2002).

RECAP/EVALUATE/RETHINK

RECAP

What are humanistic approaches to treatment?

▶ Humanistic therapy is based on the premise that people have control of their behavior, that they can make choices about their lives, and that it is up to them to solve their own problems. Humanistic therapies, which take a nondirective approach, include person-centered therapy. (p. 581)

What is interpersonal therapy?

▶ Interpersonal therapy focuses on interpersonal relationships and strives for immediate improvement during short-term therapy. (p. 582)

How does group therapy differ from individual types of therapy?

▶ In group therapy, several unrelated people meet with a therapist to discuss some aspect of their psychological functioning, often centering on a common problem. (p. 582)

How effective is therapy, and which kind of therapy works best in a given situation?

▶ Most research suggests that, in general, therapy is more effective than no therapy, although how much more effective is not known. (p. 583)

▶ The answer to the more difficult question of which therapy works best is even less clear, in part because therapies are so qualitatively different and in part because the definition of *cure* is so vague. Clearly, particular kinds of therapy are more appropriate for some problems than for others. (p. 584)

EVALUATE

1. Match each of the following treatment strategies with the statement you might expect to hear from a therapist using that strategy.
   1. Group therapy
   2. Unconditional positive regard
   3. Behavioral therapy
   4. Nondirective counseling

a. "In other words, you don't get along with your mother because she hates your girlfriend, is that right?"
b. "I want you all to take turns talking about why you decided to come and what you hope to gain from therapy."
c. "I can understand why you wanted to wreck your friend's car after she hurt your feelings. Now tell me more about the accident."
d. "That's not appropriate behavior. Let's work on replacing it with something else."

2. _____ therapies assume that people should take responsibility for their lives and the decisions they make.

3. One of the major criticisms of humanistic therapies is that
   a. They are too imprecise and unstructured.
   b. They treat only the symptom of the problem.
   c. The therapist dominates the patient-therapist interaction.
   d. They work well only on clients of lower socioeconomic status.

4. In a controversial study, Eysenck found that some people go into _____ _____, or recovery without treatment, if they are simply left alone instead of treated.

5. Treatments that combine techniques from all the theoretical approaches are called _____ procedures.

RETHINK

1. How can people be successfully treated in group therapy when individuals with the "same" problem are so different? What advantages might group therapy offer over individual therapy?

2. List some examples of behavior that might be considered abnormal by members of one cultural or economic group and normal by members of a different cultural or economic group. Suppose most therapies had been developed by psychologists from minority culture groups and with lower socioeconomic status; how might they differ from current therapies?

Answers to Evaluate Questions

1. 1-b, 2-c, 3-d, 4-a; 2. humanistic; 3. a; 4. spontaneous remission; 5. eclectic

KEY TERMS

Biomedical Therapy: Biological Approaches to Treatment

How are drug, electroconvulsive, and psychosurgical techniques used today in the treatment of psychological disorders?

If you get a kidney infection, your doctor gives you an antibiotic, and with luck, about a week later your kidney is as good as new. If your appendix becomes inflamed, a surgeon removes it and your body functions normally once more. Could a comparable approach, focusing on the body's physiology, be taken with psychological disturbances?

According to biological approaches to treatment, the answer is yes. Therapists routinely use biomedical therapies. This approach suggests that rather than focusing on a patient's psychological conflicts or past traumas, or on environmental factors that may produce abnormal behavior, focusing treatment directly on brain chemistry and other neurological factors may be more appropriate. To do this, therapists can use drugs, electric shock, or surgery to provide treatment.

▲ ▲ ▲

Drug Therapy

Drug therapy, the control of psychological disorders through drugs, works by altering the operation of neurotransmitters and neurons in the brain. Some drugs operate by inhibiting neurotransmitters or receptor neurons, reducing activity at particular synapses, the sites where nerve impulses travel from one neuron to another. Other drugs do just the opposite: They increase the activity of certain neurotransmitters or neurons, allowing particular neurons to fire more frequently (see Figure 1 and try **Interactivity 53–1.**)

ANTIPSYCHOTIC DRUGS

Probably no greater change has occurred in mental hospitals than the successful introduction in the mid-1950s of **antipsychotic drugs**—drugs used to reduce severe symptoms of disturbance, such as loss of touch with reality and agitation. Previously, the typical mental hospital fulfilled all the stereotypes of the nineteenth-century insane asylum, giving mainly custodial care to screaming, moaning, clawing patients who displayed the most bizarre behaviors. Suddenly, in just a matter of days after hospital staff members administered antipsychotic drugs, the wards became considerably calmer environments in which professionals could do more than just try to get patients through the day without causing serious harm to themselves or others.

This dramatic change came about through the introduction of a drug called *chlorpromazine.* That drug, along with others of a similar nature, rapidly became the most popular and successful treatment for schizophrenia. Today drug therapy is the preferred treatment for most cases of severely abnormal behavior and, as such, is used for most patients hospitalized with psychological disorders. The drugs *clozapine* and *Zyprexa* represent the current generation of antipsychotics (Anand & Burton, 2003).

How do antipsychotic drugs work? Most operate by blocking dopamine receptors at the brain's synapses. Some newer drugs, such as clozapine, increase dopamine

Drug therapy: Control of psychological disorders through the use of drugs.

INTERACTIVITY 53–1

Drug therapy

Antipsychotic drugs: Drugs that temporarily reduce psychotic symptoms such as agitation, hallucinations, and delusions.

FIGURE I The major classes of drugs used to treat psychological disorders have different effects that are produced by several biological processes.

Drug Treatments			
Class of Drug	**Effects of Drug**	**Primary Action of Drug**	**Examples**
Antipsychotic Drugs	Reduction in loss of touch with reality, agitation	Block dopamine receptors	Chlorpromazine (Thorazine) Clozapine (Clozaril) Haloperidol (Haldol)
Antidepressant Drugs			
Tricyclic antidepressants	Reduction in depression	Permit rise in neurotransmitters such as norepinepherine	Trazodone (Desyrel), Amitriptyline (Elavil), Desipramine (Norpamin)
MAO inhibitors	Reduction in depression	Prevent MAO from breaking down neurotransmitters	Phenelzine (Nardil), Tranylcypromine (Parnate)
Selective serotonin reuptake inhibitiors	Reduction in depression	Inhibit reuptake of serotonin	Fluoxetine (Prozac), Luvox, Paxil, Celexa, Zoloft, Nefazodone (Serzone)
Mood Stabilizers			
Lithium	Mood stabilization	Can alter transmission of impulses within neurons	Lithium (Lithonate), Depakote, Tegretol
Antianxiety Drugs	Reduction in anxiety	Increase activity of neurotrasmitter GABA	Benzodiazepines (Valium, Xanax)

PowerWeb: Are Medications for Treating Depression Harmful?

www.mhhe.com/feldmanup7

levels in certain parts of the brain, such as those related to planning and goal-directed activity (Moghaddam & Adams, 1998; Sawa & Snyder, 2002).

Despite the effectiveness of antipsychotic drugs, they do not produce a "cure" in the same way that, say, penicillin cures an infection. Most of the time, when the drug is withdrawn, the original symptoms reappear. Furthermore, such drugs can have long-term side effects, such as dryness of the mouth and throat, dizziness, and sometimes tremors and loss of muscle control, that may continue after drug treatments are stopped (Shriqui & Annable, 1995).

ANTIDEPRESSANT DRUGS

Antidepressant drugs: Medications that improve a severely depressed patient's mood and feeling of well-being.

As you might guess from the name, **antidepressant drugs** are a class of medications used in cases of severe depression to improve the moods of patients. They were discovered by accident: Medical doctors found that patients with tuberculosis who received the drug iproniazid suddenly became happier and more optimistic. When researchers tested that drug on people with depression, a similar result occurred, and these drugs became an accepted form of treatment for depression (Shuchter, Downs, & Zisook, 1996).

Most antidepressant drugs work by changing the concentration of particular neurotransmitters. For example, *tricyclic drugs* increase the availability of norepinepherine at the synapses of neurons, whereas *MAO inhibitors* prevent the enzyme monoamine oxidase (MAO) from breaking down neurotransmitters. Newer antidepressants— such as Lexapro—are *selective serotonin reuptake inhibitors (SSRIs)*. SSRIs target the neurotransmitter serotonin, permitting it to linger at the synapse. One of the latest antidepressants, Nefazodone (Serzone), blocks serotonin at some receptor sites but not others (see Figure 2; Berman, Krystal, & Charney, 1996; Williams et al., 2000; Anand, 2002).

Although antidepressant drugs may produce side effects such as drowsiness and faintness, their overall success rate is quite good. Unlike antipsychotic drugs, antidepressants can produce lasting, long-term recovery from depression. In many cases,

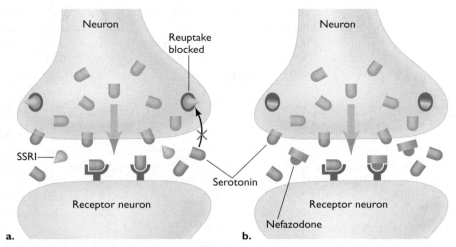

FIGURE 2 In (a), selective serotonin reuptake inhibitors (SSRIs) reduce depression by permitting the neurotransmitter serotonin to remain in the synapse. In (b), a newer antidepressant, Nefazodone (Serzone), operates more selectively, blocking serotonin at certain sites but not others, helping to reduce the side effects of the drug. (Source: Based on Mischoulon, 2000.)

even after patients stop taking the drugs, their depression does not return (Zito, 1993; Julien, 1995).

Consumers spend billions of dollars each year on antidepressant drugs, and sales are increasing more than 20 percent a year. In particular, the antidepressant *Fluoxetine*, sold under the trade name *Prozac*, has been highlighted on magazine covers and has been the topic of best-sellers.

Does Prozac deserve its acclaim? In some respects, yes. Despite its high expense—each daily dose costs around $2—it has significantly improved the lives of thousands of depressed individuals. Compared with other antidepressants, Prozac (along with its cousins Luvox, Paxil, Celexa, and Zoloft) has relatively few side effects. Furthermore, many people who do not respond to other types of antidepressants do well on Prozac. However, like all drugs, Prozac does not agree with everyone. For example, 20 to 30 percent of users report experiencing nausea and diarrhea, and a smaller number report sexual dysfunctions (Kramer, 1993; Glenmullen, 2000).

Another drug that has received a great deal of publicity is *St. John's wort*, an herb that some have called a "natural" antidepressant. Although it is widely used in Europe for the treatment of depression, the U.S. Food and Drug Administration considers it a dietary supplement, and therefore the substance is available here without a prescription.

Despite the popularity of St. John's wort, definitive clinical tests have found that the herb is ineffective in the treatment of depression. However, because some research shows that the herb successfully reduces certain symptoms of depression, some proponents argue that using it is reasonable. Clearly, people should not use St. John's wort to medicate themselves without consulting a mental health care professional (Maidment, 2000; Williams et al., 2000; Shelton et al., 2002).

LITHIUM

The drug **lithium,** a form of mineral salts, has been used very successfully in patients with bipolar disorders. Although no one knows definitely why, it and drugs such as *Depakote* and *Tegretol* effectively reduce manic episodes. However, they do not effectively treat depressive phases of bipolar disorder, so antidepressants are usually prescribed during those phases (Dubovsky, 1999).

Prozac is a widely prescribed—but still controversial—antidepressant.

Lithium: A drug comprised of mineral salts used to treat bipolar disorders.

Lithium and drugs similar to it have a quality that sets them apart from other drug treatments: They can be a *preventive* treatment, blocking future episodes of manic depression. Often, people who have been subject to bipolar disorder episodes can take a daily dose of lithium that prevents a recurrence of their symptoms. In contrast, most other drugs are useful only after symptoms of psychological disturbance occur.

ANTIANXIETY DRUGS

Antianxiety drugs: Drugs that reduce the level of anxiety a person experiences, essentially by reducing excitability and increasing feelings of well-being.

As the name implies, **antianxiety drugs** reduce the level of anxiety a person experiences and increase feelings of well-being. They are prescribed not only to reduce general tension in people who are experiencing temporary difficulties but also to aid in the treatment of more serious anxiety disorders (Zito, 1993).

Antianxiety drugs such as Xanax and Valium are among the medications most frequently prescribed by physicians. In fact, more than half of all U.S. families have someone who has taken such a drug at one time or another.

Although the popularity of antianxiety drugs suggests that they hold few risks, they can produce a number of potentially serious side effects. For instance, they can cause fatigue, and long-term use can lead to dependence. Moreover, when taken in combination with alcohol, some antianxiety drugs can be lethal. But a more important issue concerns their use to suppress anxiety. Almost every therapeutic approach to psychological disturbance views continuing anxiety as a signal of some other sort of problem. Thus, drugs that mask anxiety may simply be hiding other difficulties. Consequently, rather than confronting their underlying problems, people may be hiding from them through the use of antianxiety drugs.

Electroconvulsive Therapy (ECT)

> Martha Manning had contemplated all kinds of suicide—by pills, hanging, even guns. Her depression was so deep that she lived each minute "afraid I [wouldn't] make it to the next hour." But she balked when her therapist recommended electroconvulsive therapy, commonly known as "shock treatment." Despite her training and practice as a clinical psychologist, Manning immediately flashed to scenes from *One Flew Over the Cuckoo's Nest*, "with McMurphy and the Chief jolted with electroshock, their bodies flailing with each jolt" (Guttman, 1995, p. 16).

The reality, it turned out, was quite different. Although it did produce some memory loss and temporary headaches, the procedure also brought Manning back from the brink of suicide.

Electroconvulsive therapy (ECT): A procedure in which an electric current of 70 to 150 volts is briefly administered to a patient's head, causing a loss of consciousness and often causing seizures.

First introduced in the 1930s, **electroconvulsive therapy (ECT)** is a procedure in which an electric current of 70 to 150 volts is briefly administered to a patient's head, causing a loss of consciousness and often causing seizures. Usually health professionals sedate patients and give them muscle relaxants before administering the current, and this helps reduce the intensity of muscle contractions produced during ECT. The typical patient receives about ten such treatments in the course of a month, but some patients continue with maintenance treatments for months afterward (Nierenberg, 1998b; Fink, 1999).

ECT is a controversial technique. Apart from the obvious distastefulness of a treatment that evokes images of electrocution, side effects occur frequently. For instance, after treatment patients often experience disorientation, confusion, and sometimes memory loss that may remain for months. Furthermore, ECT often does not produce long-term improvement; one study found that without follow-up medication, depression returned in most patients who had undergone ECT treat-

PowerWeb: Does Electroshock Therapy Cure Depression?

www.mhhe.com/feldmanup7

ments. Finally, even when ECT does work, we do not know why, and some critics believe it may cause permanent brain damage (Valente, 1991; Sackeim et al., 2001; Frank, 2002).

In light of the drawbacks to ECT, why do therapists use it at all? Basically, they use it because, in many severe cases of depression, it offers the only quickly effective treatment. For instance, it may prevent depressed, suicidal individuals from committing suicide, and it can act more quickly than antidepressive medications.

The use of ECT has risen in the last decade, with more than 100,000 people undergoing it each year. Still, ECT tends to be used only when other treatments have proved ineffective (Sackheim et al., 1996; Fink, 2000; Eranti & McLoughlin, 2003).

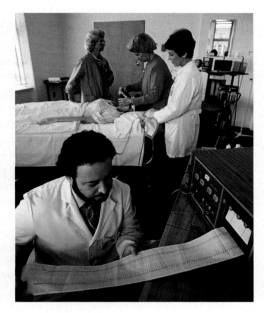

Dr. Richard B. Weiner of Duke University Medical Center reads a patient's electroencephalogram as technicians administer electroconvulsive therapy. ECT is a controversial treatment, but it does help some people whose severe depression has not responded to other approaches.

Psychosurgery

If ECT strikes you as a questionable procedure, the use of **psychosurgery**—brain surgery in which the object is to reduce symptoms of mental disorder—probably appears even more dubious. A technique used only rarely today, psychosurgery was introduced as a "treatment of last resort" in the 1930s.

The initial form of psychosurgery, a *prefrontal lobotomy,* consisted of surgically destroying or removing parts of a patient's frontal lobes, which, surgeons thought, controlled emotionality. In the 1930s and 1940s, surgeons performed the procedure on thousands of patients, often with little precision. For example, in one common technique, a surgeon would jab an ice pick under a patient's eyeball and swivel it back and forth (Miller, 1994).

Psychosurgery often did improve a patient's behavior—but not without drastic side effects. Along with remission of the symptoms of the mental disorder, patients sometimes experienced personality changes, becoming bland, colorless, and unemotional. In other cases, patients became aggressive and unable to control their impulses. In the worst cases, treatment resulted in the death of the patient.

With the introduction of effective drug treatments—and the obvious ethical questions regarding the appropriateness of forever altering someone's personality—psychosurgery became nearly obsolete. However, it is still used in very rare cases when all other procedures have failed and the patient's behavior presents a high risk to the patient and others. Today, surgeons sometimes use a more precise form of psychosurgery called a *cingulotomy* in rare cases of obsessive-compulsive disorder. Occasionally, dying patients with severe, uncontrollable pain also receive psychosurgery. Still, even these cases raise important ethical issues, and psychosurgery remains a highly controversial treatment (Miller, 1994; Baer et al., 1995; Jenike, 1998).

Psychosurgery: Brain surgery once used to reduce the symptoms of mental disorder but rarely used today.

Biomedical Therapies in Perspective

In some respects, no greater revolution has occurred in the field of mental health than biological approaches to treatment. As previously violent, uncontrollable patients have been calmed by the use of drugs, mental hospitals have been able to concentrate more on actually helping patients and less on custodial functions. Similarly, patients whose lives have been disrupted by depression or bipolar episodes have been able to function normally, and other forms of drug therapy have also shown remarkable results.

The use of biomedical therapy for everyday problems is rising. For example, one survey of users of a college counseling service found that from 1989 to 2001, the proportion of students receiving treatment who were taking medication for psychological disorders increased from 10 percent to 25 percent (Benton et al., 2003).

However, biomedical therapies do not represent a cure-all for psychological disorders. For one thing, critics charge that such therapies merely provide relief of the *symptoms* of mental disorder; as soon as the drugs are withdrawn, the symptoms return. Although it is considered a major step in the right direction, biomedical treatment may not solve the underlying problems that led a patient to therapy in the first place. Moreover, biomedical therapies can produce side effects, ranging from physical reactions to the development of *new* symptoms of abnormal behavior.

Still, biomedical therapies—sometimes alone and more often in conjunction with psychotherapy—have permitted millions of people to function more effectively. Furthermore, although biomedical therapy and psychotherapy appear distinct, research shows that biomedical therapies ultimately may not be as different from talk therapies as one might imagine, at least in terms of their consequences.

Specifically, measures of brain functioning as a result of drug therapy compared with psychotherapy show little difference in outcomes between the two. For example, one study compared the reactions of patients with major depression who received either an antidepressant drug or psychotherapy. After six weeks of either therapy, activity in the portion of the brain related to the disorder—the basal ganglia—had changed in similar ways, and that area appeared to function more normally. Although such research is not definitive, it does suggest that at least for some disorders, psychotherapy may be just as effective as biomedical interventions—and vice versa. Research also makes it clear that no single treatment is effective universally, and that each type of treatment has both advantages and disadvantages (Brody et al., 2001; Hollon, Thase, & Markowitz, 2002; DeRubeis, Hollon, & Shelton, 2003).

Community Psychology: Focus on Prevention

Each of the treatments we have reviewed has a common element: It is a "restorative" treatment, aimed at alleviating psychological difficulties that already exist. However, an approach known as **community psychology** has a different aim: to prevent or minimize the incidence of psychological disorders.

Community psychology came of age in the 1960s, when mental health professionals developed plans for a nationwide network of community mental health

Community psychology: A branch of psychology that focuses on the prevention and minimization of psychological disorders in the community.

centers. Those centers would provide low-cost mental health services, including short-term therapy and community educational programs. In another development since the 1970s, the population of mental hospitals has plunged as drug treatments have made physical restraint of patients unnecessary. This transfer of former mental patients out of institutions and into the community—a process known as **deinstitutionalization**—further spurred the community psychology movement (see Figure 3). Proponents of deinstitutionalization wanted to ensure not only that deinstitutionalized patients received proper treatment but also that their civil rights were maintained (Melton & Garrison, 1987).

Unfortunately, the promise of deinstitutionalization has not been met, largely because insufficient resources are provided to deinstitutionalized

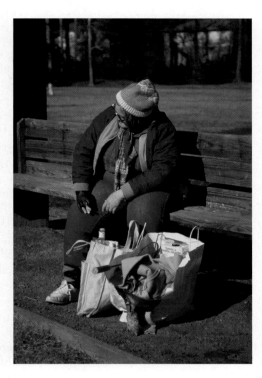

While deinstitutionalization has had many successes, it has also contributed to the release of mental patients into the community with little or no support. As a result many have become homeless.

Deinstitutionalization: The transfer of former mental patients from institutions into the community.

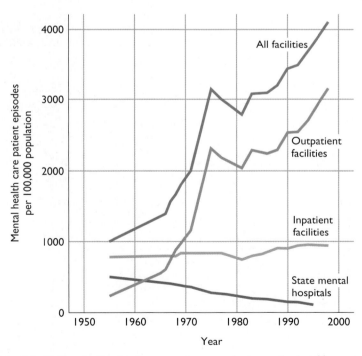

FIGURE 3 As deinstitutionalization has become more prevalent over the last fifty years, the number of patients being treated in state mental hospitals has declined significantly, while the number of outpatient facilities has increased. (Source: National Mental Health Information Center, U.S. Department of Health and Human Services, reprinted in *Scientific American*, December, 2002, p. 38.)

patients. What started as a worthy attempt to move people out of mental institutions and into the community ended, in many cases, with former patients being dumped into the community without any real support. Many became homeless—between a third and a half of all homeless adults are thought to have a major psychological disorder—and some became involved in illegal acts caused by their disorders. In short, many people who need treatment do not get it, and in some cases care for people with psychological disorders has simply shifted from one type of treatment site to another (Kiesler & Simpkins, 1993; Torrey, 1997; Doyle, 2002).

On the other hand, the community psychology movement has had some positive outcomes. Telephone "hot lines" are now common. At any time of the day or night, people experiencing acute stress can call a trained, sympathetic listener who can provide immediate—although obviously limited—treatment (Blewett, 2000; Reese, Conoley, & Brossart, 2002).

College and high school crisis centers are another innovation that grew out of the community psychology movement. Modeled after suicide prevention hot-line centers (services that enable potential suicide victims to call and speak to someone about their difficulties), crisis centers give callers an opportunity to discuss life crises with a sympathetic listener, who is often a volunteer.

BECOMING AN INFORMED CONSUMER of Psychology

Choosing the Right Therapist

If you decide to seek therapy, you're faced with a daunting task. Choosing a therapist is not a simple matter. One place to start the process of identifying a therapist is at the "Help Center" of the American Psychological Association at http://helping.apa.org/ or 1-800-964-2000. And if you start therapy, several general guidelines can help you determine whether you've made the right choice:

▶ *You and your therapist should agree on the goals for treatment.* They should be clear, specific, and attainable.

FIGURE 4 For most clients improvements in psychological functioning occur relatively soon after therapy has begun. (Source: Howard et al., 1986a.)

▶ *You should feel comfortable with your therapist.* You should not be intimidated by, or in awe of, a therapist. Instead, you should trust the therapist and feel free to discuss even the most personal issues without fearing a negative reaction. In sum, the "personal chemistry" should be right.

▶ *Therapists should have appropriate training and credentials and should be licensed by appropriate state and local agencies.* Check therapists' membership in national and state professional associations. In addition, the cost of therapy, billing practices, and other business matters should be clear. It is not a breach of etiquette to put these matters on the table during an initial consultation.

▶ *You should feel that you are making progress after therapy has begun, despite occasional setbacks.* If you have no sense of improvement after repeated visits, you and your therapist should discuss this issue frankly. Although there is no set timetable, the most obvious changes resulting from therapy tend to occur relatively early in the course of treatment. For instance, half of patients in psychotherapy improve by the eighth session, and three-fourths by the twenty-sixth session (see Figure 4). The average number of sessions with college students is just five (Crits-Cristoph, 1992; HMHL, 1994b; Lazarus, 1997).

"Looking good!"

Be aware that you will have to put in a great deal of effort in therapy. Although our culture promises quick cures for any problem, in reality, solving difficult problems is not easy. You must be committed to making therapy work and should know that it is you, not the therapist, who must do most of the work to resolve your problems. The effort has the potential to pay off handsomely—as you experience a more positive, fulfilling, and meaningful life.

RECAP/EVALUATE/RETHINK

RECAP

How are drug, electroconvulsive, and psychosurgical techniques used today in the treatment of psychological disorders?

▶ Biomedical treatment approaches suggest that therapy should focus on the physiological causes of abnormal behavior, rather than considering psychological factors. Drug therapy, the best example of biomedical treatments, has brought about dramatic reductions in the symptoms of mental disturbance. (p. 589)

▶ Antipsychotic drugs such as chlorpromazine very effectively reduce psychotic symptoms. Antidepressant drugs such as Prozac reduce depression so successfully that they are used very widely. Antianxiety drugs, or minor tranquilizers, are among the most frequently prescribed medications of any sort. (p. 590)

▶ In electroconvulsive therapy (ECT), used only in severe cases of depression, a patient receives a brief electric current of 70 to 150 volts. (p. 592)

▶ Psychosurgery typically consists of surgically destroying or removing certain parts of a patient's brain. (p. 593)

▶ The community psychology approach stimulated deinstitutionalization, in which previously hospitalized mental patients were released into the community. (p. 594)

EVALUATE

1. Antipsychotic drugs have provided effective, long-term, and complete cures for schizophrenia. True or false?

2. One highly effective biomedical treatment for a psychological disorder, used mainly to arrest and prevent manic-depressive episodes, is
   a. Chlorpromazine
   b. Lithium
   c. Librium
   d. Valium

3. Psychosurgery has grown in popularity as a method of treatment as surgical techniques have become more precise. True or false?

4. The trend toward releasing more patients from mental hospitals and into the community is known as _____.

RETHINK

1. One of the main criticisms of biological therapies is that they treat the symptoms of mental disorder without uncovering and treating the underlying problems from which people are suffering. Do you agree with this criticism? Why?

2. If a dangerously violent person could be "cured" of violence through a new psychosurgical technique, would you approve the use of that technique? Suppose the person agreed to—or requested—the technique? What sort of policy would you develop for the use of psychosurgery?

Answers to Evaluate Questions

1. false; schizophrenia can be controlled, but not cured, by medication; 2. b; 3. false; psychosurgery is now used only as a treatment of last resort. 4. deinstitutionalization

KEY TERMS

drug therapy p. 589
antipsychotic drugs p. 589
antidepressant drugs p. 590
lithium p. 591

antianxiety drugs p. 592
electroconvulsive therapy
(ECT) p. 592

psychosurgery p. 593
community psychology
p. 594

deinstitutionalization
p. 595

Looking Back

Psychology on the Web

1. Investigate computer-assisted psychotherapy on the Web. Locate (a) a computerized therapy program, such as ELIZA, which offers "therapy" over the Internet, and (b) a report on "cybertherapy," in which therapists use the Web to interact with patients. Compare the two approaches, describing how each one works and relating it to the therapeutic approaches you have studied.

2. Find more information on the Web about deinstitutionalization. Try to find pro and con arguments about it and summarize the arguments, including your judgment of the effectiveness and advisability of deinstitutionalization as an approach to dealing with mental illness.

3. After completing Interactivity 53–1 on drug therapies, investigate new drug therapies for a specific disorder of your choosing, such as schizophrenia, bipolar disorder, or panic attacks. Summarize how the drugs operate, their effectiveness, and any side effects.

Epilogue

We have examined how psychological professionals treat people with psychological disorders. We considered a range of approaches, including both psychologically based and biologically based therapies. Clearly, the field has made substantial progress in recent years both in terms of treating the symptoms of mental disorders and in terms of understanding their underlying causes.

Before we leave the topic of treatment of psychological disorders, turn back to the Prologue, in which several people who had had schizophrenia held a belated prom to celebrate their liberation from that disorder. On the basis of your understanding of the treatment of psychological disorders, consider the following questions.

1. The prom goers in the story were treated with drug therapy. How would their treatment have proceeded if they had undergone Freudian psychoanalysis? What sorts of issues might a psychoanalyst have examined?

2. Do you think any behavioral therapies would have been helpful in treating the prom goers' schizophrenia? Could behavioral therapies have helped them control the outward exhibition of symptoms?

3. Would cognitive or humanistic approaches have had any effect on schizophrenia? In what ways might such approaches have fallen short?

4. Do you think that people who recover from schizophrenia can reenter the world quickly and calmly and take up their lives as if nothing had happened to them? What sorts of adjustments might lifelong sufferers now in their thirties have to make?

5. Antipsychotic drugs sometimes have the side effect of numbing emotional responses. If it could have been known ahead of time that the prom goers would eventually experience this side effect, do you think the drug therapy would still have been advisable? Why or why not?

Social Psychology

Prologue

Everyday Heroes

It was 2 o'clock on July 12 in tiny Cut Off, Louisiana, and auto repairmen Lonnie Chouest, Tucker Scioneaux, and Kim Plaisance were doing the usual—talking about fishing and their love lives. Then they heard a heavy thud and a muffled splash and knew that a car had plunged into Bayou Lafourche across the highway. The pals, all of whom work at Ken's Body Shop, dashed across the road. When they reached the water, says Scioneaux, "the car was upside down, four tires up."

The men momentarily relaxed when Stacey Rogers, 21, Opel Lovette, 20, and Joni LeBlanc, 15, emerged from the sinking car, which had hit a hole in the rail-sliced road, flown into the air and struck two trees before landing in the bayou. But relief turned to horror when two of the women began screaming, "Our babies are still in the car!" . . .

The men, fathers all, kicked off their shoes and dove in. It took several minutes to pry the doors of the 1998 Kia Sephia. Visibility was so poor that the trio then had to find the babies by feel. Plaisance surfaced and yelled for a knife. Chouest quickly dug one out of his pocket, and Plaisance used it to cut [one of the baby's] restraining belts. By the time he emerged with the unconscious boy and handed him to Scioneaux, Plaisance recalls, "Both sides of the bayou were filled with worried people." (Charles et al., 2001, p. 90).

The three rescuers and the infants they saved.

After a number of additional dives, both babies were saved. Although one of the infants had water in his lungs and later developed pneumonia, he, along with the other child, recovered completely from the ordeal. As to the three rescuers, each rejected the title "hero," saying that the important thing was that the two infants had survived the crash.

What led the three rescuers to behave so heroically? Was it simply the circumstances, or was it something about who they were? What, in general, spurs some people to help others—and, in contrast, why do some people show no concern for the welfare of others? More broadly, how can we improve social conditions to help people live together in harmony?

Looking Ahead

We can fully answer each of these questions only by taking into account findings from the field of social psychology, the branch of psychology that focuses on the aspects of human behavior that unite—and separate—us from one another. **Social psychology** is the scientific study of how people's thoughts, feelings, and actions are affected by others. Social psychologists consider the nature and causes of individual behavior in social situations.

The broad scope of social psychology is conveyed by the kinds of questions social psychologists ask, such as: How can we convince people to change their attitudes or adopt new ideas and values? In what ways do we come to understand what others are like? How are we influenced by what others do and think? Why do some people display so much violence, aggression, and cruelty toward others that people throughout the world live in fear of annihilation at their hands? And why, in comparison, do some people place their own lives at risk to help others? In exploring these and other questions, we also discuss strategies for confronting and solving a variety of problems and issues that all of us face—ranging from achieving a better understanding of persuasive tactics to forming more accurate impressions of others.

We begin with a look at how our attitudes shape our behavior and how we form judgments about others. We'll discuss how we are influenced by others, and we will consider prejudice and discrimination, focusing on their roots and the ways in which we can reduce them. After examining what social psychologists have learned about the ways in which people form friendships and relationships, we'll conclude with a look at the determinants of aggression and helping.

Social psychology: The scientific study of how people's thoughts, feelings, and actions are affected by others.

Attitudes and Social Cognition

What do Tiger Woods, Britney Spears, and Jay Leno have in common?

Each has appeared—frequently—in advertisements designed to mold or change our attitudes. Such commercials are part of the barrage of messages we receive each day from sources as varied as politicians, sales staff in stores, and celebrities, all meant to influence us.

(▲)(▲)(▲)

Persuasion: Changing Attitudes

Persuasion is the process of changing attitudes, one of the central concepts of social psychology. **Attitudes** are learned evaluations of a particular person, behavior, belief, or thing (Eagly & Chaiken, 1995; Perloff, 2003).

The ease with which attitudes can be changed depends on a number of factors, including:

▶ *Message source.* The characteristics of a person who delivers a persuasive message, known as an *attitude communicator*, have a major impact on the effectiveness of that message. Communicators who are physically and socially attractive produce greater attitude change than those who are less attractive. Moreover, the expertise and trustworthiness of a communicator are related to the impact of a message—except in situations in which the audience believes the communicator has an ulterior motive (Hovland, Janis, & Kelly, 1953; Ziegler, Diehl, & Ruther, 2002).

▶ *Characteristics of the message.* It is not just *who* delivers a message but *what* the message is like that affects attitudes. Generally, two-sided messages—which include both the communicator's position and the one he or she is arguing against—are more effective than one-sided messages, assuming the arguments for the other side can be effectively refuted and the audience is knowledgeable about the topic. In addition, fear-producing messages ("If you don't practice safer sex, you'll get AIDS") are generally effective when they provide the audience with a means for reducing the fear. However, If the fear aroused is too strong, messages may evoke people's defense mechanisms and be ignored (Rosenthal, 1997; Perloff, 2003).

▶ *Characteristics of the target.* Once a communicator has delivered a message, characteristics of the *target* of the message may determine whether the message will be accepted. For example, intelligent people are more resistant to persuasion than are those who are less intelligent. Gender differences in persuasibility also seem to exist. In public settings, women are somewhat more easily persuaded than men, particularly when they have less knowledge about the message's topic. However, they are as likely as men to change their private attitudes. In fact, the magnitude of the differences between men and women is not large (Wood & Stagner, 1994; Guadagno & Cialdini, 2002).

What are attitudes, and how are they formed, maintained, and changed?

How do we form impressions of what others are like and of the causes of their behavior?

What are the biases that influence the ways in which we view others' behavior?

Attitude: A learned evaluation of a particular person, behavior, belief, or thing.

Companies use sports stars such as Tiger Woods to persuade consumers to buy their products. Can celebrities really affect the purchasing habits of consumers? How?

Cards like these were distributed in Iraq by U.S. Armed Forces during the 2003 war. Do you believe they could be effective in changing the attitudes and beliefs of the Iraqi people?

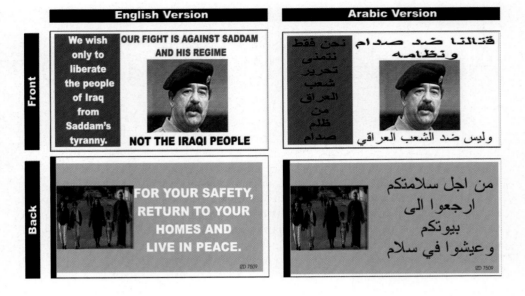

Central route processing: Message interpretation characterized by thoughtful consideration of the issues and arguments used to persuade.

Peripheral route processing: Message interpretation characterized by consideration of the source and related general information rather than of the message itself.

Recipients' receptiveness to persuasive messages relates to the type of information-processing they use. Social psychologists have discovered two primary information-processing routes to persuasion: central route and peripheral route processing. **Central route processing** occurs when the recipient thoughtfully considers the issues and arguments involved in persuasion. **Peripheral route processing,** in contrast, occurs when people are persuaded on the basis of factors unrelated to the nature or quality of the content of a persuasive message. Instead, factors that are irrelevant or extraneous to the issue, such as who is providing the message and how long the arguments are, influence them (Petty, Cacioppo, Strathman, & Priester, 1994; Petty, Wheeler, & Tormala, 2003).

In general, people who are highly involved and motivated use central route processing to comprehend a message. However, if a person is uninvolved, unmotivated, bored, or distracted, the nature of the message becomes less important, and peripheral factors become more critical (see Figure 1). Although both central route and peripheral route processing lead to attitude change, central route processing generally leads to stronger, more lasting attitude change.

Are some people more likely than others to use central route processing rather than peripheral route processing? The answer is yes. People who have a high *need*

FIGURE I Routes to persuasion. Targets who are highly involved, motivated, and attentive use central route processing when they consider a persuasive message, which leads to a more lasting attitude change. In contrast, uninvolved, unmotivated, and inattentive targets are more likely to use peripheral route processing, and attitude change is likely to be less enduring. Can you think of particular advertisements that try to produce central route processing?

The Need for Cognition

Which of the following statements apply to you?

1. I really enjoy a task that involves coming up with new solutions to problems.
2. I would prefer a task that is intellectual, difficult, and important to one that is somewhat important but does not require much thought.
3. Learning new ways to think doesn't excite me very much.
4. The idea of relying on thought to make my way to the top does not appeal to me.
5. I think only as hard as I have to.
6. I like tasks that require little thought once I've learned them.
7. I prefer to think about small, daily projects rather than long-term ones.
8. I would rather do something that requires little thought than something that is sure to challenge my thinking abilities.
9. I find little satisfaction in deliberating hard and for long hours.
10. I don't like to be responsible for a situation that requires a lot of thinking.

Scoring: The more you agree with statements 1 and 2, and disagree with the rest, the greater the likelihood that you have a high need for cognition.

FIGURE 2 This simple questionnaire will give you a general idea of the level of your need for cognition. (Source: Cacioppo et al., 1996.)

for cognition, a person's habitual level of thoughtfulness and cognitive activity, are more likely to employ central route processing. Consider the statements shown in Figure 2. People who agree with the first two statements and disagree with the rest have a relatively high need for cognition (Cacioppo et al., 1996).

People who have a high need for cognition enjoy thinking, philosophizing, and reflecting on the world. Consequently, they tend to reflect more on persuasive messages by using central route processing, and are likely to be persuaded by complex, logical, and detailed messages. In contrast, those who have a low need for cognition become impatient when forced to spend too much time thinking about an issue. Consequently, they usually use peripheral route processing and are persuaded by factors other than the quality and detail of messages (Haugtvedt, Petty, & Cacioppo, 1992; Dollinger, 2003).

THE LINK BETWEEN ATTITUDES AND BEHAVIOR

Not surprisingly, attitudes influence behavior. The strength of the link between particular attitudes and behavior varies, of course, but generally people strive for consistency between their attitudes and their behavior. Furthermore, people hold fairly consistent attitudes. For instance, you would probably not hold the attitude that eating meat is immoral and still have a positive attitude toward hamburgers (Kraus, 1995; Ajzen, 2002; Conner et al., 2003).

Interestingly, the consistency that leads attitudes to influence behavior sometimes works the other way around, for in some cases it is our behavior that shapes our attitudes. Consider, for instance, the following incident:

> You've just spent what you feel is the most boring hour of your life, turning pegs for a psychology experiment. Just as you finally finish and are about to leave, the experimenter asks you to do him a favor. He tells you that he needs a helper for future experimental sessions to introduce subsequent participants to the peg-turning task. Your specific job will be to tell them that turning the pegs is an interesting, fascinating experience. Each time you tell this tale to another participant, you'll be paid $1.

If you agree to help the experimenter, you may be setting yourself up for a state of psychological tension called **cognitive dissonance**. According to a major social

PowerWeb: A Theory of Cognitive Dissonance

www.mhhe.com/feldmanup7

Cognitive dissonance: The conflict that occurs when a person holds two contradictory attitudes or thoughts (referred to as *cognitions*).

psychologist, Leon Festinger (1957), **cognitive dissonance** occurs when a person holds two contradictory attitudes or thoughts (referred to as *cognitions*).

If you participate in the situation just described, it leaves you with two contradictory thoughts: (1) I believe the task is boring, but (2) I said it was interesting with little justification ($1). These two thoughts should arouse dissonance. How can you reduce such dissonance? You cannot deny having said that the task is interesting without breaking with reality. Relatively speaking, it is easier to change your attitude toward the task—and thus the theory predicts that participants will reduce dissonance by adopting more positive attitudes toward the task (Harmon-Jones, Peterson, & Vaughn, 2003; Storch & Storch, 2003).

A classic experiment (Festinger & Carlsmith, 1959) confirmed this prediction. The experiment followed essentially the same procedure outlined earlier, in which a participant was offered $1 to describe a boring task as interesting. In addition, as a control, a condition was included in which participants were offered $20 to say that the task was interesting. The reasoning behind this condition was that $20 was so much money that participants in this condition had a good reason to be conveying incorrect information; dissonance would *not* be aroused, and *less* attitude change would be expected. The results supported this notion. Participants who were paid $1 changed their attitudes more (becoming more positive toward the peg-turning task) than participants who were paid $20.

We now know that dissonance explains many everyday events involving attitudes and behavior. For example, smokers who know that smoking leads to lung cancer hold contradictory cognitions: (1) I smoke, and (2) smoking leads to lung cancer. The theory predicts that these two thoughts will lead to a state of cognitive dissonance. More important, it predicts that—assuming that they don't change their behavior by quitting smoking—smokers will be motivated to reduce their dissonance by one of the following methods: (1) modifying one or both of the cognitions, (2) changing the perceived importance of one cognition, (3) adding cognitions, or (4) denying that the two cognitions are related to each other. Hence, a smoker may decide that he really doesn't smoke all that much or that he'll quit soon (modifying the cognition), that the evidence linking smoking to cancer is weak (changing the importance of a cognition), that the amount of exercise he gets compensates for the smoking (adding cognitions), or that there is no evidence linking smoking and cancer (denial). Whichever technique the smoker uses results in reduced dissonance (see Figure 3).

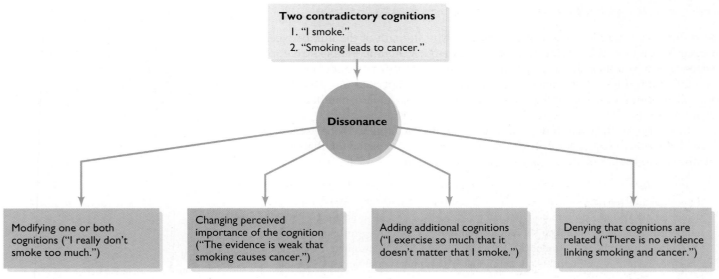

FIGURE 3 Cognitive dissonance. The simultaneous presence of two contradictory cognitions ("I smoke" and "Smoking leads to cancer") produces dissonance, which may be reduced through several methods. What are additional ways in which dissonance can be reduced?

Social Cognition: Understanding Others

Regardless of Bill Clinton's personal transgressions and impeachment trial, many Americans genuinely *liked* him when he was president, and his popularity remained high throughout his term in office. Cases like this illustrate the power of our impressions and attest to the importance of determining how people develop an understanding of others. One of the dominant areas in social psychology during the last few years has focused on learning how we come to understand what others are like and how we explain the reasons underlying others' behavior.

UNDERSTANDING WHAT OTHERS ARE LIKE

Consider for a moment the enormous amount of information about other people to which we are exposed. How can we decide what is important and what is not and make judgments about the characteristics of others? Social psychologists interested in this question study **social cognition**—the way people understand and make sense of others and themselves. Those psychologists have learned that individuals have highly developed **schemas,** sets of cognitions about people and social experiences. Those schemas organize information stored in memory, represent in our minds the way the social world operates, and give us a framework to recognize, categorize, and recall information relating to social stimuli such as people and groups (Fiske & Taylor, 1991; Kunda, 2000).

We typically hold schemas for particular types of people. Our schema for "teacher," for instance, generally consists of a number of characteristics: knowledge of the subject matter he or she is teaching, a desire to impart that knowledge, and an awareness of the student's need to understand what is being said. Or we may hold a schema for "mother" that includes the characteristics of warmth, nurturance, and caring. Regardless of their accuracy, schemas are important because they organize the way in which we recall, recognize, and categorize information about others. Moreover, they help us predict what others are like on the basis of relatively little information, because we tend to fit people into schemas even when we do not have much concrete evidence to go on (Bargh et al., 1995; Ruscher, Fiske, & Schnake, 2000).

IMPRESSION FORMATION

How do we decide that Sayreeta is a flirt, Jacob is obnoxious, or Hector is a really nice guy? The earliest work on social cognition examined *impression formation*, the process by which an individual organizes information about another person to form an overall impression of that person. In a classic study, for instance, students learned that they were about to hear a guest lecturer (Kelley, 1950). Researchers told one group of students that the lecturer was "a rather warm person, industrious, critical, practical, and determined," and told a second group that he was "a rather cold person, industrious, critical, practical, and determined."

The simple substitution of "cold" for "warm" caused drastic differences in the way the students in each group perceived the lecturer, even though he gave the same talk in the same style in each condition. Students who had been told he was "warm" rated him considerably more positively than students who had been told he was "cold."

The findings from this experiment led to additional research on impression formation that focused on the way in which people pay particular attention to certain unusually important traits—known as **central traits**—to help them form an overall impression of others. According to this work, the presence of a central trait alters the meaning of other traits. Hence, the description of the lecturer as "industrious" presumably meant something different when it was associated with the central trait

Social cognition: The cognitive processes by which people understand and make sense of others and themselves.

Schemas: Sets of cognitions about people and social experiences.

Central traits: The major traits considered in forming impressions of others.

"warm" than it meant when it was associated with "cold" (Asch, 1946; Widmeyer & Loy, 1988).

Other work on impression formation has used information-processing approaches to develop mathematically oriented models of how individual personality traits combine to create an overall impression. Generally, the results of this research suggest that in forming an overall judgment of a person, we use a psychological "average" of the individual traits we see, just as we would find the mathematical average of several numbers (Anderson, 1996; Mignon & Mollaret, 2002).

Of course, as we gain more experience with people and see them exhibiting behavior in a variety of situations, our impressions of them become more complex. However, because our knowledge of others usually has gaps, we still tend to fit individuals into personality schemas that represent particular "types" of people. For instance, we may hold a "gregarious person" schema, made up of the traits of friendliness, aggressiveness, and openness. The presence of just one or two of those traits may be sufficient to make us assign a person to a particular schema.

However, our schemas are susceptible to error. For example, mood affects how we perceive others. Happy people form more favorable impressions and make more positive judgments than people who are in a bad mood (Forgas & Bower, 2001).

Even when schemas are not entirely accurate, they serve an important function: They allow us to develop expectations about how others will behave. Those expectations permit us to plan our interactions with others more easily and serve to simplify a complex social world.

ATTRIBUTION PROCESSES: UNDERSTANDING THE CAUSES OF BEHAVIOR

Consider the following case:

> When Barbara Washington, a new employee at the Ablex Computer Company, completed a major staffing project two weeks early, her boss, Yolanda, was delighted. At the next staff meeting, she announced how pleased she was with Barbara and explained that *this* was an example of the kind of performance she was looking for in her staff. The other staff members looked on resentfully, trying to figure out why Barbara had worked night and day to finish the project not just on time but two weeks early. She must be an awfully compulsive person, they decided.

Most of us have, at one time or another, puzzled over the reasons behind someone's behavior. Perhaps it was in a situation similar to the one above, or it may have been in more formal circumstances, such as serving as a judge on a student judiciary board in a cheating case. In contrast to theories of social cognition, which describe how people develop an overall impression of others' personality traits, **attribution theory** seeks to explain how we decide, on the basis of samples of an individual's behavior, what the specific causes of that person's behavior are.

The general process we use to determine the causes of behavior and other social occurrences proceeds in several steps, as illustrated in Figure 4. After first noticing that something unusual has happened—for example, golf star Tiger Woods has played a miserable round of golf—we try to interpret the meaning of the event. This leads us to formulate an initial explanation (maybe Woods stayed up late the night before the match). Depending on the time available, the cognitive resources on hand (such as the attention we can give to the matter), and our motivation (determined in part by how important the event is), we may choose to accept our initial explanation or seek to modify it (Woods was sick, perhaps). If we have the time, cognitive resources, and motivation, the event triggers deliberate problem solving as we seek a fuller explanation. During the problem formulation and resolution stage, we may try out several possibilities before we reach a final explanation that seems satisfactory to us (Krull & Anderson, 1997).

Attribution theory: The theory of personality that seeks to explain how we decide, on the basis of samples of an individual's behavior, what the specific causes of that person's behavior are.

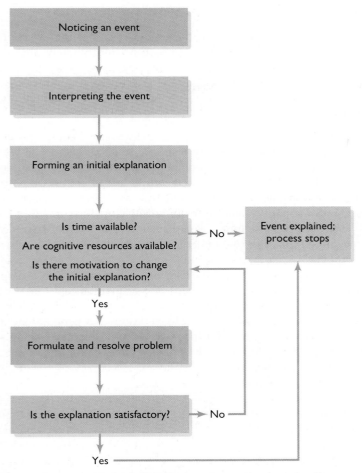

FIGURE 4 Determining why people behave the way they do. The general process we use to determine the causes of others' behavior proceeds in several steps. The kind of explanation we come up with depends on the time available to us, our cognitive resources, and our degree of motivation to come up with an accurate explanation. If time, cognitive resources, and motivation are limited, we'll make use of our first impression, which may be inaccurate. (Source: Adapted from Krull & Anderson, 1997, p. 2.)

In seeking an explanation for behavior, we must answer one central question: Is the cause situational or dispositional (Heider, 1958)? **Situational causes** are those brought about by something in the environment. For instance, someone who knocks over a quart of milk and then cleans it up probably does it not because he or she is necessarily a neat person but because the *situation* requires it. In contrast, a person who spends hours shining the kitchen floor probably does so because he or she *is* a neat person—hence, the behavior has a **dispositional cause,** prompted by the person's disposition (his or her internal traits or personality characteristics).

In our example involving Barbara, her fellow employees attributed her behavior to her disposition rather than to the situation. But from a logical standpoint, it is equally plausible that something about the situation caused the behavior. If asked, Barbara might attribute her accomplishment to situational factors, explaining that she had so much other work to do that she just had to get the project out of the way, or that the project was not all that difficult and so it was easy to complete ahead of schedule. To her, then, the reason for her behavior might not be dispositional at all; it could be situational.

Situational causes (of behavior): Perceived causes of behavior that are based on environmental factors.

Dispositional causes (of behavior): Perceived causes of behavior that are based on internal traits or personality factors.

BIASES IN ATTRIBUTION: TO ERR IS HUMAN

If we always processed information in the rational manner that attribution theory suggests, the world might run a lot more smoothly. Unfortunately, although attribution theory generally makes accurate predictions, people do not always process information about others in as logical a fashion as the theory seems to suggest. In fact, research reveals consistent biases in the ways people make attributions. Typical ones include the following:

- *The halo effect.* Harry is intelligent, kind, and loving. Is he also conscientious? If you were to guess, your most likely response probably would be yes. Your guess reflects the **halo effect,** a phenomenon in which an initial understanding that a person has positive traits is used to infer other uniformly positive characteristics. The opposite would also hold true. Learning that Harry was unsociable and argumentative would probably lead you to assume that he was lazy as well. However, because few people have either uniformly positive or uniformly negative traits, the halo effect leads to misperceptions of others (Larose & Standing, 1998; Feeley, 2002).

- *Assumed-similarity bias.* How similar to you—in terms of attitudes, opinions, and likes and dislikes—are your friends and acquaintances? Most people believe that their friends and acquaintances are fairly similar to themselves. But this feeling goes beyond just people we know to a general tendency— known as the **assumed-similarity bias**—to think of people as being similar to oneself, even when meeting them for the first time. Given the range of people in the world, this assumption often reduces the accuracy of our judgments (Watson, Hubbard, & Wiese, 2000).

- *The self-serving bias.* When the team wins, coaches usually feel that the team's success is due to their coaching. But when they coach a losing team, coaches may think it's due to the poor skills of their players. Similarly, if you get an A on a test, you may think it's due to your hard work, but if you get a poor grade, it's due to the professor's inadequacies. The reason is the **self-serving bias,** the tendency to attribute success to personal factors (skill, ability, or effort) and attribute failure to factors outside of oneself (Spencer et al., 2003).

- *The fundamental attribution error.* One of the more common attribution biases is the tendency to overattribute others' behavior to dispositional causes and the

Halo effect: A phenomenon in which an initial understanding that a person has positive traits is used to infer other uniformly positive characteristics.

Assumed-similarity bias: The tendency to think of people as being similar to oneself, even when meeting them for the first time.

Self-serving bias: The tendency to attribute personal success to personal factors (skill, ability, or effort) and to attribute failure to factors outside oneself.

The assumed-similarity bias leads us to believe that others hold similar attitudes, opinions, and likes and dislikes.

corresponding failure to recognize the importance of situational causes. Known as the **fundamental attribution error,** this tendency is quite prevalent in Western cultures. We tend to exaggerate the importance of personality characteristics (dispositional causes) in producing others' behavior, minimizing the influence of the environment (situational factors). For example, we are more likely to jump to the conclusion that someone who is often late to work is too lazy to take an earlier bus (a dispositional cause) than to assume that the lateness is due to situational factors, such as the bus always running behind schedule.

Why is the fundamental attribution error so common? One reason pertains to the nature of information available to the people making an attribution. When we view the behavior of another person in a particular setting, the most conspicuous information is the person's behavior. Because the individual's immediate surroundings remain relatively unchanged and less attention-grabbing, we center our attention on the person whose behavior we're considering. Consequently, we are more likely to make attributions based on personal, dispositional factors and less likely to make attributions relating to the situation (Ross & Nisbett, 1991; Hansen, Kimble, & Biers, 2001; Follett & Hess, 2002). To learn more about the fundamental attribution error, complete **Interactivity 54–1.**

Despite the importance of the fundamental attribution error in shaping the perceptions of members of western cultures, it turns out that it's not so fundamental when one looks at non-western cultures, as we discuss next.

Fundamental attribution error: A tendency to overattribute others' behavior to dispositional causes and the corresponding minimization of the importance of situational causes.

INTERACTIVITY 54–1

Fundamental attribution error

Attribution biases do not affect all of us in the same way. The kind of culture in which we are raised clearly plays a role in the way we attribute others' behavior.

Take, for example, the fundamental attribution error, the tendency to overestimate the importance of personal, dispositional factors and underattribute situational causes in determining the causes of others' behavior. The error is pervasive in Western cultures and not in Asian societies.

Specifically, social psychologist Joan Miller (1984) found that adult experimental participants in India were more likely to use situational attributions than dispositional ones in explaining events. These findings are the opposite of those for experimental participants in the United States, and they contradict the fundamental attribution error.

Miller suggested that we can discover the reason for these results by examining the norms and values of Indian society, which emphasize social responsibility and societal obligations to a greater extent than in Western societies. She also suggested that the language spoken in a culture may lead to different sorts of attributions. For instance, a tardy person using English may say "I am late," suggesting a personal, dispositional cause ("I am a tardy person"). In contrast, users of Spanish who are late say, "The clock caused me to be late." Clearly, the statement in Spanish implies that the cause is a situational one (Zebrowitz-McArthur, 1988).

Cultural differences in attributions may have profound implications. For example, parents in Asia tend to attribute good academic performance to effort and hard work (situational factors). In contrast, parents in Western cultures tend to deemphasize the role of effort and attribute school success to innate ability (a dispositional factor). As a result, Asian students may strive harder to achieve and ultimately outperform U.S. students in school (Stevenson, Chen, & Lee, 1993; Lee, Hallahan, & Herzog, 1996).

Exploring DIVERSITY

Attributions in a Cultural Context: How Fundamental Is the Fundamental Attribution Error?

Students in Asian societies may perform exceptionally well in school because the culture emphasizes academic success and perseverance.

RECAP/EVALUATE/RETHINK

RECAP

What are attitudes, and how are they formed, maintained, and changed?

- ▶ Social psychology is the scientific study of the ways in which people's thoughts, feelings, and actions are affected by others and the nature and causes of individual behavior in social situations. (p. 602)
- ▶ Attitudes are learned evaluations of a particular person, behavior, belief, or thing. (p. 603)
- ▶ Cognitive dissonance occurs when an individual simultaneously holds two cognitions—attitudes or thoughts—that contradict each other. To resolve the contradiction, the person may modify one cognition, change its importance, add a cognition, or deny a link between the two cognitions, thereby bringing about a reduction in dissonance. (p. 606)

How do we form impressions of what others are like and of the causes of their behavior?

- ▶ Social cognition involves the way people understand and make sense of others and themselves. People develop schemas that organize information about people and social experiences in memory and allow them to interpret and categorize information about others. (p. 607)
- ▶ People form impressions of others in part through the use of central traits, personality characteristics that receive unusually heavy weight when we form an impression. (p. 607)
- ▶ Information-processing approaches have found that we tend to average sets of traits to form an overall impression. (p. 608)
- ▶ Attribution theory tries to explain how we understand the causes of behavior, particularly with respect to situational or dispositional factors. (p. 608)

What are the biases that influence the ways in which we view others' behavior?

- ▶ Even though logical processes are involved, attribution is prone to error. For instance, people are susceptible to the halo effect, assumed-similarity bias, self-serving bias, and fundamental attribution error (the tendency to overattribute others' behavior to dispositional causes and the corresponding failure to recognize the importance of situational causes). (p. 610)

EVALUATE

1. A learned evaluation of a particular person, behavior, belief, or thing is called a(n) _____.
2. One brand of peanut butter advertises its product by describing its taste and nutritional value. It is hoping to persuade customers through _____ route processing. In ads for a competing brand, a popular actor happily eats the product—but does not describe it. This approach hopes to persuade customers through _____ route processing.
3. Cognitive dissonance theory suggests that we commonly change our behavior to keep it consistent with our attitudes. True or false?
4. Sopan was happy to lend his textbook to a fellow student who seemed bright and friendly. He was surprised when his classmate did not return it. His assumption that the bright and friendly student would also be responsible reflects the _____ effect.

RETHINK

1. Suppose you were assigned to develop a full advertising campaign for a product, including television, radio, and print ads. How might theories of persuasion guide your strategy to suit the different media?
2. Joan sees Annette, a new coworker, act in a way that seems abrupt and curt. Joan concludes that Annette is unkind and unsociable. The next day Joan sees Annette acting kindly toward another worker. Is Joan likely to change her impression of Annette? Why or why not? Finally, Joan sees several friends of hers laughing and joking with Annette, treating her in a very friendly fashion. Is Joan likely to change her impression of Annette? Why or why not?

Answers to Evaluate Questions

1. attitude; 2. central, peripheral; 3. false; we typically change our attitudes, not our behavior, to reduce cognitive dissonance; 4. halo

KEY TERMS

social psychology p. 602
attitude p. 603
central route processing p. 604
peripheral route processing p. 604

cognitive dissonance p. 606
social cognition p. 607
schemas p. 607
central traits p. 607
attribution theory p. 608

situational causes (of behavior) p. 609
dispositional causes (of behavior) p. 609
halo effect p. 610

assumed-similarity bias p. 610
self-serving bias p. 610
fundamental attribution error p. 611

Social Influence

What are the major sources and tactics of social influence?

You have just transferred to a new college and are attending your first class. When the professor enters, your fellow classmates instantly rise, bow to the professor, and then stand quietly, with their hands behind their backs. You've never encountered such behavior, and it makes no sense to you. Is it more likely that you will (1) jump up to join the rest of the class or (2) remain seated?

On the basis of what research has told us about **social influence,** the process by which the actions of an individual or group affect the behavior of others, a person would almost always choose the first option. As you undoubtedly know from your own experience, pressures to conform can be painfully strong, and can bring about changes in behavior that otherwise never would have occurred.

Social influence: The process by which the actions of an individual or group affect the behavior of others.

▲▲▲

Conformity: Following What Others Do

Conformity is a change in behavior or attitudes brought about by a desire to follow the beliefs or standards of other people. Subtle or even unspoken social pressure results in conformity.

The classic demonstration of pressure to conform comes from a series of studies carried out in the 1950s by Solomon Asch (Asch, 1951). In the experiments, the participants thought they were taking part in a test of perceptual skills with a group of six other people. The experimenter showed the participants one card with three lines of varying length and a second card that had a fourth line that matched one of the first three (see Figure 1). The task was seemingly straightforward: Each of the participants had to announce aloud which of the first three lines was identical in length to the "standard" line on the second card. Because the correct answer was always obvious, the task seemed easy to the participants.

Indeed, because the participants all agreed on the first few trials, the procedure appeared to be quite simple. But then something odd began to happen. From the perspective of the participant in the group who answered last on each trial, all the answers of the first six participants seemed to be wrong—in fact, unanimously wrong. And this pattern persisted. Over and over again, the first six participants provided answers that contradicted what the last participant believed to be correct. The last participant faced the dilemma of whether to follow his or her own perceptions or follow the group by repeating the answer everyone else was giving.

As you might have guessed, this experiment was more contrived than it appeared. The first six participants were actually confederates (paid employees of the experimenter) who had been instructed to give unanimously erroneous answers in many of the trials. And the study had nothing to do with perceptual skills. Instead, the issue under investigation was conformity.

Asch found that in about one-third of the trials, the participants conformed to the unanimous but erroneous group answer, with about 75 percent of all participants

Conformity: A change in behavior or attitudes brought about by a desire to follow the beliefs or standards of other people.

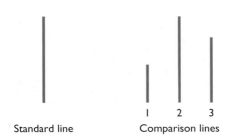

Standard line   Comparison lines

FIGURE 1 Which of the three comparison lines is the same length as the "standard" line? In Asch's conformity experiment, there was always a clear, correct answer, yet participants often conformed to the answers of the other group members. In what ways could participants in the study have avoided being influenced by pressure from the group?

conforming at least once. However, he found strong individual differences. Some participants conformed nearly all the time, whereas others never did.

Since Asch's pioneering work, literally hundreds of studies have examined conformity, and we now know a great deal about the phenomenon. Significant findings focus on:

Status: The social rank held within a group.

▶ *The characteristics of the group.* The more attractive a group appears to its members, the greater is its ability to produce conformity (Hogg & Hardie, 1992). Furthermore, a person's relative **status,** the social rank held within a group, is critical: The lower a person's status in the group, the greater the power of the group over that person's behavior.

▶ *The situation in which the individual is responding.* Conformity is considerably higher when people must respond publicly than it is when they can do so privately, as the founders of the United States noted when they authorized secret ballots in voting.

▶ *The kind of task.* People working on ambiguous tasks and questions (ones having no clear answer) are more susceptible to social pressure. Asked to give an opinion, such as what type of clothing is fashionable, a person will more likely yield to conformist pressures than he or she will if asked a question of fact. In addition, tasks at which an individual is less competent than others in the group make conformity more likely. For example, a person who is an infrequent computer user may feel pressure to conform to an opinion about computer brands when in a group of experienced computer users.

Social supporter: A group member whose dissenting views make non-conformity to the group easier.

▶ *Unanimity of the group.* Groups that unanimously support a position show the most pronounced conformity pressures. But what of the case in which people with dissenting views have an ally in the group, known as a **social supporter,** who agrees with them? Having just one person present who shares the minority point of view is sufficient to reduce conformity pressures (Levine, 1989; Prislin, Brewer, & Wilson, 2002).

Why can conformity pressures in groups be so strong? For one reason, groups, and other people generally, play a central role in our lives. Most of us seek social approval, and we know that groups develop and hold *norms,* expectations regarding behavior appropriate to the group. Furthermore, we understand that not adhering to group norms can result in retaliation from other group members, ranging from being ignored to being overtly derided or even being rejected or excluded by the group. Thus, people conform to meet the expectations of the group (Van Knippenberg, 1999; Baumeister, Twenge, & Nuss, 2002; Twenge, Catanese, & Baumeister, 2002).

GROUPTHINK: CAVING IN TO CONFORMITY

Although we usually think of conformity in terms of our individual relations with others, in some instances conformity pressures in organizations can lead to disastrous effects with long-term consequences. For instance, consider NASA's determination that the falling foam that hit the space shuttle *Columbia* when it took off in 2003 would pose no significant danger when it was time for the *Columbia* to land. Despite the misgivings of some engineers, a consensus formed that the foam was not dangerous to the shuttle. Ultimately, that consensus proved wrong: The shuttle came apart as it attempted to land, killing all the astronauts on board (Schwartz & Wald, 2003).

In hindsight, NASA's decision was clearly wrong. How could such a poor decision have been made?

A phenomenon known as groupthink provides an explanation. *Groupthink* is a type of thinking in which group members share such a strong motivation to achieve consensus that they lose the ability to critically evaluate alternative points of view. Groupthink is most likely to occur when a popular or powerful leader is surrounded by people of lower status—obviously the case with any U.S. president and his

The poor decisions that led to the destruction of the space shuttle *Columbia* may have been due to groupthink.

advisers, but also true in a variety of other organizations (Janis, 1989; Eaton, 2001; Kowert, 2002).

The phenomenon of groupthink is likely to happen when the following conditions exist:

- ⏵ The group appears invulnerable and incapable of making major errors in judgment.
- ⏵ Information contradictory to the dominant group view is ignored, discounted, or minimized.
- ⏵ Group members feel pressure to conform to the majority view—although the pressure may be relatively subtle.
- ⏵ The pressure to conform discourages minority viewpoints from coming before the group; consequently, the group *appears* to be unanimous, even if this is not really the case.
- ⏵ The group views itself as representing something just and moral, leading members to assume that any judgment the group reaches will also be just and moral.

Groupthink almost always produces negative consequences. Groups tend to limit the list of possible solutions to just a few, and spend relatively little time considering any alternatives once the leader seems to be leaning toward a particular solution. In fact, group members may completely ignore information that challenges a developing consensus. Because historical research shows that many disastrous decisions reflect groupthink, it is important for groups to be on guard (Tetlock et al., 1993; Cline, 1994; Schafer & Crichlow, 1996; Park, 2000).

Compliance: Submitting to Direct Social Pressure

When we refer to conformity, we usually mean a phenomenon in which the social pressure is subtle or indirect. But in some situations social pressure is much more obvious, with direct, explicit pressure to endorse a particular point of view or behave

Compliance: Behavior that occurs in response to direct social pressure.

in a certain way. Social psychologists call the type of behavior that occurs in response to direct social pressure **compliance.**

Several specific sales tactics represent attempts to gain compliance. Those frequently employed include:

▶ *The foot-in-the-door technique.* A salesperson comes to your door and asks you to accept a small sample. You agree, thinking you have nothing to lose. A little later comes a larger request, which, because you have already agreed to the first one, you have a hard time turning down.

The salesperson in this case is using a tried-and-true strategy that social psychologists call the foot-in-the-door technique. According to the *foot-in-the-door technique*, you ask a person to agree to a small request and later ask that person to comply with a more important one. It turns out that compliance with the more important request increases significantly when the person first agrees to the smaller favor.

Researchers first demonstrated the foot-in-the-door phenomenon in a study in which a number of experimenters went door to door asking residents to sign a petition in favor of safe driving (Freedman & Fraser, 1966). Almost everyone complied with that small, benign request. A few weeks later, different experimenters contacted the residents and made a much larger request: that the residents erect a huge sign reading "Drive Carefully" on their front lawns. The results were clear: 55 percent of those who had signed the petition agreed to the request to put up a sign, whereas only 17 percent of the people in a control group who had not been asked to sign the petition agreed to put up a sign.

Why does the foot-in-the-door technique work? For one reason, involvement with the small request leads to an interest in an issue, and taking an action—any action—makes the individual more committed to the issue, thereby increasing the likelihood of future compliance. Another explanation revolves around people's self-perceptions. By complying with the initial request, individuals may come to see themselves as people who provide help when asked. Then, when confronted with the larger request, they agree in order to maintain the kind of consistency in attitudes and behavior that we described earlier. Although we don't know which of these two explanations is more accurate, it is clear that the foot-in-the-door strategy is effective (Burger, 1999; Guadagno et al., 2001; Gueguen, 2002).

▶ *The door-in-the-face technique.* A fund-raiser asks for a $500 contribution. You laughingly refuse, telling her that the amount is way out of your league. She then asks for a $10 contribution. What do you do? If you are like most people, you'll probably be a lot more compliant than you would be if she hadn't asked for the huge contribution first. In this tactic, called the *door-in-the-face technique*, someone makes a large request, expecting it to be refused, and follows it with a smaller one. Clearly this strategy, which is the opposite of the foot-in-the-door approach, has also proved to be effective (Abrahams & Bell, 1994; Millar, 2002).

In a field experiment that demonstrates the success of this approach, experimenters stopped college students on the street and asked them to agree to a substantial favor—acting as unpaid counselors for juvenile delinquents two hours a week for two years (Cialdini et al., 1975). Not surprisingly, no one agreed to make such an enormous commitment. But when they were later asked the considerably smaller favor of taking a group of delinquents on a two-hour trip to the zoo, half the people complied. In comparison, only 17 percent of a control group of participants who had not first received the larger request agreed.

The use of this technique is widespread. You may have tried it at some point yourself, perhaps by asking your parents for a large increase in your allowance and later settling for less. Similarly, television writers, by sometimes sprinkling their scripts with obscenities that they know will be cut out by network censors, hope to keep other key phrases intact (Cialdini, 2000).

▶ *The that's-not-all technique.* In this technique, a salesperson offers you a deal at an inflated price. But immediately after the initial offer, the salesperson offers an incentive, discount, or bonus to clinch the deal.

Although it sounds transparent, this practice can be quite effective. In one study, the experimenters set up a booth and sold cupcakes for 75 cents each. In one condition, the experimenters directly told customers that the price was 75 cents. But in another condition, they told customers that the price was originally $1 but had been reduced to 75 cents. As the that's-not-all technique would predict, more people bought cupcakes at the "reduced" price—even though it was identical to the price in the other experimental condition (Burger, 1986).

▶ *The not-so-free sample.* If you ever receive a free sample, keep in mind that it comes with a psychological cost. Although they may not couch it in these terms, salespeople who provide samples to potential customers do so to instigate the norm of reciprocity. The *norm of reciprocity* is the well-accepted societal standard dictating that we should treat other people as they treat us. Receiving a *not-so-free sample*, then, suggests the need for reciprocation—in the form of a purchase, of course (Cialdini, 1988; Spiller & Wymer, 2001).

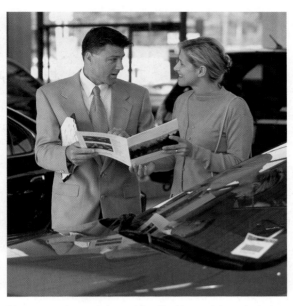

The persuasive techniques identified by social psychologists can be seen in practice at auto dealerships.

Companies seeking to sell their products to consumers often use the techniques identified by social psychologists for promoting compliance. But employers also use them to bring about compliance and raise the productivity of employees in the workplace. In fact, a close cousin to social psychology, **industrial-organizational (I/O) psychology,** considers issues such as worker motivation, satisfaction, safety, and productivity. I/O psychologists also focus on the operation and design of organizations, asking questions such as how decision making can be improved in large organizations and how the fit between workers and their jobs can be maximized.

Industrial-organizational (I/O) psychology: The branch of psychology focusing on work and job-related issues, including worker motivation, satisfaction, safety, and productivity.

Obedience: Following Direct Orders

Compliance techniques are used to gently lead people toward agreement with a request. In some cases, however, requests aim to produce **obedience,** a change in behavior in response to the commands of others. Although obedience is considerably less common than conformity and compliance, it does occur in several specific kinds of relationships. For example, we may show obedience to our bosses, teachers, or parents merely because of the power they hold to reward or punish us.

To acquire an understanding of obedience, consider for a moment how you might respond if a stranger said to you:

Obedience: A change in behavior in response to the commands of others.

> I've devised a new way of improving memory. All I need is for you to teach people a list of words and then give them a test. The test procedure requires only that you give learners a shock each time they make a mistake on the test. To administer the shocks you will use a "shock generator" that gives shocks ranging from 30 to 450 volts. You can see that the switches are labeled from "slight shock" through "danger: severe shock" at the top level, where there are three red X's. But don't worry; although the shocks may be painful, they will cause no permanent damage.

FIGURE 2 This impressive-looking "shock generator" led participants to believe they were administering electric shocks to another person, who was connected to the generator by "electrodes" that were attached to the skin. (Source: Copyright 1965 by Stanley Milgram. From the film *Obedience*, distributed by the New York University Film Library and Pennsylvania State University, PCR.)

PowerWeb: Behavioral Study of Obedience

www.mhhe.com/feldmanup7

Presented with this situation, you would be likely to think that neither you nor anyone else would go along with the stranger's unusual request. Clearly, it lies outside the bounds of what we consider good sense.

Or does it? Suppose the stranger asking for your help were a psychologist conducting an experiment. Or suppose it were your teacher, your employer, or your military commander—all people in authority with a seemingly legitimate reason for the request.

If you still believe it unlikely that you would comply—think again. The situation presented above describes a now-classic experiment conducted by social psychologist Stanley Milgram in the 1960s (Milgram, 1974). In the study, an experimenter told participants to give increasingly stronger shocks to another person as part of a study on learning (see Figure 2). In reality, the experiment had nothing to do with learning; the real issue under consideration was the degree to which participants would comply with the experimenter's requests. In fact, the "learner" supposedly receiving the shocks was a confederate who never really received any punishment.

Most people who hear a description of the experiment feel that it is unlikely that *any* participant would give the maximum level of shock—or, for that matter, any shock at all. Even a group of psychiatrists to whom the situation was described predicted that fewer than 2 percent of the participants would fully comply and administer the strongest shocks.

However, the actual results contradicted both experts' and nonexperts' predictions. Some 65 percent of the participants eventually used the highest setting on the shock generator—450 volts—to shock the learner. This obedience occurred even though the learner, who had mentioned at the start of the experiment that he had a heart condition, demanded to be released, screaming, "Let me out of here! Let me out of here! My heart's bothering me. Let me out of here!" Still, despite the learner's pleas, most participants continued to administer the shocks.

Why did so many individuals comply with the experimenter's demands? The participants, who were extensively interviewed after the experiment, said they obeyed primarily because they believed that the experimenter would be responsible for any potential ill effects that befell the learner. The participants accepted the experimenter's orders, then, because they thought that they personally could not be held accountable for their actions—they could always blame the experimenter (Darley, 1995; Blass, 1996).

Although most participants in the Milgram experiment said later that they felt the knowledge gained from the study outweighed the discomfort they may have felt, the experiment has been criticized for creating an extremely trying set of circumstances for the participants, thereby raising serious ethical concerns. (Undoubtedly, the experiment could not be conducted today because of ethical considerations.) Other critics have suggested that Milgram's methods were ineffective in creating a situation that actually mirrored real-world obedience. For example, how often are people placed in a situation in which someone orders them to continue hurting a victim, while the victim's protests are ignored (Miller, Collins, & Brief, 1995; Blass, 2000)?

Despite these concerns, Milgram's research remains the strongest laboratory demonstration of obedience. We need only consider actual instances of obedience to authority to witness some frightening real-life parallels. For instance, after World War II, the major defense that Nazi officers gave to excuse their participation in atrocities during the war was that they were "only following orders." Milgram's experiment, which was motivated in part by his desire to explain the behavior of everyday Germans during World War II, forces us to ask ourselves this question: Would we be able to withstand the intense power of authority? (To explore the Milgram study more thoroughly, complete **Interactivity 55–1.**)

INTERACTIVITY 55–1
Milgram obedience experiment

RECAP/EVALUATE/RETHINK

RECAP

What are the major sources and tactics of social influence?

- ▶ Social influence is the area of social psychology concerned with situations in which the actions of an individual or group affect the behavior of others. (p. 613)
- ▶ Conformity refers to changes in behavior or attitudes that result from a desire to follow the beliefs or standards of others. (p. 613)
- ▶ Compliance is behavior that results from direct social pressure. Among the ways of eliciting compliance are the foot-in-the-door, door-in-the-face, that's-not-all, and not-so-free-sample techniques. (p. 615)
- ▶ Obedience is a change in behavior in response to the commands of others. (p. 617)

EVALUATE

1. A _____ _____, or person who agrees with the dissenting viewpoint, is likely to reduce conformity.

2. Who pioneered the study of conformity?
   a. Skinner
   b. Asch
   c. Milgram
   d. Fiala

3. Which of the following techniques asks a person to comply with a small initial request to enhance the likelihood that the person will later comply with a larger request?
   a. Door-in-the-face
   b. Foot-in-the-door
   c. That's-not-all
   d. Not-so-free sample

4. The _____ _____ _____ _____ technique begins with an outrageous request that makes a subsequent, smaller request seem reasonable.

5. _____ is a change in behavior that is due to another person's orders.

RETHINK

1. Because persuasive techniques like those described in this section are so powerful, should the use of such techniques be outlawed? Should people be taught defenses against such techniques? Is the use of such techniques ethically and morally defensible? Why?

2. Why do you think the Milgram experiment is so controversial? What sorts of effects might the experiment have had on participants? Do you think the experiment would have had similar results if it had been conducted not in a laboratory setting, but among members of a social group (such as a fraternity or sorority) with strong pressures to conform?

Answers to Evaluate Questions

1. social supporter; 2. b; 3. b; 4. door-in-the-face; 5. obedience

KEY TERMS

social influence p. 613
conformity p. 613
status p. 614

social supporter p. 614
compliance p. 616

industrial-organizational
(I/O) psychology p. 617

obedience p. 617

Prejudice and Discrimination

What do you think when someone says, "He's African American," "She's Chinese," or "That's a woman driver"?

If you're like most people, you'll probably automatically form some sort of impression of what that person is like. The views that the speaker expressed represent **stereotypes,** generalized beliefs and expectations about social groups and their members. Stereotypes, which may be negative or positive, grow out of our tendency to categorize and organize the vast amount of information we encounter in our everyday lives. All stereotypes share the common feature of oversimplifying the world: We view individuals not in terms of their unique, personal characteristics, but in terms of characteristics we attribute to all the members of their particular group.

Stereotypes can lead to **prejudice,** negative (or positive) evaluations of groups and their members. For instance, racial prejudice occurs when a member of a racial group is evaluated in terms of race and not because of his or her own characteristics or abilities. Although prejudice can be positive ("I love the Irish"), social psychologists have focused on understanding the roots of negative prejudice ("I hate immigrants").

Common stereotypes and forms of prejudice involve racial, religious, and ethnic categories. Over the years, various groups have been called "lazy" or "shrewd" or "cruel" with varying degrees of regularity by those who are not group members. Even today, despite major progress toward reducing legally sanctioned forms of prejudice such as school segregation, stereotypes remain (Johnston, 1996; Madon et al., 2001).

Even people who on the surface appear to be unprejudiced may harbor hidden prejudice. For example, when white participants in experiments are shown faces on a computer screen so rapidly that they cannot consciously perceive the faces, they react more negatively to black than to white faces—an example of what has been called *modern racism.* You can get a sense of this phenomenon in yourself by going to the website http://implicit.harvard.edu/implicit/demo/index.jsp (Dovidio, Kawakami, & Gaertner, 2002; Greenwald et al., 2002).

Although usually backed by little or no evidence, stereotypes have harmful consequences. Acting on negative stereotypes results in **discrimination**—behavior directed toward individuals on the basis of their membership in a particular group. Discrimination can lead to exclusion from jobs, neighborhoods, and educational opportunities, and may result in members of particular groups receiving lower salaries and benefits. For an example, see the *Applying Psychology in the 21st Century* box.

⊛⊛⊛

Stereotyping not only leads to overt discrimination, it can also *cause* members of stereotyped groups to behave in ways that reflect the stereotype through a phenomenon known as the *self-fulfilling prophecy.* Self-fulfilling prophecies are expectations about the occurrence of a future event or behavior that act to increase the likelihood that the event or behavior *will* occur. For example, if people think that members of a particular group lack ambition, they may treat them in a way that actually brings

Stereotypes: Generalized beliefs and expectations about social groups and their members.

Prejudice: Negative (or positive) evaluations of groups and their members.

Discrimination: Behavior directed toward individuals on the basis of their membership in a particular group.

621

Discrimination in the Workplace: Can Your Name (or Hat) Cost You a Job?

Imagine you are in charge of hiring at your company. Each day, dozens of résumés arrive in your in box. Because your company receives many more résumés than there are job openings, you must determine quickly whether a particular résumé merits a follow-up phone call or e-mail. How would you decide which job candidates were worth pursuing? Would you look closely at each person's educational background and focus on his or her job experiences or skills? Or would you simply make a decision based on a person's name?

Surprisingly, people's names have a significant influence on hiring decisions, according to the results of new research. The names that may help land a job are stereotypically "white" names such as Brad, Kristen, Jay, and Carrie. The names that may hurt one's chances include Kareem, Keisha, Rasheed, and Aisha—stereotypically "black" names. In short, the research suggests that stereotypically "white" names may increase the likelihood that your résumé will be noticed positively, whereas stereotypically "black" names increase the likelihood that a potential employer will not respond (Krueger, 2002).

The research study that identified this phenomenon was carried out by Marianne Bertrand of the University of Chicago and Sendhil Mullainathan of the Massachusetts Institute of Technology. It involved sending out around 5,000 fake résumés in response to over 1,300 job advertisements placed in the *Chicago Tribune* and the *Boston Globe*. The researchers carefully crafted four distinct types of fake résumés, and all potential employers received one of each type: a highly qualified person with a white-sounding name, a highly qualified person with a black-sounding name, a less-qualified person with a white-sounding name, and a less-qualified person with a black-sounding name (Hearn, 2003).

After the researchers totaled all the follow-up letters, e-mails, and telephone calls they received for each fake applicant, they found that employers requested job interviews from 10.1 percent of the fictional applicants who had white-sounding names; only 6.7 percent of the applicants with black-sounding names were invited to an interview. In addition, among the 232 employers who requested an interview from at least one of the fictional applicants, 28 percent asked for interviews from equal numbers of fictional applicants with white- and black-sounding names. However, 51 percent requested an interview from more applicants with white-sounding names than from those with black-sounding names. Only 22 percent of employers requested an interview from more fictional applicants with black-sounding names than from those with white-sounding names (Bertrand & Mullainathan, 2002; Krueger, 2002).

Perhaps even more problematic is the fact that the qualifications of applicants with black-sounding names did not seem to matter. Highly qualified applicants with black-sounding names were not much more likely to earn interviews than were less-qualified applicants with black-sounding names. In contrast, highly qualified applicants with white-sounding names stood a much better chance of being contacted than did less-qualified applicants with white-sounding names (Krueger, 2002).

Names are not the only basis for discrimination in hiring. Social psychologists have examined a wide range of hiring discrimination, including problems related to age, gender, and sexual orientation. For example, in a recent study by researchers at Rice University in Houston, students were sent into mall stores to ask to fill out a job application. Half the students were given hats that said "Texan and Proud," and the other half wore "Gay and Proud" hats.

Although potential employers allowed almost as many students with "Gay" hats as "Texan" hats to complete an application, the employers spent less time talking with the "Gay" students than with the "Texan" students, and the employers were rated as more standoffish, nervous, and hostile by "Gay" students than by "Texan" students (Hebl et al., 2002). Unfortunately, whatever employers' reasons for discrimination, some job applicants seem to have an unfair advantage over others: Even the writing on your hat or the name on your birth certificate can help or harm your chances of being hired.

RETHINK

What do you think causes name-based discrimination? How might its effects be reduced? Do you think government agencies should send fake résumés and fake job applicants as part of their efforts to enforce antidiscrimination laws? Why or why not?

about a lack of ambition (Madon, Jussim, & Eccles, 1997; Oskamp, 2000; Edwards, 2001).

The Foundations of Prejudice

No one has ever been born disliking a particular racial, religious, or ethnic group. People learn to hate, in much the same way that they learn the alphabet.

According to *social learning approaches* to stereotyping and prejudice, the behavior of parents, other adults, and peers shapes children's feelings about members of various groups. For instance, bigoted parents may commend their children for expressing prejudiced attitudes. Likewise, young children learn prejudice by imitating the behavior of adult models. Such learning starts at an early age, as children as young as 3 years of age begin to show preferences for members of their own race (Katz, 1976; Yenerall, 1995; Olson & Fazio, 2001).

The mass media also provide a major source of information about stereotypes, not just for children but for adults as well. Even today, some television shows and movies portray Italians as Mafia-like mobsters, Jews as greedy bankers, and African Americans as promiscuous or lazy. When such inaccurate portrayals are the primary source of information about minority groups, they can lead to the development and maintenance of unfavorable stereotypes (Graves, 1999; Coltraine & Messineo, 2000).

Other explanations of prejudice and discrimination focus on how being a member of a particular group helps to magnify one's sense of self-esteem. According to *social identity theory*, we use group membership as a source of pride and self-worth. Slogans such as "gay pride" and "black is beautiful" illustrate that the groups to which we belong furnish us with a sense of self-respect (Tajfel, 1982; Rowley et al., 1998).

Like father, like son: Social learning approaches to stereotyping and prejudice suggest that attitudes and behaviors toward members of minority groups are learned through the observation of parents and other individuals. How can this cycle be broken?

However, the use of group membership to provide social respect produces an unfortunate outcome. In an effort to maximize our sense of self-esteem, we may come to think that our own group (our *ingroup*) is better than groups to which we don't belong (our *outgroups*). Consequently, we inflate the positive aspects of our ingroup—and, at the same time, devalue outgroups. Ultimately, we come to view members of outgroups as inferior to members of our ingroup (Turner et al., 1992). The end result is prejudice toward members of groups of which we are not a part.

Neither the social learning nor the social identity approach provides a full explanation for stereotyping and prejudice. For instance, some psychologists argue that prejudice results when there is perceived competition for scarce societal resources. Thus, when competition exists for jobs or housing, members of majority groups may believe (however unjustly or inaccurately) that minority group members are hindering their efforts to attain their goals, and this can lead to prejudice. In addition, other explanations for prejudice emphasize human cognitive limitations that lead us to categorize people on the basis of visually conspicuous physical features such as race, sex, and ethnic group. Such categorization can lead to the development of stereotypes and, ultimately, to discriminatory behavior (Bobo & Hutchings, 2001; Dovidio, 2001; Fiske, 2002). (To learn more about prejudice and discrimination, complete **Interactivity 56–1.**)

INTERACTIVITY 56–1

Prejudice

Reducing the Consequences of Prejudice and Discrimination

How can we diminish the effects of prejudice and discrimination? Psychologists have developed several strategies that have proved effective, including these:

- ▶ *Increasing contact between the target of stereotyping and the holder of the stereotype.* Research has shown that increasing the amount of interaction between people can reduce negative stereotyping. But only certain kinds of contact are likely to reduce prejudice and discrimination. Situations in which contact is relatively intimate, the individuals are of equal status, or participants must cooperate with one another or are dependent on one another are more likely to reduce stereotyping (Gaertner et al., 1996; Oskamp, 2000; Pettigrew & Tropp, 2000).

- ▶ *Making values and norms against prejudice more conspicuous.* Sometimes just reminding people about the values they already hold regarding equality and fair treatment of others is enough to reduce discrimination Similarly, people who hear others making strong, vehement antiracist statements are subsequently more likely to strongly condemn racism (Blanchard, Lilly, & Vaughn, 1991; Dovidio, Kawakami, & Gaertner, 2000).

- ▶ *Providing information about the objects of stereotyping.* Probably the most direct means of changing stereotypical and discriminatory attitudes is education: teaching people to be more aware of the positive characteristics of targets of stereotyping. For instance, when the meaning of puzzling behavior is explained to people who hold stereotypes, they may come to appreciate the true significance of the behavior—even though it may still appear foreign and perhaps even threatening (Schaller et al., 1996; Isbell & Tyler, 2003).

- ▶ *Reducing stereotype vulnerability.* Social psychologist Claude Steele suggests that many African Americans suffer from *stereotype vulnerability*, obstacles to performance that stem from their awareness of society's stereotypes regarding minority group members. He argues that African American students who receive instruction from teachers who may doubt their abilities and set up special remedial programs to assist them may come to accept society's stereotypes and believe that they are prone to fail (Steele, 1992, 1997; Steele, Spencer, & Aronson, 2002).

Such beliefs can have devastating effects. When confronted with an academic task, African American students may fear that their performance will simply confirm society's negative stereotypes. The immediate consequence of this fear is anxiety that hampers performance. But the long-term consequences may be even worse: Doubting their ability to perform successfully in academic environments, African Americans may decide that the risks of failure are so great that it is not worth the effort even to attempt to do well. Ultimately, they may "disidentify" with academic success by minimizing the importance of academic endeavors (Steele, 1997; Stone, 1999, 2002).

However, Steele's analysis suggests that African Americans may be able to overcome their predicament. Specifically, schools can design intervention programs to teach minority group members about their vulnerability to stereotypes and illustrate that the stereotypes are inaccurate. Members of minority groups, convinced that they have the potential to be academically successful, may become immune to the potentially treacherous consequences of negative stereotypes.

RECAP/EVALUATE/RETHINK

RECAP

What is the distinction among stereotypes, prejudice, and discrimination?

- ▶ Stereotypes are generalized beliefs and expectations about social groups and their members. (p. 621)
- ▶ Prejudice is the negative (or positive) evaluation of groups and their members. (p. 621)
- ▶ Stereotyping and prejudice can lead to discrimination, behavior directed toward individuals on the basis of their membership in a particular group. (p. 621)
- ▶ Self-fulfilling prophecies are expectations about the occurrence of future events or behaviors that act to increase the likelihood that the events or behaviors will actually occur. (p. 621)
- ▶ According to social learning approaches, children learn stereotyping and prejudice by observing the behavior of parents, other adults, and peers. Social identity theory suggests that group membership is used as a source of pride and self-worth, and this may lead people to think of their own group as better than others. (p. 623)

How can we reduce prejudice and discrimination?

- ▶ Among the ways of reducing prejudice and discrimination are increasing contact, demonstrating positive

values against prejudice, and providing information about the target of the attribution or stereotype. (p. 624)
- ▶ Stereotype vulnerability relates to the obstacles to performance that stem from minority group members' awareness of society's stereotypes regarding them. (p. 624)

EVALUATE

1. Any expectation—positive or negative—about an individual solely on the basis of that person's membership in a group can be a stereotype. True or false?
2. The negative (or positive) evaluations of groups and their members is called
   a. Stereotyping
   b. Prejudice
   c. Self-fulfilling prophecy
   d. Discrimination
3. Paul is a store manager who does not expect women to succeed in business. He therefore offers important, high-profile responsibilities only to men. If the female employees fail to move up in the company, this could be an example of a _____-_____ prophecy.

RETHINK

1. How are stereotypes, prejudice, and discrimination related? In a society committed to equality, which of the three should be changed first? Why? Will changing one of these things lead to changes in the other two?

2. Do you think women can be victims of stereotype vulnerability? In what topical areas might this occur? Can men be victims of stereotype vulnerability? Why?

Answers to Evaluate Questions

1. true; 2. b; 3. self-fulfilling

KEY TERMS

stereotypes p. 621

prejudice p. 621

discrimination p. 621

Positive and Negative Social Behavior

Are people basically good or bad?

Like philosophers and theologians, social psychologists have pondered the basic nature of humanity. Is it represented mainly by the violence and cruelty we see throughout the world, or does something special about human nature permit loving, considerate, unselfish, and even noble behavior as well?

We turn to two routes that social psychologists have followed in seeking answers to these questions. We first consider what they have learned about the sources of our attraction to others, and we end with a look at the two sides of the coin of human behavior: aggression and helping.

⚆⚆⚆

Why are we attracted to certain people, and what progression do social relationships follow?

What factors underlie aggression and prosocial behavior?

Liking and Loving: Interpersonal Attraction and the Development of Relationships

Nothing is more important in most people's lives than their feelings for others, and consequently, it is not surprising that liking and loving have become a major focus of interest for social psychologists. Known more formally as the study of **interpersonal attraction** or **close relationships**, this area addresses the factors that lead to positive feelings for others.

Interpersonal attraction (or close relationship): Positive feelings for others; liking and loving.

HOW DO I LIKE THEE? LET ME COUNT THE WAYS

By far the greatest amount of research has focused on liking, probably because it is easier for investigators conducting short-term experiments to produce states of liking in strangers who have just met than to instigate and observe loving relationships over long periods. Consequently, research has given us a good deal of knowledge about the factors that initially attract two people to each other (Harvey & Weber, 2002). The important factors considered by social psychologists are the following:

- ▶ *Proximity.* If you live in a dormitory or an apartment, consider the friends you made when you first moved in. Chances are, you became friendliest with those who lived geographically closest to you. In fact, this is one of the more firmly established findings in the literature on interpersonal attraction: *Proximity* leads to liking (Festinger, Schachter, & Back, 1950; Burgoon et al., 2002).
- ▶ *Mere exposure.* Repeated exposure to a person is often sufficient to produce attraction. Interestingly, repeated exposure to *any* stimulus—a person, picture, compact disc, or virtually anything—usually makes us like the stimulus more. Becoming familiar with a person can evoke positive feelings; we then transfer the positive feelings stemming from familiarity to the person himself or herself. There are exceptions, though. In cases of strongly negative initial interactions,

"I'm attracted to you, but then I'm attracted to me, too."

627

repeated exposure is unlikely to cause us to like a person more. Instead, the more we are exposed to him or her, the more we may dislike the individual (Kruglanski, Freund, & Bar Tal, 1996; Zajonc, 2001).

▶ *Similarity.* Folk wisdom tells us that birds of a feather flock together. However, it also maintains that opposites attract. Social psychologists have come up with a clear verdict regarding which of the two statements is correct: We tend to like those who are similar to us. Discovering that others have similar attitudes, values, or traits promotes our liking for them. Furthermore, the more similar others are, the more we like them. One reason similarity increases the likelihood of interpersonal attraction is that we assume that people with similar attitudes will evaluate us positively. Because we experience a strong **reciprocity-of-liking effect** (a tendency to like those who like us), knowing that someone evaluates us positively promotes our attraction to that person. In addition, we assume that when we like someone else, that person likes us in return (Metee & Aronson, 1974; Bates, 2002).

▶ *Physical attractiveness.* For most people, the equation *beautiful = good* is quite true. As a result, physically attractive people are more popular than are physically unattractive ones, if all other factors are equal. This finding, which contradicts the values that most people say they hold, is apparent even in childhood—with nursery-school-age children rating their peers' popularity on the basis of attractiveness—and continues into adulthood. Indeed, physical attractiveness may be the single most important element promoting initial liking in college dating situations, although its influence eventually decreases when people get to know each other better (Langlois et al., 2000; Aharan et al., 2001; Marcus & Miller, 2003). (To learn more about how our first impressions affect liking, try **Interactivity 57–1.**)

These factors alone, of course, do not account for liking. For example, surveys have sought to identify the factors critical in friendships. In a questionnaire answered by some 40,000 respondents, people identified the qualities most valued in a friend as the ability to keep confidences, loyalty, and warmth and affection, followed closely by supportiveness, frankness, and a sense of humor (Parlee, 1979). The results are summarized in Figure 1.

Reciprocity-of-liking effect: A tendency to like those who like us.

INTERACTIVITY 57–1

First impressions and attraction

FIGURE I These are the key qualities looked for in a friend according to some 40,000 respondents to a questionnaire.

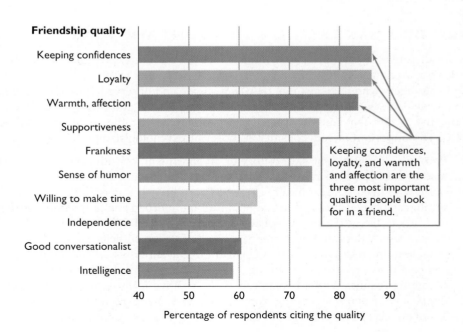

HOW DO I LOVE THEE? LET ME COUNT THE WAYS

Whereas our knowledge of what makes people like one another is extensive, our understanding of love is more limited in scope and recently acquired. For some time, many social psychologists believed that love is as a phenomenon too difficult to observe and study in a controlled, scientific way. However, love is such a central issue in most people's lives that eventually social psychologists could not resist its allure.

As a first step, researchers tried to identify the characteristics that distinguish between mere liking and full-blown love. They discovered that love is not simply a greater quantity of liking, but a qualitatively different psychological state. For instance, at least in its early stages, love includes relatively intense physiological arousal, an all-encompassing interest in another individual, fantasizing about the other, and relatively rapid swings of emotion. Similarly, love, unlike liking, includes elements of passion, closeness, fascination, exclusiveness, sexual desire, and intense caring. We idealize partners by exaggerating their good qualities and minimizing their imperfections (Murray & Holmes, 1997; Garza-Guerrero, 2000).

Other researchers have theorized that there are two main types of love: passionate love and companionate love. **Passionate (or romantic) love** represents a state of intense absorption in someone. It includes intense physiological arousal, psychological interest, and caring for the needs of another. In contrast, **companionate love** is the strong affection we have for those with whom our lives are deeply involved. The love we feel for our parents, other family members, and even some close friends falls into the category of companionate love (Baumeister & Bratslavsky, 1999; Regan, 2000; Masuda, 2003).

Psychologist Robert Sternberg makes an even finer differentiation between types of love. He proposes that love consists of three parts: a *decision/commitment component*, encompassing the initial cognition that one loves someone and the longer-term feelings of commitment to maintain love; an *intimacy component*, encompassing feelings of closeness and connectedness; and a *passion component*, made up of the motivational drives relating to sex, physical closeness, and romance. These three components combine to produce the different types of love (Barnes & Sternberg, 1997; Sternberg, Hojjat, & Barnes, 2001; see Figure 2).

Is love a necessary ingredient in a good marriage? Yes, if you live in the United States. In contrast, it's considerably less important in other cultures. Although mutual attraction and love are the two most important characteristics desired in a mate by men and women in the United States, men in China rated good health as most

PowerWeb: Is Love a Mechanism of Evolution?

www.mhhe.com/feldmanup7

PowerWeb: Finding Real Love

www.mhhe.com/feldmanup7

Passionate (or romantic) love: A state of intense absorption in someone that includes intense physiological arousal, psychological interest, and caring for the needs of another.

Companionate love: The strong affection we have for those with whom our lives are deeply involved.

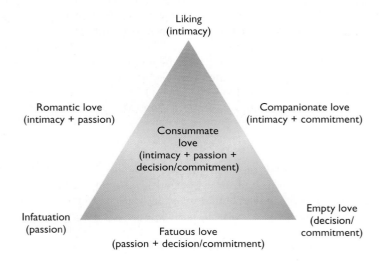

FIGURE 2 According to Sternberg, love has three main components: intimacy, passion, and decision/commitment. Different combinations of these components can create other types of love. Nonlove contains none of the three components.

FIGURE 3 Although love may be an important factor in choosing a marriage partner if you live in the United States, other cultures place less importance on it. (Source: Buss et al., 1990.)

Rank Ordering of Desired Characteristics in a Mate						
	United States		China		South Africa Zulu	
	Females	Males	Females	Males	Females	Males
Mutual attraction—love	1	1	8	4	5	10
Emotional stability and maturity	2	2	1	5	2	1
Dependable character	3	3	7	6	1	3
Pleasing disposition	4	4	16	13	3	4
Education and intelligence	5	5	4	8	6	6
Good health	9	6	3	1	4	5
Good looks	13	7	15	11	16	14
Sociability	8	8	9	12	8	11
Desire for home and children	7	9	2	2	9	9
Refinement, neatness	12	10	10	7	10	7
Ambition and industriousness	6	11	5	10	7	8
Similar education	10	12	12	15	12	12
Good cook and housekeeper	16	13	11	9	15	2
Favorable social status or rating	14	14	13	14	14	17
Similar religious background	15	15	18	18	11	16
Good financial prospect	11	16	14	16	13	18
Chastity (no prior sexual intercourse)	18	17	6	3	18	13
Similar political background	17	18	17	17	17	15

important, and women there rated emotional stability and maturity as most important. Among the Zulu in South Africa, men rated emotional stability first and women rated dependable character first (Buss et al., 1990; see Figure 3).

Liking and loving clearly show a positive side of human social behavior. Now we turn to behaviors that are just as much a part of social behavior: aggression and helping behavior.

Aggression and Prosocial Behavior: Hurting and Helping Others

Drive-by shootings, carjackings, and abductions are just a few examples of the violence that seems all too common today. Yet we also find examples of generous, unselfish, thoughtful behavior that suggest a more optimistic view of humankind. Consider, for instance, people such as Mother Teresa, who ministered to the poor in India. Or contemplate the simple kindnesses of life: lending a valued compact disc, stopping to help a child who has fallen off her bicycle, or merely sharing a candy bar with a friend. Such instances of helping are no less characteristic of human behavior than are the distasteful examples of aggression (Miller, 1999).

HURTING OTHERS: AGGRESSION

We need look no further than the daily paper or the nightly news to be bombarded with examples of aggression, both on a societal level (war, invasion, assassination) and on an individual level (crime, child abuse, and the many petty cruelties humans are capable of inflicting on one another). Is such aggression an inevitable part of the human condition? Or is aggression primarily a product of particular circumstances that, if changed, could lead to its reduction?

Is This Aggression?

To see for yourself the difficulties involved in defining aggression, consider each of the following acts and determine whether it represents aggressive behavior—according to your own definition of aggression.

1. A spider eats a fly. Yes ___ No ___
2. Two wolves fight for the leadership of the pack. Yes ___ No ___
3. A soldier shoots an enemy at the front line. Yes ___ No ___
4. The warden of a prison executes a convicted criminal. Yes ___ No ___
5. A man viciously kicks a cat. Yes ___ No ___
6. A man, while cleaning a window, knocks over a flower pot, which, in falling, injures a pedestrian. Yes ___ No ___
7. Mr. X, a notorious gossip, speaks disparagingly of many people of his acquaintance. Yes ___ No ___
8. A man mentally rehearses a murder he is about to commit. Yes ___ No ___
9. An angry son purposely fails to write to his mother, who is expecting a letter and will be hurt if none arrives. Yes ___ No ___
10. An enraged boy tries with all his might to inflict injury on his antagonist, a bigger boy, but is not successful in doing so. His efforts simply amuse the bigger boy. Yes ___ No ___
11. A senator does not protest the escalation of bombing to which she is normally opposed. Yes ___ No ___
12. A farmer beheads a chicken and prepares it for supper. Yes ___ No ___
13. A hunter kills an animal and mounts it as a trophy. Yes ___ No ___
14. A physician gives a flu shot to a screaming child. Yes ___ No ___
15. A boxer gives his opponent a bloody nose. Yes ___ No ___
16. A Girl Scout tries to assist an elderly woman but trips her by accident. Yes ___ No ___
17. A bank robber is shot in the back while trying to escape. Yes ___ No ___
18. A tennis player smashes her racket after missing a volley. Yes ___ No ___
19. A person commits suicide. Yes ___ No ___
20. A cat kills a mouse, parades around with it, and then discards it. Yes ___ No ___

FIGURE 4 What is aggression? It depends on how the word is defined and in what context it is used. (Source: Adapted from Benjamin, 1985, p. 41.)

The difficulty of answering such knotty questions becomes apparent as soon as we consider how best to define the term *aggression.* Depending on the way we define the word, many examples of inflicted pain or injury may or may not qualify as aggression (see Figure 4). For instance, a rapist is clearly acting with aggression toward his victim. On the other hand, it is less certain that a physician carrying out an emergency medical procedure without an anesthetic, thereby causing incredible pain to the patient, should be considered aggressive.

Most social psychologists define aggression in terms of the intent and the purpose behind the behavior. **Aggression** is intentional injury of or harm to another person (Berkowitz, 1993). By this definition, the rapist is clearly acting aggressively, whereas the physician causing pain during a medical procedure is not.

We turn now to several approaches to aggressive behavior developed by social psychologists (Berkowitz, 1993; Geen & Donnerstein, 1998).

Instinct Approaches: Aggression as a Release. If you have ever punched an adversary in the nose, you may have experienced a certain satisfaction, despite your better judgment. Instinct theories, noting the prevalence of aggression not only in humans but in animals as well, propose that aggression is primarily the outcome of innate—or inborn—urges.

Sigmund Freud was one of the first to suggest, as part of his theory of personality, that aggression is a primary instinctual drive. Konrad Lorenz, an ethologist

Aggression: Intentional injury of or harm to another person.

Catharsis: The process of discharging built-up aggressive energy.

(a scientist who studies animal behavior), expanded on Freud's notions by arguing that humans, along with members of other species, have a fighting instinct, which in earlier times ensured protection of food supplies and weeded out the weaker of the species (Lorenz, 1966, 1974). Lorenz's instinct approach led to the controversial notion that aggressive energy constantly builds up within an individual until the person finally discharges it in a process called **catharsis.** The longer the energy builds up, says Lorenz, the greater will be the amount of the aggression displayed when it is discharged.

Probably the most controversial idea to come out of instinct theories of aggression is Lorenz's proposal that society should provide acceptable means of permitting catharsis. For example, he suggested that participation in aggressive sports and games would prevent the discharge of aggression in less socially desirable ways. However, little research has found evidence for the existence of a pent-up reservoir of aggression that needs to be released. In fact, some studies flatly contradict the notion of catharsis, leading psychologists to look to other explanations for aggression (Anderson & Bushman, 2001; Bushman, Baumeister, & Phillips, 2001; Bushman, 2002).

Frustration-Aggression Approaches: Aggression as a Reaction to Frustration. Suppose you've been working on a paper that is due for a class early the next morning, and your computer printer runs out of ink just before you can print out the paper. You rush to the store to buy more ink, only to find the sales clerk locking the door for the day. Even though the clerk can see you gesturing and begging him to open the door, he refuses, shrugging his shoulders and pointing to a sign that indicates when the store will open the next day. At that moment, the feelings you experience toward the sales clerk probably place you on the verge of real aggression, and you are undoubtedly seething inside.

Frustration: The thwarting or blocking of some ongoing, goal-directed behavior

Frustration-aggression theory tries to explain aggression in terms of events like this one. When first put forward, the theory said flatly that frustration *always* leads to aggression of some sort, and that aggression is *always* the result of some frustration, where **frustration** is defined as the thwarting or blocking of some ongoing, goal-directed behavior (Dollard et al., 1939). More recent formulations, however, have modified the original theory, suggesting instead that frustration produces anger, leading to a *readiness* to act aggressively. Whether actual aggression occurs depends on the presence of *aggressive cues*, stimuli that have been associated in the past with actual aggression or violence and that will trigger aggression again. In addition, frustration produces aggression to the degree to which it produces negative feelings (Berkowitz, 1989, 1990).

What kinds of stimuli act as aggressive cues? They can range from the most overt, such as the presence of weapons, to the subtlest, such as the mere mention of the name of an individual who behaved violently in the past. For example, in one experiment, angered participants behaved significantly more aggressively when in the presence of a rifle and a revolver than they did in a comparable situation in which no guns were present (Berkowitz & LePage, 1967). Similarly, frustrated participants in an experiment who had viewed a violent movie were more physically aggressive toward a confederate with the same name as the star of the movie than they were toward a confederate with a different name (Berkowitz & Geen, 1966). It appears, then, that frustration does lead to aggression, at least when aggressive cues are present (Carlson, Marcus-Newhall, & Miller, 1990).

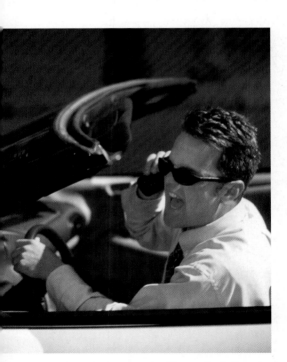

Is road rage a result of frustration? According to frustration-aggression approaches, frustration is a likely cause.

Observational Learning Approaches: Learning to Hurt Others. Do we learn to be aggressive? The observational learning (sometimes called social learning) approach to aggression says that we do. Taking an almost opposite view from instinct theories, which focus on innate explanations of aggression, observational learning theory emphasizes that social and environmental conditions can teach individuals to be aggressive. The theory sees aggression not as inevitable, but rather as a learned response that can be understood in terms of rewards and punishments.

Observational learning theory pays particular attention not only to direct rewards and punishments that individuals themselves receive, but also to the rewards and punishments that models—individuals who provide a guide to appropriate behavior—receive for their aggressive behavior. According to observational learning theory, people observe the behavior of models and the subsequent consequences of that behavior. If the consequences are positive, the behavior is likely to be imitated when observers find themselves in a similar situation.

Suppose, for instance, a girl hits her younger brother when he damages one of her new toys. Whereas instinct theory would suggest that the aggression had been pent up and was now being discharged, and frustration-aggression theory would examine the girl's frustration at no longer being able to use her new toy, observational learning theory would look to previous situations in which the girl had viewed others being rewarded for their aggression. For example, perhaps she had watched a friend get to play with a toy after he painfully twisted it out of the hand of another child.

Observational learning theory has received wide research support. For example, nursery-school-age children who have watched an adult model behave aggressively and then receive reinforcement for it later display similar behavior themselves if they have been angered, insulted, or frustrated after exposure. Furthermore, a significant amount of research links watching television shows containing violence with subsequent viewer aggression (Bandura, 1983; Anderson & Dill, 2000; Huesmann, Moise-Titus, Podolski, & Eron, 2003).

PowerWeb: Taking Sides
www.mhhe.com/feldmanup7

HELPING OTHERS: THE BRIGHTER SIDE OF HUMAN NATURE

Turning away from aggression, we move now to the opposite—and brighter—side of the coin of human nature: helping behavior. Helping behavior, or **prosocial behavior** as it is more formally known, has been considered under many different conditions. However, the question that psychologists have looked at most closely relates to bystander intervention in emergency situations. What are the factors that lead someone to help a person in need?

One critical factor is the number of others present. When more than one person witnesses an emergency situation, a sense of diffusion of responsibility can arise among the bystanders. **Diffusion of responsibility** is the tendency for people to feel that responsibility for acting is shared, or diffused, among those present. The more people who are present in an emergency, the less personally responsible each individual feels—and therefore the less help he or she provides (Latané & Nida, 1981; Markey, 2000; Barron & Yechiam, 2002).

Although most research on helping behavior supports the diffusion-of-responsibility formulation, other factors are clearly involved in helping behavior. According to a model developed by Latané and Darley (1970), the process of helping involves four basic steps (see Figure 5):

▶ *Noticing a person, event, or situation that may require help.*
▶ *Interpreting the event as one that requires help.* Even if we notice an event, it may be sufficiently ambiguous for us to interpret it as a nonemergency situation (Shotland, 1985; Harrison & Wells, 1991). It is here that the presence of others first affects helping behavior. The presence of inactive others may indicate to us that a situation does not require help—a judgment we do not necessarily make if we are alone.
▶ *Assuming responsibility for helping.* It is at this point that diffusion of responsibility is likely to occur if others are present. Moreover, a bystander's particular expertise is likely to play a role in determining whether he or she helps. For instance, if people with training in medical aid or lifesaving techniques are present, untrained bystanders are less likely to intervene

Prosocial behavior: Helping behavior.

Diffusion of responsibility: The tendency for people to feel that responsibility for acting is shared, or diffused, among those present.

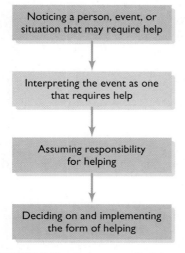

FIGURE 5 The basic steps of helping. (Source: Based on Latané & Darley, 1970).

because they feel they have less expertise. This point was well illustrated in a study by Jane and Irving Piliavin (1972), who conducted a field experiment in which an individual seemed to collapse in a subway car with blood trickling out of the corner of his mouth. The results of the experiment showed that bystanders were less likely to help when a person (actually a confederate) who appeared to be a medical intern was present than when the "intern" was not present.

▶ *Deciding on and implementing the form of helping.* After we assume responsibility for helping, we must decide how to provide assistance. Helping can range from very indirect forms of intervention, such as calling the police, to more direct forms, such as giving first aid or taking the victim to a hospital. Most social psychologists use a *rewards-costs approach* for helping to predict the nature of the assistance a bystander will choose to provide. The general notion is that the rewards for helping, as perceived by the bystander, must outweigh the costs if helping is to occur, and most research tends to support this notion (Bell et al., 1995).

After we determine the nature of the assistance needed, one step remains: the implementation of the assistance. A rewards-costs analysis suggests that we are most likely to use the least costly form of implementation. However, this is not always the case: In some situations, people behave altruistically. **Altruism** is helping behavior that is beneficial to others but clearly requires self-sacrifice. For example, people who helped strangers escape from the burning World Trade Center towers during the September 11, 2001, terrorist attack in New York City, putting themselves at mortal risk, would be considered altruistic (Batson, 1991; Shapiro & Gabbard, 1994; Krueger, Hicks, & McGue, 2001).

People who intervene in emergency situations tend to possess certain personality characteristics that differentiate them from nonhelpers. For example, helpers are more self-assured, sympathetic, emotionally understanding, and have greater *empathy* (a personality trait in which someone observing another person experiences the emotions of that person) than are nonhelpers (Sibicky, Schroeder, & Dovidio, 1995; Batson, Ahmad, Lishner, & Tsang, 2002).

Still, most social psychologists agree that no single set of attributes differentiates helpers from nonhelpers. For the most part, temporary situational factors (such as

Altruism: Helping behavior that is beneficial to others but clearly requires self-sacrifice.

Altruism is often the only bright side of a natural disaster.

the mood we're in) determine whether we will intervene in a situation requiring aid (Eisenberg, 1991; Knight et al., 1994; Bersoff, 1999).

At one time or another, almost everyone feels angry. The anger may have come as a result of a frustrating situation, or it may be due to the behavior of another individual. The way we deal with such anger may determine the difference between a promotion and a lost job or a broken relationship and one that mends itself.

BECOMING AN INFORMED CONSUMER of Psychology

Dealing Effectively with Anger

Social psychologists who have studied the topic suggest several good ways to deal with anger, strategies that maximize the potential for positive consequences (Deffenbacher, 1988, 1996; Bass, 1996; Nelson & Finch, 2000). Among the most useful strategies are the following:

▶ *Look again at the anger-provoking situation from the perspective of others.* By taking others' point of view, you may be able to understand the situation better, and with increased understanding you may become more tolerant of the apparent shortcomings of others.

▶ *Minimize the importance of the situation.* Does it really matter that someone is driving too slowly and that you'll be late to an appointment as a result? Reinterpret the situation in a way that is less bothersome.

▶ *Fantasize about getting even—but don't act on it.* Fantasy provides a safety valve. In your fantasies, you can yell at that unfair professor all you want and suffer no consequences at all. However, don't spend too much time brooding: Fantasize, but then move on.

▶ *Relax.* By teaching yourself the kinds of relaxation techniques used in systematic desensitization (see Figure 2 in Module 51), you can help reduce your reactions to anger. In turn, your anger may dissipate.

No matter which of these strategies you try, above all, don't ignore your anger. People who always try to suppress their anger may experience a variety of consequences, such as self-condemnation, frustration, and even physical illness (Engebretson & Stoney, 1995; Sharma, Ghosh, & Spielberger, 1995).

RECAP/EVALUATE/RETHINK

RECAP

Why are we attracted to certain people, and what progression do social relationships follow?

▶ The primary determinants of liking include proximity, exposure, similarity, and physical attractiveness. (p. 627)

▶ Loving is distinguished from liking by the presence of intense physiological arousal, an all-encompassing interest in another, fantasies about the other, rapid swings of emotion, fascination, sexual desire, exclusiveness, and strong feelings of caring. (p. 629)

▶ Love can be categorized into two broad types: passionate and companionate. In addition, love has several components: intimacy, passion, and decision/commitment. (p. 629)

What factors underlie aggression and prosocial behavior?

▶ Aggression is intentional injury of or harm to another person. (p. 630)

▶ Explanations of aggression include instinct approaches, frustration-aggression theory, and observational learning. (p. 631)

▶ Helping behavior in emergencies is determined in part by the phenomenon of diffusion of responsibility, which results in a lower likelihood of helping when more people are present. (p. 633)

▶ Deciding to help is the outcome of a four-stage process consisting of noticing a possible need for help, interpreting the situation as requiring aid, assuming responsibility for taking action, and deciding on and implementing a form of assistance. (p. 633)

EVALUATE

1. We tend to like people who are similar to us. True or false?
2. Which of the following sets are the three components of love proposed by Sternberg?
   a. Passion, closeness, sexuality
   b. Attraction, desire, complementarity
   c. Passion, intimacy, decision/commitment
   d. Commitment, caring, sexuality
3. Based on research evidence, which of the following might be the best way to reduce the amount of fighting a young boy does?
   a. Take him to the gym and let him work out on the boxing equipment.
   b. Make him repeatedly watch violent scenes from the film *The Matrix Reloaded* in the hope that it will provide catharsis.
   c. Reward him if he doesn't fight during a certain period.
   d. Ignore it and let it die out naturally.
4. If a person in a crowd does not help in an apparent emergency situation because many other people are present, that person is falling victim to the phenomenon of _____ _____.

RETHINK

1. Can love be studied scientifically? Is there an elusive quality to love that makes it at least partially unknowable? How would you define "falling in love"? How would you study it?
2. How would the aggression of Timothy McVeigh, convicted of blowing up a federal building in Oklahoma City, be interpreted by proponents of the three main approaches to the study of aggression: instinct approaches, frustration-aggression approaches, and observational learning approaches? Do you think any of these approaches fits the McVeigh case more closely than the others?

Answers to Evaluate Questions

1. true; 2. c; 3. c; 4. diffusion of responsibility

KEY TERMS

interpersonal attraction (or close relationship) p. 627
reciprocity-of-liking effect p. 628

passionate (or romantic) love p. 629
companionate love p. 629
aggression p. 631

catharsis p. 632
frustration p. 632
prosocial behavior p. 633

diffusion of responsibility p. 633
altruism p. 634

Looking Back

Psychology on the Web

1. Find examples on the Web of advertisements or other persuasive messages that use central route processing and peripheral route processing. What type of persuasion appears to be more prevalent on the Web? For what type of persuasion does the Web appear to be better suited? Is there a difference between Web-based advertising and other forms of advertising?

2. Is "hate crimes legislation" a good idea? Use the Web to find at least two discussions of hate crimes legislation—one in favor and one opposed—and summarize in writing the main issues and arguments presented. Using your knowledge of prejudice and aggression, evaluate the arguments for and against hate crimes legislation. State your opinion about whether this type of legislation is advisable.

3. After completing Interactivity 56–1 on prejudice, use the Web to identify two recent incidents in the news in which prejudice played a role. Summarize the incidents and discuss the ways such prejudice might have been prevented.

Epilogue

We have touched on some of the major ideas, research topics, and experimental findings of social psychology. We examined how people form, maintain, and change attitudes and how they form impressions of others and assign attributions to them. We also saw how groups, through conformity and tactics of compliance, can influence individuals' actions and attitudes. Finally, we discussed interpersonal relationships, including both liking and loving, and looked at the two sides of a coin that represent the extremes of social behavior: aggression and prosocial behavior.

Turn back to the Prologue to this set of modules, which describes how three bystanders rescued two infants trapped in a car. Use your understanding of social psychology to consider the following questions.

1. What factors would a social psychologist consider in examining why the rescuers helped out?

2. If there had been more than the three men present when the car plunged into the bayou, would it have been more or less likely that someone would have helped? Why?

3. Given what social psychologists know about the factors that lead people to be helpful, do you believe that the men's helpfulness was caused by situational factors or that it had more to do with their personalities? Why?

4. What are some ways in which the incidence of helping behavior can be increased and the incidence of aggressive and antisocial behavior can be discouraged?

1 Social Influence is Part of Everyday Life

In many aspects of life, including sales, politics, and even romance, people try to influence your beliefs and behavior. Psychologists have identified a number of these social influence techniques that increase conformity and the ease with which you are persuaded.

2 Attractiveness and Status

Groups exert pressure that causes you to conform and change your opinions to match the group norms. You are more likely to conform when a group consists of attractive and high-status individuals.

3 Public Proclamations

You are also more likely to conform to a group when you make subjective judgments and when you are asked to declare your opinion publicly.

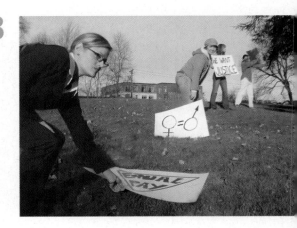

4 Groupthink

Groupthink is an extreme form of group conformity that occurs when a group has a strong desire to achieve consensus. Groupthink occurs when the group forms an early consensus and when the members believe that the group is nearly invulnerable and occupies the high moral ground. NASA is often cited as an organization in which groupthink has occurred. Groupthink might have contributed to the explosion of the space shuttle *Challenger* in 1986 and, more recently, the loss of the crew of the *Columbia*.

Foot-in-the-Door Technique 5

The foot-in-the-door technique begins with a small, easily-agreed-to request. After agreement, though, you are more likely to agree to a larger subsequent request.

6 Door-in-the-Face Technique

The door-in-the-face technique begins with a large request, which you are likely to immediately refuse. However, you may feel guilty and then become likely to agree to a smaller follow-up request.

7 And That's Not All!

A salesman using this technique begins with an overpriced offer but then sweetens the deal with a series of "discounts" and "bonuses."

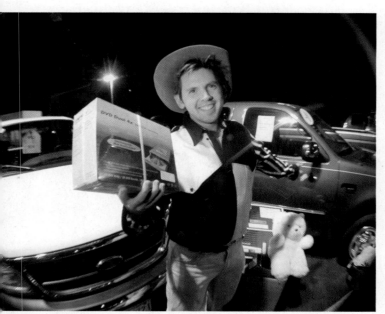

The Not-So-Free Gift Technique 8

Receipt of a "free" gift makes you feel indebted to the giver and makes it more likely that you will later comply with a request from that person.

Appendix:
Going by the Numbers:
Statistics in Psychology

Prologue

Selma Vorwerk

As the boat moved nearer to shore, the outline of the Statue of Liberty was plainly visible in the distance. Closer and closer it came, sending a chill down the spine of Selma Vorwerk. A symbol of America, the statue represented the hopes she carried from her native Europe in the early 1900s—hopes of liberty, of success, of a life free of economic and social strain.

Yet as the boat sailed closer to Ellis Island, the first point of arrival in the United States, Vorwerk did not realize that her very presence—and that of the other thousands of immigrants seeking their fortune in a land of opportunity—was threatened. A strong political movement was growing in the country on which she was pinning her hopes. That movement sought, by using information collected by psychologists, to stem the flow of immigrants through "scientific" analysis of data.

The major claim of the group was that a flood of "mentally deficient" immigrants was poisoning the intellectual capacity of the United States. To supporters of that view, unless drastic measures were taken, it would not be too many years before Western civilization collapsed from a lack of intelligence.

To support this assertion, Lathrop Stoddard, a member of the anti-immigration movement, reported the results of a study of intelligence in which tests were administered to a group of 82 children and 400 adults. On the basis of those test results, he concluded that the average mental age of people in the United States was only 14 years—proof to him that unlimited immigration had already produced a serious decline in the country's intelligence.

Fortunately for immigrants such as Selma Vorwerk, observers in favor of immigration pointed out the fallacy of using data from a relatively small sample—when a considerably larger set of intelligence test data was available. The U.S. Army had been collecting intelligence data for years and had the test scores of 1.7 million men available. When those scores were analyzed, it immediately became apparent that the claim that the average mental age of American adults was 14 years was completely without merit.

A debate reminiscent of this one rages today, as some observers suggest that an unre-strained flow of immigrants—this time from Latin America and Asia—will seriously damage the United States. This time, though, the debate is based more on analyses of social and

Looking Ahead

economic statistics, with opponents of immigration suggesting that the social fabric of the country will be changed and that jobs are being taken away from longer-term residents because of the influx of immigrants. Equally vehement proponents of immigration suggest that the relevant statistics are being misinterpreted, and that *their* analyses of the situation result in a very different conclusion.

Statistics, the branch of mathematics concerned with collecting, organizing, analyzing, and drawing conclusions from numerical data, is a part of all of our lives. For instance, we are all familiar with the claims and counterclaims regarding the effects of smoking. The U.S. government requires that cigarette manufacturers include a warning that smoking is dangerous to people's health on every package of cigarettes and in their advertisements; the govern-ment's data show clear statistical links between smoking and disease. At the same time, the tobacco industry has long minimized the negative effects of smoking.

Statistics: The branch of mathematics concerned with collecting, organizing, analyzing, and drawing conclusions from numerical data.

"*Meaningless statistics were up one-point-five percent this month over last month.*"

Statistics is also at the heart of a considerable number of debates in the field of psychology. How do we determine the nature and strength of the effects of heredity on behavior? What is the relationship between learning and schedules of reinforcement? How do we know if the "double standard" regarding male and female sexual practices has shifted over time? These questions, and most others of interest to psychologists, cannot be answered without a reliance on statistics (Leblanc, 2004).

In this set of modules, we consider the basic approaches to statistical measurement. We first discuss approaches to summarizing data that allow us to describe sets of observations. Next, we consider techniques for deciding how different one set of scores is from another. Finally, we exam-ine approaches to measuring the relationship between two sets of scores.

Descriptive Statistics

Suppose, as an instructor of college psychology, you wanted to evaluate your class's performance on its initial exam. Where might you begin?

You would probably start by using **descriptive statistics,** the branch of statistics that provides a means of summarizing data, presenting the data in a usable and convenient form. For instance, you might first simply list the scores the pupils had received on the test:

72	78	78	92	69	73
85	49	86	86	72	59
58	85	89	80	83	69
78	90	90	96	83	

Viewed in this way, the scores are a jumble of numbers of which it is difficult to make any sense. However, there are several methods by which you could begin to organize the scores in a more meaningful way. For example, you might sort them in order of highest score to lowest score, as is done in Figure 1. By indicating the number of people who obtained each score, you would have produced what is called a **frequency distribution,** an arrangement of scores from a sample that indicates how often a particular score is present.

Another way of summarizing the scores is to consider them visually. For example, you could construct the **histogram,** or bar graph, shown in Figure 2. In that histogram, the number of people obtaining a given score is represented pictorially. The scores are ordered along one dimension of the graph, and the number of people obtaining each score along the other dimension.

Arranging the scores from the highest to the lowest allows us to visually inspect the data. Most often, however, visual inspection is insufficient. For one thing, there may be so many scores in a sample that it is difficult to construct a meaningful visual representation. For another, our interpretations of patterns on a graph or table are often biased and inaccurate; more precise, mathematically based measures would seem to be preferable. In cases in which a precise means of summarizing the data is desirable, psychologists turn to measures of central tendency. **Central tendency** is an index of the central location within a distribution of scores. There are three major measures of central tendency: the mean, the median, and the mode.

The Mean: Finding the Average

The most familiar measure of central tendency is the mean. A **mean** is the technical term for an average, which is simply the sum of all the scores in a set, divided by the number of scores making up the set. For example, to calculate the mean of the sample we have been using, begin by adding each of the numbers (96 + 92 + 90 + 90 + 89 + · · · and so forth). When you have the total, divide that sum by the number

A Sample Frequency Distribution

Test Score	Number of Students Attaining That Score
96	1
92	1
90	2
89	1
86	2
85	2
83	2
80	1
78	3
73	1
72	2
69	2
59	1
58	1
49	1

FIGURE 1 Example of a frequency distribution, which arranges scores from a sample and indicates how often a particular score is present.

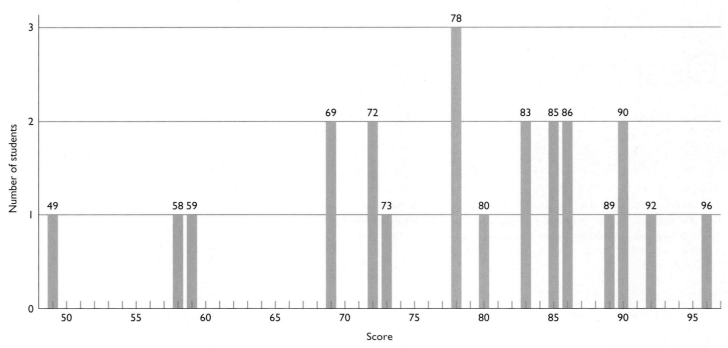

FIGURE 2 In this histogram, the number of students obtaining each score is represented by a bar.

Mean: The average of all scores, arrived at by adding scores together and dividing by the number of scores.

of scores, which is 23. This calculation, 1,800/23 = 78.26, produces a mean score, or average, for our sample.

In general, the mean is an accurate reflection of the central score in a set of scores; as you can see from the histogram in Figure 1, our mean of 78.26 falls roughly in the center of the distribution of scores. Yet the mean does not always provide the best measure of central tendency. For one thing, the mean is very sensitive to extreme scores. As an example, imagine that we added two scores of 20 and 22 to our sample scores. The mean would now become 1,842/25, or 73.68, a drop of almost five points. Because of its sensitivity to extreme scores, then, the mean can sometimes present a deceptive picture of a set of scores, especially in cases where the mean is based on a relatively small number of scores.

The Median: Finding the Middle

Median: The point in a distribution of scores that divides the distribution exactly in half when the scores are listed in numerical order.

A measure of central tendency that is less sensitive to extreme scores than the mean is the median. The **median** is the point in a distribution of scores that divides the distribution exactly in half. If we arrange all the scores in order from the highest to the lowest, the median lies in the middle of the distribution.

For example, consider a distribution of five scores: 10, 8, 7, 4, and 3. The point that divides the distribution exactly in half is the score 7: Two scores in the distribution lie above the 7 score, and two scores lie below it. If there are an even number of scores in a distribution—in which case there will be no score lying in the middle—the two middle scores are averaged. If our distribution consisted of scores of 10, 8, 7, 6, 4, and 3, then, we would average the two middle scores of 7 and 6 to form a median of 7 + 6 divided by 2, or 13/2 = 6.5.

In our original sample test scores, there are twenty-three scores. The score that divides the distribution exactly in half will be the twelfth score in the frequency distribution of scores, because the twelfth score has eleven scores above it and eleven below it. If you count down to the twelfth score in the distribution depicted in Figure 1, you will see that the score is 80. Therefore, the median of the distribution is 80.

One feature of the median as a measure of central tendency is that it is insensitive to extreme scores. For example, adding the scores of 20 and 22 to our distribution would change the median no more than would adding scores of 48 and 47 to the distribution. The reason is clear: The median divides a set of scores in half, and the magnitude of the scores is of no consequence in this process.

The median is often used instead of the mean when extreme scores might be misleading. For example, government statistics on income are typically presented using the median as the measure of central tendency, because the median corrects for the small number of extreme cases of very wealthy individuals, whose high incomes might otherwise inflate the mean income.

The Mode: Finding What Is Most Frequent

The final measure of central tendency is the mode. The **mode** is the most frequently occurring score in a set of scores. If you return to the distribution in Figure 1, you can see that three people scored 78, and the frequency of all the other scores is either 2 or 1. The mode for the distribution, then, is 78.

Some distributions, of course, may have more than one score occurring most frequently. For instance, we could imagine that if the distribution had a score of 86 added to the two that are already there, there would be two most frequently occurring categories: 78 and now 86. In this instance, we would say there are two modes— a case known as a *bimodal distribution*.

The mode is often used as a measure of preference or popularity. For instance, if teachers wanted to know who was the most popular child in their elementary school classrooms, they might develop a questionnaire that asked the students to choose someone with whom they would like to participate in some activity. After the choices were tallied, the mode probably would provide the best indication of which child was the most popular.

Mode: The most frequently occurring score in a set of scores.

Comparing the Three M's: Mean versus Median versus Mode

If a sample is sufficiently large, there is generally little difference between the mean, median, and mode. The reason is that with large samples, scores typically form what is called a normal distribution. A **normal distribution** is a distribution of scores that produces a symmetrical, bell-shaped curve, such as the one displayed in Figure 3, in which the right half mirrors the left half, and in which the mean, median, and mode all have the same value.

Normal distribution: A distribution of scores that produces a symmetrical, bell-shaped curve in which the right half mirrors the left half and in which the mean, median, and mode all have the same value.

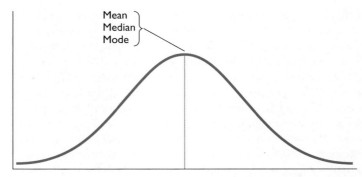

FIGURE 3 In a normal distribution, the mean, median, and mode are identical, falling at the center of the distribution.

Most large distributions, those containing many scores, produce a normal curve. For instance, if you asked a large number of students how many hours a week they studied, you might expect to find that most studied within a similar range of hours, and there would be a few who studied many, many hours, and a very few who studied not at all. There would be many scores hovering around the center of the distribution of scores, then, and only a few at the extremes—producing a normal distribution. Many phenomena of interest to psychologists produce a normal curve when graphed. For example, the distribution of IQ scores among the general population falls into a normal distribution.

The mean, median, and mode fall at exactly the same point in a normal distribution. This means that in a normal distribution of scores, the mean score will divide the distribution exactly in half (making it the median), and it will be the most frequently occurring score in the distribution (making it the mode).

The mean, median, and mode differ, however, when distributions are not normal. In cases in which the distributions are *skewed,* or not symmetrical, there is a "hump" at one end or the other (see Figures 4 and 5). For instance, if we gave a calculus exam to a group of students enrolled in an elementary algebra class, we would expect that most of the students would fail the test, leading to low scores being over-

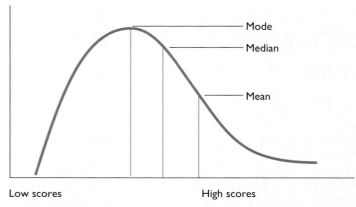

FIGURE 4 In this skewed distribution, most scores are low.

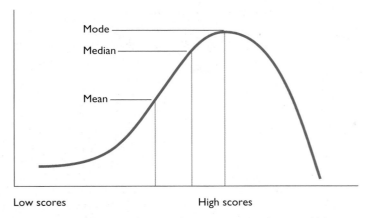

Low scores   High scores

FIGURE 5 In this example of a skewed distribution, there tend to be more high scores than low scores.

represented in the distribution, as in Figure 4. On the other hand, if we gave the same students a test of elementary addition problems, the scores would probably form a distribution in which high scores predominated, as in Figure 5. Both distributions are skewed, although in opposite directions, and the mean, median, and mode are different from one another.

RECAP/EVALUATE/RETHINK

RECAP

What measures can we use to summarize sets of data?

- ▶ Statistics is concerned with collecting, organizing, analyzing, and drawing conclusions from numerical data. (p. A–2)
- ▶ Descriptive statistics provides a means of summarizing data and presenting the data in a usable and convenient form. (p. A–3)
- ▶ A frequency distribution arranges scores from a sample by indicating how often a particular score is presented. A histogram, or bar graph, presents the same data pictorially. (p. A–3)
- ▶ Central tendency is the most representative score in a distribution of scores. The mean (or average) is generally the best measure of central tendency. The median is the point or score in a distribution that divides the distribution in half so that half the scores are higher and half are lower. The third measure of central tendency is the mode, the most frequently occurring score in a distribution of scores. (p. A–3)

EVALUATE

1. A frequency distribution of numbers could be displayed pictorially by constructing a bar graph, or _____.

2. Match each item in the left-hand column with the corresponding item in the right-hand column.
   - 1. Mean = 10.0   a. 2, 8, 10, 12, 13, 18
   - 2. Median = 11   b. 4, 5, 10, 10, 15, 16
   - 3. Mode = 12   c. 4, 5, 12, 12, 12, 16

3. The mean, median, and mode are measures of _____ _____.

4. Professor Garcia explains to the class that most of the forty exam scores fell within a B range, but there were two extremely high scores. Should she report the median or the mean as a measure of central tendency?

5. The mean, median, and mode will differ in a normal distribution. True or false?

RETHINK

1. Government statistics on family income are presented in a variety of ways. What would be the most useful way of providing a summary of family incomes across the country: the mean, median, or mode? Why might providing only the mean be misleading?

Answers to Evaluate Questions

1. histogram; 2. 1-b, 2-a, 3-c; 3. central tendency; 4. the median; the mean is too sensitive to extreme scores; 5. false; they will be equal

KEY TERMS

statistics p. A–2
descriptive statistics p. A–3
frequency
distribution p. A–3

histogram p. A–3
central tendency p. A–3

mean p. A–4
median p. A–4

mode p. A–5
normal distribution p. A–5

Measures of Variability

Although measures of central tendency provide information about where the center of a distribution lies, often this information is insufficient. For example, suppose a psychologist was interested in determining the nature of people's eye movements while they were reading in order to perfect a new method to teach reading. It would not be enough to know how *most* people moved their eyes (information that a measure of central tendency would provide); it would also be important to know how much individual people's eye movements differed or varied from one another.

A second important characteristic of a set of scores provides this information: variability. **Variability** is a term that refers to the spread, or dispersion, of scores in a distribution. Figure 1 contains two distributions of scores that have identical means but differ in variability. Measures of variability provide a way to describe the spread of scores in a distribution.

Variability: The spread, or dispersion, of scores in a distribution.

▲▲▲

The Range: Highest Minus Lowest

The simplest measure of variability is the range. The **range** is the difference between the highest score in a distribution and the lowest score. In the set of scores

Range: The difference between the highest score and the lowest score in a distribution.

96	92	90	90	89	86
86	85	85	83	83	80
78	78	78	73	72	72
69	69	59	58	49	

the distribution has a range of 47 (96 − 49 = 47).

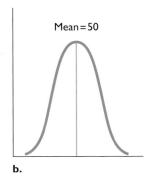

FIGURE 1 Although the mean is identical in these two distributions, the variability, or spread of scores, is very different. Specifically, the variability is considerably greater in (a) than in (b).

The fact that a range is simple to calculate is about its only virtue. The problem with this particular measure of variability is that it is based entirely on extreme scores, and a single score that is very different from the others in a distribution can distort the picture of the distribution as a whole. For example, the addition of a score of 20 to the test score distribution we are considering would almost double the range, even though the variability of the remaining scores in the distribution would not have changed at all.

The Standard Deviation: Differences from the Mean

The most frequently used method of characterizing the variability of a distribution of scores is the standard deviation. The standard deviation bears a conceptual relationship to a mean. You will recall that the mean is the average score in a distribution

FIGURE 2 How to calculate a standard deviation.

Calculating a Standard Deviation

1. The calculation of a standard deviation begins with the calculation of the mean of distribution. In the following distribution of scores on a psychology student's weekly quizzes, the mean is 84.5: 82, 88, 71, 86, 96, 84. (As you recall, the mean is the sum of the scores divided by the number of scores in the distribution, or 507 ÷ 6 = 84.5.)
2. The next step is to produce a deviation score for each score in the distribution. A deviation score is simply an original score minus the mean of all the scores in a distribution. This has been done in the second column below:

Original Score	Deviation Score*	Deviation Score Squared
82	−2.5	6.25
88	3.5	12.25
71	−13.5	182.25
86	1.5	2.25
96	11.5	132.25
84	−.5	.25

3. In the third step, the deviation scores are squared (multiplied by themselves) to eliminate negative numbers. This has been carried out in the third column above.
4. The squared deviation scores are then added together, and this sum is divided by the number of scores. In the example above, the sum of the squared deviation scores is 6.25 + 12.25 + 182.25 + 2.25 + 132.25 + .25 = 335.50, and 335.50 ÷ 6 = 55.916.
5. The final step is to take the square root of the resulting number. The square root of 55.916 is 7.4777—which is the standard deviation of the distribution of scores.
6. To summarize, the standard deviation is calculated using the formula

$$\sqrt{\frac{\Sigma(\text{score}-\text{mean})^2}{N}}$$

*Original score minus the mean of 84.5

(Note: Because this formula provides the standard deviation for a sample, the sum of the deviation scores is divided by the number of scores, N. However, in some cases, in which we might wish to generalize beyond the specific sample to a larger population, the standard deviation is calculated by using the number of scores minus 1, or N − 1.)

of scores. A **standard deviation** is an index of the average deviation of a set of scores from the center of the distribution.

> Standard deviation: An index of the average deviation of a set of scores from the center of the distribution.

Consider, for instance, the distributions in Figure 1. The distribution on the left is widely dispersed, and on the average an individual score in the distribution can be thought of as deviating quite a bit from the center of the distribution. Certainly the scores in the distribution on the left are going to deviate more from the center of the distribution than those in the distribution on the right.

In contrast, in the distribution on the right, the scores are closely packed together and there is little deviation of a typical score from the center of the distribution. On the basis of this analysis, then, it would be expected that a good measure of variability would yield a larger value for the distribution on the left than it would for the one on the right—and, in fact, a standard deviation would do exactly this by indicating how far away a typical score lies from the center of the distribution.

In a normal distribution, 68 percent of the scores fall within one standard deviation of the mean (34 percent on either side of it), 95 percent of the scores fall within two standard deviations, and 99.7 percent fall within three standard deviations. In the general population, IQ scores of intelligence fall into a normal distribution, and they have a mean of 100 and a standard deviation of 15. Consequently, an IQ score of 100 does not deviate from the mean, whereas an IQ score that is three standard deviations above the mean (or 145) is very unusual (higher than 99 percent of all IQ scores).

The calculation of the standard deviation follows the logic of calculating the difference of individual scores from the mean of the distribution (see Figure 2). Not only does the standard deviation provide an excellent indicator of the variability of a set of scores, it provides a means for converting initial scores on standardized tests such as the SAT (the college admissions exam) into the scales used to report results. In this way, it is possible to make a score of 585 on the verbal section of the SAT exam, for example, equivalent from one year to the next, even though the specific test items differ from year to year.

RECAP/EVALUATE/RETHINK

RECAP

How can we assess the variability of a set of data?

▶ The range and standard deviation are two measures of variability, which is the spread, or dispersion, of scores in a distribution. The range is the distance between the largest score in a distribution and the smallest score. The standard deviation is an index of the extent to which the average score in a distribution deviates from the center of the distribution. (p. A–9)

EVALUATE

1. A measure of variability based solely on the distance between the most extreme scores is the
   a. Spread
   b. Standard deviation
   c. Deviation score
   d. Range
2. By simply eyeing the following sets of numbers, predict which will have a higher standard deviation and why:
   a. 6, 8, 10, 10, 11, 12, 13
   b. 2, 5, 8, 11, 16, 17, 18
3. Calculate the mean and standard deviation for sets **a** and **b** in Question 2.

RETHINK

1. If you were interested in understanding the number of people living below the poverty line in the United States, why might the range and the standard deviation provide you with a better understanding of the extent of poverty than would measures of central tendency (the mean, median, and mode)?

Answers to Evaluate Questions

1. d; 2. b, because the numbers are more widely dispersed; 3a. mean = 10, standard deviation = 2.20; 3b. mean = 11, standard deviation = 5.80

KEY TERMS

variability p. A–9   range p. A–9   standard deviation p. A–11

Using Statistics to Answer Questions: Inferential Statistics and Correlation

Suppose you were a psychologist who was interested in whether there is a relationship between smoking and anxiety. Would it be reasonable to simply look at a group of smokers and measure their anxiety by using some rating scale? Probably not. It clearly would be more informative if you compared their anxiety with the anxiety exhibited by a group of nonsmokers.

Once you decided to observe anxiety in two groups of people, you would have to determine just who would be your subjects. In an ideal world with unlimited resources, you might contact *every* smoker and nonsmoker, because these are the two populations with which you are concerned. A **population** consists of all the members of a group of interest. Obviously, however, this would be impossible because of the all-encompassing size of the two groups; instead, you would limit your subjects to a sample of smokers and nonsmokers. A **sample,** in formal statistical terms, is a subgroup of a population of interest that is intended to be representative of the larger population. Once you had identified samples representative of the population of interest to you, it would be possible to carry out your study, yielding two distributions of scores—one from the smokers and one from the nonsmokers (Fowler, 2001).

The obvious question is whether the two samples differ in the degree of anxiety displayed by their members. The statistical procedures that we discussed earlier are helpful in answering this question, because each of the two samples can be examined in terms of central tendency and variability. The more important question, though, is whether the magnitude of difference between the two distributions is sufficient to conclude that the distributions truly differ from one another, or if, instead, the differences are attributable merely to chance.

To answer the question of whether samples are truly different from one another, psychologists use inferential statistics. **Inferential statistics** is the branch of statistics that uses data from samples to make predictions about a larger population, permitting generalizations to be drawn. To take a simple example, suppose you had two coins that both were flipped 100 times. Suppose further that one coin came up heads forty-one times and the other came up heads sixty-five times. Are both coins fair? We know that a fair coin should come up heads about fifty times in 100 flips. But a little thought would also suggest that it is unlikely that even a fair coin would come up heads exactly fifty times in 100 flips. The question is, then, how far a coin could deviate from fifty heads before that coin would be considered unfair.

Questions such as this—as well as whether the results found are due to chance or represent unexpected, nonchance findings—revolve around how "probable" certain events are. Using coin flipping as an example, fifty-three heads in 100 flips would be a highly probable outcome because it departs only slightly from the expected outcome of fifty heads. In contrast, if a coin was flipped 100 times and ninety of those times it came up heads, that would be a highly improbable outcome. In fact, ninety heads out of 100 flips should occur by chance only once in 2 million trials of 100 flips

How do we generalize from data?

How can we determine the nature of a relationship, and the significance of differences, between two sets of scores?

Population: All the members of a group of interest.

Sample: A representative subgroup of a population of interest.

Inferential statistics: The branch of statistics that uses data from samples to make predictions about the larger population from which the sample is drawn.

of a fair coin. Ninety heads in 100 flips, then, is an extremely improbable outcome; if ninety heads did appear, the odds would be that the coin or the flipping process was rigged.

Inferential statistics are used to mathematically determine the probability of observed events. By using inferential statistics to evaluate the result of an experiment, psychologists are able to calculate the likelihood that the difference is a reflection of a true difference between populations. For example, suppose we find that the mean on an anxiety scale is 68 for smokers and 48 for nonsmokers. Inferential statistical procedures allow us to determine whether this difference is really meaningful, or whether we might expect the same difference to occur merely because of chance factors (Cohen & Lea, 2003).

The results of inferential statistical procedures are described in terms of measures of significance. To a psychologist, a **significant outcome** is one in which the observed outcome would be expected to have occurred only by chance with a probability of .05 or less. Put another way, a significant difference between two means says that there are only five chances out of 100 (or less) that the difference an experimenter has found is due to chance, rather than to an actual difference between the means.

Obtaining a significant outcome in a study does not necessarily imply that the results of an experiment have real-world importance. An experiment may demonstrate that two groups differ significantly from one another, but the meaning of the differences in terms of what occurs outside the laboratory may be limited. Still, finding a significant outcome tells us something important: The differences a researcher has found are overwhelmingly likely to be true differences, not only due to chance (Lehmann & Romano, 2004).

Ⓐ Ⓐ Ⓐ

Significant outcome: An outcome in which the observed outcome would be expected to have occurred by chance with a probability of .05 or less.

The Correlation Coefficient: Measuring Relationships

How do we know if television viewing is related to aggression, if reading romance novels is related to sexual behavior, or if mothers' IQs are related to their daughters' IQs?

Each of these questions revolves around the issue of the degree of relationship between two variables. One way of answering them is to draw a *scatterplot*, a means of graphically illustrating the relationship between two variables. We would first collect two sets of paired measures and assign one score to the horizontal axis (variable x) and the other score to the vertical axis (variable y). Then we would draw a dot at the place where the two scores meet on the graph. The first two scatterplots in Figure 1 present typical situations. In (a) and (b), there is a **positive relationship,** in which high values of variable x are associated with high values of variable y and low values of x are associated with low values of y. In (c) and (d), there is a **negative relationship:** As values of variable x increase, the values of variable y decrease. In (e), no clear relationship exists between variable x and variable y.

It is also possible to consider scores in terms of their mathematical relationship to one another, rather than simply the way they appear on a scatterplot. Suppose, for example, a psychologist was interested in the degree to which a daughter's IQ was related to her mother's IQ—specifically, if a mother with a high IQ tended to

Positive relationship: A relationship established by data that shows high values of one variable corresponding with high values of another, and low values of the first variable corresponding with low values of the other.

Negative relationship: A relationship established by data that shows high values of one variable corresponding with low values of the other.

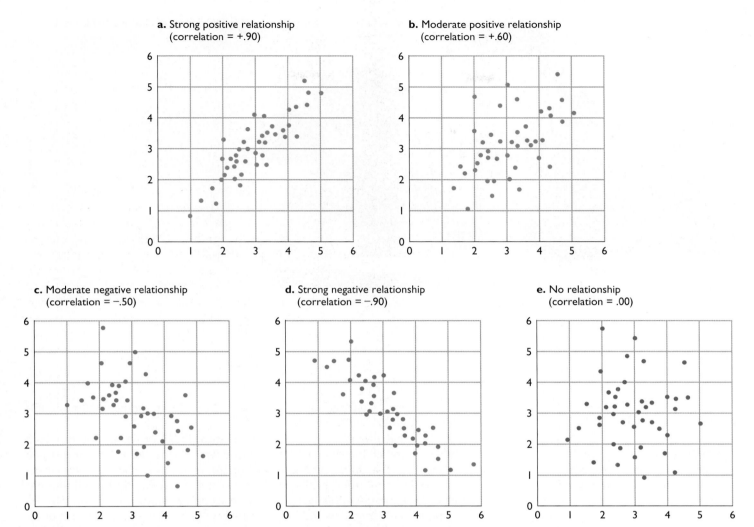

FIGURE 1 These scatterplots show relationships of different strengths. In (a) and (b), the relationships are positive, although in (a) the relationship is considerably stronger than in (b). In contrast, the relationships in (c) and (d) are negative, with (d) representing a stronger negative relationship. Finally, (e) illustrates a case where no systematic relationship exists between the variables.

have a daughter who also had a high IQ, and whether a mother with a low IQ tended to have a daughter with a low IQ. To examine the issue, suppose the psychologist measured the IQs of ten mothers and daughters and arranged their IQs as presented in Figure 2.

Looking at the data in the table, it is obvious that mothers and daughters do not have identical IQs. Moreover, they do not even have IQs that are rank-ordered the same in the two columns. For example, the mother with the highest IQ does not have the daughter with the highest IQ, and the mother with the lowest IQ does not have the daughter with the lowest IQ. It is apparent, then, that there is not a *perfect* relationship between the IQ of a mother and the IQ of a daughter. However, it would be a mistake to conclude that there is a *zero,* or no, relationship between the IQs of the mothers and daughters, because it is clear that there is a tendency for mothers

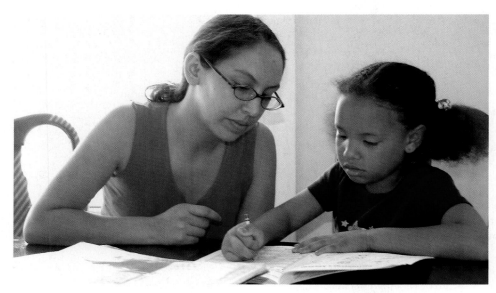

IQ Scores of Mothers and Daughters

Mother's IQ	Daughter's IQ
135	122
128	130
125	110
120	132
114	100
110	116
102	108
96	89
90	84
86	92

FIGURE 2 In this distribution, each mother's IQ score is compared to her daughter's IQ score. Using a correlation coefficient, we can calculate the strength of the relationship between the set of pairs of scores.

Correlation coefficient: A numerical measure that indicates the extent of the relationship between two variables.

who have high IQs to have daughters with high IQs, and that mothers with low IQs tend to have daughters with low IQs.

The statistic that provides a precise mathematical index of the degree to which two variables are related is the correlation coefficient. A **correlation coefficient** is a numerical measure that indicates the extent of the relationship between two variables. It ranges in value from +1.00 to −1.00. A value of +1.00 would indicate that two variables had a perfect positive relationship with one another, meaning that the highest score on one variable would be associated with the highest score on the other variable, the second highest score on the first variable would be associated with the second highest score on the second variable, and so on. A value of −1.00 would indicate that there was a perfect negative relationship between the two variables; the highest score on the first variable would be associated with the lowest score on the second variable, the second highest score would be associated with the second lowest score, and so forth.

Correlation coefficients at or only slightly greater or slightly less than zero indicate that there is no relationship between the two variables. In such cases, there is no tendency for high values on one variable to be associated with either high or low values on the second variable.

Correlation coefficients that range between zero and ±1.00 reflect varying degrees of relationship between the two variables. For instance, a value of +.20 or −.20 would indicate that there was a slight relationship between the two variables, a value of around +.50 or −.50 would indicate a moderate relationship, and a value of +.80 or −.80 would indicate a relatively strong relationship. As an example, if we were to calculate the correlation of the two sets of variables in Figure 2 (most advanced calculators do the necessary calculations automatically), we would find a correlation that is quite strong: The coefficient is +.86.

It is important to note that finding a strong correlation between two variables does *not* in any way indicate that changes in one variable *cause* changes in another—only that the variables are associated with one another. Although it may seem plausible to us, for example, that it is the mother's intelligence that causes higher intelligence in a daughter, it is just as possible that a daughter's intelligence affects how the mother performs on an IQ test. (Perhaps the daughter's behavior affects the general home environment, influencing the mother's performance on IQ tests.) It is even plausible that some unmeasured—and previously unconsidered—third variable is causing both mother's and daughter's IQs to increase or decrease simultaneously. In a clear example of this possibility, even if we found that ice cream sales and rates of violent crime are positively correlated with one another (as they happen to be), we would not presume that they are causally related. In this case, it is likely that both are influenced by a third factor— the weather.

The crucial point is that even if we find a perfect correlation between two sets of variables, we will not be able to say that the two variables are linked causally— only that they are strongly related to one another (Good, 2003).

RECAP/EVALUATE/RETHINK

RECAP

How do we generalize from data?

▶ Inferential statistics—techniques that use data from samples to make predictions about a larger population—are useful in deciding whether differences between distributions of data are attributable to real differences or to chance variation. (p. A–13)

How can we determine the nature of a relationship, and the significance of differences, between two sets of scores?

▶ Measures of relationship provide a numerical index of the extent to which two variables are related. The correlation coefficient ranges in value from $+1.00$ to -1.00, with $+1.00$ indicating a perfect positive relationship and -1.00 indicating a perfect negative relationship. Correlations close to or at zero indicate there is little or no relationship between two variables. (p. A–14)

EVALUATE

1. Researchers would like to estimate the level of stress for first-year college students for a given year at a large university. A stress index is given to a randomly assigned group of 500 first-year students. The class size is 6,000 for that year. In this example the group of 500 is known as a _____, and the entire class of first-year students is known as the _____.

2. Dr. Sanders states that the results of his experiment show a difference between the two groups, and that there is a 90 percent probability that the results are due to a true difference between the groups and not to chance. Are his results statistically significant in the way the term *significant* typically is used by psychologists?

3. A hypothetical set of data drawn from a sample of college sophomores at a university found that as the rate of caffeine consumption increases, the amount of sleep decreases. The scatterplot for these data is apt to show a _____ relationship.

4. What would the value of the correlation coefficient be for the following?
   a. A perfect negative relationship
   b. A perfect positive relationship
   c. No relationship

5. If we observed a correlation coefficient of $-.90$ in Question 3, we would probably be safe in saying that caffeine consumption *causes* lack of sleep in college students. True or false?

6. The researchers in Question 3 decide to extend the findings they obtain from their sample of college sophomores to all adults. Would you accept their generalization? Why or why not?

RETHINK

1. For many years, cigarette manufacturers argued that because the data linking smoking and disease was correlational, one could not infer that there was a causal connection between them and therefore no reason not to smoke. Did the manufacturers have a valid argument? How could you refute their argument?

Answers to Evaluate Questions

1. sample, population; 2. no, at least not at the .05 level typically required by psychologists who wish to claim a result is significant; 3. negative; 4. a. −1.00, b. +1.00, c. 0; 5. false; we cannot assume a causal relation, only an association; 6. no; the sample (drawn from college sophomores) does not represent the population (all adults)

KEY TERMS

population p. A–13
sample p. A–13
inferential statistics p. A–13

significant outcome p. A–14
positive relatiohship
p. A–14

negative
relationship p. A–14

correlation
coefficient p. A–16

Psychology on the Web

1. Search the Web for the results of a recent survey, such as one conducted by the Gallup polling organization (www.gallup.com). Describe the results, summarizing the methodology and the sample size for the survey. How does the sample address the population to which the survey is being generalized?

Epilogue

In this group of modules, we've seen how statistical methods are used by psychologists to summarize data and support hypotheses. Return, for a moment, to the Prologue about Selma Vorwerk, who immigrated to this country in the early 1900s, and use the statistical concepts that we covered to answer the following questions.

1. What was the sample size used by anti-immigrationist Lathrop Stoddard, and to what population was he generalizing?

2. What are the statistical flaws in the arguments made by critics of immigration in the early 1900s?

3. What statistical methods would you find useful in refuting Stoddard's conclusions about immigrants?

Glossary

absolute threshold The smallest intensity of a stimulus that must be present for the stimulus to be detected (Module 10)

achievement test A test designed to determine a person's level of knowledge in a given subject area (Module 26)

acquired immune deficiency syndrome (AIDS) A fatal, sexually transmitted disease caused by a virus that destroys the body's immune system (Module 36)

action potential An electric nerve impulse that travels through a neuron when it is set off by a "trigger," changing the neuron's charge from negative to positive (Module 7)

activation-synthesis theory Hobson's theory that the brain produces random electrical energy during REM sleep that stimulates memories lodged in various portions of the brain (Module 14)

activity theory of aging A theory that suggests that the elderly who age most successfully are those who maintain the interests and activities they had during middle age (Module 41)

adaptation An adjustment in sensory capacity following prolonged exposure to stimuli (Module 10)

addictive drugs Drugs that produce a biological or psychological dependence in the user and withdrawal from them leads to a craving for the drug that, in some cases, may be nearly irresistible (Module 16)

adolescence The developmental stage between childhood and adulthood (Module 40)

age of viability The point at which the fetus can survive if born prematurely (Module 38)

aggression Intentional injury or harm to another person (Module 57)

algorithm A rule which, if applied appropriately, guarantees a solution to a problem (Module 23)

all-or-none law The rule that neurons are either on or off (Module 7)

altruism Helping behavior that is beneficial to others but clearly requires self-sacrifice (Module 57)

Alzheimer's disease A progressive brain disorder that leads to a gradual and irreversible decline in cognitive abilities (Module 41)

anal stage According to Freud, a stage from 12–18 months to 3 years of age, in which a child's pleasure is centered on the anus (Module 42)

androgen Male sex hormones secreted by the testes (Module 34)

androgynous Characterized by gender roles that encompass psychological and behavioral traits thought typical of both sexes (Module 33)

anorexia nervosa A severe eating disorder in which people may refuse to eat, while denying that their behavior and appearance—which can become skeletonlike—are unusual (Module 30)

anorgasmia (an or GAZ mee uh) A female's lack of orgasm (Module 36)

antianxiety drugs Drugs that reduce the level of anxiety a person experiences, essentially by reducing excitability and increasing feelings of well-being (Module 53)

antidepressant drugs Medication that improves a depressed patient's mood and feeling of well-being (Module 53)

antipsychotic drugs Drugs that temporarily reduce psychotic symptoms such as agitation, overactivity, hallucinations, and delusions (Module 53)

antisocial personality disorder A disorder in which individuals tend to display no regard for the moral and ethical rules of society or the rights of others (Module 49)

anxiety disorder The occurrence of anxiety without obvious external cause, affecting daily functioning (Module 49)

aptitude test A test designed to predict a person's ability in a particular area or line of work (Module 26)

archival research Research in which existing data, such as census documents, college records, or newspaper clippings, are examined to test a hypothesis (Module 5)

arousal approaches to motivation The belief that we try to maintain a certain level of stimulation and activity, increasing or reducing them as necessary (Module 29)

association areas One of the major areas of the brain, the site of the higher mental processes such as thought, language, memory, and speech (Module 9)

associative models of memory A technique of recalling information by thinking about related information (Module 20)

assumed-similarity bias The tendency to think of people as being similar to oneself, even when meeting them for the first time (Module 54)

attachment The positive emotional bond that develops between a child and a particular individual (Module 39)

attention-deficit hyperactivity disorder (ADHD) A learning disability marked by inattention, impulsiveness, a low tolerance for frustration, and a great deal of inappropriate activity (Module 49)

attitude A learned evaluation of a particular person, behavior, belief, or thing (Module 54)

attribution theory The theory of personality that seeks to explain how we decide, on the basis of samples of an individual's behavior, what the specific causes of that person's behavior are (Module 54)

authoritarian parents Parents who are rigid and punitive and value unquestioning obedience from their children (Module 39)

authoritative parents Parents who are firm, set clear limits, reason with their children, and explain things to them (Module 39)

autobiographical memories Our recollections of circumstances and episodes from our own lives (Module 21)

autonomic division The part of the peripheral nervous system that controls involuntary movement (the actions of the heart, glands, lungs, and other organs) (Module 8)

autonomy-versus-shame-and-doubt stage The period during which, according to Erikson, toddlers (ages 18 months to 3 years) develop independence and autonomy if exploration and freedom are encouraged, or shame and self-doubt if they are restricted and overprotected (Module 39)

axon The part of the neuron that carries messages destined for other neurons (Module 7)

babble Speechlike but meaningless sounds made by children from the ages of around 3 months through 1 year (Module 25)

background stressors ("daily hassles") Everyday annoyances, such as being stuck in traffic, that cause minor irritations that may have long-term ill effects if they continue or are compounded by other stressful events (Module 45)

basilar membrane A vibrating structure that runs through the center of the cochlea, dividing it into an upper and a lower chamber, and containing sense receptors for sound (Module 12)

behavior modification A formalized technique for promoting the frequency of desirable behaviors and decreasing the incidence of unwanted ones (Module 19)

behavioral assessment Direct measures of an individual's behavior used to describe characteristics indicative of personality (Module 44)

behavioral genetics The study of the effects of heredity on behavior (Module 8)

behavioral neuroscientists (or biopsychologists) Psychologists who specialize in considering the ways that biological structures and functions of the body affect behavior (Module 7)

behavioral perspective The approach that suggests that observable behavior should be the focus of study (Module 2)

behavioral perspective on psychological disorders The perspective that looks at the behavior itself as the problem (Module 48)

behavioral treatment approaches Treatment approaches that build upon the basic processes of learning, such as reinforcement and extinction (Module 51)

biofeedback A procedure in which a person learns to control through conscious thought internal physiological processes such as blood pressure, heart and respiration rate, skin temperature, sweating, and constriction of particular muscles (Module 9)

biological and evolutionary approaches to personality The theory which suggests that important components of personality are inherited (Module 43)

biomedical therapy Therapy that relies on drugs and other medical procedures to improve psychological functioning (Module 51)

bipolar disorder A disorder in which a person alternates between periods of euphoric feelings of mania and periods of depression (Module 49)

bisexuals Persons who are sexually attracted to people of the same *and* the opposite sex (Module 35)

borderline personality disorder A disorder in which individuals have difficulty in developing a secure sense of who they are (Module 49)

bottom-up processing Perception that consists of recognizing and processing information about the individual components of the stimuli (Module 13)

bulimia A disorder in which a person binges on incredibly large quantities of food (Module 30)

Cannon-Bard theory of emotion The belief that both physiological and emotional arousal are produced simultaneously by the same nerve stimulus (Module 31)

case study An in-depth, intensive investigation of an individual or small group of people (Module 5)

cataclysmic events Strong stressors that occur suddenly, affecting many people at once (e.g., natural disasters) (Module 45)

catharsis The process of discharging built-up aggressive energy (Module 57)

central core The "old brain" which controls such basic functions as eating and sleeping and is common to all vertebrates (Module 9)

central nervous system (CNS) The part of the nervous system that includes the brain and spinal cord (Module 8)

central route processing Message interpretation characterized by thoughtful consideration of the issues and arguments used to persuade (Module 54)

central tendency An index of the central location within a distribution of scores; the most representative score in a distribution of scores (the mean, median, and mode are measures of central tendency) (Module 58)

central traits The major traits considered in forming impressions of others (Module 54)

cerebellum (ser ub BELL um) The part of the brain that controls bodily balance (Module 9)

cerebral cortex The "new brain," responsible for the most sophisticated information processing in the brain; contains the lobes (Module 9)

chromosomes Rod-shaped structures that contain the basic hereditary information (Module 38)

chunk A meaningful grouping of stimuli that can be stored as a unit in short-term memory (Module 20)

circadian rhythms Biological processes that occur repeatedly on approximately a twenty-four-hour cycle (Module 14)

classical conditioning A type of learning in which a neutral stimulus comes to bring about a response after it is paired with a stimulus that naturally brings about that response (Module 17)

cochlea (KOKE lee uh) A coiled tube in the ear filled with fluid that vibrates in response to sound (Module 12)

cognitive approaches of motivation The theory suggesting that motivation is a product of people's thoughts and expectations—their cognitions (Module 29)

cognitive development The process by which a child's understanding of the world changes as a function of age and experience (Module 39)

cognitive dissonance The conflict that occurs when a person holds two attitudes or thoughts (referred to as *cognitions*) that contradict each other (Module 54)

cognitive perspective The approach that focuses on how people think, understand, and know about the world (Module 2)

cognitive perspective on psychological disorders The perspective that suggests that people's thoughts and beliefs are a central component of abnormal behavior (Module 48)

cognitive psychology The branch of psychology that focuses on the study of cognition (Module 23)

cognitive treatment approaches Approaches to treatment that teach people to think in more adaptive ways by changing their dysfunctional cognitions about the world and themselves (Module 51)

cognitive-behavioral approach An approach used by cognitive therapists that attempts to change the way people think through the use of basic principles of learning (Module 51)

cognitive-social learning theory The study of the thought processes that underlie learning (Module 19)

collective unconscious A set of influences we inherit from our own particular ancestors, the whole human race, and even animal ancestors from the distant past (Module 42)

community psychology A branch of psychology that focuses on the prevention and minimization of psychological disorders in the community (Module 53)

companionate love The strong affection that we have for those with whom our lives are deeply involved (Module 57)

compliance Behavior that occurs in response to direct social pressure (Module 55)

compulsion An irresistible urge to repeatedly carry out some act that seems strange and unreasonable (Module 49)

concepts Categorizations of objects, events, or people that share common properties (Module 23)

concrete operational stage According to Piaget, the period from 7 to 12 years of age that is characterized by logical thought and a loss of egocentrism (Module 39)

conditioned response (CR) A response that, after conditioning, follows a previously neutral stimulus (e.g., salivation at the ringing of a bell) (Module 17)

conditioned stimulus (CS) A once-neutral stimulus that has been paired with an unconditioned stimulus to bring about a response formerly caused only by the unconditioned stimulus (Module 17)

cones Cone-shaped, light-sensitive receptor cells in the retina that are responsible for sharp focus and color perception, particularly in bright light (Module 11)

conformity A change in behavior or attitudes brought about by a desire to follow the beliefs or standards of other people (Module 55)

consciousness The awareness of the sensations, thoughts, and feelings being experienced at a given moment (Module 14)

constructive processes Processes in which memories are influenced by the meaning that we give to events (Module 21)

continuous reinforcement schedule Behavior that is reinforced every time it occurs (Module 18)

control group A group participating in an experiment that receives no treatment (Module 5)

convergent thinking The ability to produce responses that are based primarily on knowledge and logic (Module 24)

conversion disorder A major somatoform disorder that involves an actual physical disturbance, such as the inability to use a sensory organ or the complete or partial inability to move an arm or leg (Module 49)

coping The efforts to control, reduce, or learn to tolerate the threats that lead to stress (Module 45)

correlation coefficient A numerical measure that indicates the relationship between two variables (Module 60)

correlational research Research in which the relationship between two sets of variables is examined to determine whether they are associated, or "correlated" (Module 5)

creativity The combining of responses or ideas in novel ways (Module 24)

cross-sectional research A research method in which people of different ages are compared at the same point in time (Module 37)

crystallized intelligence The accumulation of information, skills, and strategies learned through experience and that can be applied in problem-solving situations (Module 26)

cue-dependent forgetting Forgetting that occurs when there are insufficient retrieval cues to rekindle information that is in memory (Module 22)

culture-fair IQ test A test that does not discriminate against members of any minority group (Module 28)

date rape Rape in which the rapist is either a date or a romantic acquaintance (Module 36)

daydreams Fantasies that people construct while awake (Module 14)

decay The loss of information in memory through its nonuse (Module 22)

declarative memory Memory for factual information: names, faces, dates, and the like (Module 20)

defense mechanisms Unconscious strategies people use to reduce anxiety by concealing its source from themselves and others (Module 42, 45)

deinstitutionalization The transfer of former mental patients from institutions into the community (Module 53)

dendrites A cluster of fibers at one end of a neuron that receive messages from other neurons (Module 7)

dependent variable The variable that is measured and is expected to change as a result of changes caused by the experimenter's manipulation of the independent variable (Module 5)

depressants Drugs that slow down the nervous system (Module 16)

descriptive statistics The branch of statistics that provides a means of summarizing data (Module 58)

determinism The idea that people's behavior is produced primarily by factors outside their willful control (Module 3)

developmental psychology The branch of psychology that studies the patterns of growth and change occurring throughout life (Module 37)

Diagnostic and Statistical Manual of Mental Disorders, Fourth Edition (DSM-IV-TR) A system devised by the American Psychiatric Association used by most professionals to diagnose and classify abnormal behavior (Module 48)

difference threshold The smallest level of stimulation required to sense that a *change* in stimulation has occurred (Module 10)

diffusion of responsibility The tendency for people to feel that responsibility for acting is shared, or diffused, among those present (Module 57)

discrimination Behavior directed toward individuals based on their membership in a particular group (Module 56)

disengagement theory of aging A theory that suggests that aging is a gradual withdrawal from the world on physical, psychological, and social levels (Module 41)

display rules The guidelines that govern the appropriateness of showing emotion nonverbally (Module 32)

dispositional causes (of behavior) A perceived cause of behavior that is based on internal traits or personality factors (Module 54)

dissociative amnesia A disorder in which a significant, selective memory loss occurs (Module 49)

dissociative disorder Psychological dysfunctions characterized by the separation of critical personality facets that are normally integrated, allowing stress avoidance by escape (Module 49)

dissociative fugue A form of amnesia in which people take sudden, impulsive trips, sometimes assuming a new identity (Module 49)

dissociative identity disorder (or multiple personality) A disorder in which a person displays characteristics of two or more distinct personalities (Module 49)

double standard The view that premarital sex is permissible for males but not for females (Module 35)

dreams-for-survival theory The theory suggesting that dreams permit information that is critical for our daily survival to be reconsidered and reprocessed during sleep (Module 14)

drive Motivational tension, or arousal, that energizes behavior in order to fulfill some need (Module 29)

drive-reduction approaches to motivation A theory suggesting that when people lack some basic biological requirement such as water, a drive to obtain that requirement (in this case, the thirst drive) is produced (Module 29)

drug therapy Control of psychological problems through drugs (Module 53)

eardrum The part of the ear that vibrates when sound waves hit it (Module 12)

echoic memory Memory which stores auditory information coming from the ears (Module 20)

eclectic approach to therapy An approach to therapy that uses techniques taken from a variety of treatment methods, rather than just one (Module 52)

ego The part of the personality that provides a buffer between the id and the outside world (Module 42)

egocentric thought A way of thinking in which the child views the world entirely from his or her own perspective (Module 39)

ego-integrity-versus-despair stage According to Erikson, a period from late adulthood until death during which we review life's accomplishments and failures (Module 40)

electroconvulsive therapy (ECT) A procedure in which an electric current of 70 to 150 volts is briefly administered to a patient's head, causing a loss of consciousness and often seizures (Module 53)

embryo A developed zygote that has a heart, a brain, and other organs (Module 38)

emotional intelligence The set of skills that underlie the accurate assessment, evaluation, expression, and regulation of emotions (Module 26)

emotions Feelings that generally have both physiological and cognitive elements and that influence behavior (Module 31)

endocrine system A chemical communication network that sends messages throughout the body via the bloodstream (Module 8)

episodic memory Memory for the biographical details of our individual lives (Module 20)

erectile dysfunction The inability of a male to achieve or maintain an erection (Module 36)

erogenous zones Areas of the body that are particularly sensitive because of the presence of an unusually rich array of nerve receptors (Module 34)

estrogen Female sex hormones (Module 34)

evolutionary psychology The branch of psychology that seeks to identify behavior patterns that are a result of our genetic inheritance from our ancestors (Module 8)

excitatory message A chemical message that makes it more likely that a receiving neuron will fire and an action potential will travel down its axon (Module 7)

excitement phase The interval at which an arousing stimulus begins a sequence that prepares the genitals for sexual intercourse (Module 34)

experiment The investigation of the relationship between two (or more) variables by deliberately producing a change in one variable in a situation and observing the effects of that change on other aspects of the situation (Module 5)

experimental bias Factors that distort how the independent variable affects the dependent variable in an experiment (Module 6)

experimental group Any group participating in an experiment that receives a treatment (Module 5)

experimental manipulation The change that an experimenter deliberately produces in a situation (Module 5)

explicit memory Intentional or conscious recollection of information (Module 20)

extinction One of the basic phenomena of learning that occurs when a previously conditioned response decreases in frequency and eventually disappears (Module 17)

extramarital sex Sexual activity between a married person and someone who is not his or her spouse (Module 35)

facial-affect program The activation of a set of nerve impulses that make the face display the appropriate expression (Module 32)

facial-feedback hypothesis The hypothesis that facial expressions not only *reflect* emotional experience, they also help *determine* how people experience and label emotions (Module 32)

family therapy An approach that focuses on the family and its dynamics (Module 52)

feature analysis A theory of perception according to which we perceive a shape, pattern, object, or scene by reacting first to the individual elements that make it up (Module 13)

feature detection The activation of neurons in the cortex by visual stimuli of specific shapes or patterns (Module 11)

fetus A developing child, from eight weeks after conception until birth (Module 38)

fixation Conflicts or concerns that persist beyond the developmental period in which they first occur (Module 42)

fixed-interval schedule A schedule that provides reinforcement for a response only if a fixed time period has elapsed, making overall rates of response relatively low (Module 18)

fixed-ratio schedule A schedule whereby reinforcement is given only after a certain number of responses are made (Module 18)

flashbulb memories Memories centered around a specific, important, or surprising event that are so vivid it is as if they represented a snapshot of the event (Module 21)

fluid intelligence Intelligence that reflects information processing capabilities, reasoning, and memory (Module 26)

formal operational stage According to Piaget, the period from age 12 to adulthood that is characterized by abstract thought (Module 39)

free will The idea that behavior is caused primarily by choices that are made freely by the individual (Module 3)

frequency distribution An arrangement of scores from a sample that indicates how often a particular score is present (Module 58)

frequency theory of hearing The theory that the entire basilar membrane acts like a microphone, vibrating as a whole in response to a sound (Module 12)

frustration The thwarting or blocking of some ongoing, goal-directed behavior (Module 57)

functional fixedness The tendency to think of an object only in terms of its typical use (Module 24)

functionalism An early approach to psychology that concentrated on what the mind does—the functions of mental activity—and the role of behavior in allowing people to adapt to their environments (Module 2)

fundamental attribution error A tendency to attribute others' behavior to dispositional causes and the tendency to minimize the importance of situational causes (Module 54)

g or g-factor The single, general factor for mental ability, assumed to underlie intelligence in some early theories of intelligence (Module 26)

gate-control theory of pain The theory that particular nerve receptors lead to specific areas of the brain related to pain (Module 12)

gender roles The set of expectations, defined by a particular society, that indicate what is appropriate behavior for men and women (Module 33)

gender schema A mental framework that organizes and guides a child's understanding of information relevant to gender (Module 33)

gender The perception of being male or female (Module 33)

general adaptation syndrome (GAS) A theory developed by Selye that suggests that a person's response to stress consists of three stages: alarm and mobilization, resistance, and exhaustion (Module 45)

generalized anxiety disorder The experience of long-term, persistent anxiety and worry (Module 49)

generativity-versus-stagnation stage According to Erikson, a period in middle adulthood during which we take stock of our contributions to family and society (Module 40)

genes The parts of the chromosomes through which genetic information is transmitted (Module 38)

genetic preprogramming theories of aging Theories that suggest there is a built-in time limit to the reproduction of human cells, and that after a certain time they are no longer able to divide (Module 41)

genital stage According to Freud, the period from puberty until death, marked by mature sexual behavior (i.e., sexual intercourse) (Module 42)

genitals The male and female sex organs (Module 34)

gestalt laws of organization A series of principles that describe how we organize bits and pieces of information into meaningful wholes (Module 13)

gestalt (geh SHTALLT) psychology An approach to psychology that focuses on the organization of perception and thinking in a "whole" sense, rather than on the individual elements of perception (Module 2)

gestalt therapy An approach to therapy that attempts to integrate a client's thoughts, feelings, and behavior into a unified whole (Module 52)

grammar The system of rules that determine how our thoughts can be expressed (Module 25)

group therapy Therapy in which people discuss problems in a group (Module 52)

habituation The decrease in the response to a stimulus that occurs after repeated presentations of the same stimulus (Module 39)

hair cells Tiny cells covering the basilar membrane that, when bent by vibrations entering the cochlea, transmit neural messages to the brain (Module 12)

hallucinogen A drug that is capable of producing hallucinations, or changes in the perceptual process (Module 16)

halo effect A phenomenon in which an initial understanding that a person has positive traits is used to infer other uniformly positive characteristics (Module 54)

hardiness A personality characteristic associated with a lower rate of stress-related illness, consisting of three components: commitment, challenge, and control (Module 45)

health psychology The branch of psychology that investigates the psychological factors related to wellness and illness, including the prevention, diagnosis, and treatment of medical problems (Module 45)

hemispheres Two symmetrical left and right halves of the brain that control the side of the body opposite to their location (Module 9)

heritability A measure of the degree to which a characteristic is related to genetic, inherited factors (Module 28)

heterosexuality Sexual attraction and behavior directed to the opposite sex (Module 35)

heuristic A cognitive shortcut that may lead to a solution (Module 23)

histogram Bar graph (Module 58)

homeostasis The body's tendency to maintain a steady internal state (Module 29)

homosexuals Persons who are sexually attracted to members of their own sex (Module 35)

hormones Chemicals that circulate through the blood and affect the functioning or growth of other parts of the body (Module 8)

humanistic approaches to personality The theory that emphasizes people's basic goodness and their tendency to grow to higher levels of functioning (Module 43)

humanistic perspective The perspective that emphasizes the responsibility that people have for their own behavior, even when such behavior is abnormal (Module 48)

humanistic perspective The approach that suggests that all individuals naturally strive to grow, develop, and be in control of their lives and behavior (Module 2)

humanistic therapy Therapy in which the underlying assumption is that people have control of their behavior, can make choices about their lives, and are essentially responsible for solving their own problems (Module 52)

hypnosis A trancelike state of heightened susceptibility to the suggestions of others (Module 15)

hypochondriasis A disorder in which people have a constant fear of illness and a preoccupation with their health (Module 49)

hypothalamus A tiny part of the brain, located below the thalamus of the brain, that maintains homostasis and produces and regulates vital, basic behavior such as eating, drinking, and sexual behavior (Module 9)

hypothesis A prediction, stemming from a theory, stated in a way that allows it to be tested (Module 4)

iconic memory Memory which reflects information from our visual system (Module 20)

id The raw, unorganized, inborn part of personality, whose sole purpose is to reduce tension created by primitive drives related to hunger, sex, aggression, and irrational impulses (Module 42)

identical twins Twins who are genetically identical (Module 37)

identification The process of trying to be like another person as much as possible, imitating that person's behavior and adopting similar beliefs and values (Module 42)

identity The distinguishing character of the individual: who each of us is, what our roles are, and what we are capable of (Module 40)

identity-versus-role-confusion stage According to Erikson, a time in adolescence of major testing to determine one's unique qualities (Module 40)

implicit memory Memories of which people are not consciously aware, but which can affect subsequent performance and behavior (Module 20)

incentive approaches to motivation The theory suggesting that motivation stems from the desire to obtain valued external goals, or incentives (Module 29)

independent variable The variable that is manipulated by an experimenter (Module 5)

industrial-organizational (I/O) psychology The branch of psychology focusing on work and job-related issues, including productivity, job satisfaction, decision-making, and consumer behavior (Module 55)

industry-versus-inferiority stage According to Erikson, the last stage of childhood during which children ages 6 to 12 years may develop positive social interactions with others or may feel inadequate and become less sociable (Module 39)

inferential statistics The branch of statistics that uses data from samples to make predictions about the larger population from which the sample is drawn (Module 60)

inferiority complex According to Adler, a situation in which adults have not been able to overcome the feelings of inferiority that they developed as children, when they were small and limited in their knowledge about the world (Module 42)

information processing The way in which people take in, use, and store information (Module 39)

informed consent A document signed by participants affirming that they have been told the basic outlines of the study and are aware of what their participation will involve (Module 6)

inhibited ejaculation The inability of a male to ejaculate when he wants to, if at all (Module 36)

inhibited sexual desire A sexual dysfunction in which the motivation for sexual activity is restrained or lacking entirely (Module 36)

inhibitory message A chemical message that prevents or decreases the likelihood that a receiving neuron will fire (Module 7)

initiative-versus-guilt stage According to Erikson, the period during which children ages 3 to 6 years experience conflict between independence of action and the sometimes negative results of that action (Module 39)

insight A sudden awareness of the relationships among various elements that had previously appeared to be independent of one another (Module 24)

instincts Inborn patterns of behavior that are biologically determined rather than learned (Module 29)

intellectually gifted Two to 4 percent of the population who have IQ scores greater than 130 (Module 27)

intelligence The capacity to understand the world, think rationally, and use resources effectively when faced with challenges (Module 26)

intelligence quotient (IQ) A score that takes into account an individual's mental *and* chronological ages (Module 26)

intelligence tests Tests devised to identify a person's level of intelligence (Module 26)

interference The phenomenon by which information in memory displaces or blocks out other information, preventing its recall (Module 22)

interneurons Neurons that connect sensory and motor neurons, carrying messages between the two (Module 8)

interpersonal attraction (or close relationship) Positive feelings for others; liking and loving (Module 57)

intimacy-versus-isolation stage According to Erikson, a period during early adulthood that focuses on developing close relationships (Module 40)

introspection A procedure used to study the structure of the mind, in which subjects are asked to describe in detail what they are experiencing when they are exposed to a stimulus (Module 2)

James-Lange theory of emotion The belief that emotional experience is a reaction to bodily events occurring as a result of an external situation ("I feel sad because I am crying") (Module 31)

just noticeable difference The minimum stimulation required to detect the difference between two stimuli (Module 10)

language The communication of information through symbols arranged according to systematic rules (Module 25)

language-acquisition device A neural system of the brain hypothesized to permit understanding of language (Module 25)

latency period According to Freud, the period between the phallic stage and puberty during which children's sexual concerns are temporarily put aside (Module 42)

latent content of dreams According to Freud, the "disguised" meanings of dreams, hidden by more obvious subjects (Module 14)

latent learning Learning in which a new behavior is acquired but is not demonstrated until some incentive is provided for displaying it (Module 19)

lateralization The dominance of one hemisphere of the brain in specific functions (Module 9)

learned helplessness A state in which people conclude that unpleasant or aversive stimuli cannot be controlled—a view of the world that becomes so in-grained that they cease trying to remedy the aversive circumstances, even if they actually can exert some influence (Module 45)

learning A relatively permanent change in behavior brought about by experience (Module 17)

learning-theory approach The theory suggesting that language acquisition follows the principles of reinforcement and conditioning (Module 25)

levels-of-processing theory The theory of memory that emphasizes the degree to which new material is mentally analyzed (Module 21)

life review The process by which people examine and evaluate their lives (Module 41)

limbic system The part of the brain located outside the "new brain" that controls eating, aggression, and reproduction (Module 9)

lithium A drug comprised of mineral salts used to treat bipolar disorders (Module 53)

lobes The four major sections of the cerebral cortex: frontal, parietal, temporal, and occipital (Module 9)

longitudinal research A research method that investigates behavior as participants age (Module 37)

long-term memory Memory that stores information on a relatively permanent basis, although it may be difficult to retrieve (Module 20)

major depression A severe form of depression that interferes with concentration, decision making, and sociability (Module 49)

mania An extended state of intense, wild elation (Module 49)

manifest content of dreams According to Freud, the overt story line of dreams (Module 14)

masturbation Sexual self-stimulation (Module 35)

mean The average of all scores, arrived at by adding scores together and dividing by the number of scores (Module 58)

means-ends analysis Repeated testing for differences between the desired outcome and what currently exists (Module 24)

median The point in a distribution of scores that divides the distribution exactly in half when the scores are listed in numerical order (Module 58)

medical perspective The perspective that suggests that when an individual displays symptoms of abnormal behavior, the root cause will be found in a physical examination of the individual, which may reveal a hormonal imbalance, a chemical deficiency, or a brain injury (Module 48)

meditation A learned technique for refocusing attention that brings about an -altered state of consciousness (Module 15)

memory The process by which we encode, store, and retrieve information (Module 20)

memory trace An actual physical change in the brain that occurs when new material is learned (Module 22)

menopause The point at which women stop menstruating and are no longer fertile (Module 41)

mental age The average age of individuals who achieve a particular level of performance on a test (Module 26)

mental images Representations in the mind that resemble the object or event being represented (Module 23)

mental retardation Identified by significantly below-average intellectual functioning accompanied by limitations in at least two areas of adaptive functioning (Module 27)

mental set The tendency for old patterns of problem solving to persist (Module 24)

metabolism The rate at which food is converted to energy and expended by the body (Module 30)

metacognition An awareness and understanding of one's own cognitive processes (Module 39)

Minnesota Multiphasic Personality Inventory-2 (MMPI-2) A test used to identify people with psychological difficulties as well as to predict such behavior as job performance (Module 44)

mode The most frequently occurring score in a set of scores (Module 58)

mood disorder Disturbances in emotional feeling strong enough to interfere with everyday living (Module 49)

motivation The factors that direct and energize the behavior of humans and other organisms (Module 29)

motor area The part of the cortex that is largely responsible for the voluntary

movement of particular parts of the body (Module 9)

motor (efferent) neurons Neurons that communicate information from the nervous system to muscles and glands of the body (Module 8)

myelin sheath A protective coat of fat and protein that wraps around the axon (Module 7)

narcissistic personality disorder A personality disturbance which is characterized by an exaggerated sense of self-importance (Module 49)

narcotics Drugs that increase relaxation and relieve pain and anxiety (Module 16)

naturalistic observation Research in which an investigator simply observes some naturally occurring behavior and does not make a change in the situation (Module 5)

nature-nurture issue The issue of the degree to which environment and heredity influence behavior (Module 37)

need for achievement A stable, learned characteristic in which satisfaction is obtained by striving for and attaining a level of excellence (Module 30)

need for affiliation An interest in establishing and maintaining relationships with other people (Module 30)

need for power A tendency to seek impact, control, or influence over others, and to be seen as a powerful individual (Module 30)

need-complementarity hypothesis The hypothesis that people are attracted to others who fulfill their needs (Module 57)

negative reinforcer An unpleasant stimulus whose removal leads to an increase in the probability that a preceding response will occur again in the future (Module 18)

negative relationship A relationship established by data that shows high values of one variable corresponding with low values of the other (Module 60)

neo-Freudian psychoanalysts Psychoanalysts who were trained in traditional Freudian theory but who later rejected some of its major points (Module 42)

neonate A newborn child (Module 39)

neurons Nerve cells, the basic elements of the nervous system (Module 7)

neuroscience perspective The approach that views behavior from the perspective of the brain, nervous system, and other biological functions (Module 2)

neurotransmitters Chemicals that carry messages across the synapse to the dendrite (and sometimes the cell body) of a receiver neuron (Module 7)

neutral stimulus A stimulus that, before conditioning, does not naturally bring about the response of interest (Module 17)

normal distribution A distribution of scores that produces a bell-shaped, symmetrical curve (Module 58)

norms Standards of test performance that permit the comparison of one person's score on the test to the scores of others who have taken the same test (Module 26)

obedience A change in behavior due to the commands of others (Module 55)

obesity The state of being more than 20 percent above the average weight for a person of a given height (Module 30)

object permanence The awareness that objects—and people—continue to exist even if they are out of sight (Module 39)

observational learning Learning through observing the behavior of another person called a *mode* (Module 19)

obsession A persistant, unwanted thought or idea that keeps recurring (Module 49)

obsessive-compulsive disorder A disorder characterized by obsessions or compulsions (Module 49)

Oedipal conflict A child's sexual interest in his or her opposite-sex parent, typically resolved through identification with the same-sex parent (Module 42)

operant conditioning Learning in which a voluntary response is strengthened or weakened, depending on its favorable or unfavorable consequences (Module 18)

operationalization The process of translating a hypothesis into specific, testable procedures that can be measured and observed (Module 5)

opponent-process theory of color vision The theory that receptor cells are linked in pairs, working in opposition to each other (Module 11)

optic nerve A bundle of ganglion axons that carry visual information (Module 11)

oral stage According to Freud, a stage from birth to 12–18 months, in which an infant's center of pleasure is the mouth (Module 42)

orgasm The peak of sexual excitement during which rhythmic muscular contractions occur in the genitals (Module 34)

otoliths Tiny, motion-sensitive crystals within the semicircular canals that sense body acceleration (Module 12)

overgeneralization The phenomenon whereby children apply rules even when the application results in an error (Module 25)

ovulation The point at which an egg is released from the ovaries (Module 34)

panic disorder Anxiety that reveals itself in the form of panic attacks that last from a few seconds to as long as several hours (Module 49)

parasympathetic division The part of the autonomic division of the nervous system that acts to calm the body after the emergency situation is resolved (Module 8)

partial (or intermittent) reinforcement schedule Behavior that is reinforced some but not all of the time (Module 18)

passionate (or romantic) love A state of intense absorption in someone that includes intense physiological arousal, psychological interest, and caring for the needs of another (Module 57)

perception The sorting out, interpretation, analysis, and integration of stimuli involving our sense organs and brain (Module 10)

peripheral nervous system The part of the nervous system that includes the autonomic and somatic subdivisions; made up of long axons and dendrites, it branches out from the spinal cord and brain and reaches the extremities of the body (Module 8)

peripheral route processing Message interpretation characterized by consideration of the source and related general information rather than of the message itself (Module 54)

permissive parents Parents who give their children lax or inconsistent direction and, although warm, require little of them (Module 39)

personal stressors Major life events, such as the death of a family member, that have immediate negative consequences which generally fade with time (Module 45)

personality The pattern of enduring characteristics that differentiate people—those behaviors that make each individual unique (Module 42)

personality disorder A mental disorder characterized by a set of inflexible, maladaptive personality traits that keep a person from functioning properly in society (Module 49)

person-centered therapy Therapy in which the goal is to reach one's potential for self-actualization (Module 52)

phallic stage According to Freud, a period beginning around age 3 during which a child's interest focuses on the genitals (Module 42)

phobias Intense, irrational fears of specific objects or situations (Module 49)

phonemes The smallest basic sound units (Module 25)

phonology The study of the smallest sound units, called phonemes (Module 25)

pituitary gland The "master gland," the major component of the endocrine system, which secretes hormones that control growth (Module 8, Module 9)

place theory of hearing The theory that different areas of the basilar membrane respond to different frequencies (Module 12)

placebo A false treatment, such as a pill, "drug," or other substance without any significant chemical properties or active ingredient (Module 6)

plateau phase The period in which the maximum level of arousal is attained, the penis and clitoris swell with blood, and the body prepares for orgasm (Module 34)

population All the members of a group of interest (Module 60)

positive reinforcer A stimulus added to the environment that brings about an increase in a preceding response (Module 18)

positive relationship A relationship established by data that shows high values of one variable corresponding with high values of another, and low values of the first variable corresponding with low values of the other (Module 60)

posttraumatic stress disorder (PTSD) A phenomenon in which victims of major catastrophes reexperience the original stress event and associated feelings in vivid flashbacks or dreams (Module 45)

practical intelligence Intelligence related to overall success in living (Module 26)

prejudice The negative (or positive) evaluations of groups and their members (Module 56)

premature ejaculation The inability of a male to delay orgasm as long as he wishes (Module 36)

preoperational stage According to Piaget, the period from 2 to 7 years of age that is characterized by language development (Module 39)

priming A phenomenon in which exposure to a word or concept (called a *prime*) later makes it easier to recall related information, even when there is no conscious memory of the word or concept (Module 20)

principle of conservation The knowledge that quantity is unrelated to the arrangement and physical appearance of objects (Module 39)

procedural memory Memory for skills and habits, such as riding a bike or hitting a baseball, sometimes referred to as "nondeclarative memory" (Module 20)

progesterone Female sex hormone (Module 34)

projective personality test A test in which a person is shown an ambiguous stimulus and asked to describe it or tell a story about it (Module 44)

prosocial behavior Helping behavior (Module 57)

prototypes Typical, highly representative examples of a concept (Module 23)

psychoactive drugs Drugs that influence a person's emotions, perceptions, and behavior (Module 16)

psychoanalysis Psychodynamic therapy that involves frequent sessions and often lasts for many years (Module 51)

psychoanalytic perspective The perspective that suggests that abnormal behavior stems from childhood conflicts over opposing wishes regarding sex and aggression (Module 48)

psychoanalytic theory Freud's theory that unconscious forces act as determinants of personality (Module 42)

psychodynamic perspective The approach based on the belief that behavior is motivated by unconscious inner forces over which the individual has little control (Module 2)

psychodynamic therapy First suggested by Freud, therapy that is based on the premise that the primary sources of abnormal behavior are unresolved past conflicts and the possibility that unacceptable unconscious impulses will enter consciousness (Module 51)

psychological tests Standard measures devised to assess behavior objectively and used by psychologists to help people make decisions about their lives and understand more about themselves (Module 44)

psychology The scientific study of behavior and mental processes (Module 1)

psychoneuroimmunology (PNI) The study of the relationship among psychological factors, the immune system, and the brain (Module 45)

psychophysics The study of the relationship between the physical aspects of stimuli and our psychological experience of them (Module 10)

psychophysiological disorders Medical problems influenced by an interaction of psychological, emotional, and physical difficulties (Module 45)

psychosocial development Development of individuals' interactions and understanding of each other and of their knowledge and understanding of themselves as members of society (Module 39)

psychosurgery Brain surgery once used to reduce symptoms of mental disorder but rarely used today (Module 53)

psychotherapy Treatment in which a trained professional—a therapist—uses psychological techniques to help someone overcome psychological difficulties and disorders, resolve problems in living, or bring about personal growth (Module 51)

puberty The period at which maturation of the sexual organs occurs, begins at about age 11 or 12 for girls and 13 or 14 for boys (Module 40)

punishment A stimulus that decreases the probability that a previous behavior will occur again (Module 18)

random assignment to condition A procedure in which participants are assigned to different experimental groups or "conditions" on the basis of chance and chance alone (Module 5)

range The difference between the highest and lowest score in a distribution (Module 59)

rape The act whereby one person forces another to submit to sexual activity (Module 36)

rapid eye movement (REM) sleep Sleep occupying 20 percent of an adult's sleeping time, characterized by increased heart rate, blood pressure, and breathing rate; erections; eye movements; and the experience of dreaming (Module 14)

rational-emotive behavior therapy A form of therapy that attempts to restructure a person's belief system into a more realistic, rational, and logical set of views (Module 51)

reactance A disagreeable emotional and cognitive reaction that results from the restriction of one's freedom and that can be associated with medical regimens (Module 47)

reciprocity-of-liking effect A tendency to like those who like us (Module 57)

reflexes Automatic, involuntary response to an incoming stimulus (Module 8)

reflexes Unlearned, involuntary responses that occur automatically in the presence of certain stimuli (Module 39)

refractory period A temporary period following the resolution stage during which the male cannot be sexually aroused again (Module 34)

rehearsal The repetition of information that has entered short-term memory (Module 20)

reinforcement The process by which a stimulus increases the probability that a preceding behavior will be repeated (Module 18)

reinforcer Any stimulus that increases the probability that a preceding behavior will occur again (Module 18)

reliability The concept that tests measure consistently what they are trying to measure (Module 26)

replication The repetition of research, sometimes using other procedures, settings, and other groups of participants, in order to increase confidence in prior findings (Module 5)

resolution stage The interval following orgasm in which the body returns to its normal state, reversing the changes brought about by arousal (Module 34)

resting state The state in which there is a negative electrical charge of about -70 millivolts within the neuron (Module 7)

reticular formation The part of the brain from the medulla through the pons made up of groups of nerve cells that can immediately activate other parts of the brain to produce general bodily arousal (Module 9)

retina The part of the eye that converts the electromagnetic energy of light into useful information for the brain (Module 11)

reuptake The reabsorption of neurotransmitters by a terminal button (Module 7)

rods Thin, cylindrical receptor cells in the retina that are highly sensitive to light (Module 11)

Rorschach test A test developed by Swiss psychiatrist Hermann Rorschach that consists of showing a series of symmetrical stimuli to people who are then asked what the figures represent to them (Module 44)

sample A subgroup of a population of interest (Module 60)

Schachter-Singer theory of emotion The belief that emotions are determined jointly by a nonspecific kind of physiological arousal and its interpretation, based on environmental cues (Module 31)

schedules of reinforcement The frequency and timing of reinforcement following desired behavior (Module 18)

schemas Organized bodies of information stored in memory that bias the way new information is interpreted, stored, and recalled (Module 21)

schemas Sets of cognitions about people and social experiences (Module 54)

schizophrenia A class of disorders in which severe distortion of reality occurs (Module 49)

scientific method The approach through which psychologists systematically acquire knowledge and understanding about behavior and other phenomena of interest (Module 4)

self-actualization A state of self-fulfillment in which people realize their highest potential in their own unique way (Module 29)

self-actualization According to Rogers, a state of self-fulfillment in which people realize their highest potential (Module 43)

self-report measures A method of gathering data about people by asking them questions about a sample of their behavior (Module 44)

self-serving bias The tendency to attribute personal success to personal factors (skill, ability, or effort) and to attribute failure to factors outside of oneself (Module 54)

semantic memory Memory for general knowledge and facts about the world, as well as memory for the rules of logic that are used to deduce other facts (Module 20)

semantics The rules governing the meaning of words and sentences (Module 25)

semicircular canals Three tubelike structures of the inner ear containing fluid that sloshes through them when the head moves, signaling rotational or angular movement to the brain (Module 12)

sensation The processes by which our sense organs receive information from the environment (Module 10)

sensorimotor stage According to Piaget, the stage from birth to 2 years during which a child has little competence in representing the environment using images, language, or other symbols (Module 39)

sensory (afferent) neurons Neurons that transmit information from the perimeter of the body to the central nervous system (Module 8)

sensory area The site in the brain of the tissue that corresponds to each of the senses, with the degree of sensitivity relating to the amount of tissue (Module 9)

sensory memory The initial, momentary storage of information, lasting only an instant (Module 20)

sequential research A research method that combines cross-sectional and longitudinal research by considering a number of different age groups and examining them over several points in time (Module 37)

sexism Negative attitudes and behavior toward a person based on that person's gender (Module 33)

sexually transmitted disease (STD) A disease acquired through sexual contact (Module 36)

shaping The process of teaching a complex behavior by rewarding closer and closer approximations of the desired behavior (Module 18)

short-term memory Memory that holds information for 15 to 25 seconds (Module 20)

significant outcome An outcome expected to occur by chance less than 5 percent of the time (Module 60)

significant outcome Meaningful results that make it possible for researchers to feel confident that they have confirmed their hypotheses (Module 5)

situational causes (of behavior) A perceived cause of behavior that is based on environmental factors (Module 54)

skin senses The senses that include touch, pressure, temperature and pain (Module 12)

social cognition The cognitive processes by which people understand and make sense of others and themselves (Module 54)

social cognitive approaches to personality The theory that emphasizes the influence of a person's cognitions—thoughts, feelings, expectations, and values—in determining personality (Module 43)

social influence The process by which the actions of an individual or group affect the behavior of others (Module 55)

social psychology The study of how people's thoughts, feelings, and actions are affected by others (Module 54)

social support A mutual network of caring, interested others (Module 45)

social supporter A person who shares an unpopular opinion or attitude of another group member, thereby encouraging nonconformity (Module 55)

sociocultural perspective The perspective that makes the assumption that people's behavior—both normal and abnormal—is shaped by the kind of family group, society, and culture in which they live (Module 48)

somatic division The part of the peripheral nervous system that specializes in the control of voluntary movements and the communication of information to and from the sense organs (Module 8)

somatoform disorder Psychological difficulties that take on a physical (somatic) form, but for which there is no medical cause (Module 49)

sound The movement of air molecules brought about by the vibration of an object (Module 12)

spinal cord A bundle of nerves that leaves the brain and runs down the length of the back and is the main means for transmitting messages between the brain and the body (Module 8)

split-brain patient A person who suffers from independent functioning of the two halves of the brain, as a result of which the sides of the body work in disharmony (Module 9)

spontaneous recovery The re-emergence of an extinguished conditioned response after a period of rest (Module 17)

spontaneous remission Recovery without treatment (Module 52)

stage 1 sleep The state of transition between wakefulness and sleep, characterized by relatively rapid, low-voltage brain waves (Module 14)

stage 2 sleep A sleep deeper than that of stage 1, characterized by a slower, more regular wave pattern, along with momentary interruptions of "sleep spindles" (Module 14)

stage 3 sleep A sleep characterized by slow brain waves, with greater peaks and valleys in the wave pattern (Module 14)

stage 4 sleep The deepest stage of sleep, during which we are least responsive to outside stimulation (Module 14)

standard deviation An index of the average deviation of a set of scores from the center of the distribution (Module 59)

statistics The branch of mathematics concerned with collecting, organizing, analyzing, and drawing conclusions from numerical data (Module 58)

status The social rank held within a group (Module 55)

stereotypes Generalized beliefs and expectations about social groups and their members (Module 56)

stimulants Drugs that affect the central nervous system by causing a rise in heart rate, blood pressure, and muscular tension (Module 16)

stimulus Energy that produces a response in a sense organ (Module 10)

stimulus discrimination The ability to differentiate between stimuli (Module 17)

stimulus generalization Response to a stimulus that is similar to but different from a conditioned stimulus; the more similar the two stimuli, the more likely generalization is to occur (Module 17)

stress The response to events that are threatening or challenging (Module 45)

structuralism Wundt's approach that focuses on the fundamental elements that form the foundation of thinking, consciousness, emotions, and other kinds of mental states and activities (Module 2)

subjective well-being An approach by which people evaluate their lives in terms of both their thoughts and emotions (Module 47)

superego According to Freud, the final personality structure to develop that represents the rights and wrongs of society as handed down by a person's parents,

teachers, and other important figures (Module 42)

survey research Research in which people chosen to represent some larger population are asked a series of questions about their behavior, thoughts, or attitudes (Module 5)

syllogistic reasoning Formal reasoning in which people draw a conclusion from a set of assumptions (Module 23)

sympathetic division The part of the autonomic division of the nervous system that acts to prepare the body in stressful emergency situations, engaging all the organism's resources to respond to a threat (Module 8)

synapse The space between two neurons where the axon of a sending neuron communicates with the dendrites of a receiving neuron using chemical messages (Module 7)

syntax The rules that indicate how words and phrases can be combined to form sentences (Module 25)

systematic desensitization A behavioral technique in which gradual exposure to anxiety-producing stimulus is paired with relaxation in order to extinguish the response of anxiety (Module 51)

telegraphic speech Sentences that sound as if they were part of a telegram, in which words not critical to the message are left out (Module 25)

temperament A basic, innate disposition that emerges early in life (Module 39, 43)

teratogens Environmental agents such as a drug, chemical, virus, or other factors that produce a birth defect (Module 38)

terminal buttons Small bulges at the end of axons that send messages to other neurons (Module 7)

test standardization A technique used to validate questions in personality tests by studying the responses of people with known diagnoses (Module 44)

thalamus The part of the brain located in the middle of the central core that acts primarily as a busy relay station, mostly for information concerning the senses (Module 9)

Thematic Apperception Test (TAT) A test consisting of a series of pictures about which a person is asked to write a story (Module 44)

theories Broad explanations and predictions concerning phenomena of interest (Module 4)

thinking The manipulation of mental representations of information (Module 23)

tip-of-the-tongue phenomenon The inability to recall information that one realizes one knows—a result of the difficulty of retrieving information from long-term memory (Module 21)

top-down processing Perception that is guided by higher-level knowledge, experience, expectations, and motivations (Module 13)

trait theory A model of personality that seeks to identify the basic traits necessary to describe personality (Module 43)

traits Enduring dimensions of personality characteristics along which people differ (Module 43)

treatment The manipulation implemented by the experimenter (Module 5)

trichromatic theory of color vision The theory that there are three kinds of cones in the retina, each of which responds primarily to a specific range of wavelengths (Module 11)

trust-versus-mistrust stage According to Erikson, the first stage of psychosocial development, occurring from birth to 18 months of age, during which time infants develop feelings of trust or lack of trust (Module 39)

Type A behavior pattern A pattern of behavior characterized by competitiveness, impatience, tendency toward frustration, and hostility (Module 46)

Type B behavior pattern A pattern of behavior characterized by cooperation, patience, noncompetitiveness, and nonaggression (Module 46)

unconditional positive regard An attitude of acceptance and respect on the part of an observer, no matter what a person says or does (Module 43)

unconditioned response (UCR) A response that is natural and needs no training (e.g., salivation at the smell of food) (Module 17)

unconditioned stimulus (UCS) A stimulus that brings about a response without having been learned (Module 17)

unconscious A part of the personality of which a person is not aware, and which is a potential determinant of behavior (Module 42)

unconscious wish fulfillment theory Sigmund Freud's theory that dreams represent unconscious wishes that dreamers desire to see fulfilled (Module 14)

uninvolved parents Parents who show little interest in their children and are emotionally detached (Module 39)

universal grammar Noam Chomsky's theory that all the world's languages share a similar underlying structure (Module 25)

uplifts Minor positive events that make one feel good (Module 45)

validity The concept that tests actually measure what they are suppose supposed to measure (Module 26)

variability The spread, or dispersion, of scores in a distribution (Module 59)

variable Behaviors, events, or other characteristics that can change, or vary, in some way (Module 5)

variable-interval schedule A schedule whereby the time between reinforcements varies around some average rather than being fixed (Module 18)

variable-ratio schedule A schedule whereby reinforcement occurs after a varying number of responses rather than after a fixed number (Module 18)

visual illusions Physical stimuli that consistently produce errors in perception (Module 13)

wear-and-tear theories of aging Theories that suggest that the mechanical functions of the body simply stop working efficiently (Module 41)

Weber's law One of the basic laws of psychophysics, that a just noticeable difference is in constant proportion to the intensity of an initial stimulus (Module 10)

weight set point The particular level of weight that the body strives to maintain (Module 30)

working memory A set of active, temporary memory stores that rehearse information (Module 20)

zone of proximal development (ZPD) According to Vygotsky, the level at which a child can almost, but not fully, comprehend or perform a task on his or her own (Module 39)

zygote The new cell formed by the union of an egg and sperm (Module 38)

References

Abbot, A. (2002). Neurobiology: Music, maestro, please! *Nature, 416*, 12–14.

Ablon, J. S., & Jones, E. E. (2002). Validity of controlled clinical trials of psychotherapy: Findings from the NIMH Treatment of Depression Collaborative Research Program. *American Journal of Psychiatry, 159*, 775–783.

Abrahams, M. F., & Bell, R. A. (1994). Encouraging charitable contributions: An examination of three models of door-in-the-face compliance. *Communication Research, 21*, 131–153.

Abramson, L. Y., Alloy, L. B., Hogan, M. E., Whitehouse, W. G., Donova, P., Rose, D. T., Panzarella, C., & Raniere, D. (2002). Cognitive vulnerability to depression: Theory and evidence. In R. L. Leahy & E. T. Dowd (Eds.), *Clinical advances in cognitive psychotherapy: Theory and Application*, pp. 75–92. New York: Springer.

Abt, S. (1999, July 26). Armstrong wins tour and journey. *The New York Times*, pp. D1, D4.

Ackard, D. M., & Neumark-Sztainer, D. (2002). Date violence and date rape among adolescents: Associations with disordered eating behaviors and psychological health. *Child Abuse and Neglect, 26*, 455–473.

Adair, J. G., & Vohra, N. (2003). The explosion knowledge, references, and citations: Psychology's unique response to a crisis. *American Psychologist, 58*, 15–23.

Adams, B., & Parker, J. D. (1990). Maternal weight gain in women with good pregnancy outcome. *Obstetrics and Gynecology, 76*, 1–7.

Ader, R., Felten, D., & Cohen, N. (2001). *Psychoneuroimmunology* (3rd ed.). San Diego: Academic Press.

Adler, J. (1984, April 23). The fight to conquer fear. *Newsweek*, pp. 66–72.

Adolphs, R. (2002). Neural systems for recognizing emotion. *Current Opinion in Neurobiology, 12*, 169–177.

Adolphs, R., Denburg, N. L., & Tranel, D. (2001). The amygdala's role in long-term declarative memory for gist and detail. *Behavioral Neuroscience, 115*, 983–992.

Advances in Telepsychology/Telehealth. (2000). *Professional Psychology: Research and Practice*, 31 (2).

Affleck, G., Tennen, H., Urrows, S., & Higgins, P. (1994). Person and contextual features of daily stress reactivity: Individual differences in relations of undesirable daily events with mood disturbance and chronic pain intensity.

Journal of Personality and Social Psychology, 66, 329–340.

Aghajanian, G. K. (1994). Serotonin and the action of LSD in the brain. *Psychiatric Annals, 24*, 137–141.

Agras, W. S., & Berkowitz, R. I. (1996). Behavior therapy. In R. E. Hales & S. C. Yudofsky (Eds.), *The American Psychiatric Press synopsis of psychiatry*. Washington, DC: American Psychiatric Press.

Aharon, I., Etcoff, N., Ariely, D., Chabris, C. F., O'Connor, E., & Breiter, H. C. (2001). Beautiful faces have variable reward value: fMRI and behavioral evidence. *Neuron, 32*, 537–551.

Ahissar, M., Ahissar, E., Bergman, H., & Vaadia, E. (1992). Encoding of sound-source location and movement: Activity of single neurons and interactions between adjacent neurons in the monkey auditory cortex. *Journal of Neurophysiology, 67*, 203–215.

Ahrons, C. (1995). *The good divorce: Keeping your family together when your marriage comes apart.* New York: HarperPerennial.

Aiken, L. (2000). *Dying, death, and bereavement* (4th ed.). Mahwah, NJ: Erlbaum.

Aiken, L. R. (1996). *Assessment of intellectual functioning* (2nd ed.). New York: Plenum.

Aiken, L. R. (1997). *Psychological testing and assessment* (9th ed.). Boston: Allyn & Bacon.

Ainsworth, M. D. S., Blehar, M. C., Waters, E., & Wall, S. (1978). *Patterns of attachment: A psychological study of the strange situation.* Hillsdale, NJ: Erlbaum.

Ajzen, I. (2002). Residual effects of past on later behavior: Habituation and reasoned action perspectives. *Personality and Social Psychology Review, 6*, 107–122.

Akil, H., & Morano, M. I. (1996). The biology of stress: From periphery to brain. In S. J. Watson (Ed.), *Biology of schizophrenia and affective disease.* Washington, DC: American Psychiatric Press.

Akman, I., Ozek, E., Bilgen, H., Ozdogan, T., & Cebeci, D. (2002). Sweet solutions and pacifiers for pain relief in newborn infants. *Journal of Pain, 3*, 199–202.

Akutsu, P. D., Sue, S., Zane, N. W. S., & Nakamura, C. Y. (1989). Ethnic differences in alcohol consumption among Asians and Caucasians in the United States: An investigation of cultural and physiological factors. *Journal of Studies on Alcohol, 50*, 261–267.

Alford, B. A., & Beck, A. T. (1997) *The integrative power of cognitive therapy.* New York: Guilford Press.

Allan, G., & Harrison, K. (2002). Marital affairs. In R. Goodwin, et al. (Eds.), *Inappropriate relationships: The unconventional, the disapproved, and the forbidden: LEA's series on personal relationships*, pp. 45–63. Mahwah, NJ: Erlbaum.

Allen, M. (1999, September 19). Help wanted: The not-too-high-Q standard. *The New York Times*, p. 3.

Alloy, L. B., Jacobson, N. S., & Acocella, J. (1999). *Abnormal psychology* (8th ed.). New York: McGraw-Hill.

Allport, G. W. (1961). *Pattern and growth in personality.* New York: Holt, Rinehart and Winston.

Allport, G. W. (1966). Traits revisited. *American Psychologist, 21*, 1–10.

Allport, G. W., & Postman, L. J. (1958). The basic psychology of rumor. In E. D. Maccoby, T. M. Newcomb, & E. L. Hartley (Eds.), *Readings in social psychology* (3rd ed.). New York: Holt, Rinehart and Winston.

Almer, E. (2000, April 22). Online therapy: An arm's length approach. *The New York Times*, pp. A1, A11.

Alonso, A., Alonso, S., & Piper, W. (2003). Group psychotherapy. In G. Stricker & T. A. Widiger, et al. (Eds.), *Handbook of psychology: Clinical psychology*, Vol. 8. New York: Wiley.

Altman, N. (1996). The accommodation of diversity in psychoanalysis. In R. P. Foster, M. Moskowitz, & R. A. Javier (Eds.), *Reaching across boundaries of culture and class: Widening the scope of psychotherapy.* Northvale, NJ: Jason Aronson.

American Academy of Pediatrics. (1999a). Media Education (RE9911). *Pediatrics, 104*, 341–343.

American Academy of Pediatrics. (1999b, July 26). *Circumcision: Information for parents. www.aap.org/family/circ.htm.*

American Association of Mental Retardation (AAMR). (2002). *Mental retardation: Definition, classification, and systems of supports* (10th ed.). Washington, DC.: AAMR.

American Association of University Women (AAUW). (1992). *How schools shortchange women: The A.A.U.W. Report.* Washington, DC: AAUW Educational Foundation.

American Association of University Women (AAUW). (1993). *Hostile hallways: The AAUW survey on sexual harassment in*

American schools. Washington, DC. AAUW Educational Foundation.

American College Health Association. (1989). *Guidelines on acquaintance rape.* Washington, DC: American College Health Association.

American Psychiatric Association. (2000). Diagnostic and statistical manual of mental disorders DSM-IV-TR (Text Revision). 4th ed. Arlington, VA: American Psychiatric Association.

American Psychological Association (APA). (2002, August 21). *APA Ethics Code, 2002.* Washington, DC: American Psychological Association.

American Psychological Association Task Force on Intelligence, (1996). *Intelligence: Knowns and unknowns.* Washington, DC: American Psychological Association.

American Psychological Association. (APA). (1993, January/February). Subgroup norming and the Civil Rights Act. *Psychological Science Agenda, 5,* 6.

Anand, G. (2002, June 12). Approval is near on a new drug for depression. *The Wall Street Journal,* p. D1.

Anand, G., & Burton, T. M. (2003, April 11). Drug debate: New antipsychotics pose a quandary for FDA, doctors. *The Wall Street Journal,* pp. A1, A8.

Anastasi, A., & Urbina, S. (1997). *Psychological Testing* (7th ed.). Englewood Cliffs, NJ: Prentice Hall.

Andersen, B. L., Kiecolt-Glaser, J. K., & Glaser, R. (1994). A biobehavioral model of cancer stress and disease course. *American Psychologist, 49,* 389–404.

Anderson, B. F. (1980). *The complete thinker: A handbook of techniques for creative and critical problem solving.* Englewood Cliffs, NJ: Prentice Hall.

Anderson, C. A., & Dill, K. E. (2000). Video games and aggressive thoughts, feelings, and behavior in the laboratory and in life. *Journal of Personality and Social Psychology, 78,* 772–790.

Anderson, C. A., & Bushman, B. J. (2001). Effects of violent video games on aggressive behavior, aggressive cognition, aggressive affect, physiological arousal, and prosocial behavior: A meta-analytic review of the scientific literature. *Psychological Science, 12,* 353–359.

Anderson, C. A., & Bushman, B. J. (2002, March 29). The effects of media violence on society. *Science, 295,* 2377–2378.

Anderson, C. A., Carnagey, N. L., & Eubanks, J. (2003). Exposure to violent media: The effects of songs with violent lyrics on aggressive thoughts and feelings. *Journal of Personality and Social Psychology, 84,* 960–971.

Anderson, J. (1988). Cognitive styles and multicultural populations. *Journal of Teacher Education, 39,* 2–9.

Anderson, J. A., & Adams, M. (1992). Acknowledging the learning styles of diverse student populations: Implications for instructional design. *New Directions for Teaching and Learning, 49,* 19–33.

Anderson, J. R. (1981). Interference: The relationship between response latency and response accuracy. *Journal of Experimental Psychology: Human Learning and Memory, 7,* 311–325.

Anderson, J. R., & Bower, G. H. (1972). Recognition and retrieval processes in free recall. *Psychological Review, 79,* 97–123.

Anderson, K. B., Cooper, H., & Okamura, L. (1997). Individual differences and attitudes toward rape: A meta-analytic review. *Personality and Social Psychology Bulletin, 23,* 295–315.

Anderson, N. H. (1996). *A functional theory of cognition.* Mahwah, NJ: Erlbaum.

Anderson, T., & Magnusson, D. (1990). Biological maturation in adolescence and the development of drinking habits and alcohol abuse among young males: A prospective longitudinal study. *Journal of Youth and Adolescence, 19,* 33–42.

Andreasen, N. C., Arndt, S., Swayze II, V., Cizadlo, T., Flaum, M., O'Leary, D., Ehrhardt, J. C., & Yuh, W. T. C. (1994, October 14). Thalamic abnormalities in schizophrenia visualized through magnetic resonance image averaging. *Science, 266,* 294–298.

Andrews, F. M. & Withey, S. B. (1976). *Social indicators of well-being: Americans' perceptions of life quality* (pp. 207, 306). New York: Plenum.

Angier, N. (1991, January 22). A potent peptide prompts an urge to cuddle. *The New York Times,* p. C1.

Angier, N. (1996, November 1). Maybe gene isn't to blame for thrill-seeking manner. *The New York Times,* p. A12.

Angoff, W. H. (1988). The nature-nurture debate, aptitudes, and group differences. *American Psychologist, 43,* 713–720.

Ansaldo, A. I., Arguin, M., & Roch, L. A. (2002). The contribution of the right cerebral hemisphere to the recovery from aphasia: A single longitudinal case study. *Brain Languages, 82,* 206–222.

Antonucci, T. C., Lansford, J. E., Akiyama, H., Smith, J., Baltes, M. M., Takahashi, K., Fuhrer R., & Dartigues, J-F. (2002). Differences between men and women in social relations, resource deficits, and depressive symptomatology during later life in four nations. *Journal of Social Issues, 58,* 767–783.

Antony, M. M., Brown, T. A., & Barlow, D. H. (1992). Current perspectives on panic and panic disorder. *Current Directions in Psychological Science, 1,* 79–82.

American Psychological Association (APA). (1999). *Talk to someone who can help.* Washington, DC: American Psychological Association.

American Psychological Association (APA). (1988). *Behavioral research with animals.* Washington, DC: American Psychological Association.

American Psychological Association (APA). (1993). *Employment survey.* Washington, DC: American Psychological Association.

American Psychological Association (APA). (1994). *Careers in psychology.* Washington, DC: American Psychological Association.

American Psychological Associaton (APA). (1996). *Psychology careers for the twenty-first century.* Washington, DC: American Psychological Association.

Apanovitch, A. M., McCarthy, D., & Salovey, P. (2003). Using message framing to motivate HIV resting among low-income, ethnic minority women. *Health Psychology, 22,* 88–94.

Aponte, J. F., & Wohl, J. (2000). *Psychological intervention and cultural diversity.* Needham Heights, MA: Allyn & Bacon.

Appelhans, B. M., & Schmeck, R. R. (2002). Learning styles and approach versus avoidant coping during academic exam preparation. *College Student Journal, 36,* 157–160.

Arafat, I., & Cotton, W. L. (1974). Masturbation practices of males and females. *Journal of Sex Research, 10,* 293–307.

Arambula, P., Peper, E., Kawakami, M., & Gibney, K. H. (2001). The physiological correlates of Kundalini yoga meditation: A study of a yoga master. *Applied Psychophysiology & Biofeedback, 26,* 147–153.

Archambault, D. L. (1992). Adolescence: A physiological, cultural, and psychological no man's land. In G. W. Lawson & A. W. Lawson (Eds.), *Adolescent substance abuse: Etiology, treatment, and prevention.* Gaithersburg, MD: Aspen.

Archer, J., & Lloyd, B. B. (2002). *Sex and gender* (2nd ed.). New York: Cambridge University Press.

Arena, J. M. (1984, April). A look at the opposite sex. *Newsweek on Campus,* p. 21.

Arlin, P. K. (1989). The problem of the problem. In J. D. Sinnott (Ed.), *Everyday problem solving: Theory and applications.* New York: Praeger.

Armstrong, T. (2000). *Multiple intelligences in the classroom* (2nd ed.). Washington, DC: Association for Supervision & Curriculum Development.

Armstrong, T. (2003). *The multiple intelligences of reading and writing: Making the words come alive* (2nd ed.). Washington, DC: Association for Supervision & Curriculum Development.

Aronow, E., Reznikoff, M., & Moreland, K. (1994). *The Rorschach technique: Perceptual basics, content interpretation, and applications.* Boston: Longwood.

Aronson, E. (1988). *The social animal* (3rd ed.). San Francisco: Freeman.

Asch, S. E. (1946). Forming impressions of personality. *Journal of Abnormal and Social Psychology, 41,* 258–290.

Asch, S. E. (1951). Effects of group pressure upon the modification and distortion of judgments. In H. Guetzkow (Ed.), *Groups, leadership, and men.* Pittsburgh: Carnegie Press.

Asher, S. R., & Parker, J. G. (1991). Significance of peer relationship problems in childhood. In B. H. Schneider, G. Attili, J. Nadel, & R. P. Weissberg (Eds.), *Social competence in developmental perspective.* Amsterdam: Kluwer Academic.

Aspinwall, L. G., & Taylor, S. E. (1997). A stitch in time: Self-regulation and proactive coping. *Psychological Bulletin, 121,* 417–436.

Astbury-Ward, E. (2002). From Kama Sutra to dot.com: The history, myths and management of premature ejaculation. *Sexual and Relationship Therapy, 17,* 367–380.

Atel, D. R., Pratt, H. D., & Greydanus, D. E. (2003). Treatment of adolescents with anorexia nervosa, *Journal of Adolescent Research. Special Issue: Eating disorders in adolescents, 18,* 266–260.

Atkinson, H. (Ed.). (1997, January 21). Understanding your diagnosis. *HealthNews,* p. 3.

Atkinson, J. W., & Feather, N. T. (1966). *Theory of achievement motivation.* New York: Krieger.

Atkinson, J. W., & Shiffrin, R. M. (1971, August). The control of short-term memory. *Scientific American,* pp. 82–90.

Atkinson, R. C., & Shiffrin, R. M. (1968). Human memory: A proposed system and its control processes. In K. W. Spence & J. T. Spence (Eds.), *The psychology of learning and motivation: Advances in research and theory* (Vol. 2, pp. 80–195). New York: Academic Press.

Atran, S. (2003). Genesis of suicide terrorism. *Science, 299,* 1534–1539.

Austin, L. S. (2000). *What's holding you back?: Eight critical choices for women's success.* New York: Basic Books.

Averill, J. R. (1975). A semantic atlas of emotional concepts. *Catalog of Selected Documents in Psychology, 5,* 330.

Averill, J. R. (1994). Emotions are many splendored things. In P. Ekman & R. J. Davidson (Eds.), *The nature of emotion: Fundamental questons.* New York: Oxford University Press.

Aycan, Z. (2000). Cross-cultural industrial and organizational psychology: Contributions, past developments, and future directions. *Journal of Cross-Cultural Psychology, 31,* 110–128.

Ayyash-Abdo, H. (2002). Adolescent suicide: An ecological approach. *Psychology in the Schools, 39,* 459–475.

Babkina, A. M., & Bondi, K. M. (Eds.). (2003). *Affirmative action: An annotated bibliography* (2nd ed.). New York: Nova Science.

Baddeley, A., & Wilson, B. (1985). Phonological coding and short-term memory in patients without speech. *Journal of Memory and Language, 24,* 490–502.

Baddeley, A., Chincotta, D., & Adlam, A. (2001). Working memory and the control of action: Evidence from task switching. *Journal of Experimental Psychology, 130,* 641–657.

Baddeley, A., Gathercole, S., & Papagno, C. (1998). The phonological loop as a language learning device. *Psychological Review, 105,* 158–173.

Baddeley, A. D. (1990). *Human memory: Theory and practice.* Boston: Allyn & Bacon.

Baer, J. (1993). *Creativity and divergent thinking: A task-specific approach.* Hillsdale, NJ: Erlbaum.

Baer, L., Rauch, S. L., Callantine, T., Martuza, R., et al. (1995). Cingulotomy for intractable obsessive-compulsive disorder: Prospective

long-term follow-up of 18 patients. *Archives of General Psychiatry, 52,* 384–392.

Bahrick, H. P., Hall, L. K., & Berger, S. A. (1996). Accuracy and distortion in memory for high school grades. *Psychological Science, 7,* 265–269.

Bailey, J. M., Pillard, R. C., Kitzinger, C., & Wilkinson, S. (1997). Sexual orientation: Is it determined by biology? In M. R. Walsh (Ed.), *Women, men, and gender: Ongoing debates.* New Haven, CT: Yale University Press.

Baird, J. C. (1997), *Sensation and judgment: Complementarity theory of psychophysics.* Mahwah, NJ: Erlbaum.

Baker, R. A. (1998, February). A view of hypnosis. *The Harvard Mental Health Letter,* pp. 5–6.

Baker, S. P., Lamb, M. W., Li, G., & Dodd, R. S. (1993). Human factors in crashes of commuter airplanes. *Aviation, Space, and Environmental Medicine, 64,* 63–68.

Bakermans-Kranenburg, M. J., van IJzendoorn, M. H., & Juffer, F. (2003). Less is more: Meta-analyses of sensitivity and attachment interventions in early childhood. *Psychological Bulletin, 129,* 195–215.

Balaban, C. D. (2002). Neural substrates linking balance control and anxiety. *Physiology and Behavior. Special Issue: The Pittsburgh special issue, 77,* 469–475.

Ball, E. M., Simon, R. D., Tall, A. A., Banks, M. B., Nino-Murcia, G., & Dement, W. C. (1997, February 24). Diagnosis and treatment of sleep apnea within the community. *Archives of Internal Medicine, 157,* 419–424.

Ballinger, C. B. (1981). The menopause and its syndromes. In J. G. Howells (Ed.), *Modern perspectives in the psychiatry of middle age.* New York: Brunner/Mazel.

Baltes, P. B., & Kunzmann, U. (2003). Wisdom. *Psychologist, 16,* 131–133.

Bandura, A. (1977). *Social learning theory.* Englewood Cliffs, NJ: Prentice Hall.

Bandura, A. (1983). Psychological mechanisms of aggression. In R. G. Geen & E. I. Donnerstein (Eds.), *Aggression: Theoretical and empirical reviews, Vol. 1: Theoretical and methodological issues.* New York: Academic Press.

Bandura, A. (1986). *Social foundations of thought and action: A social cognitive theory.* Englewood Cliffs, NJ: Prentice Hall.

Bandura, A. (1988). Self-regulation of motivation and action through goal systems. In V. Hamilton and H. Gordon (Eds.), *Cognitive perspectives on emotion and motivation.* Dordrecht, Netherlands: Kluwer Academic.

Bandura, A. (1994). Social cognitive theory of mass communication. In J. Bryant, & D. Zillmann (Eds.), *Media effects: Advances in theory and research: LEA's communication series.* Hillsdale, NJ: Erlbaum.

Bandura, A. (1997). *Self-Efficacy: The exercise of control.* New York: W. H. Freeman.

Bandura, A. (1999). Social cognitive theory of personality. In D. Cervone & Y. Shod (Eds.), *The coherence of personality.* NY: Guilford.

Bandura, A. (2000). Self-efficacy: The foundation of agency. In W. J. Perrig and A. Grob

(Eds.), *Control of human behavior, mental processes, and consciousness: Essays in honor of the 60th birthday of August Flammer.* Mahwah, NJ: Erlbaum.

Bandura, A., Grusec, J. E., & Menlove, F. L. (1967). Vicarious extinction of avoidance behavior. *Journal of Personality and Social Psychology, 5,* 16–23.

Bandura, A., Ross, D., & Ross, S. (1963a). Imitation of film-mediated aggressive models. *Journal of Abnormal and Social Psychology, 66,* 3–11.

Bandura, A., Ross, D., & Ross, S. (1963b). Vicarious reinforcement and imitative learning. *Journal of Abnormal and Social Psychology, 67,* 601–607.

Banich, T., & Heller, W. (1998). Evolving perspectives on lateralization of function. *Current Directions in Psychological Science, 7,* 1–2.

Bannon, L. (2000, February 14). Why boys and girls get different toys. *The Wall Street Journal,* pp. B1, B4.

Barber, J. (2001). Freedom from smoking: Integrating hypnotic methods and rapid smoking to facilitate smoking cessation. *International Journal of Clinical & Experimental Hypnosis, 49,* 257–266.

Barber, S., & Lane, R. C. (1995). Efficacy research in psychodynamic therapy: A critical review of the literature. *Psychotherapy in Private Practice, 14,* 43–69.

Bargh, J. A., Raymond, P., Pryor, J. B., & Strack, F. (1995). Attractiveness of the underling: An automatic power sex association and its consequences for sexual harassment and aggression. *Journal of Personality and Social Psychology, 68,* 768–781.

Barinaga, M. (1997, May 30). How much pain for cardiac gain? *Science, 276,* 1324–1327.

Barkley, R. (2000). *Taking charge of ADHD* (Rev. ed.). New York: Guilford Press.

Barkley, R. A. (1998a). *Attention-deficit hyperactivity disorder: A handbook for diagnosis and treatment.* New York: Guilford Press.

Barkow, J. H., Cosmides, L., & Tooby, J. (Eds.). (1992). *The adapted mind.* New York: Oxford University Press.

Barnard, N. D. , & Kaufman, S. R. (1997, Febraury). Animal research is wasteful and misleading. *Scientific American, 276,* 80–82.

Barnes, M. L., & Sternberg, R. J. (1997). A hierarchical model of love and its prediction of satisfaction in close relationships. In R. J. Sternberg, & M. Hojjat (Eds.), *Satisfaction in close relationships,* pp. 79–101. New York: Guilford Press.

Barrett, M. (1999). *The development of language.* Philadelphia: Psychology Press.

Barringer, T. A., & Weaver, E. M. (2002). Does long-term bupropion (Zyban) use prevent smoking relapse after initial success at quitting smoking? *Journal of Family Practice, 51,* 172.

Barron, F. (1990). *Creativity and psychological health: Origins of personal vitality and creative freedom.* Buffalo, NY: Creative Education Foundation.

Barron, G. & Yechiam, E. (2002). Private e-mail requests and the diffusion of responsibility. *Computers in Human Behavior, 18*, 507–520.

Bartecchi, C. E., MacKenzie, T. D., & Schrier, R. W. (1995, May). The global tobacco epidemic. *Scientific American*, pp. 44–51.

Bartholow, B. D., & Anderson, C. A. (2001). Effects of violent video games on aggressive behavior: Potential sex differences. *Journal of Experimental Social Psychology, 38*, 283–290.

Bartlett, F. (1932). *Remembering: A study in experimental and social psychology.* Cambridge, England: Cambridge University Press.

Bartoshuk, L. (2000, July/August). The bitter with the sweet. *APS Observer, 11*, 33.

Bartoshuk, L., & Beauchamp, G. K. (1994). Chemical senses. *Annual Review of Psychology, 45*, 419–449.

Bartoshuk, L., & Drewnowski, A. (1997, February). Symposium presented at the annual meeting of the American Association for the Advancement of Science, Seattle.

Bartoshuk, L., & Lucchina, L. (1997, January 13). Are you a supertaster? *U.S. News & World Report*, pp. 58–59.

Bartzokis, G., Nuechterlein, K. H., Lu, P. H., Gitlin, M., Rogers, S., & Mintz, J. (2003). Dysregulated brain development in adult men with schizophrenia: A magnetic resonance imaging study. *Biological Psychiatry, 53*, 412–421.

Baruss I. (2003a). Psychedelics. In I. Baruss, *Alterations of consciousness: An empirical analysis for social scientists*, pp. 161–185. Washington, DC: American Psychological Association.

Baruss, I. (2003b). Sleep. In I. Baruss, *Alterations of consciousness: An empirical analysis for social scientists* (pp. 51–78). Washington, DC: American Psychological Association.

Basch, M. F. (1996). Affect and defense. In D. L. Nathanson (Ed.), *Knowing feeling: Affect, script, and psychotherapy.* New York: W. W. Norton.

Bass, A. (1996, April 21). Is anger good for you? *Boston Globe Magazine*, pp. 20–41.

Bates, P. E., Cuvo, T., Miner, C. A., & Korabek, C. A. (2001). Simulated and community-based instruction involving persons with mild and moderate mental retardation. *Research in Developmental Disabilities, 22*, 95–115.

Bates, R. (2002). Liking and similarity as predictors of multi-source ratings. *Personnel Review, 31*, 540–552.

Batson, C. D. (1991). *The altruism question: Toward a social-psychological answer.* Hillsdale, NJ: Erlbaum.

Batson, C. D., Ahmad, N., Lishner, D. A., & Tsang, J. A. (2002). Empathy and altruism. In C. R. Snyder & S. J. Lopez (Eds.), *Handbook of positive psychology*, pp. 485–498. London: Oxford University Press.

Bauer, P. J. (1996). What do infants recall of their lives? Memory for specific events by one- to two-year-olds. 102nd Annual Convention of the American Psychological Association. (1994, Los Angeles, California, US). *American Psychologist, 51*, 29–41.

Baum, A. (1994). Behavioral, biological, and environmental interactions in disease processes. In S. Blumenthal, K. Matthews, & S. Weiss (Eds.), *New research frontiers in behavioral medicine: Proceedings of the National Conference.* Washington, DC: NIH Publications.

Baum, A. S., Revenson, R. A., & Singer, J. E. (Eds.). (2002). *Handbook of health psychology.* Mahwah, NJ: Erlbaum.

Baumeister, A. A., & Francis, J. L. (2002). Historical development of the dopamine hypothesis of schizophrenia. *Journal of the History of the Neurosciences, 11*, 265–277.

Baumeister, R. F. (1998). The self. In D. T. Gilbert & S. T, Fiske (Eds.), *The handbook of social psychology*, Vol. 1 (4th ed.). Boston: McGraw-Hill.

Baumeister, R. F. (2000). Gender differences in erotic plasticity: The female sex drive as socially flexible and responsive. *Psychological Bulletin, 126*, 347–374.

Baumeister, R. F., & Twenge, J. M. (2002). Cultural suppression of female sexuality. *Review of General Psychology, 6*, 166–203.

Baumeister, R. F. Twenge, J. M., & Nuss, C. K. (2002). Effects of social exclusion on cognitive processes: Anticipated aloneness reduces intelligent thought. *Journal of Personality and Social Psychology, 83*, 817–827.

Baumeister, R. F., & Bratslavsky, E. (1999). Passion, intimacy, and time: Passionate love as a function of change in intimacy. *Personality and Social Psychology Review, 3*, 49–67.

Baumeister, R. F., Catanese, K. R., & Vohs, K. D. (2001). Is there a gender difference in strength of sex drive? Theoretical views, conceptual distinctions, and a review of relevant evidence. *Personality and Social Psychology Review, 5*, 242–273.

Baumgartner, F. (2002). The effect of hardiness in the choice of coping strategies in stressful situations. *Studia Psychologica, 44*, 69–75.

Baumrind, D., Larzelere, R. E., & Cowan, P. A. (2002). Ordinary physical punishment: Is it harmful? Comment on Gershoff (2002).

Baumrind, D. (1971). Current patterns of parental authority. *Developmental Psychology Monographs, 4* (1, pt. 2).

Baumrind, D. (1980). New directions in socialization research. *Psychological Bulletin, 35*, 639–652.

Bayer, D. L. (1996). Interaction in families with young adults with a psychiatric diagnosis. *American Journal of Family Therapy, 24*, 21–30.

Bayhill, A. T., & Karnavas, W. J. (1993). The perceptual illusion of baseball's rising fastball and breaking curveball. *Journal of Experimental Psychology: Human Perception and Performance, 19*, 3–14.

Baynes, K., Eliassenk J. C., Lutsep, H. L., & Gazzaniga, M. S. (1998, May 8). Modular organization of cognitive systems marked by interhemispheric integration. *Science, 280*, 902–905.

Bazell, B. (1998, August 25). Back pain goes high-tech. *Slate*, pp. 1–4.

Bear, M. F., Connors, B. W., & Paradiso, M. A. (2000). *Neuroscience: Exploring the brain.* Philadelphia: Lippincott Williams & Wilkins.

Beatty, J. (2000). *The human brain: Essentials of behavioral neuroscience.* Thousand Oaks, CA: Sage.

Beatty, W. W. (2002). Sex difference in geographical knowledge: Driving experience is not essential. *Journal of the International Neuropsychological Society, 8*, 804–810.

Beck, A. P., & Lewis, C. M. (Eds.). (2000). *The process of group psychotherapy: Systems for analyzing change.* Washington, DC: American Psychological Association.

Beck, A. T. (1991). Cognitive therapy: A 30-year perspective. *American Psychologist, 46*, 368–375.

Beck, A. T. (1995). Cognitive therapy: Past, present, and future. In M. J. Mahoney (Ed.), *Cognitive and constructive psychotherapies: Theory, research, and practice.* New York: Springer.

Beck, A. T., & Emery, G., with Greenberg, R. L. (1985). *Anxiety disorders and phobias: A cognitive perspective.* New York: Basic Books.

Beck, M. (1992, May 25). Menopause. *Newsweek*, pp. 71–79.

Becker, T. (2003). Is emotional intelligence a viable concept? *Academy of Management Review, 28*, 192–195.

Beckham, E. E., & Leber, W. R. (Eds.). (1997). *Handbook of Depression* (2nd ed.). New York: Guilford Press.

Bedard, W. W., & Parsinger, M. A. (1995). Prednisolone blocks extreme intermale social aggression in seizure-induced, brain-damaged rats: Implications for the amygdaloid central nucleus, corticotrophin-releasing factor, and electrical seizures. *Psychological Reports, 77*, 3–9.

Begg, D., & Langley, J. (2001). Changes in risky driving behavior from age 21 to 26 years. *Journal of Safety Research, 32*, 491–499.

Begley, S. (1998b, July 13). You're OK, I'm terrific: "Self-esteem" backfires. *Newsweek*, p. 69.

Begley, S. (2002, March 11). The schizophrenic mind. *Time*, pp. 44–51.

Begley, S. (2002, September 13) The memory of September 11 is seared in your mind; But is it really true? *The Wall Street Journal*, p. B1.

Begley, S. (2003, April 4). Likely suicide bombers include some profiles you'd never suspect. *The Wall Street Journal*, p. B1.

Beilin, H. (1996). Mind and meaning: Piaget and Vygotsky on causal explanation. *Human Development, 39*, 277–286.

Bell, J., Grekul, J., Lamba, N., & Minas, C. (1995). The impact of cost on student helping behavior. *Journal of Social Psychology, 135*, 49–56.

Bell, R., Matthews, S. R., Lassister, L. & Leverett, K. (2002). Validity of the Wonderlic Personnel Test as a measure of fluid or crystallized intelligence: Implications for career assessment. *North American Journal of Psychology, 4*, 113–120.

Bella, M., DePaulo, B. M., Lindsay, J. J., Malone, B. E., Muhlenbruck, L. Charlton, K., &

Cooper, H. (2003). Cues to deception. *Psychological Bulletin, 129*, 74–118.

Bellack, A. S., Hersen, M., & Kazdin, A. E. (1990). *International handbook of behavior modification and therapy.* New York: Plenum.

Bellezza, F. S., Six, L. S., & Phillips, D. S. (1992). A mnemonic for remembering long strings of digits. *Bulletin of the Psychonomic Society, 30*, 271–274.

Belsky, J. (2002). Quantity counts: Amount of child care and children's socioemotional development. *Journal of Developmental and Behavioral Pediatarics, 23*, 167–170.

Belsky, J., & Rovine, M. (1988). Nonmaternal care in the first year of life and infant-parent attachment security. *Child Development, 59*, 157–167.

Bem, D. J., & Honorton, C. (1994). Does psi exist? Replicable evidence for an anomalous process of information transfer. *Psychological Bulletin, 115*, 4–18.

Bem, D. J., (1996). Exotic becomes erotic: A developmental theory of sexual orientation. *Psychological Review, 103*, 320–335.

Bem, S. L. (1993). *Lenses of gender.* New Haven, CT: Yale University Press.

Bem, S. L. (1998). *An unconventional family.* New Haven, CT: Yale University Press.

Benbow, C. P., Lubinski, D., & Hyde, J. S. (1997). Mathematics: Is biology the cause of gender differences in performance? In M. R. Walsh (Ed.), *Women, men, and gender: Ongoing debates.* New Haven, CT: Yale University Press.

Benjamin, L. T., Jr., (2001). American psychology's struggles with its curriculum. *American Psychologist, 56*, 735–742.

Benjamin, L. T., Jr. (1985, February). Defining aggression: An exercise for classroom discussion. *Teaching of Psychology, 12* (1), 40–42.

Benjamin, L. T., Jr. (1997). The psychology of history and the history of psychology: A historiographical introduction. In L. T. Benjamin (Ed.), *A history of psychology: Original sources and contemporary research* (2nd ed.). New York: McGraw-Hill.

Bennett, M. R. (2000). The concept of long term potentiation of transmission of synapses. *Progress in Neurobiology, 60*, 109–137.

Benson, E. (2003, April). The science of sexual arousal. *Monitor on Psychology,* pp. 50–56.

Benson, H. (1993). The relaxation response. In D. Goleman & J. Guerin (Eds.), *Mind-body medicine: How to use your mind for better health.* Yonkers, NY: Consumer Reports Publications.

Benson, H., & Friedman, R. (1985). A rebuttal to the conclusions of Davis S. Holme's article, "Meditation and somatic arousal reduction." *American Psychologist, 40*, 725–726.

Benson, H., Kornhaber, A., Kornhaber, C., LeChanu, M. N., et al. (1994). Increases in positive psychological characteristics with a new relaxation-response curriculum in high school students. *Journal of Research and Development in Education, 27*, 226–231.

Bentall, R. P. (1992). The classification of schizophrenia. In D. J. Kavanagh (Ed.), *Schizophrenia: An overview and practical handbook.* London: Chapman & Hall.

Benton, S. A., Robertson, J. M., Tseng, W-C., Newton, F. B., & Benton, S. L. (2003). Changes in counseling center client problems across 13 years. *Professional Psychology: Research and Practice, 34*, 66–72.

Bergeson, T. R., & Trehub, S. E. (2002). Absolute pitch and tempo in mothers' songs to infants. *Psychological Science, 13*, 72–75.

Bergin, A. E., & Garfield, S. L. (Eds.). (1994). *Handbook of psychotherapy and behavior change* (4th ed.). New York: Wiley.

Berguier, A., & Ashton, R. (1992). Characteristics of the frequent nightmare sufferer. *Journal of Abnormal Psychology, 101*, 246–250.

Berkowitz, C. D. (2000). The long-term medical consequences of sexual abuse. In R. M. Reece, et al. (Eds.), *Treatment of child abuse: Common ground for mental health, medical, and legal practitioners.* Baltimore: Johns Hopkins University Press.

Berkowitz, L. (1989). Frustration-aggression hypothesis. *Psychological Bulletin, 106*, 59–73.

Berkowitz, L. (1990). On the formation and regulation of anger and aggression: A cognitive-neoassociationistic analysis. *American Psychologist, 45*, 494–503.

Berkowitz, L. (1993). *Aggression: Its causes, consequences, and control.* New York: McGraw-Hill.

Berkowitz, L., & Geen, R. G. (1966). Film violence and the cue properties of available targets. *Journal of Personality and Social Psychology, 3*, 525–530.

Berkowitz, L., & LePage, A. (1967). Weapons as aggression-eliciting stimuli. *Journal of Personality and Social Psychology, 7*, 202–207.

Berliner, L., & Elliott, D. M., (2002). Sexual abuse of children. In J. E. B. Myers & L. Berliner, et al. (Eds.), *The APSAC handbook on child maltreatment* (2nd ed.), pp. 55–78. Thousand Oaks, CA: Sage.

Berlyne, D. (1967). Arousal and reinforcement. In D. Levine (Ed.), *Nebraska symposium on motivation.* Lincoln: University of Nebraska Press.

Berman, A. L. (1991). *Adolescent suicide: Assessment and intervention.* Washington, DC: American Psychological Association.

Berman, A. L., & Jobes, D. A. (1991). *Adolescent suicide: Assessment and intervention.* Washington, DC: American Psychological Association.

Berman, R. M., Krystal, J. H., & Charney, D. S. (1996). Mechanism of action of antidepressants: Monoamine hypotheses and beyond. In S. J. Watson (Ed.), *Biology of schizophrenia and affective disease.* Washington, DC: American Psychiatric Press.

Bernal, G., Trimble, J. E., Burlew, A. K., & Leong, F. T. (Eds.) (2002). *Handbook of racial and ethnic minority psychology.* Thousand Oaks, CA: Sage.

Bernard, L. L. (1924). *Instinct: A study in social psychology.* New York: Holt.

Berrettini, W. H. (2000). Are schizophrenic and bipolar disorders related?: A review of family and molecular studies. *Biological Psychiatry: Special issue: A special issue on bipolar disorder, 48*, 531–538.

Berrios, G. E. (1996). *The history of mental symptoms: Descriptive psychopathology since the nineteenth century.* Cambridge, England: Cambridge University Press.

Bersoff, D. M. (1999). Why good people sometimes do bad things: Motivated reasoning and unethical behavior. *Personality and Social Psychology Bulletin, 25*, 28–39.

Berthoud, H. R. (2002). Multiple neural systems controlling food intake and body weight. *Neuroscience and Biobehavioral Reviews, 26*, 393–428.

Bertrand, M., & Mullainathan, S. (2002). Are Emily and Brendan more employable than Lakisha and Jamal? A field experiment on labor market discrimination. Unpublished manuscript.

Betancourt, H., & Lopez, S. R. (1993). The study of culture, ethnicity, and race in American Psychology. *American Psychologist, 48*, 1586–1596.

Beutler, L. E., Brown, M. T., Crothers, L., Booker, K., et al. (1996). The dilemma of factitious demographic distinctions in psychological research. *Journal of Consulting and Clinical Psychology, 64*, 892–902.

Beyene, Y. (1989). *From menarche to menopause: Reproductive lives of peasant women in two cultures.* Albany, NY: State University of New York Press.

Bianchi, S. M., Casper, L. M. (2000). American Families. *Population Bulletin, 55*, (4).

Biederman, I. (1981). On the semantics of a glance at a scene. In M. Kubovy & J. R. Pomerangtz (Eds.), *Perceptual organization.* Hillsdale, NJ: Erlbaum.

Biederman, I. (1987). Recognition-by-components: A theory of human image understanding. *Psychological Review, 94*, 115–147.

Biederman, I. (1990). Higher-level vision. In D. N. Osherson, S. Kosslyn, & J. Hollerbach (Eds.), *An invitation to cognitive science: Visual cognition and action.* Cambridge, MA: MIT Press.

Binet, A., & Simon, T. (1916). *The development of intelligence in children (The Binet-Simon Scale).* Baltimore: Williams & Wilkins.

Binstock, R., & George, L. K. (Eds.). (1996). *Handbook of aging and the social sciences* (4th ed.). San Diego, CA: Academic Press.

Birch, H. G. (1945). The role of motivation factors in insightful problem solving. *Journal of Comparative Psychology, 38*, 295–317.

Birren, J. E. (Ed.). (1996). *Encyclopedia of gerontology: Age, aging and the aged.* San Diego, CA: Academic Press.

Bjork, D. W. (1993). *B. F. Skinner: A life.* New York: Basic Books.

Bjork, E. L., & Bjork, R. A. (Eds.). (1996). *Memory.* New York: Academic Press.

Bjork, R. A., & Richardson-Klarehn, A. (1989). On the puzzling relationship between environmental context and human memory. In

C. Izawa (Ed.), *Current issues in cognitive processes: The Tulane-Floweree symposium on cognition.* Hillsdale, NJ: Erlbaum.

Bjorklund, D. F. (1997). In search of a metatheory for cognitive development (or, Piaget is dead and I don't feel so good myself). *Child Development, 68,* 144–148.

Black, P. H., & Barbutt, L. D. (2002). Stress, inflammation and cardiovascular disease. *Journal of Psychosomatic Research, 52,* 1–23.

Blakeslee, S. (1991, August 7). Levels of caffeine in various foods. *The New York Times.*

Blakeslee, S. (1992, August 11). Finding a new messenger for the brain's signals to the body. *The New York Times,* p. C3.

Blakeslee, S. (2000, January 4). A decade of discovery yields a shock about the brain. *The New York Times,* p. D1.

Blakeslee, S. (2002, September 22). Exercising toward repair of the spinal cord. *The New York Times,* p. 25.

Blanchard, F. A., Lilly, R., & Vaughn, L. A. (1991). Reducing the expression of racial prejudice. *Psychological Science, 2,* 101–105.

Blass, T. (1996). Attribution of responsibility and trust in the Milgram obedience experiment. *Journal of Applied Social Psychology, 26,* 1529–1535.

Blass, T. (Ed.) (2000). *Obedience to authority: Current perspectives on the Milgram Paradigm.* Mahwah, NJ: Erlbaum.

Blau, Z. S. (1973). *Old age in a changing society.* New York: New Viewpoints.

Blewett, A. E. (2000). Help cards for patients. *Psychiatric Bulletin, 24,* 276.

Blood, A. J., & Zatorre, R. J. (2001). Intensely pleasurable responses to music correlate with activity in brain regions implicated in reward and emotion. *Proceedings of the National Academy of Sciences, 98,* 11818–11823.

Blum, D. (2002). *Love at goon park: Harry Harlow and the science of affection.* Cambridge, MA: Perseus.

Blume, S. B. (1998, March). Alcoholism in women. *The Harvard Mental Health Letter,* pp. 5–7.

Bobo, L., & Hutchings, V. L. (2001). Perceptions of racial group competition: Extending Blumer's theory of group positions to a multiracial social context. In M. A. Hogg & D. Abrams (Eds.), *Intergroup relations: Essential readings. Key readings in social psychology.* Philadelphia: Psychology Press.

Bock, R. I. (2000). Effects of frequent marijuana use on brain tissue volume and composition. Neuroreport, 11, 491–496.

Boehm, K. E., & Campbell, N. B. (1995). Suicide: A review of calls to an adolescent peer listening phone service. *Child Psychiatry and Human Development, 26,* 61–66.

Bolger, N., Zuckerman, A., & Kessler, R. C. (2000). Invisible support and adjustment to stress. *Journal of Personality and Social Psychology, 79,* 953–961.

Bolla, K. I., Cadet, J. L., & London, E. D. (1998). The neuropsychiatry of chronic cocaine abuse. *Journal of Neuropsychiatry and Clinical Neurosciences, 10,* 280–289.

Borbely, A. (1986). *Secrets of sleep* (p. 43, graph). New York: Basic Books.

Bornstein, M. H. & Arterberry, M. (1999). Perceptual development. In M. Bornstein & M. Lamb, *Developmental Psychology.* Mahwah, NJ: Erlbaum.

Bornstein, R. F. (2001). The impending death of psychoanalysis. *Psychoanalytic Psychology, 18,* 3–20.

Bortfeld, H. & Whitehurst, G. J. (2001). Sensitive periods in first language acquisition. In D. B. Bailey, Jr., J. T. Bruer, et al. (Eds.), *Critical thinking about critical periods,* pp. 173–192. Baltimore, MD: Paul H. Brookes.

Bosma, H., van Boxtel, M. P. J., Ponds, R. W. H. M., Houx, P. J. H., & Jolles, J. (2003). Education and age-related cognitive decline: The contribution of mental workload. *Educational Gerontology, 29,* 165–173.

Bosma, H., van Boxtel, M. P. J., Ponds, R. W. H. M., Houx, P. J. H., Burdorf, A., & Jolles, J. (2002). Mental work demands protect against cognitive impairment: MAAS prospective cohort study. *Experimental Aging Research, 29,* 33–45.

Botting, J. H., & Morrison, A. R. (1997, February). Animal research is vital to medicine. *Scientific American, 276.* 83–86.

Bouchard, C., & Bray, G. A. (Eds.). (1996). *Regulation of body weight: Biological and behavioral mechanisms.* New York: Wiley.

Bourne, L. E., Dominowski, R. L., Loftus, E. F., & Healy, A. F. (1986). *Cognitive processes* (2nd ed.). Englewood Cliffs, NJ: Prentice Hall.

Bower, G. H., Thompson, S. S., & Tulving, E. (1994). Reducing retroactive interference: An interference analysis. *Journal of Experimental Psychology Learning, Memory, and Cognition, 20,* 51–66.

Boyle, G. J., Goldman, R., Svoboda, J. S., & Fernandez, E. (2002). Male circumcision: Pain, trauma and psychosexual sequelae. *Journal of Health Psychology, 7,* 329–343.

Bozarth, J. D., Zimring, F. M., & Tausch, R. (2002). Client-centered therapy: The evolution of a revolution. In D. J. Cain (Ed.), *Humanistic psychotherapies: Handbook of research and practice,* pp. 147–188. Washington, DC: American Psychological Association.

Braff, D. L. (1993). Information processing and attention dysfunctions in schizophrenia. *Schizophrenia Bulletin, 19,* 233–259.

Brasic, J. R. (2002). Conversion disorder in childhood. *German Journal of Psychiatry, 5,* 54–61.

Braun, A. R. (1998). *Brain image.* Washington, DC: National Institutes of Health.

Brazelton, T. B. (1969). *Infants and mothers: Differences in development.* New York: Dell.

Breakwell, G. M., Hammond, S., & Fife-Schaw, C. (Eds.). (1995). *Research methods in psychology.* Newbury Park, CA: Sage.

Brehm, J. W., & Self, E. A. (1989). The intensity of motivation. *Annual Review of Psychology, 40,* 109–131.

Breland, K., & Breland, M. (1961). Misbehavior of organisms. *American Psychologist, 16,* 681–684.

Brendgen, M., Vitaro, F., & Bukowski, W. M. (2000). Stability and variability of adolescents' affiliation with delinquent friends: Predictors and consequences. *Social Development, 9,* 205–225.

Brewer, J. B., Zhao, Z., Desmond, J. E., Glover, G. H., & Gabrieli, J. D. E. (1998, August 21). Making memories: Brain activity that predicts how well visual experience will be remembered. *Science, 281,* 1185–1187.

Brislin, R. (1993). *Understanding culture's influence on behavior.* Fort Worth, TX: Harcourt Brace Jovanovich.

Brody, A. L., Saxena, S., Stoessel, P., Gillies, L. A., Fairbanks, L. A., Alborzian, L., Phelps, M. E., Huang, S-C., Wu, H-M., Ho, M. L., Ho, M. K., Au, S. C., Maidment, K., & Baxter, L. R., Jr. (2001). Regional brain metabolic changes in patients with major depression treated with either paroxetine or interpersonal therapy. *Archives of General Psychiatry, 58,* 631–640.

Brody, N. (1990). Behavior therapy versus placebo: Comment on Bowers and Clum's meta-analysis. *Psychological Bulletin, 107,* 106–109.

Bronner, E. (1998, November 24). Study casts doubt on the benefits of S.A.T. coaching courses. *The New York Times,* p. A19.

Brookhiser, R. (1997, January 13). Lost in the weed. *U.S. News & World Report,* p. 9.

Brooks-Gunn, J., Han, W., & Waldfogel, J. (2002). Maternal employment and child cognitive outcomes in the first three years of life: The NICHD study of early child care. *Child Development, 73,* 1052–1072.

Brown, A. S., Susser, E. S., Butler, P. D., Andrews, R. R., et al. (1996). Neurobiological plausibility of prenatal nutritional deprivation as a risk factor for schizophrenia. *Journal of Nervous and Mental Disease, 184,* 71–85.

Brown, D. C. (1994). Subgroup norming: Legitimate testing practice or reverse discrimination? *American Psychologist, 49,* 927–928.

Brown, E. (2001, September 17). The World Health Organization takes on big tobacco (but don't hold your breath): Anti-smoking advocates are mounting a global campaign: It's going to be a long, hard fight. *Forbes,* pp. 37–41.

Brown, L. S., & Pope, K. S. (1996). *Recovered memories of abuse: Assessment, therapy, forensics.* Washington, DC: American Psychological Association.

Brown, P. K., & Wald, G. (1964). Visual pigments in single rod and cones of the human retina. *Science, 144,* 45–52.

Brown, R. (1958). How shall a thing be called? *Psychological Review, 65,* 14–21.

Brown, S. (2003). Providing social support may be more beneficial than receiving it: Results from a prospective study of mortality. *Psychological Science* (accepted for publication).

Brown, S. I., & Walter, M. I. (Eds.). (1993). *Problem posing: Reflections and applications.* Hillsdale, NJ: Erlbaum.

Bruce, B., & Wilfley, D. (1996). Binge eating among the overweight population: A serious and prevalent problem. *Journal of the American Dietetic Association, 96*, 58–61.

Bruce, V., Green, P. R., & Georgeson, M. (1997). *Visual perception: Physiology, psychology and ecology* (3rd ed.). Mahwah, NJ: Erlbaum.

Bruer, J. T. (2001). A critical and sensitive period primer. In D. B. Bailey, Jr., J. T. Bruer, et al. (Eds.), *Critical thinking about critical periods,* pp. 173–192. Baltimore, MD: Paul H. Brookes.

Brzustowicz, L. M., Hodgkinson, K. A., Chow, E. W. C., Honer, W. G., & Bassett, A. S. (2000, April 28). Location of major susceptibility locus for familial schizophrenia on chromosome 1q21-q22. *Science, 288*, 678–682.

Buck, L., & Axel, R. (1991, April 5). A novel multigene family may encode odorant receptors: A molecular basis for odor recognition. *Cell, 65*, 167–175.

Buckout, R. (1974). Eyewitness testimony. *Scientific American, 231*, 23–31.

Bukowski, W. M., Newcomb, A. F., & Hartup, W. W. (Eds.). (1996). *The company they keep: Friendship in childhood and adolescence.* New York: Cambridge University Press.

Bulik, C. M., Tozzi, F., Anderson, C., Mazzeo, S. E., Aggen, S., & Sullivan, P. F. (2003). The relation between eating disorders and components of perfectionism. *American Journal of Psychiatry, 160*, 366–368.

Bulmahn, G., & Krakel, M. (2002). Overeducated workers as an insurance device. *Labour, 16*, 383–402.

Burchinal, M. R., Roberts, J. E., & Riggins, R., Jr. (2000). Relating quality of center-based child care to early cognitive and language development longitudinally. *Child Development, 71*, 338–357.

Burger, J. M. (1986). Increasing compliance by improving the deal: The that's-not-all technique. *Journal of Personality and Social Psychology, 51*, 277–283.

Burger, J. M. (1999). The foot-in-the-door compliance procedure: A multiple-process analysis and review. *Personality and Social Psychology Review, 3*, 303–325.

Burgess, D., & Borgida, E. (1997). Sexual harassment: An experimental test of sex-role spillover theory. *Personality and Social Psychology Bulletin, 23*, 63–75.

Burgoon, J. K., & Dillman, L. (1995). Gender, immediacy, and nonverbal communication. In P. J. Kalbfleisch & M. J. Cody (Eds.), *Gender, power, and communication in human relationships. LEA's communication series.* Hillsdale, NJ: Erlbaum.

Burgoon, J. K., Bonito, J. A., Ramirez, A. J. R., Dunbar, N. E., Kam, K., & Fischer, J. (2002). Testing the interactivity principle: Effects of mediation, propinquity, and verbal and nonverbal modalities in interpersonal interaction. *Journal of Communication, Special Issue: Research on the relationship between verbal and nonverbal communication: Emerging integrations, 52*, 657–677.

Burns, A., & Scott, C. (1994). *Mother-headed families and why they have increased.* Hillsdale, NJ: Erlbaum.

Bush, P. J., & Osterweis, M. (1978). Pathways to medicine use. *Journal of Health and Social Behavior, 19*, 179–189.

Bushman, B. J. (1993). Human aggression while under the influence of alcohol and other drugs: An integrative research review. *Current Directions in Psychological Science, 2*, 148–152.

Bushman, B. J. (2002). Does venting anger feed or extinguish the flame? Catharsis, rumination, distraction, anger, and aggressive responding. *Personality and Social Psychology Bulletin, 28*, 724–731.

Bushman, B. J., & Anderson, C. A. (2001). Media violence and the American public: Scientific facts versus media misinformation. *American Psychologist, 56*, 477–489.

Bushman, B. J., & Anderson, C. A. (2002). Violent video games and hostile expectations: A test of the General Aggression Model. *Personality and Social Psychology Bulletin, 28*, 1679–1689.

Bushman, B. J., Baumeister, R. F., Phillips, C. M. (2001). Do people aggress to improve their mood? Catharsis beliefs, affect regulation opportunity, and aggressive responding. *Journal of Personality and Social Psychology, 81*, 17–32.

Buss, D. M. (2000). The evolution of happiness. *American Psychologist, 55*, 15–23.

Buss, D. M. (2001). Human nature and culture: An evolutionary psychological perspective. *Journal of Personality, 69*, 955–978.

Buss, D. M. (2003) *The evolution of desire: Strategies of human mating.* New York: Basic Books

Buss, D. M., & Kenrick, D. T. (1998). Evolutionary social psychology. In D. T. Gilbert, S. T. Fiske, & G. Lindzey (Eds.), *The handbook of social psychology.* (4th ed., Vol. 2). Boston: McGraw-Hill.

Buss, D. M., Larsen, R. J., Westen, D., & Semmelroth, J. (1992). Sex differences in jealousy: Evolution, physiology, and psychology. *Psychological Science, 3*, 251–255.

Butcher, J. N. (1995). Interpretation of the MMPI-2. In L. E. Beutler, & M. R. Berren (Eds.), *Integrative assessment of adult personality.* New York: Guilford Press.

Butcher, J. N. (1999). *A beginner's guide to the MMPI-2.* Washington, DC: American Psychological Association.

Butcher, J. N., Graham, J. R., Dahlstrom, W. G., & Bowman, E. (1990). The MMPI-2 with college students. *Journal of Personality Assessment, 54*, 1–15.

Byne, W. (1996). Biology and homosexuality: Implications of neuroendocrinological and neuroanatomical studies. In R. P. Cabaj & T. S. Stein (Eds.), *Textbook of homosexuality and mental health.* Washington, DC: American Psychiatric Press.

Byrne, B. M., & Watkins, D. (2003). The issue of measurement invariance revisited. *Journal of Cross-Cultural Psychology, 34*, 155–175.

Cabanac, M., & Frankham, P. (2002). Evidence that transient nicotine lowers the body weight set point. *Physiology & Behavior, 76*, 539–542.

Cacioppo, J. T., Tassinary, L. G., & Bernston, G. G. (Eds.). (2000). *Handbook of psychophysiology* (2nd ed.). New York: Cambridge University Press.

Cacioppo, J. T., Berntson, G. G., & Crites, S. L., Jr. (1996). Social neuroscience: Principles of psychophysiological arousal and response. In E. T. Higgins & A. W. Kruglanski (Eds.), *Social psychology: Handbook of basic principles.* New York: Guilford.

Cain, D. J. (Ed.). (2002). *Humanistic psychotherapies: Handbook of research and practice.* Washington, DC: American Psychological Association.

Calderon, M. E., & Minaya-Rowe, L. (2003). *Designing and implementing two-way bilingual programs: A step-by-step guide for administrators, teachers, and parents.* Thousand Oaks, CA: Corwin Press.

Calmes, J. (1998, March 5). Americans retain puritan attitudes on matters of sex. *The Wall Street Journal,* p. A12.

Cameron, O. G. (2002). *Visceral sensory neuroscience: Interoception.* London: Oxford University Press.

Campbell, J. J., Lamb, M. E., & Hwang, C. P. (2000). Early child-care experiences and children's social competence between 1.5 and 15 years of age. *Applied Developmental Science, 4, Special issue: The effects of quality care on child development*, 166–175.

Campbell, T. S., & Ditto, B. (2002). Exaggeration of blood pressure-related hypoalgesia and reduction of blood pressure with low frequency transcutaneous electrical nerve stimulation. *Psychophysiology, 39*, 473–481.

Campfield, L. A., Smith, F. J., Rosenbaum, M., & Hirsch, J. (1996). Human eating: Evidence for a physiological basis using a modified paradigm. [Special issue: Society for the Study of Ingestive Behavior, Second Independent Meeting.] *Neuroscience and Biobehavioral Reviews, 20*, 133–137.

Cannon, T. D. (1998). Genetic and perinatal influences in the etiology of schizophrenia: A neurodevelopmental model. In M. F. Lenzenweger & R. H. Dworkin (Eds.), *The origins and development of schizophrenia: Advances in Experimental Psychopathology.* Washington, DC: American Psychological Association.

Cannon, W. B. (1929). Organization for physiological homeostatics. *Physiological Review, 9*, 280–289.

Canteras, N. S. (2002). The medial hypothalamic defensive system: Hodological organization and functional implications. *Pharmacology, Biochemistry and Behavior. Special Issue: Functional role of specific systems within the extended amygdala and hypothalamus, 71*, 481–491.

Cantwell, R. H., & Andrews, B. (2002). Cognitive and psychological factors underlying secondary school students' feelings towards group work. *Educational Psychology, 22,* 75–91.

Capaldi, E. D. (Ed.). (1996). *Why we eat what we eat: The psychology of eating.* Washington, DC: American Psychological Association.

Carli, L. L. (1990). Gender, language, and influence. *Journal of Personality and Social Psychology, 59,* 941–951.

Carlson, M., Marcus-Newhall, A., & Miller, N. (1989). Evidence for a general construct of aggression. *Personality and Social Psychology Bulletin, 15,* 377–389.

Carlson, S. (2002, November 15). Virtual counseling: As campus psychologists go online, they reach more students, but may also risk lawsuits. *The Chronicle of Higher Education,* pp. A35–A36.

Carnegie Council on Adolescent Development. (1995). *Great transitions: Preparing adolescents for a new century.* New York: Carnegie Corporation of New York.

Carnegie Task Force on Meeting the Needs of Young Children. (1994). *Starting points: Meeting the needs of our youngest children.* New York: Carnegie Corporation.

Carney, R. N., & Levin, J. R. (1998). Coming to terms with the keyword method in introductory psychology: A "neuromnemonic" example. *Teaching of Psychology, 25,* 132–135.

Carney, R. N., Levin, J. R., Levin, M. E., & Schoen, L. M. (2000). Improving memory. In M. E. Ware, D. E. Johnson, et al. (Eds.), *Handbook of demonstrations and activities in the teaching of psychology: Physiological-comparative, perception, learning, cognitive, and developmental,* (2nd ed., Vol. II). Mahwah, NJ: Erlbaum.

Carpenter, S. (2001). Sleep deprivation may be undermining teen health. *APA Monitor, 32,* 42–45.

Carpenter, S. (2002, April). What can resolve the paradox of mental health disparities? *APA Monitor, 33,* 18.

Carr, A. (2002). *Avoiding risky sex in adolescence.* New York: Blackwell.

Carroll, J. M., & Russell, J. A. (1997). Facial expressions in Hollywood's portrayal of emotion. *Journal of Personality and Social Psychology, 72,* 164–176.

Carson, R. C., Butcher, J. N., & Coleman, J. C. (1992). *Abnormal psychology and modern life* (9th ed.). New York: HarperCollins.

Carter, A. S., Pauls, D. L., & Leckman, J. F. (1995). The development of obsessionality: Continuities and discontinuities. In D. Cicchetti & D. J. Cohen (Eds.), *Developmental psychopathology, Vol. 2: Risk, disorder, and adaptation.* New York: Wiley.

Carter, R. T. (2003). Becoming racially and culturally competent: The racial-cultural counseling laboratory. *Journal of Multicultural Counseling and Development, 31,* 20–30.

Carver, C. S., Harris, S. D., Lehman, J. M., Durel, L. A., Antoni, M. H., Spencer, S. M., & Pozo-Kaderman, C. (2000). How important is the perception of personal control?

Studies of early stage breast cancer patients. *Personality and Social Psychology Bulletin, 26,* 139–149.

Case, R., & Okamoto, Y. (1996). The role of central conceptual structures in the development of children's thought. *Monographs of the Society for Research in Child Development, 61,* v–265.

Casey, B. J. (2002, May 24). Windows into the human brain. *Science, 296,* 1408–1409.

Caspi, A., Henry, B., McGee, R. O., Moffitt, T. E., & Silva, P. A. (1995). Temperamental origins of child and adolescent behavior problems: From age three to age fifteen. *Child Development, 66,* 55–68.

Cassel, W. S., Roebers, C. E. M., & Bjorklund, D. F. (1996). Developmental patterns of eyewitness responses to repeated and increasingly suggestive questions. *Journal of Experimental Child Psychology, 61,* 116–133.

Cattell, R. B. (1965). *The scientific analysis of personality.* Chicago: Aldine.

Cattell, R. B. (1987). *Intelligence: Its structure, growth, and action.* Amsterdam: North-Holland.

Cattell, R. B., Cattell, A. K., & Catell, H. E. P. (1993). *Sixteen personality factor questionnaire; (16PF)* (5th ed.). San Antonio, TX: Harcourt Brace.

Cattell, R. B., Cattell, A. K., & Cattell, H. E. P. (2000). *The Sixteen Personality Factor™ (16PF®) questionnaire.* Champaign, IL: Institute for Personality and Ability Testing.

Cattell, R. B., Eber, L. & Tatsuoka, M. (1970, 1988, 1992). *Handbook for the 16PF.* Institute for Personality and Ability Testing. Champaign, IL: Institute for Personality and Ability Testing.

Centers for Disease Control (CDC). (1992). *Most students sexually active: Survey of sexual activity.* Atlanta, GA: Centers for Disease Control.

Centers for Disease Control (CDC). (2000). *Suicide prevention fact sheet, National Center for Injury Prevention and Control.* Atlanta, GA: Centers for Disease Control and Prevention.

Center on Addiction and Substance Abuse. (1994). *Report on college drinking.* New York: Columbia University.

Chamberlain, K., & Zika, S. (1990). The minor events approach to stress: Support for the use of daily hassles. *British Journal of Psychology, 81,* 469–481.

Chamberlin, J. (1998, June). Help for students of color. *APA Monitor,* p. 37.

Chamberlin, J. (2000, February). Where are all these students coming from? *Monitor on Psychology,* pp. 32–34.

Chandler, M. J. (1976). Social cognition and life-span approaches to the study of child development. In H. W. Reese & L. P. Lipsitt (Eds.), *Advances in child development and behavior* (Vol 11). New York: Academic Press.

Chang, S-W., & Ansley, T. N. (2003). A comparative study of item exposure control methods in computerized adaptive testing. *Journal of Educational Measurement, 40,* 71–103.

Chao, R. K. (2000). Cultural explanations for the role of parenting in the school success of Asian-American children. In R. D. Taylor & M. C. Wang (Eds.), *Resilience across contexts: Family, work, culture, and community,* pp. 333–363. Mahwah, NJ: Erlbaum.

Chapman, L. J., & Chapman, J. P. (1973). *Disordered thought in schizophrenia.* New York: Appleton-Century-Crofts.

Charles, N., Cheakalos, C., Hubbard, K., Miller, S., & Schindehette, S. (2001, December 10). Beyond the call. *People,* pp. 88–106.

Charles, S. T., Reynolds, C. A., & Gatz, M. (2001). Age-related differences and change in positive and negative affect over 23 years. *Journal of Personality and Social Psychology, 80,* 136–151.

Charters, L. (2000, July 15). Microelectronic device continues to show promise. *Ophthalmology Times, 25,* 1.

Chase, M. (1993, October 13). Inner music: Imagination may play role in how the brain learns muscle control. *Wall Street Journal,* pp. A1, A6.

Chastain, G. & Landrum, R. E. (Eds.). (1999). *Protecting human subjects: Departmental subject pools and institutional review boards.* Washington, DC: American Psychological Association.

Cheakalos, C., & Breu, G. (2002, September 9). The one-pound wonder. *People,* pp. 60–64.

Cheakalos, C., & Heyn, E. (1998, November 2). Mercy mission. *People Weekly,* pp. 149–150.

Chechile, R. A. (2003). Elements of psychophysical theory. *Journal of Mathematical Psychology, 47,* 385.

Chen, C., & Stevenson, H. W. (1995). Motivation and mathematics achievement: A comparative study of Asian-American, Caucasian-American, and East Asian high school students. *Child Development, 66,* 1215–1234.

Cheney, C. D. (1996). Medical nonadherence: A behavior analysis. In J. R. Cautela & W. Ishaq (Eds.), *Contemporary issues in behavior therapy: Improving the human condition: Applied Clinical Psychology.* New York: Plenum Press.

Cheng, H., Cao, Y., & Olson, L. (1996, July 26). Spinal cord repair in adult paraplegic rats: Partial restoration of hind limb function. *Science, 273,* 510–513.

Cherlin, A. (1993). *Marriage, divorce, remarriage.* Cambridge, MA: Harvard University Press.

Cherry, B. J., Buckwalter, J. G., & Henderson, V. W. (1996). Memory span procedures in Alzheimer's disease. *Neuropsychology, 10,* 286–293.

Cheston, S. E. (2002). A new paradigm for teaching counseling theory and practice. *Counselor Education & Supervision, 39,* 254–269.

Chi-Ching, Y., & Noi, L. S. (1994). Learning styles and their implications for cross-cultural management in Singapore. *Journal of Social Psychology, 134,* 593–600.

Chin, S. B., & Pisoni, D. B. (1997). *Alcohol and speech.* New York: Academic Press.

Cho, A. (2000, June 16). What's shakin' in the ear? *Science, 288,* 1954–1955.

Chomsky, N. (1968). *Language and mind.* New York: Harcourt Brace Jovanovich.

Chomsky, N. (1969). *The acquisition of syntax in children from five to ten.* Cambridge, MA: MIT Press.

Chomsky, N. (1978). On the biological basis of language capacities. In G. A. Miller & E. Lennenberg (Eds.), *Psychology and biology of language and thought.* New York: Academic Press.

Chomsky, N. (1991). Linguistics and cognitive science: Problems and mysteries. In A. Kasher (Ed.), *The Chomskyan turn.* Cambridge, MA: Blackwell.

Chow, A. Y., Pardue, M. T., Chow, V. Y., Peyman, G. A., Liang, C., Perlman, J. I., & Peachey, N. S. (2001). Implantation of silicon chip microphotodiode arrays into the cat subretinal space. *IEEE Transactions on Rehabilitation Engineering, 9,* 86–95.

Christensen, A. J., & Johnson, J. A. (2002). Patient adherence with medical treatment regimens: An interactive approach. *Current Directions in Psychological Science, 11,* 94–101.

Churchland, P. S., & Ramachandran, V. S. (1995). Filling in: Why Dennett is wrong. In B. Dahlbom (Ed.), *Dennett and his critics: Demystifying mind: Philosophers and their critics.* Oxford, England: Basil Blackwell.

Cialdini, R. (2000). *Influence: Science and practice.* Boston: Allyn & Bacon.

Cialdini, R. B. (1984). *Social influence.* New York: William Morrow.

Cialdini, R. B. (1988). *Influence: Science and practice* (2nd ed.). Glenview, IL: Scott, Foresman.

Cialdini, R. B., Schaller, M., Houlihan, D., Arps, K., Fultz, J., & Beaman, A.L. (1975). Reciprocal concessions procedure for inducing compliance: The door-in-the-face technique. *Journal of Personality and Social Psychology, 31,* 206–215.

Cicero, F. R., & Pfadt, A. (2002). Investigation of a reinforcement-based toilet training procedure for children with autism. *Research in Developmental Disabilities, 23,* 319–331.

Clancy, S. A., Schacter, D. L., McNally, R. J., & Pitman, R. K. (2000). False recognition in women reporting recovered memories of sexual abuse. *Psychological Science, 2,* 26–33.

Clark, L., & Watson, R. (1999). Temperament. In L.A. Pervin & O.P. John (Eds.), *Handbook of personality: Theory and research* (2nd ed.). New York: Guilford.

Clark, R. E., & Squire, L. R. (1998, April 3). Classical conditioning and brain systems: The role of awareness. *Science, 280,* 77–81.

Clark, R., Anderson, N. B., Clark, V. R., & Williams, D. R. (1999). Racism as a stressor for African Americans: A biopsychosocial model. *American Psychologist, 54,* 805–816.

Clarke-Stewart, K. A., & Friedman, S. (1987). *Child development: Infancy through adolescence.* New York: Wiley.

Clarkin, J. F., & Lenzenweger, M. F. (Eds.) (1996). *Major theories of personality disorder.* New York: Guilford.

Clay D. L. (2000). Commentary: Rethinking our interventions in pediatric chronic pain and treatment research. *Journal of Pediatric Psychology, 25,* 53–55.

Clay, R. A. (April 2002). Overcoming barriers to pain relief. *Monitor on Psychology,* pp. 58–60.

Clayton, R. R., Cattarello, A. M., & Johnstone, B. M. (1996). The effectiveness of Drug Abuse Resistance Education (project DARE): 5-year follow-up results. *Preventative Medicine, 25,* 307–318.

Clements, M. (1994). Making love, how old, how often. *Parade* magazine, August 7, 1994. New York: Parade Publications.

Cloud, J. (2000, June 5). The lure of ecstasy. *Time,* pp. 60–68.

Council of National Psychological Associations for the Advancement of Ethnic Minority Interests (CNPAAEMI). (2000, January). *Guidelines for research in ethnic minority communities.* Washington, DC: American Psychological Association.

Coats, E. J., & Feldman, R. S. (1996). Gender differences in nonverbal correlates of social status. *Personality and Social Psychology Bulletin, 22,* 1014–1022.

Coats, E. J., Feldman, R. S., & Schwartzberg, S. (1994). *Crticial thinking: General prinicples and case studies.* New York: McGraw-Hill.

Cobos, P. Sanchez, M., Garcia, C., Vera, M. N., & Vila, J. (2002). Revisiting the James versus Cannon debate on emotion: Startle and autonomic modulation in patients with spinal cord injuries. *Biological Psychology, 61,* 251–269.

Cochran, S. D. (2000). Emerging issues in research on lesbians' and gay men's mental health: Does sexual orientation really matter? *American Psychologist, 56,* 33–41.

Coffey, C. E., Saxton, J. A., & Ratcliff, G. (1999). Relation of education to brain size in normal aging: Implications for the reserve hypothesis. *Neurology, 53,* 189–196.

Cohen, B. H., & Lea, R. B. (2003). *Essentials of statistics for the social and behavioral sciences.* New York: Wiley.

Cohen, B. H. (2002). *Explaining psychological statistics* (2nd ed.). New York: Wiley.

Cohen, D. (1996). Law, social policy, and violence: The impact of regional cultures. *Journal of Personality and Social Psychology, 70,* 961–978.

Cohen, J. (2003). Things I have learned (so far). In A. E. Kazdin (Ed.), *Methodological issues and strategies in clinical research* (3rd ed.). Washington, DC: American Psychological Association.

Cohen, P., Slomkowski, C., & Robins, L. N. (Eds.). (1999). *Historical and geographical influences on psychopathology.* Mahwah, NJ: Erlbaum.

Cohen, S., Hamrick, N., & Rodriguez, M. (2002). Reactivity and vulnerability to stress-associated risk for upper respiratory illness. *Psychosomatic Medicine, 64,* 302–310.

Colapinto, J. (2000). *As nature made him: The boy who was raised as a girl.* New York: HarperCollins.

Coleman, E. (2002). Masturbation as a means of achieving sexual health. *Journal of Psychology and Human Sexuality, 14,* 5–16.

Coles, R., & Stokes, G. (1985). *Sex and the American teenager.* New York: Harper & Row.

Coles, R., (1997). *The moral intelligence of children.* New York: Random House.

Collins, A. M., & Loftus, E. F. (1975). A spreading-activation theory of semantic processing. *Psychological Review, 82,* 407–428.

Collins, A. M., & Quillian, M. R. (1969). Retrieval times from semantic memory. *Journal of Verbal Learning and Verbal Behavior, 8,* 240–247.

Coltraine, S., & Messineo, M. (2000). The perpetuation of subtle prejudice: Race and gender imagery in 1990s television advertising. *Sex Roles, 42,* 363–389.

Committee to Review the Scientific Evidence on the Polygraph. (2003). *The polygraph and lie detection.* Washington, DC: National Academies Press.

Comuzzie, A. G., & Allison, D. B. (1998, May 29). The search for human obesity genes. *Science, 280,* 1374–1377.

Conger, R. D., Wallace, L. E., Sun, Y., Simons, R. L., McLoyd, V. C., & Brody, G. H. (2002). Economic pressure in African American families: A replication and extension of the family stress model. *Developmental Psychology, 38,* 179–193.

Conner, M., Povey, R., Sparks, P., James, R., & Shepherd, R. (2003). Moderating role of attitudinal ambivalence within the theory of planned behaviour. *British Journal of Social Psychology, 42,* 75–94.

Conte, H. R., & Plutchik, R. (Eds.). (1995). *Ego defenses: Theory and measurement.* New York: Wiley.

Conway, M. A. (1997). *Cognitive models of memory.* Cambridge, MA: MIT Press.

Cooper, N. R., Kalaria, R. N., McGeer, P. L., & Rogers, J. (2000). Key issues in Alzheimer's disease inflammation. *Neurobiology of Aging, 21,* 451–453.

Copolov, D. L., Seal, M. L., Maruff, P., Ulusoy, R., Wong, M. T. H., Tochon-Danguy, H. J., & Egan, G. F. (2003). Cortical activation associated with the human experience of auditory hallucinations and perception of human speech in schizophrenia: A PET correlation study. *Psychiatry Research: Neuroimaging, 123,* 139–152.

Corbetta, M., Miezin, F. M., Shulman, G. L., & Petersen, S. E. (1993, March). A PET study of visuospatial attention. *Journal of Neuroscience, 13,* 1202–1226.

Coren, S. (1992b). The moon illusion: A different view through the legs. *Perceptual and Motor Skills, 75,* 827–831.

Coren, S., & Aks, D. J. (1990). Moon illusion in pictures: A multimechanism approach. *Journal of Experimental Psychology: Human Perception and Performance, 16,* 365–380.

Coren, S., & Ward, L. M. (1989). *Sensation and perception* (3rd ed.). San Diego, CA: Harcourt Brace Jovanovich.

Coren, S., Porac, C., & Ward, L. M. (1979). *Sensation and perception*. New York: Academic Press.

Coren, S., Porac, C., & Ward, L. M. (1984). *Sensation and perception* (2nd ed.). New York: Academic Press.

Cornelius, M. D., Taylor, P. M., Geva, D., & Day, N. L. (1995). Prenatal tobacco and marijuana use among adolescents: Effects on offspring gestational age, growth, and morphology. *Pediatrics, 95,* 57–68.

Cornelius, S. W., & Caspi, A. (1987). Everyday problem solving in adulthood and old age. *Psychology and Aging, 2,* 144–153.

Cornell, T. L., Fromkin, V. A., & Mauner, G. (1993). A linguistic approach to language processing in Broca's aphasia: A paradox resolved. *Current Directions in Psychological Science, 2,* 47–52.

Correll, J., Park, B., Judd, C. M., & Wittenbrink, B. (2002). The police officer's dilemma: Using ethnicity to disambiguate potentially threatening individuals. *Journal of Personality and Social Psychology, 83,* 1314–1329.

Corvin, A., & Gill, M. (2003). Psychiatric genetics in the post-genome age. *British Journal of Psychiatry, 182,* 95–96.

Cosser, C. (2002). Hypnosis in the treatment of chronic pain: An ecosystemic approach. *Australian Journal of Clinical and Experimental Hypnosis, 30,* 156–169.

Costa, P. T., Jr., & Widiger, T. A. (Eds.). (2002). *Personality disorders and the five-factor model of personality* (2nd ed.). Washington, DC: American Psychological Association.

Cothran, M. M., & White, J. P. (2002). Adolescent behavior and sexually transmitted diseases: The dilemma of human papillomavirus. *Health Care for Women International. Special Issue: Adolescent women's health, 23,* 306–319.

Cotton, P. (1993, July 7). Psychiatrists set to approve DSM-IV. *Journal of the American Medical Association, 270,* 13–15.

Coventry, K. R., Venn, S. F., Smith, G. D., & Morley, A. M. (2003). Spatial problem solving and functional relations. *European Journal of Cognitive Psychology, 15,* 71–99.

Cowan, N., Towse, J. N., Hamilton, Z., Saults, J. S., Elliott, E. M., Lacey, J. F., Moreno, M. V., & Hitch, G. J. (2003). Children's working-memory processes: A response-timing analysis. *Journal of Experimental Psychology: General, 132,* 113–132.

Cowley, G. (2000b, January 31). Alzheimer's: Unlocking the mystery. *Time,* pp. 46–54.

Cox, J. (2003, May 6). How far would you go to save your life? *Denver Post,* p. F1.

Consumer Reports (CR). (1995, November). Mental health: Does therapy help? pp. 734–739.

Consumer Reports (CR). (1993, June). Dieting and weight loss, p. 347.

Craig, R. J. (1999). *Interpreting personality tests: A clinical manual for the MMPI-2, MCMI-III, CPI-R, and 16PF.* New York: Wiley.

Craik, F. I. M. (1990). Levels of processing. In M. E. Eysenck (Ed.), *The Blackwell dictionary of cognitive psychology.* London: Blackwell.

Craik, F. I., & Lockhart, R. S. (1972). Levels of processing: A framework for memory research. *Journal of Verbal Behavior, 11,* 671–684.

Cramer, J. A. (1995). Optimizing long-term patient compliance. *Neurology, 45,* s25–s28.

Cramer, P. (1996). *Storytelling, narrative, and the Thematic Apperception Test.* New York: Guilford Press.

Cramer, P. (2000). Defense mechanisms in psychology today: Further process for adaptation. *American Psychologist, 55,* 637–646.

Crandall, C. S., D'Anello, S., Sakalli, N., Lazarus, E., Wieczorkowska, G., & Feather, N. T. (2001). An attribution-value model of prejudice: Anti-fat attitudes in six nations. *Personality and Social Psychology Bulletin, 27,* 30–37.

Crapo, L. (1985). *Hormones, the messengers of life.* New York: Freeman.

Crawford, M. (1995). *Talking difference: On gender and language.* Thousand Oaks, CA: Sage.

Crawford, N. (2002). Science-based program curbs violence in kids. *APA Monitor, 33,* 38–39.

Crews, F. (1996). The verdict on Freud. *Psychological Science, 7,* 63–68.

Crits-Christoph, P. (1992). The efficacy of brief dynamic psychotherapy: A meta-analysis. *American Journal of Psychiatry, 149,* 151–158.

Csikszentmihalyi, M. (1997). *Creativity: Flow and the psychology of discovery and invention.* New York: BasicBooks/ Mastermind Series.

Cullinane, C. A., Chu, D. Z. J., & Mamelak, A. N. (2002). Current surgical options in the control of cancer pain. *Cancer Practice, 10,* s21–s26.

Cummings, E., & Henry, W. E. (1961). *Growing old.* New York: Basic Books.

Cummings, J., & Hall, C. (2002). Athletes' use of imagery in the off-season. *Sport Psychologist, 16,* 160–172.

Cwikel, J., Behar, L., & Rabson-Hare, J. (2000). A comparison of a vote count and a meta-analysis review of intervention research with adult cancer patients. *Research on Social Work Practice, 10,* 139–158.

Czeisler, C. A., Duffy, J. F., Shanahan, T. L., Brown, E. N., Mitchell, J. F., Rimmer, D. W., Ronda, J. M., Silva, E. J., Allan, J. S., Emens, J. S., Dijk, D. J., & Kronauer, R. E. (1999, June 25). Stability, precision, and near-24-hour period of the human circadian pacemaker. *Science, 284,* 2177–2181.

D'Antoni, T. (1999, February 21). Stop the clock. *The New York Times Magazine,* p. 26.

D'Argembeau, A., Comblain, C., & Van der Linden, M. (2003). Phenomenal characteristics of autobiographical memories for positive, negative, and neutral events. *Applied Cognitive Psychology, 17,* 281–294.

Daftary, F., & Meri, J. W. (2002). *Culture and memory in medieval Islam.* London: I. B. Tauris.

Daitz, B. (2002, December 3). In pain clinic, fruit, candy and relief. *The New York Times,* pp. 1–6.

Daley, E. M., McDermott, R. J., Brown, K. R., & Kittelson, M. J. (2003). Conducting Web-based survey research: A lesson in Internet designs. *American Journal of Health Behavior, 27,* 116–124.

Damasio, A. (1999). *The feeling of what happens: Body and emotion in the making of consciousness.* New York: Harcourt Brace.

Damon, W. (1999, August). The moral development of children. *Scientific American,* pp. 72–78.

Danner, D. D., Snowdon, D. A., & Friesen, W. V. (2001). Positive emotions in early life and longevity: Findings from the Nun Study. *Journal of Personality and Social Psychology, 80,* 804–813.

Darley, J. M. (1995). Constructive and destructive obedience: A taxonomy of principal-agent relationships. *Journal of Social Issues, 51,* 125–154.

Darwin, C. J., Turvey, M. T., & Crowder, R. G. (1972). An auditory analogue of the Sperling partial-report procedure: Evidence for brief auditory storage. *Cognitive Psychology, 3,* 255–267.

Davidson, J. E., Deuser, R., & Sternberg, R. J. (1994). The role of metacognition in problem solving. In J. Metcalfe & A. P. Shimamura (Eds.), *Metacognition: Knowing about knowing.* Cambridge, MA: MIT Press.

Davidson, P. S. R., & Glisky, E. L. (2002). Is flashbulb memory a special instance of source memory? Evidence from older adults. *Memory, 10,* 99–111.

Davidson, R. J., Gray, J. A., LeDoux, J. E., Levenson, R. W., Pankseep, J., & Ekman, P. (1994). Is there emotion-specific physiology? In P. Ekman & R. J. Davidson (Eds.), *The nature of emotion.* New York: Oxford University Press.

Davis, A., Pereira, J., & Bulkeley, W. M. (2002, August 15). Security concerns bring new focus on body language. *The Wall Street Journal,* pp. A1, A6.

Day, A. L., & Livingstone, H. A. (2003). Gender differences in perceptions of stressors and utilization of social support among university students. *Canadian Journal of Behavioural Science, 35,* 73–83.

de Fockert, J. W., Rees, G., Frith, C. D., & Lavie, N. (2001, March 2). The role of working memory in visual selective attention. *Science, 291,* 1803–1806.

de Valois, R. L., & de Valois, K. K. (1993). A multi-stage color model. *Vision Research, 33,* 1053–1065.

de Waal, F. B. M. (1999, December). The end of nature versus nurture. *Scientific American,* pp. 94–99.

DeAngelis, T. (2000, April). Is Internet addiction real? *APA Monitor,* pp. 24–27.

DeAngelis, T. (2002, March). Promising treatments for anorexia and bulimia. *Monitor on Psychology,* pp. 38–41.

Deary, I. J. (1996). Intelligence and inspection time: Achievements, prospects, and problems. *American Psychologist, 51,* 599–608.

Deaux, K. (1995). How basic can you be? The evolution of research on gender stereotypes. *Journal of Social Issues, 51,* 11–20.

deCharms, R. C., Blake, D. T., & Merzenich, M. M. (1998, May 29). Optimizing sound features for cortical neurons. *Science, 280,* 1439–1440.

Deci, E. L., Koestner, R., & Ryan, R. M. (2001). Extrinsic rewards and intrinsic motivation in education: Reconsidered once again. *Review of Educational Research, 71,* 1–27.

DeCoster, V. A. (2003). Predicting emotions in everyday social interactions: A test and comparison of affect control and social interactional theories. *Journal of Human Behavior in the Social Environment, 6,* 53–73.

Deffenbacher, J. L. (1988). Cognitive relaxation and social skills treatments of anger: A year later. *Journal of Consulting Psychology, 35,* 309–315.

Deffenbacher, J. L. (1996). Cognitive-behavioral approaches to anger reduction. In K. S. Dobson & K. D. Craig (Eds.), *Advances in cognitive-behavioral therapy,* Vol 2. Thousand Oaks, CA: Sage Publications.

DeGaton, J. F., Weed, S., & Jensen, L. (1996). Understanding gender differences in adolescent sexuality. *Adolescence, 31,* 217–231.

deGroot, A. D. (1966). Perception and memory versus thought: Some old ideas and recent findings. In B. Kleinmuntz (Ed.), *Problem solving: Research, method, and theory.* New York: Wiley.

Delahanty, D., & Baum, A. (2000). Stress and breast cancer. In A. S. Baum, R. A. Revenson, & J. E. Singer (Eds.), *Handbook of health psychology.* Mahwah, NJ: Erlbaum.

Dement, W. C., & Wolpert, E. A. (1958). The relation of eye movements, body mobility, and external stimuli to dream content. *Journal of Experimental Psychology, 55,* 543–553.

Dement, W.C. (1999). *The promise of sleep.* New York: Delacorte Press.

Dempster, F. N. (1981). Memory span: Sources for individual and developmental differences. *Psychological Bulletin, 89,* 63–100.

Denmark, G. L., & Fernandez, L. C. (1993). Historical development of the psychology of women. In F. L. Denmark & M. A. Paludi (Eds.), *A handbook of issues and theories.* Westport, CT: Greenwood Press.

Dennett, D. C. (2003). *Freedom evolves.* New York: Viking.

Dennis, T. A., Cole, P. M., Zahn-Waxler, C., & Mizuta, I. (2002). Self in context: Autonomy and relatedness in Japanese and U.S. mother-preschooler dyads. *Child Development, 73,* 1803–1817.

Dentzer, S. (1986, May 5). Can you pass the job test? *Newsweek,* pp. 46–53.

DePaulo, B. M., Lindsay, J. J., Malone, B. E., Muhlenbruck, L., Charlton, K., & Cooper, H. (2003). Cues to deception. *Psychological Bulletin, 129,* 74–118.

Deregowski, J. B. (1973). Illusion and culture. In R.L. Gregory & G.H. Combrich (Eds.), *Illusion in nature and art,* pp. 161–192. New York: Scribner.

DeRubeis, R., Hollon, S., & Shelton, R. (2003, May 23). Presentation, American Psychiatric Association meeting, Philadelphia.

Desimone, R. (1992, October 9). The physiology of memory: Recordings of things past. *Science, 258,* 245–255.

DeSteno, D. A., & Salovey, P. (1996). Evolutionary orgins of sex differences in jealousy? Questioning the "fitness" of the model. *Psychological Science, 7,* 367–372.

Detterman, D. K., Gabriel, L. T., & Ruthsatz, J. M. (2000). Intelligence and mental retardation. In R. J. Sternberg, et al. (Eds.), *Handbook of intelligence.* New York: Cambridge, University Press.

Devi, G. (2002). *Take a measure of your memory.* Dr. Gayatri Devi.

deVilliers, J. G., & deVilliers, P. A. (1999). Language development. In M. H. Bronstein & M. E. Lamb (Eds.), *Developmental psychology.* Mahwah, NJ: Erlbaum.

Dey, E. L., Astin, A. W., Korn, W. S., & Berz, E. R. (1990). *The American freshman: National norms for fall, 1990.* Los Angeles: Higher Education Research Institute, Graduate School of Education, UCLA.

Diamond, M., & Sigmundson, H. K. (1997). Sex reassignment at birth: Long-term review and clinical implications. *Archives of Pediatrics and Adolescent Medicine, 15,* 298–304.

Diaz-Guerrero, R. (1979). Culture and personality revisited. *Annals of the New York Academy of Sciences, 285,* 119–130.

DiCano, P., & Everitt, B. J. (2002). Reinstatement and spontaneous recovery of cocaine-seeking following extinction and different durations of withdrawal. *Behavioural Pharmacology, 13,* 397–406.

Dickens, W. T., & Flynn, J. R. (2001). Heritability estimates versus large environmental effects: The IQ paradox resolved. *Psychological Review, 108,* 291–310.

Diefendorff, J. M. & Richard, E. M. (2003). Antecedents and consequences of emotional display rule perceptions. *Journal of Applied Psychology, 88,* 284–294.

Diener, E. (2000). Subjective well-being: The science of happiness and a proposal for a national index. *American Psychologist, 55,* 34–43.

Diener, E., & Biswas-Diener, R. (2002). Will money increase subjective well-being? *Social Indicators Research, 57,* 119–169.

Diener, E., & Clifton, D. (2002). Life satisfaction and religiosity in broad probability samples. *Psychological Inquiry, 13,* 206–209.

Diener, E., & Seligman, M. E. P. (2002). Very happy people. *Psychological Science, 18,* 81–84.

Diener, E., Lucas, R. E., & Oishi, S. (2002). Subjective well-being: The science of happiness and life satisfaction. In C. R. Snyder & S. J. Lopez (Eds.), *Handbook of positive psychology,* pp. 463–73. London: Oxford University Press.

DiGiovanna, A. G. (1994). *Human aging: Biological perspectives.* New York: McGraw-Hill.

DiLorenzo, P. M., & Yougentob, S. L. (2003). Olfaction and taste. In M. Gallagher & R. J. Nelson, *Handbook of psychology: Biological psychology,* Vol 3. New York: Wiley.

DiMatteo, M. R. (1997). Health behaviors and care decisions: An overview of professional-patient communications. In D. S. Gochman (Ed.), *Handbook of health behavior research.* New York: Plenum.

Dinges, D. F., Pack, F., Wiliams, K., Gillen, K. A., Powell, J. W., Ott, G. E., Aptowicz, C., & Pack, A. I. (1997). Cumulative sleepiness, mood disturbance, and psychomotor vigilance performance decrements during a week of sleep restricted to 4–5 hours per night. *Sleep, 20,* 267–273.

Dishman, R. K. (1997, January). Brain monoamines, exercise, and behavioral stress: Animal models. *Medical Science Exercise, 29,* 63–74.

Dixon, R. A., & Cohen, A. L. (2003). Cognitive development in adulthood. In R. M. Lerner, M. A. Easterbrooks, et al. (Eds.), *Handbook of psychology: Developmental psychology,* Vol. 6, pp. 443–461. New York: Wiley.

Dobbins, A. C., Jeo, R. M., Fiser, J., & Allman, J. M. (1998, July 24). Distance modulation of neural activity in the visual cortex. *Science, 281,* 552–555.

Dobelle, W. H. (2000). Artificial vision for the blind by connecting a television camera to the visual cortex. *ASAIO Journal, 46,* 3–9.

Doi, T. (1990). The cultural assumptions of psychoanalysis. In J. W. Stigler, R. A. Shweder, & G. Herdt (Eds.), *Cultural psychology: Essays on comparative human development.* New York: Cambridge University Press.

Dolan, R. J. (2002, November 8). Emotion, cognition, and behavior. *Science, 298,* 1191–1194.

Dollard, J., Doob, L., Miller, N., Mower, O. H., & Sears, R. R. (1939). *Frustration and aggression.* New Haven, CT: Yale University Press.

Dollinger, S. J. (2003). Need for uniqueness, need for cognition and creativity. *Journal of Creative Behavior, 37,* 99–116.

Domhoff, G. W. (1996). *Finding meaning in dreams: A quantitative approach.* New York: Plenum Press.

Domhoff, G. W. (2001). A new neurocognitive theory of dreams. *Dreaming, 11,* 13–33.

Domhoff, G. W. (2003). *The scientific study of dreams: Neural networks, cognitive development, and content analysis.* Washington, DC: American Psychological Association.

Dorion, A. A. (2000). Hemispheric asymmetry and corpus callosum morphometry: A magnetic resonance imaging study. *Neuroscience Research, 36,* 9–13.

Dortch, S. (1996, October). Our aching heads. *American Demographics,* pp. 4–8.

Doty, R. L., Green, P. A., Ram, C., & Yankell, S. L. (1982). Communication of gender from human breath odors: Relationship to perceived intensity and pleasantness. *Hormones and Behavior, 16,* 13–22.

Dovidio, J. F. (2001). On the nature of contemporary prejudice: The third wave. *Journal of Social Issues, 57,* 829–849.

Dovidio, J. F., Kawakami, K., & Gaertner, S. L. (2000). Reducing contemporary prejudice: Combating explicit and implicit bias at the individual and intergroup level. In S. Oskamp (Ed.), *Reducing prejudice and discrimination: The Claremont Symposium on Applied Social Psychology,* pp. 137–163. Mahwah, NJ: Erlbaum.

Dovidio, J. F., Kawakami, K., & Gaertner, S. L. (2002). Implicit and explicit prejudice and interracial interaction. *Journal of Personality and Social Psychology, 82,* 62–68.

Doyle, K. A. (2002). Rational Emotive Behavior Therapy and its application to women's groups. In W. Dryden, & M. Neenan (Eds.), *Rational emotive behaviour group therapy.* London: Whurr Publishers.

Dreman, S. (1997). *The family on the threshold of the 21st century.* Mahwah, NJ: Erlbaum.

Dressler, W. W., & Oths, K. S. (1997). Cultural determinants of health behavior. In D. S. Gochman (Ed.), *Handbook of health behavior research.* New York: Plenum.

Druckman, D., & Bjork, R. A. (1991). *In the mind's eye: Enhancing human performance.* Washington, DC: National Academy Press.

Drummond, D. C., Tiffany, S. T., Glautier, S., & Remington, B. (Eds.). (1995). *Addictive behaviour: Cue exposure theory and practice.* Chichester, England: Wiley.

Dryden, W. (1999). *Rational emotive behavior therapy: A training manual.* New York: Springer.

Dryden, W. (2003). *Overcoming depression.* London: Sheldon Press.

DuBois, J. M. (2002). When is informed consent appropriate in educational research? *IRB: A Review of Human Subjects Research, 24,* 1–8.

Dubovsky, S. (1999, February 25). Tuning in to manic depression. *HealthNews, 5,* p. 8.

Duffy, M., Gillig, S. E., Tureen, R. M., & Ybarra, M. A. (2002). A critical look at the DSM-IV. *Journal of Individual Psychology, 58,* 363–373.

Dugger, C. W. (1996, December 28). Tug of taboos: African genital rite vs. U.S. law. *The New York Times,* pp. 1, 9.

Duke, M., & Nowicki, S., Jr. (1979). *Abnormal psychology: Perspectives on being different.* Monterey, CA: Brooks/Cole.

Duncan, J., & Miller, E. K. (2002). Cognitive focus through adaptive neural coding in the primate prefrontal cortex. In D. T. Stuss & R. T. Knight (Eds.), *Principles of frontal lobe function,* pp. 278–291. London: Oxford University Press.

Duncan, J., Seitz, R. J., Kolodny, J., Bor, D., Herzog, H., Ahmed, A., Newell, F. N., & Emslie, H. (2000, July 21). A neural basis for general intelligence. *Science, 289,* 457–459.

Duncan, P. D., et al. (1985). The effects of pubertal timing on body image, school behavior, and deviance. [Special Issue: Time of maturation and psychosocial functioning in adolescence: I.] *Journal of Youth and Adolescence, 14,* 227–235.

Duncker, K. (1945). On problem solving. *Psychological Monographs, 58* (5, whole no. 270).

Dunham, R. M., Kidwell, J. S., & Wilson, S. M. (1986). Rites of passage at adolescence: A ritual process paradigm. *Journal of Adolescent Research, 1,* 139–153.

Dutton, D. G., & Aron, A. P. (1974). Some evidence for heightened sexual attraction under conditions of high anxiety. *Journal of Personality and Social Psychology, 30,* 510–517.

Dworkin, J. B., Larson, R., & Hansen, D. (2003). Adolescents' accounts of growth experiences in youth activities. *Journal of Youth and Adolescence, 32,* 17–26.

Eagles, J. M. (2001). SAD—help arrives with the dawn? *Lancet, 358,* p. 2100.

Eagly, A. H. & Wood, W. (1999). The origins of sex differences in human behavior. *American Psychologist, 54,* 408–423.

Eagly, A. H., & Chaiken, S. (1993). *The psychology of attitudes.* Fort Worth, TX: Harcourt Brace Jovanovich.

Earley, J. (1999). *Interactive group therapy: Integrating interpersonal, action-oriented and psychodynamic approaches.* New York: Brunner/Mazel.

Eaton, J. (2001). Management communication: The threat of groupthink. *Corporate Communications, 6,* 183–192.

Ebbinghaus, H. (1885/1913). *Memory: A contribution to experimental psychology.* (H. A. Roger & C. E. Bussenius, Trans.). New York: Columbia University Press.

Ebstein, R. P., Benjamin, J., & Belmaker, R. H. (2003). Behavioral genetics, genomics, and personality. In R. Plomin & J. C. DeFries (Eds.), *Behavioral genetics in the postgenomic era,* pp. 365–388. Washington, DC: American Psychological Association.

Eccles, J. S., Lord, S. E., & Roeser, R. W. (1996). Round holes, square pegs, rocky roads, and sore feet: The impact of stage-environment fit on young adolescents' experiences in schools and families. In D. Cicchetti & S. L. Toth (Eds.), *Adolescence: Opportunities and challenges: Rochester symposium on developmental psychopathology,* Vol. 7. Rochester, NY: University of Rochester Press.

Eccleston, C., & Crombez, G. (1999). Pain demands attention: A cognitive-affective model of the interruptive function of pain. *Psychological Bulletin, 125,* 356–366.

Ecenbarger, W. (1993, April 1). America's new merchants of death. *The Reader's Digest,* p. 50.

Ecklund, A. (1999, July 12). Cochlear implant. *People Weekly,* p. 68.

Edgette, J. H., & Edgette, J. S. (1995). *The handbook of hypnotic phenomena in psychotherapy.* New York: Brunner/Mazel.

Edingre, J. D., Wohlgemuth, W. K., Radtke, R. A., Marsh, G. R., & Quillian, R. E. (2001). Cognitive behavioral therapy for treatment of chronic primary insomnia A randomized controlled trial. *Journal of the American Medical Association, 285,* 1856–1864.

Edwards, J. C. (2001). Self-fulfilling prophecy and escalating commitment: Fuel for the Waco fire. *Journal of Applied Behavioral Science, 37,* 343–360.

Egeth, H. E., & Yantis, S. (1997). Visual attention: Control, representation, and time course. *Annual Review of Psychology, 48,* 269–297.

Eichenbaum, H. (1993, August 20). Thinking about brain cell assemblies. *Science, 261,* 993–994.

Eichenbaum, H. (1997). Declarative memory: Insights from cognitive neurobiology. *Annual Review of Psychology, 48,* 547–572.

Eid, M., & Diener, E. (2001). Norms for experiencing emotions in different cultures: Inter- and intranational differences. *Journal of Personality and Social Psychology, 81,* 869–885.

Einarsson, C., & Granstroem, K. (2002). Gender-biased interaction in the classroom: The influence of gender and age in the relationship between teacher and pupil. *Scandinavian Journal of Educational Research, 46,* 117–127.

Eisenberg, N. (1991). Meta-analytic contributions to the literature on prosocial behavior. *Personality and Social Psychology Bulletin, 17,* 273–282.

Ekman, P. (1972). Universals and cultural differences in facial expressions of emotion. In J. Cole (Ed.), *Darwin and facial expression: A century of research in review,* (pp. 169–222). New York: Academic Press.

Ekman, P. (1994a). All emotions are basic. In P. Ekman & R.J. Davidson (Eds.), *The nature of emotion: Fundamental questions.* New York: Oxford University Press.

Ekman, P. (1994b). Strong evidence for universals in facial expressions: A reply to Russell's mistaken critique. *Psychological Bulletin, 115,* 268–287.

Ekman, P. (2003). *Emotions revealed: Recognizing faces and feelings to improve communication and emotional life.* New York: Times Books.

Ekman, P., & O'Sullivan, M. (1991). Facial expression: Methods, means, and moues. In R. S. Feldman & B. Rimé (Eds.), *Fundamentals of nonverbal behavior.* Cambridge, England: Cambridge University Press.

Ekman, P., Davidson, R. J., & Friesen, W. V. (1990). Emotional expression and brain physiology: II. The Duchenne smile. *Journal of Personality and Social Psychology, 58,* 342–353.

Ekman, P., Levenson, R. W., & Friesen, W. V. (1983, September 16). Autonomic nervous system activity distinguishes among emotions. *Science, 223,* 1208–1210.

Elfenbein, H. A., & Ambady, N. (2002). On the universality and cultural specificity of emotion recognition: A meta-analysis. *Psychological Bulletin, 128,* 203–235.

Elkins, I. J., McGue, M., & Iacono, W. G. (1997). Genetic and environmental influences on parent-son relationships: Evidence for increasing genetic influence during adolescence. *Developmental Psychology, 33,* 351–363.

Elliott, A. (2002). *Psychoanalytic theory: An introduction* (2nd ed.). Durham, NC: Duke University Press.

Elliott, J., Berman, H., & Kim, S. (2002). Critical ethnography of Korean Canadian women's menopause experience. *Health Care for Women International, 23,* 377–388.

Ellis, A. (1974). *Growth through reason.* Hollywood, CA: Wilshire Books.

Ellis, A. (2002). *Overcoming resistance: A rational emotive behavior therapy integrated approach* (2nd ed.). New York: Springer.

Ellyson, S. L., Dovidio, J. F., & Brown, C. E. (1992, April). Visual dominance of behavior in mixed-sex interaction: A meta-analysis. Paper presented at the annual meeting of the Eastern Psychological Association, Boston.

Embretson, S. E. (1996). Multidimensional latent trait models in measuring fundamental aspects of intelligence. In I. Dennis & P. Tapsfield (Eds.), *Human abilities: Their nature and measurement*. Mahwah, NJ: Erlbaum.

Enard, W., Przeworski, M., Fisher, S. E., Lai, C. S. L., Wiebe, V., Kitano, T., Monaco, A. P., & Paabo, S. (2002, August 14). Molecular evolution of FOXP2, a gene involved in speech and language. *Nature, 388,* 14.

Engebretson, T. O., & Stoney, C. M. (1995). Anger expression and lipid concentrations. *International Journal of Behavioral Medicine, 2,* 281–298.

Engen, T. (1987, September–October). Remembering odors and their names. *American Scientist, 75,* 497–503.

Engle, R. W. (2002). Working memory capacity as executive attention. *Current Directions in Psychological Science, 11,* 19–23.

Engle-Friedman, M., Baker, A., & Bootzin, R. R. (1985). Reports of wakefulness during EEG identified stages of sleep. *Sleep Research, 14,* 152.

Engler, J., & Goleman, D. (1992). *The consumer's guide to psychotherapy*. New York: Simon & Schuster.

Enserink, M. (1999, April 9). Can the placebo be the cure? *Science, 284,* 238–240.

Enserink, M. (2000, April, 21). Are placebo-controlled drug trials ethical? *Science, 288,* 416.

Epstein, R. (1987). The spontaneous inter-connection of four repertoires of behavior in a pigeon. *Journal of Comparative Psychology, 101,* 197–201.

Epstein, R. (1996). *Cognition, creativity, and behavior: Selected essays*. Westport, CT: Praeger/Greenwood.

Eranti, S. V., & McLoughlin, D. M. (2003). Electroconvulsive therapy: State of the art. *British Journal of Psychiatry, 182,* 8–9.

Erikson, E. H. (1963). *Childhood and society* (2nd ed.). New York: Norton.

Estes, W. K. (1991). Cognitive architectures from the standpoint of an experimental psychologist. *Annual Review of Psychology, 42,* 1–28.

Evans, R. B. (December 1999). So, what will the next century bring? *Monitor: American Psychological Association, 29.*

Eysenck, H. J. (1990). Biological dimensions of personality. In L. A. Pervin (Ed.), *Handbook of personality: Theory and research,* p. 246. New York: Guilford Press.

Eysenck, H. J. (1994). The Big Five or giant three: Criteria for a paradigm. In C. F. Halverson, Jr., G. A. Kohnstamm, & R. P. Martin (Eds.), *The developing structure of temperament and personality from infancy to adulthood*. Hillsdale, NJ: Erlbaum.

Eysenck, H. J. (1995). *Eysenck on extraversion*. New York: Wiley.

Ezzell, C. (September 2002). Clocking cultures. *Scientific American,* pp. 74–75.

Fagan, J. F., & Holland, C. R. (2002). Equal opportunity and racial differences in IQ. *Intelligence, 30,* 361–387.

Falk, D., Forese, N., Sade, D. S., & Dudek, B. C. (1999). Sex differences in brain/body relationships of Rhesus monkeys and humans. *Journal of Human Evolution, 36,* 233–238.

Farber, B. A., Brink, D. C., & Raskin, P. M. (Eds.). (1996). *The psychotherapy of Carl Rogers: Cases and commentary*. New York: Guilford Press.

Farley, F. (1986, May). The big T in personality. *Psychology Today,* pp. 44–52.

Faroqi-Shah, Y. (2003). Effect of lexical cues on the production of active and passive sentences in Broca's and Wernicke's aphasia. *Brain and Language, 85,* 409–426.

Fearing, V. G., & Clark, J. (Eds.). (2000). Individuals in context: A practical guide to client-centered practice. Chicago: Slack Publishing.

Fee, E., Brown, T. M., Lazarus, J., & Theeman, P. (2002). Exploring acupuncture: Ancient ideas, modern techniques. *American Journal of Public Health, 92,* 1592.

Feeley, T. H. (2002). Comment on halo effects in rating and evaluation research. *Human Communication Research. Special Issue: Statistical and methodological issues in communication research, 28,* 578–586.

Feinberg, A. W. (2002, April). Homocysteine may raise Alzheimer's risk: A physician's perspective. *HealthNews,* p. 4.

Feingold, A. (1994). Gender differences in personality: A meta-analysis. *Psychological Bulletin, 116,* 429–456.

Feldman Barrett, L., & Barrett, D. J. (2001). Computerized experience-sampling: How technology facilitates the study of conscious experience. *Social Science Computer Review, 19,* 175–185.

Feldman, D. H. (2003). Cognitive development in childhood. In R. M. Lerner, M. A. Easterbrooks, et al. (Eds.), *Handbook of psychology: Developmental psychology,* Vol. 6, pp. 195–210. New York: Wiley.

Feldman, R. S. (2003). *P.O.W.E.R. Learning*. New York: McGraw-Hill.

Feldman, R. S. (Ed.). (1982). *Development of nonverbal behavior in children*. New York: Springer-Verlag.

Feldman, R. S. (Ed.). (1993) *Applications of nonverbal behavioral theories and research*. Hillsdale, NJ: Erlbaum.

Feldman, R. S., Coats, E. J., & Schwartzberg, S. (1994). *Case studies and critical thinking about psychology*. New York: McGraw-Hill.

Feldman, R. S. (2003). *P.O.W.E.R. Learning* (2nd ed.). New York: McGraw-Hill.

Feldt, L. S. (2003). Estimating test score reliability when no examinee has taken the complete test. *Educational and Psychological Measurement, 63,* 193–203.

Festinger, L. (1957). *A theory of cognitive dissonance*. Stanford, CA: Stanford University Press.

Festinger, L., & Carlsmith, J. M. (1959). Cognitive consequences of forced compliance. *Journal of Abnormal and Social Psychology, 58,* 203–210.

Festinger, L., Schachter, S., & Back, K.W. (1950). *Social pressure in informal groups*. New York: Harper.

Fields-Meyer, T. (1999, October 25). The whiz kids. *People,* pp. 59–63.

Fields-Meyer, T., & Haederle, M. (1996, June 24). Married to a stranger. *People,* pp. 48–51.

Fields-Meyer, T., & Wihlborg, U. (2003). Gender jump. *People,* pp. 109–111.

Fine, L. (1994). Personal communication.

Fine, R., & Fine, L. (2003). *Basic chess endings*. New York: Random House.

Fineran, S. (2002). Adolescents at work: Gender issues and sexual harassment. *Violence Against Women, 8,* 953–967.

Fink, A. & Kosecoff, J. (1998). *How to conduct surveys: A step-by-step guide*. Thousand Oaks, CA: Sage.

Fink, G. (Ed.). (2000) *Encyclopedia of stress*. New York: Academic Press.

Fink, M. (1999). *Electroshock: Restoring the mind*. New York: Oxford University Press.

Fink, M. (2000). Electroshock revisited. *American Scientist, 88,* 162–167.

Finke, R. A. (1995). Creative insight and preinventive forms. In R. J. Sternberg & J. E. Davidson (Eds.), *The nature of insight*. Cambridge, MA: MIT Press.

Finkelhor, D. (1984). *Child sexual abuse: New theory and research*. New York: Free Press.

Finlay, F. O., Jones, R., & Coleman, J. (2002). Is puberty getting earlier? The views of doctors and teachers. *Child: Care, Health and Development, 28,* 205–209.

Firestein, B. A. (Ed.). (1996). *Bisexuality: The psychology and politics of an invisible minority*. Thousand Oaks, CA: Sage.

Fischer, K. W., Shaver, P. R., & Carnochan, P. (1990). How emotions develop and how they organize development. *Cognition and Emotion, 4,* 81–127.

Fish, J. M. (Ed.) (2002). *Race and intelligence: Separating science from myth*. Mahwah, NJ: Erlbaum.

Fisher, C. B. (2003). *Decoding the ethics code: A practical guide for psychologists*. Thousand Oaks, CA: Sage.

Fisher, C. B., Hoagwood, K., Boyce, C., Duster, T., Frank, D. A., Grisso, T., Levine, R. J., Macklin, R., Spencer, M. B., Takanishi, R., Trimble, J. E., & Zayas, L. H. (2002). Research ethics for mental health science involving ethnic minority children and youths. *American Psychologist, 57,* 1024–1040.

Fisk, J. E., & Sharp, C. (2002). Syllogistic reasoning and cognitive ageing. *Quarterly Journal of Experimental Psychology: Human Experimental Psychology, 55A,* 1273–1293.

Fiske, S. T. (2002). What we know now about bias and intergroup conflict, the problem of the century. *Current Directions in Psychological Science, 11*, 123–128.

Fiske, S. T., & Taylor, S. E. (1991). *Social cognition* (2nd ed.). New York: McGraw-Hill.

Fitzgerald, H., Mann, T., Cabrera, N., & Wong, M. M. (2003). Diversity in caregiving contexts. In R. M. Lerner, M. A. Easterbrooks, et al. (Eds.), *Handbook of psychology: Developmental psychology,* Vol. 6, pp. 135–167. New York: Wiley.

Fitzgerald, L. F. (1993). Sexual harassment: Violence against women in the workplace. *American Psychologist, 48*, 1070–1076.

Flam, F. (1991, June 14). Queasy riders. *Science, 252*, 1488.

Flannery, D. J., Vazsonyi, A. T., & Liau, A. K. (2003). Initial behavior outcomes for the PeaceBuilders universal school-based violence prevention program. *Developmental Psychology: Special issue: Violent children, 39*, 292–308.

Flavell, J. H. (2002). Development of children's knowledge about the mental world. In W. W. Hartup & R. K. Silbereisen (Eds.), *Growing points in developmental science: An introduction,* pp. 102–122. Philadelphia: Press.

Fleming, J. (2000). Affirmative action and standardized test scores. *Journal of Negro Education, 69*, 27–37.

Flynn, J. R. (1999). Searching for justice: The discovery of IQ gains over time. *American Psychologist, 54*, 5–20.

Flynn, J. R. (2000). IQ gains and fluid g. *American Psychologist, 55*, 543.

Foderaro, L. W. (1993, July 19). With reforms in treatment, shock therapy loses shock. *The New York Times*, pp. A1, B2.

Fogarty, J. S., & Young, G. A., Jr. (2000). Patient-physician communication. *Journal of the American Medical Association, 289*, 92.

Fogg, L. F., & Rose, R. M. (1999). Use of personal characteristics in the selection of astronauts. *Human Performance in Extreme Environments, 4*, 27–33.

Folkman, S., & Moskowitz, J. T. (2000). Stress, positive emotion, and coping. *Current Directions in Psychological Science, 9*, 115–118

Follett, K., & Hess, T. M. (2002). Aging, cognitive complexity, and the fundamental attribution error. *Journal of Gerontology: Series B: Psychological Sciences and Social Sciences, 57B*, P312–P323.

Ford, C. S., & Beach, F. A. (1951). *Patterns of sexual behavior.* New York: Harper.

Forer, B. (1949). The fallacy of personal validation: A classroom demonstration of gullibility. *Journal of Abnormal and Social Psychology, 44*, 118–123.

Forgas, J. P., & Bower, G. H. (2001). Mood effects on person-perception judgments. In W. G. Parrott (Ed.), *Emotions in social psychology: Essential readings,* pp. 204–215. Philadelphia: Psychology Press.

Fowler, F. J., Jr. (2001). *Survey research methods.* Thousand Oaks, CA: Sage.

Fowler, R. D. (February 2002). APA's directory tells us who we are. *Monitor on Psychology,* 9.

Fox, S., & Spector, P. E. (2000). Relations of emotional intelligence, practical intelligence, general intelligence, and trait affectivity with interview outcomes: It's not all just "G." *Journal of Organizational Behavior, 21*, 203–220.

Frances, A., First, M. B., & Pincus, H. A. (1995). *DSM-IV guidebook.* Washington, DC: American Psychiatric Press.

Frank, L. R. (2002). Electroshock: A crime against the spirit. *Ethical Human Sciences and Services, 4*, 63–71.

Frankenberg, W. K., et al., 1992. *Denver II training manual.* Denver: Denver Developmental Materials.

Franzek, E., & Beckmann, H. (1996). Gene-environment interaction in schizophrenia: Season-of-birth effect reveals etiologically different subgroups. *Psychopathology, 29*, 14–26.

Frasure-Smith, N., Lesperance, F., & Talajic, M. (2000). The prognostic importance of depression, anxiety, anger, and social support following myocardial infarction: Opportunities for improving survival. In P. M. McCabe, N. Schneiderman, T. M. Field, & A. R. Wellens (Eds.), *Stress, coping, and cardiovascular disease.* Mahwah, NJ: Erlbaum.

Fredrickson, B. L., Tugade, M. M., & Waugh, C. E. (2003). What good are positive emotions in crisis? A prospective study of resilience and emotions following the terrorist attacks on the United States on September 11th, 2001. *Journal of Personality & Social Psychology, 84*, 365–376.

Free, M. L. (2000). *Cognitive therapy in groups: Guidelines and resources for practice.* New York: Wiley.

Freedman, D. S. (1995). The importance of body fat distribution in early life. *American Journal of the Medical Sciences, 310*, S72–S76.

Freedman, J. L., & Fraser, S. C. (1966). Compliance without pressure: The foot-in-the-door technique. *Journal of Personality and Social Psychology, 4*, 195–202.

Freeman, P. (1990, December 17) Silent no more. *People Weekly*, pp. 94–104.

French, H. W. (1997, February 2). Africa's culture war: Old customs, new values. *The New York Times*, pp. 1E, 4E.

Freud, S. (1900). *The interpretation of dreams.* New York: Basic Books.

Freud, S. (1922/1959). *Group psychology and the analysis of the ego.* London: Hogarth.

Friedman, A. F., Lewak, R., Nichols, D. S., & Webb, J. T. (2000). *Psychological assessment with the MMPI-2.* Mahwah, NJ: Erlbaum.

Friedman, J. M. (2003, February 7). A war on obesity, not the obese. *Science, 299*, 856–858.

Fritsch, J. (1999, October 5). Scientists unmask diet myth: Willpower. *The New York Times*, pp. D1, D9.

Fromkin, V. A. (2000). On the uniqueness of language. In K. Emmorey, H. Lane, et al. (Eds.), *The signs of language revisited: An anthology to honor Ursula Bellugi and Edward Klima.* Mahwah, NJ: Erlbaum.

Fromm, E., & Nash, M. (Eds.) (1992). *Contemporary hypnosis research.* New York: Guilford.

Frost, L. E., & Bonnie, R. J. (Eds.). (2001). *The evolution of mental health law.* Washington, DC: American Psychological Association.

Frost, R. O., & Steketee, G. (Eds.). (2002). *Cognitive approaches to obsessions and compulsions: Theory, assessment, and treatment.* New York: Pergamon Press.

Funder, D. C. (1991). Global traits: A neo-Allportian approach to personality. *Psychological Science, 2*, 31–39.

Funder, D. C. (1997). *The personality puzzle.* New York: W. W. Norton.

Funk, M. S. (1996). Development of object permanence in the New Zealand parakeet (*Cyanoramphus auriceps*). *Animal Learning and Behavior, 24*, 375–383.

Furnham, A. (1995). The relationship of personality and intelligence to cognitive learning style and achievement. In D. H. Saklofske & M. Zeidner (Eds.), *International handbook of personality and intelligence. Perspectives on individual differences.* New York: Plenum.

Furnham, A., Pallangyo, A. E., & Gunter, B. (2001). Gender-role stereotyping in Zimbabwean television advertisements. *South African Journal of Psychology, 31*, 21–29.

Furst, P. T. (1977). "High states" in culture-historical perspective. In N. E. Zinberg (Ed.), *Alternate states of consciousness.* New York: Free Press.

Furumoto, L., & Scarborough, E. (2002). Placing women in the history of psychology: The first American women psychologists. In W. E. Pickren (Ed.), *Evolving perspectives on the history of psychology,* pp. 527–543. Washington, DC: American Psychological Association.

Gaertner, S. L., Rust, M. C., Dovidio, J. F., Bachman, B. A., et al. (1996). The contact hypothesis: The role of a common ingroup identity on reducing intergroup bias among majority and minority group members. In J. L. Nye & A. M. Brower (Eds.), *What's social about social cognition? Research on socially shared cognition in small groups.* Thousand Oaks, CA: Sage.

Gagnon, G. H. (1977). *Human sexualities.* Glenview, IL: Scott, Foresman.

Galanter, E. (1962). Contemporary psychophysics. In R. Brown, E. Galanter, E. Hess, & G. Maroler (Eds.), *New directions in psychology,* pp. 87–157. New York: Holt.

Galanter, M., & Kleber, H. D. (Eds.). (1999). *The American Psychiatric Press textbook of substance abuse: Abuse treatment* (2nd ed.), Washington, DC: American Psychiatric Press.

Galatzer-Levy, R. M., & Cohler, B. J. (1997). *Essential psychoanalysis: A contemporary introduction.* New York: Basic Books.

Galavotti, C., Saltzman, L. E., Sauter, S. L., & Sumartojo, E. (1997, February). Behavioral science activities at the Center for Disease Control and Prevention: A selected overview of exemplary programs. *American Psychologist, 52*, 154–166.

Galef, D. (2001, April 27). The information you provide is anonymous, but what was your name again? *The Chronicle of Higher Education, 47*, B5.

Gallagher, D. J. (1996). Personality, coping, and objective outcomes: Extraversion, neuroticism, coping styles, and academic performance. *Personality & Individual Differences, 21*, 421–429.

Gallagher, J. J. (1994). Teaching and learning: New models. *Annual Review of Psychology, 45*, 171–195.

Gallagher, M., & Rapp, R. R. (1997). The use of animal models to study the effects of aging on cognition. *Annual Review of Psychology, 48*, 339–370.

Gallup News Service (1998). *Adults who find that premarital sex is not wrong.* Washington, DC: Gallup News Service.

Gallup Poll. (2001, June 8). *American's belief in psychic and paranormal phenomena is up over last decade.* Washington, DC: The Gallup Organization.

Ganong, L. H. & Coleman, M. (1999). *Changing families, changing responsibilities: Family obligations following divorce and remarriage.* Mahwah, NJ: Erlbaum.

Gao, J., Parsons, L. M., Bower, J. M., Xiong, J., Li, J., & Fox, P. T. (1996, April 26). Cerebellum implicated in sensory acquisition and discrimination rather than motor control. *Science, 272*, 545–547.

Garb, H. N. (2002). Practicing psychological assessment. *American Psychologist, 57*, 990–991.

Garb, H. N. (2003). Observations on the validity of neuropsychological and personality assessment testing. *Australian Psychologist, 38*, 14–21.

Garber, J., & Horowitz, J. L. (2002). Depression in children. In I. H. Gotlib & C. L. Hammen (Eds.), *Handbook of depression.* New York: Guilford Press.

Garcia, J. (1990). Learning without memory. *Journal of Cognitive Neuroscience, 2*, 287–305.

Garcia, J., Hankins, W. G., & Rusiniak, K. W. (1974). Behavioral regulation of the milieu intern in man and rat. *Science, 185*, 824–831.

Garcia, S. M., Weaver, K., Moskowitz, G. B., & Darley, J. M. (2002). Crowded minds: The implicit bystander effect. *Journal of Personality and Social Psychology, 83*, 843–853.

Garcia-Andrade, C., Wall, T. L., & Ehlers, C. L. (1997). The firewater myth and response to alcohol in Mission Indians. *Journal of Psychiatry, 154*, 983–988.

Gardner, E. P., & Kandel, E. R. (2000). Touch. In E. R. Kandel, J. H. Schwartz, & T. M. Jessell (Eds.), *Principles of neural science* (4th ed.). New York: McGraw-Hill.

Gardner, H. (1975). *The shattered mind: The person after brain damage.* New York: Knopf.

Gardner, H. (1999). *Intelligence reframed: Multiple intelligences for the 21st century.* New York: Basic Books.

Gardner, H. (2000). *Intelligence reframed: Multiple intelligences for the 21st century.* New York: Basic Books.

Gardner, R. A., & Gardner, B. T. (1969). Teaching sign language to a chimpanzee. *Science, 165*, 664–672.

Garza-Guerrero, C. (2000). Idealization and mourning in love relationships: Normal and pathological spectra. *Psychoanalytic Quarterly, 69*, 121–150.

Gass, C. S., Luis, C. A., Meyers, T. L., & Kuljis, R. O. (2000). Familial Creutzfeldt-Jakob disease: A neuropsychological case study. *Archives of Clinical Neuropsychology, 15*, 165–175.

Gatchel, R. J., & Baum, A. (1983). *An introduction to health psychology.* Reading, MA: Addison-Wesley.

Gatchel, R. J., & Turk, D. C. (Eds.). (1996). *Psychological Approaches to Pain Management: A Practioner's Handbook.* New York: Guilford.

Gathchel, R. J., & Oordt, M. S. (2003). Obesity. In R. J. Gathchel & M. S. Oordt, *Clinical health psychology and primary care: Practical advice and clinical guidance for successful collaboration*, pp. 149–167. Washington, DC: American Psychological Association.

Gathercole, S. E., & Baddeley, A.D. (1993). *Working memory and language processing.* Hillsdale, NJ: Erlbaum.

Gawin, F. H. (1991, March 29). Cocaine addiction: Psychology and neurophysiology. *Science, 251*, 1580–1586.

Gazzaniga, M. S. (1998, July). The split brain revisited. *Scientific American*, 50–55.

Gazzaniga, M. S. (Ed.). (1994). *The cognitive neurosciences.* Cambridge, MA: MIT Press.

Gazzaniga, M. S., Ivry, R. B., & Mangun, G. R. (2002). *Cognitive neuroscience: The biology of the mind* (2nd Ed.). New York: W. W. Norton.

Ge, X., Conger, R. D., & Elder, Jr., G. H. (1996). Coming of age too early: Pubertal influences on girls' vulnerability to psychological distress. *Child Development, 67*, 3386–3400.

Geary, D. C., & Bjorklund, D. F. (2000). Evolutionary developmental psychology. *Child Development, 71*, 57–65.

Geen, R. G., & Donnerstein, E. (1983). *Aggression: Theoretical and empirical reviews.* New York: Academic Press.

Geiselman, R. E., Fisher, R. P., MacKinnon, D. P., & Holland, H. L. (1985). Eyewitness memory enhancement in the police interview: Cognitive retrieval mnemonics versus hypnosis. *Journal of Applied Psychology, 70*, 401–412.

Gelfand, M. M. (2000). Sexuality among older women. *Journal of Women's Health and Gender Based Medicine, 9, Suppl 1*, S15–S20.

Gelman, D. (1994, April 18). The mystery of suicide. *Newsweek*, pp. 44–49.

Gelman, R., & Baillargeon, R. (1983). A review of some Piagetian concepts. In J. H. Flavell & E. M. Markman (Eds.), *Handbook of child psychology, Vol. 3: Cognitive development* (4th ed.). New York: Wiley.

Gelman, R., & Kit-Fong Au, T. (Eds.). (1996). *Perceptual and cognitive development.* New York: Academic Press.

Genuis, M., & Violato, C. (2000). Attachment security to mother, father, and the parental unit. In C. Violato, & E. Oddone-Paolucci (Eds.), *The changing family and child development.* Aldershot, England: Ashgate Publishing Ltd.

Gentner, D., Goldin, S., & Goldin-Meadow, S. (Eds.). (2003). *Language in mind: Advances in the study of language and cognition.* Cambridge, MA: MIT Press.

George, M. S., Wassermann, E. M., Williams, W. A., Callahan, A., et al. (1995). Daily repetitive transcranial magnetic stimulations (rTMS) improves mood in depression. *Neuroreport: An International Journal for the Rapid Communication of Research in Neuroscience, 6*, 1853–1856.

George, T. P. (1999) Design, measurement, and analysis in developmental research. In M. Bornstein & M. Lamb, *Developmental psychology.* Mahwah, NJ: Erlbaum.

Gershoff, E. T. (2002). Corporal punishment by parents and associated child behaviors and experiences: A meta-analytic and theoretical review. *Psychological Bulletin, 128*, 539–579.

Getner, D., & Holyoak, K. J. (1997, January). Reasoning and learning by analogy. *American Psychologist, 52*, 32–34.

Gevirtz, R. (2000). The physiology of stress. In D. T. Kenny, J. G. Carlson, et al. (Eds.), *Stress and health: Research and clinical applications*, pp. 53–71. Amsterdam, Netherlands: Harwood Academic.

Ghaemi, S. N. (2003). *Mood disorders: A practical guide.* Practical Guides in Psychiatry. New York: Lippincott Williams & Wilkins.

Ghazvini, A., & Mullis, R. L. (2002). Center-based care for young children: Examining predictors of quality. *Journal of Genetic Psychology, 163*, 112–125.

Gibbons, A. (1990, July 13). New maps of the human brain. *Science, 249*, 122–123.

Gibbs, W. W. (2002, August.) From mouth to mind. *Scientific American*, p. 26.

Gibson, B. (1997). Smoker-nonsmoker conflict: Using a social psychological framework to understand a current social controversy. *Journal of Social Issues, 53*, 97–112.

Gibson, E. J. (1994). Has psychology a future? *Psychological Science, 5*, 69–76.

Gibson, H. B. (1995). A further case of the misuse of hypnosis in a police investigation. *Contemporary Hypnosis, 12*, 81–86.

Gilberson, T. A., Damak, S., & Margolskee, R. F. (2000). The molecular physiology of taste transduction. *Current Opinion in Neurobiology, 10*, 519–527.

Gilbert, B. (1996). New ideas in the air at the National Zoo. *Smithsonian*, pp. 32–43.

Gilbert, D. G. (1995). *Smoking: Individual differences, psychopathology, and emotion.* Philadelphia: Taylor & Francis.

Gilbert, D. T., McNulty, S. E., Guiliano, T. A., & Benson, J. E. (1992). Blurry words and fuzzy deeds: The attribution of obscure behavior. *Journal of Personality and Social Psychology, 62*, 18–25.

Gilbert, D. T., Miller, A. G., & Ross, L. (1998). Speeding with Ned: A personal view of the correspondence bias. In J. M. Darley & J. Cooper (Eds.), *Attribution and social interaction: The legacy of Edward E. Jones.* Washington, DC: American Psychological Association.

Gilger, J. W. (1996). How can behavioral genetic research help us understand language development and disorders? In M. L. Rice (Ed.), *Toward a genetics of language.* Mahwah, NJ: Erlbaum.

Gilligan, C. (1996). The centrality of relationships in psychological development: A puzzle, some evidence, and a theory. In G. G. Noam & K. W. Fischer (Eds.), *Development and vulnerability in close relationships.* Hillsdale, NJ: Erlbaum.

Gillyatt, P. (1997, February). When the nose doesn't know. *Harvard Health Letter,* pp. 6–7.

Gilovich, T., Griffin, D., & Kahneman, D. (Eds.). (2002). *Heuristics and biases: The psychology of intuitive judgment.* Cambridge, England: Cambridge University Press.

Gladwell, M. (2002, August 5). The naked face: Can you read people's thoughts just by looking at them? *The New Yorker,* pp. 38–49.

Gladwin, T. (1964). Culture and logical process. In N. Goodenough (Ed.), *Explorations in cultural anthropology: Essays in honor of George Peter Murdoch.* New York: McGraw-Hill.

Glassman, A. H., & Koob, G. F. (1996, February 22). Neuropharmacology: Psychoactive smoke. *Nature, 379,* 677–678.

Glenmullen, J. (2000). *Prozac backlash: Overcoming the dangers of Prozac, Zoloft, Paxil, and other antidepressants with safe, effective alternatives.* New York: Simon & Schuster.

Glick, P., & Fiske, S. T. (1996). The Ambivalent Sexism Inventory: Differentiating hostile and benevolent sexism. *Journal of Personality and Social Psychology, 70,* 491-512.

Gluck, M. E., & Geliebter, A. (2002). Racial/ethnic differences in body image and eating behaviors. *Eating Behaviors, 3,* 143–151.

Gold, P. E., Cahill, L., & Wenk, G. L. (2002). Ginkgo biloba: A cognitive enhancer? *Psychological Science in the Public Interest, 3,* 2–7.

Golding, J. M. (1999). Sexual-assault history and long-term physical health problems: Evidence from clinical and population epidemiology. *Current Directions in Psychological Science, 8,* 191–193.

Goldner, E. M., Cockell, S. J., & Srikameswaran, S. (2002). Perfectionism and eating disorders. In G. L. Flett & P. L. Hewitt (Eds.), *Perfectionism: Theory, research, and treatment,* pp. 319–340. Washington, DC: American Psychological Association.

Goldstein, E. B. (1984). *Sensation and Perception* (2nd Ed.). Pacific Grove, CA: Brooks/Cole.

Goldstein, G., Beers, S. R., Longmore, S., & McCue, M. (1996). Efficacy of memory training: A technological extension and replication. *Clinical Neuropsychologist, 10,* 66–72.

Goldstein, I. (2000). Female sexual arousal disorder: new insights. *International Journal of Impotence Research, 12, Suppl. 4,* S152–S157.

Goldstone, R. L., & Kersten, A. (2003). Concepts and categorization. In A. F. Healy & R. W. Proctor (Eds.), *Handbook of psychology: Experimental psychology,* Vol. 4, pp. 599–621. New York: Wiley.

Goleman, D. (1988, January 21). Physicians may bungle key part of treatment: The medical interview. *The New York Times,* p. B-16.

Goleman, D. (1993a, July 21). "Expert" babies found to teach others. *The New York Times,* p. C-10.

Goleman, D. (1995). *Emotional intelligence.* New York: Bantam.

Golombok, S., & Tasker, F. (1996). Do parents influence the sexual orientation of their children? Findings from a longitudinal study of lesbian families. *Developmental Psychology, 32,* 3–11.

Good, P. I. (2003). *Common errors in statistics and how to avoid them.* New York: Wiley.

Goode, E. (1999, April 13). If things taste bad, "phantoms" may be at work. *The New York Times,* pp. D1–D2.

Goode, E. (2001, September 12). Suicide attackers are sane, not suicidal in the normal sense, experts say. *The New York Times,* p. A13.

Goode, E. (2003a, February 11). Wanted in space: Gregarious loners who take risks, cautiously. *The New York Times,* p. F1.

Goode, E. (2003b, January 28). Even in the age of Prozac, some still prefer the couch. *The New York Times,* Section F, p. 1.

Goodglass, H. (1993). *Understanding aphasia.* San Diego: Academic Press.

Goodman, G. S., Batterman-Faunce, J. M., Schaaf, J. M., & Kenney, R. (2002). Nearly 4 years after an event: Children's eyewitness memory and adults' perceptions of children's accuracy. *Child Abuse and Neglect, 26,* 849–884.

Goodman, W. K., Rudorfer, M. V., & Maser, J. D. (1999). *Obsessive-compulsive disorder: Contemporary issues in treatment.* Mahwah, NJ: Erlbaum.

Goodwin, R. D., & Hamilton, S. P. (2003). Lifetime comorbidity of antisocial personality disorder and anxiety disorders among adults in the community. *Psychiatry Research, 117,* 159–166.

Goosens, L., Beyers, W., Emmen, M., & van Aken, M. (2002). The imaginary audience and personal fable: Factor analyses and concurrent validity of the "New Look" measures. *Journal of Research on Adolescence, 12,* 193–215.

Gordon, E. F. (2000). *Mockingbird years: A life in and out of therapy.* New York: Basic Books.

Gordon, J. W. (1999, March 26). Genetic enhancement in humans. *Science, 283,* 2023–2024.

Gorman, J. M., Papp, L. A., & Coplan, J. D. (1995). Neuroanatomy and neurotransmitter function in panic disorder. In S. P. Roose & R. A. Glick (Eds.), *Anxiety as symptom and signal.* Hillsdale, NJ: Analytic Press.

Gottesman, I. I. (1991). *Schizophrenia genesis: The origins of madness.* New York: Freeman.

Gottesman, I. I., & Moldin, S. O. (1998). Genotypes genes, genesis, and pathogenesis in schizophrenia. In M. F. Lenzenweger & R. H. Dworkin (Eds.), *The origins and development of schizophrenia: Advances in experimental psychopathology.* Washington, DC: American Psychological Association.

Gottesman, I. I. (1997, June 6). Twin: En route to QTLs for cogniton. *Science, 276,* 1522–1523.

Gould, E., Reeves, A. J., Graziano, M. S. A., & Gross, C. G. (1999, October 15). Neurogenesis in the neocortex of adult primates. *Science,* pp. 548–552.

Gould, R. L. (1978). *Transformations.* New York: Simon & Schuster.

Gouras, P. (1991). Color vision. In E. R. Kandel, J. H. Schwartz, & T. M. Jessell (Eds.), *Principles of neural science* (3rd ed.). New York: Elsevier.

Gowing, L. R., Henry-Edwards, S. M., Irvine, R. J., & Ali, R. L. (2002). The health effects of ecstasy: A literature review. *Drug and Alcohol Review, 21,* 53–63.

Grady, D. (2002, November 26). Why we eat (and eat and eat). *The New York Times,* pp. D1, D4.

Graf, P. (1990). Life-span changes in implicit and explicit memory. *Bulletin of the Psychonomic Society, 28,* 353–358.

Graf, P., & Masson, M. E. J. (Eds.). (1993). *Implicit memory: New directions in cognition, development, and neuropsychology.* Hillsdale, NJ: Erlbaum.

Graffin, N. F., Ray, W. J., & Lundy, R. (1995). EEG concomitants of hypnosis and hypnotic susceptibility. *Journal of Abnormal Psychology, 104,* 123–131.

Graham, J. R. (1999). *MMPI-2: Assessing personality and psychopathology,* (3rd ed.). New York: Oxford University Press.

Graham, S. (1992). "Most of the subjects were white and middle class": Trends in published research on African Americans in selected APA journals, 1970–1989. *American Psychologist, 47,* 629–639.

Graham, S. (2001, November 12). 9/11: The psychological aftermath. Scientific American website: www.sciam.com/explorations/2001/111201anxiety/index.html.

Grammer, K. (1996, June). Sex and olfaction. Paper presented at the annual meeting of the Human Behavior and Evolution Society, Evanston, Illinois.

Graugaard, P. K., Eide, H., & Finset, A. (2003). Interaction analysis of physician-patient communication: The influence of trait anxiety on communication and outcome. *Patient Education and Counseling, 49,* 149–156.

Graves, S. B. (1999). Television and prejudice reduction: When does television as a vicarious experience make a difference? *Journal of Social Issues, 55,* 707–725.

Gray, J. R., Chabris, C. F., & Braver, T. S. (2003, February 18). Neural mechanisms of general fluid intelligence. *Nature: Neurosciences,* www.nature.com/cgitaf/DynaPage.taf?file=/neuro/journal/vaop/ ncurrent/abs/nn1014.html

Gray, R. (2002). "Markov at the bat": A model of cognitive processing in baseball batters. *Psychological Science, 13*, 542–547.

Graziano, M. S., Taylor, C. S., & Moore, T. (2002). Complex movements evolved by microstimulation of precentral cortex. *Neuron, 34*, 841–851.

Green, J. S., Henderson, F. R., & Collinge, M. D. (2003). *Prevention and control of wildlife damage: Coyotes,* http://wildlifedamage. unl.edu/handbook/handbook/carnivor/ca_c51.pdf. Lincoln: University of Nebraska, Institute of Agriculture and Natural Resources.

Greenberg, R. L. (2000). The creative client in cognitive therapy. *Journal of Cognitive Psychotherapy, 14: Special issue: Creativity in the context of cognitive therapy.* 163–174.

Greene, B., & Herek, G. (1994). *Lesbian and gay psychology: Theory, research, and clinical applications.* Newbury Park, CA: Sage.

Greene, J. D., Sommerville, R. B., Nystrom, L. E., Darley, J. M., & Cohen, J. D. (2001, September 14). An fMRI investigation of emotional engagement in moral judgment. *Science, 293*, 2105–2108.

Greene, R. L., & Clopton, J. R. (1994). Minnesota Multiphasic Personality Inventory-2. In M.E. Maruish (Ed.), *The use of psychological tests for treatment planning and outcome assessment.* Hillsdale, NJ: Erlbaum.

Greenfield, P. M. (1997). You can't take it with you: Why ability assessments don't cross cultures. *American Psychologist, 52*, 1115–1124.

Greenlaw, P. S., & Jensen, S. S. (1996). Race-norming and the Civil Rights Act of 1991. *Public Personnel Management, 25*, 13–24.

Greeno, J. G. (1978). Natures of problem-solving abilities. In W. K. Estes (Ed.), *Handbook of learning and cognitive processes.* Hillsdale, NJ: Erlbaum.

Greenwald, A. G., Banaji, M. R., Rudman, L. A., Farnham, S. D., Nosek, B. A., & Mellott, D. S. (2002). A unified theory of implicit attitudes, stereotypes, self-esteem, and self-concept. *Psychological Review, 109*, 3–25.

Greenwald, A. G., Draine S. C., & Abrams, R. L. (1996, September 20). Three cognitive markers of unconscious semantic activation. *Science, 272*, 1699–1702.

Greenwald, A. G., Spangenberg, E. R., Pratkanis, A. R., & Eskenzai, J. (1991). Double-blind tests of subliminal self-help audiotapes. *Psychological Science, 2*, 119–122.

Greenwood, C. R., Carta, J. J., Hart, B., Kamps, D., Terry, B., Arreaga-Mayer, C., Atwater, J., Walker, D., Risley, T., & Delquadri, J. C. (1992). Out of the laboratory and into the community: 26 years of applied behavior analysis at the Juniper Gardens children's project. *American Psychologist, 47*, 1464–1474.

Gregory, R. L. (1978). *The psychology of seeing* (3rd ed.). New York: McGraw-Hill.

Gregory, S. (1856). *Facts for young women.* Boston.

Gregory, S. S. (1994, March 21). At risk of mutilation. *Time,* pp. 45–46.

Greist-Bousquet, S., & Schiffman, H. R. (1986). The basis of the Poggendorff effect: An additional clue for Day and Kasperczyk. *Perception and Psychophysics, 39*, 447–448.

Grigorenko, E. L. (2000). Heritability and intelligence. In R. J. Sternberg, et al. (Eds.), *Handbook of intelligence.* New York: Cambridge University Press.

Grillner, S. (1996, January). Neural networks for vertebrate locomotion. *Scientific American,* pp. 64–69.

Grilo, C. M., Sanislow, C. A., Skodol, A. E., Gunderson, J. G., Stout, R. L., Shea, M. T., Zanarini, M. C., Bencer, D. S., Morey, L. C., Dyck, I. R., & McGlashan, T. H. (2003). Do eating disorders co-occur with personality disorders? Comparison groups matter. *International Journal of Eating Disorders, 33*, 155–164.

Grohol, J. M. & Zuckerman, E. L. (2002). *The insider's guide to mental health resources online* (2002/2003 edition). New York: Guilford Press.

Grossi, G., Semenza, C., Corazza, S., & Volterra, V. (1996). Hemispheric specialization for sign language. *Neuropsychologia, 34*, 737–740.

Groth-Marnat, G. (1990). *Handbook of psychological assessment* (2nd ed.). New York: Wiley.

Groth-Marnat, G. (1996). *Handbook of psychological assessment* (3rd ed.). Somerset, NJ: Wiley.

Grube, J. W., Rokeach, M., & Getzlaf, S.B. (1990). Adolescents' value images of smokers, ex-smokers, and nonsmokers. *Addictive Behaviors, 15*, 81–88.

Gruneberg, M. M., & Pascoe, K. (1996). The effectiveness of the keyword method for receptive and productive foreign vocabulary learning in the elderly. *Contemporary Educational Psychology, 21*, 102–109.

Grunwald, T. Boutros, N. N., Perzer, N., von Oertzen, J., Fernandez, G., Schller, C., & Elger, C. E. (2003). Neuronal substrates of sensory gating within the human brain. *Biological Psychiatry, 53*, 511–519.

Guadagno, R. E., & Cialdini, R. B. (2002). Online persuasion: An examination of gender differences in computer-mediated interpersonal influence. *Group Dynamics: Special Issue: Groups and Internet, 6*, 38–51.

Guadagno, R. E., Asher, T., Demaine, L. J., & Cialdini, R. B. (2001). When saying yes leads to saying no: Preference for consistency and the reverse foot-in-the-door effect. *Personality and Social and Social Psychology Bulletin, 27*, 859–867.

Gualtiere, C. T. (2003). Brain injury and mental retardation: Psychopharmacology and neuropsychiatry. *Human Psychopharmacology: Clinical and Experimental, 18*, 151.

Gueguen, N. (2002). Foot-in-the-door technique and computer-mediated communication. *Computers in Human Behavior, 18*, 11–15.

Gullotta, T., Adams, G., & Markstrom, C. (1999). *The adolescent experience.* Orlando, FL: Academic Press.

Gupta, S., & Petersen, K. (2002, June 13). Could bionic eye end blindness? CNN, www.cnn.com.

Gur, R. C., Gur, R. E., Obrist, W. D., Hungerbuhler, J. P., Younkin, D., Rosen, A. D., Skilnick, B. E., & Reivich, M. (1982). Sex and handedness differences in cerebral blood flow during rest and cognitive activity. *Science, 217*, 659–661.

Gur, R. C., Mozley, L. H., Mozley, P. D., Resnick, S. M., Karp, J. S., Alavi, A., Arnold, S. E., & Gur, R. E. (1995, January 27). Sex differences in regional cerebral glucose metabolism during a resting state. *Science, 267*, 528–531.

Gur, R. C., Turetsky, B. I., Matsui, M., Yan, M., Bilker, W., Hughett, P., & Gur, R. E. (1999). Sex differences in brain gray and white matter in healthy young adults: Correlations with cognitive performance. *Journal of Neuroscience, 19*, 4065–4072

Gur, R. C. (1996, March). Paper presented at the annual meeting of the American Association for the Advancement of Science, Baltimore, Maryland.

Guralnick, M. J., Connor, R. T., Hammond, M., Gottman, J. M., et al. (1996). Immediate effects of mainstreamed settings on the social interactions and social integration of preschool children. *American Journal on Mental Retardation, 100*, 359–377.

Gutek, B. A., Cohen, A. G., & Tsui, A. (1996). Reactions to perceived sex discrimination. *Human Relations, 49*, 791–813.

Guterl, F. (2002, November 11). What Freud got right. *Newsweek,* pp. 50–51.

Guthrie, R. V. (1998). *Even the rat was white: A historical view of psychology* (2nd ed.). Needham Heights, MA: Allyn and Bacon.

Guttman, M. (1995, March 3–5). She had electroshock therapy. *USA Weekend,* p. 16.

Gwynn, M. I., & Spanos, N. P. (1996). Hypnotic responsiveness, nonhypnotic suggestibility, and responsiveness to social influence. In R. G. Kunzendorf, N. P. Spahos, & B. Wallace (Eds.), *Hypnosis and imagination.* Amityville, NY: Baywood.

Haber, R. N. (1983). Stimulus information processing mechanisms in visual space perception. In J. Beck, B. Hope, & A. Rosenfeld (Eds.), *Human and machine vision.* New York: Academic Press.

Hackett, T. A., & Kaas, J. H. (2003). Auditory processing in the primate brain. In M. Gallagher, & R. J. Nelson (Eds.), *Handbook of psychology: Biological psychology,* Vol. 3, New York: Wiley.

Hagan, E., Sattler, J. M., & Thorndike, R. L. (1985). *Stanford-Binet test.* Chicago: Riverside.

Hagekull, B., & Bohlin, G. (1995). Day care quality, family and child characteristics and socioemotional development. *Early Childhood Research Quarterly, 10*, 505–526.

Haier, R. J. (1993). Cerebral glucose metabolism and intelligence. In P.A. Vernon (Ed.), *Biologic contributions to the study of human intelligence.* Norwood, NJ: Ablex.

Haley, W. E., Clair, J. M., & Saulsberry, K. (1992). Family caregiver satisfaction with medical care of their demented relatives. *Gerontologist, 32*, 219–226.

Halgin, R. P., & Whitbourne, S.K. (1994). *Abnormal psychology.* Fort Worth, TX: Harcourt Brace.

Hall, G. C. N. (1996). *Theory-based assessment, treatment, and prevention of sexual aggression.* New York: Oxford University Press.

Hall, G. C. N., & Barongan, C. (1997). Prevention of sexual aggression: Sociocultural risk and protective factors. *American Psychologist, 52*, 5–14.

Hall, J. A., Roter, D. L., & Katz, N. R. (1988). Task versus socioemotional behaviors in physicians. *Medical Care, 25*, 399–412.

Hall, R. E. (2002). *The Bell Curve*: Implications for the performance of black/white athletes. *Social Science Journal, 39*, 113–118.

Halling, S., & Goldfarb, M. (1996). The new generation of diagnostic manuals (DSM-III, DSM-III-R, and DSM-IV): An overview and a phenomenologically based critique. *Journal of Phenomenological Psychology, 27*, 49–71.

Halpern, D. F. (1998). Teaching critical thinking for transfer across domains. *American Psychologist, 53*, 449–455.

Halpern, D. F. (2000). *Sex differences in cognitive abilities* (3rd ed.). Mahwah, NJ: Erlbaum.

Halpern, D., & Riggio, H. (2002). *Thinking critically about critical thinking.* Mahwah, NJ: Erlbaum.

Halpert, J. (2003, April 28). What do patients want? *Newsweek*, pp. 63–64.

Hamann, S. (2001). Cognitive and neural mechanisms of emotional memory. *Trends in Cognitive Sciences, 5*, 394–400.

Hamann, S. B., Ely, T. D., Hoffman, J. M., & Kilts, C. D. (2002). Ecstasy and agony: Activation of human amygdala in positive and negative emotion. *Psychological Science, 13*, 135–141.

Hamel, S., Leclerc, G., & Lefrancois, R. (2003). A psychological outlook on the concept of transcendent actualization. *International Journal of the Psychology of Religion, 13*, 3–15.

Hamer, D. H., Hu, S., Magnuson, V. L., Hu, N., & Pattatucci, A. M. L. (1993, July 16). A linkage between DNA markers on the X chromosome and male sexual orientation. *Science, 261*, 321–327.

Hamilton, C. E. (2000). Continuity and discontinuity of attachment from infancy through adolescence. *Child Development, 71*, 690–694.

Hanley, S. J., & Abell, S. C. (2002). Maslow and relatedness: Creating an interpersonal model of self-actualization. *Journal of Humanistic Psychology, 42*, 37–56.

Hanna, J. L. (1984). Black/white nonverbal differences, dance, and dissonance: Implications for desegregation. In A. Wolfgang (Ed.), *Nonverbal behavior: Perspectives, applications, intercultural insights.* Lewiston, NY: Hogrefe.

Hansen, E. M., Kimble, C. E., & Biers, D. W. (2001). Actors and observers: Divergent attributions of constrained unfriendly behavior. *Social Behavior and Personality, 29*, 87–104.

Harden, B. (2000, January 9). Very young, smart, and restless. *New York Times Education Life*, pp. 28–31.

Hardy, J., & Selkoe, D. J. (2002, July 19). The amyloid hypothesis of Alzheimer's disease: Progress and problems on the road to therapeutics. *Science, 297*, 353–356.

Harlow, H. F., & Zimmerman, R. R. (1959). Affectional responses in the infant monkey. *Science, 130*, 421–432.

Harlow, J. M. (1869). Recovery from the passage of an iron bar through the head. *Massachusetts Medical Society Publication, 2*, 329–347.

Harlow, R. E., & Cantor, N. (1996). Still participating after all these years: A study of life task participation in later life. *Journal of Personality and Social Psychology, 71*, 1235–1249.

Harmon-Jones, E., Peterson, H., & Vaughn, K. (2003). The dissonance-inducing effects of an inconsistency between experienced empathy and knowledge of past failures to help: Support for the action-based model of dissonance. *Basic and Applied Social Psychology, 25*, 69–78.

Harold, G. T., Fincham, F. D., Osborne, L. N., & Conger, R. D. (1997). Mom and dad are at it again: Adolescent perceptions of marital conflict and adolescent psychological distress. *Developmental Psychology, 33*, 333–350.

Harper, T. (1978, November 15). It's not true about people 65 or over. *Green Bay Press-Gazette* (Wisconsin), p. D-1.

Harris Interactive. (2002, April 2). *Beyond spring break: What college students do with the rest of their leisure time?* www.harrisinteractive.com/news/allnewsbydate.asp?NewsID=441.

Harris Poll. (2000 February 2). *The power of tobacco addiction.* New York: Harris Interactive, Inc.

Harris, C. R., & Christenfeld, N. (1996). Gender, jealousy, and reason. *Psychological Science, 7*, 364–366.

Harrison, J. A., & Wells, R. B. (1991). Bystander effects on male helping behavior: Social comparison and diffusion of responsibility. *Representative Research in Social Psychology, 19*, 53–63.

Hart, B. & Risley, T. R. (1997). Use of language by three-year-old children. Courtesy of Drs. Betty Hart and Todd Risley, University of Kansas.

Hart, B., & Risley, T. R. (1995). *Meaningful differences.* Baltimore, MD: Brookes.

Hartmann, E. (1967). *The biology of dreaming.* Springfield, IL: Thomas.

Harton, H. C., & Lyons, P. C. (2003). Gender, empathy, and the choice of the psychology major. *Teaching of Psychology, 30*, 19–24.

Hartung, C. M., & Widiger, T. A. (1998). Gender differences in the diagnosis of mental disorders: Conclusions and controversies of the DSM-IV. *Psychological Bulletin, 123*, 260–278.

Harvey, E. (1999). Short-term and long-term effects of early parental employment on children of the National Longitudinal Survey of Youth. *Developmental Psychology, 35*, 445–459.

Harvey, J. H., & Weber, A. L. (2002). *Odyssey of the heart: Close relationships in the 21st century*, (2nd ed.). Mahwah, NJ: Erlbaum.

Hastings, R. P., & Oakford, S. (2003). Student teachers' attitudes towards the inclusion of children with special needs. *Educational Psychology, 23*, 87–94.

Haugtvedt, C. P., Petty, R. E., & Cacioppo, J. T. (1992). Need for cognition and advertising: Understanding the role of personality variables in consumer behavior. *Journal of Consumer Psychology, 1*, 239–260.

Hauri, P. J. (Ed.). (1991). *Case studies in insomnia.* New York: Plenum.

Hauser, M. D. (2000). The sound and the fury: Primate vocalizations as reflections of emotion and thought. In N. L. Wallin & B. Merker (Eds.), *The origins of music.* Cambridge, MA: MIT Press.

Hauser, M. D., Chomsky, N., & Fitch, W. T. (2002, November, 22). The faculty for language: What is it, who has it, and how did it evolve? *Science, 298*, 1569–1579.

Haviland-Jones, J., & Chen, D. (1999, April 17). *Human olfactory perception.* Paper presented at the Association for Chemoreception Sciences, Sarasota, Florida.

Hawke, J. M., Jainchill, N., & De Leon, G. (2000). The prevalence of sexual abuse and its impact on the onset of drug use among adolescents in therapeutic community drug treatment. *Journal of Child & Adolescent Substance Abuse, 9*, 35–49

Haxby, J. V., Gobini, M. I., Furey, M. L., Ishai, A., Schouten, J. L., & Pietrini, P. (2001, September 28). Distributed and overlapping representations of faces and objects in ventral temporal cortex. *Science, 293*, 2425–2430.

Hayes, J. R. (1966). Memory, goals, and problem solving. In B. Kleinmuntz (Ed.), *Problem solving: Research, method, and theory.* New York: Wiley.

Hayflick, L. (1994). *How and why we age.* New York: Ballatine.

Health Pages. (2003, March 13). Just what the doctor ordered. www.thehealthpages.com/articles/ar-drord.html.

Hearn, K. (2003, January 28). Names may trigger hiring bias. *Christian Science Monitor*, p. 19.

Heath, A. C., & Madden, P. A. F. (1995). Genetic influences on smoking behavior. In J. R. Turner, L. R. Cardon, & J. K. Hewitt (Eds.), *Behavior genetic approaches in behavioral medicine: Perspectives on individual differences.* New York: Plenum.

Hebl, M. R. & Hetherton, T. F. (1998). The stigma of obesity in women: The difference is black and white. *Personality and Social Psychology Bulletin, 24*, 417–426.

Hebl, M. R., Foster, J. B., Mannix, L. M., & Dovidio, J. F. (2002). Formal and interpersonal discrimination: A field study of bias toward homosexual applicants. *Personality and Social Psychology Bulletin, 28*, 815–825.

Hedges, L. V., & Nowell, A. (July 7, 1995). Sex differences in mental test scores, variability, and numbers of high-scoring individuals. *Science, 269*, 41–45.

Heider, F. (1958). *The psychology of interpersonal relations*. New York: Wiley.

Heikkinen, H., Nutt, J. G., & LeWitt, P. A. (2001). The effects of different repeated doses of entacapone on the pharmacokinetics of L-dopa and on the clinical response to L-dopa in Parkinson's disease. *Clinical Neuropharmacology, 24*, 150–157.

Hellmich, N. (2000, March 28). A teen thing: Losing sleep. *USA Today*, p. A1.

Helms, J. E. (1992). Why is there no study of cultural equivalence in standardized cognitive ability testing? *American Psychologist, 47*, 1083–1101.

Helmuth, L. (2000, August 25). Synapses shout to overcome distance. *Science, 289*, 1273.

Helmuth, L. (2001, September 14). Moral reasoning relies on emotion. *Science, 293*, 1971–1972.

Helps, S., Fuggle, P., Udwin, O., & Dick M. (2003). Psychosocial and neurocognitive aspects of sickle cell disease, *Child and Adolescent Mental Health, 8*, 11–17.

Henderlong, J., & Lepper, M. R. (2002). The effects of praise on children's intrinsic motivation: A review and synthesis. *Psychological Bulletin, 128*, 774–795.

Henderson, N. D. (1982). Correlations in IQ for pairs of people with varying degrees of genetic relatedness and shared environment. *Annual Review of Psychology, 33*, 219–243.

Herman, D., Vansteenwegen, D., Crombez, G., Baeyens, F., & Eelen, P. (2002). Expectancy-learning and evaluative learning in human classical conditioning: Affective priming as an indirect and unobtrusive measure of conditioned stimulus valence. *Behaviour Research and Therapy, 40*, 217–234.

Hermann, D., Raybeck, D., & Gruneberg, M. M. (2002). *Improving memory and study skills: Advances in theory and practice*. Cambridge, MA: Hogrefe & Huber.

Herrington, D. M., & Howard, T. D. (2003). From presumed benefit to potential harm—Hormone therapy and heart disease. *New England Journal of Medicine, 349*, 519–521.

Herrnstein, R. J., & Murray, D. (1994). *The bell curve*. New York: Free Press.

Heshka, S., Anderson, J. W., Atkinson, R. L., Greenway, F. L., Hill, J. O., Phinney, S. D., Kolotkin, R. L., Miller-Kovach, K., & Pi-Sunyer, F. X. (2003). Weight loss with self-help compared with a structured commercial program: A randomized trial. *Journal of the American Medical Association, 289*, 1792–1798.

Hetherington, E. M. (Ed.). (1999). *Coping with divorce, single parenting, and remarriage: A risk and resiliency perspective*. Mahwah, NJ: Erlbaum.

Heward, W. L., & Orlansky, M. D. (1988). *Exceptional children* (3rd ed.). Columbus, OH: Merrill.

Hewitt, B., Gose, S. G., & Birkbeck, M. (2000, December 11). House divided. *People Weekly, 54*, 138–144.

Hewitt, B., Heyman, J.D., Lambert, P., Rogers, P., & Tresniowski, A. (2003, February 17). Seven became one. *People*, pp. 92–104.

Heyman, G. D., & Diesendruck, G. (2002). The Spanish ser/estar distinction in bilingual children's reasoning about human psychological characteristics. *Developmental Psychology, 38*, 407–417.

Heyward, W. L., & Curran, J. W. (1988, October). The epidemiology of AIDS in the U.S. *Scientific American*, pp. 72–81.

Hicks, T. V., & Leitenberg, H. (2001). Sexual fantasies about one's partner versus someone else: Gender differences in incidence and frequency. *Journal of Sex Research, 38*, 43–50.

Hilgard, E. (1992). Dissassociation and theories of hypnosis. In E. Fromm & M. E. Nash (Eds.), *Contemporary hypnosis research*. New York: Guilford.

Hilgard, E. R. (1975). Hypnosis. *Annual Review of Psychology, 26*, 19–44.

Hill, J. O., & Peters, J. C. (1998). Environmental contributions to the obesity epidemic. *Science, 280*, 1371–1374.

Hill, J. O., Wyatt, H. R., Reed, G. W., & Peters, J. C. (2003, February 7). Obesity and the environment: Where do we go from here? *Science, 299*, 853–855.

Hill, M. L., & Craig, K. D. (2002). Detecting deception in pain expressions: The structure of genuine and deceptive facial displays. *Pain, 98*, 135–144.

Hines, M., Golombok, S., Rust, J., Johnston, K. J., Golding, J., & Avon Longitudinal Study of Parents and Children Study Team. (2002). Testosterone during pregnancy and gender role behavior of preschool children: A longitudinal, population study. *Child Development, 73*, 1678–1687.

Hinshaw, S. P., Zupan, B. A., Simmel, C., Nigg, J. T., & Melnick, S. (1997). Peer status in boys with and without attention-deficit hyperactivity disorder: Predictions from overt and covert antisocial behavior, social isolation, and authoritative parenting beliefs. *Child Development, 68*, 880–896.

Hipkiss, R. A. (1995). *Semantics: Defining the discipline*. Mahwah, NJ: Erlbaum.

Hirsh, I. J., & Watson, C. S. (1996). Auditory psychophysics and perception. *Annual Review of Psychology, 47*, 461–484.

Hitt, J. (2000, February 20). The second sexual revolution. *The New York Times Magazine*, pp. 34–62.

Harvard Mental Health Letter (HMHL). (1994b, March). Brief psychodynamic therapy—Part I. *Harvard Mental Health Letter*, p. 10.

Harvard Mental Health Letter (HMHL). (1996, November). Suicide. *Harvard Mental Health Letter, 13*, 1–5.

Hobfoll, S. E., Freedy, J. R., Green B. L., & Solomon, S. D. (1996). Coping in reaction to extreme stress: The roles of resource loss and resource availability. In M. Zeidner & N. S. Endler (Eds.), *Handbook of coping: Theory, research, applications*. New York: Wiley.

Hobson, J. A. (1988). *The dreaming brain*. New York: Basic Books.

Hobson, J. A., & Silverstri, L. (1999, February). Parasomnias. *The Harvard Mental Health Letter*, pp. 3–5.

Hobson, J. A. (1996, February). How the brain goes out of its mind. *Harvard Mental Health Letter*, pp. 3–5.

Hochschild, A. (2001, February). A Generation without public passion. *Atlantic Monthly*, pp. 33–42.

Hochschild, A. R. (1990). The second shift: Employed women and putting in another day of work at home. *Utne Reader, 38*, 66–73.

Hochschild, A. R., & Machung, A. (1990). *The second shift: Working parents and the revolution at home*. New York: Viking.

Hoeller, K. (Ed.). (1990). *Readings in existential psychology & psychiatry*. Seattle, WA: Review of Existential Psychology & Psychiatry.

Hoff, E. (2003). Language development in childhood. In R. M. Lerner, M. A. Easterbrooks, et al. (Eds.), *Handbook of psychology: Developmental psychology*, Vol. 6, pp. 171–193. New York: Wiley.

Hoffman, E. (2001). *Psychological testing at work: How to use, interpret, and get the most out of the newest tests in personality, learning style, aptitudes, interests, and more!* New York: McGraw-Hill.

Hoffman, J. P., Baldwin, S. A., & Cerbone, F. G. (2003). Onset of major depressive disorder among adolescents. *Journal of the American Academy of Child and Adolescent Psychiatry, 42*, 217–224.

Hogan, R., Hogan, J., & Roberts, B. W. (1996). Personality measurement and employment decisions: Questions and answers. *American Psychologist, 51*, 469–477.

Hogg, M. A., & Hardie, E. A. (1992). Prototypicality, conformity and depersonalized attraction: A self-categorization analysis of group cohesiveness. *British Journal of Social Psychology, 31*, 41–56.

Holden, G. W. (2002). Perspectives on the effects of corporal punishment: Comment on Gershoff (2002). *Psychological Bulletin, 128*, 590–595.

Holden, R. R. (2000). Are there promising MMPI substitutes for assessing psychopathology and personality? Review and prospect. In R. H. Dana, (Ed), et al. *Handbook of cross-cultural and multicultural personality assessment. Personality and clinical psychology series*. Mahwah, NJ: Lawrence Erlbaum.

Holland, J. C., & Lewis, S. (2001). *The human side of cancer: Living with hope, coping with uncertainty*. New York: Quill.

Hollingworth, H. L. (1943/1990). *Leta Stetter Hollingworth: A biography*. Boston: Anker.

Hollis, K. L. (1997, September). Contemporary research on Pavlovian conditioning: A "new" functional analysis. *American Psychologist, 52*, 956–965.

Hollon, S. D., Thase, M. E., & Markowitz, J. C. (2002). Treatment and prevention of depression. *Psychological Science in the Public Interest, 3*, 39–77.

Holmes, C. T., Keffer, R. L. (1995). A computerized method to teach Latin and Greek root words: Effect on verbal SAT scores. *Journal of Educational Research, 89*, 47–50.

Holowka, S., & Pettito, L. A. (2002, August 30). Left hemisphere cerebral specialization for babies while babbling. *Science, 297*, 1515.

Holy, T. E., Dulac, C., & Meister, M. (2000, September 1). Responses of vomeronasal neurons to natural stimuli. *Science, 289*, 1569–1572.

Hong, E., Milgram, R. M., & Gorsky, H. (1995). Original thinking as a predictor of creative performance in young children. *Roeper Review, 18*, 147–149.

Hong, S. (2000). Exercise and psychoneuroimmunology. *International Journal of Sport Psychology. Special Issue: Exercise psychology, 31*, 204–227.

Hong, Y., Morris, M., Chiu, C., & Benet-Martinez, V. (2000). Multicultural minds. *American Psychologist, 55*, 709–720.

Horgan, J. (1993, December). Fractured functions: Does the brain have a supreme integrator? *Scientific American*, pp. 36–37.

Horgan, J. (1995, November). Get smart, take a test. *Scientfic American*, pp. 12–14.

Horgan, J. (1996, December). Why Freud isn't dead. *Scientific American*, pp. 106–111.

Horn, J. L. (2002). Selections of evidence, misleading assumptions, and oversimplifications: The political message of *The Bell Curve*. In J. M. Fish (Ed.), *Race and intelligence: Separating science from myth*, pp. 297–325. Mahwah, NJ: Erlbaum.

Horney, K. (1937). *Neurotic personality of our times*. New York: Norton.

Hovland, C., Janis, I., & Kelly, H. H. (1953). *Communication and persuasion*. New Haven, CT: Yale University Press.

Howard, A., Pion, G. M., Gottfredson, G. D., Flattau, P. E., Oskamp, S., Pfafflin, S. M., Bray, D. W., & Burstein, A. D. (1986). The changing face of American psychology: A report from the committee on employment and human resources. *American Psychologist, 41*, 1311–1327.

Howe, C. J. (2002). The countering of overgeneralization. *Journal of Child Language, 29*, 875–895.

Howe, M. L. (1999). *The fate of early memories: Developmental science and the retention of childhood experiences*. Washington, DC: American Psychological Association.

Howells, J. G., & Osborn, M. L. (1984). *A reference companion to the history of abnormal psychology*. Westport, CT: Greenwood Press.

Howitt, D., & Cramer, D. (2000). *First steps in research and statistics: A practical workbook for psychology students*. Philadelphia: Psychology Press.

Hsu, B., Koing, A., Kessler, C., Knapke, K., et al (1994). Gender differences in sexual fantasy and behavior in a college population: A ten-year replication. *Journal of Sex and Marital Therapy, 20*, 103–118.

Hubbard, K., O'Neill, A., & Cheakalos, C. (1999, April 12). Out of control. *People*, pp. 52–72.

Hubble, M. A., Duncan, B. L., & Miller, S. D. (Eds.). (1999). *The heart and soul of change: What works in therapy*. Washington, DC: American Psychological Association.

Hubel, D. H., & Wiesel, T. N. (1979). Brain mechanisms of vision. *Scientific American*, pp. 150–162.

Hudson, W. (1960). Pictorial depth perception in subcultural groups in Africa. *Journal of Social Psychology, 52*, 183–208.

Hudspeth, A. J. (2000). Hearing. In E. R. Kandel, J. H. Schwartz, & T. M. Jessell (Eds.), *Principles of neural science* (4th ed.). New York: McGraw-Hill.

Huesmann, L. R., Moise-Titus, J., Podolski, C. L., & Eron, L. D. (2003). Longitudinal relations between children's exposure to TV violence and their aggressive and violent behavior in young adulthood: 1977–1992. *Developmental Psychology. Special Issue: Violent children, 39*, 201–221.

Huffman, C. J., Matthews, T. D., & Gagne, P. E. (2001). The role of part-set cuing in the recall of chess positions: Influence of chunking in memory. *North American Journal of Psychology, 3*, 535–542.

Hugdahl, K, & Davidson, R. J. (Eds.) (2002). *The assymetrical brain*. Cambridge, MA: Bradford.

Hull, C. L. (1943). *Principles of behavior*. New York: Appleton-Century-Crofts.

Humphreys, G. W., & Müller, H. (2000). A search asymmetry reversed by figure-ground assignment. *Psychological Science, 11*, 196–200.

Humphreys, J. (2003). Resilience in sheltered battered women. *Issues in Mental Health Nursing, 24*, 137–152.

Hunt, E. (1983). On the nature of intelligence. *Science, 219*, 141–146.

Hunt, E. (1994). Problem solving. In R. J. Sternberg (Ed.), *Thinking and problem solving: Handbook of perception and cognition* (2nd ed.). San Diego, CA: Academic Press.

Hunt, M. (1974). *Sexual behaviors in the 1970s*. New York: Dell.

Hunt, M. (1999). *How science takes stock: The story of meta-analysis*. New York: Russell Sage Foundation.

Huston, A. C., Donnerstein, E., Fairchild, H. H., Feshback, N. D., Katz, P., Murray, J. P., Rubinstein, E. A., Wilcox, B. L., & Zuckerman, D. (1992). Big world, small screen: The role of television in American society. Omaha, NE: University of Nebraska Press.

Hyde, J. S. (1994). *Understanding human sexuality* (5th ed.). New York: McGraw-Hill.

Hyde, J. S., & Linn, M. C. (1988). Gender differences in verbal ability: A meta-analysis. *Psychological Bulletin, 104*, 53–69.

Hyde, J. S., Fennema, E., & Lamon, S.J. (1990). Gender differences in mathematics performance: A meta-analysis. *Psychological Bulletin, 107*, 139–155.

Hyman, R. (1994). Anomaly or artifact? Comments on Bem and Honorton. *Psychological Bulletin, 115*, 19–24.

Ihler, E. (2003). Patient-physician communication. *Journal of the American Medical Association, 289*, 92.

Ikonomidou, C., Bittigau, P., Ishimaru, M. J., Wozniak, D. F., Koch, C., Genz, K., Price, M. T., Stefovska, V., Hörster, F., Tenkova, T., Dikranian, K., & Olney, J. W. (2000, February 11). Ethanol-induced apoptotic neurodegeneration and fetal alcohol syndrome. *Science, 287*, 1056–1060.

Inglefinger, F. J. (1944). The late effects of total and subtotal gastrectomy. *New England Journal of Medicine, 231*, 321–377.

Isay, R. A. (1990). *Being homosexual: Gay men and their development*. New York: Avon.

Isbell, L. M., & Tyler, J. M. (2003). Teaching students about in-group favoritism and the minimal groups paradigm. *Teaching of Psychology, 30*, 127–130.

Ishikura, R., & Tashiro, N. (2002). Frustration and fulfillment of needs in dissociative and conversion disorders. *Psychiatry and Clinical Neurosciences, 56*, 381–390.

Iversen, L. L. (2000). *The science of marijuana*. Oxford, England: Oxford University Press.

Iverson, P., Kuhl, P. K., Reiko, A. Y., Diesch, E., Tohkura, Y., Ketterman, A., & Siebert, C. (2002). A perceptual interference account of acquisition difficulties for non-native phonemes. *Cognition, 87*, B47–B57.

Izard, C. E. (1990). Facial expressions and the regulation of emotions. *Journal of Personality and Social Psychology, 58*, 487–498.

Izard, C. E. (1994). Innate and universal facial expressions: Evidence from developmental and cross-cultural research. *Psychological Bulletin, 115*, 288–299.

Jackson, T. L. (Ed.). (1996). *Acquaintance rape: Assessment, treatment, and prevention*. Sarasota, FL: Professional Resource Press/Professional Resource Exchange.

Jacobson, P. D., Wasserman, J., & Anderson, J. R. (1997). Historical overview of tobacco legislation and regulation. *Journal of Social Issues, 53*, 75–95.

Jaffe, S., & Hyde, J. S. (2000). Gender differences in moral orientation: A meta-analysis. *Psychological Bulletin, 126*, 703–726.

James, J. E. (1997). *Understanding caffeine: A biobehavioral analysis*. Newbury Park, CA: Sage.

James, W. (1890). *The principles of psychology*. New York: Holt.

Jamison, K. R. (1993). *Touched with fire: Manic depressive illness and the artistic temperament*. New York: Free Press.

Jamison, K.R. (1995a). *An unquiet mind: A memoir of moods and madness*. New York: Knopf.

Jamison, K.R. (1995b, February). Manic-Depressive illness and creativity. *Scientific American*, pp. 62–67.

Janata, P., Tillman, B., & Bharucha, J. J. (2002). Listening to polyphonic music recruits domain-general attention and working memory circuits. *Cognitive, Affective & Behavioral Neuroscience, 2*, 121–140.

Janis, I. L. (1989). *Crucial decisions: Leadership in policy-making management*. New York: Free Press.

Jaret, P. (1992, November/December). Mind over malady. *Health*, pp. 87–94.

Jaroff, L. (1996, Fall). Keys to the kingdom. *Time*, pp. 24–29.

Jenike, M. A. (1998). Neurosurgical treatment of obsessive-compulsive disorder. *British Journal of Psychiatry, 173(Suppl 35)*, 79–90.

Jenkins, A. M., Albee, G. W., & Paster, V. S. (2003). In D. K. Freedheim (Ed.), *Handbook of psychology: History of psychology*, Vol. 1. New York: Wiley.

Jenkins, C. D., Zyzanski, S. J., & Rosenman, R. H. (1978). Coronary-prone behavior: One pattern or several? *Psychosomatic Medicine, 40*, 25–43.

Jenkins, L. S., & Gortner, S. R. (1998). Correlates of self-efficacy expectation and prediction of walking behavior in cardiac surgery elders. *Annals of Behavioral Medicine, 20*, 99–103.

Jenkins, S. R. (1994). Need for power and women's careers over 14 years: Structural power, job satisfaction, and motive change. *Journal of Personality and Social Psychology, 66*, 155–165.

Jensen, A. R. (2002). Galton's legacy to research on intelligence. *Journal of Biosocial Science, 34*, 145–172.

Jensen, A. R. (2003). Do age-group differences on mental tests imitate racial differences? *Intelligence, 31*, 107–121.

Jequier, E. (2002). Pathways to obesity. *International Journal of Obesity and Related Metabolic Disorders, 26*, S12–S17.

Jerome, L., DeLeon, P., James, L., & Gedney, J. (2000). The coming of age of telecommunications in psychological research practice. *American Psychologist, 55*, 128–133.

Jhally, S., Goldman, R., Cassidy, M., Katula, R., Seiter, E., Pollay, R. W., Lee, J. S., Carter-Whitney, D., Steinem, G., et al. (1995). Advertising. In G. Dines & J. M. Humez (Eds.), *Gender, race, and class in media: A text-reader*. Thousand Oaks, CA: Sage.

Johnson, D. M., Parrott, G. R., & Stratton, R. P. (1968). Production and judgment of solutions to five problems. *Journal of Educational Psychology Monograph Supplement, 59* (6, pt. 2).

Johnson, G. B. (2000). *The Living World*, p. 600. Boston: McGraw-Hill.

Johnson, J. G., Cohen, P., Smailes, E. M., Kasen, S., & Brook, J. S. (2002, March 29). Television viewing and aggressive behavior during adolescence and adulthood. *Science, 295*, 2468–2471.

Johnson, J. T., Cain, L. M., Falke, T. L., Hayman, J., & Perillo, E. (1985). The "Barnum Effect" revisited: Cognitive and motivational factors in the acceptance of personality descriptions. *Journal of Personality and Social Psychology, 49*, 1378–1391.

John-Steiner, V., & Mahn, H. (2003). Sociocultural contexts for teaching and learning. In W. M. Reynolds & G. E. Miller (Eds.), *Handbook of psychology: Educational psychology*, Vol. 7, pp. 125–151. New York: Wiley.

Johnston, L. (1996). Resisting change: Information-seeking and stereotype change. *European Journal of Social Psychology, 26*, 799–825.

Johnston, L. D., O'Malley, P. M., & Bachman. J. G. (2002, December 16). *Ecstasy use among American teens drops for the first time in recent years, and overall drug and alcohol use also decline in the year after 9/11*. Ann Arbor, MI: University of Michigan News and Information Services. www.monitoringthefuture.org; accessed December 26, 2002.

Johnston, L. D., O'Malley, P. M., & Bachman, J. G. (2003). *Monitoring the future: National results on adolescent drug use: Overview of key findings, 2002*. Bethesda MD: National Institute on Drug Abuse.

Joiner, T. E., & Wagner, K. D. (1995). Attribution style and depression in children and adolescents: A meta-analytic review. *Clinical Psychology Review, 15*, 777–798.

Joiner, T., & Coyne, J. C. (Eds.). (1999). *The interactional nature of depression: Advances in interpersonal approaches*. Washington, DC: American Psychological Association.

Jones, A., & Crandall, R. (Eds.). (1991). Handbook of self-actualization. *Journal of Social Behavior and Personality, 6*, 1–362.

Jones, J. C., & Barlow, D. H. (1990). Self-reported frequency of sexual urges, fantasies, and masturbatory fantasies in heterosexual males and females. *Archives of Sexual Behavior, 19*, 269–279.

Jones, J. E., & Corp, E. S. (2003). Effect of naltrexone on food intake and body weight in Syrian hamsters depends on metabolic status. *Physiology and Behavior, 78*, 67–72.

Jorgenson, L. M., & Wahl, K. M. (2000). Psychiatrists as expert witnesses in sexual harassment cases under Daubert and Kumho. *Psychiatric Annals, 30*, 390–396.

Joseph, R. (1996). *Neuropsychiatry, neuropsychology, and clinical neuroscience: Emotion, evolution, cognition, language, memory, brain damage, and abnormal behavior* (2nd ed.). Baltimore: Williams & Wilkins.

Joyce, J. (1934). *Ulysses*. New York: Random House.

Julesz, B. (1986). Stereoscopic vision. *Vision Research, 26*, 1601–1612.

Julien, R. M. (1995). *Primer of drug action* (7th ed.). New York: Freeman.

Julien, R. M (2001). *A primer of drug action* (9th ed.). New York: Freeman.

Jung, C. G. (1961). *Freud and psychoanalysis*. New York: Pantheon.

Jung, J. (2002). *Psychology of alcohol and other drugs: A research perspective*. Thousand Oaks, CA: Sage.

Juster, F. T., Ono, H., & Stafford, F. (2002). *Report on housework and division of labor*. Ann Arbor, MI: Institute for Social Research.

Kaasinen, V., & Rinne, J. O. (2002). Functional imaging studies of dopamine system and cognition in normal aging and Parkinson's disease. *Neuroscience & Biobehavioral Reviews, 26*, 785–793.

Kahn, R. S., Davidson, M., & Davis, K. L. (1996). Dopamine and schizophrenia revisited. In S. J. Watson (Ed.), *Biology of schizophrenia and affective disease*. Washington, DC: American Psychiatric Press.

Kahneman, D., Diener, E., & Schwarz, N. (1998). *Well-being: The foundations of hedonic psychology*. New York: Russell Sage Foundation.

Kakigi, R., Matsuda, Y., & Kuroda, Y. (1993). Effects of movement-related cortical activities on pain-related somatosensory evoked potentials following CO_2 laser stimulation in normal subjects. *Acta Neurologica Scandinavica, 88*, 376–380.

Kalb, C. (2001a, April 9). Playing with pain killers. *Newsweek*, pp. 45–48.

Kalb, C. (2001b, February 26). DARE checks into rehab. *Newsweek*, pp. 56.

Kamieniecki, G. W., & Lynd-Stevenson, R. M. (2002). Is it appropriate to use United States norms to assess the "intelligence" of Australian children? *Australian Journal of Psychology, 54*, 67–78.

Kanas, N., Salnitskiy, V., Grund, E. M., Gushin, V., Weiss, D. S., Kozerenko, O., Sled, A., & Marmar, C. R. (2002). Lessons learned from shuttle/Mir: Psychosocial countermeasures. *Aviation, Space, & Environmental Medicine, 73*, 607–611.

Kandell, E. R., Schwartz, J. H., & Jessell, T. M. (Eds.) (2000). *Principles of neural science* (4th ed.). New York: McGraw-Hill

Kane, M. J., & Engle, R. W. (2002). The role of prefrontal cortex in working-memory capacity, executive attention, and general fluid intelligence: An individual-differences perspective. *Psychonomic Bulletin and Review, 9*, 637–671.

Kaniasty, K., & Norris, F. H. (1995, June). Mobilization and deterioration of social support following natural disasters. *Current Directions in Psychological Science, 4*, 94–98.

Kanner, A. D., Coyne, J. C., Schaefer, C., & Lazarus, R. (1981). Comparison of two modes of stress measurement: Daily hassles and uplifts versus major life events. *Journal of Behavioral Medicine, 4*, 14.

Kaplan, H. S. (1974). *The new sex therapy*. New York: Brunner-Mazel.

Kaplan, J. R., & Manuck, S. B. (1989). *The effect of propranolol on behavioral interactions among adult male cynomolgus monkeys (Macaca fascicularis) housed in disrupted social groupings. Psychosomatic Medicine, 51*, 449–462.

Kaplan, R. M., & Saccuzzo, D. P. (1997). *Psychological testing: Principles, applications, and issues* (4th ed.). Pacific Grove, CA: Brooks/Cole.

Kapur, S., & Remington, G. (1996). Serotonin-dopamine interaction and its relevance to schizophrenia. *American Journal of Psychiatry, 153,* 466–476.

Karni, A., Tanne, D., Rubenstein, B. S., Askenasy, J. J. M., & Sagi, D. (1994, July 29). Dependence on REM sleep of overnight improvement of a perceptual skill. *Science, 265,* 679–682.

Karni, A., Tanne, D., Rubenstein, B. S., Askenazy, J. J. M., & Sagi, D. (1992, October). No dreams—no memory: The effect of REM sleep deprivation on learning a new perceptual skill. *Society for Neuroscience Abstracts, 18,* 387.

Kassel, J. D., Stroud, L. R., & Paronis, C. A. (2003). Smoking, stress, and negative affect: Correlation, causation, and context across stages of smoking. *Psychological Bulletin, 129,* 270–304.

Katigbak, M. S., Church, A. T., Guanzon-Lapena, M. A., Carlota, A. J., & del Pilar, G. H. (2002). Are indigenous personality dimensions culture specific? Philippine inventories and the five-factor model. *Journal of Personality and Social Psychology, 82,* 89–101.

Katsiyannis, A., Zhang, D., & Archwamety, T. (2002). Place and exit patterns for students with mental retardation: An analysis of national trends. *Education and Training in Mental Retardation and Developmental Disabilities, 37,* 134–145.

Katz, A. N. (1989). Autobiographical memory as a reconstructive process: An extension of Ross's hypothesis. *Canadian Journal of Psychology, 43,* 512–517.

Katz, M. (2001). The implications of revising Freud's empiricism for drive theory. *Psychoanalysis and Contemporary Thought, 24,* 253–272.

Katz, P. A. (Ed.). (1976). *Towards the elimination of racism.* New York: Pergamon.

Kaufman, A. S., & Lichtenberger, E. O. (1999). *Essentials of WISC-III and WPPSI-R assessment.* New York: Wiley.

Kaufman, L., & Kaufman, J. H. (2000). From the cover: Explaining the moon illusion. *Proceedings of the National Academy of Science, 97,* 500–505.

Kausler, D. H. (1994). *Learning and memory in normal aging.* San Diego, CA: Academic Press.

Kavale, K. A. (2002). Mainstreaming to full inclusion: From orthogenesis to pathogenesis of an idea. *International Journal of Disability, Development & Education. Special Issue: The slow learning child: 25 years on, 49,* 201–214.

Kawasaki, C., Nugent, J. K., Miyashita, H., Miyahara, H., et al. (1994). The cultural organization of infants' sleep. Special Issue: Environments of birth and infancy. *Children's Environment, 11,* 135–141.

Kazdin, A. E. (1994). *Behavior modification in applied settings* (5th ed.). Pacific Grove, CA: Brooks/Cole.

Keating, D. P., & Clark, L. V. (1980). Development of physical and social reasoning in adolescence. *Developmental Psychology, 16,* 23–30.

Keefe, F. J., & France, C. R. (1999). Pain: Biopsychosocial mechanisms and management. *Current Directions in Psychological Science, 8,* 137–141.

Keehn, J. D. (1996). *Master builders of modern psychology: From Freud to Skinner.* New York: New York University Press.

Keillor, J. M., Barrett, A. M., Crucian, G. P., Kortenkamp, S., & Heilman, K. M. (2002). Emotional experience and perception in the absence of facial feedback. *Journal of the International Neuropsychological Society, 8,* 130–135.

Kelley, H. (1950). The warm-cold variable in first impressions of persons. *Journal of Personality and Social Psychology, 18,* 431–439.

Kelly, E. S. (1997, January 22). The latest in take-at-home tests: I.Q. *New York Times,* p. B7.

Kelly, F. D. (1997). *The assessment of object relations phenomena in adolescents: TAT and Rorschach measures.* Mahwah, NJ: Erlbaum.

Kempermann, G., & Gage, F. H. (1999, May). New nerve cells for the adult brain. *Scientific American,* pp. 48–53.

Kenshalo, D. R. (1968). *The Skin senses.* Springfield, IL: Charles C Thomas.

Kenway, L., & Wilson, M. A. (2001). Temporally structured replay of awake hippocampal ensemble activity during rapid eye movement sleep. *Neuron, 29,* 145–156.

Kess, J. F., and T. Miyamoto (1994). *Japanese Psycholinguistics.* Amsterdam: John Benjamins.

Kessler, R. C., McGonagle, K. A., Zhao, S., Nelson, C. B., Hughes, M., Eshleman, S., Wittchen, H., & Kendler, K. S. (1994). Lifetime and 12-month prevalence of DSM-III-R psychiatric disorders in the United States. *Archives of General Psychiatry, 51,* 8–19.

Ketterhargen, D., VandeVusse, L., & Berner, M. A. (2002). Self-hypnosis: Alternative anesthesia for childbirth. *American Journal of Maternal/Child Nursing, 27,* 335–341.

Key, W. B. (2003). Subliminal sexuality: The fountainhead for America's obsession. In T. Reichert & J. Lambaiase (Eds.), *Sex in advertising: Perspectives on the erotic appeal. LEA's communication series,* pp. 195–212. Mahway, NJ: Erlbaum.

Kiecolt, J. K. (2003). Satisfaction with work and family life: No evidence of a cultural reversal. *Journal of Marriage and Family, 65,* 23–35.

Kienker, P. K., Sejnowski, T. J., Hinton, G. E., & Schumacher, L. E. (1986). Separating figure from ground with a parallel network. *Perception, 15,* 197–216.

Kiesler, C. A., & Simpkins, C.G. (1993). *The unnoticed majority in psychiatric inpatient care.* New York: Plenum.

Kiesler, D. J. (1999). *Beyond the disease model of mental disorders.* Westport, CT: Praeger.

Kihlstrom, J. F., Schacter, D. L., Cork, R. C., Hurt, C. A., & Behr, S. E. (1990). Implicit and explicit memory following surgical anesthesia. *Psychological Science, 1,* 303–306.

Kilborn, P. T. (1991, May 15). "Race norming" tests become a fiery issue. *The New York Times,* p. B1.

Kilpatrick, D. G., Edmunds, C. S., & Seymour, A. K. (1992, November 13). *Rape in America: A report to the nation.* Arlington, VA: National Victims Center and Medical University of South Carolina.

Kim, H. S. (2002). We talk, therefore we think? A cultural analysis of the effect of talking on thinking. *Journal of Personality and Social Psychology, 83,* 828–842.

Kim, K. H., Relkin, N. R., Lee, K. M., & Hirsch, J. (1997, July 10). Distinct cortical areas associated with native and second languages. *Nature, 388,* 171–174.

Kim, S. Y. H., & Holloway, R. G., (2003). Burdens and benefits of placebos in antidepressant clinical trials: A decision and cost-effectiveness analysis. *American Journal of Psychiatry, 160,* 1272–1276.

Kimble, G. A. (1989). Psychology from the standpoint of a generalist. *American Psychologist, 44,* 491–499.

Kimura, D. (1992, September). Sex differences in the brain. *Scientific American,* pp. 119–125.

Kimura, D. (1999). *Sex and cognition.* Cambridge, MA: MIT Press.

King, K. C., Hyde, J. S., Showers, C. J., & Buswell, B. N. (1999). Gender differences in self-esteem: A meta-analysis. *Psychological Bulletin, 125,* 470–500.

Kinsey, A. C., Pomeroy, W. B., & Martin, C. E. (1948). *Sexual behavior in the human male.* Philadelphia: Saunders.

Kinsey, A. C., Pomeroy, W. B., Martin, C. E., & Gebhard, P. H. (1953). *Sexual behavior in the human female.* Philadelphia: Saunders.

Kirby, D. (1977). The methods and methodological problems of sex research. In J. S. DeLora & C. A. B. Warren (Eds.), *Understanding sexual interaction.* Boston: Houghton Mifflin.

Kirk, S. A. (1992). *The selling of DSM: The rhetoric of science in psychiatry.* Hawthorne, NY: Aldine de Gruyter.

Kirsch, I. (Ed.). (1999). *How expectancies shape experience.* Washington, DC: American Psychological Association.

Kirsch, I., & Braffman, W. (2001). Imaginative suggestibility and hypnotizability. *Current Directions in Psychological Science, 10,* 57–61.

Kirsch, I., & Lynn, S. J. (1995). The altered state of hypnosis: Changes in the theoretical landscape. *American Psychologist, 50,* 846–858.

Kirsch, I., & Lynn, S. J. (1998). Social-cognitive alternatives to dissociation theories of hypnotic involuntariness. *Review of General Psychology, 2,* 66–80.

Kirshner, H. S. (1995). Alexias. In H. S. Kirshner (Ed.), *Handbook of neurological speech and language disorders: Neurological disease and therapy,* Vol. 33. New York: Marcel Dekker.

Kish, S. J. (2002). Effects of dose, sex, and long-term abstention from use on toxic effects of MDMA (Ecstasy) on brain serotonin neurons: Comment. *Lancet, 359,* 1616.

Kite, M. E., Russo, N. F., Brehm, S. S., Fouad, N. A., Hall, C. C. I., Hyde, J. S., & Keita, G. P. (2001). Women psychologists in academe: Mixed progress, unwarranted complacency. *American Psychologist, 56*, 1080–1098.

Kittell, L. A., & Mansfield, P. K. (2000). What perimenopausal women think about using hormones during menopause. *Women & Health, 30*, 77–91.

Kitterle, F. L. (Ed.). (1991). *Cerebral laterality: Theory and research.* Hillsdale, NJ: Erlbaum.

Klein, M. (1998, February). Family chats. *American Demographics*, p. 37.

Kleinman, A. (1996). How is culture important for DSM-IV? In J. E Mezzich, A. Kleinman, H. Fabrega, Jr., & D. L. Parron (Eds.), *Culture and psychiatric diagnosis: A DSM-IV perspective.* Washington, DC: American Psychiatric Press.

Kleinman, A., & Cohen, A. (1997, March). Psychiatry's global challenge. *Scientific American*, pp. 86–89.

Klinke, R., Kral, A., Heid, S., Tillein, J., & Hartmann, R. (1999, September 10). Recruitment of the auditory cortex in congenitally deaf cats by long-term cochlear electrostimulation. *Science, 285*, 1729–1733.

Klinkenborg, V. (1997, January 5). Awakening to sleep. *The New York Times*, pp. 26–31, 41, 51, 55.

Kluft, R. P. (1996). Dissociative identity disorder. In L. K. Michelson & W. J. Ray (Eds.), *Handbook of dissociation: Theoretical, empirical, and clinical perspectives.* New York: Plenum Press.

Kluger, J. (2001, April 2). Fear not! *Time*, pp. 51–62.

Kmiec, E. B. (1999). Gene therapy. *American Scientist, 87*, 240–247.

Knight, G. P., Jonson, L. G., Carlo, G., & Eisenberg, N. (1994). A multiplicative model of the dispositional antecedents of a prosocial behavior: Predicting more of the people more of the time. *Journal of Personality and Social Psychology, 66*, 178–183.

Kobasa, S. C. O., Maddi, S. R., Puccetti, M. C., & Zola, M. A. (1994). Effectiveness of hardiness, exercise and social support as resources against illness. In A. Steptoe & J. Wardle (Eds.), *Psychosocial processes and health: A reader.* Cambridge, England: Cambridge University Press.

Koch, J. (2003). Gender issues in the classroom. In W. M. Reynolds & G. E. Miller (Eds.), *Handbook of psychology: Educational psychology*, Vol. 7, pp. 259–281. New York: Wiley.

Kohlberg, L. (1984). *The psychology of moral development: Essays on moral development*, Vol. 2. San Francisco: Harper & Row.

Kohlberg, L., & Ryncarz, R. A. (1990). Beyond justice reasoning: Moral development and consideration of a seventh stage. In C. N. Alexander & E. J. Langer (Eds.), *Higher stages of human development: Perspectives on adult growth.* New York: Oxford University Press.

Köhler, W. (1927). *The mentality of apes.* London: Routledge & Kegan Paul.

Kohout, J. (February 2001). Who's earning those psychology degrees? *Monitor on Psychology*, p. 42.

Kolata, G. (1998). *Clone: The road to Dolly and the path ahead.* New York: William Morrow.

Kolata, G. (2002, December 2). With no answers on risks, steroid users still say "yes." *The New York Times*, p. 1A.

Kolata, G. (2002, May 21). Runner's high? Endorphins? Fiction, some scientists say. *The New York Times*, pp. S1, S6.

Kolb, B., Gibb, R., & Robinson, T. E. (2003). Brain plasticity and behavior. *Current Directions in Psychological Science, 12*, 1–5.

Koocher, G. P. & Keith-Spiegel, P. (1998). *Ethics in psychology: Professional standards and cases* (2nd ed.). New York: Oxford University Press.

Kopelman, M. D., & Fleminger, S. (2002). Experience and perspectives on the classification of organic mental disorders. *Psychopathology, 35*, 76–81.

Koplewicz, H. (2002). *More than moody: Recognizing and treating adolescent depression.* New York: Putnam.

Kosambi, D. D. (1967). Living prehistory in India. *Scientific American*, p. 105.

Koss, M. P. (1993). Rape: Scope, impact, interventions, and public policy responses. *American Psychologist, 48*, 1062–1069.

Kosslyn, S. M., & Shin, L. M. (1994). Visual mental images in the brain: Current issues. In M. J. Farah & G. Ratcliff (Eds.), *The neuropsychology of high-level vision: Collected tutorial essays. Carnegie Mellon symposia on cognition.* Hillsdale, NJ: Erlbaum.

Kosslyn, S. M., Caciopppo, J. T., Davidson, R. J., Hugdahl, K., Lovallo, W. R., Spiegel, D., & Rose, R. (2002). Bridging psychology and biology. *American Psychologist, 57*, 341–351.

Kotre, J., & Hall, E. (1990). *Seasons of life.* Boston: Little, Brown.

Koval, J. J., Pederson, L. L., Mills, C. A., McGrady, G. A., & Carvajal, S. C. (2000). Models of the relationship of stress, depression, and other psychosocial factors to smoking behavior: A comparison of a cohort of students in Grades 6 and 8. *Preventive Medicine: an International Devoted to Practice & Theory, 30*, 463–477.

Koveces, Z. (1987). *The container metaphor of emotion.* Paper presented at the University of Massachusetts, Amherst.

Kowert, P. A. (2002). *Groupthink or deadlock: When do leaders learn from their advisors? SUNY Series on the Presidency.* Albany: State University of New York Press.

Kramer, P. (1993). *Listening to Prozac.* New York: Viking.

Kraus, S. J. (1995, January). Attitudes and the prediction of behavior: A meta-analysis of the empirical literature. *Personality and Social Psychology Bulletin, 21*, 58–75.

Krause, N., & Shaw, B. A. (2001). Role-specific feelings of control and mortality. *Psychology and Aging, 15*, 617–626.

Krause, S. S. (2003). *Aircraft safety: Accident investigations, analyses, and applications* (2nd ed.). New York: McGraw-Hill.

Kravitz, E. A. (1988). Hormonal control of behavior: Amines and the biasing of behavioral output in lobsters. *Science, 241*, 1775–1782.

Kremer, J. M. D., & Scully, D. M. (1994). *Psychology in sport.* London, England: Taylor & Francis.

Kring, J. P. (2001). Multicultural factors for international spaceflight. *Journal of Human Performance in Extreme Environments, 5*, 11–32.

Kriz, J. (1995). Naturwissenschaftliche Konzepte in der gegenwartigen Diskussion zum Problem der Ordnung (The contribution of natural science concepts to the current discussion of order). *Gestalt Theory, 17*, 153–163.

Krohne, H. W. (1996). Individual differences in coping. In M. Zeidner & N. S. Endler (Eds.), *Handbook of coping: Theory, research, applications.* New York: Wiley.

Krueger, A. B. (2002, December 12). Sticks and stones can break bones, but the wrong name can make a job hard to find. *The New York Times*, p. C2.

Krueger, R. G., Hicks, B. M., & McGue, M. (2001). Altruism and antisocial behavior: Independent tendencies, unique personality correlates, distinct etiologies. *Psychological Science, 12*, 397–402.

Kruglanski, A. W., Freund, T., & Bar Tal, D. (1996). Motivational effects in the mere-exposure paradigm. *European Journal of Social Psychology, 26*, 479–499.

Krull, D. S., & Anderson, C. A. (1997). The process of explanation. *Current Directions in Psychological Science, 6*, 1–5.

Ku, L., St. Louis, M., Farshy, C., Aral, S., Turner, C. F., Lindberg, L. D., & Sonenstein, F. (2002). Risk behaviors, medical care, and chlamydial infection among young men in the United States. *American Journal of Public Health, 92*, 1140–1143.

Kübler-Ross, E. (1969). *On death and dying.* New York: Macmillan.

Kubovy, M., Epstein, W., & Gepshtein, S. (2003). Foundations of visual perception. In A. F. Healy, & R. W. Proctor (Eds.). *Handbook of psychology: Experimental psychology*, Vol. 4, New York: Wiley.

Kubovy, M., & Wagemans, J. (1995). Grouping by proximity and multistability in dot lattices: A quantitative gestalt theory. *Psychological Science, 6*, 225–233.

Kulynych, J. J., Vladar, K., Jones, D. W., & Weinberger, D. R. (1994). Gender differences in the normal lateralization of the supratemporal cortex: MRI surface-rendering morphometry of Heschl's gyrus and the planum temporale. *Cerebral Cortex, 4*, 107–118.

Kunda, Z. (2000). The case for motivated reasoning. In D. T. Higgins & A. W. Kruglanski (Eds.), *Motivational science: Social and personality perspectives. Key readings in social psychology*, pp. 313–335. Philadelphia: Psychology Press.

Kuther, T. L. (2000). *The psychology major's handbook.* Belmont, CA: Wadsworth.

Kuther, T. L. (2003). *Your career in psychology: Psychology and the law*. New York: Wadsworth.

Kwan, V. S. Y., Bond, M. H., & Singelis, T. M. (1997). Pancultural explanations for life satisfaction: Adding relationship harmony to self-esteem. *Journal of Personality & Social Psychology, 73*, 1038–1051.

Kwon, P., & Laurenceau, J-P. (2002). A longitudinal study of the hopelessness theory of depression: Testing the diathesis-stress model within a differential reactivity and exposure framework. *Journal of Clinical Psychology: Special issue: Reprioritizing the role of science in a realistic version of the scientist-practitioner model, 50*, 1305–1321.

Lacey, M. (2002, January 6). In Kenyan family, ritual for girls still divides. *The New York Times*, p. 6.

LaFromboise, T., Coleman, H. L. K., & Gerton, J. (1995). Psychological impact of biculturalism: Evidence and theory. In N. R. Goldberger & J. B. Veroff (Eds.), *The culture and psychology reader*. New York: New York University Press.

Laird, J. D., & Bressler, C. (1990). William James and the mechanisms of emotional experience. *Personality and Social Psychology Bulletin, 16*, 636–651.

Lal, S. (2002). Giving children security: Mamie Phipps Clark and the racialization of child psychology. *American Psychologist, 57*, 20–28.

Lamal, P. A. (1979). College students' common beliefs about psychology. *Teaching of Psychology, 6*, 155–158.

Lamb, M. E. & Garretson, M. E. (2003), The effects of interviewer gender and child gender on the informativeness of alleged child sexual abuse victims in forensic interviews. *Law and Human Behavior, 27*, 157–171.

Lamb, M. E. (1996). Effects of nonparental child care on child development: An update. *Canadian Journal of Psychiatry, 41*, 330–342.

Lambert, M. J., Shapiro, D. A., & Bergin, A. E. (1986). The effectiveness of psychotherapy. In S. L. Garfield & A. E. Bergin (Eds.), *Handbook of psychotherapy and behavior change* (3rd ed.). New York: Wiley.

Lana, R. E. (2002). The cognitive approach to language and thought. *Journal of Mind and Behavior. Special issue: Choice and chance in the formation of society: Behavior and cognition in social theory, 23*, 51–57.

Landry, D. W. (1997, February). Immunotherapy for cocaine addiction. *Scientific American*, pp. 41–45.

Langer, E., & Janis, I. (1979). *The psychology of control*. Beverly Hills, CA: Sage.

Langlois, J. H., Kalakanis, L., & Rubenstein, A. J. (2000). Maxims or myths of beauty? A meta-analytic and theoretical review. *Psychological Bulletin, 126*, 390–423.

Langreth, R. (2000, May 1). Every little bit helps: How even moderate exercise can have a big impact on your health. *The Wall Street Journal*, p. R5.

Lanza, R. P., Cibelli, J. B., Faber, D., Sweeney, R. W., Henderson, B., Nevala, W., West, M. D., & Wettstein, P. J. (2001, November 30). Cloned cattle can be healthy and normal. *Science, 294*, 1893–1894.

Lanza, S. T., & Collins, L. M. (2002). Pubertal timing and the onset of substance use in females during early adolescence. *Prevention Science, 3*, 69–82.

Laqueur, T. W. (2003). *Solitary sex: A cultural history of masturbation*. New York: Zone.

Larose, H., & Standing, L. (1998). Does the halo effect occur in the elderly? *Social Behavior & Personality, 26*, 147–150.

Larson, R. K. (1990). Semantics. In D. N. Osherson & H. Lasnik (Eds.), *Language*. Cambridge, MA: MIT Press.

Larson, R. W., Richards, M. H., & Perry-Jenkins, M. (1994). Divergent worlds: The daily emotional experience of mothers and fathers in the domestic and public spheres. *Journal of Personality and Social Psychology, 67*, 1034–1046.

Lask, B., & Bryant-Waugh, R. (Eds.). (1999). *Anorexia nervosa and related eating disorders in childhood and adolescence*. New York: Brunner/Mazel.

Lasnik, H. (1990). Syntax. In D. N. Osherson & H. Lasnik (Eds.), *Language*. Cambridge, MA: MIT Press.

Latané, B., & Darley, J. M. (1970). *The unresponsive bystander: Why doesn't he help?* New York: Appleton-Century-Crofts.

Latané, B., & Nida, S. (1981). Ten years of research on group size and helping. *Psychological Bulletin, 89*, 308–324.

Laumann, E. O., Paik, A., & Rosen, R. C. (1999, February 10). Sexual dysfunction in the United States: Prevalence and predictors. *Journal of the American Medical Association, 281*, 537–544.

Lazarus, A. A. (1997). *Brief but comprehensive psychotherapy: The multimodal way*. New York: Springer.

Lazarus, R. S. (1991a). Cognition and motivation in emotion. *American Psychologist, 46*, 352–367.

Lazarus, R. S. (1991b). *Emotion and adaptation*. New York: Oxford University Press.

Lazarus, R. S. (1994). Appraisal: The long and short of it. In P. Ekman & R. J. Davidson (Eds.), *The nature of emotion: fundamental questions*. New York: Oxford University Press.

Lazarus, R. S. (1995). Emotions express a social relationship, but it is an individual mind that creates them. *Psychological Inquiry, 6*, 253–265.

Lazarus, R. S. (2000). Toward better research on stress and coping. *American Psychologist, 55*, 665–673.

Leavitt, F. (2002). The reality of repressed memories revisited and principles of science. *Journal of Trauma and Dissociation, 3*, 19–35.

Leblanc, D. C. (2004). *Statistics for science students: Concepts and applications for the sciences*. Boston: Jones and Bartlett.

Lee, F., Hallahan, M., & Herzog, T. (1996). Explaining real-life events: How culture and domain shape attributions. *Personality and Social Psychology Bulletin, 22*, 732–741.

Lee, H-J., & Kwon, S-M. (2003). Two different types of obsession: Autogenous obsessions and reactive obsessions. *Behaviour Research & Therapy, 41*, 11–29.

Lee, T-W., Wachtler, T., & Sejnowski, T. J. (2002). Color opponency is an efficient representation of spectral properties in natural scenes. *Vision Research, 42*, 2095–2103.

Lee-Chai, A. Y., Bargh, J. A. (Eds.). (2001). *The use and abuse of power: Multiple perspectives on the causes of corruption*. Philadelphia, PA: Psychology Press.

Lehar, S. (2003). *The world in your head: A Gestalt view of the mechanism of conscious experience*. Mahwah, NJ: Erlbaum.

Lehman, D. R., & Taylor, S. E. (1988). Date with an earthquake: Coping with a probable, unpredictable disaster. *Personality and Social Psychology Bulletin, 13*, 546–555.

Lehmann, E. L., & Romano, J. P. (2004). *Testing statistical hypotheses*. New York: Springer-Verlag.

Lehrer, P. M. (1996). Recent research findings on stress management techniques. In Editorial Board of Hatherleigh Press, *The Hatherleigh guide to issues in modern therapy: The Hatherleigh guides series*, Vol. 4. New York: Hatherleigh Press.

Leibel, R. L., Rosenbaum, M., Hirsch, J. (1995, March 9). Changes in energy expenditure resulting from altered body. *New England Journal of Medicine, 332*, 621–628.

Leibovic, K. N. (Ed.). (1990). *Science of vision*. New York: Springer-Verlag.

Leiter, S., & Leiter, W. M. (2003). *Affirmative action in antidiscrimination law and policy: An overview and synthesis. SUNY series in American constitutionalism*. Albany: State University of New York Press.

Leland, J. (2000, May 29). The science of women and sex. *Newsweek*, pp. 48–54.

Lemonick, M. D. (2000, December 11). Downey's downfall. *Time*, p. 97.

Lengua, L. J., & Long, A. C. (2002). The role of emotionality and self-regulation in the appraisal-coping process: Tests of direct and moderating effects. *Journal of Applied Developmental Psychology, 23*, 471–493.

Lenzenweger, M. F., & Dworkin, R. H. (Eds.). (1998). *The origins and development of schizophrenia: Advances in Experimental Psychopathology*. Washington, DC: American Psychological Association.

Leonard, B. E. (2000). Stress, depression and the immune system. *Stress Medicine, 16*, 133–137.

Leong, F. L, & Blustein, D. L. (2000). Toward a global vision of counseling psychology. *Counseling Psychologist, 28*, 5–9.

Lepore, S. J., Ragan, J. D., & Jones, S. (2000). Talking facilities cognitive-emotional processes of adaptation to an acute stressor. *Journal of Personality and Social Psychology, 78*, 499–508.

Lerner, R. M., Fisher, C. B., & Weinberg, R. A. (2000). Toward a science for and of the people: Promoting civil society through the application of developmental science. *Child Development, 71,* 11–20.

Lesch, K.-P., Bengel, D., Heils, A., Sabol, S. Z., Greenberg, B. D., Petri, S., Benjamin, J., Muller, C. R., Hamer, D. H., & Murphy, D. L. (1996, November 29). Association of anxiety-related traits with a polymorphism in the serotonin transporter gene regulatory region. *Science, 274,* 1527–1531.

Leslie, C. (1991, February 11). Classrooms of Babel. *Newsweek,* pp. 56–57.

Lester, D. (1990). *Understanding and preventing suicide: New perspectives.* Springfield, IL: Thomas.

Leuchter, A. F., Cook, I. A., Witte, E. Z., Morgan, M., & Abrams, M. (2002). Changes in brain function of depressed subjects during treatment with placebo. *American Journal of Psychiatry, 159,* 122–129.

Leung, F. K. S. (2002). Behind the high achievement of East Asian students. *Education Research and Evaluation, 8: Special Issue: Achievements in mathematics and science in an international context, 87–108.*

LeVay, S. (1993). *The sexual brain.* Cambridge, MA: MIT Press.

LeVay, S. (2000, March). Brain invaders. *Scientific American, 282,* 27.

Levenson, R. W. (1994). The search for autonomic specificity. In P. Ekman & R. J. Davidson (Eds.), *The nature of emotion: Fundamental questons.* New York: Oxford University Press.

Leventhal, H., & Cleary, P. D. (1980). The smoking problem: A review of the research and theory in behavioral risk modification. *Psychological Bulletin, 88,* 370–405.

Levine, J. M. (1989). Reaction to opinion deviance in small groups. In P. B. Paulus (Ed.), *Psychology of group influence* (2nd ed.). Hillsdale, NJ: Erlbaum.

Levine, S. C., Huttenlocher, J., Taylor, A., & Langrock, A. (1999). Early sex differences in spatial skill. *Developmental Psychology, 35,* 940–949.

Levinson, D. J. (1990). A theory of life structure development in adulthood. In C. N. Alexander & E. J. Langer (Eds.), *Higher stages of human development: Perspectives on adult growth.* New York: Oxford University Press.

Levy, B. (1996). Improving memory in old age through implicit self-stereotyping. *Journal of Personality and Social Psychology, 71,* 1092–1107.

Levy, B. R., Slade, M. D., Kunkel, S. R., & Kasl, S. V. (2002). Longevity increased by positive self-perceptions of aging. *Journal of Personality & Social Psychology, 83,* 261–270.

Levy, B., & Langer, E. (1994). Aging free from negative stereotypes: Successful memory in China and among the American deaf. *Journal of Personality and Social Psychology, 66,* 989–997.

Levy, D. A. (1997). *Tools of crtical thinking: Metathoughts for psychology.* Boston: Allyn & Bacon.

Levy, S. M., Lee, J., Bagley, C., & Lippman, M. (1988). Survival hazards analysis in first recurrent breast cancer patients: Seven-year follow-up. *Psychosomatic Medicine, 50,* 520–528.

Lewinsohn, P. M., & Essau, C. A. (2002). Depression in adolescents. In I. H. Gotlib & C. L. Hammen (Eds.), *Handbook of depression,* 541–559. New York: Guilford Press.

Lewinsohn, P. M., Petit, J. W., Joiner, T. E., Jr., & Seeley, J. R. (2003). The symptomatic expression of major depressive disorder in adolescents and young adults. *Journal of Abnormal Psychology, 112,* 244–252.

Lewis, M., Feiring, C., & Rosenthal, S. (2000). Attachment over time. *Child Development, 71,* 707–720.

Lewis, M., & Haviland-Jones, J. M. (2000). *Handbook of emotions* (2nd ed.). New York: Guilford Press.

Li, M. D., Cheng, R., Ma, J. Z., & Swan, G. E. (2003). A meta-analysis of estimated genetic and environmental effects on smoking behavior in male and female adult twins. *Addiction, 98,* 23–31.

Liben, L. S., & Bigler, R. S. (2002). The development course of gender differentiations: Conceptualizing, measuring, and evaluation constructs and pathways. *Monographs of the Society for Research in Child Development, 67,* 148–167.

Lilienfeld, S. O., & Lynn, S. J. (2003). Dissociative identity disorder: Multiple personalities, multiple controversies. In S. O. Lilienfeld & S. J. Lynn (Eds.), *Science and pseudoscience in clinical psychology,* pp. 109–142. New York: Guilford Press.

Lilienfeld, S. O., Lynn, S. J., & Lohr, J. M. (Eds.). (2003). *Science and pseudoscience in clinical psychology.* New York: Guilford Press.

Lindsay, P. H., & Norman, D. A. (1977). *Human information processing* (2nd ed.). New York: Academic Press.

Linehan, M. M., Cochran, B. N., & Hehrer, C. A. (2001). Dialectical behavior therapy for borderline personality disorder. In D. H. Barlow (Ed.), *Clinical handbook of psychological disorders: A step-by-step treatment manual* (3rd ed.), pp. 470–522. New York: Guilford Press.

Linscheid, T. R., & Reichenbach, H. (2002). Multiple factors in the long-term effectiveness of contingent electric shock treatment for self-injurious behavior: A case example. *Research in Developmental Disabilities, 23,* 161–177.

Linscheid, T. R., Iwata, B. A., Ricketts, R. W., Williams, D. E., & Griffin, J. C. (1990). Clinical evaluation of the self-injurious behavior inhibiting system (SIBIS). *Journal of Applied Behavior Analysis, 23,* 53–78.

Linszen, D. H., Dingemans, P. M., Nugter, M. A., Van der Does, A. J. W., et al. (1997). Patient attributes and expressed emotion as risk factors for psychotic relapse. *Schizophrenia Bulletin, 23,* 119–130.

Lips, H. M. (2003). *A new psychology of women: Gender, culture, and ethnicity.* New York: McGraw-Hill.

Lipsey, M. W., & Wilson, D. B. (1993). The efficacy of psychological, educational, and behavioral treatment: Confirmation from meta-analysis. *American Psychologist, 48,* 1181–1209.

Lloyd, J. W., Kameenui, E. J., & Chard, D. (Eds.). (1997). *Issues in educating students with disabilities.* Mahwah, NJ: Erlbaum.

Loehlin, J. C. (2002). The IQ paradox: Resolved? Still an open question. *Psychological Review, 109,* 754–758.

Loewenstein, G. (1994). The psychology of curiosity: A review and reinterpretation. *Psychological Bulletin, 116,* 75–98.

Lofholm, N. (2003, May 6). Climber's kin share relief: Ralston saw 4 options, they say; death wasn't one of them. *Denver Post,* p. A1.

Loftus, E. (1998, November). The memory police. *APA Observer, 3,* 14.

Loftus, E. F. (1993). Psychologists in the eyewitness world. *American Psychologist, 48,* 550–552.

Loftus, E. F. (1997). Memory for a past that never was. *Current Direcctions in Psychological Science, 6,* 60–65.

Loftus, E. F. (2003). The dangers of memory. In R. J. Sternberg (Ed.), *Psychologists defying the crowd: Stories of those who battled the establishment and won,* pp. 105–117. Washington, DC: American Psychological Association.

Loftus, E. F., & Palmer, J. C. (1974). Reconstruction of automobile destruction: An example of the interface between language and memory. *Journal of Verbal Learning and Verbal Behavior, 13,* 585–589.

Loftus, E. F., Loftus, G. R., & Messo, J. (1987). Some facts about "weapon focus." *Law and Human Behavior, 11,* 55–62.

Long, A. (1987, December). What is this thing called sleep? *National Geographic, 172,* 786–821.

Long, G. M., & Beaton, R. J. (1982). The case for peripheral persistence: Effects of target and background luminance on a partial-report task. *Journal of Experimental Psychology: Human Perception and Performance, 8,* 383–391.

López, S. R., & Guarnaccia, P. J. J. (2000). Cultural psychopathology: Uncovering the social world of mental illness. *Annual Review of Psychology, 51,* 571–598.

Lorenz, K. (1966). *On aggression.* New York: Harcourt Brace Jovanovich.

Lorenz, K. (1974). *Civilized man's eight deadly sins.* New York: Harcourt Brace Jovanovich.

Lovaas, O. I., & Koegel, R. (1973). Behavior therapy with autistic children. In C. Thoreson (Ed.), *Behavior modification and education.* Chicago: University of Chicago Press.

Lowe, M. R. (1993). The effects of dieting on eating behavior: A three-factor model. *Psychological Bulletin, 114,* 100–121.

Lowery, D., Fillingim, R. B., & Wright, R. A. (2003). Sex differences and incentive effects on perceptual and cardiovascular responses to cold pressor pain. *Psychosomatic Medicine, 65,* 284–291.

Luborsky, L. (1988). *Who will benefit from psychotherapy?* New York: Basic Books.

Luce, R. D. (1993). *Sound and hearing.* Hillsdale, NJ: Erlbaum.

Luchins, A. S. (1946). Classroom experiments on mental set. *American Journal of Psychology, 59,* 295–298.

Ludwig, A. M. (1969). Altered states of consciousness. In C. T. Tart (Ed.), *Altered states of consciousness.* New York: Wiley.

Ludwig, A. M. (1996, March). Mental disturbances and creative achievement. *The Harvard Mental Health Letter,* pp. 4–6.

Luria, A. R. (1968). *The mind of a mnemonist.* Cambridge, MA: Basic Books.

Lurie, K. (2002). *Cracking the 2003 GRE.* Burlington, MA: Princeton Review.

Luthas, S. S., Cicchetti, D., & Becker, B. (2000). The construct of resilience: A critical evaluation and guidelines for future work. *Child Development, 71,* 543–562.

Ly, D. H., Lockhart, D. J., Lerner, R. A., & Schultz, P. G. (2000, March 31). Mitotic misregulation and human aging. *Science, 287,* 2486–2492.

Lykken, D., & Tellegen, A. (1996). Happiness is a stochastic phenomenon. *Psychological Science, 7,* 181–185.

Lykken, D. T. (1995). *The antisocial personalities.* Mahwah, NJ: Erlbaum.

Lynam, D. R., Milich, R., Zimmerman, R., Novak, S. P., Logan, T. K., Martin, C. Leukefeld, M. C., & Clayton, R. (1999). Project DARE: No effects at 10-year follow-up. *Journal of Consulting and Clinical Psychology, 67,* 590–593.

Lynn, S. J., & Rhue, J. W. (1988). Fantasy-proneness: Hypnosis, developmental antecedents, and psychopathology. *American Psychologist, 43,* 35–44.

Lynn, S. J., Lock, T. G., Myers, B., & Payne, D. G. (1997). Recalling the unrecallable: Should hypnosis be used to recover memories in psychotherapy? *Current Directions in Psychological Science, 6,* 79–83.

Lynn, S. J., Neufeld, V., Green, J. P., Sandberg, D., et al. (1996). Daydreaming, fantasy, and psychopathology. In R. G. Kunzendorf, N. P. Spanos, & B. Wallace (Eds.), *Hypnosis and imagination. Imagery and human development series.* Amityville, NY: Baywood.

Macaluso, E., Frith, C. D., & Driver, J. (2000, August 18). Modulation of human visual cortex by crossmodal spatial attention. *Science, 289,* 1206–1208.

Macchi, M. M., Boulos, Z., Ranney, T., Simmons, L., & Campbell, S. S. (2002). Effects of an afternoon nap on nighttime alertness and performance in long-haul drivers. *Accident Analysis and Prevention, 34,* 825–834.

Maccoby, E. E., & Jacklin, C. N. (1974). *The psychology of sex differences.* Stanford, CA: Stanford University Press.

MacIntyre, T., Moran, A., & Jennings, D. J. (2002). Is controllability of imagery related to canoe-slalom performance? *Perceptual & Motor Skills, 94,* 1245–1250.

Mack, J. (2003). *The museum of the mind.* London: British Museum Publications.

Mackay, J., & Eriksen, M. (2002). *The Tobacco Atlas.* Geneva, Switzerland: World Health Organization.

MacKenzie, K. R., & Grabovac. A. D. (2001). Interpersonal psychotherapy group (IPT-G) for depression. *Journal of Psychotherapy Practice and Research, 10,* 46–51.

Macmillan, M. (1991). *Freud evaluated: The competed arc.* Amsterdam: North-Holland.

Macmillan, M. (2000). *An odd kind of fame: Stories of Phineas Gage.* Cambridge, MA: MIT Press.

MacPherson, K. (2002, March 17). Unfilled pink-collar jobs threaten service cuts. *Pittsburgh Post-Gazette,* p. 7.

Mader, S. S. (2000). *Biology,* p. 250. Boston: McGraw-Hill.

Madon, S., Guyll, M., Aboufadel, K., Montiel, E., Smith, A., Palumbo, P., & Jussim, L. (2001). Ethnic and national stereotypes: The Princeton Trilogy revisited and revised. *Personality and Social Psychology Bulletin, 27,* 996–1010.

Madon, S., Jussim, L., & Eccles, J. (1997). In search of the powerful self-fulfilling prophecy. *Journal of Personality and Social Psychology, 72,* 791–809.

Magley, V. J. (2002). Coping with sexual harassment: Reconceptualizing women's resistance. *Journal of Personality and Social Psychology, 83,* 930–946.

Maidment, I. (2000). The use of St John's Wort in the treatment of depression. *Psychiatric Bulletin, 24,* 232–234.

Malamuth, N. M., Linz, D., Heavey, C. L., & Barnes, G. (1995). Using the confluence model of sexual aggression to predict men's conflict with women: A 10-year follow-up study. *Journal of Personality and Social Psychology, 69,* 353–369.

Malott, R. W., Whaley, D. L., & Malott, M. E. (1993). *Elementary principles of behavior* (2nd ed.). Englewood Cliffs, NJ: Prentice-Hall.

Mann, D. (1997). *Psychotherapy: An erotic relationship.* New York: Routledge.

Manstead, A. S. R. (1991). Expressiveness as an individual difference. In R. S. Feldman, & B. Rime (Eds.), *Fundamentals of nonverbal behavior.* Cambridge, England: Cambridge University Press.

Manstead, A. S. R., & Wagner, H. L. (2004). *Experience emotion.* Cambridge, England: Cambridge University Press.

Manstead, A. S. R., Frijda, N., & Fischer, A. H. (Eds.) (2003). *Feelings and emotions: The Amsterdam Symposium.* Cambridge, England: Cambridge University Press.

Mapes, G. (1990, April 10). Beating the clock: Was it an accident Chernobyl exploded at 1:23 in the morning? *The Wall Street Journal,* pp. A1, A16.

Marcaurelle, R., Belanger, C., & Marchand, A. (2003). Marital relationship and the treatment of panic disorder with agoraphobia: A critical review. *Clinical Psychology Review, 23,* 247–276.

Marcus, D. K. & Miller, R. S. (2003). Sex differences in judgments of physical attractiveness: A social relations analysis. *Personality & Social Psychology Bulletin, 29,* 325–335.

Marcus, G. F. (1996). Why do children say "breaked"? *Current Directions in Psychological Science, 5,* 81–85.

Margolis, E., & Laurence, S. (Eds.). (1999). *Concepts: Core readings.* Cambridge, MA: MIT Press.

Maris, R. W. (2002). Suicide. *Lancet, 360,* 319–326.

Markey, P. M. Bystander intervention in computer-mediated communication. *Computers in Human Behavior, 16,* 183–188.

Markowitz, J. C. (2003). Controlled trials of psychotherapy. *American Journal of Psychiatry, 160,* 186–187.

Markowsitsch, H. J. (2000). Memory and amnesia. In M. M. Mesulam (Ed.), *Principles of behavioral and cognitive neurology* (2nd ed.). London: Oxford University Press.

Marsland, A. L., Bachen, E. A., Cohen, S., Rabin, B., & Manuck, S. B. (2002). Stress, immune reactivity and susceptibility to infectious disease. *Physiology and Behavior. Special Issue: The Pittsburgh special issue, 77,* 711–716.

Martelle, S., Hanley, C., & Yoshino K. (2003, January 28). "Sopranos" scenario in slaying? *Los Angeles Times,* p. B1.

Martin, A. J., & Marsh, H. W. (2002). Fear of failure: Friend or foe? *Australian Psychologist, 38,* 31–38.

Martin, C. L., Ruble, D. N., & Szkrybalo, J. (2002). Cognitive theories of early gender development. *Psychological Bulletin, 128,* 903–933.

Martin, L., & Pullum, G. K. (1991). *The great Eskimo vocabulary hoax.* Chicago: University of Chicago Press.

Martin, S. (April 2002). Easing migraine pain. *Monitor on Psychology,* pp. 71–73.

Martindale, C. (1981). *Cognition and consciousness.* Homewood, IL: Dorsey.

Martinez, J. L., Jr., & Derrick, B. E. (1996). Long-term potentiation and learning. *Annual Review of Psychology, 47,* 173–203.

Maruta, T., Colligan, R. C., Malinchoc, M., & Offord, K. P. (2000). Optimists vs. pessimists: Survival rate among medical patients over a 30-year period. *Mayo Clinic Proceedings, 75,* 140–143.

Maslow, A. H. (1970). *Motivation and personality* (2nd ed.). New York: Harper & Row.

Maslow, A. H. (1987). *Motivation and personality* (3rd ed.). New York: Harper & Row.

Mason, M. (1994). *The making of Victorian sexual attitudes,* Vol. 2. New York: Oxford University Press.

Mast, F. W., & Kosslyn, S. M. (2002). Visual mental images can be ambiguous: Insights from individual differences in spatial transformation abilities. *Cognition, 86,* 57–70.

Masters, W. H., & Johnson, V. E. (1966). *Human sexual response.* Boston: Little, Brown.

Masters, W. H., & Johnson, V. E. (1979). *Homosexuality in perspective.* Boston: Little, Brown.

Masters, W., & Johnson, V. (1994). *Heterosexuality.* New York: Harper Collins.

Mastropieri, M. A., & Scruggs, T. E. (1991). *Teaching students ways to remember: Strategies for learning mnemonically.* Cambridge, MA: Brookline.

Masuda, M. (2003). Meta-analyses of love scales: Do various love scales measure the same psychological constructs? *Japanese Psychological Research, 45,* 25–37.

Mataix-Cols, D., & Bartres-Fax, D. (2002). Is the use of the wooden and computerized versions of the Tower of Hanoi Puzzle equivalent? *Applied Neuropsychology, 9,* 117–120.

Matarazzo, J. D. (1992). Psychological testing and assessment in the 21st century. *American Psychologist, 47,* 1007–1018.

Matchen, J., & DeSouza, E. (2000). The sexual harassment of faculty members by students. *Sex Roles, 42,* 295–306.

Matlin, M. M. (1987). *The psychology of women.* New York: Holt.

Matlin, M. W. (2000). *The psychology of women* (4th ed.). Ft. Worth, Texas: Harcourt.

Matsumoto, D. (2002). Methodological requirements to test a possible in-group advantage in judging emotions across cultures: Comment on Elfenbein and Ambady (2002) and evidence. *Psychological Bulletin, 128,* 236–242.

Matsumoto, D. (Ed.). (2001). *The handbook of culture and psychology.* New York: Oxford University Press.

Matthews, G., Zeidner, M., & Roberts, R. D. (2003). *Emotional intelligence: Science and myth.* Cambridge, MA: MIT Press.

Maurer, D., Lewis, T. L., Brent, H. P., & Levin, A. V. (1999, October 1). Rapid improvement in the acuity of infants after visual input. *Science, 286,* 108–110.

Mauro, R., Sato, K., & Tucker, J. (1992). The role of appraisal in human emotions: A cross-cultural study. *Journal of Personality and Social Psychology, 62,* 301–317.

Mayer, J. D., Salovey, P., Caruso, D. R., & Sitarenios, G. (2003). Measuring emotional intelligence with the MSCEIT V2.0. *Emotion, 3,* 97–105.

Mayne, T. J., & Bonanno, G. A. (Eds.). (2001). *Emotions: Current issues and future directions.* New York: Guilford Press.

Mays, V. M., Rubin, J., Sabourin, M., & Walker, L. (1996). Moving toward a global psychology: Changing theories and practice to meet the needs of a changing world. *American Psychologist, 51,* 485–487.

Mazza, J. J. (2000). The relationship between posttraumatic stress symptomatology and suicidal behavior in school-based adolescents. *Suicide & Life-Threatening Behavior, 30,* 91–103.

McAdams, D. P., Diamond, A., de St. Aubin, E., & Mansfield, E. (1997). Stories of commitment: The psychosocial construction of generative lives. *Journal of Personality and Social Psychology, 72,* 678–694.

McCabe, P. M., Schneiderman, N., Field, T., & Wellens, A. R. (Eds.). (2000). *Stress, coping, and cardiovascular disease.* Mahwah, NJ: Lawrence Erlbaum.

McCaul, K. D., Johnson, R. J., & Rothman, A. J. (2003). The effects of framing and action instructions on whether older adults obtain flu shots. *Health Psychology.*

McClelland, D. C. (1985). How motives, skills, and values determine what people do. *American Psychologist, 40,* 812–825.

McClelland, D. C. (1993). Intelligence is not the best predictor of job performance. *Current Directions in Psychological Research, 2,* 5–8.

McClelland, D. C., Atkinson, J. W., Clark, R. A., & Lowell, E. L. (1953). *The achievement motive.* New York: Appleton-Century-Crofts.

McClintock, M. K., & Herdt, G. (1996). Rethinking puberty: The development of sexual attraction. *Current Directions in Psychological Science, 5,* 178–183.

McClintock, M. K., Jacob, S., Zelano, B., & Hayreh, D. J. S. (2001). Pheromones and vasanas: The functions of social chemosignals. In J. A. French & A. C. Kamil (Eds.), *Evolutionary psychology and motivation.* Vol. 47 of the Nebraska symposium on motivation. Lincoln, NB: University of Nebraska Press.

McCormick, C. G. (2003). Metacognition and learning. In W. M. Reynolds & G. E. Miller (Eds.), *Handbook of psychology: Educational psychology,* Vol. 7 pp. 79–102. New York: Wiley.

McCrae, R. R., & Costa, P. T. Jr. (1986) A five-factor theory of personality. In L. A. Pervin & O. P. John (Eds.), *Handbook of personality: Theory and research* (2nd ed.). New York: Guilford.

McCreery D. B., Yuen T. G. H., and Bullara, L. (2000). Chronic microstimulation in the feline ventral cochlear nucleus: Physiologic and histologic effects. *Hearing Research, 149,* 223–238.

McCullough, J. P., Jr. (1999). *Treatment for chronic depression: Cognitive behavioral analysis system of psychology (CBASP).* New York: Guilford Press.

McDaniel, M. A., Maier, S. F., & Einstein, G. O. (2002). "Brain specific" nutrients: A memory cure? *Psychological Science in the Public Interest, 3,* 12–18.

McDonald, C., & Murray, R. M. (2000). Early and late environmental risk factors for schizophrenia. *Brain Research Reviews, 31: Special issue: Nobel Symposium 111: Schizophrenia: Pathophysiological mechanisms,* pp. 130–137.

McDonald, H. E., & Hirt, E. R. (1997). When expectancy meets desire: Motivational effects in reconstructive memory. *Journal of Personality and Social Psychology, 72,* 5–23.

McDonald, J. W. (1999, September). Repairing the damaged spinal cord. *Scientific American,* pp. 65–73.

McDougall, W. (1908). *Introduction to social psychology.* London: Methuen.

McDowell, D. M., & Spitz, H. I. (1999). *Substance abuse.* New York: Brunner/Mazel.

McEwen, B. S. (1998, January 15). Protective and damaging effects of stress mediators [Review article]. *New England Journal of Medicine, 338,* 171–179.

McGaugh, J. L. (2000, January 14). Memory—a century of consolidation. *Science, 287,* 248–251.

McGaugh, J. L., Weinberger, N. M., & Lynch, G. (Eds.). (1990). *Brain organization and memory: Cells, systems, and circuits.* New York: Oxford University Press.

McGilvray, J. (Ed.). (2004). *The Cambridge companion to Chomsky.* Oxford, England: Cambridge University Press.

McGue, M. (1999). The behavioral genetics of alcoholism. *Current Directions in Psychological Science, 8,* 109–115.

McGuire, S. (2003). The heritability of parenting. *Parenting: Science & Practice, 3,* 73–94.

McGuire, W. J. (1997). Creative hypothesis generating in psychology: Some useful heuristics. *Annual Review of Psychology, 48,* 1–30.

McHale, S. M., Crouter, A. C., & Tucker, C. J. (1999). Family context and gender role socialization in middle childhood: Comparing girls to boys and sisters to brothers. *Child Development, 70,* 990–1004.

McKelvie, P., & Low, J. (2002). Listening to Mozart does not improve children's spatial ability: Final curtains for the Mozart effect. *British Journal of Developmental Psychology, 20,* 241–258.

McLaughlin, S., & Margolskee, R. F. (1994). The sense of taste: The internal molecular workings of the taste bud help it distinguish the bitter from the sweet. *American Scientist, 82,* 538–544.

McManus, F., & Waller, G. (1995). A functional analysis of binge-eating. *Clinical Psychology Review, 15,* 845–863.

McMillan, D. E., & Katz, J. L. (2002). Continuing implications of the early evidence against the drive-reduction hypothesis of the behavioral effects of drugs. *Psychopharmacology, 163,* 251–264.

McMullin, R. E. (2000). *The new handbook of cognitive therapy techniques.* New York: Norton.

McNally, R. J. (2003). Recovering memories of trauma: A view from the laboratory. *Current Directions in Psychological Science, 12,* 32–35.

Mead, M. (1949). *Male and female.* New York: Morrow.

Mealy, L. (2000). *Sex differences: Developmental and evolutionary strategies.* San Diego, CA: Academic Press.

Meier, R. P., & Willerman, R. (1995). Prelinguistic gesture in deaf and hearing infants. In K. Emmorey & J. S. Reilly (Eds.), *Language, gesture, and space.* Hillsdale, NJ: Erlbaum.

Mel, B. W. (2002, March 8). What the synapse tells the neuron. *Science, 295,* 1845–1846.

Mel'nikov, K. S. (1993, October–December). (On some aspects of the mechanistic approach to the study of processes of forgetting.) *Vestnik Moskovskogo Universiteta Seriya 14 Psikhologiya,* pp. 64–67.

Melton, G. B., & Garrison, E. G. (1987). Fear, prejudice, and neglect: Discrimination against mentally disabled persons. *American Psychologist, 42,* 1007–1026.

Meltzer, H. Y. (2000). Genetics and etiology of schizophrenia and bipolar disorder. *Biological Psychiatry, 47,* 171–173.

Meltzoff, A. N. (1996). The human infant as imitative generalist: A 20-year progress report on infant imitation with implications for comparative psychology. In C. M. Heyes & B. G. Galef, Jr. (Eds.), *Social learning in animals: The roots of culture.* San Diego, CA: Academic Press.

Melzack, R., & Wall, P. D. (2001). *The challenge of pain.* London: Penguin.

Merai, A. (Ed.). (1985). *On terrorism and combating terrorism.* College Park, MD: University Publications of America.

Merlin, D. (1993). Origins of the modern mind: Three stages in the evolution of culture and cognition. *Behavioral and Brain Sciences, 16,* 737–791.

Mesquita, B., & Frijda, N. H. (1992). Cultural variations in emotions: A review. *Psychological Bulletin, 112,* 179–204.

Messer, S. B., & McWilliams, N. (2003). The impact of Sigmund Freud and *The Interpretation of Dreams.* In R. J. Sternberg (Ed.), *The anatomy of impact: What makes the great works of psychology great,* pp. 71–88. Washington, DC: American Psychological Association.

Meston, C. M. (2003). Validation of the female sexual function index (FSFI) in women with female orgasmic disorder and in women with hypoactive sexual desire disorder. *Journal of Sex and Marital Therapy, 29,* 39–46.

Metcalfe, J. (1986). Premonitions of insight predict impending error. *Journal of Experimental Psychology: Learning, Memory, and Cognition, 12,* 623–634.

Metee, D. R., & Aronson, E. (1974). Affective reactions to appraisal from others. In T. L. Huston (Ed.), *Foundations of interpersonal attraction,* pp. 235–283. New York: Academic Press.

Meyer, G. J. (2000). Incremental validity of the Rorschach Prognostic Rating scale over the MMPI Ego Strength Scale and IQ. *Journal of Personality Assessment, 74,* 356–370.

Meyer, R. G., & Osborne, Y. V. H. (1987). *Case studies in abnormal behavior* (2nd ed.). Boston: Allyn & Bacon.

Meyer-Bahlburg, H. (1997). The role of prenatal estrogens in sexual orientation. In L. Ellis & L. Ebertz (Eds.), *Sexual orientation: Toward biological understanding.* Westport, CT: Praeger.

Michael, R. T., Gagnon, J. H., Laumann, E. O., & Kolata, G. (1994). *Sex in America: A definitive survey.* Boston: Little, Brown.

Middaugh, S. J., & Pawlick, K. (2002). Biofeedback and behavioral treatment of persistent pain in the older adult: A review and a study. *Applied Psychophysiology & Biofeedback, 27,* 185–202.

Middlebrooks, J. C., Clock, A. E., Xu, L., & Green, D. M. (1994, May 6). A panoramic code for sound location by cortical neurons. *Science, 264,* 842–844.

Miele, F. (2002). *Intelligence, race, and genetics: Conversations with Arthur R. Jensen.* Boulder, CO: Westview Press.

Mifflin, L. (1998, January 14). Study finds a decline in TV network violence. *New York Times,* p. A14.

Mignon, A., & Mollaret, P. (2002). Applying the affordance conception of traits: A person perception study. *Personality and Social Psychology Bulletin, 28,* 1327–1334.

Miklowitz, D. J., & Thompson, M. C. (2003). Family variables and interventions in schizophrenia. In G. Sholevar & G. Pirooz (Eds.), *Textbook of family and couples therapy: Clinical applications,* pp. 585–617. Washington, DC: American Psychiatric Publishing.

Miles, R. (2000, January 14). Diversity in inhibition. *Science, 287,* 244–246.

Miletic, M. P. (2002). The introduction of a feminine psychology to psychoanalysis: Karen Horney's legacy. *Contemporary Psychoanalysis: Special Issue: Interpersonal psychoanalysis and feminism, 38,* 287–299.

Milgram, S. (1974). *Obedience to authority.* New York: Harper & Row.

Millar, M. (2002). Effects of guilt induction and guilt reduction on door-in-the-face. *Communication Research, 29,* 666–680.

Miller, A. G., Collins, B. E., & Brief, D. E. (1995). Perspectives on obedience to authority: The legacy of the Milgram experiments. *Journal of Social Issues, 51,* 1–19.

Miller, A. G. (1999). Harming other people: Perspectives on evil and violence. *Personality and Social Psychology Review, 3,* 176–178.

Miller, D. W. (2000, February 25). Looking askance at eyewitness testimony. *The Chronicle of Higher Education,* A19–A20.

Miller, G. A. (1956). The magical number seven, plus or minus two: Some limits on our capacity for processing information. *Psychology Review, 63,* 81–97.

Miller, G., & Cohen, S. (2001). Psychological interventions and the immune system: A meta-analystic review and critique. *Health Psychology, 20,* 47–63.

Miller, J. G. (1984). Culture and the development of everyday social explanation. *Journal of Personality and Social Psychology, 46,* 961–978.

Miller, L. T., & Vernon, P. A. (1997). Developmental changes in speed of information processing in young children. *Developmental Psychology, 33,* 549–554.

Miller, M. N., & Pumariega, A. J. (2001). Culture and eating disorders: A historical and cross-cultural review. *Psychiatry: Interpersonal and Biological Processes, 64,* 93–110.

Miller, M. W. (1994, December 1). Brain surgery is back in a limited way to treat mental ills. *The Wall Street Journal,* pp. A1, A12.

Miller, N. E. (1985a, February). Rx: Biofeedback. *Psychology Today,* pp. 54–59.

Miller, N. E., & Magruder, K. M. (Eds.). (1999). *Cost-effectiveness of psychotherapy: A guide for practitioners, researchers, and policymakers.* New York: Oxford University Press.

Miller-Jones, D. (1989). Culture and testing. *American Psychologist, 44,* 360–366.

Millon, T., & Davis, R. (1999). *Personality disorders in modern life.* New York: Wiley.

Millon, T., & Davis, R. O. (1996). *Disorders of personality: DSM-IV and beyond* (2nd ed.). New York: Wiley.

Millon, T., Davis, R., & Millon, C. (2000). *Personality disorders in modern life.* New York: Wiley.

Mills, J. L. (1999). Cocaine, smoking, and spontaneous abortion. *New England Journal of Medicine, 340,* 380–381.

Mills, J. S., Polivy, J., Herman, C. P., & Tiggemann, M. (2002). Effects of exposure to thin media images: Evidence of self-enhancement among restrained eaters. *Personality and Social Psychology Bulletin, 28,* 1687–1699.

Milner, B. (1966). Amnesia following operation on temporal lobes. In C. W. M. Whitty & P. Zangwill (Eds.), *Amnesia.* London: Butterworth.

Milner, P. M. (1996). Neural representations: Some old problems revisited. *Journal of Cognitive Neuroscience, 8,* 69–77.

Milton, J., & Wiseman, R. (1999). Does psi exist? Lack of replication of an anomalous process of information transfer. *Psychological Bulletin, 125,* 387–391.

Mingo, C., Herman C. J., & Jasperse, M. (2000). Women's stories: Ethnic variations in women's attitudes and experiences of menopause, hysterectomy, and hormone replacement therapy. *Journal of Women's Health and Gender Based Medicine, 9, Suppl 2,* S27–S38.

Minuchin, S., & Nichols, M. P. (1992). *Family healing.* New York: Free Press.

Mischoulon, D. (2000, June). Antidepressants: Choices and controversy. *HealthNews,* p. 4.

Miserando, M. (1991). Memory and the seven dwarfs. *Teaching of Psychology, 18,* 169–171.

Mitchell, T. (2000, November 3–5). Extinguish your habit for good. *USA Weekend,* p. 4.

Mitchener, B. (2001, March 14). Controlling a computer by the power of thought. *Wall Street Journal,* pp. B1, B4.

Mittleman, M. A., Maclure, M., Sherwood, J. B., Mulry, R. P., Tofler, G. H., Jacobs, S. C., Friedman, R., Benson, H., & Muller, J. E. (1995, October 1). Triggering of acute myocardial infarction onset by episodes of anger. *Circulation, 92,* 1720–1725.

Miyake, K., Chen, S., & Campos, J. J. (1985). Infant temperament, mother's mode of interaction, and attachment in Japan: An interim report. *Monographs of the Society for Research in Child Development, 50,* 276–297.

Miyashita, Y. (1995, June 23), How the brain creates imagery: Projection to primary visual cortex. *Science, 268,* 1719–1720.

Moghaddam, B., & Adams, B. W. (1998, August 28). Reversal of phencyclidine effects by a group II metabotropic glutamate receptor agonist in rats. *Science, 281,* 1349–1352.

Molfese, V. J. & Molfese, D. L. (2000). *Temperament and personality development across the life span.* Mahwah, NJ: Erlbaum.

Monnier, J., Resnick, H. S., Kilpatrick, D. G., & Seals, B. (2002). The relationship between distress and resource loss following rape. *Violence and Victims, 17,* 85–92.

Montague, D. P. F., & Walker-Andrews, S. (2002). Mothers, fathers, and infants: The role of person familiarity and parental involvement in infants' perception of emotion expressions. *Child Development, 73,* 1339–1352.

Montgomery, G. M., & Bovbjerg, D. H. (2003). Expectations of chemotherapy-related nausea: Emotional and experimental predictors. *Annals of Behavioral Medicine, 25,* 48–54.

Moody, H. R. (2000). *Aging: Concepts and controversies.* Thousand Oaks, CA: Sage.

Moon, S. M., Swift, M., & Shallenberger, A. (2002). Perceptions of a self-contained class for fourth- and fifth-grade students with high to extreme levels of intellectual giftedness. *Gifted Child Quarterly, 46,* 64–79.

Moore-Ede, M. (1993). *The twenty-four hour society.* Boston: Addison-Wesley.

Moretti, M. M., & Higgins, E. T. (1990). The development of self-system vulnerabilities: Social and cognitive factors in developmental psychopathology. In R. J. Sternberg & J. Kolligian, Jr. (Eds), *Competence considered.* New Haven, CT: Yale University Press.

Morgan, R. (2002, September 27). The men in the mirror. *The Chronicle of Higher Education,* pp. A53–A54.

Morris, J. F., Waldo, C. R., & Rothblum, E. D. (2001). A model of predictors and outcomes of outness among lesbian and bisexual women. *American Journal of Orthopsychiatry, 71,* 61–71.

Morrow, J., & Wolff, R. (1991, May). Wired for a miracle. *Health,* pp. 64–84.

Motley, M. T. (1987, February). What I meant to say. *Psychology Today,* pp. 25–28.

Moutoussis, K., & Zeki, S. (1997). A direct demonstration of perceptual asynchrony in vision. *Proceedings of the Royal Society of London, B., Biological Sciences, 264,* 393–399.

Movshon, J. A., & Newsome, W. T. (1992). Neural foundations of visual motion perception. *Current Directions in Psychological Science, 1,* 35–39.

Muehlenhard, C. L., & Hollabaugh, L. C. (1988). Do women sometimes say no when they mean yes? The prevalence and correlates of women's token resistance to sex. *Journal of Personality and Social Psychology, 54,* 872–879.

Mufson, M. J. (1999, September). What is the role of psychiatry in the management of chronic pain? *The Harvard Mental Health Letter,* pp. 8–10.

Mukerjee, M. (1997, February). Trends in animal research. *Scientific American, 276,* 86–93.

Mulligan, C., Moreau, K., Brandolini, M., Livingstone, B., Beaufrere, B., & Boire, Y. (2002). Alterations of sensory perceptions in

healthy elderly subjects during fasting and refeeding: A pilot study. *Gerontology, 48,* 39–43.

Munroe, R. L., Hulefeld, R., Rodgers, J. M., Tomeo, D. L., & Yamazaki, S. K. (2000). Aggression among children in four cultures. *Cross-Cultural Research: The Journal of Comparative Social Science, 34,* 3–25.

Munson, L. J., Hulin, C., & Drasgow, F. (2000). Longitudinal analysis of dispositional influences and sexual harassment: Effects on job and psychological outcomes. *Personnel Psychology, 53,* 21–46.

Murphy, E., & Carr, A. (2000). Pediatric pain problems. In A. Carr et al. (Eds.), *What works with children and adolescents?: A critical review of psychological interventions with children, adolescents and their families,* pp. 258–279. New York: Routledge.

Murphy, K. E. (Ed.). (2003). *Validity generalization: A critical review. Applied psychology series.* Mahwah, NJ: Erlbaum.

Murphy, R. T., Wismar, K., & Freeman, K. (2003). Stress symptoms among African-American college students after the September 11, 2001 terrorist attacks. *Journal of Nervous and Mental Disease, 191,* 108–114.

Murphy, S., et al. (1998). Interference under the influence. *Personality and Social Psychology Bulletin, 24,* 517–528.

Murphy, S. T., & Zajonc, R. B. (1993). Affect, cognition, and awareness: Affective priming with optimal and suboptimal stimulus exposures. *Journal of Personality and Social Psychology, 64,* 723–739.

Murray, B. (June 2002). Good news for bachelor's grads. *Monitor on Psychology,* pp. 30–32.

Murray, J. B. (1990). Nicotine as a psychoactive drug. *Journal of Psychology, 125,* 5–25.

Murray, J. B. (1995). Evidence for acupuncture's analgesic effectiveness and proposals for the physiological mechanisms involved. *Journal of Psychology, 129,* 43–46.

Murray, J. B. (2001). Ecstasy is a dangerous drug. *Psychological Reports, 88,* 895–902.

Murray, S. L., & Holmes, J. G. (1997). A leap of faith? Positive illusions in romantic relationships. *Personality and Social Psychology Bulletin, 23,* 586–604.

Myerhoff, B. (1982). Rites of passage: Process and paradox. In V. Turner (Ed.), *Celebration: Studies in festivity and ritual.* Washington, DC: Smithsonian Institution Press.

Myers, D. G. & Diener, E. (1996, May). The pursuit of happiness: New research uncovers some anti-intuitive insights into how many people are happy—and why. *Scientific American,* pp. 70–72.

Myers, D. G. (2000). The funds, friends, and faith of happy people. *American Psychologist, 55,* 56–67.

Myerson, J., Adams, D. R., Hale, S., & Jenkins, L. (2003). Analysis of group differences in processing speed: Brinley plots, Q-Q plots, and other conspiracies. *Psychonomic Bulletin and Review, 10,* 224–237.

Mytinger, C. (2001). *Headhunting in the Solomon Islands: Around the Coral Sea.* Santa Barbara, CA: Narrative Press.

Narrow, W. E., Rae, D. S., Robins, L. N., & Regier, D. A. (2002). Revised prevalence estimates of mental disorders in the United States: Using a clinical significance criterion to reconcile 2 surveys' estimates. *Archives of General Psychiatry, 59,* 115–123.

Nash, M. R. (July 2001). The truth and hype of hypnosis. *Scientific American,* pp. 47–55.

Nathan, P. E. & Gorman, J. M. (Eds.). (1997). *A guide to treatments that work.* New York: Oxford University Press.

Nathan, P. E., Stuart, S. P., & Dolan, S. L. (2000). Research on psychotherapy efficacy and effectiveness: Between Scylla and Charybdis? *Psychological Bulletin, 126,* 964–981.

Nathans, J., Davenport, C. M., Maumenee, I. H., Lewis, R. A., Hejtmancik, J. F., Litt, M., Lovrien, E., Weleber, R., Bachynski, B., Zwas, F., Klingaman, R., & Fishman, G. (1989, August 25). Molecular genetics of human blue cone monochromacy. *Science, 245,* 831–838.

National Academy of Sciences (1999). *Marijuana and medicine: Assessing the science base.* Washington, DC: National Academy Press.

National Center on Addiction and Substance Abuse. (1996, June). *Substance abuse and the American woman.* New York: National Center on Addiction and Substance Abuse.

National Clearinghouse for Alcohol and Drug Information (NCADI). (1998). *Cocaine use.* Washington, DC: National Clearinghouse for Alcohol and Drug Information.

National Depression Screening Day. (2003, March 26). Questionnaire on website, www.mentalhealthscreening.org/dep/ dep-sample.htm#sampletest.

National Heart, Lung, and Blood Institute. (2002). *International position paper on women's health and menopause: A comprehensive approach,* to be published by the National Heart, Lung, and Blood Institute (NHLBI), National Institutes of Health (NIH).

National Institute of Child Health and Human Development (NICHD) (2002). Child-care structure → process → outcome: Direct and indirect effects of child-care quality on young children's development. *Psychological Science, 13,* 199–206.

National Institute of Child Health and Human Development (NICHD) Early Child Care Research Network. (1997). The effects of infant care on infant-mother attachment security: Results of the NICHD study of early child care. *Child Development, 68,* 860–879.

National Institute of Child Health and Human Development (NICHD) Early Child Care Research Network. (1999). Child care and mother-child interaction in the first 3 years of life. *Developmental Psychology, 35,* 1399–1413.

National Institute on Drug Abuse. (2000). *Principles of drug addiction treatment: A research-based guide.* Washington, DC: National Institute on Drug Abuse.

National Institutes of Health. (1996). Integration of behavioral and relaxation approaches into the treatment of chronic pain and insomnia. NIH Technology Assessment Panel on Integration of Behavioral and Relaxation Approaches into the Treatment of Chronic Pain and Insomnia. *Journal of the American Medical Association, 276,* 313–318.

National Sleep Foundation (2000). *Adolescent sleep needs and patterns: Research report and research guide.* Washington, DC: National Sleep Foundation.

National Sleep Foundation (2002, March). *2002 "Sleep in America" poll.* Washington, DC: National Sleep Foundation.

Natvig, G. K., Albrektsen, G., & Ovarnstrom, U. (2003). Methods of teaching and class participation in relation to perceived social support and stress: Modifiable factors for improving health and wellbeing among students. *Educational Psychology, 23,* 261–274.

Navon, R., & Proia, R. L. (1989, March 17). The mutations in Ashkenazi Jews with adult G(M2) gangliosidosis, the adult form of Tay-Sachs disease. *Science, 243,* 1471–1474.

Neber, H., & Heller, K. A. (2002). Evaluation of a summer-school program for highly gifted secondary-school students: The German Pupils Academy. *European Journal of Psychological Assessment, 18,* 214–228.

Negrin, G., & Capute, A. J. (1996). Mental retardation. In R. H. A. Haslam & P. J. Valletutti (Eds.), *Medical problems in the classroom: The teacher's role in diagnosis and management* (3rd ed). Austin, TX: PRO-ED.

Neisser, U. (1982). *Memory observed.* San Francisco: Freeman.

Neisser, U. (1996, April.) Intelligence on the rise: Secular changes in IQ and related measures. Conference at Emory University. Atlanta: Emory University.

Neisser, U., Boodoo, G., Bouchard, T. J., Jr., Boykin, A. W., Brody, N., Ceci, S. J., Halpern, D. F., Loehlin, J. C., Perloff, R., Sternberg, R. J., & Urbina, S. (1996). Intelligence: Knowns and unknowns. *American Psychologist, 51,* 77–101.

Neitz, J., Neitz, M., & Kainz, P. M. (1996, November 1). Visual pigment gene structure and the severity of color vision defects. *Science, 274,* 801–804.

Nelson, D. L., & Simmons, B. L. (2003). Health psychology and work stress: A more positive approach. In J. C. Quick, & L. E. Tetrick (Eds.), *Handbook of occupational health psychology.* Washington, DC: American Psychological Association.

Nesse, R. M. (2000). Is depression an adaptation? *Archives of General Psychiatry, 57,* 14–20.

Nestler, E. J. (2001, June 22). Total recall—the memory of addiction. *Science, 292,* 2266–2267.

Newcombe, N. S., Drummey, A. B., Fox, N. A., Lie, E., & Ottinger-Alberts, W. (2000). Remembering early childhood: How much, how, and why (or why not). *Current Directions in Psychological Science, 9,* 55–58.

Newell, A., & Simon, H. (1972). *Human problem solving.* Englewood Cliffs, NJ: Prentice-Hall.

Newman, A. W., & Thompson, J. W., Jr. (2001). The rise and fall of forensic hypnosis in criminal investigation. *Journal of the American Academy of Psychiatry & the Law, 29,* 75–84.

Newman, C. F., Leahy, R. L., Beck, A. T., Reilly-Harrington, N. A., & Gyulai, L. (2002). *Bipolar disorder: A cognitive therapy approach.* Washington, DC: American Psychological Association.

Newport, E. L., Bavelier, D., & Neville, H. J. (2001). Critical thinking about critical periods: Perspectives on a critical period for language acquisition. In E. Dupoux (Ed.), *Language, brain, and cognitive development: Essays in honor of Jacques Mehler.* Cambridge, MA: MIT Press.

Newport, F., & Carroll, J. (2002, November 27). Battle of the bulge: Majority of Americans want to lose weight. *Gallup News Service,* pp. 1–9.

Nicholson, I. A. M. (2003). *Inventing personality: Gordon Allport and the science of selfhood.* Washington, DC: American Psychological Association.

Nickerson, R. S., & Adams, M. J. (1979). *Cognitive Psychology, 11,* 297.

Nicolelis, M. A. L., & Chapin, J. K. (2002). Controlling robots with the mind. *Scientific American, 287,* pp. 47–53.

Nierenberg, A. A. (1998, February 17). The physician's perspective. *HealthNews,* pp. 3–4.

Nigg, J. T., & Goldsmith, H. H. (1994). Genetics of personality disorders: Perspectives from personality and psychopathology research. *Psychological Bulletin, 115,* 346–380.

Nikles, C. D., II, Brecht, D. L., Klinger, E., & Bursell, A. L. (1998). The effects of current concern- and nonconcern-related waking suggestions on nocturnal dream content. *Journal of Personality and Social Psychology, 75,* 242–255.

National Institute of Mental Health (NIMH). (2000). *Prevention of eating disorders: Challenges and Opportunities.* Bethesda, MD: National Institute of Mental Health.

Nisbett, R. (1994, October 31). Blue genes. *New Republic, 211,* 15.

Nisbett, R. (2003). *The geography of thought.* New York: Free Press.

Nisbett, R. E. (1968). Taste, deprivation, and weight determinants of eating behavior. *Journal of Personality and Social Psychology, 10,* 107–116.

Nissle, S., & Bschor, T. (2002). Winning the jackpot and depression: Money cannot buy happiness. *International Journal of Psychiatry in Clinical Practice, 6,* 183–186.

Niu, W., & Sternberg, R. J. (2003). Societal and school influences on student creativity: The case of China. *Psychology in the Schools. Special Issue: Psychoeducational and psychosocial functioning of Chinese children, 40,* 103–114.

Noble, H. B. (1999, March 12). New from the smoking wars: Success. *The New York Times,* pp. D1–D2.

Nolen-Hoeksema, S. (2004). *Abnormal psychology,* (3rd ed.). Boston: McGraw-Hill.

Nolen-Hoeksema, S., Larson, J., & Grayson, C. (1999). Explaining the gender differences in depressive symptoms. *Journal of Personality and Social Psychology, 77,* 1061-1072.

Nosek, B. A., Banaji, M. R., & Greenwald, A. G. (2002). Math = male, me = female, therefore math ≠ me. *Journal of Personality and Social Psychology, 83,* 44–59.

Novak, M. A., & Petto, A. J. (1991). *Through the looking glass: Issues of psychological well-being in captive nonhuman primates.* Washington, DC: American Psychological Association.

Noyes, R., Jr., Stuart, S., Longley, S. L., Langbehn, D. R., & Happel, R. L. (2002). Hypochondriasis and fear of death. *Journal of Nervous and Mental Disease, 190,* 503–509.

Noyes, R., Jr., Stuart, S. P., Langbehn, D. R., Happel, R. L., Longley, S. L., Muller, B. A., & Yagla, S. J. (2003). Test of an interpersonal model of hypochondriasis. *Psychosomatic Medicine, 65,* 292–300.

Noyes, R., Kathol, R. G., Fisher, M. M., Phillips, B. M., et al. (1993). The validity of DSM-III-R hypochondriasis. *Archives of General Psychiatry, 50,* 961–970.

Nucci, L. P. (2002). The development of moral reasoning. In U. Goswami (Ed.), *Blackwell handbook of childhood cognitive development. Blackwell Handbooks of developmental psychology,* pp. 303–325. Malden, MA: Blackwell.

Nyberg, L., & Tulving, E. (1996). Classifying human long-term memory: Evidence from converging dissociations. *European Journal of Cognitive Psychology, 8,* 163–183.

O'Brien, C. P., Childress, A. R., McLellan, A. T., & Ehrman, R. (1992). Classical conditioning in drug-dependent humans. In P. W. Kalivas & H. H. Samson (Eds.), *The neurobiology of drug and alcohol addiction. Annals of the New York Academy of Sciences,* Vol. 654. New York: New York Academy of Sciences.

O'Connor, S. C., & Rosenblood, L. K. (1996). Affiliation motivation in everyday experience: A theoretical comparison. *Journal of Personality and Social Psychology, 70,* 513–522.

O'Donohue, W. (Ed.). (1997). *Sexual harassment: Theory, research, and treatment.* Boston: Allyn & Bacon.

O'Grady, W. D., & Dobrovolsky, M. (Eds.). (1996). *Contemporary linguistic analysis: An introduction* (3rd ed.). Toronto: Copp Clark Pitman.

O'Keefe, T., & Fox, K. (Eds.). (2003). Finding the real me: True tales of sex and gender diversity. San Francisco: Jossey-Bass.

Oatley, K., & Jenkins, J. M. (1996). *Understanding emotions.* Oxford, England: Blackwell Publishers.

Obermeyer, C. M. (2001, May 18). Complexities of a controversial practice. *Science, 292,* 1305–1304.

Oberstar, J. V., Bernstein, G. A., & Thuras, P. D. (2002). Caffeine use and dependence in adolescents: One-year follow-up. *Journal of Child & Adolescent Psychopharmacology, 12,* 127–135.

Oehman, A., & Mineka, S. (2003). The malicious serpent: Snakes as a prototypical stimulus for an evolved module of fear. *Current Directions in Psychological Science, 12,* 5–9.

Oezgen, E., & Davies I. R. L. (2002). Acquisition of categorical color perception: A perceptual learning approach to the linguistic relativity hypothesis. *Journal of Experimental Psychology: General, 131,* 477–493.

Offer, D., Kaiz, M., Howard, K. I., & Bennett, E. S. (2000). The altering of reported experiences. *Journal of the American Academy of Child & Adolescent Psychiatry, 39,* 735–742.

Ogbu, J. (1992). Understanding cultural diversity and learning. *Educational Researcher, 21,* 5–14.

O'Hare, D., & Roscoe, S. (1990). *Flightdeck performance: The human factor.* Ames: Iowa State University Press.

Oishi, S., & Diener, E. (2001). Goals, culture, and subjective well-being. *Personality and Social Psychology Bulletin, 27,* 1674–1682.

Oksenberg, A., Radwan, H., Arons, E., Hoffenbach, D., & Behroozi, B. (2002). Rapid eye movement (REM) sleep behavior disorder: A sleep disturbance affecting mainly older men. *Israel Journal of Psychiatry & Related Sciences, 39,* 28–35.

Okun, B. F. (1996). *Understanding diverse families: What practitioners need to know.* New York: Guilford Press.

Olds, J., & Milner, P. (1954). Positive reinforcement produced by electrical stimulation of septal area and other regions of rat brain. *Journal of Comparative and Physiological Psychology, 47,* 411–427.

Olds, M. E., & Fobes, J. L. (1981). The central basis of motivation: Intracranial self-stimulation studies. *Annual Review of Psychology, 32,* 123–129.

Oliver, M. B., & Hyde, J. S. (1993). Gender differences in sexuality: A meta-analysis. *Psychological Bulletin, 114,* 29–51.

Olshansky, S. J., Carnes, B. A., & Cassel, C. (1990, November 2). In search of Methuselah: Estimating the upper limits to human longevity. *Science, 250,* 634–639.

Olson, M. A., & Fazio, R. H. (2001). Implicit attitude formation through classical conditioning. *Psychological Science, 12,* 413–417.

Oren, D. A., & Terman, M. (1998, January 16). Tweaking the human circadian clock with light. *Science, 279,* 333–334.

Orenstein, P. (2001). Unbalanced equations: Girls, math, and the confidence gap. In R. Satow (Ed.), *Gender and social life.* Needham Heights, MA: Allyn & Bacon.

Orr, S. P., Metzger, L. J., & Pitman, R. K. (2002). Psychophysiology of posttraumatic stress disorder. *Psychiatric Clinics of North America: Special Issue: Recent advances in the study of biological alterations in post-traumatic stress disorders, 25,* 271–293.

Orth-Gomer, K., Chesney, M. A., & Wenger, N. K. (Eds.). (1996). *Women, stress and heart disease.* Mahwah, NJ: Erlbaum.

Ortony, A., & Turner, T. J. (1990). What's basic about basic emotions? *Psychological Review, 97,* 315–331.

Orwin, R. G., & Condray, D. S. (1984). Smith and Glass' psychotherapy conclusions need further probing: On Landman and Dawes' re-analysis. *American Psychologist, 39,* 71–72.

Oskamp, S. (Ed.). (2000) *Reducing prejudice and discrimination.* Mahwah, NJ: Erlbaum.

Owens, R. E., Jr. (2001) *Language development: An introduction* (5th ed.). Boston: Allyn & Bacon.

Ozer, E. J., Best, S. R., & Lipsey, T. L. (2003). Predictors of posttraumatic stress disorder and symptoms in adults: A meta-analysis. *Psychological Bulletin, 129,* 52–73.

Pääbo, S. (2001, February 16). The human genome and our view of ourselves. *Science, 291,* 1219–1220.

Paivio, A. (1971). *Imagery and verbal processes.* New York: Holt, Rinehart & Winston.

Paivio, A. (1975). Perceptual comparison through the mind's eye. *Memory and Cognition, 3,* 635–647.

Pajares, F. (2003). Self-efficacy beliefs, motivation, and achievement in writing: A review of the literature. *Reading and Writing Quarterly: Overcoming Learning Difficulties, 19,* 139–158.

Paludi, M. A. (Ed.). (1996). *Sexual harassment on college campuses: Abusing the ivory power.* Albany: State University of New York Press.

Paniagua, F. A. (2000). *Diagnosis in a multicultural context: A casebook for mental health professionals.* Thousand Oaks, CA: Sage.

Park, W-W. (2000). A comprehensive empirical investigation of the relationships among variables of the groupthink model. *Journal of Organizational Behavior, 21,* 873–887.

Parke, B. N. (2003). *Discovering programs for talent development.* Thousand Oaks, CA: Corwin Press.

Parke, R. D. (2002). Punishment revisited—Science, values, and the right question: Comment on Gershoff (2002). *Psychological Bulletin, 128,* 596–601.

Parker-Pope, T. (2003, April 22). The diet that works. *The Wall Street Journal,* pp. R1, R5.

Parlee, M. B. (1979, October). The friendship bond. *Psychology Today,* pp. 43–45.

Parrott, A. C. (2002). Recreational Ecstasy/MDMA, the serotonin syndrome, and serotonergic neurotoxicity. *Pharmacology, Biochemistry & Behavior: Special Issue: Serotonin, 71,* 837–844.

Parrott, A. C., Buchanan, T., Scholey, A. B., Heffernan, T., Ling, J., & Rodgers, J. (2002). Ecstasy/MDMA attributed problems reported by novice, moderate and heavy recreational users. *Human Psychopharmacology Clinical & Experimental, 17,* 309–312.

Pascual-Leone, A., et al. (1995). Modulation of muscle responses evoked by transcranial magnetic stimulation during the acquisition of new fine motor skills. *Journal of Neurophysiology 74,* 1037–1045.

Patel, D. R., Pratt, H. D., & Greydanus, D. E. (2003). Treatment of adolescents with anorexia nervosa. *Journal of Adolescent Research: Special issue: Editing disorders in adolescents, 18,* 244–260.

Patzwahl, D. R., Zanker, J. M., & Altenmuller, E. O. (1994). Cortical potentials reflecting motion processing in humans. *Visual Neuroscience, 11,* 1135–1147.

Paunonen, S. V. (2003). Big Five factors of personality and replicated predictions of behavior. *Journal of Personality and Social Psychology, 84,* 411–422.

Pavlides, C., & Winson, J. (1989). Influences of hippocampal place cell firing in the awake state on the activity of these cells during subsequent sleep episodes. *Journal of Neuroscience, 9,* 2907–2918.

Pavlidis, I., Eberhardt, N. L., & Levine, J. A. (2002). Seeing through the face of deception. *Nature, 415,* 35.

Pavlov, I. P. (1927). *Conditioned reflexes.* London: Oxford University Press.

Pawlik, K., & d'Ydewalle, G. (1996). Psychology and the global commons: Perspectives of international psychology. *American Psychologist, 51,* 488–495.

Payne, D. G. (1986). Hyperamnesia for pictures and words: Testing the recall level hypothesis. *Journal of Experimental Psychology: Learning, Memory, and Cognition, 12,* 16–29.

Pedersen, D. M. (2002). Intrinsic-extrinsic factors in sport motivation. *Perceptual & Motor Skills, 95,* 459–476.

Pedersen, P. B., Draguns, J. G., Lonner, W. J., & Trimble, J. E. (Eds.). (2002). *Counseling across cultures,* (5th ed.). Thousand Oaks, CA: Sage.

Peiro, J. M., & Lunt, I. (2002). The context for a European framework for psychologists' training. *European Psychologist, 7,* 169–179.

Penley, J. A., Tomaka, J., & Wiebe, J. S. (2002). The association of coping to physical and psychological health outcomes: A meta-analytic review. *Journal of Behavioral Medicine, 25,* 551–603.

Penn, D. L., Corrigan, P. W., Bentall, R. P., Racenstein, J. M., & Newman, L. (1997). Social cognition in schizophrenia. *Psychological Bulletin, 121,* 114–132.

Penney, J. B., Jr. (2000). Neurochemistry. In B. S. Fogel, R. B. Schiffer, et al. (Eds.), *Synopsis of neuropsychiatry.* New York: Lippincott Williams & Wilkins.

Pennington, B. F. (2002). *The development of psychopathology: Nature and nurture.* New York: Guilford Press.

Pennisi, E. (1997b, October 24). Enzyme linked to alcohol sensitivity in mice. *Science, 278,* 573.

Pennisi, E., & Vogel, G. (2000, June 9). Animal cloning. Clones: A hard act to follow. *Science, 288,* 1722–1727.

Penzel, F. (2000). *Obsessive-compulsive disorders: A complete guide to getting well and staying well.* New York: Oxford University Press.

Peretz, I. (2001). Brain specialization for music: New evidence from congenital amusia. In R. J. Zatorre & I. Peretz (Eds.). *The biological foundations of music. Annals of the New York*

Academy of Sciences, Vol. 930, pp. 153–165. New York: New York Academy of Sciences.

Perez, R. M., DeBord, K. A., & Bieschke, K. J. (Eds). (2000). *Handbook of counseling and psychotherapy with lesbian, gay, and bisexual clients.* Washington, DC: American Psychological Association.

Perkins, D. N. (1983). Why the human perceiver is a bad machine. In J. Beck, B. Hope, & A. Rosenfeld (Eds.), *Human and machine vision.* New York: Academic Press.

Perloff, R. M. (2003). *The dynamics of persuasion: Communication and attitudes in the 21st century* (2nd ed.). Mahwah, NJ: Erlbaum.

Pert, C. B. (2002). The wisdom of the receptors: Neuropeptides, the emotions, and bodymind. *Advances in Mind-Body Medicine, 18,* 30–35.

Pervin, L. A. &. John, O. P. (Eds.). (1999). *Handbook of personality: Theory and research.* (2nd ed.) New York: Guilford.

Peterson, A. (1985). Pubertal development as a cause of disturbance: Myths, realities, and unanswered questions. *Genetic, Social and General Psychology Monographs, 111,* 205–232.

Peterson, C. (2000). The future of optimism. *American Psychologist, 55,* 44–55.

Peterson, C., Maier, S. F., & Seligman, M. E. P. (1993). *Learned helplessness: A theory for the age of personal control.* New York: Oxford University Press.

Peterson, L. R., & Peterson, M. J. (1959). Short-term retention of individual items. *Journal of Experimental Psychology, 58,* 193–198.

Peterson, S. E. (2001). *PET Scans.* Washington University.

Petersen, S. E., & Fiez, J. A. (1993). The processing of single words studied with positron emission tomography. *Annual Review of Neuroscience, 16,* 509–530.

Petri, H. L. (1996). *Motivation: Theory, research, and applications* (4th ed.). Pacific Grove, CA: Brooks/Cole.

Pettigrew, T., & Tropp, L. (2000). *Reducing prejudice and discrimination.* Mahwah, NJ: Erlbaum.

Pettingale, K. W., Morris, T., Greer, S., & Haybittle, J. L. (1985). Mental attitudes to cancer: An additional prognostic factor. *Lancet,* p. 750.

Pettit, G. S., & Dodge, K. A. (2003). Violent children, bridging development, intervention and public policy. *Developmental Psychology: Special issue: Violent children, 39,* 187–188.

Pettito, L. A. (1993). On the ontogenetic requirements for early language acquisition. In B. de Boysson-Bardies, S. de Schonen, P. W. Jusczyk, P. McNeilage, & J. Morton (Eds.), *Developmental neurocognition: Speech and face processing in the first year of life. NATO ASI series D: Behavioural and social sciences,* Vol. 69. Dordrecht, Netherlands: Kluwer Academic.

Pettito, L. A., & Marentette, P. F. (1991, March 22). Babbling in the manual mode: Evidence for the ontogeny of language. *Science, 251,* 1493–1496.

Petty, R. E., Cacioppo, J. T., Strathman, A. J., & Priester, J. R. (1994). To think or not to think: Exploring two routes to persuasion. In S. Savitt & T. C. Brock (Eds.), *Persuasion: Psychological insights and perspectives.* Boston: Allyn & Bacon.

Petty, R. E., Wheeler, S. C., & Tormala, Z. L. (2003). Persuasion and attitude change. In T. Millon & M. J. Lerner (Eds.), *Handbook of psychology: Personality and social psychology,* Vol. 5. New York: Wiley.

Pezdek, K., & Taylor, J. (2002). Memory for traumatic events in children and adults. In M. L. Eisen (Ed.), *Memory and suggestibility in the forensic interview: Personality and clinical psychology series,* pp. 165–183. Mahwah, NJ: Erlbaum.

Phillips, E. L., Greydanus, D. E., Pratt, H. D., & Patel, D. R. (2003). Treatment of bulimia nervosa: Psychological and psychopharmacologic considerations. *Journal of Adolescent Research: Special Issue: Eating disorders in adolescents, 18,* 261–279.

Phinney, J. S. (1996). When we talk about American ethnic groups, what do we mean? *American Psychologist, 51,* 918–927.

Piaget, J. (1970). Piaget's theory. In P. H. Mussen (Ed.), *Carmichael's manual of child psychology* (3rd ed., Vol. I). New York: Wiley.

Piaget, J., & Inhelder, B. (1958). *The growth of logical thinking from childhood to adolescence* (A. Parsons & S. Seagrin, Trans.). New York: Basic Books.

Piasecki, T. M., Kenford, S. L., Smith, S. S., Fiore, M. C., & Baker, T. B. (1997). Listening to nicotine: Negative affect and the smoking withdrawal conundrum. *Psychological Science, 8,* 184–189.

Picchioni, D., Goeltzenleucher, B., Green, D. N., Convento, M. J., Crittenden, R., Hallgren, M., & Hick, R. A. (2002). Nightmares as a coping mechanism for stress. *Dreaming: Journal of the Association for the Study of Dreams, 12,* 155–169.

Pich, E. M., Pagliusi, S. R., Tessari, M., Talabot-Ayer, D., Hooft van Huijsduijnen, R., & Chiamulera, C. (1997, January 3). Common neural substrates for the addictive properties of nicotine and cocaine. *Science, 275,* 83–86.

Piechowski, M. M. (2003). From William James to Maslow and Dabrowski: Excitability of character and self-actualization. In D. Ambrose, L. M. Cohen, et al. (Eds.), *Creative intelligence: Toward theoretic integration: Perspectives on creativity,* pp. 283–322. Cresskill, NJ: Hampton Press.

Pihlgren, E. M., Gidycz, C. A., & Lynn, S. J. (1993). Impact of adulthood and adolescent rape experiences on subsequent sexual fantasies. *Imagination, Cognition and Personality, 12,* 321–339.

Piliavin, J. A., & Piliavin, I. M. (1972). Effect of blood on reactions to a victim. *Journal of Personality and Social Psychology, 23,* 353–362.

Pillard, R. C. (1996). Homosexuality from a familial and genetic perspective. In R. P. Cabaj & T. S. Stein (Eds.), *Textbook of homosexuality and mental health.* Washington, DC: American Psychiatric Press.

Pincus, T., & Morley, S. (2001). Cognitive-processing bias in chronic pain: A review and integration. *Psychological Bulletin, 127,* 599–617.

Pinel, J. P. J., Assanand, S., & Lehman, D. R. (2000). Hunger, eating and ill health. *American Psychologist, 55,* 1105–1116.

Pinker, S. (1994). *The language instinct.* New York: William Morrow.

Pinker, S. (2002). *The Blank Slate: The Modern Denial of Human Nature.* New York: Viking.

Pinkerton, S. D., Bogart, L. M., Cecil, H., & Abramson, P. R. (2002). Factors associated with masturbation in a collegiate sample. *Journal of Psychology and Human Sexuality, 14,* 103–121.

Pinkerton, S. D., Cecil, H., Bogart, L. M., & Abramson, P. R. (2003). The pleasures of sex: An empirical investigation. *Cognition and Emotion, 17,* 341–353.

Pi-Sunyer, X. (2003). A clinical view of the obesity problem. *Science, 299,* 859–860.

Plomin, R. (2003). General cognitive ability. In R. Pomin, J. C. DeFries, et al. (Eds.), *Behavioral genetics in the postgenomic era.* Washington, DC: American Psychological Association.

Plomin, R., & Caspi, R. (1999). Behavioral genetics and personality. In L. A. Pervin & O. P. John (eds.), *Handbook of personality: Theory and research.* (2nd ed.). New York: Guilford.

Plomin, R., & McClearn, G. E. (Eds.) (1993). *Nature, nurture and psychology.* Washington, DC: American Psychological Association.

Plomin, R., & McGuffin, P. (2003). Psychopathology in the postgenomic era. *Annual Review of Psychology, 54,* 205–228.

Plomin, R., & Neiderhiser, J. M. (1992). Genetics and experience. *Current Directions in Psychological Science, 1,* 160–163.

Plomin, R., & Petrill, S. A. (1997). Genetics and intelligence: What's new? *Intelligence, 24,* 53–77.

Plomin, R., & Walker, S. O. (2003). Genetics and educational psychology. *British Journal of Educational Psychology, 73,* 3–14.

Plomin, R., DeFries, J. C., Craig, I. W., & McGuffin, P. (2003). *Behavioral genetics in the postgenomic era.* Washington, DC: American Psychological Association.

Plous, S. (1996a). Attitudes toward the use of animals in psychological research and education: Results from a national survey of psychologists. *American Psychologist, 51,* 1167–1180.

Plous, S. (1996b). Attitudes toward the use of animals in psychological research and education: Results from a national survey of psychology majors. *Psychological Science, 7,* 352–358.

Plous, S., & Herzog, H. A. (2000, October 27). Poll shows researchers favor lab animal protection. *Science, 290,* 711.

Plutchik, R. (1980). *Emotion, a psychorevolutionary synthesis.* New York: Harper & Row.

Pogarsky, G., & Piquero, A. R. (2003). Can punishment encourage offending? Investigating the "resetting" effect. *Journal of Research in Crime and Delinquency, 40*, 95–120.

Polivy, J., & Herman, C. P. (1991). Good and bad dieters: Self-perception and reaction to a dietary challenge. *International Journal of Eating Disorders, 10*, 91–99.

Polivy, J., & Herman, C. P. (2002). Causes of eating disorders. *Annual Review of Psychology, 53*, 187–213.

Polk, N. (1997, March 30). The trouble with school testing systems. *The New York Times*, p. CN3.

Pollack, A. (2000, May 30). Neural cells, grown in labs, raise hopes on brain disease. *The New York Times*, pp. D1, D6.

Pollack, M. H., & Marzol, P. C. (2000). Panic: Course, complications and treatment of panic disorder. *Journal of Psychopharmacology, 14*, S25–S30.

Polyakov, A., & Pratt, H. (2003). Electrophysiologic correlates of direction and elevation cures for sound localization in the human brainstem. *International Journal of Audiology, 42*, 140–151.

Pomerlau, O. F. (1995). Individual differences in sensitivity to nicotine: Implications of genetic research on nicotine dependence. [Special issue: Genetic, environmental, and situational factors mediating the effects of nicotine.] *Behavior Genetics, 25*, 161–177.

Pomponio, A. T. (2002). *Psychological consequences of terrorism*. New York: Wiley.

Poniewozik, James (2002, June 17). Hollywood, the mob and John Gotti. *Time*, p. 37.

Ponterotto, J. G., Gretchen, D., Chauhan, R. V. (2001). Cultural identity and multicultural assessment: Quantitative and qualitative tools for the clinician. In L. A. Suzuki, & J. G. Ponterotto (Eds.), *Handbook of multicultural assessment: Clinical, psychological, and educational applications* (2nd ed.). San Francisco: Jossey-Bass/Pfeiffer.

Porkka-Heiskanen, T., Strecker, R. E., Thakkar, M., Bjorkum, A. A., Greene, R. W., & McCarley, R. W. (1997, May 23). Adensosine: A mediator of the sleep-inducing effects of prolonged wakefulness. *Science, 276*, 1265–1268.

Porte, H. S., & Hobson, J. A. (1996). Physical motion in dreams: One measure of three theories. *Journal of Abnormal Psychology, 105*, 329–335.

Porter, C. L., & Hsu, H. C. (2003). First-time mothers' perceptions of efficacy during the transition to motherhood: Links to infant temperament. *Journal of Family Psychology, 17*, 54–64.

Porter, R. H., Cernich, J. M., & McLaughlin, F. J. (1983). Maternal recognition of neonates through olfactory cues. *Physiology and Behavior, 30*, 151–154.

Porter, S., & Birt, A. R. (2001). Is traumatic memory special? A comparison of traumatic memory characteristics with memory for other emotional life experiences. *Applied Cognitive Psychology, 15*, S101–S117.

Posner, M. I., & DiGirolamo, G. J. (2000). Cognitive neuroscience: Origins and promise. *Psychological Bulletin, 126*, 873–889.

Potheraju, A., & Soper, B. (1995). A comparison of self-reported dream themes for high school and college students. *College Student Journal, 29*, 417–420.

Powell, L. H., Shaker, L. A., & Jones, B. A. (1993). Psychosocial predictors of mortality in 83 women with premature acute myocardial infarction. *Psychosomatic Medicine, 55*, 426–433.

Praisner, C. L. (2003). Attitudes of elementary school principals toward the inclusion of students with disabilities. *Exceptional Children, 69*, 135–145.

Pratt, H. D., Phillips, E. L., Greydanus, D. E., & Patel, D. R. (2003). Eating disorders in the adolescent population: Future directions. *Journal of Adolescent Research: Special issue: Eating disorders in adolescents, 18*, 297–317.

Pratt, S. I., & Moreland, K. L. (1996). Introduction to treatment outcome: Historical perspectives and current issues. In S. I. Pfeiffer (Ed.), *Outcome assessment in residential treatment*. New York: Haworth Press.

Pressley, M. (1987). Are keyword method effects limited to slow presentation rates? An empirically based reply to Hall and Fuson (1986). *Journal of Educational Psychology, 79*, 333–335.

Pressman, M. R., & Orr, W. C. (1997). *Understanding sleep: The evaluation and treatment of sleep disorders*. Washington, DC: American Psychological Association.

Price, D. D. (2000, June 9). Psychological and neural mechanisms of the affective dimension of pain. *Science, 288*, 1769–1772.

Prieto, S. L., Cole, D. A., & Tageson, C. W. (1992). Depressive self-schemas in clinic and nonclinic children. *Cognitive Therapy and Research, 16*, 521–534.

Prince, R. J., & Guastello, S. J. (1990). The Barnum effect in a computerized Rorschach interpretation system. *Journal of Personality, 124*, 217–222.

Prislin, R., Brewer, M., & Wilson, D. J. (2002). Changing majority and minority positions within a group versus an aggregate. *Personality and Social Psychology Bulletin, 28*, 650–647.

Prokasy, W. F., Jr., & Hall, J. F. (1963). Primary stimulus generalization. *Psychological Review, 70*, 310–322.

Pulvirenti, L., & Koob, G. F. (1994). Lisuride reduces intravenous cocaine self-administration in rats. *Pharmacology, Biochemistry and Behavior, 47*, 819–822.

Purves, D., Augustine, G. J., Fitzpatrick, D., Katz, L. C., LaMantia, A., & McNamara, J. O. (Eds.) (1997). *Neuroscience*. Sunderland, MA: Sinauer.

Putnam, F. W. (1995a). Development of dissociative disorders. In D. Cicchetti & D. J. Cohen (Eds.), *Developmental psychopathology, Vol. 2: Risk, disorder, and adaptation*. Wiley series on personality processes. New York: Wiley.

Putnam, F. W. (1995b). Traumatic stress and pathological dissociation. In G. P. Chrousos, R. McCarty, K. Pacak, G. Cizza, E. Sternberg, P. W. Gold, & R. Kvetnansky (Eds.), *Stress: Basic mechanisms and clinical implications. Annals of the New York Academy of Sciences*, Vol. 771. New York: New York Academy of Sciences.

Quadros, P. S., Goldstein, A. Y., De Vries, G. J., & Wagner, C. K (2000). Regulation of sex differences in progesterone receptor expression in the medial preoptic nucleus of postnatal rats. *Journal of Neuroendocrinology, 14*, 761–767.

Rabasca, L. (2000, April). Taking telehealth to the next step. *APA Monitor, 31*, 4.

Rachman, S., & deSilva, P. (1996). *Panic disorder*. Oxford, England: Oxford University Press.

Rakoff, V. M. (1995). Trauma and adolescent rites of initiation. In R. C. Marohn & S. C. Feinstein (Eds.), *Adolescent psychiatry: Developmental and clinical studies*, Vol. 20. Annals of the American Society for Adolescent Psychiatry. Hillsdale, NJ: Analytic Press.

Ramachandran, V. S. (1995). Filling in gaps in logic: Reply to Durgin et al. *Perception, 24*, 841–845.

Rampon, C., Jiang, C. H., Dong, H., Tang, Y., Lockhart, D. J., Schultaz, P. G., et al. (2000). Effects of environmental enrichment on gene expression in the brain. *Proceedings of the National Academy of Sciences, 97*, 12880–12884.

Ramsay, M. C., Reynolds, C. R., & Kamphaus, R. W. (2002). *Essentials of behavioral assessment*. New York: Wiley.

Raskin, N. J., & Rogers, C. R. (1989). Person-centered therapy. In R. J. Corsini, & D. Wedding (Eds.), *Current psychotherapies* (4th ed.). Itasca, IL: F. E. Peacock.

Ratcliff, R., & McKoon, G. (1989). Memory models, text processing, and cue-dependent retrieval. In H. L. Roediger III & F. I. M. Craik (Eds.), *Varieties of memory and consciousness: Essays in honour of Endel Tulving*. Hillsdale, NJ: Erlbaum.

Rauscher, F. H. (2002). Mozart and the mind: Factual and fictional effects of musical enrichment. In J. Aronson (Ed.), *Improving academic achievement: Impact of psychological factors on education*, pp. 267–278. San Diego: Academic Press.

Ravindran, A. V., Matheson, K., Griffiths, J., Merali, Z., & Anisman, H. (2002). Stress, coping, uplifts, and quality of life in subtypes of depression: A conceptual framework and emerging data. *Journal of Affective Disorders, 71*, 121–130.

Rawsthorne, L. J., & Elliot, A. J. (1999). Achievement goals and intrinsic motivation: A meta-analytic review. *Personality and Social Psychology Review, 3*, 326–344.

Ray, W. J. (2000). *Methods: Toward a science of behavior and experience* (6th ed.). Belmont, CA: Wadsworth.

Raymond, J. (2003, March 24.). Now for a breath of fresh air. *Newsweek*, p. 67.

Redding, G. M. (2002). A test of size-scaling and relative-size hypotheses for the moon illusion. *Perception and Psychophysics, 64,* 1281–1289.

Redding, G. M., & Hawley, E. (1993). Length illusion in fractional Muller-Lyer stimuli: An object-perception approach. *Perception, 22,* 819–828.

Reed, S. K. (1996). *Cognition: Theory and applications* (4th ed.). Pacific Grove, CA: Brooks/Cole.

Reese, R. J., Conoley, C. W., & Brossart, D. F. (2002). Effectiveness of telephone counseling: A field-based investigation. *Journal of Counseling Psychology, 49,* 233–242.

Reichman, W. E., Rabins, P. V. (1996). Schizophrenia and other psychotic disorders. In W. E. Reichman, & P. R. Katz, (Eds.), *Psychiatric care in the nursing home.* New York: Oxford University Press.

Reif, A., & Lesch, K-P. (2003). Toward a molecular architecture of personality. *Behavioural Brain Research, 139,* 1–20.

Reijonen, J. H., Pratt, H. D., Patel, D. R., & Greydanus, D. E. (2003). Eating disorders in the adolescent population: An overview. *Journal of Adolescent Research: Special Issue: Eating disorders in adolescents, 18,* 209–222.

Reisberg, D. (1997). *Cognition: Exploring the science of the mind.* New York: W. W. Norton.

Reitman, J. S. (1965). *Cognition and thought.* New York: Wiley.

Relier, J. P. (2001). Influence of maternal stress on fetal behavior and brain development. *Biology of the Neonate, 79,* 168–171.

Rescorla, R. A. (1988). Pavlovian conditioning: It's not what you think it is. *American Psychologist, 43,* 151–160.

Reyna, V. F. (1997). Conceptions of memory development with implications for reasoning and decision making. In R. Vasta (Ed.), *Annals of child development: A research annual,* Vol. 12, pp. 87–118. London: Jessica Kingsley.

Reynolds, C. R., & Ramsay, M. C. (2003). Bias in psychological assessment: An empirical review and recommendations. In J. R. Graham & J. A. Naglieri (Eds.), *Handbook of psychology: Assessment psychology,* Vol. 10 pp. 67–93. New York: Wiley.

Reynolds, R. I., & Takooshian, H. (1988, January). Where were you August 8, 1985? *Bulletin of the Psychonomic Society, 26,* 23–25.

Rhue, J. W., Lynn, S. J., & Kirsch, I. (Eds.). (1993). *Handbook of clinical hypnosis.* Washington, DC: American Psychological Association.

Ricciuti, H. N. (1993). Nutrition and mental development. *Current Directions in Psychological Science, 2,* 43–46.

Rice, G., Anderson, C., Risch, N., & Ebers, G. (1999, April 23). Male homosexuality: Absence of linkage to microsatellite markers at Xq28. *Science, 284,* 665–667.

Rice, V. H. (Ed.). (2000). *Handbook of stress, coping and health.* Thousand Oaks, CA: Sage.

Richardson, B. (2002, September 30). Light-bulb moments. *The Wall Street Journal,* p. R7.

Riedel, G., Platt, B., & Micheau, J. (2003). Glutamate receptor function in learning and memory. *Behavioural Brain Research, 140,* 1–47.

Rieder, R. O., Kaufmann, C. A., & Knowles, J. A. (1996). Genetics. In R. E. Hales & S. C. Yudofsky (Eds.), *The American Psychiatric Press synopsis of psychiatry.* Washington, DC: American Psychiatric Press.

Rierdan, J. (1996). *Adolescent suicide: One response to adversity.* In R. S. Feldman (Ed.)., *The psychology of adversity.* Amherst, MA: University of Massachusetts Press.

Ringold, D. J. (1996). Social criticisms of target marketing: Process or product? In R. P. Hill (Ed.), *Marketing and consumer research in the public interest.* Thousand Oaks, CA: Sage.

Riniolo, T. C., Koledin, M., Drakulic, G. M., & Payne, R. A. (2003). An archival study of eyewitness memory of the Titanic's final plunge. *Journal of General Psychology, 130,* 89–95.

Rinn, W. E. (1984). The neuropsychology of facial expression: A review of neurological and psychological mechanisms for producing facial expressions. *Psychological Bulletin, 95,* 52–77.

Rinn, W. E. (1991). Neuropsychology of facial expression. In R. S. Feldman & B. Rimé (Eds.), *Fundamentals of nonverbal behavior.* Cambridge, England: Cambridge University Press.

Rioult-Pedotti, M-S., Friedman, D., & Donoghue, J. P. (2000, October 20). Learning-induced LTP in neocortex. *Science, 290,* 533–536.

Risley, R. C., & Rescorla, R. A. (1972). Associations in higher order conditioning and sensory pre-conditioning. *Journal of Comparative and Physiological Psychology, 81,* 1–11.

Rizza, M. G., & Morrison, W. F. (2003). Uncovering stereotypes and identifying characteristics of gifted students and students with emotional/behavioral disabilities. *Roeper Review, 25,* 73–77.

Robbins, T. W. (1988). Arresting memory decline. *Nature, 336,* 207–208.

Robert-McComb, J. J. (2001). Physiology of stress. In J. J. Robert-McComb (Ed.), *Eating disorders in women and children: Prevention, stress management, and treatment,* pp. 119–146. Boca Raton, FL: CRC Press.

Roberts, S. M. (1995). Applicability of the goodness-of-fit hypothesis to coping with daily hassles. *Psychological Reports, 77,* 943–954.

Robertson, T. (2000, January 21.) The bystanders' dilemma: When to stand back, when to assist. *Boston Globe,* pp. A1, A30.

Robins, R. W., Gosling, S. D., & Craik, K. H. (1999). An empirical analysis of trends in psychology. *American Psychologist, 54,* 117–128.

Robinson, N. M., Zigler, E., & Gallagher, J. J. (2000). Two tails of the normal curve: Similarities and differences in the study of mental retardation and giftedness. *American Psychologist, 55,* 1413–1424.

Roccas, S., Sagiv, L., Schwartz, S. H., & Knafo, A. (2002). The Big Five personality factors and personal values. *Personality and Social Psychology Bulletin, 28,* 789–801.

Rock, A. (1999, January). Quitting time for smokers. *Money,* pp. 139–141.

Roediger, H. L., III, & McDermott, K. B. (2000). Tricks of memory. *Current Directions in Psychological Science, 9,* 123–127.

Roehricht, F., & Priebe, S. (2002). Do cenesthesias and body image aberration characterize a subgroup in schizophrenia? *Acta Psychiatrica Scandinavica, 105,* 276–282.

Roffwarg, H. P., Munzio, J. N., & Dement, W. C. (1996). Ontogenic development of the human sleep-dream cycle. *Science, 152,* 604–619.

Rogers, C. R. (1951). *Client-centered therapy.* Boston: Houghton-Mifflin.

Rogers, C. R. (1971). A theory of personality. In S. Maddi (Ed.), *Perspectives on personality.* Boston: Little, Brown.

Rogers, C. R. (1980). *A way of being.* Boston: Houghton Mifflin.

Rogers, M. (1988, February 15). The return of 3-D movies — on TV. *Newsweek,* pp. 60–62.

Rogers, P. (2002, August 2). Too much, too soon. *People,* pp. 79–82.

Rogers, P., & Eftimiades, M. (1995, July 24). *People Weekly,* pp. 42–43.

Rogler, L. H. (1999). Methodological sources of cultural insensitivity in mental health research. *American Psychologist, 54,* 424–433.

Roizen, N. J., & Patterson, D. (2003). Down's syndrome. *Lancet, 361,* 1281–1289.

Rolland, J. S., & Walsh, F. (1996). Family therapy: Systems approaches to assessment and treatment. In R. E. Hales & S. C. Yudofsky (Eds.), *The American Psychiatric Press synopsis of psychiatry.* Washington, DC: American Psychiatric Press.

Romano, E., Tremblay, R. E, Vitaro, E., Zoccolillo, M., & Pagani, L. (2001.) Prevalence of psychiatric diagnoses and the role of perceived impairment: Findings from an adolescent community sample. *Journal of Child Psychology and Psychiatry and Allied Disciplines, 42,* 451–461.

Rorschach, H. (1924). *Psychodiagnosis: A diagnostic test based on perception.* New York: Grune & Stratton.

Rose, N., & Blackmore, S. (2002). Horses for courses: Tests of a psychic claimant. *Journal of the Society for Psychical Research, 66,* 29–40.

Rose, S. A., Feldman, J. F., & Jankowski, J. J. (2002). Processing speed in the 1st year of life: A longitudinal study of preterm and full-term infants. *Developmental Psychology, 38,* 895–902.

Rosen, D. (1999, May 10). Dieting disorder: A physician's perspective. *Harvard Mental Health Newsletter,* p. 4.

Rosenberg, D., & Bai, M. (1997, October 13). Drinking and dying. *Newsweek,* p. 69.

Rosenberg, L., & Park, S. (2002). Verbal and spatial functions across the menstrual cycle in healthy young women. *Psychoneuroendocrinology, 27,* 834–841.

Rosenbloom, T., & Wolf, Y. (2002). Sensation seeking and detection of risky road signals: A developmental perspective. *Accident Analysis and Prevention, 34*, 569–580.

Rosenhan, D. L. (1973). On being sane in insane places. *Science, 179*, 250–258.

Rosenman, R. H. (1990). Type A behavior pattern: A personal overview. *Journal of Social Behavior and Personality, 5*, 1–24.

Rosenstein, D. S., & Horowitz, H. A. (1996). Adolescent attachment and psychopathology. *Journal of Consulting and Clinical Psychology, 64*, 244–253.

Rosenthal, E. (1996, January 10). From lives begun in a lab, brave new joy. *The New York Times*, pp. A1, B8.

Rosenthal, J. (1997, March 9). The age boom. *The New York Times Magazine*, pp. 39–43.

Rosenthal, R. (2002). Covert communication in classrooms, clinics, courtrooms and cubicles. *American Psychologist, 57*, 838–849.

Rosner, H. (2001, April 30). The science of O. *New York*, pp. 25–31.

Rosnow, R. L., & Rosenthal, R. (1997). *Turn away influences that undermine scientific experiments*. New York: Freeman.

Ross, C. A. (1996). *Dissociative identity disorder: Diagnosis, clinical features, and treatment of multiple personality*. Somerset, NJ: Wiley.

Ross, E. (2000, October). New approaches to treating a perplexing pain disorder. *New England Journal of Medicine Health News*. pp. 1–2.

Ross, H. E. (2000). Sensation and perception. In D. S. Gupta, S. Deepa, & R. M. Gupta, (Eds.), et al. *Psychology for psychiatrists*. (pp. 20–40). London: Whurr Publishers.

Ross, L., & Nisbett, R. E. (1991). *The person and the situation*. New York: McGraw-Hill.

Ross, M., & Newby, I. R. (1996). Distinguishing memory from fantasy. *Psychological Inquiry, 7*, 173–177.

Rossiter, J. R., Silberstein, R. B., Harris, P. G., & Nield, G. (2001). Brain-imaging detection of visual scene encoding in long-term memory for TV commercials. *Journal of Advertising Research, 41*, 13–21.

Roter, D. L., Hall, J. A., & Aoki, Y. (2002). Physician gender effects in medical communication: A meta-analytic review *Journal of the American Medical Association, 288*, 756–764.

Roth, A., & Fonagy, P. (1996). *What works for whom? A critical review of psychotherapy research*. New York: Guilford Press.

Rothblum, E. D. (1990). Women and weight: Fad and fiction. *Journal of Psychology, 124*, 5–24.

Rothman, A. J., & Salovey, P. (1997). Shaping perceptions to motivate healthy behavior: The role of message framing. *Psychological Bulletin, 121*, 3–19.

Roughton, R. E. (2002). Rethinking homosexuality: What it teaches us about psychoanalysis. *Journal of the American Psychoanalytic Association, 50*, 733–763.

Roush, W. (1995, September 1). Can "resetting" hormonal rhythms treat illness? *Science, 269*, 1220–1221.

Routtenberg, A., & Lindy, J. (1965). Effects of the availability of rewarding septal and hypothalamic stimulation on bar pressing for food under conditions of deprivation. *Journal of Comparative and Physiological Psychology, 60*, 158–161.

Rovee-Collier, C. (1993). The capacity for long-term memory in infancy. *Current Directions in Psychological Science, 2*, 130–135.

Rowe, J. B., Toni, I., Josephs, O., Frackowiak, R. S. J., & Passingham, R. E. (2000, June 2). The prefrontal cortex: Response selection or maintenance within working memory? *Science, 288*, 1656–1660.

Rowley, S. J., Sellers, R. M., Chavous, T. M., & Smith, M. A. (1998). The relationship between racial identity and self-esteem in African American college and high school students. *Journal of Personality and Social Psychology, 74*, 715–724.

Royzman, E. B., Cassidy, K. W., & Baron, J. (2003). "I know, you know": Epistemic egocentrism in children and adults. *Review of General Psychology, 7*, 38–65.

Rozin, P. (1990). The importance of social factors in understanding the acquisition of food habits. In E. D. Capaldi & T. L. Powley (Eds.), *Taste, experience, and feeding*. Washington, DC: American Psychological Association.

Rubenstein, C. (1982, July). Psychology's fruit flies. *Psychology Today*, pp. 83–84.

Rubin, D. C. (1985, September). The subtle deceiver: Recalling our past. *Psychology Today*, pp. 39–46.

Rubin, D. C. (1995). *Memory in oral traditions*. New York: Oxford University Press.

Rubin, D. C. (1999). *Remembering our past: Studies in autobiographical memory*. New York: Cambridge University Press.

Ruby, C. L. (2002). Are terrorists mentally deranged? *Analyses of Social Issues and Public Policy, 2*, 15–26.

Rudman, L. A., & Glick, P. (2001). Prescriptive gender stereotypes and backlash toward agentic women. *Journal of Social Issues, 57*, 743–762.

Runco, M. A., & Sakamoto, S. O. (1993). Reaching creatively gifted students through their learning styles. In R. M. Milgram, R. S. Dunn, & G. E. Price (Eds.), *Teaching and counseling gifted and talented adolescents: An international learning style perspective*. Westport, CT: Praeger/Greenwood.

Ruscher, J. B., Fiske, S. T. & Schnake, S. B. (2000). The motivated tactician's juggling act: Compatible vs. incompatible impression goals. *British Journal of Social Psychology, 39*, 241–256.

Russell, J. A. (1991). Culture and the categorization of emotion. *Psychological Bulletin, 110*, 426–450.

Russell, J. A., & Sato, K. (1995). Comparing emotion words between languages. *Journal of Cross Cultural Psychology, 26*, 384–391.

Russo, N. (1981). In L. T. Benjamin, Jr., & K. D. Lowman (Eds.), *Activities handbook for the teaching of psychology*. Washington, DC: American Psychological Association.

Russo, R., & Parkin, A. J. (1993). Age differences in implicit memory: More apparent than real. *Memory & Cognition, 21*, 73–80.

Rutter, M. (2002). Nature, nurture, and development: From evangelism through science toward policy and practice. *Child Development, 73*, 1–21.

Ryan, M. (1991, January 27). *Parade*, p. 14.

Ryan, R. M. & Deci, E. L. (2000). Intrinsic and extrinsic motivations: Classic definitions and new directions. *Contemporary Educational Psychology, 25*, 54–67.

Rychlak, J. (1997). *In defense of human consciousness*. Washington, DC: American Psychological Association.

Ryff, C. D., & Singer, B. (2003). Flourishing under fire: Resilience as a prototype of challenged thriving. In C. L. Keyes & J. Haidt (Eds.). *Flourishing: Positive psychology and the life well-lived*, pp. 15–36. Washington, DC: American Psychological Association.

Rymer, J., Wilson, R., & Ballard, K. (2003). Making decisions about hormone replacement therapy. *British Medical Journal, 326*, 322–326.

Rymer, R. (1994). *Genie: A scientific tragedy*. New York: Penguin

Saab, C. Y., & Willis, W. D. (2003). The cerebellum: Organization, functions and its role in nociception. *Brain Research Reviews, 42*, 85–95.

Saad, L. (2002, May 16). "Cloning" humans is a turn off to most Americans. New York: Gallup News Service.

Saariluoma, P., & Laine, T. (2001). Novice construction of chess memory. *Scandinavian Journal of Psychology, 42*, 137–146.

Sackeim, H. A., Haskett, R. F., Mulsant, B. H., Thase, M. E., Mann, J. J., Pettinati, H. M., Greenberg, R. M., Crowe, R. R., Cooper, T. B., & Prudic, J. (2001). Continuation pharmacotherapy in the prevention of relapse following electroconvulsive therapy: A randomized controlled trial. *Journal of the American Medical Association, 285*, 1299–1307.

Sackheim, H. A., Luber, B., Katzman, G. P., et al. (1996, September). The effects of electroconvulsive therapy on quantitative electroencephalograms. *Archives of General Psychiatry, 53*, 814–824.

Sacks, O. (2003, July 28). The mind's eye. *New Yorker*, pp. 48–59.

Sadker, M., & Sadker, D. (1994). *Failing at fairness: How America's schools cheat girls*. New York: Scribners.

Saffran, E. M., & Schwartz, M. F. (2003). Language. In M. Gallagher & R. J. Nelson (Eds.), *Handbook of psychology: Biological psychology*, Vol. 3, pp. 595–636. New York: Wiley.

Sagi, A., Koren-Karie, N., Gini, M., Ziv, Y., & Joels, T. (2002). Shedding further light on the effects of various types and quality of early child care on infant-mother attachment relationship: The Haifa Study of Early Child Care. *Child Development, 73*, 1166–1186.

Sales, B. D., & Folkman, S. (Eds.) (2000). *Ethics in research with human participants*. Washington, DC: American Psychological Association.

Salovey, P., Rothman, A. J., Detweiler, J. B., & Steward, W. T. (2000). Emotional states and physical health. *American Psychologist, 55*, 110–121.

Salthouse, T. A. (1996, July). The processing-speed theory of adult age differences in cognition. *Psychological Review, 103*, 403–428.

Samantaray, S. K., Srivastava, M., & Mishra, P. K. (2002). Fostering self concept and self actualization as bases for empowering women in national development: A challenge for the new millennium. *Social Science International, 18*, 58–63.

Sams, M. Hari, R., Rif, J., & Knuutila, J. (1993). The human auditory memory trace persists about 10 sec: Neuromagnetic evidence. *Journal of Cognitive Neuroscience, 5*, 363–370.

Samuda, R. J. (1998). *Psychological testing of American minorities: Issues and consequences*. Thousand Oaks, CA: Sage.

Sandoval, J., Frisby, C. L., Geisinger, K. F., Scheuneman, J. D., & Grenier, J. R. (Eds.). (1998). *Test interpretation and diversity: Achieving equity in assessment*. Washington, DC: American Psychological Association.

Sansone, C., & Haracklewicz, J. M. (Eds.). (2000). *Intrinsic and extrinsic motivation*. Orlando, FL: Academic Press.

Sapolsky, R. M. (1996, August 9). Why stress is bad for your brain. *Science, 273*, 749–750.

Saudino, K. J., & Plomin, R. (1996). Personality and behavioral genetics: Where have we been and where are we going? *Journal of Research in Personality, 30*, 335–347.

Savage-Rumbaugh, E. S., Murphy, J., Sevcik, R. A., Williams, S., Brakke, K., & Rumbaugh, D. M. (1993). Language comprehension in ape and child. *Monographs of the Society for Research in Child Development, 58*, (3, 4).

Savage-Rumbaugh, S., & Brakke, K. E. (1996). Animal language: Methodological and interpretive issues. In M. Bekoff & D. Jamieson (Eds.), *Readings in animal cognition*. Cambridge, MA: MIT Press.

Sawa, A., & Snyder, S. H. (2002, April 26). Schizophrenia: Diverse approaches to a complex disease. *Science, 296*, 692–695.

Sayette, M. A. (1993). An appraisal disruption model of alcohol's effects on stress responses in social drinkers. *Psychological Bulletin, 114*, 459–476.

Saywitz, K., & Goodman, G. (1990). Unpublished study reported in Goleman, D. (1990, November 6). Doubts rise on children as witnesses. *The New York Times*, pp. C-1, C-6.

Scarr, S. (1992). Developmental theories for the 1990s: Development and individual differences. Biennial Meetings of the Society for Research in Child Development Presidential Address (1991, Seattle, Washington). *Child Development, 63*, 1–19.

Scarr, S. (1993). Genes, experience, and development. In D. Magnusson, P. Jules, &

M. Casaer (Eds.), *Longitudinal research on individual development: Present status and future perspectives. European network on longitudinal studies on individual development, 8*. Cambridge, England: Cambridge University Press.

Scarr, S., & Weinberg, R. A. (1976). I.Q. test performance of black children adopted by white families. *American Psychologist, 31*, 726–739.

Schaaf, J. M., Alexander, K. W., Goodman, G. S., Ghetti, S., Edelstein, R. S., & Castelli, P. (2002). Children's eyewitness memory: True disclosures and false reports. In B. L. Bottoms, M. Bull Kovera, et al. (Eds.), *Children, social science, and the law*, pp. 342–377. New York: Cambridge University Press.

Schab, F. R. (1991). Odor memory: Taking stock. *Psychological Bulletin, 109*, 242–251.

Schab, F. R., & Crowder, R. G. (Eds.). (1995). *Memory for odors*. Mahwah, NJ: Erlbaum.

Schachter, S. (1971). Some extraordinary facts about obese humans and rats. *American Psychologist, 26*, 129–144.

Schachter, S., & Singer, J. E. (1962). Cognitive, social, and physiological determinants of emotional state. *Psychological Review, 69*, 379–399.

Schacter, D. L. (1994, May). Harvard conference on false memories. Cambridge, MA.

Schacter, D. L. (1995). Implicit memory: A new frontier for cognitive neuroscience. In M. S. Gazzaniga (Ed.), *The cognitive neurosciences*. Cambridge, MA: MIT Press.

Schacter, D. L. (1998, April 3). Memory and awareness. *Science, 280*, 59–60.

Schacter, D. L., Chiu, C-Y. P., & Ochsner, K. N. (1993). Implicit memory: A selective review. *Annual Review of Neuroscience, 16*, 159–182.

Schacter, D. L., Wagner, A. D., & Buckner, R. L. (2000). Memory systems of 1999. In E. Tulving, F. I. Craik, I. M. Fergus, et al. (Eds.), *The Oxford handbook of memory*. New York: Oxford University Press.

Schaefer, R. T. (2000). *Sociology: A brief introduction* (3rd ed.). Boston: McGraw-Hill.

Schafer, M., & Crichlow, S. (1996). Antecedents of groupthink: A quantitative study. *Journal of Conflict Resolution, 40*, 415–435.

Schaie, K. W. (1991). Developmental designs revisited. In S. H. Cohen & H. W. Reese (Eds.), *Life-span developmental psychology: Methodological innovations*. Hillsdale, NJ: Erlbaum.

Schaie, K. W. (1993). The Seattle longitudinal studies of adult intelligence. *Current Directions in Psychological Science, 2*, 171–175.

Schaie, K. W. (1994). The course of adult intellectual development. *American Psychologist, 49*, 304–313.

Schaller, M., Asp, C. H., Rosell, M. C., & Heim, S. J. (1996). Training in statistical reasoning inhibits the formation of erroneous group stereotypes. *Personality and Social Psychology Bulletin, 22*, 829–844.

Schapira, A. H. V. (1999). Clinical review: Parkinson's disease. *British Medical Journal, 318*, 311–314.

Scharf, M. (1999, October 1). A new option for insomnia. *HealthNews*, p. 4.

Schatz, J., Finke, R. L., Kellett, J. M., & Kramer, J. H. (2002). Cognitive functioning in children with sickle cell disease: A meta-analysis. *Journal of Pediatric Psychology, 27*, 739–748.

Schedlowski, M. & Tewes, U. (Eds.) (1999). *Psychoneuroimmunology: An interdisciplinary introduction*. New York: Plenum.

Scheff, T. J. (1999). *Being mentally ill: A sociological theory* (3rd ed.). Hawthrone, NY: Aldine de Gruyter.

Scheier, M. F., Carver, C. S., & Bridges, M. W. (1994). Distinguishing optimism from neuroticism (and trait anxiety, self-mastery, and self-esteem): A revision of the Life Orientation Test. *Journal of Personality and Social Psychology, 67*, 1063–1078.

Schiffman, S. S., Graham, B. G., Sattely-Miller, E. A., & Zervakis, J. (2002). Taste, smell and neuropsychological performance of individuals at familial risk for Alzheimer's disease. *Neurobiology of Aging, 23*, 397–404.

Schlenger, W. E., Caddell, J. M., Ebert, L., Jordan, B. K., Rourke, K. M., Wilson, D., et al. (2002). Psychological reactions to terrorist attacks: Findings from the National Study of Americans' Reactions to September 11. *Journal of the American Medical Association, 288*, 581–588.

Schmidt, D. (1999). Stretched dream science: The essential contribution of long-term naturalistic studies. *Dreaming: Journal of the Association for the Study of Dreams, 9*, 43–69.

Schmolck, H., Buffalo, E. A., & Squire, L. R. (2000). Memory distortions develop over time: Recollections of the O. J. Simpson trial verdict after 15 and 32 months. *Psychological Science, 11*, 39–45.

Schneider, A., & Domhoff, G. W. (2002). *The quantitative study of dreams*. Retrieved December 26, 2002 from *www.dreamresearch.net/*.

Schoen, L. M. (1996). Mnemopoly: Board games and mnemonics. *Teaching of Psychology, 23*, 30–32.

Schoenpflug, U. (2003). The handbook of culture and psychology. *Journal of Cross-Cultural Psychology, 34*, 481–483.

Schofield, W., & Vaughan-Jackson, P. (1913). *What a boy should know*. New York: Cassell.

Schorr, A. (2001). Appraisal: The evolution of an idea. In K. R. Scherer, A. Schorr, et al. (Eds.), *Appraisal processes in emotion: Theory, methods, research. Series in affective science*, pp. 20–34. London: Oxford University Press.

Schretlen, D., Pearlson, G. D., Anthony, J. C., Aylward, E. H., Augustine, A. M., Davis, A., & Barta, P. (2000). Elucidating the contributions of processing speed, executive ability, and frontal lobe volume to normal age-related differences in fluid intelligence. *Journal of the International Neuropsychological Society, 6*, 52–61.

Schutt, R. K. (2001). *Investigating the social world: The process and practice of research*. Thousand Oaks, CA: Sage.

Schwartz, B. L. (2001). The relation of tip-of-the-tongue states and retrieval time. *Memory & Cognition, 29*, 117–126.

Schwartz, B. L. (2002). The phenomenology of naturally-occurring tip-of-the-tongue states: A diary study. In S. P. Shohov (Ed.), *Advances in psychology research*, Vol. 8, pp. 73–84. Huntington, NY: Nova.

Schwartz, B. L., Travis, D. M., Castro, A. M., & Smith, S. M. (2000). The phenomenology of real and illusory tip-of-the-tongue states. *Memory & Cognition, 28*, 18–27.

Schwartz, J. M., & Begley, S. (2002). *The mind and the brain: Neuroplasticity and power of mental force*. New York: ReganBooks.

Schwartz, J., & Wald, M. L. (2003). NASA's curse?: "Groupthink" is 30 years old, and still going strong. *The New York Times.*

Schwartz, S., & Maquet, P. (2002). Sleep imaging and the neuro-psychological assessment of dreams. *Trends in Cognitive Science, 6*, 23–30.

Schwarz, N., Bless, H., Strack, F., Klumpp, G., et al. (1991). Ease of retrieval as information: Another look at the availability heuristic. *Journal of Personality and Social Psychology, 61*, 195–202.

Scullin, M. H., Kanaya, T., & Ceci, S. J. (2002). Measurement of individual differences in children's suggestibility across situations. *Journal of Experimental Psychology: Applied, 8*, 233–246.

Sears, D. O. (1986). College sophomores in the laboratory: Influences of a narrow data base on social psychology's view of human nature. *Journal of Personality and Social Psychology, 51*, 515–530.

Sears, R. R. (1977). Sources of life satisfaction of the Terman gifted men. *American Psychologist, 32*, 119–128.

Sebel, P. S., Bonke, B., & Winograd, E. (Eds.). (1993). *Memory and awareness in anesthesia*. Englewood Cliffs, NJ: Prentice-Hall.

Secker-Walker, R. H., & Vacek, P. M. (2003). Relationships between cigarette smoking during pregnancy, gestational age, maternal weight gain, and infant birthweight. *Addictive Behaviors, 28*, 55–66.

Seeley, R., Stephens, T., & Tate, P. (2000). *Anatomy & Physiology*, (5th ed.), p. 384. Boston: McGraw-Hill.

Segal, N. L. (1993). Twin, sibling, and adoption methods: Tests of evolutionary hypotheses. *American Psychologist, 48*, 943–956.

Segall, M. H., Campbell, D. T., & Herskovits, M. J. (1966). *The influence of culture on visual perception*. New York: Bobbs-Merrill.

Seidenberg, M. S., & Petitto, L. A. (1987). Communication, symbolic communication, and language: Comment on Savage-Rumbaugh, McDonald, Sevcik, Hopkins, & Rupert (1986). *Journal of Experimental Psychology: General, 116*, 279–287.

Seligman, M. E. P. (1975). *Helplessness: On depression, development, and death*. San Francisco: Freeman.

Seligman, M. E. P. (1988, October). Baby boomer blues. *Psychology Today*, p. 54.

Seligman, M. E. P. (1995, December). The effectiveness of psychotherapy: The *Consumer Reports* study. *American Psychologist, 50*, 965–974.

Seligman, M. E. P. (1996, October). Science as an ally of practice. *American Psychologist, 51*, 1072–1079.

Seligmann, J. (1991, June 17). A light for poor eyes. *Newsweek*, p. 61.

Selikowitz, M. (1997). *Down syndrome: The facts.* (2nd ed.). New York: Oxford University Press.

Selkoe, D. J. (1997, January 31). Alzheimer's disease: Genotypes, phenotype, and treatments. *Science, 275*, 630–631.

Selkoe, D. J. (2002). Alzheimer's disease is a synaptic failure. *Science, 298*, 789–791.

Sells, R. (1994, August). *Homosexuality study.* Paper presented at the annual meeting of the American Statistical Assocation, Toronto.

Selsky, A. (1997, February 16). African males face circumcision rite. *The Boston Globe*, p. C7.

Seltzer, L. (1986). *Paradoxical strategies in psychotherapy*. New York: Wiley.

Selye, H. (1976). *The stress of life*. New York: McGraw-Hill.

Selye, H. (1993). History of the stress concept. In L. Goldberger & S. Breznitz (Eds.), *Handbook of stress: Theoretical and clinical aspects* (2nd ed.). New York: Free Press.

Seppa, N. (1996, May). A multicultural guide to less spanking and yelling. *APA Monitor*, p. 37.

Serpell, R. (2000). Intelligence and culture. In R. Sternberg (Ed.), *Handbook of intelligence*. Cambridge, England: Cambridge University Press.

Seventh U.S. Circuit Court of Appeals. (2001). *Chicago Firefighters Local 2, et al. v. City of Chicago, et al.* Nos. 00-1272, 00-1312, 00-1313, 00-1314, and 00-1330. Chicago, IL.

Seyfarth, R., & Cheney, D. (1996). Inside the mind of a monkey. In M. Bekoff & D. Jamieson (Eds.), *Readings in animal cognition*. Cambridge, MA: MIT Press.

Seyfarth, R. M., & Cheney, D. L. (1992, December). Meaning and mind in monkeys (vocalizations and intent). *Scientific American, 267*, 122–128.

Shadish, W. R., Cook, T. D., & Campbell, D. T. (2002). *Experimental and quasi-experimental designs for generalized causal inference*. Boston: Houghton Mifflin.

Shapiro, A. P. (1996). *Hypertension and stress: A unified concept*. Mahwah, NJ: Erlbaum.

Shapiro, Y. & Gabbard, G. O. (1994). A reconsideration of altruism from an evolutionary and psychodynamic perspective. *Ethics & Behavior, 4*, 23–42.

Shappell, S., & Wiegmann, D. A. (2003). *A human error approach to aviation accident analysis: The human factors analysis and classification system*. Aldershot, England: Ashgate.

Sharma, J., Angelucci, A., & Sur, M. (2000). Induction of visual orientation modules in auditory cortex. *Nature, 404*, 841–847.

Sharma, S., Ghosh, S. N., & Spielberger, C. D. (1995). Anxiety, anger expression and chronic gastric ulcer. *Psychological Studies, 40*, 187–191.

Shaughnessy, J. J., Zechmeister, E. B., & Zechmeister, J. S. (2000). *Research methods in psychology* (5th ed.). New York: McGraw-Hill.

Shaywitz, B. A., Shaywitz, S. E., Pugh, K. R., Constable, R. T., Skudlarski, P., Fulbright, R. K., Bronen, R. A., Fletcher, J. M., Shankweller, D. P., Katz, L., & Gore, J. C. (1995, February 16). Sex differences in the functional organization of the brain for language. *Nature, 373*, 607–609.

Shear, J. (Ed.). (1997). *Explaining consciousness: The hard problem*. Cambridge, MA: MIT Press.

Sheehan, S. (1982). *Is there no place on earth for me?* Boston: Houghton Mifflin.

Shelton, R. C., Keller, M. B., Gelenberg, A., Dunner, D. L., Hirschfeld, R. M. A., Thase, M. E., Russell, J., Lydiard, R. B., Crits-Cristoph, P., Gallop, R., Todd, L., Hellerstein, D., Goodnick, P., Keitner, G., Stahl, S. M., & Halbreich, R. U. (2002). The effectiveness of St. John's wort in major depression: A multi-center, randomized placebo-controlled trial. *Journal of the American Medical Association, 285*, 1978–1986.

Shepard, R. N., Metzler, J., Bisiach, E., Luzzati, C., Kosslyn, S. M., Thompson, W. L., Kim, I., & Alpert, N. M. (2000). Part IV: Imagery. In M. S. Gazzaniga et al. (Eds.), *Cognitive neuroscience: A reader*. Malden, MA: Blackwell.

Shepard, R., & Metzler, J. (1971). Mental rotation of three dimensional objects. *Science, 171*, 701–703.

Shier, D., Butler, J., & Lewis, R. (2000). *Hole's essentials of human anatomy and physiology* (7th ed.), p. 283. Boston: McGraw-Hill.

Shimono, K. & Wade N. J. (2002). Monocular alignment in different depth planes. *Vision Research, 42*, 1127–1135.

Shnek, Z. M., Foley, F. W., LaRocca, N. G., Smith, C. R., et al. (1995). Psychological predictors of depression in multiple sclerosis. *Journal of Neurologic Rehabilitation, 9*, 15–23.

Shotland, R. L. (1985, June). When bystanders just stand by. *Psychology Today*, pp. 50–55.

Shouler, K. (1992, August). The empire returns. *Sky*, pp. 40–44.

Shrique, C. L. & Annable, L. (1995). Tardive dyskinesia. In C. L. Shriqui & H. A. Nasrallah (Eds.), *Contemporary issues in the treatment of schizophrenia*. Washington, DC: American Psychiatric Press.

Shuchter, S. R., Downs, N., & Zisook, S. (1996). *Biologically informed psychotherapy for depression*. New York: Guilford Press.

Shultz, S. K., Scherman, A., & Marshall, L. J. (2000). Evaluation of a university-based date rape prevention program: Effect on attitudes and behavior related to rape. *Journal of College Student Development, 41*, 193–201

Shurkin, J. N. (1992). *Terman's kids: The ground-breaking study of how the gifted grow up.* Boston: Little, Brown.

Shweder, R. (2003). *Why do men barbecue? Recipes for cultural psychology.* Cambridge, MA: Harvard University Press.

Shweder, R. A. (1994). "You're not sick, you're just in love": Emotion as an interpretive system. In P. Ekman & R. J. Davidson (Eds.), *The nature of emotion: Fundamental questions.* New York: Oxford.

Sibicky, M. E., Schroeder, D. A., & Dovidio, J. F. (1995). Empathy and helping: Considering the consequences of intervention. *Basic and Applied Social Psychology, 16,* 435–453.

Siddle, R., Haddock, G., Tarrier, N., & Faragher, E. B. (2002). Religious delusions in patients admitted to hospital with schizophrenia. *Social Psychiatry and Psychiatric Epidemiology, 37,* 130–138.

Siderowf, A., & Stern, M. (2003). Update on Parkinson disease. *Annals of Internal Medicine, 138,* 651–658.

Siegel, B. (1996b). *The world of the autistic child: Understanding and treating autistic spectrum disorders.* New York: Oxford University Press.

Siegel, J. M. (1990). Stressful life events and use of physician services among the elderly: The moderating role of pet ownership. *Journal of Personality and Social Psychology, 58,* 1081–1086.

Siegel, J. M. (1993). Companion animals: In sickness and in health. *Journal of Social Issues, 49,* 157–167.

Siegel, J. M. (2000, January). Narcolepsy. *Scientific American,* pp. 76–81.

Siegel, R. K. (1989). *Life in pursuit of artificial paradise.* New York: Dutton.

Siegert, R. J., & Ward, T. (2002). Clinical psychology and evolutionary psychology: Toward a dialogue. *Review of General Psychology, 6,* 235–259.

Siegler, R. S. (1998). *Children's thinking.* (3rd ed.). Upper Saddle River, NJ: Prentice Hall.

Sigman, M. (1995). Nutrition and child development: More food for thought. *Current Directions in Psychological Science, 4,* 52–55.

Sigmund, J. A. (2002). Sildenafil advertising and the realities of sildenafil treatment. *Journal of Clinical Psychiatry, 63,* 1183.

Silber, M. H. (2001). Sleep disorders. *Neurologic Clinics, 19,* 173–186.

Sills, S. J., & Song, C. (2002). Innovations in survey research: An application of web-based surveys. *Social Science Computer Review, 20,* 22–30.

Silverman, J. (2001, August 1). Dating violence against adolescent girls linked with teen pregnancy, suicide attempts, and other health risk behaviors. *Journal of the American Medical Association, 286,* 15–20.

Silverman, K., Evans, S. M., Strain, E. C., & Griffiths, R. R. (1992, October 15). Withdrawal syndrome after the double-blind cessation of caffeine consumption. *New England Journal of Medicine, 327,* 1109–1114.

Silverman, K., Mumford, G. K., & Griffiths, R. R. (1994). Enhancing caffeine reinforcement by behavioral requirements following drug ingestion. *Psychopharmacology, 114,* 424–432.

Simcock, G., & Hayne, H. (2002). Breaking the barrier? Children fail to translate their preverbal memories into language. *Psychological Science, 13,* 225–231.

Simmons, R., & Blyth, D. (1987). *Moving into adolescence.* New York: Aldine de Gruyter.

Simonton, D. K. (2000). Creativity: Cognitive, personal, developmental, and social aspects. *American Psychologist, 55,* 151–158.

Sinclair, J. D. (1990). Drugs to decrease alcohol drinking. *Annals of Medicine, 22,* 357–362.

Singer, J. L. (1975). *The inner world of daydreaming.* New York: Harper & Row.

Singh, S., & Darroch, J. E. Trends in sexual activity among adolescent American women: 1982–1995. *Family Planning Perspectives, 31,* 212–219.

Sizemore, C. C. (1989). *A mind of my own: The woman who was known as Eve tells the story of her triumph over multiple personality disorder.* New York: Morrow.

Skinner, B. F. (1957). *Verbal behavior.* New York: Appleton-Century-Crofts.

Skinner, B. F. (1975). The steep and thorny road to a science of behavior. *American Psychologist, 30,* 42–49.

Slater, A. (1996). The organization of visual perception in early infancy. In F. Vital-Durand, J. Atkinson, & O. J. Braddick (Eds.), *Infant vision. The European brain and behaviour society publication series,* Vol. 2. Oxford, England: Oxford University Press.

Slater, A., Mattock, A., & Brown, E. (1990). Size constancy at birth: Newborn infants' responses to retinal and real size. *Journal of Experimental Child Psychology, 49,* 314–322.

Slater, E., & Meyer, A. (1959). Contributions to a pathography of the musicians. *Confinia Psychiatrica.* Reprinted in K. R. Jamison, *Touched with fire: Manic-depressive illness and the artistic temperament.* New York: Free Press.

Sleek, S. (1997 June). Can "emotional intelligence" be taught in today's schools? *APA Monitor,* p. 25.

Sloan, E. P., Hauri, P., Bootzin, R., Morin, C., et al. (1993). The nuts and bolts of behavioral therapy for insomnia. *Journal of Psychosomatic Research, 37,* (Suppl), 19–37.

Smith, C. A., & Lazarus, R. S. (2001). Appraisal components, core relational themes, and the emotions. In W. G. Parrott (Ed.), *Emotions in social psychology: Essential readings,* pp. 94–114. Philadelphia: Psychology Press.

Smith, D. (October 2001). Can't get your 40 winks? Here's what the sleep experts advise. *Monitor on Psychology, 37.*

Smith, D. V., & Margolskee, R. F. (March 2001). Making sense of taste. *Scientific American,* pp. 32–39.

Smith, E. (1988, May). Fighting cancerous feelings. *Psychology Today,* pp. 22–23.

Smith, E. E. (2000). Neural bases of human working memory. *Current Directions in Psychological Science, 9,* 45–49.

Smith, K. A., Williams, C., & Cowen, P. J. (2000). Impaired regulation of brain serotonin function during dieting in women recovered from depression. *British Journal of Psychiatry, 176,* 72–75.

Smith, L. C., Friedman, S., & Paradis, C. (2002). Panic disorder with agoraphobia: Women's issues. In F. Lewis-Hall & T. S. Williams (Eds.), *Psychiatric illness in women: Emerging treatments and research,* pp. 31–55. Washington, DC: American Psychiatric Publishing.

Smith, M. L., Glass, G. V., & Miller, T. J. (1980). *The benefits of psychotherapy.* Baltimore: Johns Hopkins University Press.

Smith, M. V. (1996). Linguistic relativity: On hypotheses and confusions. *Communication and Cognition, 29,* 65–90.

Smith, M., & Lin, K. M. (1996). Gender and ethnic differences in the pharmacogenetics of psychotropics. In M. F. Jensvold, U. Halbreich, & J. A. Hamilton (Eds.), *Psychopharmacology and women: Sex, gender, and hormones.* Washington, DC: American Psychiatric Press.

Smith, S. L., & Boyson, A. R. (2002). Violence in music videos: Examining the prevalence and context of physical aggression. *Journal of Communication, 52,* 61–83.

Snieder, H., Harshfield, G. A., Barbeau, P., Pollock, D. M., Pollock, J. S., & Treiber, F. A. (2002). Dissecting the genetic architecture of the cardiovascular and renal stress response. *Biological Psychology, 61,* 73–95.

Snyder, C. R. (1999). *Coping: The psychology of what works.* New York: Oxford University Press.

Snyder, M. (2002). Applications of Carl Rogers' theory and practice to couple and family therapy: A response to Harlene Anderson and David Bott. *Journal of Family Therapy, 24,* 317–325.

Sohn, D. (1996). Publication bias and the evaluation of psychotherapy efficacy in reviews of the research literature. *Clinical Psychology Review, 16,* 147–156.

Solso, R. L. (1991). *Cognitive psychology* (3rd ed.). Boston: Allyn & Bacon.

Sommer, R., & Sommer, B. (2001). *A practical guide to behavioral research: Tools and techniques.* (5th ed.). New York: Oxford University Press.

Sommerhof, G. (2000). *Understanding consciousness: Its function and brain processes.* Thousand Oaks, CA: Sage.

Sorenson, S. B., & Siegel, J. M. (1992). Gender, ethnicity, and sexual assault: Findings from a Los Angeles study. *Journal of Social Issues, 48,* 93–104.

Southwick, S., & Friedman, M. J. (2001). Neurobiological models of posttraumatic stress disorder. In E. Gerrity, T. M. Keane, et al. (Eds.), *The mental health consequences of torture. Plenum series on stress and coping,* pp. 73–87. Dordrecht, Netherlands: Kluwer Academic.

Spangler, W. D. (1992). Validity of questionnaire and TAT measures of need for achievement: Two meta-analyses. *Psychological Bulletin, 112,* 140–154.

Spanos, N. P., Burgess, C. A., Roncon, V., Wallace-Capretta, S., et al., (1993). Surreptitiously observed hypnotic responding in simulators and in skill-trained and untrained high hypnotizables. *Journal of Personality and Social Psychology, 65,* 391–398.

Spear, L. P., (2002). The adolescent brain and the college drinker: Biological basis of propensity to use and misuse alcohol. *Journal of Studies on Alcohol: Special issue: College drinking, what it is, and what to do about it: Review of the state of the science, Suppl, 14,* 71–81.

Spearman, C. (1927). *The abilities of man.* London: Macmillan.

Spence, M. J., & DeCasper, A. J. (1982, March). *Human fetuses perceive maternal speech.* Paper presented at the meeting of the International Conference on Infant Studies, Austin, TX.

Spencer, S. J., Fein, S., Zanna, M. P., & Olson, J. M. (Eds.) (2003). *Motivated social perception: The Ontario Symposium,* Vol. 9. Mahwah, NJ: Erlbaum.

Sperling, G. (1960). The information available in brief visual presentation. *Psychology Monographs, 74* (whole no. 498).

Sperry, R. (1982). Some effects of disconnecting the cerebral hemispheres. *Science, 217,* 1223–1226.

Spiegel, D. (1993). Social support: How friends, family, and groups can help. In D. Goleman & J. Gurin (Eds.), *Mind-body medicine.* Yonkers, NY: Consumer Reports Books.

Spiegel, D. (1996a). Dissociative disorders. In R. E. Hales & S. C. Yudofsky (Eds.), *The American Psychiatric Press synopsis of psychiatry.* Washington, DC: American Psychiatric Press, Inc.

Spiegel, D. (1996b). Hypnosis. In R. E. Hales & S. C. Yudofsky (Eds.), *The American Psychiatric Press synopsis of psychiatry.* Washington, DC: American Psychiatric Press.

Spiegel, D. (1996c, July). Cancer and depression. *British Journal of Psychiatry, 168,* 109–116.

Spiegel, D. (Ed.). (1999). *Efficacy and cost-effectiveness of psychotherapy.* New York: American Psychiatric Press.

Spiegel, D., & Cardena, E. (1991). Disintegrated experience: The dissociative disorders revisited. *Journal of Abnormal Psychology, 100,* 366–378.

Spiegel, D., Frischholz, E. J., Fleiss, J. L., & Spiegel, H. (1993). Predictors of smoking abstinence following a single-session restructuring intervention with self-hypnosis. *American Journal of Psychiatry, 150,* 1090–1097.

Spiegel, R. (1989). *Psychopharmacology: An Introduction.* New York: Wiley.

Spiller, L. D., & Wymer, W. W., Jr. (2001). Physicians' perceptions and use of commercial drug information sources: An examination of pharmaceutical marketing to physicians. *Health Marketing Quarterly, 19,* 91–106.

Spillmann, L., & Werner, J. (Eds.). (1990). *Visual perception: The neurophysiological foundations.* San Diego: Academic Press.

Spira, J. (Ed.). (1997). *Group therapy for medically ill patients.* New York: Guilford Press.

Spitz, H. H. (1987). Problem-solving processes in special populations. In J. G. Borkowski & J. D. Day (Eds.), *Cognition in special children: Comparative approaches to retardation, learning disabilities, and giftedness.* Norwood, NJ: Ablex.

Spitzer, R. L., Skodol, A. E., Gibbon, M., & Williams, J. B. W. (1983). *Psychopathology: A case book.* New York: McGraw-Hill.

Sprecher, S., & Hatfield, E. (1996). Premarital sexual standards among U.S. college students: Comparison with Russian and Japanese students. *Archives of Sexual Behavior, 25,* 261–288.

Sprecher, S., & McKinney, K. (1993). *Sexuality.* Newbury Park, CA: Sage.

Sprenkle, D. H., & Moon, S. M. (Eds.). (1996). *Research methods in family therapy.* New York: Guilford Press.

Squire, L. R. (1993). The hippocampus and spatial memory. *Trends in Neurosciences, 6,* 56–57.

Srivastava, A., Locke, E. A., & Bartol, K. M. (2001). Money and subjective well-being: It's not the money, it's the motives. *Journal of Personality and Social Psychology, 80,* 959–971.

St. Onge, S. (1995a). Systematic desensitization. In M. Ballou (Ed.), *Psychological interventions: A guide to strategies.* Westport, CT: Praeger/Greenwood.

St. Onge, S. (1995b). Modeling and role-playing. In M. Ballou (Ed.), *Psychological interventions: A guide to strategies.* Westport, CT: Praeger/Greenwood.

Staddon, J. E. R., & Cerutti, D. T. (2003). Operant conditioning. *Annual Review of Psychology, 54,* 115–144.

Stankov, L. (2003). Complexity in human intelligence. In R. J. Sternberg, J. Lautrey, et al. (Eds.), *Models of intelligence: International perspectives,* pp. 27–42. Washington, DC: American Psychological Association.

Stanton, A. L., Danoff-Burg, S., Cameron, C. L., Bishop, M., Collins, C. A., Kirk, S. B., Sworowski, L. A., & Twillman, R. (2000). Emotionally expressive coping predicts psychological and physical adjustment to breast cancer. *Journal of Consulting and Clinical Psychology, 68,* 875–882.

Stanton, H. E. (1994). Sports imagery and hypnosis: A potent mix. *Australian Journal of Clinical and Experimental Hypnosis, 22,* 119–124.

Staudinger, U. M., Fleeson, W., & Baltes, P. B. (1999). Predictors of subjective physical health and global well-being: Similarities and differences between the United States and Germany. *Journal of Personality and Social Psychology, 76,* 305–319.

Steadman, H., McGreevy, M. A., Morrissey, J. P., et al. (1993). *Before and after Hinckley: Evaluating insanity defense reform.* New York: Guilford.

Steblay, N. M. (1992). A meta-analytic review of the weapon focus effect. *Law and Human Behavior, 16,* 413–424.

Steele, C. M. (1992, April). Race and the schooling of black America. *Atlantic Monthly,* pp. 37–53.

Steele, C. M. (1997). A threat in the air: How stereotypes shape intellecutal identity and performance. *American Psychologist, 52,* 613–629.

Steele, C. M., & Josephs, R. A. (1990). Alcohol myopia: Its prized and dangerous effects. *American Psychologist, 45,* 921–933.

Steele, C. M., Spencer, S. J., & Aronson, J. (2002). Contending with group image. The psychology of stereotype and social identity threat. In M. P. Zanna (Ed.), *Advances in experimental social psychology,* Vol. 34, pp. 379–440. San Diego: Academic Press.

Steen, R. G. (1996). *DNA and destiny: Nature and nurture in human behavior.* New York: Plenum Press.

Stegerwald, F., & Janson, G. R. (2003). Conversion therapy: Ethical considerations in family counseling. *Family Journal—Counseling and Therapy for Couples and Families, 11,* 55–59.

Stein, N. L., Brainerd, C., Ornstein, P. A., Tversky, B. (Eds.). (1996). *Memory for everyday and emotional events.* Mahwah, NJ: Erlbaum.

Stein, N. L., Ornstein, P. A., Tversky, B., & Brainerd, C. (Eds.). (1997). *Memory for everyday and emotional events.* Mahwah, NJ: Erlbaum.

Steinberg, L., & Dornbusch, S. (1991). Negative correlates of part-time employment during adolescence: Replication and elaboration. *Developmental Psychology, 27,* 304.

Steinmetz, J. E., Kim, J., & Thompson, R. F. (2003). Biological models of associative learning. In M. Gallagher & R. J. Nelson (Eds.), *Handbook of psychology: Biological psychology,* Vol. 3, pp. 499–541. New York: Wiley.

Stern, E. & Silbersweig, D. A. (2001). Advances in functional neuroimaging methodology for the study of brain systems underlying human neuropsychological function and dysfunction. In D.A. Silbersweig & E. Stern (Eds.), *Neuropsychology and functional neuroimaging: Convergence, advances and new directions.* Amsterdam, Netherlands: Swets and Zeitlinger.

Stern, P. (2001, November 2). Sweet dreams are made of this. *Science, 294,* 1047.

Stern, R. M., & Koch, K. L. (1996). Motion sickness and differential susceptibility. *Current Directions in Psychological Science, 5,* 115–120.

Sternberg, R. J., & Jarvin, L. (2003). Alfred Binet's contributions as a paradigm for impact in psychology. In R. J. Sternberg (Ed.), *The anatomy of impact: What makes the great works of psychology great*, pp. 89–107. Washington, DC: American Psychological Association.

Sternberg, J. (2000, July 21). The holey grail of general intelligence. *Science, 289*, 499–501.

Sternberg, R. J. (1982). Reasoning, problem solving, and intelligence. In R. J. Sternberg (Ed.), *Handbook of human intelligence*, pp. 225–307. Cambridge, MA: Cambridge University Press.

Sternberg, R. J. (1990). *Metaphors of mind: Conceptions of the nature of intelligence.* New York: Cambridge University Press.

Sternberg, R. J. (2000). Intelligence and wisdom. In R. J. Sternberg et al. (Eds.), *Handbook of intelligence.* New York: Cambridge University Press.

Sternberg, R. J. (2001). What is the common thread of creativity? Its dialectical relation to intelligence and wisdom. *American Psychologist, 56*, 360–362.

Sternberg, R. J. (2002a). Individual differences in cognitive development. In U. Goswami (Ed.), *Blackwell handbook of childhood cognitive development. Blackwell handbooks of developmental psychology*, pp. 600–619 Malden, MA: Blackwell.

Sternberg, R. J. (Ed.). (2002b). *Why smart people can be so stupid.* New Haven, CT: Yale University Press.

Sternberg, R. J., & Beall, A. E. (1991). How can we know what love is? An epistemological analysis. In G. J. O. Fletcher & F. D. Fincham (Eds.), *Cognition in close relationships.* Hillsdale, NJ: Erlbaum.

Sternberg, R. J., & Frensch, P. A. (1991). *Complex problem solving: Principles and mechanisms.* Hillsdale, NJ: Erlbaum.

Sternberg, R. J., & Grigorenko, E. (1997). Are cognitive styles still in style? *American Psychologist, 52*, 700–712.

Sternberg, R. J., & Hedlund, J. (2002). Practical intelligence, "g", and work psychology. *Human Performance, 15*, 143–160.

Sternberg, R. J., & Jarvin, L. (2003). Alfred Binet's contributions as a paradigm for impact in psychology. In R. J. Sternberg (Ed.), *The anatomy of impact: What makes the great works of psychology great.* Washington, DC: American Psychological Association.

Sternberg, R. J., & O'Hara, L. A. (2000). Intelligence and creativity. In R. Sternberg et al. (Eds.), *Handbook of intelligence.* New York: Cambridge University Press.

Sternberg, R. J., Hojjat, M., & Barnes, M. L. (2001). Empirical aspects of a theory of love as a story. *European Journal of Personality, 15*, 1–20.

Sternberg, R. J., Wagner, R. K., Williams, W. M., & Horvath, J. A. (1995). Testing common sense. *American Psychologist, 50*, 912–927.

Sternberg, R. J. (1998). *Successful intelligence: How practical and creative intelligence determine success in life.* New York: Plume.

Stetsenko, A., Little, T. D., Gordeeva, T., Grasshof, M., & Oettingen, G. (2000).

Gender effects in children's beliefs about school performance: A cross cultural study. *Child Development, 71*, 517–527.

Stevahn, L., Johnson, D. W., Johnson, R. T., Oberle, K., & Wahl, L. (2000). Effects of conflict resolution training integrated into a kindergarten curriculum. *Child Development, 71*, 772–784.

Stevens, C. F. (1979, September). The neuron. *Scientific American*, p. 56.

Stevens, G., & Gardner, S. (1982). *The women of psychology: Pioneers and innovators*, Vol. 1. Cambridge, MA: Schenkman.

Stevens, H. W., Chen, C., & Lee, S. Y. (1993). A comparison of the parent-child relationship in Japan and the United States. In L. L. Roopnarine & D. B. Carter (Eds.), *Parent-child socialization in diverse cultures.* Norwood, NJ: Ablex.

Steward, E. P. (1995). *Beginning writers in the zone of proximal development.* Hillsdale, NJ: Erlbaum.

Stewart, D. W., & Kamins, M. A. (1993). *Secondary research: Information sources and methods.* (2nd ed.). Newbury Park, CA: Sage.

Stickgold, R., Hobson, J. A., Fosse, R., & Fosse, M. (2001, November 2). Sleep, learning, and dreams: Off-line memory reprocessing. *Science, 294*, 1052–1057.

Stier, H., & Lewin-Epstein, N. (2000). Women's part-time employment and gender inequality in the family. *Journal of Family Issues, 21*, 390–410.

Stix, G. (1996, January). Listening to culture. *Scientific American*, pp. 16–17.

Stolberg, S. G. (2001, August 15). Researchers discount a caution in debate over cloned humans. *The New York Times*, p. A18.

Stompe, T., Ortwein-Swoboda, G., Ritter, K., & Schanda, H. (2003). Old wine in new bottles? Stability and plasticity of the contents of schizophrenic delusions. *Psychopathology, 36*, 6–12.

Stone, J. (2002). Battling doubt by avoiding practice: The effects of stereotype threat on self-handicapping in white athletes. *Personality and Social Psychology Bulletin, 28*, 1667–1678.

Storch, E. A., & Storch, J. B. (2003). Academic dishonesty and attitudes towards academic dishonest acts: Support for cognitive dissonance theory. *Psychological Reports, 92*, 174–176.

Storm, L., & Ertel, S. (2001). Does psi exist? Comments on Milton and Wiseman's (1999) meta-analysis of Ganzfeld's research. *Psychological Bulletin, 127*, 424–433.

Strathern, A., & Stewart, P. J. (2003). *Landscape, memory and history: Anthropological perspectives.* London: Pluto Press.

Strauss, E. (1998, May 8). Writing, speech separated in split brain. *Science, 280*, 287.

Streissguth, A. P., Barr, H. M., Bookstein, F. L., Sampson, P. D., & Olson, H. C. (1999). The long-term neurocognitive consequences of prenatal alcohol exposure: A 14-year study. *Psychological Science, 10*, 186–190.

Strickland, B. R. (1992). Women and depression. *Current Directions in Psychological Science, 1*, 132–135.

Striegel-Moore, R. H., & Smolak, L. (Eds.) (2001). *Eating disorders: Innovative directions in research and practice.* Washington, DC: American Psychological Association.

Stroebe, M. S., Stroebe, W., & Hansson, R. O. (Eds.). (1993). *Handbook of bereavement: Theory, research, and intervention.* Cambridge, England: Cambridge University Press.

Stronski, S. M., Ireland, M., & Michaud, P. (2000). Protective correlates of stages in adolescent substance use: A Swiss national study. *Journal of Adolescent Health, 26*, 420–427.

Strube, M. (Ed.). (1990). Type A behavior [Special issue]. *Journal of Social Behavior and Personality, 5.*

Strupp, H. H. (1996, October). The tripartite model and the *Consumer Reports* study. *American Psychologist, 51*, 1017–1024.

Strupp, H. H., & Binder, J. L. (1992). Current developments in psychotherapy. *The Independent Practitioner, 12*, 119–124.

Sue, D. (1979). Erotic fantasies of college students during coitus. *Journal of Sex Research, 15*, 299–305.

Sue, D. W., & Sue, D. (1990). *Counseling the culturally different: Theory and practice* (2nd ed.). New York: Wiley.

Sue, D. W., & Sue, D. (1999). *Counseling the culturally different: Theory and practice* (3rd ed.). New York: Wiley.

Sue, D. W., Bingham, R. P., Porché-Burke, L., & Vasquez, M. (1999). The diversification of psychology: A multicultural revolution. *American Psychologist, 54*, 1061–1069.

Sue, D. W., Sue, D., & Sue, S. (1990). *Understanding abnormal behavior* (3rd ed.). Boston: Houghton-Mifflin.

Suh, E. M. (2002). Culture, identity consistency, and subjective well-being. *Journal of Personality & Social Psychology, 83*, 1378–1391.

Sulzer-Azaroff, B., & Mayer, R. (1991). *Behavior analysis and lasting change.* New York: Holt.

Sundin, O., Ohman, A., Palm, T., & Strom, G. (1995). Cardiovascular reactivity, Type A behavior, and coronary heart disease: Comparisons between myocardial infarction patients and controls during laboratory-induced stress. *Psychyophysiology, 32*, 28–35.

Super, C. M. (1980). Cognitive development: Looking across at growing up. In C. M. Super & S. Harakness (Eds.), *New directions for child development: Anthropological perspectives on child development*, pp. 59–69. San Francisco: Jossey-Bass.

Surette, R. (2002). Self-reported copycat crime among a population of serious and violent juvenile offenders. *Crime & Delinquency, 48*, 46–69.

Susser, E. S., Herman, D. B., & Aaron, B. (2002, August). Combating the terror of terrorism. *Scientific American*, pp. 70–77.

Suzuki, K. (1991). Moon illusion simulated in complete darkness: Planetarium experiment reexamined. *Perception & Psychophysics, 49,* 349–354.

Svarstad, B. (1976). Physician-patient communication and patient conformity with medical advice. In D. Mechanic (Ed.), *The growth of bureaucratic medicine.* New York: Wiley.

Svartdal, F. (2003). Extinction after partial reinforcement: Predicted vs. judged persistence. *Scandinavian Journal of Psychology, 44,* 55–64.

Swanson, H. L., Harris, K. R., & Graham, S. (Eds.). (2003). *Handbook of learning disabilities.* New York: Guilford Press.

Swets, J. A., & Bjork, R.A. (1990). Enhancing human performance: An evaluation of "new age" techniques considered by the U.S. Army. *Psychological Science, 1,* 85–96.

Szasz, T. (1982). The psychiatric will: A new mechanism for protecting persons against "psychosis" and psychiatry. *American Psychologist, 37,* 762–770.

Szasz, T. S. (1994). *Cruel compassion: Psychiatric control of society's unwanted.* New York: Wiley.

Szegedy-Maszak, M. (2003, January 13). The sound of unsound minds. *U.S. News & World Report,* pp. 45–46.

Tabakoff, B., & Hoffman, P. L. (1996). Effect of alcohol on neurotransmitters and their receptors and enzymes. In H. Begleiter, & B. Kissin (Eds.), *The pharmacology of alcohol and alcohol dependence. Alcohol and alcoholism, No. 2.* New York: Oxford University Press.

Tajfel, H. (1982). *Social identity and intergroup relations.* London: Cambridge University Press.

Talwar, S. K., Xu, S., Hawley, E. S., Weiss, S. A., Moxon, K. A., & Chapin, J. K. (2002). Behavioural neuroscience: Rat navigation guided by remote control. *Nature, 417,* 37–38.

Tan, V. L., & Hicks, R. A. (1995). Type A-B behavior and nightmare types among college students. *Perceptual and Motor Skills, 81,* 15–19.

Tanner, J. M. (1978). *Education and physical growth* (2nd ed.). New York: International Universities Press.

Tanner, J. M. (1990). *Foetus into man: Physical growth from conception to maturity* (rev. ed.). Cambridge, MA: Harvard University Press.

Tattersall, I. (2002). *The monkey in the mirror: Essays on the science of what makes us human.* New York: Harcourt.

Taubes, G. (1998, May 29). Weight increases worldwide? *Science, 280,* 1368.

Tavris, C. (1992). *The mismeasure of woman.* New York: Simon & Schuster.

Taylor, C. B., & Luce, K. H. (2003). Computer- and Internet-based psychotherapy interventions. *Current Directions in Psychological Science, 12,* 18–22.

Taylor, C. B., Jobson, K. O., Winzelberg, A., & Abascal, L. (2002). The use of the Internet to provide evidence-based integrated treatment programs for mental health. *Psychiatric Annals, 32,* 671–677.

Taylor, J., & Turner, R. J. (2002). Perceived discrimination, social stress and depression in the transition to adulthood: Racial contrasts. *Social Psychology Quarterly, 65,* 213–225.

Taylor, M. (1996). A theory of mind perspective on social cognitive development. In R. Gelman, & T. K-F. Au (Eds.), *Perceptual and cognitive development: Handbook of perception and cognition* (2nd ed.). San Diego: Academic Press.

Taylor, S. E. (1995). Quandary at the crossroads: Paternalism versus advocacy surrounding end-of-treatment decisions. *American Journal of Hospital Palliatory Care, 12,* 43–46.

Taylor, S. E., & Aspinwall, L. G. (1996). Mediating and moderating processes in psychosocial stress: Appraisal, coping, resistance, and vulnerability. In H. B. Kaplan (Ed.), *Psychosocial stress: Perspectives on structure, theory, life-course, and methods.* San Diego: Academic Press.

Taylor, S. E., Kemeny, M. E., Reed, G. M., Bower, J. E., & Gruenewald, T. L. (2000). Psychological resources, positive illusions, and health. *American Psychologist, 55,* 99–109.

Tekcan, A. I. (2001). Flashbulb memories for a negative and a positive event: News of Desert Storm and acceptance to college. *Psychological Reports, 88,* 323–331.

Tellegen, A., Lykken, D. T., Bouchard, T. J., Jr., Wilcox, K. J., Segal, N. L., & Rich, S. (1988). Personality similarity in twins reared apart and together. *Journal of Personality and Social Psychology, 54,* 1031–1039.

Tenenbaum, H. R., & Leaper, C. (2002). Are parents' gender schemas related to their children's gender-related cognitios? A meta-analysis. *Developmental Psychology, 38,* 615–630.

Tennant, N. (2002). The future with cloning: On the possibility of serial immortality. In J. H. Fetzer (Ed.), *Consciousness evolving. Advances in consciousness research,* pp. 223–237. Amsterdam, Netherlands: John Benjamins.

Tenopyr, M. L. (2002). Theory versus reality: Evaluation of 'g' in the workplace. *Human Performance, 15,* 107–122.

Teodorov, E., Salzgerber, S. A., Felicio, L. F., Varolli, F. M. F., & Bernardi, M. M. (2002). Effects of perinatal picrotoxin and sexual experience on heterosexual and homosexual behavior in male rats. *Neurotoxicology and Teratology, 24,* 235–245.

Tepperman, L., & Curtis, J. (1995). A life satisfaction scale for use with national adult samples from the USA, Canada and Mexico. *Social Indicators Research, 35,* 255–270.

Terman, L. M., & Oden, M. H. (1947). *Genetic studies of genius: IV. The gifted child grows up.* Stanford, CA: Stanford University Press.

Terry, W. S. (2003). *Learning and memory: Basic principles, processes, and procedures* (2nd ed.). Boston: Allyn & Bacon.

Tetlock, P. E., Hoffmann, S., Janis, I. L., Stein, J. G., Kressel, N. J., & Cohen, B. C. (1993). The psychology of international conflict. In N. J. Kressel (Ed.), *Political psychology: Classic and contemporary readings.* New York: Paragon House.

Tharp, R. G. (1989). Psychocultural variables and constants: Effects on teaching and learning in schools. [Special issue: Children and their development: Knowledge base, research agenda, and social policy application.] *American Psychologist, 44,* 349–359.

Thiffault, P., & Bergeron, J. (2003). Fatigue and individual differences in monotonous simulated driving. *Personality and Individual Differences, 34,* 159–176.

Thomas, D. (2003). *Improving your memory.* NY: Penguin.

Thombs, D. L. (1999). *Introduction to addictive behaviors* (2nd ed.). New York: Guilford Press.

Thompson, B. (2002). *Score reliability: Contemporary thinking on reliability issues.* Thousand Oaks, CA: Sage.

Thompson, J. (2000, June 18). "I was certain, but I was wrong." *The New York Times,* p. E14.

Thompson, J. K., & Smolak, L. (Eds.). (2001). *Body image, eating disorders and obesity in youth: Assessment, prevention, and treatment.* Washington, DC: American Psychological Association.

Thompson, K. M., & Hanninger, K. (2001). Violence in e-rated video games. *Journal of the American Medical Association, 286,* 591–598.

Thorndike, E. L. (1932). *The fundamentals of learning.* New York: Teachers College.

Thorndike, R. L., Hagan, E., & Sattler, J. (1986). *Stanford-Binet* (4th ed.). Chicago: Riverside.

Thornton, A., & Young-DeMarco, L. (2001). Four decades of trends in attitudes toward family issues in the United States: The 1960s through the 1990s. *Journal of Marriage and the Family, 63,* 1009–1037.

Thrash, T. M., & Elliot, A. J. (2002). Implicit and self-attributed achievement motives: Concordance and predictive validity. *Journal of Personality, 70,* 729–755.

Time. (1982, October 4). "We're sorry: A case of mistaken identity," *Time,* p. 45.

Titone, D. A. (2002). Memories bound: The neuroscience of dreams. *Trends in Cognitive Science, 6,* 4–5.

Tkachuk, G. A., & Martin, G. L. (1999). Exercise therapy for patients with psychiatric disorders: Research and clinical implications. *Professional Psychology: Research and Practice, 33,* 275–282.

Tolman, E. C., & Honzik, C. H. (1930). Introduction and removal of reward and maze performance in rats. *University of California Publications in Psychology, 4,* 257–275.

Tomasello, M. (2000). Culture and cognitive development. *Current Directions in Psychological Science, 9,* 37–40.

Tomlinson-Keasey, C. (1985). *Child development: Psychological, sociological, and biological factors.* Homewood, IL: Dorsey.

Tonidandel, S., Quinones, M. A., & Adams, A. A. (2002). Computer-adaptive testing: The impact of test characteristics on perceived performance and test takers' reactions. *Journal of Applied Psychology, 87,* 320–332.

Torrey, E. F. (1997, June 13). The release of the mentally ill from institutions: A well-intentioned disaster. *Chronicle of Higher Education,* pp. B4–B5.

Toth, J. P., & Reingold, E. M. (1996). *Beyond perception: Conceptual contributions to unconscious influences of memory.* Oxford, England: Oxford University Press.

Trehub, S. E. (2001). Musical predispositions in infancy. In R. J. Zatorre & I. Peretz (Eds.)., *The biological foundations of music. Annals of the New York Academy of Sciences,* Vol. 930, (pp. 1–16). New York: New York Academy of Sciences.

Trehub, S. E., & Nakata, T. (2001–02). Emotion and music in infancy. [Musicae scientiae: Special issue.] *Current Trends in the Study of Music and Emotion,* pp. 37–61.

Treisman, A. (1988). Features and objects: The Fourteenth Bartlett Memorial Lecture. *Quarterly Journal of Experimental Psychology, 40,* 201–237.

Treisman, A. (1993). The perception of features and objects. In A. D. Baddeley & L. Weiskrantz (Eds.), *Attention: Selection, awareness, and control: A tribute to Donald Broadbent.* Oxford, England: Oxford University Press.

Troxel, W. M., Matthews, K. A., Bromberger, J. T., & Sutton-Tyrell, K. (2003). Chronic stress burden, discrimination, and subclinical carotid artery disease in African American and Caucasian women. *Health Psychology, 22,* 300–309.

Trudel, G. (2002). Sexuality and marital life: Results of a survey. *Journal of Sex and Marital Therapy, 28,* 229–249.

Trull, T. J., & Widiger, T. A., (2003). Personality disorders. In. G. Stricker, T. A. Widiger, et al. (Eds.), *Handbook of psychology: Clinical psychology,* Vol. 8, pp. 149–172. New York: Wiley.

Trull, T. J., Stepp, S. D., & Durrett, C. A. (2003). Research on borderline personality disorder: An update. *Current Opinion in Psychiatry, 16,* 77–82.

Tryon, W. W., & Bernstein, D. (2003). Understanding measurement. In J. C. Thomas & M. Hersen (Eds.), *Understanding research in clinical and counseling psychology.* Mahwah, NJ: Erlbaum.

Tsunoda, T. (1985). *The Japanese brain: Uniqueness and universality.* Tokyo: Taishukan Publishing.

Tucker, C. M., & Herman, K. C. (2002). Using culturally sensitive theories and research to meet the academic needs of low-income African American children. *American Psychologist, 57,* 762–773.

Tucker, J. A., Donovan, D. M., & Marlatt, G. A. (Eds.). (1999). *Changing addictive behavior: Bridging clinical and public health strategies.* New York: Guilford Press.

Tuerlinckx, F., De Boeck, P., & Lens, W. (2002). Measuring needs with the Thematic Apperception Test: A psychometric study. *Journal*

of Personality and Social Psychology, 82, 448–461.

Tulving, E. (1993). What is episodic memory? *Current Directions in Psychological Science, 2,* 67–70.

Tulving, E. (2000). Concepts of memory. In E. Tulving, F. I. M. Craik, et al. (Eds.). *The Oxford handbook of memory.* New York: Oxford University Press.

Tulving, E., & Psotka, J. (1971). Retroactive inhibition in free recall: Inaccessibility of information available in the memory store. *Journal of Experimental Psychology, 87,* 1–8.

Tulving, E., & Schacter, D. L. (1990, January 19). Priming and human memory systems. *Science, 247,* 301–306.

Tulving, E., & Thompson, D. M. (1983). Encoding specificity and retrieval processes in episodic memory. *Psychological Review, 80,* 352–373.

Turk, D. C. (1994). Perspectives on chronic pain: The role of psychological factors. *Current Directions in Psychological Science, 3,* 45–49.

Turkel, R. A. (2002). From victim to heroine: Children's stories revisited. *Journal of the American Academy of Psychoanalysis, 30,* 71–81.

Turkewitz, G. (1993). The origins of differential hemispheric strategies for information processing in the relationships between voice and face perception. In B. de Boysson-Bardies, S. de Schonen, P. W. Jusczyk, P. McNeilage, & J. Morton (Eds.), *Developmental neurocognition: Speech and face processing in the first year of life. NATO ASI series D: Behavioural and social sciences,* Vol. 69. Dordrecht, Netherlands: Kluwer Academic.

Turner, M. E., Pratkanis, A. R., Probasco, P., & Leve, C. (1992). Threat, cohesion, and group effectiveness: Testing a social identity maintenance perspective on groupthink. *Journal of Personality and Social Psychology, 63,* 781–796.

Turner, W. J. (1995). Homosexuality, Type 1: An Xq28 phenomenon. *Archives of Sexual Behavior, 24,* 109–134.

Tversky, A., & Kahneman, D. (1987). Rational choice and the framing of decisions. In R. Hogarth & M. Reder (Eds.), *Rational choice: The contrast between economics and psychology.* Chicago: University of Chicago Press.

Twenge, J. M., Catanese, K. R., & Baumeister, R. F. (2002). Social exclusion causes self-defeating behavior. *Journal of Personality and Social Psychology, 83,* 606–615.

Twenge, J. M. & Crocker, J. (2002). Race and self-esteem revisited: Reply to Hafdahl and Gray-Little. *Psychological Bulletin, 128,* 417–420.

U.S. Bureau of the Census. (2000). *Census 2000.* Accessed on American Fact Finder at http://factfinder.census.gov/servlet/BasicFactsServlet.

U.S. Bureau of Labor Statistics. (2003). Women's weekly earnings as a percentage of men's earnings. Washington, DC: U.S. Bureau of Labor Statistics.

Ubell, E. (1993, January 10). Could you use more sleep? *Parade,* pp. 16–18.

Uchino, B. N., Cacioppo, J. T., & Kiecolt-Glaser, J. K. (1996). The relationship between social support and physiological processes: A review with emphasis on underlying mechanisms and implications for health. *Psychological Bulletin, 119,* 488–531.

Udolf, R. (1981). *Handbook of hypnosis for professionals.* New York: Van Nostrand.

Ullman, S. (1996). *High-level vision: Object recognition and visual cognition.* Cambridge, MA: MIT Press.

UNAIDS. (2002). *AIDS epidemic update, 2002.* Geneva, Switzerland: World Health Organization.

Underwood, G. D. M. (Ed.). (1996). *Implicit cognition.* Oxford, England: Oxford University Press.

Uylings, H. B. M., & Vrije, U., (2002). About assumptions in estimation of density of neurons and glial cells. *Biological Psychiatry, 51,* 840–842.

Valencia, R. R., & Suzuki, L. A. (2003). *Intelligence testing and minority students: Foundations, performance factors, and assessment issues.* Thousand Oaks, CA: Sage.

Valente, S. M. (1991). Electroconvulsive therapy. *Archives of Psychiatric Nursing, 5,* 223–228.

Van De Graaff, K. (2000). *Human Anatomy* (5th ed.). Boston: McGraw-Hill.

van Eck, M., Nicolson, N. A., & Berkhof, J. (1998). Effects of stressful daily events on mood states: Relationship to global perceived stress. *Journal of Personality and Social Psychology, 75,* 1572–1585.

Van Knippenberg, D. (1999). Social identity and persuasion: Reconsidering the role of group membership. In D. Abrams & M.A. Hogg (Eds.), *Social identity and social cognition.* Malden, MA: Blackwell.

van Wel, F., Linssen, H., & Abma, R. (2000). The parental bond and the well-being of adolescents and young adults. *Journal of Youth & Adolescence, 29,* 307–318.

Vance, E. B., & Wagner, N. W. (1976). Written descriptions of orgasm: A study of sex differences. *Archives of Sexual Behavior, 5,* 87–98.

VanLehn, K. (1996). Cognitive skill acquisition. *Annual Review of Psychology, 47,* 513–539.

Vaughn, L. A., & Weary, G. (2002). Roles of the availability of explanations, feelings of ease, and dysphoria in judgments about the future. *Journal of Science and Clinical Psychology, 21,* 686–704.

Veasey, S., Rosen, R., Barzansky, B., Rosen, I., & Owens, J. (2002). Sleep loss and fatigue in residency training: A reappraisal. *Journal of the American Medical Association, 288,* 1116–1124.

Veltman, M. W. M., & Browne, K. D. (2001). Three decades of child maltreatment research: Implications for the school years. *Trauma Violence and Abuse, 2,* 215–239.

Veniegas, R. C. (2000). Biological research on women's sexual orientations: Evaluating the scientific evidence. *Journal of Social Issues, 56,* 267–282.

Verfaellie, M., & Keane, M. M. (2002). Impaired and preserved memory processes in amnesia.

In L. R. Squire & D. L. Schacter (Eds.), *Neuropsychology of memory* (3rd ed.). New York: Guilford Press.

Verhaeghen, P., Marcoen, A., & Goossens, L. (1992). Improving memory performance in the aged through mnemonic training: A meta-analytic study. *Psychology and Aging, 7,* 242–251.

Vernon, P. A., Jang, K. L., Harris, J. A., & McCarthy, J. M. (1997). Environmental predictors of personality differences: A twin and sibling study. *Journal of Personality and Social Psychology, 72,* 177–183.

Victor, S. B., & Fish, M. C. (1995). Lesbian mothers and the children: A review for school psychologists. *School Psychology Review, 24,* 456–479.

Vihman, M. M. (1996). *Phonological development: The origins of language in the child.* London, England: Blackwell.

Villarosa, L. (2002, December 3). To prevent sexual abuse, abusers step forward. *The New York Times,* p. B1.

Violani, C., & Lombardo, C. (2003). Peripheral temperature changes during rest and gender differences in thermal biofeedback. *Journal of Psychosomatic Research, 54,* 391–397.

Vital-Durand, F., Atkinson, J., & Braddick, O. J. (Eds.). (1996). *Infant vision. The European brain and behaviour society publication series,* Vol. 2. Oxford, England: Oxford University Press.

Vogel, G. W., Feng, P., & Kinney, G. G. (2000). Ontogeny of REM sleep in rats: Possible implications for endogenous depression. *Physiology & Behavior, 68,* 453–461.

Voicu, H., & Schmajuk, N. (2002). Latent learning, shortcuts and detours: A computational model. *Behavioural Processes, 59,* 67–86.

Volterra, V., Caselli, M. C., Capirci, O., Tonucci, F., & Vicari, S. (2003). Early linguistic abilities of Italian children with Williams syndrome. *Developmental Neuropsychology: Special issue: Williams syndrome, 23,* 33–58.

von Restorff, H. (1933). Uber die wirking von bereichsbildungen im Spurenfeld. In W. Kohler & H. von Restorff, *Analyse von vorgangen in Spurenfeld: I. Psychologische forschung, 18,* 299–342.

Vrij, A. (2001). Detecting the liars. *Psychologist, 14,* 596–598.

Vygotsky, L. S. (1926/1997). *Educational psychology.* Delray Beach, FL: St. Lucie Press.

Wachtel, P. L., & Messer, S. B. (Eds.). (1997). *Theories of psychotherapy: Origins and evolution.* Washington, DC: American Psychological Association.

Wagner, B. M. (1997). Family risk factors for child and adolescent suicidal behavior. *Psychological Bulletin, 121,* 246–298.

Wagner, E. F., & Atkins, J. H. (2000). Smoking among teenage girls. *Journal of Child & Adolescent Substance Abuse, 9,* 93–110.

Wagner, R. K. (2000). Practical intelligence. In R. J. Sternberg et al. (Eds.). *Handbook of intelligence.* New York: Cambridge University Press.

Wahlstrom, K. L., Davison, M. L., Choi, J., & Ross, J. N. (2001, August). *School start time study: Executive summary.* Minneapolis: University of Minnesota, Center for Applied Research and Educational Improvement.

Wainer, H., Dorans, N. J., Eignor, D., Flaugher, R., Green, B. E., Mislevy, R. J., Steinberg, L., & Thissen D. (2000). *Computerized adaptive testing: A primer* (2nd ed.). Mahwah, NJ: Erlbaum.

Walcott, D. M. (2000). Repressed memory still lacks scientific reliability. *Journal of the American Academy of Psychiatry & the Law, 28,* 243–244.

Wald, M. L. (2002, June 23). For air crash detectives, seeing isn't believing. *The New York Times,* p. WK5.

Waldrep, D., & Waits, W. (2002). Returning to the Pentagon: The use of mass desensitization following the September 11, 2001 attack. *Military Medicine: Special issue: The mental health response to the 9-11 attack on the Pentagon, 167,* 58–59.

Waldrop, M. W. (1989, September 29). NIDA aims to fight drugs with drugs. *Science, 245,* 1443–1444.

Walker, M. P., Brakefield, T., Morgan, A., Hobson, J. A., & Stickgold R. (2002). Practice with sleep makes perfect: Sleep-dependent motor skill learning. *Neuron, 35,* 205–211.

Wall, P. D., & Melzack, R. (1989). *Textbook of pain* (2nd ed.). New York: Churchill Livingstone.

Wall, P. D., & Melzack, R. (Eds.) (1984). *Textbook of pain.* Edinburgh: Churchill Livingstone.

Wallace, M. S. (2002). Treatment options for refractory pain: The role of intrathecal therapy. *Neurology: Special issue: Advances in understanding chronic pain: Mechanisms of pain modulation and relationship to treatment, 59,* S18–S24.

Wallis, C., & Willwerth, J. (1992, July 6). Schizophrenia: A new drug brings patients back to life. *Time,* pp. 52–57.

Walter, H. J., Vaughan, R. D., & Wynder, E. L. (1994). Primary prevention of cancer among children: Changes in cigarette smoking and diet after six years of intervention. In A. Steptoe & J. Wardle (Eds.), *Psychosocial processes and health: A reader.* Cambridge, England: Cambridge University Press.

Walter, J. H., White F. J., Hall, S. K. MacDonald, A., Rylance, G., Boneh, A., Francis, D. E., Shortland, G. J., Schmidt, M., & Vail, A. (2002). How practical are recommendations for dietary control in phenylketonuria? *Lancet, 360,* 55–57.

Wang, A., & Clark, D. A. (2002). Haunting thoughts: The problem of obsessive mental intrusions. *Journal of Cognitive Psychotherapy: Special issue on intrusions in cognitive behavioral therapy, 16,* 193–208.

Wang, O. (2003). Infantile amnesia reconsidered: A cross-cultural analysis. *Memory, 11,* 65–80.

Ward, W. C., Kogan, N., & Pankove, E. (1972). Incentive effects in children's creativity. *Child Development, 43,* 669–677.

Wark, G. R., & Krebs, D. L. (1996). Gender and dilemma differences in real-life moral judgement. *Developmental Psychology, 32,* 220–230.

Wasserman, E. A., & Miller, R. R. (1997). What's elementary about associative learning? *Annual Review of Psychology, 48,* 573–607.

Waters, E., & Beauchaine, T. P. (2003). Are there really patterns of attachment? Comment on Fraley and Spieker (2003). *Developmental Psychology, 39,* 417–422.

Waters, E., Hamilton, C. E., & Weinfield, N. S. (2000). The stability of attachment security from infancy to adolescence and early adulthood: General introduction. *Child Development, 71,* 678–683.

Watson, D., Hubbard, B., & Wiese, D. (2000). Self-other agreement in personality and affectivity: The role of acquaintanceship, trait visibility, and assumed similarity. *Journal of Personality and Social Psychology, 78,* 546–558.

Watson, J. B. (1924). *Behaviorism.* New York: Norton.

Watson, J. B., & Rayner, R. (1920). Conditioned emotional reactions. *Journal of Experimental Psychology, 3,* 1–14.

Waugh, C. E., & Larkin, G. R. (2003). What good are positive emotions in crises? A prospective study of resilience and emotions following the terrorist attacks on the United States on September 11th, 2001. *Journal of Personality and Social Psychology, 84,* 365–376.

Webb, W. B. (1992). *Sleep: The gentle tyrant* (2nd ed.). Boston: Anker.

Wechsler, H., Davenport, A., Dowdall, G., Moeykens, B., & Castillo, S. (1994). Health and behavioral consequences of binge drinking in college. A national survey of students at 140 campuses. *Journal of the American Medical Association, 272,* 1672–1677.

Wechsler, H., Kuo, M., Lee, H., & Dowdall, G. W. (2000). *Environmental correlates of underage alcohol use and related problems of college students.* Cambridge, MA: Harvard School of Public Health.

Wechsler, H., Lee, J. E., Nelson, T. F., & Kuo, M. (2002). Underage college students' drinking behavior, access to alcohol, and the influence of deterrence policies. *Journal of American College Health, 50,* 223–236.

Weeks, G. R., & Gambescia, N. (2000). *Erectile dysfunction: Integrating couple therapy, sex therapy, and medical treatment.* New York: W. W. Norton.

Weinberg, M. S., Williams, C. J., & Pryor, D. W. (1991, February 27). Personal communication. Indiana University, Bloomington.

Weiner, B.A., & Wettstein, R. (1993). *Legal issues in mental health care.* New York: Plenum Press.

Weiner, I. B. (1998). *Principles of Rorschach interpretation.* Mahwah, NJ: Erlbaum.

Weintraub, M. (1976). Intelligent noncompliance and capricious compliance. In L. Lasagna (Ed.), *Patient compliance.* Mt. Kisco, NY: Futura.

Weissman, M. M., Bland, R. C., Canino, G. J., Faravelli, C., Greenwald, S., Hwu, H. G.,

Joyce, P. R., Karam, E. G., Lee, C. K., Lellouch, J., Lepine, J. P., Newman, S. C., Rubio-Stipec, M., Wells, J. E., Wickramarante, P. J., Wittchen, H., & Yeh, E. K. (1996, July 24–31). Cross-national emidemiology of major depression and bipolar disorder. *Journal of the American Medical Association, 276,* 293–299.

Weissman, M. W., & Olfson, M. (1995, August 11). Depression in women: Implications for health care research. *Science, 269,* 799–801.

Weitzenhoffer, A. M. (1999). *The practice of hypnotism* (2nd ed.). New York: Wiley.

Welch, K. C. (2002). *The Bell Curve* and the politics of Negrophobia. In J. M. Fish (Ed.), *Race and intelligence: Separating science from myth* pp. 177–198. Mahwah, NJ: Erlbaum.

Welkowitz, L. A., Struening, E. L., Pittman, J., Guardino, M. & Welkowitz, J. (2000). Obsessive-compulsive disorder and comorbid anxiety problems in a national anxiety screening sample. *Journal of Anxiety Disorders, 14,* 471–482.

Wells, G. L., Olson, E. A., & Charman, S. D. (2002). The confidence of eyewitnesses in their identifications from lineups. *Current Directions in Psychological Science, 11,* 151–154.

Wenar, C. (1994). *Developmental psychopathology: From infancy through adolescence* (3rd ed.). New York: McGraw-Hill.

Werner, E. E. (1995). Resilience in development. *Current Directions in Psychological Science, 4,* 81–85.

Wertheimer, M. (1923). Untersuchungen zur Lehre von der Gestalt. II. *Psychol. Forsch., 5,* 301–350. In R. Beardsley and M. Wertheimer (Eds.). (1958), *Readings in perception.* New York: Van Nostrand.

West, R. L. (1995). Compensatory strategies for age-associated memory impairment. In A. D. Baddeley, B. A. Wilson, & F. N. Watts (Eds.), *Handbook of memory disorders.* Chichester, England: Wiley.

West, R. L., Thorn, R. M., Bagwell, D. K. (2003). Memory performance and beliefs as a function of goal setting and aging. *Psychology & Aging, 18,* 111–125.

Westen, D., & Gabbard, G. O. (1999). Psychoanalytic approaches to personality. In L. A. Pervin & O. P. John (Eds.), *Handbook of personality: Theory and research.* (2nd ed.). New York: Guilford.

Wetter, D. W., Fiore, M. C., Gritz, E. R., Lando, H. A., Stitzer, M. L., Hasselblad, V., & Baker, T. B. (1998). The Agency for Health Care Policy and Research. Smoking cessation clinical practice guideline: Findings and implications for psychologists. *American Psychologist, 53,* 657–669.

Whaley, B. B. (Ed.). (2000). *Explaining illness: Research, theory, and strategies.* Mahwah, NJ: Erlbaum.

Wheeler, M. E., Petersen, S. E., & Buckner, R. L. (2000). Memory's echo: Vivid remembering reactivates sensory-specific cortex. *Proceedings of the National Academy of Sciences, 97,* 11125–11129.

Whelan, H. T., Smits, R. L., Buchmann, E. V., Whelan, N. T., Turner, S. G., Margolis, D. A., Cevenini, V., Stinson, H., Ignatius, R., Martin, T., Cwiklinski, J., Philippi, A. F., Graf, W. R., Hodgson, B., Gould, L., Kane, M., Chen, G., & Caviness, J. (2001). Effect of NASA light-emitting diode (LED) irradiation on wound healing. *Journal of Clinical Laser Medicine and Surgery, 19,* 305–314.

Whisenant, W. A., Pedersen, P. M., & Obenour, B. L. (2002). Success and gender: Determining the rate of advancement for intercollegiate athletic directors. *Sex Roles, 47,* 485–491.

Whitbourne, S. K. (2000). The normal aging process. In S. K. Whitbourne, Susan Krauss, (Ed.), *Psychopathology in later adulthood.* New York: Wiley.

Whitbourne, S. K., & Wills, K. (1993). Psychological issues in institutional care of the aged. In S. B. Goldsmith (Ed.), *Long-term care.* Gaithersburg, MD: Aspen Press.

Whitbourne, S. K., Zuschlag, M. K., Elliot, L. B., & Waterman, A. S. (1992). Psychosocial development in adulthood: A 22-year sequential study. *Journal of Personality and Social Psychology, 63,* 260–271.

Whorf, B. L. (1956). *Language, thought, and reality.* New York: Wiley.

Wickelgren, I. (1998a, June 26). Teaching the brain to take drugs. *Science, 280,* 2045–2047.

Wickelgren, I. (2001, March, 2). Working memory helps the mind focus. *Science, 291,* 1684–1685.

Wickens, C. D. (1984). *Engineering psychology and human performance.* Columbus, OH: Merrill.

Widiger, T. A., & Clark, L. A. (2000). Toward *DSM-V* and the classification of psychopathology. *Psychological Bulletin, 126,* 946–963.

Widmeyer, W. N., & Loy, J. W. (1988). When you're hot, you're hot! Warm-cold effects in first impressions of persons and teaching effectiveness. *Journal of Educational Psychology, 80,* 118–121.

Wielgosz, A. T., & Nolan, R. P. (2000). Biobehavioral factors in the context of ischemic cardiovascular disease. *Journal of Psychosomatic Research, 48,* 339–345.

Wigfield, A., & Eccles, J. S. (2000). Expectancy-value theory of achievement motivation. *Contemporary Educational Psychology, 25,* 68–81.

Wiggins, J. S. (1997). In defense of traits. In R. Hogan, J. Johnson, & S. Briggs (Eds.), *Handbook of personality psychology.* Orlando, FL: Academic Press.

Wildavsky, B. (2000, September 4). A blow to bilingual education. *U.S. News & World Report,* pp. 22–28.

Wilgoren, J. (1999, October 22). Quality day care, early, is tied to achievements as an adult. *The New York Times,* p. A16.

Williams, J. E., & Best, D. L. (1990). *Measuring sex stereotypes: A multinational study.* Newbury Park, CA: Sage.

Williams, J. E., Paton, C. C., Siegler, I. C., Eigenbrodt, M. L., Nieto, F. J., & Tyroler, H. A. (2000). Anger proneness predicts coronary heart disease risk: Prospective analysis from the Atherosclerosis Risk in Communities (ARIC) Study. *Circulation, 101,* 2034–2039.

Williams, J. W., Mulrow, C. D., Chiquette, E., Noel, P. H., Aguilar, C., & Cornell, J. (2000). A systematic review of newer pharmacotherapies for depression in adults: Evidence report summary. *Annals of Internal Medicine, 132,* 743–756.

Willis, S. L., & Nesselroade, C.S. (1990). Long-term effects of fluid ability training in old-old age. *Developmental Psychology, 26,* 905–910.

Willis, S. L., & Schaie, K. W. (1994). In C. B. Fisher & R. M. Lerner (Eds.), *Applied developmental psychology.* New York: McGraw-Hill.

Wilson, G. T., & Agras, W. S. (1992). The future of behavior therapy. *Psychotherapy, 29,* 39–43.

Wilson, G. T., & Fairburn, C. G. (2002). Treatments for eating disorders. In P. E. Nathan, & J. M. Gorman (Eds.), *A guide to treatments that work* (2nd ed.), pp. 559–592. London: Oxford University Press.

Wilson, J. P., & Keane, T. M. (Eds.). (1996). *Assessing psychological trauma and PTSD.* New York: Guilford.

Wilson, M. A. (2002). Hippocampal memory formation, plasticity and the role of sleep. *Neurobiology of Learning & Memory, 78,* 565–569.

Windholz, G. (1997, September). Ivan P. Pavlov: An overview of his life and psychological work. *American Psychologist, 52,* 941–946.

Windholz, G., & Lamal, P. A. (2002). Koehler's insight revisited. In R. A. Griggs (Ed.), *Handbook for teaching introductory psychology, Vol. 3: With an emphasis on assessment,* pp. 80–81. Mahwah, NJ: Erlbaum.

Winkler, K. J. (1997, July 11). Scholars explore the blurred lines of race, gender, and ethnicity. *Chronicle of Higher Education,* pp. A11–A12.

Winner, E. (1997). *Gifted children: Myths and realities.* New York: BasicBooks.

Winner, E. (2000). The origins and ends of giftedness. *American Psychologist, 55,* 159–169.

Winningham, R. G., Hyman, I. E., Jr., & Dinnel, D. L. (2000). Flashbulb memories? The effects of when the initial memory report was obtained. *Memory, 8,* 209–216.

Winson, J. (1990, November). The meaning of dreams. *Scientific American,* pp. 86–96.

Winter, D. G. (1973). *The power motive.* New York: Free Press.

Winter, D. G. (1987). Leader appeal, leader performance, and the motive profile of leaders and followers: A study of American presidents and elections. *Journal of Personality and Social Psychology, 52,* 196–202.

Winter, D. G. (1988). The power motive in women—and men. *Journal of Personality and Social Psychology, 54,* 510–519.

Winter, D. G. (1995). *Personality: Analysis and interpretation of lives.* New York: McGraw-Hill.

Wiseman, R., & Greening, E. (2002). The mind machine: A mass participation experiment into the possible existence of extra-sensory perception. *British Journal of Psychology, 93,* 487–499.

Witelson, S. (1989, March). *Sex differences.* Paper presented at the annual meeting of the New York Academy of Sciences, New York.

Witmans, M. B., & Kirk, V. G. (2002). Infancy onset of symptoms of narcolepsy in a child. *Clinical Pediatrics, 41,* 609–612.

Wixted, J. T., & Ebbesen, E. B. (1991). On the form of forgetting. *Psychological Science, 2,* 409–415.

Wolfe, D. A. (1999). *Child abuse: Implications for child development and psychopathology.* Thousand Oaks, CA: Sage.

Wolpe, J. (1990). *The practice of behavior therapy.* Boston: Allyn & Bacon.

Wolters, G. (1995). Het geheugen. Functie, structuur en processen. (Memory: Its function, structure, and processes.) *Psycholoog, 30,* 369–374.

Wonderlic (2003, February 9). *Wonderlic Personnel Test.* http://www.wonderlic.com/products/product.asp? prod_id=4.

Wonderlic. (2000, March 7). Wonderlic Personnel Test. www.wonderlic.com/ wpt.html.

Wong, M. M., & Csikszentmihalyi, M. (1991). Affiliation motivation and daily experience: Some issues on gender differences. *Journal of Personality and Social Psychology, 60,* 154–164.

Wood, E., Desmarais, S., & Gugula, S. (2002). The impact of parenting experience on gender stereotyped toy play of children. *Sex Roles, 47,* 39–49.

Wood, J. M., & Bootzin, R. (1990). The prevalence of nightmares and their independence from anxiety. *Journal of Abnormal Psychology, 99,* 64–68.

Wood, J. M., Nezworski, M. T., Lilienfeld, S. O., & Garb, H. N. (2003). *What's wrong with the Rorschach? Science confronts the controversial inkblot test.* New York: Wiley.

Wood, W., & Eagly, A. H. (2002). A cross-cultural analysis of the behavior of women and men: Implications for the origins of sex differences. *Psychological Bulletin, 128,* 699–727.

Wood, W., & Stagner, B. (1994). Why are some people easier to influence than others? In S. Savitt & T. C. Brock (Eds.), *Persuasion: Psychological insights and perspectives.* Boston: Allyn & Bacon.

Woodruff-Pak, D. S. (1999). New directions for a classical paradigm: Human eyeblink conditioning. *Psychological Science, 10,* 1–7.

Woods, S. C., & Seeley, R. J. (2002). Hunger and energy homeostasis. In H. Pashler & R. Gallistel (Eds.). *Steven's handbook of experi-*

mental psychology (3rd ed.), *Vol. 3: Learning, motivation, and emotion* pp. 633–668. New York: Wiley.

Woods, S. C., Schwartz, M. W., Baskin, D. G., & Seeley, R. J. (2000). Food intake and the regulation of body weight. *Annual Review of Psychology, 51,* 255–277.

Woods, S. C., Seeley, R. J., Porte, D., Jr., & Schwartz, M. W. (1998, May 29). Signals that regulate food intake and energy homeostasis. *Science, 280,* 1378–1383.

Woods, S. J. (2000). Prevalence and patterns of posttraumatic stress disorder in abused and postabused women. *Issues in Mental Health Nursing, 21,* 309–324.

Wozniak, R. H., & Fischer, K. W. (Eds.). (1993). *Development in context: Acting and thinking in specific environments.* Hillsdale, NJ: Erlbaum.

Wright, K. (September 2002). Times of our lives. *Scientific American,* pp. 59–65.

Writing Group for the Women's Health Initiative Investigators. (2000). Risks and benefits of estrogen plus progestin in healthy postmenopausal women: Principal results from the Women's Health Initiative Randomized Controlled Trial. *Journal of the American Medical Association, 288,* 321–333.

Wuethrich, B. (2001, March 16). Does alcohol damage female brains more? *Science, 291,* 2077–2079.

Wurtz, R. H., & Kandel, E. R. (2000). Central visual pathways. In E. R. Kandel, J. H. Schwartz, & T. M. Jessell (Eds.), *Principles of neural science* (4th ed.). New York: McGraw-Hill.

Wyatt, G. E. (1992). The sociocultural context of African American and white American women's rape. *Journal of Social Issues, 48,* 77–92.

Wynn, K. (1995). Infants possess a system of numerical knowledge. *Current Directions in Psychological Science, 4,* 172–177.

Wynn, K. (2000). Findings of addition and subtraction in infants are robust and consistent: Reply to Wakeley, Rivera, and Langer. *Child Development, 71,* 1535–1536.

Wynn, K., Bloom, P., & Chiang, W-C. (2002). Enumeration of collective entities by 5-month-old infants. *Cognition, 83,* B55–B62.

Yalom, I. D. (1997). *The Yalom reader: On writing, living, and practicing psychotherapy.* New York: Basic Books.

Yan, H., Kinzler, K. W., & Vogelstein, B. (2000, September 15). Genetic testing—present and future. *Science, 289,* 1890–1892.

Yang, S., & Sternberg, R. J. (1997). Taiwanese Chinese people's conceptions of intelligence. *Intelligence, 25,* 21–36.

Yee, A. H., Fairchild, H. H., Weizmann, F., & Wyatt, G. E. (1993). Addressing psychology's problem with race. *American Psychologist, 48,* 1132–1140.

Yenerall, J. D. (1995). College socialization and attitudes of college students toward the elderly. *Gerontology and Geriatrics Education, 15,* 37–48.

Yost, W. A. (2000). *Fundamentals of hearing* (4th ed.). New York: Academic Press.

Young, M. W. (2000, March). The tick-tock of the biological clock. *Scientific American,* pp. 64–71.

Yuskauskas, A. (1992). Conflict in the developmental disabilities profession: Perspectives on treatment approaches, ethics, and paradigms. *Dissertation Abstracts International, 53,* 1870.

Zajonc, R. B. (1985). Emotion and facial efference: A theory reclaimed. *Science, 228,* 15–21.

Zajonc, R. B. (2001). Mere exposure: A gateway to the subliminal. *Current Directions in Psychological Science, 10,* 224–228.

Zajonc, R. B., & McIntosh, D. N. (1992). Emotions research: Some promising questions and some questionable promises. *Psychological Science, 3,* 70–74.

Zalsman, G., & Apter, A. (2002). Serotonergic metabolism and violence/aggression. In J. Glicksohn (Ed.), *The neurobiology of criminal behavior: Neurobiological foundation of aberrant behaviors,* pp. 231–250. Dordrecht, Netherlands: Kluwer Academic.

Zamarra, J. W., Schneider, R. H., Besseghini, I., Robinson, D. K., & Salerno, J. W. (1996). Usefulness of the transcendental meditation program in the treatment of patients with coronary artery disease. *American Journal of Cardiology, 77,* 867–870.

Zarren, J. I., & Eimer, B. N. (2002). *Brief cognitive hypnosis: Facilitating the change of dysfunctional behavior.* New York: Springer.

Zatorre, R. J., Belin, P., & Penhune, V. B. (2002). Structure and function of auditory cortex: Music and speech. *Trends in Cognitive Sciences, 6,* 37–46.

Zautra, A. J., Reich, J. W., & Guarnaccia, C. A. (1990). Some everyday life consequences of disability and bereavement for older adults. *Journal of Personality and Social Psychology, 59,* 550–561.

Zebrowitz-McArthur, L. (1988). Person perception in cross-cultural perspective. In M. H. Bond (Ed.), *The cross-cultural challenge to social psychology.* Newbury Park, CA: Sage.

Zeidner, M., & Endler, N. S. (Eds.). (1996). *Handbook of coping: Theory, research, applications.* New York: Wiley.

Zevon, M., & Corn, B. (1990). Paper presented at the annual meeting of the American Psychological Association, Boston.

Ziegler, R., Diehl, M., & Ruther, A. (2002). Multiple source characteristics and persuasion: Source inconsistency as a determinant of message scrutiny. *Personality and Social Psychology Bulletin, 28,* 496–508.

Zigler, E. F., Finn-Stevenson, M., & Hall, N. W. (2002). The first three years and beyond: Brain development and social policy. In E. F. Zigler, M. Finn-Stevenson, & N. W. Hall, *Current perspectives in psychology.* New Haven, CT: Yale University Press.

Zigler, E., Bennett-Gates, D., Hodapp, R., & Henrich, C. (2002). Assessing personality traits of individuals with mental retardation.

American Journal on Mental Retardation, 107, 181–193.

Zika, S., & Chamberlain, K. (1987). Relation of hassles and personality to subjective well-being. *Journal of Personality and Social Psychology, 53,* 155–162.

Zilbergeld, B., & Ellison, C. R. (1980). Desire discrepancies and arousal problems in sex therapy. In S. R. Leiblum & L. A. Pervin (Eds.), *Principles and practices of sex therapy.* New York: Guilford.

Zimprich, D., & Martin, M. (2002). Can longitudinal changes in processing speed explain longitudinal age changes in fluid intelligence? *Psychology and Aging, 17,* 690–695.

Zito, J. M. (1993). *Psychotherapeutic drug manual* (3rd ed., rev.). New York: Wiley.

Zuckerman, M. (1978). The search for high sensation. *Psychology Today,* pp. 30–46.

Zuckerman, M. (1994). *Behavioral expression and biosocial expression of sensation seeking.* Cambridge, England: Cambridge University Press.

Zuckerman, M. (2002). Genetics of sensation seeking. In J. Benjamin, R. P. Ebstein, et al. (Eds.), *Molecular genetics and the human personality,* pp. 193–210. Washington, DC: American Psychiatric Publishing.

Zuckerman, M., & Kuhlman, D. M. (2000). Personality and risk-taking: Common biosocial factors, *Journal of Personality: Special issue:*

Personality processes and problem behavior, 68, 999–1029.

Zuger, A. (1998, June 2). The "other" drug problem: Forgetting to take them. *The New York Times,* pp. C1, C5.

Zurbriggen, E. L. (2000). Social motives and cognitive power–sex associations: Predictors of aggressive sexual behavior. *Journal of Personality and Social Psychology, 78,* 559–581.

Credits

Unit 1

Module 1: Figure 1: From Lamal, P. A. Students common beliefs about psychology. *Teaching of Psychology, 6,* Copyright © 1979 Lawrence Erlbaum Associates. **Figure 3:** From *Psychology, Careers for the Twenty-First Century.* Washington, DC: American Psychological Association. Copyright © 1996 by the American Psychological Association. Adapted with permission. **Figure 4:** From *Origin of Published Research.* Washington, DC: American Psychological Association. Copyright © 1991 American Psychological Association. Adapted with permission. **Figure 5:** From *The Psychology Major's Handbook,* 1st Edition by Kuther. © 2003 with permission of Wadsworth, a division of Thomson Learning: www.thomsonrights.com. Fax 800-730-2215.

Unit 2

Module 5: Figure 4: Darley, J. M., & Latané, B. (1968). Bystanders intervention in emergencies: Diffusion of responsibility. *Journal of Personality and Social Psychology, 8,* 377–383. Copyright © 1968 American Psychological Association. Adapted with permission.

Unit 3

Module 7: Figure 1: From *Human Anatomy,* 5th edition, by K. Van DeGraaff, p. 339. Copyright © 2000 by The McGraw-Hill Companies. **Figure 2:** From C. F. Stevens, "The Neuron" *Scientific American,* September 1979, page 56. Reprinted with permission of Carol Donner. **Figure 3:** From *Human Biology,* 6th edition, by S. Mader, page 250. Copyright © 2000 by The McGraw-Hill Companies. **Figure 4a:** From *Human Biology,* 6th edition, by S. Mader, page 250. Copyright © 2000 by The McGraw-Hill Companies. **Figure 4b:** From *The Living World,* 2nd edition, by G. B. Johnson, page 600. Copyright © 2000 by The McGraw-Hill Companies.
Module 8: Figure 2: From *Psychology,* 4th edition, by E. Loftus and C. Wortmann, pg. 63. Copyright © 1989 by The McGraw-Hill Companies. **Figure 4:** From *Human Biology,* 6th edition, by S. Mader, page 250. Copyright © 2000 by The McGraw-Hill Companies.
Module 9: Figure 2: From *Anatomy & Physiology,* 5th edition, by R. Seeley, T. Stephens, and P. Tate, p. 384. Copyright © 2000 by The McGraw-Hill Companies. **Figure 3:** From *The Living World,* 2nd edition, by G. B. Johnson, page 600. Copyright © 2000 by The McGraw-Hill Companies. **Figure 4a:** From *Elements of Physiological Psychology,* by A.M. Schneider and B. Tarshis. Copyright © 1995 by The McGraw-Hill Companies. **Figure 4b:** Courtesy of Dr. Robert B. Livingston, University of California-San Diego, and Philip J. Mercurio, Neurosciences Institute. **Figure 7:** Used with the permission of Dr. Edward G. Jones, University of California at Davis Center for Neuroscience.

Unit 4

Module 11: Figure 1: From *Psychology,* 5th edition, by C. Wortman, E. Loftus, and C. Weaver, p. 113. Copyright © 1999 by The McGraw-Hill Companies. **Figure 3:** From *Hole's Essentials of Human Anatomy and Physiology, 7th edition,* by D. Sheir, J. Butler, and R. Lewis, p. 283. Copyright © 2000 by The McGraw-Hill Companies. **Figure 5:** From *Human Biology,* 6th edition, by S. Mader, page 250. Copyright © 2000 by The McGraw-Hill Companies.
Module 12: Figure 1: From *Anatomy & Physiology,* 5th edition, by R. Seeley, T. Stephens, and P. Tate, p. 384. Copyright © 2000 by The McGraw-Hill Companies. **Figure 2:** From *Anatomy & Physiology,* 5th edition, by R. Seeley, T. Stephens, and P. Tate, p. 384. Copyright © 2000 by The McGraw-Hill Companies. **Figure 3:** From Better Hearing Institute, 1998 Better Hearing Institute: Washington, DC. **Figure 4:** Adapted from S. Brownlee and T. Watson, "The Senes," *US News & World Report,* January 13, 1997, pp. 51–59. Reprinted with permission of Linda M. Bartoshuk. **Figure 5:** From Kenshalo, *the Skin Senses,* 1968. Courtesy of Charles C. Thomas, Publisher, Ltd. Springfield, Illinois.
Module 13: Figure 1c: From *Mind Sights* by Roger N. Shepard © 1990 by Roger N. Shepard. Reprinted by permission of Henry Holt & Company. **Figure 4:** From *Sensation & Perception, 2nd edition,* by E. Goldstein © 1984. Reprinted with permission of Wadsworth, an imprint of the Wadsworth Group, a division of Thomson Learning. **Figure 5:** I. Biederman, Higher level vision. In D.N. Osherson, S. Kosslyn and J. Hollerback (eds.), *An Invitation to Cognitive Science: Visual Cognition and Action,* 1990. Reprinted with permission of MIT Press. **Figure 6:** Reprinted from *Vision Research, 26,* Julesz, B., Stereoscopic vision, pgs 1601–1602. Copyright © 1986 with kind permission from Elsevier Science Ltd., The Boulevard, Langford Lane, Kidlington OX5 1GN, UK. **Figure 7:** Figure from *Sensation and Perception,* 3rd edition, by Stanley Coren and Lawrence M. Ward, copyright © 1989 by John Wiley & Sons reproduced by permission of the publisher. **Figure 8 a–d:** Figure from *Sensation and Perception,* 3rd edition, by Stanley Coren and Lawrence M. Ward, copyright © 1989 by John Wiley & Sons, reproduced by permission of the publisher. **Figure 9a:** Figure from *Sensation and Perception,* 3rd edition, by Stanley Coren and Lawrence M. Ward, copyright © 1989 by John Wiley & Sons, reproduced by permission of the publisher. **Figure 12:** From Gregory and Gombrich, *Illusion in Nature and Art,* Figure 5-16. Copyright © 1973, by permission of Gerald Duckworth & Co., Ltd.

Unit 5

Module 14: Figure 1: From Palladino, J.J. & Carducci, B.J. Students knowledge of sleep and dreams. *Teaching of Psychology, 11,* 189–191. Copyright © 1984 Lawrence Erlbaum Associates. **Figure 2:** Fig 1 from *Sleep* by J.

Allan Hobson © 1989 by J. Allan Hobson. Reprinted by permission of Henry Holt & Co. **Figure 3:** From E. Hartmann, *The Biology of Dreaming,* 1967. Courtesy of Charles C Thomas, Publisher, Ltd., Springfield, Illinois. **Figure 4:** From *Secrets of Sleep* by Alexander Borbely. English translation copyright © 1986 by Basic Books, Inc, copyright © 1984 by Deutsche Verlag-Anstalt GmbH, Stuttgart. Reprinted by permission of Basic Books, a member of Perseus Books, L.L.C. **Figure 5:** Reprinted with permission from H.P. Roffwarg, J. N. Munzio and W. C. Dement, "Ontogenic Development of the Human Sleep-Dream Cycle," *Science,* 152, p. 604–619. Copyright © 1996 American Association for the Advancement of Science. **Figure 6:** Used with the permission of G. William Domhof, Dreamresearch.net.
Module 15: Figure 1: From *The Relaxation Response* by Herbert Benson, M.D., with Miriam Z. Klipper. Copyright © 1975 by William Morrow & Company, Inc. Reprinted by permission of Harper-Collins Publishers.
Module 16: Figure 1: Monitoring the Future Study 2002. University of Michigan, Ann Arbor. **Figure 2:** From *Human Biology,* 6th edition, by S. Mader, page 250. Copyright © 2000 by The McGraw-Hill Companies. **Figure 3:** Copyright © 1991 by The New York Times Co. Reprinted by permission. **Figure 5:** Gawin, F. H., & Kleber, H. D. (Mar 29, 1991). Cocaine abstinence phases. *Science.* Copyright © 1991 American Association For the Advancement of Science. **Figure 6:** Adapted from Wechsler, H., et al. (2000). College binge drinking in the 1990s: a continuing problem: results of the Harvard School f Public Health 1999 College Health alcohol Study. Reprinted with permission of Henry Wechsler. **Figure 8:** Monitoring the Future Study 2002. University of Michigan, Ann Arbor.

Unit 6

Module 19: Figure 1: E.C. Tolman, & C.H. Honzik, (1930). Introduction and removal of reward and maze performance in rats. *University of California Publications in Psychology,* 4, 257—275. **Figure 2:** From Anderson, J. A., & Adams, M. (1992). Acknowledging the learning styles of diverse student populations: Implications for instructional design. *New Directions for Teaching and Learning,* 49, 19–33. © Copyright 1992 Jossey Bass Publications.

Unit 7

Module 20: Figure 2: Used with permission of Dr. Gayatri Devi. **Figure 3:** Figure from "Human Memory: A Proposed System and Its Control Processes," by R. C. Atkinson and R. M. Shiffrin, from *The Psychology of Learning and Motivation: Advances in Research and Theory,* Volume 2, edited by K. W. Spence and J. T. Spence, copyright © 1968. Reprinted with permission from Elsevier. **Figure 4:** From "Perception and Memory Versus Thought: Some Old Ideas and Recent Findings," by A. D. deGroot in *Problem Solving: Research, Method &*

Theory, by B. Kleinmuntz (ed.). Copyright © 1966 John Wiley & Sons, Inc. Reprinted by permission of John Wiley & Sons, Inc. **Figure 5:** From Gathercole, S. E., & Baddeley, A.D. (1993). *Working memory and language processing*. Hillsdale, NJ: Erlbaum. **Figure 7:** Adapted from "Retrieval times from semantic memory," by A.M. Collins and M.R. Quillian in *Journal of Verbal Learning and Verbal Behavior*, Volume 8, 240–247, copyright © 1969 by Academic Press, reproduced by permission of the publisher.
Module 21: Figure 3: From D. C. Rubin "The subtle deceiver recalling," *Psychology Today*, September 1995. Reprinted with permission from *Psychology Today* Magazine. Copyright 1995 Sussex Publishers, Inc. **Figure 4:** From Loftus, E. F., & Palmer, J. C. (1974). Reconstruction of automobile destruction: An example of the interface between language and memory. *Journal of Verbal Learning and Verbal Behavior, 13*, 585–589, copyright © 1974 by Academic Press, reproduced by permission of the publisher. **Figure 5:** From H. P. Bahrick, L.. K. Hall & S. A.. Berger, "Accuracy and distortion in memory for high school grades," *Psychological Science*, Volume 7, 265–269. Reprinted with permission of Blackwell Publishers.
Module 22: Figure 2: Figure from R. S. Nickerson, & M. J. Adams, *Cognitive Psychology*, Volume 11, pg. 297. Copyright © 1979 by Academic Press, used by permission of the publisher. **Figure 4:** From *Human Anatomy*, 5th edition, by K. Van DeGraaff, p. 339. Copyright © 2000 by The McGraw-Hill Companies. **Figure 6:** Used with the permission of Dr. Paul Thompson, UCLA Laboratory of Neural Imaging.

Unit 8

Module 23: Figure 1: Reprinted with permission from R. Shepard and J. Metzler, "Mental Rotation of Three Dimensional Objects," *Science*, 171 701–703. Copyright 1971 American Association for the Advancement of Science. **Figure 2:** Republished with permission of American Physiological Society, from *Journal of Neurophysiology*, by Alvaro Pascual-Leone, September 1995; permission conveyed through Copyright Clearance Center. **Figure 3:** From "Family Resemblances: Studies in the Internal Structure of Categories," by E. Rosch and C. Mervis in *Cognitive Psychology*, Volume 7, 573–605, copyright © 1975 by Academic Press, reproduced by permission of the publisher.
Module 24: Figure 2: From R. Solso, *Cogntive Psychology*, 3rd edition. Copyright © 1991 by Allyn & Bacon. Reprinted/Adapted with permission. **Figure 4:** Reprinted with permission of Barry F. Anderson.
Module 25: Figure 1: Courtesy of Drs. Betty Hart and Todd Risley. **Figure 2:** From *Time Magazine*, January 30, 1995. Copyright © 1995 Time, Inc. Reprinted by permission. **Figure 3:** Used with the permission of Nature, Copyright © 1997, http://www.nature.com/nature/.

Unit 9

Module 26: Figure 1: From *Intelligence Reframed: Multiple perspectives for the 21st Century* by Howard Gardner. Copyright © 1999 by Howard Gardner. Reprinted by permission of Basic Books, a member of Perseus Books, L.L.C. **Figure 3:** Reprinted with permission from R. Sternberg, The Holy Grail of general intelligence. *Science, 289*, p. 389.Copyright 2000 American Association for the Advancement of Science. **Figure 7:** Reprinted with permission of Wonderlic, Inc, Libertyville, Illinois.
Module 28: Figure 1: Adapted from Familial studies of intelligence: A review, by T.J. Bouchard and M. McGue, *Science*, 212, 1981, pp. 1055–1059. **Figure 2:** Reprinted

with permission of Dmitry Schildovsky.
Module 29: Figure 2: From M. Zuckerman, The search for high sensation, *Psychology Today*, February 1978. Reprinted with permission of *Psychology Today* Magazine. Copyright © 1978, Sussex Publishers, Inc. **Figure 3:** *Motivation and Personality*, by A. Maslow, © 1998 Reprinted by Permission of Prentice Hall, Inc. Upper Saddle River, NJ.
Module 30: Figure 2: From *Anatomy & Physiology*, 5th edition, by R. Seeley, T. Stephens, and P. Tate, p. 384. Copyright © 2000 by The McGraw-Hill Companies. **Figure 3:** From *Time* Magazine, July 22, 1997. Copyright © 1997 Time Inc. Reprinted by permission.

Unit 10

Module 31: Figure 1: K. W. Fischer, P. R. Shaver, and P. Carnochan, How emotions develop and how they organize development, *Cognition and Emotion*, 1990. Reprinted by permission of Psychology Press Limited, Hove, UK.

Unit 11

Module 33: Figure 1: From J. E. Williams and D. L. Best, Measuring sex stereotypes: A multinational study. Copyright © 1990 by Sage Publications. Reprinted by permission of Sage Publications. **Figure 2:** U.S. Bureau of Labor Statistics. **Figure 3:** Hostile Hallways: The AAUW survey on sexual harassment in American Schools. 1993. Reprinted with permission of the American Association of University Women Educational Foundation. **Figure 4:** From Dey, E .L., Astin, A. W., Korn, W. S., & Berz, E. R. (1990). *The American Freshman: National Norms for Fall, 1990*. Reprinted with permission of Higher Education Research Institute. **Figure 5:** Republished with permission of *The Wall Street Journal* from February 14, 2000. Permission conveyed through the Copyright Clearance Center.
Module 34: Figure 2: Republished with permission of Society for the Scientific Study of Sexuality, from *Journal of Sex Research*, D. Sue, Erotic fantasies of college students during coitus, 1979. Permission conveyed through Copyright Clearance Center. **Figure 3:** E. E. Vance & N. W. Wagner, Written descriptions of orgasm: A study of sex differences, *Archves of Sexual Behavior, 6*, 1976, 87–98. Reprinted with permission of Kluwer Academic/Plenum Publishers. **Figure 4:** W. H. Masters & V. E. Johnson, 1966, *Human sexual response*. Boston: Little, Brown.
Module 35: Figure 1: Republished with permission of Society for the Scientific Study of Sexuality, from *Journal of Sex Research*, I. Arafat & W. L. Cotton, Masturbation practices of males and females, 1974. Permission conveyed through Copyright Clearance Center. **Figure 2:** Source: © 1972-1998 The Gallup Organization. All rights reserved. Reprinted with permission from www.gallup.com . **Figure 3:** From M. Clements, Making love, how old, how often. *Parade Magazine*, August 7, 1994. p. 5. **Figure 4:** From Kinsey, Pomeroy and Martin, *Sexual Behavior in the Male*, 1948. Reprinted with permission of W. B. Saunders Company.
Module 36: Figure 1: Used with permission of Dr. David Finkelhor, Director, Crimes Against Children Research Center, University of New Hampshire.

Unit 12

Module 39: Figure 1: Reproduced with permission from *Pediatrics*, Vol. 89, Pages 91–97, 1992 **Figure 3:** National Center for Health Statistics, 2000. Boys and Girls stature for age and weight for age percentiles. Washington, DC. **Figure 4:** Figure adapted from W. J. Robbins, 1929, *Growth*, New Haven, CT:

Yale University Press. Copyright Yale University Press. **Figure 6:** Used with the permission of Dr. Carol Tomlinson-Keasey. **Figure 10:** From Judith A. Schickendanz, et al. *Understanding Children and Adolescents*, 4th edition. © 2001 by Allyn & Bacon. Used with permission. **Figure 11:** Adapted from F. N. Dempster. Memory span: Sources for individual and developmental differences. *Psychological Bulletin, 89*, 63–100. Copyright © 1981 by the American Psychological Association. Adapted by permission.
Module 40: Figure 1: Reprinted from *Education and Physical Growth*, Tanner. Copyright © 1978 by International Universities Press. **Figure 2:** Used with the permission of David A. Goslin. **Figure 4:** K. E. Boehm and N. B. Campbell, Suicide: A review of calls to an adolescent peer listing phone service, *Child Psychiatry and Human Development*, 1996, 26, 61–66. Reprinted with permission of Kluwer Academic/Plenum Publishers.
Module 41: Figure 1: Statistical Office of the European Communities. **Figure 2:** U.S. Bureau of the Census. Census Population Survey, 2000. **Figure 3:** From K. W. Schaie, The course of adult intellectual development, *American Psychologist*, 49, 304–313. Copyright © 1994 by the American Psychological Association. Reprinted with permission.

Unit 13

Module 43: Figure 1: Data derived from Cattell, Eber and Tatsuoka: *Handbook for the 16PF*, Copyright © 1970, 1988, 1992 by the Institute for Personality and Ability Testing, Inc, Champaign, Illinois, USA. All rights reserved. **Figure 2:** From H. J. Eysenck, Biological dimensions of Personality. In L.. A. Pervin (ed.), *Handbook of Personality: Theory & Research*, 1990, p. 246. Reprinted with permission of Guilford Press. **Figure 3:** From L. .A. Pervin (ed.), *Handbook of Personality: Theory & Research*, 1990, Reprinted with permission of Guilford Press. **Figure 5:** From A. Tellegen, D. T. Lykken, T. J. Bouchard, Jr., K. J, Wilcox, N. L. Segal, & S. Rich. Persoality similarity in twins reared apart and together, *Journal of Personality and Social Psychology, 54*, 1031–1039. Copyright © 1988 by the American Psychological Association. Reprinted with permission.
Module 44: Figure 1: From Scheier, M. F., Carver, C. S., & Bridges, M. W. (1994). Distinguishing optimism from neuroticism (and trait anxiety, self-mastery, and self-esteem): A revision of the Life Orientation Test. *Journal of Personality and Social Psychology, 67*, 1063–1078. Copyright © 1994 by the American Psychological Association. Adapted with permission. **Figure 2:** Based on R. P. Halgin & S. K. Whitbourne, 1994, *Abnormal Psychology*, Fort Worth, TX: Harcourt Brace, and *Minnesota Multiphasic Personality Inventory, 2*, University of Minnesota.

Unit 14

Module 45: Figure 1: Adapted from Cohen, S., Kamarck, T. & Mermelstein, R. (1983). A global measure of perceived stress. *Journal of Health and Social Behavior, 24*, 385–396. **Figure 2:** From *The Stress of Life*, by H. Selye. Copyright © 1976 by The McGraw-Hill Companies. **Figure 5 (hassles):** From Chamberlain, K., & Zika, S. (1990). The minor events approach to stress: Support for the use of daily hassles. *British Journal of Psychology, 81*, 469–481. **Figure 5 (uplifts):** From, Comparison of two modes of stress measurement: Daily hassles and uplifts versus major life events. *Journal of Behavioral Medicine, 4*, 14, by A.D., Kanner, J. C. Coyne, C. Schaefer, & R. Lazarus. 1981, New York, Plenum. Copyright 1976 by Kluwer Academic/Plenum.
Module 46: Figure 2: Reprinted with permission from Elsevier. Pettingale, K. W., Morris, T., Greer, S., & Haybittle, J. L.. (1985). Mental attitudes to cancer: An

additional prognostic factor. *Lancet*, 750. **Figure 3:** From Morbidity and Mortality Weekly Report, July 9, 1993. Centers for Disease Control. **Figure 4:** Monitoring the Future Study 2002. University of Michigan, Ann Arbor. **Figure 5:** U.S. Department of Agriculture, 1998.

Module 47: Figure 2: Drawn from *Social Indicators of Well-Being: Americans' Perceptions of Life Quality* (p. 207 and p. 306), by F. M. Andrews and S. B. Withey, 1976, New York, Plenum. Copyright 1976 by Kluwer Academic/Plenum.

Unit 15

Module 49: Figure 2: From *Anxiety Disorders and Phobias: A Cognitive Perspective* by Aaron T. Beck and Gary Emery, with Rith L. Greenberg. Copyright © by Aaron T. Beck, MD & Gary Emery, PhD. Reprinted with permission of Basic Books, a member of Perseus Books, L.L.C. **Figure 4:** Personal communication with W. Hill. 1992. Public Affairs Network Coordinator for the American Psychiatric Association. **Figure 5:** Copyright © 1993 By The New York Times Co. Reprinted by permission. **Figure 10:** From *Schizophrenia Genesis* by Irving I. Gottesman © 1991 by Irving I. Gottesman. Used with permission of Henry Holt and Company. **Figure 11:** Reprinted with permission of Dr. Nancy C. Andreasen, University of Iowa Hospitals and Clinics. **Module 50: Figure 1:** From Benton, S. A., et al. (2003). Changes in counseling center client problems across 13 years. *Professional Psychology: Research and Practice, 34,* 66–72. Copyright © 2003 by the American Psychological Association. Adapted with permission.

Unit 16

Module 51: Figure 2: Reprinted by permission of Dr. Herbert Benson, Beth Israel Deaconess Medical Center, Boston, MA.

Module 52: Figure 1: Smith, Mary, Lee, Gene V. Glass, and Thomas I. Miller. *The Benefits of Psychotherapy,* pp. 89, Table 5-1. © 1980 (Copyright holder). Adapted with permission of The Johns Hopkins University Press. **Figure 2:** Mental Health: Does Therapy Help? © 1995 by Consumers Union of U.S., Inc., Yonkers, NY 10703-1057, a nonprofit organization. Reprinted with permission from the November 1995 issue of CONSUMER REPORTS ® for educational purposes only. No commercial use or photocopying/transmitting permitted. To subscribe, call 1 800-234-1645 or log on to www.ConsumerReports.org.

Module 53: Figure 2: From Antidepressants: Choices and Controversy. Health News, June 2000. Content © 2000 Massachusetts Medical Society. Published by Englander Communications LLC, an affiliate of Belvoir Publications, Inc. **Figure 3:** From National Mental Health Information Center, U.S. Dept. of Health and Human Services, 2002. **Figure 4:** From Howard, A., Pion, G. M., Gottfredson, G. D., Flattau, P. E., Oskamp, S., Pfafflin, S. M., Bray, D. W., & Burstein, A.. D. (1986). The changing face of American psychology: A report from the committee on employment and human resources. *American Psychologist, 41,* 1311–1327. Copyright © 1986 by the American Psychological Association. Adapted with permission.

Unit 17

Module 54: Figure 2: Adapted from Cacioppo, Bernston, & Crites, "Social Neuroscience: Principles of psychophysiological arousal and response. In E. T. Higgins & A. W. Kruglanski (Eds.), *Social Psychology: Handbook of Basic Principles,* 1996 Guilford Press. **Figure 4:** Adapted from Anderson, C. A., Krull, D. S., & Weiner, B. (1996). Explanations: Processes and consequences. In E. T. Higgins & A. W. Kruglanski (Eds.), *Social Psychology: Handbook of basic principles* (pp. 271–296). NY: Guilford Press. (The figure is adapted from the one shown on pg. 274.)

Module 57: Figure 2: From Sternberg, R. J. (1986). Triangular theory of love. *Psychological Review, 93,* 119–135. Copyright © 1986 by the American Psychological Association. Adapted with permission. **Figure 3:** From D. M. Buss International preferences in selecting mates: A study of 37 cultures, *Journal of Cross-Cultural Psychology, 21,* pp. 5–47. Copyright © 1990 by Sage Publications. Reprinted by permission of Sage Publications, Inc. **Figure 4:** From Benjamin, L. T., Jr. (1985, February). Defining aggression: An exercise for classroom discussion. *Teaching of Psychology, 12.* Copyright © 1985 Lawrence Erlbaum Associates. **Figure 5:** *Motivation and Personality* 3/e by Maslow, © 1998 Reprinted by Permission of Prentice Hall, Inc. Upper Saddle River, NJ.

Photos

Contents

Photos are credited as the first image of each unit below.

Unit 1

p. 2: © Jon Riley/Getty Images; **p. 3:** Photo by John Kanengieter, Courtesy, National Outdoor Leadership School (NOLS); **p. 4:** © Jon Riley/Getty Images; **p. 7 (top):** © Jeff Greenberg/Photo Researchers, Inc.; **p. 7 (center):** © Chuck Keeler/Getty Images; **p. 7 (bottom):** © Zigy Kaluzny/Getty Images; **p. 8:** © Laura Dwight/Photo Edit; **p. 16 (top, bottom left):** © Bettmann/Corbis Images; **p. 16 (center left):** © Photo Researchers; **p. 16 (center right):** © The Granger Collection; **p. 17 (top left):** Courtesy, Wellesley College Archives. Photographed by Notman; **p. 17 (top center):** © Culver Pictures; **p. 17 (top right, bottom right):** © The Granger Collection; **p. 17 (bottom left):** © Bettmann/Corbis Images; **p. 19:** © Bettmann/Corbis Images; **p. 21:** © 2002 Newsweek, Inc. All rights reserved. Reprinted by permission. Photo: Sheron Norman/AP; **p. 25 (left):** © Richard T. Nowitz/National Geographic Image Collection; **p. 25 (right):** © Frank Herholdt/Getty Images.

Unit 2

p. 30, 32: © Bob Daemmrich/Image Works; **p. 38:** © Robert I. M. Campbell/National Geographic Image Collection; **p. 40 (both):** Correll, J., Park, B., Judd, C.M., & Wittenbrink, B. (2002). The police officer's dilemma: Using ethnicity to disambiguate potentially threatening individuals. *Journal of Personality and Social Psychology,* 83, 1314–1329. Images courtesy, Josh Correll.; **p. 42:** © Bill Aron/Photo Edit; **p. 43:** © James Wilson/Woodfin Camp; **p. 46 (top):** © Spencer Grant/Photo Edit; **p. 46 (bottom):** © Jonathan Nourok/Photo Edit; **p. 50:** © Tom Stewart/Corbis Images; **p. 52:** © Douglas Faulkner/Photo Researchers; **p. 56 (left):** © Spencer Grant/Photo Edit; **p. 56 (top right):** © Erik Anderson/Stock Boston; **p. 56 (bottom right):** © Comstock; **p. 57 (top right):** © Comstock; **p. 57 (left):** © Image Source; **p. 57 (bottom right):** © Comstock.

Unit 3

p. 58: © Alexander Tsiaras/Stock Boston; **p. 59:** © AP/Wide World Photos; **p. 60:** © Alexander Tsiaras/Stock Boston; **p. 62:** © Dennis Kunkel/Visuals Unlimited; **p. 67 (both):** © Moonrunner Design Ltd.; **p. 68:** © AP/Wide World Photos; **p. 77:** © Reuters NewMedia Inc./Corbis Images; **p. 79:** © Leonard Lessin/Peter Arnold; **p. 80(a, b):** © Science Photo Library/Science Source/Photo Researchers; **p. 80(c):** © Mehau Kulyk/Science Photo Library/Photo Researchers; **p. 80(d):** © Dan McCoy/Rainbow; **p. 80(e):** © Roger Ressmeyer/Corbis Images; **p. 81:** Artificial Intelligence Laboratory, MIT. Image courtesy, Michael Leventon; **p. 82:** Courtesy, SUNY Downstate Medical Center ; **p. 83:** © AP/Wide World Photos; **p. 87:** Courtesy, Trustees of the British Museum, Natural History; **p. 89 (top):** From: Damasio H, Grabowski, T, Frank R, Galaburda AM, Damasio AR: The return of Phineas Gage: Clues about the brain from the skull of a famous patient. Science, 264:1102–1105, 1994. Department of Neurology and Image Analysis Facility, University of Iowa.; **p. 89 (bottom):** Courtesy, Center for Neuroscience, University of California, Davis; **p. 92:** B.A. Shaywitz et al., 1995. NMR/Yale Medical School.

Unit 4

p. 98, 100: © Martine Mouchy/Getty Images; **p. 102:** © Curtis Myers/Stock Connection/Picturequest; **p. 106 (both):** © Biophoto Associates/Photo Researchers; **p. 111 (all):** © Joe Epstein/Design Conceptions; **p. 116:** © VideoSurgery/Photo Researchers; **p. 118:** © NASA; **p. 119:** © AP/Wide World Photos; **p. 120:** © NASA; **p. 121:** © Prof. P. Motta/Dept. of Anatomy/University "La Sapienza", Rome/SPL/Photo Researchers; **p. 122:** © Omikron/Photo Researchers; **p. 126:** ©Lisa M. McGeady/Corbis Images; **p. 132 (both):** Courtesy, Bela Julesz; **p. 134:** ©Cary Wolinsky/Stock Boston; **p. 136:** © Jeff Greenberg/Stock Boston; **p. 137:** © John G. Ross/Photo Researchers; **p. 138 (both):** © Innervisions; **p. 140:** © AP/HO/Wide World Photos; **p. 144:** © PhotoDisc/Getty Images.

Unit 5

pp. 146, 148: © Nicholas Devore III/Network Aspen; **p. 152 (all):** © Ted Spagna/Photo Researchers; **p. 156:** PhotoDisc/Getty Images; **p. 160:** © Jose Carrillo/Stock Boston; **p. 164:** © AP, Midland Daily News/Wide World Photos; **p. 169:** © Suzanne Opton; **p. 172:** © Corbis Images; **p. 174:** © Dr. Dennis Kunkel/PhotoTake; **p. 177 (top left):** © Bob Daemmrich/Stock Boston; **p. 177 (top right):** © IT Int'l/eStock Photography/PictureQuest; **p. 178:** © Lawrence Migdale/Stock Boston; **p. 180:** © Kal Muller/Woodfin Camp.

Unit 6

pp. 184, 186: © Joanna B. Penneo/Aurora/PictureQuest; **p. 188:** © Culver Pictures; **p. 190:** PhotoDisc/Getty Images; **p. 193 (both):** © Stuart Ellins; **p. 196:** © Nina Leen/Time Life Pictures/Getty Images; **p. 198 (left):** © PhotoDisc/Getty Images; **p. 198 (center):** © PhotoDisc/Getty Images; **p. 198 (right):** © John Henley/CORBIS; **p. 204:** © AP/Wide World Photos; **p. 205:** Courtesy, Dr. Marian Bailey; **p. 211:** Courtesy, Albert Bandura; **p. 212 (left):** © Spencer Grant/Stock Boston; **p. 212 (right):** From Meltzhoff, A.N. (1988). Imitation of Televised Models by Infants. Child Development, 59, 1221–1229. Photo Courtesy, A.N. Meltzhoff & M. Hanak.; **p. 213:** © Kobal Collection/ HBO; **p. 214:** © PhotoDisc/Getty Images; **p. 216 (top):** © PhotoDisc/Getty Images; **p. 216 (bottom):** © John Henley/Corbis; **p. 217 (top left):** © PhotoDisc/Getty Images; **p. 217 (top right):** © Banana Stock; **p. 217 (bottom):** Image 100.

Unit 7

p. 220: © Steve Raymer/Corbis Images; **p. 221:** © Adolphe Pierre-Louis Photo; **p. 222:** © Steve Raymer/Corbis Images; **p. 227:** © Bob Wallace/Stock Boston; **p. 228:** © F. Dewey Webster/Sovfoto/Eastfoto/PictureQuest; **p. 231:** PhotoDisc/Getty Images; **p. 232 (top):** PhotoDisc/Getty Images; **p. 232 (bottom):**

Name Index

Note to readers: "A-" page numbers refer to the Appendix, which follows page 639.

Subject Index